International Disaster Response Law

Andrea de Guttry · Marco Gestri
Gabriella Venturini
Editors

International Disaster Response Law

T·M·C·ASSER PRESS

Springer

Editors
Andrea de Guttry
DIRPOLIS Institute
Scuola Superiore Sant'Anna
Pisa
Italy

Gabriella Venturini
Department of International Studies
University of Milan
Milan
Italy

Marco Gestri
Dipartimento di Scienze Giuridiche
Università di Modena e Reggio Emilia
Modena
Italy

ISBN 978-90-6704-881-1 ISBN 978-90-6704-882-8 (eBook)
DOI 10.1007/978-90-6704-882-8

Library of Congress Control Number: 2012941633

Published by T.M.C. Asser Press, The Hague, The Netherlands www.asserpress.nl
Produced and distributed for T.M.C. Asser Press by Springer-Verlag Berlin Heidelberg

Printed on acid-free paper

Springer is part of Springer Science+Business Media (www.springer.com)

Foreword

We are living in an increasingly fragile world. The frequency and intensity of natural disasters has increased dramatically over the recent decades. Last year alone brought massive floods in Australia, Thailand, and Pakistan, devastating earthquakes in Japan and New Zealand as well as famine at the Horn of Africa. The tsunami that hit Japan showed the vulnerability even of the most highly developed countries. And we should never think that Europe is in some way immune from natural disasters. Between 1999 and 2009, 100,000 Europeans were killed by natural disasters that cost the European economy €150 billion.

Experience shows that the effective implementation of disaster management policies leads to fewer deaths and less damage. In 2009, the Lisbon Treaty gave the EU important new responsibilities in this area: most notably a formal legal base to both humanitarian and civil protection policies. At the operational level, the European Commission brought together its humanitarian aid and civil protection instruments in an expanded DG ECHO in 2010. This has resulted in a single delivery platform that can deploy assistance immediately and in a coherent manner. Making this portfolio the responsibility of a single European Commissioner has also ensured a higher political visibility for disaster management inside the EU system.

The instruments we have work well—but there is still room for further improvement. In the area of civil protection we have recently tabled legislation that would move Europe away from the current ad hoc response to one which is preplanned, predictable, and immediate. Our proposals include the development of reference scenarios for the main types of disasters, the identification and mapping of key existing assets that could be made available, and the development of contingency plans for the deployment of these assets. It also includes the development of a European Emergency Response Capacity in the form of a voluntary pool of Member States' assets that are on call for operations under the Mechanism.

Response is only one part of disaster management. I believe our citizens can benefit best from a holistic approach where disaster preparedness and prevention are also fully covered. This is why our legislative proposals also call on Member States to draw up risk management plans by 2016.

The growing frequency of disasters has increased the political focus on disaster management. It has also increased the attention paid by academia. This is something that is very welcome. As we look to develop robust policies that can stand up to the challenges of the future we need critical analysis of what we have been doing—and we need creative thinking to inspire the new policy initiatives that can build a more resilient society.

This book covers the whole range of legal issues related to disaster management. As such it is an essential contribution to a debate that could not be more urgent.

Kristalina Georgieva
European Commissioner for International Cooperation
Humanitarian Aid and Crisis Response

Preface and Acknowledgments

Over the last three decades natural and technological disasters have been increasing in terms of frequency, size, number of people affected, and material damage caused. Between 1980 and 2011, 9.916 natural disasters have occurred killing some 2.5 million people across the world (according to the data collected and elaborated by the Centre for Research on the Epidemiology of Disasters at the University of Louvain).[1] The number of those affected by these phenomena—i.e. individuals requiring immediate assistance during a period of emergency, such as the provision of food, water, shelter, sanitation and immediate medical assistance—is even more impressive, as it reaches a figure close to 6 billion. The material damage produced has been reckoned to amount to 2.2 billion USD. Statistics are less astonishing, but still disturbing, with respect to the 6,603 technological disasters reported. In the time span considered, over 250.000 persons have died because of such events, while 4.4 million have been affected with estimated damages amounting to over 25 million USD. To provide a term of comparison, in the three decades between 1950 and 1980 the number of individuals affected by natural or technological disaster was around 730 million, while the combined economic losses caused by these events were just under 780 million USD. The total number of disasters reported in those years was 2,216 as opposed to the 16,519 registered from 1980 to nowadays, with an increase of 745 %. Hydrological and meteorological disasters represented about 80 % of the total disaster occurrence in the last decade while geophysical disasters accounted for about 7 % in the same period. As far as the regional distribution of disaster is concerned, in the last decade Asia accounted for about 30 % of the number of all reported disasters, the Americas 25 %, Europe and Africa about 20 % each, and Oceania less than 4 %.

---

[1] Guha-Sapir D, Vos F, Below R and Ponserre S, Annual Disaster Statistical Review 2010: The numbers and trends, Centre for Research on the Epidemiology of Disasters (CRED), Université Catholique de Louvain—Brussels, Belgium, 2011.

While most of these disasters were relatively small scale and only a rather small number of large disaster caught the attention of the media and public opinion, there is growing awareness of the potentially devastating consequences of the increase in frequency and scope of disasters especially for those areas most vulnerable to climate change and environmental stress. According to the Intergovernmental Panel on Climate Change, major impacts of climate change on human health are likely to occur in the next future via changes in the magnitude and frequency of extreme events, which trigger a natural disaster or emergency. As consequence, in recent years national budgets for emergency response, disaster preparedness, and mitigation have experienced rapid growth as have the activities of international agencies and NGOs directly involved in policy development related to disasters prevention and mitigation and in operational disaster response. For instance, according to OECD data on Official Development Assistance, from 1995 to 2009 financial commitments for emergency response has increased by 400 %.

Heightened awareness about the plight of disaster victims has called attention to the importance of adequate national and international legal rules and structures for disaster prevention, mitigation, and response. International Disaster Response Law has developed significantly in recent years, as shown by the increasing number of relevant treaties which have been signed and ratified worldwide. The codification of norms addressing various aspects related to disaster prevention, management, and post-disaster recovery occurred over a strikingly short period of time, very often as a reaction to new kinds of disasters. This resulted in *ad hoc* developments of IDRL, which sometimes caused significant overlapping and contradictions. The need for better synchronization and co-ordination of codification activities has been highlighted several times by scholars, and this inspired the International Law Commission to focus its attention on these issues. A special rapporteur, Mr. Eduardo Valencia-Ospina, has been therefore appointed to deal with the protection of persons in the event of disasters and so far the ILC has examined seven reports and agreed on about 10 articles.

IDRL has also attracted increasing attention from both practitioners and the public. This growing awareness is due to the new complex challenges facing international relief operations as well as to the magnitude and incidence of natural and man-made disasters. As it often occupies a center-stage position under close public scrutiny, the relief organizations and the humanitarian community have discovered the importance of better international and internal regulation of their activities, which is essential to be able to perform in a more professional manner, to deliver the requested relief services on time, and to act in a more accountable way.

IDRL, however, is not a self-contained regime, growing in isolation from general international law. On the contrary, it shares a number of fundamental tenets with the legal discipline of other areas that in various ways contribute to shape its form and content. This relationship may be aptly described in terms of mutual support and cross-fertilization. While the general principles and rules belonging to related branches of international law influence and stimulate the progress of IDRL, the latter may in turn enhance their implementation. It is the opinion of the editors and the authors of this volume that in order to fully benefit from this productive relationship, IDRL should be constructed and applied taking into account the interpretation and implementation of Human Rights Law, International Humanitarian Law, refugee law, global health law, international environmental law, international criminal law, and the law of international development.

The editors and authors of this book wish to contribute to identify the existing international rules and normative gaps, and to share reflections about the best way to address the numerous issues at stake.

To achieve these goals the book is divided into five parts: Part I presents recent trends in natural and made-made disasters and offers a survey of the present state of IDRL, while positioning this emerging body of norms within existing International Law. Special attention is devoted to the work of the International Law Commission as well to a special type of disaster, subject to *ad hoc* legal rules, namely nuclear accidents.

In Part II the focus is on EU disaster response law. As the European Union has become a major actor in dealing with disasters, the relevant decision-making mechanisms and rules are examined, regarding both disasters within and outside Europe.

In Part III the emphasis is put on issues related to liability and compensation, and on the rights and duties of States in preventing and mitigating a disaster, in facilitating access to their territory by humanitarian relief actors, both in times of peace and war. The existing obligations incumbent on disaster-affected nations relating to the hosting of international missions are carefully examined.

Disasters usually have a serious effect on human rights. Human rights obligations of the greatest importance in such situations include (but are not limited to) the right to life, the right to personal liberty and security, the right to humane treatment, the right to food, the right to health. Those rights must be respected in accordance with the fundamental principle of nondiscrimination, i.e., without any adverse distinction, and special measures need to be undertaken to protect the most vulnerable groups. Part IV examines these issues more deeply and analyzes the potential relevance of international criminal law.

The natural impulse to offer support to the population affected by a disaster has contributed to the proliferation of new players in the international humanitarian arena ready to offer their services. The development of these relief actions poses several challenges related to the design and implementation of a disaster response field operation and to the controversial and so far unresolved issue of coordination among the many actors involved. Additional topics such as the customs barriers to relief consignments (which very often delay the full operational capacity of the missions), the use of civilian and military defence assets in emergency situations, the mechanisms and procedures available to offer financial support for recovery and rehabilitation efforts, the challenges related to offering risk insurance, and the issue of corruption during disaster-related activities are specifically addressed in Part V.

In the Conclusions it clearly emerges that it is now time for fine words in treaties to be transformed into concrete measures which will achieve real co-operation and synergies in the interests of the people suffering the consequences of ever more frequent natural and man-made disasters.

This book is the result of a joint research project carried out by the Scuola Superiore Sant'Anna, the University of Milan and the University of Modena and Reggio Emilia. It has involved about 30 researchers from several Universities and a number of independent researchers/scholars. Research began at the end of 2010 and its first results were presented and discussed during an international Conference on IDRL which took place in Rome, at the Headquarters of the Italian Civil Protection Department, in November 2011. The authors of the various contributions benefited tremendously from the comments and discussions which took place during that conference, which inspired the revision and finalization of the contributions published in this volume.

We are indebted to all those who contributed to this research, and in particular to Kristalina Georgieva (EU Commissioner for International Cooperation, Humanitarian Aid and Crisis Response), who agreed to write the foreword to this Volume; to Franco Gabrielli, Head of the Italian Civil Protection Department, who strongly supported our research since the very beginning and hosted the IDRL Conference in Rome; to Emanuele Sommario for his invaluable support from the preliminary stages of the design of the research project; to Michele Gonnelli for his support in the technical preparation of the manuscript, and to Marco Colucci for the preparation of the analytical indexes.

Pisa, Modena, Milan, May 2012

Andrea de Guttry
Marco Gestri
Gabriella Venturini

Contents

Part III Rights and Duties of States

Part IV The Human Rights Dimension

Appendices

Abbreviations

AADMER	ASEAN Agreement on Disaster Management and Emergency Response
AASTMT	Arab Academy for Science, Technology and Maritime Transport
ACDM	ASEAN Committee on Disaster Management
ACHR	American Convention on Human Rights
ACP States	African, Caribbean and Pacific States
ACSAD	Arab Centre for the Studies of Arid Zones and Dry Lands
ADB	Asian Development Bank
ADPC	Asian Disaster Preparedness Centre
AECID	Spanish Agency for International Development Cooperation
AHA Centre	ASEAN Co-ordinating Centre for Humanitarian Assistance
ALNAP	Active Learning Network for Accountability and Performance
AMCDRR	Asian Ministerial Conference on Disaster Risk Reduction
AMM	Aceh Monitoring Mission
AOSIS	Alliance of Small Island States
AP1	Additional Protocol I to the 1949 Geneva Conventions
AP2	Additional Protocol II to the 1949 Geneva Conventions
ARPDM	ASEAN Regional Programme on Disaster Management
ASEAN	Association of South-East Asian Nations
ASP	Assembly of States Parties
AU	African Union
BNPB	Badan Nasional Penanggulangan Bencana
BP	British Petroleum
BSEC	Black Sea Economic Cooperation
CAP	Consolidated Appeal Process
CAPRADE	Comité Andino para la Prevención y Atención de Desastres
CARE	Citizens Consular Assistance Regulation in Europe
CARICOM	Caribbean Community
CAS	Country Assistance Strategy
CAT bonds	Catastrophic Risk bonds

CDEMA	Agencia Caribeña para el Manejo de los Desastres y la Emergencia
CDM	Comprehensive Disaster Management
CEA	European Insurance and Reinsurance Federation
CECIS	Common Emergency Communication and Information System
CEPREDENAC	Centro de Co-ordinación Para la Prevención de Desastres Naturales en América central
CERF	Central Emergency Response Fund
CESCR	Committee on Economic, Social and Cultural Rights
CFSP	Common Foreign and Security Policy
CHFs	Common Humanitarian Funds
CMCoord	UN Humanitarian Civil Military Coordination
COCON	EU Consular Working Group
CONRED	Coordinadora Nacional para la Reducción de Desastres
CoOL	Consular On Line
COREU	Correspondance Européenne
CPFI	Civil Protection Financial Instrument
CPM	Community Civil Protection Mechanism
CPR	Civil and Political Rights
CRED	Centre for Research on the Epidemiology of Disasters
CRID	Regional Disaster Information Centre (Centro Regional de Información sobre Desastres, América Latina y El Caribe)
CRSR	Convention Relating to the Status of Refugees
CSI	Commonwealth of Independent States
CWGER	Cluster Working Group on Early Recovery
DAC	Development Assistance Committee
DG ECHO	Directorate General for Humanitarian Aid and Civil Protection
DHA	Department of Humanitarian Affairs
DOS	Department of State
DPO	Disabled Persons Organization
DRC	Democratic Republic of Congo
DRR	Disaster Risk Reduction
DRRM	Disaster Risk Reduction and Management
EAC	East African Community
EADRCC	Euro-Atlantic Disaster Response Coordination Centre
EADRU	Euro-Atlantic Disaster Response Unit
EAPC	Euro-Atlantic Partnership Council
ECHO	Humanitarian Aid and Civil Protection Department of the European Commission
ECHR	European Convention on Human Rights (Convention for the Protection of Human Rights and Fundamental Freedoms)
ECommHR	European Commission of Human Rights
ECtHR	European Court of Human Rights
ECJ	European Court of Justice
ECLAC	Economic Commission for Latin America and the Caribbean

ECO	Economic Cooperation Organization
ECOWAS	Economic Community of West African States
ECR	European Court Reports
EDF	European Development Fund
EDR	European Disaster Response
EEA	European Environment Agency
EEAS	European External Action Service
EEC	European Economic Community
EECC	Eritrea-Ethiopia Claims Commission
EECR	European Emergency Response Centre
EIA	Environmental Impact Assessment
ELD	Environmental Liability Directive
ELN	National Liberation Army (Ejército de Libéración Nacional, Colombia)
EM-DAT	Emergency Events Database
ENDA	Emergency Natural Disaster Assistance
EPPR	Emergency Prevention, Preparedness and Response Working Group of the Arctic Council
ERC	Emergency Relief Coordinator
ESCR	Economic, Social and Cultural Rights
ESDP	European Security and Defence Policy
EU	European Union
EUHR	European Union High Representative for Foreign Affairs and Security Policy
EUMS	EU Military Staff
EUFFTR	EU Forest Fire Tactical Reserve
EUSC	EU Satellite Centre
EUSF	European Union Solidarity Fund
EVAC	Evacuation Operation Exercise Study
FAFA	Financial and Administrative Framework Agreement
FAO	United Nations Food and Agriculture Organization
FARC	Revolutionary Armed Forces of Colombia (Fuerzas Armadas Revolucionarias de Colombia)
FEMA	Federal Emergency Management Agency
FTCA	Federal Tort Claims Act
GAM	Gerakan Aceh Merdeka
GBV	Gender-Based Violence
GC I	1949 Geneva Convention I
GC II	1949 Geneva Convention II
GC III	1949 Geneva Convention III
GC IV	1949 Geneva Convention IV
GCCF	Gulf Costal Claims Facility
GDP	Gross Domestic Product
GHD	Good Humanitarian Donorship
GRECO	Group of States Against Corruption

GTPL	General Third Party Liability
GURI	Gazzetta Ufficiale della Repubblica Italiana
HAR	Humanitarian Aid Regulation
HFA	Hyogo Framework for Action
HRC	Human Rights Committee
HCT	Humanitarian Country Team
IAC	International Armed Conflict
IACAC	Inter-American Convention Against Corruption
IACommHR	Inter-American Commission on Human Rights
IAEA	International Atomic Energy Agency
IASC	Inter-Agency Standing Committee
IBRD	International Bank for Reconstruction and Development
ICC	International Criminal Court
ICCPR	International Covenant on Civil and Political Rights
ICESCR	International Covenant on Economic, Social and Cultural Rights
ICISS	International Commission on Intervention and State Sovereignty
ICJ	International Court of Justice
ICPAC	IGAD Climate Prediction and Application Centre
ICRC	International Committee of the Red Cross
ICTY	International Criminal Tribunal for former Yugoslavia
ICTR	International Criminal Tribunal for Rwanda
IDA	International Development Association
IDI	Institut de Droit International
IDLO	International Development Law Organisation
IDPs	Internally Displaced Persons
IDRL	International Disaster Response Law
IEC	Incident and Emergency Centre
IEL	International Environmental Law
IFI	International Financing Institution
IFRC	International Federation of Red Cross and Red Crescent Societies
IGAD	Intergovernmental Authority on Development
IHL	International Humanitarian Law
IHR	International Health Regulations
ILA	International Law Association
ILC	International Law Commission
ILO	International Labour Organization
IMF	International Monetary Fund
INES	International Nuclear Events Scale
INSARAG	International Search And Rescue Advisory Group
IOs	International Organisations
IOM	International Organization for Migration
IRA	Irish Republican Army

IRFs	Impulse Response Functions
IRU	International Relief Union
LEMA	Local Emergency Management Authority
LRRD	Linking Relief, Rehabilitation and Development
LTTE	Liberation Tigers of Tamil Eelam
MCDA	Military and Civil Defence Assets
MDGs	Millennium Development Goals
MIC	Monitoring and Information Centre
MINUSTAH	United Nations Stabilization Mission in Haiti
MoU	Memorandum of Understanding
NATO	North Atlantic Treaty Organisation
NDMC	Natural Disaster Management Commission
NDRI	Natural Disaster Risk Index
NGHA	Non-Governmental Humanitarian Agency
NGO	Non-Governmental Organization
NIAC	Non-International Armed Conflict
NIMS	National Incident Management System
NSCI	Nuclear Safety Cooperation Instrument
OAS	Organization of American States
OAU	Organization for African Unity
OCHA	United Nations Office for the Coordination of Humanitarian Affairs
ODA	Official Development Assistance
OECD	Organization for Economic Cooperation and Development
OHCHR	Office of the High Commissioner for Human Rights
OJEU	Official Journal of the European Union
OJEC	Official Journal of the European Communities
OP	Occupying Power
OPOL	Offshore Pollution Liability Association Limited
OSOCC	On Site Coordination Centre
OSPRAG	United Kingdom Oil Spill Prevention and Response Advisory Group
POWs	Prisoners of War
PRGT	Poverty Reduction and Growth Trust
PRST	Poverty Reduction and Strategy Paper
R2P	Responsibility To Protect
RABIT	Rapid Border Intervention Team
RCD	Rassemblement Congolais pour la Démocratie
RCF	Rapid Credit Facility
REHU	Reunión Especializada de Reducción de Riesgos de Desastres Socionaturales, la Defensa Civil, la Protección Civil y la Asistencia Humanitaria del MERCOSUR
RFI	Rapid Financing Instrument
SAARC	South Asian Association for Regional Co-operation
SADC	Southern African Development Community

SADKN	South Asian Disaster Knowledge Network
SAR	Search and Rescue
SASOP	ASEAN Standard Operating Procedure for Regional Standby Arrangements and Coordination of Joint Disaster Relief and Emergency Response Operations
SDMC	SAARC Disaster Management Centre
SEGEPLAN	General Secretariat of the Executive Branch for Planning and Programming (Secretaría de Planificación y Programmación de la Presidencia, Guatemala)
SICA	Sistema de la Integración Centroamericana
SIDS	Small Island Developing States
SIPRI	Stockholm International Peace Research Centre
SITCEN	Joint Situation Centre
SOFA	Status of Forces Agreement
SOPAC	Pacific Islands Applied GeoScience Commission
SOPs	Standard Operating Procedures
SPDC	State Peace and Development Council
SPILL	Securing Protections for the Injured from Limitations of Liability Act
SRSG	Special Representative of the Secretary General
TCG	Tripartite Core Group
TEC	Treaty Establishing the European Community
TEU	Treaty on European Union
TFEU	Treaty on the Functioning of the European Union
TI	Transparency International
UCPM	Union Civil Protection Mechanism
UN	United Nations
UNAMA	United Nations Assistance Mission to Afghanistan
UNCAC	United Nations Convention Against Corruption
UNCLOS	United Nations Convention on the Law of the Sea
UNCT	United Nations Country Team
UNDAC	United Nations Disaster Assessment and Coordination
UNDP	United Nations Development Programme
UNDP BCPR	United Nations Development Programme Bureau for Crisis Prevention and Recovery
UNDRO	United Nations Disaster Relief Organization
UNECOSOC	United Nations Economic and Social Council
UNEP	United Nations Environment Programme
UNESCO	United Nations Educational, Scientific and Cultural Organization
UNFCCC	United Nations Framework Convention on Climate Change
UNFPA	United Nations Population Fund
UNHCR	United Nations High Commissioner for Refugees
UNICEF	United Nations Children's Fund
UNISDR	United Nations International Strategy for Disaster Reduction

UNODC	United Nations Office on Drug and Crime
US	United States
USAID	United States Agency for International Development
VFA	Visiting Forces Agreement
WB	World Bank
WCDR	World Conference on Disaster Reduction
WCO	World Custom Organization
WFP	World Food Programme
WHO	World Health Organisation

Contributors

Giovanna Adinolfi Associate Professor of International Law, University of Milan, Milan, Italy

Mariangela Bizzarri Consultant on Gender, Protection and Gender-Based Violence, Founder and Managing Director at Gender Consult, Milan, Italy

Enrico Calossi Research Fellow at the Observatory on Political Parties and Representation (OPPR), European University Institute, Florence, Italy

Piero Calvi-Parisetti Professor of Emergencies and Humanitarian Action, Istituto per gli Studi di Politica Internazionale, Milan, Italy

Sara Cannizzo Research Fellow, Scuola Superiore Sant'Anna, Pisa, Italy

Federico Casolari Assistant Professor of International Law, University of Bologna, Bologna, Italy

Milena Costas Trascasas Research Fellow, University of Milan, Milan, Italy

Annalisa Creta Research Fellow, Scuola Superiore Sant'Anna, Pisa, Italy

Giovanni De Siervo International Relations Officer, Department of Civil Protection, Presidenza del Consiglio dei Ministri, Rome, Italy

Andrea de Guttry Professor of International Law, Scuola Superiore Sant'Anna, Pisa, Italy

Antonio Donini Senior Researcher Feinstein International Center, Tufts University, Boston, MA, USA

Federico Forni Lecturer in International Law, University of Modena and Reggio Emilia, Modena, Italy

Marco Gestri Professor of International Law, University of Modena and Reggio Emilia, Modena, Italy

Andrea Gioia Professor of International Law, University of Modena and Reggio Emilia, Modena, Italy

Alessandra La Vaccara LL.M in International Humanitarian Law, Graduate Institute of International and Development Studies, Geneva, Geneva

Marina Mancini Assistant Professor of International Law, Mediterranean University of Reggio Calabria, Reggio Calabria, Italy

Barbara Nicoletti Research Fellow, Scuola Superiore Sant'Anna, Pisa, Italy

Ingrid Nifosi-Sutton Adjunct Professor of Law, Washington College of Law, American University, Washington, DC, USA

Ivana Palandri Assistant Professor of International Organizations Law, University of Modena and Reggio Emilia, Modena, Italy

Natalino Ronzitti Professor of International Law, Associate Member of the Institut de Droit International, Rome, Italy

Francesca Russo PhD candidate in Public International Law, Scuola Superiore Sant'Anna, Pisa, Italy

Salvatore Sberna Research Fellow, University of Pisa, Pisa, Italy

Emanuele Sommario Assistant Professor of International Law, Scuola Superiore Sant'Anna, Pisa, Italy

Tullio Scovazzi Professor of International Law, University of Milan-Bicocca, Milan-Bicocca, Italy

Stefano Silingardi Lecturer in International Law, University of Modena and Reggio Emilia, Modena, Italy

Leopoldo Trieste Research Fellow, Scuola Superiore Sant'Anna, Pisa, Italy

Giuseppe Turchetti Associate Professor of Economics and Management, Scuola Superiore Sant'Anna, Pisa, Italy

Alberto Vannucci Associate Professor of Political Science, University of Pisa, Pisa, Italy

Gabriella Venturini Professor of International Law, University of Milan, Milan, Italy

Flavia Zorzi Giustiniani Assistant Professor of International Law, International Telematic University Uninettuno, Rome, Italy

Part I
Positioning International Disaster Response Law Within Existing International Law

Chapter 1
Surveying the Law

Andrea de Guttry

Abstract International Disaster Response Law has developed significantly in the last decades, as clearly proven by the increasing number of relevant treaties which have been signed and ratified worldwide. The codification of various aspects related to disaster prevention, management, and post-disaster recovery did happen in a pretty short time, very often just as a reaction to new typologies of disasters, sometimes in a confused and unco-ordinated manner, very often causing significant overlapping and contradictions. A closer investigation of the various legal texts makes evident that there are significant differences in the terminology used, discrepancies and inconsistencies between the various treaties and among the various treaty levels (bilateral, regional, universal), different stages of development of the rules regulating international co-operation in disaster prevention and management (very sophisticated and comprehensive rules in Latin America, less detailed legal regulation in the African continent), ongoing confusion and uncertainty about the borders between soft law and positive law (in disaster prevention and management soft law has a proven record of great influence and importance in orienting the behavior of international actors). The need for a better synchronization and co-ordination of the codification activities is inevitably and dramatically emerging. The author focuses the attention on how current international instruments are directly or indirectly addressing disaster prevention, management, and recovery response. He describes what the legal picture looks like at universal and at regional level and finally addresses existing problems in terms of co-ordination of legal instruments adopted at various levels (bilateral, regional, and universal).

A. de Guttry (✉)
Scuola Superiore Sant'Anna, Piazza Martiri della Libertà 33,
56127, Pisa, Italy
e-mail: deguttry@sssup.it

A. de Guttry et al. (eds.), *International Disaster Response Law*,
DOI: 10.1007/978-90-6704-882-8_1,

Keywords International Disaster Response Law · Codification · Regional disaster management mechanisms · State's Rights and obligations during disasters

Contents

1.1 Introductory Remarks and Purpose of the Paper

International Disaster Response Law has developed significantly in recent decades, as clearly proven by the increasing number of relevant treaties which have been signed and ratified worldwide.[1] Various aspects of disaster prevention, management, and post-disaster recovery were codified rapidly, sometimes in a confused and unco-ordinated manner, very often causing significant overlapping and contradictions. This anarchic accumulation of treaties and rules is due to the fact that most international regulations have been agreed upon and enacted without reference to each other, and sometimes as a reaction to new kinds of disasters, most often related to natural or man-made circumstances such as climate change or nuclear incidents. There are now more than 200 international treaties (universal, regional, and even bilateral) regulating various matters related to the prevention, management of disasters, and post-disaster rehabilitation and reconstruction.[2]

[1] Harper 2009, p. 15.

[2] There are various archives containing disaster-related agreements: see for example http://www.ifrc.org/en/what-we-do/idrl/publication/); the UN Treaty Collection (http://treaties.un.org/); the IDRL legal database, a collection of international and national legal documents such as treaties, resolutions, laws and regulations relevant to international disaster response operations, which was promoted and is managed by the International Federation of Red Cross and Red Crescent Societies (the OCHA Disaster Response Preparedness Toolkit available at http://ocha.unog.ch/drptoolkit/PNormativeandLegalInstruments.html; the various regional organizations websites listing the

A closer investigation of the various treaties makes it clear that they are far from uniform: they show differences in the terminology used; discrepancies and inconsistencies between individual treaties and different treaty levels (bilateral, regional, universal); different stages of development of the rules regulating international co-operation in disaster prevention and management (very sophisticated and comprehensive rules in Latin America, less detailed legal regulations on the African continent); ongoing confusion and uncertainty about the borders between soft law and positive law (in disaster prevention and management soft law, guidelines and resolutions have a proven record of great influence and importance in orienting the behavior of international actors). Many of these aspects have already attracted the attention of scholars, and increased attention has been paid to developments in IDRL generally.[3]

The areas touched upon in the various treaties are extremely diversified and include issues such as information sharing, creation of early warning mechanisms, regulations for the activation of emergency support, rules governing the entry and exit of goods and human resources, liability, compensation for damages, cost sharing, status of relief workers, assistance to persons with special needs, etc.

In more recent times this trend to codify an increasing number of issues related to emergency operations has received full support and encouragement from the UN Secretary-General Ban Ki-Moon[4] and various regional organizations,[5] and has

(Footnote 2 continued)
relevant agreements adopted in that framework, the websites of the national authorities in charge of disaster management (see for example the data bank of Italian Civil Protection Department listing the bilateral agreements signed by Italy: http://www.protezionecivile.gov.it/jcms/it/accordi_internazionali.wp;jsessionid=97F26DEA445C2A38A66A20869F891FE1); the ECOLEX Databank, operated jointly by FAO, IUCN and UNDEP, providing the most comprehensive, global source of information on environmental law which lists most of the relevant emergency management treaties (http://www.ecolex.org/start.php), including those related to the management of forest fire (more than 30 treaties: on these treaties see also FAO, Forest Protection Working Papers, Legal Frameworks for Forest Fire Management: International Agreements and National Legislation, Follow-up Report to FAO/ITTO International Expert Meeting on Forest Fire Management, March 2001, available at http://www.fao.org/docrep/009/ag044e/ag044e00.htm). All the above mentioned web sites have been accessed on 28 February 2012.

[3] Contributions on the theoretical aspects are cited in the References, at the end of this contribution.

[4] On July 6, 2010 UN Secretary-General Ban Ki-Moon paid an official visit to the International Federation of the Red Cross during which he underlined the importance of IDRL. See: http://www.ifrc.org/docs/news/07/07060801/. Accessed 20 February 2012.

[5] The OAS General Assembly underlined the importance of IDRL in its Resolution 2314, adopted on June 7, 2007, expressing its commitment to 'eliminate obstacles to humanitarian assistance…, with particular emphasis on strengthening the necessary legal framework.' See http://www.oas.org/37ag/english/default.asp. Accessed 28 February 2012.

attracted the attention of the International Federation of the Red Cross, the scientific community, and the International Law Commission.[6]

This is the background for this chapter, which aims to define the major challenges of the present heterogeneous and complex situation and to indicate possible paths to overcome the current contradictions in international disaster response law. Before this can be attempted, some terminology will need to be clarified, as different treaties use identical terms, including technical ones, with sometimes different meanings.

1.2 Definition of Relevant Terms

In a recent article, Isabelle Reinecke stated that IDRL includes '…the body of rules and principles for international humanitarian assistance in the wake of peacetime disasters of natural, technological or industrial origin. …. Unlike IHL, IDRL applies to (usually) unintended disasters in a co-operative peacetime context when states or intergovernmental humanitarian or other organisations offer, request, provide or accept cross-border disaster assistance.'[7] This definition seems only partially satisfactory, as it refers mainly to the acute phase of a disaster and does not include other aspects which have become more and more relevant in recent times, such as the prevention of disaster, disaster risk reduction (DRR), the creation of the environment necessary to implement DRR, as well as those measures which are usually implemented for the early recovery. It is the opinion of the present author that all these aspects should be included in an updated concept of IDRL in which the term "response" has to be interpreted in a more flexible manner to include as well all those activities aimed at preventing the disaster and managing the early recovery activities.

Further clarification is needed for the notion of disaster, which is obviously essential for an accurate profile of IDRL. A closer examination of the content of several conventions makes it possible to argue that the definitions of the term 'disaster,' where provided in the treaties, are almost identical or at least do not differ in any significant manner. One example is the definition contained in the 1998 Tampere Convention on the Provision of Telecommunication Resources for Disaster Mitigation and Relief Operations, whose Article 1(6) states that disaster is

> A serious disruption of the functioning of society, posing a significant, widespread threat to human life, health, property or the environment, whether caused by accident, nature or human activity, and whether developing suddenly or as the result of complex, long-term processes.

---

[6] At its 2006 session the International Law Commission specified the topic Protection of persons in the event of disasters for inclusion in its long-term programme of work. For more on the work carried out so far within the ILC, see Chap. 3 by Zorzi Giustiniani in this volume.

[7] Reinecke 2010, p. 145.

Similar wording is found in the 1997 Agreement between the Republic of Argentina and the Republic of Chile on co-operation in case of catastrophes, according to which disaster/catastrophe is

> any event considered as such by any one Party, which shall produce risks to the life, health, essential services or property of the population, or to the environment.

Finally, the 1994 Agreement by and between the Government of the Finnish Republic and the Government of the Russian Federation about co-operation to avert disasters and to prevent their consequences states that

> 'A disaster is understood to be an industrial accident, an explosion, a fire, a cave-in, an earthquake, a flood, or another comparable event or natural catastrophe, which causes or may cause injury or damage to people, property or the environment'.

The definition of "disaster" adopted by the International Commission clearly confirms this trend, although adding a reference to the consequences of the disaster:

> '"Disaster" means a calamitous event or series of events resulting in widespread loss of life, great human suffering and distress, or large-scale material or environmental damage, thereby seriously disrupting the functioning of society'.[8]

The specific elements of the definition of 'disaster' can, therefore, be summed up in the following manner: (a) it is a man-made or a natural event; (b) its consequences produce risks or cause significant injuries or widespread damage; (c) persons, property, and/or the environment are affected.

This definition implies that the various treaties will also usually be applicable in circumstances where there is no risk or damage to human beings and related property, but the risks or the damage affect solely the environment, which is considered to have an intrinsic worth, needing protection.

Finally, in cases of man-made disasters, the possible deliberate nature of the act or omission triggering the emergency is of no consequence for the application of the relevant treaties. Intentionally caused disasters are treated no differently from those attributable to negligence or to events beyond human control.

Key features of the definition of IDRL are therefore:

(a) *Nature of disasters which are relevant for IDRL*: man-made or natural events the consequences of which produce risks or cause significant injuries or widespread damage to persons, property, or the environment regardless of the intentionality of the act (in the case of a man-made disaster);

---

[8] ILC, Protection of persons in the event of disasters, Draft Articles 1–5, Document A/CN.4/629. See more in Chap. 3 by Zorzi Giustiniani in this volume.

(b) *Phases in response to disasters, regulated by International Disaster Response Law*: IDRL regulates the various phases of a disaster management cycle, including prevention,[9] disaster risk reduction (DRR),[10] and mitigation, the creation of an environment enabling DRR measures,[11] an immediate humanitarian assistance phase (sometimes also defined as rescue or relief),[12] early recovery,[13] recovery (or restoration).[14] The subsequent activities (in a

---

[9] UN 2004: 'Measures to avoid completely the adverse impact of hazards and means to minimize related environmental, technological and biological disasters.'

[10] UNISDR 2009, p. 4: 'Disaster risk reduction (DRR)' refers to the 'concept and practice of reducing disaster risks through systematic efforts to analyze and manage the causal factors of disasters, including through reduced exposure to hazards, lessened vulnerability of people and property, wise management of land and the environment, and improved preparedness for adverse events.'

[11] See more on this concept Chap. 9 by La Vaccara in this volume, as well as Brinkerhoff 2007, p. 86.

[12] According to the Resolution on Humanitarian Assistance adopted by the Institut de Droit International at its Bruges Session, 2 September 2003, humanitarian assistance includes

> All acts, activities and the human and material resources for the provision of goods and services of an exclusively humanitarian character, indispensable for the survival and the fulfillment of the essential needs of the victims of disasters.

[13] In its Guidance Note on Early Recovery, published in 2008, the Cluster Working Group on Early Recovery (CWGER), led by the UNDP Bureau for Crisis Prevention and Recovery, defines 'early recovery' as: 'a multidimensional process of recovery that begins in a humanitarian setting. It is guided by development principles that seek to build on humanitarian programmes and catalyze sustainable development opportunities. It aims to generate self sustaining, nationally owned, resilient processes for post-crisis recovery. It encompasses the restoration of basic services, livelihoods, shelter, governance, security and rule of law, environment and social dimensions, including the reintegration of displaced populations.' The document is available at http://www.undp.org/cpr/iasc/content/docs/CWGER_Tools/Doc1.pdf. Accessed 23 February 2012. More on this in the UNDP Post-Disaster Recovery Guidelines, available at http://www.undp.org/cpr/disred/documents/publications/regions/america/recovery_guidelines_eng.pdf. Accessed 23 February 2012.

[14] A convincing definition of recovery is to be found in the Glossary of the International Recovery Platform (available at http://www.recoveryplatform.org/resources/glossary/R, accessed 23 February 2012), which defines recovery as

> The restoration, and improvement where appropriate, of facilities, livelihoods and living conditions of disaster-affected communities, including efforts to reduce disaster risk factors.
>
> The recovery task of rehabilitation and reconstruction begins soon after the emergency phase has ended, and should be based on pre-existing strategies and policies that facilitate clear institutional responsibilities for recovery action and enable public participation. Recovery programmes, coupled with the heightened public awareness and engagement after a disaster, afford a valuable opportunity to develop and implement disaster risk reduction measures and to apply the 'build back better' principle.

It seems clear and evident that there is significant overlapping between the definitions of early recovery and recovery (which also includes the facilities, livelihood, and living conditions of disaster-affected communities) but this overlapping does not have any concrete consequences.

chronological perspective) such as rehabilitation, or reconstruction,[15] and development are regulated by the general rules of international law and will not receive any special attention in this volume. This comprehensive approach to disaster management, from prevention to reconstruction, has acquired pivotal importance in recent decades, as repeatedly underlined in almost all relevant international forums (intergovernmental, NGO's, academic and scientific community, etc.).[16]

(c) *Issues regulated by IDRL*: IDRL covers a wide array of issues which become relevant during the various phases of a disaster. These issues include: (a) the rules defining the obligation of the States to prevent or mitigate a disaster and to appropriately assist the affected persons and to fight against corruption, which has become a major problem in disaster management activities[17]; (b) the rules regulating the relations between the disaster-affected State and other States or international organizations, including such matters as modality of requesting and offering assistance, status of the personnel sent on a mission, cost sharing, chain of command of a mission, relations with local authorities, liabilities, claims, and compensation regime in an emergency mission, entry and exit of goods and personnel; (c) the rules dealing with the protection of human rights (civil and political as well as economic, social, and cultural rights, the rights of vulnerable groups, and the rights of children).

(d) *Relations with the host State*: generally speaking IDRL is applicable when the State in which the disaster took place (host State), is ready to co-operate with the international community to alleviate the sufferings of those directly affected by the disaster. Only in exceptional cases, when the local State is unable or unwilling to co-operate, the relevance of the consent of the local State to carry out a humanitarian/relief operation diminishes and new rules of IDRL are slowly emerging, closely following the notions of 'responsible sovereignty' and 'responsibility to protect' as they have evolved recently.

(e) *Applicability at particular times*: IDRL governs, as a general rule, disasters occurring in peacetime. While a few treaties regulating specific aspects of the management of disaster contain *ad hoc* rules stating that the treaty is applicable only in peacetime (see for example the 1989 Agreement between

---

[15] The operation and decisions after a disaster and after the previous activities, with the view to restoring to the stricken country, communities, families, and individuals the former living conditions, whilst at the same time encouraging and facilitating the necessary adjustments to the changes caused by the disaster or emergency.

[16] In its Resolution 64/250 of 2010, the UN General Assembly reiterated clearly the need for a continued high level of support for and commitment to the immediate humanitarian relief phase, early recovery, rehabilitation, reconstruction and development efforts, including in the medium and long terms, that reflect the spirit of international solidarity and co-operation in addressing the disaster.

[17] Fenner and Mahlstein 2009, p. 143.

Denmark, Finland, Norway, Sweden on co-operation across State frontiers to prevent or limit damage to persons or property or to the environment in the case of accidents[18]) this is not the case in many other treaties. This raises the sensitive problem of the applicability of IDRL during armed conflicts: although this aspect is complex, there seems to be wide consensus that IDRL does not regulate disasters which are immediate and direct consequences of military activities carried out during wartime; for wartime disasters IHL is the main normative source. However, IDRL remains applicable, at least among those parties to an IDRL treaty which are not involved in the conflict, for the regulation of unintended and indirect consequences of warfare, such as a massive outflow of refugees leaving the country to escape the war.[19] In other words, unless there is a specific convention stating the contrary, multilateral treaties dealing with IDRL remain applicable in time of war among those member States not party to the conflict. Finally, considering the specific architecture of almost all the IDRL treaties, which require an active attitude of the affected State requesting the assistance and a co-operative attitude of the intervening State, it seems obvious that should these two States be at war with each other, almost all of the relevant IDRL treaties will remain suspended in the relations between these States during the war period on the assumption that they are incompatible by their very nature with the situation of war, and the future destiny of the bilateral treaties will be decided at the end of the armed conflict.

In this book careful attention will also be devoted to various issues related to IHL owing to the many gray areas at the borderline between peace and war, and to the fact that some of the principles of IHL must be considered the minimum standard in any situation whatsoever.

(f) *Typology of rules*: IDRL is composed not only by rules codified in international treaties and customary law[20] but also by principles (or soft law). In the specific area of disaster management, soft law principles have acquired a significant importance owing to the special nature of the issues at stake and the way codification of IDRL has developed. Soft law has undoubtedly influenced the codification of IDRL.

---

[18] In the preamble of the Convention it is clearly stated that the parties agreed to sign the Convention

> Being convinced of the need for cooperation between the competent authorities of the Contracting States for the purpose of facilitating the necessary reciprocal assistance *in the case of accidents in peacetime* and of expediting the dispatch of emergency squads and materials (emphasis added).

[19] In similar cases other branches of international law, such as refugees' law, may be also applicable.

[20] For more on this see the Conclusions by Ronzitti in this volume.

1.3 The Codification of IDRL: (a) Bilateral Agreements

The number of bilateral agreements, however labeled,[21] aimed at regulating mutual co-operation in cases of major natural or man-made disaster is extremely high and extends throughout almost all continents. Although in most cases these bilateral treaties have been signed between neighboring States with the aim of establishing effective systems of mutual co-operation between the contracting parties in the event of natural disasters, in several instances treaties have been concluded between States far away from each other. In such cases the treaties are often instrumental in reinforcing the capacity of one State to deal with major disaster through capacity building initiatives sponsored and promoted by the counterpart.[22] In addition, there are an increasing number of bilateral treaties between a State and an international organization.

Bilateral agreements on the issue in question seem very popular in almost all areas of the world, although they are most common in Europe and America and have a lower incidence on the African and Asian continents.

There are various commonalities, and even though the bilateral treaties sometimes present unique features it seems possible to classify them according to their specific characteristics.

The following distinctions can be made in the *typology of disasters regulated* by these treaties:

(a) treaties regulating all kinds of major natural and/or man-made disasters;
(b) treaties restricted to specific kinds of natural disasters, such as forest fire control,[23] earthquakes,[24] etc.;

---

[21] The terms used in the different agreements vary: Treaty, Agreement, Arrangement, Memorandum of Understanding (very popular), Protocol, Administrative MoU, Declarations of intent. With the exception of Declarations of Intent all the other agreements are, from a legal and formal point of view, international agreements, and as such their life is regulated by the 1969 Vienna Convention on the Law of Treaties. The frequent use of the term MoU is very often due to the fact that the agreements are not subject to a specific ratification process, as they usually come into force at the time the MoU is signed.

[22] See for example, the 2007 MoU between Italy and Venezuela on bilateral co-operation in civil protection issues.

[23] See the 1995 Agreement on Joint Control of Forest Fire between China and Russia or the 2001 Wildfire Arrangement between the Department of the Interior and the Department of Agriculture of the USA and the National Rural Fire Authority of New Zealand which is designed to create a regulatory framework enabling the Parties to request wildfire suppression resources from the other contracting Party.

[24] See for example the 2006 MoU between the China Earthquake Administration and the Italian Civil Protection Department on Co-operation in the field of Seismic Risk Mitigation and Emergency Management.

(c) treaties regulating disasters occurring only in very specific and predefined areas (such as, for example, disasters occurring in mountainous areas,[25] maritime disasters affecting the area of the seas or lakes at the border between the two countries, or disasters occurring in the border regions).[26]

As to *the areas of co-operation* regulated in the agreements, it seems possible to establish the following subcategories:

(a) agreements with a wide definition of the areas of co-operation including, for example, risk assessment and reduction, damage and loss assessment, monitoring systems, education and training, emergency management and planning, study of the effects of megacities, engineering and social problems, technological information exchanges, etc.;
(b) agreements with a narrow definition of the areas of co-operation, i.e., treaties devoted only to the preparation of emergency operations in response to a specific disaster, or dealing only with the preparation and execution of projects of scientific and technical co-operation in the area of civil protection.[27]

With regard to modalities regulating *the functioning of the co-operation in an emergency situation*, almost all the treaties under consideration provide an institutional framework for the exchange of information, request of assistance, and mutual assistance. In all cases, however, the request of the affected State is essential for the activation of co-operation. Finally, the request of assistance is, generally speaking, to be presented through diplomatic channels[28] or through the competent national authorities specified in the agreement.[29] A few treaties are so detailed in this respect that they even provide the contact details (including telephone and fax numbers) of the person/office to be called in case assistance is needed.[30]

---

[25] See for example the 2007 Administrative agreement between Italy and France on transboundary co-operation in mountainous areas in situations of emergency (text available at: http://www.protezionecivile.gov.it/resources/cms/documents/Francia_cooptransfrontaliera.pdf). Accessed 15 February 2012.

[26] As an example we can cite the 1999 Wildfire protection Agreement between the Department of Agriculture of the USA and the Secretariat for Environment Natural Resources and Fisheries of the United Mexican States for the common border, and the 2007 Italy–France agreement which is applicable exclusively for events occurring in three Italian regions (Lombardy, Piedmont, and Aosta Valley) and in five French Departments.

[27] 1993 Protocol between the Kingdom of Spain and the Republic of Portugal regarding technical co-operation and mutual assistance in Civil Protection.

[28] 1977 Agreement between Argentina and Chile on co-operation in cases of catastrophes; 1970 Agreement on Mutual Assistance between the French and Monegasque relief and civil defence services.

[29] 2001 Wildfire Arrangement between the Department of the Interior and the Department of Agriculture of the USA and the National Rural Fire Authority of New Zealand.

[30] See for example the 2007 Italy–France Administrative MoU on cross border co-operation in emergency situations in mountainous areas.

Once the request has been issued it is quite usual that *the chain of command of the operation* is regulated as follows:

> The operations shall be directed by the authorities of the territory where the catastrophe takes place, nevertheless the assisting teams though acknowledging their objectives and missions to the Chief of Expedition, will act under their original superiors.[31]

Another topic which is usually dealt with in the bilateral agreements concerns the sensitive issue of the *division of the costs associated to the deployment and functioning of an emergency mission.* The content of the rules at this regard varies significantly and the following models of cost repartition or sharing can be traced:

(a) the sending State is responsible for all the costs,[32]
(b) the receiving/host State has to pay back all the expenses incurred by the sending State providing the operation,[33]
(c) costs are shared between the sending State and the host nation according to pre-defined rules,[34]

---

[31] Article 3.7 of the 1993 Protocol between the Kingdom of Spain and the Portuguese Republic regarding technical co-operation and mutual assistance in the field of civil defense.

[32] 1999 Wildfire Protection Agreement between the Department of the Interior and the Department of Agriculture of the United States of America and the Secretariat of Environment, Natural Resources, and Fisheries of the United Mexican States for the common border; 1970 Agreement on Mutual Assistance between the French and Monegasque relief and civil defense services.

[33] 2001 Wildfire Arrangement between the Department of the Interior and the Department of Agriculture of the USA and the National Rural Fire Authority of New Zealand; 1994 Agreement by and between the government of the Finnish Republic and the government of the Russian Federation on co-operation to avert disasters and to prevent their consequences. Article 12 of this agreement states that 'The assistance requesting contracting party shall compensate the assistance giving contracting party for the costs caused by the assistance, including the expenses of medical care, unless agreed differently by the contracting parties in view of the nature and proportions of the disaster. The assistance requesting contracting party may cancel their request for the assistance at any time. In that case, the assistance giving party is entitled to compensation for the costs caused to them. If not agreed differently between the contracting parties, the costs shall be compensated immediately after the assistance giving contracting party has demanded this to the assistance requesting party.'

[34] In the 1997 agreement between Argentina and Chile on co-operation in case of catastrophes, for example, the sending State will take care of the transportation cost for the mission, while the receiving State will be responsible for all the local costs. Similar terms are also used in the drafting of Article 5 of the 1962 Agreement on Mutual Assistance between French and Luxemburg Fire and Emergency Services and Article 4 of the Agreement of 14 July 1959 on mutual assistance between the French and Spanish services against fire and assistance. Article 4 of the Spain-Morocco Agreement on technical co-operation and mutual assistance in civil protection states that 'The expense of furnishing the assistance equipment and materials during the operations, shall be covered by the Assisted Party. The Assisted Party shall cover the expense of maintenance or substitutions due to loss, destruction or deterioration of aircraft, ground vehicles or assistance materials caused as a consequence of the rescue operations.'

(d) each State covers its own costs.[35]

The cost sharing model (c) is used much more frequently than the other models.

Several bilateral treaties devote special attention to another very sensitive aspect related to *liabilities, claims, and compensation regime in an emergency mission.* The rules devoted to this specific topic are, once more, fairly diverse, although there is a trend to provide very specific rules limiting the liability of the sending State and to regulate the topic in a very detailed manner.[36] Only in a very limited number of treaties is the assisting party considered fully responsible for any illegal act of its personnel arising as a consequence of assistance after catastrophes.[37] More frequently treaty rules provide that:

- each party waives its claims against the other party for compensation in the case of death occurring as a consequence of the assistance[38];
- any damage to a third party caused as a consequence of the assistance, will be covered by the assisted party, even in case of human and technical error;

---

[35] 1999 Memorandum of Understanding between the Government of the Republic of Ghana and the Government of the Province of British Columbia.

[36] As an example of an extremely detailed manner of regulating the issue under discussion, please refer to the 2001 Wildfire Arrangement between the Department of the Interior and the Department of Agriculture of the USA and the National Rural Fire Authority of New Zealand.

[37] Article of the 1997 Agreement between Argentina and Chile on co-operation in case of catastrophes.

[38] In several cases, the treaties even provide for total immunity from civil and criminal jurisdiction for the members of the international missions: see for example the 1997 Agreement between Argentina and Chile on co-operation in case of catastrophes as well as the 1994 Agreement between the Government of the Finnish Republic and the Government of the Russian Federation about Co-operation to avert disasters and to prevent their consequences whose Article 13 reads as follows: 'Both contracting parties waive all demands for compensation from the other contracting party on account of a death or a bodily injury, or for other damages caused to the health of their experts or other personnel, or to their personal property, if these events have taken place while carrying out duties relating to the implementation of this Agreement. The assistance giving contracting party shall take out insurance, according to the regulations effective in their country, for their personnel taking part in the assistance operation. The insurance costs are included in the general costs for the assistance and the assistance requesting contracting party shall pay them as provided for in this Agreement. If a member of the assistance giving party's relief team, while carrying out duties relating to the implementation of this Agreement, should cause damage to a third party in the territory of the assistance requesting state, the assistance requesting contracting party shall pay the damages under the legislative provisions that would be applied if the damage had been caused by their own relief troops. The assistance requesting contracting party shall have the right of recourse to file a lawsuit for any compensation, paid under this article, against a member of the relief team who has caused the damage intentionally or by gross negligence. The contracting parties' competent authorities shall exchange pertinent information about the situation in which the damage referred to in this article took place.'

- any damage to a third party during the transport of the means of assistance, will be covered by the party in whose territory the accident occurred and
- the assisting party will only be responsible in the case of criminal negligence.[39]

Another set of rules which is quite commonly found in the bilateral treaties under consideration is devoted *to border crossing of persons*, which might represent a major issue during disaster management activities. In several treaties, including almost all those dealing with co-operation in fire prevention and management, there are detailed rules regulating cross border movement of emergency personnel. In most cases, the parties are required to undertake all reasonable steps to facilitate entry and exit from their territory, without entry fees[40] and without payment of any duties or taxes. The authorities of both parties must ensure prompt opening of their respective borders for assistance whenever required. Both parties shall seek practical means of opening alternative temporary border crossing points to facilitate the assistance to the receiving party, as well as border crossings in zones without a permanent frontier customs house.[41] Sometimes, special categories of emergency personnel are even allowed to cross the border without passports and residence permits.[42] Only in very special cases, and when the treaty is between States which do not have a significant tradition of mutual co-operation, the rules provide that if the emergency staff needs to cross borders it shall observe the formalities, in accordance with bilateral agreements and the respective current laws of both parties.[43]

As far as the *free movement of emergency equipment and goods* is concerned, the treaties foresee generally that the parties are obliged to undertake all reasonable steps and use their best efforts, within applicable laws and internal regulations, to facilitate the admission of all supplies, aircraft, vehicles, specialized machinery, or other equipment whether owned or contracted, that are used or intended for use in a disaster management operation[44] without payment of any duties or taxes imposed by reason of importation.[45] In a limited number of treaties,

39 1992 Spain-Morocco Agreement on technical co-operation and mutual assistance in civil protection: Article 4.

40 1997 Agreement between Argentina and Chile on co-operation in case of catastrophes.

41 1992 Spain–Morocco Agreement on technical co-operation and mutual assistance in civil protection: Article 2.

42 1992 Spain–Morocco Agreement on technical co-operation and mutual assistance in civil protection: Article 2.5.

43 Article II. 5 of the 1995 Agreement of Joint Control on Forest Fire between the Government of the People's Republic of China and the Government of the Russian Federation.

44 Article VI of the 1999 Wildfire protection agreement between the Department of the Interior and the Department of Agriculture of the United States of America and the Secretariat of Environment, Natural Resources, and Fisheries of the United Mexican States for the common border.

45 1955 USA and Korea Relief Supplies and Equipment: Duty-Free Entry and Exemption From Internal Taxation Agreement. Article VI of the 1999 Wildfire protection agreement between the Department of the Interior and the Department of Agriculture of the United States of America and

however, the regulations of the import and re-export of emergency equipment are much stricter: in the 1994 Agreement by and between the Government of the Finnish Republic and the Government of the Russian Federation concerning co-operation to avert disasters and to prevent their consequences, it is stated that it is not permitted to bring into the country equipment or materials, the importing of which into the country is forbidden, except if specifically agreed case by case, and that a complete list, signed by the team leader, of the relief team's equipment and relief supplies shall be submitted to the customs authorities. *Ad hoc* rules are sometimes formulated to regulate the importing and re-exporting of medical first-aid kits carried by the relief teams.[46]

Another aspect which emerges from the examination of bilateral agreements is the new attitude by States to promoting and enhancing co-operation in matters relating to disaster management among local authorities. In Europe, the legal framework to develop co-operation among local authorities is offered by the 1980 European Outline Convention on Transfrontier Co-operation between Territorial Communities or Authorities promoted by the Council of Europe. On the basis of this convention a significant number of bilateral agreements have been signed by border towns and regions all over Europe, but especially along the border between Germany and the Benelux countries.[47] Very often these agreements have proved quite effective, promoting the sharing of experiences at the local level, raising awareness among the population and, should an emergency occur, delivering timely assistance.

Finally, it should be mentioned that in recent decades a new trend may be observed in the nature of the parties to bilateral agreements. If in the past these treaties were signed among States, in recent times there are an increasing number of bilateral agreements between a State and an international organizations (be it regional or universal). As an example of this trend we can quote the 2006 Scientific Co-operation Agreement on Co-operation in Hydro-Meteorological

(Footnote 45 continued)
the Secretariat of Environment, Natural Resources, and Fisheries of the United Mexican States for the common border.

[46] Should they include medical preparations which contain narcotics, the leaders of the relief teams must report these to the customs officials who shall allow their free entry into the country. Such preparations may only be used by the competent medical staff of the assistance giving contracting party in accordance with the legislation of the assistance giving contracting party. At the termination of the rescue operations, the remaining preparations which contain narcotics shall be taken out of the country and a consumption report, signed by the team leader and the doctor, shall be submitted to the customs; this report shall specify the consumption of the preparations and it must be certified by a representative of the assistance requesting party's competent authority: see more in Article 4 of the 1994 Agreement by and between the Government of the Finnish Republic and the Government of the Russian Federation about co-operation to avert disasters and to prevent their consequences.

[47] See more on this in The Netherlands Red Cross 2010. Several studies on these typologies of agreements among local authorities, especially in Europe, have been carried out by the IFRC and are available at: http://www.ifrc.org/en/what-we-do/idrl/research-tools-and-publications/country-and-regional-studies/. Accessed 10 February 2012.

Monitoring, Natural Disaster Prevention and Early Warning between Italy and the Caribbean Community (CARICOM)[48] or the 1998 Agreement between Italy and the UN Economic Commission for Latin America on Disaster Prevention in Latin America and in the Caribbean aimed at providing financial support to various specific activities in the area of disaster prevention and mitigation.

1.4 The Codification of IDRL: (b) Regional and Subregional Agreements

It has often been suggested that there be better regional regulations to increase the efficacy and efficiency of disaster prevention and management activities. A strong boost to further develop regional and subregional co-operation in disaster management was given by the World Conference on Disaster Reduction held in Kobe Japan in January 2005 and the 'Hyogo Framework of Action: Building the Resilience of Nations and Communities to Disasters' that was adopted at the Conference by the 168 participating States. The Hyogo Framework for Action requested regional organizations to undertake several specific tasks, one of them being precisely 'to support the development of regional mechanisms and capacities for early warning to disasters, including tsunami….'

These regional agreements have become popular on almost all continents except Africa. The level of co-operation and the institutional architecture provided in these regional treaties vary significantly, however. This suggests that we should briefly describe the regional and subregional treaties and mechanisms and, especially in those areas where there are no formal treaties, present the current political initiatives which might be a prelude to the codification of future treaties. To do so it might be wise to start with the agreements covering the entire American continent, as this region has been very proactive in this matter, and then to examine the treaties applicable on other continents. At the end of this paragraph we will then make a few general remarks on emerging trends in the regional codification of IDRL.

1.4.1 American Continent: Continental-Level Agreements

Under the auspices of the Organization of American States, the Inter-American Convention to Facilitate Disaster Assistance, a specific agreement covering the

---

[48] This Agreement, which is no longer in force, was aimed at preparing a joint feasibility study in preparation for the development of a project proposal for donor financing toward the establishment of a modern hydro-meteorological monitoring system with real time transmission of data for the benefit of CARICOM and its member States.

entire continent, was signed as early as 1991. This comprehensive convention, which becomes applicable whenever a State party furnishes assistance in response to a request from another State party, contains very detailed rules regulating the modalities of requesting, offering, and accepting assistance, names the relevant national authorities, confirms that unless otherwise agreed, the overall direction, control, co-ordination, and supervision of the assistance within its territory shall be the sole responsibility of the assisted State. It regulates the entry of personnel and goods, establishes the *status* of the emergency workers sent to another country, and provides a framework for claims and compensation for losses and damages caused by the international operation. Finally, a specific rule states that in general terms the assistance shall be provided at the expense of the assisting State, without cost to the assisted State, except where these States agree otherwise. The Convention is drafted in a fairly innovative manner (considering that is was signed in 1991), and its various rules have influenced subsequent international practice. It is unfortunate, however, that only five member States of OAS have ratified the Convention[49] which came into force in 1996 (5 years after it was signed). The limited number of ratifications may be considered one of the reasons why subregional agreements on this issue have proliferated on the American continent.

Caribbean and Central American regions. The Caribbean region, being an area which frequently suffers major natural disasters, was among the first[50] to be actively involved in creating and developing regional mechanisms and structures to deal with natural and man-made disasters. As early as 1981, a Pan Caribbean Disaster Preparedness and Prevention Project was launched in Costa Rica to increase interest in and awareness of the threat of hazards and the potential of low-cost mitigation measures.[51] Later, in 1991, the countries of the region concluded the 1991 Agreement establishing the Caribbean Disaster Emergency Response Agency (CDEMA) as a response to the need to complement the initiatives of the Pan Caribbean Disaster Preparedness and Prevention Project. The 1991 agreement, which creates several new internal bodies aimed at reinforcing the co-operation,[52] provides extremely detailed rules for

(a) making an immediate and co-ordinated response by means of emergency disaster relief to an affected Participating State;
(b) securing, co-ordinating, and channeling to interested intergovernmental and non-governmental organizations reliable and comprehensive information on disasters affecting a Participating State;
(c) mobilizing and co-ordinating disaster relief from governmental and non-governmental organizations for affected Participating States;

[49] Dominican Republic, Nicaragua, Panama, Peru, and Uruguay are the States which have ratified the 1991 Convention.

[50] See more in Poncelet 1997, p. 267.

[51] Poncelet 1997, p. 269.

[52] The bodies created in the Agreement are the following: (a) The Council (b) The Board of Directors (c) The Coordinating Unit.

(d) mitigating or eliminating, as far as practicable, the immediate consequences of disasters in Participating States;
(e) promoting the establishment, enhancement, and maintenance on a sustainable basis adequate emergency disaster response capabilities among the Members of the Agency.

While most of the treaty's obligations on members concern the improvement of the national early warning and recovery systems, Article 13(s) indicates that States are also requested 'to identify, maintain in a state of readiness and make available immediately on request by the Co-ordinator relevant material and human resources in the event of disaster.'

The agreement also regulates the sending of an early recovery mission to the host nation upon a formal request for assistance, the sharing of the cost of providing assistance,[53] the privileges and immunities of the sending State and personnel, the transit of personnel, and the issue of claims and compensation.

A few years later, in 1999, an additional agreement between the Member States and associate members of the Association of the Caribbean States for regional co-operation was signed in Santo Domingo (Dominican Republic): this treaty set up a quite complex institutional structure and reiterated provisions already codified in the previous agreement. It also introduced the innovative concept of Highly Vulnerable Areas, to be identified in all the Member States according to a specific procedure. Owing to their particular situation, these areas will receive special attention and increased co-operation from the participating States.

Considering the specific needs and problems of the area, which is surrounded by the sea, a new Convention for the Protection and Development of the Marine Environment of the Wider Caribbean Region was signed in Cartagena de Indias (Colombia) in 1993. On the basis of this agreement, the contracting parties are requested to co-operate in taking all necessary measures to respond to pollution emergencies in the Convention area, whatever the cause of such emergencies, and to control, reduce, or eliminate resulting pollution or the threat of pollution. Should a contracting party become aware of cases in which the Convention area has been polluted or is in imminent danger of being polluted, it shall immediately notify other States likely to be affected by such pollution, as well as the competent international organizations. Furthermore, it shall inform, as soon as feasible, such other States and competent international organizations of measures it has taken to minimize or reduce pollution or the threat of pollution.

There are two other relevant actors actively involved in the institutional structure in the Caribbean region aimed at disaster prevention and management.

One is *the CRID (Regional Disaster Information Center)* a co-ordination and intersectoral collaborative platform for disaster information management located in San Jose, Costa Rica, sponsored by six organizations that decided to join forces

[53] Article 19 of the Agreement states that 'Except as may otherwise be agreed between them, the expenses incurred by a sending State in providing assistance to a requesting State shall be defrayed by the sending State.'

to ensure the compilation and dissemination of disaster-related information in Latin America and the Caribbean. The CRID goals are to

- improve compilation, processing, and dissemination of disaster-related information, offering quality information services to a wide range of users in Latin America and the Caribbean Region;
- strengthen subregional (Central America, South America, and the Caribbean), national and local capacities to establish and maintain disaster information and documentation centers;
- promote the use of electronic technology for the provision of information services;
- contribute to the development of the Regional Disaster Information System.

The other is *the Co-ordination Center for Natural Disaster Prevention in Central America (CEPREDENAC)* operating at a subregional level (Central America). Based on an agreement promoted in the framework of the Sistema de la Integración Centroamericana (SICA), the Center aims at strengthening the subregional co-operation in the prevention and management of natural disasters, while reinforcing the resilience of the local population and the effectiveness of intrastate co-operation. Although the agreement does not impose detailed obligations on the parties, it does create a sophisticated organizational structure which includes about six different institutions (from the Council of the member States to the Executive Secretariat).

Andean subregion. In July 2002, the Andean Council of Ministers[54] created the Comité Andino para la Prevención y Atención de Desastres (CAPRADE), as an instrument to contribute to the reduction of risk and the impact of natural and man-made disasters in the territories of the Andean subregion. The means include political co-ordination and lobbying, strategy and planning, the promotion of disaster prevention, mitigation, preparedness, relief, and reconstruction, as well as facilitating co-operation, mutual assistance, and exchange of experience in this area. A few years later the Comité Andino adopted its Internal Rules[55] which regulate in a detailed manner the tasks and working methodologies of the Committee.

MERCOSUR subregion. In July 2004, in Iguazu, the member States of MERCOSUR signed the Protocolo Adicional al Acuerdo Marco sobre Medio Ambiente del MERCOSUR en Materia de Cooperación y Asistencia Frente a Emergencias Ambientales[56] which contains very precise rules regulating all

[54] Decision 529 of July 7, 2002 of the Andean Council of Foreign Ministers.

[55] The Reglamento interno del Comité Andino para la prevenciòn y atención de desastres (CAPRADE) is available at http://www.caprade.org/caprade/index.php?option=com_content&view=article&id=25. Accessed 22 February 2012.

[56] The text is available at http://www.mre.gov.py/dependencias/tratados/mercosur/registro%20mercosur/Acuerdos/2004/español/71.%20Protocolo%20Adicional%20al%20Acuerdo%20Marco%20sobre%20Medio%20Ambiente%20del%20Mercosur%20-%20Emergencias%20Ambientales.pdf. Accessed 23 February 2012.

aspects of disaster management (from prevention to early recovery and reconstruction). It is most unfortunate that so far the protocol has not come into force, as only two States (Argentina and Paraguay) have ratified it. However, in this region the institutional structures to promote co-ordination in disaster management include the meeting of the ministers of MERCOSUR member States in charge of Civil Protection, Humanitarian Affairs, and Risk Management (Reunión Especializada de Reducción de Riesgos de Desastres Socionaturales, la Defensa Civil, la Protección Civil y la Asistencia Humanitaria del MERCOSUR——REHU).

Co-ordination structures in Latin America among the various subregional institutions/mechanisms. In order to improve the synergetic approach and exchange of information among the various bodies active on these issues in Latin America, a special forum has been created: the Foro de coordinaciòn y cooperacion de los mecanismos Sub-regionales de Gestiòn del Riesgo de Desasters de la Amerìca which brings together the four existing subregional mechanism: Comitê Andino para a Prevenção e Atenção aos Desastres (CAPRADE), the Centro de Coordinación para la Prevención de los Desastres Naturales en América Central (CEPREDENAC), the Agencia Caribeña para el Manejo de los Desastres y la Emergencia (CDEMA), and the Reunión Especializada de Reducción de Riesgos de Desastres Socionaturales, la Defensa Civil, la Protección Civil y la Asistencia Humanitaria del MERCOSUR (REHU).

1.4.2 Arctic and Antarctic Regions

Considering the particular situation of the Arctic region and its very delicate environmental equilibrium, together with the constant increase in human activity in this area and the effects of the global warming which will allow navigation in part of the Arctic waters, the eight Arctic Nations (United States, Canada, Russia, Denmark, Iceland, Sweden, Finland, and Norway), agreed in 2011 to sign a brand new agreement on Co-operation on Aeronautical and Maritime Search and Rescue in the Arctic.[57] This agreement establishes areas where each state will take responsibility for search and rescue operations in the event of an accident or natural or man-made disaster. Specific rules define the responsibilities of the States and the mechanisms for activating co-operation; they also describe the modalities of conducting search and rescue operations. This treaty is the forerunner of another treaty, for which negotiations have just started in the framework of the recently created Emergency Prevention, Preparedness, and Response (EPPR) Working Group of the Arctic Council. This WG has been given two tasks which are relevant to our discussion: to develop an international instrument on Arctic marine oil pollution preparedness and response, and to develop a set of recommendations or best practices in the area of prevention of marine oil pollution.

[57] The text of the Agreement is available at http://arctic-council.org/filearchive/Arctic_SAR_Agreement_EN_FINAL_for_signature_21-Apr-2011.pdf. Accessed 23 February 2012.

As to the Antarctic region, the 1991 Protocol on Environmental Protection to the Antarctic Treaty contains a specific article devoted to emergency response actions, which clearly defines the obligations of the Parties should an environmental emergency occur in the area concerned.[58]

1.4.3 Asia

As Asia is a region which regularly suffers natural disasters of different kinds, regional organizations in Asia have promoted significant instruments and mechanisms to reinforce co-operation in the area of disaster management. The main achievement has been, so far, the creation in 1998 of the Asian Disaster Reduction Centre located in Kobe, Hyogo prefecture.[59] Its mission is to enhance disaster resilience of the 29 member countries (from Armenia to Papua New Guinea),[60] to build safe communities, and to create a society where sustainable development is possible. Another instrument which has proved to be quite successful at the Asian continental level is the biennial Asian Ministerial Conference on Disaster Risk Reduction (AMCDRR): meetings of this Conference have been held since 2005 and are open to participation by national governments, international interested institutions and other stakeholders, including representatives of relevant NGO and Civil Society organizations, and have been effective in promoting public awareness of the need for increased co-operation and speeding up the preparation of national action plans.

South-East Asia subregion. Subregions of Asia have been much more active in this area than the Asian continent as a whole. The Association of South-East Asian Nations (ASEAN) decided in 2003 to create, first of all, the Committee on Disaster Management (ACDM) as a tool to strengthen the previous forms of regional co-operation, which were fairly vague. The ACDM consists of heads of national agencies responsible for disaster management of ASEAN Member Countries and assumes overall responsibility for co-ordinating and implementing regional activities. One of the major results achieved by the ACDM has been the launching of an ASEAN Regional Programme on Disaster Management (ARPDM) to provide a framework for co-operation and to create a platform for co-operation and collaboration between ASEAN and other relevant international organizations, such as the Pacific Disaster Centre, the United Nations Office for Co-ordination of Humanitarian Affairs (OCHA), UN High Commissioner for Refugees (UNHCR), UNICEF, IFRC, Asian Disaster Preparedness Centre (ADPC), etc.

---

[58] See Article 15 of the Protocol.

[59] See more at: http://www.adrc.asia/aboutus/index.html. Accessed 23 February 2012.

[60] Armenia, Azerbaijan, Bangladesh, Bhutan, Cambodia, China, India, Indonesia, Japan, Kazakhstan, Kyrgyz, Laos PDR, Malaysia, Maldives, Mongolia, Myanmar, Nepal, Pakistan, Papua New Guinea, Philippines, Republic of Korea, Russian Federation, Singapore, Sri Lanka, Tajikistan, Thailand, Uzbekistan, Viet Nam, Yemen.

The signing of the ASEAN Agreement on Disaster Management and Emergency Response in 2005 represented another major achievement in that area with the objective of providing an

> effective mechanisms to achieve substantial reduction of disaster losses in lives and in the social, economic and environmental assets of the Parties, and to jointly respond to disaster emergencies through concerted national efforts and intensified regional and international co-operation.

To this end, the Agreement, which came into force in 2009 after having been ratified by all ten ASEAN member States, provides detailed rules concerning disaster prevention, preparedness, obligations of member States, national and joint emergency response, privileges and immunities to be given to relief workers, management of claims, burden sharing, etc. All these rules seem similar to those codified in other regional treaties. The treaty contains two notable innovations: first of all, in order to ensure preparedness for effective response, the Agreement provides for the establishment of the ASEAN Standby Arrangements for Disaster Relief and Emergency Response (Article 9). On a voluntary basis, each party earmarks assets and capacities available for the regional standby arrangements for disaster relief and emergency response, such as emergency response/search and rescue directories, military and civilian assets, emergency stockpiles of disaster relief items, and disaster management expertise and technologies. This mechanism aims to identify and, at a later stage, mobilize available assets and capacities for disaster management. To achieve this goal, an online inventory has been created, giving the focal points of the ASEAN Committee on Disaster Management (ACDM) rapid access to all the needed information and provides a clear picture of the resources ASEAN Member States could make available for an emergency operation.

The second innovative element of the Treaty is the decision to create an ASEAN Co-ordinating Centre for Humanitarian Assistance for the purpose of facilitating co-operation and co-ordination not only among the ASEAN Member States, but with relevant United Nations and international organizations.

South Asia subregion. Developments similar to those occurring in the ASEAN region have also been taking place in South Asia, where the South Asian Association for Regional Co-operation (SAARC), which groups several States of that region, most of which suffered serious consequences of natural and man-made disasters.[61] As has been noted,

> Six out of eight member states of SAARC are located, partly or fully, on the Himalayas and its associated ranges, which are still adjusting to tectonic movements. This had triggered some of the worst earthquakes and the probability of even more disastrous earthquakes poses a grave threat to human lives, livelihoods and infrastructure in the region.

---

[61] Afghanistan, Bangladesh, Bhutan, India, Maldives, Nepal, Pakistan, and Sri Lanka are the member States of SAARC.

> The Himalayas have the largest deposits of glaciers outside the polar region, which are melting due to climate change. The immediate consequence has been the increasing incidence of flash floods, glacial lake outburst floods and riverine floods.... South Asia's long coastline faces cyclonic storms, storm surge and inundation regularly.[62]

For the appropriate management of these events, the SAARC Disaster Management Centre (SDMC) was set up in October 2006 at the premises of National Institute of Disaster Management in New Delhi. The Centre has the mandate to serve member countries of SAARC by providing policy advice and facilitating capacity building services including strategic learning, research, training, system development, and exchange of information for effective disaster risk reduction and management in South Asia. The Centre conducts studies and research, organizes workshops and training programs, publishes its reports and documents, and provides various policy advisory services to the member countries. The Centre has promoted the creation of the South Asian Disaster Knowledge Network (SADKN), which provides information on disaster risk management in South Asia. Its web portal is a valuable common platform for sharing knowledge and information among the multiple stakeholders of the member countries of the SAARC on the multidisciplinary and multisectoral issues of disaster management.[63]

Finally, the SAARC has been working on an agreement outlining a Natural Disaster Rapid Response Mechanism. The agreement, which has been negotiated under the auspices of the SAARC Disaster Management Centre, provides for the establishment of a disaster response division and an emergency operation unit at the Centre. It has been signed in Addu City, the Maldives, on 11 November 2011 during the Seventeenth Summit of the South Asian Association for Regional Co-operation.

Central Asia subregion. In central Asia, the only subregional organization actively involved in promoting co-operation in disaster management is the Economic Co-operation Organization (ECO), an intergovernmental regional organization which brings together Iran, Pakistan, Afghanistan, Azerbaijan, Kazakhstan, Kyrgyzstan, Tajikistan, Turkmenistan, Uzbekistan and Turkey for the purpose of promoting economic, technical, and cultural co-operation among its member states. Article II of the 1996 Izmir Treaty establishing ECO specified the objective of 'facilitating cooperation in the fields of ecological and environmental protection within the region,' among the many objectives of the organization. Using this as their legal basis, at their Ninth Summit in Baku in 2006 ECO leaders called for regional programmes for early warning and practical steps for disaster preparedness. Since

---

[62] Message from H.E. Uz. Fathimath Dhiyana Saeed, Secretary-General of SAARC, at the InterGovernmental Meeting to Finalize the Draft SAARC Agreement on Rapid Response to Natural Disasters - Maldives, 25–26 May 2011, available at http://www.saarc-sec.org/2011/05/25/news/Message-from-H.E.-Uz.-Fathimath-Dhiyana-Saeed-Secretary-General-of-SAARC–at-the-Inter-Governmental-Meeting-to-Finalize-the-Draft-SAARC-Agreement-on-Rapid-Response-to-Natural-Disasters—Maldives-25-26-May-2011/60/. Accessed 10 February 2012.

[63] See for more info on the Center: http://saarc-sadkn.org/about.aspx. Accessed 10 February 2012.

then, ECO has organized several conferences and workshops, and a Memorandum of Understanding between ECO and UN/ISDR was signed in 1997.[64]

The Regional Centre for Risk Management of disasters caused by natural hazards is another potentially interesting initiative affiliated to ECO. The Centre was established in Mashhad in 2007 by the Government of Iran to develop early warning mechanisms, to monitor disaster caused by natural hazards, weather and environmental conditions, and to help member states in capacity- building. Unfortunately, the centre has not yet been as active as expected.

The five core Central Asian States have nevertheless been trying to improve co-operation among themselves. In 1998, they signed a Co-operation Agreement for Prevention and Liquidation of Emergencies. This was to include 'a range of activities carried out well in advance, aimed at reducing to the maximum possible extent the risk of an emergency as well as preserving human health, reducing the extent of environmental damage and material losses in case an emergency occurs.'

In addition, representatives of Azerbaijan, Iran, Kazakhstan, the Russian Federation, and Turkmenistan met in Tehran in 2003, and agreed on the text of the Framework Convention for the Protection of the Marine Environment of the Caspian Sea; Article 13 is specifically devoted to the management of environmental emergencies.

Finally, according to a recent ESCAP report, three States in the region, Kyrgyzstan, Tajikistan, and Uzbekistan met in Osh in Kyrgyzstan in 2008 and 2009 to reach a common understanding and co-operate on a number of disaster concerns. They agreed to:

> 'Establish early warning systems;
> Make or revise inter-state agreements between the customs offices, ministries of internal affairs, and border security forces;
> Train professional search-and-rescue teams;
> Exchange information, including hydro-meteorological data;
> Establish a working group for disaster risk management for the Ferghana Valley.'[65]

West Asia and Arab States. So far the West Asia subregion has not been actively involved in promoting reinforced forms of co-operation at subregional level, although there are ongoing efforts, especially by the Gulf Co-operation Council, to create a Disaster Centre. In 2008, the Arab League signed a Memorandum of Understanding (MoU) between the General Secretariat of the League of Arab States and the United Nations International Strategy for Disaster Reduction (UNISDR), and approved the creation of the Arab Academy for Science, Technology, and Maritime Transport (AASTMT). The tasks given to the new centre are quite ambitious: promoting integration of DRR in regional and national sustainable

---

[64] Text available at: http://www.ecosecretariat.org/. Accessed 15 February 2012.

[65] UN Economic and Social Commission for Asia and the Pacific, The Asia-Pacific Disaster Report, 2010, Protecting Development Gains, Reducing Disaster Vulnerability and Building Resilience in Asia and the Pacific, available at http://www.unescap.org/idd/pubs/Asia–PacificDisaster-Report%20-2010.pdf. Accessed 23 February 2012.

development policies, strategies and plans; enhancing regional and national capacities in the field of DRR research, education, and training; contributing to the development and harmonization of regional DRR methodologies and tools, including databases and guidelines; promoting networking and partnership building with a multistakeholder approach to accelerate the implementation of the Hyogo Framework of Action.[66]

Another important part of the League of Arab States structure devoted to the management of disaster is the decision to establish a Regional Early Warning system for drought monitoring and forecasting by the Arab Centre for the Studies of Arid Zones and Dry Lands (ACSAD), which has become a major tool supporting regional and country activities on climate change adaptation strategies, food security and land use, and planning.

Finally, it should be noted that special efforts have been carried out in this region to protect the marine environment from pollution: in the 1978 Kuwait Regional Convention for Co-operation on the Protection of the Marine Environment from Pollution there are special rules dealing with pollution emergencies.[67]

1.4.4 Pacific Islands

In the Pacific islands there have been a few relevant initiatives; they have been mainly at the political level and have not led to the conclusion of an international treaty. Nevertheless, it seems appropriate to mention briefly the main ongoing initiatives, as they reflect the level of awareness and interest of the States in the region.

The Pacific island countries have developed a regional framework for disaster risk management known as 'An Investment for Sustainable Development in the Pacific Island Countries—Disaster Risk Reduction and Disaster Management A Framework for Action 2005–2015: Building the Resilience of Nations and Communities to Disasters.' One of the first concrete outcomes of this new framework was the creation of the Pacific Disaster Risk Management Partnership Network. The Network was launched in February 2006, by Pacific Islands GeoScience Commission (SOPAC) with the support of several regional development partners. The main aim of the Network is to strengthen Pacific Island Countries in the development and implementation of DRM National Action Plans (NAP).

The Alliance of Small Island States (AOSIS) has done valuable work in actively promoting the specific needs of Small Island developing States (SIDS) within the United Nations system. AOSIS is a coalition of small islands and low-lying coastal countries that share similar development challenges and concerns about the environment, especially their vulnerability to the adverse effects of global climate change.[68]

---

[66] More on the Centre at: http://www.rcdrr.org. Accessed 23 February 2012.

[67] See Article IX of the 1978 Kuwait Convention.

[68] For more details visit: http://www.sidsnet.org/aosis/about.html. Accessed 23 February 2012.

1.4.5 The African Continent and its Subregions

As in the case of the Pacific islands region, the African continent has not (yet) been very active in promoting regional or subregional legal instruments to promote a wider and deeper co-operation in the prevention and management of natural and man-made disasters. The sole exception is the question of marine pollution, which is among the few topics to have received significant attention and to have been regulated by several regional treaties, most of which contain a specific rule to deal with emergency situations.[69] As in the Pacific region, the emphasis on the African continent has been at the political level, and there are several interesting documents which clearly prove the increasing awareness in Africa of addressing disaster management issues. As early as 2003–2004, the first African Regional Strategy for Disaster Risk Reduction (the African strategy) was developed by the African Union, together with the NEPAD Secretariat and with the support of several institutional partners. The Strategy was favorably noted by the 2004 African Union Summit, which called for the formulation of the Programme of Action for the Implementation of the Africa Strategy (2005–2010). On the basis of this request, the African Ministers responsible for disaster risk management held the first AU Ministerial Conference on Disaster Risk Reduction (DRR) in December 2005 and developed the African Programme of Action for DRR, which was later approved by the AU Executive Council, in Khartoum, Sudan, in December 2005.[70] After a long period of silence, the issue was once more placed among the main priorities on the agenda, and a Second AU Ministerial Conference in Disaster Risk Reduction was convened in Kenya in April 2010. It approved an Extended Programme of Action for the Implementation of the Africa Regional Strategy for Disaster Risk Reduction (2006–2015). The AU Executive Council meeting in 2010 fully endorsed that extended programme and requested all AU member States to implement it as soon as possible.[71]

The African subregions followed the AU with similar measures: ECOWAS, for example, developed its own DRR Strategy, which was adopted at the 31st Ordinary Summit of Heads of States and Governments in Ouagadougou on January 19, 2007. At the institutional level, ECOWAS decided to create an internal DRR Division and a special ECOWAS Working Group on Disaster Risk Reduction which began meeting in March 2009. On the other side of the African continent, the East African

[69] See Article 12 of the 1981 Convention for Co-operation in the Protection and Development of the Marine and Coastal Environment of the West and Central African Region, and Article 11 of the 1985 Nairobi Convention of the Protection, Management and Development of the Marine and Coastal Environment of the Eastern African Region.

[70] Decision EX.CL/Dec 250—VIII, 'Implementation of the strategy rests at the sub-regional and national levels. (ECOWAS, ECOWAS policy for Disaster Risk Reduction, 2006,' available at http://www.preventionweb.net/files/4037_ECOWASpolicyDRR.pdf. Accessed 23 February 2012.

[71] Decision on the Report of the second Ministerial Conference on Disaster Risk Reduction, Doc. EX.CL/589(XVII), available at: http://www.preventionweb.net/files/18734_1838517947ex.cldec.600643edecisiono.pdf. Accessed 23 February 2012.

Community recently created a special working group called the EAC's Partner States Heads of Disaster Risk Reduction and Management Co-ordination, which had its first meeting in April 2011. During the inaugural meeting, the EAC Deputy Secretary-General urged the delegates 'to propose practical and affordable mechanisms for co-operation in disaster preparedness and response across the region.'[72] A more active attitude has been shown by the Intergovernmental Authority on Development (IGAD) which has created three important mechanisms: the Ministerial Committee in charge of disaster risk management institutions of the member states, which provides policy and political guidance; the Technical Advisory Panel drawn from member states, which assists in technical matters during the implementation period; and the IGAD Climate Prediction and Applications Centre (ICPAC). This centre has been given the responsibility of coordinating all issues related to climate risk reduction in the Region. The mission of ICPAC is to provide climate information, prediction, timely early warning for operations to support of environmental management, disaster risk reduction, and sustainable development in the IGAD Region.[73]

1.4.6 The Commonwealth of Independent States Region

The Commonwealth of Independent States (CIS) region has been very active in promoting legal instruments for increased co-operation in disaster management. There are at least three very important agreements which regulate in a detailed manner all the relevant issues: (a) the Intergovernmental agreement on interaction in the field of the prevention and reduction of consequences of natural and technological disasters (Minsk, 1993); (b) the Agreement on co-operation and interaction in the field of study of earthquakes and forecasting of seismic danger of the countries of the CIS (Moscow, 1993) and (c) the Agreement on interaction of the States—participants of the Commonwealth of Independent States in case of evacuation of their citizens from third countries in the event of the occurrence of natural disasters (Moscow, 1996). The last of these three agreements is very innovative, as so far it is the only existing treaty devoted exclusively to the regulation of the evacuation of citizens in case of natural disaster.

Beside the regional agreements, there are also several treaties concluded among a limited number of member States of the CIS: examples are the Agreement between the Governments of the Republic of Kazakhstan, the Kyrgyz Republic, and the Republic of Uzbekistan on co-operation and interaction in the field of research on earthquakes and forecasting of seismic danger (Bishkek, 1995), the Agreement between the Government of the Republic of Kazakhstan and the

[72] Available at: http://www.eac.int/component/k2/item/605-press-release-eac-heads-of-disaster-management-meet-in-dar.html. Accessed 10 February 2012.

[73] More at: http://www.icpac.net/. Accessed 23 February 2012.

Government of the Russian Federation on co-operation in the field of prevention of industrial failures, accidents, acts of nature and the reduction of their consequences (Moscow, 1994), the Agreement between the Republic of Kazakhstan, Kyrgyz Republic, Republic of Tajikistan, and Republic of Uzbekistan about co-operation in the field of prevention and liquidation of emergencies (Cholpon-Ata, 1998).

1.4.7 The European Continent

On the European continent the issue of disaster prevention and management has received a high level of attention from the various regional and subregional organizations. The focus, here, will not be on the significant activities carried out at EU level, as this is the main topic of the contribution by Gestri in this Volume, nor on the regional treaties for the protection of the marine environment, which often devote specific articles to the management of emergency situations.[74] We will be focusing attention on the specific activities of the Economic Commission for Europe and the Council of Europe, and on the relevant treaties adopted at subregional level aimed at reinforcing mutual co-operation in disaster management.

The activities of the UN Economic Commission for Europe. The UN Economic Commission for Europe recognized the importance and urgency of preventing serious adverse effects of industrial accidents on human beings and the environment, and sought to expedite all measures that encourage the rational, economic, and efficient use of preventive, preparedness, and response measures to enable environmentally sound and sustainable economic development. It promoted a specific Convention on the Transboundary Effects of Industrial Accidents adopted at Helsinki on March 17, 1992. This Convention, although focused on the environmental aspects, contains several relevant rules aimed at regulating the prevention duties of the States, the notification of incidents, assistance in an emergency situation, and the responsibility for damaging the environment.

---

[74] For example Article 9 of the 1976 Barcelona Convention for the Protection of The Mediterranean Sea Against Pollution (revised in Barcelona, Spain, on 10 June 1995 as the Convention for the Protection of the Marine Environment and the Coastal Region of the Mediterranean) states that

> 1. The Contracting Parties shall co-operate in taking the necessary measures for dealing with pollution emergencies in the Mediterranean Sea area, whatever the causes of such emergencies and reducing or eliminating damage resulting therefrom.
> 2. Any Contracting Party which becomes aware of any pollution emergency in the Mediterranean Sea area shall without delay notify the Organization and, either through the Organization or directly, any Contracting Party likely to be affected by such emergency.

Similar rules are provided in the 1992 Bucharest Convention on the Protection of the Black Sea Against Pollution.

The activities of Council of Europe. In 1987, the Committee of Ministers of the Council of Europe adopted Resolution (87) creating the EUR-OPA Major Hazards Agreement. Notwithstanding the rather ambitious title, EUR-OPA is simply a co-operating group concerned with major natural disasters occurring in Europe and Southern Mediterranean countries. It aims to develop means of preventing disasters, protecting against them when they occur, and organizing relief in their aftermath. Participation in this Group is open to member States of the Council of Europe, to the European Commission, and any other interested State. The Group's field of competence covers knowledge of major natural and technological disasters, prevention, risk management, post-crisis analysis, and rehabilitation.[75] It has 26 member States to date. During the 12th Ministerial Session of the Agreement, which took place in September 2010 in Saint Petersburg (Russian Federation), a new 'Action Plan 2011–2015 working together in Europe and the Mediterranean for the prevention of disasters, preparedness, and response' was adopted.[76] The three priorities for 2011–2015 emerging from the Action Plan are: (1) focusing on preparedness for emergencies; (2) using information to save lives and help victims and using knowledge to reduce vulnerability and (3) placing people at the heart of disaster risk reduction, improving prevention and preparedness, and promoting good governance.

Central Europe. In 1992 Austria, Croatia, Hungary, Italy, Poland, and Slovenia signed a Co-operation Agreement on the Forecast, Prevention, and Mitigation of Natural and Technological Disasters.[77] The treaty, which is phrased in a very cautious language, makes manifest the intention of the contracting parties to further expand the level of co-operation, although no specific procedure or mechanisms are indicated in the agreement. Article 3 indicates that 'all procedures for stronger co-operation and tighter solidarity will be agreed upon by the Joint Committee mentioned in Article 2.'

Nordic Countries. As early as 1963, the Nordic Countries and the International Atomic Energy Agency (IAEA) signed an innovative Nordic Mutual Emergency Assistance Agreement in Connection with Radiation, with the aim of prescribing the best ways to assist each other in the event of an incident involving damage from ionizing radiation, and to establish the terms under which a contracting State requesting assistance may use the assistance provided by another Contracting State or by the IAEA.

In addition, in 1989 Denmark, Finland, Norway, and Sweden signed an agreement on co-operation across State frontiers to prevent and limit damage to persons or property or to the environment in the case of accidents, to facilitate the

---

[75] See more on EUR-OPA at: http://www.coe.int/T/DG4/MajorHazards/Default_en.asp. Accessed 23 February 2012.

[76] The text of the Action Plan is available at http://www.coe.int/t/dg4/majorhazards/ressources/Apcat2010/StPetersburg/APCAT2010_05rev2_MediumTermPlan2011-2015_EN.pdf. Accessed 10 February 2012.

[77] The text of the Cooperation Agreement is available at www.mae.it/trattati. Accessed 23 February 2012.

necessary reciprocal assistance in the case of accidents, and to expedite the dispatch of emergency squads and materials.

Subsequently, in 2002, a Nordic public health preparedness agreement between Denmark, Finland, Iceland, Norway, and Sweden, was signed.[78] This is a very important agreement which restates the commitment of the participating countries to

(1) provide assistance to one another upon request, as far as possible under the provisions of this Agreement;
(2) inform one another, as promptly as possible, of measures they plan to implement, or are implementing, that will have or are expected to have a significant impact on the other Nordic countries;
(3) promote co-operation and as far as possible remove obstacles in national legislation, regulations, and other rules of law;
(4) provide opportunities for the exchange of experience, co-operation, and competence-building;
(5) promote the development of co-operation in this area;
(6) inform one another of relevant changes in the countries' preparedness regulations, including amendments of legislation.[79]

Black Sea States. Another very relevant and sophisticated agreement was signed in 1998 by the governments of the participating States of the Black Sea Economic Co-operation (BSEC) on collaboration in emergency assistance and emergency response to natural and man-made disasters.[80] Interestingly enough, this agreement is drafted in a very detailed manner, and most of its rules can be considered to be immediately applicable. The treaty regulates the rights and duties of States should an emergency situation arise in the region,[81] the transit and border crossing procedures, the export and re-import procedures. It identifies the

[78] The text of the agreement is available at http://www.norden.org/en/about-nordic-co-operation/agreements/treaties-and-agreements/social-and-health-care/nordic-public-health-preparedness-agreement. Accessed 23 February 2012.

[79] Article 4 of the Agreement.

[80] The text of the agreement is available at http://www.bsec-organization.org/documents/LegalDocuments/agreementmous/agr4/Documents/Emergencyagreement%20071116.pdf. Accessed 23 February 2012.

[81] Article 3 of the Agreement states that

> 3.2. If a Party needs assistance in case of natural or man-made disasters which has occurred on the territory of its State, this Party can require Assistance from the other Party(s) by forwarding the national appeal. The Assisting Party(s) shall help the Requesting Party by means and measures aimed at preventing and/or eliminating consequences of the Disaster.
> 3.3 The Parties shall render one another Assistance according to their possibilities. The Assistance shall be of granted at no cost unless otherwise agreed by the Parties.
> 3.4 The Requesting Party shall ensure unobstructed receipt and distribution of goods of assistance exclusively among the afflicted population. The goods of assistance shall be distributed without any discrimination based on race, religion, language, political, or other factors.

competent national bodies and focal points to be activated in cases of emergencies and clarifies the damage and compensation procedures.

The survey of existing regional and subregional agreements and policies shows that regional co-operation has taken place in four different but closely interrelated domains.

The first is *co-operation among sovereign states of the region* (or subregion) through legally established regional treaties, very often creating *ad hoc* institutions or mechanisms to deal with emergencies. These include the 1991 Inter-American Convention to Facilitate Disaster Assistance, the 1995 ASEAN Agreement on Disaster Management and Emergency Response, the 1993 Intergovernmental agreement on interaction in the field of the prevention and reduction of consequences of natural and technological—signed by CIS member States, the 1998 Treaty among the governments of the participating States of the Black Sea Economic Co-operation (BSEC) on Collaboration in Emergency Assistance and Emergency Response to natural and man-made disasters etc. as well as the EU mechanisms. These treaties, usually drafted in a very detailed manner, regulate all the relevant aspects of emergency operations, and most of the rules are drafted in very similar terms.

The second domain, a looser one compared to the first, is based mainly on political commitments and documents (and not on treaties) of the regional organizations and/or member States, very often in close co-operation with the United Nations and its various agencies (ESCAP and UNISDR). In this connection, we can quote as significant examples the Extended Programme of Action for the Implementation of the Africa Regional Strategy for Disaster Risk Reduction (2006–2015) and the Pacific Disaster Risk Management Partnership Network.

The third domain of regional collaboration is a *pan regional* phenomenon of more recent origin 'where all the stakeholders of regional co-operation—the national governments, the regional and subregional organizations, the non-governmental organizations including the scientific, technical and academic institutions, the media, the corporate sector and the humanitarian agencies and the international organizations and the multi-financial institutions have joined together to support the movement for regional co-operation.'[82] A concrete example of his type of domain of regional collaboration is found in the 2005 ASEAN Agreement on Disaster Management and Emergency Response in which an ASEAN Co-ordinating Centre for Humanitarian Assistance was created for the purpose of facilitating co-operation and co-ordination among the parties and with relevant United Nations and international organizations, in promoting regional collaboration.

The fourth domain includes *intra-regional co-operation*, i.e., an attempt to create a structure of co-ordination of the various efforts carried out in different regions or subregions. The most significant instances are undoubtedly the Foro de coordinación y cooperación de los mecanismos Sub-regionales de Gestión del

[82] See more on this in The Asia–Pacific Disaster Report, Protecting Development Gains, Reducing disaster vulnerability and Building Resilience in Asia and the Pacific, 96 ff., available at http://www.unescap.org/idd/pubs/Asia–Pacific-Disaster-Report%20-2010.pdf. Accessed 3 February 2012.

Riesgo de Desasters de la América which brings together all the relevant Latin American subregional mechanisms and, to a more limited extent, the EUR-OPA Major Hazards Agreement, which is a co-operation group open not only to members States of the Council of Europe but also to the European Commission and other interested States.

1.5 The Codification of IDRL: (c) Universal Agreements

While the dramatic issues related to the management of the consequences of wars attracted the attention of the international community, as early as 1856 when the Paris Declaration Respecting Maritime Law was agreed upon, the international community only became interested in disaster-related issues at the beginning of the twentieth century.[83] Early evidence of this new interest was the signing of the Convention Establishing the International Relief Union (IRU) in 1927. In the preamble, member States declared their willingness and commitment

> to render aid to each other in disasters, to encourage international relief by a methodical co-ordination of available resources, and to further the progress of international law in this field.

The 1927 Convention, which was agreed upon after lengthy preparatory work,[84] mandated the IRU with various tasks, including the co-ordination of the international assistance in case of disaster and the promotion of scientific studies on the causes of natural calamities, with a view to counteracting or limiting their effects. To carry out this ambitious mandate the Convention established a Council of Member States and the Executive Committee, an executive organ in which the ICRC and the League of Red Cross Societies each had two representatives. This first attempt of the international community to create a multilateral mechanism dealing with the various phases of disaster management unfortunately proved to be a failure. As there was no natural disaster in which the IRU played a role, it concentrated mainly on the publication of a scientific journal. After the Second World War, member States of the IRU used the withdrawal clause foreseen in the Agreement to abandon the IRU, whose real impact and usefulness had been questioned repeatedly both inside the UN and the ICRC. All this led to the Secretariat of the IRU being shut down in 1982. Its scientific activities, focusing mainly on the study of natural disasters, were transferred to UNESCO as early as 1968. In the following years, the 1971 UNGA Resolution 2816(XXVI) finally created the Office of the United Nations Disaster Relief Coordinator (later replaced

[83] Inter-State co-operation in the fight against the international community only becameemergency related issues dealt with in international treaties, both at bilateral and multilateral level: as an example see the 1912 International Sanitary Convention later updated in 1926.

[84] On the preparatory steps and the negotiation of the IRU Treaty and on its content see Toman 2006, 1 ff.

by OCHA), an internal body of the UN whose function was to become a catalyst and co-ordinator of donors of aid and services and to assist governments in preventing disasters or mitigating their effects by contingency planning.

The negative experience of the IRU had a significant impact on the international community: on the one hand, as noted in the previous sections, it represented an important incentive to develop regional and subregional agreements. On the other hand, the idea of a specific universal treaty comprehensively regulating disaster prevention, management, and recovery was no longer considered feasible, and was therefore postponed *sine die*. As a consequence, the strategy of the international community changed significantly, and a new trend emerged: in several universal treaties which regulated in general terms issues such as the transport of goods by sea[85] or air,[86] customs,[87] health regulations,[88] human rights,[89] waste management,[90] the protection of the safety and security of international personnel involved in emergency operations[91] and especially the safeguarding of the envi-

[85] See for e.g., the 1965 London Convention on Facilitation of International Maritime Traffic, containing a specific section F devoted to Natural Disaster Relief Work according to which

> '5.11 Standard. Public authorities shall facilitate the arrival and departure of vessels engaged in natural disaster relief work.
> 5.12 Standard. Public authorities shall to the greatest extent possible, facilitate the entry and clearance of persons and cargo arriving in vessels referred to in Standard 5.11.'

[86] See letter C of Chapter 3 of International Standards and Recommended Practices, Facilitation, Annex 9 of 1997 to the Convention on International Civil Aviation: letter C is entirely devoted to Relief flights following man-made and natural disasters which seriously endanger human health or the environment and similar emergency situations where UN assistance is required.

[87] See for e.g., the 1961 Customs Convention on the Temporary Importation of professional equipment, the 1973 International Convention on the simplification and harmonization of Customs procedures (Kyoto Convention), Revised Kyoto Convention 2000, the 1990 Istanbul Convention on Temporary Admission. For a more detailed comment of these treaties please see Chap. 22 by Adinolfi in this volume.

[88] WHO, International Health Regulations, (2005) Second Edition available at http://whqlibdoc.who.int/publications/2008/9789241580410_eng.pdf. Accessed 3 February 2012.

[89] Most of the international (both Universal and regional) HR Conventions contain specific rules dealing with the issue of protecting human rights '..in time of public emergency which threatens the life of the nation and the existence of which is officially proclaimed' (Article 4 of the 1966 International Covenant on Civil and Political Rights). See more on this in Chap. 14 by Sommario in this volume.

[90] 1989 Basel Convention on the Control of Transboundary Movement of Hazardous Wastes and their disposal.

[91] See the 2005 Optional Protocol to the Convention on the Safety of United Nations and Associated Personnel. This protocol, which has been adopted considering that United Nations operations conducted for the purposes of delivering emergency humanitarian assistance entail particular risks for United Nations and associated personnel, extended the scope of legal protection under the Convention to such emergency personnel. Unfortunately the Protocol has not yet entered into force.

ronment,[92] *ad hoc* rules were included to prescribe the specific duties for States in the event of a natural or man-made disaster.

In more recent times, the proposal of negotiating universal treaties devoted to disaster management has regained momentum, although it has been limited to the regulation of specific issues (as opposed to the earlier unsuccessful IRU attempt to regulate in a comprehensive manner all the aspects related to emergency situations). The 1986 Convention on Early Notification of a Nuclear Accident, the 1986 Convention on Assistance in the Case of Nuclear Accident or Radiological Emergency, the 1992 Convention on the Transboundary Effects of Industrial Incidents,[93] the 1992 United Nations Framework Convention on Climate Change, and the 1997 Kyoto protocol thereto, the 1998 Tampere Convention on the Provision of Telecommunication Resources for Disaster Mitigation and Relief Operations, the 1999 Food Aid Convention, the 2000 Framework Convention in Civil Defence Assistance,[94] the 2005 Revision of the International Health Regulations, as well as the 2005 Optional Protocol to the 1994 Convention on the Safety of United Nations and Associated Personnel,[95] are just a few expressions of the international community's new attitude. As most of these treaties will be commented upon in a more detailed manner in other chapters of this volume, there is no need for deeper analysis of their content in this section. In any case, these newer

[92] The number of Treaties regulating the protection of the environment and containing specific rules dealing with emergency situations is very impressive: as an example one may cite the 1969 Bruxelles International Convention Relating to Intervention on the High Seas in Cases of Oil Pollution Casualties Intervention, the 1990 International Convention on Oil Pollution Preparedness, Response and Co-operation and the London 2000 Protocol on Preparedness, Response and Co-operation to Pollution Incidents by Hazardous and Noxious Substances.

[93] Article 1 of this Convention states that the Convention itself shall apply

> 'to the prevention of, preparedness for and response to industrial accidents capable of causing transboundary effects, including the effects of such accidents caused by natural disasters, and to international co-operation concerning mutual assistance, research and development, exchange of information and exchange of technology
> in the area of prevention of, preparedness for and response to industrial accidents.

[94] The Framework Convention, which came into force in 2001, has been ratified by only 10 States. The text is available at http://www.icdo.org/files/framework-convention.pdf. Accessed 23 February 2012.

[95] The 2005 Protocol clearly states, at Article II, that the 1994 Convention is applicable

> 'in respect of all other United Nations operations established by a competent organ of the United Nations in accordance with the Charter of the UN and conducted under United Nations authority and control for the purpose of…
> b) Delivering emergency humanitarian assistance.

The following para 3 of the same Article II allows, however, a member State to make a declaration to the UN Secretary-General that it shall not apply this protocol with respect to a UN operation which is carried out with the sole purpose of responding to a natural disaster. See more on this specific issue in IFRC 2010; Bourloyannis-Vrailas 1995, p. 560; Bloom 1995, p. 621; Lepper 1995, p. 359.

treaties, some of which have been concluded very recently, are concerned only with very specific issues related to disaster management or to categories of actors intervening in emergency situations, and contain very detailed regulations which aim to offer a coherent and comprehensive legal framework to address all the potential problems which might occur in an emergency situation. By way of example, the Tampere Convention contains detailed rules concerning the appointment of the co-ordinator of an emergency operation and the nature of his/her mandate; rights and duties of the States (both the State affected by the disaster and those States ready to offer their assistance); privileges, immunities, and facilities to be granted to the organization/States taking part in the relief operation and to their personnel; payment or reimbursement of costs and fees; reduction of regulatory barriers which might hamper the work of the relief mission.

Beside this new approach, typical of the work of the international community in this area during recent decades, we must recall that in the same period another conspicuous trend has developed: the soft law approach. During the last three decades, States, international organizations, NGOs, the scientific community and the IFRC have promoted the preparation and subsequent adoption of soft law instruments on relevant issues, very often in the format of guidelines, handbooks, principles etc. Concrete outcomes of these initiatives were, amongst others, the 1969 IFRC Declaration of principles for international humanitarian relief to the civilian population in disaster situations,[96] the Principles and Good Practice of Humanitarian Donorship (1973),[97] the 1970 Customs Council Recommendation to Expedite the Forwarding of Relief Consignments, the 1990 Turku Declaration of Minimum Humanitarian Standards,[98] the 1997 Measures to expedite relief,[99] adopted by both ICRC and ECOSOC, the 2004 Code of Conduct for The International Red Cross and Red Crescent Movement, and NGOs in Disaster Relief,[100] the 2007 IFRC Guidelines for the Domestic Facilitation and Regulation of International Disaster Relief and Initial Recovery Assistance,[101] the 2008 Operational Guidelines and Field Manual on Human Rights Protection in Situations of Natural Disaster,[102] the recent 2011 Sphere Handbook.[103] All of these had an important impact, as they were instrumental in reinforcing global awareness of the

[96] Available at http://www.ifrc.org/Docs/idrl/I49EN.pdf. Accessed 23 February 2012.

[97] Available at http://www.cgiar.org/changemanagement/pdf/wg4_Principles%20and%20Good%20Practice%20of%20Humanitarian%20Donorship.pdf. Accessed 23 February 2012.

[98] Available at http://www.ifrc.org/Docs/idrl/I149EN.pdf. Accessed 23 February 2012.

[99] Available at http://www.ifrc.org/Docs/idrl/I82EN.pdf. Accessed 23 February 2012.

[100] Available at http://www.ifrc.org/en/publications-and-reports/code-of-conduct/. Accessed 23 February 2012.

[101] Available at http://www.ifrc.org/Docs/pubs/idrl/guidelines/introduction-guidelines-en.pdf. Accessed 23 February 2012.

[102] Available at http://www.brookings.edu/reports/2008/spring_natural_disasters.aspx. Accessed 23 February 2012.

[103] Available at http://www.sphereproject.org/content/view/720/200/lang,english/. Accessed 23 February 2012.

importance of the different issues at stake, and also prompted the codification of specific treaties.

These soft law instruments, together with numerous more political activities carried out in different contexts during recent decades,[104] have contributed to raising awareness and creating a sense of urgency in the UN family about a more strategic approach in dealing with disaster. It is within this context that on December 19, 1991, the UN General Assembly, further expanding and complementing the initiatives already undertaken with the creation of UNDRO, adopted the landmark Resolution 46/182 Strengthening of the co-ordination of humanitarian emergency assistance of the United Nations, which established the framework within which international disaster relief activities are undertaken, and provided, beside the innovative guiding principles for humanitarian assistance, the normative basis for the creation of the Inter-Agency Standing Committee (IASC), the Consolidated Appeals Process (CAP), the Central Emergency Revolving (now Response) Fund (CERF), the Central Register of Disaster Management Capacities, and the position of Emergency Relief Coordinator (ERC) at USG-level.[105]

Finally, it is interesting to note that in the UN family interest in disaster prevention and mitigation arose even before the historic UNGA Resolution 46/182: already in 1989 the UN General Assembly passed Resolution 44-236, International Decade for Natural Disaster Reduction, in which the UNGA adopted the international Framework for Action calling on member States and relevant institutions to expand their capacity to deal with major natural disasters and to increase the resilience and mitigation capacity of the local population. This Resolution was an important starting point and subsequently prompted several significant activities, both at UN level[106] (with the launching of the UN International Strategy for Risk Reduction[107]) and at regional level. One of the main achievements reached in this framework is undoubtedly the World Conference on Disaster Reduction which took place in Kobe, Hyogo, Japan in 2005. The Conference offered a unique opportunity

---

[104] See for example the very interesting and comprehensive 2003 Resolution of the Inter-Parliamentary Union on International Co-operation for the prevention and management of Transborder Natural Disaster (available at http://www.ipu.org/conf-e/108-2.htm: accessed 23 February 2012) in which IPU

> *Encourages* the international community to co-operate more closely in mitigating the adverse effects of transborder natural disasters through improved preparedness, risk reduction, and effective response, and to strengthen coordination mechanisms among States at the regional and international levels, including improved donor response coordination and harmonisation.

[105] See more on this in Chap. 20 by De Siervo in this volume.

[106] See, for e.g., the 1999 UN General Assembly Resolution 54/219, International Decade for Natural Disaster Reduction: successor arrangements. From that year on, the UN General Assembly adopts regularly on an annual basis a specific Resolution on the risk reduction strategy: the more recent Resolution is the 65/157 International Strategy for Risk Reduction adopted on February 25, 2011.

[107] See more at: http://www.unisdr.org/. Accessed 23 February 2012.

to the international community to promote a strategic, systematic, and synergetic approach to disaster risk reduction and to strengthen the disaster resilience of local communities. At the end of the Conference the 'Hyogo Framework for Action 2005–2015: Building the resilience of nations and communities to disasters'[108] was adopted with a view to addressing the following aspects:

- challenges posed by disasters
- the Yokohama Strategy: lessons learned and gaps identified
- WCDR: Objectives, expected outcomes, and strategic goals
- priorities for action 2005–2015
- implementation and follow-up.

1.6 Major Findings from Surveying IDRL: Gaps, Overlapping, and Inconsistencies

Our analysis of existing international conventions at bilateral, regional, and universal level permits a number of conclusions and observations.

First, the accumulation of treaties regulating disaster management is very impressive, at least from a quantitative point of view; their content ranges from mere generic commitments to co-operate in researching fields of common interest, to detailed rules concerning the rights and duties of a State should a major natural or man-made disaster occur.

It is worth highlighting a major difference between regional and universal agreements: at regional (and subregional) level there are numerous treaties regulating in a comprehensive manner all the relevant issues related to disaster prevention, mitigation, management, and early recovery, but at universal level this does not apply. As clearly emerges from Sect. 1.5, after the negative experience of the International Relief Union the preferred approach at universal level has been to deal with specific issues (telecommunication, protection of the personnel, customs, transports of emergency goods etc.), or to reinforce UN mechanisms, while the more general rules on the modality of intervention of the international community have been added to the regional, subregional, and bilateral conventions. This specific situation undoubtedly explains why there are so many regional and subregional agreements dealing with the management of man-made and natural disasters. On the other hand it is more difficult to explain the co-existence on the same continent of regional and several subregional agreements, very often dealing with identical issues, and sometimes regulating them in a different and contradictory manner. We may cite the situation in Latin America where there is a very comprehensive and detailed continental agreement, the 1991 Inter-American

[108] Available at http://www.preventionweb.net/english/professional/publications/v.php?id=1037&pid:3&pif:3. Accessed 3 February 2012.

Convention to Facilitate Disaster Assistance, but there are several subregional agreements regulating the same issues (for example the 1991 Agreement establishing the Caribbean Disaster Emergency Response Agency—CDERA-, the 2004 Protocolo Adicional al Acuerdo Marco sobre Medio Ambiente del MERCOSUR en Materia de Cooperación y Asistencia Frente a Emergencias Ambientales and the Comité Andino para la Prevención y Atención de Desastres). This overlapping of legal instruments, with their potential contradictions, may create political and legal difficulties. As a concrete case, let us consider the rules dealing with the sharing of the costs of an international emergency operation contained in the 1991 Inter-American Convention to Facilitate Disaster Assistance and in the 2004 Protocolo Adicional al Acuerdo Marco sobre Medio Ambiente del MERCOSUR en Materia de Cooperación y Asistencia Frente a Emergencias Ambientales (which has not yet come into force). While the Inter-American Convention states that

> Except for the provisions of Articles IX and XII, the assistance shall be provided at the expense of the assisting state, without cost to the assisted state, except where these states agree otherwise[109]

article 8 of the MERCOSUR Treaty states exactly the opposite:

> Los gastos que ocasionen la misión de asistencia serán de responsabilidad del Estado Parte que la solicite, a menos que se acuerde otra modalidad.

Obviously if the two States involved agree in the specific situation on the sharing of the costs of assistance, no problem arises, as both treaties provide that the cost sharing issue can be regulated on an *ad hoc* basis between the States involved. But what happens if there is no specific bilateral agreement at this regard? Once both treaties come into force, which one would apply to the States which are parties to both of them—the more recent one, or the one chosen by the States involved at the time the emergency procedure commenced? Article XV of the 1991 Inter-American Convention to Facilitate Disaster Assistance, concerned with regulating the relationship to existing agreements, does not provide a solution, as it merely states that

> If there is any discrepancy between this Convention and other international agreements on the subject to which the assisting and assisted states are parties, the provision that affords the greatest degree of assistance in the event of disaster and favors support and protection to personnel providing assistance shall take precedence.

Other similar treaties would probably lead to the same conclusion—that treaty rules dealing with the problem being considered here are irrelevant. One such is Article 10 of the Tampere Convention, which in this connection state merely

> This Convention shall not affect the rights and obligations of States Parties deriving from other international agreements or international law.

[109] Article XIV of the 1991 Inter-American Convention.

It is the opinion of the present author that the solution of the problem is to apply the relevant rules of the treaty under which the affected State activated the international assistance mechanism. If several mechanisms are activated, and there is a multiplicity of international actors providing their services to the State affected by the natural disaster, the rules to be applied might be diverse depending under which framework the specific event occurs.

The reason for this overlapping of regulations on the American continent might be that (a) the 1991 Inter-American Convention to Facilitate Disaster Assistance treaty has been ratified, so far, by only five American States; (b) subregional treaties very often allow a more detailed regulation of the various issues, and sometimes they are used to expand the area of co-operation (including, for example, joint training activities, joint researches in specific areas of common interest, the organization of field exercises to test the real reaction capability etc.) owing to the advantages of the physical proximity of the partners; (c) the subregional organizations need a higher level of visibility, and disaster management undoubtedly provides this visibility.

If a comparison of regional and subregional treaties reveals significant overlapping and inconsistencies, the problem is even greater when multilateral treaties are compared with bilateral ones. A closer look at these bilateral agreements, as in Sect. 1.3, shows that there is frequent contradiction of valid regional or subregional agreements and bilateral treaties in the following matters: status of personnel, cost sharing of the operation, access to the affected territory, claims and compensation. In similar cases, the rules which apply should be, once more, those provided in the treaty invoked by the affected States when they request the assistance of other States.

An additional issue which deserves to be mentioned here is the high (perhaps excessive) number of bilateral treaties, considering the universal, regional, and subregional legal frameworks which exist on almost all continents (with the exception of Africa). The number of bilateral treaties may sometimes be validly explained and justified, especially where the treaties are between neighboring States sharing similar specific problems and wishing to go beyond the subregional or regional co-operation modalities for the sake of effectiveness of mutual co-operation should a natural or man-made disaster occur. This is the case, for example, with various bilateral treaties dealing with specific kinds of disaster, such as fire in mountainous zones, which undoubtedly require additional specific regulations in bilateral treaties to guarantee that the emergency mission is completely effective. It must be stressed, however, that in many other cases the bilateral treaties seem to be motivated by the need to guarantee a higher level of visibility to specific forms of bilateral co-operation in the sharing of experiences and technology, promotion of joint projects, and common training activities, etc. In such cases, one might seriously doubt if the signing of an international treaty is really the best instrument to achieve the given purpose of a reinforced co-operation between States.

Looking at the overall picture, one may wonder if it would be wise to further reinforce existing regional agreements in the future and to restrict the use of bilateral agreements to very specific situations where their use is dictated by the nature of the potential disaster. This would promote a more standardized approach which would benefit everyone.

The present author suggests that there are at least two areas among the topics covered by various relevant treaties which would benefit from receiving additional attention.

The first is the relationship between the protection of the environment and the management of natural and man-made disasters.[110] Although the two issues should go hand in hand, this is not always the case, and stronger links would be extremely beneficial. While most of the more recent disaster management treaties clearly consider the threat or damage to the environment as one of the prerequisites for the applicability of the treaty itself,[111] there are still several treaties which become applicable only if there is serious damage, or potential damage, to human beings or to their property.[112] Environmental treaties, on the other hand, focus their attention on the protection of the environment as such, irrespective of any damage to the property of the local population. These different prerequisites for the application of the various sets of conventions should be overcome for the sake of the highest level of protection of both human beings and the environment.

The second topic is the use of military resources to address natural or man-made disasters. It is a very sensitive and controversial issue which has been neglected for too long, and would benefit immensely from additional attention and development of new rules by the international community. The first timid but promising steps undertaken so far are the creation within the framework of the Euro-Atlantic Partnership Council (EAPC) in 1998 of the Euro-Atlantic Disaster Response Co-ordination Centre, together with the Euro-Atlantic Disaster Response Unit, a non-standing multinational force of civil and military elements, which can be deployed in the event of a major natural or man-made disaster in an EAPC country. The Centre, which works in close co-operation with the United Nations Office for the Co-ordination of Humanitarian Affairs (UN-OCHA), is mandated to co-ordinate the response of NATO and partner countries to natural or man-made disasters within the Euro-Atlantic area. The Centre has been actively involved in

---

[110] Farber, Chen, Verchick, Sun 2009, p. 165.

[111] There are however many disaster-related treaties which are applicable on the occurrence of a natural disaster which might affect only the environment, even without damaging personal property or threatening the life of individuals: see for example the 2005 Tampere Convention. Another relevant example is given by the 1992 Cooperation agreement on the forecast, prevention and mitigation of natural and technological disaster among Austria, Croatia, Hungary, Italy, Poland and Slovenia which extends the treaty to the 'Cooperation in the field of forecast and prevention of major risks, entailing serious consequences for the safety of people, assets *and environment*...' (Emphasis added).

[112] In the Preamble of the 1991 Inter-American Convention to Facilitate Disaster Assistance, reference is made to

> .... disasters, catastrophes, and calamities that take and threaten the lives, safety, and property of the inhabitants of the American hemisphere.

more than fifty emergencies, including fighting floods and forest fires and dealing with the aftermath of earthquakes. Similar efforts to reinforce civil-military co-operation in the management of emergencies have also been made within ASEAN.[113]

The increasing importance of the issue is confirmed by the adoption in 2004 (with a revision in 2007) of the Oslo Guidelines on the Use of Foreign Military and Civil Defence Assets in Disaster Relief, which aims

> to establish the basic framework for formalizing and improving the effectiveness and efficiency of the use of foreign military and civil defense assets in international disaster relief operations.

Much controversy surrounds these questions: is it really appropriate for military and civil defense forces to be used in man-made or natural disaster emergency situations? To what extent does the presence of military forces impact on the ability to deliver professional emergency assistance by the traditional 'civilian' actors? The sensitive problems arising through the use of military resources in emergency operations, both from a political and an operational perspective (cost sharing, status of the military personnel, etc.), would clearly benefit from a higher level of interest by the international community, and from more detailed rules to govern an increasingly complex phenomenon.[114]

Finally, this survey of international disaster response law, which has demonstrated that there is already a very significant number of international treaties regulating the various aspects of disaster prevention, mitigation, management, and recovery, highlights the extraordinary importance of closer relations and more effective forms of co-operation among the different actors involved in this area.[115] The UN established the framework for international disaster relief activities, in particular with the landmark 1991 General Assembly Resolution 46/182 'Strengthening of the co-ordination of humanitarian emergency assistance of the United Nations,' which represented a serious and well conceived attempt to encourage closer co-ordination of all relevant international actors involved in disaster management, but it is the opinion of the present author that more could and should be done. In many regional treaties there are interesting and very promising commitments to reinforce co-operation with other relevant actors: as an example we could cite Article 17 of the Agreement among the Governments of the Participating States of the Black Sea Economic Co-operation (BSEC) on collaboration in Emergency Assistance and Emergency Response to natural and man-made Disasters, which states that

---

[113] See the ASEAN document entitled The Use of Asean Military Assets and Capacities in Humanitarian Assistance and Disaster Relief, Concept Paper, available at http://www.asean.org/18471-d.pdf. Accessed 23 February 2012.

[114] See more on this issue in Chap. 24 by Calvi Parisetti in this volume and SIPRI 2008.

[115] Marshall 2008, p. 184.

> On the basis of mutual arrangement the relevant Parties may invite the interested international and national organizations/institutions to join the activities, connected with the implementation of the present Agreement.

The 1997 Memorandum of Understanding between Economic Co-operation Organization (ECO) and UN/ISDR as well as the Foro de coordinación y cooperación de los mecanismos Sub-regionales de Gestión del Riesgo de Desasters de la America are positive attempts to move in the same direction.

An appeal for more rapid progress towards the same goal was also formulated by the UN General Assembly in its recent Resolution 65/157, adopted on December 20, 2010, in which the UNGA

> 7. *Welcomes* the national, subregional, and regional initiatives undertaken by Member States, in particular developing countries, to achieve disaster risk reduction, and reiterates the need to further develop regional initiatives and risk reduction capacities of regional mechanisms where they exist, to strengthen them and to encourage the use and sharing of all existing tools, and requests the regional commissions, within their mandates, to support the efforts of Member States in this regard, in close co-ordination with implementing entities of the United Nations system.

It is now time for fine words in treaties to be transformed into concrete measures which will achieve real co-operation and synergies in the interests of the people suffering the consequences of increasing natural and man-made disasters.

References

Antoniadis A, Schutze R, Spaventa E (eds) (2011) The European Union and global emergencies: a law and policy analysis. Hart Publishing, Oxford

Bannon V (2006) Strengthening disaster response laws, rules and principles: overview of the current system and a new way forward. In: Kumar CR, Srivastava K (eds) Tsunami and disaster management: law and governance. S & M Asia, Hong Kong, pp 9–41

Bannon V (2008) International Disaster Response Law and the Commonwealth: answering the call to action. Commonw Law Bulletin 34:843–857

Bannon V, Fisher D (eds) (2006) Legal lessons in disaster relief from the tsunami, the Pakistan earthquake and Hurricane Katrina. ASIL Insights 10(6). Available at www.asil.org/insights060315.cfm

Bloom ET (1995) Protecting peacekeepers: the convention on the safety of United Nations and associated personnel. AJIL 89:621–631

Bothe M (2000) Relief actions. In: Bernhardt R (ed) Encyclopedia of Public International Law, vol 4. Elsevier Science Publishers, Amsterdam, pp 168–182

Bourloyannis-Vrailas Ch (1995) The convention on the safety of United Nations and associated personnel. ICLQ 44:560–590

Brinkerhoff DW (2007) The enabling environment for achieving the millennium development goals: government actions to support NGOs. In: Brinkerhoff DW, Smith SC, Teegen H (eds) NGOs and the millennium development goals: citizen action to reduce poverty. Palgrave MacMillan, New York, pp 86–107

Caron D, Leben C (eds) (2001) International aspects of natural and industrial Catastrophies/Les aspects Internationaux des Catastrophes Naturelles et Industrielles. Martinus Nijhoff, Leyden

Farber DA, Chen J, Verchick R, Sun L (eds) (2000) Disaster law and policy. Aspen Publisher, Washington

Fenner G, Mahlstein M (2009) Curbing the risks of and opportunities for corruption in natural disaster situations. In: Harper E (ed) International Law and standards applicable in natural disaster situations. IDLO, Rome, pp 243–250

Fidler DP (2005) Disaster relief and governance after the Indian Ocean tsunami: what role for international law? Melb J Int Law 6:458–473

Fischer H (2003) International disaster response law treaties: trends, patterns, and lacunae. In: Bannon V (ed) IFRC, International Disaster Response Laws, Principles and Practice: reflections, prospects, and challenges. International Federation of the Red Cross and Red Crescent Societies, Geneva, pp 24–44

Fisher D (2007) Law and legal issues in international disaster response: a desk study. International Federation of Red Cross and Red Crescent Societies, Geneva

IFRC (2010) Will the optional protocol to the UN safety convention matter in disaster relief operations? IDRLE-Newsletter 26. www.ifrc.org/global/publications/inrl/resources/newsletter/october_2010/optional-protocol.pdf

Harper E (2009) International Law and standards applicable in natural disaster situations. IDLO, Rome

Hoffman M (2003) What is the scope of international disaster response law? In: IFRC, International Disaster Response Laws, Principles and Practice: reflections, prospects, and challenges. International Federation of the Red Cross and Red Crescent Societies, Geneva, pp 13–20

Jakovljević B (2004) International disaster relief law. Israel Yearb Human Rights 34:251–286

Leben C (2001) Vers un droit international des catastrophes. In: Caron D, Leben C (eds) The international aspects of natural and industrial catastrophes. Martinus Nijhoff Publishers, The Hague, pp 31–91

Lepper SJ (1995) The legal status of military personnel in United Nations peace operations: one delegate's analysis. Houst J Int Law 18:359–464

Macalister-Smith P (ed) (1985) International humanitarian assistance: disaster relief actions in international law and organization. Springer, Heidelberg

Marshall LW (2008) International disaster response law: an introduction. Am J Disaster Medicine 3:181–184

Poncelet JL (1997) Disaster management in the Caribbean. Disaster 21:267–279

Reinecke I (2010) International Disaster Response Law and the co-ordination of international organisations. ANU Undergrad Res J 2:143–163

Samuels JW (2003) The relevance of international law in the prevention and mitigation of natural disasters. In Tenon LH (ed) International legal mechanisms regulating disaster response in countries of the Mediterranean region. International Federation of Red Cross and Red Crescent Societies, Geneva

The Netherland Red Cross (2010) Legal aspects of international disaster response in Dutch emergencies and crisis situation. International Federation of Red Cross and Red Crescent Societies, Geneva

Sarat A, Lezaun J (eds) (1999) Catastrophe: law politics and the humanitarian impulse. University of Massachusetts Press, Boston

SIPRI (2008) The effectiveness of foreign military assets in natural disaster response: a report by SIPRI. SIPRI, Stockholm

Toman J (1989) Towards disaster relief law: legal aspects of disaster relief operations. In: Kalshoven F (ed) Assisting the victims of armed conflicts and other disasters: papers delivered at the international conference on humanitarian assistance in armed conflict, The Hague, 22–24 June 1988. Martinus Nijhoff Publishers, Dordrecht, pp 181–199

Toman J (2006) International Disaster Response Law: treaties, regulations and remaining gaps, pp 1–12 http://ssrn.com/abstract=1312787

United Nations (2004) Living with risk: a global review of disaster reduction initiatives, vol 1. International Strategy for Disaster Reduction, New York. http://www.unisdr.org/files/657_lwr1.pdf

UNISDR (2009) Terminology on disaster risk reduction. http://www.unisdr.org/eng/library/lib-terminology-eng.htm

Chapter 2
International Disaster Response Law in Relation to Other Branches of International Law

Gabriella Venturini

Abstract This chapter examines the relationship between international disaster response law (IDRL) and some other branches of public international law that variously contribute to shape its form and substance. It is argued that IDRL should be construed and implemented along the lines of Human Rights Law, International Humanitarian Law, Refugee Law, Global Health Law, International Environmental Law, and the Law of International Development. The IDRL rules stem from traditional sources of public international law, such as custom and treaties, however, general principles and soft law play a major role in its gradual development. Under IDRL, the traditional principle of State sovereignty is being challenged by the duty of cooperating to assist disaster victims. Human Rights Law, as a corpus of basic rules applying to all situations, provides a catalog of non-derogable rights. International Humanitarian Law extensively stipulates how persons in need of assistance are to be treated. It is also the basis of the fundamental principles governing humanitarian assistance, i.e., humanity, impartiality, and neutrality. Especially, humanity prompts the expansion of the scope of the principle of non-refoulement to persons forced to migrate in the wake of disaster. State obligations regarding public health and environmental protection contribute to the avoidance of health emergencies and environmental harm, thus making disaster prevention and disaster response easier. Disaster Risk Reduction is a critical component of both IDRL and the Millennium Development Goals set by the international community in order to take decisive steps against poverty and to boost development.

G. Venturini (✉)
Università degli Studi di Milano, Via Conservatorio 7, 20122, Milan, Italy
e-mail: gabriella.venturini@unimi.it

A. de Guttry et al. (eds.), *International Disaster Response Law*,
DOI: 10.1007/978-90-6704-882-8_2,

Keywords Sovereignty · Human rights · International humanitarian law · Humanitarian assistance · Soft law · Refugee law · Global health law · International environmental law · Development

Contents

2.1 Introduction

Since the second half of the twentieth century, international law has progressively evolved from the legal regulation of coexistence among sovereign States, to a system of co-operation covering the entire range of international relations. Bilateral and multilateral treaties have been concluded in all fields of State competence, and international organizations have been established in order to bring about institutional co-operation.[1] Under customary law, however, States do not have a general duty to co-operate. Rather, they freely choose their partner States as well as the object of co-operation. Yet, treaty law often stipulates obligations to co-operate in the subject matter of the agreement. This equally applies to disaster situations, either natural or man-made, where a great number of treaties provide for rights and obligations relating to assistance and relief between or among the parties.[2] As a consequence, both domestic and international response to disasters must be organized in accordance with international law as far as it is applicable. Under customary law, the State in whose territory a disaster occurs is bound to respect a number of obligations (e.g., those concerning human rights and the treatment of aliens) in carrying out relief and recovery. It is also entitled to demand respect for

[1] Dupuy 1998, Abbott and Snidal 2004.

[2] For a review of the existing treaty law concerning IDRL see Chap. 1 by de Guttry in this volume.

its own rights (e.g., in terms of access to territory or imports of goods and services) by foreign States, intergovernmental, and non-governmental organizations providing assistance. Bilateral and multilateral treaties establish other relevant obligations and corresponding rights. Therefore, international disaster response law (IDRL) largely builds upon the existing customary and conventional law. The IFRC Desk Study[3] identifies several areas related to IDRL, i.e., human rights, armed conflicts, refugees and internally displaced persons, privileges and immunities, customs, transport, telecommunications, donations, civil defense, health, the environment, weapons control, outer space, and humanitarian personnel.

Further discussion on most of the above-mentioned topics may be found in subsequent chapters of this volume. The scope of this contribution is to consider a number of rules, principles, and procedures already existing in the realm of public international law that inspire and influence the development of IDRL. For the sake of clarity, a distinction should be made between customary international law, treaty law, general principles, and soft law. While it is undisputed that the first two categories establish the legal regulation of States' behavior, the meaning of general principles is often ambiguous, and the nature of soft law is still questioned. For the purposes of IDRL, general principles may be relevant either in the procedural sense (as 'a method of creating rules of international law') or in the material sense (as 'the intrinsic value or the substantive content of a given rule').[4] Soft law has been described as a 'grey area' of international law 'between the white space of law and the black territory of non-law.'[5] Given their considerable importance in the making of IDRL, due attention should be paid to both general principles and soft law, with a view to explaining how they work and interact with positive rules.

This contribution first examines the principle of State sovereignty together with the related principles of non-intervention and consent that must be respected while carrying out international response to disasters. The following sections concisely discuss the relevant aspects of human rights law (HRL), international humanitarian law (IHL), and the principles of humanitarian assistance. There follows an appraisal of soft law. The author then focuses on refugee law, health law, environmental law, and the law of international development with a view to detecting those rules and principles that are essential in shaping IDRL and ensuring its effectiveness.

2.2 State Sovereignty, Non-Intervention, and Consent

At the turn of the twentieth century, public international law is firmly grounded on the principle of State sovereignty, which implies that every sovereign State has the right to conduct its affairs without interference from foreign States. As a consequence, the prohibition of intervention in domestic affairs is recognized as a

---

[3] IFRC 2007, Law and Legal Issues in International Disaster Response, 34–52.

[4] van Hoof 1983, 148–150.

[5] Id. at 188.

customary rule having general application. This has been reflected in a number of well-known declarations and resolutions adopted by the United Nations bodies and international conferences,[6] as well as in the jurisprudence of the International Court of Justice.[7] In principle, the exercise by a State of any elements of sovereignty in the territory of a foreign State is a wrongful act. Only valid consent may preclude such wrongfulness.[8]

The sovereignty principle clearly suggests that disaster response falls within the jurisdiction of the State in whose territory the catastrophic event has occurred. Whenever assistance from foreign States or international organizations (IOs) is needed, it has to be requested. Consent could arguably take the form of acquiescence, i.e., acceptance of relief provided without a request. In any case, States and IOs providing assistance must keep within the limits of the consent given. Current treaties dealing with co-operation in the event of accidents and disasters are constantly based on those principles.[9] All the more so if assistance is offered by non-governmental organizations (NGOs) or other private foreign entities: the territorial State is free to admit them or to refuse entrance; admission entails their duty to abide by the laws and regulations of that State.

Nevertheless, contemporary international law presents a number of situations where a State may be under obligation to accept assistance from abroad. On the one hand, a duty to accept assistance is established by a number of treaties, either bilateral or within the framework of regional organizations. On the other hand, the Security Council could authorize or even mandate an intervention with the purpose of providing assistance to disaster victims. This should require that the consequences of the catastrophic event (e.g., a massive flow of refugee toward and across international borders) might be qualified as a threat to international peace and security in a given region.[10]

More generally, it should be considered that the principle of non-intervention aims to preclude those policies that essentially endanger the sovereignty and political independence of States, such as recourse to the threat or use of force, aggression, military occupation, the escalation of the military presence or intimidation. Clearly, assistance to disaster response falls short of those situations. Rather, it corresponds to the duty of States to co-operate with one another, called for by many resolutions and declarations. The principle of co-operation covers,

---

[6] Declaration on the Inadmissibility of Intervention in the Domestic Affairs of States and the Protection of their Independence and Sovereignty, A/RES/2131(XX) of 21 December 1965; Declaration on the Inadmissibility of Intervention and Interference in the Internal Affairs of States, A/RES/36/103 of 9 December 1981.

[7] Case concerning the military and paramilitary activities in and against Nicaragua (Nicaragua v. United States of America) Judgment of 27 June 1986, ICJ Rep. 1986, paras 202–209.

[8] Draft Articles on Responsibility of States for Internationally Wrongful Acts adopted by the International Law Commission at its fifty-third session (2001), ILC Yearbook 2001 II Part Two, Article 20.

[9] See Chap. 1 by de Guttry in this volume.

[10] See Chap. 10 by Costas Trascasas in this volume, Sects. 10.3 and 10.4.

inter alia, such matters as economic stability and progress, the general welfare of nations, human rights, and fundamental freedoms.[11] The Convention Establishing the International Relief Union (IRU) has adopted that perspective ever since 1927.[12] More recently, the International Law Commission draft articles on the Protection of persons in the event of disasters took the same approach. Article 5, as provisionally adopted by the ILC Drafting Committee, states the duty of States to co-operate among themselves, and with the UN and intergovernmental and non-governmental organizations. Article 10 lays the obligation with the State affected by a disaster to seek assistance if the situation exceeds its national capacity. Finally, Article 11, while restating the requirement of consent to external assistance, recognizes that such consent shall not be refused arbitrarily.[13] As a consequence, IDRL puts sovereignty back in its right perspective and commits States to effectively co-operate whenever the dimension of a disaster so requires.

2.3 IDRL and Human Rights Law

Human rights law (HRL) sets out the general legal framework for disaster response as being primarily incumbent upon the territorial State, but equally binding on States providing assistance. HRL incorporates customary rules as well as a great number of treaty commitments in the field of civil, political, social, economic, and cultural rights. A catalog of human rights obligations of the greatest importance in IDRL includes (although it is not limited to) the right to life, liberty, and security of persons, the right to personal identity, the right to humane treatment, the right to food and water, and the right to health. Those rights must be respected in accordance with the fundamental principle of non-discrimination, i.e., with no adverse distinction based on race, color, sex, language, religion, political or other opinion, national or social origin, property, birth or any other status. Non-discrimination is also a core principle of IDRL and it shapes the rules of conduct for those providing assistance and relief in disasters.

Human rights, however, are subject to limitations and derogations. Limitation clauses allow States to restrict the exercise of certain civil and political rights (CPR) in the interest of national security or public safety, public order, public

---

[11] Declaration on Principles of International Law concerning Friendly Relations and Co-operation among States in accordance with the Charter of the United Nations, A/RES/2625(XXV) of 24 October 1970; Strengthening of the co-ordination of humanitarian emergency assistance of the United Nations, A/RES/46/182 of 19 December 1991, 5–7; Article 5 as provisionally adopted by the Drafting Committee of the International Law Commission on Protection of Persons in the Event of Disasters A/CN.4/L.758 of 24 July 2009.

[12] Preamble to the 1927 Convention Establishing an International Relief Union. See Macalister-Smith 1981.

[13] A/CN.4/L.758 of 24 July 2009, A/CN.4/L.794 of 20 July 2011. See Chap. 3 by Zorzi Giustiniani in this volume.

health or morals or the protection of the rights and freedoms of others. Examples of rights that may be restricted are the liberty of movement, the freedom to manifest one's religion, the freedom of expression, the right of assembly, and the freedom of association.[14] Furthermore, in a time of public emergency threatening the life of the nation the international instruments concerning civil and political human rights allow States to derogate from their obligations. Derogations must be temporary and non-discriminatory; they are subject to the requirement of proportionality, and States willing to avail themselves of derogation must abide by some procedural requirements.[15] In order to mitigate the effects of derogations, HRL has established a set of non-derogable rights including among others the right to life, the right to humane treatment, and the right to juridical personality.[16]

Economic, social, and cultural rights (ESCR) may be limited by law 'only in so far as this may be compatible with the nature of these rights and solely for the purpose of promoting the general welfare in a democratic society.'[17] But under the ICESCR, States' obligations regarding the rights covered are subject to an inherent limitation insofar as they are to be realized 'progressively' and 'to the maximum of available resources.'[18] Therefore, derogations from ESCR may arguably be justified in times of emergency.[19]

As a matter of fact, when a catastrophic event strikes a country, the ability of a government to ensure full respect of a number of CPRs and ESCRs may be seriously impaired. To cite an example, the liberty of movement or the right of assembly may sometimes prove incompatible with the management of assistance and relief. In extreme cases, floods of persons forced to abandon a disaster area could even threaten the life of a weak State. In situations such as these, restrictions or derogations based on emergency laws are likely to be implemented by the affected State.[20] For this reason, IDRL should build its own discipline of non-derogable rights taking into account the rules contained in human rights treaties as well as their implementation. Since a number of social, economic, and cultural rights are particularly relevant for the victims of a disaster, the core of non-derogable rights in IDRL should be expanded to include obligations to ensure the basic needs of human beings in terms of food, water, health, and the protection of vulnerable groups.

---

[14] 1966 International Covenant on Civil and Political Rights (ICCPR) Articles 12 para 3, 18 para 3, 21 and 22 para 2.

[15] 1950 Convention for the Protection of Human Rights and Fundamental Freedoms (ECHR) Article 15 para 1; ICCPR Article 4 para 1; 1969 American Convention on Human Rights (ACHR) Article 27 para 1. See Oraá 1992, 96; Svensson-McCarty 1998, 371; Beyani 2000, 131–144; Viarengo 2005, 983; de Schutter 2010, 513.

[16] ECHR Article 15 para 2; ICCPR Article 4 para 2; ACHR Article 27 para 2.

[17] 1966 International Covenant on Economic, Social and Cultural Rights (ICESCR) Article 4.

[18] ICESCR Article 1 para 1.

[19] Cotula and Vidar 2002, 6.

[20] See Chap. 14 by Sommario in this volume, Sect. 14.3.

2.4 IDRL and International Humanitarian Law

As the IFRC Desk Study argues, 'it is instructive to look to IHL by way of analogy where it addresses the same issues confronted by IDRL, particularly in light of the fact that some of the origins of IDRL can be traced to the rise of IHL.'[21] Certainly, IHL gives a fundamental contribution to the development of IDRL. Except for combat law, which applies to the material conduct of armed hostilities, the remaining corpus of IHL includes plenty of principles and rules that meet the needs of individuals affected by disaster. In effect, like the victims of armed conflict, disaster victims are wounded, sick, displaced, in danger, and in need of protection.

The application of IHL and IDRL to situations where a disaster occurs during an armed conflict will be discussed in a separate chapter in this volume.[22] Here some general considerations will be made regarding the IHL principles and rules that are of particular interest to IDRL.

A significant set of such rules concerns the protection of the wounded and sick. The Geneva Conventions (GCs) I and II of 1949, as well as the two Additional Protocols (APs) of 1977 include a great number of provisions on this subject.[23] The fundamental principle of non-discrimination applies as expressed by Article 9 of Additional Protocol I. The wording is in line with HRL, but in IHL (as well as in IDRL) distinctions founded on medical grounds are particularly relevant. Detailed IHL provisions related to the respect and protection of medical personnel, material and transports, offer a blueprint for the safeguarding of those providing disasters assistance and relief, as well as of humanitarian units and transports.[24]

Generally, IHL rules pertaining to the protection of civilian persons in time of war, such as those on the protection of the whole of the population, place obligations, and bestow the corresponding rights on belligerent States.[25] Some stipulations, however, are more precisely drafted in terms of individual rights, e.g., the exchange of family news, that 'all persons' ... 'shall be enabled to give', the application to relief organization that protected persons 'shall have every facility for making' and the right of aliens to leave the territory.[26] Those provisions

---

[21] IFRC 2007, Law and Legal Issues in International Disaster Response, 36.

[22] See Chap. 11 by Venturini in this volume.

[23] 1949 Convention (I) for the Amelioration of the Condition of the Wounded and Sick in Armed Forces in the Field, Articles 12–18; 1949 Convention (II) for the Amelioration of the Condition of Wounded, Sick and Shipwrecked Members of Armed Forces at Sea, Articles 12–21; 1977 Protocol Additional to the Geneva Conventions (Protocol I), Articles 10–11; 1977 Protocol Additional to the Geneva Conventions (Protocol II), Articles 7–12.

[24] GC I Articles 24–37, GC II Articles 36–40, AP I Articles 12–17.

[25] GC IV Articles 13–46. E.g., the duty to allow the free passage of consignments of medical and hospital stores (Article 23), to take the necessary measures to ensure child welfare (Article 24) and to facilitate enquiries made by members of dispersed families (Article 26).

[26] GC IV Articles 25, 30, 35.

demonstrate how IHL directly benefits individuals. For this reason, they provide useful reference for IDRL.

IHL applicable to occupied territories also embraces a number of principles appropriate to IDRL, such as the prohibition of forcible transfers (except when evacuation is required for the security of the population), the delivery of food and medical supplies to the population, and the maintenance of medical and hospital services, public health and hygiene 'with particular reference to the adoption and application of the prophylactic and preventive measures necessary to combat the spread of contagious diseases and epidemics.'[27] Furthermore, the regulations for the treatment of internees offer clear patterns for IDRL in terms of accommodation, medical attention, administration, and relief.[28]

Clearly, the above-mentioned standards may not be applied as such in IDRL. Disaster is different from armed conflict, and the basic rationale for the rules pertaining to the law of international armed conflict, i.e., the opposition between the duty bearers (belligerent States) does not exist in disaster situations. The law of non-international armed conflict as codified by Article 3 common to the GCs and by Additional Protocol II may seem to be closer to IDRL. Most regrettably, it offers little contribution to this end. On the one hand, the fundamental guarantees established by the said instruments are far weaker than those provided by HRL. On the other hand, they lack the precision of the provisions pertaining to the law of international armed conflict, whereas detailed rules of conduct are acutely needed in troublesome situations such as disasters. Therefore, the development of IDRL should mainly be pursued by taking into account the principles underlying the protection of victims of international armed conflict.

2.5 Principles of Humanitarian Assistance as Applicable to Disaster Response

It is widely recognized that humanitarian assistance, as outlined by IHL instruments, is based on three main principles: humanity, impartiality, and neutrality. Since these principles are inferred from treaty provisions, their content is often poorly explained. Among the most convincing definitions are those given by the twenty-fifth International Conference of the Red Cross included in the preamble of the Movement's Statutes. The principle of humanity is understood as demanding respect for the human being in all circumstances, protecting life and health as well as 'mutual understanding, friendship, co-operation, and lasting peace amongst all peoples.' Impartiality requires that assistance make no discrimination among the

[27] GC IV Articles 79, 55, 56.

[28] GC IV Articles 79–135. The Commentaries to the Geneva Conventions and their Additional Protocols provide explanations and further elaboration of the rules cited in the text (http://www.icrc.org/ihl.nsf/CONVPRES?OpenView, accessed 16 February 2012).

victims on grounds of nationality, race, religion, class, or political ideology, always giving priority to the most urgent cases of distress. Neutrality applies to those providing assistance, which must abstain from taking sides in hostilities or in controversies of a political, racial, religious, or ideological nature.[29]

Since the paramount purpose of disaster response is the provision of relief to victims, arguably the principles of humanity, impartiality, and neutrality are inherent in IDRL. Humanity is deeply rooted both in HRL and IHL and it inspires most of their basic rules. Impartiality is the preliminary condition for non-discrimination and as such it obviously must govern any assistance and relief.[30] As regards neutrality, its precondition is the existence of an armed conflict where it prevents support being given to one party to the detriment of the other. Therefore, this principle fully plays its role whenever disaster assistance occurs during armed conflicts. The question is, what might the meaning of the principle of neutrality in IDRL be in peacetime? On the one hand, when assistance to the affected State is provided by another State, the principle of consent implies that the public interest of the recipient State should not be harmed. On the other hand, where non-State entities are involved, they are bound to respect the laws and regulations of the territorial State. In both cases, the government clearly has the power to control and to direct assistance. Is this consistent with neutrality in tensions of a political, racial, religious, or ideological nature that may oppose the government to groups of its own citizens? In such situations, neutrality plays more like an attitude, or a state of mind that could hardly generate legal rules.

Be it as it may, the principles of humanity, impartiality, and neutrality actually represent the common denominator of HRL, IHL, and IDRL. As such they offer guidance to States, IOs, NOGs, and emergency workers alike when conducting disaster response. For this reason they are recurrently restated by numerous soft law instruments existing on this subject matter.

2.6 The Role of Soft Law

Soft law designates a number of non-binding instruments aimed at directing the conduct of international actors such as States, governmental, and non-governmental organizations, and other private entities, in fields where customary or treaty-based rules are not established or where, for various reasons, binding agreements may not be accepted. Soft law includes declarations and resolutions, action plans, codes of conduct, guidelines, and principles adopted by intergovernmental bodies or conferences as well as NGOs and other private associations.

[29] See ICRC 1965, Pictet 1985, 61–71.

[30] Impartiality and non-discrimination are referred to separately by the current ILC draft: see Article 6 as provisionally adopted by the Drafting Committee of the International Law Commission on Protection of Persons in the Event of Disasters A/CN.4/L.7576 of 14 July 2010. See Chap. 3 by Zorzi Giustiniani in this volume.

Though not binding, and therefore not supplemented by systems of sanctions, soft law is deemed to have a legal scope and indeed it has practical effects based on voluntary compliance. There appears to be broad consensus that the complex character of contemporary international relations justifies increasing resort to soft law for creating international norms.[31] First, soft law as an alternative to treaties facilitates the wording of more detailed provisions and it enables States to eschew the lengthy and often unpredictable ratification process. Second, revising or replacing a soft law instrument is easier than amending a treaty.[32] Finally, soft law may initiate a law-making process gradually leading to a formal agreement or even to the development of customary law.[33] That said, it should be mentioned that a minority of scholars question the usefulness of the concept of soft law arguing that it may encourage arbitrariness on the part of institutions, and unduly stretches the limits of international law.[34]

A discussion of the merits of those opposing opinions falls beyond the scope of this work. Suffice it to say that IDRL extensively relies on soft law, but this label refers to various different kinds of instruments.

Of primary interest are those instruments adopted by the bodies of international organizations or by intergovernmental conferences with a view to influencing the behavior of States. A number of important resolutions on humanitarian emergency assistance and disaster-related issues were passed by the United Nations General Assembly, especially recognizing the responsibility of States to protect their populations in the event of disaster, but also stressing the principle of consent and respect of the territorial sovereignty of the State receiving assistance from abroad.[35] In these resolutions, soft law coexists with the restatement of existing rules belonging to customary law. Furthermore, as a result of international conferences, a number of strategies and frameworks have been endorsed by States concerning the prevention of natural disasters and disaster risk reduction.[36] These programs are innovative in nature inasmuch as they devise new rules that impact on both international relations and State's domestic activities.

A second group of soft IDRL instruments consists of guidelines and codes of conduct also adopted by intergovernmental bodies and directed at regulating the practical organization of relief and assistance in the field. To cite but a few examples, since 1998 the United Nations Economic and Social Council has

---

[31] See Boyle 1999, Hillgenberg 1999, Chinkin 2000, O'Connell 2000, Boyle and Chinkin 2007, 211–212.

[32] Boyle 1999, 903.

[33] Chinkin 2000, 31–32.

[34] Klabbers 1998, d'Aspremont 2008.

[35] The archetype resolution being that on Strengthening of the Co-ordination of Humanitarian Emergency Assistance, A/RES/46/82 of 19 December 1991. See Chap. 15 by Creta in this volume, Sect. 15.2.4.

[36] Such as the 1994 Yokohama Strategy for a Safer World, the 2005 Hyogo Declaration and the 2005–2015 Hyogo Framework for Disaster Reduction. See Chaps. 8, 9 and 15 by Nicoletti, La Vaccara and Creta in this volume, Sects. 8.3, 9.3.2.1 and 15.2.4, respectively.

established a normative framework for the protection of persons displaced within a country's territory, including disaster situations.[37] The Inter-Agency Standing Committee (IASC, a co-ordination forum involving UN as well as non-UN humanitarian partners) has laid down procedures on co-ordination in the use of military and civil defense assets in response to natural and man-made disasters and in complex emergencies.[38] IASC has also recently adopted guidelines to assist aid workers in implementing a rights-based approach to assistance in situations of natural disaster, including protection of vulnerable groups.[39]

Finally, IDRL guidelines and codes of conduct have been, and are being set out by NGOs in co-operation with States. Those are the most interesting and innovative IDRL instruments that closely resemble voluntary self-regulation or co-regulation by transnational associations and networks. Hence the development of standards for water, sanitation and hygiene, food security and food aid, nutrition and health services.[40] In addition, model guidelines have been issued to regulate the system of legal facilities for disaster relief personnel,[41] and procedures for making use of civil and military defense assets in emergency situations have been provided.[42]

The advantages and disadvantages of the soft law approach to IDRL may be roughly summarized as follows. UN resolutions and programs are worthy of merit since they coalesce consensus by States and direct their course of action. Spontaneous observance of guidelines and codes of conduct by governmental as well as by private actors ensures implementation notwithstanding the non-binding nature of those instruments. Soft law, however, may jeopardize the status of certain obligations and rights that are already established by customary or treaty law. For example, including the prohibition of discrimination based on sex in a soft law instrument runs the risk of downgrading the rank of that rule (that is positively binding upon States and individuals) in the perception of the recipient subjects. For this reason, soft law on disaster response should be resorted to only in those areas where customary or treaty rules of international law either do not exist or need to be specified. IDRL may then be seen as a legal laboratory where customary law, treaty law, and soft law coexist and intermingle in order to achieve the best regulation for international disaster response.

---

[37] United Nations Economic and Social Council, Commission on Human Rights, Guiding Principles on Internal Displacement, E/CN.4/1998/53/Add.2 of 11 February 1998.

[38] Civil-Military Relationship in Complex Emergencies, An IASC Reference Paper (2004). See Chap. 24 by Calvi Parisetti in this volume, Sect. 24.3.1.

[39] IASC (2011). On the IASC Guidelines and similar non-governmental instruments see Chap. 16 by Bizzarri in this volume, Sect. 16.2.3.

[40] The Sphere Project was launched in 1997 by a group of humanitarian NGOs and the Red Cross and Red Crescent Movement. See Chap. 16 by Bizzarri in this volume, Sect. 16.3.3 and Chap. 20 by De Siervo, Sect. 20.3.3.

[41] IFRC (2007) Guidelines. See Chap. 23 by Silingardi in this volume, Sect. 23.3.2.

[42] Such as the Oslo Guidelines (1994) and the MCDA Guidelines (2003). See Chap. 24 by Calvi Parisetti in this volume, Sect. 24.3.1.

2.7 Disaster-Induced Migration: The Case for Non-Refoulement

The hundreds of natural or man-made disasters that occur every year around the world cause the forced movement of millions people. Either these are displaced within their own country, or they migrate across international borders to seek shelter in foreign territory.[43] In both cases, their situation is critical and often desperate since they have limited or no access to food, education or health care.

In principle, internal displacement falls within the domain of a State's domestic jurisdiction, and it must be dealt with in the context of human rights. Whenever internal displacement is triggered by a disaster, the related responsibility rests with national governments; it is not an international concern. The works of the Human Rights Commission and of the UN Special Representative on internally displaced persons (IDPs) have devised standards for the treatment of IDPs,[44] but these have seldom been included in international treaties and are not universally accepted as customary law. International responses to internal displacement have mainly been considered in relation to conflict-induced displacement and sovereignty issues.[45]

Regarding cross-border migration, the 1951 Refugee Convention and its 1967 Protocol that removed its geographic and temporal limitations[46] protect those persons who are outside their country of nationality 'owing to well-founded fear of being persecuted for reasons of race, religion, nationality, membership of a particular social group, or political opinion.'[47] Persons fleeing their country due to a natural or man-made disaster do not fall into those categories.[48] As a consequence, they might not avail themselves of the rule of non-refoulement that constitutes the fundamental component of international refugee protection applying both to persons within a State's territory and to those who arrive at its borders.[49] Nevertheless, established State practice has given extra-Convention refugees various forms of so-called complementary or subsidiary protection preventing involuntary return, while not creating a status recognized in domestic law.[50] Although the topic has been primarily discussed with reference to the protection of persons fleeing

---

[43] The terms 'environmental refugees' or 'environmentally displaced persons' are often used to refer to those people who have been forced to leave their traditional habitat because of an environmental disruption, either natural or man-made (de Moor and Cliquet 2009, 8).

[44] Luopajärvi 2003, 706–712; OCHA (2004); Phuong 2005, 56–65. See also Chap. 16 by Bizzarri in this volume, Sect. 16.2.3.

[45] Luopajärvi 2003, 687–691, Phuong 2005, 117–141.

[46] 1951 Convention Relating to the Status of Refugees (CRSR); 1967 Protocol Relating to the Status of Refugees.

[47] CRSR Article 1 para A (2).

[48] Unless their government willfully deprived them of assistance on one of the grounds set out in the refugee definition: see Kolmannskog and Myrstad 2009, 314 n 8.

[49] CRSR Article 33 para 1.

[50] Mandal 2005, 31–60, Betts 2010, 219 and 223.

conflict areas or serious violations of human rights,[51] there are no legal reasons not to extend at least the basic protection to individuals for whom a disaster is the cause for their displacement.

It is widely recognized that nowadays the principle of non-refoulement corresponds to a rule of customary international law. Recent practice demonstrates that when a major catastrophe occurs, States are prepared to temporarily accept the displaced persons and to delay their return to the affected regions in the aftermath.[52] This paves the way for the application and interpretation of the principle of non-refoulement as a fundamental component of IDRL. Further guidance could be offered by soft law, which might develop specific frameworks for the temporary protection of people fleeing from natural disasters.[53]

2.8 IDRL and Global Health Law: A Parallel Development

Disasters have a serious impact on public health. Besides death and injuries, natural catastrophes often bring about the outbreak of infectious diseases, in addition to the immediate and long-term consequences of man-made disasters.[54]

Contemporary globalization has increased awareness about the international character of public health issues.[55] As a consequence, a body of legal norms labeled either 'global health law' or 'international health law' has been established through treaty commitments, regulations issued by a number of international organizations, and soft law instruments. The purpose of these norms is to foster the worldwide growth of health with the participation of public and private actors, with a view to building a system of global health governance.[56] The World Health Organization (WHO), one of the main agencies of the United Nations, is expanding its activities accordingly. Indeed, the constitution of the WHO empowers the board of the organization to 'take emergency measures within the functions and financial resources of the organization to deal with events requiring immediate action' as well as to 'authorize the director-general to take the necessary steps to combat epidemics, to participate in the organization of health relief to victims of a calamity…'[57] and in 2005 the IASC designated the WHO as the lead agency for the

[51] McAdam 2006 n 9 and accompanying text.

[52] See Kolmannskog and Myrstad 2009, 322 with reference to the UNCHR call for the suspension of return to the areas affected by the 2004 tsunami.

[53] Betts 2010, 211 and 226.

[54] World Health Organization (2006); see Keim 2011.

[55] Fidler 1998, Jost 2004, 146.

[56] Gostin 2008, 240; Acconci 2011, 8–10.

[57] 1948 Constitution of the World Health Organization, Article 28(i).

Global Health Cluster.[58] In the same year, the World Health Assembly adopted the new International Health Regulations (IHR) designed 'to prevent, protect against, control and provide a public health response to the international spread of disease in ways that are commensurate with and restricted to public health risks, and which avoid unnecessary interference with international traffic and trade.'[59]

Although IHR do not explicitly address disaster issues, they are strictly connected with disaster response. States commit themselves to develop, strengthen, and maintain the capacity to detect, assess, notify, and report public health events occurring in their territory that may constitute a public health emergency of international concern; they also undertake to develop, strengthen, and maintain the capacity to respond promptly and effectively to public health risks and public health emergencies of international concern.[60] On the basis of relevant information provided by member States, WHO bodies make recommendations on the appropriate health measures to be implemented.[61] Clearly, good governance in public health is critical for reducing disaster impact and delivering effective response in disasters.[62]

The IHR and other relevant international agreements should be interpreted as compatible without affecting the rights and obligations of States parties deriving from other international agreements.[63] However, the public health measures States may adopt, e.g., on the basis of Part V of IHR might possibly hinder access to their territory by emergency workers in the event of disaster. For this reason, it is essential that Global Health Law and IDRL concurrently develop within domestic legislation as well as in international practice, implementing IHR and disaster response.

2.9 IDRL and Environmental Law: A Synergy for Disaster Prevention

The frequency and intensity of environment-related hazards has been constantly increasing during the past two decades, and their relationship with climate change

58 See Fidler and Gostin 2006; Acconci 2011, 352–354. On the UN Cluster Approach see Chap. 20 by De Siervo in this volume, Sect. 20.2.3.

59 World Health Organization, International Health Regulations (2005) Second Edition, Article 21. According to the WHO Constitution, regulations adopted by the Health Assembly are binding upon all WHO members except for those that notify rejection or reservations. The 2005 IHR entered into force on 15 June 2007 and they have since then acquired universal acceptance. See http://www.who.int/ihr/legal_issues/states_parties/en/index.html. Accessed 10 February 2012.

60 IHR (2005) Articles 5 and 13. See Gostin 2008, 245–254, Rodier 2008, and Acconci 2011, 170–172.

61 IHR (2005) Articles 15, 16.

62 Sixty-fourth World Health Assembly, Strengthening national health emergency and disaster management capacities and resilience of health systems WHA64.10, 24 May 2011.

63 IHR (2005) Article 57 para 1.

has been strongly highlighted in international fora.[64] Therefore, national activities and regulations aimed at preventing environmental harm, as well as States' international commitments in environmental matters are very closely associated with disaster response.

International environmental law (IEL) consists of a multitude of instruments, such as treaties and agreements, declarations, recommendations, guidelines, and codes of conduct focusing on the interactions of humans and the natural world.[65] While the existence of customary rules is still debated, a number of general principles are widely recognized as inspiring States' activities in environmental matters, such as the prevention principle, the 'polluter pays' principle, the principle of sustainable development, the principle of common but differentiated responsibilities, and the precautionary principle.[66]

The prevention principle is deep-rooted in a number of treaties aimed at preventing environmental harm such as, *inter alia*, the 1979 Geneva Convention on long-range trans-boundary air pollution and related protocols, the 1989 Basel Convention on the trans-boundary movements of hazardous wastes, the 1992 UN Convention on climate change, and the related 1997 Kyoto Protocol, the 1994 UN Convention to combat desertification, and the 2001 Stockholm Convention on persistent organic pollutants.[67] With these instruments playing a fundamental role in averting natural and man-made disasters, the prevention principle is the very foundation of disaster risk reduction.[68]

The 'polluter pays' principle underlies domestic regulations requiring polluters to bear the real costs of their pollution. Several treaties dealing with the civil liability for hazardous activities are based on the principle of the owner's responsibility, while the Council of Europe has promoted a convention on the protection of the environment through criminal law for harmonizing member States' legislation in the field of environmental offenses.[69] The fact that the latter Convention is not yet in force suggests that the civil liability approach may better

---

[64] Recently, the Nansen Conference on Climate Change and Displacement in the Twenty-first Century of 6–7 June 2011 focused on vulnerability, resilience and capacity for adaptation of communities in areas prone to disaster due to climate change as well as on the protection of displaced people. See http://www.nansenconference.no/. Accessed 18 October 2011.

[65] Bodanski 2010, 9–15.

[66] Kamminga 1995, 111–131; Lang 1999, 157–172; Sands 2003, 231–290.

[67] 1979 Convention on Long-range Transboundary Air Pollution; 1989 Basel Convention on the Control of Transboundary Movements of Hazardous Wastes and their Disposal; 1992 United Nations Framework Convention on Climate Change; 1994 United Nations Convention to Combat Desertification in Those Countries Experiencing Serious Drought and/or Desertification, Particularly in Africa; 1997 Kyoto Protocol to the United Nations Framework Convention on Climate Change; 2001 Stockholm Convention on persistent organic pollutants.

[68] See Chap. 8 by Nicoletti in this volume.

[69] 1998 Convention on the protection of the environment through criminal law, Council of Europe Treaty Series no. 172, http://conventions.coe.int/. Accessed 16 February 2012.

enhance IDRL to the extent that compensation to victims of man-made disasters is involved.[70]

While sustainable development and common, but differentiated responsibilities are important elements of the concept of natural hazard mitigation, as well as disaster resilience, the precautionary principle remains more controversial. The EU strongly advocates that where scientific data do not permit complete evaluation of the risk, recourse to this principle allows policy makers to take action to protect the public from exposure to harm.[71] The same principle is included in the UN Global Compact principles.[72] Although this view is not universally shared, the adoption of the precautionary principle may certainly enhance strategies to reduce the damages caused by natural as well as by man-made hazards.

2.10 Strategies for Disaster Risk Reduction Within the Millennium Development Goals

Disasters adversely affect development, especially when they hit countries with extreme poverty and weak institutions. At the onset of the twenty-first century, the international community has undertaken unprecedented commitments in order to enhance development. On 8 September 2000, the UN General Assembly adopted the Millennium Declaration by consensus, setting out an international agenda for human development.[73] Eight Millennium Development Goals (MDGs) were agreed upon: eradicating extreme poverty and hunger, achieving universal primary education, promoting gender equality and empowering women, reducing child mortality, improving maternal health, combating HIV/AIDS, malaria, and other diseases, ensuring environmental sustainability, and developing a global partnership for development. Each MDG includes specific targets supported by quantitative indicators for measuring progress.[74]

Reducing disaster risk may greatly contribute to the achievement of MDGs. Indeed, disasters deplete assets needed to combat hunger; they destroy schools, and drain domestic resources to be devoted to education; women, and children are

[70] See Chap. 17 by Nifosi-Sutton in this volume.

[71] Commission of the European Communities, Communication from the Commission on the precautionary principle, Brussels, 2 February 2000, COM(2000) 1 final.

[72] Principle 7 of the United Nations Global Compact's Ten principles (http://www.unglobalcompact.org/AboutTheGC/, accessed 16 February 2012). The Global Compact is a UN initiative directed to businesses to align their operations and practices with ten universally recognized principles in the fields of human rights, labor, environment and combating corruption. See Sahlin-Andersson 2004.

[73] A/Res/55/2 (http://www.un.org/millennium/declaration/ares552e.pdf, accessed 16 February 2012). Section IV of the Millennium Declaration, entitled "Protecting Our Common Future", explicitly recommends collective efforts to reduce the effects of natural and man-made disasters.

[74] http://www.un.org/millenniumgoals/. Accessed 16 February 2012.

particularly vulnerable to the consequences of disasters; destruction related to environmental hazards prevents sustainable urban or rural development. International co-operation is a prerequisite for reducing risk from natural hazards.[75] The close relationship between MDGs and disaster risk reduction has been explained, *inter alia*, by the Secretary-General's Report to the General Assembly of 6 September 2001 recommending strategies that include developing early warning systems, supporting interdisciplinary and intersectoral research on the causes of natural disasters, encouraging governments to address the man-made determinants of disasters, and to incorporate disaster risk reduction into national planning processes.[76]

Although reports praise significant progress toward the MDGs, it is highly doubtful that the 2015 deadline may be met. Empowering women and girls, promoting sustainable development and protecting the most vulnerable are the most critical issues.[77] For this very reason, the relationship between MDGs and IDRL is one of mutual need. On the one hand, IDRL may benefit from the commitments that UN members have assumed to boost development. The systematic evaluation of the targets reached helps shape timely action by States on disaster-related matters. On the other hand, disaster risk policy is instrumental to the fight against poverty. As a consequence, appropriate measures of disaster risk reduction will speed up and bolster efforts to achieve the MDGs.

2.11 Conclusions

IDRL as it is taking shape in contemporary practise is not a self-contained regime, growing in isolation from general international law. On the contrary, it shares a number of fundamental tenets with the legal discipline of other areas that in various ways contribute to molding its form and content. This relationship may be aptly described in terms of mutual support and cross-fertilization. While the general principles and rules belonging to related branches of international law influence and stimulate the progress of IDRL, the latter may in turn enhance their implementation. In order to fully benefit from this productive relationship, IDRL should be construed and applied, taking into account the interpretation and implementation of HRL, IHL, refugee law, global health law, international environmental law, and the law of international development.

Customary international law plays an important, though indirect role with regard to IDRL insofar as customary HRL and IHL provisions apply to disaster response as

[75] UNDP 2004, 16.

[76] Road map towards the implementation of the United Nations Millennium Declaration, Report of the Secretary–General, 6 September 2011, A/56/326. See also Chap. 9 by La Vaccara in this volume.

[77] The Millennium Development Goals Report 2011, United Nations, New York 2011, 4–5.

appropriate. IDRL itself is essentially based on bilateral and multilateral agreements, as well as on a variety of soft law instruments aimed at translating treaty law and general principles into practice. The interplay of these sources may sometimes veil the precise content of the rules governing international disaster response. The presence of multiple actors such as States, intergovernmental, and non-governmental organizations further complicates the picture.

This situation reveals the emergence of a body of law where the traditional principles of State sovereignty and consent are confronted with the need to guarantee assistance to disaster victims, and where co-operation among States tends to be envisaged as a duty instead of a free choice. IDRL stands at the crossroads of multiple pathways. It draws from HRL, IHL, and refugee law to direct the conduct of governmental and non-State actors in disaster relief activities, as well as to establish appropriate standards of treatment for disaster victims. It relies on environmental protection, global health and development to both prevent and mitigate the consequences of disasters. It includes well-settled customary rules together with recognized principles and a variety of agreements and soft law documents. Combining those diverse sources into a coherent system is one of the challenges to which international law must rise in the twenty-first century.

References

Abbott KW, Snidal D (2004) Pathways to international cooperation. In: Benvenisti E, Hirsch M (eds) The impact of international law on international cooperation: theoretical perspectives. Cambridge University Press, Cambridge, pp 50–84

Acconci P (2011) Tutela della salute e diritto internazionale. CEDAM, Padova

Betts A (2010) Towards a 'soft law' framework for the protection of vulnerable irregular migrants. Int J Refug Law 22(2):209–236

Beyani C (2000) Human rights standards and the movement of people within states. Oxford University Press, Oxford

Bodanski D (2010) The art and craft of international environmental law. Harvard University Press, Cambridge

Boyle A (1999) Some reflections on the relationship of treaties and soft law. Int Comp Law Q 48(4):901–913

Boyle A, Chinkin C (2007) The making of international law. Oxford University Press, Oxford

Chinkin C (2000) Normative development in the international legal system. In: Shelton D (ed) Commitment and compliance: the role of non-binding norms in the international legal system. Oxford University Press, Oxford, pp 21–42

Cotula L, Vidar M (2002) The right to adequate food in emergencies. Food and Agriculture Organization of the United Nations, Rome

d'Aspremont J (2008) Softness in international law: a self-serving quest for new legal materials. Eur J Int Law 19(5):1075–1093

de Moor N, Cliquet A (2009) Environmental displacement: a new security risk for Europe? http://biblio.ugent.be/input/download?func=downloadFile&fileOId=923105

de Schutter O (2010) International human rights law: cases, materials, commentary. Cambridge University Press, Cambridge

Dupuy P-M (1998) International law: torn between coexistence, cooperation and globalization. General conclusions. Eur J Int Law 9:278–286

Fidler DP (1998) The future of the World Health Organization: what role for international law? Vanderbilt J Trans Law 31:1079–1126
Fidler DP, Gostin GO (2006) The new international health regulations: an historic development for international law and public health. J Law Med Ethics 34:85–94
Gostin GO (2008) Public health law. Power, duty, restraint. University of California Press, Berkeley
Hillgenberg H (1999) A fresh look at soft law. Eur J Int Law 3:499–515
IASC (2011) Operational guidelines on the protection of persons in situations of natural disasters. http://ochanet.unocha.org/p/Documents/Operational%20Guidelines.pdf
ICRC (1965) The fundamental principles of the Red Cross and Red Crescent. http://www.icrc.org/eng/assets/files/other/icrc_002_0513.pdf
IFRC (2007) Guidelines for the domestic facilitation and regulation of international disaster relief and initial recovery assistance. http://www.ifrc.org/global/publications/idrl/resources/guidelines.asp
IFRC (2007b) Law and legal issues in international disaster response: a desk study. International Federation of Red Cross and Red Crescent Societies, Geneva
Jost TS (2004) Comparative and international health law. Health Matrix 14:141–147
Kamminga K (1995) Principles of international environmental law. In: Blowers A, Glasbergen P (eds) Environmental policy in an international context, vol 1. Elsevier Butterworth-Heinemann, Oxford, pp 111–131
Keim ME (2011) The public health impact of industrial disasters. Am J Disaster Med 6:265–272
Klabbers J (1998) The undesirability of soft law. Nord J Int Law 67:381–391
Kolmannskog V, Myrstad F (2009) Environmental displacement in European asylum law. Eur J Migr Law 11:313–326
Lang W (1999) UN—principles and international environmental law. Max Planck Yearb U N Law 3:157–172
Luopajärvi K (2003) Is there an obligation on states to accept international humanitarian assistance to internally displaced persons under international law? Int J Refug Law 15(4):678–714
Macalister-Smith P (1981) The International Relief Union of 1932. Disasters 5(2):147–154
Mandal R (2005) Protection mechanisms outside the 1951 Convention ('Complementary Protection'), Legal and Protection Policy Research Series No. 9, UNHCR, Geneva
McAdam J (2006) The Refugee Convention as a rights blueprint for persons in need of international protection, New Issues in Refugee Research, Research Paper No. 125, UNCHR, Geneva
OCHA (2004) Guiding principles on internal displacement, E/CN.4/1998/53/Add.2, United Nations, New York
O'Connell ME (2000) The role of soft law in the global order. In: Shelton D (ed) Commitment and compliance: the role of non-binding norms in the international legal system. Oxford University Press, Oxford, pp 100–114
Oraá J (1992) Human rights in states of emergency in international law. Oxford University Press, Oxford
Phuong C (2005) The international protection of internally displaced persons. Cambridge University Press, Cambridge
Pictet J (1985) Development and principles of international humanitarian law. Martinus Nijhoff Publishers, Dordrecht
Rodier G (2008) Le Règlement Sanitaire International Revisé, in Société Française pour le Droit International. Colloque de Nanterre, La Responsabilité de Protéger, Pedone, Paris
Sahlin-Andersson K (2004) Emergent cross-sectional soft regulations: dynamics at play in the global compact initiative. In: Mörth U (ed) Soft law in governance and regulation. An interdisciplinary analysis. Edward Elgar Publishing Limited, Cheltenham
Sands P (2003) Principles of international environmental law, 2nd edn. Cambridge University Press, Cambridge

Svensson-McCarty A-L (1998) The international law of human rights and states of exception. Martinus Nijhoff Publishers, Dordrecht
United Nations Development Programme (2004) Reducing disaster risk. A challenge for development, UNDP, New York, 2004
van Hoof GJH (1983) Rethinking the sources of international law. Kluwer Law and Taxation Publishers, Deventer
Viarengo I (2005) Deroghe e restrizioni alla tutela dei diritti umani nei sistemi internazionali di garanzia. Rivista di diritto internazionale 41:955–996
World Health Organization (2005) International health regulations second edition, http://whqlibdoc.who.int/publications/2008/9789241580410_eng.pdf
World Health Organization (2006) Communicable diseases following natural disasters: risk assessment and priority interventions. http://www.who.int/diseasecontrol_emergencies/guidelines/CD_Disasters_26_06.pdf

Chapter 3
The Works of the International Law Commission on 'Protection of Persons in the Event of Disasters'. A Critical Appraisal

Flavia Zorzi Giustiniani

Abstract This chapter is focused on the works of the International Law Commission (ILC) on the topic 'Protection of persons in the event of disasters' and it aims at presenting and critically evaluating what the Commission has done so far. After a brief introduction, the analysis will concentrate on the Special Rapporteur's rights-based approach to the topic, and proceed by assessing its pros and cons at both the theoretical and practical levels. Specific attention will be devoted to the key aspects of the ILC's study: the primary responsibility of the affected State, the rules and principles that regulate the delivery of humanitarian relief, and the (ambiguous) role assigned to the international community.

Keywords Codification · Human rights · Needs · Access · Consent · Cooperation

Contents

F. Zorzi Giustiniani (✉)
Università Telematica Internazionale UNINETTUNO, Rome, Italy
e-mail: f.zorzigiustiniani@uninettunouniversity.net

A. de Guttry et al. (eds.), *International Disaster Response Law*,
DOI: 10.1007/978-90-6704-882-8_3,

3.1 Introductory Remarks

The survey of International Disaster Response Law clearly shows a tendency to regulate each and every specific issue involved at regional or, more frequently, bilateral level. On the contrary, universal agreements in recent times have been recurred to very seldom to deal with some particular issue or setting.[1] The end result is a patchwork of rules and systems which is characterized by overlapping and gaps.

The lack of a coherent and complete framework covering the various phases of a disaster prompted the oldest disaster relief organization—the International Federation of Red Cross and Red Crescent Societies (IFRC)[2]—to launch in 2001 the so-called International Disaster Response Laws, Rules, and Principles (IDRL) Programme. The main objectives of this program were to create a legal database focused on international and national instruments dealing with disaster relief and recovery and, through national Societies, to assist governments in developing appropriate rules and policies on the various issues involved.

The IDRL Programme also led to the development of the Guidelines for the Domestic Facilitation and Regulation of International Disaster Relief and Initial Recovery Assistance, a soft-law instrument instructing governments how to be prepared for disasters and regulate the common problems arising in international disaster relief operations. These Guidelines were unanimously adopted by States parties to the Geneva Conventions and by all the Red Cross and Red Crescent components at the thirteenth International Conference of the Red Cross and Red Crescent Movement in 2007.[3] This instrument, although it is not binding, is extremely important not just for being the first of its kind, but also for its global reach. In fact, a great number of the States parties of the international community consented to it and the UN General Assembly has encouraged its use as a means able to improve the international cooperation in disaster relief.[4]

The importance of the work undertaken by the Red Cross Movement has also been recognized by the UN Secretariat, which referred in its Memorandum on the

---

[1] A case in point is the Tampere Convention on the provision of telecommunication resources for disaster mitigation and relief operations. See Chap. 1 by de Guttry in this volume.

[2] Its institution dates back to 1919; its name at the time was the League of Red Cross Societies.

[3] The text of the ICRC's Guidelines is available at: http://www.ifrc.org/global/publications/idrl/resources/guidelines.asp. Accessed on February 15, 2012.

[4] Strengthening of the coordination of emergency humanitarian assistance of the United Nations, UN Doc. A/RES/63/139, 5 March 2009; International cooperation on humanitarian assistance in the field of natural disasters, from relief to development, UN Doc. A/RES/63/141, 10 March 2009; Strengthening emergency relief, rehabilitation, reconstruction and prevention in the aftermath of the Indian Ocean tsunami disaster, UN Doc. A/RES/63/137, 3 March 2009. See also the following resolutions adopted by the Economic and Social Council: Strengthening of the coordination of emergency humanitarian assistance of the United Nations, E/RES/2008/36, 25 July 2008; Strengthening of the coordination of emergency humanitarian assistance of the United Nations, E/RES/2009/3, 22 July 2009.

Protection of persons in the event of disasters to the 2007 IDRL Guidelines as one of the most recent and significant developments of an 'expanding regulatory framework.'[5] Thus, it is possible to say that the IFRC Guidelines constituted a primary reference point for the International Law Commission (ILC) since the beginning of its work on this topic.

The first proposal to study the topic at issue, entitled 'International protection of persons in critical situations', was formulated in 2004 by Mr. M. Kamto and it was submitted to the consideration of the Working Group on the Long-Term Programme of Work.[6] The topic was recommended to the attention of the ILC in 2006, and put it on its agenda starting from the following year under the heading 'Protection of persons in the event of disasters.' The ILC endorsed it by emphasizing its being as one of the 'new developments in international law and pressing concerns of the international community as a whole' and taking into account the growing demands from the disaster relief community towards its systematization.[7] In the same year, the Secretariat was invited by the Commission to prepare a background study detailing the existing legal instruments and texts that apply to disaster prevention, relief assistance, and the protection of persons.[8] The topic was then assigned to Mr. Eduardo Valencia-Ospina as Special Rapporteur.

Since the beginning the Commission was well aware of that it would embark on an exercise *de lege ferenda*. In fact, as was correctly remarked by an author, '[m]any aspects of disaster response are subject to disparate practice by states, and therefore any efforts to establish clear rules in this area will require a drafter to engage in progressive development of the law, rather than strict codification of existing custom.'[9]

The inclusion of the topic in the ILC's programme of work was generally welcomed by States, which in 2007, during the debates held within the Sixth Committee, remarked the timeliness of such a study.[10] The only dissenting voice

---

5 Protection of persons in the event of disasters: Memorandum by the Secretariat, UN Doc. A/CN.4/590, 11 December 2007, para 6.

6 Within the UN context, several attempts of codification had already been made during the 1970s and 1980s. In particular, in 1984 the Office of the UNDRO submitted a 'Draft Convention on Expediting the Delivery of Emergency Assistance' (UN Doc. A/39/267/Add.2, 18 June 1984), whose overall objective was to smooth the technical barriers of relief operations. The initiative received some support by governments, but in the end the Council never took action on it. In fact, the view prevailed that times were not yet ripe for such an enterprise (see Bettati 1991, 653).

7 Report of the International Law Commission on the work of its fifty-eighth session (1 May to 9 June and 3 July to 11 August 2006) UN Doc. A/61/10, Annex C para 1.

8 The Secretariat released its Memorandum on the topic on 11 December 2007 (cf. UN Doc. A/CN.4/590).

9 Benton Heath 2011, 424.

10 See the statements made by Benin (A/C.6/62/SR.18 para 47), Egypt (A/C.6/62/SR.18 para 71), Guatemala (A/C.6/62/SR.19 para 12), United Kingdom of Great Britain and Northern Ireland (A/C.6/62/SR.19 para 42), Sri Lanka (A/C.6/62/SR.19 para 55), India (A/C.6/62/SR.19 para 107), Poland (A/C.6/62/SR.20 para 1), United States of America (A/C.6/62/SR.20 para 23), Hungary (A/C.6/62/SR.21 para 7), Greece (A/C.6/62/SR.21 para 53), Romania (A/C.6/62/SR.21 para 78),

came from Portugal, whose representative put in doubt the appropriateness of engaging in codification works of the subject.[11]

The scope of the topic *ratione materiae* was initially focused on natural disasters or natural disaster components of broader emergencies; in fact, it was considered that 'the more immediate need may be for a consideration of activities undertaken in the context of a natural disaster'.[12] Yet, various factors militated against such a narrow focus. In particular, it was soon acknowledged that establishing a clear-cut distinction between natural and man-made catastrophes was both practically and logically difficult. As a matter of fact, it is not a coincidence that a generally accepted definition of the term 'disaster' in international law is lacking. The Special Rapporteur remarked that an examination of treaty law shows two opposing trends: while some treaties deliberately omit to define disasters, others adopt an all-encompassing definition.[13]

In his Preliminary Report Mr. Valencia-Ospina aptly observed that many calamitous events cannot be ascribed to a unique causal factor, and also considered inappropriate to distinguish among various types of disasters because of different origin. 'The need for protection'—he noted—'can be said to be equally strong in all disaster situations.'[14] As a consequence, he proposed to widen the scope of the analysis, considering all kinds of disasters with the exception of armed conflicts, and his proposal met with no particular opposition.

In conformity with this approach, Draft Article 3, as provisionally adopted by the Drafting Committee, gives the following definition of disaster: "Disaster" means a calamitous event or series of events resulting in widespread loss of life, great human suffering and distress, or large-scale material or environmental damage, thereby seriously disrupting the functioning of society.'[15]

Remarkably this definition, despite the focus of the work being on the protection of persons, also comprises those calamitous events which do not cause deaths but only provoke destruction or loss of goods or property or also deterioration of the environment. Moreover, it is not required that the event provokes a transboundary effect.[16]

(Footnote 10 continued)
Israel (A/C.6/62/SR.21 para 99), Kenya (A/C.6/62/SR.21 para 112), Sierra Leone (A/C.6/62/SR.24 para 100) and New Zealand (A/C.6/62/SR.25 para 19).

11 A/C.6/62/SR.19, para 77.

12 UN Doc. A/61/10, Annex C para 2. In a similar vein, the Secretariat's Memorandum acknowledged that '[w]hile the bulk of the study pertains to disasters emanating from natural phenomena, few of the legal instruments and texts cited maintain a clear distinction between natural and man-made disasters' (UN Doc. A/CN.4/590 para 8).

13 Preliminary report on the protection of persons in the event of disasters, 5 May 2008, UN Doc. A/CN.4/598 para 47. For an extensive survey of the state of the art on the issue see Chap. 1 by de Guttry in this volume.

14 UN Doc. A/CN.4/598 para 49.

15 Cf. draft Article 3.

16 Report of the International Law Commission on the work of its sixty-second session (3 May to 4 June and 5 July to 6 August 2010), UN Doc. A/65/10, 11.

In his Preliminary Report the Rapporteur also referenced to the Responsibility to protect doctrine and noted that the debate on its applicability to disaster response at international level was echoed in the first debates on the topic at the ILC and the Sixth Committee. Considering the widespread political resistance to extending such doctrine to natural disasters, and also recalling the position taken by the Secretary-General,[17] he deemed it necessary to exclude it from the scope of the topic.[18]

Concerning the objective of the work, the Special Rapporteur noted that the ILC intended to elaborate a text which would serve as a legal framework for the conduct of international disaster relief activities, clarifying the core legal principles and concepts necessary for the creation of a legal 'space' in which such a disaster relief work could take place on a secure footing. Then the final form could be either a convention or a declaration incorporating a model or guidelines.[19] Nevertheless, in order not to duplicate the previous efforts already undertaken by the IFRC in the subject area, only the adoption of a treaty could be said to have a real added value to existing instruments.[20]

3.2 The Concept of Protection of Persons: A Human Rights-Based Approach?

Addressing the general scope of the topic, the Special Rapporteur analyzed the concept of protection by distinguishing an all-encompassing notion, which includes the more specific concepts of response, relief or assistance, and protection in a strict sense, which is also covered by the first notion and denotes a rights-based approach.[21] Considering that the focus on the individual as a victim of a disaster implied that certain rights accrued to that individual, he then concluded affirming the need to address the topic under review with the said rights-based approach.[22]

---

[17] In fact, the Secretary-General in his 2009 report on implementing the responsibility to protect clarified that the concept is not applicable to calamities such as natural disasters (Implementing the responsibility to protect: report of the Secretary-General, 12 January 2009, UN Doc. A/63/677 para 10 (b)). But see Chap. 10 by Costas Trascasas in this volume, para 10.4.1–2.

[18] The discussion on the opportunity to apply the concept of 'responsibility to protect' to natural disasters was launched after the Nargis typhoon which devastated Myanmar in 2008.

[19] UN Doc. A/CN.4/598 para 264.

[20] The need to avoid duplications was highlighted, inter alia, by the Dutch representative (see International Law Commission: Legal Adviser Dr. Liesbeth Lijnzaad addresses the Sixth Committee (Part III) 31 October 2008, available at http://www.netherlandsmission.org/article.asp?articleref=AR00000476EN&categoryvalue=statements&subcategoryvalue=). Accessed on February 26 2012.

[21] UN Doc. A/CN.4/598, para 51.

[22] UN Doc. A/CN.4/598, para 218. See also the Secretariat's Memorandum, wherein it is affirmed that '[e]xisting international human rights obligations lie at the core of the content of protection in the context of disasters.' (UN Doc. A/CN.4/590, 3).

The rights-based approach propounded by the Special Rapporteur has met with no particular opposition neither within the Commission nor by States in the Sixth Committee. Nevertheless, some members lamented the lack of a general understanding of what was meant by such an approach for the purposes of the present topic. Doubts on the appropriateness of a rights-based approach were expressed by a few other members. On the one hand they remarked that it would require addressing the issue of rights' enforcement, and on the other they contended that the real focus of the work ought rather to be on the obligations that would be taken to facilitate action to protect such persons.[23]

The human rights-based approach has been defined by the OHCHR as follows:

> '[A] conceptual framework for the process of human development that is normatively based on international human rights standards and operationally directed to promoting and protecting human rights. It seeks to analyze inequalities which lie at the heart of development problems and redress discriminatory practices and unjust distributions of power that impede development progress.'[24]

This approach has first been conceptualized within the field of development, when it was realized that human rights should guide the processes involved in development projects and not just the results achieved. The failure to incorporate rights in such processes could in fact prejudice the fulfillment of human rights of those affected by the projects once built.[25] Central to this conceptual change is the position of the human being. The meaning of development changed this perception insofar as it clearly described the human being as the *subject*, not the *object* of development.[26]

The main feature of this approach is thus the existence of a duty-bearer—the State—and on the opposite side rights-holders—those affected by the disaster. It therefore emphasizes the realizing of rights as opposed to meeting needs. In other words, 'victims' or 'beneficiaries' become 'rights-holders' and, because of that, they are entitled to assert legitimate claims to protection and assistance. Participation and empowerment in fact became key concepts in development.

From the development context the rights-based approach was subsequently applied to emergency humanitarian response. Traditionally, humanitarian organizations arriving in a disaster context were focused on the distribution of life-essentials, overlooking on the importance of monitoring the observance of human rights of those affected by the disaster. Over time, the charitable and essentially depoliticized response to need, featuring the so-called needs-based approach, has

---

[23] Report of the International Law Commission on the work of its sixtieth session (5 May to 6 June and 7 July to 8 August 2008), UN Doc. A/63/10 paras 227–229.

[24] Office of the High Commissioner on Human Rights 2006.

[25] Several United Nations agencies have developed a 'Common Understanding' of the human rights-based approach to programming (United Nations Development Group, UN Statement of Common Understanding on Human Rights-Based Approaches to Development Cooperation and Programming, May 2003). Among the NGOs, BRAC, Oxfam, Save the Children Alliance, and World Vision are the leaders in the rights-based approach to development.

[26] Gready and Ensor 2005, 18.

though been challenged by an approach that asserts legitimate claims to protection and assistance.[27] As a consequence, an increasing number of humanitarian organizations adhered to their own set of guidelines and standards,[28] including some form of rights-based standards.[29]

The rights-based approach was initially elaborated and adhered upon with enthusiasm by humanitarian organizations, which understood themselves to be directly fulfilling the human rights of beneficiaries. Nevertheless, assuming the responsibility to provide services does not automatically transform the previously mentioned organizations into duty-bearers and in fact two distinct and yet interrelated problems emerged. The first consisted in the direct lack of accountability of humanitarian agencies to the beneficiaries of their services. A *leitmotiv* of the standards adopted is in fact that, while the content of the rights is set out clearly, the corresponding obligation to fulfill those rights is not articulated as binding on any specific body.[30]

A rights-based approach to humanitarian aid, if adopted by humanitarian agencies, could also have the disadvantage of shifting responsibility for fulfilling beneficiaries' rights to the former and away from other stakeholders, *in primis* host States. As a matter of fact, while the (host) State's capacity may be diminished by the cause of the emergency itself, it nevertheless remains the primary guarantor of rights. Therefore, humanitarian organizations cannot and should not assume human rights obligations *in lieu* of the territorial State.

The affirmation of the rights-based approach in the humanitarian community also had the effect of creating an unhelpful and misleading dichotomy between needs and rights. Instead, there is no necessary incompatibility between needs-based and rights-based approaches:

---

[27] The systematic integration of human rights standards into operational humanitarian assistance programming tools can be traced to humanitarians' distress about their role in several well-known emergencies, especially the famine in Somalia in the early 1990s and the aftermath of the Rwandan genocide in 1994. In relation to Rwanda, the Joint Evaluation of Emergency Assistance to Rwanda identified the need for humanitarian organizations to set up self-regulation schemes aimed at improving performance. See Relief and Rehabilitation Network 1996, Recommendation 11.

[28] In fact humanitarian organizations often tailored human rights standards on their needs and ultimately their discretion.

[29] The rights to which a given organization abides are generally included in codes of conduct or standards, such as the Code of Conduct of the International Red Cross and Red Crescent Movement in Disaster Relief, the Humanitarian Charter, the People in Aid Code of Practice in the Management and Support of Aid Personnel, the Sphere Project's Minimum Standards in Disaster Response, and the HAP Standard. More recently, in 2009, the International Development Law Organization (IDLO) published the Manual on International Law and Standards Applicable in Natural Disaster Situations.

[30] In order to come up with this problem, by 1996 humanitarian organizations had set up the Active Learning Network for Accountability and Performance (ALNAP) and the 'Standards Project', which later became the Sphere Project, aimed at formulating standards for humanitarian assistance. Members of the humanitarian aid system identified the need to ensure their accountability to beneficiaries and other stakeholders.

> 'A statement about need (or, better, risk) may be essential to defining the 'what' of programming, and is of itself value neutral, and not a moral statement. In traditional humanitarian terms, it acquires moral force when the need is of a certain kind, by reference to the principle of humanity and the 'humanitarian imperative'. A statement about rights involves a moral (and perhaps a legal) claim about entitlements, and is as significant for its identification of related responsibilities as for the rights claim itself. While such language may be used alongside or in place of an appeal to the humanitarian imperative, it cannot in any sense be said to supersede the language of needs.'[31]

For our purposes, this implies that both approaches maintain their validity and thus can be applied in disaster response, but their content should necessarily vary depending on the stakeholder involved (humanitarian organization, host State, third State). These reflections, though, are not adequately reflected in the ILC work.

Taking into account the comments received within the ILC, the Rapporteur clarified that the rights-based approach proposed was not exclusive and had to be informed by other considerations when appropriate, including the needs of disaster victims. 'Needs and rights'—he added—'were two sides of the same coin'.[32] The rights-based approach had thus to be understood in two senses: 'requiring particular attention be paid to the needs and concerns of individuals who are suffering; and as a reminder that people have legal rights when disaster strikes, thereby reaffirming the place of international law in the context of disasters.'[33]

Moreover, he remarked that the ILC was dealing at once with traditional reciprocal relationships between States and with rights and obligations of States toward affected persons. These clarifications were reflected in draft Article 1 (Scope), which reads as follows: 'The present draft articles apply to the protection of persons in the event of disasters, in order for States to ensure the realization of the rights of persons in such an event, by providing an adequate and effective response to their needs in all phases of a disaster.'[34]

Following the suggestions arisen during the plenary debate, the article was divided into two draft articles, the first dealing with the scope proper (i.e., the protection of persons in the event of disasters) and the second addressing the purpose. Draft Article 2, as provisionally adopted by the Commission at its sixty-second session, locates the purpose in the facilitation of 'an adequate and effective response to disasters that meets the essential needs of the persons concerned, with full respect for their rights'. It is evident that this last formulation slightly shifts the focus from rights to needs.[35] This was the result of an 'elegant compromise'

---

[31] Darcy and Hoffman 2003, 5.

[32] Report of the International Law Commission on the work of its sixty-first session (4 May to 5 June and 6 July to 7 August 2009), UN Doc. A/64/10 para 155.

[33] UN Doc. A/64/10 para 178.

[34] UN Doc. A/63/677 para 10 (b).

[35] The Commission also decided to delete the general statement on the obligation of States to ensure an adequate and effective response, deeming it more appropriate to specifically address the different obligations incumbent on the various States involved (affected States, assistance-providing States etc.) in subsequent articles.

between two opposing views militating for a focus either on needs or on rights.[36] Moreover, the ILC in the Commentary has affirmed to understand 'rights' as an all-encompassing notion, which contains not just internationally recognized human rights but also rights acquired under domestic law.[37] The continuing adherence to the rights-based approach would nonetheless seem to be justified by the insertion of an article—draft Article 8—dealing specifically with human rights. The text of this provision, though, stands out for its generic nature, affirming that: 'Persons affected by disasters are entitled to respect for their human rights.'

In a similar vein, Article 7 addresses the principle of human dignity in disaster response, and requires all the actors involved (States, competent intergovernmental organizations, and relevant non-governmental organizations) to respect and protect such core principle.

The assertion that people affected by disasters shall be protected and respected in their dignity and rights is at least vague and adds nothing to what should be taken for granted. As a consequence, also unexplored is the ability of rights-holders to claim their rights, which is one of the key features of rights-based as opposed to needs-based approaches.

From the work under discussion one would instead expect an unambiguous reference to those rights which are particularly relevant for the protection of persons in a disaster-like situation and hence should be prioritized over others.[38] The step back is even more evident if one considers that the working group's proposals were clearly formulated in terms of specific rights of the victims, in particular the right to protection, safety and security, and the right to access to disaster relief and basic needs.[39]

In addition to that, the primary responsibility of the affected State in protecting people's rights is not adequately reflected in the draft articles. As a matter of fact, except that in case of State's collapse, the affected State's responsibility to protect, respect, and fulfill people's rights also involves taking measures to ensure that third parties (private actors, NGOs, and humanitarian/intergovernmental organizations) not infringe on rights. Far from clarifying the different roles and responsibilities of the various stakeholders, draft Articles 7 and 8 end in a rhetorical affirmation of the need to protect human rights and dignity of those affected by a disaster. In this respect the ILC limited itself to specify, in the Commentary, that 'distinct obligations will be held by affected States, assisting States, and various other assisting actors respectively.'[40]

---

[36] Third report on the protection of persons in the event of disasters, UN Doc. A/CN.4/629, 31 March 2010 para 9.

[37] Cf. Commentary to draft Article 2, UN Doc. A/65/10 para 331.

[38] However, a reference to the importance, in case of disasters, of economic and social rights is made in the Commentary to Article 10, Report of the International Law Commission on the work of its sixty-third session (26 April to 3 June and 4 July to 12 August 2011), UN Doc. A/66/10, para 289.

[39] Cf. UN Doc. A/61/10, 481.

[40] Commentary, draft Article 8, UN Doc. A/66/10 para 289.

Ultimately, despite the initial intentions the draft articles cannot be said to be informed by a rights-based approach.

3.3 A Missed Opportunity: The Failure to Recognize the Right to Humanitarian Assistance for Victims of Disasters

One of the most crucial problems of disaster relief (and of relief in general) concerns the humanitarian access to people in need and the boundaries of discretion within which the affected State can legitimately deny it. In its preliminary report Mr. Valencia-Ospina acknowledged the importance, from the standpoint of disaster victims, of the existence of a right to humanitarian assistance.[41] At the same time, though, he remarked that such a right, on whose existence he did not take a position, would contrast with the traditional understanding of sovereignty and non-intervention.[42] After the elaboration of the rights-based approach he then concentrated, in his third report, on the principles directly relevant to the protection of persons and on the primary responsibility of the affected State for protecting persons under its territorial jurisdiction.

Concerning humanitarian principles, the Rapporteur proposed the following provision: 'Response to disasters shall take place in accordance with the principles of humanity, neutrality and impartiality.'[43]

He recalled that these principles find their roots in international humanitarian law and the fundamental principles of the Red Cross, but in time have come to characterize humanitarian action irrespective of the context (armed conflict, natural disasters, etc.) and hence are generally required from all the assisting actors involved. In particular, their significance in disaster situations was highlighted by the notorious GA resolution 46/182 back in 1991 and most recently reaffirmed in different contexts.[44] These principles can thus be considered as being the fundamental and distinguishing features of humanitarian action.[45] As was correctly

---

[41] On the issue see Chap. 15 by Creta in this volume.

[42] UN Doc. A/CN.4/598 para 54.

[43] Cf. draft Article 6, reading 'Humanitarian principles in disaster response.'

[44] Cf. *inter alia*: GA resolutions 63/139 (5 March 2009), 63/141 (10 March 2009), 64/74 (27 January 2010) and 64/76 (2 February 2010); Guidelines on the Use of Foreign Military and Civil Defence Assets in Disaster Relief, revised on 1 November 2007, paras 1, 20, 22, 79, 80, 93 and 95; International Federation of Red Cross and Red Crescent Societies, Guidelines for the Domestic Facilitation and Regulation of International Disaster Relief and Initial Recovery Assistance, 2007, Article 4 para 2; AU Kampala Convention for the Protection and Assistance of Internally Displaced Persons in Africa, adopted 22 October 2009, Article 5 para 8.

[45] While humanity and impartiality indisputably apply to any kind of disaster situations, neutrality at first sight could seem a context-specific principle, inextricably connected to the idea of a conflict or contrast among opposing parties. Nevertheless, as was noted by Mr. Valencia-

remarked by the Special Rapporteur, 'response to disasters in all stages is conditioned on these humanitarian principles so as to preserve the legitimacy and effectiveness of that response'.[46]

The reference to the said principles found support within the ILC and, despite some concerns regarding the feasibility of their transposition to the present topic, was subsequently approved by the Drafting Committee without any major change.[47]

Then the Special Rapporteur analyzed the role and responsibility of the affected State. Doing it, he focused the attention on the traditional principles of State sovereignty and non-intervention. In his view, these principles imply that 'a State affected by a disaster has the freedom to adopt whatever measures it sees fit to ensure the protection of the persons found within its territory. As a consequence, no other State may legally intervene in the process of response to a disaster in a unilateral manner: third parties must instead seek to cooperate with the affected State in accordance with Article 5, as provisionally adopted by the Drafting Committee'.[48]

Despite his initial focus on a very traditional conception of sovereignty, he then admitted that States' domestic sphere is 'by no means absolute' and that regarding the life, health, and bodily integrity of individuals 'humanitarian law and human rights law demonstrate that principles such as sovereignty and non-intervention constitute a starting point for the analysis, not a conclusion'.[49] In his understanding, the principles of sovereignty and non-intervention in the context of disasters find expression in the primary responsibility of the affected State for the protection of persons in its territory. From this primacy two consequences would flow:

(Footnote 45 continued)
Ospina, in disaster situations other than armed conflict neutrality should be understood as implying that 'those responding to disasters should abstain from any act which might be interpreted as interference with the interests of the State. Conversely, the affected State must respect the humanitarian nature of the response activities and 'refrain from subjecting it to conditions that divest it of its material and ideological neutrality.' Neutrality can thus be considered as 'a key operational principle to ensure access to those adversely affected by disasters in an impartial manner' (UN Doc. A/CN.4/629 paras 29–30).

46 UN Doc. A/CN.4/629 para 25.

47 Draft Article 6, entitled 'Humanitarian principles in disaster response', reads as follows:
'Response to disasters shall take place in accordance with the principles of humanity, neutrality and impartiality, and on the basis of non-discrimination, while taking into account the needs of the particularly vulnerable.'
With respect to the draft originally proposed, the text as approved makes explicit reference to non-discrimination. Admittedly, this addition is unnecessary because the principle at issue already finds expression in the principles of impartiality and neutrality, and in fact most instruments relating to humanitarian assistance do not separately mention it.

48 UN Doc. A/CN.4/629 para 74.

49 UN Doc. A/CN.4/629 paras 74–75.

> 'First is the recognition that the affected State bears the ultimate responsibility for protecting disaster victims on its territory and that it has the primary role in facilitating, coordinating and overseeing relief operations on its territory. The other general conclusion is that international relief operations require the consent of the affected State.'[50]

From an overview of provisions contained in several IDRL agreements and soft-law documents, he then concluded that both States and humanitarian actors converge in recognizing the principle of the primary responsibility of the affected State. Accordingly, he proposed a draft article, entitled 'Primary responsibility of the affected State', whose first paragraph so provides:

> 'The affected State has the primary responsibility for the protection of persons and provision of humanitarian assistance on its territory. The State retains the right, under its national law, to direct, control, coordinate and supervise such assistance within its territory.'

However, the principle of primary responsibility has not survived in the draft text provisionally adopted by the Drafting Committee. In fact, some ILC members opposed it since it implies the existence of 'secondary' duties and could hence lead to unwarranted intervention.[51] The text provisionally adopted, more neutrally entitled 'Role of the affected State', reads as follows:

> '1. The affected State, by virtue of its sovereignty, has the duty to ensure the protection of persons and provision of disaster relief and assistance on its territory.
>
> 2. The affected State has the primary role in the direction, control, coordination and supervision of such relief and assistance.'

While at first sight the new formulation, in affirming unambiguously the *duty* of the affected State to assist and protect disaster victims, would seem more progressive, on one hand the direct connection of such a duty with the principle of sovereignty and, on the other hand, the distinct provision on the State's primary role in the overall direction and control of relief operations[52] reveal instead a very traditional and conservative understanding of State sovereignty.[53]

---

[50] Un Doc. A/CN.4/629 para 78.

[51] UN Doc. A/65/10 para 318.

[52] A direct connection between the State's duty to protect and its primary role in the control and supervision of humanitarian actions taking place on its territory is affirmed in the 2003 IDI resolution on humanitarian assistance (hereinafter Bruges resolution), which states that:

'The affected State has the duty to take care of the victims of disaster in its territory and has *therefore* the primary responsibility in the organization, provision and distribution of humanitarian assistance. As a result, it has the duty to take the necessary measures to prevent the misappropriation of humanitarian assistance and other abuses'. (Institut de Droit International, Humanitarian assistance, 2 September 2003, Bruges Session, Article III.1, emphasis added).

[53] The said view is confirmed by the Commentary, where it is clearly recognized that 'As a whole, draft Article 9 is premised on the core principles of sovereignty and non-intervention respectively, as enshrined in the Charter of the United Nations, and recognized in numerous international instruments' (UN Doc. A/66/10 para 289).

Concerning the 'external' aspect of the State's primary responsibility—i.e., the affected State's relationships with other international actors in the wake of a disaster—the Rapporteur expressed the view that consent is a necessary requirement for disaster relief.[54] Accordingly, he proposed that: 'External assistance may be provided only with the consent of the affected State.'[55]

This formulation is directly inspired by the corresponding provision contained in General Assembly resolution 46/182. Nevertheless, while the latter affirmed that assistance *should* be provided with the State's consent, the proposed provision, as was remarked by Mr. Valencia-Ospina himself, establishes 'a clear requirement'.[56]

Within the ILC the intransigency of the rule, though gaining some support, also raised the concerns of several members, who noted *inter alia* that in exceptional circumstances the affected State could be unable to give formal consent within a timescale needed to react to an overwhelming disaster.[57]

The consent requirement is nonetheless accompanied by two corollary obligations that somewhat limit its rigidity. These obligations are dealt with extensively in the fourth and last report released so far by Mr. Valencia-Ospina, and concern, respectively, (1) the affected State's responsibility to seek assistance where its national response capacity is exceeded and (2) the affected State's duty not to arbitrarily withhold its consent to external assistance.

Concerning the first obligation, the Rapporteur considered that where the national response capacity is overwhelmed by a disaster, seeking international assistance may be an element of the fulfillment of an affected State's primary responsibilities under international human rights instruments and customary international law.[58] He then proposed a provision affirming that:

'The affected State has the duty to seek assistance, as appropriate, from among third States, the United Nations, other competent intergovernmental organizations

---

[54] The Rapporteur recalled that such a requirement is present in several treaties governing disaster relief as well as in humanitarian law conventions. The reference to humanitarian law is though incomplete. The Rapporteur in fact refers to the basic provisions regulating the delivery of humanitarian assistance in international and non-international armed conflicts, forgetting instead to mention the ones dealing with relief in an occupied territory. Far from being too context-specific, these latter provisions deal with a situation—that of occupation—which is the most similar to that occurring in peacetime in an emergency context. In both cases the territorial State/Occupying Power is assigned the primary responsibility to take care of the victims of the emergency. In fact the Occupying Power, while not having sovereignty on the territory it occupies, nonetheless has towards the occupied population obligations that are similar to those of a sovereign entity. That is why, not coincidentally, Article 59 IV Geneva Convention unambiguously requires that: 'If the whole or part of the population of an occupied territory is inadequately supplied, the Occupying Power *shall agree* to relief schemes' (emphasis added). See also Chap. 2 by Venturini in this volume.

[55] Cf. draft Article 8, para 2 (UN Doc. A/CN.4/629 para 96).

[56] UN Doc. A/CN.4/629 para 100.

[57] UN Doc. A/65/10 para 323.

[58] Fourth report on the protection of persons in the event of disasters, UN Doc. A/CN.4/643, 11 May 2011.

and relevant non-governmental organizations if the disaster exceeds its national response capacity.'[59]

An obligation to seek or request assistance can be found in some non-binding instrument such as the 2003 IDI Resolution on humanitarian assistance (so-called Bruges Resolution)[60] and the IFRC guidelines on disaster relief and, as was recognized in the Secretariat's Memorandum, there is a growing recognition of a positive duty in this respect.[61]

The Special Rapporteur considered that in this context a duty to 'seek' assistance is more appropriate than a duty to 'request' assistance because it implies a broader, negotiated approach to the provision of relief.[62] Conversely, a duty to 'request' assistance would carry an implication that an affected State's consent is granted upon acceptance of that request by a third actor.[63]

The duty to seek assistance, which was supported by the majority of ILC members and hence provisionally adopted,[64] constitutes an important acknowledgement of the broad scope of the primary responsibility of the affected State to protect disaster victims. In the Commentary to draft Article 10 the Commission correctly remarked that the said duty 'derives from an affected State's obligations under international human rights instruments and as such therefore it can be argued that the said obligation reflects customary law, irrespective of the context (peace or wartime) and the type of disaster.'[65]

However, the recognition of such a duty seems to have come to the detriment of the right to humanitarian assistance, whose consecration by the ILC would instead be most consistent with the proclaimed rights-based approach to the topic.

According to the UN Secretariat, the duty to seek assistance 'would likewise constrain [the affected State's] ability to decline offers of assistance, and would suggest that consent should not be arbitrarily withheld.'[66] Failing an express

---

[59] Cf. draft Article 10 entitled Duty of the affected State to seek assistance (UN Doc. A/66/10 para 289).

[60] Article III para 3, Bruges resolution.

[61] UN Doc. A/CN.4/590 para 57.

[62] UN Doc. A/CN.4/643 para 44. According to Benton Heath, this would not necessarily be the case since '[a]n equally reasonable interpretation [of the right to request assistance] would be that international law requires an affected state to put out a call for offers of assistance, while leaving it the plenary right to refuse any offer for any reason' (Benton Heath 2011, 454–455).

[63] UN Doc. A/CN.4/643 para 44; ILC Commentary, Article 10 (UN Doc. A/66/10 para 289). The formulation of the article was directly inspired by the corresponding provision of the Bruges resolution.

[64] The text as adopted contains only a minor change with respect to the original draft and reads as follows: 'To the extent that a disaster exceeds its national response capacity, the affected State has the duty to seek assistance from among other States, the United Nations, other competent intergovernmental organizations and relevant nongovernmental organizations, as appropriate'.

[65] ILC Commentary, Article 10, UN Doc. A/66/10 para 289. It then referred to some of the rights which are directly implicated in the context of a disaster, such as the right to life, the right to food, and the right to health and medical services.

[66] UN Doc. A/CN.4/590 para 65.

limitation to the consent rule, though, this suggestion could well remain unheard. And in fact the Special Rapporteur, after reminding the importance of consent for preserving State sovereignty, also recognized the need to introduce a provision limiting the general rule on consent when the territorial State is unable or unwilling to protect and assist disaster victims.[67] The rule proposed so declares: 'Consent to external assistance shall not be withheld arbitrarily. When an offer of assistance is extended in accordance with the present draft articles, the affected State shall, whenever possible, make its decision regarding the offer known'.

In the Special Rapporteur's view, this rule would permit to put the consent requirement in line with the purpose of the work, as defined in draft Article 2. During the last session it was provisionally adopted by the Commission and inserted in draft Article 11, which so establishes 'a qualified consent regime' in the field of disaster relief operations.[68]

In contrast to the duty to seek assistance, whose customary nature is generally recognized, the status of the rule prohibiting arbitrary refusals of aid offers is controversial. During the debates preceding the adoption of the Bruges resolution, several members of the *Institut de Droit International* expressed the opinion that such rule can only be considered *lex ferenda*,[69] while a few others viewed it with skepticism. In this regard, the argument is sometimes made that a positive discipline is only provided by international humanitarian law, and that its extension to peacetime disasters could conflict with the principle of non-intervention.

The major problem with this obligation concerns the determination of what is meant by arbitrary and who can legitimately evaluate the arbitrariness of a refusal. In deliberations of the *Institut*, several reasons were proposed that would justify a refusal without being arbitrary.[70] Along the same lines the Special Rapporteur, followed by the Commission in the Commentary, affirmed that even though the 'arbitrary' character of a refusal must be determined on a case-by-case basis,[71] some valid reasons for a refusal could be adduced. This should be the case, in particular: where a State is capable of providing, and willing to provide, an adequate and effective response with its own resources; if an affected State has accepted appropriate and sufficient assistance from elsewhere; if the relevant offer

---

[67] UN Doc. A/CN.4/643 para 70.

[68] *Sic* Commentary, Article 11, UN Doc. A/66/10 para 289.

[69] See, e.g., Institut de Droit International 2003, 161.

[70] Institut de Droit International 2003, 420 (Orrego Vicuña), 446 (Schermers), 562 (Rapporteur Vukas); Tome II 164 (Cassese) and 178 (Ress).

[71] Kolb remarks that 'L'interdiction de l'arbitraire a été perçue par certains comme un principe général du droit international, qui se rattache à l'interdiction de l'abus de droit et, de manière médiate, au principe de la bonne foi'. According to him, 'on peut dire que l'interdiction de l'arbitraire constitue un standard pour des actes gravement viciés au regard des idées directrices de l'ordre juridique et de la justice, un standard qui se compose de divers volets non exhaustifs: (1) des actes manifestement injustifiés au regard des faits; (2) l'exercice manifestement et objectivement choquant d'un droit; (3) les actes violant la conscience juridique; (4) les actes en fraude à la loi ou au droit; (5) certains exercices discriminatoires de droits; (6) l'exercice déraisonnable de droits, y compris les actes dépourvus d'utilité réelle.' (Kolb 2004, 868–9).

is not extended in accordance with the present draft articles. Moreover, draft Article 11 also requires that: 'When an offer of assistance is extended in accordance with the present draft articles, the affected State shall, whenever possible, make its decision regarding the offer known.'[72]

The said obligation would thus seem to imply that the absence of reasons may act to support an inference that the withholding of consent is arbitrary.[73] The consequences of an arbitrary refusal have though remained unexplored.[74]

3.4 International Cooperation and the Role Assigned to the International Community

When disaster strikes, it is incumbent upon the affected State to take care of the victims. Nonetheless, as was remarked by the Rapporteur, other actors have a role to play on the basis of the principles of international solidarity and cooperation:

> 'The underlying principles in the protection of persons in the event of disasters are those of solidarity and cooperation, both among nations and among individual human beings. It is in the solidarity inspired by human suffering that the Commission's mandate finds *telos*, as an expression of our common heritage in a global context.'[75]

In fact the Rapporteur recalled that cooperation is a fundamental principle of international law, enshrined in the Charter of the United Nations and in the Declaration on Friendly Relations, and that its importance in combating the effects of disasters had been affirmed in numerous General Assembly resolutions as well as in international instruments. Regarding solidarity, he argued that it is 'an international legal principle, and distinct from charity, [which] gives rise to a system of cooperation in furtherance of the notion that justice and the common good are best served by policies that benefit all nations'.[76] While cautioning that the cooperation imperative should not be stretched to trespass on the sovereignty

---

[72] Cf. Article 11, para 3 as provisionally adopted by the ILC (UN Doc. A/66/10 para 289).

[73] Cf. ILC Commentary Article 11, ibid. Referring to the UN Guiding Principles on Internal Displacement, Cohen and Bradley affirm that '[r]efusal without good reason constitutes arbitrariness and a violation of the right to life.' (Cohen and Bradley 2010, 34). On the need to give reasons for a refusal the same opinion was expressed by Cassese (see Institut de Droit International 2003, 535).

[74] The issue is specifically dealt with by Costas Trascasas in Chap. 10 of this volume.

[75] Second report on the protection of persons in the event of disasters, UN Doc. A/CN.4/615 para 50.

[76] UN Doc. A/CN.4/615 para 54. A definition of solidarity can be found in GA resolution 56/151 of 19 December 2001, which states that solidarity is 'a fundamental value, by virtue of which global challenges must be managed in a way that distributes costs and burdens fairly, in accordance with basic principles of equity and social justice, and ensures that those who suffer or benefit the least receive help from those who benefit the most' (see para 3 *f*).

of affected States, the Special Rapporteur affirmed that the said principles also involve non-State actors, in particular relief organizations and civil society. Accordingly, he proposed the following article on the duty to cooperate:

> 'For the purposes of the present draft articles, States shall cooperate among themselves and, as appropriate, with:
>
> (a) competent international organizations, in particular the United Nations;
> (b) the International Federation of Red Cross and Red Crescent Societies; and
> (c) civil society.'

The text proposed was not the object of major contestations within the ILC, which therefore recognized the core importance of the duty it enshrined for the topic under discussion. Nevertheless, several members expressed the need to make a sharper difference between the duty on Member States to cooperate with the UN under the Charter and duties owed to other organizations and entities. Some concern was also voiced over the phrase 'civil society' which, it was remarked, is not a legal category and should better be substituted with NGOs.[77]

The new formulation of the article, as provisionally adopted by the Drafting Committee, duly takes account of the quoted remarks affirming that:

'In accordance with the present draft articles, States shall, as appropriate, cooperate among themselves, and with the United Nations and other competent intergovernmental organizations, the International Federation of the Red Cross and Red Crescent Societies and the International Committee of the Red Cross, and with relevant non-governmental organizations.'[78]

Then the role of international cooperation in disaster situations was expressed, in more concrete terms, in Article 12 concerning the right to offer assistance: 'In responding to disasters, States, the United Nations, other competent intergovernmental organizations and relevant non-governmental organizations shall have the right to offer assistance to the affected State.'

This provision was introduced with the purpose 'to acknowledge *the legitimate interest* of the international community to protect persons in the event of a disaster' and was to be viewed, as remarked by Mr. Valencia-Ospina, 'in the broader context of the primary responsibility of the affected State to protect persons affected by disasters'. As a consequence, offers of assistance were conceived by the Rapporteur as 'an expression of solidarity, based on the principles of humanity, neutrality, impartiality and non-discrimination.'[79]

---

[77] UN Doc. A/64/10 paras 173 ff.

[78] Cf. Article 5. Duty to cooperate (Texts of draft Article 1, 2, 3, 4, and 5 as provisionally adopted by the Drafting Committee, 24 July 2009, UN Doc. A/CN.4/L.758). Note that Article 5 was adopted, two years before Articles 10 and 11, on the understanding that a provision on the primary responsibility of the affected State would be included in the future in the set of draft Articles.

[79] UN Doc. A/CN.4/643 para 96.

Article 12 was commented upon within the ILC during its last session. In that occasion, a general support was expressed for the idea that genuine offers of humanitarian assistance should not be viewed as interference. Some members, though, pointed to the difficulties in referring to the 'right' to offer, especially when it came to non-governmental organizations, since it implied that the latter enjoyed the same rights as the States. It was thus suggested that the article merely provided an authorization and not a right.[80]

Conceived as a right or as a mere authorization, it is doubtless that the offer of humanitarian services is quite a reductive task for the international community to play. The said entitlement does not in fact extend to the provision of relief.

It is well known that the right of third parties to *offer and provide* assistance is generally characterized *as a corollary to the right of victims to humanitarian assistance*.[81] Failing to recognize the latter right, the Rapporteur instead limited the entitlement of third actors to the *offer* of relief. As a consequence the international community, while having a *legitimate interest* to protect disaster victims, is not assigned a corresponding *responsibility* when the affected State is unable or unwilling to comply with its primary obligations.

This approach is unnecessarily restrictive and, in the end, contradictory. Despite of the proclaimed human rights approach, the draft articles proposed and approved so far are framed in the context of purely horizontal relationships between the affected State and assisting States and organizations. In this way, the victims of disasters are conceived as mere beneficiaries of aid. In addition to that, the ILC has failed to recognize to third parties the right to provide assistance, so underestimating the values at stake. In fact, by virtue of their *erga omnes* character, the basic subsistence rights, which are at issue in a disaster-like situation, like all fundamental human rights entail State obligations which are owed to the international community as a whole. As a consequence, 'all States can be held to have a legal interest in their protection'.[82] While it is generally excluded that *erga omnes* obligations can trigger a duty to act on foreign States,[83] the latter are however entitled to act to protect the community interest.[84] In the case at hand, the right to

---

[80] Report of the International Law Commission on the work of its sixty-third session (26 April to 3 June and 4 July to 12 August 2011) UN Doc. A/66/10 paras 279 ff.

[81] Cf. Stoffels 2004, 521; Kolb 2004, 864.

[82] Barcelona Traction, Light and Power Company, Limited (Belgium v. Spain), Judgement of 5 February 1970, ICJ Rep. 1970, para 33.

[83] Skogly 2006, 81.

[84] Boisson de Chazournes speaks in this respect of the 'horizontal dimension' of solidarity, conceived as 'a means of rescuing a population encountering serious dangers that cannot be protected by its own State. This is a form of solidarity where the relationship is between States and populations of other States (and between international organisations and populations), hence 'vertical'' (Boisson de Chazournes 2010, 102).

provide humanitarian aid could thus be considered as the logical counterpart of the duty not to arbitrarily deny access to external aid.[85]

3.5 Final Remarks

The ILC works so far have resulted in the elaboration of a set of draft articles that touches upon delicate questions of principle. The overall result is rather disappointing, especially if considered in light of the expectations.

The Special Rapporteur had initially proposed to carry out the work with a rights-based approach to the topic. Nonetheless, the lack of a clear understanding of the said approach, coupled with the resistances coming from within (and also outside) the Commission, has resulted in the practical denial of the premised centrality of the individual. The tensions between the protection of the affected persons' rights and the respect for State sovereignty and the principle of non-intervention in internal affairs—constantly evoked during the plenary debates of the ILC and by States in the Sixth Committee—have in fact been solved to the detriment of the former's rights. As was shown, no reference is made in the draft articles to the rights which are most relevant for disaster victims, much less to the right to humanitarian assistance, whose importance was though recognized by the same Rapporteur. Instead, a qualified consent regime is set up which shifts the focus from human rights to States' rights and obligations.

Moreover, the draft text also fails to adequately conceptualize the role of third actors and of the international community. The specter of the responsibility to protect doctrine in fact haunted the debates within the ILC averting a thorough and calm reflection on the responsibilities connected to a modern conception of sovereignty.[86]

It remains to be seen if in the following work the ILC will engage and, most importantly, succeed in proposing adequate solutions to the more concrete legal problems which consistently recur in disaster relief operations and undercut their speed and efficiency. Considering the highly technical nature of the issues involved, which require specialized competence, this cannot be taken for granted and in turn raises legitimate doubts on the expediency for the ILC of embarking in such an undertaking.[87]

---

[85] And in fact it was so conceived by the Institut de Droit International, which in Article IV of the Bruges resolution, entitled 'Droit d'offrir et de fournir une assistance humanitaire', affirms that:

'Les États et les organisations ont le droit de fournir une assistance humanitaire aux victimes se trouvant sur le territoire des États affectés, sous réserve du consentement de ces derniers' (para 2).

[86] It must in fact be recalled in this respect that the concept of sovereignty as responsibility dates back well before the responsibility to protect doctrine and was first conceptualized by Francis Deng with respect to the protection of internally displaced persons (cf. Cohen and Deng 1998, 251).

[87] Furthermore, the topic here reviewed does not seem to have attracted much interest from States. This is shown by the fact that following a request, back in 2008, addressed to States to submit information on their practice under this topic, so far only three States responded (UN Doc. A/66/10 para 284).

References

Benton Heath J (2011) Disaster, relief and neglect: the duty to accept humanitarian assistance and the work of the International Law Commission. Int Law Politics 43:419–477

Bettati M (1991) Un droit d'ingérence? RGDIP 45:639–670

Boisson de Chazournes L (2010) Responsibility to protect: reflecting solidarity? In: Wolfrum R, Kojima C (eds) Solidarity: a structural principle of international law. Springer Verlag, Heidelberg, pp 93–109

Cohen R, Bradley M (2010) Disasters and displacement: gaps in protection. J Int Human Legal Stud 1:95–142

Cohen R, Deng FM (1998) Masses in flight: the global crisis of internal displacement. Brookings Institution Press, Washington

Darcy J, Hoffman C-A (2003) According to need? Needs assessment and decision-making in the humanitarian sector, HPG Report 15

Gready P, Ensor J (eds) (2005) Reinventing development? translating rights-based approaches from theory into practice. Zed Books, London

Institut de Droit International (2003) Annuaire de l'Institut de droit international, vol 70, Tome 1, Session de Bruges

Kolb R (2004) De l'assistance humanitaire: la resolution sur l'assistance humanitaire adoptée par l'Institut de droit international à sa session de Bruges en 2003. Int Rev Red Cross 86(856):853–878

Office of the High Commissioner on Human Rights (2006) Frequently asked questions on a human rights-based approach to development cooperation

Relief and Rehabilitation Network (1996) The joint evaluation of emergency assistance to Rwanda: study III principal findings and recommendations. Overseas Development Institute, London

Skogly S (2006) Beyond national borders: States' human rights obligations in international cooperation. Intersentia, Antwerp

Stoffels A (2004) Legal regulations of humanitarian assistance in armed conflict: achievements and gaps. Int Rev Red Cross 86(855):515–546

Chapter 4
Nuclear Accidents and International Law

Andrea Gioia

Abstract This chapter outlines the main features of international treaties adopted in order to deal with nuclear accidents, both from the point of view of their prevention and from the point of view of their consequences. International nuclear law, intended as a set of legally binding rules creating States' rights and obligations relating to the conduct of activities related to the use of atomic energy, has mainly evolved as a result of the Chernobyl nuclear accident in 1986. These rules relate to nuclear safety and security, emergency preparedness and response and liability for nuclear damage. However, the nuclear accident at the Fukushima Daiichi nuclear power station in 2011 has shown that nuclear accidents can still happen, even in a highly developed State. As a result, the effectiveness of international nuclear law, in particular as regards the legal framework for nuclear safety and for emergency preparedness and response, is currently under review.

Keywords International nuclear law · Nuclear activities · Nuclear safety · Nuclear security · Emergency preparedness and response · International atomic energy agency · Nuclear liability

Contents

A. Gioia (✉)
Dipartimento di Giurisprudenza, Università di Modena e Reggio Emilia,
Via San Geminiano 3, 41121, Modena, Italy
e-mail: andrea.gioia@unimore.it

A. de Guttry et al. (eds.), *International Disaster Response Law*,
DOI: 10.1007/978-90-6704-882-8_4,

4.1 Introduction

The complex international problems of both law and legal policy raised by the civil uses of atomic energy stem from a number of features such as the great potentialities of atomic energy, the relatively great hazards involved in the operation of nuclear installations, the high degree of scientific and technical development required for nuclear industry. In order to deal with these issues and tackle the problems derived therefrom, a number of specific legally binding rules have emerged at the international level; these rules constitute international nuclear law, a highly specialized branch of international law.

Until relatively recently, the international legal framework for nuclear energy—apart from the constitutive instruments of international organizations (such as the Statute of the International Atomic Energy Agency (IAEA)), the bilateral treaties concluded between States and the agreements concluded by international organizations with one another or with other entities (such as member States or third States)—mainly consisted of non-binding recommendations, with the exception of the multilateral conventions relating to liability for nuclear damage and to the physical protection of nuclear material.[1] The Chernobyl nuclear accident in 1986 raised States' awareness of the international dimension of nuclear energy, in particular as regards the potential transboundary impact of a nuclear accident, and brought about the revision of the existing treaties and to the adoption of new ones relating, in particular, to nuclear safety and to emergency preparedness and response. These multilateral treaties are now the most important sources of international nuclear law and will be briefly examined in this chapter, to the exclusion of the non-legally binding instruments adopted at the international level.

International law deals with nuclear accidents from three different perspectives: first of all, the perspective of nuclear safety and security, in order to adopt measures intended to exclude or limit the possibility of nuclear accidents and of damage therefrom; second, the perspective of emergency preparedness and response, in order to adopt measures intended to deal with an emergency situation and to mitigate the consequences of a nuclear accident; and third, the perspective of liability for nuclear damage, in order to adopt measures intended to guarantee an acceptable level of compensation of damage caused by a nuclear accident. All three aspects of international nuclear law will be briefly analyzed in this chapter.

---

[1] See Arangio-Ruiz 1963.

On the other hand, this chapter intends to analyze the specific international legal rules relating to accidents involving nuclear facilities and nuclear materials associated with the nuclear fuel cycle, i.e., with the production of nuclear power, to the exclusion of other radioactive materials and of facilities associated therewith. Nuclear facilities and materials associated with the nuclear fuel cycle are in fact those that create the greatest risk of an accident with potentially grave consequences and transboundary effects. Moreover, most of the multilateral treaties so far adopted at the international level apply to nuclear facilities and materials associated with the nuclear fuel cycle, whereas most of the international rules relating to other radioactive material and to facilities associated therewith are still contained in non-legally binding instruments.

4.2 Nuclear Safety and Nuclear Security

Measures designed to exclude or limit the possibility of nuclear accidents or their consequences are often considered as pertaining to nuclear safety or nuclear security. Whereas 'nuclear safety' is an expression widely used to cover all measures designed to prevent nuclear accidents or to limit their consequences, 'nuclear security' is a much more ambiguous expression which is often used in the context of efforts to prevent the proliferation of nuclear weapons[2] but which will be used in this chapter in a specific sense to cover the prevention and detection of, and response to, theft, sabotage, or other unauthorized acts involving nuclear material or facilities associated thereto.[3] Although a nuclear accident, intended as a release of ionizing radiation that leads to significant consequences for people, property, or the environment, can be caused by a number of factors, the term 'nuclear security' as used in this chapter specifically covers measures designed to prevent accidents caused by 'the malevolent use of nuclear materials and technology or sabotage of nuclear facilities by sub-national criminal or terrorist elements',[4] i.e., non-state actors.

---

[2] This is especially, though not exclusively, true in the case of the earlier studies relating to international nuclear law: see, in particular, Arangio-Ruiz 1963, 560–574.

[3] According to a working definition adopted within the IAEA by the Agency's Advisory Group on Nuclear Security, 'nuclear security' means: 'the prevention and detection of, and response to, theft, sabotage, unauthorized access, illegal transfer or other malicious acts involving nuclear material, other radioactive substances or their associated facilities' (see: IAEA Doc. GOV/2005/50).

[4] Stoiber 2010, 219.

4.2.1 Nuclear Safety

In the area of nuclear safety, two conventions relevant for the prevention of nuclear accidents have been adopted dealing, respectively, with the safety of land-based civil nuclear power plants, and with the safety of spent fuel and radioactive waste management. The Convention on Nuclear Safety[5] was adopted on 17 June 1994, entered into force on 24 October 1996 and, as of 31 December 2011, has 74 Contracting Parties. The Joint Convention on the Safety of Spent Fuel Management and on the Safety of Radioactive Waste Management[6] was adopted on 5 September 1997, entered into force on 18 June 2001 and, as of 31 December 2011, has 63 Contracting Parties. Although in the Preamble of the first of those two conventions there is a reference to the usefulness of technical work in connection of other parts of the nuclear fuel cycle which ‘may, in time, facilitate the development of current or future international instruments’ (para (x)), no such instruments have been adopted in the form of binding international treaties. As regards, for example, research reactors, a non-binding code of conduct was adopted within the IAEA in 2004.[7]

The Convention on Nuclear Safety applies to ‘the safety of nuclear installations’ (Article 3), but these are narrowly defined in Article 2 to mean ‘for each Contracting Party any land-based civil nuclear power plant under its jurisdiction’; storage, handling, and treatment facilities for radioactive materials are only included inasmuch as they are ‘on the same site and are directly related to the operation of’ such a nuclear power plant. Furthermore, under the definition, a nuclear power plant ceases to be a ‘nuclear installation’ covered by the Convention ‘when all nuclear fuel elements have been removed permanently from the reactor core and have been stored safely in accordance with approved procedures and a decommissioning programme has been agreed by the regulatory body’.

The main obligations of the Contracting Parties are laid down in Chap. 2 of the Convention (Articles 4–19). In addition to a few general obligations, to which I shall revert later, a number of substantive obligations specifically relate, first of all, to the area of ‘legislation and regulation’ and deserve to be referred to in detail. Under Article 7, each Contracting Party is to ‘establish and maintain a legislative and regulatory framework to govern the safety of nuclear installations’ providing for: the establishment of applicable national nuclear safety requirements and regulations; a system of licensing, and the prohibition of operating an installation without a license; a system of regulatory inspection and assessment of nuclear installations to ascertain compliance with applicable regulations and the terms of

---

[5] IAEA Doc. INFCIRC/449.

[6] IAEA Doc. INFCIRC/546.

[7] The Code of Conduct on the Safety of Research Reactors was adopted by the IAEA Board of Governors on 8 March 2004 (IAEA Doc. GOV/OR.1088). In resolution GC(48)/RES/10, the 2004 IAEA General Conference endorsed the code of conduct and encouraged member States to apply the guidance therein to the management of research reactors.

licenses; the enforcement of applicable regulations and the terms of licences, including suspension, modification, or revocation. In addition, under Article 8, each Contracting Party is to establish or designate a 'regulatory body entrusted with the implementation of the legislative and regulatory framework envisaged in Article 7, and provided with adequate authority, competences and financial, and human resources to fulfill its assigned responsibilities'; an 'effective separation' between the functions of the regulatory body and those of organizations concerned with 'the promotion of nuclear energy' is to be ensured. Finally, under Article 9, each Contracting Party is to ensure that 'the primary responsibility for the safety of a nuclear installation lies with the holder of the relevant licence' and that each such license holder meets this responsibility.

Other substantive obligations are labeled as 'general safety considerations' (Articles 10–16). Among these, mention must be made, in particular, of the obligations relating to: the need for all organizations engaged in activities directly related to nuclear installations to establish policies that give 'due priority to nuclear safety' (Article 10); the carrying out of comprehensive and systematic safety assessments, not only before the construction and commissioning of a nuclear facility but also 'throughout its life', as well as of verification by analysis, surveillance, testing, and inspection to ensure that the physical state and the operation of a nuclear installation continue to be in accordance with safety requirements (Article 14); and the preparation and routine testing of on-site and off-site emergency plans that cover the activities to be carried out in the event of an emergency (Article 16). In this context, it is important to point out that the need for the preparation and testing of emergency plans is also envisaged for 'Contracting Parties which do not have a nuclear installation on their territory, insofar as they are likely to be affected in the event of a radiological emergency at a nuclear installation in the vicinity' (Article 16, para 3).

Finally, specific obligations on the 'safety of installations' relate to the siting (Article 17), design and construction (Article 18), and operation (Article 19) of nuclear installations. One obligation relating to siting is especially noteworthy in that it relates to the consultation of 'Contracting Parties in the vicinity of a proposed nuclear installation, insofar as they are likely to be affected by that installation', as well as to the provision to such Contracting Parties, upon request, of the 'necessary information' in order 'to enable them to evaluate and make their own assessment of the likely safety impact on their own territory of the nuclear installation' (Article 17 (iii)).

Among the 'general provisions' contained in Chap. 2 of the Convention on Nuclear Safety, mention must be made, first of all, of a general obligation for each Contracting Party 'to take, within the framework of its national law, the legislative, regulatory and administrative measures and other steps necessary for implementing its obligations' under the Convention (Article 4). Second, of particular importance is the obligation of each Contracting Party to submit for review 'a report on the measures it has taken to implement each of the obligations' under the Convention (Article 5). In fact, one of the most important features of the Convention on Nuclear Safety is the 'peer review' mechanism envisaged in Chap. 3 (Articles 20–28), whereby all Contracting Parties are obliged to participate in regular 'review meetings', to be held at intervals not exceeding three year, for the purpose of reviewing the national reports submitted under Article 5: at such review meetings, each Contracting Party 'shall have a reasonable opportunity to discuss the reports submitted by other Contracting Parties and to seek clarification of such reports' (Article 20, para 3). 'Extraordinary meetings' can also be held if so agreed by a majority of the Contracting Parties present and voting at a meeting (Article 23).

The Joint Convention on the Safety of Spent Fuel Management and on the Safety of Radioactive Waste Management (Joint Convention) combines, as its title suggests, two discrete subject matters. Pursuant to Article 3, the Joint Convention applies to: (i) the safety of spent fuel management, defined in Article 2 as 'all activities that relate to the handling or storage of spent fuel, excluding off-site transportation', when the spent fuel results from the operation of civilian nuclear reactors, but does not apply to spent fuel held at reprocessing facilities as part of a reprocessing process, unless the interested Contracting Party declares reprocessing to be part of spent fuel management; and to (ii) the safety of radioactive waste management, defined in Article 2 as 'all activities, including decommissioning activities, that relate to the handling, pre-treatment, treatment, conditioning, storage, or disposal of radioactive waste, excluding off-site transportation', when the radioactive waste results from civilian applications.

Despite the exclusion of the safety of management of spent fuel and radioactive waste from military or defense programs, under Article 3 the Joint Convention applies to (iii) the safety of management of spent fuel and radioactive waste resulting from military or defense programs, if and when such materials are transferred permanently to and managed within exclusively civilian programs, or when declared as spent fuel or radioactive waste for the purpose of the convention by the interested Contracting Party.

Finally, under Article 3 the Joint Convention also applies to (iv) to 'discharges', defined in Article 2 as 'planned and controlled releases into the environment, as a legitimate practice, within limits authorized by the regulatory body, or liquid or gaseous radioactive materials that originate from regulated nuclear facilities during normal operation'.

As for the substantive obligations of Contracting Parties, these are largely based on those relating to nuclear power plants, which I have already outlined when discussing the Convention on Nuclear Safety, and there is, therefore, no need to describe them in detail. Obligations relating to legislation and regulation are common to spent fuel management and radioactive waste management and are laid down in Chap. 4 of the Joint Convention, entitled 'General Safety Provisions', together with the requirements relating to human and financial resources, quality assurance, operational radiation protection, emergency preparedness, and decommissioning. Chaps. 2 and 3 contain parallel sets of specific requirements governing, respectively, the 'Safety of Spent Fuel Management' and the 'Safety of Radioactive Waste Management'.

In addition, despite the exclusion of 'off-site transportation' from the definitions of both 'spent fuel management' and 'radioactive waste management' (Article 2)-

and, therefore, from the scope of application of the Joint Convention (Article 3), Chap. 5, entitled 'Miscellaneous Provisions', contains a provision (Article 27)[8] obliging each Contracting Party involved in 'trans-boundary movement', defined in Article 2 as 'any shipment of spent fuel or radioactive waste from a State of origin to a State of destination', to 'take the appropriate steps to ensure that such movement is undertaken in a manner consistent with the provisions of this Convention and relevant international instruments'. In addition, specific obligations are imposed on the State of origin and the State of destination, whereas 'trans-boundary movement through States of transit shall be subject to those international obligations which are relevant to the particular mode of transport utilized', thus leaving unaffected, inter alia, the relevant provisions of the international law of the sea.[9]

Finally, apart from the main substantive obligations of the Contracting Parties, the Joint Convention 'mirrors' the Convention on Nuclear safety in respect of the 'peer review' mechanism envisaged in Chap. 6 (Articles 29–37). In fact, in addition to the general obligation for each Contracting Party to 'take, within the framework of its national law, the legislative, regulatory and administrative measure and other steps necessary for implementing its obligations' under the Joint Convention (Article 18), each Contracting Party is also obliged to submit for review a report on the measures it has taken to implement each of those obligations, and to attend regular 'review meetings', to be held at intervals not exceeding 3 years, for the purpose of reviewing those national reports. As in the case of the Convention on Nuclear safety, 'extraordinary meetings' can also be held.

4.2.2 Nuclear Security

In the specific area of nuclear security, one convention relevant for the prevention of nuclear accidents has been adopted under the auspices of the IAEA, namely the Convention on the Physical Protection of Nuclear Material.[10] This convention was opened for signature on 3 March 1980, entered into force on 8 February 1987 and, as of 31 December 2011, has 145 Parties. The Convention is usually listed among the numerous counter-terrorism conventions that have been adopted at the global level and, as a result of the events of 11 September 2001 and of the ensuing efforts

---

[8] Apart from Article 27, Chap. 5 also contains a provision (Article 28) relating to 'disused sealed sources', which are outside the scope of this chapter. In principle, under Article 3, the Joint Convention does not apply to 'waste that contains only naturally occurring radioactive material and that does not originate from the nuclear fuel cycle, unless it constitutes a disused sealed source or is declared as radioactive waste for the purposes of this Convention by the Contracting Party'. A 'sealed source' is defined in Article 2 as 'radioactive material that is permanently sealed in a capsule or closely bonded and in a solid form, excluding reactor fuel elements'.

[9] See Gioia 2002.

[10] IAEA Doc. INFCIRC/274/Rev.1.

to enhance the global counter-terrorism regime, an Amendment to the Convention was adopted on 8 July 2005.[11] The Amendment to the Convention is, however, not yet in force: in accordance with Article 20 of the Convention, the Amendment will enter into force upon ratification by two-thirds of the States Parties to the Convention. Pending the entry into force of the 2005 Amendment, the IAEA General Conference has repeatedly encouraged the Parties to the Convention to act in accordance with its objectives and purposes of the Amendment.[12]

The Convention on the Physical Protection of Nuclear Material has three main objectives, namely to ensure, as its title suggests, the physical protection of nuclear material, to ensure the prevention, detection, and punishment of offenses relating to nuclear material, and to facilitate international co-operation to those ends. The 2005 Amendment is designed to enhance the Convention in all of these three respects.

As far as the physical protection of nuclear material[13] are concerned, the provisions of the Convention as at present in force exclusively apply to 'nuclear material used for peaceful purposes while in international nuclear transport', whereas the other provisions of the Convention also apply to such material 'while in domestic use, storage and transport' (Article 2). Each State Party is, in particular, obliged to 'take the appropriate steps within the framework of its national law and consistent with international law to ensure that, during international nuclear transport, nuclear material within its territory, or on board a ship or aircraft under its jurisdiction insofar as such ship or aircraft is engaged in the transport to or from that State, is protected at the levels described in Annex I' to the Convention (Article 3). In addition, each State Party is required not to import, export, or authorize the import or export or transit of, nuclear material unless it has received assurances that such material will be protected during the international nuclear transport at the levels described in Annex I (Article 4).

Upon entry into force of the 2005 Amendment, these provisions will be complemented by additional provisions (in Article 2 A) relating to the physical protection of nuclear material in domestic use, storage and transport, and to the physical protection of nuclear facilities, widely defined (in Article 1 (d)) so as to cover all facilities where nuclear material is produced, processed, used, handled, stored, or disposed of, but excluding nuclear material used or retained for military purposes and nuclear facilities containing such material (Article 2). Such provisions will include measures aimed at protecting nuclear material and nuclear facilities against 'sabotage', defined (in Article 1 (e)) as 'any deliberate act directed against a nuclear facility or nuclear material in use, storage or transport which could directly or indirectly endanger the health and safety of personnel, the

[11] IAEA Doc. GOV/INF/2005/10-GC(49)/INF/6.

[12] See, for example, the latest resolution on nuclear security adopted on 23 September 2001: IAEA Doc. GC(55)/RES/10.

[13] 'Nuclear Material' is defined so as to exclude radioactive material not associated with the nuclear fuel cycle (Article 1 (a)).

public or the environment by exposure to radiation or release of radioactive substances'.

As far as the prevention, detection, and punishment of offences relating to nuclear material are concerned, the Convention, as at present in force, exclusively covers offenses related to nuclear material (Article 7), whereas the entry into force of the 2005 Amendment will enhance the provisions of the Convention by covering offenses related to both nuclear material and nuclear facilities, including acts directed against nuclear material or nuclear facilities that cause or are likely to cause damage to the environment.

Each State Party is obliged to establish jurisdiction over such offenses both when the offense is committed in its territory, or on board a ship or aircraft registered therein, and when the alleged offender is one of its nationals; in addition, it also has to establish jurisdiction in cases where the alleged offender is present in its territory and is not extradited to either the State in whose territory the offense was committed or the State of nationality of the alleged offender, thus giving effect to the well-known principle *aut dedere aut judicare*(Article 8). The Convention does not, however, exclude other cases where criminal jurisdiction is exercised in accordance with national law, and in fact specifically authorizes each State Party involved in international nuclear transport of nuclear material as the exporting or importing State to establish jurisdiction over the offenses relating to such material. Specific provisions relate to the prosecution of alleged offenders (Article 10) and to their extradition (Article 11).

Finally, the provisions relating to international co-operation and assistance relate to both the physical protection of nuclear material and its recovery in the case of theft, robbery, or any other unlawful taking (Article 5), and to criminal proceedings brought in respect of the offenses set forth in the Convention (Article 13). The entry into force of the 2005 Amendment will enhance these provisions, in particular, by covering the sabotage of nuclear material and of nuclear facilities.

But the picture relating to the international legal framework for nuclear security would not be complete without at least a brief reference to a number of legally binding international instruments adopted outside the context of the IAEA. First and foremost among such instruments is of course the International Convention for the Suppression of Acts of Nuclear Terrorism, adopted by the United Nations General Assembly on 13 April 2005 and entered into force on 7 July 2007. Unlike the IAEA Convention on the Physical protection of Nuclear Material, this convention is primarily an international criminal law instrument designed to establish certain act as offenses in the national criminal law of the Contracting Parties and to oblige these to establish their jurisdiction over such offenses and to prosecute or extradite the alleged offenders, as appropriate. On the other hand, within this limited ambit, the convention has a wider scope that the IAEA Convention on the Physical protection of Nuclear Material, in that it also covers criminal acts involving radioactive material other than nuclear material and associated facilities, as well as nuclear material and facilities used or retained for military purposes.

Other counter-terrorism conventions that have a bearing on nuclear security are the International Convention for the Suppression of Terrorist Bombing, also adopted by the UN General Assembly on 15 December 1997, and a number of important conventions adopted under the auspices of the International Maritime Organization: the 1988 Convention on the Suppression of Unlawful Acts against the Safety of Maritime Navigation and the related 1988 Protocol on the Suppression of Unlawful Acts against the Safety of Fixed Platforms located on the Continental Shelf, as well as the two Protocols adopted in 2005 to amend these two conventions. Last but not least, mention must be made of two important and well-known UN Security Council resolutions that are binding on UN member States by virtue of Chapter VII of the UN Charter: Resolution 1373 (2001) relating to the prevention and suppression of the financing and preparation of acts of terrorism in general and, especially, Resolution 1540 (2004) specifically relating to the proliferation of nuclear weapons and their means of delivery, in particular as concerns non-State actors.

4.3 Emergency Preparedness and Response

The conventions examined in the previous paragraph comprise a handful of provisions that are relevant for emergency preparedness and response. As far as nuclear power plants are concerned, it was pointed out above that the Convention on Nuclear Safety provides for the preparation and routine testing of on-site and off-site emergency plans that cover the activities to be carried out in the event of an emergency, for both States that have such power plants on their territory and those that have none, 'insofar as they are likely to be affected in the event of a radiological emergency at a nuclear power plant in the vicinity'; each Contracting Party is to take the appropriate steps to ensure that, 'insofar as they are likely to be affected by a radiological emergency, its own population and the competent authorities of the States in the vicinity of the nuclear installation, are provided with appropriate information for emergency planning and response' (Article 16). In addition, as was also pointed out above, the Joint Convention on the Safety of Spent Fuel Management and of Radioactive Waste Management has similar provisions for spent fuel and radioactive waste management facilities (Article 25). Finally, in the area of nuclear security, the Convention on the Physical Protection of Nuclear Material provides for international co-operation in the event of 'theft, robbery or any other unlawful taking of nuclear material or of credible threat thereof' for the recovery and protection of such material (Article 5), irrespective of whether or not such a situation has lead to a release of radiation.

However, the two most important treaties relevant in the area of emergency preparedness and response are the Convention on Early Notification of a Nuclear Accident and the Convention on Assistance in the Case of a Nuclear Accident or Radiological Emergency, both adopted by the IAEA General Conference meeting in special session on 26 September 1986 in the aftermath of the Chernobyl accident.

The Convention on Early Notification of a Nuclear Accident[14] entered into force on 27 October 1986 and, as of 31 December 2011, has 113 Parties. Under Article 1, the Convention applies in the event of any accident involving specified facilities or activities of a State Party or of persons or legal entities under its jurisdiction or control, 'from which a release of radioactive material occurs or is likely to occur and which has resulted or may result in an international trans-boundary release that could be of radiological safety significance for another State'. Facilities and activities covered are: any reactor wherever located; any nuclear fuel facility, any radioactive waste management facility, the transport and storage of nuclear fuels or radioactive wastes; but also the manufacture, use, storage, disposal, and transport of radioisotopes for agricultural, industrial, medical, and related scientific and research purposes, as well as the use of radioisotopes for power generation in space objects.

In the event of a nuclear accident covered by Article 1, Article 2 of the convention obliges the State Party concerned to 'forthwith' notify, directly or through the IAEA, those States which are or may be physically affected and the Agency itself of the nuclear accident, its nature, the time of its occurrence and its exact location 'where appropriate', as well as to 'promptly' provide to the same States and the Agency with such available information relevant to minimizing the radiological consequences in those States, as specified in Article 5. In addition, Article 6 requires the State Party providing information, 'as far as is reasonably practicable', to respond 'promptly' to requests for further information or consultation by an affected Party with a view to minimizing the radiological consequences in that State.

Article 3 provides that, 'with a view to minimizing the radiological consequences, States Parties may notify in the event of nuclear accidents other than those specified in Article 1'. The relevance of such a voluntary notification becomes apparent when a closer look is given to the scope of application of the convention under Article 1: in fact, doubts as to the applicability of the convention may arise in a given situation, in particular as to whether or not a release that has occurred or is likely to occur 'has resulted or may result in an international trans-boundary release that could be or radiological significance for another State'; in addition, despite the apparently very comprehensive enumeration of facilities and activities covered, which has lead at least one commentator to state that 'whether the use of nuclear energy is for civil or military purposes is, as far as the application of the convention is concerned, immaterial', the same commentator also states that the list in Article 1 does not include 'plants and activities connected with nuclear weapons and the testing of such weapons'.[15] On this latter point, the *travaux préparatoires* of the convention, as well as declarations made to the Depository after its adoption, suggest that the nuclear weapons States are willing

---

[14] IAEA Doc. INFCIRC/335.

[15] Moser 1986, 12–13.

to notify accidents involving military activities such as those involving nuclear weapons on the basis of Article 3 of the convention only.[16]

The Convention on Assistance in the Case of a Nuclear Accident or Radiological Emergency[17] entered into force on 26 February 1987 and, as of 31 December 2011, has 108 Parties. Like the Early notification Convention, the Assistance Convention does not only apply to accidents originating in nuclear installations, but also applies to accidents caused by radioactive material other than nuclear material. In addition, as its title suggests, the convention does not only apply to 'nuclear accidents' but also to 'radiological emergencies'. Although the two terms are not defined in the convention, it is reasonable to assume that the term 'nuclear accident' has the same meaning as in the Early Notification Convention, which was adopted at the same time. On the other hand, the term 'radiological emergency' is not used in the Early Notification Convention and, in the absence of a definition, may be taken to include a situation where there has not (yet) been any damage. Moreover, it could be taken to apply to installations or activities not covered by the Early Notification Convention, including those connected with nuclear weapons or the testing of such weapons.[18]

The most important provisions in the Assistance Convention relate to the preconditions for, and the scope of, the measures of assistance: under Article 1, States Parties are to co-operate between themselves and with the IAEA to facilitate the prompt assistance in the event of a nuclear accident or radiological emergency, in order to minimize its consequences and to protect life, property, and the environment from the effects of radioactive releases, Article 2 specifies that a State Party needing assistance, irrespective of whether or not it is the State of the accident, may call for such assistance from any other State Party, directly or through the IAEA, and from the IAEA itself or, where appropriate, other intergovernmental organizations, and that the scope and type of assistance are to be specified by the requesting State. Article 2 also provides that the requested States Parties have to 'promptly' decide and notify the requesting State, directly or through the IAEA, whether they are in a position to render the assistance required, whereas State Parties in general are required, within the limits of their capabilities, to identify and notify the IAEA of experts, equipment and materials which could be made available for the provision of assistance to other States in the event of an accident or radiological emergency, as well as the terms under which such assistance could be provided.

Article 3 specifies that the overall direction, control, direction, co-ordination, and supervision of assistance shall be the responsibility, within its territory, of the requesting State, which is also responsible for the protection of personnel, equipment and materials brought into its territory by or on behalf of the assisting Parties. Article 6 relates provides for an obligation to protect confidential

---

[16] See Adede 1987, 3, 16–25, and 136–140.

[17] IAEA Doc. INFCIRC/336.

[18] See Moser 1986, 14.

information on the part of both the requesting State and the assisting party. Under Article 11 termination of assistance may be requested at any time by the requesting State, after appropriate consultations and notification in writing. Arrangements for the proper conclusion of assistance have thereafter to be made in consultation with the interested States.

A number of other provisions in the convention relate to questions of reimbursement of costs of compensation (Article 7), to privileges, immunities, and facilities to be afforded by the requesting State to personnel of the assisting party and personnel acting on its behalf (Articles 8 and 9), as well as to claims for compensation arising out of the assistance activities carried out in the territory of the requesting State (Article 10).

One of the most significant features of both the Early Notification Convention and the Assistance Convention is the role assigned to the IAEA. Under Article 4 of the Early Notification Convention, the Agency is required to inform States Parties, member States, other States which are or may be physically affected by the accident, and relevant international intergovernmental organizations of a notification received pursuant to Article 1 of the convention. Upon request, the Agency is also required to provide States Parties, member States, and relevant international organizations (though not other States that may be physically affected) with the additional information received from the State of the accident pursuant to Article 2. Under Article 8, the Agency is also required, upon request, to assist a State without nuclear installations but bordering on a State having an active nuclear program but not Party to the convention to conduct investigations on the feasibility and establishment of an appropriate radiation monitoring system.

Under the Assistance Convention, the IAEA, acting within the framework of its Statute, is requested to use its best endeavors to promote, facilitate, and support the co-operation between States Parties provided for in the convention (Article 1). In addition, the IAEA itself is required to respond to requests for assistance, including by States Parties which are not members of the Agency, by making available appropriate resources, transmitting promptly such requests to other States and international organizations, and even co-ordinating the assistance at the international level, if requested by the requesting State (Article 2). The Agency is also required to collect and disseminate information relating to the types of assistance that could be made available in the event of nuclear accidents or radiological emergencies, to assist a State Party or a member State, when requested, in the area of emergency preparedness and response, to make resources available to the requesting State for conducting an initial assessment of the accident or emergency, to offer its good offices in the event of an accident or emergency, as well as to liaise with relevant international organizations for obtaining and exchanging relevant information and data (Article 5).

A number of practical arrangements and mechanisms have been developed within the IAEA since the adoption of the two conventions in 1986, and these have substantially contributed to the international nuclear emergency preparedness and response framework. Although these practical arrangements and mechanisms are outside the scope of this chapter, mention must at least be made of the Agency's

Incident and Emergency Centre (IEC), which was established as a 24-h warning and operational focal point for acting on notifications and/or advisory messages by States and relevant international organizations, of nuclear accidents or radiological emergencies, as well as responding to requests for information or assistance during such emergencies, regardless of their cause. The IEC is also concerned with promoting, facilitating, and supporting co-operation among Parties to the 1986 conventions and establishing and maintaining liaison with relevant international organizations.

4.4 Liability for Nuclear Damage

The picture relating to the international law of nuclear accidents would not be complete without a brief description of the conventions relating to civil liability for nuclear damage. These consist at the moment of the Paris Convention on Third Party Liability in the Field of Nuclear Energy of 29 July 1960 (the Paris Convention), as amended by Protocols of 1964 and 1982,[19] and of the Vienna Convention on Civil Liability for Nuclear Damage of 21 May 1963 (the Vienna Convention),[20] which was also amended after the Chernobyl accident by a Protocol of 12 September 1997 (the Vienna Protocol).[21] The Paris Convention is only open to OECD member States and, as of 31 December 2011, has 16 Contracting Parties, whereas the Vienna regime, adopted under the auspices of the IAEA, is potentially open to all States but, as of 31 December 2011, has comparatively few Contracting Parties: 38 for the Vienna Convention, and only 9 for the Vienna Protocol. No State is currently a Party to both the Paris Convention and the Vienna Convention (or the Vienna Protocol).

Despite the existence of these two distinct treaty regimes aiming at harmonizing the national law of the Contracting Parties in the field of civil liability for nuclear damage, both contain similar rules and are based on common basic principles. The uniform rules apply to nuclear damage arising out of nuclear accidents at certain nuclear installations (land-based reactors, factories for the production or processing of nuclear material, facilities where nuclear material is stored unless storage is incidental to transport), or in the course of transport of nuclear material (nuclear fuel, excluding natural or depleted uranium, and radioactive products or waste) to or from such installations. Nuclear damage is defined to cover, as a minimum, loss of life and personal injury, and loss of or damage to property, but the 1997 Vienna Protocol adds a number of additional heads of damage in order to

[19] The Paris Convention will be further amended by a Protocol adopted in 2004, but not yet in force, in order to bring it in line with the modernized regime envisaged in the 1997 Vienna Protocol, and in order to provide for a higher minimum limit of compensation.

[20] IAEA Doc. INFCIRC/500. The Vienna Convention entered into force on 12 November 1977.

[21] IAEA Doc. INFCIRC/566. The Vienna Protocol entered into force on 4 October 2003.

cover the costs of preventive measures and of measures of reinstatement of a significantly impaired environment, as well as loss of income deriving from an economic interest in the use or enjoyment of a significantly impaired environment.

The basic principles of international nuclear liability law are: (i) exclusive liability of the operator of the nuclear installation (i.e., to the exclusion of any other person who might otherwise be liable under general torts law); (ii) strict liability and minimization of the causes of exoneration from liability (armed conflict, civil war, hostilities or insurrection, and a grave natural disaster of an exceptional character, except that this latter cause of exoneration is no longer envisaged by the Vienna Protocol); (iii) minimum amount of liability (except for the Paris Convention which at present provides for a maximum limit); (iv) minimum liability coverage by insurance or other financial security; (v) limitation of liability in time (10 years and, under the Vienna Protocol, 30 years but only for claims relating to loss of life and personal injury); (v) equal treatment of victims, irrespective of nationality, domicile, or residence; (vi) uniform rules on jurisdictional competence; and (vii) recognition and enforcement of final judgments.

Despite their common principles and the similarity of their uniform rules, the coexistence of distinct treaty regimes has proved so far impossible to overcome, mainly because of the different amounts of compensation envisaged therein. At the regional level, the Paris Convention at present provides for a maximum liability limit of 15 million SDRs and is supplemented by a Supplementary Convention (the Brussels Convention) which envisages the provision of additional public funds (not only by the State of the liable operator, but also by all the Contracting Parties) to compensate nuclear damage in the event that the compensation provided on the basis of the Paris Convention proves insufficient. Furthermore, amending Protocols adopted in 2004, but not yet in force, are expected to raise the liability limit in the Paris Convention to 700 million EUR (and change it to a minimum limit) and to also raise the compensation based on the public funds envisaged in the Brussels Convention, so that the compensation available under the combined Paris-Brussels regime would amount to not less than 1.5 billion EUR. At the global level, the Vienna Convention only provides for a mandatory minimum limit of 5 million US $, although the definition of the US$ refers to its value under the gold standard at the time of the adoption of the convention and may thus be interpreted to require a much higher limit as of today. The Vienna Protocol raises the minimum amount of compensation that has to be made available to 300 million SDRs.

The absence of treaty relations among the Parties to the Paris Convention, on the one hand, and the Parties to the Vienna Convention or the Vienna Protocol, on the other, causes a number of problems. Some of these problems are very technical in nature and relate to the determination of the operator liable, and of the State whose courts have jurisdiction, in transport cases: without going into unnecessary details, it is worth pointing out that the uniform rules differentiate between transport between operators in Contracting Parties and transport between one operator in a Contracting Party and one in a non-contracting State, and Contracting Parties to different conventions are obviously to be considered as non-contracting States in their mutual relations. But perhaps a more important problem caused by the absence of treaty relations derives from the fact that the conventions do not provide for mandatory coverage of nuclear damage suffered in non-contracting States: even the modernized nuclear liability regime embodied in the Vienna Protocol provides for mandatory coverage of nuclear damage 'wherever suffered' as a matter of principle, but then allows for the exclusion of damage suffered in nuclear non-contracting States that do not afford reciprocal benefits.

In order to establish treaty relations between the Parties to the Paris Convention and the Vienna Convention, both defined as including any amendment thereto, a specific treaty was adopted on 21 September 1988, in the aftermath of the Chernobyl incident, under the joint auspices of the IAEA and the OECD: the Joint Protocol Relating to the Application of the Vienna Convention and the Paris Convention (the Joint Protocol), which entered into force on 27 April 1992 and, as of 31 December 2011, has 26 Contracting Parties. More recently, another treaty aiming at creating a truly global nuclear liability regime was adopted under the auspices of the IAEA at the same time as the Vienna Protocol: the Convention on Supplementary Compensation for Nuclear Damage (CSC) but, unfortunately, this latter convention has not yet entered into force.

The CSC is considerably more ambitious that the Joint Protocol: on the one hand, it is open not only to States that are Parties to either the Vienna Convention or the Paris Convention (including amendments thereto) but also to States that are Parties to neither convention, provided that their national law complies with the basic principles of nuclear liability, as outlined above, which are reflected in uniform rules contained in an Annex to the Convention; on the other, it also aims at establishing a minimum compensation amount of 300 million SDRs at the national level and at increasing the amount of compensation available, in the event that the national compensation amount is insufficient, by obliging all Contracting Parties to make public funds available on the basis of a formula whereby more than 90 % of the contributions will come from nuclear-power-generating States. On 21 May 2008 the CSC was ratified by the United States of America, which is not a Party to either the Vienna Convention or the Paris Convention, and it is hoped that this important development will contribute to an early entry into force of the CSC.

4.5 Conclusions

As was pointed out at the outset, until the Chernobyl accident, the legal framework for nuclear energy was constituted, for the most part, by international technical recommendations, which could only be made binding through their incorporation in national law or in bilateral or multilateral treaties (e.g., in the area of maritime transportation). After Chernobyl, the international community was able to react to the accident in an effective way and adopt binding international treaties in the areas of nuclear safety and of emergency preparedness and response, as well as to modernize the international legal regime for nuclear liability. After the events of 11 September 2001, the international community's attention shifted from the area of nuclear safety to the area of nuclear security, but the recent nuclear accident at the Fukushima Daiichi nuclear power plant in Japan has brought its attention back to nuclear safety and emergency preparedness ad response.

The Fukushima accident showed that, despite the efforts to improve nuclear safety that were made after Chernobyl, nuclear accidents can still take place, even in the developed world. The questions now are whether the treaties that were adopted as a result of the Chernobyl accident provide an effective basis for nuclear safety and emergency preparedness and response and whether improvements are necessary. This is particularly true for the conventions relating to nuclear safety, which fall short of making the IAEA safety standards binding on Contracting Parties; in addition, they are often labeled as 'incentive conventions' because the obligations they create for Contracting Parties are mainly obligations *de moyens* rather than obligations of result, and much of their effectiveness depends on the peer-review mechanism they have established. But the conventions relating to emergency preparedness and response also have their flaws and are currently under scrutiny, and so are the various conventions relating to nuclear liability, which have so far failed to establish a truly global legal regime.

In light of the serious consequences of the Fukushima accident, a Ministerial Conference on Nuclear Safety took place in Vienna under the auspices of the IAEA in June 2011, in order to direct, under the leading role of the IAEA, the process of learning and of acting upon lessons to strengthen nuclear safety, emergency preparedness and radiation protection of people and the environment worldwide. On 20 June 2011, the conference adopted a Declaration[22] which inter alia reiterated 'the importance of universal adherence and effective implementation and continuous review of the relevant international instruments on nuclear safety' and considered 'the possibility of strengthening the international legal framework in this area'; the Declaration also recognized 'the need for a global nuclear liability regime that addresses the concerns of all States that might be affected by a nuclear accident with a view to providing appropriate compensation for nuclear damage'. As requested by the Declaration, the IAEA Secretariat drew up an Action Plan on Nuclear Safety,[23] which was approved by the Agency's Board of Governors and endorsed by the IAEA General Conference at their September 2011 meetings. The Action Plan envisages a number of actions, one of which focuses on the improvement of the international legal framework, including in the area of nuclear liability.

It is a well-known fact that the use of nuclear energy in most States is a matter of public concern, and in many States people are skeptical or even strongly opposed to this form of energy. However, whereas some States have decided not to use or to phase out nuclear energy, other States still consider nuclear power as a viable option in meeting their energy needs, as was recognized in the June 2011 IAEA Ministerial Declaration in the aftermath of the Fukushima accident. Taking

[22] IAEA Doc. INFCIRC/821.

[23] IAEA Doc. GOV/2011/59-GC(55)/14.

this into account, the current efforts, in particular under the auspices of the IAEA, to enhance the existing international legal framework are seen by many States as essential in order to enhance nuclear safety throughout the world and regain public confidence in the safety of nuclear activities.

References

Adede AO (1987) The IAEA notification and assistance conventions in case of a nuclear accident. Graham & Trotman/Martinus Nijhoff, London

Arangio-Ruiz A (1963) Some international legal problems of the civil uses of nuclear energy. In: 107 collected courses of the Hague Academy of International Law, 1962-III, pp 499–637

Baer A, Pelzer N, Stoiber C, Tonhauser W (2004) Handbook on nuclear law. IAEA, Vienna

Gioia A (2002) The international law of the sea and the transport of spent nuclear fuel and radioactive waste. In: Pelzer N (ed) Rechtsfragen des Umgangs mit abgebrannten Brennelementen und radioaktiven Abfällen. Nomos, Baden-Baden, pp 75–94

Gioia A (2009) The International Atomic Energy Agency, nuclear security and the fight against international terrorism. Italian Yearb Int Law 2008 18:139–157

Handl G (2003) The IAEA nuclear safety conventions: an example of successful treaty management? Nucl Law Bull 72:7–27

Jankowitsch-Prevor O (2006) The convention on nuclear safety. In: International nuclear law in the post-Chernobyl period, OECD-NEA, Paris, pp 155–168

Kuş S (2011) International nuclear law in the 25 years between Chernobyl and Fukushima and beyond. Nucl Law Bull 87:7–26

Moser B (1986) The IAEA conventions on early notification of a nuclear accident and on assistance in the case of a nuclear accident or radiological emergency. Nucl Law Bull 38:10–23

Pelzer N (2006) Learning the hard way: did the lessons taught by the Chernobyl nuclear accident contribute to improving nuclear law? In: International nuclear law in the post-Chernobyl period, OECD-NEA, Paris, pp 73–118

Rautenbach J, Tonhauser W, Wetherall A (2006) Overview of the international legal framework governing the safe and peaceful uses of nuclear energy—some practical steps. In: International nuclear law in the post-Chernobyl period, OECD-NEA, Paris, pp 7–36

Schwartz J (2010) Liability and compensation for third party damage resulting from a nuclear incident. In: International nuclear law: history, evolution and outlook, OECD-NEA, Paris, pp 307–354

Stoiber C (2010) Nuclear security: Legal aspects of physical protection, combating illicit trafficking and nuclear terrorism. In: International nuclear law: history, evolution and outlook, OECD-NEA, Paris, pp 219–242

Tonhauser W, Jankowitsch-Prevor O (2006) The Joint convention on the safety of spent fuel management and on the safety of radioactive waste management. In: International nuclear law in the post-Chernobyl period, OECD-NEA, Paris, pp 201–214

Tonhauser W, Wetherall A (2010) The international legal framework on nuclear safety: developments, challenges and opportunities. In: International nuclear law: history, evolution and outlook, OECD-NEA, Paris, pp 157–169

Part II
The EU Legal Framework

Chapter 5
EU Disaster Response Law: Principles and Instruments

Marco Gestri

Abstract This chapter aims at analyzing the legal framework governing disaster prevention, preparedness and response at EU level, with specific regard to emergencies occurring inside the Union. First, the origin and the development of the European cooperation in the field of civil protection are illustrated. Such a cooperation has led to important results, notably to the establishment of the Civil Protection Mechanism (CPM) which has acted successfully in an ever increasing number of emergencies. However, before the entry into force of the Treaty of Lisbon the further development of a European response capacity was limited by the absence of an adequate legal basis. The Lisbon Treaty has opened up new opportunities *in subiecta materia*, introducing into primary law a new 'clause of solidarity' (Article 222 TFEU) and a specific EU competence in the area of civil protection (Article 196 TFEU). The author analyzes the scope and legal effects of the solidarity clause, both *vis-à-vis* the EU and its Member States, arguing that the norm provides a binding legal obligation of assistance, even if characterized by a margin of discretion as to its actual implementation. The possible relevance of Article 222 either for the establishment of a new machinery dealing with disasters or for enhancing the existing mechanism for civil protection is also assessed. As for the new competence in the area of civil protection, the opportunities stemming from the new provisions are discussed as well as the limitations deriving from its classification as a 'complementary' or 'supporting' competence (Article 6 TFEU). Finally, the chapter describes the initiatives recently undertaken in order to review, and reinforce, the current CPM: the most delicate issues are discussed and possible solutions are outlined.

M. Gestri (✉)
Dipartimento di Giurisprudenza, Università di Modena e Reggio Emilia,
via San Geminiano 3, 41121, Modena, Italy
e-mail: marco.gestri@unimore.it

A. de Guttry et al. (eds.), *International Disaster Response Law*,
DOI: 10.1007/978-90-6704-882-8_5,

Keywords European Union · Lisbon Treaty · Solidarity clause · Civil protection · Complementary competence · Union civil protection mechanism

Contents

5.1 Origin and Historical Development of Civil Protection Cooperation at the European Level

In the face of disasters a sense of solidarity develops immediately and spontaneously among human beings. This natural impulse can only be stronger among individuals and peoples belonging to the 'European family'. Furthermore, having regard to the current development of European integration, it is normal for every European citizen to look at the European Union (EU) in order to seek help in case of disasters. In effect, according to a recent survey, approximately 90 % of the European citizens expect the EU to do more for helping their country when hit by disasters.[1]

On the European plane, the first step toward the introduction of forms of cooperation on civil protection was a meeting held in Rome, at ministerial level, in May 1985.[2] Further to that meeting, the Council and the representatives of the Governments of the Member States adopted a number of resolutions laying down the initial bases for developing Community cooperation in the field of civil

[1] See European Commission, Communication 'Towards a stronger European disaster response: the role of civil protection and humanitarian assistance', COM (2010) 600, 26 October 2010, 4.

[2] See also BIICL 2010, 6.

protection.[3] The implementation of these resolutions led to the development of a number of mechanisms for facilitating operational cooperation among Member States in the areas of disaster preparedness and response; however, the impact of these acts was limited by their non-binding nature.[4]

An important policy instrument was the Community action program in the field of civil protection, established in 1997 by a Council Decision and terminated in 2006.[5] The program provided financial support for major projects of interest for all Member States, or a number of them, in the field of civil protection and for training and information activities.

In order to strengthen the forms of cooperation and as a consequence 'to ensure even better protection in the event of natural, technological, radiological and environmental emergencies', in 2001 the Council adopted a decision establishing a Community Civil Protection Mechanism (CPM).[6] In the following years, the CPM has rather successfully operated in respect of a great number of major emergencies, both within the EU and in third States.[7] In the wake of the 2004 Tsunami in the Indian Ocean, the CPM was subject to a review and a reappraisal,[8] which led to the adoption of the recast Council decision 2007/779/EC, Euratom of 8 November 2007.[9] Overall, the recast decision confined itself to Introducing some ameliorations to the existing regulatory framework,[10] without radically reforming it. An important innovation was in any case the development of the modular approach.[11]

---

[3] Resolution of 25 June 1987 on the introduction of Community cooperation on civil protection, *OJ* 1987 C 176/1; Resolution of 13 February 1989 on the new developments in Community cooperation on civil protection, *OJ* 1989 C 44/3; Resolution of 23 November 1990 on Community cooperation on civil protection, *OJ* 1990 C 315/1; Resolution of 8 July 1991 on improving mutual aid between Member States in the event of natural or technological disasters, *OJ* 1991 C 198/11; Resolution of 31 October 1994 on strengthening Community cooperation on civil protection, *OJ* 1994 C 33/1; Resolution of 26 February 2001 on strengthening the capabilities of the EU in the field of civil protection, *OJ* 2001 C 82/11.

[4] See also Cremona 2011, 12.

[5] Council Decision 98/22/EC of 19 December 1997 establishing a Community Action Program in the field of Civil Protection, *OJ* 1998 L 8/20. A first 2-year Action Program (1998–1999) was followed by a second 5-year Action Program (2000–2004)—Council Decision 1999/847/EC of 9 December 1999, *OJ* 1999 L 327/53—extended till 2006.

[6] Council Decision 2001/792/EC, Euratom of 23 October 2001 establishing a Community mechanism to facilitate reinforced cooperation in civil protection assistance interventions, *OJ* 2001 L 297/7.

[7] See European Commission, Communication 'Improving the Community Civil Protection Mechanism', COM (2005) 137, 20 May 2005, 2. See also Missiroli 2005.

[8] Ibid.

[9] *OJ* 2007 L 314/9.

[10] House of Lords 2009, 6.

[11] See *infra*, Sect. 5.3.

In the absence of a specific legal basis for the adoption of EC legislation on civil protection,[12] the decisions on the establishment of the Community Action Programme and the CPM were adopted under the former article 308 TEC (so-called 'flexibility provision'). As is known, such a provision empowered the Council to take whatever measures were necessary, in order to attain one of the objectives of the Community, when the Treaty did not provide the necessary powers. An important limitation derived from the requirement of unanimity within the Council. Apart from that, recourse to such a procedure in the field at issue did not raise particular problems. In this connection, it has to be recalled that the Treaty of Maastricht of 7 February 1992 introduced into Article 3 TEC, listing the activities that the Community was empowered to carry out for the purposes set out in Article 2 TEC, a reference to 'measures in the spheres of energy, civil protection and tourism'.[13] However, on the one hand such a reference did not constitute in itself a legal basis for the adoption of EC measures in the three spheres. On the other hand, Article 3(t) TEC was not accompanied by any other provision in the Treaty articulating the objectives of the measures to be adopted in the areas in question and, more importantly, establishing appropriate legal bases for the adoption of normative acts; with the consequence that the Community competence in the sphere of civil protection was left 'hanging in the air'. Action in that field could be pursued thanks only to the flexibility provision or to the legal bases offered by provisions concerning other EC policies.[14]

The ambiguity of such a legal picture, evidently stemming from a compromise, was expressly acknowledged by the Member States, which, in the Declaration no. 1 annexed to the Maastricht Treaty, committed them to re-examine the question of introducing into the TEC specific titles on energy, civil protection, and tourism, in particular in the framework of the 1996 Intergovernmental Conference. This notwithstanding, until the Treaty of Lisbon, the legal picture deriving from Community primary law remained unchanged.

---

[12] On the concept of 'legal basis', in the light of the 'principle of conferral', see also, with specific regard to civil protection, Cremona 2011, 11–12.

[13] Article 3(t), later becoming Article 3(u).

[14] In the European Convention, there was a general feeling that 'it was an anomaly to have subject matters mentioned in TEC Article 3 without having any corresponding Treaty article setting out the policy objectives and the competence': Final report of Working Group V 'Complementary Competencies', CONV 375/1/02, 4 November 2002, 15. A number of measures having a bearing on disaster management and response were adopted under the legal bases offered by the Treaty provisions concerning other policies, such as environmental protection (Article 174 TEC) and health safety or by the Euratom Treaty as regards nuclear safety. See also Cremona 2011, *passim* and Chap. 4 by Gioia, in this volume.

5.2 Civil Protection After the Treaty of Lisbon

5.2.1 The Solidarity Clause (Article 222 TFEU)

The entry into force of the Lisbon Treaty, on 1 December 2009, has determined important innovations in the European legal framework concerning civil protection. On the one hand, Article 6(f) of Treaty on the Functioning of the European Union (TFEU) sets forth in general terms a competence of the Union 'to carry out actions to support, coordinate or supplement the actions of the member States' *inter alia* in the area of 'civil protection'. Such a competence is more precisely spelled out in Title XXIII of the TFEU, entitled 'civil protection' and consisting of Article 196. This provision signals the definitive acknowledgment of a specific legal basis in EU primary law for the actions carried out by the Union in the field of civil protection.

On the other hand, the Lisbon Treaty has also introduced into EU primary law a 'solidarity clause', precisely in Article 222 TFEU. The latter provides a general duty of the Union and its Member States to 'act jointly in a spirit of solidarity if a member State is the object of a terrorist attack or the victim of a natural or man-made disaster'.

The significance of such innovations has now to be fully assessed, starting from the solidarity clause.

5.2.1.1 Origin of the Solidarity Clause

The idea of a solidarity clause was first articulated in the European Convention, which prepared the 2003 draft Treaty establishing a Constitution for Europe, notably in its Working Group VIII 'Defence'.[15] Originally, the solidarity clause was intended as a sort of complement to the mutual defense clause, now enshrined in Article 42(7) TEU.[16] In particular, while the mutual defense clause would introduce an obligation of aid and assistance among Member States in the event of 'armed aggression' against one of them, the solidarity clause would cover 'new threats' coming from non-State actors and confronting Member States, in particular that of terrorism. In fact, a first version of the clause only dealt with terrorist attacks; yet, the scope of the provision was subsequently broadened, by virtue of an initiative of the chairman of the Working Group, Michel Barnier, referring also to unintentional disasters.[17] As a consequence, the Treaty establishing a

[15] The European Convention, Final report of Working Group VIII 'Defence', CONV 461/02, 16 December 2002, 21.

[16] Sur 2007, *passim*; Myrdal and Rhinard 2010, 3.

[17] See von Ondarza and Parkes 2010, 2; Myrdal and Rhinard 2010, 4; Konstadinides 2011, 6. Notably, the final report of the WG Defence (*supra*, n. 15) stated: 'Taking this enhanced solidarity further, and to strengthen the existing Community mechanism, a situation might be

Constitution for Europe, signed in Rome on 29 October 2004, included in Article I-43 a solidarity clause, covering both terrorist attacks and natural or man-made disasters, as well as a provision (Article III-329) spelling down the detailed arrangements for the implementation of the clause. The two provisions have been re-proposed by the Lisbon Treaty, which has merged them into a single norm (Article 222), constituting Title VII of the TFEU ('Solidarity clause'). More precisely, the first paragraph of the article defines the substantive content and the scope of the clause whereas the following paragraphs (2–4) deal with the procedural aspects.

Indeed, according to Article 222(1) TFEU:

> 1. The Union and its Member States shall act jointly in a spirit of solidarity if a Member State is the object of a terrorist attack or the victim of a natural or man-made disaster. The Union shall mobilize all the instruments at its disposal, including the military resources made available by the Member States, to:
>
> (a) – prevent the terrorist threat in the territory of the Member States;
> – protect democratic institutions and the civilian population from any terrorist attack;
> – assist a Member State in its territory, at the request of its political authorities, in the event of a terrorist attack;
>
> (b) assist a Member State in its territory, at the request of its political authorities, in the event of a natural or man-made disaster.

5.2.1.2 Scope of the Solidarity Clause

The pre-requisite for the activation of the solidarity clause is the fact of a Member State being 'the victim of a natural or man-made disaster'. As regards the material scope of the provision, it is worth noting that it does not offer any definition of 'natural or man-made disaster' nor it includes any exemplification of them. As observed by Sur, the national legislations of Member States may in effect differ as to the definition of 'disaster'.[18] A more precise definition of 'natural or man-made disaster' could emerge from the acts adopted for the implementation of Article 222. In this respect, it has to be stressed that some scholars have advocated a restrictive interpretation of the notion of disaster envisaged in Article 222 TFEU. For instance, according to Sara Myrdal and Mark Rhinard, 'the solidarity clause

---

(Footnote 17 continued)
envisaged in which a pool of specialised civilian or military civil-protection units identified by the Member States undertakes joint training and intervention coordination programmes so as to facilitate more effective intervention in the event of natural or humanitarian disasters within the Union'.

[18] Sur 2007, 574.

should only apply to large-scale incidents simultaneously or consecutively affecting multiple member States'. A similar interpretation has been put forward by Nicolai von Ondarza and Roderick Parkes, justifying it with the fear of possible abuses on the part of 'accident-prone' States which 'can cry solidarity and rely upon the EU to perform tasks they should really be doing themselves'.[19] Consequently, these authors have proposed the adoption of a 'subsidiarity baseline' in the implementing arrangements or of a catalog of disasters.

In respect of these interpretations, it must be stressed that there is nothing in Article 222 TFEU indicating that the clause should find application exclusively *vis-à-vis* disasters affecting a number of Member States, or 'cross-border' emergencies. Such a restrictive reading cannot indeed be accepted, in the light not only of the text of the provision but also of its object and purpose. Moreover, given the fact that very often disasters hitting a single State have enormous consequences in terms of loss of life or damages to property, the interpretation is also clearly unreasonable. Much more in line with the text as well as with the object and purpose of the provision is a reading according to which the solidarity clause could be triggered by any type of disaster overwhelming the response capacity of the victim State.[20] In the light of that, the adoption of a more elaborated definition of disaster would probably be inopportune. To alleviate the worries of some Governments, echoed in the literature referred above, one has to consider that the right to request assistance under Article 222 TFEU should be exercised in good faith by the Member State concerned, taking into account that each Member State has a general responsibility to provide its citizens with adequate protection. In any case, the gravity of the emergency is implied in the notion of 'disaster'.[21] In this direction, mention can be made of the position expressed by the European Council in the Stockholm Programme, according to which

> Union disaster management is built on two main principles: the responsibility of Member States for providing their citizens with the necessary protection in view of the existing risks and threats, and solidarity among the Member States to assist each other before, during and after disasters, if catastrophes overwhelm national capacities or affect more than one Member State.[22]

As far as the territorial scope of Article 222 is concerned, the provision may find application only when 'a Member State' is the victim of a disaster. So, as a rule the clause should cover only disasters occurring inside the EU. Besides, Article 222(1)(b) refers to a general duty 'to assist a Member State *in its*

---

[19] von Ondarza and Parkes 2010, 3–4.

[20] See also European Commission, 'Towards a stronger European disaster response' *supra* n. 1, 5: 'The EU disaster response capacity should address all types of disasters (i.e., natural and man-made, other than armed conflicts) that overwhelm national response capacities and result in a need for EU assistance…'.

[21] See also Sur 2007, 574.

[22] European Council, 'The Stockholm Programme—An open and secure Europe serving and protecting citizens', *OJ* 2010 C 115/25.

territory'.[23] In other words, the solidarity clause is certainly focused on the territory of the Union.[24]

However, it might be asked whether the application of the clause *vis-à-vis* disasters occurring outside the EU would be completely excluded. One could notably think of an event which takes place in a third State but at the same time affects a great number of citizens of one or more Member States and, as a consequence, requires the organization of a response also in the territory of the Union.[25] Another phenomenon to be considered is the occurrence of emergencies which do not necessarily have a precise territorial dimension, as is the case of some epidemics.[26]

Besides, one has to note that although Article 222 is focused on disasters occurring inside the Union, the provision is surprisingly placed in Part V of the TFEU, dedicated to the 'External action of the Union'. This is a consequence, as pointed out by some scholars, of the fact that in the European Convention the solidarity clause was linked to the requirement of solidarity in foreign policy matters, representing 'a bridge between internal and external security'.[27] In effect, Marise Cremona has spoken of a 'dual dimension' of the clause, which is also reflected in the institutional arrangements for its implementation, involving both the Commission and the High Representative for Foreign Affairs and Security Policy (HR) and both internal and external security committees.[28]

In any case, it has to be stressed that the European Parliament has expressed itself in favor of a broader interpretation of the territorial scope of Article 222 TFEU. In the Resolution adopted on 27 September 2011 the Parliament 'invites the Commission, when setting up the European disaster response capability, to take into account the Solidarity Clause and its implementation arrangements which will ensure a more effective and coherent response to disasters inside and *outside the European Union*'.[29]

---

[23] Emphasis added.

[24] Cf. Sur 2007, 564; Cremona 2011, 14.

[25] See von Ondarza and Parkes 2010, 4. For instance, after the terrorist attacks in Mumbai the need emerged to organize the medical evacuation of a great number of EU citizens. The MIC (see *infra*) was activated in that respect and that led to the deployment of a Swedish aircraft which evacuated UK and Spanish citizens from India.

[26] See also Sur 2007, 577.

[27] Grevi 2007, 818.

[28] Cremona 2011, 29–30.

[29] European Parliament, Resolution of 27 September 2011 on 'Towards a stronger European disaster response: the role of civil protection and humanitarian assistance', doc. P7_TA-PROV(2011)0404, para 3 [emphasis added]. See also the Report of 19 July 2011 by Elisabetta Gardini (doc. A7-0283/2011).

5.2.1.3 Legal Effects Stemming from Article 222 TFEU

It is now time to assess the legal effects deriving from Article 222 TFEU. As emerges from the opening sentence of its first paragraph ('the Union and its Member States shall act jointly in a spirit of solidarity'), Article 222 addresses itself both to the EU and to its Member States. As observed, the solidarity clause is characterized by a 'supranational intent ... making it more than an intergovernmental obligation (as is the case with the mutual defense clause)'.[30] This means that the EU institutions are to be involved alongside national ones. In other words, it is possible to speak of a 'vertical dimension' of solidarity. More precisely, the first paragraph of Article 222 TFEU focuses on the Union's responsibilities whereas the second one deals with Member States duties. Apart from the broad duty to act jointly with Member States in a spirit of solidarity, Article 222(1) TFEU provides that the Union 'shall mobilise all the instruments at its disposal' ('*l'Union mobilise*'; '*l'Unione mobilita*') in order to 'assist a Member State in its territory, at the request of its political authorities'. The wording of the provision clearly expresses a legal obligation of the EU. On the other hand, it has to be noted that solidarity must be activated by a request coming from the political authorities of the victim State. In other words, the EU formally does not have a right to take the initiative in this context and the victim State is free, at least from the viewpoint of Article 222 TFEU, not to ask for Union assistance.

As to the notion of 'political authorities', the latter might appear ambiguous. In any case, it seems that one has to interpret the provision in the light of the general features of the EU institutional and legal order, according to which the EU ordinarily deals with the Member States, that is, their central governmental authorities. As a consequence, it is submitted that a regional or local authority could have the competence to request the intervention of the EU only with the consent of the central government of the State in question.

The literal language of the provision seems to confine the intervention of the Union exclusively to response actions, that is to activities carried out *ex post facto*. In this respect, one might emphasize the difference in the language used *vis-à-vis* terrorism, in relation to which Article 222 (1)(a) TFEU also spells out obligations of prevention and protection. On the other hand, one could observe that the EU must in any case prepare itself adequately in order to carry out assistance activities and 'to act jointly with States'. This would seem to imply an expansion of the obligation also toward the preparedness and prevention phase. In any case, Article 222 TFEU must be read in conjunction with Article 196 TFEU, which is focused on prevention activities.

As regards the position of the other Member States, Article 222(2) TFEU provides that, in case of a natural or man-made disaster hitting a EU State, they 'shall assist it at the request of its political authorities', adding that 'the Member States shall coordinate between themselves in the Council'. In this case too, it has

[30] Myrdal and Rhinard 2010, 6.

to be borne in mind that the assistance of the other Member States has to be requested by the victim State. As to the effects of the provision, its wording evocates a binding duty of assistance on the part of the other Member States.[31] It is worth mentioning, in this regard, that the European Parliament, in its Resolution of 27 September 2011, has affirmed that the clause under Article 222 TFEU 'establishes *the obligation* for member States to assist each other in the event of a natural or man-made disaster on EU territory'.[32]

However, account must also be taken of the 'Declaration on Article 222 of the Treaty on the Functioning of the European Union' (no. 37), annexed to the Final Act of the Lisbon Conference, according to which:

> Without prejudice to the measures adopted by the Union to comply with its solidarity obligation toward a Member State which is the object of a terrorist attack or the victim of natural or man-made disaster, none of the provisions of Article 222 is intended to affect the right of another Member State to choose the most appropriate means to comply with its own solidarity obligation toward that Member State.

On account of the importance of its content, the legal significance of that Declaration has to be clarified. Being a declaration annexed to the Final Act of the Lisbon Intergovernmental Conference, and not to the Treaties, the Declaration is not covered by Article 51 TEU; as a consequence, it does not form an integral part of EU treaty law.[33] However, such a Declaration is to be regarded as forming part of the 'context' of the EU treaties, in accordance with Article 31(2)(b) of the 1969 Vienna Convention on the law of treaties. It follows that the Declaration must be taken into consideration for the interpretation of the TFEU and of its Article 222.[34]

In the light of the above, one has to conclude that each Member State, even if under a legal obligation to assist the victim State *ex* article 222 TFEU, will maintain the right to choose, in good faith,[35] the concrete modalities of assistance. In any event, as pointed out by Myrdal and Rhinard, 'member States must actually give something in response'.[36]

With regard to the practical fulfillment of the duty of solidarity, the Member States concerned should coordinate among themselves in the Council. As noted by

[31] See also Stavros Dimas, European Commissioner for the Environment, 'The third Civil Protection Forum: developing Europe's resilience to disasters, Civil Protection Forum, Towards a more resilient society', Brussels, 25–26 November 2009, SPEECH/09/556 ('obligation of Member States to assist each other'). In the legal literature, the binding nature of the duty stemming from Article 222(2) TFEU is underlined by Sur 2007, 578; von Ondarza and Parkes 2010, 2. In the same vein, cf. Myrdal and Rhinard 2010, 8, even if they add that 'it is hard to imagine a Member State being called to the Court of Justice for violation of the clause'.

[32] *Supra*, n. 29, para J [emphasis added].

[33] See also Gaja and Adinolfi 2010, 160.

[34] See, in that direction, ECJ, Case C-193/99 *Kaur* [2001] *ECR* I-1237, para 13. See also Adam and Tizzano 2010, 121.

[35] The provision of Article 222 TFEU has to be read in conjunction with the principle of sincere cooperation envisaged in Article 4(3) TFEU. See also Konstadinides 2011, 15.

[36] Myrdal and Rhinard 2010, 6.

Sur, the intergovernmental character of the obligation in question is 'mitigated' by the institutional framework in which the coordination of the assistance has to take place.[37]

5.2.1.4 The Implementing Arrangements

According to Article 222(3) TFEU, the 'arrangements for the implementation by the Union' of the solidarity clause are to be defined by a Council Decision, adopted on the basis of a joint proposal by the Commission and the HR.[38] By virtue of the general rule of Article 16(3) TEU, the Council shall adopt such a decision by qualified majority. On the other hand, where the decision to be taken has 'defence implications', the Council has to act in accordance with Article 31(1) TEU, that is, unanimously. The Council shall be assisted both by the Political and Security Committee, with the support of the structures developed in the context of the Common Security and Defence Policy, and by the Standing Committee on Operational Cooperation on Internal Security (COSI)[39]: the two Committees may, if necessary, submit joint opinions. As to the European Parliament, it has simply to 'be informed'.

5.2.2 The New Competence in the Area of Civil Protection Under Article 196 TFEU

It has been previously mentioned that the Lisbon Treaty has inserted into primary law a new specific EU legal basis in the area of civil protection. On the other hand, as is known, the Lisbon Treaty has for the first time provided an articulation and a definition of the different categories of competence granted to the Union, namely in Article 2 TFEU. Under that classification—basically making reference to exclusive competence, shared competence, and the competence to carry out supporting actions ('complementary competence')—civil protection is one of the areas of complementary EU competence *ex* article 6 TFEU. In the fields in question, as clarified by Article 2(5) TFEU, the Union 'shall have competence to

---

[37] Sur 2007, 578.

[38] See European Commission, 'Proposal for a Decision of the European Parliament and of the Council on a Union Civil Protection Mechanism', COM (2011) 934, 20 December 2011, 3 (the Commission and the HR 'will bring forward a proposal in 2012').

[39] See Council Decision (2010/131) of 25 February 2010 on setting up the Standing Committee on operational cooperation on internal security, *OJ* 2010 L 52/50. The COSI consists of high-level officials from Member States' ministries of the interior and of Commission representatives (Eurojust, Europol, Frontex and other relevant bodies may be invited to attend meetings of the Committee as observers). Under Article 3(3) of the Decision 'the Standing Committee shall assist the Council in accordance with the provisions of Article 222 of the Treaty'.

carry out actions to support, coordinate or supplement the actions of the Member States without thereby superseding their competence in these areas'. Furthermore, even if the EU may adopt legally binding acts, those acts may not entail any harmonization of Member States' laws or regulations.[40] It can be observed that, from a substantive point of view, the new explicit competence in the area of civil protection essentially reflects the practice that developed *in subiecta materia* prior to the Lisbon Treaty, giving rise to the current mechanism of European civil protection, which is complementary in nature, not intending to replace nor radically transform national systems.[41]

The precise and detailed definition of the objectives and the scope of the new EU competence regarding civil protection is spelled out in Article 196 TFEU, providing in particular that:

> 1. The Union shall encourage cooperation between Member States in order to improve the effectiveness of systems for preventing and protecting against natural or man-made disasters.
>
> Union action shall aim to:
>
> (a) support and complement Member States' action at national, regional and local level in risk prevention, in preparing their civil protection personnel and in responding to natural or man-made disasters within the Union;
> (b) promote swift, effective operational cooperation within the Union between national civil protection services;
> (c) promote consistency in international civil protection work.

To start with, it has to be noted that the new treaty provision covers civil protection cooperation both inside and outside the EU, mirroring also in this respect the current legal framework.

Second, one has to underline the very ample scope of the new competence, covering the three phases of risk prevention, preparedness, and response to natural and man-made disasters. In the light of the new provision, the prevention component of the European civil protection will have presumably to be reinforced. In effect, there exists a general consensus in the EU in favor of the development of a comprehensive approach to disaster management, as for instance acknowledged by the Council conclusions of 30 November 2009 on a Community framework on disaster prevention within the EU.[42]

Of certain significance is the reference by Article 196 TFEU to the objective of supporting and complementing Member States' action at all levels, and particularly the explicit mention of the responsibility of regional and local authorities.

A crucial innovation deriving from the provision of an explicit legal basis for the area of civil protection is that, under the new Article 196(2) TFEU, European

---

[40] Those EU competences may be characterized as 'parallel' to those of the Member States: Gaja and Adinolfi 2010, 140.

[41] BIICL 2010, 18. See also Cremona 2011, 15–16.

[42] Doc. 15394/09. See also the European Parliament Recommendation to the Council of 14 December 2010 on setting up EU rapid response capability, INI/2010/2096, para E.

measures *in subiecta materia* will be enacted in accordance with the ordinary legislative procedure, envisaged by Article 294 TFEU. As a consequence, the relevant acts are to be adopted, upon a proposal from the Commission, in co-decision by the European Parliament and the Council, the latter deciding by qualified majority. This represents an important step forward in respect of the pre-existing legal framework, where acts of a general relevance in that policy area had to be adopted using the flexibility clause (Article 308 TEC), which required unanimity in the Council and a mere consultation of the Parliament. The new decision-making process will undoubtedly facilitate further advances in the European CPM.

Besides, the legal acts adopted under such a procedure will have legislative nature, in conformity with Article 289(3) TFEU.[43] As concerns their legal form, having regard to the fact that Article 196 TFEU speaks generically of the adoption of 'measures', one could imagine that the acts at issue might consist of Regulations, Directives and Decisions. However, it has to be recalled that in the field in question the adoption of acts implying any harmonization of Member States' laws is excluded. This obviously tends to hinder the adoption of Regulations[44] and Directives (which typically aim at substituting or harmonizing national legislation), with the consequence that the legal acts normally enacted *in subiecta materia* will be Decisions in accordance with Article 288 TFEU.

5.3 The Existing Legal and Operational Framework: The Civil Protection Mechanism

As previously seen, the European system for civil protection is currently based on two legal texts: the Council Decision of 8 November 2007 establishing a CPM (recast)[45] and that of 5 March 2007 on the Civil Protection Financial Instrument (2007/162/EC, Euratom).[46] However, it has to be borne in mind that the European Commission, after a comprehensive evaluation of the existing legislation, has recently submitted a Proposal for a decision reforming the system and giving rise to a new Union Civil Protection Mechanism (UCPM).[47] Here the current legal

---

[43] Under that provision, 'Legal acts adopted by legislative procedure shall constitute legislative acts'.

[44] One could in any case conceive the adoption of Regulations having a practical, concrete relevance, for instance for the establishment of financial programs.

[45] *Supra*, n. 9.

[46] *OJ* 2007 L 71/9. See Chap. 26 by Palandri, in this volume.

[47] *Supra*, n. 38.

picture is considered,[48] whereas the perspectives emerging from the recent *de lege ferenda* initiatives will be discussed in the following section.

The CPM is an operative mechanism, which essentially aims at facilitating the mobilization of immediate in-kind assistance for disasters both within and outside the EU. In particular, it intends to improve the preparedness of EU Member States (and of the other participating States[49]) and to favor cooperation among them and with the EU.[50]

As regards its scope of application, in accordance with Decision 2007/779 the CPM may be activated 'in the event of major emergencies, or the imminent threat thereof' (Article 1(1)). More precisely, a 'major emergency' is defined as 'any situation which has or may have an adverse impact on people, the environment or property and which may result in a call for assistance under the Mechanism' (Article 3(1)). Besides, Article 1(2) points out that the protection ensured by the CPM

> shall cover primarily people but also the environment and property, including cultural heritage, in the event of natural and man-made disasters, acts of terrorism and technological, radiological or environmental accidents, including accidental marine pollution, occurring inside or outside the Community, taking also into account the special needs of the isolated, outermost and other regions or islands of the Community.[51]

Such a definition of 'disasters' is essentially in line with that emerging from international practice.[52] This also as regards the inclusion of 'acts of terrorism'.[53] In any case, the specific reference to the protection not only of people and property, but also of the environment and cultural heritage has to be highlighted.[54] To

[48] In any case, where particularly important, reference will be made in the following footnotes to relevant provisions of the 2011 Proposal.

[49] A total of 31 States currently participate in the CPM (the 27 EU State members, Croatia, Iceland, Lichtenstein and Norway). See Article 10 of the 2007/779 Decision (*supra* n. 9) and Article 28 of the Proposal on a UCPM (*supra* n. 38), according to which the UCPM shall be open to the participation of members of the European Economic Area, acceding countries, candidate countries, and potential candidates.

[50] The increasing importance of the CPM has to be stressed. In its first year of operation (2002), the Mechanism was mobilized three times; in 2009, 27 times. Approximately half of operations have dealt with disasters occurring within the EU: see European Commission, 'Towards a stronger European disaster response', *supra* n. 1, 4.

[51] See, in the same vein, Article 1(2) of the Commission Proposal for a decision on a UCPM (*supra* n. 38) which also refers to 'acute health emergencies'.

[52] See Chap. 1 by de Guttry, in this volume.

[53] Acts of terrorism were not mentioned in the definition set forth in the 2001 Decision, but there was a general consensus that those acts could determine the activation of the CPM. See House of Lords 2009, 6.

[54] Chapter 1 by de Guttry, in this volume.

conclude, it is apparent that the definition of disasters embodied in the CPM decision has a very wide scope.[55]

As to the different phases of the disaster management cycle which are usually identified by the specialized literature,[56] the emphasis of the existing CPM is mainly on preparedness and response, even if the 2007/779 decision also envisages some rules on prevention and early warning.[57] More particularly, one could say that the European mechanism is focused on providing immediate relief in the first days of a disaster.

In practice, the CPM consists of a series of elements and actions. First of all, Member States are to identify in advance, within their competent services, intervention teams and any other form of support which might be available, or established at very short notice, and mobilized in response to an emergency (Article 2(1) and Article 4(1)). In this respect, the recast decision of 2007 has introduced the 'modular approach', by virtue of which the participating States shall develop 'modules', that is, self-sufficient task and needs-driven pre-defined arrangements of resources (Article 3(5)). Under the Decision, modules can be made up of resources from one or more States, on a voluntary basis. The technical requirements for the establishment of European civil protection modules—in terms of tasks, capacities, main components, self-sufficiency, and deployment times—have been articulated in the rules for the implementation of Decision 2007/779 adopted by the Commission.[58] Currently, a total of 17 different types of European civil protection modules are contemplated.[59]

Furthermore, the CPM provides training programs, simulation exercises, exchanges of experts as well as the organization of workshops, seminars, and pilot projects in order to enhance the capability and the inter-operability of teams and modules. The creation of assessment and co-ordination teams is also envisaged (particularly as regards emergencies outside the EU).

The central element of the CPC is the establishment of the Monitoring and Information Centre (MIC), based in Brussels, which has become the operational heart of the European civil protection.[60] *In primis*, the MIC functions as a

---

[55] The 2011 Commission Proposal (*supra* n. 38) refers to a notion of 'disaster' which basically follows that envisaged by the Decision of 2007, even if it appears more accurate (see Article 1(2) and (4)).

[56] Ibid.

[57] Decision 2007/779, *supra* n. 9, recital 7.

[58] Commission Decision 2004/227/EC, Euratom of 29 December 2003, *OJ* 2004 L 87/20, as amended by Commission Decision 2010/481/EU, Euratom of 29 July 2010, *OJ* 2010 L 236/5.

[59] High capacity pumping, Water purification, Medium urban search and rescue, Heavy urban search and rescue, Aerial forest firefighting using helicopters, Aerial forest firefighting using airplanes, Advanced medical post, Advanced medical post with surgery, Field hospital, Medical aerial evacuation of disaster victims, Emergency temporary shelter, CBRN detection and sampling, Search and rescue in CBRN conditions, Ground forest firefighting, Ground forest firefighting using vehicles, Flood containment, Flood rescue using boats (ibid.).

[60] BIICL 2010, 19. For an overview of the tasks of the MIC, see also http://ec.europa.eu/echo/civil_protection/civil/prote/mic.htm (accessed 4 March 2012).

communications hub, accessible 24 h a day and 7 days a week. Any State victim of a disaster may request assistance through the MIC (but also directly from other participating States[61]), which will immediately forward the request to a network of national contact points.[62] A State to which the request of assistance is addressed shall assess whether it is in a position to render it and shall inform the MIC (or directly the requesting State) of such determination (Article 7(3)). The MIC will collect all the information and communicate to the requesting State the assistance that is available on the part of the participating States. For these purposes, a Common Emergency Communication and Information System (CECIS) has been established by the Decision; this is a secure web-based platform for communication between the MIC and the contact points in the Member States.[63]

In any case, it is the requesting State that has to take the final decision as to the acceptance of the assistance which is offered and that will have the responsibility for directing and coordinating the interventions. More precisely, the authorities of the requesting State 'shall lay down guidelines and, if necessary, define the limits of the tasks entrusted to the intervention teams or modules', whereas the responsibility of the person in charge appointed by the State rendering assistance will be confined to the 'details of the execution of those tasks' (Article 7(4)). Moreover, the arrangements for the actual dispatch of the accepted assistance are made directly by the requesting State and the offering States: in this respect, the MIC may however play, if requested, a facilitating role.

Second, the MIC operates as a center of information. In particular, it disseminates information on civil protection preparedness and response to participating States (as well as to a wider audience of interested subjects). What is very important, the MIC also informs the participating States on the situation concerning ongoing disasters and alert them to possible or imminent emergencies. To this end, a daily bulletin (MIC Daily) is distributed to the participating States.

Third, the MIC plays an important role as regards the operational coordination of the civil protection assistance provided by the participating State, in particular in respect of emergencies occurring outside the EU.[64] In fact, as far as disasters inside the EU are concerned the coordination of the assistance, even from an operational viewpoint, is ensured by the requesting State. The MIC may in any case intervene, if requested, for facilitating or supporting the technical coordination of the assistance.

---

[61] But see Article 15 of the Proposal for a new decision on a UCPM, *supra* n. 38, under which assistance has to be requested through the ERC.

[62] It has to be noted that Article 6 of the 2007/779 Decision, *supra* n. 9, provides that a Member State in which an emergency capable of causing transboundary effects occurs is under an obligation to notify the Commission and those Member States which may be affected.

[63] The system needed a number of years to be developed, but it became operational since July 2007. On the functioning of CECIS, see the testimony of E. Dobson, House of Lords 2009, 3.

[64] See also the testimony of H. Das, Deputy Head of Unit, Civil Protection, European Commission: House of Lords 2009, Minutes of Evidence, 2.

It is also important to recall the activities carried out by the MIC in the field of disaster preparedness, that is before emergencies, notably in respect of training, exchanges of experts and experiences between national civil protection services, organization of workshops and seminars.

In the administrative apparatus of the European Commission, the CPM initially developed within the Directorate General (DG) for the Environment, due to the fact that at first the focus was mainly on environmental disasters. Recently, civil protection and humanitarian aid were brought together into one Directorate General, DG ECHO, under the responsibility of a single Commissioner responsible for International Cooperation, Humanitarian Aid and Crisis Response (currently, Kristalina Georgieva). As acknowledged by the European Parliament, this should improve the coherence of the overall disaster response of the Union.[65]

5.4 Strengthening a European Response to Disasters within the Union: From the Barnier Report to the 2011 Proposal for a New Union Civil Protection Mechanism

An assessment of the options currently debated at the EU level, in order to reinforce the European response to disasters, has to start from the 'Barnier Report'.[66] On 9 May 2006 the former French Foreign Minister and European Commissioner Michel Barnier presented a Report on European civil protection—requested by the Presidents of the Commission and of the EU Council—which has had a major influence on future discussions *in subiecta materia*. The Barnier Report moves from the consideration that the existing CPM 'relies too heavily on the help that is forthcoming spontaneously' from Member States and is penalized by the absence of an overall organization of the European response. In order to improve the current picture, the report proposes the creation of a European civil protection force ('Europe Aid'). Such a force would in reality represent a formula of compromise. On the one hand, it would not determine a real centralization of civil protection instruments at EU level. In effect, the new mechanism would basically continue using the assets of Member States. The latter would only be asked to earmark, on a voluntary basis, some resources to be employed in the framework of EU missions when the need would arise. On the other hand, according to the report the European Force should also be able to acquire and utilize additional EU-funded resources and equipment (e.g., ships, helicopters, aircraft), in particular in order to perform horizontal tasks (assessment, logistic, coordination) or to fill gaps in the civil protection capacities of Member States. The European force would have as its focal point an 'Operations Centre', formed by the present MIC

---

65 European Parliament recommendation of 14 December 2010, *supra* n. 42. See the Foreword by Commissioner Georgieva, in this volume.

66 Barnier 2006.

team with the addition of seconded national experts. The Operations Center would have the responsibility of drawing up the 'scenarios' for the different types of crises as well as the procedures or 'protocols' for their management.

Another key element of the system would be the setting up of a 'Civil Security Council', composed of the Presidents of the Council and of the Commission, the HR, the affected Member States, and the Chief of Staff of the EU. It should establish the existence of a crisis, launch the procedures drafted by the Operations Center, ensure that coordination and planning efforts are as effective as possible and keep Member States informed. The Barnier Report met with mixed reactions. The European Parliament fully supported it and repeatedly asked the Council to implement its main ideas.[67] Yet, some Member States were not prepared to accept some of the elements of the proposal, as the envisaged constitution of EU-funded common assets. That circumstance prevented any serious action on the part of the Council.[68] In any case, the June 2006 European Council reaffirmed the political imperative of improving the Union's responsiveness to emergencies, crises, and disasters, pointing out that

> while Member States are responsible for managing emergencies on their territory… the EU can, in a spirit of active solidarity, play a role by coordinating a political response and by helping to organize and coordinate available assets when requested to do so.[69]

Some of the suggestions put forward by the Barnier Report were re-launched by the European Commission in its Communication 'Towards a stronger European disaster response: the role of civil protection and humanitarian assistance' of 26 October 2010.[70] Building on the 2010 Communication, and in the light of the consultations held with the interested parties,[71] the Commission has recently presented a proposal for a decision of the European Parliament and of the Council on a UCPM.[72] The latter should replace both the decision on the CPM and that on the Civil Protection Financial Instrument. The new decision will rely on the new legal basis deriving from Article 196 TFEU. At the same time, according to the Commission the strengthened European Civil Protection will contribute to the implementation of the solidarity clause (Article 222 TFEU), which however will

---

[67] See, e.g., Resolution of 4 September 2007 on this summer's natural disasters, P6_TA (2007) 0362 para 9; Recommendation of 14 December 2010, *supra* n. 42, para 1(g).

[68] von Ondarza and Parkes 2010, 3.

[69] European Council, Presidency Conclusions, 15–16 June 2006, para 12.

[70] *Supra* n. 1.

[71] European Commission, report from the first stakeholder consultation meeting on the preparation of legislative proposals reviewing the EU Civil Protection Regulatory Framework, Brussels, 6 April 2011. See also Report from stakeholder consultation meeting: Impact Assessment for the Commission Communication on Reinforcing the EU's Disaster Response Capacity, Brussels, 22 July 2010.

[72] *Supra* n. 38. The Proposal will be here discussed exclusively as far as civil protection within the EU concerned. For the aspects concerning EU action in third States, see Chap. 6 by Casolari, in this volume.

be the object of a distinct proposal, to be presented by the Commission and the HR in 2012.

In conformity with the wide scope of Article 196 TFEU, the new instrument on a UCPM aims at developing an 'integrated approach' to disaster management including prevention, preparedness and response. As a consequence, compared with the legislation in force the new instrument gives a much greater emphasis to disaster prevention and risk management. In this regard, it has to be stressed that under its Article 2 the decision will apply to preventive and preparedness measures for 'all kinds of disasters', whereas European response assistance actions will be provided in respect of 'major disasters'.

In what follows it will not be possible to discuss every detail of the new Proposal but attention will be drawn to some of the major changes and key issues. First, the Commission envisages the establishment of a new European Emergency Response Centre (ERC), which will merge the two crisis rooms currently operating for civil protection (MIC) and humanitarian assistance (ECHO). It has to be stressed that while the MIC mainly acts as a communication platform, the proposal outlines a more active role for the ERC, notably in the field of planning and operational coordination.

Unlike the Barnier Report, the 2011 Proposal does not refer to the creation of a 'European Civil Protection Force', preferring the more prudent terminology of 'European Emergency Response Capacity' (Article 11). That even if the general thrust of the two documents is similar: rendering the European response to disasters more predictable, better planned, and coordinated.[73] To this end, in the Commission's view, it is necessary to overcome the current system based on *ad hoc* offers of assistance from the participating States.

In the first place, to improve the planning of assistance, the proposal provides for the development, by the Commission in non- with Member States, of reference scenarios for the main types of disasters, the mapping of the assets available in the Member States and the adoption of prior contingency plans for the deployment of the capacities (Article 10).

In the second place, in order to enhance the availability of key resources, the new European Emergency Response Capacity should consist of a voluntary pool of pre-committed civil protection assets from Member States, to be placed on standby for EU disaster response operations (Article 11(1)). The capacities will be made available by Member States in accordance with a certification and registration process to be managed by the Commission (Article 11(4)).

Even if the principle of establishing a pool of Member States' assets on standby for EU operations seems to be widely accepted, a number of concerns have been raised over the effective functioning of the system, notably as regards the level of

---

[73] See the statement made by Commissioner Georgieva before the European Parliament, on 27 September 2011, during the debate on the Report submitted by E. Gardini (*supra* n. 29): 'in the Barnier report, from which we have adopted a total of 12 proposals, the idea is to integrate the capabilities of Member States but there the approach was more top-down, whereas what we are coming with is bottom-up', CRE 27 September 2011.

commitment deriving from registration of assets in the pool. During the discussion of the ideas emerging from the 2010 Communication, some Governments insisted on stressing the absolutely voluntary nature of the mechanism and the right of Member States to refuse the deployment of registered assets.[74] The 2011 proposal seems to recognize, in its Article 11, the above-mentioned concerns. In particular, it points out that the identification and registration of the capacities committed by Member States to the European mechanism will occur 'on a voluntary basis'. Furthermore, it allows a Member State to inform the Commission that 'compelling reasons' prevent it from making the registered capacities available in a specific emergency. The proposal also acknowledges that the registered capacities shall remain available for national purposes when not deployed in European operations.

Another thorny issue is the possible development of EU-funded assets for civil protection, envisaged in the 2010 Communication and endorsed by the European Parliament.[75] The idea has met with the reservations of a group of Member States, worried by the potential cost of such a step and arguing that it could discourage some States from developing their own capacities.[76] In this regard, the 2011 Proposal is based on a compromise formula, reflected in its Article 12. According to it, the Commission shall determine, in co-operation with Member States, whether there are gaps in the emergency response capacities available in the Member States; then, it shall support the Member States in addressing these gaps in the most appropriate and cost-effective way. That might also include, where it is believed to be more cost-effective, the development of resources at EU level, serving as a common buffer against shared risks.

Perhaps, the most delicate point is that concerning the coordination of the assistance delivered under the European civil protection. According to the legal picture currently deriving from Decision 2007/779, a distinction has to be made between: (a) disasters outside the EU, in respect of which the overall political coordination is ensured by the State holding the Presidency of the Council whereas

---

[74] For instance, the Government of the United Kingdom 'would resist moves to prioritise EU operations over national purposes, or to introduce a legal presumption that Member States will pre-commit disaster response assets for EU operational deployment in any way limiting their right to decide how such assets should be deployed whether domestically or internationally': Explanatory Memorandum of 15 November 2010, submitted to the House of Commons by the Minister for Security at the Home Office (Baroness Neville-Jones). Moreover, during the stakeholder consultation meeting of 22 July 2010 'some participants noted that circumstances in which the Member States could refuse deploying assets committed to the pool should remain relatively broad' (*supra* n. 71). It may be worth adding that this position seems to be generally supported by regional and local authorities, as shown by the Opinion of the Committee of the Regions of 1 July 2011, *OJ* 2011 C 192/15, noting *inter alia* that 'civil protection is essentially a task for Member States and their regional and local bodies, whose authority should not be infringed upon' (para 33), and welcoming the abandonment of the idea of a European Civil Protection Force (para 34).

[75] See, e.g., the Resolution of 27 September 2011, *supra* n. 39, paras. 23–24.

[76] See for instance the Explanatory Memorandum of the UK Minister for Security at the Home Office, *supra* n. 74.

operational coordination is entrusted to the Commission; (b) those occurring inside the EU, in respect of which the operational coordination remains in the hands of the requesting Member State. The 2011 Proposal, after re-affirming that in the event of deployment the national capacities shall remain under Member States' command and direction, entrusts the Commission with the coordination among the different capacities, to be ensured through the ERC. It remains to be seen whether this idea will be accepted by the Council, having regard to the skepticism manifested by some Member States in respect of an expansion of the coordination role of the Commission.[77]

Apart from that important innovation, as regards the carrying out of EU assistance operations the 2011 Proposal basically reaffirms, in Article 15, the essential features of the current system. One has, however, to note the provision under which the requesting State 'shall take the necessary actions to ensure host nation support for the incoming assistance'.[78] The concept of 'host nation support' (HNS) is at the center of the current debate on IDRL. According to the definition envisaged by Article 4 of the Proposal, HNS refers to 'any action undertaken in the preparedness and response phases by country receiving assistance and transit countries to remove foreseeable obstacles to the delivery and use of international assistance'. At the European level, the Council expressly invited in 2010 the Commission and the Member States to step up structured work in the field of HNS, also including the possible drafting of guidelines. In effect, even within the EU—and notwithstanding the establishment of an internal market and of an area of freedom, security, and justice—a number of legal barriers to the delivery of assistance have been identified.[79] From a legal viewpoint, the new provision would establish on the requesting State a general due diligence obligation, which could certainly gain substance through the adoption of HNS guidelines.

5.5 Concluding Remarks

In order to illustrate the state of affairs concerning EU disaster response capacity, still emerging from a legal picture which developed in the framework of pre-Lisbon treaty law, it has been remarked that the existing mechanisms 'facilitate' the delivering of assistance to the victim State 'without guaranteeing European assistance'.[80] On the one hand, help to the victim is given by the other Member States voluntarily and on an *ad hoc* basis. On the other hand, as far as disasters inside the Union are concerned, the MIC still acts essentially as a communication

77 Ibid.

78 Council Conclusions on Host Nation Support of 22 September 2010 (doc. 15874/10).

79 See Commission Staff Working Paper, 'Impact Assessment—2011 review of the Civil Protection regulatory framework', doc. SEC (2011) 1632, 20 December 2011, 18.

80 ECORYS 2009, 10.

platform and a mere facilitator of inter-State non-, lacking decision-making powers and competences regarding coordination of the interventions.

If that is certainly true, it has nonetheless to be stressed that in the reality of things the CPM has operated with remarkable success and its impact has become ever more important. It is of great significance that in the practice of Member States, as observed by the Deputy Head of the Civil Protection Unit within the Commission, 'there has never been a case where a member State has requested assistance and there has not been any offered'.[81] This being said, and going back to the legal framework, it is evident that the Lisbon Treaty, by virtue of the solidarity clause and the new legal basis on civil protection, opens up new chances for further development of European disaster response law. As regards the solidarity clause, we have seen that Article 222 TFEU imposes legal obligations of assistance *vis-à-vis* the victim State both upon the EU and the other Member States. These obligations are of a general nature, basically demanding of the EU and the Member States 'to do their best' for helping the victim State. In effect, as concerns Member States, they have expressly reserved the right to choose 'the most appropriate means to comply' with that solidarity obligation. It is indeed apparent that there exists a certain tension between the duty of solidarity and the respect for national sovereignty in a field that many States still see as essentially reserved to their responsibility. In the end, much will depend on the arrangements for implementing Article 222 TFEU that will be adopted.

A thorny issue is the coordination between the solidarity clause and the new legal basis on civil protection (Article 196 TFEU). Both norms have to do with disaster response: it is not clear whether the EU solidarity system will remain distinct from the CPM and, in that case, what will be the relations between the two machineries. One has in any case to note that the TFEU envisages two completely different procedures for the implementation of Article 222 (Council Decision upon the proposal of the Commission and the HR) and of Article 196 (ordinary legislative procedure). Furthermore, the two mechanisms display a partly different territorial scope. In any case, having regard to the overlaps between the two provisions, problems concerning the correct choice of the legal basis might arise in the implementation practice.

In the light of the analysis we have made, notably of the position of some Governments, it remains to be seen whether Member States will accept a solidarity or a CPM machinery enabling the European Commission (or another EU body) to mandate the deployment of national resources for organized European assistance in case of disasters. A precedent in that direction can be found in the field of external border control,[82] notably in the Regulation establishing the FRONTEX

[81] Oral testimony of Mr Das, House of Lords 2009, 16. According to the Deputy Director, the only case in which there was a request of assistance (namely from Bulgaria) which was not matched with offers of help had to do with the forest fire season in 2007. In that case, there had been simultaneous requests from several Member States and when Bulgaria requested the assistance there was no forest fire fighting asset available.

[82] See, in this respect, Gestri 2011.

Agency, as amended in 2007 and 2011.[83] The most recent amendments envisage the setting up of European Border Guard Teams, consisting of a pool of national guards, to be employed in joint operations, rapid interventions, and pilot projects. It has to be underlined that the contribution of the Member States to the European Border Guard Teams is essentially structured on a compulsory basis and that FRONTEX also has the ability to acquire its own technical equipment (such as vessels or helicopters for border surveillance). However, one has to consider, in the first place, that the actual implementation of such mechanism has not been immune from problems and, in the second place, that the provisions on the EU competence in the matter of external border control establish a 'common European policy' (and a 'shared' competence between the EU and the Member States). A completely different situation is that of civil protection, in respect of which the new legal basis only entrusts the Union with the competence to adopt supporting or complementary measures.

References

Adam R, Tizzano A (2010) Lineamenti di diritto dell'Unione europea. Giappichelli, Turin

Antoniadis A et al (eds) (2011) The European Union and global emergencies: a law and policy analysis. Hart Publishing, Oxford

Barnier M (2006) For a European civil protection force: Europe aid, European Union. http://ec.europa.eu/archives/commission_2004-2009/president/pdf/rapport_barnier_en.pdf

BIICL-British Institute of International and Comparative Law (2010) Analysis of law in the European Union pertaining to cross-border disaster relief. Report prepared for the International Federation of Red Cross and Red Crescent Societies, Geneva

Cremona M (2011) The EU and global emergencies: competence and instruments. In: Antoniadis A et al (eds) The European Union and global emergencies. Hart, Oxford, pp 11–31

ECORYS (2009) Strengthening the EU capacity to respond to disasters: identification of the gaps in the capacity of the Community Civil Protection Mechanism to provide assistance in major disasters and options to fill the gaps—a scenario-based approach. Report committed by the European Commission. http://ec.europa.eu/echo/civil_protection/civil/prote/pdfdocs/Final%20Report%20%20scenario%20study.pdf

Gaja G, Adinolfi A (2010) Introduzione al diritto dell'Unione europea. Ed. Laterza, Bari

Gestri M (2011) La politica europea dell'immigrazione: solidarietà tra Stati membri e misure nazionali di regolarizzazione. In: Ligustro A, Sacerdoti G (eds) Problemi e tendenze del diritto internazionale dell'economia: Liber amicorum in onore di Paolo Picone. Editoriale Scientifica, Naples, pp 895–925

Grevi G (2007) The common foreign, security and defence policy. In: Amato G et al (eds) Genèse et Destinée de la Constitution Européenne: Commentaire du traité établissant une Constitution pour l'Europe à la lumière des travaux préparatoires et perspectives d'avenir. Bruylant, Brussels, pp 807–834

[83] Regulation 2007/2004/EC of 26 October 2004 establishing a European Agency for the Management of Operational Cooperation at the External Borders of the Member States of the EU (FRONTEX), *OJ* 2004 L 349/1 as amended by Regulation 863/2007/EC of 11 July 2007, *OJ* 2007 L 199/30, and Regulation 1168/2011/EU of 25 October 2011, *OJ* 2011 L 304/1.

House of Lords (2009) European Union Committee, 6th report of session 2008–09, civil protection and crisis management in the European Union. Report with evidence, 11 March 2009, HL paper 43. The Stationery Office, London

Konstadinides T (2011) Civil protection in Europe and the Lisbon 'solidarity clause': a genuine legal concept or a paper exercise, Uppsala Faculty of Law, working paper 2011:3. http://www.jur.uu.se/LinkClick.aspx?fileticket=ywEQQ722UuI%3D&tabid=3159&language=sv-SE

Missiroli A (ed) (2005) Disasters, diseases, disruptions: a new D-drive for the EU, Chaillot paper, September 2005, no. 83. Institute for Security Studies, Paris

Myrdal S, Rhinard M (2010) The European Union's solidarity: empty letter or effective tool? An analysis of article 222 of the treaty on the functioning of the European Union, Occasional papers (2/2010), Swedish Institute of International Affairs. http://www.sipri.org/research/security/euroatlantic/eu-seminar/documentation/2010_Myrdal%20Rhinard_EU%20Solidarity%20Clause_UIOP.pdf

Olsson S (ed) (2009) Crisis management in the European Union—cooperation in the face of emergencies. Springer, Dordrecht

Sur S (2007) Article I-43. In: Burgorgue-Larsen et al (eds) Traité établissant une Constitution pour l'Europe, Parties I et IV, 'Architecture constitutionnelle', Commentaire article par article, Tome 1. Bruylant, Bruxelles, pp 561–578

von Ondarza N, Parkes R (2010) The EU in the face of disaster, implementing the Lisbon Treaty's solidarity clause. SWP comments 9, April 2010. http://www.swp-berlin.org/fileadmin/contents/products/comments/2010C09_orz_pks_ks.pdf

Chapter 6
The External Dimension of the EU Disaster Response

Federico Casolari

Abstract This chapter analyses how the European Union responds to overseas natural and man-made disasters, and discusses the main legal issues involved in Union's action. The first part of the chapter is devoted to the existing instruments established by the EU institutions before the entry into force of the Lisbon Treaty. The analysis reveals a multifaceted scenario: besides some general tools, which are complementary and thus form a global platform for EU response in overseas disasters, the action of the Union has been developed through sector instruments that in some cases risk undermining the efficiency and coherence of the response. The second part of the chapter discusses the innovations introduced by the Lisbon Treaty in this domain. In particular, it shows how these innovations (such as the establishment of a general framework of the EU external action, the establishment of new co-ordinating tools and tasks, the provision of a new explicit legal basis for humanitarian aid) may contribute to ensure a more efficient and consistent management of the external dimension of the EU disaster response.

Keywords European Union · Lisbon Treaty · External action · Humanitarian aid assistance · Civil protection · Crisis management

Contents

F. Casolari (✉)
Università degli Studi di Bologna, via Zamboni 22, I-40126, Bologna, BO, Italy
e-mail: federico.casolari@unibo.it

A. de Guttry et al. (eds.), *International Disaster Response Law*,
DOI: 10.1007/978-90-6704-882-8_6,

6.1 Introduction

The European Union (EU)[1] has developed important and efficient tools for the management of disasters affecting member States.[2]

Besides, since the very beginning of the European integration process, capacities for responding to overseas emergencies have also been put in place. In this respect, the EU has developed a number of distinct instruments, responding to a variety of policies and mandates.

On the one hand, as recently pointed out by the Commission, the multifaceted scenario, and the quality, of the EU response 'helped demonstrating to EU citizens and member States the added value brought by the EU institutions' in this domain.[3] This was also due to the fact that, in some cases, the instruments covering external assistance interact with those adopted for internal response and thus form integrated capacities for disaster management.

On the other hand, that framework revealed lacks and inconsistencies, which require further steps towards a more coordinated European disaster response.

This chapter offers first a general overview of the main existing instruments the European Union may use to give assistance to third countries (Sect. 6.2). Then it concentrates on the entry into force of the Lisbon Treaty, which provides for a new legal framework for the EU external disaster response (EDR), and offers new legal bases for disaster management (Sects. 6.3 and 6.4). It ends with a summary of the main findings (Sect. 6.5).

1 On the basis of the succession of the European Union to the European Community (Article 1 TEU, as amended by the Lisbon Treaty), this chapter refers to the European Union without distinguishing between the EU and EC framework, except where that distinction is relevant.

2 See Chap. 5 by Gestri in this volume.

3 European Commission, Communication 'Towards a Stronger Disaster Response: The Role of Civil Protection and Humanitarian Assistance', COM (2010) 600, 26 October 2010, at 2.

6.2 The pre-Lisbon Instruments for Disaster Response Outside the Union

Before the entry into force of the Lisbon Treaty, the EDR had mainly been based on three pillars: (a) the Development Cooperation Policy, (b) the Civil Protection Cooperation, and (c) the Common Foreign and Security Policy (CFSP). The recourse to the instruments provided for by these policies has led to the establishment of 'horizontal tools' for the management of the assistance in the event of a natural or man-made disaster, in the sense that the instruments made available to the EU institutions and member States, which are still in force, may have different contents and objectives, varying according to both the nature and the characteristics of the emergency. Furthermore, as will be highlighted in more detail below, the measures adopted under the three pillars are often complementary and have thus paved the way for a general platform of the EU crisis and disaster response in third countries.

In addition, 'vertical tools' for overseas emergencies have been established under several EU sector policies (such as the environmental policy, the nuclear safety policy, the health policy, etc.).

The present section focuses on the characteristics of, and the interaction between, the instruments used by the Union in managing its external disaster response with a view to highlighting the shortcomings and inconsistencies for which the Lisbon Treaty has been called to make itself respondent.

6.2.1 The Development Cooperation Policy

Whereas developing countries are often vulnerable and exposed to disasters and catastrophes, the development cooperation policy has represented, to date, the major dimension of the EDR.

Despite the absence in the pre-Lisbon primary law of elements concerning the European response to overseas disasters, assistance measures have been provided in that domain since the establishment of the first contractual relations of the European Economic Community (EEC) with third countries. The Lomé Convention,[4] for instance, which was concluded in 1975 with the African, Caribbean and Pacific (ACP) States, expressly provided the establishment of a fund for exceptional aid to ACP States faced with serious difficulties resulting from natural disasters or comparable extraordinary circumstances.

Such co-operation has been reinforced in the course of time through the revision of the EU–ACP relations. The present global Partnership Agreement, signed in Cotonou in 2000,[5] provides for regional initiatives for humanitarian and emergency

[4] *OJ* 1976 L 25/2.

[5] *OJ* 2000 L 317/2.

assistance among the main fields of the co-operation. In particular, such initiatives may include the safeguard of human lives in disasters and immediate post-disaster situations, the contribution to the financing and delivery of humanitarian aid and to the direct access to it, and the assistance in setting up disaster prevention and preparedness mechanisms.

Moreover, while the EU–ACP co-operation represents the major example of EU contractual relations established under the development Cooperation policy dealing with overseas emergencies, references to disaster response are also contained in other international agreements concluded thereunder.[6]

Furthermore, several internal acts have been adopted by EU institutions under the umbrella of the development cooperation policy to manage the EU response to disasters affecting non-member countries.

6.2.1.1 The Humanitarian Aid Regulation

In particular, the Humanitarian Aid Regulation (Regulation (EC) No. 1257/96)[7] still contains today the general European Union's mandate for overseas assistance.[8]

Before focusing on the main institutional features of the Regulation, it is worth pausing to consider its scope of application, since it clearly illustrates the EU's approach in dealing with disaster response issues in light of development cooperation policy.

What is worth noting in this respect is the fact that, while adopted on the basis of Article 130 W TEC (now Article 209 TFEU), which, according to Advocate General Kokott, represents the legal basis for the 'more specific provisions for cooperation with developing countries',[9] the Regulation also covers operations concerning non-developing countries.[10]

---

6 For instance, the 1998 Framework Agreement on Co-operation between the European Community and the Cartagena Agreement and its member countries (*OJ* 1998 L 127/11) establishes that the Parties shall endeavour to work together on measures targeting, *inter alia*, research projects on disasters and their prevention.

7 *OJ* 1996 L 163/1.

8 Whilst the assistance in the event of natural and man-made disasters is mainly delivered under Regulation 1257/96, the European Union has adopted in the course of time other financial resources and financing instruments to support EU response. For a general survey of such instruments and for a more detailed analysis of the Humanitarian Aid Regulation, see Chap. 26 by Palandri, in this volume and Versluys 2009.

9 ECJ, Case C-155/07 *European Parliament v Council of the European Union* [2008] *ECR* I-08103; opinion of AG Kokott of 26 June 2008, para 36.

10 Article 1 of the Regulation stipulates that the EU humanitarian aid aims at providing assistance and relief to the victims of natural disasters or man-made crises 'in third countries, *particularly* the most vulnerable among them, *and as a priority those in developing countries*' [emphasis added].

Since, under the EC Treaty, no specific legal basis concerning humanitarian aid for third countries other than developing countries has been provided, it might be felt that the choice of the legal basis made in the case of the Regulation 1257/96 was questionable. This would, however, be premature, due to the expansive interpretation of development cooperation given (to date) by EU institutions.[11]

One prominent example of such an interpretation is provided by the ECJ's judgment in the *Portugal v Council* case, which dealt with an application for annulment of the Council Decision concerning the conclusion of the Cooperation Agreement between the European Community and India on partnership and development. In this case, the application had been made on the grounds that the Council adopted as the legal basis for the Agreement in question some provisions of the Founding Treaty concerning the development cooperation, even if the Agreement covered matters falling within the scope of other EC policies (e.g., energy, tourism, and culture). In the judgment, the Court, in affirming the validity of the contested Decision, held that the objectives of the development cooperation policy

> are broad… in the sense that it must be possible for the measures required for their pursuit to concern a variety of specific matters. That is so in particular in the case of an agreement establishing the framework of such cooperation.[12]

Some 12 years later, in the *ECOWAS* case, the Court confirmed that line of reasoning. Here the question was whether a CFSP Decision on the European Union's contribution to combating the accumulation and spread of small arms and light weapons had encroached upon the Community competences under the development cooperation policy and, then, infringed Article 47 TEU (now Article 40 TEU).[13] Before stating on the validity of the contested Decision, the Court held that the provisions laid down in the EC Treaty,

> which deal with cooperation with developing countries, refer not only to the sustainable economic and social development of those countries, their smooth and gradual integration into the world economy and the campaign against poverty, but also to the development and consolidation of democracy and the rule of law, as well as to respect for human rights and fundamental freedoms.[14]

Of course, the ECJ's case-law made explicit reference only to the wide scope of the objectives of EU development cooperation policy, without mentioning the issue concerning which countries are excluded a priori from the personal scope of

---

[11] Dusepulchre 2008.

[12] ECJ, Case C-268/94 *Portuguese Republic v Council of the European Union* [1996] *ECR* I-06177, para 37.

[13] As is well known, that provision concerned the relationship between the CFSP and Community policies and provided that the Union could not have recourse to a legal basis falling within the CFSP to adopt act whose aims also felt within a competence conferred on the Community.

[14] ECJ, Case C-91/05 *European Parliament v Commission of the European Communities* [2007] *ECR* I-09045, para 65.

that policy. This notwithstanding, by confirming the expansive interpretation of development cooperation, the case-law seemed to engender the idea that its objectives may also justify the adoption of assistance measures in favour of non-developing countries.

As far as the EU disaster response is concerned, such a pragmatic approach has guaranteed the European assistance in respect of all the major disasters occurring across the globe in the last decade. It is important to note, however, that the incorporation of the humanitarian assistance into the general (and very broad) framework of the development cooperation policy risked at the same time jeopardising the specificity and thus the effectiveness of the former. It is exactly for this reason that the Lisbon Treaty, as will be seen below, rendered the humanitarian aid a self-standing policy of the Union.[15]

Turning, now, to its content, the Humanitarian Aid Regulation (HAR) establishes, first of all, the objectives and general principles of EU humanitarian aid. In this respect, Article 1 clarifies that it

> shall comprise assistance, relief and protection operations on a non-discriminatory basis to help people in third countries…, victims of natural disasters, man-made crises… or exceptional situations or circumstances comparable to natural or man-made disasters…

The common principles of EU humanitarian assistance have been further specified in the European Consensus on Humanitarian Aid,[16] a joint statement by the Council, the Representatives of the Governments of the member States meeting within the Council, the European Parliament, and the European Commission, signed in December 2007. In this respect, the Consensus stipulates that '[t]he EU is firmly committed to upholding and promoting the fundamental humanitarian principles of humanity, neutrality, impartiality and independence'.[17]

While the principles of humanity, neutrality and impartiality are commonly recognised as the leading principles for humanitarian response in disaster situations,[18] the principle of independence, which is also mentioned in several international instruments concerning disasters response,[19] may be considered as a derived principle insofar as it integrates the content of the former by requiring the autonomy of humanitarian objectives from political, economic, military or other objectives.

As will be seen below, the Lisbon Treaty has completed this framework by according to the humanitarian aid principles the same legal value as the primary law.[20]

---

[15] See *infra* 6.4.2.

[16] *OJ* 2008 C 25/1.

[17] Ibid., para 10.

[18] See Chap. 2 by Venturini in this volume.

[19] See the Third report on the protection of persons in the event of disasters by the special rapporteur of the International Law Commission, Eduardo Valencia-Ospina, doc. A/CN.4/629, 31 March 2010, paras 17–18.

[20] See *infra* 6.4.2.

Articles 3 and 4 of the HAR list the activities which may be financed to implement the humanitarian aid operations. Indeed, EU humanitarian aid shall only take the form of grants at the request of international or non-governmental organisations, from a member State, or a recipient third country, or on the initiative of the Commission.

As to the activities covered by the HAR, they comprise the implementation of humanitarian operations (including preparatory and feasibility studies, assessment and monitoring of humanitarian projects, public awareness and information campaigns, and measures to strengthen the EU's coordination with other actors involved), but also initiatives dealing with disaster's preparedness.

Among the features concerning the implementation of the HAR, one deserves to be stressed. It concerns the coordination of the Directorate General for Humanitarian Aid and Civil Protection (DG ECHO) of the European Commission, which manages EU aid, with other international organisations involved in disaster response.[21] This is a matter of great importance, given the need, widely recognised, to ensure an adequate and effective response to disasters.

In particular, it is worth mentioning the co-operation with the United Nations (UN), since it normally plays a leading role in delivering humanitarian assistance.

In 2001, the European Commission adopted a Communication containing a new strategy for improving the dialogue between the Union and the UN in the fields of development and humanitarian affairs.[22] The document pointed out a piecemeal approach in co-operation with the UN, which risked undermining the effectiveness of the EU efforts in facing humanitarian emergencies. As a result, the European Commission, acting under Article 302 TEC (now Article 220 TFEU), concluded a new comprehensive legal framework for the EU–UN co-operation in financial matters, which represents today the model of co-operation between ECHO and other international organisations.

The 2003 Financial and Administrative Framework Agreement (FAFA)[23] sets out the principles that shall be applied with regard to all the EU financial contributions to an operation, programme or project administered by the UN.

All funding decisions covered by the FAFA are managed on the basis of a Grant Agreement between the Commission and the concerned UN entity, which shall be consistent with both the FAFA and the General Conditions applicable to European Union Contribution Agreements with International Organizations for

[21] The European Union also interacts with several partners at the political/policy making level. Such cooperation, which is governed by Article 220 TFEU, includes the participation of the Union in decision-making organs and bodies and in normative fora on social, economic, humanitarian and development issues.

[22] European Commission, Communication 'Building an effective partnership with the United Nations in the fields of Development and Humanitarian Affairs', COM (2001) 231, 2 May 2001.

[23] Its text is available at: http://ec.europa.eu/echo/files/about/actors/fafa/agreement_en.pdf (accessed 15 January 2012). For a more detailed survey of the FAFA, see Baroncini 2008, 431.

Humanitarian Aid Actions that are annexed to the latter.[24] The General Conditions contain a detailed discipline which is complementary to the FAFA. In particular, it is worth mentioning the liability regime they establish. Indeed, pursuant to Article 3, under no circumstances may the Commission be held liable for damages caused by implementing partners, contractors or property of the international organisation as a result of the action's implementation. The contracting international organisation shall also discharge the Commission of all liabilities associated with any claim or action brought as a result of a violation of rules or regulations or third party's rights by the international organisation.

The importance of enhancing the relationship between the EU and the UN has been further emphasised, in 2004, through an Exchange of letters between the United Nations Office for the Coordination of Humanitarian Affairs (UNOCHA) and the European Commission on their co-operation in the framework of disaster response.[25] It establishes Standard Operational Procedures (SOPs) concerning, on one hand, the coordination between UNOCHA and the Community Mechanism for Civil Protection[26] and, on the other hand, the coordination between UNOCHA and ECHO. In this respect, the instrument requires exchange of information, strategic dialogue and mutual inclusion in training activities between the two entities. In addition, during the response/emergency phase, UNOCHA and ECHO should ensure that, whenever possible and appropriate, their teams provide joint recommendations to the respective headquarters.

6.2.2 The External Dimension of the Civil Protection Mechanism

Another fundamental legal tool for facilitating and supporting disaster response is represented by the Civil Protection Mechanism (CPM), which has been implemented within the framework of the EU initiatives on civil protection co-operation.[27]

It is important to stress at the outset that, inasmuch that the CPM shall ensure an immediate *operative* response to the affected country, it is normally conceived as a complementary instrument to humanitarian aid.

This complementarity is particularly evident in the 2010 decision by President Barroso to establish a new portfolio in the College of Commissioners

---

[24] The last version of the General Conditions has been adopted on 1 December 2009: http://ec.europa.eu/echo/files/about/actors/fafa/2010/Gen_Conds_AnnexIII_011209_en.pdf (accessed 15 January 2012).

[25] *OJ* 2005 L 52/42.

[26] See *infra* Sect. 6.2.2.

[27] For a general survey of the CPM, see Chap. 5 by Gestri in this volume.

(International Cooperation, Humanitarian Aid, and Crisis Response), which brings together the instruments for civil protection and humanitarian aid assistance.

Decision No. 2007/779/EC, establishing a Community Civil Protection Mechanism[28] provides the existing legal framework for civil protection cooperation.[29]

Under Article 8 of the Decision 2007/779, when a major emergency[30] occurs outside the Union, the CPM may be activated, on request, in order to give immediate assistance to the affected country.

When the Mechanism is used outside the Union, the overall coordination of the civil protection assistance interventions shall be ensured by the member State holding the Presidency of the Council of the Union. In particular, the Presidency shall: (a) assess the use of the Mechanism as a tool for facilitating and supporting crisis management; and, (b) where necessary, establish relations with the affected third country.

At EU level, the operational coordination is guaranteed by the European Commission. The Commission shall also ensure the complementarity and coherence of actions developed under the Mechanism with those financed under Regulation 1257/96 and guarantee the integration of the European intervention within the coordination provided by UNOCHA, where present.

In this respect, it is useful to recall the above-mentioned 2004 Exchange of letters between UNOCHA and the European Commission,[31] since it also contains, as anticipated, SOPs for the coordination between the UN body and the Community Mechanism for Civil Protection. Besides requiring information exchanges and mutual participation in training, the SOPs stipulate that UNOCHA and the European Commission shall

> alert each other as a disaster emerges and provide information on their intended response. When the activation of the Mechanism is envisaged for disasters occurring outside the EU, and where the UN and EC response systems might both be deployed, the European Commission and UNOCHA will exchange views at the earliest possible stage on the preliminary assessment of situation, relief needs and intended response…

As for the personal scope of the Mechanism, Article 8(8) of the Decision 2007/779 clarifies that the coordination roles of the Presidency and the Commission cannot affect the member States' competences and responsibility for their teams, assets and capabilities.

---

[28] *OJ* 2007 L 314/9.

[29] The review of the implementation of this act carried out by the European Commission after the entry into force of the Lisbon Treaty has led to the adoption of a Proposal reforming the Mechanism (COM (2011) 934, 20 December 2011). The details of the Proposal concerning the external dimension of civil protection operations will be spelt out later (6.4.1).

[30] Under Article 3(1) of the Decision, 'major emergency' means 'any situation which has or may have an adverse impact on people, the environment or property and which may result in a call for assistance under the Mechanism'.

[31] See *supra* n. 25.

Furthermore, Decision 779/2007 stipulates that the Mechanism shall be open to EU candidate countries and third countries or other international organisations with which agreements enabling their participation have been concluded.[32]

Civil cooperation issues may also be covered by non- treaty-based initiatives the Union takes part in (e.g., the Union for the Mediterranean, the Council of the Baltic Sea States, the Central European Initiative, and the 1987 EUROPA Major Hazards Agreement).

6.2.3 The Crisis Management Tool

As acknowledged by Article 43(1) TEU, humanitarian tasks in emergency situations may also fall within the scope of application of the European Security and Defence Policy (ESDP), which is an integral part of the CFSP. Similarly to the action developed under the civil protection cooperation, the crisis management operations launched under the ESDP are conceived as complementary to the other pillars of the EDR. In particular, they show a strict link to the civil protection cooperation: this has become apparent since the European Council of Feira, which, in considering the crises Europe had had to face, pointed out that civil protection represents one of the priority areas of the EU crisis management operations.[33]

The interaction between the EU crisis management and civil protection assistance shows a twofold scenario.

First, civil protection assets may be used as a tool for facilitating and supporting the EU civilian crisis management missions.

In this respect, the Union could decide to launch an intervention exclusively under the former second pillar, using member States' civil protection assets. However, as made clear by the Council, the activation of the CPM represents the most appropriate solution.[34] Details concerning the operational dimension of involving CPM in crisis management are laid down in a Joint Declaration by the Council and the Commission on the use of the Common Civil Protection Mechanism in Crisis Management adopted in 2003.[35] According to that Declaration,

> [w]here the Commission receives a request from a third State for civil protection assistance…, it will… immediately inform the Presidency of the Council of the European Union… If the Presidency considers that the assistance requested might fall within EU crisis management, it will so inform member States and the Commission. In those cases

---

[32] Besides the Exchange of Letters with UNOCHA and the 1992 Agreement on the European Economic Area (*OJ* 1994 L 1/3), specific bilateral arrangements have been concluded with Croatia, Russia and Ukraine.

[33] Cf. European Council, Presidency Conclusions Santa Maria da Feira European Council Meeting, Part II of Annex I, 19–20 June 2000; see also Olsson 2009 and Marhic 2011.

[34] Council of the European Union, Civil Protection in the framework of crisis management—draft concept, doc. 10882/1/02, 16 September 2002.

[35] Cf. Council doc. 10639/03, 17 June 2003.

> the Presidency, following consultations with the member States and the Commission..., may establish that the assistance requested falls within EU crisis management and may request, on behalf of the Council, civil protection assistance under the Community Mechanism, either to launch an EU crisis management operation or to add a civil protection component to a pre-existing EU crisis management operation.[36]

When an integrated EU crisis management operation has been launched, the Presidency appoints the Civil Protection Coordination Head. He or she is a civil protection expert from a member State who is responsible for leading the assessment and coordination teams. Furthermore, he or she shall liaise with the affected country and the Presidency of the Council and coordinate with other parts of the EU crisis management: this confirms that integrated EU crisis management operations provide distinct in-field reporting lines for the different crisis management components.[37] At headquarters level, coordination between the civil protection component and the military component is ensured by the Crisis Response Co-ordinating Team,[38] while the political control and strategic direction of the operation is exercised by the Political and Security Committee (PSC) envisaged by Article 38 TEU.

The legal position of EU crisis management operations abroad is normally governed by the so-called Status of Mission Agreements (SOMAs), which are concluded with the third State concerned.[39]

Furthermore, EU-led civilian crisis management operations may include the participation of third countries. Generally speaking, the conditions governing the participation of a third country in specific EU civilian crisis management operations are enshrined in bilateral accords concluded with the Union. In addition to these specific arrangements, framework participation agreements, which refer to the same issues that may arise in the case of participation of third countries in specific EU operations,[40] may be concluded.[41]

---

[36] At the time of writing, the only case of operation directly linked to a natural disaster, which has been launched by the Union, is represented by the Aceh Monitoring Mission (AMM). However, the AMM, deployed after the massive Indian Ocean tsunami occurred in December 2004, was mainly designed to monitor the implementation of several aspects of the Memorandum of Understanding signed on 15 August 2005 between the Free Aceh Movement and the Government of Indonesia: its mandate did not contain any reference to tasks concerning disaster response. Cf. Council Joint Action No. 2005/643/CFSP on the European Union Monitoring Mission in Aceh (Indonesia), *OJ* 2005 L 234/13.

[37] All EU instruments in the field may be coordinated by an EU Special Representative, when appointed. It is interesting to note that the articulation of tasks in integrated EU crisis management operations looks similar to that of UN complex operations: see Chap. 19 by Silingardi, in this volume.

[38] Cf. Council of the European Union, Use of the Community Civil Protection Mechanism in the context of civilian crisis management outside the Union, doc. 13728/02, 4 November 2002.

[39] Sari 2008.

[40] Framework participation agreements do not imply the automatic participation of the third contracting party in EU operations and are without prejudice to the decision-making autonomy of the European Union.

[41] For a detailed analysis of the content of participation agreements, see Koutrakos 2012, 167.

The second scenario dealing with the interaction between civil protection assistance and crisis management consists in deploying EU military assets in order to support the Civil Protection Mechanism. In such cases, as made clear by the Decision 779/2007, it is for the Council to set out procedures and criteria for making military assets for the protection of civilian populations available to the Mechanism.[42]

In this respect, in 2004, practical modalities for making the Military Database[43] available to the CPM were established by the Council.[44] Originally conceived for the effects of terrorist attacks, the use of the Military Database by CPM has then been extended to all types of emergencies (including natural and man-made disasters).

Some 2 years later, the General Secretariat of the Council laid down the arrangements for the military support to EU overseas disaster response.[45] The Secretariat document first clarifies the general principles on the coordination of the use of military assets and capabilities:

- the primary responsibility of the affected State to make a request for external support and to be responsible for co-ordinating the relief activities within its borders;
- the respect for the principles of humanity, neutrality and impartiality;
- the leading role of UNOCHA, when present;
- the complementary nature of military support to civilian efforts;
- the use of military assets and capabilities as a last resort when civilian resources are overstretched or inadequate; and
- the fact that the use of military assets and capabilities should be limited in time and focus on initial immediate relief, and should not extend to more structural support.

Then it establishes the operational arrangements: in particular, it stipulates that, in the context of Community Civil Protection Mechanism interventions outside the EU, the Presidency, when informed by the Commission of a request, shall consider military assistance and the possible requirement for the Council Secretariat assistance with the facilitation of military support to EU disaster response. In all cases of requests received for military support, immediate consultation shall take place between the Presidency, the Commission and the Secretariat. The latter shall guarantee the coordination of member States' military contributions through information exchange, provision of military expertise and liaison officers, and clearing house mechanisms.

---

42 Cf. recital 19 of the Decision.

43 The Database contains a compilation of voluntary contributions from member States.

44 General Secretariat of the Council, Draft report on the database of military assets and capabilities relevant to the protection of civilian populations, doc. 8587/06, 24 April 2006.

45 General Secretariat of the Council, Military support to EU disaster response: Identification and coordination of available assets and capabilities, doc. 9462/3/06 REV 3, 25 October 2006.

The Consensus on Humanitarian Aid, after having confirmed the exceptional nature of the recourse to military assets for humanitarian assistance, has pointed out that the use of such assets cannot alter the civilian nature of the humanitarian operation:

> this means that, while military assets will remain under military control, the humanitarian operation as a whole must remain under the overall authority and control of the responsible humanitarian organization.[46]

6.2.4 The External Dimension of the EU Sector Policies Dealing with Natural and Man-made Disasters

Although the external dimension of the Union disaster response is largely based on the above-mentioned pillars, a specific role is also played in this respect by the (vertical) initiatives linked to the sector policies of the organisation. In this regard, the treaty-based initiatives established by the Union reflect the same trends showed by international law practice: on the one hand, specific disaster-related clauses have been inserted in the international treaties concluded by the Union and regulating general issues; on the other hand, the Union has entered into treaties facing specific aspects related to disaster management.[47]

First, since disasters often cause damages affecting the environment or have environmental implications, the Union has contributed to disaster response challenges through the external dimension of its environmental policy.

Besides participating in many environmental-related fora, the European Union is party to several bilateral, regional, or universal environmental agreements containing provisions dealing with the management of emergency situations.

As for its bilateral relations, the Union has concluded several co-operation agreements containing a standard clause on environmental co-operation dealing with disaster response, which states that the environmental co-operation shall also take place through disaster planning and other emergencies situations.[48] A more detailed cooperation mechanism is laid down in the Stabilisation and Association Agreements. The related clause stipulates that:

> In the field of protection against natural disasters, the Parties will cooperate to ensure the protection of people, animals, property and environment against man-made disasters. To this end the co-operation could include the following areas:

---

[46] Para 63.

[47] See Chap. 1 by de Guttry in this volume.

[48] See, for instance, Article 56(3) of the Partnership and Cooperation Agreement between the European Communities and their member States, of the one part, and the Republic of Azerbaijan, *OJ* 1999 L 246/3.

- the exchange of the outcome of scientific and research development projects;
- mutual and early notification and warning systems on hazards, disasters and their consequences;
- rescue and relief exercises and assistance systems in case of disasters;
- exchange of experience in rehabilitation and reconstruction after disaster.[49]

At regional level, the most relevant environmental agreements dealing with disaster/emergency scenarios to which the Union is a party are: the 1976 Barcelona Convention for the Protection of the Mediterranean Sea against pollution[50] and its Protocols[51]; the 1983 Agreement for co-operation dealing with the pollution of the North Sea by oil and other harmful substances[52]; the 1990 Cooperation Agreement for the protection of the coasts and waters of the North-East Atlantic against pollution[53]; the 1992 Convention on the Protection of the marine environment of the Baltic Sea Area[54]; the 1992 Convention for the protection of the marine environment of the North-East Atlantic (OSPAR Convention)[55]; the 1992 Convention on the transboundary effects of industrial accidents[56]; the 1992 Convention on the protection and use of transboundary watercourses and international lakes[57]; and the 1994 Convention on co-operation for the protection and sustainable use of the river Danube.[58]

Amongst the universal instruments facing emergency issues (or containing specific clauses concerning environmental emergencies) concluded by the Union one has to mention: the 1982 UN Convention on the Law of the Sea[59]; the 1992 United Nations Framework Convention on Climate Change[60] and the 1997 Kyoto Protocol[61]; the 1985 Vienna Convention for the protection of the ozone layer and the 1987 Montreal Protocol on the substances that deplete the ozone layer.[62]

---

[49] Cf. Article 103(3) of the Stabilisation and Association Agreement concluded with the former Yugoslav Republic of Macedonia, *OJ* 2004 L 84/13.

[50] *OJ* 1977 L 240/3.

[51] Protocol concerning co-operation in combating pollution of the Mediterranean Sea by oil and other harmful substances in cases of emergency, *OJ* 1981 L 162/6; Protocol to the Barcelona Convention for the Protection of the Mediterranean Sea against Pollution, concerning co-operation in preventing pollution from ships and, in cases of emergency, combating pollution of the Mediterranean Sea, *OJ* 2004 L 261/41; Protocol on Integrated Coastal Zone Management in the Mediterranean to the Convention for the Protection of the Marine Environment and the Coastal Region of the Mediterranean *OJ* 2009 L 34/19.

[52] *OJ* 1984 L 188/9.

[53] *OJ* 1993 L 267/22.

[54] *OJ* 1994 L 73/20.

[55] *OJ* 1998 L 104/2.

[56] *OJ* 1998 L 326/6.

[57] *OJ* 1995 L 186/44.

[58] *OJ* 1997 L 342/19.

[59] *OJ* 1998 L 179/3.

[60] *OJ* 1994 L 33/13.

[61] *OJ* 2002 L 130/4.

[62] *OJ* 1988 L 297/10.

Another policy area covered by the Union which is strictly linked to disaster response is represented by the nuclear safety domain. Here, the major legal tool developed by the Union is the Nuclear Safety Cooperation Instrument (NSCI), established by Regulation No. 300/2007.[63]

Under the NSCI, the Euratom provides financial, economic and technical assistance to third countries to support the promotion of a high level of nuclear safety, radiation protection and the application of efficient and effective safeguards of nuclear materials. In particular, amongst the measures supported by the NSCI, it is worth mentioning the 'establishment of effective arrangements for the prevention of accidents with radiological consequences as well as the mitigation of such consequences should they occur, and for emergency-planning, preparedness and response, civil protection and rehabilitation measures'.[64] Moreover, Regulation 300/2007 establishes that actions financed under the NCSI shall be complementary to any assistance provided by the European Commission under the HAR.

Specific contractual relations have also been established by the Union with third countries in that domain.

At multilateral level, reference has to be made to the 1986 Convention on Assistance in the case of a Nuclear Accident or Radiological Emergency,[65] the 1994 Convention on Nuclear Safety,[66] and the 2003 Agreement between the European Atomic Energy Community and non-member States of the European Union on the participation of the latter in the Community arrangements for the early exchange of information in the event of radiological emergency (Ecurie).[67]

As for the bilateral relations, several general cooperation agreements concluded by the Union lay down standard provisions on nuclear safety,[68] while *ad hoc* cooperation agreements in the field of nuclear safety have been concluded with some third countries (such as Ukraine[69] and the Russian Federation[70]).

Of course, co-operation with third countries in disaster response also faces health-related issues. As recently pointed out by the European Commission in its 2010 Communication on the EU Role in Global Health, the European Union is committed to supporting the global and third countries' national capacities of early prediction, detection and response to global health threats. In this respect, a leading role should be played by the International Health Regulations implemented within the framework of the World Health Organization.[71] On the other hand, the Union

---

63 *OJ* 2007 L 81/1.

64 Article 2(d) of the Regulation 300/2007.

65 *OJ* 2005 L 314/28.

66 *OJ* 1999 L 318/21.

67 *OJ* 2003 C 102/2.

68 See, for instance, Article 103(4) of the Stabilisation and Association Agreement with the former Yugoslav Republic of Macedonia (*supra* n. 49).

69 *OJ* 2002 L 322/33.

70 *OJ* 2001 L 287/24.

71 COM (2010) 128, 31 March 2010.

is also involved in supporting the access to health services for populations under stress in fragile contexts.

Other areas of the external action of the Union where reference has been made to co-operation in disaster response are represented by customs co-operation,[72] agricultural policy,[73] and transport policy.[74]

It is beyond the scope of this chapter to analyse the specific features of the external dimension of the EU sector policies facing disaster response. Nonetheless, two general issues deserve to be stressed.

First, aside from some exceptions (e.g., the NSCI), actions undertaken by the Union mark a significant shift from the model of interaction, which characterizes the horizontal legal tools implementing the EDR.

Indeed, the former contain neither coordination mechanisms nor explicit reference to the need of complementarity with other disaster response instruments and, in particular, with those analysed in the first part of this section. This risks jeopardising (and thus weakening) the Union's disaster response capacity.

Second, the majority of the multilateral agreements binding the Union in disaster-related domains have been concluded as mixed treaties. As is well known, such a practice raises several questions dealing with the allocation of competences between the Union and its member States and the international responsibility for failure to fulfil the obligations stemming from those treaties. In this respect, despite the Eurocentric case-law of the Court of Justice on mixed agreements and the increasing role played in this context by the general principle of loyal co-operation between Member States and European institutions,[75] 'mixity' still remains a factor which complicates the management of EU external action and thus risks further undermining the efficiency of the Union's overseas disaster response.

---

[72] So, for instance, the Union is party to the 1990 Convention relating to temporary admission (*OJ* 1993 L 130/4), which contains specific provisions on relief consignments means (i.e., all goods, such as vehicles and other means of transport, blankets, tents, prefabricated houses or other goods of prime necessity, forwarded as aid to those affected by natural disaster and similar catastrophes). Specific provisions on emergency situations are also contained in the EU Customs Code. For more details, see Chap. 22 by Adinolfi, in this volume.

[73] Suffice to mention the International Treaty on Plant Genetic Resources for Food and Agriculture (*OJ* 2004 L 378/3), which stipulates that, in emergency disasters situations, the Parties agree 'to provide facilitated access to appropriate plant genetic resources for food and agriculture… for the purpose of contributing to the re-establishment of agricultural systems, in co-operation with disaster relief coordinators' (Article 12(6)).

[74] For example, crisis measures in the event of a natural disaster are provided for by the Agreement between the European Community and the Swiss Confederation on the Carriage of Goods and Passengers by Rail and Road, *OJ* 2002 L 114/91.

[75] According to the Court, this principle requires member States to facilitate the achievement of the EU's tasks and to abstain from any measure which could jeopardise the attainment of the objectives of the Treaty. Furthermore, the member States and the EU institutions have an obligation of close co-operation in fulfilling the commitments undertaken by them under joint competence when they conclude a mixed agreement. See ECJ/GC, Case C-459/03 *Commission of the European Communities v Ireland* [2006] *ECR* I-04635, paras 174–175, and Neframi 2010 and 2012.

6.3 The Path to Lisbon

In the light of the multifaceted framework analysed above, it should not be surprising that the need to improve the existing instruments, their efficiency and overall coherence has represented one of the recurring themes of the discussion on the European disaster response capacity, which has been taking place during the last years at EU political level.

Some traces of such a discussion emerge from the work of the Convention on the future of Europe, which paved the way for the reform of the European Union legal order. In particular, mention should be made of the Final Report of the Working Group VII 'External Action', which, after having stressed, in general terms, the enhancing of coherence and efficiency of the external action of the Union, discussed 'the urgent need to clarify both the purpose and role of the EC's/EU's development policy, both in relation to those of member States and in relation to other external policies'.[76] In this respect, the Group first called attention to the importance of simplifying the piecemeal framework of administrative and legal instruments for managing EU development programmes and underlined the need to ensure coherence between the development cooperation policy and other aspects of EU external action. Then the Group

> noted the *specific* nature of humanitarian aid, on which the principles of independence and impartiality applied, not only because of international obligations but also to ensure that aid is delivered effectively and without additional risks to the lives of the providers.[77]

In doing so, the Group suggested the idea that humanitarian aid should be conceived as a self-standing policy of the Union. Such a conception has also been stressed by the 2007 European Consensus on Humanitarian Aid, which provided, for the first time, a joint declaration by EU institutions and member States on the shared objectives and principles governing the EU emergency assistance.

In parallel, the need to improve the coherence and efficiency of the EU disaster response has been highlighted in several occasions by the EU institutions.

In 2005, after the unprecedented disaster in Asia, the European Commission adopted a Communication on the EU Disaster and Crisis Response in Third Countries,[78] which identified several practical measures to strengthen existing EU instruments and their linkages to (and coherence with) the EU and international response. In 2008, a new Communication on Reinforcing the Union's Disaster Response Capacity was adopted by the European Commission.[79] The document proposed the implementation of specific actions concerning, *inter alia*, the inter-institutional co-operation, the reinforcement of European humanitarian aid, the

---

[76] European Convention, Final report of the Working Group VII on External Action, CONV 459/02, 16 December 2002, para 53.

[77] Doc. CONV 459/02, *supra* n. 76, para 57; emphasis added.

[78] COM (2005) 153, 20 April 2005; see also Glasius 2006.

[79] COM (2008) 130, 5 March 2008.

improvement of the European Civil Protection Mechanism, and the strengthening of an integrated approach across EU policies and instruments facing disaster response.

6.4 The Lisbon Age: A New Legal Framework for the EU External Disaster Response

In the light of the above-mentioned debate, the Lisbon Treaty has deeply amended the pre-existing legal framework of the EDR. This section will elaborate on the new EDR architecture and the main institutional changes.

6.4.1 The External Disaster Response as Part of the New Union's External Action

First, the Treaty introduces a general legal framework for EU external action which is also applicable when the Union provides assistance to third countries in the event of a natural or man-made disaster. More precisely, the Lisbon Treaty reform leads to the emergence of an integrated EU external policy, of which the EDR is a part.

In this respect, Article 21(1) TEU specifies the principles which shall guide the Union's action on the international scene: democracy, the rule of law, the universality and indivisibility of human rights and fundamental freedoms, respect for human dignity, the principles of equality and solidarity, and respect for the principles of the United Nations Charter and international law. Article 21(2) TEU sets out the objectives of the EU external action. It stipulates that the Union shall define and pursue common policies and actions, and shall work for a high degree of cooperation in all fields of international relations, in order to, *inter alia*, 'assist populations, countries and regions confronting natural or man-made disasters': this is the first time that the Union's overseas disaster response is expressly mentioned in EU primary law.

The provision adds then that:

> [t]he Union shall ensure consistency between the different areas of its external action and between these and its other policies. The Council and the Commission, assisted by the High Representative of the Union for Foreign Affairs and Security Policy, shall ensure that consistency and shall cooperate to that effect.[80]

[80] Article 21(3) TEU. That provision shall be read in conjunction with Article 7 TFEU, which states that '[t]he Union shall ensure consistency between its policies and activities, taking all of its objectives into account and in accordance with the principle of conferral of powers'.

Whilst already contained in the primary law since the 1986 Single European Act, the reference to the need of coherence becomes one of the distinctive features of the new institutional balance,[81] which is destined to deeply influence the implementation of the legal tools for the management of disaster response.

Of course, the difficulties of ensuring coherence between the different strands of the EU external action do not disappear with the entry into force of the Lisbon Treaty: in particular, concerns on the interaction between the institutional actors having co-ordinating tasks under the Lisbon Treaty (namely, the President of the European Council, the High Representative for Foreign Affairs and Security Policy and the Presidency of the Council of European Union) have been expressed by many commentators.[82] This notwithstanding, the new framework seems to have already led to the attainment of positive effects in the implementation of EU disaster response policies.

The establishment by the President of the European Commission of a single portfolio on International Cooperation, Humanitarian Aid and Crisis Response has already been mentioned as a practical example of ensuring coordination between different aspects of the EDR. On the other hand, also the High Representative for Foreign Affairs and Security Policy has effectively showed her co-ordinating tasks. In response to the devastating earthquake that struck Haiti in 2010, she convened, in close coordination with the Spanish Presidency, an extraordinary meeting of the Foreign Affairs Council to discuss the situation and the EU's response, from immediate relief measures to medium and longer term needs.[83] Similar actions have been put in place, more recently, on the occasion of other overseas disasters (for instance, in the case of the 2010 emergency resulting from the floods in Pakistan).

An important co-ordinating role should also be played by the European External Action Service (EEAS). Conceived as a supporting body of the High Representative (Article 27(3) TEU), the EEAS intervenes, indeed, transversally to the different strands of the external action, irrespective of most traditional obstacles to its coherence. Furthermore, as rightly pointed out by Cremona, it is 'intended to bridge the gap between … competitive policy services within the Commission and the Council Secretariat but also, through the involvement of the national diplomatic services, to encourage vertical cohesion'.[84]

The Council Decision establishing the EEAS[85] contains textual indications of the potential co-ordinating tasks of the Service in disaster response.

[81] Cremona 2011b, and Duke 2011.

[82] Craig 2010, 426.

[83] European Union, Press release 'Catherine Ashton: Rebuilding Haiti is a priority for the EU', IP/10/24, 15 January 2010.

[84] Cremona 2011b, 57.

[85] Council Decision No. 2010/427/EU of the Council establishing the organisation and functioning of the European External Action Service, *OJ* 2010 L 201/30.

First, under Article 9(3) of the Decision, the EEAS shall contribute to the programing and management cycle for most of the EU financial instruments involved in disaster assistance (such as the Development Cooperation Instrument, the European Development Fund, the European Neighbourhood and Partnership Instrument, the Instrument for Stability, and the Instrument for Nuclear Safety). In particular, it shall have responsibility for preparing the decisions of the Commission regarding the strategic, multiannual steps within the programing cycle of these tools. In doing so, it should thus ensure more complementarity between the different instruments and between these and the HAR.

Second, a member of the EEAS chairs the Political and Security Committee, which, as already mentioned, exercises political control and strategic direction of the crisis management operations of the Union.[86] On the other hand, the Service comprises the bodies supporting the PSC: the Crisis Management and Planning Directorate, the EU Military Staff and the Civilian Planning Conduct Capability.[87] Such a participation should thus lead to a more coherent implementation of the crisis management tool *vis-à-vis* the other pillars of the EDR.

Third, the EU delegations, which are now part of the EEAS structure, can provide for the liaison between the crisis response in the field and the diplomatic missions of third and member States.

The fact that the EEAS may play a strategic role in co-ordinating the EU overseas action in disaster management has also been illustrated by the practice of the political institutions.

The central position of the Service has been firstly emphasised by the High Representative, who, in December 2010, decided to appoint an EEAS Managing Director for Crises Response and Operational Coordination.[88] In the same year, in its Communication 'Towards a stronger European disaster response', the Commission has outlined the opportunities offered by the EEAS 'to improve consistency between disaster response and possible political and security related elements of the EU's overall crisis response', and proposed the development of working arrangements between EU bodies and the EEAS with the aim 'of ensuring complementarity and of using synergies between the ways in which disaster relief and civilian and military crisis management operations are managed.'[89]

The co-ordinating role of the EEAS has also been stressed, more recently, by the Commission in its 2011 Proposal for a Decision on a Union Civil Protection Mechanism, which should replace the existing legal tools concerning the civil protection cooperation.[90] The Proposal contains a new provision on overseas

---

[86] Article 4(4) of the Council Decision 2010/427.

[87] Article 4(3) of the Council Decision 2010/427.

[88] See European Union, Press release 'EU High Representative Catherine Ashton appoints EEAS Managing Director for Crisis Response', A 244/10, 2 December 2010.

[89] COM (2010) 600, *supra* n. 3, 3 and 8, respectively.

[90] COM (2011) 934. For a general survey of the content of the Proposal, see Chap. 5 by Gestri, in this volume.

interventions (Article 16), which has been significantly entitled ‘Promoting consistency in the response to major disaster outside the Union’, stating that the European External Action Service should ensure the consistency between the civil protection operation and the overall Union relations with the affected country.[91]

This element represents an important innovation of the existing framework, insofar as it suggests that the overall coordination of the civil protection assistance, which is today ensured by the Presidency of the Council of the European Union, could be exercised in the future by the EEAS. This should ensure a more efficient coordination within the Commission, which, according to the Proposal, should take charge of all operational coordination duties concerning the activation of the Mechanism.

The discussion thus far has considered the linkages between the different components of the EDR. It should, however, be noted that the new general provisions on the EU external action impose the respect of consistency with regard to all measures adopted by the Union. It is thus clear that also consistency between the EDR and the instruments established to face emergencies affecting member States should be ensured.

6.4.2 The New Legal Bases for Humanitarian Assistance

Another major legal innovation introduced by the Lisbon Treaty is represented by the establishment of new legal bases for the EU response in overseas emergencies.

First, the Reform Treaty introduces a specific provision in the Treaty on the Functioning of the European Union dealing with civil protection (Article 196), which expressly recognises, *inter alia*, the need to ‘promote consistency in international civil-protection work’. According to Article 6(f) TFEU, such a competence will be exercised by EU institutions only to carry out actions to support, coordinate or supplement the actions of the member States. This textual indication is confirmed by the 2011 Proposal for the establishment of a Union Civil Protection Mechanism, which has been adopted by the Commission on the basis of the new Treaty Article 196. As seen above, the Proposal actually aims at reinforcing the consistency of the civil protection response outside the Union and expressly makes clear that the Union’s action ‘shall not affect the member States’ competences and responsibility for their teams, modules and other support, including military capacities’.[92]

But the most important innovation is represented by the establishment of an explicit legal basis for humanitarian assistance outside the Union, Article 214 TFEU, which clearly separates, as envisaged by the Working Group VII ‘External

[91] Article 16 also specifies that the Union Delegations shall provide logistical support to the civil protection expert teams and ensure contacts with the government of the affected country.

[92] Article 16(10).

Action' of the Convention on the future of Europe, humanitarian aid from the EU development cooperation policy.

In particular, Article 214(1) stipulates that:

> The Union's operations in the field of humanitarian aid shall be conducted within the framework of the principles and objectives of the external action of the Union. Such operations shall be intended to provide *ad hoc* assistance and relief and protection for people in third countries who are victims of natural or man-made disasters, in order to meet the humanitarian needs resulting from these different situations. The Union's measures and those of the member States shall complement and reinforce each other.

Although its wording is very broad, this extract reveals some elements, which shall be stressed.

First, it makes clear that, although conceived as a self-standing policy, the EU humanitarian aid does not represent a self-contained regime; it is an integral part of the legal framework concerning the external action of the Union and shall thus ensure the respect of its principles and objectives.

Second, the passage sets a new demarcation between EU competences involved in managing emergency situations, which should help in overcoming some of the difficulties shown by the pre-existing legal framework. On the one hand, whereas measures adopted under Article 214 TFEU shall only be designed for supporting first relief ('*ad hoc* assistance and relief and protection') in the event of emergencies, the provision makes clear that long-term assistance should fall outside its scope of application, and should be governed by Articles 208 and 212 TFEU (devoted, respectively, to development co-operation and the economic, financial and technical co-operation with non-developing countries).[93] It is clear, moreover, that the establishment of a self-standing policy on humanitarian aid should lead to a narrower interpretation of the material and personal scope of the development cooperation policy than was the case with the former Treaties. Furthermore, the new legal basis suggests quite unambiguously that urgent humanitarian measures cannot be covered by the emergency clause contained in Article 213 TFEU, which provides that '[w]hen the situation in a third country requires urgent financial assistance from the Union, the Council shall adopt the necessary decisions on a proposal from the Commission'. Indeed, the recourse to such a provision for humanitarian aid would necessarily deprive Article 214 of its scope of application. Finally, since humanitarian aid should meet 'the humanitarian needs' of people victims of disasters, such a field of competence cannot be invoked for actions having a political or security dimension. In such cases, the EU action should be covered by the CFSP umbrella.[94]

---

[93] Cremona 2011a, 13 and Dashwood 2011, 38.

[94] This conclusion is reinforced by the fact that the new Treaty provision concerning the demarcation of competences between the CFSP and other domains of EU action (Article 40 TEU) introduces a mutual non-affectation clause, according to which also the implementation of the other policies of the Union shall not affect the exercise of the EU competences under the CFSP.

Third, the last sentence of the above-mentioned phrasing, '[t]he Union's measures and those of the member States shall complement and reinforce each other', provides some indications on the nature of EU humanitarian aid action. In this respect, Article 214(1) should be interpreted in light of Article 4(4) TFEU, which states that

> [i]n the are[a] of... humanitarian aid, the Union shall have competence to carry out activities and conduct a common policy; however, the exercise of that competence shall not result in member States being prevented from exercising theirs.

Whereas Article 4 TFEU lists EU areas falling within the category of shared competence, the formula used in Article 214 may be interpreted as reflecting the shared nature of EU humanitarian action. Having said this, it should also be noted that, due to the caveat contained in the second part of Article 4(4) TFEU, in this case the pre-emption principle, which is generally applicable within the context of EU shared competence,[95] does not act. This can also be inferred from the provision contained in Article 214(4), which confers a treaty-making power to the Union to conclude agreements with third countries and competent international organisations for the achievement of the objectives of the humanitarian assistance. Such a treaty-making power shall, indeed, be without prejudice to member States' competence to negotiate in international bodies and to conclude agreements.

Craig interprets the above-mentioned provisions, and the emphasis given to the fact that the Commission may take, under Article 214 TFEU, any useful initiative in order to enhance the efficiency and the complementarity of Union and national humanitarian assistance,[96] in the sense that a clear demarcation between the EU competence in humanitarian assistance and the supporting, co-ordinating, and supplementary actions listed in Article 6 TFEU cannot be easily delineated.[97] However, this representation of the EU competence in humanitarian aid does not alter the fact that the limitations imposed to the EU action in that domain shall be balanced by the implementation of the 'loyalty clause' enshrined in Article 4(3) TEU, which requires member States not to jeopardise the assistance measures put in place by the Union.

Another distinctive feature of the new Treaty provision is represented by the incorporation of the principles governing EU humanitarian assistance (namely, impartiality, neutrality and non-discrimination), which acquire the rank of primary law. It thus follows that such principles will act as criteria for determining the validity of EU secondary law.

In this respect, two considerations deserve to be mentioned.

First, the provision enshrined in Article 214 referring to such principles states that '[h]umanitarian aid operations shall be conducted in compliance with the principles of international law and with the principles of impartiality, neutrality and non-discrimination'. It thus engenders the idea that the latter are formally

---

95 According to that principle, '[t]he member States shall exercise their competence to the extent that the Union has not exercised its competence': Article 2(2) TFEU.

96 Article 214(6).

97 Craig 2010, 394–395.

separated and independent from the principles stemming from international law.[98] In reality, as duly explained in this volume,[99] the principles governing disaster response originate from International Humanitarian Law, and are fully part of the international legal order.

Second, the principles mentioned in the Treaty do not perfectly correspond to the guiding principles governing disaster response that are contained in the main international instruments devoted to humanitarian assistance and in the European Consensus on Humanitarian Aid. In particular, the Treaty does not make reference to the principles of humanity and independence.[100]

This notwithstanding, it is difficult to maintain that only the principles expressly mentioned in Article 214 could be considered as binding over the EU institutions involved in the implementation of humanitarian aid. On the one hand, principles which are not mentioned in the Treaty may be covered by the expression 'principles of international law' contained in that article. On the other hand, the binding nature of some of these principles may also be inferred from Article 1 of the EU Charter of fundamental rights[101] enshrining the inviolability of human dignity, which constitutes the real basis of fundamental rights and lies at the core of several international instruments dealing with humanitarian assistance.[102] That is particularly true with regard to the principle of humanity, which represents the most prominent principle of humanitarian aid and stipulates that human suffering must be addressed wherever it is found.

This conclusion is supported by the practice of the EU institutions. In particular, it is worth noting that the 2011 Proposal on the Union Civil Protection Mechanism makes it clear that:

> [w]hen assistance under the Mechanism contributes to a wider Union humanitarian response, actions receiving financial assistance under this Decision *shall be consistent with the humanitarian principles referred to in the European Consensus on Humanitarian Aid.*[103]

It thus follows that all the principles mentioned in the European Consensus (namely, humanity, impartiality, neutrality and independence) shall be considered as binding (and guiding) all actors (including EU institutions) involved in humanitarian assistance operations.

---

98 A similar approach has been taken by the framers of the Lisbon Treaty in the formulation of Article 21(1) TEU, which distinguishes the respect of international law from that for the principles of the United Nations Charter.

99 See Chap. 2 by Venturini.

100 Besides, Article 214 explicitly mentions the principle of non-discrimination as a general principle of disaster relief even if such a principle is commonly considered as a component of the principle of impartiality: doc. A/CN.4/629, *supra* n. 19, paras 31–34.

101 According to Article 6(1) TEU, the Charter shall have the same legal value as the Treaties.

102 Cf. doc. A/CN.4/629, *supra* n. 19, para 59. Note that the respect for human dignity is also mentioned among the principles which shall govern the external action of the Union (Article 21(1) TEU).

103 Article 26(3) of the Proposal [emphasis added].

Finally, it is worth pointing out that Article 214(7) repeats what the pre-existing practice already stressed: EU aid operations shall be coordinated and consistent with those of other international organisations involved in disaster response, in particular those forming part of the UN system.

6.5 Concluding Remarks

This chapter has attempted to give a global overview of the EU action in external disaster response.

In this respect, the Lisbon Treaty has paved the way for a general reform process of existing mechanisms with a view to strengthening their efficiency and coherence.

While some of the Treaty innovations have already shown their potential role in ensuring the consistency and effectiveness of the EDR, other new clauses will be applied only in the next months.

In particular, the new legal bases introduced by the Lisbon Treaty should lead to the adoption of legislative acts on disaster response partially replacing the existing legal framework.[104] Only the actual implementation of these Treaty provisions will thus permit an overall assessment of the new legal framework of the EDR.

In any case, what emerges from the initial practice of the EU institutions is that the need of ensuring coherence and efficiency in this domain seems generally to focus only on the interaction between the horizontal tools for disaster management (i.e., humanitarian aid, civil protection cooperation, and civilian crisis management),[105] which, as the analysis in Sect. 6.2 clearly illustrates, already show a high level of mutual coordination.[106]

Whilst fundamental for the EU external assistance, those instruments have been accompanied in the course of time by several sector activities, which may play a significant role for overseas emergencies.[107] Of course, the new legal framework of the external action of the Union and the co-ordinating tasks conferred to some EU actors in this context should also ensure a more consistent interaction between

---

[104] Besides the Proposal on the EU CPM (*supra* n. 90), the Commission should adopt legislative proposals on the EU humanitarian aid and the establishment of the European Voluntary Aid Corps.

[105] For instance, the Proposal on the new CPM stipulates that '[s]ynergies shall be sought with other instruments of the Union, *in particular*, with actions financed under Regulation (EC) No 1257/96'. Cf. Article 16(11) [emphasis added].

[106] The asymmetrical character of coherence in disaster response also emerges from the European Consensus on Humanitarian Aid. The Document highlights the need to ensure coherence and complementarity in response to crisis, making the most effective use of the various instruments mobilised. However, it significantly only refers to the interaction between EU humanitarian aid and instruments related to crisis management, civil protection and consular assistance (para 22).

[107] See *supra* 6.2.4.

the sector policies involved in disaster response and between these policies and the horizontal instruments of the EDR. This notwithstanding, a more comprehensive approach in disaster management, integrating the horizontal instruments with its vertical dimension, would be preferable.

References

Baroncini E (2008) Il *treaty-making power* della Commissione europea. Editoriale Scientifica, Naples

Craig P (2010) The Lisbon Treaty—Law, Politics, and Treaty Reform. Oxford University Press, Oxford

Cremona M (2011a) The EU and global emergencies: competence and instruments. In: Antoniadis et al (eds) The European Union and global emergencies. A Law and Policy Analysis, Hart Publishing, Oxford and Portland, 11–31

Cremona M (2011b) Coherence in European Foreign Relations Law. In: Koutrakos P (ed) European Foreign Policy—Legal and Political Perspectives. Edward Elgar, Cheltenham, pp 55–92

Dashwood A (2011) Conflicts of competence in responding to global emergencies. In: Antoniadis et al (eds) The European Union and global emergencies. A Law and Policy Analysis, Hart Publishing, Oxford and Portland, 33–48

Duke S (2011) Consistency, coherence and European Union external action: the path to Lisbon and beyond. In: Koutrakos P (ed) European Foreign Policy—Legal and Political perspectives. Edward Elgar, Cheltenham, pp 15–54

Dusepulchre G (2008) Dimension politique de la politique communautaire de coopération au développement, quelle cohérence? In: Dony M, Rossi LS (eds) Démocratie, cohérence et transparence: vers une constitutionnalisation de l'Union Européenne? Editions de l'Université de Bruxelles, Bruxelles, pp 265–286

Glasius M (2006) The EU response to the Tsunami and the need for a Human security approach. Eur Foreign Aff Rev 11:353–378

Koutrakos P (2012) International agreements in the area of the EU's common security and Defence Policy. In: Cannizzaro et al (eds) International Law as Law of the European Union, Martinus Nijhoff Publishers, Leiden, 157–187

Marhic G (2011) Common security and Defence Policy Crisis management missions: an effective tool for EU response to emergencies. In: Antoniadis et al (eds) The European Union and global emergencies. A Law and Policy Analysis, Hart Publishing, Oxford and Portland, 247–260

Neframi E (2012) Mixed Agreements as a source of European Union Law. In: Cannizzaro et al (eds) International Law as Law of the European Union, Martinus Nijhoff Publishers, Leiden, 325–349

Neframi E (2010) The duty of loyalty: rethinking its scope through its application in the field of EU external relations. Common Market Law Rev 47:323–359

Olsson S (ed) (2009) Crisis management in the European Union—cooperation in the face of emergencies. Springer, Dordrecht

Sari A (2008) Status of forces and status of mission agreements under the ESDP: the EU's evolving practice. Eur J Int Law 19:67–100

Versluys H (2009) European humanitarian aid: lifesaver or political tool? In: Orbie J (ed) Europe's global role—external policies of the European Union. Ashgate, Aldershot, pp 91–116

Chapter 7
The Consular Protection of EU Citizens during Emergencies in Third Countries

Federico Forni

Abstract This chapter focuses on the consular protection that the member States and the EU can offer in third countries to EU citizens involved in disasters. The analysis aims to assess the legal framework applicable to the assistance granted by Article 23 TFEU and by its implementing acts. Decision 95/553 and the Council guidelines on consular protection do not apply solely to routine problems of individuals as they also contain rules and procedures coordinating the intervention of the member States' diplomatic and consular missions during catastrophes involving a large number of EU citizens. The repatriation of distressed EU citizens is included in the cases where the member States have to give consular protection in accordance with Decision 95/553. The EU countries generally seem willing to co-operate in evacuating EU citizens, even if the practice shows some cases in which the diplomatic missions did not take the principle of non-discrimination on grounds of nationality into serious account. From a practical point of view, the dynamic process of the EU crisis management could offer a high degree of assistance. However, the efficacy of the consular cooperation in third countries is strictly connected to the capacity of the diplomatic missions on the ground, as well as to the resources available for managing emergencies. To evaluate the effective content of the consular protection granted by EU law in third countries, this chapter analyzes the four stages of crisis management: prevention, mitigation, relief and recovery. The contribution underlines both strengths and critical aspects of each phase, highlighting the co-ordinating role of the EU Presidency and the 'Lead State' in ensuring assistance to individuals. The author argues that the current problems could be overcome by the evolution of the external dimension of EU citizenship. In fact, the importance of the assistance interventions carried out

F. Forni (✉)
Dipartimento di Scienze Giuridiche, Università di Modena e Reggio Emilia,
via San Geminiano 3, I-41121, Modena, MO, Italy
e-mail: fedeforni@libero.it

A. de Guttry et al. (eds.), *International Disaster Response Law*,
DOI: 10.1007/978-90-6704-882-8_7,

in third countries could allow the Union to become a reference point for distressed citizens.

Keywords EU citizenship · Consular protection · Consular cooperation · Evacuation · EU Presidency · Lead State · Terrorist attacks

Contents

7.1 Introduction

In the event of disasters,[1] persons need assistance from public authorities as they cannot singlehandedly face problems 'caused by a natural phenomenon, such as a cyclone, tornado, earthquake, volcanic eruption, flood or forest fire, or by a technological accident, such as pollution by hydrocarbons, toxic or radioactive substances'.[2] The affected country is responsible, by virtue of its sovereignty, for assisting people, including aliens, who might need help.[3] Nevertheless, it cannot be reasonably foreseen that the particular needs of aliens can be fully satisfied by States facing dangerous contexts. Hence, the national States of the aliens can assist their citizens by means of their diplomatic and consular missions. In fact, these representations can offer consular protection to their nationals abroad by

[1] For the purpose of this chapter, the term disaster is intended as defined in Chap. 1 by de Guttry in this volume. See also International Law Commission, Protection of persons in the event of disasters, Texts of draft Articles 1, 2, 3, 4 and 5 as provisionally adopted by the Drafting Committee, UN Doc. A/CN.4/L.758, 24 July 2009, Article 3.

[2] 2000 Charter on cooperation to achieve the coordinated use of space facilities in the event of natural or technological disasters, Rev. 3, Article 1.

[3] International Law Commission, Protection of persons in the event of disasters, Texts of draft Articles 6, 7, 8 and 9 provisionally adopted by the Drafting Committee on 6, 7 and 8 July 2010, UN Doc. A/CN.4/L.776, 14 July 2010, Article 9(1). For a comment on these provisions see Chap. 3 by Zorzi Giustiniani in this volume.

'providing (…) [them] with information and advice, helping them in their relations with the authorities of the receiving State (…), facilitating their repatriation, etc'.[4]

However, a State is not represented everywhere outside its borders since the establishment and maintenance of a consular network represents a high financial burden. For instance, all 27 member States are represented outside the EU only in the People's Republic of China, Russia, and the USA.[5] Therefore, when a disaster involves EU citizens, it is most likely that some member States will not be able to promptly assist their nationals within that territory.

To overcome this drawback, the drafters of the Maastricht Treaty introduced a norm (Article 8c) according to which '[e]very citizen of the Union shall, in the territory of a third country in which the Member State of which he is a national is not represented, be entitled to protection by the diplomatic or consular authorities of any Member State, on the same conditions as the nationals of that State'. This provision became Article 20 TEC after the Amsterdam revision and is currently stated in Article 23 TFEU by means of the Treaty of Lisbon.[6] The practical importance of the norm is evident if one considers that about 2 million EU citizens are living in third countries and 7 million travel every year to third countries where their national States do not have consular or diplomatic representations.[7]

Generally, the measure is discussed while analyzing the right of unrepresented EU citizens to request protection from the diplomatic or consular authorities of another member State to solve routine problems of the individual.[8] However, Article 23 TFEU is the legal base which also allows an EU country to give assistance when crisis situations affect a significant number of EU citizens.[9] In these circumstances, the represented member States might be unable to assist even their own nationals due to the capacities of their missions being

[4] Economidès 1992, 772. Consular protection is distinguished from diplomatic protection which 'consists of the invocation by a State, through diplomatic action or other means of peaceful settlement, of the responsibility of another State for an injury caused by an international wrongful act of that State to a natural or legal person that is a national of the former State with a view to the implementation of such responsibility' (United Nations, Diplomatic Protection: resolution adopted by the General Assembly, A/RES/62/67, 8 January 2008, Article 1).

[5] European Commission, Communication from the Commission to the European Parliament and the Council, Consular protection for EU citizens in third countries: State of play and way forward, COM(2011) 149 final, Brussels, 23 March 2011, 3.

[6] The first sentence of Article 23 TFEU is reproduced in Article 46 of the EU Charter of Fundamental Rights with slight variations that do not affect the meaning of the provision. The Committee on migration, refugees and demography of the Council of Europe proposed to extend the measure to Council of Europe countries (Council of Europe, Parliamentary Assembly, Link between Europeans living abroad and their countries of origin, Doc. 8339, 5 March 1999, 13, para 98).

[7] Commission of the European Communities, Commission staff working document, Accompanying document to the Communication from the Commission to the European Parliament, the Council and the European Economic and Social Committee–Effective consular protection in third countries: the contribution of the European Union–Action Plan 2007–2009–Impact Assessment, SEC(2007) 1600 final, Brussels, 5 December 2007, 13.

[8] See, for instance, Battini 2011, 177–181.

[9] Lindström 2009, 110.

overwhelmed. Owing to these difficulties, it is advisable for the member States to co-operate given that the large number of EU citizens involved in disasters 'made it obvious that even the best, widest and most resourceful consular services could not cope on their own'.[10] Therefore, the Union has outlined a common European response to reinforce the action of single EU countries.[11] This approach is coherent with Article 5 of the ILC project regarding the protection of persons in the event of disasters, stating the impossibility for a single State to give effective assistance to all people involved in the catastrophe.[12]

On the basis of these premises, the present chapter aims to assess the legal framework applicable to the protection granted by Article 23 TFEU during crisis situations caused by a disaster affecting a third country. The analysis will assess the behavior of the member States vis-à-vis EU citizens who are in need of assistance during emergencies without stressing the application of the provision to issues affecting routine problems of individuals. In the course of the exposition, this paper will try to foresee the role of the Union in 'helping and assisting'[13] EU citizens during disasters, especially in the light of the recent establishment of the European External Action Service (EEAS). As few documents on exceptional consular assistance in natural or man-made disasters are publicly available, the analysis will assess also how the EU consular cooperation has faced the consequences of conflicts and terrorist attacks. The examination of such events is consistent with the purposes of this volume as the member States' diplomatic and consular missions assist the EU citizen involved in terrorist or conflict situations following the same legal rules applied in disasters.[14]

---

[10] Porzio 2008, 94.

[11] European Commission, Communication from the Commission to the European Parliament and the Council, Towards a stronger European disaster response: the role of civil protection and humanitarian assistance, COM(2010) 600 final, Brussels, 26 October 2010, 4.

[12] International Law Commission, Protection of persons in the event of disasters, *supra* footnote 1, Article 5.

[13] According to Article 5(e) of the 1963 Vienna Convention on Consular Relations, one of the consular functions consists in 'helping and assisting nationals, both individuals and bodies corporate, of the sending State.'

[14] The analysis of EU documents can support the thesis that the action of the member States in favor of EU citizens in third countries is governed by the same rules regardless of the event (natural or man-made disaster, conflict or terrorist attack). For example, the European Economic and Social Committee stated that '[t]he Commission has (…) submitted a number of measures for discussion in its Green Paper, aimed at strengthening the principle of protection for EU citizens in third countries as an important right for every Member State citizen resulting from their EU citizenship. The measures also take account of the experiences from the aftermath of natural disasters such as the tsunami and Hurricane Katrina, the conflicts in the Balkans and Lebanon and terrorist attacks on Bali and in Sharm El Sheikh' [opinion on the Green Paper on diplomatic and consular protection of Union citizens in third countries, COM(2006) 712 final, *OJ* 2007 C 161/75-79, 13 July 2007, point 2.7]. Moreover, this approach is coherent with the recent non-legal scholarly writings suggesting that terrorism should be treated as an hazard and should be analyzed similarly to the way in which natural hazards are handled (Slovic 2002, 425; King et al. 2003, 789–798; Bulleit and Drewek 2011, 205).

7.2 Decision 95/553 and Crisis Situations Caused by Disasters

The current legal framework on consular protection is characterized by Decision 95/553.[15] This EU act, which might be replaced by the Directive recently proposed by the Commission,[16] grants unrepresented EU citizens the right to be treated as if they were nationals of the member States represented by the diplomatic and consular missions to which they address.[17]

According to Decision 95/553, the diplomatic and consular representations must provide consular assistance in the situations identified by Article 5(1), offering help in the instance of a grave accident, serious illness, or even death; intervening in favor of detainees; aiding victims of violent crimes and repatriating distressed EU citizens.[18] The entitlement to consular protection does not extend into other fields. In fact, even though Article 5(2) of this act affirms that the member States may also assist every EU citizen 'in other circumstances', the exhortative rather than the binding nature of Article 5(2) prevents individuals from invoking the provision in case the assistance is denied in a situation not provided for within the first paragraph of the provision.[19]

The situations included in Article 5(1) might initially be intended to manage problems involving a (small) number of EU citizens, which does not cause difficulties to the staff and resource capacities of the missions.[20] As time passed, the practice brought about circumstances in which a large number of citizens needed the intervention of the diplomatic and consular representations. It is obvious, in fact, that the number of EU citizens involved in a calamitous event exceeded the threshold of a single European mission.[21]

---

[15] Decision 95/553/EC of the Representatives of the Governments of the Member States meeting within the Council of 19 December 1995 regarding protection for citizens of the European Union by diplomatic and consular representations, *OJ* 1995 L 314/73-76, 28 December 1995.

[16] Commission proposal for a Council Directive on consular protection for citizens of the Union abroad, COM(2011) 881 final, Brussels, 14 December 2011.

[17] Decision 95/553, Article 3.

[18] Article 6(2) of the recent proposal for a Directive on consular protection, *supra* footnote 16, does not extend the material scope of the assistance. The draft provision just adds to the present list the issue of emergency travel documents currently regulated by Decision 96/409/CFSP of the Representatives of the Governments of the Member States, meeting within the Council of 25 June 1996 on the establishment of an emergency travel document, *OJ* 1996 L 168/4-11, 6 July 1996.

[19] The draft Directive on consular protection, *supra* footnote 16, does not explicitly mention the existence of 'other circumstances' in which the diplomatic and consular representations may give assistance.

[20] For instance, the United Kingdom emphasizes a relatively low number of requests of assistance presented to its consular network from unrepresented EU citizens in third countries compared to those advanced by British nationals (about 750 on more than 114,000 in the time period from 2003 to 2007). House of Commons, European Scrutiny Committee, Twenty-Sixth Report of Session 2007–2008, The Stationery Office, London, 17 June 2008, 36.

[21] Porzio 2008, 94.

As a consequence, it was necessary to involve a large number of member States regardless of this choice creating management problems related to sharing information, handling relations with the media, decision making and co-ordinating the response.[22] To adapt to these coordination necessities, the Council adopted the guidelines on consular protection which are continuously updated.[23] These legally non-binding rules are aimed at enhancing EU consular cooperation to improve assistance offered to EU citizens in dangerous situations within a third country.[24] These guidelines were undertaken on the basis of former Article 20 TEU (now Article 35 TEU), according to which the diplomatic and consular representations of the member States and the EU delegations shall contribute to the implementation of the right to consular assistance in third countries.[25]

In crisis situations, the member States seem generally willing to co-operate in the repatriation of distressed EU citizens, given that this form of assistance is included in Article 5(1) of Decision 95/553. Such willingness is confirmed by the procedures suggesting the arrangement of joint transportation of EU citizens to the nearest safe place on the basis of evacuation plans,[26] whose contents, previously prepared and regularly updated, are not divulged to the general public as they are considered confidential by the Commission.[27]

On the contrary, the relief phase is widely known by public opinion since it is highlighted by media as the intervention in an emotional event could allow the member States' governments to gain consent. For instance, the German press gave emphasis to the consular assistance in the evacuation given by the German embassy during the 2008 Georgian crisis in Tbilisi.[28] Similarly, the media reported

---

[22] For an analysis of the difficulties arising from crisis management during disasters, see Quarantelli 1988, 373–385.

[23] For the latest version, see Council of the European Union, Guidelines on consular protection of EU citizens in third countries, Doc. 15613/10, Brussels, 5 November 2010.

[24] At present the implementation of the guidelines is left to the discretion of the Heads of the diplomatic and consular missions according to the situation in the third country. Articles 7–16 of the draft Directive on consular protection, *supra* footnote 16, aim to give a binding force to these coordination and cooperation measures.

[25] Article 35(3) TEU reads: 'They [diplomatic and consular missions of the member States and the Union delegations in third countries] shall contribute to the implementation of the right of citizens of the Union to protection in the territory of third countries as referred to in Article 20(2)(c) of the Treaty on the Functioning of the European Union and of the measures adopted pursuant to Article 23 of that Treaty.'

[26] Joint framework for EU cooperation and coordination in relation to emergencies in Japan, 6 December 2006, 3.

[27] Answer given by Mr Nielson on behalf of the Commission on 18 July 2000 to the written question E-1916/00 by G. Podestà, subject: 'War in Ethiopia and Eritrea', *OJ* 2001 C 89 E/112-113, 20 March 2001.

[28] Germany offers to evacuate EU citizens in Georgia, *Deutsche Welle*, 11 August 2008 (http://www.dw.de/dw/article/0,3554820,00.html, accessed 12 February 2012).

the role played by a Dutch warship in bringing logistic and medical support to the French navy during the evacuation of EU citizens from the Ivory Coast.[29]

These interventions cannot be highlighted only due to their promotional impact, but also for their great importance from a practical point of view of the EU citizens involved. In fact, the significance of the numerical data seems to confirm that the member States did not only give assistance exclusively to their own nationals during the evacuation from crisis areas. For instance, an Irish aircraft safely evacuated 16 EU citizens from Tripoli, among whom only three were Irish.[30] As well as this, the United Kingdom also evacuated nearly 230 non-British EU citizens from Libya.[31]

The reported practice seems to indicate not only that the ‘space on transportation used for an evacuation is maximised and (…) rotations are optimised’,[32] but also that the principle of non-discrimination on grounds of nationality is taken into account during a disaster. At the same time, despite this legal obligation, the practice also shows episodes that might contrast with this duty enshrined in primary law. In fact, the Commission pointed out that the member States, during the recent crises in Northern Africa and Japan, were inclined to repatriate unrepresented EU citizens only when their own nationals had available places left on aircrafts.[33] Hence, it is necessary to deepen the concrete behavior of the member States in order to evaluate whether EU law imposes upon the diplomatic and consular representations to apply the principle of non-discrimination or whether they are still bound to a national concept of solidarity.[34]

---

29 Netherlands sends warship to Ivory Coast, *The Guardian*, 24 December 2010 (http://www.guardian.co.uk/world/2010/dec/24/netherlands-warship-ivory-coast, accessed 12 February 2012).

30 Irish team leads evacuation of 16 EU citizens from Libya, *The Journal*, 27 February 2011 (http://www.thejournal.ie/irish-team-leads-evacuation-of-16-eu-citizens-from-libya-2011-02, accessed 12 February 2012).

31 http://www.publications.parliament.uk/pa/cm201011/cmhansrd/cm110307/text/110307w0004.htm, accessed 12 February 2012.

32 Council of the European Union, Guidelines on consular protection of EU citizens in third countries, *supra* footnote 23, 7, para 12.9.

33 European Commission, Consular protection for EU citizens in third countries: State of play and way forward, *supra* footnote 5, 12, para 3.3.1. This event is not the only one reported in the practice. During the 2006 Lebanon crisis, Denmark offered to EU citizens only vacant places in a ferry for Cyprus and in a bus convoy (CARE Project, Citizens Consular Assistance Regulation in Europe, Consular and Diplomatic Protection. Legal framework in the EU Member States, Istituto di teoria e tecniche dell’informazione giuridica del CNR, Firenze, 2010, 150).

34 The Heads of cabinet of the Commissioners seem to have a different interpretation on the solidarity clause introduced by the Lisbon Treaty (see Chap. 5 by Gestri in this volume, Sect. 5.2.1). According to Ms Åsenius (Head of cabinet, Commissioner for Home Affairs) the clause operates mainly within Europe, while Ms Fink-Hooijer (Head of cabinet, Commissioner for International Cooperation, Humanitarian Aid and Crisis Response) is inclined to include in the norm also the evacuation of EU nationals from third countries (Conference Proceedings, Searching for solidarity: developing EU capacities for crisis and disaster management, Brussels, 24 March 2011, 11 and 14).

7.3 Granting an Effective Implementation of the Non-Discrimination Principle

From a political point of view, it is understandable that States might give preference to their own nationals since no government would risk the consent of its electors by evacuating unrepresented EU citizens while leaving its own nationals in difficulty. On the other hand, any preferences shown towards nationals contrasts with the principle of non-discrimination, as stated in Article 23 TFEU, which reproduces the equality of treatment imposed by Article 18 TFEU within the EU's external sphere.[35]

A first perplexity is raised by the financial conditions established for giving assistance during times of crisis. The guidelines of the Council specify that the 'Member States will reimburse those Member States which act on their behalf for expenses incurred in securing the safety of their nationals (e.g., where provision of a radio network is necessary, hiring of vehicles to transport persons to a safe area, etc.), in a pragmatic way'.[36] Thus, the principle of non-discrimination does not seem to be applied strictly if consular protection is compared to the domestic citizens' rights, such as free movement of persons which 'accepts a certain degree of financial solidarity (…) [among] nationals of (…) [the] Member States, particularly if the difficulties (…) are temporary'.[37]

Besides the lack of financial solidarity, formal interpretations can be used as a plausible excuse for justifying discrimination on grounds of nationality–even in seriously dangerous situations. Such a case occurred during the 2008 Mumbai terrorist attacks. In this event, a German diplomat attempted to save only its nationals without giving assistance to EU citizens of other nationalities. However, the Council raised no objections against this behavior since Article 23 TFEU limits the possibility to invoke this right to cases in which the national country is not represented. Thus, the provision could not impose any duty of non-discrimination on the German consulate in Mumbai since the States of the nationals concerned had their own missions on the ground.[38]

---

[35] Closa 1992, 1164; O'Leary 1992, 383.

[36] Council of the European Union, Guidelines on consular protection of EU citizens in third countries, *supra* footnote 23, 7, para 12.8. See also on the same page para 12.10 according to which '[w]here EU nationals being evacuated are asked to pay the costs of the evacuation as well as other expenses related thereto (see point 12.8 above), payment arrangements should be made from Member State to Member State, on a pro-rata basis. It will then be the responsibility of the requesting Member State to pursue repayment from its nationals.'

[37] European Court of Justice (ECJ), Case C-184/99 Grzelczyk, Judgment of 20 September 2001, [2001] ECR I-6193, para 44.

[38] See the intervention of Alexandr Vondra, President-in-Office of the Council, during the debate at the European Parliament (Debates, Wednesday 4 February 2009, Strasbourg, 13. Consular protection of citizens of the European Union in third countries, http://www.europarl.europa.eu/sides/getDoc.do?pubRef=-//EP//TEXT+CRE+20090204+ITEM-013+DOC+XML+V0//EN, accessed 12 February 2012).

Although the behavior of the German diplomat was formally correct, this episode proves that a restrictive interpretation can discriminate against EU citizens on the basis of their nationalities. Hence, it is possible to affirm that the Mumbai affair calls for a flexible interpretation of the meaning of 'accessible representation'[39] in the light of the proportionality principle in order to prevent such a situation from occurring again. The term 'accessible' is, in practice, difficult to be determined a priori since it depends on the concrete local situations. Thus, it should be evaluated on a case-by-case basis, imposing on member States' consulates to give assistance to EU citizens even when their States of nationality are represented, but their missions are difficult to reach owing to acute problems connected with certain disasters.[40]

7.4 The Coordination of Providing Assistance to EU Citizens During Crisis

To understand the concrete implementation of the consular protection on the basis of Article 23 TFEU, it is necessary to examine the functioning of the EU consular cooperation during disasters. From a general point of view, crisis management is not limited to responding to emergencies, but rather it is a dynamic process that begins with the forecast of the critical events and also continues after the conclusion of the crisis. Hence, it can be described as a procedure developed over four stages: prevention, mitigation, relief, and recovery—[41] each one requiring a different approach.

[39] Decision 95/553, Article 1.

[40] The proposal for a Directive on consular protection, *supra* footnote 16, underlines the absence of a 'common understanding about when an embassy or consulate is accessible' (3). To clarify the meaning of 'accessible representation, draft Article 3(2) affirms that '[a]n embassy or consulate established on a permanent basis is accessible if it can effectively provide protection and can be reached safely within convenient travel distance and reasonable time. Citizens of the Union at least need to be able to reach the embassy or consulate and return to their place of departure the same day, via means of transport commonly used in the third country, unless the urgency of the matter requires swifter assistance. The embassy or consulate is not accessible if it is temporarily not in a position to effectively provide protection, in particular if it is temporarily closed in case of crisis.' The provision is coherent with the recital 8 of the draft Directive.

[41] See Chap. 1 by de Guttry in this volume. The four phases can be identified with different names. For instance, a legal commentator indicates these stages as prevention, preparation, response and recovery phases (Lindström 2009, 110). According to other academic contributions (Naghdi et al. 2008, 1671–1676) and some public agencies (Crisis and emergency management: a guide of the public service in Canada, Canadian Centre for Management Development, 2004), the disaster management cycle is divided into mitigation, preparedness, response and recovery.

7.4.1 The Prevention Phase

Prevention activities aim at identifying possible situations of crisis in advance so as to avoid EU citizens from being subjected to predictable dangers. These actions consist in offering travel information through concise statements that clearly delineate the situation in a third country. In order to reduce the number of accidents, the EU has recently created a website which reports the advice that each member State addresses to its nationals intending to travel outside the EU.[42] Search results on the site point out the absence of agreement among the member States in evaluating local situations.[43]

These findings are actually not puzzling, since in most cases it would be difficult to impose a single 'European' assessment for each third country, despite the existence of common sources of information elaborated by the Joint Situation Center (SITCEN) and available to EU countries.[44] The contrasting advice might also be attributed to the fact that some member States feel more linked to some third nations than to other EU countries. In this respect, Ireland pointed out the differences in its evaluation, emphasizing that 'travelling public tend to congregate with citizens of those countries [Australia, New Zealand and the USA] abroad and hence our advice is often similar to those countries'.[45]

The welcome of a EU citizen in a nation outside the Union may be different depending on the perception of his/her national State by the local population owing to historical and cultural links or to the current political situation. The evaluation could be the same only when all of the member States are involved in a dispute with a third nation; in case of epidemics or due to an armed conflict in the country.

---

[42] The website (http://ec.europa.eu/consularprotection/index.action, accessed 12 February 2012) is the practical implementation of recital 8 of the Commission Recommendation of 5 December 2007 on reproducing the text of Article 20 TEC in passports (*OJ* 2008 L 118/30-31, 6 May 2008, 31) which suggested 'to create a website dedicated to consular protection to publish practical information, e.g., updated contact details of Member States' representations in third countries'.

[43] On 12 February 2012, for instance, the results for a hypothetical travel to Burkina Faso showed differing opinions. Belgium and Slovenia recommended 'caution' and other member States (Denmark, France, Spain, etc.) invited to 'avoid non-essential travel'. Czech Republic, Germany, Italy, Netherlands ('Some areas may be dangerous'), Austria, the UK ('Avoid all travel to certain areas') and Sweden ('Avoid non-essential travel to certain areas') indicated the presence of danger only in certain regions, while other EU countries (Finland, Greece, Hungary, Ireland, etc.) did not foresee any 'specific travel advice.'

[44] Written question E-4121/09 by M. Ehrenhauser to the Council (11 August 2009), subject: 'Joint Situation Centre products,' *OJ* 2011 C 10 E/39, 14 January 2011.

[45] Ireland's 'Comments on the Commission Green Paper "Diplomatic and Consular Protection of Union citizens in third countries"' (http://www.careproject.eu/database/upload/EIcomments/EIcommentsText.pdf, accessed 12 February 2012).

7.4.2 The Mitigation Phase

After having identified a predictable disaster, it is essential to develop a mitigation phase which renders the respondent member States ready to act if and when the emergency actually occurs. Problem solving requires planning interventions and mobilization of suitable resources for temporary sheltering of injured persons, for their evacuation to safe areas and for rescue operations. Being aware that good planning is essential in order to make the relief phase effective, the diplomatic and consular missions of the member States in a third country co-operate in drawing up shared contingency plans before a possible crisis.[46]

In this way, the represented EU countries exchange their emergency plans in order to establish joint and more efficient procedures, such as drawing up the instructions that EU citizens must follow when the disaster occurs and deciding in which locations supplies and resources will be available.[47] Moreover, the States can make common emergency drills,[48] since practical exercises and the communication of some aspects of the plan will allow EU citizens to learn how they should behave. This is probably the reason why the Finnish embassy in Greece sent a plan with instructions to follow in case of a crisis to its own nationals who were living in Greece and Albania at the time.[49] As part of the EU consular cooperation, Denmark and Austria released advice to be followed by EU citizens in case of a major crisis (natural disaster, plane crash or bus accident) in Bhutan.[50]

The Council guidelines strive as much as possible to improve this coordination during the mitigation phase since they advise the Heads of the diplomatic and consular missions in third countries to schedule at least one meeting every 3 months in order to discuss issues that may be a threat to the safety of EU citizens.[51]

Obviously, the necessity to point out the critical aspects of the procedures in order to have validated protocols suggests exercise studies based on a hypothetical scenario according to which evacuation plans and operations are tested with the coordination of the consular authorities.[52]

---

[46] Council of the European Union, Guidelines on consular protection of EU citizens in third countries, *supra* footnote 23, 3, para 6.

[47] Ibid., 6, para 12.3.

[48] Ibid., 6, paras 12.1 and 12.4.

[49] Written question E-2133/08 by G. Georgiou to the Council (15 April 2008), subject: 'Crisis evacuation plan for Finnish citizens,' *OJ* 2009 C 40/14, 18 February 2009.

[50] http://bhutan.um.dk/en/travel-and-residence/emergency-advice, accessed 28 February 2012.

[51] Council of the European Union, Guidelines on consular protection of EU citizens in third countries, *supra* footnote 23, 4, para 9.1.

[52] Council of the European Union, EU Evacuation Operation Exercise Study (EVAC 06) 5 April 2006, Press Release, 8093/06, Brussels, 3 April 2006.

7.4.3 The Relief Phase

The member States' information cannot predict the sudden outbreak of an unexpected crisis or disaster such as a natural or technological catastrophe, nor a sudden popular riot or a coup d'état. In these events, it is hard for a person in distress to quickly obtain any information concerning the presence of their own diplomatic and consular authorities in the territory of a third country. Therefore, many governments have taken national initiatives in order to update the general public. For instance, the Italian Ministry of Foreign Affairs activated an operational telephone exchange which can be contacted everyday from Italy or abroad.[53] In the same way, the Netherlands established a Crisis Telephone Team in The Hague which 'offers a rapid, organized response to telephone calls from potential victims of crises and their family members'.[54] However, a mere telephonic support might not be sufficient to assist people in difficulty, even if it is also essential at the beginning of the crisis to respond efficiently and to share information with other member States in order to successfully assist EU citizens.

For this reason, the Council guidelines suggest to improve the quality of the intervention by easing the flow of acquired information during a disaster through the *Correspondance Européenne* (COREU), by sending e-mails and using the Consular On Line (CoOL) website.[55] Sometimes the responsibility of organizing information sharing is carried out by the Presidency-in-office of the EU together with the incoming Presidency and the EU delegation within the affected third country.[56] In this context, the member States can also choose to collect resources to handle relations with the press and media.[57]

A relevant form of consular assistance in responding fully to a crisis situation is the evacuation of EU citizens from the places where the disaster has occurred.

In individual cases, Article 23 TFEU does not limit the possibility for unrepresented EU citizens to choose the member State's missions to which they should address since it does not seem logical to limit a citizens' fundamental right with an additional condition that is not provided for within the provision. On the contrary, organizational reasons impose fixing certain rules which determine in advance which EU country must intervene in a situation of crisis involving a large number of EU citizens. For instance, the representatives of a member State might be designated to carry out the evacuation in a certain area or appointed to be

[53] http://www.viaggiaresicuri.mae.aci.it/index.php?62, accessed 12 February 2012.

[54] Jones-Bos and Daalen van 2008, 91.

[55] Council of the European Union, Guidelines on consular protection of EU citizens in third countries, *supra* footnote 23, 8, para 14.1. Also recital 13 of the draft Directive on consular protection, *supra* footnote 16, points out the importance of 'the secure website of the European External Action Service (Consular On-Line).'

[56] Joint framework for EU cooperation and coordination in relation to emergencies in Japan, *supra* footnote 26, 2.

[57] Ibid., 3.

responsible for a specific assembly point. These arrangements enable the saving of public resources, but they have the drawback of making it extremely difficult for the EU citizens involved to know which State is responsible for the evacuation.[58] This problem was, in part, overcome by inviting the EU citizens living in a third country to indicate their address, to give their consent for the diffusion of their personal data to other member States and to receive communication on the assembly points as well as on the procedure established in case of an evacuation.[59] The information collected allows the represented member States to be aware of the number of EU citizens living in the different areas of a third country. However, practical problems may arise when individuals who are temporarily present on the territory are not advised of the member State responsible, having not previously informed their national State about their travel plans. In these cases, they have to find out which member State is able to give adequate information on action plans from within the territory. In every case, the missions of the member States can use both the media and local contacts to alert all EU citizens in the affected third nation. Recently, Britain and France assumed this behavior during the June 2011 outburst of violence in Yemen, urging Europeans to leave the country immediately.[60]

Evidently, no rules can be established to determine the State which is responsible for providing emergency assistance to EU citizens as the decision depends on the actual local circumstances and the agreement among the member States.

7.4.3.1 The Role of the EU Presidency

The State holding the Presidency of the Union has an important function in co-ordinating a response to the crisis, since it holds the Chair of the EU Consular Working Group (COCON). For instance, Hungary, as the State holding the rotating Presidency, played a key role in allowing EU citizens to leave Libya safely after the 2011 civil war,[61] as did the Netherlands during the Asian

---

[58] The proposal for a Directive on consular protection, *supra* footnote 16, points out at 4 the necessity to 'clarif[y] which Member State has to assist an unrepresented EU citizen and how assistance is to be coordinated with the citizen's Member State of nationality. This lack of clarity causes delays and does not safeguard efficient protection under the same conditions as for nationals.'

[59] Council of the European Union, Guidelines on consular protection of EU citizens in third countries, *supra* footnote 23, 12, Annex III.

[60] EU to coordinate evacuation of citizens from Yemen: Ashton, *EUbusiness*, 3 June 2011. Article 15(1) of the draft Directive on consular protection, *supra* footnote 16, affirms that member States 'shall agree on respective tasks to (...) inform unrepresented citizens on crisis preparedness arrangements under the same conditions as nationals.'

[61] Irish Department of Foreign Affairs and Trade, Taoiseach praises successful evacuation of Irish citizens from Libya, 2 March 2011 (http://www.dfa.ie/home/index.aspx?id=86575, accessed 12 February 2012).

tsunami.[62] However, this function might be excessive for the small member States which do not have many resources or do not possess an extensive diplomatic and consular network. The absence of a representative of the Presidency in a particular third country can allow the assigning of duties of the Presidency to the member State 'next in line' or by rotation among the represented EU countries.[63] According to this rule, in 2008, French diplomatic missions held the local Presidency of the EU in 110 third countries on behalf of Slovenia,[64] which is currently represented in only 20 nations outside the Union.[65]

Even large member States can meet with difficulties in a period in which the EU Presidency has to face a large number of emergencies. This situation might be more and more frequent in the future considering that the 'annual number of disasters has increased fivefold from 78 in 1975 to nearly 400 today [2010]'.[66] To give an idea of just how a single State can be overloaded it can be pointed out that the Finnish Presidency (July–December 2006) had to respond 'to such crises as the Lebanon evacuations (July and August); Turkey bombings (August); a military coup in Thailand (September); and an earthquake (…) in Japan (November)'.[67] One may wonder whether the effort requested from Finland to assist the EU citizens involved was proportionate to its available means in those territories. Only the Finnish State could answer this question. This rationale could be the basis of the EU guidelines, according to which the Presidency is the main body in charge of deciding whether the support of the EU delegation is necessary to improve national capacities.[68] In this way, the EEAS could also play a key role since Article 5(10) of Council Decision 2010/427[69] affirms that '[t]he Union delegations shall, (…) upon request by Member States, support the Member States in their role of providing consular protection to citizens of the Union in third countries'. Besides

[62] European Commission mobilises the Civil Protection Mechanism for victims of the earthquake and tsunami in South Asia, IP/04/1543, Brussels, 27 December 2004.

[63] Determining the representation of the Presidency in Third Countries (Noted by the Council of 19 December 2006—Doc. 16568/06) in Council of the European Union, 'CFSP Guide'– compilation of relevant texts, Doc. 16074/1/06 REV 1, Brussels, 21 March 2007, 9, para 5.

[64] http://ambafrance-gh.org/spip.php?Article910, accessed 12 February 2012.

[65] http://ec.europa.eu/consularprotection/search.action, accessed 12 February 2012.

[66] European Commission, Communication from the Commission to the European Parliament and the Council, Towards a stronger European disaster response: the role of civil protection and humanitarian assistance, *supra* footnote 11, 3. For an analysis of the trend of disasters, see Chap. 21 by Donini in this volume.

[67] WorldReach Software Newsletter, Consularis, April 2007, Coordinating consular response on behalf of the Council of the European Union, 1.

[68] Council of the European Union, Guidelines on consular protection of EU citizens in third countries, *supra* footnote 23, 17, para 2.2.

[69] Council Decision 2010/427/EU of 26 July 2010 establishing the organisation and functioning of the European External Action Service, *OJ* 2010 L 201/30-40, 3 August 2010, 30.

the logistical support of the EU delegations, the SITCEN can also provide staff (1 or 2 persons) to assist the Presidency in local management.[70]

The joint action of the member States and EU institutions can be summarized by the data which emerged during the recent crisis in Libya, where the efforts of the consular missions were supported by SITCEN, which monitors and assesses the situation in real time, also thanks to the imagery provided from the EU Satellite Center (EUSC), from the EU Military Staff (EUMS)[71] and from the Monitoring, and Information Center (MIC) for the practical aspects related to the evacuation.[72] The involvement of several agencies is not surprising since '[b]oth EU institutions and member states have used agency creation to demonstrate political will and decisiveness, especially in the wake of disasters and emergencies confronting the EU'.[73]

7.4.3.2 The 'Lead State'

Some member States could come up against problems when assisting EU citizens even with the support of the local EU delegation and the SITCEN staff, due to the lack of experience to manage a certain crisis or delicate relations with the authorities of the affected country.[74]

To overcome these problems, it would be better to adopt a flexible solution in determining the assisting State, instead of rigidly imposing this duty without considering the means available to protect distressed EU citizens. However, at the same time certain rules must exist, as otherwise determining the country in charge of offering assistance would be excessively uncertain.

For this reason, the Council introduced the notion of 'Lead State', suggesting with this term that this country would carry out coordination functions in situations of consular crisis[75] and offer protection to all the individuals entitled to consular

---

[70] Council of the European Union, Guidelines on consular protection of EU citizens in third countries, *supra* footnote 23, 17, para 2.2.

[71] Council Decision 2011/210/CFSP of 1 April 2011 on a European Union military operation in support of humanitarian assistance operation in response to the crisis situation in Libya (EUFOR Libya), *OJ* 2011 L 89/17-20, 5 April 2011.

[72] European Commission, Developments in Libya: an overview of the EU's response, 10 March 2011 (http://ec.europa.eu/news/external_relations/110310_1_en.htm, accessed 12 February 2012).

[73] Groenleer 2009, 103.

[74] In the case of a breach of diplomatic relations, the EU countries usually delegate the protection of their interests in a third nation to a second member State. Non-member States are invited to act as protecting Power only when the breach involves all the member States, as happened during the 1998 NATO airstrikes in Serbia when Brazil was asked to provide assistance to British nationals [Roberts (ed) 2010, 408, para 27.15].

[75] Council of the European Union, Stocktaking Report on the implementation of measures to increase the efficiency, coherence and visibility of EU external policies, and future work, Doc. 15822/1/06 REV 1, Brussels, 5 December 2006, 13; Council of the European Union, Reinforcing the European Union's emergency and crisis response capacities, Doc. 16642/06, Brussels, 12 December 2006, 6, para 16.

assistance from a member State.[76] The concept of 'Lead State' was applied for the first time in February 2008, in Chad.[77] In this case, France—which was one of the two represented member States in the African country—evacuated more than 1,200 citizens from 12 member States and also third country nationals,[78] thus proving the willingness to effectively apply Articles 23 TFEU and 35 TEU during crisis situations.

Despite this successful application of consular protection, a problem derives from the fact that it is unclear which basic criteria to use in order to determine the member State that will hold this position in advance. Even the European Parliament questioned the Council to gain clarification on the matter due to the need to ensure 'that the more frequently represented embassies or consulates of certain (larger) Member States are not overburdened compared with Member States that are less often represented abroad'.[79] This issue was not merely hypothetical, since it is not incidental that France had to evacuate a large number of EU citizens during the Presidency of a small State like Slovenia. Nevertheless, the problem does not seem to have been clarified by the reply of the Council, which pointed out that:

> 'the role of the Lead State is voluntary and requires the active support and participation of all Member States. The criteria for determining which Member State will take the lead in any third country will be established by the Member States on a case-by-case basis, depending, inter alia, on local conditions. Member States will ensure that an appropriate share of the burden is allotted to each mission present in that third country'.[80]

Even in this context, the EU Presidency seems involved since '[t]he Lead State concept provides for coordination by the Lead State, in consultation with the Presidency-in-office'.[81]

It is unquestionable that, during the relief phase, the 'Lead State' is responsible for the evacuation operations taking EU citizens, even if represented, to a safe

---

[76] Council of the European Union, European Union guidelines on the implementation of the consular Lead State concept, *OJ* 2008 C 317/6-8, 12 December 2008, 6, para 3.1. The absence of a strict reference to 'EU citizens' implies that the beneficiaries of the assistance can be also third country nationals who are long-term residents or family members of a EU citizen when the rules of the member State of residence assure them consular assistance (Vermeer-Künzli 2011, 979).

[77] Council of the European Union, Stocktaking report: Measures to increase the effectiveness, coherence, and visibility of EU external policies, Doc. 10612/08, Brussels, 13 June 2008, 10.

[78] Slovenian Presidency of the EU 2008, Evacuation of EU citizens from Chad and application of the consular Lead State concept, Press Release, 11 February 2008 (http://www.eu2008.si/en/News_and_Documents/Press_Releases/February/0211MZZ_Chad.html, accessed 12 February 2012).

[79] Written question E-2865/07 by S. Kaufmann to the Council (5 June 2007), subject: 'Consular and diplomatic protection of Union citizens in third countries—the concept of lead nation,' *OJ* 2008 C 45/138, 16 February 2008.

[80] Reply on 27 September 2007 to the written question E-2865/07 by S. Kaufmann to the Council, *OJ* 2008 C 45/138, 16 February 2008. Even the draft Directive on consular protection, *supra* footnote 16, does not clarify this matter, as Article 16 does not include criteria able to determine the 'Lead State.'

[81] Ibid.

place without having the obligation to accompany them to any other country.[82] The practice confirms that the statement is applied, as shown by the case in Chad.

The solidarity of the member States is not limited to EU citizens as emerged in a resolution of the European Parliament[83] and recently confirmed by the Hungarian action that repatriated nearly 200 Chadian citizens blocked in Libya[84] and also by Greece which transported Chinese and Egyptians from Tripoli to a safe area.[85]

Sometimes, the consular cooperation on crisis management is founded on a reciprocal basis to the advantage of both EU citizens and third country nationals. This joint assistance is evident considering that China helped to evacuate nearly 500 EU citizens from Libya[86] 3 days after the assistance of Greece in favor of Chinese nationals. This cooperation with third countries has not recently started with the uprisings in North Africa, since it was far back considered as a means to improve the probabilities of success.[87] This mutual help was already implemented during the terrorist attacks in Sharm-El-Sheikh and Bali and the crisis in Lebanon, wherein the EU evacuated US nationals and the USA evacuated EU citizens.[88]

7.4.4 The Recovery Phase

Finally, the recovery phase involves the evaluation of the results achieved through the consular cooperation in crisis management, thus giving the EU and the member States the opportunity to learn from their successes and failures. Hence, the diplomatic and consular services can review all the procedures identifying and correcting the weaknesses in the measures for the protection of EU citizens.

---

[82] Ibid.

[83] European Parliament, Resolution on the situation in Congo-Brazzaville, *OJ* 1997 C 200/180, 30 June 1997. The English version underlines that 'France has sent 800 soldiers to reinforce its troops in Brazzaville to protect French citizens,' but other linguistic (e.g., French, Italian, German and Spanish) versions affirm that the rescue operation was done in order to protect aliens.

[84] Hungarian Presidency of the Council of the European Union, Libya: Chadians repatriated with Hungarian assistance, 29 April 2011 (http://www.eu2011.hu/news/libya-chadians-repatriated-hungarian-assistance, accessed 12 February 2012).

[85] Greece sends ships to evacuate Chinese, Europeans, and Egyptians from Libya, *Keep Talking Greece*, 22 February 2011 (http://www.keeptalkinggreece.com/2011/02/22/greece-sends-ships-to-evacuate-chinese-europeans-and-egyptians-from-libya/, accessed 12 February 2012).

[86] European states evacuate nationals from Libya, *China Daily*, 25 February 2011 (http://www.chinadaily.com.cn/world/2011-02/25/content_12075158.htm/, accessed 12 February 2012).

[87] Rodt and Wolff 2008, 269.

[88] Ministry for Foreign Affairs of Finland, EU troika, and US ready to increase cooperation in consular crisis management, 5 October 2006 (http://formin.finland.fi/public/Print.aspx?contentid=81583&nodeid=15148&culture=en-US&contentlan=2, accessed 12 February 2012). The participation of non-EU States is formalized in treaties, as shown, for instance, by the recent agreements with USA (*OJ* 2011 L 143/2-6, 31 May 2011) and Serbia (*OJ* 2011 L 163/2-7, 23 June 2011).

Obviously, the recovery phase is not limited to internal scrutiny given that the critical analysis from the media,[89] the European Parliament,[90] the national Parliaments[91] and scholarly comments[92] can inform the public about any failures in the action.

7.5 Conclusion

According to the practice, the member States are generally willing to co-operate when disasters affect a third country in which EU citizens live or travel. This evidence seems to confirm the interpretation, according to which Article 23 TFEU could guarantee the same consular services that EU citizens could obtain from their own national States, which then allows the member States to reduce public expenses.[93] In fact, a member State could rely on this form of protection to close a diplomatic or consular mission in a third country.

Nevertheless, this reflection does not consider that an embassy constitutes the symbol of a State abroad and its closing might be interpreted by the nationals of that country as a lack of interest towards them in case they ever need help. In fact, the distressed EU citizens, when assisted by a member State other than that of their own nationality, are grateful for the protection received, however, once home, will complain about the absence of their national country.[94] Moreover, the member States have difficulties in delegating the representation of their nationals to the Presidency or to the 'Lead State' since they fear that the diplomats of some member States might be more inclined to protect the interests of their nationals rather than assisting all EU citizens without any discrimination.

Another problem is that an effective European solidarity in consular cooperation is destined to foster the small member States with a limited number of diplomatic and consular missions, thus exploiting the resources of the most represented EU countries. This observation is confirmed by the practice showing

---

[89] Egypt and the mirage of European unity, *Warsaw Business Journal*, 15 February 2011 (http://www.stratfor.com/other_voices/20110215-egypt-and-mirage-european-unity/, accessed 12 February 2012).

[90] Debates, Wednesday 4 February 2009, Strasbourg, 13. Consular protection of citizens of the European Union in third countries, *supra* footnote 38.

[91] French Senate, Written question n° 823 by Mr R. Yung, subject: 'Coopération européenne en matière de protection consulaire,' *JO Sénat*, 12 July 2007/1225.

[92] See *inter alia* Hyde-Price 2002, 57, who emphasizes 'the failure of EU Member States to take common action during the Albanian crisis of April-August 1997.' The scholar refers to operation 'Alba' 'spearheaded by Italy, leading a multinational force' (European Parliament, Resolution on the role the Union in the world: implementation of the common foreign and security policy for 1997, *OJ* 1998 C 195/35, 22 June 1998).

[93] Koslowski 2000, 122–123.

[94] Porzio 2008, 95.

that 'France, Germany and the United Kingdom are the three countries most often appointed as Lead States'.[95] On the other hand, it is difficult to reallocate assistance functions, since the less represented EU countries are definitely not interested in increasing the number of their representations, as long as they can lean on the missions of the most represented States.

These complaints could be overcome by the evolution of the external dimension of EU citizenship. This development is not a mere hypothesis. In fact, the importance of the protection actions in favor of EU citizens during disasters could weaken the link which binds the individuals to the national State, allowing the EU to become a reference point for distressed citizens in third countries. Hence, the EU would be perceived as being closer to individuals, increasing the sense of belonging to the Union.

During crisis situations, the absence of international agreements with third countries to assure consular protection to EU citizens does not prevent the enforcement of Article 23 TFEU since the exercise of the delegated consular assistance does not require the explicit consent of the receiving State.[96] The lack of objections is not surprising. Third countries affected by a disaster are inclined to accept the intervention of the EU and therefore they do not oppose if member States assist also EU citizens that are not their nationals. Moreover, the consular protection during emergencies, on the basis of Article 23 TFEU, does not affect the national interests of non-EU countries.[97]

The full attention of the member States towards EU citizens could push through the recognition of EU citizenship by the third countries. The well-established enforcement of Article 23 TFEU during crisis could determine the recognition of the competence of each member State in offering assistance to each and every EU citizen, as well as solving routine problems of individuals in normal situations.[98] If accepted, this broad interpretation of Article 23 TFEU would allow the literal meaning of the provision to be surmounted, removing the condition that requires the absence of the diplomatic and consular missions of the national State. This approach would assure an effective implementation of the non-discrimination principle, thus preventing episodes like the behavior of the German mission in the Mumbai affair in future situations.

---

[95] Lindström 2009, 117.

[96] 1963 *Vienna Convention on Consular Relations*, Article 8: 'Upon appropriate notification to the receiving State, a consular post of the sending State may, unless the receiving State objects, exercise consular functions in the receiving State on behalf of a third State.' See also International Law Commission, Protection of persons in the event of disasters, Texts of draft Articles 10 and 11 provisionally adopted by the Drafting Committee on 19 July 2011, UN Doc. A/CN.4/L.794, 20 July 2011, Article 10(2) according to which the '[c]onsent to external assistance shall not be withheld arbitrarily.'

[97] Stein 2002, 34.

[98] Szczekalla 1999, 331.

References

Battini S (2011) The impact of EU law and globalization on consular assistance and diplomatic protection. In: Chiti E, Mattarella BG (eds) Global administrative law and EU administrative law relationships Legal issues and comparison. Springer, Berlin, pp 173–186

Bulleit WM, Drewek MW (2011) Agent-based simulation for human-induced hazard analysis. Risk Anal 31:205–216

Closa C (1992) The concept of citizenship in the treaty of European Union. CMLRev 29:1137–1169

Economidès C (1992) Consuls. In: Bernhardt (ed), Encyclopedia of Public International Law, vol. I, North-Holland, Amsterdam, London, New York ,Tokyo, 770–776

Groenleer M (2009) The autonomy of European Union agencies. Eburon, Delft

Hyde-Price A (2002) Decision-making under the second pillar. In: Arnull A, Wincott D (eds) Accountability and legitimacy in the European Union. Oxford University Press, New York, pp 41–62

Jones-Bos R, van Daalen M (2008) Trends and developments in consular services: the dutch experience. The Hague J Dipl 3:87–92

King SA, Adib HR, Drobny J, Buchanan J (2003) Earthquake and terrorism risk assessment: Similarities and differences. In: Beavers JE (ed), Proceedings of the 6th US conference and workshop on lifeline earthquake engineering, American Society of Civil Engineering, Reston, 789–798

Koslowski R (2000) Migrants and citizens: demographic change in the European state system. Cornell University Press, Ithaca

Lindström M (2009) EU consular cooperation in crisis situations. In: Olsson S (ed) Crisis management in the European Union. Spinger, Berlin, pp 109–126

Naghdi K, Mansourian A, Valadanzoej MJ, Saadatseresht M (2008) Evacuation planning in earthquake disasters, using RS & GIS, in International Archives of the Photogrammetry, Remote Sensing and Spatial Information Sciences, vol 24, Part B4, 1671–1676

O'Leary S (1992) Nationality Law and Community citizenship: a tale of two uneasy bedfellows, 12 Yearbook of European Law, 353–384

Porzio G (2008) Consular assistance and protection: an EU perspective. The Hague J Dipl 3: 93–97

Quarantelli EL (1988) Disaster crisis management: a summary of research findings. J Manag Stud 25:373–385

Roberts I (ed) (2010) Satow's diplomatic practice, 6th edn. Oxford University Press, New York

Rodt AP, Wolff S (2008) The EU and the management of ethnic conflict, in Institutions for the management of ethnopolitical conflict in central and eastern Europe. Council of Europe Publishing, Strasbourg, pp 245–271

Slovic P (2002) Terrorism as hazard: a new species of trouble. Risk Anal 22:425–426

Stein T (2002) Interim report on 'Diplomatic protection under the European Union Treaty', in International Law Association, New Delhi Conference, 32–39

Szczekalla P (1999) Die Pflicht der Gemeinschaft und der Mitgliedstaaten zum diplomatischen und konsularischen Schutz. Europarecht 34:325–342

Vermeer-Künzli A (2011) Where the law becomes irrelevant: consular assistance and the European Union. Int Comp Law Q 60:965–995

Part III
Rights and Duties of States

Chapter 8
The Prevention of Natural and Man-Made Disasters: What Duties for States?

Barbara Nicoletti

Abstract Prevention within IDRL is both a well-accepted concept which permeates politically relevant soft law documents and a specific obligation based on bilateral and multilateral treaties. However, the experience of the concept and the practice of prevention in IDRL is too limited in time to have reached the level of sophistication which the same concept has reached in international environmental law (IEL) and to allow for both establishing a general duty of prevention and spelling out its specific contents. Although the reference to IEL is indispensable in order to identify whether and how the content of the prevention obligation in this area can be relevant for the affirmation of a general duty to disaster prevention, other branches of international law are contributing to the progressive expansion of the scope of application of the duty to prevent disasters.

Keywords IDRL · Disaster prevention · Duty to prevent · Prevention principle · International environmental law · Right to life · Development planning

Contents

B. Nicoletti (✉)
Scuola Superiore Sant'Anna, Piazza Martiri della Libertà, 33, 56127, Pisa, Italy
e-mail: b.nicoletti@sssup.it

A. de Guttry et al. (eds.), *International Disaster Response Law*,
DOI: 10.1007/978-90-6704-882-8_8,

8.1 Introduction

The main set of current projects on IDRL has been prioritizing the evaluation of the dispersed body of existing international and national norms relating to disaster relief and response in view of its systematization. Still the concern for prevention soon started to emerge, especially for those categories of disasters brought on or exacerbated by human activities, in which a causal link between the disaster and previous environmental degradation could easily be identified. In such cases, the emergence of international duties under international environmental law (IEL) has helped the identification of the obligation on States to prevent that environmental damage is produced in neighboring countries. More recently, State responsibility to prevent disasters also in the face of its own citizens has been affirmed by invoking that State failure to take feasible measures to prevent or mitigate the consequences of foreseeable disasters amounts to a violation of the right to life. The concept of disaster prevention has also been used for the identification of comprehensive development policies in which risk management practices have been judged an essential part of sustainable development.

This contribution aims at investigating the relevance of the concept of prevention within international disaster response law (IDRL), and the importance that prevention has assumed in the systematization of IDRL as an autonomous *corpus juris*. The pursued objective is that of trying to identify the elements of an autonomous general duty for States to put in place preventive measures in order to avoid disasters or mitigate their effects. In order to do this, the discussion on the concept of prevention and its operationalization in IEL will be paired with the analysis of more recent trends which affirm the relevance of prevention for the purposes of international development and human rights law.

8.2 Prevention as a Principle of International Law

Prevention is a well-established principle of IEL[1] that has gradually affirmed itself as the consciousness about the need to secure the protection of the environment gradually emerged. In the words of the International Law Commission (ILC) 'the principle of prevention is known to international law' and it '[i]nvolves an obligation to act in a setting where the imperative to do so is not necessarily present'.[2] Although the expression 'known to international law' does not exclusively attach the principle to the specific environmental law sector, the principle of prevention has only recently started to be discussed for its relevance in domains of international law outside the environmental sector, and precisely in the ambit of the branch of IDRL which is in the process of consolidation.

In fact, it was the advent of IEL in the second half of the twentieth century that brought about the acknowledgment of the concept of prevention, which firstly inspired normative action at the international level with regard to industrial disasters.[3] However, well before the need for an international legal regime for the protection of the environment was recognized, the principle of prevention predominantly served the interests of international law to regulate the consequences of transboundary catastrophes, mainly in terms of State responsibility. The principle of prevention that is mentioned as a 'well-established principle' by the ILC is in fact the principle which inspired case and treaty laws aimed at the identification of liability of States for hazardous—although not prohibited—activities spreading their consequences on the territory of other States. However, as it is clearly pointed out by Romano, 'l'obligation de prévention n'est pas uniquement la base servant a apprécier la responsabilité *ex post facto*. Il s'agit à l'heure actuelle d'une obligation ben définie et autonome de prévention et de contrôle diligents'.[4] We will see whether this latter affirmation holds true by looking at how the foundations of the prevention principle have expanded over time.

---

[1] For a discussion on the principle of prevention, see Judge Cançado Trinidade separate opinion on ICJ, *Case Concerning Pulp Mills on the River Uruguay*, Judgment, 20 April 2010. Available at http://www.icj-cij.org/docket/files/135/15885.pdf. Accessed 8 February 2012.

[2] UN Doc. A/CN.4/590 (2007), ILC, Memorandum of the Secretariat, Protection of persons in the event of disasters, 24.

[3] International action on the prevention of natural disasters developed mainly after the launch of the International Decade on Natural Disaster Reduction by the Assembly General Resolution 44/263 of 22 December 1989.

[4] Romano 2001, 279.

8.2.1 *The Principle of Prevention in the Stockholm Declaration of 1972*

It is commonly held that the concept of prevention finds its first pronouncement in Principle 21 of the 1972 Declaration of the United Nations Conference on the Human Environment (usually referred to as the Stockholm Declaration) that reads:

'States have, in accordance with the Charter of the United Nations and principles of international law, the sovereign right to exploit their own resources pursuant to their own environmental policies, and the responsibility to ensure that activities within their jurisdiction or control do not cause damage to the environment of other States or of areas beyond the limits of national jurisdiction'.[5]

Despite its collocation within a Declaration that has been referred to as the 'foundation of modern international environmental law'[6] and despite being invoked by many as the codification of the principle of prevention in international law, Principle 21 seems to reveal a stronger preoccupation for States' traditional 'interests' than for the preservation of the environment and the prevention of harmful consequences of polluting activities as such. By looking at the two distinct parts which make up Principle 21, the primary aim seems to be the affirmation, on the one hand, of the sovereign right of the State to exploit its natural resources and, on the other hand, the affirmation of its responsibility to respect the territorial integrity of other States while enjoying this right. Building upon the principle according to which the use of one's own property cannot injure that of another, reaffirmed by both the Trail Smelter Arbitration of 1941 and the ICJ's pronouncement on the Corfu Channel Case (1949),[7] Principle 21 roots the duty to prevent transboundary harms into the idea of territorial integrity, although it offers entry points for forward looking.[8]

8.2.2 *The Evolution of the Principle from Stockholm to Rio*

The United Nations Conference on Environment and Development that was organized in Rio in 1992 as the natural follow-up to Stockholm was much more

[5] UN Doc. A/CONF.48/14&Corr. 1 (1973), UN Declaration on the Human Environment, June 16, 1972, Principle 21.

[6] Vessey 1998, 184.

[7] *Trail Smelter Case*, International Arbitral Award, 16 April 1938 and 11 March 1941, Part Three and ICJ, *Corfu Channel Case*, Judgment, 9 April 1949, 22.

[8] The Principle includes a concern for the environment as such, with no State-related connotations when it places upon the States the responsibility to ensure that no harm comes to 'areas beyond the limits of national jurisdiction' (that is areas such as the atmosphere, deep see, and Antarctica).

focused on development than on the environment. As a consequence, the whole Declaration is permeated with developmental concerns, which also reverberate on Principle 2 devoted to prevention. Although the enunciation of the Stockholm Principle 21 was only slightly changed by adding the reference to developmental policies in its first clause, the very presence in the Declaration of an article devoted to its reformulation signaled, according to Vessey, the discontinuity in the development of law along those lines identified in Stockholm, despite the non-binding nature of the Declaration itself and the principles contained therein. Furthermore, for those who spouse the view according to which the Stockholm Principle 21 (and by extension Rio Principle 2) is made up of two reciprocally balancing clauses,[9] the Rio reformulation of the prevention principle 'alters the nature of one side of the scale'[10] and gives more opportunities for 'overemphasizing resource exploitation at the expense of the environment of foreign states'.[11] According to this view, rather than expanding the scope of prevention for the purposes of sustainable development promotion, the new formulation seems to put greater restraints on the opportunity to invoke a violation of the duty to prevent transboundary harms, by including the pursuit of developmental policies among the factors which exclude State responsibility.

Since the Rio formulation, ambiguities over the interpretation of the Prevention Principle have not been eliminated. Although prevention is said to be a principle of international law, still uncertainty exists over the pre or post-Rio wording as well as with regard to the interpretation of the relationship between its two clauses; this jeopardizes the possibility to affirm an absolute standard of prevention for all States.[12]

8.3 Prevention Within the International Instruments on Disaster Response

The idea of prevention—as one of the constituting elements of any effective strategy of response to disasters—imposed itself in the 1990s in the wake of the growing awareness of the devastating effects of natural disasters in terms of loss of lives, destruction, and missed opportunities for development.[13] As a consequence of the predominant attention which at that time was given to natural disasters, 'that

---

[9] In the sense that the State right to exploit its own resources is balanced by the obligation not to cause transboundary harm.

[10] Vessey 1998, 192.

[11] Ibid.

[12] In case the two clauses are considered as balancing each other, then the rights of the States to pursue environmental and developmental policies may lawfully temper the duty to prevent. On the contrary, in case they are separated, the second clause would impose an absolute standard of prevention.

[13] UNISDR 2004, 9 (vol. I).

extend beyond individual countries and recognize no single sovereignty' and for which 'the simple determination of causes and effects can prove very difficult',[14] 'prevention came to be conceived as a question of disaster risk management and reduction'.[15] Following the proclamation of the International Decade for Natural Disaster Reduction, the Yokohama Strategy for a Safer World adopted in 1994[16] testifies the international community's commitment to integrate prevention into a comprehensive strategy towards natural disasters.[17]

Principle 2 of the Yokohama Strategy affirms that '[d]isaster prevention and preparedness are of primary importance in reducing the need for disaster relief', while Principle 3 provides that '[d]isaster prevention and preparedness should be considered integral aspects of development policy and planning at national, regional, bilateral, multilateral and international levels for reducing disaster relief needs as well as for reducing the vulnerability of populations'. Furthermore, Principle 9 stresses the importance of the link between environmental protection, sustainable development and the prevention of natural disasters,[18] thus contributing to clarifying both the scope, and the content of the recommended preventive action.

Interestingly, Yokohama's Principle 10 places on each country 'the primary responsibility for protecting its people, infrastructure, and other national assets from the impact of natural disasters', and gives a primary role to national measures in the prevention of natural disasters. Although the scope of this Principle is affected by the non-binding nature of the Declaration in which it is contained, the relevance it may assume in the progressive identification of a widespread responsibility to implement mechanisms for disaster prevention cannot be ignored. The multi-level approach to prevention proposed—when this same Principle affirms that '[p]reventive measures are most effective when they involve participation at all levels from the local community through the national government to the regional and international level'[19]—might well be used to support the need for

---

[14] United Nations doc. A/CONF.206/L.I, Review of the Yokohama Strategy and Plan of Action for a Safer World, 6.

[15] United Nations, doc. A/CN.4/590, *supra* n. 2, 25. For a definition of Disaster Risk Reduction see Chap. 1 by de Guttry in this volume.

[16] Yokohama Strategy and Plan of Action for a Safer World. Guidelines for Natural Disaster Prevention, Preparedness and Mitigation World Conference on Natural Disaster Reduction Yokohama, Japan, 23–27 May 1994. Available at http://www.ifrc.org/Docs/idrl/I248EN.pdf. Accessed 21 February 2012

[17] 'Experience has demonstrated that, although not a part of the mandate of the Decade, the concept of disaster reduction should be enlarged to cover natural and other disaster situations including environmental and technological disasters (NaTechs) and their interrelationship which can have a significant impact on social, economic, cultural and environmental systems, in particular in developing countries'. Ibid., 8.

[18] Principle 9 states that '[e]nvironmental protection as a component of sustainable development consistent with poverty alleviation is imperative in the prevention and mitigation of natural disasters'.

[19] Principle 10, Yokohama Strategy and Plan of Action for a Safer World, *supra* n. 16.

complementary rules which are able to address both the international and the national/local dimensions of disaster prevention.

The principles enunciated in the Yokohama Strategy were transformed into a Plan of Action and then submitted to review in 2004. The Review, in particular, reconfirms the validity of the 'multisectoral and multi-stakeholder emphasis foreseen by the Yokohama Strategy'[20] and echoes the recommendation to not only take into consideration natural disasters, highlighting the 'need for greater attention to the interaction between natural and human-induced hazard' and the importance of a whole-of-risks approach, irrespective of the fact that triggering events are related to natural, human induced, environmental, or technological emergencies.[21]

The shift to a concept of disaster which encompasses disasters caused by hazards of natural origin and related environmental and technological hazards is clearly spelled out in the Preamble of the Hyogo Framework for Action 2005–2015 adopted at the World Conference on Disaster Reduction held at Kobe, Hyogo in January 2005. On this occasion, the significant reduction in losses of lives and social, economic, and environmental assets caused by disasters was identified as the objective to be achieved by 2015. In addition, prevention, mitigation, preparedness, and vulnerability reduction were proposed as instruments for integrating 'disaster risk considerations into sustainable development policies, planning and programming at all levels'.[22]

Besides these documents containing enunciations of principles and recommendations for action at the UN level, declarations supporting the strengthening of prevention and mitigation of risks and natural disasters have also been adopted at the regional level.[23] However, most of the existing multilateral legislative instruments dealing with the prevention of disasters have a non-binding nature. Only two are in fact the universal open treaties which have been concluded in the twentieth century, namely the ill-fated Convention and Statute Establishing an International Relief Union[24] and the 1998 Tampere Convention on the Provision of Telecommunication Resources for Disaster Mitigation and Relief Operations.

At the multilateral level, the 2000 Framework Convention on Civil Defence Assistance is, as reported by the ILC in the December 2007 Secretariat's

---

[20] United Nations doc. A/CONF.206/L.I, *supra* n. 14, 6.

[21] Ibid., 10.

[22] United Nations doc. A/CONF.206/6, Final Report of the World Conference on Disaster Reduction, 3. See more extensively on this Chap. 9 by La Vaccara in this volume.

[23] See the Declaration of Panama of 29 July 2005 by the Association of Caribbean States, para 20; the Busan Declaration of November 2005 by the 13th Asia–Pacific Economic Cooperation (APEC) Leaders' Meeting; The Dhaka Declaration on South Asia's Environmental Challenges and Natural Disasters of November 2005 by the 13th Summit of the South Asian Association for Regional Cooperation, paras 33–35; the Guatemala Declaration of October 1999 by the 20th Ordinary Meeting of the Presidents of Central America, the Dominican Republic and Belize.

[24] The International Relief Union was terminated in 1968 when the UNESCO took over. See Fidler 2005.

Memorandum, '[t]he closest contemporary global international convention dealing with the prevention and mitigation of disasters (including disaster risk reduction)',[25] in which prevention is pursued by means of the mutual assistance duty identified for the Civil Defence Services of the States Parties. Even in the Tampere Convention, cooperation among States and with non-state and intergovernmental organizations in the area of telecommunication in humanitarian assistance is required with the objective of implementing disaster mitigation measures as 'measures designed to prevent, predict, prepare for, respond to, monitor and/or mitigate the impact of disasters'.[26]

At the regional level too, the focus has also gradually shifted from the aspects of response to disasters to those of prevention and mitigation, as in the case of the 1999 Agreement between Member States and Associate Members of the Association of Caribbean States for Regional Cooperation on Natural Disasters; its objective is to establish 'a network of legally binding mechanisms that promote cooperation for prevention, mitigation and management of natural disasters'[27] and includes a specific provision on prevention and mitigation.[28] The requirement for the States Parties to 'give priority to prevention and mitigation, and thus to take precautionary measures to prevent, monitor and mitigate disasters',[29] is contained in the 2005 ASEAN Agreement on Disaster Management and Emergency Response. Here the States parties are called to co-operate in order to adopt preventive measures, such as the implementation of risk assessment activities, the development of legislative and other regulatory measures for the monitoring of hazards with transboundary effects, the exchange of information.[30] Furthermore, this same Agreement, like many other legal instruments dealing with the issues of disaster prevention and mitigation,[31] sets up its own institutional mechanism for the implementation of the specific duties of prevention and mitigation it provides for its States Parties.

Prevention is also a component of multilateral instruments dealing with man-made disasters. Prevention of industrial accidents is requested to States parties 'as far as possible', as in the 1992 Convention on Transboundary Effects of Industrial

---

[25] United Nations doc. A/CN.4/590, *supra* n. 2, 29.

[26] See Article 1 of the 1998 Tampere Convention on the Provision of Telecommunication Resources for Disaster Mitigation and Relief Operations.

[27] See Article 2 of the 1999 Agreement between Member States and Associate Members of the Association of Caribbean States for Regional Cooperation on Natural Disasters.

[28] Ibid., Article 8.

[29] See Article 3.4 of the 2005 ASEAN Agreement on Disaster Management and Emergency Response.

[30] Ibid., Article 4. Monitoring, assessment and early warning systems are mentioned among these measures.

[31] See the 2005 Additional Protocol to the Agreement among the governments of Participating States of the Black Sea Economic Cooperation on Collaboration in Emergency Assistance and Emergency Response to Natural and Man-made Disasters as well as the 2005 ASEAN Agreement on Disaster Management and Emergency Response.

Accidents,[32] or by means of 'all appropriate measures' as provided for by the 1993 ILO Prevention of Major Industrial Accidents Convention.[33] For example, instruments giving practical application to the obligation of prevention are identified in the adoption of legislation or guidelines on safety measures and standards, the identification of hazardous activities which require specific preventive actions, the assessment of risks, the provision of information to competent authorities, the application of the most appropriate technology.[34] In the same vein, specific indications of activities to be undertaken by member States in order to fulfill their prevention and preparedness obligations are contained in the decision establishing the EU Civil Protection Mechanism.[35]

As for the bilateral agreements with a prevention component, a number of these exist and they are usually mutual cooperation treaties, in many cases establishing technical cooperation on issues related to monitoring, early warning, and exchange of information in view of ensuring mutual assistance in the event of disasters and the prevention of the same.[36]

This brief overview on how the issue of prevention has been addressed by both soft law and binding international legal instruments shows the growing political commitment to the prevention of the devastating effects of disasters as well as the efforts to practically regulate those specific areas in which prevention can more appropriately be operationalized. Unlike the process through which the principle of prevention initially affirmed itself within IEL, prevention in IDRL has been more willingly accepted as an operational concept to be used within binding legislative instruments; from the very beginning prevention has been intended as a set of mechanisms of national and international relevance, whose adoption must be ensured by means of inclusion in binding bilateral and multilateral instruments.

In the following paragraphs an attempt will be made to identify the content of a general duty of prevention which could be adopted within IDRL as the basis for taking preventive action in the face of any kind of disaster, irrespective of both its nature and the existence of specific treaties regulating states' response to it. In this effort, the reference to IEL will be indispensable in order to identify when and how the content of the prevention obligation in this area can be relevant for the affirmation of a general duty to disaster prevention. Actually, the provisions contained within the above-analyzed declarations and agreements do not make explicit

[32] See Article 3 of the Convention.

[33] See the Preamble of the Convention.

[34] These are only a few of the instruments listed in Annex IV to the abovementioned 1992 Convention on Transboundary Effects of Industrial Accidents.

[35] Among these activities we find training, monitoring, the establishment of emergency communication, and information systems. See Council Decision of 8 November 2007 establishing a Community Civil Protection Mechanism, 2007/779/EC, Euratom. OJ L 314, 01/12/2007. On the issue see Chap. 5 by Gestri in this volume.

[36] For a selection of bilateral treaties specifically devoted to disaster prevention and preparedness or including significant aspects of prevention see UN doc. A/CN.4/590, *supra* n. 2, 33.

reference to the existence of a general obligation of prevention, as instead is the case in IEL. This circumstance seems to tell us about the perception of prevention as a general consolidated principle (whose reaffirmation is not deemed to be needed) rather than tell us about the recognition of the inapplicability of the environmental law experience to the area of disaster response. However, in addition to strong environmental influences, other branches of international law are contributing to the progressive expansion of the scope of application of the duty to prevent disasters.[37]

8.4 The Content of the Duty to Prevent in International Environmental Law and Corollary Obligations: Between State Sovereignty and Environmental Protection

The principle of prevention permeates legislative instruments—multilateral conventions and bilateral agreements—as well as jurisprudence within IEL. The obligation of prevention is mentioned in many international instruments on the protection of the environment and according to the ICJ, 'in the field of environmental protection, vigilance and prevention are required on account of the often irreversible character of damage to the environment and of the limitations inherent in the very mechanism of reparation of this type of damage'.[38]

As explained above, the duty of prevention was born mainly out of the need to manage the consequences of hazardous activities outside the territory of a State in terms of State liability, in situations in which the possibility of identifying the causal links between human activities and environmental damages existed.

The preventive principle has later been used within treaties devoted to the protection of the environment in general, in order 'to avoid harm irrespective of whether or not there are transboundary impacts'.[39] However, the project of ILC Draft Articles, which was adopted in 2001, testifies that the issue of prevention of transboundary harms has provided an important corpus of accepted norms on which the General Assembly could accomplish its task of 'encouraging the progressive development of international law and its codification'.[40] In the cases mentioned in draft Article 1, namely 'activities non prohibited by international law which involve a risk of causing significant transboundary harm through their

[37] See Romano 2001, 387.

[38] ICJ, *Gabcíkovo–Nagymaros Project*, Judgment, 25 September 1997, para 140.

[39] Shelton and Kiss 1997, 91. See Article 192 of the 1982 UN Convention on the Law of the Sea and Article 20 of the 1997 UN Convention on Non-Navigational Uses of International Watercourses.

[40] UN doc. A/56/10 Supp. No. 10 (2001), Report of the ILC on the Work of its Fifty-Third Session, Chap. V, International Liability for Injurious Consequences Arising out of Acts Non Prohibited by International Law, 149.

physical consequences', States are called upon by draft Article 3 to take all 'appropriate measures' in order to avoid transboundary harm and, in case this is not fully possible, in order to 'minimize the risk thereof'. As made clear by the commentary to Article 3 '[t]he modalities whereby the State of origin may discharge the obligation of prevention which have been established include, for example, legislative, administrative or other action'.[41] However, more in general, the delimitation of the content of the prevention duty is provided by the due diligence rule, according to which 'l'Etat sous la juridiction duquel le dommage est causée est dans l'obligation d'adopter les mesures de précaution nécessaires et réalisables, seulement la ou existe un risque raisonnable'.[42] The rule of due diligence is a guiding criterion which has been widely used in most international legal instruments for the protection of the environment, in which the obligation to take all 'necessary or appropriate measures'[43] formula is often used to identify the content of the prevention duty (although quite vaguely). In fact, in the effort to make the rule of due diligence more objective, international minimum standards have been established in a number of sectors so as to give indication on the type of legislation and control required in each sector and in specific circumstances. The pursued objective is to avoid the State being 'garant absolu de la prévention des dommages'[44]: this is done either by the inclusion of minimum standards in treaties and protocols or by reference to other legal instruments and acts of international organizations.

The discussion over the due diligence rule and its function in delimitating the content of the prevention duty in IEL also highlights an important feature of the duty itself, which will also be confirmed in the following analysis of corollary duties. The duty of prevention, as it is codified today in most international binding instruments, poses obligations to States as for the activities to be undertaken but not for the result to be achieved. The use of due diligence for the prevention of a damage to the environment or a transboundary harm as well as the recourse to 'best possible efforts' to minimize ensuing risks do not guarantee that the harm will not occur, thus making prevention mainly a procedural duty within IEL.

---

[41] Ibid., 153.

[42] Romano 2001, 388.

[43] See, *inter alia*, the 1982 UN Convention on the Law of the Sea (Article 194); the 1972 Convention on the Prevention of Marine Pollution by Dumping of Wastes and Other Matter (Article 1); the 1992 Helsinki Convention on Transboundary Effects of Industrial Accidents (Article 3).

[44] Romano 2001, 391.

8.4.1 *The Precautionary Principle: Preventive Measures When There is a Plausible Risk*

According to Article 2 of the ILC Draft Articles, the above illustrated duty to prevent by using due diligence does not exist in the face of any type of activity, but only when 'the risk of causing significant transboundary harm [...] takes the form of a high probability of causing significant transboundary harm and a low probability of causing disastrous transboundary harm'.[45] Such a risk 'refers to the combined effect of the probability of the occurrence of an accident and the magnitude of its injurious impact'. Thus being 'the combined effect of "risk" and "harm" which sets the threshold'. In order to ascertain whether the above indicated threshold is reached, a series of assessments need to be made, which are, by admission of the ILC itself, of an ambiguous nature. However, the ILC puts forward the criterion of the 'high probability of significant harm' as the threshold for imposing 'reasonable' obligations of prevention on States.[46] The fact that the risk must be foreseeable and not necessarily foreseen, opens the way to a discussion over the relationship between the duty of prevention and the well-known Precautionary Principle.

The general formulation of the Precautionary Principle can be found in Principle 15 of the Rio Declaration where it is said that '[i]n order to protect the environment, the precautionary approach shall be widely applied by States according to their capabilities. Where there are threats of serious or irreversible damage, lack of full scientific certainty shall not be used as a reason for postponing cost-effective measures to prevent environmental degradation'.[47] According to this principle, preventive action must also be taken in those situations where there is no conclusive scientific evidence available concerning the risk in question, thus amplifying the scope of prevention to those risks that are neither immediately foreseen nor foreseeable.

The relevance of the Precautionary Principle within IEL is widely recognized to the point that it is considered a principle of 'customary international *environmental* law'.[48] The principle is said to cover all types of environmental harm (although not all level of harm, according to the above-mentioned threshold scale), and therefore covers the environment as a whole irrespective of any jurisdictional boundaries, in all issue areas and for all potentially harmful human activities. However, the principle's reach does not extend beyond the environmental sphere, and its customary status under other branches of international law is still disputed.[49]

---

[45] UN doc. A/56/10 Supp. No. 10 (2001), *supra* n. 42. Article 2 (a).

[46] Ibid., commentary to Article 2.

[47] UN doc. A/CONF.151/26 (Vol. I), Report of the United Nations Conference on Environment and Development, Rio de Janeiro, 3–14 June 1992.

[48] Trouwborst 2007, 189. See also Romano 2001, 396

[49] In this sense see Trouwborst 2007, 190 and Thacher 1992, 97–100.

8.4.2 Duty to Co-operate

Whatever the supreme objective, whether the avoidance of transboundary harm—and the safeguard of territorial integrity—or the protection of the environment with no jurisdictional limits, cooperation is recognized as the best modality for implementing preventive action. This is the widespread approach adopted in international bilateral and multilateral conventions in different areas of environmental protection, as well as in soft law instruments, and the approach affirmed by judgments of international courts.[50] Cooperation is also required by Article 7 of the ILC Draft Articles, where it is said that 'States concerned shall co-operate in good faith and, as necessary, seek the assistance of one or more competent international organizations in preventing significant transboundary harm'. Draft Article 7 and its reference to the 'good faith' requisite for international cooperation is the element which would confirm the existence of a real obligation of cooperation. The good faith principle is in fact recognized as one of the 'basic principles governing the creation and performance of legal obligations, whatever their source',[51] including unilateral acts.[52]

The existence of an obligation to co-operate in the ambit of environmental protection is indeed confirmed by the fact that a number of bilateral and multilateral agreements exist in which cooperation features prominently or which include cooperation activities as a component. The 1992 Convention on the Protection and Use of Transboundary Watercourses and International Lakes, for example, is almost completely built around the principle of the 'cooperation between member countries in regard to the protection and use of transboundary waters' which is operationalized by means of exchange of information, joint assessment of risks, and monitoring.[53] The 1996 Agreement between Argentina and Brazil on the Early Notification and Mutual Assistance in the Case of a Nuclear Accident or Radiological Emergency also provides for the parties to 'cooperate with a view to the establishment of measures and procedures which will help to prevent or mitigate the damage which might result from a nuclear accident or radiological emergency'. On the basis of this widespread presence in legal instruments providing for the prevention of transboundary harm, commentators see the obligation of co-operation as a corollary duty to that of prevention.[54]

---

[50] For an overview see Romano 2001.

[51] ICJ, *Nuclear Tests Case*, Judgment, 20 December 1974, para 46.

[52] UN doc. A/56/10 Supp. No. 10 (2001), *supra* n. 41, 156.

[53] 1992 Convention on the Protection and Use of Transboundary Watercourses and International Lakes, Articles 11–13

[54] See n. 80–87 in Romano 2001 for international agreements dealing with co-operation on prevention of transboundary harm.

8.4.3 Duty to Warn

Another duty which has been put beside that of prevention (and equally attributed the status of customary environmental law) is the duty to warn.[55] The existence of such an obligation is already affirmed by the pronouncement of the International Court of Justice in the Corfu Channel Case[56] and widely confirmed by its spreading into international instruments of different nature: in Principle 9 of the UNEP Environmental Law Guidelines and Principles on Shared Natural Resources, which States that 'States have a duty urgently to inform other States which may be affected (a) [o]f any emergency situation arising from the utilization of a shared natural resource which might cause sudden harmful effects on their environment, (b) [o]f any sudden grave natural events related to a shared natural resource which may affect the environment, of such States'; in treaties dealing with pollution affecting marine environment such as in the 1976 Barcelona Convention for the protection of the Mediterranean (and its Protocols) and the 1982 Montego Bay Convention on the Law of the Sea; in treaties dealing with activities having transboundary effects such as the 1991 Convention on Environmental Impact Assessment (EIA) in a Transboundary Context and the 1992 Convention on the Transboundary Effects of Industrial Accidents; in Principle 19 of the Rio Declaration which imposes on the States to 'provide prior and timely notification and relevant information to potentially affected States'. Following the 1986 Chernobyl explosion and the Sandoz spill, the duty of notification, which in none of these two circumstances had been observed by the affecting States, has been further reinforced,[57] leading to the 'cristallisation en coutume internationale de l'obligation pour les Etats de notifier rapidement tout risque appréciable de dommage transfrontalier'.[58] On the basis of this corpus of legislative and non-legislative international instruments, the obligation has eventually been codified in ILC draft Article 8 on 'Notification and information', which reads that 'the State of origin shall provide the State likely to be affected with timely notification of the risk and the assessment and shall transmit to it the available technical and all other relevant information on which the assessment is based'.

---

[55] Hand 2003, 154.

[56] 'The obligations incumbent upon the Albanian authorities consisted in notifying, for the benefit of shipping in general, the existence of a minefield in Albanian territorial waters and in warning the approaching British warships of the imminent danger to which the minefield exposed them'. ICJ, *Corfu Channel Case*, Judgment, 9 April 1949, 22. Such a duty is equally confirmed by the Court in ICJ, *Military and Paramilitary Activities in and against Nicaragua*, Judgment, 27 June 1986, para 239.

[57] See the 1986 IAEA Convention on Early Notification of a Nuclear Accident.

[58] Romano 2001, 407.

8.4.4 *Duty to Assess Risks*

As evident from the wording of the above-mentioned draft Article 8, in order for the risk of harm to be notified, it has to be first assessed. The ILC draft Article 7 states that '[a]ny decision in respect of the authorization of an activity within the scope of the present article shall, in particular, be based on an assessment of the possible transboundary harm caused by that activity, including any environmental impact assessment'.

EIA techniques have been widely used since the 1980s in order to identify the extent and the nature of the environmental risk involved in an activity and the type of preventive measures that are to be undertaken. Since then, the requirement of carrying out this type of assessment has been included in many international agreements, such as the 1982 UN Convention on the Law of the Sea,[59] the 1985 ASEAN Convention on the Conservation of Nature and Natural Resources[60] and the most relevant 1991 Convention on EIA. The requirement of an assessment of risks for activities that are likely to have a significant impact on the environment is also contemplated by Principle 17 of the Rio Declaration and has been reaffirmed by means of judicial pronouncements. In particular, after that the Trail Smelter Case arbitration 'emphasized the importance of an assessment of the consequences of an activity causing significant risk',[61] the recent judgment of the ICJ on the Pulp Mills case in 2010 has eventually recognized EIA to be a practice that has become an obligation of general international law in cases regarding risks of transboundary harm.[62]

8.5 Development and Human Rights Law Contributions in the Identification of Prevention Obligation in the Face of Disasters

As demonstrated in previous paragraphs, prevention within IDRL is both a well-accepted concept which permeates politically relevant soft law documents as well a specific treaty-based duty within bilateral and multilateral legislative instruments. However, the experience of the concept and the practice of prevention in IDRL is too limited in time to have reached the level of sophistication the same concept has reached in IEL and to allow for both establishing a general duty of prevention and spelling out of its specific contents. Also, no judicial

59 See 1982 UN Convention on the Law of the Sea, Article 206.

60 ASEAN Agreement on the Conservation of Nature and Natural Resources, Kuala Lumpur, 9 July 1985, Article 14. Available at http://www.aseansec.org/1490.htm. Accessed 10 February 2012.

61 See UN doc. A/56/10 Supp. No. 10 (2001), *supra* n. 41.

62 ICJ, *Case Concerning Pulp Mills on the River Uruguay*, Judgment, 20 April 2010, para 205.

pronouncement has so far explicitly addressed the issue of the existence of an obligation of States to prevent or reduce the risks of disasters, let alone has pronounced itself on the nature of such a duty.

As for the opportunity to regulate the issue of disaster prevention by directly applying the relevant rules of IEL, commentators like Hand highlight the limits of applying a *corpus juris* which focuses mainly on ensuring that remedies are provided after the damage has occurred. However, opportunities have been identified, making it possible to overcome the traditional IEL reactive stance in the face of environmental damage,[63] so as to highlight how this branch of IL can provide a relevant set of operationalizing instruments which assume great relevance for the prevention of disasters if proactively used. The duty of international co-operation, for instance, includes procedures and conducts through which the effectiveness of prevention can be significantly increased. International co-operation for the prevention and the reduction of disaster effects ideally implies a shared management of risks through procedures such as consultations, notifications, and assessments that by their nature are capable of avoiding the occurrence of disasters and allowing a more effective mitigation of their effects.[64]

However, the transposition of duties from the environmental field to that of disaster response may have little effect in terms of the real avoidance of harmful events or the reduction of risks if these remain purely procedural duties. As Hand points out, '[o]nce the originating state has analyzed the potential effects [through an EIA], notified the potentially injured state [fulfilling the notification duty] and consulted with them, it has no substantive duty to forgo the project or even to modify it to prevent injury, including disasters'.[65] This is even more significant if we consider that environmental degradation which causes disasters is in many cases the result of failing to plan or regulate and to take broader decisions at the program and policy level more than at the level of single projects. In particular, in those countries where developmental concerns are high in the priorities of both the population and decision makers, the danger of an underestimation of the effects of speed pace and unregulated development over the environment exists.

This annotation brings additional considerations into the discussion with regard to the relationship between development planning and disaster prevention/disaster risk reduction. Such a connection has been clearly identified in Chapter 7 of Agenda 21,[66] in which the link between effective disaster prevention and sustainable development is clearly marked. Pre-disaster planning is here proposed as a tool for assessing the 'vulnerability of human settlements and settlement infrastructure' and

[63] See for instance Popiel 1995, 7.

[64] See on this the Yokohama Message, included in the Yokohama Strategy and Plan of Action for a Safer World, *supra* n. 16, Point 4.

[65] Hand 2003, 158.

[66] Agenda 21 together with the Rio Declaration on Environment and Development, and the Statement of principles for the Sustainable Management of Forests were adopted by more than 178 Governments in 1992 at the UN Conference on Environment and Development.

establishing measures for the reduction of disaster effects on populations and settlements by increasing their resilience. In addition, practices of development planning would also be highly important in the identification of probable contents of a general duty to prevent disasters. Focusing on the recognition that the features of development processes have themselves the potential of greatly influencing the occurrence and the effects of disasters, a UNDP–BCPR report affirms that '[i]n development planning, many countries and international funding agencies include elements of environmental and social impact assessment for large projects. These assessments could take into account the potential impact of developments on disaster risk. This would allow for greater transparency in the power of large infrastructure developments to reshape where people live and what they do to make a living, and so to contribute to changing patterns of disaster risk'.[67]

A widespread diffusion of assessment requirements for development plans in terms of environmental and social sustainability, accompanied by an element of *opinio juris* as for the binding character of the requirement may thus help the identification of specific contents to the obligation of prevention in an autonomous disaster response law sector.[68]

The principal duty of preventing environmental harm of transboundary nature—along with the side duties to perform EIA, to consult and inform and ultimately to warn other nations of potential disasters—may well be applied to the prevention of those disasters that are referable to environmental degradation and have the potential to affect the territory and the citizens of another State. What should then be the specificity of a general obligation for States to prevent disasters of whatever nature and their consequences, or to mitigate their effects? In our opinion such specificity would consist in the identification of a duty of prevention irrespective of whether a disaster affects the territory and citizens of another State or those of the same State of origin. For the time being, when the causative environmental degradation occurs within the same country, the main regulating instruments[69] are either relevant IDRL/IEL treaties addressing the specific case or norms of international human rights law.[70]

Leaving aside the rules which may be binding for States in case of disaster on their own territory in virtue of the treaties to which they are parties, it seems interesting to identify what the contribution of international human rights law to the identification of a general duty to prevent disasters is. Although this branch of international law does not explicitly address the right to protection from disasters,

---

[67] UNDP–BCPR Global Report 'Reducing Disaster Risk, A Challenge for Development' 2004. Available at http://www.undp.org/cpr/whats_new/rdr_english.pdf. Accessed February 12 2012.

[68] An interesting example is the Strategic Environmental Assessment provided for by the Protocol on Strategic Environmental Assessment signed by 35 countries on 21 May 2003 during the Ministerial 'Environment for Europe' Conference (Kyiv). See Hand 2003, 158.

[69] Ibid., 159.

[70] See on this Chap. 15 by Creta in this volume.

this objective has become considered as 'clearly implied'[71] by it and explicitly confirmed by international human rights courts' judgments. As pointed out by Hand, State obligation to prevent and mitigate natural disasters would be part of the responsibility issuing from Article 11 of the International Covenant on Economic, Social and Cultural Rights, which recognizes 'the right of everyone to an adequate standard of living for himself and his family, including adequate food, clothing and housing, and to the continuous improvement of living conditions'.[72] The existence of such a State duty would also rely on Article 3 of the Universal Declaration of Human Rights, which provides that '[e]veryone has the right to life, liberty, and security of person', as well as on Article 25 which provides for 'the right to security in the event of unemployment, sickness, disability, widowhood, old age or other lack of livelihood in circumstances beyond his control',[73] such as in disaster situations. Furthermore, the existence of a human right to a healthy environment as part of the right to life, rooted in the aforementioned basic instruments of international human rights law, has been strongly affirmed in the wake of the Rio Conference of 1992[74] with consequences also reverberating in the IDRL. Making reference to Article 3 of the Universal Declaration of Human Rights and the Article 6 of the International Covenant on Civil and Political Rights, the World Disaster Report 2000 suggests that '[...] calculated neglect in the wake of natural or technological disaster may well constitute a de facto death sentence',[75] thus corresponding to a violation of human rights. According to this perspective the right not to be subjected to catastrophic events able to cause loss of life and harm for individual health and well-being would be upgraded to a core human right.

International jurisprudence has moved along this path, as confirmed, in particular, by the pronouncements of the European Court of Human Rights called to address the question as to whether and when deaths caused by a man-made or natural disaster can amount to a human rights' violation by the State.[76]

Both in the Budayeva[77] and in the Öneryildiz[78] cases, claims of this nature were rejected by national courts, which argued that the causes of death could not have been foreseen or prevented since they were natural and the State could not be held responsible. In both cases, the European Court of Human Rights instead found that both States taken to Court were responsible for violation of their duty to protect

---

71 Kent 2001, 137–138.

72 Hand 2003, 159–160.

73 1948 Universal Declaration of Human Rights, UN General Assembly Resolution 217 A (III).

74 See Hand 2003, 160.

75 IFRC, World Disaster Report 2000, available at http://www.ifrc.org/en/publications-and-reports/general-publications/. Accessed 15 February 2012.

76 Proceedings before the Court aimed at the ascertainment of the States' responsibility in order to mandate the State to compensate the survivors.

77 ECHR, *Case of Budayeva and others v. Russia*, Judgement, 29 September 2008.

78 ECHR, *Case of Öneryildiz v. Turkey*, Judgment, 30 November 2004.

life, having failed to take preventive measures. The Court affirmed that the right to life 'does not solely concern deaths resulting from the use of force by agent of the State but also [...] lays down a positive obligation on States to take appropriate steps to safeguard the lives of those within their jurisdiction' and stressed that '[t]his positive obligation entails above all a primary duty on the State to put in place a legislative and administrative framework designed to provide effective deterrence against threats to the right to life'.[79]

According to the Court a causal link existed among national authorities' actions or omissions and the deaths of the victims. In the Court's words deaths occurred 'because the authorities neglected their duty to take preventive measures when a natural hazard had been clearly identifiable and effective means to mitigate the risk were available to them'.[80]

Leaving aside the recent important debate on the relationship between human rights and climate change and on the progressive affirmation of environmental rights,[81] the relevant point to be highlighted in this discussion over the development of a general obligation for States to endeavor to prevent disasters is the contribution that human rights law can offer in identifying a content for such a duty which is free from exclusively territorial and environmental considerations. Human rights law and the interpretation currently given by both jurisprudence and commentators with regard to the content of the specific right to life may in fact help the identification of a State's obligation to act preventively in order to ensure that life is protected in all situation of potential disaster.

8.6 Conclusions

The traditional perception of natural and man-made disaster as episodic events, requiring first and foremost circumscribed humanitarian responses by both affected and helping States, delayed the development of international law on response to and prevention of disasters in general. Only in recent times disasters have in fact begun to be considered as events touching upon the 'persistent' interests of States to such an extent and with such costly consequences that international legislative action regulating State response to disasters, including prevention, has flourished.

Within the developing branch of IDRL, prevention has been affirmed both by means of political commitments undertaken by States in international fora and through the declaration of principles and binding procedural duties specifically contained in legislative instruments. Despite disagreement regarding the existence of a general principle of prevention, the developing disaster response branch of International Law, of which disaster prevention and mitigation is a constitutive

[79] Ibid., paras 128–129.

[80] Kalin and Haenni 2008, 31–32.

[81] See Boyle 2010 and Pedersen 2009.

element, appears to be inherently founded on such a principle and on its environmentally related constitutive elements.

As illustrated in the paragraphs above, the duty to prevent is well established in IEL and has been over time subjected to further specification and practical operationalization especially by means of corollary obligations. In trying to broaden the field of application of such State duties to the field of disaster prevention, in general, we may well affirm that the contribution of environmental law is mainly seen when identifying procedures and mechanisms which could be easily applied for preventing either the occurrence of disasters or the mitigation of their effects.

However, both the principle and the content of the duty to prevent as developed by IEL do not constitute completely appropriate foundations for the identification of analogous principles and obligations for States to act preventively in the face of natural and man-made disasters. While, on the one hand, a proactive interpretation of the instruments developed in the environmental domain is needed, especially with regard to the application of procedural preventive obligations, on the other hand, other-than-environmental elements are to be included in the identification of comprehensive preventive obligations capable of addressing the complexity of the dimensions affected in situations of disaster.

Instruments such as assessment, information, and notification procedures, as well as other corollary instruments which regulate prevention under IEL need to be proactively interpreted in order to be usefully and effectively applied in the face of all types of disasters. However, the comprehensive scope which prevention has within IDRL calls for developmental and human rights considerations (which have recently been expressed by means of international courts judgments), to be explicitly accepted and further developed within binding legal instruments.

The duty to prevent natural and man-made disasters is in fact a duty which States must have in the face of both other States and their population as well as their own citizens. The issue of international liability of States for hazardous activities with transboundary effects is in fact only limited to identifying out-of-territory responsibility of States. Excluding State responsibility for lack of prevention in the face of its own population ignores the multidimensional effects of disasters. Harm caused by natural and man-made disasters is not only environmental: disasters must also be prevented because human health, human rights, sustainable development are menaced and State responsibility comes into play under several domains of international law. If prevention of disasters is to be proactive rather than reactive, the developmental and human rights concerns expressed by recent judgments of international courts need to be incorporated into the newly consolidating corpus of IDRL, thus making prevention a general obligation which transcends the pure and simple defense of State interests; interests affected in situation of disasters go well beyond those of States.

References

Boyle A (2010) Human rights and the environment: a reassessment, paper presented at the United Nations Environment Programme (UNEP) and Office of the High Commissioner for Human Rights (OHCHR) High-level Expert Meeting 'The New Future of Human Rights and Environment: Moving the Global Agenda Forward', Nairobi, 30 November–1 December 2009

Fidler DP (2005) Disaster relief and governance after the Indian Ocean Tsunami: what role for international law? Melb J Int L 6(2):458

Hand J (2003) Disaster prevention presentation. Santa Clara J Int L 1:147. www.scu.edu/scjil

International Federation of Red Cross and Red Crescent Societies (2000) World disaster report 2000. www.ifrc.org/en/publications-and-reports/general-publications/

International Federation of Red Cross and Red Crescent Societies (2003) International disaster response laws, principles and practice: reflections, prospects and challenges

Kalin W, Haenni Dale C (2008) Disaster risk mitigation—why human rights matter. Forced Migr Rev 31:31–32

Kent G (2001) The human right to disaster mitigation and relief. Environ Hazards 3(2001): 137–138

Pedersen OW (2009) The role of human rights in national climate change strategies. www.law.ed.ac.uk/europa/files/OP%20Draft.pdf

Popiel BR (1995) From customary law to environmental impact assessment: a new approach to avoiding transboundary environmental damage between Canada and the United States. BC Environ Aff L Rev 22:447. http://lawdigitalcommons.bc.edu/ealr/vol22/iss2/8

Samuels JW (2003) The relevance of international law in the prevention and mitigation of natural disasters. In Tenon LH (ed) International legal mechanisms regulating disaster response in countries of the Mediterranean region. International Federation of Red Cross and Red Crescent Societies, Geneva

Romano CP (2001) L'obligation de prévention des catastrophes industrielles et naturelles. In Caron D, Leben C (eds) The international aspects of natural and industrial catastrophes. Martinus Nijhoff Publishers, The Hague, 379–428

Shelton D, Kiss A (1997) A guide to international environmental law. Martinus Nijhoff Publishers, Leiden

Thacher PS (1992) Changing requirements for international information. In: Brown Weiss E (ed), Environmental change and international law. United Nations University Press, Tokyo

Trouwborst A (2007) The precautionary principle in general international law: combating the Babylonian confusion. Rev Eur Community Int Environ L 16(2):185–195

UN doc. A/CONF.48/14&Corr. 1 (1973) Declaration of the UN on the human environment, 16 June 1972

UN doc. A/CONF.151/26, Vol. I (1992) Report of the UN conference on environment and development, Rio de Janeiro, 3–14 June 1992

UN doc. A/56/10 Supp. No. 10 (2001), Report of the international law commission the work of its fifty-third session, Chap. V. International liability for injurious consequences arising out of acts non prohibited by international law

UN doc. A/CONF.206/6 (2005) Final report of the world conference on disaster reduction

UN doc. A/CONF.206/L.I (2005) Review of the Yokohama strategy and plan of action for a safer world

UN doc. A/CN.4/590 (2007) International law commission, memorandum by the secretariat, protection of persons in the event of disasters

UNDP–BCPR Global Report (2004) Reducing disaster risk, a challenge for development. www.undp.org/cpr/whats_new/rdr_english.pdf

UNDP Evaluation Office (2010) Reduction vulnerabilities. An assessment of UNDP contribution to disaster prevention and recovery

UNISDR (2004) Living at risk: a global review of disaster reduction initiatives, vol. I. www.unisdr.org/we/inform/publications/657

Vessey J (1998) The principle of prevention in international law. Austrian Rev Int Eur L 3:181–207

World Conference on Natural Disaster Reduction Yokohama (1994) Yokohama strategy and plan of action for a safer world. Guidelines for natural disaster prevention, preparedness and mitigation, Japan, 23–27 May 1994. www.preventionweb.net/files/8241_doc6841contenido1.pdf

Chapter 9
An Enabling Environment for Disaster Risk Reduction

Alessandra La Vaccara

Abstract Definitions of the concept of enabling environment are numerous, and range from all-encompassing to narrow ones. This chapter intends to highlight the current understandings of how an enabling environment works with and through Disaster Risk Reduction (DRR) and to pinpoint its components. To this aim, a deductive approach seems to be the most appropriate: the focus on the general concept will be followed by the analysis of specific applications to the DRR case. An enabling environment for DRR entails the action and participation of different actors. A brief review of the existing literature on the topic helps identify the actors most involved in its implementation and define their specific role in the enabling environment formation process. DRR activities serve both to build resilience to hazards and to ensure that development efforts do not increase vulnerability to those hazards. The achievement of such objectives is also linked to a legal follow-up at the international and national level. This chapter intends to identify the international legal basis of the concept and questions whether establishing an enabling environment for DRR is an international obligation.

Keywords: Enabling environment · Disaster risk reduction · Hyogo framework for action · Capacity development · Disaster risk governance · Non-conventional concerted act

Contents

A. La Vaccara (✉)
Scuola Superiore Sant'Anna, Piazza Martiri della Libertà, 33, 56127, Pisa, Italy
e-mail: a.lavaccara@sssup.it

A. de Guttry et al. (eds.), *International Disaster Response Law*,
DOI: 10.1007/978-90-6704-882-8_9,

9.1 Introductory Remarks

An enabling environment is a multi-level system which entails the concurrent actions of different actors from either the public sector or the private one and, as such produces positive effects in the medium and long term. It should be set up for the management of complex phenomena like disasters. The purpose of this chapter is two-fold: highlighting the current understandings of how an enabling environment works with and through disaster risk reduction (hereafter, DRR) and exploring its legal basis. A deductive approach will be adopted: the focus on the general concept of enabling environment will be followed by the analysis of its specific applications to DRR. For the purpose of this chapter, the term DRR is intended as defined by the United Nations International Strategy for Disaster Reduction (hereafter UNISDR), i.e., 'the concept and practice of reducing disaster risks through systematic efforts to analyze and manage the causal factors of disasters, including through reduced exposure to hazards, lessened vulnerability of people and property, wise management of land and the environment, and improved preparedness for adverse events.'[1]

In order to explain the interaction between such a concept and DRR and to detect the legal basis of the concept, the chapter proceeds in five sections. After this introduction, Sect. 9.2 provides an overview of the history of the concept of 'enabling environment,' identifies the current understandings of the concept against DRR, and pinpoints the measures which contribute to the establishment of an enabling environment for DRR. Section 9.3 discusses the legal foundation of the concept and clarifies how an enabling environment for DRR interacts with the existing soft law framework set down by the UN, i.e., the Hyogo framework for Action (hereafter, HFA). Section 9.4 questions whether the States' commitment to the HFA has a legal dimension and impacts on the establishment of an enabling environment for DRR. Finally, Sect. 9.5 identifies the current legal nature of the concept in international law and draws some conclusions as to whether the establishment of an enabling environment for DRR is a legal and/or political commitment.

[1] See Chap. 1 by de Guttry in this volume.

9.2 The Concept of 'Enabling Environment'

In its broadest sense, the concept of enabling environment is similar to that of institutional environment which was defined by *Davis and North* as follows: 'the set of fundamental political, social and legal ground rules that establishes the basis for production, exchange and distribution.'[2] According to *Brinkerhoff*, 'a quick scan of printed and electronic sources reveals the ubiquity of the term. [...] However, [it] exhibits an apparent clarity that masks the underlying complexity inherent in the conceptual territory it subsumes.'[3]

Due to its connection with development, governance, and economics, the concept has different facets. For instance, the hybrid concept of enabling environment capacity dates back to the 1990s. Different approaches to institutional capacity development[4] can be discerned in the literature over the last 50 years: institution building in the 1950s, institutional strengthening between the 1960s and the 1970s, development management in the 1970s, institutional development in the 1980s, and enabling environment capacity in the 2000s.[5]

The 'ubiquity' of the concept is determined by the possibility to link it to different sectors and to narrow or broaden its scope against the features of such sectors. In the policy domain, the concept refers to basic elements related to good governance. For instance, an enabling environment for power decentralization in the local arena is based on the level of legal reform involved, the scale and number of layers of local government, the kinds of local authorities being engaged, the mix of powers and obligations devolved, and the aim of governments to launch reforms.[6] Likewise, an enabling environment for the private sector development is perceived as a complex system including rules, regulations, physical and financial infrastructures, research, and development, education, and training created outside the company but affecting operations inside the company.[7]

The international organizations' standpoint on the concept of enabling environment puts forward additional features. The International Labour Organization (ILO) makes use of this concept in various fields, e.g., women growth enterprise, decent work country programs, sustainable enterprise development, freedom of

---

[2] Davis and North 1971, 6. See also Tripp 2003, 1.

[3] Brinkerhoff 2007, 84.

[4] UNDP defines capacity as 'the ability of individuals, institutions, and societies to perform functions, solve problems, and set and achieve objectives in a sustainable manner. Capacity development is the "how" of making development work better and is, in essence, about making institutions better able to deliver and promote human development,' UNDP 2010a, 2. The UNDP includes in its definition the notion that 'capacity development processes must improve the ability to assess and react to future needs and thus maintain relevance and effectiveness over time.' Horton et al. 2003, 31.

[5] OECD—Development Assistant Committee 2000, 119.

[6] Ribot 2002, 3.

[7] Mortensen et al. 2003, 249. On the enabling environment for social entrepreneurship, see Fulgence and Mori 2009.

association, and informal economy. An enabling environment for sustainable enterprise development is based on fundamental conditions, such as peace and political stability, good governance, social dialog, trade, and sustainable economic integration, legal and regulatory frameworks, implementation and enforcement of labor, and environmental standards.[8] The UNDP refers to the concept of enabling environment as the core subject of national policy-makers' actions which determines the necessary conditions to secure the financial resources for investment. Its establishment entails the attainment of growth and equitable development, mainly in the developing countries.[9] Finally, the Organization for Economic Co-operation and Development (OECD)'s definition of the concept is reflected in principle 5 of the OECD principles for private sector participation in infrastructure:

> a sound and enabling environment for infrastructure investment, [...] implies high standards of public and corporate governance, transparency and the rule of law, including protection of property and contractual rights, [and] is essential to attract the participation of the private sector.[10]

9.2.1 DRR-Oriented Measures to Put the Concept into Practice

In the literature, some authors propose implementing policies and developing a legal framework for the creation of an enabling environment[11] and attribute a leading role to national governments in such activities. However, DRR is based on a continuous strategy of vulnerability and risk assessment which entails the involvement of different actors.[12] The increasing participation of the private sector in functions formerly provided by the government confirms that 'there is nothing inherent in aspects such as warning systems or disaster management to make them exempt from this general trend.'[13] A joint effort is, therefore, required in order to address the 'underlying risk drivers'[14] which bring about the disaster risk–poverty nexus (see Fig. 9.1). Indeed, a range of underlying risk drivers, such as poor urban and local governance, vulnerable rural livelihoods and ecosystem decline, contribute to the translation of poverty and everyday risk into disaster risk, in a context of broader economic, and political processes.[15]

---

[8] ILO 2007, 3, 7. See also ILO 2008.

[9] UNDP (Commission on the Private Sector and Development) 2004, 47–48.

[10] OECD 2009, 18.

[11] Noya and Clarence 2007, 10.

[12] UNISDR 2004, 13.

[13] Britton 2006, 365.

[14] The 'underlying risk drivers' are major factors which drive disaster risk and contribute to catastrophe risk, especially in impoverished communities. See UNISDR 2009a, 87 ff.

[15] Ibid., 9.

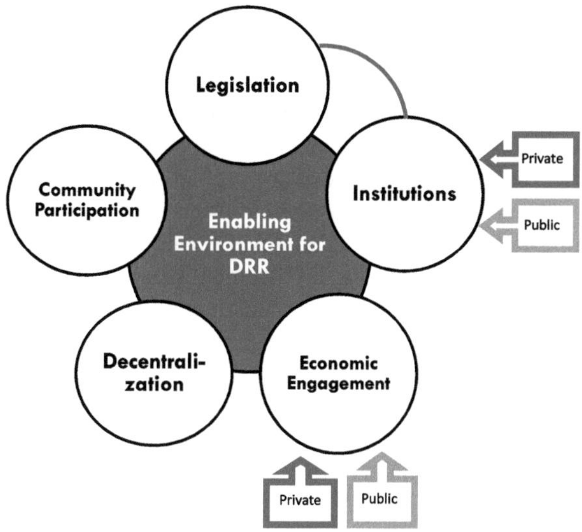

Fig. 9.1 An enabling environment for DRR entails a multilevel interaction among different actors both in the public and private sphere, with the participation of local communities

In order to establish an enabling environment for DRR, the adoption of high-level development policy frameworks facilitates the management of risk, builds on the capacities of urban and local governments, and effectively addresses the underlying drivers of risk.[16] A development initiative is based on different steps: initially, the analysis of the existing policies along with an assessment of their adequacy[17]; then, the review of the existing laws concerning DRR; finally, the approval of a sound disaster-related legislation.[18]

The urban and local governments' capacities need to be improved through the integration of DRR-related matters into a national strategy[19] which entails the devolution of powers and adequate resources to subnational levels of governments.[20] Thus, the decentralization should result in a better promotion of exchange of experience, common problems and good practices among stakeholders, and experts dealing with DRR.[21] The country's capacity development can be fostered through the empowerment of those affected by bad governance and poverty, the respect for human rights, the promotion of participatory decision making, the adoption of effective measures to combat corruption, the undertaking of judicial reforms, and an equal opportunity to access resources.[22]

---

[16] Point no. 4 of the 20-point plan to reduce risk, see ibid. 176.

[17] ILO/AfDB 2007, 57.

[18] UNDP 2010b, 3.

[19] Such measure is inferred from the 2009 Global Assessment Report on DRR which outlines different recommendations for action as to DRR and sums them up in the 20-point plan to reduce risk. In particular, see Point no. 5 of the 20-point plan to reduce risk, UNISDR 2009a, 177.

[20] Brinkerhoff 2007, 87.

[21] WHO-Europe 2010, 5.

[22] Ibid. 83.

Investing in natural resource management, infrastructure development, livelihood generation, and social protection reduces vulnerability and strengthens resilience[23] of rural community livelihoods.[24] In order to endorse enabling environment's measures, DRR investments should be enhanced by a specific policy on the elimination of investment obstacles such as criminality which affects investors, the red tape, and unnecessary regulations.[25]

Governments are required to promote a culture of planning and implementation of DRR[26] which builds on government/civil society partnerships and is supportive of local actions.[27] The involvement of a wide range of stakeholders is achievable through the adoption of a mainstreaming approach to DRR[28] with the support of a co-ordination mechanism (e.g., the national platforms[29]). The linkages between the organizations generating early warnings and those responsible for disaster preparedness and response[30] involve a proper communication system for the promotion of DRR-oriented partnerships.[31] The improvement of existing systems for public administration enhances the incorporation of innovations into the governance of DRR.[32]

Finally, as a complex framework, an enabling environment for DRR needs a structured system of responsibility vested in the highest level of political authority and explicitly incorporated into national plans and budget.[33] The respect for the rule of law, which mirrors the goodness of governance,[34] facilitates the development of such a system.

For the purpose of this chapter though, the aforementioned measures need to be customized because measures that succeed in reducing risk in one setting may not

---

[23] The term resilience refers to 'the ability of a system, community or society exposed to hazards to resist, absorb, accommodate to and recover from the effects of a hazard in a timely and efficient manner, including through the preservation and restoration of its essential basic structures and functions'. UNISDR 2009b, 24.

[24] Point no. 6 of the 20-point plan to reduce risk. See *supra,* op. cit. n.19.

[25] Brinkerhoff 2007, 87.

[26] White 1999, 73.

[27] Point no. 9 of the 20-point plan to reduce risk. See *supra,* op. cit. n.19.

[28] 'Mainstreaming of DRR is a governance process enabling the systematic integration of DRR concerns into all relevant development spheres. In other words, responsive, accountable, transparent and efficient governance structures underwrite the environment where DRR can be institutionalized as an underlying principle of sustainable development'. UNDP 2010b, 1.

[29] National Platforms are national mechanisms for co-ordination and policy guidance on DRR that are multi sectoral and inter-disciplinary in nature, with public, private, and civil society participation involving all concerned entities within a country. UNISDR 2009b, 20.

[30] Point no. 15 of the 20-point plan to reduce risk. See *supra,* op. cit. n.19.

[31] Misuraca 2007, 55 et seq.

[32] UNISDR 2011, 177.

[33] Point no. 10 of the 20-point plan to reduce risk. See *supra,* op. cit. n. 19.

[34] Hope defines good governance as 'the existence—within States—of political accountability, bureaucratic transparency, the exercise of legitimate power, […], sound fiscal management and public financial accountability, respect for the rule of law […]'. Hope 2009, 81.

work in others.[35] Indeed, the great diversity of political, socio economic, cultural environments, and hazard circumstances among States requires the implementation of policies and activities that are appropriate for the local context.

9.3 The International Legal Basis

The analysis of legally binding DRR instruments and non-binding documents intends to elucidate whether establishing an enabling environment for DRR is an international obligation. Although the concept of enabling environment is not in use in international law, the purpose of this section is to pinpoint the founding components of an enabling environment[36] in DRR-related treaties and to delineate its legal basis.

9.3.1 The Enabling Environment for DRR in the Existing DRR International Legal Tools

International regulation on DRR exists, but regulation in this area occurs primarily at the domestic level.[37] DRR is taken into account as a core component of national strategies and domestic laws.[38] Nonetheless, a limited number of bilateral and regional disaster risk management agreements have been recently ratified.[39]

At the international level, the 1992 *Convention on the transboundary effects of industrial accidents*[40] (hereafter, the Convention on industrial accidents) requires States Parties to 'take appropriate legislative, regulatory, administrative and financial measures for the prevention of, preparedness for [...] industrial accidents.'[41] Article 6 reiterates the obligation for States Parties to set up 'appropriate measures for the prevention of industrial accidents, including measures to induce

[35] UNISDR 2008, 5.

[36] See *supra* Sect. 9.2.1.

[37] United Nations International Law Commission, "Protection of persons in the event of disasters", Memorandum by the Secretariat, UN doc. A/CN.4/590 (2007), para 33.

[38] Pronto 2008–2009, 453.

[39] The International Law Commission's memorandum on 'the Protection of persons in the event of disasters' has identified a number of legal instruments on disaster response and disaster management wherein prevention and mitigation feature prominently or which include risk reduction and mitigation activities as components. See United Nations International Law Commission, 'Protection of persons in the event of disasters' [...], op. cit., para 34.

[40] 1992 Convention on the Transboundary Effects of Industrial Accidents.

[41] Ibid. Article 3 (4).

action by operators to reduce the risk of industrial accidents.'[42] Specifically, States Parties should adopt legislative and guidance documents on safety measures and standards; identify those hazardous activities requiring special preventive measures; evaluate risk analyzes for hazardous activities; produce an action plan for the implementation of necessary measures; provide the competent authorities with the information needed to assess risks; undertake the appropriate training of all persons engaged in hazardous activities; and monitor hazardous activities.[43] The downside of such Convention resides in the lack of an effective responsibility system. Article 13 affirms that all 'Parties shall support appropriate international efforts to elaborate rules, criteria, and procedures in the field of responsibility and liability.' There is a wide degree of discretion bestowed to States Parties. The absence of compliance with the Convention provisions does not entail any sanction for State Parties and can hinder the effectiveness of an enabling environment for reducing disaster risk. However, in the field of environmental protection, the obligation to undertake vigilance and disaster prevention activities, like those required by the Convention on industrial accidents, is internationally confirmed on the basis of 'the often irreversible character of damage to the environment and of the limitations inherent in the very mechanism of reparation of this type of damage. [...].'[44]

The 1998 *Tampere Convention on the Provision of Telecommunication Resources for Disaster Mitigation and Relief Operations* (hereafter, the Tampere Convention)[45] requires States Parties to set up the enabling environment components. The use of telecommunication resources for disaster mitigation[46] along with

[42] Ibid. Article 6 (1). Other provisions contribute to lay out some of the founding components of an enabling environment such as the adoption of legislative and regulatory measures, the decision making (Article 7), the emergency preparedness (Article 8), the information to and participation of the public (Article 9), response measures in the event of an industrial accident (Article 11), and the exchange of technology (Article 16).

[43] Ibid. Annex IV.

[44] This was the position hold by the International Court of Justice (ICJ) in the case *Gabcíkovo-Nagymaros Project.* The case arose out of the signature, on 16 September 1977, by the Hungarian People's Republic and the Czechoslovak People's Republic, of a treaty concerning the construction and operation of the Gabcíkovo-Nagymaros System of Locks. The ICJ found that Hungary was not entitled to suspend and subsequently abandon, in 1989, its part of the works in the dam project, as laid down in the aforesaid Treaty; it also found that Czechoslovakia was entitled to start, in November 1991, preparation of an alternative provisional solution (called 'Variant C'), but not to put that solution into operation in October 1992 as a unilateral measure. As to the future conduct of the Parties, the ICJ, *inter alia,* underlined that two provisions of the aforesaid Treaty—Articles 15 and 19—not only allowed, but even prescribed 'to evaluate the environmental risks'. Indeed, both provisions provided for the obligation 'to maintain the quality of the water of the Danube and to protect nature.' ICJ, *Gabcíkovo-Nagymaros Project (Hungary* v. *Slovakia),* Judgment, 25 September 1997, para 140. See also Chap. 8 by Nicoletti in this volume.

[45] 1998 Tampere Convention on the Provision of Telecommunication Resources for Disaster Mitigation and Relief Operations.

[46] Ibid. Article 3 (1).

'measures designed to prevent, predict, prepare for, respond to, monitor and/or mitigate the impact of, disasters'[47] concur to implement an enabling environment for reducing disaster risk.

As for climate change, '[it] is a direct result of the same unsustainable development processes that have led to the existing accumulations of disaster risk.'[48] In coming decades, 'it will become one of the primary drivers of disaster risk.'[49] Therefore, the 1992 *United Nations Framework Convention on Climate Change* (hereafter, UNFCCC)[50] can be considered as a DRR-oriented tool. States Parties to the UNFCCC should implement constitutive measures of an enabling environment for DRR in order to cope with the combined effects of climate change and disaster risk. Specifically, they have to formulate, implement, publish and regularly update national and regional programs including climate change considerations; co-operate in preparing for adaptation to the impacts of climate change; develop and elaborate appropriate and integrated plans for coastal zone management, water resources and agriculture, and for the protection and rehabilitation of areas affected by drought and desertification, as well as floods; promote and co-operate in the full, open and prompt exchange of relevant scientific, technological, technical, socio economic and legal information related to the climate system, and climate change [...]; enhance education, training and public awareness related to climate change, and encourage the widest participation in this process.[51]

As for the regional level, the European Union's (EU) involvement in the implementation of the DRR approach is proved by the normative activities which have been recently carried out at the EU level. The lack of a legally binding document on DRR does not impinge on the ongoing construction of a European enabling environment for DRR. In 2008, the European Commission approved the communication on reinforcing the EU's disaster response capacity[52] which has been the preliminary effort to pave the way towards an EU approach to DRR. In 2009, the Commission has adopted two communications related to DRR: 'A community approach on the prevention of natural and man-made disasters,' and 'A strategy for supporting DRR in developing countries.'[53] Despite its non-binding

---

[47] Ibid. Article 1 (7).

[48] Wallström 2009, 154.

[49] Ibid. 155.

[50] 1992 United Nations Framework Convention on Climate Change.

[51] UNFCCC, Article 4 (1), a–j.

[52] Commission (EC), 'Reinforcing the Union's Disaster Response Capacity' (Communication) COM (2008) 130 final, 5 March 2008. For a legal perspective on the EU's disaster response capacity, see Chap. 5 by Gestri in this volume.

[53] Commission (EC), 'A Community approach on the prevention of natural and man-made disasters' (Communication) COM (2009) 82 final, 23 February 2009; Commission (EC), 'EU Strategy for supporting Disaster Risk Reduction in developing countries' (Communication) COM (2009) 84 final, 23 February 2009.

nature, 'a communication [i.e., a non-standard or atypical act in the EU law] is an important first step launching a long term process'[54] for EU's DRR actions. The communication on a community approach—also known as 'the Prevention Communication'—plays a fundamental role in the EU effort towards a common enabling environment for DRR. In particular, it identifies specific areas where action at the EU level could provide added value[55]: establishing a Community-level inventory of existing information and best practices; developing guidelines on hazards and risk mapping; linking actors and policies throughout the disaster management cycle; improved access to early warning systems; and more efficient targeting of community funds.[56] Under the communication, the implementation of such measures 'will take account of actions already undertaken by the Community, thus creating the necessary conditions for bringing the latter together under a consistent and effective Community framework.'[57] The economic impacts of disasters may adversely affect the economic growth and competitiveness of EU regions (and hence the EU as a whole).[58] As a matter of fact, the overall economic impact of disasters in Europe has been estimated at €15 billion yearly.[59] A regional enabling environment for reducing disaster risk, therefore, requires the endorsement of all EU member States. The communication launching a strategy for supporting DRR in developing countries reveals an external EU's involvement in promoting the creation of an enabling environment for DRR in such countries.[60] In order to implement the strategy, the EU intends to foster the development of DRR-oriented institutional frameworks, especially within national platforms, and the allocation of adequate financial resources for DRR activities.[61]

In the Asia–Pacific region, the 2005 *ASEAN Agreement on Disaster Management and Emergency Response*[62] (hereafter, the ASEAN agreement) aims to 'provide effective mechanisms to achieve substantial reduction of disaster losses in lives and in the social, economic and environmental assets of the State Parties, and to jointly respond to disaster emergencies [...]' (Article 2). Apparently, the ASEAN Agreement adopts a comprehensive approach including disaster management, DRR, and disaster response.[63] Its three main principles, which sum up the

[54] Press Release, Stavros Dimas - Former European commissioner for environment, ReliefWeb 'Commission focuses on disaster prevention and reduction of risks at home and abroad', 23 February 2009 http://reliefweb.int/node/298691. Accessed 12 February 2012.

[55] Ibid.

[56] Commission (EC), 'A Community approach…', op. cit. n. 53, 4–6.

[57] Ibid. 4.

[58] Ibid.

[59] Ibid.

[60] Commission (EC), 'EU strategy for supporting…', op. cit. n. 53, 2–5.

[61] Ibid. 6.

[62] ASEAN Agreement on Disaster Management and Emergency Response of 26 July 2005, ASEAN Documents Series 2005.

[63] For a definition of disaster response see Chap. 1 by de Guttry in this volume; for a definition of disaster management see Chap. 8 by Nicoletti in this volume.

core components of an enabling environment for DRR, read as follows: the adoption of precautionary measures to prevent, monitor, and mitigate disasters,[64] the mainstreaming of DRR efforts into sustainable development policies, and the involvement of all stakeholders including local communities, non-governmental organizations, and private enterprises[65] in addressing disaster risks. As for the normative obligations, State Parties are required to develop and implement legislative and regulatory measures for the disaster prevention and mitigation, as well as policies, plans, programs, and strategies.[66] A National Focal Point[67] and one or more Competent Authorities for the purpose of the implementation of the Agreement[68] have to be designated. The fulfillment of the aforementioned obligations contributes to establish a multilevel enabling environment which comprises a national and regional dimension.

At a bilateral level, some examples of bilateral treaties, which have been singled out on the basis of their relevance against the topic, show how States collaborate in order to establish an enabling environment. The 2001 *Protocol of intentions between the United States of America and the Republic of the Philippines on the cooperation in disaster prevention and management*[69] includes specific provisions which encompass the enabling environment components. For instance, Article 1(1) provides for co-operation mechanisms that, if implemented, strengthen the National Disaster Coordinating Council of the Philippines, i.e., the focal inter-institutional organization in disaster-risk management. Both States intend to organize the exchange of emergency management professionals and practitioners in order to facilitate the development of programs and activities, including the sharing of expertise, experience, and information as well as the transfer of new technology in emergency management.[70] The Protocol partly contributes to the step-by-step process which jointly leads to an enabling environment. Furthermore, the 1992 *Convention in the area of the prediction and prevention of major risks and on mutual assistance in the event of natural or man–made disasters* between Italy and France[71] establishes an information exchange system and intends to develop joint training programs on disaster prediction and prevention.[72] Likewise, the co-operation for disaster preparedness and prevention between Spain and Argentina is sanctioned by a bilateral agreement on disaster

[64] ASEAN Agreement, Article 3 (4).

[65] Ibid. Article 3, (5–6).

[66] Ibid. Article 6 (2) a.

[67] The National Focal Point is an entity designated and authorized by each Party to receive and transmit information pursuant to the provisions of this Agreement. See ibid. Article 1 (8).

[68] Ibid. Article 22 (1).

[69] 2001 Protocol of Intentions between the Government of the United States of America and the Republic of the Philippines Concerning Co-operation and Disaster Prevention and Management.

[70] Ibid. Article 1(2).

[71] 1992 Convention between Italy and France in the Area of the Prediction and Prevention of Major Risks and on Mutual Assistance in the Event of Natural or Man-Made Disasters.

[72] Ibid. Article 2.

preparedness, prevention, and mutual assistance.[73] Co-operation for disaster preparedness and prevention includes the development of the enabling environment's components. Specifically these are: the exchange of information, documentation, publications and teaching materials of a scientific and technical nature; training specialists in disaster preparedness and prevention and the provision of emergency aid; taking part in the design and implementation of exercises in the other State; transferring state-of-the-art technology; dispatching experts to provide consultancy or advisory services; and jointly preparing and implementing specific DRR programs and projects.[74]

The international and regional legal instruments feature the international efforts for a systematic approach to DRR. Their purpose is mainly to facilitate the role of national governments in setting down the necessary enabling conditions for reducing disaster risk. Regional and bilateral agreements on DRR-related matters consolidate the legal basis of the enabling environment core components and of the DRR approach *per se* as well.

9.3.2 The Soft Law Dimension of an Enabling Environment for DRR

The DRR rationale has been incorporated in the HFA, which 'does not need to constitute a binding treaty before it can exercise an influence in international politics.'[75] Although the soft law dimension of the HFA is meant to indicate that the instrument in question is not of itself 'law,' the use of such document is significant in indicating the evolution and establishment of guidelines, 'which can be converted into legally binding rules.'[76] Indeed, the soft law contributes to international law development and can be equivalent to what—in Roman law—is known as '*lex ferenda.*'

9.3.2.1 The Normative Impact of the Hyogo Framework for Action

The pivotal international instrument on the prevention and reduction of disasters is the 2005–2015 Hyogo Framework for Action (HFA) adopted at the World Conference on Disaster Reduction (hereafter, WCDR).[77] The HFA, lays down five

[73] 1988 Argentina-Spain Agreement on Cooperation on Disaster Preparedness and Prevention, and Mutual Assistance in the Event of Disasters.

[74] Ibid. Article IV.

[75] Shaw 2003, 111.

[76] Ibid.

[77] 168 UN member States, 78 observer organizations and 161 NGOs participated in the WCDR. See UNISDR (2005a), 96.

priorities for action which set forth the main components of an enabling environment for reducing disaster risk. In 2006, the United Nations General Assembly backed the HFA by means of a non-legally binding resolution whose recommendatory nature is reflected in the wording employed: 'the *General Assembly [...] endorses* [emphasis added] the Hyogo Declaration and the HFA 2005–2015 [...].'[78]

Though not legally binding, the HFA points out that:

> 'each State has the primary responsibility for its own sustainable development and for taking effective measures to reduce disaster risk [...]. At the same time, in the context of increasing global interdependence, concerted international cooperation and an enabling international environment are required to stimulate and contribute to developing the knowledge, capacities and motivation needed for disaster risk reduction at all levels.'[79]

The HFA's priorities define the path which States have to follow with the aim to establish an enabling environment for DRR. According to the Priority for action 1, States should 'ensure that [DRR] is a national and a local priority with a strong institutional basis for implementation.' The development of policy, legislative, and institutional frameworks for [DRR] along with national mechanisms apt to track progress through specific and measurable indicators lead to manage risks and to achieve widespread consensus for, engagement in and compliance with DRR measures across all sectors of society.[80] Three key activities put this Priority into practice: improving national institutional and legislative frameworks; allocating new resources; and promoting community participation. States are required to implement a comprehensive national DRR plan and/or policy which, *inter alia,* includes the integration of risk reduction into development policies; the adoption and/or modification of DRR legislation; the recognition of the importance and specificity of local risk patterns and trends; and the decentralization of responsibilities and resources for DRR. According to the 'Guide for Implementing the Hyogo Framework' national governments should also allocate new resources, eliminate the investment barriers, and enhance the participation of other actors involved in the sector concerned.[81]

The following four priorities for action, likewise, contribute to develop a multilevel enabling system for reducing disaster risk: identify, assess and monitor

---

[78] UNGA Res. "International Strategy for Disaster Reduction", UN doc. A/RES/60/195 (2006), para 2.

[79] UNISDR 2005b, para 13 (b), 4. The Yokohama Strategy for a Safer World adopted in 1994, whose gaps have been addressed in the HFA, called for the UN member States, through their respective legislative bodies, to improve their preparedness postures in the face of natural disasters. It also recognized that '[...] *in the context of increasing global interdependence, concerted international cooperation and an enabling international environment are vital for the success of these national efforts'.* See Yokohama Strategy for a safer World: Guidelines for Natural Disaster Prevention, Preparedness and Mitigation Containing the Principles, the Strategy and the Plan of Action, Yokohama, Japan, 23–27 May 1994.

[80] UNISDR 2005b, para 16.

[81] UNISDR 2007, 7 et seq.

disaster risks and enhance early warning (Priority 2); use knowledge, innovation and education to build a culture of safety and resilience at all levels (Priority 3); reduce the underlying risk factors (Priority 4); and strengthen disaster preparedness for effective response at all levels (Priority 5).

Along the same lines, through the Hyogo Declaration–a further outcome of the WCDR—States have affirmed that:

> '[...] it is vital to give high priority to disaster risk reduction in national policy, consistent with their capacities and the resources available to them. [...] [S]trengthening community level capacities to reduce disaster risk at the local level is especially needed, considering that appropriate disaster reduction measures at that level enable the communities and individuals to reduce significantly their vulnerability to hazards [...].'[82]

Both the declaration and the HFA reflect the political will to increase attention to DRR and put the DRR rationale into practice with the aim to reduce human vulnerability.[83] The importance of 'political will' for DRR both at national and local level is repeatedly cited as a crucial element for national strategies as well as a local enabling environment.[84] The HFA spells out that a national enabling environment has to be backed by an enabling international environment, and therefore includes an external and internal dimension in the concept of enabling environment. The normative importance of the HFA and the Hyogo declaration is also proved by the fact that both have been recalled in the preamble of the ASEAN Agreement[85] which points out the importance of regional co-operation 'to prepare for and ensure rapid and effective disaster response in situations that exceed national coping capacities.' Furthermore, at the EU level, the Prevention Communication[86] affirms that 'it contributes to the implementation of the [HFA] 2005–2015.'

In order to understand whether States commit to the HFA and how their commitment is put into practice, the Global Platform provides the necessary explanatory tools (see *infra* Sect. 9.4). Indeed, the Global Platform, established in 2007, is mandated to assess progress made in the implementation of the HFA[87] and identify the remaining gaps and actions in order to accelerate the national and local implementation.

---

[82] UNISDR 2005c, para 4.

[83] UNISDR 2005a, 97.

[84] See Pelling 2007; Pro Vention 2009.

[85] See *supra* Sect. 9.3.1.

[86] Ibid.

[87] UNGA, Res. "International Strategy for Disaster Reduction", UN doc. A/RES/62/192 (2007), para 15.

9.4 The Commitment of States to the HFA Through the Establishment of an Enabling Environment for DRR

Declarations and statements made during the main international forum on DRR—the Global Platform–confirm the normative impact of both the HFA and Hyogo declaration and mirror a growing State practice as to the enhancement of DRR measures. The Global Platform–a biennial forum for accelerating worldwide momentum on DRR through the information exchange, the discussion of latest development and knowledge and the partnership building across sectors[88]–provides strategic guidance for implementing the HFA and for sharing DRR experiences and expertise. This section intends to chart the components of the enabling environment for DRR in a selected number of State declarations made during the three sessions of the Global Platform (i.e., in 2007, 2009, 2011). Such declarations have been singled out on the basis of two main criteria: the commitment of a State to the HFA backed by national implementing measures and the extent of the impact of recent disasters on the country taken into account.

In 2007, Romania[89] put forward a set of concrete actions which contributed to the implementation of the HFA. Such actions *inter alia* include the adoption of the national strategy for prevention against disasters (2006), the national strategy for flood risk management (2005), the national strategy on climate change for 2005–2007 (2005), the national plan for action regarding climate change, and the national strategy for public information and education in emergency situations (2006), which is part of a national campaign launched by 'The project for diminishing the losses associated to calamities and training in emergency situations' (2004).[90]

The commitment of Australia[91] to the HFA[92] turned into concrete measures in 2009 when the Australian Government announced the launch of the DRR policy

---

[88] As the primary gathering for the world's disaster risk community, the Global Platform brings together governments, UN, international regional organizations and institutions, NGOs, scientific/academic institutions and the private sector. See PreventionWeb, 'Global Platform for Disaster Risk Reduction,' http://www.preventionweb.net/english/hyogo/GP/. Accessed 12 February 2012.

[89] Romania is rated as a 'medium risk' country in the Natural Disasters Risk Index (hereafter, NDRI). The NDRI, compiled by the global risk advisory firm, Maplecroft, was developed to enable businesses and insurance companies to identify risk to international assets. Such an index is calculated by measuring the human impact of natural disasters, in terms of deaths per annum and per million of population, plus the frequency of events over the last 30 years. See PreventionWeb, 'Natural Disasters Risk Index 2010', http://www.preventionweb.net/english/professional/maps/v.php?id=14169. Accessed 12 April 2011.

[90] PreventionWeb 2007, Contributions and Statements, Global Platform for DRR, First Session.

[91] Australia is rated as a 'medium risk' country in the NDRI. See *supra* n. 89. In 2010, eight natural disasters were reported in the country, see PreventionWeb '2010 Disasters in number' released by UNISDR, USAID, and CRED http://www.preventionweb.net/files/17615_confpress2010.pdf. Accessed 12 February 2012.

[92] PreventionWeb 2007, Contributions and Statements, Global Platform for DRR, First Session.

'*Investing in a Safer Future.*'[93] Through such a policy, Australia has articulated its commitment to the HFA in four areas: (1) integrating DRR across Australia's development and humanitarian programs; (2) supporting international and regional stakeholders for targeted DRR programs in line with the HFA; (3) enhancing leadership and advocacy for DRR to encourage greater consideration for and investment in efforts that will minimize disasters; and (4) ensuring the co-ordination and the coherence of the Australia's policies and programs for DRR and climate change adaptation.[94] In 2011, Australia announced the adoption of a new National Strategy for Disaster Resilience aiming to make DRR a shared responsibility of governments, business, communities, and individuals.[95]

In 2007, Pakistan declared its commitment to the goals of the HFA[96] which was backed by the promulgation of the National Disaster Management Ordinance (2006) and the establishment of the National Disaster Management Commission (hereafter, NDMC) and Authority. The second session of the Platform gave Pakistan the opportunity to explain its national involvement in implementing the HFA and the NDMC's key initiatives against the establishment of a comprehensive disaster management system in the country. These activities consisted in the formulation of the National Disaster Risk Management Framework in order to guide the work of the entire system in the area of disaster risk management, the establishment of the National Disaster Management Fund, and the launch of the National Institute of Disaster Management Project and the Composite Risk Assessment and National Emergency Response System Project.[97] In 2011, Pakistan made clear that the legal basis of the national disaster risk management system–the 2010 National Disaster Management Act–put the DRR strategy into practice through the use of local potential.[98]

In 2007, India,[99] which during the last decade faced four 'mega disasters,'[100] shared its national experience as to the development of a strong disaster management system in the country. As a matter of fact, the former relief approach has been changed into a holistic approach to disaster management which, therefore,

---

93 PreventionWeb 2009, Country Statements, Global Platform for DRR, Second Session.

94 Ibid.

95 PreventionWeb 2011, Official Statements, Global Platform for DRR, Third Session.

96 PreventionWeb 2007, Contributions and Statements, Global Platform for DRR, First Session. Pakistan is rated as "extreme risk" in the NDRI, see *supra* n. 89. In 2010, seven natural disasters were reported in the country, see *supra* n. 91.

97 PreventionWeb 2009, Country Statements, Global Platform for DRR, Second Session. As for the status of emergency workers in Pakistan, see Chap. 23 by Silingardi in this volume.

98 PreventionWeb 2011, Official Statements, Global Platform for DRR, Third Session.

99 India is rated as an 'extreme risk' country in the NDRI, see *supra* n. 89. In 2010, 16 natural disasters were reported in the country, see *supra* n. 91.

100 PreventionWeb 2007, Contributions and Statements, Global Platform for DRR, First Session.

encompasses prevention, mitigation, preparedness, response, relief, and rehabilitation. The government enacted the Disaster Management Act (2005) which provides for the necessary institutional, financial and legal framework at the national, and provincial levels.[101]

In 2009, despite the lack of a clear commitment to the HFA, China[102] showed a strong involvement in implementing DRR measures. As a matter of fact, the Chinese government issued the '11th five year-plan on comprehensive disaster reduction' with the aim to integrate disaster reduction into national development plans and social policies.[103] China also declared to promote the community level capacity building in disaster reduction by means of a community-based disaster response system and to enhance the DRR culture through, *inter alia,* the designation of May 12 as national 'Disaster Prevention and Reduction Day.'[104]

In 2007, Mozambique[105] announced to mainstream DRR in the national plan for poverty reduction.[106] The HFA was considered as the basis for the launch of a 10-year National Master Plan for DRR, and consequently DRR was integrated into the overall development planning process. In 2009, the second session of the Global Platform[107] gave the possibility to better define the purpose of the 10-year National Master Plan, i.e., the implementation of HFA-oriented measures such as the reform of legal and institutional framework enhancing the mandate of the National Institute for Disasters Management to coordinate all DRR activities; the establishment of the National Operative Centers for Emergency, at the national and regional levels; and, the decentralization of disaster risk issues to local levels.[108]

Along the same lines, the United States of America's declarations substantiate the normative impact of the HFA on national policies and legislation. In 2009, the USA[109] declared its commitment to strengthening the UNISDR and acknowledged that reducing the loss of life and property depends on successful implementation of the HFA. The principles of the HFA have been included in the USA's domestic policies and practices.[110] As part of the commitment to the HFA, the US Agency for International Development and the Federal Management Agency have supported DRR measures in developing countries through the improvement of

---

[101] Ibid.

[102] China is rated as 'extreme risk' country in the Natural Disasters Risk Index, see *supra* n. 89. In 2010, 22 natural disasters were reported in the country, see *supra* n. 91. On the protection of persons in the event of disasters in China, see Chap. 15 by Creta in this volume.

[103] PreventionWeb 2009, Country Statements, Global Platform for DRR, Second Session.

[104] Ibid.

[105] Mozambique is rated as an 'extreme risk' country in the NDRI, see *supra* n. 89.

[106] PreventionWeb 2007, Contributions and Statements, Global Platform for DRR, First Session.

[107] PreventionWeb 2009, Country Statements, Global Platform for DRR, Second Session.

[108] Ibid.

[109] In 2010, 12 natural disasters were reported in the country, see *supra* n. 91.

[110] PreventionWeb 2009, Country Statements, Global Platform for DRR, Second Session.

mitigation and response capacities. In 2011, the USA explained that DRR is an important component towards building a sustainable future and confirmed the endorsement of the HFA's goals and principles and the effort to foster DRR both at home and abroad.[111]

National efforts in reducing disaster risk confirm the normative impact of the HFA and contribute to create an enabling environment which includes prevention and preparedness,[112] mitigation, response, and rehabilitation considerations. From States' declarations we infer that establishing an enabling environment clearly has the two-fold purpose of improving resilience to disasters and strengthening the DRR capacity at a local, national, and international level.

9.5 Conclusions: Establishing an Enabling Environment for DRR as a Political and Legal Commitment?

An enabling environment is a multi-level system for the management of disasters whose positive impact becomes apparent in the medium and long term with the concurrent action and involvement of different actors. National governments in collaboration with other stakeholders are required to implement a set of measures in so far as their aim is to develop a national enabling environment for DRR (see Fig. 9.1). Specifically, they should:

- improve a DRR-related legislative and regulatory framework;[113]
- enhance the institutional capacity across sectors at various levels;
- establish a range of accountability mechanisms;[114]
- mobilize and allocate public resources and investments[115] for DRR activities;
- enhance (DRR) governance;[116]
- invest in training and specialized technical assistance with the aim to foster local capacity development;
- strengthen the DRR capacity of communities and individuals in order enable them to recognize and reduce risks in their localities;[117]
- promote the dialog with the DRR international environment;

---

[111] A National Disaster Recovery Framework has been developed along with the recommendation for national climate change adaptation strategies which prioritize the most vulnerable and apply the best-available science. See PreventionWeb 2011, Official Statements, Global Platform for DRR, Third Session. On the US' Legal Framework Governing Disaster Response, see Chap. 12 by Mancini in this volume.

[112] See Chap. 8 by Nicoletti in this volume.

[113] ILO 2008, 17.

[114] Brinkerhoff 2007, 86.

[115] Ibid.

[116] Van Dijk and Savenije 2009, 89.

[117] UNISDR 2008, 4.

- focus on the political, social, and cultural aspects of DRR;
- and address national DRR-related economic and financial challenges.[118]

As a matter of fact, these national measures partly have a legal basis in the provisions of the aforementioned treaties and conventions.[119] For instance, international treaties include programmatic obligations[120] regarding the implementation of DRR-oriented legislative, administrative, and economic frameworks (e.g., the UNFCCC, the Convention on the transboundary effects of industrial accidents). The analysis of bilateral agreements reveals that States endeavor to strengthen the bilateral co-operation for the enhancement of an enabling environment and make use of the bilateral agreement in order to mutually implement DRR actions. Along the same lines, the ASEAN Agreement fosters the establishment of a regional enabling system based on the partnerships and co-operation among States Parties. Likewise, the EU Prevention Communication, specifically addressed to the EU member States, propose integrating the DRR rationale in national policies and/or legislation and achieving the HFA's goals.

A treaty-based obligation to establish an enabling environment for DRR does not exist to date. Neither does a customary rule which comprises such obligation exist. However, as this chapter shows, the establishment of a multi-level system, which enables a country to cope with disaster risk, is the result of a set of measures which may subsumed under the existing DRR-related treaties and conventions.

The development of a national enabling environment is required by the HFA which features an apparent normative intent and effect. The analysis of States' declarations made during the Global Platform[121] has highlighted the ongoing process towards the attainment of the HFA's goals of reducing disaster losses by 2015 and building resilience to disasters. The HFA can be considered as a 'non-conventional concerted act,' i.e., 'a recognized and legitimate mean for States to express their intentions, policies, and political commitments without entering into a legally binding engagement.'[122] As such, the HFA must be distinguished from treaties or custom accepted as law. Nonetheless, 'when States enter into a non-legal commitment, they generally assume a political obligation to carry it out in good faith.'[123] According to *Schachter*, 'a State assuming such an international political commitment may (under the requirement of good faith) be considered to have given up its prior right under international law to declare the matter in question as exclusively domestic.'[124] Indeed, further factors confirm what have

118 Ibid.

119 See *supra* Sect. 9.3.1.

120 On the programmatic and incremental approach to climate change, see Bodansky 1993.

121 The number of UN member States participating in the Global Platform amounted to 168 at the 3rd session in 2011(121 States participated in the 1st session in 2007 and 140 in the 2nd session).

122 Schachter 1991, 268.

123 Ibid. 267.

124 Ibid. 268.

been underlined so far. A growing number of States, which endorsed the HFA, are reporting to the UNISDR on the degree of implementation of the HFA.[125] They are, likewise, engaged in establishing and/or strengthening their national platforms which reflect the commitment of governments to implement national and local DRR activities while linking up with international efforts.[126]

The main international DRR framework, the HFA, provides the necessary tools and guidelines to develop the components of an enabling environment for DRR. Therefore, the connection between the implementation of the HFA's five priorities[127] and the establishment of an enabling environment for DRR is consolidating even further. The ongoing international trend leads to affirm that the HFA includes diverse levels of State involvement. In other terms, it is not only a (potential) legal commitment which puts an enabling environment for DRR into practice, but also political, social, and economic considerations play a pivotal role. In international *fora,* States have affirmed their commitment to develop an enabling environment for reducing disaster risk and have made their engagement effective through the adoption of legislative measures (e.g., in Pakistan, Romania), the establishment of *ad hoc* institutions (e.g., in Pakistan, Mozambique, USA), and the allocation of funds for DRR activities at the national and international level (e.g., in Australia, USA). Such an international conduct puts forward the legal facet of the (political) duty to establish an enabling environment for DRR and contributes to build the resilience of nations to disasters.

References

Bodansky D (1993) The United Nations framework convention on climate change: a commentary. Yale J Int L 18:451–558

Brinkerhoff DW (2007) The enabling environment for achieving the millennium development goals: government actions to support NGOs. In: Brinkerhoff J et al (eds) NGOs and the millennium development goals: citizen action to reduce poverty, Palgrave MacMillan, New York, pp 83–101

Britton N R (2006) National planning and response: national systems. In: Rodrìguez H et al (eds) Handbook of disaster research, Springer, New York, pp 347–367

Davis L, North D (1971) Institutional change and American economic growth. Cambridge University Press, Cambridge

Fulgence K, Mori N (2009) Social entrepreneurship in Tanzania: assessment of enabling environment, 2nd EMES conferences—selected papers series. Available at http://www.emes.net. Accessed 4 Feb 2012

[125] The HFA—Monitor is an online tool which assists the countries to monitor and review their progress and challenges in the implementation of disaster risk reduction and recovery actions undertaken at the national level, in accordance with the HFA's priorities. See PreventionWeb, HFA Monitor 2009–2011, http://www.preventionweb.net/english/hyogo/hfa-monitoring/hfa-monitor/. Accessed 4 February 2012.

[126] See *supra* footnote 29.

[127] See *supra* Sect. 9.3.2.1.

Hope KR (2009) Capacity development for good governance in developing societies: lessons from the field. Dev Pract 19:79–86

Horton D et al (2003) Evaluating capacity development: experiences from research and development organizations around the world, International Service for National Agricultural Research (ISNAR), The Netherlands; International Development Research Centre (IDRC), Canada, ACP-EU Technical Centre for Agricultural and Rural Cooperation, The Netherlands

ILO (2007) Conclusions concerning the promotion of sustainable enterprises (International Labour Conference), Geneva

ILO (2008) Freedom of Association in Practice: lessons learned, global report under the follow-up to the ILO declaration on fundamental principles and rights at work. ILO, Geneva

ILO/AfDB (2007) Assessing the enabling environment for women in growth enterprises: an AfDB/ILO integrated framework assessment guide, ILO, Geneva. http://www.ilo.org/empent/Publications/WCMS_116163/lang–en/index.htm

Misuraca GC (2007) E-Governance in Africa from theory to action—a handbook on ICTs for local governance, Africa World Press, Inc., International Development Research Centre, Ottawa. http://www.idrc.ca/en/ev-113398-201-1-DO_TOPIC.html

Mortensen JB et al (2003) Foreign aid and private sector development. In: Tarp F (ed) Foreign aid and development: lessons learned and direction for the future, Routledge, London, pp 242–257

Noya A, Clarence E (2007) The social economy: building inclusive economies, OECD, Paris. http://www.oecd.org/document/62/0,3746,en_2649_34417_40127998_1_1_1_1,00.html

OECD—Development Assistant Committee (2000) Donor support for institutional capacity development in environment: lessons learned, OECD, Paris. http://www.oecd.org/

OECD (2009) Private sector participation in water infrastructure. Checklist for public action, (e-book), OECD, Paris. http://www.oecd.org/document/31/0,3343,en_2649_34893_42362271_1_1_1_1,00.html

Pelling M (2007) Learning from others: scope and challenges for participatory disaster risk assessment. Disasters 31:373–385

PreventionWeb (2007) Contributions and statements, Global Platform for DRR, First Session, Geneva, Switzerland. http://www.preventionweb.net/globalplatform/2007/first-session/gp_1st_statements.html#delegations_w, 5–7 June 2007

PreventionWeb (2009) Country Statements, Global Platform for DRR, Second Session, Geneva, Switzerland. http://www.preventionweb.net/globalplatform/2009/programme/statements/, 16–19 June 2009

PreventionWeb (2010) 2010 Disasters in number' released by UNISDR, USAID, and CRED. http://www.preventionweb.net/files/17615_confpress2010.pdf

PreventionWeb (2011) Official statements, Global Platform for DRR, Third Session, Geneva, Switzerland. http://www.preventionweb.net/globalplatform/2011/programme/statements/, 8–13 May 2011

PreventionWeb 'Global Platform for Disaster Risk Reduction' (2012) http://www.prevention web.net/english/hyogo/GP/

PreventionWeb, 'Natural Disasters Risk Index 2010', http://preventionweb.net/go/14169

Pronto A (2008–2009) Consideration of the protection of persons in the event of disasters by the International Law Commission. ILSA J Int Comp Law 15 :449–457

ProVention (2009) ProVention forum 2009—risk and governance: bridging national enabling environments and local action. ProVention Consortium, Geneva

Ribot JC (2002) African decentralization: local actors, powers and accountability, UNRISD/International Development Research Centre Paper no.8. http://www.unrisd.org

Schachter O (1991) Non-conventional concerted acts. In Bedjaoui M (ed) International law: achievements and prospects, UNESCO, Parigi; Martinus Nijhoff Publishers, Dordrecht, Boston, London, pp 266–269

Shaw MN (2003) International law, 5th edn. Cambridge University Press, Cambridge

Tripp R (2003) Strengthening the enabling environment for agricultural technology development in Sub-Saharan Africa, Overseas Development Institute Working Paper no 212. http://www.odi.org.uk/resources/download/1777.pdf

UNDP (2010a) Capacity development. Measuring capacity. UNDP, New York. http://www.beta.undp.org/content/undp/en/home/librarypage/capacity-building.html

UNDP (2010b) Disaster risk reduction, governance and mainstreaming. UNDP, New York. http://www.undp.org/cpr/documents/disaster/4Disaster%20Risk%20Reduction%20-%20Governance.pdf

UNISDR (2004) Living with risk. A global review of disaster reduction initiatives, vol 1. UNISDR, New York and Geneva

UNISDR (2005a) World conference on disaster reduction 18–22 January 2005, Kobe, Hyogo, Japan. In: Proceedings of the conference 'Building the resilience of nations and communities to disasters'. http://www.unisdr.org/2005/wcdr/thematic-sessions/WCDR-proceedings-of-the-Conference.pdf

UNISDR (2005b) Hyogo framework for action 2005–2015: building the resilience of Nations and communities to disasters, extract from the final report of the World Conference on Disaster Reduction, 18–22 Jan 2005, Kobe, Hyogo, Japan. http://www.unisdr.org/2005/wcdr/intergover/official-doc/L-docs/Hyogo-framework-for-action-english.pdf

UNISDR (2005c) Hyogo declaration, extract from the final report of the World Conference on Disaster Reduction, 18–22 Jan 2005, Kobe, Hyogo, Japan. http://www.unisdr.org/2005/wcdr/intergover/official-doc/L-docs/Hyogo-declaration-english.pdf

UNISDR (2007) Words into action: a guide for implementing the Hyogo framework, UNISDR, Geneva. http://www.unisdr.org/files/594_10382.pdf

UNISDR (2008) Disaster preparedness for effective response. Guidance and indicator package for implementing priority five of the Hyogo framework, Geneva and New York, UNISDR

UNISDR (2009a) Risk and poverty in a changing climate. 2009 Global assessment report on disaster risk reduction, United Nations, Geneva. http://www.preventionweb.net/english/hyogo/gar/report/index.php?id=1130&pid:34&pih:2

UNISDR (2009b) Terminology on disaster risk reduction. UNISDR, Geneva

UNISDR (2011) Revealing risk, redefining development. Global assessment report on DRR 2011, United Nations, Geneva

Van Dijk K, Savenije H (2009) Towards national financing strategies for sustainable forest management in Latin America: overview of the present situation and the experience in selected countries. FAO, Rome

Wallström M (2009) Disaster risk and its reduction: who is responsible? Fletcher Forum World Aff J 33(2):153–158

White S (1999) Create an enabling environment for micro and small enterprise (MSE) development in Thailand, ILO/UNDP working paper 3. http://www.ilo.org/public/english/region/asro/bangkok/library/pub10.htm

WHO-Europe (2010) Progress and challenges on water health: the role of the protocol on water health, WHO-Europe, Copenhagen. http://www.euro.who.int/__data/assets/pdf_file/0014/100940/Parma_water_BD3.pdf

Chapter 10
Access to the Territory of a Disaster-Affected State

Milena Costas Trascasas

Abstract Facilitation of the entry of personnel of assisting relief organizations to the territory of a disaster-affected State as well as the provision of goods and services to the victims constitute two critical elements that are reliant on the consent of national authorities. Nevertheless, the introduction of the protection of persons in disasters as a necessary component of the IDRL has provided the basis for limiting, to some extent, the role that consent by the affected State is called to play in disaster relief. This article analyzes two important developments that are taking place in this regard. Firstly, it deals with progress in the work of the International Law Commission on constructing the duty of the affected State to accept humanitarian relief when it is deemed to be 'unable' or 'unwilling' to protect persons that are under its jurisdiction. The second part is devoted to analyzing the 'Responsibility to Protect' doctrine and the advantages or disadvantages of extending its scope to disaster situations. It finally analyzes progressive developments in UN Security Council practice in order to establish under what circumstances it would be justified for this body to take coercive measures in the context of disasters, with the aim of 'coercing' a government to accept access by international relief, and the consequences of such a course of action.

Keywords Sovereignty · Human rights · Humanitarian assistance · Access to territory · Use of force · Responsibility to protect

M. Costas Trascasas (✉)
Università degli Studi di Milano, Via Conservatorio 7, 20122, Milan, Italy
e-mail: milena.costas@unimi.it

A. de Guttry et al. (eds.), *International Disaster Response Law*,
DOI: 10.1007/978-90-6704-882-8_10,

Contents

10.1 Introductory Remarks

The question of access to the territory of a disaster-affected State is a key issue in disaster relief. Facilitation of the entry of personnel of assisting relief organizations as well as the provision of goods and services to the victims constitute two critical elements that are reliant on the consent of national authorities. The fundamental principles of sovereignty and non-intervention tend to preserve the right of a State to control the provision of humanitarian relief within its territory at any stage of the disaster response (initiation, organization, co-ordination, and implementation).[1] Nevertheless, the introduction of the protection of persons as a necessary component of the IDRL has provided a basis for limiting, to some extent, the role that the affected State is called to play. In fact, by underscoring the 'primary responsibility' of the State, the focus has now been shifted from a right-oriented to a duty-oriented approach.[2] In accordance with this new perspective, sovereignty is to be interpreted more as a responsibility than a privilege and this applies, in particular, with respect to the role national authorities must play in the protection of persons under its jurisdiction.[3] By insisting on the general

[1] See A/RES/38/202, 20 December 1983 para 2; A/RES/46/182, 19 December 1991 Annex, para 4. The International Law Commission Special Rapporteur has considered that: 'the primary responsibility of the affected State, as expressed through its operational control of disaster relief and through the consent requirement, constitutes a general rule governing humanitarian assistance.' *Third report on the protection of persons in the event of disasters*, UN Doc. A/CN.4/629, 31 March 2010 para 96.

[2] It is to be noted that the ILC has tried to avoid any kind of terminological misunderstandings by privileging in its text of draft articles the use of the term 'duty' instead of that of 'responsibility'.

[3] In this context it has been acknowledged the urgency of a growing consensus among States to redefine their sovereignty by means of a 'constructive use of international law.' *Preliminary report on the protection of persons in the event of disasters*, UN Doc. A/CN.4/598, 5 May 2008 para 55.

responsibility and on the more particular duties which lie with the affected State, such a conceptual shift would contribute in some way to resolving existing legal difficulties in the recognition and specification of both the 'right' of the victims to receive humanitarian assistance and the 'right' of assisting actors to make aid offers.

As far as the regulation of disaster relief is concerned, this kind of re-conceptualization of State sovereignty is evident in two important developments that are taking place in international law. Firstly, the work that the International Law Commission (ILC) is carrying out for the codification of IDRL confirms the emergence of various concepts that deal with duties of protection burdening both States and, subsidiarily, the international community. Attempts to construct the duty of the affected State to accept humanitarian relief when it is deemed to be 'unable' or 'unwilling' to fulfill its primary role in protecting those that are under its jurisdiction reflect the challenges the idea of a 'responsible exercise of power' poses to the traditional State approach to sovereignty. In the event of disaster, if a State demonstrates a clear lack of collaboration, inefficiency, or inability to confront the humanitarian catastrophe it is now being held that it is under a duty to accept offers of aid, or even, an obligation to seek external aid. Conversely, an offer of assistance that is met with refusal, under certain conditions, might be considered as constituting a violation of the right to life. As a corollary of this approach, if the State does not undertake all the means at its disposal to provide the necessary humanitarian relief then the international community is called to intervene subsidiarily.

The second noticeable development impacting the field of disaster relief is the emergence as part of the UN Security Council action of an incipient practice allowing for recourse to coercive measures in cases of humanitarian catastrophes. This course of action can be seen as the starting point of an embryonic 'collective responsibility' to deal with grave humanitarian crisis caused by the 'inability' or 'unwillingness' of the concerned State to exercise its primary responsibility. The question is whether current international law offers the basis for supporting the idea that the 'international community' (in assuming that such an entity does exist) can 'replace' or 'overpass' State consent and, if it does, under what circumstances and for what purposes.

In this context, attempts to extend the doctrine of so-called 'Responsibility to Protect' (R2P) to situations of disaster underscores the same idea that the international community should intervene in cases where the State is 'manifestly' failing to protect its population. The question of 'coercing' the State to consent to the entry into its territory of external humanitarian aid and personnel was notably raised in 2008 when, despite widespread and severe human suffering caused by the Cyclone Nargis to the population of Myanmar, the government refused international offers of aid without providing very convincing reasons. A close analysis of this case shows that the R2P doctrine continues to generate significant controversy not only regarding its unclear content but also regarding its legal scope, and further on the way in which it can be implemented in practice. More particularly, the risk of R2P becoming a kind of 'Trojan horse,' allowing external interventions for humanitarian purposes, must not be underestimated. In fact, it has been noted that what is presented as an emerging norm is not anything new, but rather a re-conceptualization of the old humanitarian intervention presented in a more 'attractive' way.[4] Concerns on whether claims of extending this doctrine to disaster situations can serve to legitimize interference by the great powers in the internal affairs of the weak, or to circumvent the UN Security Council authority over and monopoly on the use of coercive powers, must therefore be carefully considered.[5]

10.2 State Consent as a Prerequisite for Humanitarian Access

It is well known that the principles of territorial sovereignty and non-intervention constitute fundamental principles of international law regulating access to the territory of a disaster-affected State.[6] As a result, disaster relief provided by assisting actors is subject to the consent of the affected State that bears primary responsibility for the protection of persons in its territory (or subject to its jurisdiction or control during a disaster).[7] The key UN General Assembly Resolution 46/182 (1991) underlines this approach when underscoring that 'humanitarian assistance is to be provided with the consent of the affected country and in principle on the basis of an appeal.'[8]

A relevant study on the practice of States, undertaken under the auspices of the International Federation of Red Cross and Red Crescent Societies in 2007, demonstrates that most disasters are addressed domestically and that States normally only make recourse to request for international assistance for the most massive disasters.[9] Thus, it is to be expected that under such exceptional circumstances States may be willing to seek—and accept—international aid and that only in very rare cases would they be unwilling to permit access by any humanitarian relief or external actors. Still, because consent is a *conditio sine qua non* for the initiation of a humanitarian operation the concerned State should always manifest its agreement in some way. This authorization usually takes the form of a request for assistance and subsequent acceptance of an offer made by another State or international organization. The request—offer dialog is the traditional process provided by most relevant instruments in the field, even if State practice shows that there are

---

[4] See Boisson de Chazournes and Condorelli 2007, 6. See also Jackson 2010.

[5] Bellamy 2010, 152. See also Weissman 2010.

[6] The need to respect the territorial sovereignty of the State is clearly established in most multilateral treaties governing disaster relief and further recognized by relevant principles guiding the provision of humanitarian assistance in such situations. See also Chap. 1 by de Guttry and Chap. 2 by Venturini in this volume.

[7] ILC, *Protection of persons in the event of disasters. Memorandum by the Secretariat*, UN Doc. A/CN.4/590, 11 December 2007 para 22.

[8] A/RES/46/182, 19 December 1991, para 3.

[9] Fisher 2007, 89.

cases where States may give a kind of 'blanket consent' by announcing in quite general terms that international assistance is welcomed. Although the non-specific nature of this announcement may pose some problems, the trend is to interpret this practice as amounting to the grant of advance consent to international assistance, including that from States and other entities that are not parties to any of the agreements to which the affected State is a party. In the same vein, it has been suggested that when States are unwilling or unable to issue specific requests for international assistance in a timely manner (because of domestic barriers), other considerations may intercede 'allowing for the lawful circumvention of the established mode for determining consent.' But, even in those cases, it remains the State's basic right to control the provision of assistance, including the freedom to reject that which it deems inappropriate.[10]

A further consequence of the State's consent is the freedom to select the legal framework governing the provision of assistance. Access by operational organizations to the affected areas for the rapid provision of emergency assistance might be legitimately impeded by national authorities under certain circumstances, especially when they have reasons to believe that the humanitarian action will not be implemented strictly on the basis of humanitarian needs but for other purposes (i.e., political, economic, or military).[11] Particularly in the current context, where a great number and variety of international actors (including third States, international organizations, and non-governmental organizations) respond to major disasters, States must maintain some margin of discretion in the selection of those to whom they grant access. In fact, the right of the State not to allow entry into its territory of any humanitarian assistance or relief personnel is generally perceived—and accepted—as a natural right arising out of State sovereignty. Accordingly, current international law does not, in principle, limit the discretion of States to accept international relief or impose on them an obligation to justify their decision not to permit access by external aid or personnel to their territory. In this context, the passage of the Nicaragua case where the International Court of Justice stated that 'the provision of strict humanitarian aid to persons or forces in another country, whatever their political affiliation or objectives, cannot be regarded as unlawful intervention or as in any other way contrary to international law' is frequently quoted.[12] Based on the reasoning of the Court, it follows that the offering State should provide guarantees of non-intervention by providing evidence that the offer is limited to alleviating suffering and protecting the life and

[10] ILC *Protection of persons in the event of disasters. Memorandum by the Secretariat*, UN Doc. A/CN.4/590, 11 December 2007 para 58.

[11] In other cases, practice shows that States can also impose several obstacles to both the humanitarian actors' ability to reach populations in need and to operations that aim to provide services and assistance to those affected, for example, through the establishment of unnecessary bureaucratic restrictions on personnel and humanitarian supplies. For a further discussion on this issue see Chap. 23 by Silingardi in this volume.

[12] Case concerning the military and paramilitary activities in and against Nicaragua (Nicaragua v. United States of America) Judgment of 27 June 1986, ICJ Rep. 1986 para 242.

health of the victims. However, because international actors act for various reasons that tend to converge with those that are purely humanitarian, a requirement whereby aid offers must be exclusively intended for humanitarian purposes, although desirable, is not very realistic.[13]

International practice shows that there are a number of reasons that can be raised by States for the purposes of refusing international assistance from others.[14] The State might reject aid in an attempt to preserve its image of national pride or because it wishes to appear as a State that does not need outside assistance. In other cases, governments may decide not to accept offers coming from non-friendly governments or international organizations,[15] or they may simply seek to avoid both the entry of outsiders within State borders or confusion caused by the flow of a large quantity of international assistance. In the aftermath of the Hurricane Katrina in 2005, the US initially decided to reject financial donations and other forms of assistance, including many beneficial supplies offered by several countries, such as medical assistance from Cuba.[16] Also, refusal by India of some international aid following both the 2004 tsunami and a major 2005 South Asian Earthquake, because of its long history of reluctance to request international aid, constitutes a good example of a government's discretion in accepting relief offers.[17] More recently, the expulsion of aid agencies from Sudan in March 2009 underlines the extent to which the whole aid relief system relies on the acquiescence and support of the host government.[18]

---

[13] A good example of how humanitarian action in the context of a natural disaster can converge with other objectives is the relief operation launched by NATO in response to the Pakistan earthquake in 2005. There seems to be little doubt that while the operation was mainly motivated by humanitarian considerations, these were most probably mixed with security interests particularly linked with the fight against international terrorism. The scale of the response was in fact perceived to be part of the security agenda of the United States and its allies in the framework of the fight against international terrorism. Some in the media commented that the main purpose of the US and NATO troops was not taking part in the relief and rehabilitation work but to 'hunt' for Osama-Bin-Laden and other Al-Quaeda leaders. See Jochems 2006.

[14] States may have also used consent to relief as an instrument for political purposes: while accepting the offer of relief from other States can be seen as a way of strengthening the diplomatic relationship, refusal of the offers will usually have an adverse effect. Examples include the Unites States offering aid to Iran following the 26 December 2003 Earthquake and Iran offering aid to the United States following Hurricane Katrina in August 2005; the India-Pakistan rapprochement following the 8 October 2005 Earthquake; or the Ethiopia-Eritrea interaction during droughts from 1999–2000. For these cases see Kelman 2006, 223–224.

[15] After the Earthquake in April 1989 China declared that it welcomed any appropriate emergency assistance from 'friendly' governments and international organizations. China—Earthquake UNDRO Situation Report 2, 18 May 1989, http://reliefweb.int/node/35113. Accessed 2 March 2012.

[16] Kelman 2006, 288; Penuel and Statler 2011, 322–324.

[17] Harvey 2009, 1.

[18] Sudan Tribune, Khartoum's Expulsion of Humanitarian Organizations (March 4, 2009), http://www.sudantribune.com/Khartoum-s-Expulsion-of,30643. Accessed 2 March 2012.

There are some examples where States have completely refused offers of external relief. This has occurred particularly when the host State had grounded—or sometimes exacerbated—motives to suspect that the offer of aid made by third parties concealed an intention to intervene in its internal affairs. In some striking examples, national authorities were manifestly unable to provide aid to victims within their own territories and have also been unwilling either to accept any international offer of aid or to promptly permit humanitarian assistance from outside. In 1990 in the aftermath of the earthquake that hit the Gilan province, causing more than 50,000 victims, the Iranian Government was slow to ask for international assistance, appealing to its people 'to pass this test with pride through patience, endeavour and cooperation.'[19] Although Iran eventually sought assistance from the international community, the government initially forbade direct rescue flights and the entry of aid workers. Myanmar's block on foreign aid and on aid workers entering the country in the crucial days after the Cyclone Nargis is another frequently quoted example.

If the co-operative attitude of the host State is, for operative reasons, essential for the effective delivery and distribution of humanitarian aid to victims, it is difficult to imagine how humanitarian relief operations can take place without consent from national authorities.[20] Indeed, humanitarian actors need to move goods and personnel, implement distributions, provide health services and carry out other operations to meet the basic needs of the affected population; and all these activities presuppose full and unimpeded access to the affected areas. Without the authorization of national authorities, humanitarian personnel would be compelled to work clandestinely in a hostile environment and the conditions necessary to engage in their activities, and this would obviously compromise the achievement of the humanitarian objectives. As has been rightly observed: 'For better or worse, the work of international aid actors depends on the consent of States: whether a State is strong or weak, abusive or concerned for its citizen's welfare, it is still the central determinant of whether or not humanitarian actors can be present in crisis.'[21]

---

[19] Hardcastle and Chua 1998, 634.

[20] Some authors have suggested this possibility as a feasible way of delivering aid to victims under certain circumstances. States willing to provide humanitarian aid could opt to launch a 'clandestine operation' in the territory of the State or to put aid at the disposal of humanitarian organizations, which then cross the State's borders without authorization. It has been noted in this regard that this was common practice in conflicts such as those in Ethiopia, Sudan, Iraq, and the former Yugoslavia. See Abril Stoffels 2004, 536; Bothe 1989, 96.

[21] Harvey 2009, 1.

10.3 Constructing the Duty of an Affected State to Accept Humanitarian Relief

This strict interpretation is now being challenged by the idea that the requirement of consent must not be considered in isolation but rather in light of the responsibilities of the State in exercising its sovereignty. Such an approach would be consistent with contemporary arguments concerning the protection of persons in the context of disasters. In this regard, it should be noted that recent non-binding texts on disaster response tend to meld operational concerns present in treaties with humanitarian ones.[22] Such obligations would arise out of both the relationship the affected State has with the international community and in relation to the people that had suffered the disaster and are under its jurisdiction, and compel the concerned State not to arbitrarily withhold the consent, particularly when it is *unable or unwilling* to provide the required humanitarian assistance.[23] The question arises as to what extent the international community (or other actors such as non-governmental organizations) ought to engage in protection activities in the context of disasters. In other words, can it be acknowledged that the international community has a legitimate interest to protect persons in the event of disaster and, if yes, under what circumstances? This question must necessarily be addressed in the broader context of the lack of fulfillment by the State of its primary responsibility to ensure the protection of persons within its territory.

10.3.1 The State is 'Unable' to Assist its Population

In this regard, it is necessary to note the emerging consensus on the fact that where the domestic response capacity of a State is overwhelmed, rendering the receiving State totally or partially '*unable*' (i.e., incapable)[24] of meeting the needs of persons

---

[22] For example, the Mohonk Criteria for Humanitarian Assistance in Complex Emergencies, 1995, establish that: '[w]here the government or other authority is *unable or manifestly unwilling* to provide life-sustaining aid, the international community has the right and obligation to protect and provide relief to affected and threatened civilian populations in conformity with the principles of international law.' (Section II.4). See Ebersole 1995, 192. Also the 1998 Guiding Principles on Internal Displacement introduce the same idea when establishing that: '[i]nternational humanitarian organizations and other appropriate actors have the right to offer their services in support of the internally displaced. Such an offer shall not be regarded as an unfriendly act or interference in a State's internal affairs and shall be considered in good faith.' Report of the Representative of the Secretary-General, Mr. Francis M. Deng, submitted pursuant to Commission resolution 1997/39. Addendum, *Guiding Principles on Internal Displacement,* E/CN.4/1998/53/Add.2, 11 February 1998, Guiding principle 25 para 2 *in fine*.

[23] ILC, *Report on the work of its sixty-third session*, UN Doc. A/66/10, para 276.

[24] It should be stressed that the ILC draft article dealing with consent by the affected State does not use the 'unable or unwilling' formulation present in other texts to trigger an obligation to accept relief, but rather mainly focuses on the first variation.

within its territory, outside actors may play a significant role.[25] Cases targeted would primarily be those where States are not able to meet their responsibilities to assist and protect their population due to their limited resources as well as those where States may be found to be unable to respond to and fulfill their responsibilities in directing and co-ordinating the relief efforts, due to total disintegration of the governmental authority or the lack of effective control over the territory (so-called 'failed States').[26] For those particular cases, the ILC draft article 10 establishes the duty of the affected State to the extent that a disaster exceeds its national response capacity 'to seek assistance among other States, the United Nations, other competent intergovernmental organizations and relevant non-governmental organizations, as appropriate.'[27]

However, the practical implementation of this duty might be difficult because as it has been observed: 'a general obligation to unconditionally accept all offers of assistance would undermine the co-ordinating role held by the affected State which implies the freedom to choose the assistance that is considered the most appropriate to cover its specific needs.'[28] Moreover, a major concern is that of how the State's inability can be established and demonstrated in practice. If the aim is to help those States that cannot provide relief because they do not have the economic resources to render the assistance required, and therefore to secure the survival of their citizens, it is clear that further developments of this 'duty' into objective criteria (or indicators) are required; otherwise it is unclear under what circumstances it can be held that a certain State is failing in providing relief to its population.[29] However, it might be recognized that the main value of the proposal of developing the State's duty to seek assistance is that of underlining the complementary role international community has to play when the affected State is

---

[25] ILC, *Protection of persons in the event of disasters. Memorandum by the Secretariat*, UN Doc. A/CN.4/590, 11 December 2007 para 250. The Committee on Economic, Social and Cultural Rights has maintained that 'whether an individual or group is unable, for reasons beyond their control, to enjoy the right to adequate food by the means at their disposal, States have the obligation to fulfil (provide) that right directly. This obligation also applies for persons who are victims of natural or other disasters.' General Comment n 12 (E/C.12/1999/5) para 15. Also in considering in 1999 article 11 of the Covenant (Right to adequate food), it commented that: (a) 'States had a core obligation to take the necessary action to mitigate and alleviate hunger, even in times of natural or other disasters,' (b) 'the State had to demonstrate that every effort had been made to use all the resources at its disposal,' and (c) that if it was unable to carry out its obligation, it had the burden of proving that this was the case and that it had 'unsuccessfully sought to obtain international support.' General comment n 13 (E/C.12/1999/10) paras 6 and 17.

[26] The complete collapse of Haiti's infrastructure after the 2010 Earthquake provides a paradigmatic example of this type of State 'inability' to provide disaster response. On January 12, 2010, a massive earthquake struck Haiti destroying the Haitian government infrastructure. For an analysis of this case in the light of the 'Responsibility to Protect' doctrine see Malone 2010.

[27] ILC, *Report on the work of its sixty-third session*, A/66/10, 261.

[28] Benton Heath 2011, 462.

[29] It has been stressed that this is more than a technical question: 'making such an assessment is an inherently political act, and political considerations often weigh heavily as donors governments decide whether and how to intervene.' Harvey 2009, 2.

unable to fulfill its primary duties.[30] Still, international relief should always remain as a last resort, and therefore situations where the international community inappropriately replaces the State in violation of its sovereignty or undermining its local capacities should be avoided.[31] Rather than by concentrating on 'inability' the focus should be on the supporting role the international community should play by encouraging and supporting States to fulfill their responsibilities of assisting and protecting their own population in times of disaster.[32] By fostering national ownership of and local capacities for humanitarian and development strategies the risk of interpreting the 'inability' of the State as a way to legitimize illicit interventions would be avoided. In fact, it has rightly been pointed out that it is difficult to see how the primary duty of the State to seek assistance can be specified without establishing a correlative duty of cooperation for the international community. Besides, it has been noted that a more adequate—and constructive—approach to this question should go in the direction of developing a legal basis for the international community to assume its 'common responsibility to assist' rather than justifying a non-centralized 'right to assist.'[33] Otherwise, this interpretation could lead to a violation of the principle that upholds equality among States allowing for the subordination of one State to others.

10.3.2 The State is 'Unwilling' to Assist its Population

Although the unwillingness of the State is mentioned by recent non-binding texts as justification for the 'right' of the international community to deliver international assistance, the meaning of this expression and the consequences of this course of action have not yet been deeply addressed by scholars. In fact, while the inability of a State can be assessed according to objective capacities from the very outset of the disaster, the 'unwillingness' requirement introduces a subjective criterion that is not easy to determine.[34] Recent developments in IDRL in this

---

[30] Zorzi Giustiniani 2008, 248.

[31] Boisson de Chazournes 2008, 151.

[32] Harvey 2009, 3.

[33] Although in these cases it has been held that the international community may in some way act, it has to be noted that articulation of the willingness of the States to provide assistance as a 'right' might be controversial as it does not necessarily imply the conceptual development of the correlative obligation on States unable to provide adequate assistance to accept aid given by international organizations.

[34] Some authors have attempted to figure out the following 'indicators of unwillingness': (a) there is regular failure on the part of the State to deliver humanitarian aid, development aid, or social services to a particular geographic area, or to a particular gender, ethnic or political group, or religious section; (b) there has been an unjustified delay in the delivery of assistance which in the circumstances is inconsistent with an attempt to meet the needs of the affected population; (c) assistance is not being delivered in accordance with internationally recognized principles of humanity, neutrality, impartiality, and non-discrimination. See Benton Heath 2011, 472.

connection demonstrate a tendency to consider that this requirement would be fulfilled when a State refuses the entry of aid and relief personnel to its territory without providing valid reasons. In an attempt at progressive development, ILC draft article 11 introduces some kind of qualified consent regime in the field of disaster relief operations, by requiring that consent to external assistance shall not be withheld arbitrarily and that the State must make its decision regarding an offer of assistance known, whenever possible.

A decision as to whether the withholding of consent is not arbitrary is an assessment that, in principle, can only be carried out on a case-by-case basis and this would normally lead to difficulties in the practical application of this emerging rule. In fact, it seems much easier to identify cases where denial of the consent is valid rather than those when it is not. It is generally accepted that States have valid reasons for not accepting international relief if they are capable of providing an adequate and effective response to a disaster on the basis of their own resources, or when they have accepted appropriate and sufficient assistance elsewhere.[35] But outside these situations, i.e., when an offer is made in accordance with the principles of humanity, impartiality and neutrality and no alternate sources of assistance are available, there would be a strong inference that a decision to withhold consent is arbitrary.

The inclusion of this element of progressive development in the ILC draft of articles must be recognized as a positive step, even if a closer examination of this new rule shows that ultimate discretion as to whether to accept any offers of assistance continues to lie with the affected State.[36] By focusing on the primary role of the State, pursuant to the ILC draft text of articles an offer of assistance that is met with refusal can, under certain conditions, be interpreted as a possible violation of the right to life.[37] This would potentially permit individuals to introduce complaints before the human rights monitoring bodies, but would also raise the question of whether, in extreme cases of failure by the State to adopt the positive measures needed to provide assistance to the population, the adoption of collective measures for the enforcement of delivery of humanitarian assistance would be justified.[38] In this regard, it must be noted that the ICSS Report on the

---

[35] ILC, *Report on the work of its sixty-third session*, A/66/10, 270.

[36] In the ILC proposed draft article, the main burden of proving that it has good reasons not to accept the offer lies with the affected State, which should clarify these reasons when it refuses. Although the requirement for public justification is a positive step, the ILC has highlighted this burden on considering that a rigid duty to formally respond to every offer of assistance would place an excessive burden on the affected State and that at the current stage a 'wide decision regarding all offers of assistance, specifying its decision would be a satisfactory solution.' (Ibid.).

[37] In supporting this view it is necessary to recall the Human Rights Committee, General Comment n° 6 to the ICCPR in interpreting that the protection of the right to life also contains a positive obligation on States to adopt positive measures together with General Assembly Resolutions 43/131 (8 December 1988) and 45/100 (14 December 1990) stating that 'the abandonment of the victims of natural disasters and similar emergency situations without humanitarian assistance constitutes a threat to human life and an offence to human dignity.'

[38] Benton Heath 2011, 474–475. See also Sandoz 1992, Kent 2010.

'Responsibility to Protect' supported this view also in relation to 'overwhelming natural or environmental catastrophes' by establishing that: '[w]hile the State whose people are directly affected has the default responsibility to protect, a residual responsibility also lies with the broader community of States. This fall-back responsibility is activated when a particular State is clearly either *unwilling or unable* to fulfil its responsibility to protect or is itself the actual perpetrator of crimes or atrocities; or where people living outside a particular State are directly threatened by actions taking place there. This responsibility also requires that in some circumstances action must be taken by the broader community of States to support populations that are in jeopardy or under serious threat.'[39]

Indeed, it is one thing to recognize that IDRL rules are being reinterpreted in the light of human rights obligations and another very different thing to claim that this development can provide the basis for a broad doctrine of humanitarian intervention embracing disaster situations.[40] As we have seen, without going so far as to justify coercive humanitarian intervention, the ILC efforts have focused on the development of the international law by defining a rule outlining situations in which a State is required to consent to international humanitarian assistance.[41] Rather than being established on a modern reinterpretation of sovereignty based upon the notion of a 'Responsibility to Protect,' the ILC theoretical justification in supporting the obligation of States to accept disaster relief relies on the traditional principles of international cooperation, solidarity, and human rights.

10.4 Coercing the State to Consent to Humanitarian Relief

Recourse to coercive action authorized by the Security Council to protect the population of a disaster-affected State has been claimed for those cases in which it has been made evident that failure on the part of the State to deliver aid or to promptly seek external assistance results in human suffering on a wide scale. This extreme solution was raised, for example, as a way of overcoming lack of consent to international aid by the Government of Myanmar in the aftermath of the

---

[39] ICISS, *The Responsibility to Protect*. Report of the International Commission on Intervention and State Sovereignty, December 2001, available at http://responsibilitytoprotect.org/ICISS%20Report.pdf, para 2.31. Accessed February 11, 2012.

[40] In relation to the application of the R2P the general vision of the members of the Commission is that the formulation of this concept has not been conceived to apply to these situations. The ILC Special Rapporteur has recognized that 'even if the responsibility to protect were to be recognized in the context of protection and assistance of persons in the event of disasters, its implications would be unclear.' *Preliminary report on the protection of persons in the event of disasters*, UN Doc. A/CN.4/598, 5 May 2008 para 55; *Protection of persons in the event of disasters. Memorandum by the Secretariat*, UN Doc. A/CN.4/590, 11 December 2007 para 250.

[41] Benton Heath 2011, 423.

Cyclone Nargis (2008), and more recently to deal with the lack of national capacity to respond to the 2010 Earthquake in Haiti.[42]

Focusing on the possibility of forcible intervention in the context of an extreme humanitarian emergency following a natural disaster, it is necessary to determine under which circumstances it can be presumed that a threshold allowing for collective action encompassing the use of force has been reached.[43] In view of the gradual expansion of the UN Security Council practice of what constitutes a 'threat to peace, breach of the peace, or an act of aggression', together with various criteria that have been proposed for enacting the R2P, it is possible to outline circumstances in which collective forcible action could be justified and legitimated in the context of natural or man–made disasters.

10.4.1 The Responsibility to Protect: A New Paradigm?

An assessment of the adequacy of extending the application of this doctrine to cases of disaster relief requires some preliminary remarks regarding the content and the scope of the R2P doctrine. Even if the starting point of this new concept is usually identified in the 2001 report by the International Commission on Intervention and State Sovereignty (ICSS), the idea goes back to general reflections on the 'dilemma of intervention' launched by the UN Secretary-General Kofi Annan after the international community's failure to respond to the human tragedies of Rwanda and the Kosovo in the 1990s.[44] Notably, in the Millennium Report, the Secretary-General observed that 'no legal principle—not even sovereignty—can ever shield crimes against humanity. Where such crimes occur and peaceful attempts to halt them have been exhausted, the Security Council has a moral duty to act on behalf of the international community.' In his opinion 'armed intervention must always remain the option of last resort, but in the face of mass murder it is an option that cannot be relinquished.'[45] The Canadian Government

[42] See Evans and Sahnoun 2002, 99; Malone 2010.

[43] *Preliminary report on the protection of persons in the event of disasters*, UN Doc. A/CN.4/598, 5 May 2008 para 47. See Massingham 2009.

[44] A general reflection on the 'dilemma' of humanitarian intervention was launched by the Secretary–General Kofi Annan in his 1999 Report to the General Assembly. In his opinion the core challenge to the Security Council and to the United Nations as a whole in the next century was that of forging unity behind the principle that massive and systematic violations of human rights—wherever they may take place—should not be allowed to stand. *Secretary–General presents his Annual Report to the General Assembly*, 20 September 1999, https://www.un.org/News/ossg/sg/stories/statments_search_full.asp?statID=28. Accessed 2 March 2012.

[45] *We the People: the role of the United Nations in the twenty-first century. Report of the Secretary-General*, A/54/2000, para 219.

endorsed these concerns and in 2001 established an international commission in charge of finding some new common ground on the issue.[46]

In reality, as many authors have observed, the core idea of the R2P is nothing more than an updated version of the old doctrine on 'humanitarian intervention.' The revisited concept of sovereignty shifts the focus from the 'right' to intervene to the idea that the international community can subsidiarily undertake the responsibility when the State is unwilling or unable to act. Focusing attention on the needs of the potential beneficiaries the R2P becomes a less confrontational doctrine, also allowing the introduction of a need for prior preventive or subsequent building efforts. The primary responsibility of the affected State to decide what is best for its people is encompassed by the residual responsibility that also lies with the broader community of the States and requires that in some circumstances action be taken to support populations that are in jeopardy or under serious threat.

For those cases where the affected State neglects its own responsibility, the report articulates this subsidiary responsibility as embracing a *continuum* of responses ranging from the responsibility 'to prevent' (addressing the root causes and direct causes of internal conflict and other man-made crises), to the responsibility 'to react' (respond to situations of compelling human need with appropriate measures, which may include coercive measures and in extreme cases military intervention), including the responsibility 'to rebuild' (provide full assistance with recovery, reconstruction and reconciliation, particularly after a military intervention). Similar importance allocated to each of these three pillars has not prevented public opinion and scholars from focusing on the most controversial innovation of the new approach: the 'responsibility to react to situations of compelling need for human protection.' In fact, by admitting 'resort to military action by other members of the broader community of States' when preventive measures fail to resolve or contain the situation and when a single State is unable or unwilling to redress the situation, the ICSS report paves the way for both unilateral and collective intervention in countries experiencing 'large-scale loss of life' or 'ethnic cleansing', even in the absence of a UN Security Council authorization.[47] Although presented as a last resort solution, this has been by far the most criticized aspect of the R2P doctrine.[48]

The UN has generally endorsed the R2P approach even if significantly limiting the scope of the doctrine, with regard to the original ICSS report, in two ways. First, by underscoring that the collective international 'responsibility to protect' can only be exercised within the scope of the UN Charter (i.e., military intervention can only take place by way of authorization from the Security Council as a

---

[46] *Secretary–General presents his Annual Report to the General Assembly*, *supra* n 44.

[47] ICISS, *The Responsibility to Protect* op. cit. n. 39, para 4.19.

[48] It is to be recalled that among the range of situations that amount to 'just cause' for military intervention, the ICSS report includes 'overwhelming natural or environmental catastrophes, where the State concerned is either unwilling or unable to cope, or call for assistance, and significant loss of life is occurring or threatened.' Ibid. para 4.20.

last resort and in conformity with Chapter VII), and secondly by narrowing the scope of the R2P to certain specific categories of crimes.[49]

Reasons alleged by the UN Secretary-General to exclude the application of the R2P doctrine to 'other calamities such as HIV–AIDS, climate-change or the response to natural disasters' tend to consider that a broader interpretation of this concept could undermine existing political support and make its implementation more difficult.[50] Thus, the R2P would be restricted to those four mass atrocity crimes only (i.e., genocide, war crimes, ethnic cleansing, and crimes against humanity), in relation to which there is a clear consensus among the States regarding the justification of a collective reaction by the international community. Another important consequence of the way in which the R2P is being shaped is that it does not allow for unilateral non-authorized interventions.[51] As the High Level Panel on 'Threats, Challenges and Change' observed, international responsibility has come to accept that under Chapter VII and in pursuit of the emerging norm of the collective international responsibility to protect, the Security Council can always authorize military action to redress catastrophic internal wrongs if it is prepared to declare that the situation is a 'threat to international peace and security.'[52]

The restricted approach to cases for implementation of R2P has been endorsed by a recent consultation among the G-20 governments carried out by the International Federation of the Red Cross and the Red Crescent Societies, demonstrating that most of the States consulted emphasized that primary responsibility for addressing needs and leading the response during a natural disaster lies with national authorities. Canada and Australia showed a more flexible position on admitting that the international community has a role to play in supporting and—where appropriate—supplementing these efforts when the needs of people and communities affected by natural disasters and complex emergencies exceed the capacity of their government and local agencies to respond. It is to be noted that only one State—the United States—expressly supported the R2P doctrine by affirming that 'when local governments are unable or unwilling to protect their

[49] At the 2005 Word Summit Outcome, the Heads of State and government unanimously affirmed that: '[e]ach individual State has the responsibility to protect its populations from genocide, war crimes, ethnic cleansing and crimes against humanity.' They agreed, as well, that the international community should assist States in exercising that responsibility and in building their protection capacities. Furthermore, in cases where a State is 'manifestly failing' to protect its population from specified crimes and violations the document confirmed that the international community is prepared to take collective action in a 'timely and decisive manner' through the Security Council and in accordance with the Charter of the United Nations. A/RES/60/1, 24 October 2005, para 139.

[50] *Implementing the responsibility to protect*, A/63/677, 12 January 2009 para 10 (b).

[51] Determining whether the R2P constitutes an emerging international customary norm built on the States practice would only be relevant when the position is taken that they can act unilaterally in case of inoperability of the Security Council. See Venturini and Costas Trascasas 2009, Poli 2011.

[52] *A more secure world: Our shared responsibility, Report of the Secretary General's High-level Panel on Threats, Challenges and Change,* UN Doc. A/59/565 para 202.

own citizens, there has to be some sort of an international action.'[53] The overwhelming opposition by the States when faced with claims of application of this doctrine to natural disasters was also confirmed following the Cyclone Nargis crisis in Myanmar in 2008.[54]

10.4.2 The 2008 Myanmar Cyclone: A Case-Test for the Applicability of R2P to Disasters

Controversy that followed the Government of Myanmar's refusal of external aid in the aftermath of the Cyclone Nargis (2008) constitutes the most representative and interesting case study on this issue. Restrictions imposed by the government on external humanitarian aid, despite the scale of the emergency, inflamed debate on the possibility of using R2P doctrine to justify an intervention by the international community using coercive means.

Cyclone Nargis struck Myanmar on 2 and 3 May 2008 causing widespread devastation and loss of life in the Ayeyarwady Delta region and the inland areas, as a consequence of floods. On 2 May 2008, the official death toll was 84,537, and UN assessments indicated that 2.4 million people were severely affected and in need of humanitarian assistance.[55] The national response started quickly but it was soon clear that the cyclone overwhelmed the capacity of national response. The Government of Myanmar declared early on and informally that it would be open to international assistance, but no immediate steps were taken by the authorities to facilitate access by international humanitarian staff. On the contrary, the facts demonstrate that Myanmar authorities gave preference to a national response supported by bilateral aid rather than any form of international relief operations.

---

[53] IFRC, Believe in Humanity. A Consultation with G20 governments, November 2009, 11, 17–19. Available at http://www.ifrc.org/Global/Publications/volunteers/G20_Consultation_Report_Nov2009.pdf. Accessed 2 March 2012. However, a different position seems to flow from discussions held before the ILC where the representative of the United States underlined his government's 'reservations about taking a rights-based approach to the topic and its objections to incorporating the concept of the responsibility to protect the Commission should focus on areas of the law that would have the most significant practical impact in mitigating the effects of disasters, including, for example, the development of practical tools to facilitate coordination among providers of disaster assistance or the drafting of model bilateral agreements to facilitate access of people and equipment to affected areas.' ILC *Report on the work of its sixtieth session* UN Doc. A/C.6/63/SR.23, para 86.

[54] The increasing demand for a right to access disaster victims is in fact causing the States to place greater emphasis on the role of sovereignty and non-intervention in international law. Specifically, States that face potentially adverse consequences from a disaster have stressed sovereignty rather than consent to legal rules requiring them to accept foreign aid. See Benton Heath 2011, 432. See also the discussions before the UN General Assembly Sixth Committee, and in particular the positions of China (A/C.6/63/SR.23, para 31), Japan (A/C.6/63/SR.23, para 42); and Russia (A/C.6/63/SR.24, para 5).

[55] For an accurate account of the facts see Chap. 18 by Russo, Sect. 18.4.

On insisting that the government would distribute the aid itself, it imposed several restrictions on external personnel regarding the issue of visas and limited access to most affected areas. Although local agencies and personnel did not face restrictions and could work normally on the ground, the lack of key staff led to delays in getting reliable data on needs and in strengthening co-ordination and response capacity.[56]

As it became clear that the authorities were not immediately allowing international access to the affected areas, international community pressure began. Growing concerns regarding the consequences of failing to deliver the assistance to those in need, together with frustration caused by the government's refusal to accept assistance offered by the international community, paved the way for an intense debate among experts and scholars on the convenience of making recourse to military means to quickly solve the humanitarian emergency. In this context, France's Foreign Minister Bernard Kouchner invoked the R2P doctrine calling on the UN Security Council to pass a resolution authorizing recourse to force to impose the delivery of aid to survivors of the cyclone on national authorities.[57] The proposal was flatly rejected by China arguing that the R2P did not apply to natural disasters and that Myanmar could not be coerced on this basis into accepting humanitarian assistance.[58] Following this suggestion experts, diplomats and academics discussed the moral, legal, and political justification of such an action and the current advantages or disadvantages of invoking the R2P doctrine in the context of natural disasters.[59]

While the legal debate among academics has revolved around the convenience or otherwise of extending the concept of the R2P to disasters and on legal

---

[56] *Post Nargis Joint Assessment*, July 2008, http://www.aseansec.org/21765.pdf. Accessed 2 March 2012.

[57] Burma—Joint press briefing given by M. Bernard Kouchner, Minister of Foreign and European Affairs, and M. Jean–Pierre Jouyet, Minister of State responsible for European Affairs, 25 May 2008 (excerpts), available at: http://www.ambafrance-uk.org/Bernard-Kouchner-on-Burma-disaster.html. Accessed 2 March 2012. The EU's High Representative for Common Foreign and Secure Policy, Javier Solana, also affirmed: 'We have to use all the means to help those people. The UN Charter opens some avenues if things cannot be resolved in order to get humanitarian aid into a country that has had a catastrophe, as in the case of Burma/Myanmar, where the leaders of the country do not allow the fast and well organised arrival of aid. By "all means" we mean all the means that are provided for in the UN Charter—whatever is necessary in order to help the people who are suffering.' Remarks by Javier Solana, EU High Representative for the CFSP, on the latest developments in Burma/Myanmar, Brussels, 13 May 2008, S165/08, available at http://www.consilium.europa.eu/ueDocs/cms_Data/docs/pressdata/EN/discours/100322.pdf. Accessed 2 March 2012. The EU Council has subsequently endorsed the R2P doctrine but only restricted to certain categories among which situations of natural or man-made disaster are not included. Report on the Implementation of the European Security Strategy—Providing Security in a Changing Word, Brussels, 11 December 2008, S407/08.

[58] Bellamy 2010, 152. See also the document of the Asia–Pacific Center for the Responsibility to Protect, 'Cyclone Nargis and the Responsibility to Protect', available at: http://www.r2pasiapacific.org/documents/Burma_Brief2.pdf, p 9. Accessed 2 March 2012.

[59] Thakur 2008, Ozerdem 2011, OCRtoP 2008.

arguments as to the qualification of conduct by governments as included within the concept of 'crimes against humanity,'[60] civil society has considered the question more pragmatically. On one side, human rights organizations such as Amnesty International and Human Rights Watch have focused on the State's failure to respond in an effective and timely fashion by generally supporting the idea that the UN Security Council should take action when national authorities deny the full and unimpeded access of humanitarian relief.[61] On the other side, humanitarian organizations such as the International Committee of the Red Cross and Médecins sans Frontières have taken a much more cautious position, pointing out the risks of invoking the R2P incorrectly in the context of disaster relief. In their view, claiming the use of force in such circumstances could become a counterproductive argument that would lead to a further obstacle to access to the victims. Other similar concerns about the risks of politicizing the delivery of humanitarian aid have also been expressed by arguing that military measures can involve long lead times and do not necessarily result in improved aid to those in need.[62]

The majority of commentators conclude that the crisis was solved in the best way possible and that the various initiatives pursued led to the desired result: enhanced access to affected areas and close cooperation with national authorities.[63] It is clear that the delay of several weeks certainly increased the risk of further fatalities, but there are no guarantees that pursuing a different strategy could have contributed to reducing this delay. As has been rightly noted, a more forceful strategy most probably would not have led to the same positive working environment and could also have had an ultimately detrimental effect on humanitarian aid.[64] Also in his 2008 report on the human rights situation in Myanmar the UN Secretary-General stressed the need to separate the humanitarian response from political considerations, in order to be able to provide assistance to those in need as a matter of urgency and promoted a pragmatic solution that led to resolution of the crisis through the involvement of a regional organization, the ASEAN.[65] By bringing together representatives of the Government of Myanmar, the Association of Southeast Asian Nations (ASEAN), and the United Nations, a 'Tripartite Core Group' (TCG) was formed that proved to be an efficient platform for trust building

---

60 Barber 2009, Wong 2009, Evans 2008, 2009, Thakur 2008.

61 Amnesty International Myanmar Briefing: Human rights concerns a month after Cyclone Nargis, 5 June 2008, AI Index: ASA 16/013/2008; Human Rights Watch, Burma, time for UN Security Council to Act, http://www.hrw.org/news/2008/05/19/burma-time-un-security-council-act. Accessed 2 March 2012.

62 Médecins Sans Frontières (2011) Humanitarian Negotiations Revealed: The MSF Experience http://www.msf-crash.org/livres/en/humanitarian-negociations-revealed; strengthening coordination of UN humanitarian and disaster relief assistance: the ICRC statement to the United Nations, 2011 (14 December 2011), available at: http://www.icrc.org/eng/resources/documents/statement/united-nations-humanitarian-coordination-statement-2011-12-14.htm. Accessed 2 March 2012.

63 See Belanger and Horsey 2008, 4–5.

64 Ibid.

65 *Situation of human rights in Myanmar,* A/63/356, 17 September 2008, para 29.

and facilitated agreement with the national authorities for the purposes of an effective large-scale humanitarian response.[66]

While this case was not, overall, very helpful in the short term in consolidating support for the R2P as an emerging norm, at least it has generated serious debate that has apparently advanced international understanding of the scope and limits of this doctrine along the lines suggested, and served to clarify the burden of proof that needs to be satisfied in order to successfully invoke this doctrine to justify coercive measures.[67] Moreover, it can be concluded that the misapplication of the R2P to this case has led to an increasing skepticism among some Security Council's permanent members, particularly China, and Russia, regarding the possibility of launching a collective response in cases of natural disaster, making it more than ever unlikely that a consensus authorizing the use of force will be reached.

10.4.3 Acting Under Chapter VII of the UN Charter in Case of Disaster

Despite their capacity to cause significant damage, situations of natural disaster are still perceived as a social and economic issue that is incapable of endangering the maintenance of international peace and security. For this reason, cases in which the UN Security Council will authorize the recourse to coercive measures in the context of a natural disaster are expected to be exceptional even after verifying that the denial of access has resulted in widespread human suffering and increased the risk of loss of lives.[68] The extension of the mandate of the UN Stabilization Mission in Haiti (MINUSTAH) in the aftermath of the 2010 Haiti Earthquake probably constitutes the only clear example of application of the Security Council powers under UN Charter Chapter VII in the context of a disaster.

The UN mission was established by the Security Council resolutions 1529 (2004) and 1542 (2004), following the appeal of the new President of Haiti for the urgent support of the international community to assist in restoring peace and security in the country and with the aim of supporting the Transitional government to ensure a secure and stable environment to facilitate the constitutional and political process in Haiti. In determining that 'the situation in Haiti constitutes a threat to international peace and security, and to stability in the Caribbean, especially through the potential outflow of people to other States in the subregion,' the Security Council authorized the immediate deployment of a Multinational Interim Force (MIF) and the members States participating therein 'to take all

66 See Turner et al. 2008. Accessed 2 March 2012.

67 Evans 2009.

68 A/RES/63/245, 23 January 2009.

necessary measures to fulfil its mandate.'[69] The original mandate of the peacekeeping mission consisting of a civilian and military component was complemented after the 2010 devastating earthquake by an additional deployment of peacekeepers to support the immediate recovery, reconstruction, and stability efforts in the country.[70]

Although Security Council coercive measures must be clearly distinguished from the establishment of peacekeeping operations that are generally based on a State's consent, this case might well constitute a precedent of the Security Council's action under Chapter VII in case of disaster relief. It further demonstrates the potential relationship that can be established among the maintenance of international peace and security, and the role to be played by the international community in supporting national relief efforts and post-disaster reconstruction. It is to be noted that even if the disaster took place in a situation of evident fragility for the State's institutions, after recognizing the significant devastation that has been suffered by the government, far from underlining the inability of the State to comply with its duties of protection the Security Council underlined 'the ownership and primary responsibility of the Government and the people of Haiti over all aspects of the country's stabilization,' and therefore the need for relief operations to take place in a framework of full cooperation with national authorities. In this regard, it recognizes the supporting role of MINUSTAH and the need for expanded assistance by the international community 'in order to allow State institutions to continue operations, provide basic services and build State capacity.'[71]

10.4.3.1 Humanitarian Catastrophe as a Threat to International Peace and Security

Even if exceptionally, the possibility of a disaster relief operation being undertaken in the context of invocation of Chapter VII coercive measures is not to be excluded, when taking into account the Security Council's practice of declaring a humanitarian crisis to be a threat to international peace and security.[72]

In fact, there is a consistent UN Security Council practice indicating that the magnitude of human tragedy caused by conflict, further exacerbated by obstacles being created to the distribution of humanitarian assistance, constitutes a threat to

---

[69] See S/RES/1529(2004), 29 February 2004, preamble para 9 and operative para 6.

[70] S/RES 1908 (2010), 19 January 2010, preamble para 5 and operative para 3.

[71] In this context, Resolution 1927 (2010), 4 June 2010, clearly outlines the role international community can play in disaster relief situations. See preamble, para 5 and operative para 3.

[72] See *Preliminary report on the protection of persons in the event of disasters*, UN Doc. A/CN.4/598, 5 May 2008 para 250.

international peace, and security.[73] The first and most striking example was the UN action in Somalia (1992–1995). The Security Council in 'recognizing the unique character of the situation (...) and mindful of its deteriorating, complex and extraordinary nature, requiring an immediate and exceptional response' took action *responding to urgent calls from Somalia* for the international community to ensure the delivery of humanitarian assistance. By acknowledging the deterioration in the humanitarian situation and the urgent need for the quick delivery of humanitarian assistance in the whole country, it was assumed that impediments to the delivery of humanitarian assistance can trigger authorization to 'use all necessary means to establish as soon as possible a secure environment for humanitarian relief' by means of the coercive use of force.[74] Also, in dealing with the magnitude of the humanitarian crisis in Rwanda, in 1994, the Security Council decided to set up a temporary multinational operation for humanitarian purposes. The operation under national command and control aimed at contributing to the security and protection of displaced persons, refugees, and civilians at risk and providing security and support for the distribution of relief supplies and humanitarian relief operations.[75] A similar solution was adopted in eastern Zaire, in 1996, when the situation demanded an 'urgent response by the international community.' The Security Council, also acting under Chapter VII, authorized the establishment for strictly humanitarian purposes of a temporary multinational force to facilitate the immediate return of humanitarian organizations and the effective delivery of humanitarian aid by civilian relief organizations to alleviate the immediate suffering of displaced persons, refugees, and civilians at risk in the Great Lakes region.[76] In the same spirit, the aim of facilitating the safe and prompt delivery of humanitarian assistance and to help create a secure environment for the missions of international organizations, including those providing humanitarian assistance, was included within the mandate of the multinational protection force that was authorized in the context of internal violence taking place in Albania in 1997.[77] In the most recent situation in Darfur in Sudan, the Security Council has also intervened, explicitly enacting the R2P, for the provision of humanitarian

---

[73] In the case of Somalia, the Security Council declares to be '[d]ismayed by the continuation of conditions that impede the delivery of humanitarian supplies to destinations within Somalia, and in particular reports of looting of relief supplies destined for starving people, attacks on aircraft and ships bringing in humanitarian relief supplies, and attacks on the Pakistani UNOSOM contingent in Mogadishu.' S/RES/794 (1992), 3 December 1992.

[74] In the case of Somalia (1992), Rwanda (1994), Zaire (1996) and Albania (1997), the Security Council has authorized the States to undertake military measures in order to reach humanitarian objectives. S/RES/794 (1992); S/RES/929 (1994), 22 June 1994; S/RES/1080 (1996), 15 November 1996; S/RES/1114 (1997), 19 June 1997.

[75] This included the establishment and maintenance, where feasible, of secure humanitarian areas. See S/RES/925 (1994), 8 June 1994 and S/RES/929 (1994).

[76] See S/RES/1080 (1996).

[77] S/RES/1101 (1997), 28 March 1997 and S/RES/1114 (1997).

assistance, and acting under Chapter VII has decided to authorize the United Nations Mission in Sudan (UNMIS) 'to use all necessary means.'[78]

These precedents show that the Security Council has, with increasing frequency, authorized the international community to provide aid within a receiving State for humanitarian purposes. The requirement of the previous consent of national authorities, generally needed for the launching of a peacekeeping mission, could be circumvented in cases where the need to adopt coercive measures is endorsed by the Security Council.[79] In fact, what these practice shows is that the imposition of the entry of humanitarian assistance by means of the use of force in situations other than armed conflict is not to be excluded as a possible evolution of the Security Council action.[80] This would be particularly true for those cases where the response capability of the affected State is exceeded by the magnitude and the duration of the emergency, and the action or inaction on the part of national authorities results in a humanitarian catastrophe. More particularly, a complete refusal to allow any kind of humanitarian aid to victims of an emergency when national capacities are overwhelmed and in the absence of a co-operative attitude by national authorities or in the absence of such authority, would constitute a *justa causa* allowing for the international community to undertake collective action. It is clear that this should be an exceptional situation where a government is notoriously failing to give humanitarian organizations unrestricted access to the victims of the natural disaster and non-coercive means have been exhausted or are invalid due to the urgency of the situation. Possible scenarios in which the unwillingness of the State to co-operate could contribute to jeopardizing the lives of its own population or exacerbate the transboundary effects of a disaster would be, for example, cases of an epidemic, a nuclear or environmental disaster or other kinds of disaster that can be the cause of a massive exodus of people.

---

[78] See S/RES 1706 (2006), 31 August 2006, and S/RES/1769 (2007), 31 July 2007.

[79] See S/RES/688 (1991), 5 April 1991 para 3 (with respect to the grant of access to international humanitarian organizations in Iraq), S/RES/770 (1992), 13 August 1992 para 2 (with respect to the provision of humanitarian assistance in Bosnia and Herzegovina), S/RES/794 (1992), 3 December 1992 para 10 (concerning humanitarian relief operations in Somalia) and S/RES/929 (1994), 22 June 1994 para 3 (authorizing distribution of relief supplies in Rwanda).

[80] This possibility is recognized in the resolution on humanitarian assistance, adopted by the Institute of International Law in 2003, which states that 'if a refusal to accept a bona fide offer of humanitarian assistance or to allow access to the victims, leads to a threat to international peace and security, the Security Council may take the necessary measures under Chapter VII of the Charter of the United Nations.' Principle 7 of the Guiding Principles on the Right to Humanitarian Assistance, adopted by the Council of the International Institute of Humanitarian Law in April 1993, states: 'The competent United Nations organs and regional organisations may undertake necessary measures, including coercion, in accordance with their respective mandates, in case of severe, prolonged and mass suffering of populations, which could be alleviated by humanitarian assistance. These measures may be resorted to when an offer has been refused without justification, or when the provision of humanitarian assistance encounters serious difficulties.' See Chap. 3 by Zorzi Giustiniani, Sect. 3.4.

10.4.3.2 Criteria Legitimizing the Collective Use of Force

Indeed, the enforcement of humanitarian aid in the context of a disaster would constitute an exceptional situation if one bears in mind that the Security Council has to consider that there are elements leading to qualify the situation as a threat to international peace and security. As it is well known, this determination should be made on a case-by-case basis and would be necessarily a selective decision since the political nature of the Security Council in practice may give rise to omissions and inconsistencies.[81] For this reason, it must be underlined that an extensive interpretation of the Security Council's coercive powers for the provision of assistance when urgent humanitarian action is needed should be complemented with clear rules and means aiming to avoid the potential misuse of this instrument as some kind of modern humanitarian intervention.

A brief analysis of disaster situations, in consideration of the basic criteria of legitimacy put forward by the 2004 High Level Panel as guidelines to be taken into account by the Security Council when deciding whether to authorize or endorse the use of coercive means, can help us to understand under what circumstances this body could justifiably authorize the use of force in the context of natural disasters 'as a matter of good conscience and good sense.'[82] For an intervention to be considered adequate: (1) the threat to the State of human security of any kind has to be sufficiently clear and serious as to justify *prima facie* the use of military force; (2) the primary purpose must be that of stopping or averting the threat in question; (3) all non-military means must have been exhausted; (4) the intervention must be proportional to the threat and; (5) the consequences of the action must not be likely to be worse than the consequences of inaction.[83]

As pointed out before, authorization of the use of force would only be justified in cases of extreme humanitarian emergency where a government fully blocks and not only restricts humanitarian relief, resulting in an otherwise preventable humanitarian catastrophe.[84] Even by admitting that humanitarian protection is rarely the sole motive for intervention, this should constitute the main objective and other non-compatible objectives (such as overthrowing a political regime) should be clearly excluded. Likewise, coercive measures should finish as soon as the situation returns to normality and would not justify any kind of unilateral and non-authorized intervention or occupation. Difficulties on determining the primary purpose were clear in the case of Myanmar, where suspicions by the Government of Myanmar that the international community may not have been exclusively motivated by the desire to deliver aid to the survivors of the cyclone may not have

---

81 Dungel 2004, 12; Viotti 2007, 131.

82 *A more secure world: Our shared responsibility, Report of the Secretary General's High-level Panel on Threats, Challenges and Change,* UN Doc. A/59/565 para 206.

83 Ibid, para 207.

84 Barber 2009, 22. For some authors the gravity of the situation should be comparable to the categories of crimes listed in the International Criminal Court Statute, causing great suffering, or serious injury. Benton Heath 2011, 476.

been entirely unfounded.[85] Because the disaster struck at a very politically sensitive moment (the government was focusing on a national referendum) fears that international humanitarian assistance would be used as a way to influence the country's political agenda was logically amplified by the threat of carrying out a coercive intervention under the R2P. Yet, it might be recognized that the threat of possible coercive action under the R2P, although inappropriate and premature in practice, produced the desired effect.

Consideration of matters such as the extent and urgency of humanitarian needs and the potential consequences of denying humanitarian assistance make it difficult to determine at what time it can be said that all non-coercive measures have been exhausted and that there are reasonable grounds for believing that other measures will not succeed before resorting to coercive measures. As a matter of fact, the case of Myanmar particularly illustrates the success of disaster diplomacy: together with the UN Secretary-General good offices, the involvement of ASEAN was a key factor for succeeding in facilitating trust and co-operation between the Government of Myanmar and the international community. This course of action shows that at the time that the forcible intervention was suggested as a possible response to the humanitarian emergency in Myanmar, other possible means, particularly diplomatic and economic means, still had to be explored. Moreover, everything seems to indicate that the crisis of the Cyclone Nargis has paved the way for opening the Myanmar regime to a constructive and more co-operative dialog with the UN that is starting to produce some concrete results.[86] Still, one may question what would have been the solution to the crisis if Myanmar's inaction and resistance to external help, instead of giving way to eventual significant co-operation, had continued to the extent that a large number of people would actually suffer and begin to die in significant numbers.[87]

Finally, the requirement of proportionality, i.e., that the scale, duration, and intensity of the proposed military actions be the minimum necessary to meet the threat, raises the question of whether there could be other minor uses of force that might be more appropriate in cases where the State does not consent to the delivery of aid. In this perspective, it has been suggested that other less invasive

---

[85] The deployment of a US naval group, a French navy vessel and a British frigate with aid supplies to waters bordering on territorial waters certainly contributed to increasing suspicion by the Junta that humanitarian assistance was being used to conceal an external intervention.

[86] In his 2010 report on the Myanmar's situation UN Secretary-General affirms: 'I am glad to report that, today, 15 United Nations agencies, 50 international organizations and a similar number of local non-governmental organizations are now operating inside the country and are working not only in the Ayeyarwaddy delta, but in all regions of Myanmar. Looking forward, the United Nations and the Government of Myanmar have reached an agreement to collaborate on a two-year joint humanitarian initiative (2010–2011) on northern Rakhine State, a border area whose population faces a particularly difficult combination of socio-economic and humanitarian factors. I welcome this initiative, as it aims to provide a unified response to meet the immediate needs of the region's populations while focusing on longer-term developmental objectives and goals.' UN Doc. A/65/367, para 37.

[87] Evans 2009.

means than a coercive intervention, such as airdrops or the dispatch of aid workers without the approval of the government, may help to temporarily solve the situation.[88] But significantly, such a possibility has not received much support from humanitarian relief personnel in the field, who are aware of the difficulties of delivering humanitarian aid by air, not only because deliveries are notoriously imprecise but also because it is unlikely that airdrops could deliver sufficient assistance.[89]

More generally, criticism has been raised regarding the sending of foreign troops to deliver aid without the consent of the government: apart from provoking practical difficulties it could be counterproductive as it could provoke a hostile reaction from national authorities. Thus, the use of force in disaster situations for humanitarian purposes could paradoxically increase rather than mitigate the number of civilian causalities and further pose a greater risk to humanitarian workers and wider efficient aid delivery. As it has been rightly observed, the main problem with these kinds of approaches is that they 'threaten to divert attention from the delivery of humanitarian relief, making co-operation with the local authorities more difficult, regional support less forthcoming and ultimately delaying assistance to those in need.'[90] Whether the imposition of humanitarian aid by enacting the Security Council coercive powers can actually be effective in addressing the humanitarian needs of the affected population is in fact a question that may be posed before a decision to resort to military means, in assessing that the consequences of action are not likely to be worse than the consequences of inaction.[91]

10.5 Concluding Remarks

A few general conclusions can be drawn regarding cases where a State fails to provide or permit the entry into its territory of sufficient humanitarian relief in the wake of a natural disaster. Even if human rights considerations tend to limit the State's discretion to arbitrarily withhold its consent under certain circumstances,

---

[88] The United Nations considered this possibility to reach the victims of the Cyclone Nargis in Myanmar. US Considers Air Drops for Burma Cyclone Victims, http://articles.economictimes.indiatimes.com/2008-05-09/news/28410161_1_myanmar-devastating-cyclone-relief-supplies. Accessed 2 March 2012.

[89] Oxfam Canada, Discounting Aid Drops, http://oxfam.ca/news-and-publications/news/discounting-aid-drops. Accessed 2 March 2012.

[90] Asia–Pacific Center for the Responsibility to Protect, 'Cyclone Nargis and the Responsibility to Protect', available at: http://www.r2pasiapacific.org/documents/Burma_Brief2.pdf, 11. Accessed 2 March 2012. See also Ozerdem2011, 706–709; Holmes, Disaster Lessons, Washington Post, August 6 2008; available at: http://www.washingtonpost.com/wp-dyn/content/article/2008/08/05/AR2008080502924.html. Accessed 2 March 20120.

[91] *A more secure world: Our shared responsibility, Report of the Secretary General's High-level Panel on Threats, Challenges and Change,* UN Doc. A/59/565 para 207.

international law generally recognizes the right of the States not to accept offers of international relief for various grounds. Likewise, practice shows that States usually make recourse to a request for international assistance only for the most massive disasters and that only in very exceptional cases have some governments entirely rejected access to their territory by international aid and personnel.

In this context, developments in the ILC's work on the protection of the person in disaster situations, aiming at articulating the State's duty to accept humanitarian offers of assistance, and the duty not to arbitrarily withhold consent to external assistance, must be welcomed. Still, further developments are required in order to establish a set of reasonable criteria outlining when and through what mechanisms States would be expected to accept humanitarian aid on behalf of their population, when an offer is contrary to international law, and under what circumstances it can be held that there are 'valid reasons' to refuse assistance. The logical development of the duty of the State to accept international offers should simultaneously be complemented by a more rational development of the correlative principle of solidarity on behalf of the international community and the subsequent 'obligation' to provide international humanitarian assistance in certain cases.

As to whether or not it is convenient to extend the notion of the R2P to natural disasters where the State's refusal to accept international relief causes serious harm to its population, two questions should be clarified. In the first place, many doubts can be raised on the current scope and legal value of this doctrine. Recent developments within the United Nations indicate that rather than being an 'emerging norm' the R2P is becoming a 'political guideline' that can be attached to a particular crisis in order to generate the will and consensus necessary to mobilize a decisive international response in cases of genocide, war crimes, ethnic cleansing, and crimes against humanity. Although some steps have been taken during the last years in this direction, the great challenge remains how to implement the R2P, taking into consideration the fact that there is still no general consensus regarding those situations in which such a coercive intervention is justified nor on the procedure for enacting this collective responsibility. Rather, profound disagreements regarding the function, meaning and proper use of the R2P raise the question as to whether this doctrine has the potential to introduce any real value to the existing legal framework.

In fact, widespread skepticism among the States regarding the concept and the legal scope of this doctrine prevents the R2P being considered of any help in the emergence of a norm recognizing that there are certain situations in which unilateral military intervention for human rights purposes would be justified. On the contrary, States generally assume that the use of force may only be legitimated through the Security Council authorization and that the R2P does not provide the basis for automatic justification for coercive intervention in the event of a humanitarian crisis. Under these circumstances, the R2P doctrine does not add anything new to the UN Charter other than preferring a softer interpretation in accordance with which the Security Council can qualify situations of humanitarian catastrophe as a threat to international peace and security allowing for coercive action.[92] This shows that over the last few years, the R2P has become more a part of the language used to debate and frame collective responses to humanitarian emergencies than a legal norm.[93] Nevertheless, it might be recognized that it has decisively contributed to focusing attention on the need to develop the institutions and capacities for effective response to certain atrocities within the prevailing normative framework in a 'timely and decisive manner.'

Secondly, it must be noted that in reality discussions regarding the precise outline of this notion and the advantages or disadvantages of the extension of the R2P to natural disasters are quite sterile due to the political and non-legal nature of this notion. The activation of the R2P, in the sense of urging a prompt response by the international community, does not depend on the situation but on the magnitude of the violations taking place so, potentially, certain disaster situations could trigger coercive measures under Chapter VII. Thus, a broader formulation of this concept embracing disasters would not be contrary to the UN Security Council practice insofar as a potential humanitarian catastrophe provoked by the inaction of a State could arise in a situation suitable of being qualified as a threat to international peace and security, taking into account the grave human and natural consequences or the potential transboundary effects of the crisis. However, until clear procedures and criteria guiding the Security Council's action are agreed upon, any decision in this direction will probably continue to be essentially political, and therefore selective.

References

Abril Stoffels R (2004) Legal regulation of humanitarian assistance in armed conflict: achievements and gaps. Int Rev Red Cross 86(855):515–545

Barber R (2009) The responsibility to protect the survivors of natural disaster. J Confl Secur Law 14(1):3–34

Belanger J, Horsey R (2008) Negotiating humanitarian access to cyclone-affected areas of Myanmar: a review. Humanit Exch Mag 41:2–5. http://www.odihpn.org/report.asp?id=2964

Bellamy AJ (2010) The responsibility to protect—five years on. Ethics Int Aff 24:143–169

Benton Heath J (2011) Disasters, relief, and neglect: the duty to accept humanitarian assistance and the work of the International Law Commission. N Y Univ J Int Law Politics 43(2):419–477

Boisson de Chazournes L, Condorelli L (2007) La responsabilità di proteggere: una nuova veste per una nozione già acquisita. In: Papanicolopulu I, Scovazzi T (a cura di), Conflitti armati e situazioni di emergenza: la risposta del diritto internazionale, Giuffrè, Milano, pp 5–12

Boisson de Chazournes L (2008) Responsabilité de protéger et catastrophes naturelles: l'émergence d'un régime? In: Société Française pour le droit international. Colloque de Nanterre, Pedone, Paris, pp 149–152

Bothe M (1989) Relief actions: the position of the recipient State. In: Kalshoven F Assisting the victims of armed conflict and other disasters, papers delivered at the International Conference

[92] Corten 2008, 777.

[93] Bellamy 2010, 158.

on Humanitarian Assistance in Armed Conflict, The Hague, 22–24 June 1988, Martinus Nijhoff Publishers, Dordrecht-Boston-London, pp 91–97

Corten O (2008) Le droit contre la guerre. L'interdiction du recours à la force en droit international contemporain, Pedone, Paris

Dungel J (2004) A right to humanitarian assistance in internal armed conflicts respecting sovereignty, neutrality and legitimacy: practical proposals to practical problems. J Humanit Assist. http://sites.tufts.edu/jha/archives/838

Ebersole JM (1995) Mohonk criteria for humanitarian assistance in complex emergencies. Human Rights Q 17:192–208

Evans G (2008) Facing up to our responsibilities. The Guardian, 12 May 2008. http://www.responsibilitytoprotect.org/index.php?option=com_content&view=article&id=1665

Evans G (2009) The responsibility to protect in environmental emergencies. Presentation to American Society of International Law (ASIL) 103rd annual meeting, Washington DC, 26 March 2009. http://www.gevans.org/speeches/speech312.html

Evans G, Sahnoun M (2002) The responsibility to protect. Foreign Affairs 81(6):99–110

Fisher D (2007) Law and legal issues in international disaster response: a desk study. International Federation of Red Cross and Red Crescent Societies, Geneva

Hardcastle RJ, Chua ATL (1998) Humanitarian assistance: towards a right of access of victims of natural disasters. Int Rev Red Cross 325:633–655

Harvey P (2009) Towards good humanitarian government. The role of the affected State in disaster response. Humanit Policy Group Policy Brief 37 http://www.odi.org.uk/resources/details.asp?id=4196&title=good-humanitarian-government-affected-state-disaster-response

Jackson TR (2010) Bullets for beans: humanitarian intervention and the responsibility to protect in natural disasters. Naval Law Rev 59:1–20

Jochems M (2006) NATO's growing humanitarian role, NATO Review, Spring 2006. http://www.nato.int/docu/review/2006/issue1/english/art4.html

Kelman I (2006) Acting on disaster diplomacy. J Int Affairs 59(2):215–240

Kent G (2010) Disasters and 'responsibility to protect'—should nations force aid on others? Disaster Prev Manag 19(2):155–174

Malone LA (2010) The responsibility to protect Haiti. Am Soc Int Law Insight 14(7). http://www.asil.org/insights100310.cfm

Massingham E (2009) Military intervention for humanitarian purposes: does the responsibility to protect doctrine advance the legality of the use of force for humanitarian ends? Int Rev Red Cross 91:803–831

OCRtoP (2008) The responsibility to protect and its application to the situation in Burma. http://www.responsibilitytoprotect.org/index.php/former-r2pcs-project/reports-and-statements/2234-r2pcs-commentary-on-the-crisis-in-burma

Ozerdem A (2011) The 'responsibility to protect' in natural disasters: another excuse for interventionism? Nargis Cyclone, Myanmar. Confl. Secur Dev 10(5):673–713

Penuel KB, Statler M (2011) Encyclopedia of disaster relief. SAGE Publications, Los Angeles

Poli L (2011) La responsabilità di proteggere e il ruolo delle organizzazioni internazionali regionali. Nuove prosopettive dal continente africano, Edizioni Scientifiche Italiane, Napoli

Sandoz Y (1992) 'Droit' or 'devoir d'ingérence' and the right to assistance: the issues involved. Int Rev Red Cross 74(288):215–227

Thakur R (2008) To invoke of not to invoke R2P in Burma, The Hindu (India), Tuesday, 20 May 2008. http://www.cigionline.org/print/articles/2008/05/invoke-or-not-invoke-r2p-burma

Turner R, Baker J, Myo Oo Z, Soe Aye N (2008) Inter-agency real time evaluation of the response to Cyclone Nargis. 17 December 2008. Available at http://ochanet.unocha.org/p/Documents/IA_RTE_Nargis_Response_Final_Report_with_pics[1].pdf

Venturini G, Costas Trascasas M (2009) Intervento umanitario e Responsibility to Protect secondo il diritto internazionale. In: Bilotta BM, Cappelletti FA, Scerbo A (eds) Pace, Guerra, Conflitto nella Società dei Diritti, Giappichelli, Torino, pp 183–219

Viotti A (2007) In search of symbiosis: the Security Council in the humanitarian domain. Int Rev Red Cross 89(865):131–153

Weissman F (2010) 'Not in our name': why Médecins Sans Frontières does not support the 'Responsibility to Protect'. Crim Justice Ethics 29(2):194–207
Wong J (2009) Reconstructing the responsibility to protect in the wake of cyclones and separatism. Tulane Law Review 84(2):219–263

Chapter 11
Disasters and Armed Conflict

Gabriella Venturini

Abstract It is widely held in current opinion that in the event of disaster occurring in conflict-affected countries (the so-called mixed situations) International Humanitarian Law (IHL) exclusively governs humanitarian assistance and relief. This work explores the content and extent of the rights and obligations of the parties to an international or non-international armed conflict in the event of disaster. It focuses on humanitarian assistance and the relief provisions included in the Geneva Conventions and Additional Protocols, with special regard to Article 70 of Additional Protocol I and Article 18 of Additional Protocol II. Based on a survey of relevant international practice, the author finds that IHL plays a limited role in facilitating disaster assistance and relief, and that one important reason for this is that the rule of consent, constantly reaffirmed by pertinent treaties and agreements, may seriously obstruct assistance and relief. It is then argued that in mixed situations, IHL and IDRL should be considered complementary rather than alternative. The choice of which body of special rules to apply should be made on the basis of the respective degree of appropriateness for the specific situation, taking into consideration the clarity and precision of the pertinent provisions.

Keywords Armed conflict · International humanitarian law · Humanitarian assistance · Relief actions · Consent · Eritrea · Ethiopia · Colombia · Democratic Republic of the Congo · Indonesia · Sri Lanka

G. Venturini (✉)
Università degli Studi di Milano, Via Conservatorio 7, 20122, Milan, Italy
e-mail: gabriella.venturini@unimi.it

A. de Guttry et al. (eds.), *International Disaster Response Law*,
DOI: 10.1007/978-90-6704-882-8_11,

Contents

11.1 Introductory Remarks

International Humanitarian Law (IHL) as codified in the four Geneva Conventions (GCs) of 12 August 1949, and in the two Additional Protocols (APs) of 8 June 1977, strives to mitigate the consequences of armed conflict by protecting war victims, i.e., the wounded, sick and shipwrecked, prisoners of war (POWs) and civilian persons not participating in hostilities. IHL comprises both the law applicable to international armed conflict (IAC) and the law applicable to non-international armed conflict (NIAC).[1] Armed conflict often aggravates the incidence of disasters such as droughts and floods and during NIACs armed groups may seize relief aid consignments to enhance their position, hence rekindling hostilities.[2] Armed conflict may also originate disaster due to the use of indiscriminate means or methods of warfare such as weapons of mass destruction or scorched earth tactics. Conversely, disasters often foster conflict by prompting struggle for resources which are likely to become insufficient.[3]

It is recognized that IHL governs humanitarian relief when natural or man-made disasters strike conflict-affected countries (so-called mixed situations).[4] The IDRL Guidelines adopted on November 2007 by the International Conference of the Red Cross and Red Crescent 'are not intended to apply to situations of armed conflict or to disasters that occur during armed conflicts, or to imply changes in any rules governing relief in those contexts.'[5] Likewise Article 4 as provisionally adopted by the Drafting Committee of the International Law Commission (ILC) on

[1] NIACs, often arising from disputes over resources, currently characterize many developing countries especially in Africa and in Asia. See Ballentine, Sherman 2003, 259–283.

[2] UNDP 2004, 72; Blouin et al. 2008, 548.

[3] Brancati 2007, 725.

[4] Fisher 2007, 368. See also Chap. 1 by de Guttry in this volume.

[5] IFRC 2008, 10.

the Protection of Persons in the Event of Disasters reads: 'The present draft articles do not apply to situations to which the rules of international humanitarian law are applicable.'[6] These assertions, however, are open to discussion. The International Court of Justice (ICJ) defined IHL as *lex specialis* in relation to human rights law (HRL) admitting that some situations may come under both these branches on international law.[7] Therefore, at least those IDRL obligations that belong to HRL must be respected in all armed conflict. This is especially relevant in the context of NIACs, where multilateral mechanisms such as UN peace operations are often involved.

The purpose of this paper is to discuss whether IHL rules, the scope of which is to protect the victims of war, are also appropriate to the specific circumstances of disaster in order to ensure that assistance and relief are provided in the most efficient way. To this purpose the relevant obligations codified in the GCs as well as in the APs will be analyzed, including those concerning situations of belligerent occupation or internal armed conflict. The principle of humanitarian initiative in IHL will also be examined as well as the role of third States. Subsequently some examples of the relevant international practice will be reviewed with a view to evaluating the attitude of States regarding disaster response in time of armed conflict. Finally, the possible implications of applying IDRL instruments in armed conflict situations will be considered.

11.2 Rights and Obligations of the Parties to the Conflict in Case of Disaster

Both Article 1 common to the four GCs and Article 1 para 1 of Additional Protocol I (AP I) applicable in IAC commit the contracting parties to 'respect and to ensure respect' for the pertinent treaties 'in all circumstances.' The aim of those provisions is to prohibit States from invoking any reason not to respect IHL for any legal or other reason.[8] Although the drafters of the GCs and AP I most probably did not have disasters in mind, the ordinary meaning of such language envisages the application of the Geneva Conventions and Protocols in such events between the beginning and end of their temporal scope.

Indeed, IHL applicable in IAC includes plenty of rules able to safeguard protected persons who happen to be affected by disaster. GCs I and II place detailed obligations on belligerent States as to the protection and care of the wounded, sick and shipwrecked, medical establishments and units, hospital zones and localities.

---

[6] A/CN.4/L.758 of 24 July 2009.

[7] ICJ, Legality of the Threat or Use of Nuclear Weapons, Advisory Opinion of 8 July 1996, ICJ Rep. 1996, 240 at para 25. See also ICJ, Legal Consequences of the Construction of a Wall in the Palestinian Occupied Territory, Advisory Opinion, 9 July 2004, para 106.

[8] Uhler, Coursier 1958, 25; Sandoz et al. 1987, 33 at paras 47–51.

These provisions are able to ensure assistance and relief to disaster victims, who are protected persons under the said Conventions, i.e., members of the armed forces in the field and at sea. However, the wounded, sick, and shipwrecked not belonging to the armed forces hit by a catastrophic event unrelated to armed military activities, would fall outside their scope.[9]

Since the GC III obligations concerning POW maintenance, evacuation, food, clothing, medical attention, and general conditions apply in all circumstances, they must be observed even on the occurrence of a disaster. However, it would be difficult to implement these much detailed regulations in a situation where the hardships of war are gravely worsened by the disruption of the detaining power's organization. Similar considerations may be made when considering the protection of civilians in time of war. GC IV provisions on the general protection of civilian populations[10] aim to mitigate the consequences of war, not those of disaster. Moreover, they are supposed to apply mostly outside the immediate theater of hostilities, i.e., in areas where risk is not extreme. An extensive interpretation may possibly expand their scope to meet the needs of disaster victims, provided that the catastrophe is somehow related to the conflict. It seems unlikely, however, that they could protect citizens in the event of disasters in their own territory but not connected with the war.

Protection in disaster situations may prove especially critical in occupied territories. Indeed, under Article 55 GC IV, the occupying power 'has the duty of ensuring the food and medical supplies of the population' by bringing in foodstuffs, medical, and other articles if the resources of the occupied territory are inadequate. Article 69 AP I further puts the occupying power under the obligation to ensure the provision of clothing, bedding, means of shelter, other supplies essential to the survival of the civilian population, and items necessary for religious worship. These obligations must be fulfilled 'to the fullest extent of the means available.' Since a catastrophic event would severely reduce the 'means available', the provisions on the consignment of medical supplies, food and clothing might prove impracticable just when they are most needed. Moreover, military necessity plays a considerable role in IHL applicable to IAC, and often adversely affects the treatment of civilians under belligerent occupation, regarding *inter alia*, repatriation, deportation, transfer and evacuation.[11] It is not unreasonable to presume that its operation may hinder assistance to disaster victims as well. For example, military necessity may allow the detaining power to limit the quantity of shipments bound for internee use containing foodstuffs, clothing and medical supplies.[12]

The protection of the victims of non-international armed conflict, as laid down by Article 3 common to the 1949 Geneva Conventions and by Additional Protocol

---

[9] Gavshon 2009, 250.

[10] General protection of the wounded and sick, evacuation, protection of hospital, medical staff and transportation, consignments of medical supplies, food and clothing, measures related to child welfare, family news and dispersed families: see GC IV Articles 13–26.

[11] GC IV Articles 48–49.

[12] GC IV Article 108.

II of 1977 (AP II), does not contain comparable rules that could be expanded to include assistance to disaster victims. Indeed provisions on protection and care are vague and undetermined,[13] their main purpose being to prevent assistance to victims harming in any way the State in whose territory the armed conflict is taking place. The advantage of common Article 3 resides in its binding effect on 'each party to the conflict', i.e., both the government and non-State actors, 'by the mere fact of that party's existence and of the existence of an armed conflict between it and the other party'.[14] There is no reciprocity clause. As a consequence, while disaster response during NIAC falls short of the main body of IHL obligations, the basic humanitarian provisions are always applicable 'as a minimum' in such a situation.

11.3 Humanitarian Assistance in IHL

The problems faced by States in implementing their obligations on the protection of war victims have prompted the development of a large number of rules on humanitarian assistance during armed conflict.

Concerning the Geneva Conventions, a common article applicable in international armed conflict[15] establishes that the provisions of the GCs 'constitute no obstacle to the humanitarian activities which the International Committee of the Red Cross or any other impartial humanitarian organization may, subject to the consent of the Parties to the conflict concerned,' undertake for the protection and relief of wounded, sick and shipwrecked persons, medical personnel and chaplains, prisoners of war, and civilian persons. Humanitarian activities may take the form of representations, interventions, suggestions, and practical measures affecting the protection accorded under the Conventions, including the sending of medical and other personnel and equipment, the sending and distribution of foodstuffs, clothing and medicaments. For example, if military operations prevent a belligerent power fulfilling its obligation to ensure the delivery of shipments to civilian internees, the Protecting Powers or, in their absence, the ICRC or any other organization accepted as substitute, may undertake the transportation of such shipments.[16]

Common Article 3 to the GCs relating to non-international armed conflict also recognizes that 'an impartial humanitarian body, such as the International Committee of the Red Cross, may offer its services to the Parties to the conflict.' Article 18 AP II further provides that relief societies located in the territory of the State where an internal conflict occurs may offer their services for the protection of the victims of the armed conflict.

---

[13] GCs Article 3 para 2, AP II Articles 7–11.

[14] Uhler, Coursier 1958, 51.

[15] GC I, GC II and GC III Article 9, GC IV Article 10.

[16] GC IV Article 111.

The above-mentioned provisions create a right of humanitarian initiative to which any impartial humanitarian organization is entitled under certain conditions.[17] First, the term 'organization' clearly refers to entities other than States, such as the International Committee of the Red Cross (ICRC), which is by far the most active in humanitarian assistance during armed conflicts. Second, the intervening organization has to be humanitarian, that is to say, it must be concerned with human beings as such and must not be influenced by political or military considerations. Third, it must also be impartial, i.e., it is required to adopt the same attitude toward all parties to the conflict and act exclusively in the interest of individuals needing assistance. Neither GCs nor APs require the humanitarian organizations in question to be neutral, nevertheless neutrality may be seen as a prerequisite for impartiality, as the ICRC doctrine strongly advocates.[18]

Last, but not least, humanitarian activities by impartial organizations are subject to the consent of the Parties to the conflict. This condition implies that a belligerent power is free to admit or to refuse access to its territory. Prisoners of war, however, are entitled to receive foodstuffs, clothing, medical supplies and other articles[19]; in the absence of agreement between belligerents on the delivery, the prisoner's representatives are allowed to directly distribute collective relief shipments for which they are responsible.[20]

GCs entrust a significant role in humanitarian assistance to neutral States. Neutral countries are required to authorize national entities to lend the assistance of their medical personnel and units to a belligerent without being deemed to be interfering in the conflict.[21] Assistance and relief to the benefit of protected persons are also among the prerogatives of the Protecting Powers (PPs) which monitor the application of the Conventions in order to safeguard the interests of the parties to the conflict.

11.4 Relief Actions

International co-operation to meet the needs of the victims of armed conflicts is codified by a number of provisions in IHL treaties under the label of relief actions.

GC IV includes a number of important articles relating to relief actions. Article 23 (applicable to the whole of the populations of the countries in conflict) provides that State parties to the Convention have a duty to allow free passage of 'all consignments of medical and hospital stores and objects for religious worship intended only for civilians' 'as rapidly as possible' as well as 'all consignments of

[17] Sandoz 1979, 368; Moir 2004, 63.

[18] Uhler, Coursier 1958, 97–98; Plattner 1996.

[19] GC III Article 72.

[20] GC III Article 73 and Annex III.

[21] GC I Article 27; GC II Article 25.

essential foodstuffs, clothing, and tonics intended for children under 15, expectant mothers and maternity cases' directed to another State party. This obligation is incumbent upon all State parties to the Convention, including the belligerents. Any State allowing free passage is entitled to 'prescribe the technical arrangements under which such passage is allowed' and to require that the related items be distributed under the supervision of the PPs. A State may not refuse to allow passage unless it has serious reasons for fearing

'(a) that the consignments may be diverted from their destination, (b) that the control may not be effective, or (c) that *a definite advantage may accrue to the military efforts or economy of the enemy* through the substitution of the above-mentioned consignments for goods which would otherwise be provided or produced by the enemy or through the release of such material, services, or facilities as would otherwise be required for the production of such goods.' [emphasis added].

While the reasons under (a) and (b) may be alleged by any State, (c) clearly refers to a belligerent wanting to prevent the enemy from improving its military strength. As a consequence, in that case, free passage is subject to military assessment and especially to military necessity.

Article 59 GC IV is applicable in occupied territories. It was inspired by the relief actions carried out by the ICRC in occupied Greece during World War II.[22] It requires the occupying power to accept plans of action meant to deliver foodstuffs, medical articles, clothing, and like materials to the civilian populations of an occupied territory that is inadequately supplied.[23] Relief actions may be undertaken either by States or by impartial humanitarian organizations. All States (including enemies) must allow the transit and transport, free of charge, and guarantee protection of relief consignments.[24] A belligerent, however, has the right to search the consignments, to regulate their passage and to be 'reasonably satisfied' that the shipments are used for the population in need and are not redirected to the benefit of the occupying power. The occupying power must not 'divert relief consignments from the purpose for which they are intended, except in cases of urgent necessity, in the interests of the occupied territory and with the consent of the Protecting Power'.[25] This provision notably refers to the necessities of occupied territory; it does not mention the military necessity of the occupying power, which may play a role in restricting only the delivery of individual relief consignments.[26] In any case, the condition of the consent of the PP has little meaning since that institution is not commonly resorted to armed conflicts. For the same reason, the distribution of relief consignments is usually delegated to the ICRC.

---

22 Uhler, Coursier 1958, 319.

23 The obligation to accept relief implies the duty to give consent: see Bothe 1989, 93; Fisher 2007, 349–350; Gavshon 2009, 252.

24 GC IV Article 61.

25 GC IV Article 60. See Patrnogic 1984, 925.

26 GC I Article 62.

AP I applicable in international armed conflict expands the scope of relief actions. They are to be undertaken to provide the civilian population of territories under the control of a party to the conflict, other than occupied territories, with bedding, means of shelter and other supplies essential to survival besides foodstuffs, medical stores, and clothing.[27] Article 70 of the said Protocol still calls for the agreement of the parties concerned, i.e., the sending State, the State(s) through whose territory relief consignments pass, and the receiving State. This provision is interpreted as meaning that consent may not be arbitrarily withheld.[28] It is supplemented by the requirement that both belligerents and third parties 'shall allow and facilitate rapid and unimpeded passage' of all relief consignments, equipment and personnel.[29] Offers of relief 'shall not be regarded as interference in the armed conflict or as unfriendly acts'.[30] This strengthens the right of initiative of third States and impartial humanitarian organizations.

In line with State practice, Article 70 AP I is presently deemed to correspond to customary international law.[31] However, determination of priorities in the distribution of relief consignments is limited to 'expectant mothers, maternity cases and nursing mothers'.[32] IDRL has developed a more detailed list of priority beneficiaries including older people, persons with disabilities, minorities, and indigenous people.[33] These criteria should complement IHL when delivering assistance to disaster victims in a mixed situation.

Article 71 AP I takes into account the status of personnel participating in relief actions. This provision essentially envisages persons participating in the transportation and distribution of relief consignments, subject to the approval of the receiving State. The latter must respect, protect, and assist relief personnel in carrying out their mission, however it may restrict their activities and movements for reasons of (imperative) military necessity.[34]

As usual, rules applicable to non-international armed conflict are far less stringent. Article 18 AP I, while giving priority to the action of relief societies located in the territory of the State where the internal conflict is occurring, mandates relief actions (subject to the consent of the government in power) to be undertaken to the benefit of the civilian population which is suffering a lack of supplies essential for its survival. Although the entities that will carry out such relief actions are not identified, the provision implicitly refers to impartial

---

27 AP I Articles. 69–71.

28 Sandoz et al. 1987, 819 at para 2805; Fisher 2007, 350.

29 AP I Aticle 70 para 2. States allowing passage retain the right to prescribe the related technical arrangements, including search, and to make permission conditional on the distribution of assistance being made under the local supervision of a Protecting Power (Article 70 para 3).

30 AP I Article 70, para 1.

31 Henckaerts, Doswald Beck 2005, Rule 55.

32 AP I Article 70 para 1.

33 See Chap. 16 by Bizzarri in this volume.

34 Bothe 1989, 95.

humanitarian organizations and particularly to the ICRC. An extensive interpretation holds that the State concerned cannot refuse relief without good reasons. Indeed, a refusal would correspond to a violation of AP II Article 14 prohibiting the starvation of civilians as a method of combat.[35] However, when relief consignments must be forwarded to areas under the control of non-State armed groups, States' obligations may prove ineffective. For this reason it is argued that if it is in the interests of the victims, consent may be presumed when it is impossible to ascertain which authorities are in control of a given territory.[36]

11.5 A Look at International Practice

11.5.1 Eritrea–Ethiopia (1998–2000)

When an international armed conflict broke out between Eritrea and Ethiopia in May 1998, both countries were facing a harsh drought. Drought is endemic in the Horn of Africa, but the fact that several places in Eritrea and Ethiopia had been without rain for the preceding 2–3 years triggered a severe famine. For decades, internal and inter-State conflicts have devastated the area and the interrelationships among drought, famine and conflict have been persuasively demonstrated.[37]

In May 1998, a number of humanitarian food cargoes directed to Ethiopia were waiting for delivery in the Eritrean port of Assab. After the war began, all shipment of cargo to Ethiopia ended. It was reported that Ethiopia repeatedly dismissed offers by Eritrea to open a humanitarian corridor from Assab as aid agencies were advocating.[38] When the two States eventually concluded a peace treaty on 20 December 2000, they entrusted an arbitral tribunal, the Eritrea–Ethiopia Claims Commission (EECC) to decide all claims relating to the conflict and resulting from violations of IHL.[39]

In one of its awards, the EECC offered a rare judicial interpretation of Article 23 GC IV relating to the consignment of humanitarian supplies. Since Eritrea did not ratify the Geneva Conventions until the end of hostilities, the EECC applied the corresponding customary IHL, including Article 23 GC IV as an exception to the right of a belligerent to restrict or terminate trade and commerce between itself

---

[35] Sandoz et al. 1987, 1479 at para 4885.

[36] Idem at para 4884.

[37] Keller 1992, Meedan Mekkonen 2006.

[38] Eritrea/Ethiopia Disaster Diplomacy, http//www.disasterdiplomacy.org/Eritreaethiopia.html. Accessed 26 September 2011. See also Kelman 2012, 34–36.

[39] Agreement between the Government of the Federal Democratic Republic of Ethiopia and the Government of the State of Eritrea, Algiers 12 December 2000, Article 5 para 1. The text of the agreement is available on the website of the Permanent Court of Arbitration: http://www.pca-cpa.org/upload/files/Algiers%20Agreement.pdf. Accessed 26 October 2011.

and the enemy that 'has been clearly established, and is evidenced by extensive State practice during the twentieth century.'[40] Ethiopia contended that Eritrea had blocked humanitarian consignments directed to Ethiopia from the port of Assab, thus violating the obligations stated by Article 23. The EECC held that 'While some medical supplies may have been included in the mass of property remaining at Assab in May 1998, the record did not show that any meaningful proportion was potentially subject to Article 23, that Ethiopia requested the passage of any such goods, or that Ethiopia had any control measures in place to prevent their diversion.'[41] Since the request by the country of destination is equivalent to consent, the EECC's interpretation corresponds to both IHL and IDRL requirements.[42] As a consequence, the decision taken by a State not to ask for help has the effect of barring the free passage of relief consignments through enemy territory in mixed situations of war and disaster, seriously impairing the duty to accept assistance established by IHL.

11.5.2 Colombia (1999)

On 25 January 1999, a massive earthquake hit the Quindio Department of Colombia, in the northwestern part of the country. While the capital Armenia was the most severely affected, the disaster area extended across 5 provinces including about 20 towns; an estimated 1,000 people were killed and about 35,000 were left homeless.[43]

An internal armed conflict had been ongoing in Colombia since the mid-1960s between the government and armed guerrilla groups such as the Revolutionary Armed Forces of Colombia (FARC) and the National Liberation Army (ELN) receiving support from Colombia's rural areas. In the autumn of 1998, following informal contacts, the Colombian government and rebel groups agreed to establish a demilitarized zone in south-central Colombia. In January 1999 formal peace talks began; just a few days before the quake, however, the FARC decided to suspend participation in negotiations.

Since the disaster-affected area did not include guerrilla strongholds, disaster response was not delayed by uncertainties about control of the territory. However, the deployment of military personnel in relief operations weakened the government's ability to force the rebels to withdraw from the demilitarized zone. As a consequence, attacks by FARC and ELN intensified in several parts of the country.

---

[40] Eritrea–Ethiopia Claims Commission, Final Award, Ports, Ethiopia's claim 6, December 19, 2005 para 20, http://www.pca-cpa.org/upload/files/FINAL%20ET%20PORTS.pdf. Accessed 26 October 2011. See Heintschel von Heinegg 2009, 378–379.

[41] Loc. cit. n. 40 para 22.

[42] See Chap. 2 by Venturini in this volume.

[43] Shoaf, Rottman 2000, 58; Brancati 2007, 724.

Meanwhile, disaster relief provided by the government was slow and inadequate. Widespread looting and violence erupted in the region and the Colombian army and police were not able to effectively protect citizens.[44]

This situation did not prevent international aid from being delivered to disaster-affected zones. The ICRC and IFRC in co-operation with the Colombia Red Cross Society distributed timely emergency relief and food supplies; some European Red Cross societies with ECHO funding brought further assistance and the United States provided a million dollars in aid to the Colombian government. Several UN agencies and NGOs were also involved. It appears that Colombia's public health infrastructure adequately faced the post-quake sanitation concerns. The Colombian government obtained credits from the Inter-American development Bank and the World Bank in order to re-establish essential infrastructure. In the following months, while support to the earthquake victims lingered, international assistance turned toward disaster preparedness, reinforcement of systems, and rehabilitation.[45]

Whereas the 1999 earthquake in Colombia adversely impacted on the prospects for peace in the country, since disaster was unrelated to the ongoing internal conflict, international response did not seem to be affected. Co-operation among humanitarian actors was planned and carried out based on current patterns. Although it had been a contracting party of AP II since 1995, Colombia did not rely on its provisions concerning relief actions to obtain assistance coming from the international community.

11.5.3 The Democratic Republic of the Congo (2002)

Since 1998 most southern African countries have been involved in the Second Congo War, i.e., the conflict between the Democratic Republic of the Congo (DRC) together with the armed forces of the allied governments of Angola, Chad, Libya, Namibia, Sudan, and Zimbabwe, and the armed forces of Burundi, Rwanda, and Uganda. Most of the warring States have supported rebel groups or factions fighting in enemy territory against their own government.[46] As a consequence, international armed conflict and conflict of a non-international character have coexisted at the same time in different areas of the DRC. All belligerents were parties to the four GCs and to AP I. Most of them, including the DRC and Rwanda, were also parties to AP II.[47]

---

[44] Brancati 2007, 724–725.

[45] Shoaf, Rottman 2000, 59. Reports on IFRC operations are available on the Federation's website: http://www.ifrc.org. Accessed 26 October 2011.

[46] Reyntjens 2009, 194–201; Binder et al. 2010, 22–30.

[47] In June 1999 the Democratic Republic of the Congo brought applications before the International Court of Justice against Burundi, Rwanda and Uganda concerning the alleged perpetration of acts of armed aggression in violation of the United Nations Charter and of the Charter of the Organization of African Unity. It discontinued proceedings against Burundi and Rwanda in 2001. The Court found Uganda responsible for violations of human rights treaties and IHL, particularly as occupying power in the province of Ituri (Armed activities on the territory of the Congo, Democratic Republic of the Congo v. Uganda, Judgment of 19 December 2005, ICJ Rep. 2005).

In January 2002, eighteen kilometers north of the city of Goma, capital of the North Kivu province of the RDC, the Mount Nyiragongo volcano erupted causing severe destruction to buildings in the city and forcing most of the population to flee into neighboring Rwanda. The Rwandan-aligned Congolese Rally for Democracy (Rassemblement Congolais pour la Démocratie, RCD) was the rebel movement controlling the area at that time. Reportedly the rebels refused to accept aid from the central government, while allowing humanitarian organizations to enter their territory.[48] The UN and the Organization for African Unity (OAU, now the African Union, AU) provided further relief. The ICRC, which had been present in the area for several years, used its structures to address the humanitarian needs of the population both on the Congolese and on the Rwandan side of the border, in co-ordination with the International Federation of Red Cross and Red Crescent Societies (IFRC), the Rwandan Red Cross and other national societies present in the country.[49] Refugees in Rwanda were accommodated in three camps, however most of them were soon able to return to Goma. Within a few months the situation was no longer reported as an emergency related to the eruption.

In the face of the 2002 Mount Nyiragongo eruption, the implementation of IHL worked satisfactorily in practice. The armed group maintaining control over the affected territory recognized the right of humanitarian initiative by allowing aid organizations to access the area. Co-ordination among assisting entities was thoroughly managed. Rwanda (legally speaking, an enemy State) admitted displaced persons to its territory. In that situation, the IHL machinery proved appropriate to handle relief for disaster victims in time of armed conflict.

11.5.4 Indonesia and Sri Lanka (2004–2005)

On 26 December 2004 an undersea earthquake with its epicenter in the Indian Ocean generated a destructive tsunami along the coasts of the Bay of Bengal. The Indian Ocean tsunami significantly impacted on two long-lasting internal conflicts in the area, i.e., the insurrection of the Liberation Tigers of Tamil Eelan (LTTE) against the government of Sri Lanka and the rebellion of the separatist province of Aceh in Indonesia.

Although both States are parties to the GCs, they neither signed nor ratified the APs. As a consequence, only common Article 3 corresponding to customary international law is binding upon them. In fact, the ICRC was present in both countries in the exercise of its humanitarian mandate and it immediately undertook to distribute relief items in those parts of the countries hit by the tsunami.

---

[48] Goma Volcano in 2002, http://www.disasterdiplomacy.org/casestudies.html. Accessed 30 September 2011. See also Kelman 2012, 83–84.

[49] ICRC, Democratic Republic of the Congo (DRC), Eruption of Nyiragongo Volcano, Goma. 04.02.2002 Operational Update, http://www.icrc.org/eng/resources/documents/misc/57jrmb.htm. Accessed 3 October 2011.

Emergency supplies were delivered in co-operation with the local Red Cross Societies as well as the IFRC and other humanitarian organizations. Relief included emergency supplies, support for mobile clinics serving displaced persons, evacuating the wounded, assisting displaced families, enabling family members separated by the disaster to re-establish contact with one another, and removing mortal remains.[50] At the same time, an unprecedented global response to the Indian Ocean tsunami by foreign governments, international organizations, multilateral institutions, and private entities allocated and delivered financial and logistic assistance that largely exceeded the obligations provided by humanitarian instruments.[51]

Interestingly the post-tsunami events led to opposite outcomes. In Sri Lanka, where a ceasefire agreement was in force at the time of the disaster, in its immediate aftermath, the government and the insurgents temporarily established an operational joint structure to handle relief. This prompted a constitutional challenge before the Sri Lanka Supreme Court that eventually ruled out that mechanism.[52] Thereafter, hostilities between the LTTE and the government resumed and dramatically escalated over the following years. Between 2006 and 2008 the government launched a series of military offensives progressively taking control of all areas previously held by the LTTE. On 17 May 2009, the insurgents finally admitted defeat. While the debate over the role of post-tsunami foreign assistance in the resumption of the hostilities was inconclusive, it was argued that relief consignments 'did not appropriately match the regional distribution of damage.'[53] After the end of the conflict, the ICRC itself closed its offices outside Colombo at the request of the Sri Lankan government and it is presently conducting its operations exclusively from the capital.[54]

In Banda Aceh the Indonesian government had declared martial law since 2003. Notwithstanding several ceasefire agreements, the rebel Free Aceh Movement (Gerakan Aceh Merdeka, GAM) grew in military and financial power, expanding its territorial control of the province.[55] In the post-tsunami situation, the Indonesian government assigned the task of executing rescue and relief actions to the military. It did not, however, suspend security operations against the rebels, thus

---

[50] Sri Lanka: ICRC provides relief for tsunami victims, ICRC News Release 04/149 of 28 December 2004, http://www.icrc.org/eng/resources/documents/misc/684m43.htm. Accessed 26 October 2011. Aceh: reconstruction will take years, ICRC Press Briefing of 6 September 2005, http://www.icrc.org/eng/resources/documents/misc/tsunami-aceh-060905.htm. Accessed 30 September 2011.

[51] Kennedy et al. 2008, 26–29.

[52] Brancati 2007, 725–726; Kuhn 2009, 18; Kelman 2012, 41.

[53] Loc. cit. But see Kennedy et al., 30.

[54] The ICRC in Sri Lanka 01–05–2011 Overview, http://www.icrc.org/eng/where-we-work/asia-pacific/sri-lanka/overview-sri-lanka.htm. Accessed 30 September 2011.

[55] Ross 2003, 6.

making it difficult for aid to reach the victims. This allegedly resulted in a great deal of unnecessary deaths among the civilian populations.[56] However, during the following months, growing pressures from the international community persuaded the government to allow aid organizations and volunteers access to the province. It was argued that the disaster itself was a catalyst in diplomatic talks that ultimately led to an agreement granting the release of GAM prisoners, a status of special autonomy for Banda Aceh and several economic advantages. For its part, GAM renounced their claims of independence and handed over their weapons.[57]

Investigating the military, political, and economic grounds that may explain the different outcomes of disaster relief in the Sri Lanka and Indonesian conflicts is beyond the purpose of this work. What seems evident is the limited role that IHL played in both cases. Governments had trouble managing assistance to victims in insurrectional areas. Disaster relief was eventually made possible by the unprompted initiative of many actors whose impartiality, let alone neutrality, was somehow unclear. Therefore, it seems that when facing a major disaster in a situation of non-international armed conflict, IHL needs to be complemented by all the instruments of humanitarian assistance as they have developed in peacetime.

11.6 Concluding Remarks

Legal analysis and relevant international practice throw both light and shadow on the effectiveness of IHL provisions on assistance and relief for disasters occurring during an armed conflict. One reason is that both belligerent States and non-State actors are often reluctant to expressly refer to the IHL rules applicable during hostilities. Nonetheless, formal declarations are not a requirement in order to assess their substantive implementation. From this perspective, it seems that IHL and IDRL may be considered as complementary rather than alternative in mixed situations.

It is recognized that the existence of an international armed conflict does not *per se* terminate or suspend the operation of treaties in force between the parties to the conflict. Most importantly, treaties relating to the protection of human rights may not be terminated or suspended. This has been affirmed not only by the legal scholarship[58] but also by the ILC in the recently adopted Draft articles on the effects of armed conflicts on treaties.[59] IHL and IDRL treaties are not mutually incompatible. On the contrary, they share the very same aim, i.e., the protection of the human person in situations of danger and suffering. For that reason both are *lex*

[56] Sinitchkina 2005, 4.

[57] Gaillard et al. 2008, 511; Kelman 2012, 42–44.

[58] As expressed by the members of the Institut de Droit International (The effects of Armed Conflicts on Treaties 1985, articles 2 and 4).

[59] International Law Commission 2011, Article 3 and Annex.

specialis with respect to HRL. The choice of which body of special rules to apply should be made on the basis of its degree of appropriateness to the specific situation, taking into consideration the clarity and precision of the pertinent provisions. Agreements on the provision of assistance and relief in the event of disaster should be implemented notwithstanding the outbreak of an armed conflict between the parties, in the same way as the free passage of medical consignments must be allowed by enemy belligerents under Article 23 of GC IV.

This is even more so in the case of armed conflicts not of an international character. States in whose territory such a conflict occurs remain bound by all the treaty obligations they have accepted. Given the elusive nature and function of IHL provisions on assistance and relief in NIAC, it is essential that IDRL provisions be fully applied in the event of disaster. At that moment IHL would play a complementary role insofar as it is binding on the affected State as well as on non-State parties to the conflict.

Regrettably, upon consideration of international practice, it has to be said that the need to obtain consent from the territorial States may seriously hinder the effectiveness of assistance and relief in mixed situations. Still IHL and IDRL instruments strongly reaffirm that principle. There are, however, limits to refusing consent. On the one hand, offers of humanitarian assistance are not to be regarded as unfriendly acts. On the other hand, there must be valid justification for refusal. Last, but not least, consent could be taken as presumed in exceptional situations. Hopefully, evolving State practice will support these interpretations in good faith, thus leading to more effective aid for disaster victims.

References

Ballentine K, Sherman J (eds) (2003) The political economy of armed conflict: beyond greed and grievance. Boulder, London

Binder A, de Geoffroy V, Sokpoh B (2010) IASC cluster approach evaluation 2nd phase, country study. Democratic Republic of Congo, Global Public Policy Institute/Groupe URD, Berlin/Plaisians

Blouin M, Pallage S (2008) Humanitarian relief and civil conflict. J Confl Resolut, 52:548–565

Bothe M (1989) Relief actions: the position of the recipient state. In: Kalshoven F (ed) Assisting the victims of armed conflicts and other disasters: Papers delivered at the international conference on humanitarian assistance in armed conflict, The Hague, 22–24 June 1988. Martinus Nijhoff Publishers, Dordrecht, pp 91–97

Brancati D (2007) Political aftershocks: the impact of earthquakes on intrastate conflicts. J Confl Resolut 51:715–743

Fisher D (2007) Domestic regulation of international humanitarian relief in disasters and armed conflict: a comparative analysis. Int Rev Red Cross 866:345–372

Gaillard J-C, Clavé E, Kelman I (2008) Wave of peace? Tsunami disaster diplomacy in Aceh, Indonesia. Geoforum 39:511–526

Gavshon D (2009) The applicability of IHL in mixed situations of disaster and conflict. J Confl Secur L 14:243–263

Heintschel von Heinegg W (2009) International Economic relations and armed conflict. In: de Guttry A, Post H, Venturini G (eds) The 1998–2000 war between Eritrea and Ethiopia. T.M.C. Asser Press, The Hague, pp 371–387

Henckaerts J-M, Doswald Beck L (eds) (2005) Customary international humanitarian law, vol 1: rules. ICRC, Geneva

IFRC (2008) Introduction to the guidelines for the domestic facilitation and regulation of international disaster relief and initial recovery assistance. International Federation of Red Cross and Red Crescent Societies, Geneva

Institut de Droit International (1985) The Effects of Armed Conflicts on Treaties, Annuaire de l'Institut de Droit International 61:1–27

International Law Commission (2011) Draft articles on the effects of armed conflicts on treaties, Yearbook of the International law Commission, 2011, vol II, Part Two

Keller EJ (1992) Drought, war and the politics of famine in Ethiopia and Eritrea. J Mod Afr Stud 30:609–624

Kelman I (2012) Disaster diplomacy: how disasters affect peace and conflict. Routledge, London

Kennedy J, Ashmore J, Babister E, Kelman I (2008) The meaning of 'build back better': evidence from post–tsunami Aceh and Sri Lanka. J Contingencies Crisis Manag 16:24–36

Kuhn R (2009) Tsunami and conflict in Sri Lanka, Josef Korbel School of International Studies. http://gfdrr.org/gfdrr/sites/gfdrr.org/files/New%20Folder/Kuhn_Tsunami%26Conflict.pdf

Meedan Mekonnen (2006) Drought, famine, and conflict: case from the horn of Africa. http://www.beyondintractability.org/

Moir L (2004) The law of internal armed conflict. Cambridge University Press, Cambridge

Patrnogic J (1984) Some reflections on humanitarian principles applicable in relief actions. In: Swinarski C (ed) Studies and essays on international humanitarian law and red cross principles in honour of Jean Pictet. Martinus Nijhoff Publishers, The Hague, pp 925–936

Plattner D (1996) La neutralité du CICR et la neutralité de l'assistance humanitaire, Revue Internationale de la Croix–Rouge, 818:169–189

Reyntjens F (2009) The great African war: Congo and regional geopolitics, 1996–2006. Cambridge University Press, New York

Ross ML (2003) Resources and rebellion in Aceh, Indonesia, UCLA Department of Political Science. http://www.aceheye.org. Accessed 30 Sept 2011

Sandoz Y (1979) Le droit d'initiative du CICR, Jahrbuch für Internationales Recht 22:352–373

Sandoz Y, Swinarski C, Zimmermann B (1987) Commentary on the Additional Protocols of 8 June 1977 to the Geneva Conventions of 12 August 1949, International Committee of the Red Cross, Martinus Nijhoff Publishers, Geneva: Gasser H–P and Wenger C F (Protocol I) Eberlin P (Annex I) Junod S–S (Protocol II)

Shoaf KI, Rottman SJ (2000) Public health impact of disasters. Aust J Emerg Manag 15:58–63

Sinitchkina S (2005) Tsunami and Aceh conflict resolution, inventory of conflict and environment (ICE) case studies no 165. http://www1.american.edu/ted/ice/tsunami-aceh.htm

Uhler O, Coursier H (1958) Geneva Convention relative to the protection of civilian persons in time of war: Commentary, ICRC, Geneva

UNDP (2004) Reducing disaster risk. A challenge for development. United Nations Development Programme, New York

Chapter 12
The National Legal Frameworks Relating to Disaster Response: How is Incoming International Assistance Regulated?

Marina Mancini

Abstract This chapter focuses on the domestic legal frameworks relating to disaster response of a number of States which have been hit by major disasters in the past few years, namely Indonesia, the United States, the Philippines, Haiti, and Japan. It analyzes the provisions regulating incoming international assistance and investigates (1) how they are applied in practice and (2) whether they are consistent with the IFRC's Guidelines for the Domestic Facilitation and Regulation of International Disaster Relief and Initial Recovery Assistance and the treaty obligations of the States in question. The author finds that the legal preparedness for receiving international assistance varies significantly in the five countries taken into consideration and argues that even the legislation of those apparently best prepared can be improved. She concludes that the legal frameworks relating to disaster response in the countries considered reveal a reactive approach to regulatory problems in international relief operations and suggests instead that a proactive approach to those problems should be adopted.

Keywords Legislation · Disaster management · Disaster response · International assistance · Foreign states · International organizations · Foreign NGOs · IDRL guidelines · Treaty obligations

---

M. Mancini (✉)
Faculty of Law, Mediterranean University of Reggio Calabria,
Via dei Bianchi, 2,
89127, Reggio Calabria, Italy
e-mail: marina.mancini@unirc.it

A. de Guttry et al. (eds.), *International Disaster Response Law*,
DOI: 10.1007/978-90-6704-882-8_12,

Contents

12.1 Introduction

Over the last decade, major natural disasters, including the 2004 Indian Ocean tsunami, the 2005 hurricane Katrina, the 2010 Haiti earthquake, and the 2011 Japanese earthquake and tsunami, have focused world attention on the importance of having adequate national legal frameworks in place for disaster prevention and response. In fact, legislation plays a crucial role in promoting and supporting disaster risk reduction as well as in guaranteeing the speed and effectiveness of disaster response.

The critical importance of legislation is emphasized in the Hyogo Framework for Action 2005–2015: Building the Resilience of Nations and Communities to Disasters, which was adopted by the World Conference on Disaster Reduction in 2005.[1] It calls on States to 'adopt, or modify where necessary, legislation to support disaster risk reduction, including regulations and mechanisms that encourage compliance and that promote incentives for undertaking risk reduction and mitigation activities'.[2] Legislation is considered as a key means to achieve the first priority for action identified by the Conference, namely to 'ensure that disaster risk reduction is a national and a local priority with a strong institutional basis for implementation'.[3]

The Guidelines for the Domestic Facilitation and Regulation of International Disaster Relief and Initial Recovery Assistance (IDRL Guidelines), adopted by the 30th International Conference of the Red Cross and Red Crescent in 2007, also

[1] International Strategy for Disaster Reduction, Hyogo Framework for Action 2005–2015: Building the Resilience of Nations and Communities to Disasters, Extract from the Final Report of the World Conference on Disaster Reduction (A/CONF.206/6), United Nations, available at http://www.unisdr.org/we/inform/publications/1037. Accessed 23 January 2012. It was endorsed by the General Assembly of the United Nations in a number of resolutions, the most recent of which is—at the time of writing—resolution 65/264 of 21 June 2011.

[2] Ibid., 6.

[3] Ibid.

highlight the pivotal role of legislation.[4] The adoption of comprehensive legislation on disaster prevention and response is considered 'an essential element of a larger disaster risk reduction programme' (Para. 8(1)). Such legislation should address *inter alia* the initiation, facilitation, transit and regulation of international assistance consistent with the IDRL Guidelines (Para. 8(2)).

In the light of these developments, it is worth investigating States' legal preparedness for responding to disasters. This chapter focuses on the domestic legal frameworks relating to disaster response of a number of States which have been hit by major catastrophes over the past few years, namely Indonesia, the United States, the Philippines, Haiti, and Japan. It explores the provisions addressing the issue of international assistance in the event of disasters affecting the national territory and discusses (1) how they are applied in practice and (2) whether they are consistent with the IDRL Guidelines and the treaty obligations of the States in question.

In fact, the IDRL Guidelines are a set of recommendations to States on how to draft or revise their disaster management laws and plans so as to avoid the main problems that commonly arise in international disaster response operations, such as those relating to the quality of relief, the coordination of relief providers, the entry into the affected State and transit through other States of relief personnel, goods, and equipment.[5] They are complemented by the Model Act for the Facilitation and Regulation of International Disaster Relief and Initial Recovery Assistance (Model Act), which was developed by the International Federation of Red Cross and Red Crescent Societies, in co-operation with the United Nations Office for the Coordination of Humanitarian Affairs and the Inter-Parliamentary Union and was launched in a pilot version in November 2011.[6] The Model Act is intended to serve as a reference tool for States wishing to implement the IDRL Guidelines in their domestic legal system.[7]

As to regional treaty obligations relating to incoming international assistance, the obligations arising for Indonesia and the Philippines from the 2005 ASEAN Agreement on Disaster Management and Emergency Response[8] (AADMER) are

---

[4] IFRC, Introduction to the Guidelines for the Domestic Facilitation and Regulation of International Disaster Relief and Initial Recovery Assistance, Geneva, 2008, available at http://www.ifrc.org/en/what-we-do/idrl/idrl-guidelines/, 8 et seq. Accessed 23 January 2012. They too were endorsed by the General Assembly of the United Nations in a number of resolutions, the most recent being—at the time of writing—resolution 65/264 of 21 June 2011.

[5] Ibid., 4 et seq.

[6] IFRC, OCHA, IPU, Model Act for the Facilitation and Regulation of International Disaster Relief and Initial Recovery Assistance, Pilot Version, Geneva, November 2011, available at http://www.ifrc.org/en/what-we-do/idrl/disaster-law-at-the-31st-international-conference/. Accessed 26 January 2012.

[7] Ibid., iv.

[8] ASEAN Agreement on Disaster Management and Emergency Response, done at Vientiane (Lao People's Democratic Republic) on 26 July 2005, entered into force on 24 December 2009, available at http://www.aseansec.org/17579.htm. Accessed 26 January 2012.

worth considering. The AADMER aims *inter alia* at ensuring a joint response to disaster emergencies on the territory of the State parties 'through concerted national efforts and intensified regional and international cooperation' (Article 2). In this context, it sets forth the obligations of the State parties requesting assistance or accepting assistance offered from abroad. In particular, those States are required to set up simplified customs and immigration procedures for relief goods, equipment and personnel. Unlike Indonesia and the Philippines, the other three countries taken into consideration are not parties to any regional treaty in the field of disaster management. In this respect, it is to be noted that neither the United States nor Haiti are parties to the 1991 Inter-American Convention to Facilitate Disaster Assistance[9] and that the latter is not even a party to the 2008 Agreement Establishing the Caribbean Disaster Emergency Management Agency (CDEMA).[10]

With regard to universal treaty obligations relating to incoming international assistance, the obligations arising for Indonesia, the United States, the Philippines, and Japan from the 1986 Convention on Assistance in the Case of Nuclear Accident or Radiological Emergency[11] (CACNARE) are worth mentioning. The CACNARE aims at facilitating the provision of assistance to any requesting State party from the IAEA and the other parties in the event of nuclear accidents or radiological emergencies. To this end, it imposes a number of obligations on the requesting State party. In particular, this State shall facilitate the access to its territory of personnel, property, and equipment involved in the assistance and shall afford them some privileges and immunities. However, the possibility of a nuclear accident in Indonesia and the Philippines is remote, as there is no operational nuclear power plant in those countries. As for the other universal treaties establishing obligations in the field of incoming international assistance, it is to be stressed that none of the countries taken into consideration is a party to the 1992 Convention on the Transboundary Effects of Industrial Accidents,[12] the 1998 Tampere Convention on the Provision of Telecommunication Resources for

[9] Inter-American Convention to Facilitate Disaster Assistance, done at Santiago (Chile) on 7 June 1991, entered into force on 16 October 1996, available at http://www.oas.org/juridico/english/treaties/a-54.html. Accessed 26 January 2012.

[10] Agreement Establishing the Caribbean Disaster Emergency Management Agency (CDEMA), done at St. Johns (Antigua and Barbuda) on 1 July 2008, provisionally applied since 4 July 2008, available in the IDRL database of the International Federation of Red Crescent and Red Cross Societies at http://www.ifrc.org/en/what-we-do/idrl/publication. Accessed 26 January 2012.

[11] Convention on Assistance in the Case of Nuclear Accident or Radiological Emergency, done at Vienna on 26 September 1986, entered into force on 26 February 1987, available at http://www.iaea.org/Publications/Documents/Conventions/cacnare.html. Accessed 26 January 2012.

[12] Convention on the Transboundary Effects of Industrial Accidents, done at Helsinki on 17 March 1992, entered into force on 19 April 2000, available at http://www.unece.org/env/teia/about.html. Accessed 26 January 2012.

Disaster Mitigation and Relief Operations[13] and the 2000 Framework Convention on Civil Defence Assistance.[14]

12.2 Indonesia

The Indonesian legal framework relating to disaster response consists mainly of Law no. 24 of 2007 Concerning Disaster Management[15] and a number of implementing regulations.[16] Law no. 24 of 2007 is the outcome of a process started in the aftermath of the 2004 Indian Ocean tsunami.[17] On 26 December 2004, the tsunami generated by an earthquake off the coast of Sumatra struck the northern part of the island, causing about 170,000 people killed and over 570,000 displaced.[18] It revealed the urgent need for a new, comprehensive, and clear disaster management system.[19]

Law no. 24 of 2007 adopts a global approach to disaster management, covering natural and man-made disasters (Article 1(1)) and including disaster risk reduction, disaster prevention, emergency response and rehabilitation (Article 1(5)). It vests both the central government and the regional governments with the responsibility for disaster management (Article 5). In particular, they are responsible at their respective levels for promoting disaster risk reduction and integrating it into the development program, protecting the population against disaster impact and guaranteeing the rights of the members of the disaster affected communities (Articles 6, 8).

---

[13] Tampere Convention on the Provision of Telecommunication Resources for Disaster Mitigation and Relief Operations, done at Tampere on 18 June 1998, entered into force on 8 January 2005, available at http://www.itu.int/ITU-D/emergencytelecoms/tampere.html. Accessed 26 January 2012.

[14] Framework Convention on Civil Defence Assistance, done at Geneva on 22 May 2000, entered into force on 23 September 2001, available at http://www.icdo.org/index.php?option=com_content&view=article&id=23&Itemid=26&lang=en
. Accessed 26 January 2012.

[15] Law no. 24 of 2007 Concerning Disaster Management, available in the IDRL database of the International Federation of Red Crescent and Red Cross Societies at http://www.ifrc.org/en/what-we-do/idrl/publication. Accessed 27 January 2012.

[16] They are the following: Government Regulation no. 8 of 2008 Concerning the National Disaster Management Agency; Government Regulation no. 21 of 2008 Concerning Disaster Management Operations; Government Regulation no. 22 of 2008 Concerning Funding and Management of Disaster Assistance; Government Regulation no. 23 of 2008 Concerning Participation of International Institutions and Foreign Non-Governmental Organizations in Disaster Management. They are all available at http://drrindonesia.org/index.php?option=com_weblinks&view=category&id=43&Itemid=58. Accessed 26 January 2012.

[17] See: IFRC 2010, 5; Walker et al. 2011, 16 et seq.

[18] IFRC 2010, 4.

[19] Ibid.

Law no. 24 of 2007 directs the central government to establish the National Disaster Management Agency (Article 10) and the regional governments to set up the Regional Disaster Management Agencies (Article 18). In fact, the National Disaster Management Agency, in Indonesian 'Badan Nasional Penanggulangan Bencana' (BNPB), was set up soon after the entry into force of the law.[20] The National Disaster Management Agency and the Regional Disaster Management Agencies are tasked at their respective levels with formulating disaster management policy and coordinating disaster management activities (Articles 13, 20). It is worth noting, however, that they can mobilize personnel, logistics, and equipment to respond to disasters only when a state of emergency has been declared by the central or regional government depending on the scale of disaster (Articles 50, 51).

As regards international assistance, Law no. 24 of 2007 confines itself to stipulating that 'international institutions and foreign non-governmental organizations can participate in disaster management activities and receive Government protection for their workers' (Article 30(1)) and adds that they 'can carry out disaster management severally, jointly, and/or together with Indonesian working partner while considering the local community social, cultural, and religious backgrounds' (Article 30(2)).

Detailed provisions on international assistance are contained in Government Regulation no. 23 of 2008, which was enacted pursuant to Article 30(3) of Law no. 24 of 2007.[21] It covers participation of international organizations and foreign non-governmental organizations (NGOs) in disaster management, including emergency response, pre-disaster and post-disaster phases. With regard to the emergency response phase, this regulation is complemented by the Guideline on the Role of the International Organizations and Foreign Non-Governmental Organizations during Emergency Response, which was adopted by the Head of BNPB at the end of 2010.[22]

Under Government Regulation no. 23 of 2008, it is for the Head of BNPB to determine the participation of international organizations and foreign NGOs in disaster management (Article 4). International organizations and foreign NGOs wishing to participate in disaster management activities shall follow a standard procedure, except in the phase of emergency response (Articles 5, 6, 8(1)). During this phase, they are only required to submit the list of personnel, logistics and equipment and communicate the location of activity (Article 8(2)). The list may be sent even immediately following arrival in Indonesia (Article 8(3)). The Head of BNPB will approve the personnel, logistics and equipment included in the list, depending on needs (Article 8(4)). Where international organizations and foreign

---

[20] UNDP 2009, 21. As for the Regional Disaster Management Agencies, see Walker et al. 2011, 17.

[21] See *supra* footnote 16.

[22] The Guideline on the Role of the International Organizations and Foreign Non-Governmental Organizations during Emergency Response is available in the IDRL database of the International Federation of Red Crescent and Red Cross Societies at http://www.ifrc.org/en/what-we-do/idrl/publication. Accessed 27 January 2012.

NGOs wish to provide funds, they should be delivered or transmitted directly to BNPB (Article 8(6)). In this regard, it is worth mentioning that Law no. 24 of 2007 gives BNPB the authority to use national and international contributions (Article 12(e)).

Government Regulation no. 23 of 2008 makes it clear that international organizations and foreign NGOs shall refrain from political or security activities (Article 14(1)), and confirms that they shall respect the social, cultural and religious backgrounds of the local communities (Article 14(3)). During pre-disaster and post-disaster phases, BNPB will only coordinate their work; while, during emergency response, it will have the role of directing their operations (Article 10).

With regard to access to the country, Government Regulation no. 23 of 2008 only stipulates that, during the emergency response period, international organizations and foreign NGOs' personnel, equipment and logistics shall be granted facilitated access to the Indonesian territory (Article 9). This issue is specifically dealt with in Government Regulation no. 21 of 2008 concerning disaster management operations.[23] Under this regulation, foreign personnel who take part in emergency response operations shall be promptly provided with visa, entry permit, limited residence permit and exit permit on the recommendation of the Head of BNPB (Article 33). Similarly, equipment and logistics entering Indonesia for use in those operations shall be exempted from import duties and taxes on the recommendation of the Head of BNPB (Article 36).

The aforementioned provisions are largely consistent with the AADMER and the CACNARE, to both of which Indonesia is a party. In particular, they implement Article 12(1) and Article 14 of the AADMER. According to Article 12(1), unless otherwise agreed, the State party requesting or accepting international assistance in the event of a disaster emergency 'shall exercise the overall direction, control, coordination and supervision of the assistance within its territory'. Under Article 14, it shall 'facilitate the entry into, stay in and departure from its territory of personnel and of equipment, facilities and materials involved or used in the assistance' and exempt such equipment, facilities and materials from import taxes and duties. Moreover, the provisions of Law no. 24 of 2007 and Government Regulation no. 23 of 2008 implement Article 3(a) and Article 8(3)(a) and (5) of the CACNARE, whose content is identical to the aforementioned AADMER provisions.

The Indonesian provisions illustrated above are also in line with the IDRL Guidelines. In particular, they follow the recommendations which concern the provision of international relief in a manner sensitive to the social, cultural and religious traditions of the local communities (Para. 4(3)(d)), the designation of domestic governmental entities with responsibility and authority over international relief (Para. 8(2)), and the legal facilities to be granted to international relief personnel, goods and equipment (Paras. 16(1),(2) and 17(1)).

---

[23] See *supra* footnote 16.

That said, it should be noted that the AADMER provisions regarding emergency response and the IDRL Guidelines cover assistance provided not only by international organizations and foreign NGOs, but also by States. Similarly, the CACNARE provisions address the provision of assistance not only by the international organizations parties to that Convention, but also and foremost by the other State parties. On the contrary, Law no. 24 of 2007 and Government Regulation no. 23 of 2008 only refer to the assistance provided in the event of a disaster emergency by international organizations and foreign NGOs. With regard to assistance from other States, Government Regulation no. 23 of 2008 only stipulates that, in the event of participation of foreign States in disaster management, the Head of BNPB shall consult and coordinate with the Minister of Foreign Affairs.

12.3 The United States

The main legislative instruments regulating the United States (US) response to domestic disasters are the Homeland Security Act of 2002[24] and the Robert T. Stafford Disaster Relief and Emergency Assistance Act[25] (Stafford Act). Both these acts were significantly amended by the Post-Katrina Emergency Management Reform Act of 2006[26] (Post-Katrina Act). Hurricane Katrina, which hit Louisiana, Mississippi and Alabama in August 2005, was the greatest natural disaster in the US history. It prompted the Federal Government to enact a major reform of the national emergency management system. The Post-Katrina Act aimed at addressing the shortcomings which emerged during the preparation for and response to hurricane Katrina.[27]

The Homeland Security Act of 2002 sets out, *inter alia*, the organization and the mission of the Federal Emergency Management Agency (FEMA), which operates within the Department of Homeland Security. Under Section 503(b)(1), the primary mission of FEMA is 'to reduce the loss of life and property and protect the Nation from all hazards, including natural disasters, acts of terrorism, and other man-made disasters, by leading and supporting the Nation in a risk-based, comprehensive emergency management system of preparedness, protection, response, recovery, and mitigation'.

The Stafford Act describes the procedures and the programs by which the Federal Government will provide assistance to State and local governments, non-

---

24 Homeland Security Act of 2002, Pub. L. 107-296, Nov. 25, 2002, 116 Stat. 2135 (6 U.S.C. 101 et seq.).

25 Robert T. Stafford Disaster Relief and Emergency Assistance Act, Pub. L. 93-288, May 22, 1974, 88 Stat. 143 (42 U.S.C. 5121 et seq.).

26 Post-Katrina Emergency Management Reform Act of 2006, Pub. L. 109-295, Title VI, Oct. 4, 2006, 120 Stat. 1394.

27 See US Government Accountability Office 2008.

profit organizations and individuals, if the US President declares that a major disaster or an emergency exists. Section 102(2) defines a major disaster as 'any natural catastrophe … or, regardless of cause, any fire, flood, or explosion, in any part of the United States, which in the determination of the President causes damage of sufficient severity and magnitude to warrant major disaster assistance' under the Act. Section 401 authorizes the US President to declare that a major disaster exists on request of the governor of an affected State and specifies that the governor's request must be 'based on a finding that the disaster is of such severity and magnitude that effective response is beyond the capabilities of the State and the affected local governments and that Federal assistance is necessary'.

Section 701(b) authorizes the US President or his delegate to 'accept and use bequests, gifts, or donations of service, money, or property, real, personal, or mixed, tangible, or intangible', in furtherance of the purposes of the Act. In practice, in case of a declared major disaster, the US President has broad authority to accept gifts, both domestic and foreign. In fact, this authority has been delegated to the Administrator of FEMA.[28]

In the event of a declared major disaster, it is for FEMA to accept or request international assistance. If FEMA needs help in managing requests for and offers of international assistance, it will activate the International Assistance System.[29] This is a detailed plan for submitting requests for and processing offers of assistance from foreign States and international organizations, which was developed jointly by the Department of Homeland Security, the Department of State (DOS) and the United States Agency for International Development (USAID), and was released in October 2010. The need for such a plan was felt by the US Government following hurricane Katrina.[30] Suffice to mention that, in the weeks after that disaster, over 150 States and international organizations offered the US financial or material assistance to support relief operations.[31]

Within the International Assistance System, DOS and USAID will co-operate with FEMA in managing international assistance. FEMA will assign tasks to both of them. In general, DOS will transmit requests for international assistance, receive offers, and communicate acceptance or refusal; while USAID will provide technical support and manage logistical operations.[32]

As regards requests for international assistance, the US will strive to purchase the required supplies, equipment, and services rather than to seek donations from

[28] FEMA, Department of State, USAID, International Assistance System Concept of Operations, October 1, 2010, available at https://www.llis.dhs.gov/docdetails/details.do?contentID=47760, 9. Accessed 27 January 2012. It supplements the International Coordination Support Annex to the National Response Framework of January 2008, available at http://www.fema.gov/emergency/nrf/. Accessed 27 January 2012.

[29] Ibid., 12.

[30] Ibid., 7.

[31] Ibid., 3.

[32] Ibid., 10. See also the International Coordination Support Annex to the National Response Framework, op. cit. n. 28, 5.

other States. The underlying assumption is that purchase guarantees greater control over the technical specifications and delivery time of the required items than accepting donations. Requests for foreign personnel will be sent only as a last resort.[33]

As for offers of international assistance, financial contributions to non-governmental organizations working in the affected area will be preferred. Following the onset of a major disaster, DOS will send a cable to all the US diplomatic and consular posts abroad recommending that States wishing to assist make such contributions.[34]

Overall, the International Assistance System sets out the procedures for handling requests for and offers of international assistance and the roles of FEMA, DOS, and USAID in the event of a declared major disaster. It clearly follows the recommendation enshrined in the IDRL Guidelines regarding the designation of domestic governmental entities with responsibility and authority over international relief (Para. 8(2)). Interestingly, however, the International Assistance System only refers to the assistance provided by foreign States and international organizations and does not cover the assistance given by NGOs.

With regard to recent US practice, it is worth noting that, in the case of the 2010 Gulf of Mexico oil spill, the US President did not issue a major disaster declaration, although the incident might fall within the scope of the Stafford Act.[35] The oil spill was caused by an explosion on a drilling rig operated by the oil company British Petroleum within the US exclusive economic zone. It lasted about 3 months and was the largest accidental oil spill in history.[36]

The decision not to avail of the Stafford Act was almost certainly due to the existence of specific legislation relating to federal response to oil spills.[37] In fact, the Gulf of Mexico oil spill was addressed by the Oil Pollution Act of 1990[38] and the Federal Water Pollution Control Act, also known as the Clean Water Act.[39] Section 1321(c)(1) of the Clean Water Act, as amended by the Oil Pollution Act of 1990, provides the US President with the authority to 'ensure effective and immediate removal of a discharge, and mitigation or prevention of a substantial threat of a discharge, of oil or a hazardous substance … into or on the waters of the exclusive economic zone'. Executive Order no. 12777 of 1991 delegated this authority to the Secretary of the Department in which the Coast Guard operates,

---

33 FEMA, Department of State, USAID, International Assistance System Concept of Operations, op. cit. n. 28, 14.

34 Ibid., 13. See also the International Coordination Support Annex to the National Response Framework, op. cit. n. 28, 5.

35 Hagerty and Ramseur 2010, 45 et seq.

36 See: Hagerty and Ramseur 2010, 1; Griggs 2011, 57 et seq.

37 Hagerty and Ramseur 2010, 45 et seq.

38 Oil Pollution Act of 1990, Pub. L. 101-380, Aug. 18, 1990, 104 Stat. 484 (33 U.S.C. 2701 et seq.).

39 Federal Water Pollution Control Act, June 30, 1948, ch. 758, as added Oct. 18, 1972, Pub. L. 92-500, Sec. 2, 86 Stat. 816 (33 U.S.C. 1251 et seq.).

that is to say the Secretary of the Department of Homeland Security.[40] In practice, the Coast Guard was the lead agency in the Gulf of Mexico oil spill response and FEMA only played an auxiliary role.[41]

As regards international assistance in the Gulf of Mexico oil spill response, the US Government did not issue any appeal for assistance. However, it received offers of assistance from several countries and international organizations and accepted a number of them. DOS acted as the intermediary between the US Government and the foreign States and international organizations offering assistance.[42]

12.4 The Philippines

The Philippine legal framework relating to disaster response consists mainly of the Philippine Disaster Risk Reduction and Management Act of 2010[43] (Philippine DRRM Act) and its Implementing Rules and Regulations of the same year.[44] The typhoons that hit the country in September and October 2009 causing devastating floods convinced the Parliament of the urgent need for reform of the Philippine disaster management system.[45] The new law was enacted in May 2010.

---

40 Ex. Ord. No. 12777, Oct. 18, 1991, 56 F.R. 54757, as amended by Ex. Ord. No. 13286, para. 34, Feb. 28, 2003, 68 F.R. 10625.

41 Hagerty and Ramseur 2010, 45.

42 See: US Department of State, Office of the Spokesman, Deepwater Horizon Oil Spill: International Offers of Assistance, Media Note, June 14, 2010, PRN: 2010/794, available at http://www.state.gov/r/pa/prs/ps/2010/06/143127.htm, accessed 27 January 2012; US Department of State, Office of the Spokesman, Deepwater Horizon Oil Spill: International Offers of Assistance, Taken Question, June 14, 2010, PRN: 2010/793, available at http://www.state.gov/r/pa/prs/ps/2010/06/143125.htm, accessed 27 January 2012; US Department of State, Office of the Spokesman, Deepwater Horizon Oil Spill: International Offers of Assistance, Media Note, June 29, 2010, PRN: 2010/875, available at http://www.state.gov/r/pa/prs/ps/2010/06/143771.htm, accessed 27 January 2012.

43 Republic Act no. 10121, An Act Strengthening the Philippine Disaster Risk Reduction and Management System, Providing for the National Disaster Risk Reduction and Management Framework and Institutionalizing the National Disaster Risk Reduction and Management Plan, Appropriating Funds Therefore and for Other Purposes, May 27, 2010, available at http://ndrrmc.gov.ph/index.php?option=com_content&view=article&id=45:republic-act-no-10121&catid=17:ndrrmc-issuances&Itemid=19
. Accessed 27 January 2012.

44 Implementing Rules and Regulations of Republic Act no. 10121, also known as "An Act Strengthening the Philippine Disaster Risk Reduction and Management System, Providing for the National Disaster Risk Reduction and Management Framework and Institutionalizing the National Disaster Risk Reduction and Management Plan, Appropriating Funds Therefore and for Other Purposes", September 27, 2010, available at http://ndrrmc.gov.ph/index.php?option=com_content&view=article&id=95:implementing-rules-and-regulation-of-republicact-no-10121&catid=17:ndrrmc-issuances&Itemid=19. Accessed 27 January 2012.

45 See IFRC 2010, 9 et seq.

The Philippine DRRM Act covers both natural and man-made disasters (Section 3(h)) and provides for the development of policies and the adoption of measures regarding disaster risk reduction, disaster prevention, emergency response, and rehabilitation (Section 4). A key role is assigned to the National Disaster Risk Reduction and Management Council (National Council) and the Office of Civil Defence.[46]

The National Council is given *inter alia* the following tasks: developing the National Disaster Risk Reduction and Management Framework, which 'shall serve as the principal guide to disaster risk reduction and management efforts in the country and shall be reviewed on a 5-year interval, or as may be deemed necessary' (Section 6(a)); managing and mobilizing resources for disaster risk reduction and management (Section 6(h)); and overseeing the implementation of the disaster management treaties to which the Philippines is a party in the domestic legal order (Section 6(q)). The National Disaster Risk Reduction and Management Framework was adopted by the National Council on 16 June 2011.[47] As regards the disaster management treaties, it is worth recalling that the Philippines is a party to the AADMER and the CACNARE.

The Office of Civil Defence is charged with 'administering a comprehensive national civil defence and disaster risk reduction and management program by providing leadership in the continuous development of strategic and systematic approaches as well as measures to reduce the vulnerabilities and risks to hazards and manage the consequences of disasters' (Section 8). Interestingly, the Administrator of the Office of Civil Defence also serves as Executive Director of the National Council (Section 8), thus guaranteeing a close link between the two organs.

The Philippine DRRM Act stipulates that, in the event of a disaster, the National Council shall recommend the President of the Philippines to declare a state of calamity in the affected areas. The declaration of state of calamity is required before a call for international assistance can be issued (Section 16). Detailed provisions in this regard are contained in the Implementing Rules and Regulations. Under Rule 14, Section 1, the President of the Philippines may issue a call for international assistance on the recommendation of the Chairman of the National Council, 'depending on the scope, magnitude of damage or implications of the adverse effects of the disaster'. In such a case, the Department of Foreign Affairs shall facilitate the appeal for international assistance, through the Philippine diplomatic and consular posts abroad, and closely coordinate with the National Council for this purpose. As regards the State parties to the AADMER,

---

[46] The Philippine DRRM Act also establishes Regional Disaster Risk Reduction and Management Councils, Local Disaster Risk Reduction and Management Councils and Local Disaster Risk Reduction and Management Offices.

[47] National Disaster Risk Reduction and Management Framework, June 16, 2011, available at http://www.ndrrmc.gov.ph/index.php?option=com_content&view=article&id=227:ndrrmc-framework&catid=24:disaster-risk-reduction-and-management-laws&Itemid=39. Accessed 27 January 2012.

the Philippines may request assistance from them directly or through the ASEAN Humanitarian Assistance Centre, in accordance with Article 11(1). However, they may also appeal to other States, international organizations and NGOs for assistance.

With regard to the provision of international assistance, the Philippine DRRM Act confines itself to stipulating that 'the importation and donation of food, clothing, medicine and equipment for relief and recovery and other disaster management and recovery-related supplies' shall be exempted from all customs duties and taxes generally levied on imported items, subject to the approval of the Office of the President of the Philippines (Section 18).[48]

The aforementioned provision is consistent with Article 14(a) of the AADMER, under which the State party requesting or accepting international assistance in the event of a disaster emergency shall afford the assisting State, international organization or NGO 'exemptions from taxation, duties and charges of a similar nature on the importation and use of equipment including vehicles and telecommunications, facilities and materials ... for the purpose of the assistance'. It is also in line with Article 8(3)(a) of the CACNARE, which requires that the requesting State party afford the assisting party exemption from taxation, duties or other charges on the property and equipment brought into its territory for the purpose of the assistance.

The above mentioned provision of the Philippine DRRM Act also follows the IDRL Guidelines, which recommend the affected States to exempt disaster relief goods and equipment imported by, or on behalf of, assisting States and eligible assisting humanitarian organizations from 'all customs duties, taxes, tariffs, and governmental fees' (Para. 17(1)).

From 16 to 18 December 2011, typhoon Washi hit the Mindanao region, killing about 1,250 people and injuring more than 6,000.[49] Many States, international organizations and NGOs immediately offered the Philippines assistance in emergency response operations. On 20 December 2011, the President of the Philippines declared a state of national calamity.[50] Following that declaration, the National Council formally accepted international assistance.[51] The city of Cagayan de Oro, in Northern Mindanao, was declared point of entry for foreign donated relief goods

[48] See also Rule 14, Section 3, of the Implementing Rules and Regulations.

[49] NDRRMC Update, SitRep no. 40 re Effects of Tropical Storm "Sendong" (Washi) and Status of Emergency Response Operations, 16 January 2012, available at http://www.ndrrmc.gov.ph/index.php?option=com_content&view=article&id=358preparedness-and-response-to-the-effects-of-tropical-storm-sendong&catid=1:ndrrmc-update, 1
. Accessed 27 January 2012.

[50] President of the Philippines, Proclamation no. 303 Declaring a State of National Calamity, December 20, 2011, available at http://www.ndrrmc.gov.ph/index.php?limitstart=10. Accessed 27 January 2012.

[51] NDRRMC Update, SitRep no. 40, op. cit. n. 49, 2.

and equipment and a one-stop shop facility was established there to expedite their processing and release.[52]

12.5 Haiti

The main piece of legislation regulating disaster response in Haiti is the Law of April 15, 2010, amending the Law on the State of Emergency of 9 September, 2008.[53] In fact, the Law of 2010 consolidates the vast majority of the provisions of the Law of 2008 and contains only a few new provisions introduced to facilitate the country's recovery after the devastating earthquake of 12 January, 2010.[54] In particular, it establishes the Interim Commission for the Reconstruction of Haiti (Article 14) and authorizes the President of the Republic to extend the state of emergency declared on 16 January, 2010 for a period of 18 months (Article 16). Such extension was made by Order of the President of the Republic of 20 April, 2010.

As regards the declaration of a state of emergency, the Law of 2010 simply incorporates the provisions of the Law of 2008. Article 3 stipulates that a state of emergency shall be declared whenever a natural disaster, actual or imminent, requires an immediate action to protect people, property, environment or infrastructure, which cannot be properly performed under the ordinary rules of operation of public institutions, nor under the National Risk and Disaster Management Plan. Article 5 authorizes the President of the Republic or, if he is temporarily unable to perform his duties, the Prime Minister to declare a state of emergency on all or part of the national territory, by order adopted in a meeting of the Council of Ministers.

Article 6 provides that during a state of emergency, the Government has the authority to take all the measures it deems necessary to cope with the disaster, including the appeal for international solidarity. With regard to this, it specifies that 'les interventions se feront selon les règles de Droit international et la Loi nationale'. This provision, which appears to be extremely general, is the only one referring to international assistance. Clearly, it proved insufficient to address the massive international response to the January 2010 earthquake.[55]

---

[52] NDRRMC Memorandum no. 13, Tropical Storm "Sendong" (Washi) ONE STOP SHOP (OSS) Facility for the Acceptance and Processing of Foreign Donations, December 23, 2011, available at http://www.ndrrmc.gov.ph/index.php?option=com_content&view=article&id=394:ndrrmc-memo-order-&catid=21:one-stop-shop&Itemid=37. Accessed 29 January 2012.

[53] Loi portant amendment de la loi sur l'état d'urgence du 9 septembre 2008, 15 avril 2010, available at http://www.parlementhaitien.ht/crbst_35.html. Accessed 29 January 2012.

[54] Loi sur l'état d'urgence, 9 septembre 2008, available at http://www.parlementhaitien.ht/crbst_35.html. Accessed 29 January 2012.

[55] See: Margesson and Taft-Morales 2010; Froberg 2010.

12.6 Japan

The Japanese legal framework relating to disaster response comprises several laws enacted over the years on the basis of the lessons learnt from disaster experiences.[56] The main instrument, however, is the Disaster Countermeasures Basic Act of 1961.[57] It establishes a comprehensive disaster management system, which includes disaster prevention, emergency response and rehabilitation (Articles 1, 2(2)) and covers natural and man-made disasters (Article 2(1)).

Under the Disaster Countermeasures Basic Act, the central government and the local governments, that is to say prefectures and municipalities, are all responsible at their respective levels for disaster management. A key role is played by the Central Disaster Management Council, the Prefectural Disaster Management Councils and the Municipal Disasters Management Councils. The Central Disaster Management Council is composed of the Prime Minister, who serves as chairperson, the Minister for Disaster Management, all the other Ministers, the heads of major Japanese institutions and a number of experts (Article 12). It is charged with formulating and promoting the implementation of a basic disaster management plan and an emergency plan for major disasters (Article 11). The Prefectural Disaster Management Councils are chaired by the governors of the prefectures (Article 15) and are responsible for formulating and promoting the implementation of analogous plans with regard to the prefectures (Article 14). Similarly, the Municipal Disaster Management Councils are tasked with formulating and promoting the implementation of a disaster management plan regarding the municipalities (Article 16).

In the event of a disaster, the governor of the affected prefecture and the mayor of the affected municipality may establish the Headquarters for Disaster Response, which shall be responsible for implementing emergency response measures at the prefectural and municipal level, respectively (Article 23). Moreover, if the disaster qualifies as a major disaster, the Prime Minister may establish the Headquarters for Major Disaster Response, which shall be chaired by one of the Ministers and shall be responsible for the implementation of the emergency plan for major disasters and the overall coordination of emergency response activities (Articles 24, 25, 26). In the event of a disaster of extreme severity, the Prime Minister may establish the Headquarters for Extreme Disaster Response with analogous responsibilities, which shall be chaired by him (Articles 28-2, 28-3, 28-4).

The Disaster Countermeasures Basic Act also provides that, in the case of a disaster of extreme severity, the Prime Minister may declare a state of emergency after consultation with the Central Disaster Management Council (Articles 11(3),

[56] See: OECD 2009, 201; Cabinet Office, Government of Japan 2011a, 6 et seq.

[57] Disaster Countermeasures Basic Act, Act no. 223, November 15, 1961, available at http://www.adrc.asia/nationinformation.php?NationCode=392&Lang=en&NationNum=23. Accessed 29 January 2012.

105). Following that declaration, he shall establish the Headquarters for Emergency Disaster Response, if this has not yet been set up (Article 107).

As regards international assistance, the Disaster Countermeasures Basic Act confines itself to stipulating that both the central government and the local governments are responsible for matters relating to the acceptance of assistance in disaster prevention and emergency response from other countries (Article 8(2)) and that, in the event of a disaster, where necessary, the Cabinet may enact an ordinance in order to take the necessary steps to accept assistance from other States (Article 109-2).

Specific provisions relating to nuclear disasters are contained in the Act on Special Measures Concerning Nuclear Emergency Preparedness of 1999[58] (Act on Nuclear Emergency Preparedness). Under that Act, whenever the detected radiation dose rate outside a nuclear site exceeds the limit set by the Cabinet or an event classified by the Cabinet as an event indicating a nuclear emergency occurs, the Prime Minister shall declare a state of nuclear emergency and immediately give the governors of the affected prefectures and the mayors of the affected municipalities instructions concerning emergency response measures (Article 16). Moreover, the Prime Minister shall establish the Nuclear Emergency Response Headquarters, which shall be chaired by him and shall be responsible for the overall coordination of emergency response activities (Articles 16–18). The governors of the affected prefectures and the mayors of the affected municipalities shall set up the Headquarters for Disaster Response as provided in the Disaster Countermeasures Basic Act to face the nuclear emergency (Article 22).

It is worth noting that the issue of international assistance is not specifically addressed in the Act on Nuclear Emergency Preparedness. The absence of any provision on this matter is all the more surprising when one considers that Japan is a party to the CACNARE and, as such, it is required to comply with the provisions thereof whenever it requests assistance from other parties.

On 11 March 2011, an earthquake of magnitude 9 and a devastating tsunami struck the east coast of Japan, causing more than 15,000 deaths. The large tsunami waves severely damaged the nuclear power stations in Fukushima Prefecture, resulting in a nuclear emergency.[59] Immediately after the earthquake the Prime Minister set up the Headquarters for Extreme Disaster Response. Later on the same day, he declared a state of nuclear emergency and established the Nuclear Emergency Response Headquarters.[60] The situation was extremely trying for Japan, since it had to respond to the nuclear emergency while reacting to the

---

[58] Act on Special Measures Concerning Nuclear Emergency Preparedness, Act no. 156 of December 17, 1999, available at http://www.nisa.meti.go.jp/english/resources/legislativeframe work/index.html. Accessed 29 January 2012.

[59] See: Cabinet Office, Government of Japan, 2011b, 1 et seq., 11 et seq.; IAEA 2011, 11 et seq.; Nuclear Emergency Response Headquarters, Government of Japan 2011a, 4 et seq.

[60] See: Cabinet Office, Government of Japan, 2011b, 3, 13; Nuclear Emergency Response Headquarters, Government of Japan 2011a, 18.

broader disaster caused by the earthquake and the ensuing tsunami.[61] The country's emergency response system was unable to function properly. The local governments were not able to perform the tasks assigned to them, in many cases because their employees had been killed or were injured or missing.[62]

Assistance was immediately offered by many States and international organizations.[63] The Japanese Government, however, could not promptly respond to the offers received. No specific structure to assess whether the offers of assistance met the needs had been set up. Hence, the Ministry of Foreign Affairs had to contact the relevant ministries and agencies in respect of each offer to ascertain whether it matched their needs.[64] Japan received relief supplies from a large number of countries and international organizations. Disaster response teams from around the world operated in the affected areas, while Japan's overseas missions accepted cash donations to support relief efforts. Moreover, on the evening of 11 March, the Minister of Foreign Affairs formally asked the US Ambassador for the assistance of the US forces in Japan. Following that request, the US launched a large-scale disaster relief operation, named Operation Tomodachi, with 20 ships, 160 aircraft, and over 20,000 personnel.[65]

12.7 Conclusion

The legal frameworks relating to disaster response in the five countries considered are largely heterogeneous. However, all of them provide for the possibility of international assistance in the event of a major catastrophe occurring on the national territory.

That said, the legal preparedness for receiving international assistance varies significantly in the countries taken into consideration. Only in Indonesia and the Philippines disaster management legislation does address, to some extent, the issue of facilitating and regulating international disaster relief. In Haiti and Japan the main pieces of legislation relating to disaster response do not specifically consider that issue. In the United States, there is merely a plan on how to submit requests for and process offers of assistance from foreign States and international organizations in the event of a declared major disaster.

---

[61] Nuclear Emergency Response Headquarters, Government of Japan 2011a, 1.

[62] See: Disaster Law to Boost State's Role, Kyodo, August 14, 2011, in The Japan Times Online, available at http://www.japantimes.co.jp/text/nn20110814a4.html; IAEA 2011, 117. Accessed 29 January 2012.

[63] See the list of the States and international organizations that offered assistance on the web site of the Ministry of Foreign Affairs of Japan at http://www.mofa.go.jp/j_info/visit/incidents/index2.html#assistance. Accessed 29 January 2012.

[64] Nuclear Emergency Response Headquarters, Government of Japan 2011a, 38, VIII-3.

[65] See the information provided on the web site of the Ministry of Foreign Affairs of Japan at http://www.mofa.go.jp/j_info/visit/incidents/index2.html#assistance. Accessed 29 January 2012.

It is to be remarked that the disaster related legislation now in force in Indonesia and the Philippines and the aforementioned plan in the United States were adopted only recently and on the basis of the lessons learnt from the severe disasters, which struck those countries over the past decade. As mentioned above, they are largely consistent with the IDRL Guidelines. The former also implement a number of AADMER provisions concerning emergency response assistance, as well as certain CACNARE provisions. However, there is room for improvement. For example, the Indonesian legislation only regulates assistance from international organizations and foreign NGOs and does not cover assistance from other States. Under the Philippine legislation, the requirement that a state of calamity be declared prior to an appeal for international assistance may lead to delays in the provision of international relief, as demonstrated by the typhoon Washi experience.

As regards Haiti and Japan, it is expected that disaster management legislation will be reformed and specific rules for facilitating and managing incoming international assistance will be adopted on the basis of the lessons learnt from the January 2010 earthquake and the March 2011 catastrophe, respectively.

Overall, the legal frameworks relating to disaster response of the countries considered in this chapter reveal a reactive approach to regulatory problems in international relief operations. Instead, a proactive approach to those problems should be adopted. As hurricane Katrina in the United States and the March 2011 disaster in Japan demonstrated, any State, even the richest one, may need international assistance in responding to a major catastrophe on its territory. Therefore, it is desirable that all States adequately prepare themselves for this possibility in advance.

References

Cabinet Office, Government of Japan (2011a) Disaster management in Japan. http://www.cao.go.jp/en/disaster.html

Cabinet Office, Government of Japan (2011b) White paper on disaster management 2011. Executive summary. http://www.preventionweb.net/english/professional/publications/v.php?id=20761

Froberg M (2010) UN Panel addresses preliminary findings from IDRL study in Haiti, IDRL Newsletter No. 27. http://www.ifrc.org/en/what-we-do/idrl/latest-news/idrl-e-newsletter

Griggs JW (2011) BP Gulf of Mexico oil spill. Energy L J 32:57

Hagerty CL, Ramseur JL (2010) Deepwater horizon oil spill: selected issues for Congress, CRS report for Congress, version of July 30, 2010. http://opencrs.com/document/R41262

IAEA (2011) IAEA international fact finding expert mission of Fukushima Dai-ichi NPP accident following Great East Japan earthquake and tsunami (24 May–2 June 2011), Mission report. http://www.iaea.org/newscenter/focus/fukushima/

IFRC (2010) Disasters in Asia: the case for legal preparedness, Geneva. http://www.ifrc.org/en/what-we-do/idrl/idrl-around-the-world/idrl-around-the-world-asia-and-the-pacific

IFRC (2011) Progress in the implementation of the guidelines for the domestic facilitation and regulation of international disaster relief and initial recovery assistance: background document, Geneva. http://www.ifrc.org/en/what-we-do/idrl/disaster-law-at-the-31st-international-conference

Margesson R, Taft-Morales M (2010) Haiti earthquake: crisis and response, CRS report for Congress, version of March 8, 2010. http://opencrs.com/document/R41023

Nuclear Emergency Response Headquarters, Government of Japan (2011a) Report of the Japanese government to the IAEA ministerial conference on nuclear safety: the accident at TEPCO's Fukushima nuclear power stations, June 2011. http://www.iaea.org/newscenter/focus/fukushima/japan-report/

Nuclear Emergency Response Headquarters, Government of Japan (2011b) Additional report of the Japanese government to the IAEA: the accident at TEPCO's Fukushima nuclear power stations, September 2011. http://www.iaea.org/newscenter/focus/fukushima/japan-report2/

OECD (2009) Reviews of risk management policies. Japan: large-scale floods and earthquakes. http://www.oecd.org/document/27/0,3746,en_2649_49355626_42313947_1_1_1_1,00.html

UNDP (2009) Institutional and legislative systems for early warning and disaster risk reduction: Indonesia. http://www.snap-undp.org/elibrary/Publications/EWSReportIndonesia.pdf

US Government Accountability Office (2008) Actions taken to implement the Post-Katrina Emergency Management Reform Act of 2006, GAO-09-59R. http://www.gao.gov/products/GAO-09-59R

Walker P, Rasmussen C, Molano S (2011) International dialogue on strengthening partnership in disaster response: bridging national and international support, Background Paper 3: best practice experience at the national level, Geneva. http://www.ifrc.org/en/what-we-do/idrl/international-dialogue-on-strengthening-partnership-in-disaster-response/

Chapter 13
Maritime Accidents with Particular Emphasis on Liability and Compensation for Damage from the Exploitation of Mineral Resources of the Seabed

Tullio Scovazzi

Abstract Maritime casualties can affect both human life and the protection of the environment. The United Nations Convention on the Law of Sea binds States to effectively exercise their jurisdiction and control in administrative, technical, and social matters over ships flying their flag, conforming to generally accepted international regulations, procedures, and practices. International rules related to maritime accidents are also found in a number of specific treaties adopted at either the world or the regional level and relating to both the prevention of accidents and compensation of damage if an accident has taken place. The paper focuses on the 2010 incident caused by the explosion of the Deepwater Horizon platform in the Gulf of Mexico.

Keywords Maritime incidents · Prevention · Compensation of damages · Oil exploitation platforms

Contents

T. Scovazzi (✉)
Università di Milano-Bicocca, Piazza dell'Ateneo Nuovo 1, 20126, Milano
e-mail: tullio.scovazzi@unimib.it

A. de Guttry et al. (eds.), *International Disaster Response Law*,
DOI: 10.1007/978-90-6704-882-8_13,

13.1 Maritime Casualties in General

As other accidents, maritime casualties can affect both human life and the protection of the environment. The United Nations Convention on the Law of Sea (Montego Bay 1982)[1] binds States to effectively exercise their jurisdiction and control in administrative, technical, and social matters over ships flying their flag. In particular, under Article 94:

> '3. Every State shall take such measures for ships flying its flag as are necessary to ensure safety at sea with regard, *inter alia*, to:
>
> (a) the construction, equipment and seaworthiness of ships;
>
> (b) the manning of ships, labor conditions and the training of crews, taking into account the applicable international instruments;
>
> (c) the use of signals, the maintenance of communications and the prevention of collisions.
>
> 4. Such measures shall include those necessary to ensure:
>
> (a) that each ship, before registration and thereafter at appropriate intervals, is surveyed by a qualified surveyor of ships, and has on board such charts, nautical publications and navigational equipment and instruments as are appropriate for the safe navigation of the ship;
>
> (b) that each ship is in the charge of a master and officers who possess appropriate qualifications, in particular in seamanship, navigation, communications and marine engineering, and that the crew is appropriate in qualification and numbers for the type, size, machinery and equipment of the ship;
>
> (c) that the master, officers and, to the extent appropriate, the crew are fully conversant with and required to observe the applicable international regulations concerning the safety of life at sea, the prevention of collisions, the prevention, reduction and control of marine pollution, and the maintenance of communications by radio'.

[1] Hereinafter, UNCLOS.

In taking the above-mentioned measures, each State is required to conform to generally accepted international regulations, procedures, and practices (Article 94 para 5). As ships navigate through all the oceans and seas of the world, technical requirements relating to their design, construction, manning, or equipment need to be established at a uniform level.

In the case of artificial islands, installations and structures, under Article 60 para 3:

> 'due notice must be given of the construction of such artificial islands, installations or structures, and permanent means for giving warning of their presence must be maintained. Any installations or structures which are abandoned or disused shall be removed to ensure safety of navigation, taking into account any generally accepted international standards established in this regard by the competent international organization. Such removal shall also have due regard to fishing, the protection of the marine environment and the rights and duties of other States. Appropriate publicity shall be given to the depth, position and dimensions of any installations or structures not entirely removed'.

As far as the protection of the environment is concerned, the UNCLOS makes a distinction between six different kinds of marine pollution, namely from land-based sources, from activities in the seabed subject to national jurisdiction, from activities in the seabed beyond national jurisdiction, from dumping, from vessels and from the atmosphere. In almost all cases,[2] pollution can also result from unexpected and unintentional events, as envisaged in Article 194 para 3, which binds States to take measures designed to minimize to the fullest possible extent

> '(b) pollution from vessels, in particular measures for preventing accidents and dealing with emergencies, ensuring the safety of operations at sea, preventing intentional and unintentional discharges, and regulating the design, construction, equipment, operation and manning of vessels;
>
> (c) pollution from installations and devices used in exploration or exploitation of the natural resources of the seabed and subsoil, in particular measures for preventing accidents and dealing with emergencies, ensuring the safety of operations at sea, and regulating the design, construction, equipment, operation and manning of such installations or devices;
>
> (d) pollution from other installations and devices operating in the marine environment, in particular measures for preventing accidents and dealing with emergencies, ensuring the safety of operations at sea, and regulating the design, construction, equipment, operation and manning of such installations or devices'.

The UNCLOS also provides that when a State becomes aware of cases in which the marine environment is in imminent danger of being damaged or has been damaged by pollution, it shall immediately notify other States it deems likely to be

[2] The exception is pollution from dumping, which is defined as the deliberate disposal of wastes or other matters at sea.

affected by such damage, as well as the competent international organizations (Article 198). In this case, States in the area affected, in accordance with their capabilities, and the competent international organizations must co-operate, to the extent possible, in eliminating the effects of pollution and preventing or minimizing the damage and shall jointly develop and promote contingency plans for responding to pollution incidents in the marine environment (Article 199).

International rules related to maritime accidents are also found in a number of specific treaties adopted at either the world or the regional level. As regards co-operation in the field of prevention of accidents and their consequences, is it sufficient to mention the Convention Relating to Intervention on the High Seas in Cases of Oil Pollution Casualties (Brussels 1969) and its Protocol Relating to Intervention on the High Seas in Cases of Pollution by Substances Other than Oil (London 1973), the Convention on the International Regulations for Preventing Collisions at Sea (London 1972), the Convention for the Safety of Life at Sea (London 1974), the Convention for the Prevention of Pollution from Ships as modified by the Protocol of 1978 relating thereto (London 1978), the Convention on Standards of Training, Certification, and Watchkeeping for Seafarers (London 1978), the Convention on Maritime Search and Rescue (London 1979), the Convention on Salvage (London 1989), the Convention on Oil Pollution Preparedness, Response, and Co-operation (London 1990) and its Protocol on Preparedness, Response, and Co-operation to Pollution Incidents by Hazardous and Noxious Substances (London 2000), the Convention on the Removal of Wrecks (Nairobi 2007) and the Convention for the Safe and Environmentally Sound Recycling of Ships (Hong Kong 2009).

While it is obvious that to prevent is better than to compensate, also the existence of an adequate regime to ensure compensation for damage can ultimately be seen as an effective tool to discourage actions or omissions that are likely to determine an incident. In this regard, emphasis should be put on the Convention on Civil Liability for Oil Pollution Damage (Brussels 1969; amended in 1992), the Convention relating to Civil Liability in the Field of Maritime Carriage of Nuclear Material (London 1971), the Convention on the Establishment of an International Fund for Compensation for Oil Pollution Damage (Brussels 1971; amended in 1992 and 2003), the Convention on Liability and Compensation for Damage in connection with the Carriage of Hazardous and Noxious Substances by Sea (London 1996), and the International Convention on Civil Liability for Bunker Oil Pollution Damage (London 2001).

As it would not be possible to enter into the details of such a complex regime, this paper will focus on the question of compensation of damage resulting from so-called offshore activities that is activities of exploration and exploitation of mineral resources located in the seabed falling under national jurisdiction.

13.2 The Deepwater Horizon Incident

Pollution from offshore activities[3] is not the most serious cause of degradation of the marine environment. Nevertheless, where major incidents occur, also this kind of pollution can create devastating consequences on the marine environment,[4] as the recent disasters of the *Deepwater Horizon* reminds.

13.2.1 The Facts

On 20 April 2010 the *Deepwater Horizon*, a semi-submersible rig owned by the American corporation Transocean, exploded while it was drilling for oil from a well called *Macondo* in the Gulf of Mexico. Because of the explosion, eleven out of the 126 workers on the platform died and several others were injured. The *Deepwater Horizon* was located on the continental shelf of the United States, about 49 n.m. south-east of the Mississippi River delta. It was operating under a contract with BP (formerly British Petroleum), a British multinational corporation.

Two days after, the *Deepwater Horizon* sank in about 5;000 feet (1,500 m) of water. Crude oil gushed out of the riser, which is the pipe that connects the well at the ocean floor to the platform on the surface. For long time any attempts to shut down the flow failed. Nearly 5,000,000,000 barrels of oil spilled before it was possible, on 15 July 2010, to cap the well. The discharge of oil disrupted the economy of the entire region, damaged fisheries and critical habitats and brought to light the risks of deepwater drilling for oil and gas.

The damage arising from the incident was estimated by BP to be in excess of US$ 40,000,000,000. The environmental consequences of the largest oil spill in the history of the United States are described as follows by the Commission appointed by the President of the United States to investigate on the disaster, analyze its causes and effects, and recommend the actions necessary to minimize such risks in the future:

> (…) 'although the nation would not know the full scope of the disaster for weeks, the first of more than four million barrels of oil began gushing uncontrolled into the Gulf—threatening livelihoods, precious habitats, and even a unique way of life. A treasured American landscape, already battered and degraded from years of mismanagement, faced yet another blow as the oil spread and washed ashore. (…) The costs from this one industrial accident are not yet fully counted, but it is already clear that the impacts on the

[3] Namely the seabed subject to the regimes of maritime internal waters, the territorial sea and the continental shelf, as defined in the UNCLOS.

[4] On a serious incident that occurred in 1979 during offshore activities on the continental shelf of Mexico see Badenes Casino 2005, 65.

region's natural systems and people were enormous, and that economic losses total tens of billions of dollars'.[5]

As stated in the report by the Commission, the incident was the result of a number of concurrent technical factors, such as the insufficient integrity of the well, the undetected entrance of hydrocarbons into it, the ignition of these hydrocarbons, and the failure of the blowout preventer:

> 'The immediate cause of the Macondo blowout was a failure to contain hydrocarbon pressures in the well. Three things could have contained those pressures: the cement at the bottom of the well, the mud in the well and in the riser, and the blowout preventer. But mistakes and failures to appreciate risk compromised each of those potential barriers, steadily depriving the rig crew of safeguards until the blowout was inevitable and, at the very end, uncontrollable'.[6]

More generally, the operator BP, together with its two main contractors (the corporations Halliburton and Transocean), were to be blamed for the accident:

> 'The immediate causes of the Macondo well blowout can be traced to a series of identifiable mistakes made by BP, Halliburton, and Transocean that reveal such systematic failures in risk management that they place in doubt the safety culture of the entire industry'.[7]

13.2.2 The Response

The response to the disaster mobilized several subjects, namely the Federal Government of the United States and the governments of some of its member States (Alabama, Florida, Louisiana, and Mississippi), private companies, in particular BP acting as the 'responsible party' under the United States *Oil Pollution Act* of 1990, as well as non-profit organizations, seeking to stop the leaking well, to limit the damage and to monitor and clean-up the spilled oil.

BP committed to pay all legitimate claims made by the United States and the subjects affected. After consultation with the United States government, it established a US$ 20,000,000,000 claims fund. The Gulf Coast Claims Facility (GCCF), an independent facility administered by a Claims Administrator, was set up. The GCCF is the official way for affected individuals and business, including fishermen, oystermen and tourist operators, to file claims for cost and damages due

---

[5] National Commission on the BP Deepwater Horizon Oil Spill and Offshore Drilling, *Deep Water, The Gulf Oil Disaster and the Future of Offshore Drilling, Recommendations*, 2011, vi.

[6] National Commission on the BP Deepwater Horizon Oil Spill and Offshore Drilling, *Deep Water, The Gulf Oil Disaster and the Future of Offshore Drilling, Report to the President*, 2011, 115.

[7] National Commission on the BP Deepwater Horizon Oil Spill and Offshore Drilling, *Recommendations* op. cit. n. 5, vii.

to the spill.[8] Eligible claims include removal and clean-up costs, physical damages to real or personal property, lost profits or impairment of earning capacity, loss of subsistence use of natural resources, and physical injury or death. BP has also entered into long-term reputation-building commitments relating to response projects, research, and workers compensation.

It appears that GCCF has paid so far more than US$ 5,000,000,000 to more than 200,000 claimants. Criticism has however been raised by some individuals or groups who are not satisfied with the timeliness of compensation received for approved claims, believe that certain founded claims are being turned away or allege that GCCF is pressing claimants to accept the prompt payment of amounts which do not correspond to the whole damage suffered.[9] A number of claims for compensation against BP and other defendants are today pending before the United States District Court in New Orleans, including a lawsuit for environmental damage by the United States Department of Justice.[10]

13.2.3 The Lessons to Be Learned

A first notable lesson that can be learned from the *Deepwater Horizon* disaster is the increased risk of incidents if drilling for oil takes place in deep marine waters. As stated in the Commission report,

> 'deepwater energy exploration and production, particularly at the frontiers of experience, involve risks for which neither industry nor government has been adequately prepared, but for which they can and must be prepared in the future.[11]
>
> The industry first moved into shallow water and eventually into deepwater, where technological advances have opened up vast new reserves of oil and gas in remote areas—in recent decades, much deeper under the water's surface and farther offshore than ever before. The *Deepwater Horizon* was drilling the Macondo well under 5,000 feet of Gulf water, and then over 13,000 feet under the sea floor to the hydrocarbon reservoir below. It is a complex, even dazzling, enterprise. The remarkable advances that have propelled the move to deepwater drilling merit comparison with exploring outer space. The Commission is respectful and admiring of the industry's technological capability'.[12]

In general, the Commission was of the opinion that there is today a need for more State regulation for the activities carried out by the oil and gas industry:

---

[8] The GCCF does not pay claims brought by the government. The latter sends periodical bills to BP and other responsible parties and is reimbursed by them for response and recovery operations.

[9] 'The United States Department of Justice sent a letter to Feinberg [= the GCCF Claims Administrator] on September 17, 2010, urging expediency. In response, the Claims Facility noted that the large number of fraudulent and undocumented claims have slowed the process' (ibid. 49).

[10] The District Judge has set the trial date in February 2012.

[11] National Commission on the BP Deepwater Horizon Oil Spill and Offshore Drilling, *Recommendations* op. cit. n. 5, vii.

[12] Ibid. viii.

'The oil and gas industry—remarkable for its technological innovation and productivity—needs government oversight and regulation that can keep pace.[13]

In the years between the Exxon Valdez spill and the spring of 2010, Congress, like much of the nation, appears to have developed a false sense of security about the risks of offshore oil and gas development. Congress showed its support for offshore drilling in a number of ways, but did not take any steps to mitigate the increased perils that accompany drilling in ever-deeper water'.[14]

Other remarks relate to the liability limits provided for in the above-mentioned *Oil Pollution Act*. According to the Commission, it is important that compensation to victims is paid in full and that the process for receiving compensation is swift and efficient:

'Oil spills cause a range of harms, both economic and environmental, to individuals and ecosystems. The Oil Pollution Act makes the party responsible for a spill liable for compensating those who suffered as a result of the spill—through property damage, lost profits, and other economic injuries—and for restoring injured natural resources. The Act also provides an opportunity to make claims for compensation from a dedicated Oil Spill Liability Trust Fund. The Oil Pollution Act, however, imposes limits on both the amount for which the responsible party is liable, and the amount of compensation available through the trust fund. In the case of the *Deepwater Horizon* spill, BP (a responsible party) has placed $20 billion in escrow to compensate private individuals and businesses through the independent GCCF. But if a less well capitalized company had caused the spill, neither a multi-billion dollar compensation fund nor the funds necessary to restore injured resources, would likely have been available. It is critical that compensation to victims be paid in full, and that the process for receiving compensation is swift and efficient. The Commission offers recommendations that would increase assurances that responsible parties are able to compensate victims (and at the same time strengthens incentives to prevent accidents in the first place), and that the Oil Spill Liability Trust Fund provide any compensation not provided by responsible parties'.[15]

Under the United States legislation, liability for damages from offshore spills is capped at US$ 75,000,000. However, there is no limit to damages if it can be shown that the responsible party was guilty of gross negligence or willful misconduct, violated a federal safety regulation, or failed to report the incident, or to co-operate with removal activities. Claims up to US$ 1,000,000,000 above the cap for certain damages can be made to, and paid out of, the Oil Spill Liability Trust Fund, which is supported by an 8 % per barrel tax on domestic and imported oil. The *Oil Pollution Act* also requires responsible parties to 'establish and maintain evidence of financial responsibility' generally based on a 'worstcase discharge' estimate. In the case of offshore facilities, necessary financial responsibility ranges from US$ 35,000,000 to 150,000,000.[16]

---

[13] Ibid. 57.

[14] Ibid. 50. The American supertanker *Exxon Valdez* ran aground in 1989 in the waters off Alaska. .

[15] Ibid. 45.

[16] Ibid. 45.

An evident concern is that, in the event of future accidents, not all the responsible parties may have the financial means which were available to BP, one of the largest oil companies in the world. In the specific case, BP waived its statutory US$ 75,000,000 liability limit and accepted to establish a US$ 20,000,000,000 claims fund. According to the Commission, liability limits present two serious disadvantages, as they provide little incentive for industry to adopt precautionary measures and do not ensure full compensation for damages:

> 'There are two main problems with the current liability cap and financial responsibility dollar amounts:
>
> - Lack of Adequate Safety Incentives: A threshold problem with any damages cap that limits liability well below levels that may actually be incurred is that such a cap distorts the incentives of industry participants to adopt cost-effective safety precautions. Decisions regarding safety precautions are made for a variety of reasons, some of which cannot be influenced by policy measures. The relatively modest liability cap and financial responsibility requirements provide little incentive for oil companies to improve safety practices.
> - Inadequate Damages Compensation: BP's damages from the *Deepwater Horizon* spill will total in the tens of billions of dollars. The company has already paid claims that measure in the billions, and has waived the statutory $75 million cap. But there is no guarantee that other companies in the future will agree to waive the cap. And if an oil company with more limited financial means than BP had caused the *Deepwater Horizon* spill, that company might well have declared bankruptcy long before paying fully for all damages. In the case of a large spill, the Oil Spill Liability Trust Fund would likely not provide sufficient backup. Thus, a significant portion of the injuries caused to individuals and natural resources, as well as government response costs, could go uncompensated'.[17]

Because of this kind of considerations, the Commission recommended to the United States Congress to adopt legislation to 'significantly increase the liability cap and financial responsibility requirements for offshore facilities':

> 'To address both the incentive and compensation concerns noted above, Congress should significantly raise the liability cap. Financial responsibility limits should also be increased, because if an oil company does not have adequate resource to pay for a spill, the application of increased liability has little effect: should a company go bankrupt before fully compensating for a spill, its liability is effectively capped. If, however, the level of liability imposed and the level of financial responsibility required are set to levels that bear some relationship to potential damages, firms will have greater incentives to maximize prevention and minimize potential risk of oil spills and also have the financial means to ensure that victims of spills do not go uncompensated'.[18]

To reach this conclusion, the Commission balanced contrary arguments[19] and envisaged other options that could reduce the difficulties to be faced by the oil

[17] Ibid. 45.

[18] Ibid. 46.

[19] 'Legislative attempts to raise the cap and financial responsibility requirements to significantly higher levels have been met with the argument that these changes will cause insurance carriers to

industry, such as a mutual insurance pool,[20] the phasing in of increases in liability limits,[21] or partnerships among firms.[22] The Commission was confident that developments in the insurance market would contribute to higher safety standards:

> 'If liability and financial responsibility limits are raised, increased liabilities will be borne by insurance carriers, which will have a strong incentive to promote new safety techniques and methods, as well as to monitor risk. Insurance carriers might insist on certification of operators by an independent entity devoted to identifying best safety practices and monitoring risk, such as a self-policing safety organization for the oil and gas industry. Insurers or a self-policing safety organization for the industry also could provide a guard against unqualified companies entering the offshore drilling market'.[23]

However, it appears that efforts to raise the limit of liability have so far met with the concerns of independent operators smaller than BP, who fear to be unable to afford higher insurance premiums. The main pending legislative proposal in the United States is the *Securing Protections for the Injured from Limitations of Liability Act* (SPILL), which would have the effect of repealing limitations and expanding recovery for injured claimants. The American Senate upheld a modified version of the SPILL, known as *Fairness in Admiralty and Maritime Law Act*

(Footnote 19 continued)
drop oil pollution coverage, leading to an exodus of small and independent companies from the offshore drilling market. The counter-argument is that oil companies should bear the social costs of their activities, and if those costs are too large or unpredictable to be insurable, then it is appropriate that these companies exit the market. There is legitimacy to aspects of both arguments. A company should not be able to cause billions of dollars of damage and walk away, simply because its operations contribute to the economy of the Gulf. Nor should smaller companies that can demonstrate the ability to drill safely and to pay for damages resulting from a large spill be forced out of the market. However, smaller companies that cannot demonstrate financial responsibility and meet risk requirements set and monitored by the Department of the Interior or a third party should not be allowed to make others pay for the costs of their accidents'. (ibid. 47).

[20] 'One option for keeping competent independents in the market is a mutual insurance pool. Under such an arrangement, individual companies engaged in offshore drilling would pay premiums into a pool, which would pay out damages caused by a company as a result of a spill. A possible downside is that the mutual pool could have the effect of undercutting incentives individual firms might otherwise have to improve safety practices—but this problem could be addressed, for example, by tying premium levels to the financial and safety risk posed by an individual company's activities. This option would allow companies to demonstrate financial responsibility for the cost of spills, at least to the limit paid out by the pool'. (ibid. 47). .

[21] 'Another option would be to phase in increases in the liability cap and financial responsibility requirements, which would allow the insurance industry a period of adjustment. Although any increase in liability limits and financial responsibility requirements would test the capacity of the offshore drilling insurance market, over time such a change would almost certainly stimulate an increase in insurance capacity. A phased-in approach would allow Congress to re-assess any concerns about limited capacity in the insurance industry in light of actual experience' (ibid. 47).

[22] 'Finally, regardless of how insurance is provided, smaller firms could be encouraged to partner with firms with greater financial resources. It should be noted that 'joint ventures' between larger and smaller companies already exist; thus a policy change may not be necessary to encourage such arrangements' (ibid. 47).

[23] Ibid. 49.

(FAMLA), which excludes from limitation claims for wages, personal injury, and wrongful death, as well as claims relating to oil drilling or exploration or the discharge of oil from a vessel or offshore facility. Further, the *Consolidated Land, Energy and Aquatic Resources Act* (CLEAR) was approved in 2010 by the House of Representatives. This Act would remove the *Oil Pollution Act* limits for offshore facilities. None of these bills has been passed into law so far.[24]

13.3 Treaties on Liability and Compensation for Damage from Offshore Activities

13.3.1 The World Level

So far, offshore activities are not covered by any global or regional environmental liability and compensation regime established under an international treaty. The only treaty concluded to deal with this subject matter, that is the Convention on Civil Liability for Oil Pollution Damage resulting from Exploration for and Exploitation of Seabed Mineral Resources (London 1977) which was intended to apply to the North Sea, the Baltic Sea, and the Northern Atlantic Ocean, has not entered into force and is not likely to do so. It provided for the channeling of liability on the operator (Article 3), the right of the latter to limit his liability (Article 6), and his obligation to maintain an insurance or other financial security (Article 8).[25]

13.3.2 The Mediterranean Regional Level

A few provisions on liability and compensation for damage from offshore activities can be found at the Mediterranean regional level. One of the instruments concluded within the framework of the Convention for the Protection of the Marine Environment and the Coastal Region of the Mediterranean (Barcelona 1976, amended in 1995)[26] is the Protocol concerning Pollution Resulting from Exploration and Exploitation of the Continental Shelf, the Seabed and its Subsoil (Madrid, 14 October 1994).[27] The Offshore Prot. was opened for signature in Madrid on 14 October 1994 and entered into force on 24 March 2011. It is today

[24] Foley 2001, 515. .

[25] However, 'where the operator is a State Party, the operator shall not be required to maintain insurance or other financial security to cover its liability' (Article 8 para 5).

[26] Hereinafter: Barcelona Conv.

[27] Hereinafter: Offshore Prot. The adoption of appropriate measures in this field is envisaged by Article 7 of the Barcelona Conv. The Offshore Protocol is the result of preparatory works which have lasted for several years and were carried out on the basis of a project drafted by the International Juridical Organization for Environment and Development (IJO), a non-

binding on six parties, namely Albania, Cyprus, Libya, Morocco, Syria, and Tunisia.

The Offshore Prot. is an advanced instrument from the point of view of an enhanced protection of the marine environment.[28] The general undertaking of the parties is to take, individually or through bilateral or multilateral co-operation, all appropriate measures to prevent, abate, combat, and control pollution resulting from the activities covered by the Protocol.[29] This objective can be achieved, *inter alia*, 'by ensuring that the best available techniques, environmentally effective and economically appropriate, are used for this purpose' (Article 3 para 1).

Several provisions of the Offshore Prot. set forth obligations with respect to activities carried out by operators, who often are private persons, either natural or juridical.[30] The definition of 'operator' (Article 1.*g*) has a broad content. It includes not only the persons who are authorized to carry out activities or carry out activities (e.g., the holder of a license), but also any person who does not hold an authorization but is *de facto* in control of activities.

All activities in the Offshore Prot. area,[31] including erection on site of installations, are subjected to the prior written authorization from the competent authority of a party (Article 4). Before granting the authorization, the authority must be satisfied that the installation has been constructed according to international standards and practice, and that the operator has the technical competence and the financial capacity to carry out the activities. The authorization is refused if there are indications that the proposed activities are likely to cause significant adverse effects on the environment that could not be avoided by compliance with specific technical conditions.

Detailed provisions of the Offshore Prot. are devoted to safety measures, contingency planning, notification, and mutual assistance in cases of emergency,

---

(Footnote 27 continued)
governmental organization having its seat in Rome. See Treves 1978, 827; Sersic 1989, 161; Scovazzi 1995, 543.

[28] It is composed of a preamble and 32 articles, distributed in six sections relating to the following matters: General provisions; Authorization system; Wastes and harmful or noxious substances and materials; Safeguards; Co-operation; Final provisions. Seven annexes and an appendix complete the instrument.

[29] The activities to which the Protocol applies are defined in quite broad terms by Article 1.*d*: '(i) Activities of scientific research concerning the resources of the seabed and its subsoil; (ii) Exploration activities: Seismological activities; surveys of the seabed and its subsoil; sample taking; Exploration drilling; (iii) Exploitation activities: Establishment of an installation for the purpose of recovering resources, and activities connected therewith; Development drilling; Recovery, treatment and storage; Transportation to shore by pipeline and loading of ships; Maintenance, repair and other ancillary operations'.

[30] These obligations are to be understood in the sense that parties are bound to take the appropriate measures in order to ensure that the operators comply with the provisions of the Offshore Prot.

[31] According to Article 2 para 1, the Offshore Prot. applies to the seabed under any legal condition, be it the continental shelf or the seabed under the territorial sea or the internal maritime waters. The Parties may also extend its application to wetlands or coastal areas (Article 2 para 2). .

monitoring, removal of installations, specially protected areas. Duties of co-operation among the parties are envisaged with respect to studies and research programs, formulation of rules, standards, and recommended practices and procedures, scientific and technical assistance to developing countries, mutual information, and prevention of transboundary pollution.

Of particular interest for the purpose of this study is Article 27, relating to liability and compensation. The first paragraph of Article 27, as it is provided in other treaties relating to the protection of the environment, sets forth a future undertaking by the Parties to co-operate in the drafting of appropriate rules and procedures:

> 'The Parties undertake to co-operate as soon as possible in formulating and adopting appropriate rules and procedures for the determination of liability and compensation for damage resulting from the activities dealt with in this Protocol in conformity with Art. 12 of this Convention'.[32]

An obligation to co-operate is not devoid of legal meaning. It implies a duty to act in good faith in pursuing a common objective and in taking into account the positions expressed by the other interested States. This kind of behavior is likely to lead to the conclusion of an agreement. As remarked by the International Court of Justice in the judgments of 20 February 1969 on the *North Sea Continental Shelf* cases,

> 'The parties are under an obligation to enter into negotiations with a view to arriving at an agreement, and not merely to go through a formal process of negotiation (...); they are under an obligation so to conduct themselves that the negotiations are meaningful, which will not be the case when either of them insists upon its own position without contemplating any modification of it'.[33]

The second paragraph of Article 27 sets forth three provisional, but substantive, obligations. Waiting for the adoption of appropriate rules and procedures on liability and compensation, the parties to the Offshore Prot. are bound to take measures to ensure that, first, liability is channeled on the operators, second, they pay compensation in a prompt and adequate manner and, third, they have and maintain compulsory insurance or other financial guarantee:

> 'Pending development of such procedures, each Party

[32] Under Article 12 of the original 1976 text Barcelona Conv. 'the Contracting Parties undertake to co-operate as soon as possible in the formulation and adoption of appropriate procedures for the determination of liability and compensation for damage resulting from the pollution of the marine environment deriving from violations of the provisions of this Convention and applicable protocols'. After the amendments of 2005, the corresponding Article 16 of the present Barcelona Conv. provides as follows: 'The Contracting Parties undertake to cooperate in the formulation and adoption of appropriate rules and procedures for the determination of liability and compensation for damage resulting from pollution of the marine environment in the Mediterranean Sea Area'.

[33] ICJ Rep. 1969, para 85 of the judgment.

(a) shall take all measures necessary to ensure that liability for damage caused by activities is imposed on operators, and they shall be required to pay prompt and adequate compensation;

(b) shall take all measures necessary to ensure that operators shall have and maintain insurance cover or other financial security of such type and under such terms as the Contracting Party shall specify in order to ensure compensation for damages caused by the activities covered by this Protocol'.

As it can be seen, the Offshore Prot. does not allow the so-called 'self-insurance', a dubious euphemism that simply means the absence of any insurance or financial security to cover compensation for damage.

The strict character of the obligation set forth in Article 27 para 2, may, together with other reasons, explain why it took more than 16 years for the Offshore Prot. to enter into force and why it is now binding only on six parties. In fact, at the time of signature of the Offshore Prot., the European Community (now the European Union)[34] and France entered a reservation, "pending consideration", with specific regard to para 2 of Article 27.

Today the limited number of parties to the Offshore Prot. does create evident problems. It is unfair to burden the parties with legal obligations that make offshore activities more expensive for those who operate on their continental shelves and that are not applicable in the case of other Mediterranean coastal States. There is a need to avoid that the stricter measures adopted by some coastal States are frustrated by a tolerant and insufficient regime applied in other neighboring States. As damage caused by marine pollution cannot be confined within the boundaries artificially drawn by man at sea, the consequences of an incident could affect a high number of States, including those that have adopted a more precautionary attitude.

The only equitable development is to do every effort to achieve the broadest possible participation to the Offshore Prot. and to formulate and adopt the 'appropriate rules and procedures' provided for in Article 27 para 1 to ensure that a uniform regime is in place for the whole Mediterranean seabed and marine environment. In fact, a set of Guidelines for the Determination of Liability and Compensation for Damage Resulting from Pollution of the Marine Environment in the Mediterranean Sea Area has been adopted on 18 January 2008 at the 15th ordinary meeting of the Parties to the Barcelona Conv. But they have a general character, applying to 'to the activities to which the Barcelona Convention and any of its Protocols apply' (Guideline A para 4), and are not specific to offshore activities.[35]

---

[34] The attitude of the European Union, at least as far as the European Commission and the European Parliament are concerned, has today changed (see *infra* Sect. 13.5).

[35] Scovazzi 2009, 183.

13.4 The Main Legal Questions

13.4.1 Compensation for Environmental Damage

One of the main legal questions to be addressed when discussing the regime of liability for activities hazardous for the environment is linked to the distinction between traditional and environmental damage.

Traditional damage is intended as the damage suffered by persons, either natural or juridical, such as individuals and private or public entities, including the State. It can consist in bodily injuries or loss of life, in loss or deterioration of property, in loss or reduction of earnings, as well as in the cost of measures undertaken to clean up, restore, and reinstate the impaired environment. This damage, however consistent it might be, can be calculated in precise monetary terms. There is no doubt that traditional damage must be compensated by the liable person.[36]

But the discussion is open as regards the extent to which the other kind of damage, that is environmental damage, should be compensated. This damage, which is typical in cases of pollution of natural components, including marine waters, is suffered by the environment as such (*per se*) and is given by a negative change in the quality of a natural component. It can consist in the value of the diminution of the quality of natural components during the time when restoration is pending (compensation for interim damage) or in the cost of compensation by equivalent action to be taken elsewhere if the polluted environment cannot fully return to its previous condition (compensation for irreparable damage). This kind of damage cannot be calculated in precise monetary terms.

As far as international law is concerned, the treaties that establish uniform civil liability regimes for certain potentially polluting activities, such as the exploitation of atomic energy, shipping, carriage of dangerous goods, or transboundary trade of hazardous wastes, follow a scheme usually based on strict liability, the channeling of liability on the operator, the right of the latter to limit liability to a predetermined amount, his obligation to maintain an insurance or other financial security and, in some cases, the creation of an international fund to provide compensation if the protection already afforded is inadequate. However, these treaties are often based on the assumption that compensation must be restricted to damage that can be determined in precise monetary terms. For example, under the International Convention on Civil Liability for Oil Pollution Damage (London 1992), 'pollution damage' means

> '(a) loss or damage caused outside the ship by contamination, resulting from the escape or discharge of oil from the ship, wherever such escape or discharge may occur, provided that compensation for impairment of the environment other than loss of profit from such

[36] The adjective 'traditional' simply means that there is no discussion that this kind of damage can be compensated under well established general principles of law, which have existed for hundreds, if not thousands, of years in the legislation of most countries.

impairment shall be limited to costs of reasonable measures of reinstatement actually undertaken or to be undertaken;

(b) the costs of preventive measures and further loss or damage caused by preventive measures'. (Article 1 para 6).[37]

However, it is a matter of fact that some national enactments take the different approach that also damage to the environment that cannot be evaluated in precise monetary terms shall be compensated. For instance, under the United States *Oil Pollution Act* of 1990 (s.1002(a)) each responsible party is liable for the 'removal costs' and 'damages'. The definition of 'damages' (s.1002(b)(2)) includes different entries of traditional damage, as well as the following entry of environmental damage:

'Natural Resources—Damage for injury to, destruction of, loss of, or loss of use of, natural resources, including the reasonable costs of assessing the damage, which shall be recoverable by a United States trustee, a State trustee, an Indian tribe trustee, or a foreign trustee'.[38]

Under s.1006(d)(1) of the Act the measure of natural resource damages is:

A. 'the cost of restoring, rehabilitating, replacing, or acquiring the equivalent of, the damaged natural resources;
B. the diminution in value of those natural resources pending restoration; plus
C. the reasonable cost of assessing those damages'.

A claim to recover damage to natural resources is presented by the United States Government (or the other public entities specified in the Act) as a 'trustee of natural resources' (s.1006(b)(1)). Any costs related to natural resources damage are to be determined with respect to plans that the trustee is called to develop and implement (s.1006(d)(2)).

Relevant for the purpose of compensation for environmental damage is also Directive 2004/35/EC of the European Parliament and the Council of 21 April 2004 on environmental liability with regard to the prevention and remedying of environmental damage.[39] This instrument makes a distinction between 'primary remediation', that is 'any remedial measure which returns the damaged natural resources and/or impaired services to, or towards, baseline condition', 'complementary remediation', that is 'any remedial measure taken in relation to natural resources

[37] A similar approach is followed, *inter alia*, in the 1996 International Convention on Liability and Compensation for Damage in Connection with the Carriage of Hazardous and Noxious Substances by Sea, in the 1999 Protocol on Liability and Compensation for Damage Resulting from Transboundary Movements of Hazardous Wastes and their Disposal and in the 2001 International Convention on Civil Liability for Bunker Oil Pollution Damage.

[38] The term 'natural resources' is defined as including 'land, fish, wildlife, biota, air, water, ground water, drinking water supplies, and other such resources belonging to, managed by, held in trust by, appertaining to, or otherwise controlled by the United States (including the resources of the exclusive economic zone), any State or local government or Indian tribe, or any foreign government' (s. 1001, 20).

[39] Official Journal of the European Union No L 143 of 30 April 2004.

and/or services to compensate for the fact that primary remediation does not result in fully restoring the damaged natural resources and/or services' and 'compensatory remediation', that is 'any action taken to compensate for interim losses of natural resources and/or services that occur from the date of damage occurring until primary remediation has achieved its full effect' (Annex II, para 1, sub-paras a, b, and c).[40]

The approach taken by the United Nations Compensation Commission, established under United Nations Security Council Resolution 687 (1991) after the end of the illegal invasion and occupation of Kuwait by Iraq, also provides an important contribution to the trend to take into consideration compensation for interim and irreparable environmental damage.[41] In the report and recommendations presented in 2005, the Panel of the Commission in charge of the issue of depletion of, or damage to, natural resources[42] reached the following conclusions:

> 'The Panel does not consider that there is anything in the language or context of Security Council resolution 687 (1991) or Governing Council decision 7 that mandates or suggests an interpretation that would restrict the term 'environmental damage' to damage to natural resources which have commercial value.[43]
>
> Furthermore, the Panel does not consider that the fact that the effects of the loss of or damage to natural resources might be for a temporary duration should have any relevance to the issue of the compensability of the damage or loss, although it might affect the nature and quantum of compensation that might be appropriate. In the view of the Panel, it is not reasonable to suggest that a loss that is documented to have occurred, and is shown to have resulted from the invasion and occupation of Kuwait, should nevertheless be denied compensation solely on the grounds that the effects of the loss were not permanent'.[44]

The Panel paid little consideration to the different approach adopted in a number of international treaties establishing uniform regimes of liability and compensation:

---

[40] Interim losses are defined in the Directive as 'losses which result from the fact that the damaged natural resources and/or services are not able to perform their ecological functions or provide services to other natural resources or to the public until the primary or complementary measures have taken effect. It does not consist of financial compensation to members of the public'. (Annex II, para 1, sub-para d).

[41] The Commission (decision 7 of 1991) allowed compensation for losses or expenses resulting from '(a) Abatement and prevention of environmental damage, including expenses directly relating to fighting oil fires and stemming the flow of oil in coastal and international waters; (b) Reasonable measures already taken to clean and restore the environment or future measures which can be documented as reasonably necessary to clean and restore the environment; (c) Reasonable monitoring and assessment of the environmental damage for the purposes of evaluating and abating the harm and restoring the environment; (d) Reasonable monitoring of public health and performing medical screenings for the purposes of investigation and combating increased health risks as a result of the environmental damage; and (e) Depletion of or damage to natural resources'.

[42] Doc. S/AC.26/2005/10 of 30 June 2005.

[43] Ibid. para 55.

[44] Ibid. para 56.

'The panel does not consider that this finding is inconsistent with any principle or rule of general international law. In the view of the Panel, there is no justification for the contention that general international law precludes compensation for pure environmental damage. In particular, the panel does not consider that the exclusion of compensation for pure environmental damage in some international conventions on civil liability and compensation is a valid basis for asserting that international law, in general, prohibits compensation for such damage in all cases, even where the damage results from an internationally wrongful act'.[45]

According to the Panel, a fundamental principle of justice was at stake:

'Where the [wrongful act] itself is of such a nature as to preclude the ascertainment of the amount of damages with certainty, it would be a perversion of fundamental principles of justice to deny all relief to the injured person, and thereby relieve the wrongdoer from making any amend for his acts. In such case, while the damages may not be determined by mere speculation or guess, it will be enough if the evidence shows the extent of the damages as a matter of just and reasonable inference, although the result may be approximate'.[46]

In the case of irreparable damage, the Panel recommended compensation by equivalent, charging Iraq, for instance, for the cost of the establishment and management for 30 years of a coastal protected area:

'The Panel finds that a coastal preserve would provide appropriate compensation for the loss of shoreline resources resulting from Iraq's invasion and occupation of Kuwait. A preserve sited in shoreline habitats similar to those that have been damaged would provide ecological services similar in kind to those that were lost. In view of the Panel, such a preserve is feasible, cost-effective and poses a low risk of adverse impacts'.[47]

13.4.2 Evaluation of Environmental Damage

A different, although related, question is how to evaluate environmental damage, as it cannot be determined in precise monetary terms. Doubts and concerns have been expressed about the complexity and reliability of a number of methods used for calculating such kind of damage. For instance, in the United States

'alternatives to valuing the environment for the purpose of assessing claims include the price that the environmental resource commands in the market, the economic value attached to the use of environmental resources (such as methods of costing travel relying on expenditures made by an individual to visit and enjoy a resource, or a hedonic pricing method which takes the extra market value enjoyed by a private property with certain environmental amenities and assumes that public resources with comparable amenities have similar economic values), or contingent valuation methods to measure the

[45] Ibid. para 58.

[46] Ibid. para 80.

[47] Ibid. para 451.

willingness of individuals to pay for environmental goods such as clean air or water or the preservation of endangered species (usually taken from public opinion surveys)'.[48]

Annex II to the above-mentioned European Union Directive 2004/35 develops the following considerations:

'When determining the scale of complementary and compensatory remedial measures, the use of resource-to-resource or service-to-service equivalence approaches shall be considered first. Under these approaches, actions that provide natural resources and/or services of the same type, quality and quantity as those damaged shall be considered first. Where this is not possible, then alternative natural resources and/or services shall be provided. For example, a reduction in quality could be offset by an increase in the quantity of remedial measures (para 1.2.2).

If it is not possible to use the first choice resource-to-resource or service-to-service equivalence approaches, then alternative valuation techniques shall be used. The competent authority may prescribe the method, for example monetary valuation, to determine the extent of the necessary complementary and compensatory remedial measures. If valuation of the lost resources and/or services is practicable, but valuation of the replacement natural resources and/or services cannot be performed within a reasonable time-frame or at a reasonable cost, then the competent authority may choose remedial measures whose cost is equivalent to the estimated monetary value of the lost natural resources and/or services.

The complementary and compensatory remedial measures should be so designed that they provide for additional natural resources and/or services to reflect time preferences and the time profile of the remedial measures. For example, the longer the period of time before the baseline condition is reached, the greater the amount of compensatory remedial measures that will be undertaken (other things being equal)'. (para 1.2.3).

The already mentioned Panel of the United Nations Compensation Commission recognized that

'there are inherent difficulties in attempting to place a monetary value on damaged natural resources, particularly resources that are not traded on the market. With specific regard to HEA [= Habitat Equivalency Analysis], the Panel recognises that it is relatively a novel methodology, and that it has had limited application at the national and international levels. The Panel is also aware that there are uncertainties in HEA calculations, especially for establishing a metric that appropriately accounts for different types of service losses and for determining the nature and scale of compensatory restoration measures that are appropriate for damage to particular resources. For these reasons, the Panel considers that claims presented on the basis of HEA or similar methodologies of resource valuation should be accepted only after the Panel has satisfied itself that the extent of damage and the quantification of compensation claimed are appropriate and reasonable in the circumstances of each claim. However, the Panel does not consider that these potential difficulties are a sufficient reason for a wholesale rejection of these methodologies, or for concluding that their use is contrary to international law principles'.

It is likely that the elaboration of reliable and predictable criteria for the evaluation of environmental damage will become one of the main questions to be

48 Sands 2003, 884.

addressed in the near future at the international level, including in the case of damage resulting from offshore activities.

13.4.3 Compulsory Insurance and Compensation Fund

In domestic legislation the most usual kind of liability for polluting activities is strict liability, instead of fault based liability. For instance, under the already mentioned European Union Directive 2004/35, the operator of activities causing significant environmental damage to protected species, natural habitats, or water is strictly liable to prevent and remedy the damage and to bear the full costs of it.[49]

However, the laws of different countries greatly vary as to whether there should be a limitation to the liability to the benefit of the person, such as the operator, the licensee, or the shipowner, on whom liability is channeled. If liability is limited, it is usual to establish a compensation fund for cases in which the amount of compensation exceeds the limitation or the responsible cannot be identified. For instance, under the United States *Oil Pollution Act*, liability for damages from offshore spills is capped at US$ 75,000,000 and claims up to US$ 1,000,000,000 above the cap are paid out of the Oil Spill Liability Trust Fund.

National legislation can also establish that the operator has to be insured or has to establish an adequate financial guarantee. A certain margin of flexibility may be envisaged in this regard. This is the case, for instance, of the legislation of Norway (*Pollution Control Act* No. 6 of 3 March 1981) that provides as follows:

> 'A permit granted in accordance with this Act or regulations issued pursuant thereto may include the condition that security shall be provided in respect of possible liability to pay compensation pursuant to this chapter.
>
> The pollution control authority will decide what security shall be required.
>
> The pollution control authority may issue regulations relating to the duty to provide security for specified types of activities.
>
> The King may issue provisions concerning the establishment of separate compensation arrangements to cover claims of the types to which this chapter applies, including financing, the duty to make financial contributions, the right to bring civil action and the settlement of claims'.[50]

---

[49] Under the Directive, operators who carry out certain dangerous activities, as listed in Annex III, are strictly liable (without fault) for environmental damage. Operators carrying out other occupational activities are liable for any fault-based damage they cause to nature. Operators may benefit directly from certain exceptions and defenses (for example force majeure, armed conflict, third party intervention) and defenses introduced via transposition (for example permit defense, state of the art defense). Operators have to take preventive action if there is an imminent threat of environmental damage. They are likewise under an obligation to remedy environmental damage once it has occurred and to bear the costs (polluter-pays principle). In specific cases where the operators fail to do so, or are not identifiable, or have invoked defenses, the competent authority may carry out the necessary preventive or remedial measures.

[50] Para 63. The Norwegian relevant legislation also includes the *Petroleum Activities Act No. 72* of 29 November 1996.

On the question of financial security European Union Directive 2004/35 follows a gradual approach:

> '1. Member States shall take measures to encourage the development of financial security instruments and markets by the appropriate economic and financial operators, including financial mechanisms in case of insolvency, with the aim of enabling operators to use financial guarantees to cover their responsibilities under this Directive.
>
> 2. The Commission, before 30 April 2010 shall present a report on the effectiveness of the Directive in terms of actual remediation of environmental damages, on the availability at reasonable costs and on conditions of insurance and other types of financial security for the activities covered by Annex III. The report shall also consider in relation to financial security the following aspects: a gradual approach, a ceiling for the financial guarantee and the exclusion of low-risk activities. In the light of that report, and of an extended impact assessment, including a cost-benefit analysis, the Commission shall, if appropriate, submit proposals for a system of harmonized mandatory financial security'.[51]

In October 2010, the European Commission presented the report mentioned in Article 14 para 2.[52] It was drafted after consultation of government experts and other stakeholders, such as insurers, brokers, banks, financial institutions, and non-governmental organizations. As regard the development of financial security instruments at the national level (Article 14, para 1), it appeared that

> 'eight Member States have introduced mandatory financial security entering into force at different dates up to 2014: Bulgaria, Portugal, Spain, Greece, Hungary, Slovakia, Czech Republic and Romania. These systems are subject to risk assessment of relevant sectors and operators, and dependent on various national implementing provisions providing for issues such as ceilings, exemptions, etc. However, mandatory financial security is delayed in all three countries where it was supposed to come into effect in 2010 (Portugal, Spain, Greece) because essential provisions are not yet in place. The remaining Member States rely on voluntary financial security'.[53]

One of the most difficult issues in the implementation of the Directive is related to the complex technical requirements linked to the evaluation of damaged resources or services.[54] As regards the question of insurance,

> 'Operators aware of their environmental liabilities have tended to cover the resulting risks through a mix of environmental insurances such as General Third Party Liability—GTPL, Environmental Impairment Liability—EIL or other stand-alone insurance products. Operators were using to a much lesser extent other financial security, such as captives, bank guarantees, guarantees and funds.[55]

---

[51] Article 14.

[52] Doc. COM(2010) 581 final of 12 October 2010.

[53] Ibid. 4.

[54] 'The competent authorities judged that the most difficult issues were the complex technical requirements linked to the economic evaluation of damaged resources/services and environmental remediation methods, as well as the lack of binding thresholds for key terms such as 'significant damage'. However, Member States have started to develop guidelines and are building up their knowledge based on these questions'. (Ibid. 5).

[55] Ibid. 6.

The insurance industry reacted positively to the introduction of the ELD [= Environmental Liability Directive]. Significant work on what the ELD means for the insurance sector has been carried out and widely disseminated. The industry has gradually developed products for ELD, either specific 'stand alone' solutions, or top-ups to existing liability products. Work is in hand on practical implementation issues such as underwriting and claims management, as are efforts to develop a database of case studies to share experiences. However, there remains uncertainty at this early stage as to the readiness of existing products to deal with ELD cases. The insurance industry also reported that the recent economic crisis had resulted in a temporary drop in the industry's capacity to provide ELD cover. It can be concluded that the transposition of the ELD was slow and that implementation methods vary widely across the EU. This divergence delayed the development of financial security options at national level. Although the wide variety of national implementation methods may impair the effectiveness of the Directive, it is extremely difficult to verify exactly how'.[56]

As regards other types of financial security,

'there is a general focus on insurance products as a way to cover ELD liabilities, although a range of alternatives exist. In connection with other environmental legislation, such as that on waste management, significant experience has been gained with non-insurance instruments (bonds, bank guarantees, funds, captives, etc.). These instruments require little change to make them suitable for ELD-related liabilities. It should be noted that some alternative instruments are more appropriate for large operators with numerous operations than for SMEs [= small or medium enterprises]. The suitability of financial security instruments will depend on their efficiency in terms of remediation costs covered, their availability to operators, and their effectiveness for preventing pollution. No available instrument appears to fulfil all three requirements for all ELD liabilities and all the sectors concerned, so the choice of instrument will vary across operators'.[57]

In the light of the present situation, the opinion of the European Commission is that 'all mandatory financial security schemes should employ a form of gradual approach, provide for the exclusion of low-risk activities, and include ceilings for financial guarantees'.[58] According to the European Commission, the introduction of a harmonized system of mandatory financial security is not yet justified today. However, it is important to remark that initiatives in this direction could be justified in the specific case of oil spills from offshore activities:

---

[56] Ibid. 7.

[57] Ibid. 8.

[58] Ibid. 8. In particular 'No financial security system, be it insurance, bank guarantee or a trust fund, will provide unlimited liability. Therefore, ceilings apply both to voluntary and mandatory financial security mechanisms. A ceiling for the financial guarantee could be introduced where the risk of damage occurring above that ceiling is considered as low, and depends on the location, type and size of the operation. Spain introduced ceilings to the liability cover their operators need of up to a maximum of € 5 million. In other countries ceilings are arranged between insurers and operators. Insurance companies can also introduce ceilings to the liabilities they wish to cover, subsequently setting limits to the premiums to be paid but also in the coverage that their guarantee provides. The previous ceilings apply when determining the maximum coverage of the policies. In practice, there are also reimbursement ceilings of ELD policies, which currently range between € 1 million and € 30 million'.

'Because of the lack of practical experience in the application of the ELD, the Commission concludes that there is not sufficient justification at the present time for introducing a harmonised system of mandatory financial security. Developments in those Member States that have opted for mandatory financial security, including the gradual approach, and in the Member States that have not introduced obligatory financial security, will have to be further monitored before reliable conclusions can be drawn. The Commission will also actively monitor recent developments such as the oil spill in the Gulf of Mexico, which may provide the justification for an initiative in this area'.[59]

The European Commission will also focus on some issues that call for immediate attention, including the question of sufficiency of actual financial ceilings set for established financial security instruments with regard to accidents of potential large scale:

'The ability of existing financial security instruments to cover massive incidents needs to be assessed in connection with applicable financial ceilings and the potential of different types of instruments, such as funds, insurance, guarantees, etc. In this context, the review will aim at discovering the most efficient ways of ensuring sufficient financial resources in case of large scale incidents that involve responsible parties with mediocre or even low financial capacity'.[60]

13.5 The Initiatives for a New Regime within the European Union

The *Deepwater Horizon* incident prompted initiatives for legislative improvement also within the European Union framework. On 7 October 2010, the European Parliament adopted a Resolution on European Union action on oil exploration and extraction in Europe, based, *inter alia*, on the following considerations:

'Whereas in the light of the Deepwater Horizon oil spill in the Gulf of Mexico it is imperative for the EU and its Member States urgently to examine all aspects of oil extraction and exploration in the European Union and to take all necessary steps thereafter to ensure that such an environmental catastrophe will not occur in EU waters;

Whereas the highest levels of precaution, environmental protection and safety and security of oil operations in Europe are the principles of paramount importance which must underpin all EU action in this area;

Whereas efforts are underway to extend oil drilling and exploration into deeper and more remote parts of the sea, which involve greater risks in terms of managing and monitoring operations'.[61]

---

[59] Ibid. 10. On the Gulf of Mexico incident see *supra* Sect. 13.2.

[60] Ibid. 11.

[61] Preamble.

According to the European Parliament, offshore activities can be considered as 'hyper-hazardous' and, as such, require mandatory environmental impact assessment (EIA):

> [The European Parliament] 'calls on the Commission, in its current review of the Environmental Impact Assessment Directive, to ensure that all seabed activities are subjected to a mandatory assessment, that the quality of EIAs is guaranteed and that hyper-hazardous activities such as seabed drilling are not permitted to proceed where an EIA indicates that risks cannot be satisfactorily mitigated'.[62]

A particularly strict legislation should regulate offshore activities and should also insure "full liability" for "any damage", including environmental damage:

> [The European Parliament] 'considers furthermore that any legislative proposals must ensure a comprehensive legal framework which:
>
> prevents as far as possible potentially hazardous seabed activities from causing damage to the marine and coastal environments;
> guarantees that full liability rests with the polluter in relation to any damage caused by such activities, including damage to the terrestrial and marine environments and to the global climate;
> secures the protection of European biodiversity in marine and coastal environments;
> ensures that, before any economic activity is planned, independent experts conduct an environmental impact assessment'.[63]

The concerns expressed by the European Parliament are duly reflected in the 2010 Communication from the Commission to the European Parliament and the Council, *Facing the Challenge of the Safety of Offshore Oil and Gas Activities.*[64] The Communication acknowledges the present increase of offshore activities, including in the Mediterranean,[65] the risks that such activities entail,[66] as well as

---

[62] Para 14.

[63] Para 14.

[64] Doc. COM(2010) 560 final of 12 October 2010.

[65] 'The number of offshore installations in the North East Atlantic alone exceeds 1,000. Furthermore, while installations in the Black and Baltic Seas still only amount to single digits, there are currently over 100 installations operating in EU waters in the Mediterranean and plans to start new exploration are reported in the Maltese and Cypriot sectors. Oil and gas exploration or production also takes place in the close vicinity of the EU, off the coasts of Algeria, Croatia, Egypt, Israel, Libya, Tunisia, Turkey and Ukraine'. (ibid. 2).

[66] 'The European offshore oil and gas industry has not been immune to severe accidents in the past, as the Piper Alpha and Alexander Kielland in the North Sea have shown. As a result, a number of European countries have introduced in recent years strict safety requirements and regulatory regimes. Yet the experience of the Deepwater Horizon needs to lead to sincere reflection also in Europe on whether the current regulatory frameworks and practices are adequate in terms of safety and emergency preparedness and response. Such a reflection is also warranted by the transformation of the European oil and gas industry in response to the progressive depletion of 'easy' oil and gas reservoirs. Exploration is moving towards more complex environments characterised by high pressure/high temperature reservoirs, deeper waters and/or extreme climatic conditions that may complicate the control of subsea installations and incident

the need to ensure the fullest protection of human health and the environment.[67] The Commission looks forward to the establishment of a future uniform regime at the European Union level:

> 'A number of particular best practices exist in Member States and industry already in relation to safety, preparedness and response. However, the challenge posed by the risk of a large offshore accident requires that state of the art practices become the norm throughout the EU and its waters. Such a uniform high level of safety will elicit full public confidence and can underpin EU efforts to ensure high levels of safety, preparedness and response also beyond European borders, both in other jurisdictions and in international waters'.[68]

Rules in this field cannot be the result of either voluntary initiatives by the industry[69] or heterogeneous initiatives by single Member States.[70] There is a need for a uniform European regime that includes adequate financial security instruments to cover major incidents:

> 'The risks at stake, the need for legal certainty and the principles of 'better regulation' speak in the Commission's view in favour of a single new piece of specific legislation for offshore oil and gas activities, possibly supported by soft legal measures (guidelines). (...)
>
> Licensing stands out as the first key tool to ensure the safety of new drilling activities in complex environments. The Treaty on the Functioning of the European Union (TFEU) establishes, in the context of the establishment and functioning of the internal market and

(Footnote 66 continued)
response. At the same time, production facilities in maturing fields are ageing and often taken over by specialist operators with smaller capital bases'. (ibid. 3).

67 'The EU has an interest in maintaining indigenous oil and gas production for security of energy supply reasons as well as for keeping jobs and business opportunities in the European economy. Whilst risks cannot be totally eliminated in most human activities, including in the offshore hydrocarbon industry, the safety and integrity of operations and assurances of maximum protection of European citizens and the environment must be guaranteed'. (ibid. 3).

68 Ibid. 4.

69 'Improving the safety of citizens and the protection of the environment cannot rely on industry's discretionary initiative and self-regulation alone. The regulatory regime must ensure that industry complies with clear, robust and ambitious rules allowing only safe and sustainable operations. In addition, the regime must provide for a high level of transparency enabling the industry and public authorities to demonstrate to any interested party that activities that carry risks to life, environment or property are appropriately managed and controlled'. (ibid. 4).

70 'While international regimes for offshore oil and gas operations are either not fully developed or lack effective enforcement mechanisms, the situation in Europe is largely determined by provisions in the national legislation of individual Member States, as EU legislation either does not cover various relevant aspects of the sector or provides only performance minima. Provisions which apply to offshore activities are also often spread across different EU legislative measures. This results in licensing, operational safety and environmental protection regimes which vary from one Member State to the next. This heterogeneity complicates the understanding and management of health, safety and environmental risks in Europe and increases costs for companies. Importantly, it risks slowing down coordinated response to accidents affecting several Member States as technical standards, data formats and response procedures vary across Europe and within the same sea basin'. (ibid. 4).

with regard for the need to preserve and improve the environment, a Union policy on energy. It also recalls that Member States have the right to determine the conditions for exploiting their energy resources, their choices between different energy sources and the general structure of their energy supply, without prejudice to the environmental policy of the Union. The existing EU legislation on licensing deals only with competitive aspects of licensing procedures to ensure equal access to national bidding rounds for entities across the EU.

Consequently, each Member State issues licences and other approvals necessary for the exploration and production of hydrocarbon resources within its territory and in waters falling under its jurisdiction, setting its own requirements for license awards. Nevertheless, the approvals by individual Member States to drill off their shores may have a significant impact on other Member States. The environmental, economic and social damages caused by a major oil spill affect marine and coastal areas irrespective of national borders.

It is therefore crucial that licensing procedures anywhere in Europe conform to certain basic common criteria. National licensing procedures in all Member States should be reviewed to reflect recognized best practices and to include EU-wide obligations for safety, health and environmental performance, risk management and independent verification.

The licensing regime needs to be backed up by an unequivocal liability regime which must include adequate financial security instruments to cover major incidents. The existing financial security instruments need to be assessed with regard to financial ceilings and may be usefully complemented by other risk-coverage instruments, such as funds, insurance, guarantees, etc'.[71]

The future regime must be based on high levels of safety and environmental protection:

'To guarantee maximum safety and a level playing field for industrial operators, the requirements applicable to industry through goal-setting or, where appropriate, prescriptive legislation need to be designed according to uniform criteria, inspired by the state of the art in the sector and must be rigorously enforced. These requirements must include, in addition to the financial and technical capability, key features to protect the health and safety of workers on offshore installations, guarantee the integrity of installations, provide a high level of protection of the environment, and prevent and respond to accidents.

Not only future operations and installations but also existing ones must consistently conform to the highest levels of safety and protection. Maintenance should include requirements for regular upgrading of installations as technology evolves.

The existing environmental legislation addresses a number of issues relevant to offshore installations (e.g., environmental impact assessment) and certain aspects of offshore operations (e.g., emissions from platforms). Yet the installations are not covered by EU legislation on pollution control and major accident hazards which was mainly designed to address land-based installations and risks of major accidents on land'.[72]

---

[71] Ibid. 4.

[72] Ibid. 6.

It is not surprising that, moving from these assumptions, the Commission envisages the future participation to the Offshore Prot. by the European Union and its Member States:

> 'In the Mediterranean Sea, a large part of the marine space is made up of High Seas and co-operation between the authorities of riparian States needs to be reinforced.
>
> The EU should therefore seek that regulatory frameworks and industry supervision in jurisdictions neighbouring European waters provide equally high levels of safety and protection. There is a good example of the benefits from regional co-operation between competent authorities in the North Sea.
>
> The potential of regional conventions should be explored. This includes re-launching, in close co-operation with the Member States concerned, the process towards bringing into force the protocol combating pollution from offshore activities in the Mediterranean. This would allow involving the already existing Regional Marine Pollution Emergency Response Center for the Mediterranean Sea (REMPEC) in offshore emergency prevention, preparedness and response. Bilateral co-operation, particularly with southern Mediterranean States involved in offshore extraction activities can also be enhanced, notably through Action Plans and instruments under the European Neighbourhood Policy (ENP)'.[73]

In October 2011, the European Commission made the subsequent step by presenting a proposal for a Regulation of the European Parliament and of the Council on Safety of Offshore Oil and Gas Prospection, Exploration and Production Activities,[74] to fill the gap created by the lack of specific offshore oil and gas legislation by the European Union. The explanatory memorandum points out the dimension of the risk and the lack of adequate regulation:

> 'The risk of a major offshore oil or gas accident occurring in Union waters is significant and the existing fragmented legislation and diverse regulatory and industry practices do not provide for all achievable reductions in the risks throughout the Union.

---

[73] Ibid. 12.

[74] Doc. COM(2011) 688 final of 27 October 2011. According to the subsidiarity principle, the need for legislative action at the European Union level is explained as follows: 'Companies operate and drilling rigs like Deepwater Horizon are being moved across borders but face very different regulatory regimes along the lines of national jurisdictions. Recent reactions of the Member States suggest, that without Union action these differences are going to exacerbate as countries mainly only in the most advanced regions individually plan improvements while international initiatives make very slow progress. Moreover, without Union action, existing difficulties for comparing industry performance and sharing of intelligence and incident data will remain. Action by Member States alone would be inadequate to achieve consistent protection (including liability for pollution) of the environment, a common good, a commitment of the Union and its Member States as per the Marine Strategy Framework Directive'. (ibid. 10). The instrument lastly quoted is Directive 2008/56/EC of 17 June 2008, establishing a framework for Community action in the field of marine environmental policy. .

> The existing regulatory framework and operating arrangements do not provide for the most effective emergency response to accidents wherever they occur in Union waters, and the liabilities for clean-up and conventional damages are not fully clear.[75]
>
> The likelihood and consequences of major offshore incidents remain significant everywhere in the Union based on national reports, and risk analysis conducted by the Commission in 2011. Offshore production occurs increasingly also in the Mediterranean, the Black and even the Baltic Seas where some countries in some of these marine regions have less experience in regulating offshore operations. Still, even in the advanced regions (mainly North Sea) national action has failed to achieve common standards and comparability of data'.[76]

In this field, the disparities in laws and practices among Member States, including as regards liability provisions, also reflect the lack of relevant instruments of international law.[77] One of the general objectives of the proposal is to 'improve and clarify existing Union liability and compensation provisions'.[78] In this connection, the proposal aims at expanding the territorial applicability of environmental liability 2004/35, currently limited to the coastal strip and territorial sea in relation to water damage, to cover also all marine waters under the jurisdiction of the Member States. It foresees stronger and risk based assessment of technical and financial capacity. No 'export' of risk would be allowed:

> 'Union based companies should endeavour, and are expected, to follow the policies outlined in this regulation and not lower standards when operating outside the Union'.[79]

An interesting remark relates to some different reactions to the online public consultation on the proposal:

> 'While acknowledging improvement needs in general terms, the industry was the most conservative towards regulatory changes while preferring goal setting approaches and industry initiatives. On the other hand NGOs and the specialised companies (e.g., classification societies) were the most active in calling for changes at Union level)'.[80]

As far as liability and compensation are concerned, the preamble of the proposal of regulation points out that 'under existing liability regimes, the responsible party may not always be clearly identifiable and/or may not be able, or liable, to

---

[75] Ibid. 2.

[76] Ibid. 10.

[77] 'There are considerable disparities and fragmentation amongst Member States' laws and practices applying to offshore activities (e.g., licensing, liability provisions, equipment safety standards, public transparency and information sharing). This reflects the virtual absence of international law instruments and gaps in relevant Union law'. (ibid. 3).

[78] The others are to '1. Ensure a consistent use of best practices for major hazards control by oil and gas industry offshore operations potentially affecting Union waters or shores; 2. Implement best regulatory practices in all European jurisdictions with offshore oil and gas activities; 3. Strengthen Union's preparedness and response capacity to deal with emergencies potentially affecting Union citizens, economy or environment'. (ibid. 3).

[79] Ibid. 6.

[80] Ibid. 5.

pay all the costs to remedy the damage it has caused' (para 8) and that 'the competent authority is required to consider the technical and financial risks, and where appropriate, the previous record of responsibility, of applicants seeking exclusive exploration and production licenses'. (para 9). It is also clearly stated (para 38) that marine waters covered by the sovereignty or jurisdiction of European Union Member States form an integral part of the four marine regions, namely the Baltic Sea, the North-east Atlantic Ocean, the Mediterranean Sea, and the Black Sea, and that, for this reason, coordination should be strengthened with third countries having sovereignty or jurisdiction over waters in such marine regions. Appropriate co-operation frameworks include regional sea conventions, such as the Barcelona Conv. The preamble (para 39) acknowledges that, in relation to the Mediterranean Sea, the necessary actions are being undertaken for the accession of the European Union to the Offshore Prot.

The proposal, which is mainly focused on prevention of accidents, channels liability on the 'licensee', defined as the holder of an authorization to carry out offshore operations:

> 'The licensee is liable for the prevention and remediation of environmental damage, pursuant to Directive 2004/35/EC, caused by offshore oil and gas activities carried out by the licensee or any entity participating in the offshore oil and gas operations on the basis of a contract with the licensee. The consenting procedure for operations pursuant to this Regulation shall not prejudice the liability of the licensee'.[81]

The financial capacity of the licensee must be taken in consideration at the moment of granting an authorization:

> 'In particular, when assessing the technical and financial capacity of the entities that apply for authorisation for offshore oil and gas activities, due account shall be taken of the risk, hazards and any other relevant information related to the area concerned and the particular stage of exploration and production operations and also of the applicants' financial capacities, including any financial security and capacity to cover liabilities potentially deriving from offshore oil and gas activities in question, in particular liability for environmental damages'. (Article 4, para 2).

Neither compulsory insurance nor a compensation fund are envisaged in the proposal. However, analysis and studies in this field are expected on the basis of a prudent approach that does not exclude further developments:

> 'As no existing financial security instruments, including risk pooling arrangements, can accommodate all possible consequences of extreme accidents, the Commission should proceed with further analysis and studies of the appropriate measures to ensure adequately robust liability regime for damages related to offshore oil and gas operations, requirements on financial capacity including availability of appropriated financial security instruments or other arrangements'.[82]

Due emphasis is given in the proposal to co-operation with third States, especially within the framework of regional sea conventions:

---

[81] Article 7.

[82] Preambular para 48.

> 'The Commission, in close co-operation with the Member States, shall promote co-operation with third countries that undertake offshore oil and gas operations in the same marine regions as Member States including, where appropriate, within the framework of regional sea conventions.
>
> The Commission shall assess the safety of oil and gas operations in the waters of the third countries adjacent to waters of Member States and support a coordinated approach to mutual exchange of experience and promotion of preventive measures and regional emergency response plans.
>
> The Commission shall promote high safety standards for offshore oil and gas operations at international level at appropriate global and regional fora, including those related to Arctic waters'.[83]

Also the European Parliament, in the Resolution adopted on 13 September 2011 on *Safety of Offshore Oil and Gas Activities*, based itself on a broader vision of future developments in the field of liability and compensation, including the possible establishment of a compensation fund. By this recent instrument the Parliament

> 'Urges Member States, when considering financial guarantee mechanisms, including the necessity of third-party insurance, to pay due attention to set insurance rates on the basis of the real risk arising from drilling and exploitation difficulties, so as not to price small-and medium-sized operators out of the market whilst ensuring that liability coverage is maintained;
> Stresses that while in principle financial guarantees can be provided through either insurance or industry mutualisation, it is important to ensure that operators demonstrate that financial guarantees are in place to cover the full cost of clean-up and compensation in the case of a major disaster, and that risks and liabilities are not externalised to smaller companies that are more likely to declare insolvency in the event of an accident; calls for any joint schemes to be established in a manner that maintains incentives for avoiding risks and adheres to the highest possible safety standards in individual operations;
>
> Recognises the merit of communal funds such as OPOL in the North Sea and calls for such funds to be established in each EU sea area; calls for membership to be mandatory for operators and for legal certainty to be ensured so as to provide a safety-net mechanism designed to reassure the Member States, the maritime sector, in particular fishermen, and taxpayers[84];
> Stresses that the voluntary nature of schemes such as OPOL limit their legal control and therefore believes that these funds would be strengthened by being a mandatory licence requirement;
> Stresses that contributions should be based on, and consistent with, both the level of risk at the site concerned and contingency plans;
> Considers that the scope of the Environmental Liability Directive should be extended so that the 'polluter pays' principle and strict liability apply to all damage caused to marine waters and biodiversity, so that oil and gas companies can be held accountable for any and all environmental damage they cause, and can assume full liability;
> Calls for a revision of the Environmental Liability Directive to extend its coverage to all EU marine waters in line with the Marine Strategy Framework Directive;

---

[83] Article 28 paras from 1 to 3.

[84] As regards the OPOL see *infra* Sect. 13.6.

> Calls on the Commission, under the Environmental Liability Directive, to lower damage thresholds and to enforce a strict liability regime covering all damage to marine waters and biodiversity;
> Takes the view that the Commission should examine whether a compensation fund for oil disasters can be created within the framework of environmental liability, which would contain binding financial security provisions;
> Recommends that Member States consider adopting and strengthening deterrents against negligence and non-compliance such as fines, withdrawal of licences, and criminal liability for employees; points out however, that such a regime existed in the USA prior to the Deepwater Horizon spill;
> Stresses that the financially liable parties should be established without ambiguity prior to drilling'.[85]

The European Parliament also stresses the need to avoid the 'export of risk' by European Union companies and recalls the importance of becoming party to the Offshore Prot. It

> 'Urges the industry to employ at least EU environmental and safety standards or their equivalent wherever in the world they are operating; is aware of the enforcement issues of mandating EU-based companies to operate globally according to EU standards, but calls on the Commission to examine what mechanisms might be appropriate to ensure that EU-based companies operate globally according to at least EU safety standards; believes corporate responsibility should also be a key driver in this area and that Member State licensing regimes could take global incidents involving companies into consideration when awarding licenses, provided these incidents are accompanied by thorough reviews; calls on the Commission to promote the use of these high standards along with global partners; (...)[86];
>
> Stresses the importance of bringing fully into force the un-ratified 1994 Mediterranean Offshore Protocol, targeting protection against pollution resulting from exploration and exploitation'.[87]

13.6 Other Recent Developments

The catastrophic effects of the *Deepwater Horizon* incident stimulated also in other fora further consideration of the risks posed by potentially dangerous activities from the perspective of both prevention and compensation.

The Parties to the Convention for the Protection of the Marine Environment of the North East Atlantic (Paris 1992; so-called OSPAR Convention) adopted in 2010 a Recommendation on the Prevention of Significant Acute Oil Pollution from Offshore Drilling Activities, whereby they established a process to review existing

---

[85] Paras from 69 to 79.

[86] Para 80.

[87] Para 83.

regulatory mechanisms and associated guidance and to take in the near future additional action, if needed.

The Guidelines for the Development of Domestic Legislation on Liability, Response Action, and Compensation for Damage Caused by Activities Dangerous to the Environment, adopted in February 2010 in Bali by the UNEP Governing Council[88] can provide useful models for further normative developments in the field of liability and compensation. They allow compensation for different types of damage, among which "environmental damage"[89] is included, but only insofar as this is provided by domestic law (Guideline 8 para 2).[90] They channel liability on the operator, without however excluding the liability of other subjects:

> '1. The operator should be strictly liable for damage caused by activities dangerous to the environment.
>
> 2. Without prejudice to paragraph 1, any person should be liable for damage caused or contributed to by not complying with applicable statutory or regulatory requirements or through wrongful, intentional, reckless or negligent acts or omissions. A violation of a specific statutory obligation should be considered fault per se'.[91]

States are called to encourage or require that the operator is covered by insurance or other financial guarantees:

> 'The operator should, taking into account the availability of financial guarantees, be encouraged or required to cover liability under guideline 5, paragraph 1, for amounts not less than the minimum specified by law for the type of activity dangerous to the environment concerned and should continue to cover such liability, during the period of the time limit of liability, by way of insurance, bonds or other financial guarantees.

---

[88] The UNEP Guidelines are annexed to the Nusa Dua Declaration.

[89] 'The term "environmental damage" means an adverse or negative effect on the environment that: (a) Is measurable taking into account scientifically established baselines recognized by a public authority that take into account any other human-induced variation and natural variation; (b) Is significant, which is to be determined on the basis of factors such as: (i) Long-term or permanent change, to be understood as change that may not be redressed through natural recovery within a reasonable period of time; (ii) Extent of the qualitative or quantitative changes that adversely or negatively affect the environment; (iii) Reduction or loss of the ability of the environment to provide goods and services, either of a permanent nature or on a temporary basis; (iv) Extent of any adverse or negative effect or impact on human health; (v) Aesthetic, scientific and recreational value of parks, wilderness areas and other lands'. (Guideline 3.3).

[90] As explained in the commentary to the UNEP Guidelines, 'in addition, as regards environmental damage, domestic legislation might acknowledge such loss as being an intrinsic part of any approach to comprehensive legislation on liability, response action and compensation for environmental damage. Should domestic legislation incorporate such a comprehensive focus, domestic law might also put in place an appropriate mechanism for the assessment or valuation of compensation as a result of the loss of the use of the natural resources concerned'. (doc. UNEP/GCSS.XI/INF/6/Add.2 of 19 January 2010, 2).

[91] Guideline 5 paras 1 and 2.

The competent public authority should periodically review the availability of and the minimum limits for financial guarantees, taking into account the views of relevant stakeholders, including the specialized and general insurance industry'.[92]

Limitation of liability is envisaged under certain conditions[93] and domestic law may provide for a special fund or collective compensation mechanism:

> 'Given that the operator might be unable to meet his or her liability or that actual damages might exceed the operator's limit of liability, domestic law may provide for closure of potential compensation gaps by way of special funding or collective compensation mechanisms'.[94]

The *Deepwater Horizon* incident called for response also by the oil industry, in the form of increased co-operation to review the safety of drilling practices and contingency plans, as well as to meet financial responsibilities for potential cleanup and compensation costs arising from a major oil spill. For instance, the United Kingdom Oil Spill Prevention and Response Advisory Group (OSPRAG) has reviewed the functioning of the Offshore Pollution Liability Association Limited (OPOL), an oil industry body set up in 1975 which administers a strict liability compensation scheme to which all British offshore operators are parties.[95] In the event of a default by an operator, OPOL provides for a mutual guarantee from all of its other members for the settlement of claims up to a determined limit. In August 2010, the OPOL members increased the limit from US$ 120,000,000 to 250,000,000. According to OSPRAG, the current OPOL limit is an appropriate one, as only a small number of wells are likely to have a potential exposure above this level. Additional financial means to meet these instances are expected to be developed through OSPRAG financial responsibility guidelines that have yet to be finalized.

13.7 Conclusive Remarks

It is frequently said that many progressive developments in environmental law are the consequence of the lessons learned from disasters that heavily affect the environment and, in several cases, human life as well. This could happen also in the case of the *Deepwater Horizon* incident.

The rush towards drilling in deep waters is not likely to be halted by recent incidents, despite a number of declarations advocating for a moratorium. But the

---

92 Guideline 11 paras 1 and 2.

93 'Liability pursuant to guideline 5, para 1, may be limited in accordance with criteria established under any applicable domestic classification scheme for activities dangerous to the environment. (...) There should be no financial limit on liability arising under guideline 5, para 2'. (Guideline 10 paras 1 and 3).

94 Guideline 10 para 2.

95 See OSPRAG, *Strengthening UK Prevention and Response—Final Report*, September 2011.

public has developed an aversion to further risk of major incidents. The intention to do something to guarantee safety in oil drilling has been manifested within actors that play a pivotal role in the oil production and marketing, such as the United States and the European Union. So far offshore oil drilling has been largely characterized by self-regulation by operators, including 'self-insurance' for future damage. This also explains why there is a persistent lack of a binding instrument applicable on the world scale and relating to liability and compensation for this kind of activities.

The main lesson to be drawn from the *Deepwater Horizon* incident is that compensation is to be paid in full and through a swift and effective process. Present limitations to liability and ceilings of compensations funds, if any, are insufficient to cover the damage arising from a catastrophic event. The situation is, however, likely to change following a widespread call for more regulation at both the international and the domestic level. An evident legal gap needs to be filled and experts concur that this should be done without delay.[96]

References

Badenes Casino M (2005) Ixtoc-1. In: Juste Ruiz J, Scovazzi T (eds) La práctica internacional en materia de responsabilidad por accidentes industriales catastróficos, Tirant Lo Blanch, Valencia 65

Billé R, Druel E, Rochette J (2001) Advancing the Oceans Agenda at Rio + 20: Where We Must Go. IDDRI (Institut du Développement Durable et des Relations Internationales) Policy Brief No. 5

Chabason L (2011) Offshore oil exploitation: A new frontier for International Environmental Law, IDDRI Working Paper No. 11

Foley VJ (2001) Post-deepwater horizon: the changing landscape of liability for oil pollution in the United States, 74 Albany Law Review, 515

Sands P (2003) Principles of international environmental law, 2nd edn. Cambridge University Press, Cambridge

Schoenbaum T (2012) Liability for damages in oil spillaccidents: Evaluating the USA and international law regimes in the light of Deepwater Horizon, 22 Journal of Environmental Law 1

Scovazzi T (1995) The fifth protocol to the Barcelona convention on the protection of the mediterranean, 10 Int J Marine Coastal Law, 543

Scovazzi T (2009) The Mediterranean guidelines for the determination of environmental liability and compensation: the negotiations for the instrument and the question of damage that can be compensated, 13 Max Planck Yearbook of United Nations Law, 183

Sersic M (1989) Draft protocol for the protection of the Mediterranean sea against pollution resulting from offshore activities, Marine Policy Reports 161

Treves T (1978) La pollution résultant de l'exploration et de l'exploitation des fonds marins en droit international, 24 AFDI 827

[96] See Chabason 2011, 3; Billé et al. 2001, 1.

Part IV
The Human Rights Dimension

Chapter 14
Derogation from Human Rights Treaties in Situations of Natural or Man-Made Disasters

Emanuele Sommario

Abstract Certain natural or technological disasters may have exceptionally severe consequences that call for the adoption of extraordinary measures. Some of these may restrict individual rights and freedoms to an extent which is not compatible with the affected State's international obligations under human rights law. Yet, the existence of a public emergency of significant magnitude may temporarily exonerate States from the duty to fully respect their human rights commitments, either through the operation of specific clauses that are included in the relevant treaties (so-called "derogation clauses"), or—where no such provision is present—by invoking certain justifications recognized in international law as valid excuses for the non-performance of legal obligations. This chapter intends to look at the practice of States and treaty monitoring bodies in order to ascertain what substantial and procedural requirements States must fulfill if they deem it necessary to suspend individual rights while coping with a public emergency prompted by a natural or man-made disaster. The purpose is to ascertain what features a disaster must present in order to trigger the right to derogate, to what extent human rights may be suspended, what formal steps must be undertaken by authorities which choose to derogate from human rights treaties, and which are the legal parameters under general international law with regard to the suspension of treaties which do not explicitly provide for a right to derogate.

Keywords International disaster response law · Human rights · Derogation · Non-derogable rights · State of emergency · State responsibility

E. Sommario (✉)
Scuola Superiore Sant'Anna, Piazza Martiri della Libertà 33, 56127 Pisa, Italy
e-mail: e.sommario@sssup.it

A. de Guttry et al. (eds.), *International Disaster Response Law*,
DOI: 10.1007/978-90-6704-882-8_14,

Contents

14.1 Introduction

Just over 20 years ago, Frits Kalshoven lamented that international law concerning assistance to victims of natural disasters was characterized by "(…) the virtually total absence of generally applicable specific rules", although he immediately added that "norms of human rights" should play a central role in the matter.[1] As several contributions in the present volume show, many of the legal shortcomings in this area of international law have been (and are being) addressed. Like Kalshoven had predicted, international human rights law played an important part in this process by endeavoring to describe the legal entitlements of individuals and groups affected by natural or man-made disasters and the corresponding State obligations. Significantly, the work currently undertaken by the International Law Commission (ILC) on the protection of persons in the event of disasters is fraught with references to human rights law and other branches of international law relevant for the protection of individual and collective rights.[2]

Indeed, States have express duties under international law to guarantee the enjoyment of fundamental human rights to all individuals under their jurisdiction,

---

[1] Kalshoven 1989, p. 24.

[2] See Chap. 3 by Zorzi Giustiniani in this volume.

and these legal commitments do not lose validity in the presence of calamitous events. Yet it is widely accepted that, when facing serious public emergencies, States can temporarily suspend their obligations under certain human rights treaties and adopt exceptional measures aimed at overcoming the crisis.[3]

The present chapter intends to assess what options States have under international law to lawfully suspend the enjoyment of human rights when their territory is struck by a natural or technological disaster. The derogation regimes established under the main human rights treaties will be reviewed in order to ascertain: (a) if disaster situations can trigger a right to derogate from those treaties; and (b) what substantial and procedural limitations States must comply with when resorting to extraordinary emergency measures. It will then be assessed whether the legal principles identified are also applicable with respect to human rights treaties which do not encompass a derogation clause.

While there exists a wealth of international case law and doctrinal debate concerning derogations from civil and political rights, the legal framework appears less clear in relation to treaties which do not include a derogation clause and to instruments protecting economic, social and cultural rights. Our review will focus on the analysis of the practices of the treaty monitoring bodies established by the main universal and regional human rights treaties—with special emphasis on the pronouncements of the Human Rights Committee (HRC)[4] and the European Court of Human Rights (ECtHR)[5]—and be complemented by a perusal of relevant scholarly contributions.

We will however not address situations in which natural or man-made disasters coexist with an armed conflict, as these are regulated by the special rules of customary and positive international humanitarian law.[6] Furthermore, the study will not delve into the protection regime provided to specific vulnerable groups,

[3] For comprehensive reviews of the relevant international standards and mechanisms, see Ergec 1987, Chowdhury 1989, Oraà 1992, Fitzpatrick 1994, Premont 1996, Svensson-McCarthy 1998, Gross and Ní Aoláin 2006, Eboli 2010.

[4] The United Nations Human Rights Committee, established under Article 28 of the 1966 International Covenant on Civil and Political Rights (ICCPR), monitors compliance with the Covenant's norms by State Parties. In addition, the Committee also produces General Comments in which it sets out its view on the substantial and procedural obligations stemming from the Covenant. Through all the above activities, the Committee contributes to the elaboration of the Covenant's norms. For a recent analysis of the Committee's work see Tyagi 2011.

[5] According to Article 19 of the 1950 European Convention on Human Rights and Fundamental Freedoms (ECHR), the function of the European Court is "to ensure the observance of the engagements undertaken" by the contracting States in relation to the Convention and its protocols. Until 1998, the Court shared its supervisory function with the European Commission of Human Rights (ECommHR). For an overview of the European Human Rights system see Jacobs et al. 2010.

[6] It is understood, however, that in situations of "complex emergencies" where a man-made or natural disaster occurs in a territory affected by an armed conflict situation, the rules of International Humanitarian Law do not completely displace the applicability of other norms of international law concerning the protection of individuals and groups. See International Law Commission, *Report on the work of its sixty-second session*, in General Assembly Official

except where this is functional to highlight emerging trends and existing gaps in the legal protection afforded to all individuals as such.

14.2 Human Rights in Disaster Situations: Ordinary Limitations or Derogation?

Before moving on to describe the derogation regime under international human rights law, it is apt to recall that the exercise of most of the rights codified in international instruments may be subject to limitations.[7] The rationale behind this approach is that there are but few absolute human rights and that with respect to the exercise of many rights the individual's interest must be balanced against more general collective interests, such as the protection of national security, public order (*ordre public*), health or morals and against the rights and freedoms of others.[8] Unlike derogations, ordinary limitations can apply in times of normalcy and be of a permanent character. The exact scope of the limitations is to be determined in the light of the text of the treaty and of the interpretation given to it by State parties and by the relevant treaty monitoring bodies.

There are certain formal and substantial conditions which authorities must respect when limiting freedoms and rights.[9] The possibility for limitations must be provided for by national law that is in force at the relevant time. Even in the presence of legal underpinnings, limitations cannot be applied in an arbitrary, unreasonable or discriminatory manner. Every limitation must be necessary to attain one of the purposes listed in the relevant provision. Moreover, in order to be deemed "necessary", interferences must respond to a pressing social need, pursue a legitimate aim and be proportionate to that aim. Finally, limitation clauses shall be strictly interpreted, so as to minimize their adverse impact on the right at issue, whose essence can never be completely nullified.

Human rights treaties allow significant leeway for States to tackle disaster situations by limiting the exercise of specific rights rather than suspending them entirely.[10] For instance, the interdiction of access to areas contaminated as a result of a catastrophe would probably constitute a legitimate restriction on the right to

---

(Footnote 6 continued)
Records, Sixty-fifth session, Supplement No. 10 (A/65/10), p 327. See also Chap. 11 by Venturini in this volume.

[7] De Schutter 2010, 288; Viarengo 2005, 955–970.

[8] Lockwood et al. 1985, 35–88; Higgins 1976–1977, 283–286.

[9] See Siracusa Principles on the Limitation and Derogation Provisions in the International Covenant on Civil and Political Rights, UN Doc. E/CN.4/1984/4, Annex, 28 September 1984, principles 1–14. The requirements formulated with respect to the ICCPR may be extended to all other human rights treaties mentioned, as their limitation regime follows the same pattern, see De Schutter 2010, 290.

[10] Kiss 1981, 290.

freedom of movement, as it is aimed at protecting the public health of the population.[11] Indeed, natural calamities could call for the imposition of limitations on many of the rights and freedoms guaranteed by international treaties: freedom of expression may be curtailed to avoid panic; freedom of movement and of residence could be restricted through the adoption of forced evacuation orders; freedom from compulsory labor may be curbed to compel individuals to participate in the building of shelters or perform other kinds of tasks;[12] limitations on the right to property may be introduced if requisition of private goods is deemed necessary.[13] Yet would a very serious natural or technological disaster justify derogation from human rights treaties, i.e., an outright suspension, rather than a mere limitation, of internationally protected rights?

14.3 The Use of Derogation Clauses in Response to Disasters

Many of the most important human rights instruments recognize that certain exceptional situations call for measures that are incompatible with human rights standards applicable in ordinary situations. In the intentions of the negotiators, the treaties needed to provide States facing severe emergencies with a mechanism that would enable them "to loosen the stranglehold of their obligations without running the risk of their membership of the community of States parties being called into question".[14] The use of such "derogation clauses" exonerates the State invoking them from international responsibility for failing to fully respect its treaty obligations,[15] provided that certain substantial and procedural rules are complied with in the exercise of this prerogative.

Article 4(1) of the International Covenant for Civil and Political Rights reads as follows:[16]

---

[11] Novak 2005, 280.

[12] In this respect, however, Article 4.3(c) of the ECHR already specifies that such duties would not fall under the definition of "forced or compulsory labour" for the purposes of the Convention. Similar provisions are to be found in the ICCPR (Article 8.3(c)iii) and in the ACHR (Article 6.3(c)).

[13] Marks 1982, 186.

[14] Questiaux 1982, 11, para 37.

[15] In this respect, it must be noted that the presence of a derogation clause in a treaty qualifies the possibility to invoke *ex post facto* the plea of necessity as a circumstance precluding the wrongfulness of State conduct which is in contrast with the legal obligations imposed by that treaty. See International Court of Justice (ICJ), *Legal Consequences of the Construction of a Wall in the Occupied Palestinian Territory*, Advisory Opinion, 9 July 2004, para 140.

[16] Virtually identical provisions can be found in the ECHR at Article 15; in the 1969 American Convention on Human Rights (ACHR), Article 27; in the 1961 European Social Charter (revised in 1996), Part V, article F; in the 2004 Arab Charter on Human Rights, Article 4.

> In time of public emergency which threatens the life of the nation and the existence of which is officially proclaimed, the States Parties to the present Covenant may take measures derogating from their obligations under the present Covenant to the extent strictly required by the exigencies of the situation, provided that such measures are not inconsistent with their other obligations under international law and do not involve discrimination solely on the ground of race, colour, sex, language, religion or social origin.

As is apparent from the letter of the provision, the drafters chose to refrain from providing an exhaustive list of situations in which the right to derogate could be invoked. They preferred to place the focus on the magnitude and effects of the emergency, irrespective of its nature or origin.[17] Whereas in the vast majority of cases resort to derogation measures has been justified with reference to situations of armed conflict, severe disorders, or violent terrorist campaigns,[18] there is nothing to indicate that extreme natural or man-made disasters having the potential to severely undermine the correct functioning of the State could not amount to "public emergencies" as understood in human rights treaties. Many elements support this view.

While the preparatory works of the ECHR and ICCPR are of little assistance in clarifying this aspect,[19] the drafting history of the derogation clause in the ACHR supports the idea that disasters may justify resort to derogation. The provision explicitly mentions situations of "public danger" as one of the circumstances in which the clause may be invoked. During the negotiations, this phrasing was included following an amendment filed by El Salvador which called for the addition of the words "public calamities" in the first paragraph of the clause.[20] The amendment was finally adopted, although with the word "danger" replacing "calamities".[21]

State practice under the ICCPR and ECHR—although rather scant—also suggests the permissibility of derogations due to calamitous events. Article 4 ICCPR has been invoked by at least three States to justify derogation in cases of natural

---

[17] According to the International Law Association,"[i]t is neither desirable nor possible to stipulate in abstracto what particular type or types of events will automatically constitute a public emergency within the meaning of the term; each case has to be judged on its own merits taking into account the overriding concern for the continuance of a democratic society", International Law Association, *Paris Report*, 1984, 59, para 1.

[18] See the list of derogation notices filed by States Parties under Article 4(3) ICCPR in Novak 2005, 984–1041.

[19] However, some members of the Commission on Human Rights stressed during the negotiations leading to the adoption of the ICCPR that natural disasters "almost always justified the State in derogating from some, at least, of the rights recognized in the covenant", Report to the Economic and Social Council on the eighth session of the Commission, New York, 14 April–14 June 1952, 40, para 278.

[20] The Salvadorean delegate argued that public calamities were not necessarily threats to the internal or external security of the State, but could nonetheless warrant suspension of rights, see Doc OEA/Ser.K/XVI/1.2, Conferencia Especializada Interamericana sobre Derechos Humanos, San Josè, Costa Rica, 7–22 de noviembre de 1969, Actas y Documentos, 264.

[21] Ibid., 265.

disasters. On 23 November 1998, Guatemala notified the UN Secretary General that it intended to suspend several articles of its Constitution establishing human rights guarantees in order to tackle the "public disaster" generated by the passage of Hurricane Mitch.[22] The same State again resorted to the derogation clause when confronted with the effects of Hurricane Stan (October 2005),[23] when dealing with the "swine flu" pandemic (May 2009),[24] and when coping with the eruption of the Pacaya volcano and the devastations caused by tropical storm Agatha (May–June 2010).[25] In March 2010, Chile filed a derogation notice stating its intention to suspend freedom of movement and freedom of assembly in order to deal with the aftermath of the powerful earthquake that struck some of the country's regions.[26] The measures were publicly announced through the adoption of a decree declaring a "30-day constitutional state of disaster emergency".[27] Lastly, in March 2006 it was Georgia's turn to avail itself of Article 4 ICCPR when authorities felt they had to suspend—in one of the country's districts—constitutional guarantees related to freedom of movement and to the right to property in order to prevent further spread throughout the country of the Avian Flu virus.[28]

The lawfulness of the above derogations has not been tested by the HRC under the individual communications procedure. However, to this author's knowledge,

---

[22] The notice was accompanied by the text of the emergency decree enacted by the President describing the measures implemented. Pursuant to the decree the Government could (a) "centralize all State and privately owned public services"; (b) "establish sanitary cordons, change or maintain people's place of residence, limit vehicular traffic and prevent people from entering affected areas"; (c) "demand the necessary assistance and cooperation from members of the public to help control the affected areas"; (d) "organize the immediate evacuation of the inhabitants of affected areas" and (e) "order the civil and military authorities to take all necessary steps to protect people and property", see 2045 UNTS, 262–265.

[23] The state of emergency was declared for a period of 30 days and it restricted "the right of liberty of movement and the right of freedom of action, except for the right of persons not to be harassed for their opinions or for acts which do not violate the law", see United Nations, Multilateral Treaties Deposited with the Secretary General, Vol. I, 2009, 242.

[24] The "public health emergency" was declared throughout the national territory for a period of 30 days, with a view to "preventing and mitigating the effects of the influenza A (H1N1) epidemic". The government suspended Article 12 (right to liberty of movement), Article 19 (right to freedom of expression) and Article 21 (right of peaceful assembly) of the Covenant, see http://treaties.un.org/doc/Publication/CN/2009/CN.347.2009-Eng.pdf. Accessed 22 February 2012.

[25] With respect to the volcano eruption, a "disaster emergency" was declared for 30 days in some of the country's Departments, to safeguard the "safety and freedom from disturbance of persons and their property (…) and to prevent or reduce the impacts of the eruption". Only 2 days later a "national disaster emergency" was declared (again for 30 days) in the entire territory due to the tropical storm. The presidential decrees allowed for the "partial restriction" of Articles 12 and 21 of the Covenant, see http://treaties.un.org/doc/Publication/CN/2010/CN.788.2010-Eng.pdf. Accessed 22 February 2012.

[26] For the text of the note see http://treaties.un.org/doc/Publication/CN/2010/CN.201.2010-Eng.pdf. Accessed 23 February 2012.

[27] Ibid.

[28] The text of the note is available at http://treaties.un.org/doc/Treaties/1976/03/19760323%2006-17%20AM/Related%20Documents/CN.231.2006-Eng.pdf. Accessed 23 February 2012.

none of the UN human rights treaty monitoring bodies have so far expressed concern or disapproval over the emergency measures adopted,[29] nor have these been criticized by other State parties to the Covenant. Indeed, far from excluding the possibility of resorting to derogations in the event of disasters, the HRC has explicitly envisaged this eventuality in its latest General Comment on Article 4 of the Covenant, although it specified that situations of this kind can generally be handled through ordinary limitations to relevant rights.[30]

Turning to the ECHR, the only case of interest for our purposes is Georgia's invocation of Article 15 in 2006, made in connection to the same events recalled above. The derogation was withdrawn about 3 weeks later.[31] Again, neither the ECtHR nor other State parties to the Convention have voiced opposition to Georgia's conduct.

An additional element that militates in favor of a definition of "public emergency" that includes natural disasters is to be found in international labor conventions. Convention No. 29 on Forced Labour, for instance, provides that the term "forced and compulsory" labor does not encompass

> any work or service exacted in cases of emergency, that is to say, in the event of war or of a calamity or threatened calamity, such as fire, flood, famine, earthquake, violent epidemic or epizootic diseases, invasion by animal, insect or vegetable pests, and in general any circumstance that would endanger the existence or the well being of the whole or part of the population.[32]

While the ILO Conventions are not *per se* human rights treaties,[33] their importance in interpreting the notion of "emergency" cannot be overlooked, if nothing else because—given the high number of ratifications—they contain "relevant rules of international law applicable in the relations between the parties" that may be used in interpreting the provisions of human rights instruments having a similar membership.[34]

---

[29] This assertion is based on an examination of the concluding observations made by the HRC, the Committee on Economic, Social and Cultural Rights, the Committee on the Elimination of Racial Discrimination, the Committee on the Elimination of Discrimination against Women, the Committee against Torture and the Committee on the Rights of the Child to Nicaragua, Chile and Georgia's periodic reports filed under the respective treaties.

[30] Human Rights Committee, General Comment N. 29 ("General Comment N.29"), U.N. Doc. CCPR/C/21/Rev.1/Add.11 (2001), para 5.

[31] The text is available at http://conventions.coe.int/Treaty/Commun/ListeDeclarations.asp?NT=005&CV=0&NA = &PO = 999&CN = 8&VL = 1&CM = 9&CL = ENG. Accessed 21 February 2012.

[32] 1930 International Labour Organisation (ILO) Convention (No. 29) Concerning Forced Labour, Article 2(2)(d). Suspension clauses are present in several other ILO Conventions.

[33] But see the argument by Svensson-McCarthy, who considers these treaties as actual human rights instruments as they endow a particular group, i.e., workers, with a range of rights pertaining to their personal, economic, and social security, Svensson-McCarthy 1998, 328.

[34] 1969 Vienna Convention on the Law of Treaties (VCLT), Article 31.3(c).

Legal scholarship also endorses the view that resort to derogation clauses may be lawful in case of severe natural or man-made disasters. According to Joseph, Schultz and Castan "a severe natural disaster, such as a major flood or earthquake" could fall under the definition of public emergency for the purposes of Article 4 ICCPR.[35] Fitzpatrick maintains that "certain natural disasters might meet the criteria for derogation".[36] In commenting on the derogation clause in the ECHR, Boisson de Chazournes expresses the view that "[e]nvironmental disasters can (...) give rise to the right of derogation if the conditions of Article 15 are met".[37]

14.4 Conditions for the Exercise of the Right to Derogate

Having ascertained that natural or man-made disasters may fall under the definition of "public emergency" envisaged by the main human rights treaties, we must now determine under what circumstances these situations may trigger the right to derogate from conventional obligations and what substantial and procedural limitations States must comply with to lawfully invoke this prerogative.

14.4.1 The Principle of Exceptional Threat

As the HRC points out, "not every disturbance or catastrophe qualifies as a public emergency which threatens the life of the nation".[38] The monitoring bodies of the ECHR were the first to be called on to work out this notion when interpreting Article 15. In the *Lawless Case*, the ECtHR held the "natural and customary meaning of the words 'other public emergency threatening the life of the nation'" to be sufficiently clear and that the expression indicated "an exceptional situation of crisis or emergency which affects the whole population and constitutes a threat to the organized life of the community of which the State is composed".[39] In the *Greek Case*, the ECommHR elaborated upon the above definition, stating that a "public emergency" must possess the following features:

(1) It must be actual or imminent.
(2) Its effect must involve the whole nation.
(3) The continuance of the organised life of the community must be threatened.

---

[35] Joseph et al. 2005, 825.

[36] Fitzpatrick 1994, 56.

[37] Boisson de Chazournes 1996, 465. The same view is held by Marks 1982, 186–190; Cataldi 2001, 430; Chowdhury 1989, 16–17; Shraga 1986, 219; Hartman 1985, p 93; Svensson-McCarthy 1998, 215–216.

[38] HRC, General Comment N. 29, para 3.

[39] ECtHR, *Lawless* v. *Ireland* (*Lawless Case*), Judgment of 1 July 1961, para 22.

> (4) The crisis or danger must be exceptional, in that the normal measures or restrictions, permitted by the Convention for the maintenance of public safety, health and order, are plainly inadequate[40]

The "actual" or "imminent" nature of the emergency implies that States cannot derogate from the ECHR when the threat is merely "latent" or "perceived".[41] The same wording is used in the *Siracusa Principles on the Limitation and Derogation Provisions in the International Covenant on Civil and Political Rights*[42] ("Siracusa Principles"), which build upon the European jurisprudence.[43] This element might assume particular importance with reference to natural or man-made disasters, as it could warrant suspension of certain rights before the calamity has actually hit a particular territory (e.g., if a hurricane or a radioactive cloud is approaching).

The requirement that the emergency must involve "the whole population" or "the whole nation" has been loosened as it is accepted that the crisis situation may have a geographically limited scope while still affecting the entire population of the interested area. In *Ireland* v. *UK* the respondent State had limited the applicability of the derogation measures to the six counties of Northern Ireland and neither the ECtHR nor Ireland raised objections.[44] The *Paris Minimum Standards of Human Rights Norms In a State of Emergency*[45] ("Paris Minimum Standards") have endorsed this view, accepting that the emergency can affect "the whole population or the population of the area to which the declaration applies".[46]

---

[40] ECommHR, *Denmark, Norway, Sweden and the Netherlands* v. *Greece (Greek Case)*, Report of 5 November 1969, 12 YBECHR, 71–72, paras 152–154.

[41] See Hartman 1981, stating that derogations should not be allowed to face a danger which is "merely potential, latent or speculative", 16. See also Oraà 1992, 27–28.

[42] *Siracusa Principles on the Limitation and Derogation Provisions in the International Covenant on Civil and Political Rights*, UN Doc. E/CN.4/1984/4, Annex, 28 September 1984. The Siracusa Principles were adopted in 1984 by a group of 31 international law experts who met to examine the grounds for permissible limitations and derogations the human rights under the ICCPR. The participants considered the principles as reflecting the state of international law at the time of their adoption, see Siracusa Principles on the Limitation and Derogation Provisions in the International Covenant on Civil and Political Rights, 7 Human Rights Quarterly, 1985, 2.

[43] Ibid., 7.

[44] ECtHR, *Ireland* v. *UK*, Judgment of 18 January 1978, para 205. The Court adopted a similar stance in *Aksoy* v. *Turkey*, Judgment of 18 December 1996, para 70. See also Higgins 1976–1977, 289–290, n 5, listing a considerable number of derogations made by the UK under Article 15 with respect to some overseas colonies to which it had extended the application of the Convention in accordance with Article 63 of the treaty. Quite clearly, the disorders in those distant territories could hardly be considered to be a threat to the whole population of the United Kingdom.

[45] The Paris Minimum Standards were adopted by the International Law Association at its 61st conference held in Paris in 1984. The Standards were intended "to help ensure that, even in situations where a bona fide declaration of a state of emergency has been made, the State concerned will refrain from suspending those basic human rights which are regarded as nonderogable" in the main human rights treaties, Lillich 1985, 1072, where the text of the document is reproduced.

[46] Ibid., 1073. See also Burgenthal 1981, 80.

As to the gravity of the situation, it ought to be such that "the continuance of the organized life of the community must be threatened". According to Hartman, this implies that "some fundamental element of statehood, such as the functioning of the judiciary or legislature or the flow of crucial supplies, must be endangered".[47] In the same vein, the Siracusa Principles establish that the situation must be so serious as to imperil "the physical integrity of the population, the political independence or the territorial integrity of the State or the existence or basic functioning of institutions indispensable to ensure and protect the rights recognized in the Covenant".[48] Again, it is possible to envisage that certain major natural or technological disasters may reach—at least during their peak phase—the threshold of severity required.

Yet, where (even severe) disasters can be dealt with by using ordinary measures that are compatible with human rights standards applicable in normal situations, the danger or crisis cannot be deemed to be "exceptional" and derogation from the treaties is not allowed. Derogation measures must be the last resort and can only be enacted when all normal measures are exhausted and have not been adequate to deal with the threat. While considering the prospect of derogation from the ICCPR during a natural catastrophe or a major industrial accident, the HRC expressed the opinion that "the possibility of restricting certain Covenant rights under the terms of, for instance, freedom of movement [...] or freedom of assembly [...] is generally sufficient during such situations and no derogation from the provisions in question would be justified by the exigencies of the situation."[49]

On the basis of the legal framework outlined above, it is clear that not every calamitous event may give rise to a "public emergency" as understood under international human rights law. The notion of "exceptional threat" demands that the focus be placed on the event's repercussions on the affected population and on the maintenance of State institutions, rather than on its intensity. The more unprepared and ill-equipped States are to deal with the consequences of a disaster, the easier it will be for them to claim that the "life of the nation" is actually imperiled. This implies that the very same phenomenon can trigger a public emergency and justify derogation by States whose territory presents a high level of vulnerability, while not by others which have adopted preventive measures limiting the negative impact of such calamities.[50]

14.4.2 The Need for An "official Proclamation"

The ICCPR and the Arab Charter require that a state of emergency must be "officially proclaimed". This act usually takes the form of a decision adopted by the political organs of the State and recourse to it is normally subordinated to a

[47] Hartman 1981, 16.
[48] Siracusa Principles, N. 39.
[49] HRC, General Comment N. 29, para 5.
[50] Kalshoven 1989, 17.

number of substantive and procedural conditions. The consequences of such a move may involve not only the suspension of certain constitutional guarantees, but also a temporary modification in the allocation of powers and functions among the different State organs.[51] From a human rights law perspective, this act of publicity serves the important purpose of informing the community about possible extraordinary restrictions on the enjoyment of individual and collective rights and about the changes in the institutional settings the emergency has impelled. The rationale behind its inclusion in Article 4 ICCPR appears to have been the desire to reduce *de facto* emergencies by compelling States that intend to invoke the derogation clause to respect the formalities required by national law.[52] The HRC emphasizes that this requirement "is essential for the maintenance of the principles of legality and rule of law at times when they are most needed".[53] Both the HRC[54] and the Siracusa Principles[55] stress that the act must be adopted by a competent body and in accordance with the relevant domestic legal regime.

Neither the ECHR nor the ACHR contain a similar requirement of publicity. However, in *Cyprus* v. *Turkey* the ECommHR found that Article 15 "requires some formal and public act of derogation, such as declaration of martial law or state of emergency, and that, where no such act has been proclaimed by the High Contracting Party concerned, although it was not in the circumstances prevented from doing so, Art. 15 cannot apply".[56] In addition, the derogation clauses in both instruments require that States invoking them must respect their other obligations under international law. Therefore, State parties to regional conventions that have also ratified the ICCPR could be considered to have an "implicit" duty of official proclamation deriving from Article 4 ICCPR.[57] In all the instances of derogation motivated by natural disasters described above the principle of official proclamation appears to have been fully observed, and the derogating authorities have also made it a point of indicating that they were acting within the boundaries of municipal law.

---

[51] For a review of the emergency provisions in the municipal systems of several Council of Europe (CoE) member States see European Commission for Democracy through Law (Venice Commission), *Human Rights and the functioning of the democratic institutions in emergency situations*, Proceedings of the UniDem Seminar organized in Wrocław (Poland), 3–5 October 1996.

[52] Questiaux 1982, 12, para 43; Oraà 1992, 35.

[53] HRC, General Comment N. 29, para 2.

[54] Ibid.

[55] Siracusa Principles, N. 43.

[56] ECommHR, *Cyprus* v. *Turkey*, Report of 10 July 1976, para 527.

[57] Tremblay 1977, 10. This argument was raised by the applicants before the ECtHR in *Brannigan and Mc Bride* v. *UK*, Judgment of 25 May 1993, paras 67–73. While the Court refused to define the meaning of the terms "officially proclaimed" in Article 4 ICCPR, it found that a statement made by Secretary of State for the Home Department to the Parliament in which he detailed the reasons underlying the Government's decision to derogate "was well in keeping with the notion of an official proclamation", ibid., para 73.

14.4.3 *The Condition that Derogation Measures be "Strictly Required by the Exigencies of the Situations"*

Once it is established that a given event represents a "public emergency", it must then be asked whether the measures adopted to confront it are "strictly required by the exigencies of the situation". This requirement further clarifies that the inclusion of a derogation clause in the treaties was not intended to provide governments with full liberty of action. On the contrary, the severity of the measures resorted to must strictly depend on—and correspond to—the seriousness of the situation.

The HRC has deemed the principle of strict necessity to be "a fundamental requirement for any measures derogating from the Covenant", and one which relates "to the duration, geographical coverage and material scope of the state of emergency and any measures of derogation resorted to because of the emergency".[58]

With respect to the temporal dimension, the requirement of strict necessity stipulates that derogatory measures can only be kept in place as long as the emergency persists. In the words of the ECommHR:

> Article 15, paragraph 3, clearly means that the measures of derogation which it provides for are only justified in the circumstances defined in paragraph 1, with the result that if they remain in force after those circumstances have disappeared they represent a breach of the Convention.[59]

The principle was reaffirmed by the Inter-American Commission on Human Rights (IACommHR) in its *Report on the situation of human rights of a segment of the Nicaraguan population of Miskito origin.*[60] The case involved the forced relocation of the *Miskito Indians* from their ancestral lands to the interior of Nicaragua. The Commission's findings are of particular interest to our analysis, as forced relocation could be regarded as one of the measures called for in cases of natural or man-made disasters.[61] After reiterating the principle that "once the danger that threatens the security of the State has been overcome, the special provisions should also be terminated",[62] the IACommHR determined that a lack of assistance to the *Miskito* who intended to return to their home regions after the

---

[58] HRC, General Comment N. 29, para 4.

[59] ECommHR, *De Becker* v. *Belgium*, Report of 8 January 1960, para 271.

[60] IACommHR, *Report on the situation of human rights of a segment of the Nicaraguan population of Miskito origin*, 29 November 1983.

[61] The justification adduced for the measure was initially the promotion of the well being of the population, although the Government later justified its conduct with reference to the emergency situation generated by the military incursions of armed opposition groups from neighboring Honduras, ibid., 117–118, paras 16–18.

[62] Ibid., 117, para 14.

emergency had ended would constitute a violation of Article 27(1) of the ACHR and an undue restriction on their rights to freedom of residence and of movement.

As to its "geographic" dimension, the principle of strict necessity demands that the applicability of any derogation measure be limited to the areas where the emergency actually unfolds,[63] although one could think of situations in which certain rights may be suspended even outside said areas where this should be absolutely necessary to contain and counter the effects of the disaster. Derogation from particular aspects of the right to property, for instance, could under given circumstances be warranted even in areas of the country not directly affected by a calamity, in order to seize private goods indispensable for the survival of the disaster-stricken population.

As to the scope of the derogation measures enacted, States are again required to strike a balance between the rights and freedoms of individuals and the public interest which is imperiled by the emergency. In reviewing State compliance with the principle of "strict necessity", treaty monitoring bodies have developed a number of criteria. In the first place, it must be asked whether a specific measure is indispensable at all, in light of the fact that ordinary measures are insufficient to meet the public danger.[64] A derogation measure would fail this test if a course of action permissible under the substantive provisions of the treaties would accomplish the same end.[65] As recalled above,[66] the HRC considers that ordinary limitations should generally be sufficient to deal with natural disasters and major industrial accidents. Second, each measure of derogation must bear some relation to the threat and be apt to contribute to the solution of a specific problem which forms part of the emergency.[67] Third, when more than one measure appears acceptable after balancing the right encroached upon with the exigencies of the situation, the least interfering measure must be chosen.[68]

While assessing the requirement of strict necessity, treaty monitoring bodies have regularly referred to the availability of sufficient safeguards against the abuse of derogation measures. The need for a proper assessment of every derogation measure and for a periodic review by the legislature and by the judiciary have been identified as essential preventive factors in this respect.[69] The ECtHR deems a process of continued and permanent review of the need for emergency measures to be "implicit in the very notion of proportionality".[70] The latter aspect is

---

63 Novak 2005, 98.

64 ECtHR, *Lawless Case*, para 36.

65 O'Donnell 1985, 27.

66 *Supra*, Sect. 14.2.

67 The ECommHR maintains that "[t]here must be a link between the facts of the emergency on the one hand and the measures chosen to deal with it on the other.", *Ireland* v. *UK*, Report of 25 January 1976, 97.

68 See, e.g., the Commission's stance in *Lawless* v. *Ireland*, Report of 19 December 1959, 123 (Opinion of Mr. Waldock).

69 See ECtHR, *Lawless Case*, para 37.

70 ECtHR, *Brannigan and Mc Bride* v. *UK*, Judgment of 25 May 1993, para 54.

particularly relevant in emergencies prompted by disasters, which are inherently dynamic phenomena whose gravity can vary over time: the nature and scope of the measures adopted to deal with them must be reviewed and adjusted accordingly.[71]

14.4.4 The Prohibition on Discriminatory Measures

The derogation clauses in the ICCPR, the ACHR and the Arab Charter stipulate that measures of derogation shall not entail discrimination based "solely on the ground of race, colour, sex, language, religion or social origin". The principle of non-discrimination is not mentioned in Article 15 of the ECHR, yet, as with the principle of official proclamation, it could be argued that for State parties to the Convention that are also parties to the ICCPR the prohibition to take derogatory measures that may discriminate on one of the grounds listed in Article 4(1) ICCPR represents one of the "other obligations under international law" that must be respected when derogating from the ECHR. Oraà suggest that the omission of this principle from Article 15 is of little significance, as a differential treatment that has no objective and reasonable justification or is disproportionate to the aim it intends to achieve would most probably fail the test of "strict necessity".[72]

The HRC recalls that neither Article 26 of the ICCPR (establishing equality before the law) nor other provisions related to non-discrimination are listed among the non-derogable provisions in Article 4. However, it is of the opinion that "there are elements or dimensions of the right to non-discrimination that cannot be derogated from in any circumstances", and that the prohibition on discrimination "must be complied with if any distinctions between persons are made when resorting to measures that derogate from the Covenant".[73]

Novak suggests that the insertion of the word "solely" in the text implies that where a specific measure happens to affect only a part of the population corresponding to a certain race or ethnicity (e.g., because the emergency only concerns a specific part of the territory) the said measure cannot be deemed discriminatory, as long as it is not intentionally and exclusively directed against such group.[74] This consideration is particularly significant with respect to derogations prompted by disasters as their impact is often geographically limited.

---

[71] Oraà 1992, 142.

[72] Ibid., 181.

[73] HRC, General Comment N. 29, para 8.

[74] Novak 2005, 100; Questiaux 1982, 18, paras 65–66. Higgins similarly argues that the inclusion of the word "solely" is evidence that "derogations that inadvertently discriminate may, if the other conditions are met, be lawful", Higgins 1976–1977, 87.

14.4.5 The Requirement that Derogation Measures Be in Conformity with the State's Other Obligations Under International Law

Even if specific derogatory measures were found to comply with the criteria set out so far, a State would be barred from resorting to them if their introduction breached other international obligations by which it is bound. These will obviously vary from State to State, depending on their level of participation to multilateral and bilateral treaties. Yet, in assessing State responsibility for failure to comply with obligations stemming from other instruments, it must be borne in mind that these could include provisions allowing for their suspension or that the other parties to the treaty may agree to temporarily exonerate the derogating State from its legal commitments.[75] Furthermore, the treaty obligations could be terminated or suspended if it becomes impossible to perform them[76] or due to a fundamental change of circumstances.[77]

The requirement of consistency has generated very little case law by treaty bodies.[78] Commentators have indicated that the expression would include obligations under the UN Charter,[79] International Humanitarian Law,[80] other universal or regional Human Rights treaties,[81] European Union Treaties,[82] ILO Conventions[83] and Refugee Law treaties.[84] The HRC includes International Criminal Law as a source of possible obligations.[85] Also relevant are obligations arising under binding UN Security Council Resolutions and any rule of international law that should attain the status of *jus cogens*.[86]

---

[75] VCLT, Article 57.

[76] VCLT, Article 61. This hypothesis might assume particular relevance with respect to disaster situations as the impossibility might result "from the permanent disappearance or destruction of an object indispensable for the execution of the treaty".

[77] VCLT, Article 62.

[78] See, however the ECtHR judgment in *Brannigan and McBride* v. *UK*, paras 67–73, and the Court's pronouncement in *Marshall* v. *UK,* Application no. 41571/98, Decision on admissibility of 10 July 2001.

[79] Oraà 1992, 194, making reference to the Commission's Report in *Cyprus* v. *Turkey*, Report of 10 July 1976, paras 510, 512.

[80] Hartman 1981, 17; Svensson-McCarthy 1998, 637.

[81] Novak 2005, 99. In General Comment N. 29, the HRC makes explicit reference to the Convention on the Rights of the Child "which has been ratified by almost all States parties to the Covenant and does not include a derogation clause.", para 10, n. 5.

[82] Harris et al. 1999, p 502. See in particular Chap. 5 by Gestri in this volume.

[83] See Siracusa Principles, N. 66 and O'Donnell 1985, 31.

[84] Novak 2005, 99.

[85] General Comment N. 29, para 13.

[86] Ibid., para 11.

Treaties pertaining to the field of International Disaster Response Law are obviously of paramount importance in this respect.[87] It would be difficult for States to maintain that these instruments can be suspended during an emergency, as they are intended to find application in exactly those situations. Neither could a fundamental change of circumstances be invoked to suspend or terminate such instruments since it could not be claimed that the occurrence of a disaster was an event not foreseen when the treaty was concluded. It must be inferred that the substantial and procedural obligations under IDRL treaties are non-derogable in times of emergency, at least with respect to the situations expressly included in their material scope of application.

Also of relevance are the International Health Regulations.[88] This legally binding instrument—whose purpose is "to prevent, protect against, control and provide a public health response to the international spread of disease"—also applies to natural occurrences, accidental release or deliberate use of biological and chemical agents, or any other calamitous event which affects public health.[89] As for IDRL treaties, the particular nature of the instrument suggests that it is not subject to derogation.[90]

Reverting to the field of Human Rights, a convincing argument could be made that a State derogating under a treaty listing only a limited number of non-derogable rights, which is also a party to another treaty containing a more extensive catalog of non-derogable rights, is precluded from derogating to the supplementary rights which are included in the latter treaty.[91] In the same vein, State parties to human rights treaties which have no derogation clause and are deemed applicable in times of emergency would have to make sure that the exceptional measures they intend to adopt are consistent with the obligations established therein.[92] This is the case of the African Charter of Human and People's Rights, whose treaty monitoring body has ruled that the treaty "does not allow for State parties to derogate from their treaty obligations during emergency situations".[93]

[87] For an overview see Chap. 1 by de Guttry in this volume.

[88] The Regulations have been adopted under the auspices of the World Health Assembly in accordance with Article 21(a) of the WHO Constitution (adopted on 22 July 1946). Their latest version has been approved in 2005 and entered into force on 15 July 2007. For the text see WHO, International Health Regulations (2005), Geneva, 2008, available at http://whqlibdoc.who.int/publications/2008/9789241580410_eng.pdf. Accessed 21 February 2012.

[89] See the understanding filed by the United States, ibid., 60.

[90] O'Donnell 1985, 30.

[91] Oraà 1992, 205; Harris et al. 1999, 502.

[92] But see the discussion in para 14.6 regarding the possibility to suspend the application of human rights treaties which do not include a derogation clause.

[93] African Commission on Human and People's Rights, *Commission Nationale des Droits de l'Homme et des Libertés* v. *Chad*, Decision adopted during the 18th Ordinary session, 2–11 October 1995, para 21. Note, however, that many provisions of the African Charter contain limitation clauses which foresee fewer safeguards for individual rights than other human rights treaties. Scholars have criticized these clawback clauses, as they are deemed to open the door to sweeping restrictions of the rights protected, making a derogation clause redundant, see Wessels 2002, 132–133.

Close attention should also be paid to human rights instruments containing provisions designed to be specifically applied in situations of emergency. Article 11 of the 2006 Convention on the Rights of Persons with Disabilities, for instance, stipulates that:

> States Parties shall take, in accordance with their obligations under international law, including international humanitarian law and international human rights law, all necessary measures to ensure the protection and safety of persons with disabilities in situations of risk, including situations of armed conflict, humanitarian emergencies and the occurrence of natural disasters.

Article 23 of the 1990 African Charter on the Rights and Welfare of the Child provides that contracting States shall take all appropriate measures to ensure the protection and safety to children that are internally displaced "whether through natural disaster, internal armed conflicts, civil strife, breakdown of economic and social order or howsoever caused." For States that have ratified these treaties, these and similar commitments fall quite clearly within the ambit of their "other obligations under international law" for the purposes of the derogation clauses.

14.4.6 The Requirement of Notification

Article 15 ECHR requires a State invoking the right to derogate to keep the Secretary General of the CoE "fully informed" of the measures it has taken and of the reasons for doing so. The Secretary General then circulates the notice of derogation to other member States. The derogation clause in the ICCPR presents a slightly different wording, as it directly identifies the other State parties to the Covenant as the recipients of the relevant information and the UN Secretary General as the intermediary through which it must flow. The ACHR and the Arab Charter include the same type of obligation and ask that notifications be sent to the Secretary General of the Organization of American States and the Secretary General of the League of Arab States, respectively. The purpose of this procedural safeguard is twofold: on the one hand it allows the monitoring bodies to discharge their surveillance function over the nature and scope of the derogation measures put in place; on the other hand it permits other State parties to monitor compliance with the provisions of the treaties and to exercise their own rights accordingly.[94]

A State exercising its right of derogation under the Covenant must "immediately inform" the other State Parties of the emergency measures undertaken. The ECHR has no requirement of "immediacy", yet Article 15 has been interpreted as requiring notification "without delay" after the entry into force of the measures concerned, a standard which in the *Lawless Case* was deemed by the ECtHR to have been satisfied by a delay of 12 days.[95] In its report on the same case, the

---

[94] HRC, General Comment N.29, para 17.

[95] ECtHR, *Lawless Case*, para 47.

ECommHR had used the words "without any avoidable delay",[96] a phrasing which clearly indicates that allowance must be made for the particular impediments with which a Government might be confronted in situations of crisis. From the above it can also be inferred that the notice does not have to be transmitted prior to the derogation, as long as the notification occurs within reasonable time.[97]

With respect to the contents of the notice, the HRC demands that States include "full information about the measures taken and a clear explanation of the reasons for them, with full documentation attached regarding their law."[98] Further notifications are required when the derogation regime is subject to modifications and when the State intends to withdraw the derogation. The ICCPR, the ACHR and the Arab Charter ask States to point out which treaty provisions they intend to suspend. The ECHR only requires to describe the measures adopted. This led the ECommHR in the *Greek Case* to conclude that a Government does not need to point out the provisions from which it is derogating, as long as these can be inferred from a perusal of the documentation attached to the notice.[99] More generally, the scope and depth of the information regarding derogation measures must be such as to enable the other State parties and the monitoring bodies "to appreciate the nature and extent of the derogation from the provisions of the Convention which those measures involve".[100]

It is not clear what consequences are attached to a failure to comply with the notification requirements. The treaties do not contain any indication in this regard and the practice under the different instruments is far from conclusive. Nevertheless, in the *Lawless Case* the ECommHR made clear that under certain circumstances failure to observe the provisions regarding notification may "attract the sanction of nullity of the derogation or some other sanction."[101] Moreover, the monitoring bodies will not grant States the benefit of the derogation if no notification has occurred.[102]

The seven derogation notices (six under the ICCPR and one under the EHCR)[103] filed in the aftermath of disasters were not all in line with the formal requirements established by the treaties. Whereas all of the notices where transmitted to the competent international organs without any undue delay (and no later than 3 weeks from when the calamitous event had occurred and the national authorities had enacted emergency legislation), some did not contain precise

---

96 ECommHR, *Lawless Case*, 73.

97 Oraà 1992, 62.

98 Ibid.

99 ECommHR, *Greek Case*, 30.

100 ECommHR, *Lawless Case*, 73.

101 Ibid., 75.

102 In commenting on Sri Lanka's first periodic report, the HRC insisted that "as long as no notification or justification had been given in respect of rights permitting derogation, they must be considered in force and hence the Government must account for them as in normal situations." UNGAOR A/39/40 (1984), Report of the HRC, 21, para 104.

103 See *supra*, Sect. 14.3.

indications of the treaty provisions which were suspended.[104] However, in most cases this omission could be considered remedied through the attachment to the notice of the relevant national decrees setting out in detail the exceptional restrictions imposed on individual rights.

14.5 Non-Derogable Civil and Political Rights

One of the cornerstones of the derogation regime under human rights treaties is the principle of non-derogability, according to which certain rights can never be suspended, even in the presence of a public emergency threatening the life of the nation. The derogation clauses of the different treaties contain a catalog of these rights, which—mainly due to the lapse of time between the adoption of the instruments—display remarkable differences.[105]

Some rights are designated as non-derogable under the ICCPR, the ECHR, the ACHR and the Arab Charter alike: the right to life, the prohibition of torture and cruel, inhuman and degrading treatment and punishment, the prohibition of slavery and the prohibition of retroactive application of criminal law. These rights and freedoms are widely considered as representing norms of *jus cogens*.[106] Protocol 7 to the ECHR adds freedom from double jeopardy[107] while Protocols 6 and 13 stipulate the non-derogability of the prohibition to impose and execute the death penalty.[108] The ICCPR adds the right to legal personality, the prohibition of imprisonment for debt and freedom of thought, conscience and religion and—for the State parties to it—the abolition of the death penalty as laid down in the Second Optional Protocol to the Covenant.[109] The ACHR also includes the rights of the child and the family, the right to nationality and political rights, and also entrenches the judicial guarantees essential for the protection of non-derogable rights, as does the Arab Charter. The

---

[104] This was the case of Guatemala's notices of 1998 (*supra*, n. 22), of Chile's notification in 2010 (*supra*, n. 26), and of Georgia's notice under the ICCPR of 2006 (*supra*, n. 28).

[105] The longer lists in the ICCPR, the ACHR, and the Arab Charter are also explained by a difference in the rationale behind the inclusion of certain rights, which were added not because they were perceived as being absolutely central to the protection of the individual in emergency situations, but rather because their suspension could never be justified in times of emergency, see HRC, General Comment N.29, para 11 and Hartman 1985, 113—114.

[106] Questiaux 1982, 19.

[107] 1984 Protocol No. 7 to the Convention for the Protection of Human Rights and Fundamental Freedoms.

[108] 1983 Protocol No. 6 to the Convention for the Protection of Human Rights and Fundamental Freedoms concerning the abolition of the death penalty (this instrument still allowed for the imposition of the death penalty "in time of war or of imminent threat of war", Article 2); and 2002 Protocol No. 13 to the Convention for the Protection of Human Rights and Fundamental Freedoms, concerning the abolition of the death penalty in all circumstances.

[109] 1989 Second Optional Protocol to the International Covenant on Civil and Political Rights, aiming at the abolition of the death penalty.

latter instrument considers as non-derogable many elements of the right to fair trial, the right to habeas corpus, freedom from double jeopardy, the right to compensation for damages suffered by an indictee as the outcome of a trial in which he is found innocent, the prohibition to arbitrarily or unlawfully prevent anyone from leaving any country, including their own, or to be compelled or forbidden to reside in any part of that country, and the right to seek political asylum.

While the list of non-derogable rights is widely held to have been expanded by customary law and to include rights which go beyond the ones that are explicitly mentioned in all four of the above treaties,[110] these developments are of little consequence for our purposes. No State has in fact attempted to derogate from any of the rights that may be regarded as non-derogable under either treaty or customary international law. Moreover, no expert body or scholar has so far claimed the status of non-derogability for the rights and freedoms which have been actually suspended in times of natural or man-made disaster.

14.6 Suspending Human Rights Treaties Which Do not Envisage a Derogation Clause

A question which is central to the ascertainment of the human rights obligations of States affected by a disaster situation is whether there exists any rule of international law allowing State parties to human rights treaties not having derogation provisions to suspend their obligations under these instruments. Unlike the treaties surveyed above, the 1966 International Covenant on Economic, Social and Cultural Rights (ICESCR) and other treaties protecting both civil and political but also economic and social rights (such as the 1979 Convention on the Elimination of All Forms of Discrimination against Women, the 1989 Convention on the Rights of the Child, or the 1965 International Convention on the Elimination of All Forms of Racial Discrimination) do not contain a derogation clause. The question of whether these instruments can be suspended in emergency situations represents a legal conundrum involving complex issues of State responsibility, treaty law and the nature of the obligations they impose on State parties.[111] This part provides a brief account of possible solutions, focusing especially on economic and social rights as these are likely to be the most affected during and in the immediate aftermath of calamities.[112]

[110] See HRC, General Comment N. 29, paras 13, 15 and 16; Report of the meeting of experts on rights not subject to derogation during states of emergency, in UN Doc E/CN.4/Sub2/1995/20, pp 44–56; Siracusa Principles, NN 58–60; Paris Minimum Standards, in Lillich 1985, 1075–1081, International Commission of Jurists 1983, 440; Shraga 1986, 234–241; O'Donnell 1996, 177–189; Eboli 2010, 224–233.

[111] For an account of the different solutions offered by international organs and scholars see Eboli 2010, 42–67.

[112] See for instance the comments made by Chile, A/C.6/64/SR.20, para 28 and Thailand A/C.6/64/SR.21, para 14 during the 20th and 21st meetings of the Sixth Committee of the General Assembly in 2009.

As recalled, the absence of a derogation provision in the African Charter has prompted the African Commission to declare that the treaty remains fully applicable at all times.[113] The same conclusion was drawn by commentators with respect to the ICESCR.[114] This reading would seem in line with the *pacta sunt servanda* rule enshrined in the VCLT: if no possibility of suspension is provided by the instrument, its terms must be respected and it must be performed in good faith. Yet general international law recognizes that States may justify non-compliance with international obligations by invoking certain pleas, among which the most relevant for our analysis are *force majeure* and necessity.[115]

14.6.1 The Practice of ILO Bodies

In 1970, a Commission of Inquiry established by the ILO had to assess whether Greece was relieved from its obligations under two conventions relating to freedom of association and collective bargaining by invoking the existence of a state of emergency in the country.[116] Neither of the two instruments contains provisions authorizing derogations in situations of public emergency. In replying to the Government's claim, the Commission stated that:

> The position of pleas of emergency or necessity in international custom may be said to correspond essentially, within the peculiar framework of the international community, to the place given to pleas of *force majeure* or legitimate self-defence in national systems of law. A plea of *force majeure* generally requires a showing of irresistible force of circumstances. A plea of legitimate self-defence requires a showing both of imminent danger and of a proportionate relationship between the danger and the measures adopted for defense. Both the general principle of law derived from national practice and international custom are based on the assumption that the non-performance of a legal duty can be justified only where there is impossibility of proceeding by any other method than the one contrary to law. It must also be shown that the action sought to be justified under the plea is limited, both in extent and in time, to what is immediately necessary.[117]

A few years later, another ILO Commission used similar arguments with regard to analogous complaints brought against Poland with respect to the same

---

[113] *Supra*, n. 93.

[114] See Alston and Quinn 1987, 216–219.

[115] These excuses have been recognized by the ILC in its Draft Articles on Responsibility of States for Internationally Wrongful Acts (DARS), 2001, A/56/10, in Yearbook of the International Law Commission, 2001, Vol. II (Part Two), pp. 71–86 of the Commission's Commentary.

[116] Report of the Commission Appointed under Article 26 of the Constitution of the International Labour Organisation to Examine the Complaints concerning the Observance by Greece of the Freedom of Association and Protection of the Right to Organise Convention, 1948 (No. 87), and of the Right to Organise and Collective Bargaining Convention, 1949 (No. 98), Made by a Number of Delegates to the 52nd Session of the International Labour Conference, ILO Official Bulletin, Special Supplement, Vol. 54, No.2, 1971.

[117] Ibid., para 110.

treaties.[118] While acknowledging that Poland could in principle invoke the doctrine of *force majeure*, the expert body stressed that measures that were incompatible with the ILO Conventions could only by justified by 'circumstances of extreme gravity' and were to be 'limited in scope and in duration to what is strictly necessary given the exigencies of the situation'.[119]

Svensson-McCarthy[120] and Oraà[121] have pointed out that the two Commissions used the concepts of *force majeure* and self-defense inappropriately and that the plea of necessity is the most suitable to justify non-compliance with human rights obligations in times of emergency. The argument has some merit, as *force majeure* should only be relied upon when a State faces "an irresistible force or [...] an unforeseen event, beyond the control of the State, making it materially impossible in the circumstances to perform the obligation."[122] In other words, this excuse may be resorted to where there is no room for choosing the means to tackle the emergency and the State's only course of action is to violate its international obligation. As seen, in most crisis situations authorities are in a position to select different means and strategies to cope with the emergency and it can hardly be said that respecting a certain human right is materially impossible.[123] Instead, the plea of necessity "does not involve conduct which is involuntary or coerced",[124] but it can be invoked by a State "to safeguard an essential interest against a grave and imminent peril", and if failure to comply with its obligation "does not seriously impair an essential interest of the State or States towards which the obligation exists, or of the international community as a whole."[125] These features, along with the circumstance that necessity cannot justify non-compliance with peremptory norms of international law[126] (such as the core non-derogable human rights), prompt important authors to maintain that the principle of necessity exercises in general international law the same function derogation clauses fulfill under human rights law treaties.[127]

While this standpoint may generally be subscribed to, the possibility to rely on *force majeure* as an excuse in situations of natural disasters should not easily be

---

[118] Report of the Commission appointed under Article 26 of the Constitution of the International Labour Organisation to examine the complaints concerning the Observance by Poland of the Freedom of Association and Protection of the Right to Organise Convention 1948 (No. 87) and the Rights to Organise and Collective Bargaining Convention 1949 (No. 98), International Labour Office Official Bulletin, Special Supplement, Vol. 67, 1984.

[119] Ibid., para 479.

[120] Svensson-McCarthy 1998, 344, 348.

[121] Oraà 1992, 221–226.

[122] DARS, Article 23.

[123] Report of the meeting of experts on rights not subject to derogation during states of emergency, in UN Doc E/CN.4/Sub2/1995/20, para 27.

[124] DARS Commentary, 80.

[125] DARS, Article 25.

[126] DARS, Article 26.

[127] Ergec 1987, 53; Oraà 1992, 221.

discarded. A disaster situation squarely falls within the definition of "irresistible force" or "unforeseen event, beyond the control of the State", and its consequences may well make it materially impossible for States to perform certain human rights obligations, especially if their fulfillment imposes positive obligations requiring the provision of goods and services, as in the case of economic and social rights.[128] Oraà himself recognizes that "natural disasters correspond best with *force majeure*".[129] Describing the issue of limitations and derogations to the ICESCR, Sepulveda comments that "although the Covenant does not contain a derogation provision and makes no express provision for the case of war or other public emergencies, in extreme crisis situations a State party may refer to the notion of *force majeure* to attempt to justify not fully complying with the Covenant".[130]

Be it as it may, what can be inferred from the pronouncements of the ILO organs is that they appear to have used the principles developed by human rights treaty monitoring bodies with respect to derogation clauses to interpret the rule of impossibility to perform under ILO Conventions.[131] These are the principles of exceptionality ("irresistible force of circumstances"), of temporariness ("limited in time"), and of strict necessity/proportionality of the emergency measures implemented ("limited in extent", "proportionate relationship between the danger and the measures adopted for defence").[132] It is suggested that the same principles could be employed in assessing the suspension of human rights treaties which do not include a derogation clause.

---

[128] See Sect. 15.2.2 in this volume.

[129] Oraà 1992, 220.

[130] Sepulveda 2003, 297–298. Also admitting the relevance of *force majeure* are Rosas and Sandvik-Nylund 2001, 414. The 'Maastricht Guidelines on Violations of Economic, Social and Cultural Rights' (reprinted in 20 Human Rights Quarterly, 691–705) state in Guideline 14(f) that"[t]he calculated obstruction of, or halt to, the progressive realization of a right protected by the Covenant, unless the State is acting within a limitation permitted by the Covenant or it does so due to a lack of available resources or *force majeure*" (emphasis added). It must be recalled, however, that according to the ILC's formulation *force majeure* cannot be used as a defense where the unforeseen event "is due either alone or in combination with other factors, to the conduct of the State invoking it; or [...] the State has assumed the risk of that situation occurring". This element may call in question the relevance of the plea in certain cases of technological disaster, provided that the event can be imputed to the State.

[131] Oraà 1992, 225; Müller 2009 contending that the ILO Commission required States "to follow the same treaty law principles that are valid for derogation from the ICCPR, the ECHR and the ACHR when they wish to derogate from ILO Conventions that do not contain a derogation clause", 596–597.

[132] Oraà makes a strong argument that these principles have crystallized in rules of customary international law, Oraà 1999, 429–435.

14.6.2 Derogation from the International Covenant on Economic, Social, and Cultural Rights

The reasons for omitting a derogation clause in the text of the ICESCR are open to speculations. Alston and Quinn suggest that it could have been the result of a combination of factors, including

> (1) the nature of the rights contained in the Covenant and the fact that the case for derogation in times of emergency from, for example, the right to food or to health care would seem inherently less compelling than the case for derogation from the right to peaceful assembly or the right to vote; (2) the existence of a general limitations clause in the Covenant, unlike the approach adopted in the Covenant of Civil and Political Rights and (3) the more flexible and accommodating nature of the basic obligation contained in article 2 (1) of the Covenant.[133]

The same authors submit that the general nature of the obligation to "progressively realize" ESC rights combined with the presence of a general limitation clause allows States sufficient leeway to respond to public emergency situations.[134] However, the obligation set out in Article 2(1) of the ICESCR to achieve the full realization of Covenant rights "to the maximum of its available resources" might be heavily conditioned in the presence of disasters that severely undermine the capacity of the authorities to provide even basic assistance. It seems unrealistic to require States to fully implement all aspects of ESC rights during a disaster situation of extraordinary intensity which obliterates their material assets and seriously strains their economic and financial resources.[135] Yet, it is submitted that every suspension should be in line with the principles regulating derogations to human rights treaties.[136] Central among them is the principle that a hard core of fundamental rights is never amenable to suspension.

---

[133] Alston and Quinn 1987, 217. The limitation clause in article 4 reads: "The States Parties to the present Covenant recognize that, in the enjoyment of those rights provided by the State in conformity with the present Covenant, the State may subject such rights only to such limitations as are determined by law only in so far as this may be compatible with the nature of these rights and solely for the purpose of promoting the general welfare in a democratic society".

[134] Alston and Quinn 1987, 217–219. The redundancy of a derogation clause in ESC Rights treaties is perhaps evidenced by the fact that no State party to the European Social Charter has ever invoked article F that authorizes suspension of rights in times of public emergency, Sepulveda 2003, 294.

[135] Some commentators suggest that in situations of emergency derogations may seem appropriate at least for those rights which more closely resemble civil and political rights, i.e., the right to form and join trade unions and the right to strike, Sepulveda 2003, 296; Muller 2009, 597.

[136] See Sepulveda 2003, 302–304, providing practical examples of how the principles of non-discrimination, proportionality and conformity with the States other obligations under International law may shape the modalities of suspension of ESC rights.

14.6.3 Non-Derogability of Certain Aspects of Economic Social and Cultural Rights

Whatever stance one adopts on the precise nature and scope of the obligations imposed by the ICESCR, due consideration must be paid to the interpretation provided by its monitoring body, the Committee on Economic Social and Cultural Rights (CESCR). Interestingly, in some of its more recent General Comments the Committee points towards a rather uncompromising reading of the so-called "minimum core obligations" that States have under the Covenant.[137] These require State parties to ensure the satisfaction of minimum essential levels of each of the rights enunciated.[138] The CESCR has identified the perimeter of "core obligations" for many economic and social rights, explicitly highlighting the existence of a nucleus of non-derogable rights.[139] Core obligations can never be suspended and "continue to exist in situations of conflict, emergency and natural disaster."[140] In General Comment N. 12 on the Right to adequate food, for instance, the Committee clearly states that the progressive realization of ESC rights does not exonerate States from their duty "(…) to take the necessary action to mitigate and alleviate hunger (…) even in times of natural or other disasters."[141] A perusal of the specific obligations which constitute the core of non-derogable ESC rights has been conducted elsewhere in this book.[142] Suffice it to say that these obligations form—together with the core ICCPR rights—a nucleus of "survival rights" whose respect, protection and fulfillment must be ensured in all circumstances.[143]

It must be noted, however, that when examining compliance with the Covenant by disaster-affected States the CESCR seems prepared to show some flexibility. In describing the parameters it will be using for its review under the new Optional protocol procedure,[144] the Committee explains that these will include "the

---

[137] On the concept of "core obligations" see Ssenyonjo 2009, 65–69.

[138] CESCR, General Comment 3: The Nature of States Parties' Obligations, adopted on 14 December 1990, para 10.

[139] CESCR, General Comment N.14 on the rights to the highest attainable standard of health, adopted on 11 August 2000, para 47. See also General Comment N. 15 on the right to water, adopted on 20 January 2003, para 40.

[140] CESCR, Poverty and the International Covenant on Economic, Social and Cultural Rights, E/C.12/2001/10, 10 May 2001, para 18.

[141] CESCR, General Comment N.12 on the right to adequate food, adopted on 12 May 1999, para 6.

[142] See Sect. 15.2.2 in this volume.

[143] Rosas and Sandvik-Nylund 2001, 414.

[144] On 28 December 2008 the General Assembly adopted resolution A/RES/63/117 containing the text of an Optional Protocol to the International Covenant on Economic, Social, and Cultural Rights. Under the Protocol, individuals and groups claiming to be victims of a violation by one of the State parties to the Protocol of any of the economic, social, and cultural rights set forth in the Covenant may file a communication with the CESCR, provided that they are under the jurisdiction that State. The Protocol is not yet in force.

existence of other serious claims on the State party's limited resources; for example, resulting from a recent natural disaster or from recent internal or international armed conflict".[145] A look at the Committee's existing practice in the consideration of periodic reports confirms this approach.[146]

14.7 Conclusions

In the light of what has emerged from the above analysis, it is safe to affirm that suspension of human rights treaties by States confronting situations of natural or technological disaster is a possible occurrence, yet even in such dire situations States do not possess unfettered discretionality under international law. The relevant legal constrains are much better defined with respect to treaties on civil and political rights, as these instruments include clauses explicitly permitting the temporary suspension of certain rights in the presence of a "public emergency threatening the life of the nation". An examination of these provisions, and of the relevant jurisprudence of international bodies, has led to the definition of certain principles whose respect is essential for the lawfulness of the derogation. First among these is the principle that the menace to the State and its institutions presents a truly exceptional character such that ordinary measures do not allow the authorities to tackle it effectively. Once this element is established, further restraints define the possible courses of action. Measures derogating from conventional obligations must only be those which are strictly necessary to overcome the emergency, i.e., there must be a nexus of proportionality between the right compressed and the threat faced. In assessing this aspect, an important role is given to the establishment of effective safeguards capable of limiting the possible abuse of emergency powers. Moreover, derogatory measures cannot involve discrimination, or conflict with the derogating State's other obligations under international law. An appraisal of the latter element is a challenging task, as it requires an

[145] CESCR, An Evaluation of the Obligation to Take Steps to the 'Maximum of Available Resources' Under an Optional Protocol to the Covenant, UN Doc E/C.12/2007/1 of 10 May 2007. In one of its early General Comments the CESCR appeared inclined to condone failure to respect even the minimum core obligations, provided that a State demonstrates that "(…) every effort has been made to use all resources that are at its disposition in an effort to satisfy, as a matter of priority, those minimum obligations.", see General Comment N. 3, para 10. This discrepancy can probably be explained with the time span that separates the General Comments, over which the Committee's views on the absolute nature of at least certain obligations under the Covenant have become more entrenched.

[146] See, e.g., the Committees observations to a periodic report by Mexico, when it took note "of the natural disasters experienced by Mexico and acknowledges the limitations they impose on the Government in guaranteeing the implementation of economic, social and cultural rights to its population at all times.", CESCR, Report on the twentieth and twenty-first sessions, UN Doc. E/2000/22 - E/C.12/1999/11, para 375.

examination of both treaty law binding on the State as well as of relevant rules of general international law.

Furthermore, it is stipulated that certain rights can never be suspended, either because they are indispensable for the protection of human life and dignity or because their suspension can never be considered necessary in times of emergency. The exercise of the right to derogate is also subject to the procedural obligations of official proclamation and notification. The first guarantees that individuals are informed about the novelties introduced by the emergency regime, and that authorities do not disregard domestic legislation while implementing it. The second allows other State parties to the treaties and treaty monitoring bodies to make their own appraisal of the steps taken by the derogating State and to react accordingly. An analysis of the limited State practice concerning derogations prompted by natural catastrophes indicates that the above parameters have been generally respected.

Matters stand not much differently with respect to human rights treaties that do not include a derogation clause. While in some instances the case law of international organs upholds the stance that these instruments should remain fully applicable in times of emergency, the better view is probably that the wrongfulness of conducts incompatible with these instruments is precluded by effect of either the principle of necessity or the doctrine of *force majeure*. However, international practice and scholarly opinions support the view that the suspension of human rights treaties which are silent on their derogation should non-etheless be informed by the same substantial conditions characterizing the operation of derogation clauses. This also holds true with respect to treaties aimed at the protection of economic and social rights. While these do not contain a list of non-derogable rights, it has been shown that the notion of "minimum core obligations" developed by treaty monitoring bodies has led to the formation of a catalog of obligations that States need to respect even in emergency situations.

State practice regarding derogations to human rights treaties based on the threats posed by natural or man-made disasters is rather recent and somewhat scant. To date, neither treaty monitoring bodies nor third States have taken exception to it. Indeed, in the cases discussed resort to the derogation clauses seemed to be in compliance with the relevant procedural and substantial conditions. However, while the lawfulness of this course of action appears so far unchallenged, its desirability is more doubtful as ordinary limitations to individual rights would possibly be sufficient to tackle the effects of most disaster situations. States facing complex and urgent problems may not want to expose themselves to the risk of being found in breach of their conventional obligations and might prefer to suspend them altogether. Yet such a prudent line of action is most probably unwarranted, as legitimate interferences with individual rights would almost certainly pass muster before human rights treaty monitoring bodies, even in the absence of a derogation notice.

References

Alston P, Quinn G (1987) The nature and scope of states parties' obligations under the international covenant on economic, social and cultural rights. Hum Rights Q 9:156–229

Boisson De Chazournes L (1996) Non-derogable rights and the need to protect the environment. In: Premont D (ed) Droits intangibles et etats d'exception. Non-derogable rights and states of emergency. Editions Bruylant, Bruxelles, pp 463–476

Burgenthal T (1981) To respect and to ensure: state obligations and permissible derogations. In: Henkin L (ed) The international bill of rights: the covenant on civil and political rights. Columbia University Press, New York, pp 72–91

Cataldi G (2001) Art. 15—Deroga in caso di stato d'urgenza. In: Bartole S, Conforti B, Raimondi G (eds) Commentario alla Convenzione Europea per la tutela dei diritti dell'uomo e delle libertà fondamentali. Padua, CEDAM, pp 425–442

Chowdhury SR (1989) Rule of law in a state of emergency: the Paris minimum standards of human rights norms in a state of emergency. St. Martin's Press, New York

De Schutter O (2010) International human rights law: cases, materials, commentary. Cambridge University Press, Cambridge

Eboli V (2010) La tutela dei diritti umani negli stati d'emergenza. Giuffrè, Milan

Ergec R (1987) Les Droit de l'homme à l'épreuve des circonstances exceptionnelles—Etude sur l'article 15 de la Convention européenne des droits de l'homme. Editions Bruylant, Bruxelles

Fitzpatrick J (1994) Human rights in crisis. The international system for protecting rights during states of emergency. University of Pennsylvania Press, Philadelphia

Gross O, Ní Aoláin F (2006) Law in times of crisis: emergency powers in theory and practice. Cambridge University Press, Cambridge

Harris D, O'Boyle M, Warbrick C (1999) Law of the European convention on human rights, 2nd edn. Butterworths, London

Hartman J (1981) Derojation from human rights treaties in public emergencies. Harv Int Law J 22:1–52

Hartman J (1985) Working paper for the committee of experts on the article 4 derogation provision. Hum Rights Q 7:89–131

Higgins R (1976–1977) Derogations under human rights treaties. Br Yearb Int Law 48:281–320

International Commission of Jurists (1983) States of emergency: their impact on human rights, Geneva

Jacobs F, White R, Ovey C (2010) The European convention on human rights, 5th edn. Oxford University Press, Oxford

Joseph S, Schultz J, Castan M (2005) The international covenant on civil and political rights. Cases, materials and commentary, 2nd edn. Oxford University Press, Oxford

Kalshoven F (1989) Assistance to the victims of armed conflict and other disasters. In: Kalshoven F (ed) Assisting the victims of armed conflict and other disasters. Martinus Nijhoff, The Hague

Kiss A (1981) Permissible limitations on rights. In: Henkin L (ed) The international bill of rights: the covenant on civil and political rights. Columbia University Press, New York, pp 290–310

Lillich R (1985) The Paris minimum standards of human rights norms in a state of emergency. AJIL 79:1072–1081

Lockwood B, Finn J, Jubinsky G (1985) Working paper for the committee of experts on limitation provisions. Hum Rights Q 7:35–88

Ssenyonjo M (2009) Economic social and cultural rights in international law. Hart Publishing, Oxford

Marks S (1982) Principles and norms of human rights applicable in emergency situations: underdevelopment, catastrophes and armed conflicts. In: Vasak K, Alston P (eds) The international dimension of human rights, vol I. UNESCO, Paris, pp 175–212

Müller A (2009) Limitations to and derogations from economic, social and cultural rights. Hum Rts Law Rev 9:557–601

Novak M (2005) U.N. covenant on civil and political rights—CCPR commentary, 2nd rev ed. N.P. Engel Publisher, Kehl am Rhein

O'Donnell D (1985) Commentary by the rapporteur on derogation. Hum Rights Q 7:23–34

O'Donnell D (1996) International human rights standards concerning criminal law and procedure and derogation. In: Premont D (ed) Droits intangibles et etats d'exception. Non-derogable rights and states of emergency. Editions Bruylant, Bruxelles, pp 167–189

Oraà J (1999) The protection of human rights in emergency situations under customary international law. In: Goodwin-Gill G, Talmon S (eds) The reality of international law. Essays in honour of Ian Brownlie. Clarendon Press, Oxford

Oraà J (1992) Human rights in states of emergency in international law. Oxford University Press, Oxford

Premont D (ed) (1996) Droits intangibles et etats d'exception. Non-derogable rights and states of emergency. Editions Bruylant, Bruxelles

Questiaux N (1982) Study of the implications for human rights of recent developments concerning situations known as states of siege or emergency, Un Doc. E/CN.4/Sub.2/1982/15

Rosas A, Sandvik-Nylund M (2001) Armed conflicts. In: Eide A, Krause C, Rosas A (eds) Economic, social and cultural rights—A textbook, 2nd edn. Martinus Nijhoff, Dordrecht, pp 407–421

Sepulveda M (2003) The nature of the obligations under the international covenant on economic, social and cultural rights. Intersentia, Antwerp

Shraga D (1986) Human rights in emergency situations under the European convention on human rights. Israel Yearb Hum Rights 16:216–242

Svensson-McCarthy A (1998) The international law of human rights and states of exception. Martinus Nijhoff, The Hague

Tremblay G (1977) Les situations d'urgence qui permettent en droit international de suspendre les droits de l'homme. Les cahiers de droit 18:3–60

Tyagi Y (2011) The UN human rights committee: practice and procedures. Cambridge University Press, Cambridge

Viarengo I (2005) Deroghe e restrizioni alla tutela dei diritti umani nei sistemi internazionali di garanzia. Rivista di diritto internazionale 88:955–996

Wessels L (2002) Derogation from human rights: a possible dispensation for Africa and southern Africa. Af Yearb Int Law 27:121–139

Chapter 15
A (Human) Right to Humanitarian Assistance in Disaster Situations? Surveying Public International Law

Annalisa Creta

Abstract Current positive international law does not explicitly recognize a right to humanitarian assistance in disaster situations. The author tries to scope out the existence of such human right by carrying out a reconnoitering of hard-law instruments, a review of relevant soft-law ones and a snapshot of national practice. She also refers to authoritative doctrine on the issue. Such an examination is circumscribed to ascertaining whether such a right exists or not, for then briefly exploring the question related to its core elements by focusing on the very nature of the right (individual/collective) and trying to delineate right holders' entitlements and duty bearers' obligations using the same analytical framework applied to the right to development. She concludes that while a right to humanitarian assistance is anchored in hard law both at the conventional and customary law levels as it relates to civilians in situations of armed conflicts, the situation is not so crystal clear for those individuals victim of natural disasters in times of peace. The existence of a right to humanitarian assistance would be a sort of umbrella protection for other rights, or better a complementary entitlement to other subsistence human rights rather than a self-standing right *per se*. This is confirmed by recent human rights standard setting exercises and authoritative views of treaty monitoring bodies, which would precisely point in the direction of affirming such a right for victims of natural disasters and consider it as a set of human rights obligations.

Keywords Humanitarian assistance · Protection · Component rights, ancillary/ subsidiary right/s · Minimum core obligation/s · Complementary entitlement

---

A. Creta (✉)
Scuola Superiore Sant'Anna, Piazza Martiri della Libertà 33, 56127 Pisa, Italy
e-mail: annalisa.creta@sssup.it

A. de Guttry et al. (eds.), *International Disaster Response Law*,
DOI: 10.1007/978-90-6704-882-8_15,

Contents

15.1 Introduction

The issue as to whether a right to humanitarian assistance exists in public international law has been the object of attention in various instances in the past. The doctrine seems to be positioned on two or better three currents of thought on the specific question: those asserting that such a right exists—at least implicitly—in international law; those having a rather pessimistic view and denying its existence—in relation to the law applicable to peacetime situations and; those defining such a right not as a human rights *per se* but as a *secondary* right which comes into play when the relevant *primary* rights have been violated.

In a Memorandum prepared by the United Nations Secretariat on the protection of persons in the event of disasters for the works of the International Law Commission, the question is described as follows: 'The potential existence of a human right to humanitarian assistance during natural disasters is a *complex question.*[1] [...] [E]xisting positive law on the subject remains unclear. This situation differs markedly from the parallel question that arises during times of armed conflict, when a right to humanitarian assistance is established in conventional law'.[2]

The present chapter does not aim at reinventing the wheel but is rather meant to present an overview of the problems at stake, also in light of the recent standard setting exercises, the new soft-law instruments in place and the deliberations of United Nations legislative organs, their subsidiary organs and/or functional commissions, human rights bodies and mechanisms.

This will be done by scoping out the existence of a human right to humanitarian assistance through a reconnoitering of hard-law instruments, a review of relevant

[1] Emphasis added.

[2] A/CN.4/590, para 257.

soft-law ones and a snapshot of national practice. Such an examination will be limited to determining whether such a right exists or not, for then exploring the question related to its core elements. This latter aspect will imply an examination the very nature of the right (individual/collective) and an attempt to delineate right holders' entitlements and duty bearers' obligations using the same analytical framework applied to the right to development.

15.1.1 A Methodological Premise

The scope of the chapter is that to ascertain whether a right to humanitarian assistance does exist in public international law for victims of natural disasters. Such a task will necessarily entail a reconnoitering of relevant existing bodies of law and a review of literature on the matter. The investigation will aim at revealing whether such a right exists either explicitly or in an implicit way. The reconnoitering process will entail a phased approach: first, an analysis of hard-law instruments; second, a review of relevant soft-law ones; and finally, if and where relevant, a snapshot of national practice. The focus will also be put on authoritative doctrine on the issue.

The analysis will be circumscribed to ascertaining whether such a right exists or not, for then briefly exploring the question related to its core elements.

When referring to a right to assistance various preliminary considerations have to be made. First of all, a right to humanitarian assistance would entail that individuals meeting specific criteria enshrined in legal provisions would be entitled to receive certain services specified in the legal provisions themselves. If there is a right to receive assistance, there should also be the correlative duty to render such a service. Who are the duty bearers? From a human rights law standpoint, individuals have specific rights, and the government at stake has specific obligations to fulfill those rights. In the analysis related to the existence of a right to humanitarian assistance the rights-obligations nexus is further complicated by the role of the International Community and of third States to offer assistance and under what conditions (right/duty to offer?). Our task here is confined to the investigation related to the existence of such a right and to the identification of its core features. We will only briefly touch upon the issue of other right holders (e.g. Third States and humanitarian actors)–which is further explored in Part III of the present volume.[3]

[3] See in particular Chap. 10 by Costas Trascasas in this volume focusing precisely on the aspects related to the access to the territory of a disaster affected State. See also Chap. 3 by Zorzi Giustiniani in this volume, in her analysis related to the International Law Commission's works on "Protection of persons in the event of disasters" that *inter alia* touches upon such aspects.

15.2 Does a Right to Humanitarian Assistance Exist in International Law? Fixing the Legal Parameters

15.2.1 Terminological Clarifications First

There is no legal definition of what humanitarian assistance is and/or entails. Within the United Nations, it is generally agreed to indicate with that expression the following concept:

> Aid that seeks to save lives and alleviate suffering of a crisis-affected population. Humanitarian assistance must be provided in accordance with the basic humanitarian principles of humanity, impartiality and neutrality, as stated in General Assembly Resolution 46/182. In addition, the UN seeks to provide humanitarian assistance with full respect for the sovereignty of States. Assistance may be divided into three categories—direct assistance, indirect assistance and infrastructure support—which have diminishing degrees of contact with the affected population.[4]

As a further important specification, the terms assistance refers to:

> Aid provided to address the physical, material and legal needs of persons of concern. This may include food items, medical supplies, clothing, shelter, seeds and tools, as well as the provision of infrastructure, such as schools and roads.[5]

In the Development Assistance Committee (DAC) reporting, humanitarian aid is a sector of the Official Development Assistance (ODA) that includes: 'emergency and distress relief in cash or in kind, including emergency response, relief food aid, short-term reconstruction relief and rehabilitation, disaster prevention and preparedness. Excludes aid to refugees in donor countries.'[6]

The Principles on Good Humanitarian Donorship (GHD) adopted in Stockholm in 2003 define humanitarian assistance as follows:

> The purpose of humanitarian assistance is to save lives, alleviate suffering and maintain human dignity. For donors signing up to GHD principles, their humanitarian assistance must be allocated on the basis of need and without discrimination (impartial). It must not favour any side in a political dispute (neutral). Humanitarian objectives are autonomous from political, economic or other objectives (independent).[7]

While we will continue to use as a reference the definition adopted in 2003 by the *Institut de Droit International* (IDI), already recalled in Part I of the present volume,[8] the above definitions have been reproduced here because they will be of help in spelling out in a more detailed way the key elements of humanitarian assistance.

---

[4] OCHA 2008, 29.

[5] Ibid., 10.

[6] See ODA by sector, at http://stats.oecd.org/Index.aspx?DatasetCode=ODA_SECTOR.

[7] See Good Humanitarian Donorship (GHD), http://www.goodhumanitariandonorship.org/Libraries/Ireland_Doc_Manager/EN-23-Principles-and-Good-Practice-of-Humanitarian-Donorship.sflb.ashx. Accessed 8 February 2012.

[8] See Chap.1 by de Guttry in this volume, in particular Sect.1.2.

15.2.2 Human Rights Law

Only two international legally binding instruments applicable in any situations, so far provide an explicit reference to a right to humanitarian assistance.

The first in a chronological order is a regional instrument, namely the 1990 African Charter on the Rights and Welfare of the Child. Its Article 23 para 1 provides that State parties:

> Shall take all appropriate measures to ensure that a child who is seeking refugee status or who is considered a refugee in accordance with applicable international or domestic law shall, whether unaccompanied or accompanied by parents, legal guardians or close relatives, receive appropriate protection and humanitarian assistance in the enjoyment of the rights set out in this Charter and other international human rights and humanitarian instruments to which the States are Parties.

The same provision applies *mutatis mutandis*, as specified in para 4 of the same article, also to 'internally displaced children whether through natural disaster, internal armed conflicts, civil strife, break down of economic and social order or howsoever caused'.

The second instrument is the most recent 2006 International Convention on the Rights of Persons with Disabilities. At Article 11 it requires State parties to take:

> All necessary measures to ensure protection and safety of persons with disabilities in situations of risk, including situations of armed conflict, humanitarian emergencies and the occurrence of natural disasters.

As specified by the Committee on the Rights of Persons with Disabilities in the treaty reporting guidelines drafted for facilitating the reporting obligations for State parties to the Convention, Article 11 'obliges State Parties to ensure the protection and safety of persons with disabilities in situations of risk, such as situations resulting from armed conflicts, humanitarian emergencies or natural disasters. State Parties should report on any measures taken to ensure their protection and safety including measures taken to include persons with disabilities in national emergency protocols. State Parties should report on measures taken to ensure that humanitarian aid relief is distributed in an accessible way to people with disabilities caught in humanitarian emergency, in particular measures taken to ensure that sanitation and latrine facilities in emergency shelters and refugee camps are available and accessible for persons with disabilities.'[9]

Although the two texts refer to the reception of humanitarian assistance by persons and groups in need, their formulation does not use a *proper* (human) rights language: the wording rather puts the emphasis on States' obligations and not on

---

[9] CPRD/C/2/3, 2009, *Guidelines on treaty-specific document to be submitted by States parties under Article 35, para 1, of the Convention on the Rights of Persons with Disabilities*, 9. For an overview of States' practice in the implementation of Article 11 of the Convention refer to the States' reports available and the related concluding observations issued by the Committee accessible at http://www.ohchr.org/EN/HRBodies/CRPD/Pages/futuresessions.aspx and http://www.ohchr.org/EN/HRBodies/CRPD/Pages/Session6.aspx. Accessed 8 February 2012.

rights of individuals in need. To use the words of the International Law Commission Special Rapporteur Valencia-Ospina '[t]he nature of these provisions would, thus, seem to set public order standards for States, informed by the principle of humanity rather than that of individual rights'.[10]

At the sub-regional level, always in the African region, another instrument refers to a right to humanitarian assistance for victims of disasters. It is the agreement establishing the Intergovernmental Authority on Drought and Development (IGAD) whose Article 13-A commits members of the Organization to respect the fundamental and basic rights of the peoples of the region to benefit from emergency and other forms of humanitarian assistance and to facilitate the movement of food and emergency supplies in the event of man-made or other disasters.[11]

It is important to mention here also the 2009 Convention for the Protection and Assistance of Internally Displaced Persons (IDPs) in Africa (so called Kampala Convention—not yet in force)[12] that explicitly refer to a right to humanitarian assistance by stating that 'States shall respect the right of internally displaced persons to peacefully receive or seek protection and assistance in accordance with relevant international laws, a right for which they shall not be persecuted, prosecuted or punished'. Additionally, the 2006 Protocol on the Protection and Assistance to Internally Displaced Persons to the Pact on Security, Stability and Development in the Great Lakes region that obliges member States to adhere to the Guiding Principles on Internal Displacement indirectly crystallizes into hard law the right to humanitarian assistance contained therein.[13] Specifically, Article 3 of the Protocol is particularly relevant for our purposes. It focuses precisely on the "Responsibility for Protecting Internally Displaced Persons" and states at its para 2 that 'Member States shall, to the extent possible, mitigate the consequences of displacement caused by natural disasters and natural causes'. Paragraph 5 of same article obliges Member States to 'establish and designate organs of Government responsible for disaster emergency preparedness, coordinating protection and assistance to internally displaced persons'.[14]

For the rest, the core human rights treaties (in particular the 1966 Covenants on Civil and Political and on Economic, Social and Cultural Rights, hereinafter respectively ICCPR and ICESCR) set out rights relevant to disaster relief and recovery assistance, such as the rights to life, food and water, housing, clothing,

[10] A/CN.4/598, para 26.

[11] For the text of the agreement see http://www.iss.co.za/af/regorg/unity_to_union/pdfs/igad/AgreementEstab.pdf. Accessed 5 February 2012.

[12] The text of the Convention can be found at the following link: http://www.internal-displacement.org/8025708F004BE3B1/(httpInfoFiles)/0541BB5F1E5A133BC12576B900547976/$file/Convention(En).pdf. Accessed 5 February 2012.

[13] See Sect.15.2.4 *infra*.

[14] The text of the agreement can be retrieved at http://www.internal-displacement.org/8025708F004BE3B1/(httpInfoFiles)/29D2872A54561F66C12572FB002BC89A/$file/Final%20protocol%20Protection%20IDPs%20-%20En.pdf. Accessed 5 February 2012.

health, livelihood, and freedom from discrimination, although, with no explicit reference to a right to humanitarian assistance.

Hence, the investigation will necessary have to explore whether it can be affirmed that the right of persons in need to seek and receive protection and life-sustaining assistance is a necessary implication of the recognition, protection and promotion of such subsistence rights and—*in primis*—of the right to life.

David Fisher refers to these legal entitlements as "component rights" of the right to humanitarian assistance.[15]

As stated by the Human Rights Committee, the notion of "*inherent right to life*" cannot properly be understood in a restrictive manner, and the protection of said right requires States to also adopt positive measures[16] especially to eliminate malnutrition and epidemics.[17] In this endeavor, some have argued that States must provide life-sustaining assistance to all persons in need to protect their right to life and, the phrase "all possible measures" should be interpreted as including also acceptance of humanitarian aid to alleviate the sufferings of vulnerable groups.[18] And, this obligation would also include a duty to accept assistance from outside if the State's own resources are not sufficient to protect those in need under its jurisdiction.[19]

On the same line, the European Court of Human Rights has elaborated over the positive obligations Article 2 of the 1950 European Convention on Human Rights poses on States to take appropriate steps to safeguards the lives on those under their jurisdiction, and it has done so also for situations of disaster.[20]

In the field of subsistence rights, we can affirm that a State party to the ICESCR has additional obligations to 'take steps, individually and through international assistance and cooperation…to the maximum of its available resources, with a view to achieving progressively the full realization of the rights…'.[21] As stated by the Committee on Economic, Social and Cultural Rights (CESCR), the maximum of a State's available resources includes not only the resources existing within a State but also those available from the International Community through international cooperation and assistance.

Under Article 11 of the ICESCR, State parties also recognize the 'essential role of international cooperation'[22] for the realization of the right to an adequate standard of living, […] including adequate food, clothing and housing.[23]

---

[15] Fisher 2010, 48.

[16] CCPR, 1982, *General Comment No. 06: The right to life (Article 6)*, para 5.

[17] Ibid.

[18] Loupajarvi 2003, 693.

[19] Ibid.

[20] See European Court of Human Rights (ECtHR), *Öneryıldız v. Turkey* [GC], no. 48939/99, Judgement, 30 November 2004, para 71 ff, and; *Budayeva and Others v. Russia*, Nos. 15339/02, 21166/02, 20058/02, 11673/02 and 15343/02, Judgement, 20 March 2008, para 128–137.

[21] A/Res/2200A (XXI), Article 2(1).

[22] CESCR 1999, *General Comment No. 12, The right to adequate food (Article 11),* para 36.

[23] CESCR 1990, *General Comment No. 3, The nature of States parties obligations* (Article 2 para 1) para 13.

In the same General Comment, the Committee concluded that 'a State party in which any significant number of individuals is deprived of essential foodstuffs, of essential primary health care, of basic shelter and housing, or of the most basic forms of education is, *prima facie*, failing to discharge its obligations under the Covenant'.[24] Thus, these constitute the minimum core obligations to address survival requirements and a State must demonstrate that it has made every effort 'to use all resources that are at its disposition in an effort to satisfy, as a matter of priority, those minimum obligations'.[25] Violations of the right to food can occur, *inter alia*, through 'the prevention of access to humanitarian food aid in internal conflicts or other emergency situations'.[26]

Amongst the determinants of the right to health, as enshrined in Article 12 of the Covenant, is a right to medical care. Its para 2 requires States to take steps for the 'prevention, treatment and control of epidemic, endemic, occupational and other diseases' as well as '[t]he creation of conditions which would assure to all medical service and medical attention in the event of sickness'. In elaborating on the right to health and its components under Article 12, the Committee, in its General Comment 14 directly addresses the issue of humanitarian assistance by underlining that:

> States parties have a joint and individual responsibility, in accordance with the Charter of the United Nations and relevant resolutions of the United Nations General Assembly and of the World Health Assembly, to cooperate in providing disaster relief and humanitarian assistance in times of emergency, including assistance to refugees and internally displaced persons. Each State should contribute to this task to the maximum of its capacities. Priority in the provision of international medical aid, distribution and management of resources, such as safe and potable water, food and medical supplies, and financial aid should be given to the most vulnerable or marginalized groups of the population.[27]

Those statements can be easily applied to victims of disasters in the situations where States either deny or limit access to health services or foodstuff provided by international organizations or prevent such activities from taking place on their territory.[28]

Indeed, treaty bodies authoritative views would favor the existence of a right to humanitarian assistance as a corollary of the mentioned subsistence rights; a right which would entail the obligation for the duty bearer to accept international assistance when unable or unwilling to provide basic necessities to their population

[24] Ibid., para 10.

[25] Ibid.

[26] CESCR 1999, *General Comment No. 12*, para 19.

[27] CESCR 2000, *General Comment No. 14, The right to the highest attainable standard of health* (Article 12) para 40.

[28] Loupajarvi specifies in this regard that CESCR 'has been much more explicit in articulating the obligations of States in relation to subsistence rights such as the right to health or food and it seems that economic and social rights provide a stronger argument for a duty to accept assistance […] than does the right to life'. See Loupajarvi 2003, 698.

on its own.[29] In particular, such an obligation to accept external aid has been articulated in relation to the right to food.[30]

15.2.3 International Humanitarian Law

Yoram Dinstein insists that the assertion that 'the right to humanitarian assistance is vouchsafed by binding norms of international law (customary or conventional)'[31] is only true 'in certain contexts of armed conflict'.[32] In this regard, provisions relevant to humanitarian assistance can be classified into three clusters:

(a) Belligerents' duties *vis-à-vis* the civilian population;
(b) Civilians' right to humanitarian assistance
(c) Relief from the outside (*alias* stemming from third Parties).[33]

As a general premise, it is to be recalled that in armed conflict situations (both internal and international), the issue of humanitarian assistance chiefly arises in relation to the indispensable needs of the civilian population. Consequently, humanitarian assistance and relief are mainly confined to civilians and, relief consignments only include essentials.

Article 49 of the 1949 Convention Relative to the Protection of Civilian persons in Time of War (hereinafter GC IV) provides at para 3 that '[t]he Occupying Power undertaking … transfers or evacuations shall ensure, to the greatest practicable extent, that proper accommodation is provided to receive the protected

---

[29] In order to have a comprehensive account of core human rights applicable in disaster situations through a vulnerable group approach, see Chap.16 by Bizzarri; while a detailed analysis of minimum core human rights applicable in emergiencies situations is developed in Chap. 14 by Sommario in this volume.

[30] CESCR 1999, *General Comment No. 12, passim.* This aspect has been further examined by the International Law Commission when commenting on Article 10 of the text of the Draft Articles on the Protection of Persons in the Event of Disasters. Such article relates to the existence of a duty of the affected State to seek assistance. In this regard, the Commission 'considers that the duty to seek assistance in draft Article 10 derives from an affected State's obligations under international human rights instruments and customary international law. Recourse to international support may be a necessary element in the fulfillment of a State's international obligations towards individuals where an affected State considers its own resources are inadequate to meet protection needs. While this may occur also in the absence of any disaster, a number of human rights are directly implicated in the context of a disaster, including the right to life, the right to food, the right to health and medical services, the right to the supply of water, the right to adequate housing, clothing and sanitation, and the right to be free from discrimination'. On this see, A/66/10 Supplement n. 10, 262.

[31] Dinstein 2000, 77.

[32] Ibid.

[33] A comprehensive examination of the main features related to the first and third cluster of provisions is illustrated in Chap. 11 by Venturini and in Chap. 10 by Costas Trascasas in this volume.

persons, that the removals are effected in satisfactory conditions of hygiene, health … and nutrition.'

In parallel, Article 17 (1) of Additional Protocol II applicable in non-international armed conflicts provides that in those cases where 'displacements have to be carried out, all possible measures shall be taken in order that the civilian population may be received under satisfactory conditions of shelter, hygiene, health … and nutrition'. Moreover, during armed conflicts, States must fulfill their obligation to provide the highest attainable standard of physical and mental health by giving medical attention to the wounded and sick,[34] by seeking, permitting, and facilitating the passage of medical supplies and by ensuring the safety of medical workers.[35] Occupying powers are responsible for ensuring that local populations have food[36] and starvation as a method of warfare is prohibited.[37]

The Fourth Geneva Convention further recognizes the right of protected persons to make application to the protecting powers, the ICRC or a National Red Cross or Red Crescent Society, as well as to any organization that might assist them (Article 30 GC IV). The Commentary to the Convention specifies in this regard that '[t]he fact that the new Convention grants civilians war victims a formal and absolute right to appeal to supervising and relief agencies, a facility which up till then had depended solely on the goodwill of the Parties to the conflict, is of great significance; the certainty of being able to avoid isolation, of being able to establish contact with impartial charitable agencies, together with the hope of sympathy and relief in cases of distress, is psychologically most valuable to protected persons for the moral support it gives them'.[38]

The Additional Protocols implicitly recognize the entitlement of a civilian population in need to receive humanitarian relief as they require that relief actions "shall be undertaken" whenever a population is in need (AP I Article 70 (2) and AP II Article 18 (2)). *Common* Article 3 does not explicitly mention humanitarian assistance although it requires the parties to the conflict to treat protected persons, including civilians, *humanely*, to collect and take care of the wounded and sick and that 'an impartial humanitarian body, such as the ICRC, may offer its services to the parties to the conflict'.

[34] The relevant articles are Articles 16, 55, 56 of GC IV, Common Article 3, Article 10 of AP I, Article 7(2) and 8 of AP II.

[35] The relevant provisions are Articles 23, 50(5), 56 of GC IV; Articles 12–17 of AP I; Articles 9 and 10 of AP II.

[36] Article 55 of GC IV.

[37] Article 54(1) of AP I; Article 14 of AP II, Article 8 (2) (b) (xxv) of the International Criminal Court (ICC) Statute.

[38] ICRC, Commentary to Article 30 para 1 of 1949a, Convention (IV) relative to the Protection of Civilian Persons in Time of War.

In relation to the right to humanitarian relief of the civilian population, the ICRC has also derived a general customary law rule applicable both in international and non-international armed conflicts: Rule 55.[39]

As for relief from third parties, there are several provisions of international humanitarian law dealing with the position of the recipient State with regard to relief actions: namely Article 59 GC IV (applicable in occupied territories), Article 70 of Additional Protocol I of 1977 and Article 18 of Additional Protocol II concerning situations of non-international armed conflicts. According to the agreed understanding of the three provisions, there is an obligation for the recipient State to accept relief when all or part of its civilian population is inadequately supplied.[40]

It is also to be recalled that international humanitarian law instruments are further detailed in specifying elements of a right to relief also as it relates to another category of protected persons, namely prisoners of war. Indeed, the Third Geneva Convention contains very meticulous provisions related to the right to receive relief supplies as far as this category of right holders is concerned, elements which can play a complementary role in an attempt to identify core elements of a right to relief.

Articles 72 and 73 of the above-mentioned instrument indeed elaborate on the individual right of war prisoners to receive "relief shipments" both individually and collectively.

Article 72, in particular, establishes that '[p]risoners of war shall be allowed to receive by post or by any other means individual parcels or collective shipments containing, in particular, foodstuffs, clothing, medical supplies and articles of a religious, educational or recreational character which may meet their needs [...]'.[41]

15.2.4 Soft Law

An attempt to find additional explicit reference to a right to humanitarian assistance brings us to turn to soft-law instruments—and to instruments "even softer than soft law".[42]

---

[39] Rule 55 states that 'the parties to the conflict must allow and facilitate rapid and unimpeded passage of humanitarian relief for civilians in need, which is impartial in character and conducted without any adverse distinction, subject to their right of control'. See Customary IHL Study, Rule 55, available at: http://www.icrc.org/customary-ihl/eng/docs/v1_rul_rule55, accessed 1 September 2011.

[40] For additional details on these precise aspects refer to Chaps. 10 and 11 respectively by Costas Trascasas and Venturini in this volume.

[41] As specified by the ICRC Commentary to said articles, 'individual relief consists of parcels sent by a donor to a prisoner of war, the latter being designated by name. Collective relief is sent to prisoners of war either in standard anonymous parcels, or in the form of bulk shipments'. ICRC, Commentary to the Convention (III) relative to the Treatment of Prisoners of War. Geneva, 12 August 1949, 351 ff.

[42] This expression has been used by Kälin to define the legal nature of the Guiding Principles on Internal Displacement. See Kälin 2001, 6.

The Vienna Declaration and Programme of Action[43] adopted by the World Conference on Human Rights in Vienna on 25 June 1993 make such a reference. At para 23, '[i]n accordance with the Charter of the United Nations and the principles of humanitarian law, the World Conference on Human Rights further emphasizes the importance of and the need for humanitarian assistance to victims of all natural and man-made disaster' and, while focusing on armed conflict situations, at para 29 it 'reaffirms the right of the victims to be assisted by humanitarian organizations, as set forth in the Geneva Conventions of 1949 and other relevant instruments of international humanitarian law, and calls for the safe and timely access for such assistance.'

In the United Nations Millennium Declaration, member States of the organization affirm that they 'will spare no effort to ensure that children and all civilian populations that suffer disproportionately the consequences of natural disasters, genocide, armed conflicts and other humanitarian emergencies are given every assistance and protection so that they can resume normal life as soon as possible.'[44]

General Assembly resolutions on the issue of humanitarian emergency assistance and disasters related issues, have been constantly putting the focus on the primary responsibility to provide relief for the State concerned and on States' duties to assist rather than on individuals' right to be assisted. A cautious approach has also been taken *vis-à-vis* the existence of a sort of duty for the affected State to accept offers of humanitarian assistance. The United Nations legislative organ has repeatedly reaffirmed the primary responsibility of the concerned State to face emergencies occurring within its national borders.[45] The only emphasis on the recipients of assistance has been put while referring to the fact that 'humanitarian assistance is of cardinal importance for the victims of natural disasters and other emergencies'[46] and when declaring that the abandonment of victims of such situations without humanitarian assistance 'constitutes a threat to human life and an offense to human dignity'.[47] Instead of asserting a right of individuals to receive assistance, the Assembly's resolutions implicitly recognize a right of States, IGOs and NGOs to offer humanitarian assistance to other States in case of disaster and similar emergencies and they support the view that such offers do not constitute an

[43] A/CONF.157/23.

[44] A/Res/55/2, para 26.

[45] In General Assembly resolution 43/131 entitled *Humanitarian assistance to victims of natural disasters and similar emergencies,* the Assembly recognized 'that it is up to each State first and foremost to take care of the victims of natural disasters and similar emergency situations occurring on its territory' and reaffirmed also 'the sovereignty of affected States and their primary role in the initiation, organization, coordination and implementation of humanitarian assistance within their respective territories.' See A/Res/43/13.

[46] See A/Res/46/182, Annex.

[47] See A/Res/43/131 and A/Res/45/100.

unlawful interference in the internal affairs of these States.[48] However, they also reaffirm that the right of external actors to provide such assistance in other States depends on the consent of these States.

In conclusion, the care of victims of natural disasters is a primary responsibility of the affected State and external humanitarian assistance should be provided with the consent of the State concerned and in principle on the basis of an appeal by the same State. This rule has been expressly evoked in resolution 46/182 of the General Assembly on the *Strengthening of the Coordination of Humanitarian Emergency Assistance* where in para 3 of the Annex, the principle that assistance should be supplied only in response to an appeal from the affected State and with respect for its territorial is underlined.[49]

Nonetheless, the same member States have not always been so state-centric. Indeed, if we refer to the already mentioned Principles and Rules for Red Cross and Red Crescent Disaster Relief or to the 1994 Doha Declaration on Priorities for progressive Development of International Law in the United Nations Decade of International Law to meet the Challenges of the 21st century,[50] States have affirmed through those documents that the right of victims to humanitarian assistance should be reaffirmed as a basic human right. The Doha Declaration further specifies 'The right to humanitarian assistance implies the right of access of victims to potential donors and access of qualified national and international organizations and other donors to the victims in conformity with the relevant international instruments. Humanitarian assistance, both as regards those granting and those receiving it, should always be provided in conformity with the principles inherent in all humanitarian activities, and the principles of humanity, neutrality and impartiality'.

In the *2005 Hyogo Declaration* and the *2005–2015 Hyogo Framework for Disaster Reduction* States have acknowledged their responsibility to protect their populations in the event of a disaster and to mitigate the effects thereof through risk reduction. In particular para 4 of the Declaration affirms that:

> States have the primary responsibility to protect the people and property on their territory from hazards, and thus, it is vital to give high priority to disaster risk reduction in national policy, consistent with their capacities and the resources available to them. [...] [S]trengthening community level capacities to reduce disaster risk at the local level is especially needed, considering that appropriate disaster reduction measures at that level enable the communities and individuals to reduce significantly their vulnerability to hazards.

48 On this aspect, the ICJ in the case *Concerning Military and Paramilitary Activities in and Against Nicaragua* observed that 'there can be no doubt that the provision of strictly humanitarian aid to persons or forces in another country, whatever their policy objectives, cannot be regarded as unlawful intervention, or as in any way contrary to international law. The characteristics of such aid were indicated in the first and second of the fundamental principles declared by the 20th International Conference Red Cross'. See, International Court of Justice (ICJ), *Case Concerning Military and Paramilitary Activities in and Against Nicaragua*, Merits, 27 June 1986, in *Reports 1986*, 124.

49 See A/Res/46/182, Annex.

50 The text is available at http://www.asil.org/un21/5qatar.htm. Accessed 2 February 2012.

> Disasters remain a major threat to the survival, dignity, livelihood and security of peoples and communities, in particular the poor. Therefore there is an urgent need to enhance the capacity of disaster- prone developing countries in particular, the least developed countries and small island developing States, to reduce the impact of disasters, through strengthened national efforts and enhanced bilateral, regional and international cooperation, including through technical and financial assistance.[51]

In parallel, the Framework for Action stresses that '[...] each State has the primary responsibility for its own sustainable development and for taking effective measures to reduce disaster risk, including for the protection of people on its territory, infrastructure and other national assets from the impact of disasters'.[52]

These two documents are far-reaching insofar as they make a clear link between the responsibility of States and the protection of their population in the event of disaster (responsible sovereignty or sovereignty as a responsibility) although they restate the State-centric approach to disaster prevention and management by putting emphasis on States' role and avoiding to refer to victims' rights and needs, thus watering down what affirmed in other fora and crystallized in other documents.

The 1998 United Nations Guiding Principles on Internal Displacement make explicit reference to humanitarian assistance in several of their provisions. In particular, Principles 3(1), and 25 (1) are relevant in this regard by restating that 'the primary duty and responsibility for providing humanitarian assistance to internally displaced persons lies with national authorities'. But humanitarian assistance is not only a duty in the Guiding Principles and Principle 3(2) specifies that IDPs have a right to humanitarian assistance and are entitled to request it without fear of being victims of reprisals or persecutions.[53] Furthermore, other principles set out the scope of such a right by elaborating on its content/components: Principle 10 links it to the right to life, while Principle 18 focuses on the right to an adequate standard of living, including essential foodstuff and drinking water, housing and basic shelter, fundamental medical services and sanitation, adequate clothing. Principle 19 instead recalls the right to medical care and the need to undertake any effort to prevent contagious and infectious diseases.

The Principles and Rules for Red Cross and Red Crescent Disaster Relief provide at Principle 2.1. that 'the Red Cross and Red Crescent in its endeavor to prevent and alleviate human suffering, considers it a fundamental right of all people to both offer and receive humanitarian assistance'.[54] On a similar vein, the Mohonk Criteria state that 'everyone has the right to request and receive humanitarian aid necessary to sustain life and dignity from competent authorities or local, national or international governmental and non-governmental organizations' and call upon the States members of the United Nations to 'recognize the

---

[51] ISDR 2005a, para 2.

[52] ISDR 2005b, para 4.

[53] Fisher 2010, 50.

[54] The text of the Principles is available at http://www.ifrc.org/docs/idrl/I280EN.pdf. Accessed 2 February 2012.

right to humanitarian assistance and the responsibility to provide it'.[55] Additionally, the resolution on humanitarian assistance adopted in Bruges on 2 September 2003 by the Institute of International Law specifies 'leaving the victims of disaster without humanitarian assistance constitutes a threat to human life and an offense to human dignity and therefore a violation of fundamental human rights. The victims of disaster are entitled to request and receive humanitarian assistance'.[56] Also the Guiding Principles on the Right to Humanitarian Assistance, adopted by the Council of the International Institute of Humanitarian Law in April 1993 contain analogous concepts.[57]

15.2.5 Core Aspects of a Right to Humanitarian Assistance

If we agree that humanitarian assistance is a set of human rights obligations, or a corollary of several subsistence rights, the next step is to delineate, to the extent possible, the core aspects of such right. Is it like any other human rights, in which the duty holders are national governments and the rights holders are individuals and/or groups? Or, is it a diverse situation, implicating different rights-bearers and different duty holders? And, what are the main obligations upon duty bearers to guarantee the respect of the right for right holders?

As for the first set of questions, the following aspects come into play.

In relation to *rights holders,* the right to humanitarian assistance is surely a right of individuals. Can it be also considered a collective right of all peoples, victims of natural disasters? Some have affirmed the dual nature of the right by stating that '[t]he aim of this right is to empower individuals or people to seek humanitarian assistance, to have access to it and to receive it. This right generates the duty, in the framework and as circumscribed by legal and physical possibilities, to offer such assistance and to put no hindrances or obstacles in the way of its provision. In the same way as the right is both individual and collective, the corresponding duty

[55] The text of the *Mohonk Criteria for Humanitarian Assistance in Complex Emergencies*, adopted in 1995 by the Task Force on Ethical and Legal Issues in Humanitarian Assistance set up in 1994 by the Program on Humanitarian Assistance at the World Conference on Religion and Peace can be found at http://repository.forcedmigration.org/show_metadata.jsp?pid=fmo:2934, accessed on 30 August 2011.

[56] Institute of International Law, *Humanitarian Assistance—Resolution*, Bruges 2003/3, 2 September 2003, section II o.p. 1–3, available at http://www.idi-iil.org/idiE/resolutionsE/2003_bru_03_en.PDF, Accessed 15 September 2011.

[57] Principle 1 reads as follows: 'Every human being has the right to humanitarian assistance in order to ensure respect for the human rights to life, health, protection against cruel and degrading treatment and other human rights which are essential to survival, well being and protection in public emergencies'. See IIHL, *Guiding Principles on the Right to Humanitarian Assistance,* available at www.iihl.org/iihl/Album/GUIDING%20PRINCIPLES.doc, Accessed 30 August 2011.

is an obligation laid on all human beings, the State and the international community'.[58]

However, almost all the instruments where the right is openly provided for—except for the already mentioned Agreement establishing the IGAD—only focus on the individual aspect of the entitlement, thus not putting emphasis on its group dimension. Whenever a collective right has been affirmed and recognized, this dimension had been explicitly spelled out either in soft and/or hard-law instruments, but this is not the case, so far, for a right to humanitarian assistance—for which, however a solidarity spirit cannot be, in principle, denied. Such aspect is here deliberately left aside since there are no elements to further explore the collective nature of the right—while its individual dimension is not rebuttable.

Always in relation to *rights holders*, it is legitimate to ask whether the right to humanitarian assistance entitles other States/entities to offer humanitarian assistance. The rights—obligations nexus in relation to this right to humanitarian assistance, as already underlined, is complicated by the role, always in terms of rights and duties, of third States and other humanitarian actors. It cannot be denied that such entities have a right to offer assistance, under certain circumstances, and to a certain extent also a duty to do so. Henceforth, State obligations under this right include not only obligations of individual action with regard to individuals within the affected State's jurisdiction (classical nexus rights/duties under human rights law), but also obligations of individual action with regard to individuals outside of the State's jurisdiction (role of third States in humanitarian emergency situations) and in certain cases also obligations of collective action at regional/global level.

All this entails different types of obligations. By using the same analytical framework applied to the right to development in order to depict its core elements, we can try to classify obligations stemming from the right to humanitarian assistance as individual/internal, individual external and collective obligation of States.[59] The first type of obligations relates to how each State should act nationally with regards to his people in situations of natural disasters. On a similar note, the second category of obligations indeed insists on rights/duties of the State vis-à-vis individuals and peoples in other countries in situations of natural disasters. The collective dimension of the obligation would entail collective actions at the level of the International Community as such, involving for instance the role of the Security Council in disasters situations, processes put in place by States at the multilateral level to ensure the right at stake is guaranteed.[60]

After having established who the right holders are, an analysis of the main obligations entailed by the right to humanitarian assistance is necessary in order to

[58] Gross Espiell 1995, 19.

[59] See A/HRC/15/WG.2/TF/CPR.5, para 57 ff.

[60] On this aspect, reference should be made to Chap. 10 by Trascasas in this volume, which precisely focuses on rights and duties of States, in particular third States in situations of natural disasters.

identify the core elements of such a right. It is precisely through an analysis *a contrario* of the main obligations upon duty bearers that is possible to delineate the legal entitlements such right would grant to individuals in situations of natural disaster. This task can be carried out through the lens of the right to food and the other subsistence rights recalled in subsection 2.2, which provide for a conducive framework against which to found the core elements of the right to humanitarian assistance.

As for the economic, social and cultural rights, State obligations in relation to humanitarian assistance can be clustered into three categories: the obligation to *respect*, the obligation to *protect* and the obligation to *fulfill*. In turn, the latter includes an obligation to *facilitate* and an obligation to *provide*. This is the classification endorsed by the CESCR in its General Comment 12.

First of all, as stated by the CESCR, the obligation to *respect* existing access to adequate food requires State parties not to take any measures that result in preventing such access.[61] This is applicable in both natural and man-made disasters.[62]

The obligation to *protect* requires measures by the State to ensure that third parties do not deprive individuals of their access to adequate food.[63] It requires the adoption of measures by the State to ensure that third parties (e.g. individuals, non-State actors, business companies, etc.) do not deprive right holders of their access to adequate food. Under the obligation to protect, the State could be held accountable for violations of the right to adequate food committed by non-State actors.[64]

The obligation to *fulfill* (*facilitate*) means the State must engage in a proactive way in activities intended to strengthen access to and utilization of resources and means to ensure individuals' livelihood, including food security.[65] The obligation to facilitate implies that States adopt measures finalized at improving right holders' access to and use of resources to ensure their living. The obligation to facilitate also applies in natural and man-made emergency situations, for instance with regard to the facilitation of transit of humanitarian consignments.[66]

Whenever an individual or group is unable, for reasons beyond their control, to enjoy the right to adequate food by the means at their disposal, States have the obligation to *fulfill* (*provide*) that right directly. This obligation also applies for

---

[61] CESCR *General Comment No. 12*, para 15.

[62] FAO 2002, 27 ff.

[63] Ibid.

[64] Various judgements and reports issued by international human rights bodies (although with regard to other human rights) held States responsible because of the lack of due diligence to prevent the violation [committed by non-State actors] or to respond to it. With specific regard to the right to adequate food, CESCR listed among the examples of violations the 'failure to regulate activities of individuals or groups so as to prevent them from violating the right to food of others' (See *General Comment 12*, para 19). See also FAO 2002, 31.

[65] CESCR, *General Comment No. 12*, para 15.

[66] FAO 2002, 32.

persons who are victims of natural or other disasters.[67] The obligation to provide entails that the State, as a last resort, must provide food 'whenever an individual or group is unable, for reasons beyond their control, to enjoy the right to adequate food by the means at their disposal'.[68]

In a nutshell, a right to humanitarian assistance would entail protection actions by duty bearers aimed at stopping or preventing harm; at ensuring access for victims of disaster to relevant goods, services and opportunities; at ensuring that affected persons can claim their rights and; at combating discrimination. This summarizes what goes under the heading of a human rights-based approach to humanitarian assistance in situations of natural disaster.

A human right to humanitarian assistance would therefore involve the entitlement of individual victims of natural disaster to receive and have access to relief without discrimination of any kind on the basis of race, color, sex, language, religion, political or other opinion, national or social origin, property, birth, age, disability or other status. It would involve ensuring that, at a minimum, persons affected by disasters have a right to have access to or be provided with essential food and water; basic shelter and housing; appropriate clothing and the right to receive essential medical services and sanitation.[69]

15.3 The Academic Debate: Deniers, Advocates and 'Alternatives'

The debate over the existence of a right to humanitarian assistance in public international law is a lively one, recently revamped thanks to the attention the International Law Commission is paying to the issue of the protection of persons in the event of disasters. The doctrine is clearly divided into three main currents: those who deny the existence of such a right, even in an implicit way; those who assert the opposite advocating that there exist a human right to humanitarian assistance, and; the *alternatives*, *alias* those who refer to humanitarian assistance not as a human right *per se* but in terms of secondary right which only comes into play when the individuals' primary rights have been violated.

In the year 2000, Yoram Dinstein affirmed: 'It is impossible to assert, at the present point that a general right to humanitarian assistance has actually crystallized in positive international law. Such a general right, had it consolidated, could be invoked in all circumstances: in peacetime (either in the face of endemic problems of famine, malnutrition, and disease, or—perhaps especially—when

[67] Ibid.

[68] Ibid., 33.

[69] See in relation to a human rights-based approach to humanitarian assistance in situations of natural disasters the IASC Operational Guidelines on Human Rights and Natural Disasters, IASC 2011.

natural disasters occur) as well as in the course of armed conflicts (either international or internal). In reality, however, there is no clear-cut right under existing international law to humanitarian assistance in peacetime, not even when natural disasters strike.'[70]

Peter MacAllister-Smith shares a similar position when he affirms that '[a] legal right to humanitarian assistance already exists in certain restricted circumstances... [h]owever, extending the right to humanitarian assistance to the situations of greatest need is a difficult task which remains to be achieved'.[71]

Rohan Hardcastle and Adrian Chua do express skepticism *vis-à-vis* the idea of considering the right to humanitarian assistance as an existing one and as a human right. Such perplexity is anchored to the human rights standard setting process dynamics. Indeed they point out that '[a]scertaining whether victims of natural disasters have a right to receive humanitarian assistance in international law is problematic because it raises fundamental questions relating to the development of international human rights. In recent years, there has been a tendency on the part of United Nations organs and other international organizations to proclaim new "human rights" without giving adequate consideration to their desirability, their scope or the viability of their implementation. Although it has long been recognized that to continue to be relevant, human rights as a concept must respond to the changing needs and perceptions of individuals and the international community, the need for dynamism must be balanced against the equally important need to preserve the integrity and credibility of human rights as a 'common standard of achievement for all peoples and all nations'.[72]

Kent adds that it seems that 'there is no hard duty to provide international assistance based on explicit rights of the needy to receive assistance. There should be not only a right but also an obligation to provide international humanitarian assistance under some circumstances. In 1988 the French proposed a General Assembly resolution for disaster relief based on explicit recognition of the rights of the needy to receive assistance. That aspect disappeared by the time Resolution 43/131 of December 8, 1988 was finalized'.[73]

Heike Spieker in a recent publication on the matter concludes that '[t]here is no consistent approach to address a right of victims of non-conflict disasters to receive the best and most appropriate assistance; resolution 4 of the 30th International Conference of the Red Cross and the Red Crescent only states that the International Red Cross and Red Crescent Movement considers it' a fundamental right of all people both to offer and receive humanitarian assistance'.[74]

---

[70] Dinstein 2000, 77.

[71] Macallister-Smith 1988, 224–225.

[72] Hardcastle and Chua 1998, available at http://www.icrc.org/eng/resources/documents/misc/57jpjd.htm accessed on 19 September 2011.

[73] Kent 2000, 13.

[74] Spieker 2011, 29.

Nigel Rodley affirms that 'it seems clear [...] that there is no right to humanitarian assistance or that, even if there ought to be one and if there were in fact one, it would not be a human right.'[75] Rodley considers such a possibility as redundant and argues that 'human rights have already been flouted when a person is in this situation. And it hardly seems useful [...] to suggest that another human right has been violated, namely, the right to receive assistance'.[76]

The arguments used by Rodley to deny the existence of a right to humanitarian assistance as a human rights are indeed used by the proponents of such a legal entitlement as a human right insofar as they consider several human rights to be the "*component* rights" of that to humanitarian assistance.

David Fisher points out that '[b]eyond the few relief-specific provisions, there are a number of other human rights treaties and instruments that address what can be seen as component rights of the right to humanitarian assistance. Those component rights include the rights to life, food and water, housing, clothing and medical care'.[77]

In the same vein, Benton Heath points that humanitarian assistance is strictly linked to the individual right to life. He anchors such a statement to the interpretation the Human Rights Committee gives of the right to life as having 'both positive and negative dimensions, implying that a State must take affirmative measures to protect the lives of people on its territory'.[78] Also, he asserts that, '[w]hile the right to life may indicate some minimal right to assistance, economic and social rights create the legal space for individuals to demand the full range of humanitarian aid'.[79] Finally he considers that recent trends in human rights law to contemplate an explicit right for victims to receive relief represents a tendency of the International Community which seems to move forward toward the recognition of a distinct right to request and receive humanitarian assistance (e.g. the African Charter on the Rights and Welfare of the Child and the International Convention on the Rights of Persons with Disabilities, *supra*).[80]

An alternative voice in this debate where one takes the deniers' or the advocates' side is represented by the position expressed, in 1995 by Marie-José Domestici-Met who invited to consider the right to humanitarian assistance not as a human right *per se* but as a 'sort of procedural substitution for human rights. Just as there is a right to reparation, there is a right to assistance, if the primary rights are not fulfilled and are violated'.[81]

Although there are isolated examples of humanitarian assistance as a self-standing human right in international treaties, current international law seems

---

[75] Rodley 1995, 146.

[76] Ibid., 151.

[77] Fisher 2010, 53.

[78] Heath 2011, 439.

[79] Ibid., 440.

[80] Ibid., 441.

[81] Domestici-Met 1995, 88.

to rather entail specific obligations related to the access to humanitarian assistance. In this vein part of the doctrine advocating for the existence of such right, supported by General Comments of relevant Treaty Bodies, considers the right to receive humanitarian assistance in situations of need as an integral part of other human rights enshrined in international treaties (*supra*). Since human rights law already obliges States to protect a range of rights, which are equally applicable in disaster situations—humanitarian assistance would be a further corollary for the protection of such rights. This is the approach taken by the Inter-Agency Standing Committee in its Operational Guidelines on the Protection of Persons in Situations of Natural Disasters which grounds the basis for humanitarian assistance in a set of universally accepted human rights, thus opting for a human rights-based approach to help protect persons in situations of natural disasters.[82] This is also the position expressed by the then Secretary General Kofi Annan who defined access to humanitarian assistance and protection, or humanitarian access as 'an essential *subsidiary* or *ancillary* right that gives meaning and effect to the core rights of protection and assistance'.[83]

15.4 A Snapshot of States' Practice

An overview, although incomplete, of States' practice is the next step to follow to help solving the conundrum over the existence of a right to humanitarian assistance for victims of natural disasters. Such a reconnoitering entails an overview of relevant internal and external acts of States.

If we look at national legislation on disaster management, several countries contemplate in their legal framework specific provisions related to the rights of victims of disasters and in particular some of those refer to a right to humanitarian assistance, a right to receive aid from State's authorities and also fix the conditions for getting international assistance.

For instance, in Indonesia, the Law No. 24 of 2007 concerning Disaster Management explicitly grants—at Article 26 para 2—'[a]nybody affected by disaster [...] the right to receive aid for basic necessities'.

The Law of the Republic of Armenia on Population Protection in Emergency Situations of 2 December 1998 grants such a right in an indirect way by embodying it in the measures encompassing the concept of population protection.

The Disaster Relief Act of Japan has the precise purpose 'to protect victims of disaster and maintain social order by causing the Central Government to provide needed relief services on an emergency basis in cooperation with Local Public

[82] IASC 2011.

[83] S/1998/883, para 15. Emphasis added.

Entities and the Japan Red Cross, other entities, and the people of Japan'.[84] Its Article 23 further spells out in a concrete way the content of the right of assistance for victims of disaster by providing a precise list of items to distribute and, of services to set up.

Those countries which have proceeded to a domestication of the Guiding Principles on Internal Displacement by embodying them into their national legal frameworks—and which consider as IDPs in national laws also those persons fleeing due to natural disasters[85]—have codified in a direct or indirect way a right of internally displaced persons to apply for protection and assistance. As an example for all, the national IDPs legal framework of Azerbaijan contemplates a right to assistance *inter alia* in the Law on the Status of Forcibly Displaced Persons and in the Law on Social Protection of Forcibly Displaced Persons.[86]

The Ugandan National Policy for Internally Displaced Persons of August 2004 recalls the UN Guiding Principles on Internal Displacement as an instrument to be taken into account in implementing the policy itself thus embodying in national law the right of IDPs to request and receive humanitarian assistance. Furthermore, its chapter III spells out in a concrete way the content of such a right to assistance (and related to food security, shelter, clothing, education, health, water and sanitation, resettlement kits, rehabilitation of infrastructures…).

A landmark standpoint clarifying the existence and the extent of the right to humanitarian assistance for victims of forced displacement (also caused by disasters) in national law is that of the Constitutional Court of Colombia which, in its sentence T-830/09 elaborates on such right by stating, among others, the following:

> […] la asistencia humanitaria (…)se inscribe en esta tendencia del derecho internacional público que propende por la colaboración, auxilio y asistencia de los más pobres, incluyendo ayuda en casos de desastres naturales, hambruna, terremotos, epidemias y conflictos armados internos. La asistencia humanitaria responde al principio, al derecho y al deber de solidaridad que pretende la realización de derechos fundamentales del ciudadano incurso en una situación catastrófica y que encuentran su fundamento en principios constitucionales tales como el Estado Social de Derecho, la dignidad humana, y en derechos fundamentales que se encuentran íntimamente ligados como la vida, la dignidad humana, mínimo vital, la salud, la vivienda, entre otros.
>
> (…) debe ser entendida como un derecho radicado en cabeza de la población civil, consistente en la facultad de reclamar del Estado la ayuda necesaria para salir de la situación de emergencia en la que se encuentran los ciudadanos como consecuencia de causas naturales o humanas.

---

[84] Article 1 of the Disaster Relief Act of Japan (Law No. 108, 1947). The unofficial translation of the text of such law is available at http://www.hiroi.iii.u-tokyo.ac.jp/index-genzai_no_sigoto-jakusha-kyujohoE.htm. Accessed 2 February 2012 .

[85] Thus endorsing the definition of IDP contained in the Unitd Nations Guiding Principles.

[86] Veliyev and Asadov 2003, 280.

> (...) Con la asistencia humanitaria se pretende mejorar las condiciones mínimas de existencia de las víctimas a fin de satisfacer los derechos que fueron menoscabados y mitigar o impedir la agravación o la extensión de los efectos de los mismos. La asistencia humanitaria busca "satisfacer necesidades de carácter general de la población, en particular aquellas relacionadas con los derechos a los que la Constitución les atribuye un carácter social o cuya prestación origina gasto público social".[87]

On the international arena, the position of States has not been as linear as that crystallized in various national legislations and domestic case law. Indeed during the debates within General Assembly, States have always underlined the necessity to respect the principle of sovereignty in the delivery of humanitarian assistance and have preferred to put an emphasis on States' rights and duties in situation of disasters rather than on victims' entitlements. And, the debate in the Sixth Committee over the reports of the International Law Commission in relation to the item of the protection of victims of natural disasters, has shown how still differing are the positions both in relation to a recognition of the right of individuals to receive assistance and *vis-à-vis* the duties of States to accept offers of aid from the outside.

This shows that there is still no consolidated *opinio iuris* on the topic. States are still reluctant to affirm the existence of a right of victims of disasters to request and receive humanitarian assistance. In 1998, France tried to insert wording related to the right of victims to receive assistance in a draft resolution on assistance to victims of natural disasters[88] but the final draft tabled did not contain such language anymore—a clear signal that such a reference represented an obstacle to a consensus resolution, hence it was simply deleted.

Nowadays, the situation is still the same. Iran for instance clearly declared in the Sixth Committee that it was not convinced of the relevance of a right based approach to the protection of victims of disasters which seemed to imply that 'an affected State must accept international assistance, whereas in State practice assistance had always been provided in response to a request or authorization on the part of the affected State and was intended to supplement, rather than substitute for, action by the affected State. An affected State was obliged to assist its own population in the event of a disaster and was entitled to ensure the coordination of relief measures and to receive aid, upon request, from other States and from intergovernmental organizations. It was not, however, obliged to accept all the

[87] Corte Constitucional de Colombia, *Sentencia T-830/09*, para 6 ff, accessible at http://www.corteconstitucional.gov.co/relatoria/2009/T-830-09.htm, accessed 29 September 2011. It should be noted that with the expression *"poblaciòn civil"* the Constitutional Court did not intend to affirm that a right to humanitarian assistance is limited to the civilian population. In various other passages of the sentence, when elaborating on such a right, the Court uses wording such as "population, citizens, individuals" thus not intending to restrict the entitlement to such right only to a segment of the population. Such an expression is to be justified against the general issues at stake in the sentence itself, which related to the right to humanitarian assistance of victims of political violence in the context of the internal situation of Colombia.

[88] *Supra*, Sect. 15.3.

offers of assistance that might be forthcoming, and it could indeed refuse an ill-intentioned offer.'[89]

On the same line, China remained doubtful about the viability of a rights—or needs-based approach to the topic of protection of persons in the event of disasters [...] which inter alia 'implied that individuals were in a position to appeal for international disaster relief. In short, it not only lacked a legal basis in international law but might also contravene the principles of sovereignty and non-interference in internal affairs.'[90]

On a different note, France invited the Commission to focus 'more clearly on the rights and duties of the State in respect of both its own people, and third States and international organizations in a position to cooperate in the provision of protection. It would then be necessary to mention the rights of disaster victims, which would be consistent with the rights-based approach'.[91] Also Denmark, Finland, Iceland, Norway and Sweden were in favor of examining 'the rights and obligations of the affected State or States and of other relevant actors in addition to the rights and needs of the victims. The starting point for discussion should be the principles of solidarity and cooperation.'[92]

Again, always in relation to the works of the International Law Commissions on the protection of victims of disaster, some States have expressed views in relation to the emphasis on the topic given by the Commission by suggesting to substitute the word "protection" on the title of the relevant agenda item with the term "assistance", thus implying a change in the Commission's perspective in tackling the question and a shift in focus…more on needs and less on victims' legal entitlements.[93]

This represents in a nutshell the portrait of a debate still aligned along two opposite blocks: on one side those States considering the issue of humanitarian assistance only a matter of horizontal relationship between States and those which also put emphasis on the vertical interplays with obligations of States toward victims of disasters as subjects entitled to receive assistance and protection.

15.5 Concluding Remarks: The Right(s) to Humanitarian Assistance

A right to humanitarian assistance is anchored in hard law both at the conventional and customary level as it relates to civilians in situations of armed conflicts.

---

[89] A/C.6/64/SR.22, para 80.

[90] A/C.6/64/SR.20, para 21.

[91] A/C.6/64/SR.21, para 19.

[92] A/C.6/64/SR.20, para 7.

[93] Two of the countries at stake are Iran (Islamic Republic of) (A/C.6/64/SR.22, para 80) and the United Kingdom (A/C.6/64/SR.20, para 39).

The situation is not crystal clear for those individuals victim of natural disasters in times of peace. Indeed a patchwork of provisions scattered in various conventional and soft-law instruments would rather point toward the existence of a right to humanitarian assistance as a sort of umbrella protection for other rights, or better as a complementary entitlement to other subsistence human rights.

Even in such an endeavor, there are gray areas vis-à-vis the content of such an ancillary right and its meaning which would necessarily be twofold thus entailing the victims' right to receive assistance and third parties' right to assist said victims.

Recent human rights standard setting exercises go in the direction of affirming such a right for victims of natural disasters. Clear outputs in this regard are represented by Article 11 of the 2006 International Convention on the Rights of Persons with Disabilities or Article 9 of the Kampala Convention of 2009, which, although not yet in force, does affirm a right for internally displaced persons to seek humanitarian assistance and protection. Also human rights Treaty bodies' general comments on relevant human rights provisions seem to confirm that humanitarian assistance is part of those minimum core obligations enshrined in several economic, social and cultural rights to address survival requirements in situations of distress and also represents a positive obligations of States in relation to their duty to protect the inherent right to life.

Also, at the policy level, the Inter-Agency Standing Committee Operational Guidelines on the Protection of Persons in Situations of Natural Disasters—which embrace a human rights-based approach—do refer to humanitarian assistance in terms of legal entitlements. The Principles contained in group A and B are those composing the 'the right(s) to Humanitarian Assistance'. Indeed Group A and B of the Guidelines indicate its component rights: namely the rights related to protection of life; security and physical integrity; the protection of family ties in the context of evacuations; and those rights related to the provision of food; health; shelter; and education. This set of rights is to ensure that survivors of the disaster receive life-saving humanitarian assistance, particularly during the emergency phase.

This approach confirms the trend toward considering humanitarian assistance as a set of human rights obligations and not as a self-standing right. However, States' practice is not so linear, thus not helping to confirm such trend. Even if national legislations in many instances do refer to humanitarian assistance as a victims' right, external acts of States in various endeavors do rather put emphasis on the horizontal relationships it entails instead of on the vertical relation between duty bearer (the State) and right holder (the individual).

It will be interesting to see the approach the International Law Commission will embrace when analyzing duties of States vis-à-vis victims of disasters and when tasked with the identification of the latter ensuing related rights and redress avenues in case of violations.

References

Dinstein Y (2000) The right to humanitarian assistance. Nav War Coll Rev LIII(4):77–92
Domestici-Met MJ (1995) Interventions des partecipants. UNESCO, Le droit à l'assistance humanitaire: actes du Colloque international organisé par l'Unesco, SHS-95/Conf.85/6, pp 79–89
FAO (2002) The right to adequate food in emergencies, FAO Legislative Study 77. http://www.fao.org/DOCREP/005/Y4430E/Y4430E00.HTM
Fisher D (2010) The right to humanitarian assistance. In Kalin W, Williams RC, Koser K, Solomon A (eds) Incorporating the guiding principles on internal displacement into domestic law: issues and challenges, studies in transitional legal policy No. 41, 47–128
Gross Espiell H (1995), Legal bases of the right to humanitarian assistance, in UNESCO, Le droit à l'assistance humanitaire: actes du Colloque international organisé par l'Unesco, SHS-95/Conf.85/6, 11–21
IASC (2011) Protecting persons affected by natural disasters, IASC operational guidelines on human rights and natural disasters. http://ochanet.unocha.org/p/Documents/Operational%20Guidelines.pdf
ICRC (1949a) Commentary to the convention (III) relative to the treatment of prisoners of war. Geneva, 12 August 1949. http://www.icrc.org/ihl.nsf/WebList?ReadForm&id=375&t=com
ICRC (1949b), Commentary to convention (IV) relative to the protection of civilian persons in time of war. Geneva, 12 Aug 1949. http://www.icrc.org/ihl.nsf/WebList?ReadForm&id=380&t=com
ICRC, Customary law study. Customary IHL database. http://www.icrc.org/customary-ihl/eng/docs/v1_rul_rule55
IIHL (1993) Guiding principles on the right to humanitarian assistance. www.iihl.org/iihl/Album/GUIDING%20PRINCIPLES.doc
Institute of International Law (2003) Humanitarian assistance–resolution, Bruges 2003/3. http://www.idi-iil.org/idiE/resolutionsE/2003_bru_03_en.PDF
ISDR (2005a) Hyogo declaration, world conference on disaster reduction 18–22 January 2005, Hyogo, Japan. http://www.unisdr.org/2005/wcdr/intergover/official-doc/L-docs/Hyogo-declaration-english.pdf
ISDR (2005b) Hyogo framework for action 2005–2015: building the resilience of nations and communities to disaster, World conference on disaster reduction 18–22 January 2005, Hyogo, Japan. http://www.unisdr.org/we/coordinate/hfa
Hardcastle R, Chua A (1998) Humanitarian assistance: towards a right of access to victims of natural disasters. Int Rev Red Cross no. 325:89–609
Heath JB (2011) Distaster relief and neglect; the duty to accept humanitarian assistance and the work of the international law commission, N Y U J Int'l L.& Pol 43:419–477
Kälin W (2001) How hard is soft law? The guiding principles on internal displacement and the need for a normative framework, paper presented at the roundtable meeting Ralph Bunche institute for international studies, CUNY Graduate Center, 19 December 2001. http://www.brookings.edu/fp/projects/idp/articles/Kaelin12-19-01.pdf
Kent G (2000) The right to international humanitarian assistance. www2.hawaii.edu/~kent/assistance3.doc
Loupajarvi K (2003) Is there an obligation to accept humanitarian assistance to internally displaced persons under international law? Int J Refug Law 15(4):678–714
Macallister-Smith P (1988), The Right To Humanitarian Assistance In International Law. Revue de Droit International de Science Diplomatiques et Politiques 66:211–233
OCHA (2008) Reliefweb glossary of humanitarian terms. http://reliefweb.int/sites/reliefweb.int/files/resources/4F99A3C28EC37D0EC12574A4002E89B4-reliefweb_aug2008.pdf
Rodley N, (1995) Interventions des partecipants, in UNESCO, Le droit à l'assistance humanitaire: actes du Colloque international organisé par l'Unesco, SHS-95/Conf.85/6, 146–152

Spieker H (2011) The right to give and receive humanitarian assistance, In: Heintze HJ, Zwitter A (eds) International law and humanitarian assistance. Springer, Berlin, pp 7–31

Veliyev I, Asadov E (2003), Report on the guiding principles on internal displacement and the law of the republic of Azerbaijan. In: Cohen R, Kalin W, Mooney E (eds) The guiding principles on internal displacement and the law of the South Caucasus, studies in Transitional legal policy No. 34, 267–336

A/66/10, Report of the international law commission on the work of its sixty-third session: Supplement No. 10, 3 Oct 2011

A/CN.4/590, Protection of persons in the event of disasters, Memorandum by the Secretariat, 11 Dec 2007

A/CN.4/598, Preliminary report on the protection of persons in the event of disasters by Mr. Eduardo Valencia-Ospina, Special Rapporteur, 5 May 2008

A/C.6/64/SR.20, Sixth committee, summary record of the 20th meeting, 30 Oct 2009

A/C.6/64/SR.21, Sixth committee, summary record of the 21st meeting, 30 Oct 2009

A/C.6/64/SR.22, Sixth committee, summary record of the 22nd meeting, 2 Nov 2009

A/HRC/15/WG.2/TF/CPR.5, Bringing theory into practice: operational criteria for assessing implementation of the international right to development, Consultants report, 14 Jan 2010

S/1998/883, Report of the united nations secretary general on protection for humanitarian assistance to refugees and others in conflict situations, 22 Sept 1998

Chapter 16
Protection of Vulnerable Groups in Natural and Man-Made Disasters

Mariangela Bizzarri

Abstract Disasters do not affect all people evenly. Some people end up paying a higher price due to pre-existing conditions that influence their vulnerability. Among the key factors that determine how people are affected by disaster and able to cope with it are gender, age, disability, race, or ethnicity. Thus, women, children, older persons, people with disability and minorities, and indigenous groups are widely recognized as particularly vulnerable and in need of specific protection in disaster situation. Protection of vulnerable groups is grounded in various international human rights laws and standards. For each category of vulnerable population this chapter offers an overview of the main protection concerns commonly found in both man-made and natural disasters, the normative frameworks that provide for their protection as well as a review of the practice in disaster situations. The analysis reveals inconsistencies in relation to the amount and the extent to which international norms are actually applied across the whole disaster management cycle, that result in significant disparities in the way the needs and concerns of different categories of people are recognized and addressed. Among all, older people have received the least attention, followed by persons with disability, minorities, and indigenous groups. Lack of disaggregated data that provide evidence and guide response to the different needs and constraints different people face is one of the biggest challenges to the protection of vulnerable groups in disaster situations. Overall, despite significant advances in the past years, sensitivity to diversity and inclusiveness continues to be mostly a theoretical commitment rather than a practice in disaster management.

M. Bizzarri (✉)
GenderConsult, Milan, Italy
e-mail: mariangela.bizzarri@genderconsult.org

A. de Guttry et al. (eds.), *International Disaster Response Law*,
DOI: 10.1007/978-90-6704-882-8_16,

Keywords Protection · Vulnerabilities · Human rights · Women · Children · Older people · Persons with disabilities · Minorities and indigenous groups

Contents

16.1 Introduction

In the aftermath of a disaster, people find themselves injured, separated from their families, without a shelter, and with limited or no access to basic goods and services. Institutions and the rule of law may be weakened and unable to cope with the catastrophe left behind. Besides material loss, the lawlessness and chaos that follow disasters often leave people at risk of human rights violations and abuses. Among the most common human rights challenges in disaster situations are: lack of safety; unequal access to assistance and discrimination; abuse of children and women; forced relocation; lack of reparation and restitution; family separation, whose effects can be particularly dire on children, older persons, and persons with disabilities, among others.

The earthquakes, hurricanes, and tsunamis of recent years highlight that protection from exploitation, discrimination, and other forms of human rights abuses and violations is as important as the provision of relief. Human rights abuses further undermine people's resilience[1] as well as their ability to contribute more effectively to, and benefit fully from the opportunities offered by recovery and transition. Yet, in the rush to provide for basic needs, less attention is often

[1] Though increasingly used in the humanitarian and development spheres, there is still no accepted definition of the term 'resilience' across different disciplines. According to FAO, resilience is the ability of a system, community, or society exposed to hazards to resist, absorb, accommodate, and recover from its effects in a timely and efficient manner, including through the preservation and restoration of its essential basic structures and functions (FAO 2011).

devoted to the need for human rights protection, with negative implications for the effectiveness and long-term impacts of humanitarian response.[2]

Despite the growing attention to disasters in the last decades, it is only since mid-1990s that, recognizing the differential impact of disasters on the affected population, there has been a proliferation of studies and researches on the social, economic, and cultural factors that expose different groups within the society to different levels of risk in relation to disasters.[3] As a result, disasters are now recognized as the product of the multiple interactions between hazards, vulnerabilities, and people's coping capacity.[4]

Unfortunately, disaster figures are still for the most part not disaggregated by sex, age, and other socioeconomic factors, thus making it difficult to fully grasp the differential impact of hazards on communities and societies.[5] According to a recent study, there are almost no documented cases of collection, analysis, and use of disaggregated data across sectors of humanitarian response.[6] Lack of data disaggregated by age and sex impairs the identification of who needs what and where, and makes prioritization difficult, thus limiting the effectiveness and efficiency of disaster response. Moreover, attention to the social, cultural, and economic vulnerabilities of certain groups is rarely reflected in global disaster risks assessments.[7] This generally hampers understanding the impacts of disasters on different groups such as women, children, or older people, and impedes adequate planning.

This chapter is an attempt to illustrate the multiple human rights challenges vulnerable groups can face in disaster situations and the laws and principles that are relevant for their protection. As such, only those provisions that are aimed at addressing human rights challenges that are particularly common in disaster

---

[2] For example, human rights violations in the aftermath of the 2004 tsunami in South East Asia were widespread, and included discrimination in the provision of assistance, unequal access to aid, sexual and gender-based violence (GBV), and forced relocation of groups of people. Inadequate attention to the rights of poor, African American, the elderly, and the immigrants flawed the response to the strike of Katrina in US in 2005. http://www.brookings.edu/opinions/2010/0113_haiti_ferris.aspx. Accessed 14 September 2011. The Committee on the Rights of the Child (CRC), the Committee on the Elimination of Discrimination against Women (CEDAW), and the Committee on the Rights of Persons with Disabilities (CRPD) issued a joint statement after the 2010 Pakistan floods because discrimination in accessing relief aid and registration were found against minority communities, Afghan refugees, women, children and persons with disabilities. http://acelebrationofwomen.org/?p=30279. Accessed 14 September 2011.

[3] Just to cite an example, a contributing factor to the increased attention to women and gender roles and relations in general in disaster situations was the UN designation of the 1990s as the International Decade for Natural Disaster Reduction.

[4] Wisner 2009.

[5] See for example http://gar-isdr.desinventar.net/ and the International Disaster Database http://www.emdat.be/database. Accessed 14 September 2011.

[6] The study focuses on activities in the sectors of Agriculture/Food Security, Education, Emergency Shelter, Health and Water and Sanitation, and includes conflicts and natural disasters. See Mazurana et al. 2011.

[7] For example, vulnerable groups are not mentioned either in UNISDR 2009 or UNISDR 2011.

situations will be discussed in details. Within them, a choice was made to mainly focus on international norms and standards because of their applicability in any context, while regional and country-specific laws will be cited only when relevant.

16.2 Concepts and Frameworks

16.2.1 Protection

For protection to become a concern in disaster situations, violations, abuses, and neglect of rights should originate from the actions (and lack thereof) of a responsible party—individual/s, groups, or institutions. Protection risks are a function of the hazard, people's level of vulnerability, and the capacity they can put in place to cope with the threat they are facing, as per the following risk equation:

$$\text{Risk} = \frac{\text{Hazard} \times \text{Vulnerability}}{\text{Capacity}}$$

The length of exposure to the hazard also determines the seriousness of the risk. Experience has shown that the longer the effects of a disaster last (for example long-term displacement), the greater the risk of human rights violations.

Extensive consultations among some 50 humanitarian, human rights, and academic organizations in the late 1990s resulted in the following working definition of protection:

> 'All activities aimed at ensuring full respect for the rights of the individual in accordance with the letter and the spirit of the relevant bodies of law (i.e. human rights law, international humanitarian law and refugee law).'[8]

Activities can be conducted at three interdependent and interconnected levels: (1). *responsive*: to prevent, end the abuse, or alleviate its immediate effects; (2). *remedial*: to restore people's dignity and well being through reparation, restitution, and rehabilitation; and (3). *environment building*: to create a social, cultural, institutional, legal, and economic environment that is conducive to the full respect of human rights.[9] Non-discrimination on the basis of race, national, or ethnic origin, language, or gender lies at the heart of all protection activities.[10]

Protection does not only refer to securing the survival and physical *safety* of people, rather it is a much broader concept that also encompasses concerns for people's *dignity* and *integrity* as human beings. For example, though setting standards of minimum protection that are general enough to be valid for all, human

---

[8] Giossi Caverzasio 2001, 19.

[9] ICRC 2008.

[10] ALNAP 2005, 33.

rights allow sufficient flexibility to protect and respect cultural diversity and integrity, thus applying to the protection of persons belonging to ethnic, religious, or linguistic minorities.

Some questions help further clarifying the term protection and its application in the context of disasters. The first question is '*protection from what?*' Three sources of violations and abuses are generally indicated: *violence, coercion and deprivation. Violence* or the threat of it is a common cause of suffering for people in disasters. Factors like the breakdown of law and order, the temporary cessation of services, and the disruption of social and family support mechanisms make *violence* very likely to burst out.[11] Examples of violence that may occur in disaster situations are gender-based violence (GBV),[12] which includes domestic violence, sexual abuse, and trafficking; killing; cruel, inhuman, and degrading treatment, and violence related to the distribution of and access to humanitarian aid, among others.[13]

Rights are violated also when people are forced to do something against their will. This is the case of *coercion.* Forced prostitution, sexual slavery, sexual exploitation, forced labor, forced displacement or return, restriction of movement, prevention of return or forced relocation are all examples of coercion that can occur in the event of a disaster.[14]

Finally, *deprivation* refers to preventing people from accessing basic goods and services they need for their survival and well being. In disaster situations, people may experience deliberate assaults on their assets; possessions may be stolen; denied access to land and markets; deliberate discrimination in access to basic goods and services. These deprivations are all deliberate violations and abuses of a person's rights.

While referring to other chapters of this volume for a detailed response to the question '*who is responsible to protect?*'[15] few things need to be said here about those organizations that are specifically mandated to provide for the protection of particular aspects or specific groups of the population. Among them, the International Committee of the Red Cross (ICRC) is specifically mandated to protect prisoners of war and persons affected by armed conflict; the Office of the High

[11] WHO 2005, 1.

[12] GBV is an umbrella term for any harmful act that is perpetrated against a person's will, and that is based on socially ascribed (gender) differences between males and females. The term highlights the gender dimension of these acts that, while committed more often against women and girls, can also be experienced by boys and men. Some of the forms of GBV that may be found in disaster situations include domestic violence, sex trafficking, forced marriage, and sexual coercion. IASC 2005. GBV has been assumed to be a constituent part of protection globally. Under the UN Humanitarian Reform, UNFPA and UNICEF are mandated to coordinate efforts for the prevention of and response to GBV in emergency contexts under the Protection Cluster.

[13] See Rayner 2010 and Grant 2010.

[14] See Reyes, Charles 2010.

[15] See Chaps. 3, 10 and 12 respectively by Zorzi Giustiniani, Costas Trascasas and Mancini in this volume.

Commissioner for Human Rights (OHCHR) is responsible to promote and protect human rights; the United Nations High Commissioner for Refugees (UNHCR) works with States for the protection of refugees in their territories; the United Nations Children's Fund (UNICEF) is mandated to ensure the protection of children. Moreover in 1999, the then United Nations Secretary-General Kofi Annan asserted the UN's commitment to the protection of rights and called on all UN agencies to incorporate protection and human rights into all UN programming.[16]

Besides the State and the international community, people themselves are critical actors. Protection is something people themselves struggle for, before, during, and after any external intervention by national authorities or the international community. Thus, supporting and empowering individuals and communities in their ability to assert and claim their rights, and fostering people's resilience is at the core of any protection intervention.

One last question relates to '*who is in need of protection*' in disaster situations. While everybody is entitled to protection, there are groups of people who are understandably more vulnerable than others and require specific attention. This chapter focuses on them and the factors that make certain groups among the population particularly vulnerable in disasters.

16.2.2 Vulnerability Factors

'Vulnerability defines the characteristics of a person or group and their situation that influence their capacity to anticipate, cope with, resist and recover from the impact of a hazard'.[17] Development, governance, and power inequalities are casual factors of vulnerability. As such vulnerability precedes the event, and contributes to its severity on the affected population. A proper understanding of the vulnerabilities and their impacts on the population of concern is critical to prevent, mitigate, and respond to the human rights challenges people may face in disaster situations.

Women, children, people with disabilities, older people, and persons belonging to minorities or indigenous groups are generally regarded as particularly vulnerable in disaster situations. These groups are often at greater risk of sustaining losses and suffering, and the same vulnerabilities they experience prior to the disaster are usually amplified during and after the event had occurred.

While gender, age, ethnicity, and disability are the key vulnerability factors commonly taken into account in the event of a disaster, other aspects such as socioeconomic status and geographic location can contribute to make certain groups more in need of protection than others. For instance, a wealthy family

---

[16] UN 1997, 63–65.

[17] Wisner et al. 2004, 11.

living in a highly earthquake-resistant building will not be vulnerable to a small-scale earthquake. Similarly, a poor family living in a house with zero earthquake precautions far away from the epicenter will enjoy the same level of safety. In general however, regardless of their age, sex, or ethnicity, poor people are more likely to live in environmentally degraded areas, have less chances to accumulate assets and savings to buffer against shocks, as well as to regain them after a hazard, they hold low level of education which hinders their access to disaster preparedness activities and to early warnings, have no access to decision-making processes to express their needs in the preparedness phase; they have less adaptive capacity, and usually enjoy less legal and financial protection.[18] Loss of income opportunities and livelihoods following a disaster further increases the vulnerability of already poor people. While not suggesting that poverty, marginalization, and vulnerability should be regarded as synonymous, it is however important to consider how all these factors interrelate with each other in disasters for adequate protection to be ensured.

Finally, it is important to mention that certain groups may face additional vulnerabilities as a result of their status in the disaster-affected country. These are internally displaced persons, refugees and migrants. Among the challenges they may face are further displacement, loss of documentation, insecurity about their status, fear of forced resettlement, and lack of access to assistance.

16.2.2.1 Intersectionality

Vulnerability is a complex combination of interrelated, mutually reinforcing and dynamic factors. The relationships among different factors can be multifaceted and combine to define different levels of vulnerability. Although often treated indiscriminately in documents and reports, vulnerable groups are all but homogeneous. Not only the causes of vulnerability for women are different from those of children, but also persons within the same group do not necessarily experience the same level of vulnerability. For instance, while it is generally recognized that women are more vulnerable to sexual assaults in disaster situations, some are *de facto* more at risk than others. Among them are for example those whose family members have died following the disaster and have no mean to protect themselves in case of an assault, or those who relocated to a particularly dangerous area.[19]

The principle of non-discrimination defines the multi-layered vulnerabilities within and between different groups, and within the social structure. Again with reference to women, when gender discrimination intersects with discrimination

---

[18] See also IFRC 2010, 121; Anderson 2001.

[19] While assisting the displaced populations in the (Koshi) flood-affected districts of Sunsari and Suptari in Eastern Nepal in 2008, information gathered by the author suggested that women and girls living in temporary shelters located at the edge of the main road were more at risk of assault by strangers and people passing by than those accommodated far away.

based on ethnicity, race, age, socioeconomic conditions or disability, vulnerabilities and risks are multiplied.[20]

The goal here is not to create multiple typologies of vulnerable people but to show that there is a wide variety of scales of interaction between different vulnerabilities that combine to create relevant categories of people at risk. Among them, internally displaced, migrants and refugees can be seen as overarching groups within which to further identify vulnerabilities caused by gender, age, disability, and so forth. Furthermore, gender and age typically act as adds on to other vulnerabilities. It is in fact widely recognized that women and children, across class, caste, and ethnicity, whether migrants or refugees, are often more vulnerable among the affected population. Just to cite few examples, women and children with disabilities are often more at risk of sexual and other forms of violence than male adults with disability. In some minority's and indigenous' communities, women's health and rights are often marked down in the name of cultural identity, for example when harmful traditional practices are performed.[21] When women do migrate, they may be exposed to hazardous jobs, gender discrimination, and trafficking. Similarly, older persons with disabilities are more at risk of neglect and abandonment by both their families and the society as a whole than adult.[22]

In conclusion, vulnerability factors should not be considered in isolation, rather a holistic approach is essential to grasp the multifaceted set of interrelationships that illustrates how elaborate vulnerability can be. Such a holistic approach is also reflected in laws and policies that recognize the special vulnerabilities of, for example, indigenous elders, women, children, and persons with disabilities (articles 21–22 of the Declaration on the Rights of Indigenous People)[23]; disabled children (article 23 of the Convention on the Right of the Child[24] and article 7 of the Convention on the Rights of Persons with Disabilities)[25]; women with disabilities (article 6 of the Convention on the Rights of Persons with Disabilities) among others.

---

[20] For example, in Vietnam traditional customs and practices and language barriers contribute to the lack of knowledge about their rights among women belong to ethnic minorities. Socialist Republic of Vietnam 2005, 6.

[21] See MRG 2011, 11–12.

[22] Women's Refugee Commission 2008, 4.

[23] 2007 United Nations Declaration on the Rights of Indigenous People.

[24] 1989 Convention on the Rights of the Child.

[25] 2006 United Nations Convention on the Rights of Persons with Disabilities.

16.2.3 Legal and Policy Framework

Human rights provide a framework to analyze the vulnerability of people affected by natural and man-made disasters and the standards for appropriate and non-discriminatory humanitarian assistance to those in needs. The protection of people in disasters is grounded in the universal principles of humanity and non-discrimination as well as in a set of universally recognized human rights standards. Disasters *per se* do not discriminate. Yet, the consequences are not the same for all those affected, rather they are often determined by discrimination patterns that pre-exist the hazard and undermine the ability of certain groups to resist, accommodate, and recover from it.

This explains why special attention is generally granted to particular categories of the population such as women, children, older people, persons with disabilities, and members of minorities and indigenous groups by measures aimed to prevent, mitigate, and respond to the negative effects of a disaster. Understanding the international legal framework relevant to the needs and risks associated with disasters is the first step for ensuring people's protection.

It is important to reiterate that there is no universal treaty comprehensively regulating disaster situations. While certain aspects such as telecommunication, customs, or transport of emergency goods in situations of disaster are governed by specific international norms, for others the practice has rather been the inclusion of *ad hoc* rules in already existing treaties for application in disasters coupled with heavy reliance on soft-law instruments.[26]

This however, does not mean that the protection of persons affected by disasters rests in a legal vacuum. Domestic law is the principal legal framework for upholding the rights of persons affected by disasters within the country's territory.[27] As each legal system is unique, the laws of specific States are not considered in this chapter. In addition, irrespective of specific nationality and vulnerability, disaster-affected people are entitled to the rights and freedoms recognized by international human rights law[28] that apply to all at all times, without discrimination as to age, gender, ethnic origin, disability, language, religion, political, and other opinion, and so on. While for disasters in areas affected by an armed conflict, international humanitarian law provides a further source of legal protection.[29]

---

[26] See Chap. 1 by de Guttry in this volume, Sect. 1.7.

[27] Harper 2009, 18.

[28] This includes the Universal Declaration of Human Rights and the two Covenants on Civil and Political Rights, and Economic, Social and Cultural Rights, as well as a series of more specific treaties that will be discussed more in detail in the remaining of the chapter. For a comprehensive analysis on the role of Human Rights Law in disaster situations, refer to Chap. 15 by Creta in this volume.

[29] International Law Commission 2008, A/CN.4/598 para 22. See also Chap. 11 by Venturini in this volume.

A rights-based approach also offers the means for addressing the protection needs and concerns of migrants in destination countries hit by a disaster.[30] Evidence from various disasters in fact points to patterns of discrimination, exclusion and abuse against migrants. For example, both the Latino and the Burmese migrants in the aftermath of the Hurricane Katrina in the USA and the Indian Ocean Tsunami in Thailand, respectively faced issues such as lack of access to assistance, fear of arrest and deportation, and lack of recognition of the migrant status, among others.[31] As far as refugees are concerned, as long as they are lawfully hosted in a country hit by a disaster, they are entitled to the same treatment with respect to public relief and assistance as is accorded to nationals.[32]

In sum, in the absence of a specific convention or international treaty regulating natural or man-made disasters,[33] or specific reference to disaster situations in existing treaties, human rights and other relevant provisions of international law provide the legal framework for the protection of affected people, including particularly vulnerable groups.[34]

Besides treaty law which will be further discussed with reference to each category of vulnerable populations, there are a number of non-binding texts including resolutions, declarations, guidance, and rules and regulations (UN and others) that address protection issues in disasters.[35] Though non-binding, these tools reflect agreed upon standards by States, regional organizations, or the United Nations for the protection of rights in disaster situations.

While relying on other chapters of this book for a detailed discussion of soft-law instruments applicable in disaster situations,[36] two deserve to be mentioned here for their relevance in relation to vulnerable groups. These are the 1998 Guiding Principles on Internal Displacement[37] and the 2011 Inter-Agency

[30] Migration triggered by a disaster, both out and into disaster-affected areas, is not discussed here as the complexity of the phenomenon would require not only contextualizing the debate, but also a comprehensive overview of all the possible typologies of disaster-induced migration (voluntary vs. forced, temporary vs. permanent, internal vs. international, and so on) and the protection concerns therein. Adding to the complexity is the current unsolved debate on whether a refugee-like status should also be granted to disaster-related migrants. For a discussion of these and other relevant aspects of the migration—environment nexus see also IOM 2009.

[31] IOM 2009, 285.

[32] Article 23 of the 1951 Convention Relating to the Status of Refugees. See Chap. 2 by Venturini in this volume, Sect. 2.7. Other relevant sources of law that apply to disaster situations are detailed in Chap. 1 by de Guttry in this volume.

[33] International Law Commission 2007, A/CN.4/590.

[34] See Harper 2009, 48–70.

[35] International Law Commission 2007, A/CN.4/590.

[36] See Chap. 2, Sect. 2.6 by Venturini in this volume. See also Chap. 24 by Calvi Parisetti, Sect. 24.3.1; Chap. 20 by De Siervo, Sect. 20.3.3; Chap. 23 by Silingardi, Sect. 23.3.2 all in this volume.

[37] Guiding Principles on Internal Displacement, E/CN.4/1998/53/Add.2, 11 February 1998.

Standing Committee (IASC) Operational Guidelines on the Protection of Persons in Situations of Natural Disasters.[38]

The Guiding Principles on Internal Displacement, adopted in 1998, offer a useful normative framework for the protection of those displaced within a country's territory, including in disaster situations.[39] Although not legally binding *per se*, these principles reflect and are consistent with provisions of international humanitarian law, human rights, and refugee law, which are binding.

The principles identify the rights and guarantees relevant to the protection of internally displaced across all phases from displacement, to assistance, resettlement, and reintegration. Of relevance, first natural and man-made disasters are specifically mentioned among the possible causes of displacement. Second, principle 4 recognizes the special protection needs of particularly vulnerable categories of the population and the importance of applying the principles without discrimination on the basis of, *inter alia*, race, sex, ethnic, or social origin, age, language, religion or belief, or disability.[40] Finally, consistently with the definition provided above, protection is not limited to physical safety, but also refers to the broad range of civil, political, economic, social, and cultural rights.

The IASC Operational Guidelines on the Protection of Persons in Situations of Natural Disasters are meant to assist disaster responders in adopting a rights-based approach to assistance in situations of natural disasters, including protection of vulnerable groups. While keeping a strong operational focus, the guidelines are 'informed by and draw on relevant international human rights law, existing standards and policies pertaining to humanitarian action, and human rights guidelines on humanitarian standards in situations of natural disasters.'[41]

According to the guidelines, protection activities must respect the principles of humanity, impartiality, and neutrality.[42] In addition, they should be structured as to *do no harm* to beneficiary populations and to not expose them to further risks. The principle of non-discrimination cuts across all vulnerable groups. More specifically, among the principles that should guide the actions of all actors for the protection of vulnerable groups are: participation and consultation of all across all phases of disaster response; protection against violence, and other safety risks both during and after the emergency phase; and priority and adequate access to humanitarian goods and services.[43] Adequacy concerns the four concepts of *availability, accessibility, acceptability, and adaptability*. Of relevance to this chapter, *accessibility* requires all goods and services to be provided to everyone

[38] IASC 2011.

[39] See also the outcomes of the Oslo Conference for the 10 years of the Guiding Principles, October 2008. Most recently, they served as the basis for the 2009 Africa Union Convention for the Protection and Assistance of Internally Displaced Persons in Africa (Kampala Convention).

[40] Guiding Principles on Internal Displacement, E/CN.4/1998/53/Add.2, 11 February 1998.

[41] IASC 2011, 8.

[42] See Chap. 2 by Venturini in this volume, Sect. 2.5.

[43] IASC 2011, 61.

based on needs and without discrimination, and to be safely reached by everyone, including those with specific needs (i.e. persons with disabilities, older people, and so on). *Acceptability* on the other side commands goods and services to be culturally acceptable by, for example, members of minorities, indigenous, or religious communities, and sensitive to gender and age requirements.[44]

In addition to the general guidelines mentioned above, some group-specific guidance material has also been developed.[45] Though relevant, a comprehensive discussion of all of them is beyond the scope of this chapter.

16.3 Protection of Vulnerable Groups in Disaster Situations

Despite the growing attention to the special needs of women, children, the elderly, persons with disabilities, minorities, and indigenous groups, experience shows that vulnerable groups continue to be largely invisible, marginalized, and discriminated against in disaster management. Their inclusion in disaster preparedness, response, and recovery is not systematic, while major inequalities persist with certain groups such as women and children more frequently and better considered as compared to others.

Below is an overview of the challenges each vulnerable group can face in disaster situations and the mechanisms and standards that should (though reality shows differently) apply for their protection. While reference is made to factors such as gender, age, ethnicity, and disability, migration, displacement, and the refugee status will also be considered as contributing to the overall vulnerability of each group.

16.3.1 Women

While the poor are hit hardest, it is usually women and children within these groups that suffer the most in disaster situations.[46] Not only in disasters the death toll is generally higher for women, they also endure rape and other forms of violence, property loss, and other abuses of their rights.[47] Globally, for every one man who dies in a flood, there are 3–4 women who die.[48]

---

[44] Ibid. 29.

[45] Examples of this are Handicap International 2009, Save the Children 2007 and HelpAge International 2000.

[46] http://www.un.org/womenwatch/daw/followup/session/presskit/fs1.htm and http://www.un.org/ecosocdev/geninfo/women/women96.htm. Accessed 12 September 2011.

[47] Just to mention few examples, 1,5 times as many women as men died during the 1996 Kobe earthquake, and three times as many women as men died from the 2004 Asian tsunami. See Neumayer, Plümper 2007, 555. For regional evidence refer to ECLAC 2004; Ibarraran et al. 2007; WHO 2002; and PAHO 2001.

[48] Ferris 2008.

Women's vulnerability is deeply rooted in the gender inequalities that limit their mobility, making them less able to flee the hazard and protect themselves from the devastating consequences of the disaster. Since in many countries women are not taught how to swim, they are exposed to higher risk in the event of floods or inundations.[49] Data from the Asian Development Bank indicate that women accounted for 61 % of the deaths in cyclone Nargis, 70 % in the Indian Ocean Tsunami, and 91 % in the 1991 cyclone in Bangladesh.[50]

Gender[51] is a pervasive factor affecting various facets of vulnerabilities to natural disasters. It determines the way men and women are impacted by and respond to a disaster, which in turn is directly related to the differential roles and responsibilities, skills and capabilities, opportunities and challenges women and men had prior to it.[52]

Women tend to be generally less mobile, have less access to resources such as information, networks, and transportation, and are less likely to participate in the public sphere in which relief is organized and delivered. Their specific needs may be overlooked if relief efforts are targeted to household heads, and their contributions to reconstruction and recovery not valued. Hence, the importance of including them throughout the disaster cycle from preparedness, to response, and recovery.

In the lawlessness and chaos following the disaster, women and girls are at greater risk of violence. In the post-Noel hurricane in Dominican Republic in 2007, scarce security in temporary shelters, particularly at night, promiscuity with stranger men and women living together, and lack of security personnel have been indicated among the causes of sexual violence against women and girls in camps.[53] A survey by International Medical Corp in the post-Katrina trailer camp in 2006 found a rape rate 53.6 times higher than the highest baseline rate by the US Department of Justice in 2004.[54] Disruption of families' and communities' protection mechanisms also contributes to increased risks and negative coping mechanisms such as sexual exploitation and abuse[55] and/or survival sex for

---

[49] UNDP 2007, 77.

[50] Baez et al. 2010, 32.

[51] Gender refers to the social differences between females and males of all ages that are learned, and though deeply rooted in every culture, are changeable over time and have wide variations both within and between cultures. IASC 2006, 1. See also http://www.un.org/womenwatch/osagi/conceptsandefinitions.htm. Accessed 12 September 2011.

[52] Kumar-Range 2001, 2.

[53] Alba, Luciano 2008.

[54] IFRC 2007, 123.

[55] According to the UN Secretary-General's Bulletin on Protection from Sexual Exploitation and Abuse, ST/SGB/2003/13, *sexual exploitation* means any actual or attempted abuse of a position of vulnerability, differential power, or trust, for sexual purposes, including, but not limited to, profiting monetarily, socially, or politically from the sexual exploitation of another, while *sexual abuse* means the actual or threatened physical intrusion of a sexual nature, whether by force or under unequal or coercive conditions.

women and girls.[56] Another form of GBV that may find in disasters a fertile terrain is trafficking, particularly of women and children, for sexual and other purposes. Activists and experts from Haiti warned about a growth in trafficking and smuggling of persons since the earthquake.[57]

Women's ability to cope with the consequences of a hazard is often hampered by their lack of access to and control over basic resources,[58] such as land, and other productive assets. Following the 2004 Tsunami, women in the Aceh Province of Indonesia faced many challenges in accessing and claiming their rights. Issues included general lack of awareness about women's rights, denial of women's entitlements under Islamic inheritance law, lack of recognition of women as land owners, and lack of female lawyers.[59]

Women's care-giving role and skills as nurses, teachers, and social workers are often not identified as resources in relief and recovery efforts, meanwhile the responsibilities they often taken on in the absence of their husbands or male relatives subtract time to engage in income generating activities or act as an impediment to migration in search of new economic opportunities, as men often do.[60]

Gender-blind humanitarian assistance may fail to address the needs and concerns of a portion of the population and can possibly result in unintended harm. For instance, targeting aid to women without prior sensitization of people at the community level, can overburden them, interfere with household chores, and even increase tensions at the household level.[61] Haiti exemplifies problems that are found in many disaster settings. There, lack of understanding of the different needs of women and men of different age and of data disaggregated by sex,[62] resulted in an unequal access to relief aid. Attempts to segregate latrines have mostly failed, and early days food distribution arrangements have been criticized for putting women and girls at risk of sexual exploitation and abuse.[63]

Conversely, a sound gender analysis contributes to enhance the effectiveness and efficacy of relief aid. During the 2005 Pakistan earthquake, women, initially inhibited by the purdah norms, dramatically increased the use of medical services when female staffs were engaged.[64] Yet, integrating gender in disaster assessments and recovery plans continues to be a major challenge.[65] A careful review of some major disasters reveals the persistence of gaps such as: (1). inadequate sexual and

---

[56] Alba, Luciano 2008.

[57] Godoy 2010.

[58] See ActionAid 2004, 7 and Enarson 2000.

[59] Harper 2009, 77.

[60] Enarson 2000, 10.

[61] Houghton 2005, 3.

[62] GPPI 2010, 47.

[63] IASC Sub-Working Group on Gender 2010.

[64] Cosgrave and Herson 2008, 210.

[65] UNISDR 2011.

reproductive health services,[66] including assistance to GBV survivors; (2). inadequate design and location of shelters (i.e., lack of privacy; overcrowdings; poor lighting; and so on); and (3). lack of consultation and participation of women across the whole spectrum of disaster response.

16.3.1.1 Legal Instruments

The primary instrument for the protection of the rights of women is the 1979 Convention on the Elimination of All Forms of Discrimination Against Women (CEDAW)[67] and related Optional Protocol (1999).[68] Other relevant international instruments include the Convention on Consent to Marriage, Minimum Age for Marriage, and Registration of Marriages (1962)[69] and the 1967 Declaration on the Elimination of all Forms of Discrimination against Women.[70] Articles 6 and 8 of the CEDAW protect women against trafficking, exploitation, and prostitution. Article 5 preserves against customary and other practices that are based on the inferiority or stereotyped role of women vis-à-vis men.[71] For example non-consensual marriage, especially for those living in poverty, or unaccompanied, or widowed by the disaster, is frequently found in disaster situations.[72]

The CEDAW provides a venue for women to claim their rights to land, inheritance, and guardianship of minors (articles 14 and 15). Finally, the right to freely choose residence and domicile, including in situation of resettlement, is recognized under article 13, which ensures that decision on housing is not restricted to heads of households, a practice that for the most cases would exclude women.

The IASC operational guidelines on protection of persons in natural disasters provide a list of specific activities that should be undertaken for the protection of women and girls from, among others, family separation (principle A.2), unsafe access to humanitarian goods and services (principle B.1), dispossession and loss

---

[66] For instance, an evaluation of the assistance provided to mothers and children after the earthquake in Gujarat, India, pointed to the fact that field hospitals used during the disaster were of military origin and did not pay enough attention to the needs of women and children. See Bremer 2003, 377.

[67] 1979 Convention on the Elimination of All Forms of Discrimination against Women.

[68] 1999 Optional Protocol to the Convention on the Elimination of All Forms of Discrimination against Women.

[69] 1962 Convention on Consent to Marriage, Minimum Age for Marriage, and Registration of Marriages.

[70] 1993 United Nations Declaration on the Elimination of Violence against Women.

[71] Protection against harmful traditional practices is also provided in the 1998 Protocol to the African Charter on Human Rights and People's Rights on the Rights of Women in Africa (PACHPRA).

[72] The right to consensual marriage is also guaranteed in several international treaties such as the ICESCR, the ICCP, the Convention on the Consent to Marriage (Article 1–2), as well as in the UNDHR.

of land and other property's rights (principle C.1), and all forms of GBV both during and after the emergency phase (principle A.4).[73] Similar protection is also granted to women and girls by the IDP Guiding Principles (principles 4 and 11), which call for women's separate documentation (principle 20.3), equal participation in aid planning and distribution (principle 18.3), and access to services (principle 19.2).

16.3.2 Children

The less developed physical and mental state of children[74] as well as their social condition and dependency on adults negatively affect their ability to survive the danger or to cope with the consequences of it. In the earthquake that shook Armenia in 1998, almost two-third of the deaths were children and adolescents in schools,[75] while in the 2010 Pakistan floods half of the 20 million affected were children, of which 2.8 million under the age of 5.[76]

Outbreaks of disease following disasters hit children the hardest. Poor water, sanitation and drainage facilities, overcrowding, and the paucity of healthcare services all heighten the risk of children contracting diseases, especially if already malnourished. Diarrhea was the most common illness and cause of death among the flood-affected populations in Bangladesh in 1998, and was directly related to the increase in the proportion of severely malnourished children.[77]

Children, especially those orphaned or unaccompanied living in temporary shelters, experience heightened risks of abuses such as trafficking, forced labor, illegal adoption, sexual exploitation, and forced recruitment by armed groups and criminals. In Banda Aceh only, the 2004 Tsunami left an estimated 2,800 children orphaned. After the 2010 Haitian earthquake, more than 7,300 boys and girls have been smuggled into the Dominican Republic by traffickers profiting from hunger and desperation.[78] In post cyclone Nargis (Myanmar 2008), children were found to be vulnerable to forms of exploitation such as live-in child domestic servants, working in the fishing industry, and trafficking for labor and sexual exploitation.[79] Identification and registration, provision of immediate safe care, tracing, and

[73] For an exhaustive list see IASC 2011, 62.

[74] Children are considered persons below the age of 18 years unless under the law applicable to the child majority is attained earlier. Convention on the Rights of the Child, Article 1.

[75] http://www.aaets.org/article38.htm. Accessed 3 August 2011.

[76] Save the Children 2010b, 1.

[77] WHO 2008a, 93.

[78] http://www.worldforum2010.org/LinkClick.aspx?fileticket=GuygXDczP3s%3D&tabid=106 Accessed 16 September 2011.

[79] TCG 2009, 156.

reunification with extended family members, alerting police and community authorities, and close monitoring are key in preventing child exploitation.[80]

Children are also sold or sent away by their parents due to poverty, destruction, and destitution, and to alleviate the burden on families. Girls as young as 13 were sold as brides to much older 'tsunami widowers' in India, Sri Lanka, and Aceh.[81]

The disruption of the physical and familiar environment caused by disasters often result in trauma and distress for children and young adolescents, who need security and normalcy.[82] Psychosocial support services need to be put in place promptly, and even teachers need to be trained to be able to help re-establishing children's mental balance.

The right to education is very often threatened in the event of disasters. In Pakistan, nearly 8,000 schools were put out of use, either because damaged or taken over as temporary shelter by displaced families, by the 2010 floods.[83] Schools offer a protective environment where children can learn and play safely, going back to a normal life as part of their psychological recovery.[84]

Family reunification is of utmost importance due to children's vulnerability stemming from their dependency on adults. When this is not possible, or when parents do not have the means to care for their children and freely accept to do so, solutions for children include fostering, institutional care, guardianship, in-country and inter-country adoption.[85]

16.3.2.1 Legal Instruments

Children's rights are guaranteed in multiple international treaties and legal instruments. Among them, the 1989 Convention on the Rights of the Child (CRC),[86] and the 2000 Optional Protocol on the Sale of Children, Child Prostitution, and Child Pornography[87] deserve special consideration. Other important conventions include the 1993 Hague Convention on the Protection of Children and Co-operation in Respect of Inter-Country Adoption, and the 2000 Protocol to Prevent, Suppress, and Punish Trafficking in Persons Especially Women and Children, supplementing the United Nations Convention against Transnational Organized Crime.[88]

---

[80] CRS 2005, 16.

[81] Felten-Biermann 2006.

[82] Lazarus et al. 2003, 1.

[83] Save the Children 2010b, 2.

[84] See also Save the Children 2010a, 2010b; and UNICEF 2005.

[85] ICRC 2004.

[86] 1989 United Nations Convention on the Rights of the Child.

[87] 2000 Optional Protocol on the Sale of Children, Child Prostitution, and Child Pornography.

[88] A/RES/55/25, 15 November 2000.

While the Convention on the Rights of the Child makes explicit reference to the protection of children in armed conflict, no mention is made to man-made or natural disasters. This, however, does not mean that its general provisions do not apply to these events. For instance, article 3 affirms that States Parties shall take all appropriate legislative and administrative measures to guarantee that the children have the protection and care they need against occurrences such as abduction, physical and mental violence, and negligent treatment.

Birth registration (article 7 of the CRC) is the first step for any child's rights to be recognized. Without identity documents, children may be unable to access the goods and services they need, and may have problems with issues such as inheritance. Registration and identification are also critical to prevent abuses such as forced labor, early marriage, and trafficking.[89]

Family reunification, and/or provision of alternate care arrangements, including adoption, for those whose parents or primary care providers are dead or may pose a risk to the children (articles 9-10; 22; 7.1; 20 and 21 of the CRC) is also of particular relevance. Inter-country adoption is regulated by the 1993 Hague Convention (article 4), as well as by the CRC, the 2000 Protocol on Trafficking and the 2000 Protocol on the Sale of Children, Child Prostitution, and Child Pornography where illegal adoption is specifically criminalized.

Child labor (or labor of children below 14 years old)[90] is another key protection concern when families have lost their basic means of survival, unemployment may be heightened and schools non-operational. The girl child is at higher risk of being drawn into underage labor due to gender discrimination and industries such as sexual exploitation and pornography.[91] Protection of children against all forms of child labor is guaranteed by article 32 of the CRC, the 1999 ILO Convention 182.[92]

Finally, according to the IASC operational guidelines on protection, to the extent possible, priority should be given to evacuating children with a family member (principle A.2.1), ensuring protection from violence, including GBV and trafficking (principles A.4), while adoption arrangements should be avoided until the situation remains unsettled (principle D.3.3).[93] The IDP Guiding Principles stipulate that special attention should be granted to the needs of women and children (principle 4.2) and call for expedited family reunification's measures whenever children are involved (principle 17.3).

---

[89] Harper 2009, 139.

[90] The 1973 ILO Convention on the Minimum Age for Admission to Employment and Work No. 138 affirms that children cannot be employed before finishing their compulsory schooling, which is generally at 15. Exceptions are made possible for developing countries lowering the minimum age to 14. However, light work, which must not threaten children's health and safety or hinder their education, is allowed between 13 and 15, with exceptions for developing countries where it is allowed between 12 and 14.

[91] Harper 2009, 149.

[92] 1999 ILO Convention Concerning the Prohibition and Immediate Action for the Elimination of the Worst Forms of Child Labour No. 182.

[93] For an exhaustive list see IASC 2011, 62.

16.3.3 Older People

The term 'old age' identifies people over 60 years of age.[94] Older people comprise approximately 11 % of the world population and are expected to reach 22 % by 2050.[95] Given that roughly one in ten people is aged over 60, of the 208 million people affected by disaster in 2010, more than 20 million are estimated to be older people.

Limited mobility, chronic diseases as well as special nutritional needs can significantly constrain older people's ability to escape from harm, access aid, and cope with the hardship that results from disasters. Among those who died in Hurricane Katrina in New Orleans in 2005, 71 % were over 60 years old. This was due to the fact that evacuation plans were not in place for residential care homes housing large numbers of older persons.[96] In the Maldives, those aged 65 and over, though comprising only 3.1 % of the population, accounted for 17.3 % of the deaths during the 2004 Tsunami.[97]

Left alone by death, abandonment, and rupture of traditional support mechanisms, older people may face significant obstacles in accessing food and shelter, traveling long distances, and enduring even short periods without basic facilities.[98] According to a Red Cross official, isolation and lack of assistance, not the heat *perse* caused the death of thousands of elders in France in 2003.[99] Abuse, including of a physical, sexual, psychological, and financial nature can also become common in situation of disaster and can result in injury, illness, lost productivity, and despair.[100]

Compared to other groups, older people suffer from a general neglect in both international laws and disaster policies and practice. It is not uncommon for aid agencies to assume mismatching priorities to respond to older people's needs.[101] At the root of this are often a series of false assumptions about older people's physical, psychological, and economic vulnerability. One such misconception is that families and communities will protect and provide for them at all time. While this may be true in many contexts, reliance on families' and communities' support mechanisms also render older persons especially vulnerable when disruptions and breakdown of traditional ties occur. Another (false) assumption is that older people will be covered under general relief, thus disregarding their specific nutritional,

[94] Though there is no universally accepted numeric criterion, the UN agreed cutoff is 60+ years to refer to the older population. http://www.who.int/healthinfo/survey/ageingdefnolder/en/index.html. Accessed 19 July 2011.

[95] IASC 2008, 3.

[96] Harper 2009, 107.

[97] Baez et al. 2010, 33.

[98] HelpAge International 2000.

[99] IFRC 2007, 75.

[100] Wells 2005, 16.

[101] HelpAge International 2002.

health, and other needs. These ultimately contribute to perpetuate discrimination against older people and lack of specific attention to their needs.

Evacuation can also create specific problems. For example, during the Quebec ice storm and in the Louisiana hurricane, older people refused to evacuate to ensure the safety of their pets, while evacuation in Chernobyl resulted difficult due to strong attachment by the elderly to their place.[102]

The *Sphere Humanitarian Charter and Minimum Standards in Disaster Response* recommends 7 % of the humanitarian funds to be channeled toward older people's needs,[103] including healthcare, nutritional support, family tracing, and reunification. Yet, evidence from the 2004 Tsunami indicated that less than 1 % of the overall funding provided by major humanitarian donors was targeted to older people's needs, even though they comprise 7–10 % of the affected populations. Equally dire was the situation in the aftermath of the earthquake in Haiti. Only 5 % of the 321 projects included in the UN Flash Appeal in 2010[104] referred to older people's needs. Of these, only 0.6 % mentioned activities specifically targeted to older people, none of whom was finally funded.[105] On a similar note, a study conducted by HelpAge International indicated that only 93 (4.9 %) out of 1,912 humanitarian projects made explicit reference to older people as a specific vulnerable group, compared to 32 % for women and children.[106] Out of them, 18 included activities specifically targeted to older people, and only 5 were finally funded.[107]

Finally, another problem often experienced in disaster situations is that older people's capacities and contributions get often disregarded in recovery and reconstruction plans.[108]

16.3.3.1 Legal Instruments

As anticipated, there is no convention or legally binding instrument targeted to older people. Indeed, very few legal instruments specifically refer to older people

---

102 WHO 2008b, 14.

103 Wells 2005, 2.

104 Flash Appeals are tools for structuring a co-ordinate response for the first 3–6 months of an emergency. They are usually issued within 1 week after a disaster and identify life-saving needs and some recovery projects that can be implemented within the proposed timeframe.

105 ReliefWeb 2011, 2. Interestingly, while still very low, the percentage of projects that specifically referred to older people needs is still higher than those observed in other recent emergencies caused by natural disasters. HelpAge International 2010, 7.

106 The study analyzed the Consolidated Appeals Process (CAP) and Flash Appeals of 12 humanitarian crises since 2007, including some 7 natural disasters in Burkina Faso, El Salvador, Haiti, Honduras, Myanmar, Pakistan, and the Philippines. Ibid. 3–5.

107 Ibid. 4.

108 WHO 2008b.

as a separate category.[109] As human beings, older people's rights are guaranteed by international human rights law, while marginal protection also derives from falling into other categories such as women, minorities or indigenous groups, and people with disabilities. Interestingly, age as such is not specifically prohibited as a basis for discrimination in major human rights instruments,[110] while the gap was subsequently redressed in guidelines, policies, and major disaster response standards.[111]

The 1991 UN Principles for Older Persons provided the first authoritative framework for the right of older people to for example independence, participation, care, self-fulfillment, and dignity, among others, agreed upon by States worldwide. These gained greater impetus with the 2002 Madrid Plan of Action on Ageing (MIPAA)[112] endorsed by 159 governments, which is also the only document referring to older people that contains a specific section (54) on natural disasters and other humanitarian emergencies, including man-made disasters. At the regional level, the European Charter of Fundamental Rights[113] recognizes the rights of the elderly to conduct a life of dignity and independence and to participate in social and cultural life.

Among the most relevant actions indicated in the Plan to ensure older people's access to goods and services in emergencies are: (d) raise awareness among relief workers of the physical and health issues and needs of the elders; (g) inclusion of the elders in disaster relief plans, including disaster preparedness; (j) protection of older people from physical, economical, and sexual exploitation and abuse, with particular attention to women; and recognition of their contribution in reconstruction and rebuilding efforts.[114]

Protection and care for older people's needs are also fully reflected in the IASC operational guidelines with reference to evacuation (principle A.1), family separation (principle A.2), safety from violence (principle A.4), access to humanitarian goods and services (principle B.1), and access to livelihoods and employment

---

[109] Wells 2005, 5. Older persons are explicitly named in the Convention on the Rights of People with Disabilities, while the committee charged with the monitoring of the implementation of the CEDAW has highlighted the important role that the convention can play in protecting older women's rights. Harper 2009, 104.

[110] Wells 2005. Age, for example, is not explicitly mentioned in the UDHR, the CEDAW, the CERD, the United Nations Declaration on the Rights of Indigenous People.

[111] See for example IASC 2011.

[112] United Nations Madrid Plan of Action on Ageing, paras 54–56. The MIPAA is the final document adopted at the United Nations Second World Assembly on Ageing held in Madrid in April 2002. It is a tool to assist policymakers to integrate the rights and needs of older citizens into national and international development policies. It represents the first agreement among Governments where questions about aging are linked to other frameworks for social and economic development and human rights, most notably those agreed at the United Nations conferences and summits of the past decade.

[113] 2000 Charter of Fundamental Rights of the European Union.

[114] Ibid. paras 55–56.

opportunities (principle C.3).[115] Finally, the IDP Guiding Principles recognize the protection and assistance needs of older people by virtue of their particular conditions (principle 4).

In spite of the documents mentioned above, a need remains for more incisive norms for the protection of older people's rights.[116] The UN Secretary-General and others called for an international convention on the rights of older persons, since 'in many countries, incidents of neglect, abuse and violence against older persons are not at all rare or isolated events'.[117] While some regional conventions include specific provisions for older people, this is not done systematically and comprehensively. Such a convention would provide legal leverage for older people's rights defenders, define internationally acceptable standards against which actions (and lack thereof) can be measured, and build consensus on the need to take their rights seriously in disaster relief.

16.3.4 Persons with Disabilities

According to estimates, more than half a billion people with disabilities live in countries at risk of conflicts or emergencies caused by disasters.[118] While a specific definition of disability is missing, reference is made to persons who have long-term physical, mental, intellectual, or sensory impairments, which, in interaction with various barriers, may hinder their full and effective participation in society on an equal basis with others.[119]

Disability and poverty are linked in a vicious cycle. Among the poorest in the world, between 15 and 20 % have some kind of disability.[120] Poor people tend to have less access to health care and to work in hazardous conditions, which further increase the risk of injury and impairment.[121] Among displaced population, persons with disabilities are amongst the most hidden, marginalized, and isolated. Abandonment by family members and caretakers is a common practice in times of hardship, often leading to further destitution.

Throughout history many societies have dealt poorly with disability, with social, cultural, and religious beliefs contributing to discrimination, stigmatization,

---

115 For an exhaustive list see IASC 2011, 63.

116 See IFRC 2007 and INPEA et al. 2010.

117 NGO Committee on Aging 2008.

118 Atlas Alliansen and CBM 2011.

119 Convention on the Rights of Persons with Disabilities, Article 1.

120 Handicap International 2005, 10.

121 IFRC 2007, 87.

violence, and marginalization of those affected.[122] Only very recently, disabilities and the impacts of disasters on the disabled started being more seriously and systematically addressed.

Disability can prevent people from receiving information, getting safe, and accessing humanitarian aid. While in theory these barriers are commonly recognized, experience shows that individuals with disabilities are often left behind during evacuation due to lack of transport and other logistical facilities and services; struggle to access shelters, camps, and food distribution sites; and are often discriminated against during the whole disaster management cycle. Reduced ability to protect themselves and to develop a proper understanding of situations also put persons with disability at higher risk of sexual violence.[123]

Disasters can also lead to further disability either directly, or indirectly, due to lack of adequate care, poverty, and malnutrition. Disruption of social support services and health care facilities for example may impede people with disabilities and those who have been injured from receiving the treatment they need, and may result in worsened conditions and further disabilities. The great psychosocial distress persons with disability may suffer from is rarely tackled by relief operations and may worsen their already vulnerable condition.[124]

The World Health Organization estimates that, following a disaster, about 5–7 % of the people in camps or temporary shelters have a disability.[125] Following the earthquake in Haiti, approximately 200,000 persons are expected to live with long-term disabilities.[126] After the 1986 explosion of Chernobyl nuclear plant, nearly 150,000 people were declared disabled due to the radiation exposure.[127]

Response and recovery programs often do not cater for the specific needs and limitations of persons with disabilities. People with disabilities are not identified in registration exercises, and specialized and targeted services are often missing or poorly organized, and result in a general neglect of their rights.[128] This disregard lies in the idea that disability requires specific technical expertise, often of a medical nature,[129] and results in persons with disabilities either referred to specialized agencies, when feasible and present, or lumped together in the general 'vulnerable groups' heading rather than being considered rights-holders with

[122] This is the case for example in India, http://siteresources.worldbank.org/INDIAEXTN/Resources/295583-1171456325808/Chapter02.pdf, and in a number African, Caribbean, and Pacific and Mediterranean Basin societies, as well as Native American tribes, http://www.ntac.hawaii.edu/AAPIcourse/downloads/readings/pdf/Multiculturalism.pdf. See also http://srsg.violenceagainstchildren.org/viewpoint/2011-06-20_348. Accessed 22 September 2011.

[123] Handicap International 2005, 28.

[124] Shivji 2010, 6.

[125] Ibid.

[126] http://www.un.org/disabilities/default.asp?id=1546. Accessed 16 July 2011.

[127] UNDP et al. 2002, 32.

[128] See Handicap International 2005 and Women's Refugee Commission 2008.

[129] http://www.un.org/disabilities/default.asp?id=1546. Accessed 16 July 2011. See also Shivji 2010, 4.

specific needs and concerns.[130] Inclusion in disaster response is limited to surveys and usage of inclusion language in reports and documents, while they are almost absent in planning, decision making, and management of relief and recovery efforts. At the same time, Disabled Persons Organizations (DPOs) have usually limited capacity, and are not experienced enough to act quickly, and assertively in emergency settings.

Undoubtedly, some practical challenges to meeting the specific needs of people with disabilities in disasters do exist. Methods for communicating risks and preparedness information should be appropriate to people's impairment, i.e., sign language for the deaf or Braille and sounds for the blind. Evacuation measures should account for mobility problems, for example impediments in using stairs, moving a wheelchair over debris, or moving people bedridden, or attached to machines for the support of vital functions. When transportation means are limited, priority should be given to persons with disabilities,[131] and shelters should be designed to accommodate people's special needs. Registration itself may be problematic as many people with disabilities may not be willing to identify themselves or members of their families for fear of stigma and marginalization.[132] All the above requires an expertise and resources that are not always factored in in disaster management.

Yet, some examples exist of how few simple modifications can contribute to people with disabilities' improved access to accommodations and services. After the 2004 floods in Bangladesh, Handicap International built houses with larger doors to accommodate people in wheelchairs and installed ramps, stairs, and handrails.[133]

16.3.4.1 Legal Instruments

The 2006 Convention on the Rights of Persons with Disabilities (CRPD)[134] calls upon States Parties to ensure the protection and safety of persons with disabilities, including in situations of humanitarian emergencies and natural disasters.[135] The CRPD protects concerned individuals from any form of discrimination on the basis of the disability they suffer, while encouraging positive actions by States Parties to accelerate their de facto equality with others.[136] This is also guaranteed in the 1991 Principles for the Protection of Persons with Mental Illness, and the Improvement

---

130 Kett et al. 2005, 9.

131 IASC 2011, 17.

132 See also Simmons 2010, 11.

133 Ibid. 37.

134 2006 United Nations Convention on the Rights of Persons with Disabilities.

135 Ibid. 8.

136 The principle of non-discrimination is spread throughout the Convention on the Rights of Persons with Disabilities.

of Mental Health Care,[137] and in the 1971 Declaration on the Rights of Mentally Retarded Persons.[138]

In disaster situations for example, giving priority access to humanitarian aid to persons with disabilities is in line with the responsibility to accommodate their special needs (articles 11 and 32 of the CRPD). Protection from exploitation, violence, and abuse is also guaranteed in article 16. Significantly, the Convention recognizes the greater risk of violence, abuse, injury, neglect, maltreatment, and exploitation faced by women and girls with disabilities (article 6), whilst the specific vulnerabilities of children with disabilities are recognized under article 7.[139]

Of particular relevance, the convention marks an unprecedented shift from viewing people with disabilities as 'objects' of special medical assistance and social protection, to 'subjects' with rights and ability to claim those rights freely.

People with disabilities are fully included in the IASC operational guidelines, including evacuation (principle A.1.3), access to humanitarian goods and services (principle B.1), and access to livelihoods and skills training (principle C.3.1).[140] Finally, the IDP Guiding Principles recognize special protection and assistance to people with disabilities due to their condition (principle 4), and prompt and adequate medical care and assistance, including psychological and social support (principle 11.1).

16.3.5 Minorities and Indigenous Groups

Although no universally accepted definition of 'minority' exists in international law, the term typically refers to ethnic, religious, and linguistic groups[141] that are smaller in numbers and different from the homogeneous majority in a specific territory. Indigenous people, on the other hand, are those whose social, cultural, and economic conditions distinguish them from other sections of the national community and whose status is regulated wholly or partially by their customs or traditions or by special laws or regulations. Indigenous people are recognized based on their descent from the populations that inhabited the country at the time of conquest or colonization or establishment of present State boundaries.[142]

Natural or man-made disasters can exacerbate the social, cultural, and political challenges minorities and indigenous groups face in 'normal times' making them more vulnerable to discrimination and abuses. In the aftermath of disasters,

[137] 1991 Principles for the Protection of Persons with Mental Illness and the Improvement of Mental Health Care.

[138] 1971 Declaration on the Rights of Mentally Retarded Persons.

[139] A similar form of protection is also granted under Article 23 of the CRC.

[140] For an exhaustive list see IASC 2011, 63.

[141] http://www.minorityrights.org/548/our-work/our-work.html. Accessed 19 September 2011.

[142] 1989 ILO Convention on Indigenous and Tribal Peoples, No. 169.

language barriers, lack of identity and other documents stating land, ownership, and inheritance rights may prevent members of these groups from claiming their rights to restitution and reinstatement, and result in homelessness, landlessness, and loss of livelihoods, among others.

Though treated under the same heading, there are some differences between minorities and indigenous groups that are worth noting. While representing approximately the 6 % of the world's population, indigenous make up 15 % of the world's poor, and one-third of the 900 million extremely poor rural people.[143] Indigenous groups have won more attention than minorities in the public arena thanks to their capacity of looking for both national and international organizational support in order to put forward their needs and concerns. For instance, the Inuits' plight in relation to the melting Arctic ice has gained increased attention for the fact of having brought their case to the Inter-American Commission on Human Rights.[144] Dependence upon the environment and its resources for survival and cultural identity makes indigenous peoples particularly at risk from the consequences of disasters. Conversely, there are no clear global figures on minorities and their rights are generally less discussed in the international arena.

Yet, there are plenty of similarities in the status of discrimination both minority and indigenous groups experience, which is often perpetuated and at times even exacerbated in disaster situations. Below are some examples of how both groups have been discriminated against. In 1998, a severe flood affected a Roma community in Slovakia: 140 Roma houses were affected compared with 25 non-Roma ones, and of the 47 people who were killed, 45 were Roma as they lived in a valley at high risk of flood.[145]

Vulnerability and discrimination are also exacerbated by the way the disaster and assistance are handled. For instance, minorities and indigenous people may not be granted access to precautionary and life-saving measures, and may not be adequately targeted in relief efforts. During the 2005 Hurricane Katrina, the evacuation plan relied on personal transportation, thus depriving poor minorities of any means to escape.[146] Following the earthquake in Chile, indigenous Mapuche complained on the Internet about discrimination and lack of support from the government.[147] After the 2004 Tsunami in South East Asia, minority groups such as Dalits in India were found to suffer from discrimination in aid assistance and lacking legal protection and enforcement of their rights.[148]

---

143 UNDESA 2009, 21.

144 Petition to the Inter-American Commission on Human Rights seeking relief from violations resulting from global warming caused by acts and omissions of the United States, 7 December 2005, http://www.ciel.org/Publications/ICC_Petition_7Dec05.pdf. Accessed 24 February 2012. See Baird 2008, 2.

145 Baird 2008, 3.

146 The Brookings Institution 2009, 5. See also CPR 2005.

147 MRG 2011, 95.

148 Human Rights Centre University of California 2005, 9.

Man-made disasters such as nuclear catastrophe, chemical spillage, toxic dumping as well as global warming can also render minority and indigenous groups particularly vulnerable. Melting of the polar ice caps in the Arctic, rising sea levels in the Pacific, and desertification in some regions of Africa[149] are increasing the already existing vulnerability of minorities living in those areas. In 2010, an oil spillage in the River Maranon in Peru contaminated the water that 28 indigenous communities were using for drinking, cooking, and fishing.[150]

Minority and indigenous populations may rely on customary laws and practices, which are not always recognized by the State. This can result in land as well as marriage and inheritance rights, particularly of women, going unrecognized, with negative implications on people's ability to reinstate livelihood patterns and regain assets. A major concern of indigenous people in Chile after the 2010 quake was the struggle to regain ancestral land.[151]

Discrimination may also take the form of violence or the fear of it. In the Tsunami-affected Indian State of Tamil Nadu, some representatives of the Dalit minority wanted to be housed separately because of fear of attack from the dominant communities.[152] Another form of discrimination against Dalits that became evident during relief efforts was their employment by the authorities to carry out particularly 'dirty' jobs such as cleaning of drains and toilets and pick up of dead bodies on the shore.[153]

Communication can be life-saving in a situation of disaster. Early warning messages are often given through the media, such as television, radio, and newspapers. Minorities and indigenous groups may not have access to these alerts, either because they do not have the economic resources to own a technological apparatus, because they live in remote areas where news have difficulty to arrive[154] or because the alarms are broadcasted in a language they do not understand. In addition, lack of culturally sensitive preparedness activities may leave minorities and indigenous groups more exposed to hazards.[155]

Indigenous groups are bearers of traditional local knowledge that, originated throughout the centuries from the direct observation of their territory, has helped them coping with natural hazards. Integrating indigenous knowledge, which is accepted by local people and developed in an inclusive way, and scientific disaster management approaches can help indigenous groups prepare, mitigate, and respond to natural hazards, thus reducing their vulnerability.[156] For example, in the flood-

[149] UNDESA 2007.

[150] http://upsidedownworld.org/main/peru-archives-76/2582-oil-spill-devastates-amazon-region-in-peru. Accessed 19 September 2011.

[151] MRG 2011, 104.

[152] IFRC 2007, 24.

[153] Ibid. 48.

[154] OECD 2006, 9.

[155] Ibid. See also Socialist Republic of Vietnam 2005.

[156] Australian Red Cross 2008.

prone Dagupan City, Philippines, an alert system combined scientific knowledge and equipment with indigenous knowledge and means of communication: when the water level rises, the *kanungkong*, a traditional instrument used to relay messages within the community, is played to alert people for an imminent evacuation.[157]

16.3.5.1 Legal Instruments

As for other groups mentioned above, minorities are entitled to protection of the rights guaranteed under the ICCPR, ICESCR, and the UNDHR. More specifically, their rights are mentioned in article 27 of ICCPR. In addition, the 1963 Declaration on the Elimination of all Forms of Racial Discrimination, the 1965 Convention on the Elimination of All Forms of Racial Discrimination (CERD),[158] the 1978 Declaration on Race and Racial Prejudice, and the 1992 Declaration on the Rights of Persons Belonging to National or Ethnic, Religious, and Linguistic Minorities provide the framework for the protection of their rights, including in disasters.[159]

Specifically, article 2 of the CERD states that 'States Parties, when the circumstances so warrant, [should] take, in the social, economic, cultural, and other fields, special and concrete measures to ensure the adequate development and *protection* of certain racial groups or individuals belonging to them'[160] (italics by the author). Protection of cultural practices and identity, and of civil, economic, social, and cultural rights is also granted under article 5.

The 2007 Declaration on the Rights of Indigenous Peoples provides for the protection of indigenous populations in recognition of the injustices they suffered throughout history due to subjugation and deprivation by others. Of particular relevance to disaster situations are the right not to be forcibly moved from their lands or territories (article 10), and the right to practice their culture, traditions, language, etc. (article 11).[161] The Declaration on the Rights of Indigenous People drew upon the principles contained in the 1989 ILO Indigenous and Tribal Peoples Convention.[162] Though to date ratified by 20 states only, the ILO Convention has influenced policy documents, debates, and legal decisions at the regional and international levels on the protection and inclusion of indigenous and tribal peoples.

While the right to cultural diversity and integrity, including language, is recognized by the 1966 Covenant on Civil and Political Rights as well as by the 1992 Declaration on the Rights of Persons Belonging to National or Ethnic Minorities,

---

157 UNISDR 2008, 52–54.

158 1965 United Nations Convention on the Elimination of All Forms of Racial Discrimination.

159 There are a number of regional conventions protecting minorities' rights, namely within the European Union, America, and Africa. See Harper 2009.

160 Ibid.

161 2007 United Nations Declaration on the Rights of Indigenous People.

162 1989 ILO Convention Indigenous and Tribal Peoples, No. 169.

under-recognition of certain practices within national jurisdictions often results in discrimination, exclusion, and further harm. Risks of neglect and discrimination can be particularly high in disaster situations, with massive displacement, disruption of traditional family and community protection mechanisms, and loss of assets.

The IASC guidelines refer to indigenous people and ethnic minorities in relation to cultural adequacy of humanitarian goods and services (principle B.1), shelter (principle B.2.3) and education (principle B.2.6), traditional land property claims (principle C.1) and freedom of expression of religious beliefs and cultural traditions (principle D.4).[163] The IDP Guiding Principles, on the other hand, only ensure protection to indigenous people and minorities from being arbitrarily displaced from their lands (principle 9).

16.4 Conclusions

This chapter discussed the human rights challenges vulnerable groups face in disaster situations and the international legal, policy, and guidance material aimed at their protection. Important advances have been made in the recognition of the distinct vulnerabilities of certain categories of the population to disaster, at least in the theory and inclusion language of disaster scholars and practitioners. However, sensitivity to diversity and inclusiveness continue to be mostly a theoretical commitment rather than a practice in disaster management. This situation is further aggravated by the continuous greater attention accorded to economic loss and infrastructures damage over the human dimensions of disasters as determined by factors such as social, economic, and cultural vulnerabilities and discrimination.

Where they exist, advances have been slow and inconsistent, and have not been spread equally across the different categories of vulnerable population. Relatively speaking, protection of women and children appears far more advanced than that of other groups such as older people, persons with disabilities or minorities.[164] Just to provide an example, a review of protection projects implemented in response to major disasters between 2004 and 2010[165] reveals that out of a total of 90, only one

[163] For an exhaustive list see IASC 2011, 65.

[164] There is solid evidence of this differential attention in the global discourse and practice on disaster risk reduction. For instance, while background papers on gender issues and children have been integrated in the UNISDR Global Assessments Report on Disaster Risk Reduction 2009 and 2011, other vulnerable groups are not even referenced there.

[165] The review took in consideration Flash Appeals and CERF issued after natural disasters between 2004 and 2010. The selection included only those appeals that had 2 or more projects in the protection cluster, while other clusters such as health, nutrition, shelter and so on were not considered for selecting the appeals addressing vulnerable groups.

project was specifically targeted to persons with disability, while none was granted to older people or minority and indigenous groups. The great majority were meant for women (19) and children (43), or targeted generically to vulnerable groups (11). While analysis of sectors such as health and nutrition would probably result in more projects targeted to persons with disability, older people and ethnic and indigenous groups, it is still reasonable to expect a similar disproportion to women and children.

This is probably the result of consistent global advocacy and awareness-raising on gender equality[166] and child protection in disaster risk reduction, which unfortunately has not been seen for other categories of vulnerable populations such as minorities and indigenous groups, older people, and persons with disability.

Among others, older people are perhaps those who have received the least attention. They are not yet the subjects of a specific convention, and they are often disregarded in the practice of disaster response. This situation is further aggravated by the complete lack of data on them. While experience shows that laws do not suffice for rights to be respected and protected, a binding agreement will at a minimum raise awareness about older people's specific rights, as different from those of other vulnerable groups, and set the basis for their effective protection, including in disasters.

In most cases, challenges on the protection of vulnerable groups boil down to two main issues: discrimination and lack of participation. It is now widely recognized (and documented) that consultation with affected people and communities is still far too little. This often implies disregard for the work and expertise of local actors such as NGOs and civil society's organizations. Consultation is even less when it comes to minorities, older people, and persons with disabilities.

Drawing on the review of some recent disasters, the following factors of hindrance as leading to discrimination and lack of adequate protection for vulnerable groups can be identified: lack of disaggregated data that provide an overview of men and women of all age, race, and ethnicity and their needs in disasters; poor understanding of the linkages between gender, age, disability, and ethnicity- and minority-based vulnerabilities and disaster at conceptual and practical levels; lack of institutional and individual capacity and tools to mainstream the various vulnerabilities and their interplay in the disaster management cycle; weak laws and policies (at least for some groups), and poor implementation practices (with regard to all groups, though with wide variations from one to the other).

One of the most important factors in the exclusion of vulnerable people in disaster response is the paucity of data on who needs what, where, and why (by

[166] Elaine Enarson is widely recognized as the pioneer in the sociological research of gender aspects in disaster contexts. At the international level, the stepping stone for the integration of gender issues in disaster risk reduction was an expert group meeting on 'Environmental Management and the Mitigation of Natural Disaster: A Gender Perspective' organized by the UN Division for the Advancement of Women in collaboration with UNISDR, which focused on women's risk management capacities. However, only in 2007 at the Global Platform for Disaster Risk Reduction gender issues were finally formally addressed.

virtue of identified needs, concerns, and capacities) to inform programs and carry out monitoring and evaluation activities. Not only disaggregated data on the population of concern do not exist for disaster mitigation and prevention, but information collected during the emergency phase are often incomplete, and of poor quality. While recognizing the numerous challenges to the collection, management, and analysis of information in emergencies in terms of time, resources and understanding, having the right information at the right time is essential to the effectiveness and efficiency of disaster response and needs to be prioritized.

Poor understanding of the situation on the ground is often compounded with lack of capacity. Many agencies for example consider disability to be a specialized subject, requiring technical skill and knowledge. This often results in persons with disabilities either referred to someone else or entirely disregarded, even for those needs that are the same as for everyone else and would require only specific logistic arrangements. Time is also a constraint, as in the rush to provide for basic needs and services, the specific needs of particularly vulnerable categories of the population are often intentionally or unintentionally disregarded.

The recent experience in Haiti showcased a general incapability by the international community in adequately protecting vulnerable groups in disaster response. Regardless of the quick mobilization of an unprecedented amount of resources, both physical and financial, and of significant media attention, the lack of a comprehensive situation analysis of the different needs and concerns of the population affected the effectiveness and quality of the response provided. Not only the needs of persons with disability, the elderly,[167] and ethnic minorities were not adequately factored in disaster response, but unsafe living conditions, lack of private bathing facilities, lack of lighting, and lack of police presence have been indicated among the causes of sexual violence against women and children in camps, including sexual exploitation and abuse by humanitarian workers,[168] child trafficking and other human rights abuses.

This acts like a dog chasing its tail, as given the inadequacy of resources that often characterize emergency situations, a rigorous analysis of needs and vulnerabilities is essential for prioritization and more efficient and effective use of resources.

Finally, in relation to the disaster management cycle, it is important to mention that higher gaps are evident in relation to preparedness, also because most of the funding goes to disaster relief rather than reduction or prevention activities. This is particularly unfortunate, as better targeting pre-disaster would help greatly to prevent, mitigate, and respond to the negative effects disasters have on vulnerable groups within the population.

---

[167] See http://reliefweb.int/node/350699; and http://www.ageuk.org.uk/latest-news/archive/one-year-on-older-haitians-still-ignored-by-relief-effort/. Accessed 16 July 2011.

[168] IJDH et al. 2010, 13.

References

ActionAid (2004) Participatory vulnerability analysis: a step-by-step guide for field staff, ActionAid International, Johannesburg
Alba W, Luciano D (2008) Evaluación Rápida sobre Salud Sexual y Reproductiva, Violencia contra las Mujeres y Situación de las Personas Vulnerables Afectadas por la Tormenta Noel en la República Dominicana. UNFPA/INSTRAW, Santo Domingo
ALNAP (2005) Protection: an ALNAP guide for humanitarian agencies. Overseas Development Institute, London
Anderson MB (2001) The impacts of natural disasters on the poor: a background note. Background paper for the World Bank's WDR 2000/2001
Atlas A, CBM (2011) Disability in conflicts and emergencies. Atlas Alliansen, Oslo
Australian Red Cross (2008) Traditional knowledge and Red Cross disaster preparedness in the Pacific. Australian Red Cross, Carlton
Baez J et al (2010) Do natural disasters affect human capital? An assessment based on existing empirical evidence. IZA, Bonn
Baird R (2008) The impact of climate change on minorities and indigenous people. Minority Rights Group International, London
Bremer R (2003) Policy development in disaster preparedness and management: lessons learned from the January 2001 Earthquake in Gujarat, India. Prehospital and Disaster Medicine 18:370–382
Cosgrave J, Herson M (2008) Perception of crisis and response: a synthesis of evaluations of the response to the 2005 Pakistan Earthquake, in ALNAP Seventh Review of Humanitarian Action, London, 177–224
CPR (2005) An unnatural disaster: the aftermath of hurricane Katrina. Center for Progressive Reform, Washington
CRS (2005) Indian ocean earthquake and Tsunami: humanitarian assistance and relief operations. Congressional Research Service, Washington
ECLAC (2004) A Methodological approach to gender analysis in natural disaster assessments: a guide for the Caribbean. Economic Commission for Latin America and the Caribbean, Santiago
Enarson E (2000) Gender and natural disasters. ILO, Geneva
FAO (2011) FAO strategic objective I (SO I) Briefing Toolkit: link between SO I and Disaster risk management (DRM)-draft. FAO, Rome
Felten-Biermann C (2006) Gender and natural disaster: sexualized violence and the Tsunami. Development 49:82–86
Ferris (2008) Displacement, natural disasters and human rights. http://www.brookings.edu/speeches/2008/1017_natural_disasters_ferris.aspx
Giossi Caverzasio S (2001) Strengthening protection in war: a search for professional standards. ICRC, Geneva
Godoy E (2010) Haitian women at increased risk of trafficking. http://ijdh.org/archives/14767
GPPI (2010) Inter-agency real-time evaluation in Haiti: 3 months after the earthquake. Global Public Policy Institute, Berlin
Grant W (2010) Chile troops tackle earthquake looters, http://news.bbc.co.uk/2/hi/8542789.stm
Handicap International (2009) Mainstreaming disability into disaster risk reduction: a training manual. Handicap International, Kathmandu
Handicap International (2005) How to include disability issues in disaster management-following floods 2004 in Bangladesh. Handicap International, Dhaka
Harper E (2009) International law and standards applicable in natural disaster situations. IDLO, Geneva
HelpAge International (2010) A Study of humanitarian financing for older people. HelpAge International, London

HelpAge International (2002) Encouraging agencies to pay attention to the needs, knowledge and experience of older people. Forced Migration Review 14:4–7

HelpAge International (2000) Older people in disasters and humanitarian crises: guidelines for best practice. Help Age International, London

Houghton R (2005) Tsunami emergency—lessons from previous natural disasters. Active Learning Network for Accountability and Performance, London

Human Rights Centre University of California (2005) After the Tsunami: human rights of vulnerable populations. East–West Centre, Berkley

IASC (2011) IASC Operational guidelines on the protection of persons in situations of natural disasters, The Brookings. Bern Project on Internal Displacement, Washington

IASC (2008) Humanitarian action and older persons. IASC, Geneva/New York

IASC (2006) Women, girls, boys and men. Different needs: equal opportunities. Gender handbook in humanitarian action, IASC, Geneva/New York

IASC (2005) Guidelines for gender-based violence interventions in humanitarian settings. IASC, Geneva

IASC Sub-Working Group on Gender (2010) Addressing gender equality in early actions to humanitarian crises. IASC, Rome

Ibarraran ME et al (2007) Climate change and natural disasters: macroeconomic performance and distributional impacts, 11 Environment, Development and Sustainability, 549–569

ICRC (2008) ICRC protection policy, 90 International Review of the Red Cross. ICRC, Geneva

ICRC (2004) Inter-agency guiding principles on unaccompanied and separated children. ICRC, Geneva

IFRC (2010) World disaster report 2010. IFRC, Geneva

IFRC (2007) World disaster report. IFRC, Geneva

IJDH et al (2010) Our bodies are still trembling: Haitian women's fight against rape. Institute for Justice and Democracy in Haiti, Boston

INPEA et al (2010) Strengthening older people's rights: towards a UN convention. International Network for the Prevention of Elder Abuse, Vancouver

International Law Commission (2007) Protection of persons in the event of disasters. Memorandum by the secretariat, A/CN.4/590, UN General Assembly, New York

IOM (2009) Migration, environment and climate change: assessing the evidence. IOM, Geneva

Kett M et al (2005) Disability in conflict and emergency situations: focus on Tsunami-affected areas. IDCC, Brussels

Kumar-Range S (2001) Environmental management and disaster risk reduction: a gender perspective. EGM/NATDIS/2001/BP.1. UN, Ankara

Lazarus PJ et al (2003) Responding to natural disasters: helping children and families: information for school crisis teams. National Association of School Psychologists, Bethesda

Mazurana et al. (2011) Sex and age matter: improving humanitarian response in emergencies, Feinstein International Centre: Tufts University, Medford

MRG (2011) State of the world's minorities and indigenous people. Minority Rights Group International, London

Neumayer E, Plümper T (2007) The gendered nature of natural disasters: the impact of catastrophic events on the gender gap in life expectancy, 1981–2002. Annals of the American Association of Geographers 97:551–566

NGO Committee on Ageing (2008) A Call for a convention on the rights of older persons. NGO Committee on Ageing, New York

OECD (2006) United states disaster information needs of ethnic minorities. OECD, Paris

PAHO (2001) Género y desastres naturales. Pan American Health Organization, Washington

Rayner G (2010) Haiti earthquake: anger turns to violence on the streets, http://www.telegraph.co.uk/news/worldnews/centralamericaandthecaribbean/haiti/6999091/Haiti-earthquake-anger-turns-to-violence-on-the-streets.html

ReliefWeb (2011) Briefing Kit for HelpAge International + Haiti, http://reliefweb.int/sites/reliefweb.int/files/reliefweb_pdf/briefingkit-f250d489db81528ae21c6c19fbdce8f7.pdf

Reyes G, Charles J (2010) Trafficking, sexual exploitation of Haitian children in the Dominican Republic on the rise, http://www.miamiherald.com/2010/10/23/1888703/earthquake-survivors-are-being.html
Save the Children (2010a) Serving Haiti's children now, rebuild for their future. Six months after the massive quake, Save the Children, London
Save the Children (2010b) Three months on: Save the Children's flood relief and recovery for children in Pakistan, Save the Children, London
Save the Children (2007) Child-led disaster risk reduction: a practical guide. Save the Children Sweden, Stockholm
Shivji A (2010) Disability in displacement. Forced Migr Rev 35:4–7
Simmons KB (2010) Addressing the data challenge. Forced Migr Rev 35:10–12
Socialist Republic of Vietnam (2005) Natural disaster risk management project: ethnic minority policy framework, ministry of agriculture and rural development, Hanoi
TCG (2009) Post-Nargis joint assessment. Tripartite Core Group, Jakarta
The Brookings Institution (2009) Regional workshop on protection and response in situations of natural disaster: summary report. The Brookings Institution: Bern Project on Internal Displacement, Washington
UN (1997) Renewing the United Nations: a programme for reform, A/51/950. United Nations, New York
UNDESA (2009) State of the world's indigenous peoples. United Nations, New York
UNDESA (2007) Concept note for the international expert group meeting on indigenous peoples and protection of the environment. United Nations, New York
UNDP (2007) Human development report 2007/2008 Fighting Climate Human Solidarity in a Divided World. UNDP, New York
UNDP et al (2002) The human consequences of the Chernobyl nuclear accident: a strategy for recovery, UNDP, New York
UNICEF (2005) Building back better: a 12-month update on UNICEF's work to rebuild children's lives and restore hope since the Tsunami. UNICEF, New York
UNISDR (2011) Global assessment report on disaster risk reduction. United Nations, Geneva
UNISDR (2009) Global assessment report on disaster risk reduction. United Nations, Geneva
UNISDR (2008) Indigenous knowledge for disaster risk reduction: good practices and lessons learned from experiences in the Asia-Pacific region. UNISDR, Bangkok
Wells J (2005) Protecting and assisting older people in emergencies. Overseas Development Institute, London
WHO (2008a) Climate change and human health: risks and responses, WHO, Geneva
WHO (2008b) Older persons in emergencies: an active ageing perspective, WHO, Geneva
WHO (2005) Violence and disasters. WHO, Geneva
WHO (2002) Gender and health in disasters. WHO, Geneva
Wisner B (2009) SHINK & Swim: exploring the link between capital (Social, Human, Institutional and Natural), disaster, and disaster risk reduction. Background paper for EDRR Project, GFDRR, World Bank
Wisner B et al (2004) At risk: natural hazards people's vulnerability and disasters. Routledge, London
Women's Refugee Commission (2008) Disabilities among refugees and conflict affected populations. Women's Refugee Commission, New York

Chapter 17
Contour of Disaster Victims' Rights to a Remedy and Reparation Under International Human Rights Law

Ingrid Nifosi-Sutton

Abstract The scope of disaster victims' rights to a remedy and reparation under international law is unclear due to the fact that the legal protection of disaster-affected individuals is not the main focus of international disaster response law. This chapter endeavors to fill this gap by discussing disaster victims' rights to a remedy and reparation from the point of view of international human rights law which is relevant to the situation of disaster victims who have suffered violations of rights *ratione temporis, ratione personae,* and *ratione materiae*. The chapter outlines the contour of disaster victims' rights to a remedy and reparation through an assessment of the components of the rights to a remedy and reparation as established under international human rights law in light of disaster-affected States' practice and disaster victims' specific protection needs. The jurisprudence and practice of certain regional human rights bodies that have enforced disaster victims' rights to a remedy and reparation is also appraised. Finally, the chapter looks at the effectiveness of the redress that disaster victims could seek at the domestic level and concludes that a holistic approach, made up of a combination of those reparations provided under international human rights law, may increase the remedial scope of the relief that can be obtained domestically and should be incorporated in reparation claims by disaster victims.

Contents

I. Nifosi-Sutton (✉)
American University Washington College of Law, 4801 Massachusetts Avenue, NW, Washington, DC 20016 USA
e-mail: nifosisu@american.edu

A. de Guttry et al. (eds.), *International Disaster Response Law*,
DOI: 10.1007/978-90-6704-882-8_17,

17.1 Introduction

Disaster situations can be the setting of violations of disaster victims' rights by the disaster-affected State.[1] Basic and universal principles of the rule of law require that in these cases disaster victims use the domestic judicial system to seek redress for the harm they have suffered.

The scope of disaster victims' rights to a remedy and reparation under international law is far from straightforward due to the fact that international disaster response law (IDRL) is not specifically concerned with the legal protection of disaster-affected individuals, a gap that has prompted the UN International Law Commission to draft articles on the protection of persons in the event of disasters.[2] As the work of the Commission does not, thus far, shed light on the rights enjoyed by disaster victims, this chapter endeavors to discuss disaster victims' rights to a remedy and reparation by relying on international human rights law. It is the view of this author that such an approach is justified because international human rights law is relevant to the situation of disaster victims who have suffered injuries *ratione temporis, ratione personae,* and *ratione materiae.* Human rights law is relevant *ratione temporis* because in principle it applies always, including during disasters; human rights law applies *ratione personae* since it affords legal

[1] Violations of disaster victims' rights by third States, members of foreign NGOs or members of relief operations carried out under the auspices of international organizations are beyond the scope of this chapter.

[2] The European Union has also made clear that the work of the UN International Law Commission responds to the need to fill current gaps in the international protection regime. See Statement on behalf of the European Union by Mr. Lucio Gussetti, Director Legal Service, European Commission, at the UN General Assembly 6th Committee (legal), 66th Session on the Report of the International Law Commission on the work of its sixty-third session on Expulsion of Aliens and on Protection of Persons in the Event of Disasters, 27 October 20011, available at http://www.eu-un.europa.eu/articles/es/article_11538_es.htm. Accessed 15 February 2012. On the scope of IDRL and the work of the UN International Law Commission see also Chap. 2 by Venturini, Chap. 1 by de Guttry, and Chap. 3 by Zorzi Giustiniani in this volume.

protection to all individuals who are within the jurisdiction of a State, including therefore disaster victims; and, finally, human rights law is applicable *ratione materiae* because it provides for the rights to a remedy and reparation, two entitlements that are germane to the situation of any individual who has been subjected to violations of human rights.[3] Accordingly, it follows that if a State engages in conduct that amounts to a violation of disaster victims' human rights, disaster-affected individuals are entitled to assert, as any victim of human rights violations, the right to recourse to domestic courts and the right be afforded reparation.[4]

On these premises, Sect. 17.2 delineates the contour of disaster victims' rights to a remedy and reparation by reassessing the components of the normative content of the rights to a remedy and reparation as established under international human rights law in light of disaster-affected States' practice and disaster victims' specific protection needs. Section 17.3 focuses on the jurisprudence and practice of certain regional human rights bodies to show how disaster victims' rights to a remedy and reparation are enforced under international human rights law. The chapter concludes with an examination of the effectiveness of the redress that disaster victims could seek at the domestic level. Section 17.4 suggests that a holistic approach, made up of a combination of those reparations provided under international human rights law, may maximize the remedial scope of the relief that can be obtained domestically and should be incorporated in reparation claims by disaster victims.

17.2 Contour of Disaster Victims' Rights to a Remedy and Reparation Under International Human Rights Law

This section delineates the contour of disaster victims' rights to a remedy and reparation. The analytical pattern followed involves the elucidation of the main dimensions of the rights to a remedy and reparation as established under human rights law and their appraisal in light of the relevant practice of disaster-affected States and specific protection needs of disaster victims. For analytical purposes, the analysis is carried out in three distinct sections. Section 17.2.1 focuses on the scope of disaster victims' right to a remedy; Sect. 17.2.2 discusses restrictions to disaster victims' right to a remedy, while Sect. 17.2.3 examines disaster victims' right to reparation.

[3] It should be noted that two human rights treaties contain specific provisions that apply to the situation of certain categories of disaster victims: the 1990 African Charter on the Rights and Welfare of the Child which, in Article 23 (1) and (4), requires States to provide children with appropriate humanitarian assistance; and the 2006 UN Convention on the Rights of Persons with Disabilities which, in Article 11, obligates contracting parties to ensure protection and safety to persons with disabilities in the event of a natural disaster.

[4] For an overview of disaster victims' rights that are at stake during disasters see Chap. 15 by Creta in this volume.

17.2.1 Normative Content of Disaster Victims' Right to a Remedy

The right to a remedy is the cornerstone of the legal protection of human rights and is considered to have acquired the status of customary international law. State practice,[5] incorporation of the right to a remedy in multilateral human rights treaties,[6] reference to this right in several declarations adopted by international and regional organizations,[7] and the writing of scholars confirm this point.[8]

An analysis of relevant provisions of human rights conventions, the jurisprudence of regional and UN human rights bodies, and scholarly writings indicates that the right to a remedy has two main dimensions. One is procedural and consists of the right of access to justice, typically understood as the possibility to file a complaint with domestic courts (civil, criminal, and administrative courts).[9] As evidenced by the jurisprudence of human rights bodies and scholars, the right of access to justice has to be read together with the right to fair proceedings before

[5] For a good overview of State practice relevant to the implementation of the right to a remedy see: Bassiouni 2006, 218–223; Shelton 2006, 159–172; and Francioni 2008, 37–38.

[6] The following treaties enshrine the right to a remedy: the 1966 Covenant on Civil and Political Rights, Article 2 (3); the 1965 Convention on the Elimination of Racial Discrimination, Article 6; the 1979 Convention on the Elimination of Discrimination against Women, Article 2 (c); the 1985 Convention against Torture, Article 13; the 1990 Convention on the Protection of the Rights of All Migrant Workers and Members of their Families, Article 83; the 1950 European Convention on Human Rights (ECHR), Article 13; the 1981 African Charter on Human and Peoples' Rights, Article 7; and the 1969 American Convention on Human Rights, Article 25.

[7] See the 1948 Universal Declaration of Human Rights, GA Res. 217A (III), Article 8; the 1963 UN Declaration on the Elimination of all Forms of Racial Discrimination, GA Res. 1904 (XVIII), Article 7; the 1992 Declaration on the Protection of all Persons from Enforced Disappearances, GA Res. 47/133, Article 9; and the 1981 Muslim Universal Declaration on Human Rights, Article IV (b).

[8] Bassiouni 2006, 203–279; Shelton 2006, 105–173, Francioni 2008, 1–55; Provost 2002, 43–49; D'Ascoli and Scherr 2007; Evans 1998; and Rodley 1999, Chap. 4.

[9] See the Covenant on Civil and Political Rights, *supra* n. 6; the Convention on the Elimination of Discrimination against Women, *supra* n. 6; and the Convention on the Rights of Migrant Workers, *supra* n. 6. As far as the jurisprudence of human rights bodies and scholarly writings are concerned see: European Court of Human Rights (ECtHR), *Golder v. The United Kingdom*, Judgment of 21 February 1975; Human Rights Committee General Comment No. 32 (hereafter General Comment No. 32), CCPR/C/GC/32, paras 9 and 16; Committee on Economic Social and Cultural Rights (ESCR) General Comment No. 9 (hereafter General Comment No. 9) E/C.12/1998/24, para 9; Committee on ESCR General Comment No. 14 (hereafter General Comment No. 14), E/C.12/2000/4, paras 59–62; Inter-American Commission on Human Rights (IACHR), Access to Justice as a Guarantee of Economic, Social and Cultural Rights. A Review of the Standards Adopted by the Inter-American System of Human Rights, OEA/Ser.L/V/II.129 Doc. 4; Francioni 2008, 1–5, 30–33; and African Commission on Human and Peoples' Rights (ACHPR), Principles and Guidelines on the Right to a Fair Trial and Legal Assistance in Africa, Section C (b), available at http://www.achpr.org/english/declarations/Guidelines_Trial_en.html. Accessed 15 February 2012.

courts which are independent, competent and impartial,[10] and which also includes the right of indigent individuals who have suffered violations of rights or are charged with a criminal offense to free legal assistance.[11] The other dimension of the right to a remedy is substantive and requires that available domestic venues for recourse are effective: that is to say offer a reasonable prospect of success.[12]

State practice confirms that disaster-affected individuals have exercised the core procedural element of the right to a remedy, i.e., the right to lodge complaints before domestic courts. As shown below, the triggers of the exercise of disaster victims' right of access to justice are situations where State's negligence in managing a disaster has resulted in violations of the rights to life, adequate housing and property. As these circumstances amount to infringements of internationally recognized human rights, disaster victims are entitled to seek recourse before domestic courts as guaranteed under international human rights law. Thus, on 21 December 2011 hundreds of victims of the flood that struck Thailand in November 2011 have initiated proceedings against national authorities before the Central Administrative Court. They are represented by the Stop Global Warning Association, which is alleging that even though the government had enacted the 2007 Disaster Prevention and Mitigation Act it 'failed to enforce it for the flood-prevention and flood-relief operations',[13] and that such failure caused disaster victims

---

[10] Human Rights treaties that set forth the right to a fair hearing include: the 1966 Covenant on Civil and Political Rights, Article 14; the 1990 Convention on the Rights of Migrant Workers, Article 18; the 1969 American Convention on Human Rights, Article 8; the 1981 African Charter on Human and Peoples' Rights, Article 7; and the 1950 ECHR, Article 6. On the relationship between the right of access to justice and the right to a fair hearing see: General Comment No. 32 *supra* n. 9, paras 19–21 and 25–29; Principles and Guidelines on the Right to a Fair Trial and Legal Assistance in Africa, *supra* note 9, Section A; ECtHR, *Silver and Others v. The United Kingdom*, Judgment of 24 September 1982, para 116; Shelton 2006, 123 and 125; and Ramcharan 2011, 50–52 and 78–79.

[11] The right to legal aid is set forth in several human rights instruments including: Article 14 (3) (d) of the 1966 Covenant on Civil and Political Rights; Article 8 (e) of the 1969 American Convention on Human Rights; and Article 6 (3) (c) of the 1950 ECHR. On the relationship between the right of access to justice and the right to legal aid see: Principles and Guidelines on the Right to a Fair Trial and Legal Assistance in Africa, *supra* n. 9, Section G; Access to Justice as a Guarantee of Economic, Social and Cultural Rights, *supra* n. 9, Executive Summary, Part A; General Comment No. 32 *supra* n. 9, para 10; ECtHR, *Airey v. Ireland*, Judgment of 9 October 1979, para 26; and Francioni 2008, 1.

[12] ECtHR, *Soering v. The United Kingdom*, Judgment of 7 July 1989, para 121; ACHPR, *Jawara v. the Gambia*, Communications Nos. 147/95 and 149/96 11, May 2000, paras 32 and 38; Human Rights Committee (HRC), *Lansman* et al. *v. Finlad*, Communication No. 511/1992, 8 November 1994, para 6.2; IACHR, *Victor Nicolas Sanchez* et al. *("Operation Gatekeeper") v. United States*, Petition No. 65/99, 27 October 2005, para 67; Bassiouni 2006, 215; Sullivan 2008, 18–19 and 22; and Amerasinghe 2004, 337–339.

[13] Hundreds of Victims Sue Premier, Govt Officials over Flood Ordeal, available at http://www.nationmultimedia.com/national/Hundreds-of-victims-sue-premier-govt-officials-ove-30172332.html. Accessed 15 February 2012.

to experience prolonged flooding and damages to their properties.[14] The organization is also seeking compensation on behalf of the flood victims.[15]

In Italy relatives of persons who died during the April 2009 earthquake have instituted civil proceedings against the government in August 2010 and August 2011. They are alleging that a governmental commission's failure to give advance warning caused the death of their loved ones during the earthquake and amounts to a violation of Article 2043 of the Italian Civil Code, on principles of civil law responsibility.[16] The plaintiffs are seeking millions of Euros in compensation.[17]

In the USA Hurricane Katrina victims have instituted several legal proceedings to seek redress for violations of their rights. The most relevant lawsuit for the purposes of this chapter is *Robinson* et al., *v. United States*.[18] In this case, homeowners and owners of businesses and properties that were destroyed during Hurricane Katrina sued the US Federal Government and the US Army Corps of Engineers under the 1948 Federal Tort Claims Act (FTCA) which makes 'the United States liable for injuries caused by the negligent or wrongful act or omission of any federal employee acting within the scope of his employment'.[19] Hurricane Katrina victims contended that the canal known as MR-GO, which the US Army Corps of Engineers built in 1968 and serves as a shortcut for ships that pass through the Mississippi River and head to the Gulf of Mexico, was flawed in its design, construction and operation, and that those flaws heightened the flood damage to movable and immovable properties in the eastern parts of New Orleans and St. Bernard Parish during Katrina. They also sought damages with a view to obtain redress for violations of their property rights. The district judge concluded that the US Army Corps of Engineers was liable under the FTCA for 'monumental'[20] negligence in operating and maintaining MR-GO and that such negligence contributed to the catastrophic flood damage to the eastern parts of New Orleans and St. Bernard Parish during Katrina. Importantly, the judge awarded some Katrina victims an aggregate of $719,698 in damages to compensate them for loss or damage to property and the inconvenience caused by the flood.[21]

Another important case for the purposes of this chapter is *Claire Brou,* et al., *v. Federal Emergency Management Agency,* et al., a federal class action in the Eastern District of Louisiana involving the Federal Emergency Management

---

[14] Ibid.

[15] Ibid.

[16] Interview with Dr. Maria Teresa Di Rocco, legal counsel for the plaintiffs, 30 January 2012.

[17] Ibid.

[18] *In re Katrina Canal Breaches Consolidated Litigation*, 647 F.Supp.2d 644, 650 (E.D.La. 2009).

[19] On the FTCA see generally: Congressional Research Service, Report for Congress, Federal Tort Claims Act, 2007, Order code 95-717.

[20] *Supra* n. 18, 717.

[21] Ibid., 734–736.

Agency (FEMA)'s failure to provide accessible trailers to persons with disabilities who were displaced and rendered homeless during Katrina.[22] The plaintiffs alleged that FEMA violated the 1973 Rehabilitation Act, the 1968 Fair Housing Act and the 1988 Robert T. Stafford Disaster Relief and Emergency Assistance Act.[23] The action was filed on 17 February 2006 and settled on 15 August 2006. Under the settlement FEMA was to provide the plaintiffs with accessible trailers, make changes to trailers the plaintiffs already had or help the plaintiffs find alternative housing.[24] Accessible trailers would be equipped with a ramp; enough turning space for wheelchairs; an accessible shower or tub; and grab bars in toilets, tubs and showers.[25]

As stated above, the right of access to justice further entails that remedies are substantiated in accordance with fair hearing guarantees. Procedural fairness implies: 'the absence of any direct or indirect influence, pressure or intimidation from whatever side and for whatever motive;'[26] equality of access by women and men to judicial bodies and equality before the law in any legal proceedings; expeditiousness of legal proceedings; conduct of lawsuits orally and publicly and specific judicial guarantees for persons charged with a criminal offense.[27] More generally, as Shelton put it, the concept of fair hearing encapsulates the notion that an applicant 'must have a bona fide opportunity to have his case tested in the merits and, if appropriate, to obtain redress'.[28]

State practice shows that the implementation of disaster victims' right to fair proceedings may necessitate simplification of legal procedures and more flexible evidentiary standards given the difficulty, in some cases, to allege occurrence of violations of human rights during disaster situations or produce the relevant evidence. This last circumstance occurred in Aceh, a region of Indonesia struck by the 2004 Indian Ocean Tsunami, where determination of property ownership was fraught with problems due to the loss of official and customary land ownership records, destruction of boundary markers and land loss caused by subsidence.[29] This point is not to suggest that at present the right to a remedy incorporates an obligation to simplify legal procedures and standards in order to facilitate the exercise of disaster victims' right of access to justice. Rather, it is meant to emphasize challenges that the implementation of disaster victims' right to a remedy poses and that it would be desirable that future developments of either

---

[22] *Claire Brou* et al., *v. Federal Emergency Management Agency,* et al., Case No.: 060838, available at http://www.fema.gov/pdf/library/brou_fema.pdf. Accessed 15 February 2012.

[23] Ibid., 2. On the Stafford Act see Kromm and Sturgis 2008, 8.

[24] *Supra* n. 22, Attachment A on Accessibility Note.

[25] Ibid.

[26] General Comment No. 32 *supra* n. 9, para 25.

[27] Ibid., paras 25–29, and Principles and Guidelines on the Right to a Fair Trial and Legal Assistance in Africa *supra* n. 9, Section A (2).

[28] Shelton 2006, 125.

[29] Harper 2009, 209; UNDP 2006.

human rights law or IDRL incorporate principles, norms or even mere guidelines concerned with the scope of disaster victims' right to fair proceedings.

Although the relevant State practice considered here does not present problematic issues vis-à-vis the independence and impartiality of the courts, it is worth dwelling on these elements briefly in order to explain their possible relevance vis-à-vis disaster situations. It bears pointing out that courts' independence from the executive branch is determined in light of different factors such as the manner of appointment of the bodies' members and their term of office, whether there are safeguards against external pressure and whether the bodies present an appearance of independence from the government.[30] Impartiality reinforces the principle of the independence of the judiciary by requiring that a judicial body 'shall base its decision only on objective evidence, arguments and facts presented before it' and that '[j]udicial officers shall decide matters before them without any restrictions, improper influence, inducements, pressure, threats or interference, direct or indirect, from any quarter or for any reason'.[31] In light of the above, it would appear that the requirements of independence and impartiality would be particularly relevant in cases in which disaster victims want to allege that the State's negligent behavior has contributed to the occurrence of a disaster or the State has failed to respond to the disaster adequately, since judicial bodies that are not independent and impartial may be unwilling to establish governmental responsibility and assess complaints objectively.

The right to legal assistance may also apply to the situation of disaster victims who want to institute legal proceedings against the State. UN and regional human rights bodies have made clear that such a right is not absolute but qualified. Specifically, disaster victims would be able to claim this right if they can prove to be indigent, legal representation is compulsory, claims involve complex legal issues or the nature of the rights at stake warrants legal aid.[32]

In reality, though, the implementation of the right to legal aid may be problematic where the disaster-affected State does not have enough financial resources to provide legal services free of charge. Arguably, the practice of the USA shows how this problem could be obviated. The US federal government has developed

[30] ECtHR, *Findlay v. The United Kingdom*, Judgment of 25 February 1997, paras 73–80; ECtHR, *Cirklar v. Turkey*, Judgment of 28 October 1998; Shelton 2006, 126; General Comment No. 32 *supra* n. 9, para. 19; and Principles and Guidelines on the Right to a Fair Trial and Legal Assistance in Africa *supra* n. 10.

[31] Principles and Guidelines on the Right to a Fair Trial and Legal Assistance in Africa *supra* n. 9, Section A (5).

[32] *Airey* case *supra* n. 11; Access to Justice as a Guarantee of Economic, Social and Cultural Rights *supra* n. 9, Executive Summary, and Conclusions, para. 90; General Comment No. 32 *supra* n. 9, para 10; Principles and Guidelines on the Right to a Fair Trial and Legal Assistance in Africa *supra* n. 11; Francioni 2008, 1; and Bassiouni 2006, 218–223.

the Disaster Legal Services Programs under the auspices of the FEMA.[33] Under these programs the Young Lawyers Division of the American Bar Association, a voluntary professional association, provides free legal assistance to disaster victims.[34] Recipients of legal assistance are low-income individuals who, prior to or because of the disaster, are unable to afford legal representation adequate to meet their needs as a consequence of a major disaster. Legal assistance includes: assistance with securing FEMA and other federal and State benefits available to disaster survivors; assistance with insurance claims (life, medical, property, etc.); counseling on landlord/tenant problems; assisting in consumer protection matters, remedies, and procedures; replacement of wills and other important legal documents destroyed in a major disaster.[35] The programs have been implemented in the aftermath of Hurricane Katrina, the 2011 Iowa floods and the September 2011 Hurricane Irene.[36] Hence, the lesson that can be learned here is that disaster-affected governments could provide legal assistance to disaster victims who meet the requirements identified by human rights bodies without straining their financial resources through partnerships with associations or groups of lawyers willing to do *pro bono* work.

A pre-condition of the exercise of the right of access to justice, including in a disaster setting, is the victim's awareness of available remedies and their legal rights. While at present the practice of disaster-affected States does not shed light on this issue, it is submitted that efforts aimed at developing norms and standards on the legal protection of disaster victims should address this point because disasters may introduce profound changes to the functioning of the domestic judicial system disaster victims should be made aware of.

Finally, it has to be reiterated that the right to a remedy implies that individuals shall have access to venues for recourse that are effective. That is: remedies that offer a reasonable prospect of success, and are likely to provide effective relief.[37] The scope of damages awarded in the *Robinson* case and the fact that the plaintiffs in the *Brou* case were able to obtain housing that was tailored to their specific medical needs appear to confirm that disaster victims have enjoyed the core substantive dimension of the right to a remedy.

---

[33] The legal basis for the establishment of the programs is the Code of Federal Regulations, Title 44, Section 206.164, available at http://www.femainfo.us/Disaster_Assistance_Overview-Legal_Aid.shtml. Accessed 15 February 2012. For a description of the programs visit the following website: http://www.fema.gov/assistance/process/additional.shtm#2. Accessed 15 February 2012.

[34] Ibid.

[35] Free Legal Advice is Available to Survivors of the 2011 Iowa Floods, available at http://www.fema.gov/news/newsrelease.fema?id=59458. Accessed 15 February 2012.

[36] Ibid., Legal Help Available for Hurricane Katrina Victims, available at http://www.fema.gov/news/newsrelease.fema?id=18701. Accessed 15 February 2012. Disaster Survivors Can Get Free Legal Assistance, available at http://www.fema.gov/news/newsrelease.fema?id=58335. Accessed 15 February 2012.

[37] *Supra* n. 12.

17.2.2 Restrictions to Disaster Victims' Right to a Remedy

As State practice shows, the greatest difficulty in guaranteeing the exercise of disaster victims' right to a remedy arises in cases where the exceptionally destructive force of a disaster has damaged or destroyed facilities where domestic courts are housed. Hurricane Katrina flooded courts buildings in Louisiana prompting a twofold governmental response consisting of relocation of federal courts in a sister jurisdiction,[38] and closure of State courts from September through early November 2005.[39] In Port-au-Prince the January 2010 earthquake destroyed the Palace of Justice, a situation the government tackled by moving the court of first instance to the premises of the prosecutor office and finding alternative locations for higher courts such as the Court of Cassation and the Court of Appeal.[40]

Other difficulties are to be ascribed to 'systemic' flaws of the domestic judicial system that existed before the disaster struck and may limit the exercise of the right to a remedy by disaster victims. The situation in post-quake Haiti is a case in point. There, sexual violence against women is pervasive and occurs in and around formal and informal camps where disaster victims are sheltered.[41] Troublingly, very few cases are reported, investigated and prosecuted.[42] The reasons why not many Haitian women who have been subjected to sexual violence report sex crimes are multiple and complex: these women are not aware of their legal rights; these women do not have access to legal services and aid; judges and prosecutors, who are not trained on women rights, tend to distrust and minimize cases involving sexual violence or regard them as domestic issues with no legal relevance. Moreover, it has been reported that 'the lack of training among police and prosecutors leads to confusion and lost opportunities for women and girls to build a viable case before evidence is lost',[43] while prolonged proceedings put at risk the

---

[38] Specifically, the district and bankruptcy courts in New Orleans temporarily relocated to other federal courthouses in Louisiana, while the 5th U.S. Circuit Court of Appeals relocated to Houston. See: What Did Katrina Teach Us? available at http://www.abajournal.com/magazine/article/what_did_katrina_teach_us/. Accessed 15 February 2012.

[39] Ibid.

[40] Report of the independent expert on the situation of human rights in Haiti, A/HRC/14/44, para 42.

[41] Amnesty International, Haiti, Annual Report 2011, the State of the World's Human Rights, available at http://www.amnesty.org/en/region/haiti/report-2011. Accessed 15 February 2012. On the situation of women during disasters see Sect. 16.3.1 in this volume.

[42] Ibid.

[43] Statement submitted to the UN Commission on the Status of Women for the 56th Session Concerning the Empowerment of Rural Women and their Role in Poverty and Hunger Eradication, Development and Current Challenges in Haiti (BAI, MADRE, KOFAVIV, CGRS, SOFA Bureau of Abricots, ESCDROJ, IGLHRC), available at http://ijdh.org/wordpress/wp-content/uploads/2011/11/CSW-Statement-11_21_2011-1.pdf. Accessed 15 February 2012.

physical integrity of those women that have reported cases of sexual violence and live near the alleged offender.[44]

The above overview bears two conclusive remarks.

First, it suggests that ensuring the functioning of some components of the domestic judicial system in the immediate aftermath of very serious disasters has been part of recovery efforts carried out by some disaster-affected States. One could speculate that such a determination and resilience in getting judicial institutions back to work is rooted in those States' awareness that the right to a remedy is a crucial element of rights protection and an antidote to widespread impunity disaster situations tend unavoidably to generate. From a human rights law point of view, temporary closure of some judicial institutions while ensuring the functioning of others during disasters may amount to a limitation of the right to a remedy. As Sommario's chapter shows, in order to be lawful such limitation must comply with certain requirements, including the fact that it would have to be shown to serve the interests of public safety.

In theory, States could also derogate from the right to a remedy during a disaster situation. The possible scope of such derogation is at present unclear since, as Sommario highlights, the right to a remedy is not among the rights that disaster-affected States have derogated from under the 1950 European Convention on Human Rights (ECHR) and the 1966 Covenant on Civil and Political Rights (ICCPR). The Human Rights Committee has dwelled on the derogability of the right to a remedy and offers useful and authoritative guidance, although theoretical. A combined reading of the General Comments on Articles 4 and 14 of the ICCPR, respectively, the derogation clause and the provision on the right to a fair trial/access to court, indicates that while, in principle, the right to a remedy is derogable and the State can, during an emergency situation, 'introduce adjustments to the practical functioning of its procedures governing judicial or other remedies',[45] certain dimensions of the right to a remedy cannot be deviated from at all times. In the Committee's views these dimensions are: the above mentioned fundamental principles of fair hearing, which imply the right of access to justice, and the effectiveness of the remedy itself.[46] The African Commission on Human and Peoples' Rights has also taken the view that the fundamental guarantees of fair trial are non-derogable while the jurisprudence of the Inter-American Court of Human Rights and the European Court of Human Rights (ECtHR) includes amparo and *habeas corpus* as additional non-derogable dimensions of the right of access to justice that apply to detained individuals.[47]

---

[44] Ibid.

[45] Human Rights Committee General Comment No. 29 on States of Emergencies, CCPR/C/21/Rev.1/Add.11, para 14.

[46] Ibid., paras 11 and 14; General Comment No. 32 *supra* n. 9, paras 6 and 19. Additionally, the Committee has maintained that the 'guarantees of fair trial may never be made subject to measures of derogation that would circumvent the protection of non-derogable rights'. General Comment No. 32 *supra* n. 9, para 6.

[47] Inter-American Court of Human Rights (IACtHR), *Judicial Guarantees in States of Emergency (Articles. 27(2), 25 and 8 of the American Convention on Human Rights),* Advisory

Finally, it has to be noted that addressing challenges as those that inform judicial protection of women rights in post-quake Haiti may be a daunting task for a State that has been struck by a disaster of catastrophic dimensions or a State that does not have enough financial resources to manage a disaster situation. Nevertheless, it is submitted that the State will have to find ways to address these problems since they amount to a violation of the right to a remedy. This is not to suggest that the State must tackle these issues in the immediate aftermath of the disaster when the very priority is the provision of disaster relief. Rather, it implies that measures to enhance women's access to justice and the effectiveness of remedies they may seek will have to be adopted, progressively and provided that they are within the State's budget, once the situation has normalized. Moreover, should the State face financial problems that hinder the adoption of the above measures in the post disaster phase seeking international assistance by the UN, other international organizations, NGOs and third States may be a viable option to consider in order to implement disaster victims' right to a remedy.

17.2.3 Disaster Victims' Right to Reparation

As the right to a remedy, the right to reparation is part of customary and conventional human rights law, and constitutes a pillar of the legal protection of victims of human rights violations.[48] When applied to disaster victims whose human rights have been violated by the State in connection with a disaster situation, the right to reparation entails that these individuals shall be awarded, depending on the specific circumstances of their case and the violations at stake, with specific forms of reparation. Namely: restitution, compensation, rehabilitation, satisfaction, and guarantees of non-repetition. The above reparations have

---

(Footnote 47 continued)
Opinion, 6 October 1987; IACtHR, *Habeas Corpus in Emergency Situations (Articles. 27(2) and 7(6) of the American Convention on Human Rights),* Advisory Opinion, 30 January 1987; ECtHR, *Isayeva and Others v. Russia*, Judgment of 15 November 2007; ECtHR, *Brogan v. the United Kingdom*, Judgment of 29 November 1998; ECtHR, *Sakik and Others v. Turkey*, Judgment of 27 November 1997; Francioni 2008, 43–47; and Ní Aoláin 2008.

[48] The right to some specific forms of reparation is set forth in Article 14 of the 1985 Convention against Torture; Article 39 of the 1989 Convention on the Rights of the Child; Articles 63 (1) and 68 of the 1969 American Convention on Human Rights; Article 15 of the 1989 ILO Convention on Indigenous and Tribal Peoples in Independent Countries. See also Human Rights Committee General Comment No. 31 on the nature of the general legal obligation imposed on State parties to the Covenant, CCPR/C/21/Rev.1/Add.13, paras 16–17; ACHPR, *The Social and Economic Rights Action Center and the Center for Economic and Social Rights v Nigeria,* Communication No. 155/96, 13–27 October 2011, 13–14; ECtHR, *Z and Others v. The United Kingdom,* Judgment of 10 May 2001, paras 113–131; Bassiouni 2006, 214 and 216–217; Shelton 2006, 159–172; Echeverria 2006, 279–297; Falk 2006, 478–503; and the 2011 Report of the Special Rapporteur on Trafficking in Persons, Especially Women and Children, A/HRC/17/35, 6–11.

different remedial purposes that are relevant to the situation of disaster victims whose human rights have been violated.

Restitution, which comes from the Roman law form of redress *restituere in integrum,* aims at restoring the victim to the original situation that existed before the violation of human rights has been committed.[49] Restitution, where possible, is considered the most preferable form of reparation in so far as it avoids the scenario in which the State would pay compensation and continue to violate human rights, it avoids the 'sometimes difficult and time-consuming assessment of damages by tribunals',[50] and, more importantly, it often 'corresponds to the [real] needs and desires of the victims'.[51] As shown in Sect. 17.4, restitution may constitute a powerful tool disaster victims can use to claim their right to housing infringed by the State. This author takes the view that restitution should be construed expansively to apply to violations of rights other than the rights to property or housing. For instance, where it is possible to ascertain that the disaster-affected State has contributed to destruction of school buildings or places of worship, restitution will require that the government rebuilds these structures or provides alternative infrastructures thereby restoring disaster victims' right to education, freedom of religion and cultural rights.

Compensation, typically consisting of pecuniary and moral damages, is designed to compensate victims for the financial and moral harm they have suffered as a result of human rights violations, and provide economic opportunities to realize projects and plans hampered by the occurrence of the violations. Unlike restitution, compensation does not restore or replace rights that have been violated and depending on the cases at stake may be inadequate to fully redress the harm sustained by the victim. Nevertheless, compensation is the second-best form of redress victims can seek.[52] State practice analyzed in Sect. 17.2.1 confirms that damages are a remedial measure consistently sought by disaster victims. However, it should be emphasized that the State may find ways to delay or avoid payment of damages ordered by domestic courts, a conduct engaged by the US federal government which has appealed to the Fifth Circuit Court of Appeals with a view to challenging the district judge's findings in the above mentioned *Robinson* case.[53] The US government's decision to appeal to the Fifth Circuit Court of Appeals is thereby procrastinating the payment of compensation to Katrina victims and could

---

[49] Basic Principles and Guidelines on the Right to a Remedy and Reparation for Victims of Gross Violations of International Human Rights Law and Serious Violations of International Humanitarian Law, (hereafter Basic Principles and Guidelines), GA Res.60/147, Section IX, (19); Shelton 2006, 271–275.

[50] See Shelton 2006, 272.

[51] Ibid.

[52] Ibid., 290–294; Basic Principles and Guidelines *supra* n. 49, Section IX (20); Tortell 2006; Burgorgue-Larsen and Ubeda de Torres 2011, 232–234; Sugarman 2006.

[53] Feds Challenge Sovereign Immunity in Hurricane Katrina Lawsuit, available at http://blogs.findlaw.com/fifth_circuit/2011/11/feds-challenge-sovereign-immunity-in-hurricane-katrina-lawsuit.html. Accessed 15 February 2012.

relieve the authorities from the obligation to pay damages should the court agree with the US that sovereign immunity under the Flood Control Act of 1928 applies. The Court has heard arguments in November 2011 and is expected to rule in early 2012.[54]

Rehabilitation is awarded to victims of serious violations of the prohibition of torture and other ill-treatments and aims at restoring the individual's full health and reputation. As such it can be understood as a form of restitution.[55] Rehabilitation includes medical and psychological care such as therapy, physiotherapy, surgery, and free access to health services; and legal and social services. Given its scope and purpose, it is submitted that rehabilitation is a suitable remedial measure for victims of violations of the right to health, too. The strict interrelatedness between the prohibition of torture and other ill-treatments and the right to health, warrants such an expansive approach to rehabilitation. As shown in Sect. 17.4, disaster victims who are women could seek rehabilitation if the State has denied them access to medical aid on the ground of their sex.

Satisfaction includes measures of a general nature which vindicate human rights violations and the victims and may contribute to pave the way to legal, political and social reforms.[56] Forms of satisfaction that can be awarded to disaster victims and their next of kin include: declaratory judgments in which international and domestic courts have found that disaster-affected States have violated certain human rights; identification of disaster victims' remains; and initiatives to commemorate and honor the memory of large numbers of disaster victims died as a consequence the government's failure to prevent or mitigate the effects of certain disasters.

Guarantees of non-repetition serve a deterrent purpose in the sense that they are designed to avoid recurrence of human rights violations perpetrated in the past.[57] Disaster victims should seek this type of reparation to effect changes of the way in which disaster situations are dealt with by asking courts to order the State to: (a) amend existing domestic law on disaster relief that has proved to be ineffective before, during and in the aftermath of a disaster; (b) adopt new legal frameworks on disaster relief that embrace a human rights-based approach, and (c) develop disaster prevention and mitigation mechanisms.

Before concluding, it has to be pointed out that disaster victims' right to obtain the above reparations is not absolute and depends on the nature of the violations they allege, the specific circumstances of their cases, whether the State has already provided some forms of compensation through disaster relief schemes,[58] and the extent to which the emergency caused by disaster has hindered the State's ability to provide reparation.

---

[54] Ibid.

[55] Shelton 2006, 275 and Fassbender 1999, 251–279.

[56] Basic Principles and Guidelines *supra* n. 49, Section IX (22); Shelton 2006, 276–277; Ramcharan 2011, 186.

[57] Basic Principles and Guidelines *supra* n. 49, Section IX (23), and Shelton 2006, 278–280.

[58] ECtHR, *Budayeva and Others v. Russia*, Judgment of 20 March 2008, para 197.

17.3 The Jurisprudence and Practice of Regional Human Rights Bodies

With a view to complementing the above analysis, the following sections focus on regional human rights bodies' jurisprudence and practice relevant to disaster victims' rights to a remedy and reparation. For the purposes of this chapter, the regional human rights bodies that come under review are the ECtHR and the Inter-American Commission on Human Rights (IACHR). The analysis aims at providing concrete examples of how human rights bodies enforce disaster victims' rights to a remedy and reparation.

17.3.1 The European Court of Human Rights' Jurisprudence

The ECtHR has been concerned with the plight of disaster victims in two cases decided between 2004 and 2008: *Budayeva and Others v. Russia* and *Öneryildiz v. Turkey*.

In *Budayeva and Others v. Russia* the Court found that Russia's failure to mitigate the effects of recurring mudslides, set up an early warning system to give advance warning to residents of a mudslide-prone town and evacuate them amounted to a violation of the right to life enshrined in Article 2 of the 1950 ECHR.[59] The Court also concluded that there was a causal link between the government's failure to take the above measures and the injuries sustained by some of the applicants and the death of Mr. Budayev, Ms. Budayeva's husband.[60] The case is particularly relevant for the purposes of this chapter since the Court addressed the issue of the adequacy of domestic judicial response in cases in which the State's omissive behavior has caused the death of disaster victims. With this regard, the Court interpreted Article 2 as imposing two fundamental procedural obligations. Namely, the obligation to carry out investigations that shed light on the circumstances surrounding the deaths and ascertain whether the government's responsibility was engaged,[61] and the obligation to ensure that legal proceedings are capable of establishing the circumstances of the accident.[62] Moreover, the Court found that the absence of a proper investigation as described above frustrated the applicants' prospect of success in domestic civil proceedings by making it impossible for them to prove 'to what extent the damage attributable to the

[59] Ibid., paras 147–160.
[60] Ibid., para 158.
[61] Ibid., para 162.
[62] Ibid., para 164.

State's alleged negligence exceeded what was inevitable in the circumstances of a natural disaster'.[63] In light of the above elements the Court concluded that Russia had violated the procedural dimension of Article 2 in so far as the investigation launched by the prosecutor office and the civil proceedings instituted by Ms. Budayeva and the other applicants fell short of the above State obligations set out in Article 2.[64] The applicants also alleged a violation of Article 13 of the ECHR on the right to an effective remedy and argued that available domestic venues for recourse to complain about violations of the right to life were not effective. As the Court already dealt with the adequacy of domestic judicial response when assessing the allegations concerning Article 2 it was not deemed necessary to examine the complaint relating to Article 13 with respect to the right to life.[65] The Court awarded the applicants non-pecuniary damages acknowledging in this way the emotional harm they experienced as a result of the substantive and procedural violations of Article 2.[66]

In *Öneryildiz v. Turkey* the right to life and the right to an effective remedy were again at stake. The Grand Chamber found that Turkey violated the substantive dimension of Article 2 since it failed to prevent a methane explosion at a rubbish tip which killed nine relatives of the applicant, and to inform the applicant and other slum dwellers that lived around the tip of the risks they were running.[67] The Grand Chamber also found a violation of the procedural dimension of Article 2 because, in its view, domestic criminal proceedings did not adequately address the question of whether the authorities were responsible for the death of the applicant's nine relatives and the persons held accountable were only sentenced to derisory fines, which were eventually suspended.[68]

Subsequently, after having established that there was a violation of the applicant's right to property, mainly because the authorities' failure to prevent the methane explosion caused the destruction of the applicant's house,[69] the Grand Chamber tackled the question of whether the applicant's right to an effective remedy in respect of his complaints concerning the rights to life and property had been breached, too. The Grand Chamber did find a violation of the right at hand

---

[63] Ibid., para 163.

[64] Ibid., para 165.

[65] Ibid., paras 194–195.

[66] The applicants also alleged violations of the right to private and family life (Article 8 of the ECHR) and the right to property (Article 1 of Protocol No. 1 to the ECHR). The Court found that these provisions were not violated, Ibid., paras 171–185 and 199–201. Additionally, the applicants submitted that domestic remedies that were available to complain about alleged violations of the right to property were not effective. The Court disagreed with them and found that, in this instance, there was no violation of Article 13, Ibid., paras 196–198. Finally, the Court rejected the applicants' claims for pecuniary damages submitted to obtain compensation for loss of property sustained during the mudslides. Ibid., paras 203 and 205.

[67] ECtHR, *Öneryildiz v. Tukey,* Judgment of 30 November 2004, paras 97–110.

[68] Ibid., paras 116–118.

[69] Ibid., paras 133–138.

since the civil proceedings the applicant instituted to seek compensation on account of the death of his nine relatives and the loss of his house and household goods were too long and the government failed to pay the compensation awarded by the domestic court.[70] The applicant sought pecuniary and non-pecuniary damages. The Court awarded pecuniary damages covering funeral expenses, loss of financial support and loss of movable property resulting from the government's negligence in preventing the methane explosion.[71] Acknowledging that the applicant suffered as a result of Articles 2 and 13 violations,[72] the Court additionally awarded him non-pecuniary damages.[73]

In both the above cases, the ECtHR's declaratory judgments, in which it was found that the disaster-affected States had violated certain human rights, constitute an additional remedial measure, specifically satisfaction, which was awarded to the applicants.

17.3.2 The Inter-American Commission on Human Rights' Practice

The IACHR has endeavored to enforce disaster victims' right to a remedy through the use of its power to request States to adopt precautionary measures. The power to request precautionary measures is detailed in Article 25 of the Commission's rules of procedure and aims at preventing severe and irreparable harm to individuals and communities. The Commission is authorized to order precautionary measures vis-à-vis individuals who have initiated proceedings before it and to protect individuals from imminent harm independently of any pending petition. The Commission's request to adopt precautionary measures is binding on States.[74]

On 15 November 2010, the IACHR granted precautionary measures to protect the residents of five camps for internally displaced persons (IDPs) set up in Haiti. The request for precautionary measures alleged that disaster victims who erected tents in open fields following the destruction of their homes by the January 2010 earthquake had been forcibly evicted by the police or by private individuals aided by the police.[75] The Inter-American Commission requested the government of Haiti to undertake several steps to address such situation including: adopting a moratorium on the expulsions from the camps until a new government could take office; making sure that those who have been illegally evicted were transferred to

[70] Ibid., paras 150–157.

[71] Ibid., paras 166–170.

[72] Ibid., para 171.

[73] Ibid.

[74] Burbano Herrera 2010, 8–16; Reiter 2010, 158–163.

[75] Phillips et al. 2011, 15.

places with minimum sanitary and security conditions[76]; and, more importantly for the purposes of this chapter, 'to guarantee that those who have been internally displaced have access to effective remedies in court and before other competent authorities'.[77] Regrettably, the Haitian government has thus far failed to implement the above urgent measures.[78]

17.3.3 Analysis

Regional human rights bodies' jurisprudence and practice enforcing disaster victims' rights to a remedy and reparation add new elements to the appraisal carried out in Sect. 17.2.

Thus, the relevant case-law of the ECtHR sheds light on the normative content of disaster victims' right to a remedy in situations in which the rights to life and property have been allegedly violated by the disaster-affected State. The cases reviewed above suggest that, where individuals have allegedly died as a result of the government's negligence in mitigating or preventing a disaster, the right to a remedy necessitates the carrying out of an investigation capable of establishing the circumstances of the deaths and the government's responsibility in connection with the alleged violations of the right to life. Furthermore, in the situation in question, the right to a remedy entails that legal proceedings instituted to complain about violations of disaster victims' right to life satisfy three main requirements: (a) the proceedings must determine, as for the investigation, the circumstances in which the deaths occurred and whether the government was responsible for them; (b) the proceedings must not be unduly delayed, and (c) where appropriate, the relatives of the deceased must be compensated. The requirements that proceedings are not unduly delayed and compensation is afforded, where appropriate, also apply to civil proceedings in respect to complaints alleging that the State's negligence in preventing a disaster has caused damage to disaster victims' movable and immovable property.

The ECtHR's remedial practice further clarifies circumstances which lead to the award of pecuniary and non-pecuniary (moral) damages to disaster victims. The *Öneryildiz* case reveals that pecuniary damages can be awarded to compensate disaster victims for loss of financial support and movable property which were caused by the government's failure to prevent a disaster situation; and funeral

[76] PM 367-10—Forced Evictions from Five Camps for Displaced Persons, Haiti, available at http://www.cidh.oas.org/medidas/2010.eng.htm. Accessed 15 February 2012.

[77] Ibid. The Commission also requested the Haitian government 'to implement effective security measures to safeguard the physical integrity of the camps' inhabitants, guaranteeing in particular the protection of women and children; to train security forces on the rights of displaced persons, in particular their right not to be expelled from the camps by force; and to ensure that international co-operation agencies have access to the camps for IDPs'. Ibid.

[78] *Supra* n. 75.

expenses incurred as a consequence of the said State' omissive conduct. An examination of the *Öneryildiz* and *Budayeva* cases tells that moral damages can be used to compensate disaster victims for the emotional harm they suffered as a result of the government's negligent behavior which infringed upon their human rights.

Also, the above cases confirm that the European Court's declaratory judgments in which the disaster-affected State's responsibility has been established is a type of satisfaction that is suitable to redress violations of disaster victims' rights in so far as the purpose of these judicial decisions is to establish the truth and vindicate the victims.[79]

Finally, it bears noting that the IACHR's practice shows that provision of effective remedies may, in urgent situations, constitute a relevant precautionary measure that can avert irreparable harm to disaster victims. In the case considered in Sect. 17.3.2, the IACHR took the view that, if disaster victims were to have access to justice and courts reviewed the lawfulness of the evictions, multiple violations of disaster victims' rights could be prevented. These rights include the rights to food and health, which were satisfied in the IDPs camps through provision of food and medical care by aid agencies. State's failure to ensure that disaster victims have access to effective venues for recourse, however, defeats the preventive purposes the right to a remedy may serve in the aftermath of a disaster.

17.4 A Holistic Approach to Domestic Redress of Violations of Disaster Victims' Rights to Health, Housing and Life

This essay concludes with an analysis of the effectiveness of the relief that disaster victims can seek domestically. In this regard, this author takes the view that in order to maximize the remedial scope of redress disaster victims could obtain at the domestic level, reparation claims should incorporate a combination of some of the reparations provided by international human rights law. Where possible, reparations geared toward the redress of the specific situation of the victim should be combined with reparations that have a more general breadth, and the remedial purpose of which is to rectify human rights violations which have had a detrimental impact on entire groups or communities, and prevent recurrence of human rights infringements.

Conceived as such, reparation claims can serve different but complementary purposes: vindicate disaster victims' rights and satisfy their sense of justice; ensure that disaster victims can go on with their lives; reshape more effective disaster

[79] See *supra* n. 67, para 169 and Shelton 2006, 256. Also, it should be noted that under the ECHR once the ECtHR has delivered a declaratory judgment in which it has found violations of Convention rights the respondent State is obligated to adopt, in addition to the damages the Court may have ordered, individual and general measures to remedy the violations at stake. See Hunt 2005.

response national strategies capable of preventing recurrence of certain human rights violations during future disasters; and enable communities that have been subjected to widespread violations of human rights during a disaster to reckon with these occurrences. Domestic courts should be receptive to such claims and willing to adopt such a comprehensive remedial approach if the cases they are assessing warrant it and the disaster situation has not severely impaired the government's ability to provide reparation.

With a view to illustrating how the above holistic approach can work in practice, this section looks at certain dimensions of the normative content of the rights to health, housing and life that may be especially at stake during a disaster; identifies elements of State responsibility; and puts forward suggestions, pertaining to the substance of reparations claims disaster victims could file before domestic courts, that epitomize the proposed holistic approach.

The first right that comes under examination is the right to health.

The Committee on Economic, Social and Cultural Rights (ESCR)[80] has maintained that the right to health, enshrined in Article 12 of the 1966 Covenant on ESCR, requires that individuals have access to health care without discrimination of any kind, including discrimination based on sex and health status,[81] and that State parties' obligation to ensure non-discriminatory access to medical care is a core non-derogable duty.[82] Studies and reports show that during disasters women may be 'overlooked if relief efforts [including those aimed at providing medical aid] target programs at household heads, or focus on primary employment as the sole source of livelihoods'.[83] Also, the situation of people living with HIV/AIDS highlights criticalities, and, specifically, the fact that during disasters these persons may be denied access to health care because of their medical condition.[84] These circumstances clearly violate Article 12 and engage the responsibility of a disaster-affected State that is a party to the Covenant on ESCR. Consequently, the individuals in question could sue the government relying on Article 12 and Article 2 (2) of the Covenant on ESCR on the prohibition of discrimination, if the government has incorporated the treaty in the domestic legal system,[85] or on relevant national legislation on the right to health, including laws that have been enacted to give effect to Article 12. Reparations that could be sought include not only rehabilitation and non-pecuniary damages but

---

[80] The Committee is the body that monitors State parties' compliance with the Covenant on ESCR. It was established by ESCOSOC Resolution 1985/17 of 28 May 1985.

[81] General Comment No. 14 *supra* n. 9, paras 12 (b) (i) and 18.

[82] Ibid., paras 43 and 47.

[83] Fitzpatrick (2007). Also, on the situation of women during disasters see Sect. 16.3.1 in this volume.

[84] 2011 UN Inter-Agency Standing Committee Operational Guidelines on the Protection of Persons in Situations of Natural Disasters, B 2.5, 37.

[85] On States that have incorporated the Covenant on ESCR in the domestic legal system see General Comment No. 9 *supra* n. 9, para 6. On the importance of the incorporation of the Covenant on ESCR in the domestic legal system vis-à-vis the judicial protection of the right to health see General Comment No. 14 *supra* n. 9.

also satisfaction and guarantees of non-repetition. Rehabilitative redress would consist of immediate and non-discriminatory access to adequate medical services free of charge, whereas moral damages would aim at compensating the above individuals for the distress they experienced as a result of the disaster-affected State's neglect of their medical condition and the humiliation and sense of stigmatization they suffered as a result of the discriminatory treatment. Satisfaction would take the form of an apology by the State, a form of reparation especially suitable to cases in which the government has violated the rights of large number of individuals. Guarantees of non-repetition would consist of laws providing for enhanced protection against discrimination of persons living with HIV/AIDS and women in disaster situations, and requiring the State to take into account the specific needs of these groups when adopting disaster prevention strategies, organizing and supervising disaster relief activities, and during the reconstruction phase.

Disaster victims may also encounter problems in exercising their right to housing if, for instance, the disaster has destroyed their homes. International human rights law is well equipped to address the above situation which has to be assessed in light of the Committee on ESCR's interpretation of the general scope of State obligations under the Covenant on ESCR. In General Comment No.3 the Committee has maintained that 'a state party in which any significant number of individuals is deprived of ... basic shelter and housing ... is, *prima facie*, failing to discharge its [core] obligations under the Covenant'.[86] Such view entails, for the purposes of this chapter, that a disaster-affected State that has ratified the Covenant on ESCR is obligated to provide disaster victims who have been rendered homeless with temporary shelter and find long-term housing solutions in consultation with them. This expansive interpretation is supported by the 2011 UN Inter-Agency Standing Committee Operational Guidelines on the Protection of Persons in Situations of Natural Disasters, a valuable tool that provides guidance on how human rights should be construed during emergencies such as natural disasters.[87] Should the State fail to provide disaster victims with adequate housing, disaster victims could institute proceedings against the government by relying on the Covenant on ESCR, if the State has incorporated it in the domestic legal system, or relevant national legislation and claim that their right to housing has been violated. The reparations they could seek include restitution in the form of provision of habitable structures and moral damages compensating for the stress endured as a result of being homeless. Alternatively, disaster victims could seek pecuniary damages consisting of a sum of money to be used to buy a new house, 'government bonds, reconstruction subsidies, [....] credit for building materials'[88] or housing vouchers. These forms of compensation could be coupled, as seen above, with moral damages.

---

[86] Committee on ESCR General Comment No. 3 on the nature of State parties obligations, 12/14/1990, para. 10.

[87] See *supra* n. 84, C2, 41.

[88] Harper 2009, 205.

Another important entitlement strictly related to the right to housing is disaster victims' right to return to their places of habitual residence and repossess their homes after the disaster if their houses have not been destroyed or severely damaged. Commentators have shown that this right is a derivative of the right to leave and return to one's own Country enshrined in Article 12 (4) of the ICCPR, Article 22 of the 1969 American Convention on Human Rights and Article 12 (2) of the 1981 African Charter on Human and Peoples' Rights.[89] Therefore, if a State Party to the ICCPR, which has incorporated this treaty in its legal system, prevents disaster victims from returning to their houses without putting forward a reasonable and objective justification, disaster victims could invoke Article 12 (4) before domestic courts, argue that this provision incorporates the right to return to one's home, and ask that the property is returned to them. Seeking restitution in this case is in line with the UN Guiding Principles on Internal Displacement and the UN Principles on Housing and Property Restitution for Refugees and Displaced Persons (known as the *Pinheiro Principles*) which, according to commentators, are evidence of a trend within human rights law toward the recognition of IDPs' right to land and housing restitution as a free standing and autonomous human right.[90] Also, guarantees of non-repetition in the form of new legislation on the establishment of special commissions charged with the enforcement of housing restitution during disaster situations may be an additional remedial measure to be sought for the purposes of preventing violations of the right to return to one's home should future disasters strike.[91]

Where disaster victims' right to return to their home is hampered by significant delays due, for instance, to the redefinition of property boundaries, disaster victims could still sue the State by using Article 12 (4) and seek not only restitution but also the establishment or upgrading of an electronic cadastral system, as a measure that will guarantee that if in the future disasters will strike again relevant records concerning housing ownership will be easy to retrieve thereby preventing the occurrence of violations of the right to return to one's home.

Finally, as the *Budayeva and Öneryildiz* cases suggest, in some disaster situations the State may be responsible for violations of the right to life of disaster victims. Under the ECHR a contracting State's failure to mitigate or prevent the occurrence of a disaster that results in the death of disaster victims engages the government's responsibility. In this case the ECtHR's jurisprudence is extremely clear: the State has an obligation to ensure that the deaths are properly investigated, legal proceedings are instituted against the alleged responsible, and the families of the deceased are compensated, if appropriate. If the State fails to comply with the above obligations the family members of the deceased disaster victims are entitled to sue the State before domestic courts by relying on the ECHR or other relevant legislation. If the number of the dead is large special forms of

[89] Paglione 2008, 393 and 402; Barber 2008.

[90] See Paglione 2008.

[91] This is in line with Pinheiro Principle 20.1.

satisfaction should be claimed in addition to damages. Namely, a public apology by the State which includes acceptance of responsibility and acknowledgment of the omissive acts; commemoration and tributes such as memorials dedicated to disaster victims; and streets named after them.

17.5 Conclusions

This chapter has delineated the contour of disaster victims' rights to a remedy and reparation under international human rights law. The analysis reveals that disaster victims, whose human rights have been violated by the State in connection with a disaster situation, enjoy the most essential procedural and substantive dimensions of the right to a remedy as established under international human rights law.

Relevant State practice indicates that disaster victims have exercised the core procedural component of the right to a remedy, that is, the right of access to justice, meant as the possibility to lodge complaints with domestic courts. The inquiry also confirms that disaster victims have a right to proceedings that are fair before independent, impartial and competent courts, an entitlement that is strictly linked to the right of access to justice. With this regard, the analysis has highlighted the necessity of simplified legal procedures and evidentiary standards given the difficulty, in some cases, to allege and prove the occurrence of violations of human rights during a disaster situation. It remains to be seen whether new developments in international human rights law or IDRL will address this issue in order to guarantee a more effective protection of disaster victims' right to a fair hearing and right of access to justice. Disaster victims who are indigent may also enjoy the right to legal aid, which forms part of the normative content of the right to a fair hearing, provided that they meet requirements specified by human rights bodies. Although the implementation of this right may be problematic for States that have been struck by a disaster and do not have enough financial resources, governments may follow the lead of the United States and create partnerships with lawyers who are willing to represent indigent disaster victims in legal proceedings without being paid.

The right to a remedy also incorporates a substantive dimension which entails that victims of human rights violations use remedies that are likely to provide effective relief. The scope of reparations afforded in the cases considered in Sect. 17.2.1 confirms that disaster victims have enjoyed the right to a remedy that is effective.

However, it should be borne in mind that disaster victims' right to a remedy is not absolute. As seen in Sect. 17.2.2, the right at hand may be subject to limitations where the disaster has destroyed or damaged the buildings that housed domestic courts. State practice shows that governments have been keen to find ways to ensure that courts can carry out their functions in the aftermath of a disaster, arguably, in an effort to uphold the rule of law and avoid, to the extent that it is possible, the spreading of a climate of impunity. Other challenges in the implementation of disaster victims' right to a remedy are to be ascribed to 'systemic' flaws of the judiciary that existed before the disaster struck and which should be addressed as soon as the situation has normalized or by resorting to international assistance.

The analysis of the right to reparation has complemented the examination of disaster victims' right to a remedy, and confirms that disaster-affected individuals, whose rights have been violated by the State in connection with a disaster situation, are entitled to seek the classical reparations provided under international human rights law. Namely: restitution, compensation, rehabilitation, satisfaction and guarantees of non-repetition.

The perusal of regional human rights bodies' jurisprudence and practice has highlighted additional dimensions of disaster victims' rights to a remedy and reparation. The ECtHR's case-law indicates that where individuals have allegedly died as a result of the government's negligence in mitigating or preventing a disaster, the right to a remedy requires: (a) the carrying out of investigations and institution of legal proceedings capable of shedding light on the circumstances of the deaths and establishing the government's responsibility in connection with the alleged violations of the right to life; (b) expeditiousness of legal proceedings, and (c) compensation of the dead's relatives, if appropriate. In addition, the right to a remedy requires institution of proceedings that are not unduly delayed and, if appropriate, provision of compensation in respect to complaints involving violations of disaster victims' right to property resulting from State's failure to prevent a disaster. The Court's case-law has further shown that pecuniary damages may be awarded to compensate disaster victims for loss of financial support, loss of earnings, and loss of movable property caused by the disaster-affected State's negligent conduct vis-à-vis disaster mitigation or prevention, whereas moral damages may be ordered to compensate disaster victims for the emotional harm they experienced as a result the government's negligent behavior which infringed upon their human rights.

Interestingly, the IACHR's practice shows that provision of effective remedies may constitute a relevant precautionary measure that can avert perpetration of violations of disaster victims' human rights in the aftermath of a disaster, provided that the State complies with it.

Finally, this chapter has made the case for a holistic approach to domestic redress of violations of disaster victims' rights. Specifically, it has been argued that in order to maximize the effectiveness of the relief disaster victims could seek at the domestic level reparation claims should incorporate a combination of some of the reparations provided by international human rights law. As highlighted in Sect. 17.4, where possible, reparations geared toward the redress of the specific situation of the victim, such as rehabilitation or damages, should be combined with reparations that purport to rectify violations of human rights which have had a detrimental impact on entire groups or communities, and prevent occurrence of human rights violations in the future, such as satisfaction and guarantees of non-repetition. As seen, such an approach to domestic redress can fulfill individual and societal purposes. That is, vindicate disaster victims' rights and satisfy their sense of justice; reshape more effective disaster response national strategies capable of averting recurrence of certain human rights violations during future disasters, and enable communities that have been subjected to widespread human rights violations during a disaster to reckon with them.

References

African Commission on Human and Peoples' Rights, Principles and Guidelines on the Right to a Fair Trial and Legal Assistance in Africa. http://www.achpr.org/english/declarations/Guidelines_Trial_en.html

Amerasinghe CF (2004) Local remedies in international law. Cambridge University Press, Cambridge

Amnesty International (2011) Haiti, annual report 2011, the state of the world's human rights. http://www.amnesty.org/en/region/haiti/report-2011

Barber RJ (2008) Protecting the right to housing in the aftermath of natural disaster: standards in international human rights law. Int J Refug L 20(3):432–468

Bassiouni MC (2006) International recognition of victims' rights. Hum L Rev 6(2):203–279

Burbano Herrera C (2010) Provisional measures in the case law of the inter-American court of human rights. Intersentia, Antwerp

Burgorgue-Larsen L, Ubeda De Torres A (2011) The inter-American court of human rights: case law and commentary. Oxford University Press, Oxford

Committee on Economic Social and Cultural Rights General Comment No. 3 on the nature of State parties obligations, 12/14/1990

Committee on Economic Social and Cultural Rights General Comment No. 9 on the domestic application of the Covenant on Economic Social and Cultural Rights, E/C.12/1998/24

Committee on Economic Social and Cultural Rights General Comment No.14 on the right to health, E/C.12/2000/4

D'Ascoli S, Scherr KM (2007) The rule of prior exhaustion of local remedies in the international law doctrine and its application in the specific context of human rights protection. European University Institute, Working Paper Law No. 2007/02

Echeverria G (2006) Codifying the rights of victims in international law: remedies and reparations. In: International Bureau of the Permanent Court of Arbitration (ed) Redressing injustices through mass claims processes: innovative responses to unique challenges, Oxford University Press, New York, 279–297

Evans M (1998) Remedies in international law: the institutional dilemma. Hart Publishing, Oxford

Falk R (2006) Reparations, international law and global justice, a new frontier. In: De Greiff Pablo (ed) The handbook of reparations. Oxford Scholarship online, Oxford, pp 478–503

Fassbender B (1999) Rehabilitation and compensation of victims of human rights violations suffered in East Germany (1945–1990). In Randelzhofer A, Tomuschat C (eds), State responsibility and the individual: reparation in instances of grave violations of human rights, Martinus Nijhoff Publishers, The Hague, 251–279

Fitzpatrick D (2007) Women's rights to land and housing in Tsunami-affected Indonesia, Oxfam International Policy Paper 9, Oxford

Forst M (2010) Report of the independent expert on the situation of human rights in Haiti, A/HRC/14/44

Francioni F (2008) The right of access to justice under customary international law. In: Francioni F (ed) Access to justice as a human right. Oxford University Press, Oxford, 1–55

Harper E (2009) International law and standards applicable in natural disaster situations. International Development Law Organization, Rome

Human Rights Committee, General Comment No. 31 on the nature of the general legal obligation imposed on State parties to the Covenant, CCPR/C/21/Rev.1/Add.13
Human Rights Committee General Comment No. 32 on the right to equality before courts and tribunals and to a fair trial, CCPR/C/GC/32
Human Rights Committee General Comment No. 29 on states of emergencies, CCPR/C/21/Rev.1/Add.11
Hunt M (2005) State obligations following from a judgment of the European court of human rights. In: Christou T, Raymond JP (eds) European court of human rights: remedies and execution of judgments, British Institute of International and Comparative Law, London, 25–48
Inter-American Commission on Human Rights, Access to Justice as a Guarantee of Economic, Social and Cultural Rights. A review of the standards adopted by the inter-American system of human rights, OEA/Ser.L/V/II.129Doc. 4
Kromm C, Sturgis S (2008) Hurricane Katrina and the guiding principles on internal displacement, a global human rights perspective on a national disaster, Institute for Southern Studies, Special Report, Vol. XXXVI, No. 1 and 2
Ngozi Ezelio J (2011) Report of the special rapporteur on trafficking in persons, especially women and children, A/HRC/17/35
Ní Aoláin F (2008) The individual right of access to justice in times of crisis: emergencies, armed conflicts and terrorism. In: Francioni F (ed) Access to justice as a human right, Oxford University Press, Oxford, 57–93
Paglione G (2008) Individual property restitution: from Deng to Pinheiro and the challenges ahead. Int J Refug L 20(3):391–412
Phillips N, Bergin K, Goldsmith J, Carr L (2011) Enforcing remedies from the inter-American commission on human rights: forced evictions in post-earthquake Haiti. Hum Rts Brief 19(1):13–17
Provost R (2002) International human rights law and humanitarian law. Cambridge University Press, Cambridge
Ramcharan BG (2011) The fundamentals of international human rights treaty law. Martinus Nijhoff Publishers, Leiden
Reiter E (2010) Preventing irreparable harm: provisional measures in international human rights adjudication. Intersentia, Antwerp
Rodley N (1999) The treatment of prisoners under international law. Clarendon Press, Oxford
Saengpassa S (2011) Hundreds of victims sue premier, govt officials over flood ordeal. http://www.nationmultimedia.com/national/Hundreds-of-victims-sue-premier-govt-officials-ove-30172332.html
Shelton D (2006) Remedies in international human rights law. Oxford University Press, Oxford
Sugarman SD (2006), Roles of government in compensating disaster victims, issues in legal scholarship, Manuscript 1093
Sullivan DJ (2008) Overview of the rule requiring the exhaustion of domestic remedies under the optional protocol to CEDAW. International Women's Rights Action Watch Asia Pacific, Kuala Lumpur
Tortell LA (2006) Monetary remedies for breach of human rights: a comparative study. Hart Publishing, Oxford
UNDP (2006) Access to justice in Aceh
PM 367-10—Forced evictions from five camps for displaced persons, Haiti. http://www.cidh.oas.org/medidas/2010.eng.htm

Chapter 18
Disasters Through the Lens of International Criminal Law

Francesca Russo

Abstract In a vulnerable planet devastated by more and more frequent natural disasters and anthropogenic catastrophes the international community is called on to meet a new challenge task: to provide efficient responses to humanitarian crises. This Chapter seeks to identify the role that international criminal law could play within the emerging *corpus juris* referred to as International Disaster Response Law. A criminally-oriented perspective explores the extent to which denial, refusal, or diversion of humanitarian assistance to disaster-affected populations falls within in existing definitions of unlawful acts punishable as crimes against humanity. Hypothetically, where an inappropriate response policy results in the massive loss of life rather than massive violations of fundamental rights, may reasonable be argued that crimes against humanity were committed. Such a theoretical conclusion also underlines potential deterrent effects usually attributed to criminalization, such as preventing heinous crimes from being perpetrated even in catastrophic situations.

Keywords Disasters · Response · Crimes · Humanity · Responsibility · Myanmar · Tribunals

Contents

F. Russo (✉)
Scuola Superiore Sant'Anna Piazza, Martiri della libertà, 33, 56217 Pisa, Italy
e-mail: fr.russo@sssup.it

A. de Guttry et al. (eds.), *International Disaster Response Law*,
DOI: 10.1007/978-90-6704-882-8_18,

18.1 Introduction

Cyclone Nargis and its aftermath provide an interesting case study to test the international reaction to humanitarian emergency and revived a lively debate on the responsibility to protect (R2P) doctrine, particularly in relation to its scope. Writing on the motives for fighting wars on behalf of others, Hugo Grotius asserted that '[t]he last and most extensive motive is the common tie of one Common Nature, which alone is sufficient to oblige men to assist each other'.[1]

Those words have even been invoked to justify a military intervention aimed at imposing aid to disaster survivors facing a humanitarian crisis. Nevertheless, another approach is possible: international criminal law could be called on to determine possible individual liability for international crimes perpetrated within disaster[2] scenarios. In other words, where a state is unable or unwilling to cope with a catastrophic event, may such inability or unwillingness to properly assist the affected population incur criminal responsibility?

The overview critically explores whether an inadequate response to disasters might amount to international crimes, in particular crimes against humanity as codified in the Rome Statute[3] (RS) and interpreted in the international jurisprudence. If the refusal, denial, restriction, and diversion of humanitarian aid or the forcible transfer of victims from equipped aid camps were to satisfy either the threshold test or the non-contextual elements of murder, extermination, forcible transfer of population, persecution, or other similar inhumane acts, those acts would fall within the conduct listed in the RS as 'underlying acts' of crimes against humanity.

Shortly after the restrictions imposed by the government of Myanmar on humanitarian aid, several States did argue that the R2P concept encompasses humanitarian assistance and did envisage its application to disaster victims. In addition, the European Union (EU) Parliament called upon EU member States to trigger the International Criminal Court (ICC) through a Security Council

---

1 Hugo Grotius, on the law of war and peace, translated from the original Latin De jure belli ac pacis, 2001, Batoche Books, Kitchener, Ontario, 247.

2 See *supra* Chap. 1 by de Guttry in this volume, providing the definition of disaster and humanitarian assistance.

3 1998 Rome Statute of the International Criminal Court.

referral. What is more, invoking the intervention of the Security Council and the application of the R2P doctrine to the Myanmar case, as endorsed by the General Assembly World Summit Outcome Resolution, implicitly acknowledges that international crimes were occurring. Following this line of reasoning, policies which are inadequate to assisting disaster survivors might *in abstracto* meet all the *actus reus* and the *mens rea* requirements of crimes against humanity. Accordingly, the analysis will be focused on those particular unlawful acts committed in disaster situations which may amount to crimes against humanity. It will be further extended to the assessment of the emblematic Myanmar case.

18.2 General Insight into International Crimes in Disaster Situations

Cyclone Nargis struck the city of Yangon on May 2–3, 2008, devastating a large part of the Irrawaddy Delta, causing the deaths of tens of thousands of people and destroying food stocks and housing.[4] The storm affected over 2 million people in the region and polluted natural resources.[5]

Despite international efforts to provide life-sustaining aid, the State Peace and Development Council (SPDC) denied the gravity of the disaster. While cyclone victims were struggling for shelter and food, the SPDC blocked access to the worst-affected areas and prioritized a constitutional referendum.[6]

Faced with increasing international pressure, Myanmar's authorities finally accepted external assistance for its population. On the other hand, from May 20 onwards, the SPDC ordered more and more survivors to leave government-run camps.[7]

Traumatized by such an emergency situation, the international community echoed deep concern expressed by non-governmental organizations (NGOs) about the humanitarian catastrophe survivors who were living in Myanmar. In late may, the United Nations (UN) and the Association of Southeast Asian Nations (ASEAN) organized a multilateral meeting in Yangon, gathering 51 countries, chaired by the UN Secretary-General Ban Ki-moon and ASEAN Secretary-General Surin Pitsuwan. The UN, ASEAN, and the SPDC established a mechanism to coordinate and deliver the emergency supply of vital relief goods. Notwithstanding these steps, 2 months after the surge of the storm NGOs estimated

[4] Amnesty International 2008b, 1.

[5] Human Rights Watch 2009, 223, estimating 84,000 dead and 53,000 missing.

[6] Ibid, 224.

[7] Amnesty International 2008a, 1.

that the SPDC's obstruction prevented hundreds of people from receiving basic aid.[8]

Bernard Kouchner, the French Foreign Minister, called upon the international community to forcibly intervene through the Security Council,[9] by invoking the application of the R2P doctrine. He argued that the Junta was guilty of crimes against humanity because of the above-mentioned obstruction of relief efforts and restrictions on disaster aid.[10]

Other voices asked the Security Council to authorize delivery of aid without the Junta's consent,[11] arguing that the denial, refusal, and diversion of international aid constituted crimes punishable under international law.[12] A controversial debate ensued on the scope of the so-called R2P doctrine and its application to disaster situations where the affected State is unable or unwilling to properly assist its population.

Thus, the case raises questions on the role of international criminal law in disaster scenarios. In particular, it must be explored to what extent contemporary paradigms of genocide, war crimes, and crimes against humanity might cover inadequate responses to assist disaster victims.

Labeled the 'crime of crimes' by the International Criminal Tribunal for Rwanda[13] (ICTR), genocide is traditionally referred to as the most heinous international crime.[14] Its physical elements have been codified by Article II of the *Convention on the Prevention and Punishment of the Crime of Genocide* (*Genocide Convention*), adopted by the General Assembly on 9 December 1948.[15] Article 6 of the RS incorporates the same definition.[16] Thus the above-mentioned legal instruments list five acts which constitute genocide, if committed with the intent to destroy, in whole or in part, a national, ethnical, racial, or religious groups, as such. The Elements of Crimes, adopted by the Assembly of States Parties (ASP) specify the definitions of crimes under the ICC jurisdiction,[17] namely Articles 6, 7, and 8. Under the RS, genocide by killing means that the

---

8 Human Rights Watch 2009, 224. See also *supra* Chap. 10 by Costas Trascasas in this volume, exploring the role played by the R2P doctrine and the access to the territory of a disaster-affected State.

9 See Kouchner 2008.

10 See Parsons 2008.

11 See Maddox 2008.

12 Robert Gates, American Defense Secretary, suggested that the Junta was guilty of 'criminal neglect', in Gates accuses Myanmar of 'criminal neglect': Schmitt 2008. See also Lewis 2008.

13 *Kambanda*, (ICTR-97-23-S), Judgment and Sentence, 4 September 1998, para 16.

14 Schabas 2010, 91, for an analysis of the historical origins of the crime of genocide and its *actus reus* criteria.

15 1998 Convention on the Prevention and Punishment of the Crime of Genocide.

16 The Statutes of the ICTR (Article 2) and the International Criminal Tribunal for former Yugoslavia (Article 4) authoritatively endorsed the same provision.

17 Pursuant to Article 9 RS, the Elements of Crimes were adopted by the ASP in 2002, Doc. ICC-ASP/1/3.

'perpetrator killed one or more persons' belonging to 'a particular national, ethnical, racial, or religious group'.[18] In addition, the related footnote further clarifies that 'the term "killed" is interchangeable with the term 'caused death'.[19]

Starting from the codified definition, under which circumstances might inadequate humanitarian assistance to disaster survivors constitute genocide?

Denying, refusing, diverting, or impeding disaster relief could, *in abstracto*, fall within the enumerated categories. Nonetheless, it would be complicated to prove the causality nexus between the misconduct (cause) and the physical destruction (effect).

Even where all *actus reus* requirements are fulfilled,[20] it is even more difficult to prove that the intent of such a conduct was destruction, total or partial, of a specific group. Indeed, the genocidal intent has traditionally been considered as the hallmark element of the crime of genocide. Paradoxically, this *dolus specialis* remains the most difficult element to prove.

A case-by-case approach to the application of the mental element is suggested by the Elements of Crimes.[21] A Trial Chamber of the International Criminal Tribunal for former Yugoslavia (ICTY) opined that genocidal intent

> 'may be inferred from a number of facts such as the general political doctrine which gave rise to the acts in Article 4 [ICTY Statute] or the repetition of destructive and discriminatory acts. The intent may also be inferred from the perpetration of acts which violate, or which the perpetrators themselves consider to violate the very foundation of the group—acts which are not in themselves covered by the list in Article 4(2) but which are committed as part of the same pattern of conduct'.[22]

Although some scholars recognize that, in principle, denying humanitarian aid to disaster victims could constitute an act of genocide, inflicting conditions of life calculated to bring about the total or partial destruction of a particular group, the evidentiary limits, arising from causality nexus and the mental element requirements in particular, do narrow its practical application to disaster situations.[23]

---

[18] Article 6 (a)(3) RS, Doc. ICC-ASP/1/3.

[19] Ibid., n. 2.

[20] See also Schabas 2010, 95, for a discussion of the quantitative dimension of genocide and its relationship with the mental element: a significant number of victims, *rectius*, the number of group members, the perpetrator intended to destroy could be taken into account as proof of such a genocidal element.

[21] Article 6(a)(3), Doc. ICC-ASP/1/3: 'Notwithstanding the normal requirement for a mental element provided for in Article 30, and recognizing that knowledge of the circumstances will usually be addressed in proving genocidal intent, the appropriate requirement, if any, for a mental element regarding this circumstance will need to be decided by the Court on a case-by-case basis'.

[22] *The Prosecutor* v. *Radovan Karadzic and Ratko Mladic* (ICTY IT-95-5-R61 and IT-95-18-R61), Review of Indictment pursuant to Rule 61, 11 July 1996, para 94.

[23] Ford 2010, 275. See also, Barber 2009. Other authors focus on the intentional denial of humanitarian assistance, although disaster emergencies are not included in their analysis. See, e.g., Rottensteiner 1999, 555.

War crimes represent egregious acts which are punishable under international humanitarian law[24] (*jus in bello*) and hence entail a precondition: the existence of an armed conflict. Thus, such conduct tends to be excluded, a priori, from the debate on the application of international criminal law to catastrophic events.[25]

18.3 Assessing Crimes Against Humanity in Disaster Scenarios: Controversial Contextual and Non-Contextual Elements of Crimes

When Cyclone Nargis devastated the Irrawaddy Delta, several commentators invoked the R2P doctrine,[26] assuming that crimes against humanity were being committed in Myanmar. Gareth Evans stated:

> 'if what the generals are now doing, in effect denying relief to hundreds of thousands of people at real and immediate risk of death, can itself be characterized as a crime against humanity, then the R2P principle does indeed cut in'.[27]

Other authorities countered his position, arguing that such an interpretation would have jeopardized the efforts accomplished to shape a shared articulation of the doctrine itself. Indeed, Ramesh Thakur declared:

> 'there would be no better way to damage responsibility to protect beyond repair than to have humanitarian assistance delivered into Myanmar backed by Western soldiers fighting in the jungles of Southeast Asia again'.[28]

Since massacres are not necessarily committed with knives,[29] the first step will to assess contemporary crimes against humanity and their applicability to unusual dimensions, i.e., disaster emergencies, traditionally disregarded. In other words, might inadequate responses to disaster emergencies fit into violations which are punishable under international criminal law as crimes against humanity?

This category of crime encompasses a larger range of criminality than genocide and war crimes.[30] In this perspective, Article 7 RS will constitute the focal point,

---

[24] See *supra* Chap. 11 by Venturini in this volume, exploring the relationship between disasters and international humanitarian law principles.

[25] Ford 2010, 274–275; Barber 2009.

[26] See *infra* 18.4.

[27] See Evans 2008.

[28] See Thakur 2008.

[29] Rottensteiner 1999 quotes a refugee from Kosovo. The author explores potential prosecutions under international criminal law for denial of humanitarian assistance. Natural disasters are explicitly excluded from this analysis.

[30] The first time this criminal category was formally used was to label the atrocious massacres committed by the Turkish government against Armenians. See Schabas 2010, 98–100, for historical remarks on dealing with crimes against humanity through legal instruments.

around which the dissertation will be developed. First, the individual contextual elements will be explored through a disaster-oriented approach, and then the analysis will turn to the most relevant offenses punishable in the context of catastrophic events in which inadequate humanitarian assistance could entail individual criminal responsibility. This Section seeks to assess whether such conduct falls under international jurisdiction.

18.3.1 Threshold Test

The establishment of the ICC as an independent and permanent judicial body has marked a turning-point in the fight against impunity. The Court is mandated to try and punish the most serious crimes 'of concern to the international community as a whole'.[31] Thus, less serious misconduct which does not reach that threshold of criminality is excluded from its *ratione materiae* jurisdiction.

The *chapeau* to Article 7(1) RS codifies this jurisdictional threshold, establishing that the enumerated acts set out in the same provision constitute crimes against humanity 'when committed as part of a *widespread or systematic attack directed against any civilian population*, with knowledge of the attack' (emphasis added).[32] Thus, the definition chosen by the drafters includes several components, which deserve a more detailed explanation. The threshold requirement is considered as the internationalizing element of crimes against humanity.

Preliminary remarks should, however, be devoted to another debated issue: the nexus with armed conflict. Initial attempts to criminalize crimes against humanity also required the relevant acts to have been committed in armed conflict. The Statute of the ICTY still mentions such a nexus,[33] whereas the ICTR Statute[34] dispenses with any reference to the link with armed conflict, whether international or non-international. ICTY jurisprudence subsequently acknowledged that the nexus is 'obsolescent'.[35] Finally, the Statute adopted at the Rome Conference omits any link with armed conflict; Article 7 RS echoing the evolution of the concept of crimes against humanity. It follows that this provision applies to atrocious crimes committed in peacetime. Similarly, the introductory paragraph does not mention any specific motive, so that unlawful acts could amount to crimes

---

31 Preamble to the RS and Article 5 RS, 'The jurisdiction of the Court shall be limited to the most serious crimes of concern to the international community as a whole'.

32 These words are preceded by the expression 'for the purpose of the Statute'. As suggested by a cross-reading (Articles 10 and 22), by this premise, drafters intend to identify a definition only applicable before the Court.

33 Article 5.

34 Article 3.

35 *Prosecutor* v. *Dusko Tadic a.k.a. 'Dule'* (ICTY IT-94-1-AR72), Decision on the Defence Motion for Interlocutory Appeal on Jurisdiction, 2 October 1995, para 140.

against humanity even if they were not perpetrated on discriminatory grounds.[36] Consequently, this category of crime has been used conceived as a legal vehicle to target the widest range of atrocities. But which is the *quid pluris* elevating those acts to the threshold established by the Statute?

18.3.1.1 Widespread or Systematic Attack Directed Against any Civilian Population

The RS threshold embodies the so-called contextual element of the physical conduct set out in Article 7(1), since it imposes a connection between the unlawful acts committed by the perpetrator and the context in which they occurred. The 'widespread or systematic' raises common crimes to the international level of crimes against humanity. Para 2 expressly describes a widespread or systematic attack as 'a course of conduct involving the multiple commission of acts referred to in para 1 against any civilian population pursuant to or in furtherance of a State or organizational policy to commit such attack'.[37] Three sub-conditions are required: a multiple conduct, direction of the attack on any civilian population, connection with a State or organizational policy (policy element). The definition is further clarified by explanatory provisions contained in Article 7 of the Elements of Crimes: while re-calling the principle of legality and therefore propounding a restrictive approach,[38] para 3 explicitly states that the acts need not amount to a military attack.

A disjunctive construction means that the attack could be realized in a widespread or alternatively in a systematic manner.[39] These adjectives imply a very high threshold, ultimately aimed at the exclusion of isolated or random acts, so that the term 'widespread' requires a large-scale nature of the attack directed against a multiplicity of victims, while the term 'systematic' means that the attack must follow an organized and regular pattern.[40]

By 'directed against any civilian population' Article 7 identifies the primary object of the attack: the architecture of crimes against humanity intends to exclude

---

[36] Hall 2008, comparing different threshold requirements set out in several legal instruments which were adopted before the Court's Statute. A lengthy and detailed analysis is devoted to the nexus with armed conflict and to discriminatory grounds. In particular, the practice of the *ad hoc* tribunals has shed light on these issues from a customary standpoint: their jurisprudence leans towards the definition chosen by the drafters at the Rome Conference.

[37] Article 7(2)(a) RS.

[38] The so-called *nullum crimen sine lege* principle prohibits interpretation by analogy *in malam partem* (Article 22 RS).

[39] *Tadić, supra* n. 35, Opinion and Judgment, 7 May 1997, para 656, confirms a disjunctive approach.

[40] *Prosecutor* v. *Kunarac et al.* (ICTY IT-96-23-A), Judgment, Appeals Chamber, 12 June 2002, para 94.

single acts randomly directed against a limited number of individuals.[41] Finally, the adjective 'civilian' confirms that the category aims at protecting a broader range of victims than war crimes.

The so-called policy element is still the most disputed component of crimes against humanity set out in the RS with regard to international customary law. It requires that the acts originate from or contribute to a State or organizational policy. One interpretation argues that such a requirement reflects international customary law. The ultimate aim is to avoid the misapplication of crimes against humanity to non-State actors.[42] The diametrically opposite interpretation denies the customary character of the policy prerequisite. Recent international pronouncements support the second interpretative position, leaning toward a non-customary nature of the policy element.[43] Nonetheless, the statutory additional criteria need to be satisfied when prosecuting crimes against humanity: such a plan or policy need not have been formally articulated and may be inferred from the circumstances in which the prohibited conduct occurred.[44]

For the purpose of the present analysis, a first problematic issue related to potential disaster scenarios must be addressed: might disasters *per se* be considered attacks? Based on the afore-mentioned interpretative rationales, such an interpretation would lead to a misleading and even meaningless application of crimes against humanity.[45] In situations similar to those the aftermath of Cyclone Nargis in Myanmar in 2008 in, it may conceivably be argued that the existing

---

[41] Ibid., para 91.

[42] The ICC Statute is the first legal instrument to formalize the policy element. Bassiouni 2011, 40–42, highlights that even the extension of crimes against humanity to non-State actors, such as paramilitary groups, still imposes a policy element. Indeed, it is the requirement which distinguishes crimes against humanity from common crimes, which are punishable under domestic criminal law (e.g., organized crime and transnational organized crime groups). Such a policy condition seems to be implicitly contained in the broader contextual element, i.e., 'widespread or systematic attack', so that the specification mentioned by Article 7(2) RS may even be redundant. In conclusion, the author deems it useful to specify that the expression 'organizational policy' does not refer to the policy of a non-State actors' organization. *Contra*, more recently, the Pre-Trial Chamber II of the ICC addressed the issue in its decision on the authorization to open an investigation into the situation in the Republic of Kenya (31 March 2010), concluding that 'The Chamber finds that had the drafters of the Statute intended to exclude non-State actors from the term "organization", they would not have included this term in Article 7(2)(a) of the Statute. The Chamber thus determines that organizations not linked to a State may, for the purposes of the Statute, elaborate and carry out a policy to commit an attack against a civilian population'.

[43] The ICTY has held that that practice 'overwhelmingly supports the contention that no such requirement [a policy or plan] exists under customary international law', *Kunarac*, *Prosecutor* v. *Kunarac et al.* (ICTY IT-96-23-A), Judgment, Appeals Chamber, 12 June 2002, para 287. But Bassiouni, ibid., 41, argues that the ICTY Appeals Chambers in the *Kunarac* case mistakenly denied the customary nature of the policy requirement.

[44] *Katanga and Ngudjolo Chui* (ICC-01/04-01/07-717), Pre-Trial Chamber I, Decision on the confirmation of charges, para 396.

[45] See Ford 2010, 260.

scope of widespread and systematic attack already encompasses the consequences deriving from a government's inability or unwillingness to respond to disaster events. The direct effects caused by the calamitous event, when inadequately addressed (because of denial, refusal, or diversion of relief aid), might involve further tragic consequences and lead to a massive loss of life, perfectly consistent with the analyzed interpretation of widespread and systematic attack.[46] On the other hand, the high gravity threshold required to establish crimes against humanity constitutes the strongest obstacle against the fear of prosecuting the less serious conducts, randomly committed within disaster situations.

18.3.1.2 With Knowledge of the Attack

The second contextual requisite pertaining to the threshold element of crimes against humanity is specified in the Elements of Crimes and is common to all acts listed in Article 7 RS: the perpetrator must know that her/his acts constitute part or are intended to be part of a larger context, namely a widespread or systematic attack on the civilian population.[47] However, a precise and detailed knowledge of the plan or policy of the State or organization is unnecessary.[48] The underlying motive is equally irrelevant.[49]

Applying this element to acts committed within a disaster environment, the perpetrator's knowledge of the context is also required. In addition, in these particular situations the evidentiary test is even less stringent. Indeed, perpetrators bearing criminal responsibility under international criminal law usually coincide with the same political leaders whose actions deny or block aid to survivors. *Ergo*, they could not claim to have been unaware of the attack they contributed to.[50] All in all, extensive media coverage and international pressure symptomatically suggest awareness of an undeniable contextual dimension.

18.3.2 Specific Acts and Their Non-Contextual Elements

A provisional conclusion leads toward a potential application of threshold requisites of crimes against humanity to unlawful acts perpetrated in disaster contexts.

---

[46] Ibid.

[47] See, *inter alia*, *Kunarac*, *supra* n. 43, para 99.

[48] Article 7(2) Elements of Crimes.

[49] *Kunarac*, *supra* n. 43, para 103.

[50] Ford 2010, 261, assesses the Junta's awareness of the attack in the aftermath of Cyclone Nargis. Despite intense international pressure, the government of Myanmar did deny the gravity of an ongoing humanitarian crisis.

Once this argument is accepted, disaster scenarios raise another problematic issue: which acts are more consistent with disaster-affected scenarios?

An inadequate response to either natural or anthropologic disasters is supposed to realize through denial or refusal of humanitarian aid to the victims. Such policy reasonably risks creating inhumane living conditions for survivors, leading to their death. The Myanmar experience witnessed in 2008 has provided a wider catalogue of material options, including the diversion of relief resources and forcible transfer of survivors to unsafe areas.[51] These are the main reasons why murder, extermination, persecution, forcible transfer of population, and other inhumane acts will be scrutinized.

Before addressing specific *actus reus* requirements, it is worth clarifying that crimes against humanity can be committed either by act or omission.[52] Indeed, a policy to refrain from taking action is likely to worsen the detrimental living conditions of disaster survivors struggling for basic necessities. Denial of humanitarian aid is equally likely to increase the number of deaths. Following this line of reasoning, the failure to act in response to disasters could fall within the definition of crimes against humanity by omission.

18.3.2.1 Murder

Murder as a crime against humanity requires two *actus reus* elements: the victim's death and a causality nexus between the unlawful act or omission of the accused and the death itself.[53] This category does not, in principle, raise any interpretative issues. Since footnote 7 of the Elements of Crimes specifies that 'the term killed is inter-changeable with "caused death"', failure to provide food or medical assistance can give rise to criminal responsibility for murder, when that failure resulted in the victim's death.

In a disaster scenario, the causality link is a challenging physical requisite to prove. Nonetheless, when survivors do not receive any aid in terms of food, access to water, shelter, medical assistance, due to an obstructive policy endorsed by governmental authorities, and when some deaths occur long after the surge of a storm, there is a sufficient body of evidence to conclude that some deaths were probably caused by the acts or omission of the accused. When, despite the pressure exercised by international community, blockades obstruct humanitarian aid and rescue teams, there appears to be a reasonable basis to believe that those deaths are consequences of the denial of assistance to disaster victims. Restrictions on aid

---

[51] See *supra* Sect. 18.2.

[52] See, *inter alia*, *Akayesu* (ICTR-96-4-T), Judgment, 2 September 1998, para 589, referring to murder; *Prosecutor* v. *Kayishema* (ICTR 95-1-T), Judgment, Trial Chamber, para 147, referring to extermination.

[53] Ibid., *Akayesu*.

distribution envisage another possible factual scenario able to cause death, or at least to cause a number of deaths higher than expected.

In conclusion, it is conceivable that individuals may be held liable for murder as a crime against humanity on account of an inappropriate response to disasters, provided that the threshold conditions are met.

18.3.2.2 Extermination

The crime against humanity of extermination has not been defined by the Statute of the ICC. However, the ICTR considered that '[e]xtermination is a crime which by its very nature is directed against a group of individuals'.[54] Thus, it involves killing on a large scale, such that its *actus reus* elements include large-scale killing, directed against a targeted group of individuals.

Hence, this second category includes all objective elements of the crime of murder. International jurisprudence largely accepts that individual criminal responsibility may be incurred for extermination by omission, where the perpetrator fails to prevent others from committing the crime, provided that he or she has a duty to act in order to avoid the fatal event.[55]

Another particular requirement must also be fulfilled, namely the direction of mass killing against members of a targeted group. The concept of targeted group encompasses an open-ended variety of groups, which can be identified on, e.g., social, linguistic, or political grounds or even sexual orientation. Indeed, the concept covers collective categories which are not protected by the crime of genocide, and even groups which only exist as such in the mind of the perpetrator.

With regard to extermination, the Court's Statute provides some clarifying guidance which could assist in the assessment of disaster scenarios: the provision explicitly states that extermination includes 'the intentional infliction of conditions of life, *inter alia* the deprivation of access to food and medicine, calculated to bring about the destruction of part of a population'.[56] These words recall the provisions of the crime of genocide perpetrated by deliberately inflicting on the group conditions of life calculated to bring about its physical destruction in whole or in part. The related footnote specifies that the term 'conditions of life' may involve, but are not necessarily limited to the 'deliberate deprivation of resources

[54] See *Akayesu*, *supra* n. 52, para 591. See also para 592, in which the Chamber identified 'the essential elements of extermination as the following: (1) the accused or his subordinate participated in the killing of certain named or described persons; (2) the act or omission was unlawful and intentional; (3) the unlawful act or omission must be part of a widespread or systematic attack; (4) the attack must be against the civilian population; (5) the attack must be on discriminatory grounds, namely: national, political, ethnic, racial, or religious grounds'.

[55] *Prosecutor* v. *Rutaganira* (ICTR 95-1C-T), Judgment, Trial Chamber, 14 March 2005, para 68, elaborating on the circumstances under which the accused can be held responsible for extermination committed by indirect participation in the commission of the crime.

[56] Article 7(2)(b) RS.

indispensable for survival, such as food or medical services, or systematic expulsion from homes'.[57] Therefore, the provision assumes that such conditions of life may lead to inevitable death.[58]

The statutory provisions identify physical conduct which is perfectly consistent with a disaster scenario: disaster victims need basic assistance in order to secure access to food, basic necessities, water, sanitation, and medical care. In humanitarian crises caused by calamitous situations, the lack of proper aid inevitably leads to a massive loss of life among survivors. Such a deprivation of basic assistance may equate infliction of inhumane conditions of life falling within the formulation elaborated by the drafters of the ICC Statute. It is finally worth underlining that survivors may constitute a group under the definition analyzed above.

From this analysis, it may be concluded that depriving disaster victims of basic necessities for survival after a calamitous event may incur individual criminal responsibility for extermination, provided that there is a sufficient body of evidence that a causality link exists between the fatal events and the deliberate infliction of inhumane conditions of life.

18.3.2.3 Forcible Transfer of Population

By 'forcible transfer of population', the Statute means a forced displacement of people from one area to another within national borders.[59] As the Elements of Crimes further explain, the expression 'forcibly transferred' is interchangeable with 'forcibly displaced'.[60] The expression 'forcible transfer of population' means forcing people to move from one place to another without crossing national borders. As further specified in a footnote, the term 'forcible' is not limited to physical force, but also includes a psychological dimension of coercion, which may even arise from a coercive context.[61]

The non-contextual elements of the crime set out in the Statute also require that the individuals concerned are lawfully present in the area from which they are involuntarily removed. Finally, the compulsory displacement of civilians from a place in which they are lawfully present is not permitted on any admissible ground

---

57 Footnote 4, Article 6(c) Elements of crimes.

58 See, *inter alia*, *Kayishema*, *supra* n. 52, para 144.

59 Article 7(2)(d) RS. It is important to highlight that the crime against humanity of forcible transfer of population is coupled with the crime of deportation. Although, the Statute does not provide any distinguishing element, human rights instruments have largely clarified their legal nature. Indeed, the former prohibits compulsory internal displacement, whereas the latter prohibits transnational removal of population. However, the Statute of the ICTY and the ICTR do not list the crime of forced transfer of population among crimes against humanity. However, their jurisprudence has included acts of forced displacement under the definitions of, persecution, other inhumane acts or war crimes.

60 Footnote n. 13, Article 7(1)(d) Elements of Crimes.

61 Footnote n. 12, Article 7(1)(d) Elements of Crimes.

established within the framework of international law. Possible restrictions based on public order, national security, or public safety has to be consistent with the limits prescribed by international law.

In disaster situations, ordering the removal of survivors from government-equipped camps or other locations where they are lawfully present could might easily fall within the definition of unlawful forcible transfer of population.

It is important to bear in mind that forcing survivors to return to villages or towns in disaster-affected areas could put their lives at risk, or could amount to inflicting conditions of life presumably leading to death. Hence, such conduct could give rise to criminal responsibility for extermination, murder but also forcible transfer of population, provided that the magnitude is of the required widespread or systematic character.

18.3.2.4 Persecution

The Statute also criminalizes acts of persecution as crimes against humanity.[62] Statutory provisions reword the definition provided by the ICTY in the *Tadic* case[63] and describe persecution as intentional and severe discrimination which infringes the enjoyment of fundamental rights to which every individual is entitled. Its a*ctus reus* also requires that the violations of those fundamental rights to which every individual is entitled was committed with the discriminatory intent based on, political, racial, national, ethnic, cultural, religious, gender, or other grounds that are universally recognized as prohibited under international law.[64] Indeed, it is necessary for the victims to have been persecuted because of their membership in an identifiable group.

According to the wording of the Statute, discrimination also extends to other acts listed in para 1 as crimes against humanity, along with any crime under the Court's jurisdiction.[65] This means that if murder, extermination, or forcible transfer of population is carried out on discriminatory grounds, they are also punishable as persecution.

Where the denial of assistance to survivors is based on discriminatory grounds, the conduct comes within the definition of persecution as crime against humanity, provided that the threshold criteria are met.

---

[62] Article 7(1)(h) RS.

[63] *Tadic*, *supra* n. 34, para 697.

[64] Article 7(1)(h).

[65] Ibid.

18.3.2.5 Other Inhumane Acts

'Other inhumane acts' is the final species of conduct punishable as a crime against humanity.[66] Their non-contextual element is similar with the acts listed in the same provision, determined on the basis of the 'nature and gravity of the acts', as the Elements of Crimes expressly specify.[67] Finally, those acts must intentionally cause great suffering, or serious injury to body or to mental or physical health.[68]

Based on a so-called *ejusdem generis* interpretation, the provision appears to be an open-ended clause, which the drafters admirably intended would criminalize, through an evolving interpretation of the Statute, any conduct that Article 7 does not expressly enumerate.[69] On the other hand, authoritative scholars have, on the whole, disputed the nebulous wording of the provision and, essentially raised doubts as to its compliance with the principle of legality, summarized by the Latin maxim *nullum crimen sine lege*.[70]

However, flexible and amorphous wording does allow an extensive application of the underlying provisions, so that 'other inhumane acts' could be elevated to play a key-role with regard to disaster situations. Indeed, there is little doubt that the deprivation of shelter, clothing, food, medical attention, water, and sanitation causes psychological and/or physical suffering.[71] Such conduct could conceivably constitute a serious threat to human dignity, although its character must be determined on a case-by-case basis.[72] Consequently, it is not unreasonable to argue that an inadequate response to a humanitarian crisis caused by a disaster might fall under the definition of 'other inhumane acts', provided that the *chapeau* requirements are equally fulfilled.

---

[66] Article 7(1)(k) RS.

[67] Footnote n. 30, Article 7(1)(k), clarifying that 'it is understood that "character" refers to the nature and gravity of the act'.

[68] Article 7(1)(k) RS.

[69] The jurisprudence of the *ad hoc* tribunals has applied similar provisions contained in their Statutes. See, e.g., *Prosecutor* v. *Milosevic* (ITCY IT-02-54-T), Decision on Motion for Judgment of Acquittal, Trial Chamber, 16 June 2004, para 52, determining that the crime of forcible transfer 'could have been covered in the reference to "other inhumane acts"'.

[70] Article 22 RS. Consistency with the principle of legality also requires a strict construction of the specific conduct referred to in the statutory provisions. See Hall 2008, 230–234; Bassiouni 2011, 405–410, addressing the debated issue.

[71] For a more detailed definition of the meaning of great suffering and serious injury to body or to mental and physical health, see, *inter alia*, *Prosecutor* v. *Delalic* (also known as the *Celibici* Trail Chamber Judgment, ICTY IT-96-21-T), Judgment, Trial Chamber, 16 November 1996, paras 442 and 552.

[72] See Barber 2009, assessing the aftermath of Cyclone Nargis, the author admits that severe restrictions on humanitarian aid might satisfy the similarity test. On the other hand, this does not appear to be the case in the Myanmar's situation.

18.3.3 Mental Element

Article 30 of the Statute defines the characteristics of the so-called subjective element (also known as *mens rea*) of the crimes over which the Court has jurisdiction.

The mental element set out in the Statute encompasses different degrees of intent, which may be inferred from conduct and with respect to consequences, so that the guilty mind exists where the perpetrator willfully means to engage in the conduct, means to cause that consequence, or is aware that it will occur in the ordinary course of events.[73] Such a formulation coherently entails both a direct intent (*dolus directus*) and an indirect intent (*dolus indirectus* or *dolus eventualis*).[74] The introductory expression 'unless otherwise provided' refers to statutory provisions requiring, e.g., a specific intent (*dolus specialis*).[75]

With regard to the conduct analyzed above, the so-called *dolus eventualis* would be more consistent with a disaster context on account of the foreseeable tragic consequences caused by a total absence of or the inadequacy of assistance to the affected population.

18.4 The Aftermath of Cyclone Nargis and the Myanmar's Case

In the weeks following the outbreak of Cyclone Nargis several observers and political representatives argued that the R2P was applicable to such a devastating conscience-shocking humanitarian crisis denied by governmental authorities.[76] The government of Myanmar first underestimated the immediate effects caused by the cataclysmic event, then allegedly imposed restrictions on external aid offered by both foreign States and humanitarian organizations, and finally diverted relief resources from affected areas to the organization of a constitutional referendum

---

[73] Article 30 RS States: 'Unless otherwise provided, a person shall be criminally responsible and liable for punishment for a crime within the jurisdiction of the Court only if the material elements are committed with intent and knowledge.

For the purposes of this article, a person has intent where:

(a) In relation to conduct, that person means to engage in the conduct;
(b) In relation to a consequence, that person means to cause that consequence or is aware that it will occur in the ordinary course of events.
For the purposes of this article, 'knowledge' means awareness that a circumstance exists or a consequence will occur in the ordinary course of events. 'Know' and 'knowingly' shall be construed accordingly'.

[74] See Pisani 2004, for a detailed taxonomic description.

[75] See, e.g., genocidal intent (Article 6).

[76] See *supra* footnote 1.

which was held in late May.[77] Indeed, the Myanmar's case provides a case study[78] on which to test the interpretative theorization proposed above on the application of crimes against humanity to disaster scenarios.

First and foremost, did crimes against humanity occur in Myanmar in the aftermath of Cyclone Nargis? NGO and media reports painted a catastrophic picture, with the Myanmar Junta's members allegedly committing acts amounting to crimes against humanity: denial of aid, refusal to receive aid, diversion of aid, and the forcible removal of survivors from government-equipped camps to their hometowns and villages.

While humanitarian actors and journalists denounced the ongoing loss of life, the thousands of deaths and missing, homeless and displaced persons, the international community mobilized a swift response to care for the suffering population. Clearly, victims of disaster need water, food and other basic necessities, as well as medical assistance, shelter and clothing. Regrettably, the Myanmar's regime denied the existence of a de *facto* humanitarian crisis, refused entry visas to humanitarian aid workers, and left United States Navy ships bearing emergency relief aid off the coast.[79] Survivors were abandoned, their lives threatened, and their human dignity violated.

A first interpretative hypothesis proposes that 'other inhumane acts' is the most plausible category under which the Myanmar generals' restrictions on aid might be punished.[80] A second comprehensive approach takes into consideration other criminalized acts, namely murder, extermination, forcible transfer of population, and persecution. The Myanmar population received no water, no medical care, and no shelter. Therefore, if deaths or even deaths on a large scale were caused by the denial, or better, refusal of aid to survivors, crimes of murder and extermination were consequently occurring.[81] Similarly, the diversion of aid could clearly lead to the same consequences.[82] Press agencies and NGO reports also expressed deep concern about the phenomenon of displacement of people living in temporary government-run camps.[83] However, it does not appear that the Junta members

---

[77] See Amnesty International 2008b; Human Rights Watch 2009.

[78] See Barber 2009.

[79] See Jackson 2010, 1–3; see also Leo Lewis, *supra* footnote 11, 'By Friday the US had four planes and 23 helicopters ready in Thailand. One was allowed to drop aid yesterday and two were planned for today. The US Navy plans to have three ships in international waters off the Burmese coast today. It has 4,000 Marines on standby in Thailand. Two Indian Navy vessels docked in Rangoon last week. Despite a meeting in Burma, none of the UN's "critical" relief staff waiting in Bangkok had received visas yesterday'.

[80] See Barber 2009, acknowledging, in principle, that impeding humanitarian might fall under the *species* 'other inhumane acts', belonging to the broader *genus* 'crimes against humanity'. Nevertheless, the author argues that the Myanmar's regime imposed a partial, not total, restriction on relief aid, so that this conduct did not fulfill the required gravity.

[81] For a more detailed analysis of physical elements of specific acts, see *supra* Sect. 18.3.2.

[82] See Ford 2010.

[83] See, e.g. Amnesty International 2008b, 3, 'On 20 May the government announced that the rescue phase of the cyclone response had ended and the reconstruction phase had begun. Since

pursued their obstructive policy on the basis of any discriminatory ground, so that the crime against humanity of persecution can reasonably be excluded.[84]

A more debatable issue is that of whether the so-called *chapeau* requirements are fulfilled: were the ruling Junta's members aware of the context in which they were acting? Although there are divergent and contradictory opinions, international pressure and mobilization suggest that the Myanmar's regime could not be unaware of what was occurring in the Irrawaddy Delta region. NGO reports and press coverage confirm this.[85] Finally, it is conceivable that the Myanmar's government intentionally decided to implement an inadequate response to the cyclone, resulting in a failure to protect the affected people.

Although several interpretations differ, they unequivocally lean toward the same conclusions: crimes against humanity were allegedly committed in the aftermath of Cyclone Nargis and, in principle, an inadequate response to disaster situations falls within the scope of acts punishable as crimes against humanity.

The surge of Cyclone Nargis has also contributed to reviving the underlying interpretative debate on R2P and its application to similar cataclysmic events.[86] Actually, the UN R2P definition[87] has collocated crimes against humanity among the so-called threshold criteria justifying military intervention. As argued above, this category of crime reasonably covers absent or insufficient assistance to victims of disaster,[88] where it amounts to egregious violations which are punishable under international criminal law as crimes against humanity.

(Footnote 83 continued)
then, the government has stepped up its efforts to remove cyclone survivors from their temporary shelters and return them forcibly to their homes, in many cases in areas that are uninhabitable. The authorities have targeted emergency shelters in schools and monasteries, as both were used as polling stations for the delayed May constitutional referendum, and because the school term began on 2 June.

[84] See Ford 2010.

[85] Ibid. See also Barber 2009; Wong 2009.

[86] See Chap. 10 by Costas Trascasas in this volume.

[87] See G.A. Res. 60/1, U.N. Doc. A/RES/60/1, 2005 World Summit Outcome, 24 October 2005, para 139: 'The international community, through the United Nations, also has the responsibility to use appropriate diplomatic, humanitarian and other peaceful means, in accordance with Chapters VI and VIII of the Charter, to help to protect populations from genocide, war crimes, ethnic cleansing and crimes against humanity. In this context, we are prepared to take collective action, in a timely and decisive manner, through the Security Council, in accordance with the Charter, including Chapter VII, on a case-by-case basis and in cooperation with relevant regional organizations as appropriate, should peaceful means be inadequate and national authorities are manifestly failing to protect their populations from genocide, war crimes, ethnic cleansing and crimes against humanity. We stress the need for the General Assembly to continue consideration of the R2P populations from genocide, war crimes, ethnic cleansing and crimes against humanity and its implications, bearing in mind the principles of the Charter and international law. We also intend to commit ourselves, as necessary and appropriate, to helping States build capacity to protect their populations from genocide, war crimes, ethnic cleansing and crimes against humanity and to assisting those which are under stress before crises and conflicts break out'.

[88] See *supra* Sect. 18.3.

Provided that crimes against humanity were committed in the aftermath of Cyclone Nargis, such misconduct would give rise to individual criminal liability. Which would be the most suitable *fora* for possible trials?

Primary jurisdiction resides with the territorial State, within which the crimes occurred,[89] meaning that Myanmar's criminal tribunals could institute criminal proceedings to investigate or prosecute those acts of crimes against humanity. It is improbable that the Myanmar's government would allow its judges to proceed, since any reliable factual findings would probably lead to the incrimination of senior government members. Therefore, it is highly unlikely that criminal proceedings would be undertaken by the national authorities.

Universal jurisdiction over *delicta juris gentium* could also be invoked. Theoretically, universal jurisdiction allows every State to try cases regardless of where the crimes were committed (*forum commissi delicti*), regardless of the nationality of the perpetrator or victim (passive personality jurisdiction and active personality jurisdiction, respectively,).[90] Procedural obstacles relating to the enforcement of warrants of arrest and the gathering of evidence would render any such endeavor impracticable. That is why an ambitious solution based on universality would be unlikely and unrealistic.

Another mechanism could also take place at an international, an internationalized level: the creation of a new *ad hoc* or hybrid tribunal for Myanmar. Nevertheless, the so-called *ad-hocism* phenomenon has revealed its weaknesses, namely high costs and long-term commitment.[91] Furthermore, the establishment of hybrid tribunals[92] requires the consent/cooperation of the affected State. Clearly, the government's foreseeable opposition would paralyze any initiative to that effect.

Since the first attempts to establish an international criminal tribunal following the Treaty of Versailles, international criminal justice has evolved into the permanent institution that is the ICC.[93] Theoretically, the Court based in The Hague would represent a possible instrument to punish crimes committed in the aftermath of Cyclone Nargis.

First, insofar as they were committed after the entry into force of the RS (1 July 2002), those unlawful acts would fall under the Court's temporal jurisdiction (*ratione temporis*).[94] Nevertheless, Myanmar is not a State Party to the RS. Hence, the Court could not investigate or prosecute alleged crimes, unless Myanmar

---

89 See Schabas 2010, 58.

90 See Permanent Court of International Justice, *France* v. *Turkey*, Judgment, 7 September 1927.

91 In December 2010 the UN Security Council has decided to establish the so-called 'International Residual Mechanism for Criminal Tribunals', in order to complete the functional work of the ICTY and the ICTR ('completion strategy'). See UN Doc. S/RES/1966 (2010), 22 December 2010.

92 Hybrid tribunals are characterized by both national and international staff, to ensure independence and impartiality, but, in the meanwhile, proximity to victims. See, *inter alia*, Werle 2009, 115.

93 Ibid, 5, for a historical insight into primordial steps.

94 Article 11(1) RS.

accepts its jurisdiction by a declaration pursuant to Article 12(3) of the Statute.[95] For the same reasons mentioned above, it seems unlikely that the Myanmar's government would do so.

A last option relies upon the UN system: the Security Council, which, in accordance with Article 13(b) of the RS, and acting under Chap. 7 of the UN Charter,[96] could exert its referral power to bring the situation in Myanmar before the ICC. This option draws a connection between the R2P application and the punishment of those crimes allegedly committed in the aftermath of Cyclone Nargis. Indeed, it is not unreasonable to conceive that if the Security Council, acting under Chap. 7, had authorized a coercive intervention grounded in the R2P doctrine; the underlying situation would have been referred to the Court.[97]

However, the ICC is a permanent and independent body, mandated with prosecuting the most serious crimes of concern to the international community as a whole and it targets the highest levels of authority. Hence heinous crimes committed at lower echelons could remain unpunished. Nonetheless, the threat of prosecution embodies the undeniable deterrent that international criminal law provides.

18.5 Concluding Remarks

By approaching disasters through the lens of international criminal law, the chapter has explored to which extent the scope of crimes against humanity covers unlawful acts committed in disaster contexts by deprivation of fundamental rights. Starting from the provisions of the ICC Statute, the focal point has been further developed to determine whether, theoretically, denial of aid to or its diversion away from the victims of disaster, or the forcible removal of survivors from equipped camps might give rise to individual criminal responsibility.

The cyclone which struck Myanmar in 2008 and its consequences have provided an interesting case study. It is worth recalling the provocative message voiced in 2008 by Ramesh Thakur while facing the undeniable humanitarian crisis that was occurring:

> 'In our original report, we identified overwhelming natural or environmental catastrophes, where the State concerned is either unwilling or unable to cope, and significant loss of life is occurring or threatened as among the conscience-shocking situations justifying

[95] Schabas 2010, 67, asserting that such declarations can be retroactive.

[96] Article 13(1)(b) RS: 'A situation in which one or more of such crimes appears to have been committed is referred to the Prosecutor by the Security Council acting under Chapter VII of the Charter of the United Nations'.

[97] The Security Council, recalling the R2P principle, referred the situation to the ICC to open an investigation into the situation in Libya, since crimes against humanity were allegedly being committed. Further recalling responsibility of the Libyan authorities to protect the Libyan population, the Security Council Resolution 1973 (2011) established a ban on all flights in the Libyan airspace. See UN Doc. S/RES/1970 (2011), 26 February 2011, para 4.

> international intervention. This was not included in the 2005 UN document, but "crimes against humanity" was and would provide the necessary *legal cover* to sidestep the recalcitrant generals and give help directly to the afflicted people' [emphasis added].[98]

Confronted with the obstructive conduct of the Myanmar's authorities, the international community catalyzed a high pressure aimed at obtaining, first, cooperation. Indeed, the State affected by a natural or a man-made disaster is normally the most appropriate actor to organize and supervise rapid relief operations and coordinate both internal and external aid supply. Providing humanitarian assistance in disaster-affected territories requires a modicum of knowledge of the geographical morphology and deployable human resources. Whereas, forcible measures could not compel territorial authorities to cooperate and to provide precious support to external humanitarian workers. As the situation in Myanmar has confirmed,[99] high pressure from a united international community may achieve desirable results through peaceful means.

In this context, international criminal law plays a key-role: the threat of criminal prosecution for those responsible for unlawful acts committed against a population struck by disaster would compel governmental authorities to accept external humanitarian assistance. Hence, deterrence may prevent heinous crimes from being committed, and also achieve, as a by-product, the cooperation that emergency situations require.

References

Amnesty International (2008a) Crimes against humanity in Eastern Myanmar. www.amnesty.org/en/library/asset/ASA16/011/2008/en/72d2e8c2-b9ce-4afb-91c6-ba3391ed41e5/asa160112008en.pdf

Amnesty International (2008b) Myanmar briefing: human rights concerns a month after Cyclone Nargis. www.amnesty.org/en/library/asset/ASA16/013/2008/en/85931049-32e5-11dd-863f-e9cd398f74da/asa160132008eng.pdf

Barber R (2009) The responsibility to protect the survivors of natural disaster: cyclone Nargis, a case study. Confl Secur L 14(1):3–34

Bassiouni MC (2011) Crimes against humanity: historical evolution and contemporary application. Cambridge University Press, New York

Evans G (2008) Facing up to our responsibilities, The Guardian. http://www.guardian.co.uk/commentisfree/2008/may/12/facinguptoourresponsbilities. Accessed 12 May 2008

Ford S (2010) Is the failure to respond appropriately to a natural disaster a crime against humanity? The responsibility to protect and individual criminal responsibility in the aftermath of Cyclone Nargis. Denver J Int L Policy 38:227–276

---

[98] Ramesh Thakur, *supra* footnote 28.

[99] See Amnesty International 2008b, 1, determining that in late may, the government of Myanmar granted a limited number of entry visas to foreign humanitarian employees.

Hall CK (2008) Crimes against humanity. In: Triffterer O (ed) Commentary on the Rome statute of the international criminal court: observers' notes, article by article. C.H. Beck, Munich, pp 117–172
Human Rights Watch (2009) World Report 2009. www.hrw.org/en/publications
Jackson TR (2010) Bullets for beans: humanitarian intervention and the responsibility to protect in natural disasters. Nav L Rev 59:1–20
Kouchner B (2008) Birmanie: morale de l'extrême urgence, Le Monde, 19 May 2008. http://www.franceonu.org/spip.php?article1860
Lewis B (2008) Burma accused of 'crime' against its people, The Times. http://www.timesonline.co.uk/tol/news/world/asia/article3917681.ece. Accessed 13 May 2008
Maddox B (2008) Why it is not easy to impose help in Burma after Cyclone Nargis, The Times. http://www.timesonline.co.uk/tol/news/world/asia/article3919523.ece. Accessed 13 May 2008
Parsons C (2008) France Urges U.N. Council to act on Myanmar cyclone, Reuters. http://www.reuters.com/article/2008/05/07/idUSL07810481. Accessed 7 May 2008
Pisani N (2004) The mental element in international crime. In: Lattanzi F, Schabas WA (eds) Essays on the Rome Statute of the international criminal court, vol 2, Ripa di Fagnano Alto (AQ), Il Sirente, Italy, pp 121–142
Rottensteiner C (1999) The denial of humanitarian assistance as a crime under international law. Int Rev Red Cross 835:555–582
Schabas WA (2010) An introduction to the international criminal court. Cambridge University Press, Cambridge
Schmitt E (2008) Gates accuses Myanmar of 'criminal neglect', NY Times. http://www.nytimes.com/2008/06/02/world/asia/02gates.html. Accessed 2 June 2008
Thakur R (2008), Should the UN invoke the 'responsibility to protect'?, The Globe and Mail. http://globalr2p.org/remarks/ThakurBurmaR2P.pdf. Accessed 8 May 2008
Werle G (2009) Diritto dei crimini internazionali. Bononia University Press, Bologna
Wong J (2009) Reconstructing the responsibility to protect in the wake of cyclones and separatism. Tulane L Rev 84:219–263

Part V
Planning and Implementing Disaster Relief Actions

Chapter 19
From Theory to Practice: The Role of Disaster Response Missions

Stefano Silingardi

Abstract This chapter will be devoted to the analysis of the normative and institutional frameworks in the relevant sources of the law (at global, regional/sub-regional or domestic level) on how emergency operations should unfold on the field and which are the main issues in regard to their effective deployment. After a brief introduction, it will start with an analysis of the prescribed procedures for specific requests for assistance (Sect. 19.2). Section 19.3 will then focus on the 'command and control' paradigm in disaster response operations. In particular, we will analyse the existing tools and procedures addressing the modalities of disaster response operations through regional and sub-regional agreements, or through bilateral assistance. Finally, in Sect. 19.4 we will concentrate on the legal recognition of disaster response missions, as a necessary precursor to many of the activities that are part of a relief effort, and Sect. 19.5 will shift the focus on the prescribed procedures on termination of international assistance.

Keywords Disaster response missions · Request for assistance · Initiation of assistance · Chain of command · Legal recognition · NGOs · Termination of assistance

Contents

S. Silingardi (✉)
Dipartimento di Giurisprudenza, Università di Modena e Reggio Emilia,
Via San Geminiano 3, 41121, Modena, Italy
e-mail: stefano.silingardi@unimore.it

A. de Guttry et al. (eds.), *International Disaster Response Law*,
DOI: 10.1007/978-90-6704-882-8_19,

19.1 Introduction

When the consequences of natural disasters overwhelm the existing response capacities of disaster-affected countries, international response becomes an essential source of assistance. However, no international action can take place in the absence of a request by the local government.[1] Even when a request for international assistance has been formally made, there may be further occasional conflicts of authority and delays in decision-making due, among others, to distance, communication impediments or misunderstanding that could hamper relief efforts. Most of the times, intervening agencies even compete against each other for maximum media visibility to reach potential donors. Within this perspective, international assistance is frequently fraught with difficulties of both legal and political nature. Coordination and leadership have, therefore, been described as 'challenges from the beginning in the chaotic circumstances of disaster scenarios, where much of local capacity [has] been destroyed or disrupted, and thousands of humanitarian organisations [arrive] on the scene to provide relief to the affected communities'.[2]

19.2 The Request for International Disaster Assistance

In the event that domestic capabilities are not likely to be sufficient due to the scale of the disaster affected States may proceed with the request for international assistance. However, in the face of internal political pressure, requests for international assistance are 'normally reserved for the most massive disasters', and in some instances governments have categorically refused to request or accept international assistance even 'where the needs clearly outstripped national capacities'.[3]

---

[1] See Chap. 10 by Costas Trascasas in this volume.

[2] Bhattacharjee and Lossio (2011), 9. For more on coordination, please see Chap. 20 by De Siervo in this volume.

[3] Fischer 2007, 89.

Generally, requests for assistance should be made through diplomatic channels and, with regard to their content, they should be accompanied by information on the extent and type of assistance required and on the procedures through which assisting actors can make offers or provide assistance. For example, the Black Sea Economic Cooperation (BSEC) Agreement provides that the requesting Party should specify in its request:

> 1) Place, time, character and scale of the Disaster, and current state of the Emergency in the afflicted areas; 2) actions already carried out, specification of the required assistance, setting the priorities of the requested Disaster relief.[4]

As a general rule, each country should have a legal and policy framework for initiating or requesting international assistance in case of overwhelming disasters. However, only a few countries have legal provisions in place or set procedures on when and how international assistance should be requested, on the assessment of what type of assistance is required or on how and when it may be terminated. For example, the recently adopted 2011 Indonesian Guideline provides that the Indonesia National Board for Disaster Management (Badan Nasional Penanggulangan Bencana) should send a circular to international institutions and foreign NGOs regarding the initiation of international aid; this should contain a summary report on the disaster, indicate the length of the emergency response period, and provide information on urgently needed logistics and equipment and professional personnel required.[5]

However, not all existing disaster management laws entrust an executive authority with a full discretion to make international appeals or requests. Many existing laws require a previous formal declaration of a state of emergency or a state of disaster before international assistance can be sought; since these types of declarations have legal and political impacts well beyond international assistance, 'they can sometimes lead to significant hesitation'.[6] In the aftermath of the 2004 tsunami, for example, the Thailand's Ministry of Foreign Affairs asked the UN to avoid referring to the request of assistance as an 'international appeal';[7] and in one country, because of 'the complex, bureaucratic and politically charged process of declaring a state of calamity, coupled with outdated national legislation on foreign contributions,' the government announced that it would accept 'spontaneous gestures of solidarity from the international community, which became the basis for extensive financial and operational international assistance for the disaster'.[8]

---

[4] 1999 Agreement among the Governments of the Participating States of the BSEC on Collaboration in Emergency Assistance and Emergency Response to Natural and Man-made Disasters, Article 4.

[5] See 2011 *Guidelines on the Role of the International Organizations and Foreign NonGovernment Organisations during Emergency Response*, Chapter 2(A)(2)(c). Informal translation available at: http://www.ifrc.org/Docs/idrl/877EN.pdf. Accessed 22 February 2012.

[6] See *Model Act for the Facilitation and Regulation of International Disaster Relief and Initial Recovery Assistance (Pilot Version November 2011)*, 54.

[7] IFRC 2006c, 8.

[8] IFRC 2003, 10.

Insofar as such declarations 'can bring a host of other legal and political consequences, such as the potential for the abridgement of civil rights',[9] they could be the subject of further criticism and governments should, therefore, be extremely cautious in releasing them. For example, the decision of the Government of Sri Lanka, on 4 January 2005, to declare a state of emergency, by which the President and the armed forces were placed at the top of the relief command structure, was subject to some criticism because it suspended 'for a period the separation of powers between the legislature and the executive', and thus needed to be 'balanced and checked by the twin constraints of strict time limits and parliamentary approval'.[10]

A number of existing IDRL instruments encourage affected States to speed up the process of requesting assistance. For example, the 2000 Framework Convention on Civil Defence Assistance provides that 'offers of, or requests for, assistance shall be examined and responded to by recipient States within the shortest possible time'; and the Oslo Guidelines on the Use of Civil and Military Assets in Disaster Relief state that 'If international assistance is necessary, it should be requested or consented to by the Affected State as soon as possible upon the onset of the disaster to maximize its effectiveness'.[11]

In order to minimise potential delays and misunderstandings on this specific issue, the recently enacted Pilot Model Act of the International Federation of the Red Cross (IFRC) provides that the request for international assistance can be specifically directed to particular international actors, or it may be a general request directed to the international community as a whole. In the latter case, the request shall be directed to the relevant regional or sub-regional organisation and to the UN Emergency Relief Coordinator.[12] With this perspective, the General Assembly resolution 46/182 of 1991 also encourages States to deliver offers and requests of assistance through the Emergency Relief Coordinator (see *infra* Sect. 19.3.1).[13] However, as for the UN disaster response system, it should be noted that the evolution of quick response systems such as, in particular, UN Disaster Assessment and Coordination (UNDAC) and the International Search and Rescue Advisory Group (INSARAG) teams, has helped to undermine the notion that international assistance must take no action in the absence of a formal appeal.[14]

---

[9] Fischer 2007, 91.

[10] See IFRC 2006b, 10, citing Welikala (2005).

[11] See 2000 Framework Convention on Civil Defence Assistance, Article 3(a); and 2006 Oslo Guidelines on The Use of Foreign Military and Civil Defence Assets in Disaster Relief (Revision 1.1 November 2007), para 58. See also 1996 Convention on Assistance in the Case of a Nuclear Accident or Radiological Emergency, Article 1(1); 1998 Tampere Convention on the Provision of Telecommunication Resources for Disaster Mitigation and Relief Operations, Article 4.

[12] *Model Act*, above n. 6, Article 6.

[13] GA Res. 46/182 Strengthening of the coordination of humanitarian emergency assistance of the United Nations, 19 December 1991, Annex, para 35(a).

[14] Fischer 2007, 91. For more on UNDAC and INSARAG teams, please see Chap. 20 by De Siervo in this volume.

Over the last decade, regional and sub-regional organisations in Europe, the Americas, and Asia have also been quite active in creating regional and sub-regional mechanisms to centralise the transmission of governmental requests and offers of assistance.[15] Under the ASEAN SASOP, for example, each disaster-affected Party shall launch requests for assistance through its National Focal Point (i.e., an entity designated and authorised by each Party to receive and transmit information pursuant to the provisions of the Agreement) to any other Party directly or through the ASEAN Co-ordinating Centre for Humanitarian Assistance (commonly referred to as AHA Centre).[16] The assisting Party shall promptly acknowledge or respond to the request of assistance (preferably within 6–12 h) and, together with the National Focal Point, review the request and determine whether the type and scope of assistance can be provided; in the event that such assistance is not feasible, both parties shall explore, in consultation with the AHA Centre, other possible forms of assistance.[17]

Both the ASEAN Agreement and the Inter-American Convention to Facilitate Disaster Assistance further appear to place offers and requests on an equal footing, as long as there is consent from the affected State.[18] In case regional and sub-regional organisations are involved, also non-member States may request assistance. For example, in 2011 both Japan and New Zealand requested assistance through the EU Civil Protection Mechanism to cope, respectively, with the earthquake/tsunami destruction of 11 March and with the earthquake of 22 February 2011, the latter being the deadliest in New Zealand since 1931.

Finally, where the assistance is activated through bilateral agreements,[19] the prescribed procedures could even be well regulated. Most of such treaties specifically provide competent authorities entitled to request assistance[20]; if such authorities cannot be identified in advance, mechanisms are set up to make such

---

[15] Fischer 2007, 91.

[16] Based in the Indonesian capital Jakarta, the AHA Centre was formally launched on 27 January 2011, and will serve as the centre point for mobilisation of resources to disaster-affected areas, as well to act as the coordination engine to ensure ASEAN's fast and collective response to disasters within the ASEAN region. See ASEAN Secretariat News, *Jakarta Ready to Host ASEAN Humanitarian Assistance Centre*, January 28, 2011, at: http://www.asean.org/25743.htm#. Accessed 22 February 2012.

[17] See *Standard Operating Procedure for Regional Standby Arrangements and Coordination of Joint Disaster Relief and Emergency Response Operation* (*SASOP*), ASEAN Secretariat, November 2009, section V.

[18] Fischer 2007, 91, referring to the 2005 ASEAN Agreement on Disaster Management and Emergency Response (AADMER), Article 11(2); and the 1991 Inter-American Convention to Facilitate Disaster Assistance, Articles 1 and 2.

[19] See 2001 Agreement between the Swiss Federal Council and the Government of the Republic of the Philippines on Cooperation in the Event of Natural Disaster of Major Emergencies, Article 4(2); and also 2001 Convenio entre al Reino de Espana y la Republica Francesa en Materia de Protection y de Seguridad Civil, Article 6.

[20] See 2004 Agreement between the Republic of Austria and the Hashemite Kingdom of Jordan on Mutual Assistance in the Case of Disasters or Serious Accidents, Article 3(1).

identification possible. For neighbouring States agreements provide, for example, that, where necessary, assistance shall be requested directly and it shall granted by the competent authorities of neighbouring communes and districts.[21] A few treaties are so detailed in this respect that they indicate the language that the requesting authority shall preferably use[22] and even the contact details (including telephone and fax numbers) of the person/office to be called in case assistance is needed.[23] Other agreements, such as the Canada–United States Memorandum of Understanding of 2000, specify that these requests may be verbal or in writing and that, if verbal, the request must be confirmed in writing within 15 days.[24] As for the obligations of the assisting entities, they shall consider a request of assistance in the shortest possible time and inform the requesting State on the possibility, volume, and terms of its rendering.[25] Finally, when assistance is requested through bilateral treaties, most of them provide that affected States shall include in their requests of assistance information on the nature of the emergency, as well as specify the type and volume of personnel, equipment, materials and supplies needed, including the tasks they intend to entrust to the teams of the assisting party, with or without stating the details of their implementation.[26] In some cases, the requesting State shall also specify the length assistance and the specific place and time for staging of the assisting party's response and a contact point on site.[27]

19.3 The Initiation of International Assistance

After the rapid demise of the International Relief Union and the failure of its mandate,[28] the international community's approach to disaster relief operations

[21] See 1985 Agreement on Mutual Assistance in the Event of Disasters of Serious Accidents (with exchange of notes) between Denmark and the Federal Republic of Germany, Article 3(2); and 1981 Agreement between the Government of the French Republic and the Government of the Kingdom of Belgium on Mutual Assistance in the Event of Disasters or Serious Accidents, Article 3(2).

[22] See Austria–Jordan Agreement, above n. 20, Article 4(2). The requesting authority, in making the request, will preferably use the language of the requested party or English language.

[23] See Chap. 1 by de Guttry in this volume, citing the 2007 Italy–France Administrative Memorandum of Understaing (MoU) on cross-border cooperation in emergency situations in mountainous areas, Article 4.

[24] See 2000 International Emergency Management Assistance MoU, Article 3(2).

[25] 2000 Agreement between the Government of the Hellenic Republic and the Government of the Russian Federation on co-operation in the field of prevention and response to natural and man-made disasters, Article 7.

[26] See Swiss Federal Council–Philippines Agreement, above n. 19, Article 9(1); and 1977 Convention between the French Republic and the Federal Republic of Germany on Mutual Assistance in the Event of Disasters or Serious Accidents, Article 7(2).

[27] See Canada–United States MoU, above n. 24, Article 3(2)(b)(C).

[28] See Macalister-Smith 1986, 370.

has developed in a fragmented manner.[29] Issues of modality of intervention have been preferably managed at regional and sub-regional level, or through bilateral agreements rather than through a centralised operational agency. Thus, the specific organisations that are currently assembled for any particular disaster depend on the nature of the disaster, availability of potential participants, anticipated needs and prescribed procedures.

19.3.1 Nature of the Disaster

Unlike the damage sustained in the direct impact of a major hurricane or a massive event, such as the 2004 Asian Tsunami, there could be national disasters resulting from an accumulation of simultaneous local disasters. This is the case, for example, of tropical storm Stan, which hit Guatemala in 2005 following stationary torrential rains coming at the end of an already long and heavy wet season. In such a case, there is no clear 'day one' and this goes some way toward explaining why both the domestic declaration of a national emergency and the response operations could seem slow to start.[30]

19.3.2 Anticipated Needs

Needs assessment is 'a fundamental tool in ensuring that relief and recovery efforts are appropriately targeted and designed' as well as to determine 'whether international assistance is required to supplement national efforts'.[31] The failure of a quality needs assessment could, therefore, result in a serious handicap of the entire disaster relief effort, both in the immediate emergency response and on long-term recovery and reconstruction phases (see *infra*, Sect. 19.5). Insofar as, for example, the OCHA was unable to fulfil any systematic needs assessments during the response to the Haiti earthquake, US and Canadian armies already stationed in affected areas relied more on some of the assessment information from their military command, and different IOs used their own mechanisms to conduct individual assessments. Under this light, it has, therefore, been noted that during the response to the Haiti earthquake this failure meant a loss of opportunities for the humanitarian community to influence the role of military in humanitarian response as well as in planning of recovery and reconstruction plans.

[29] Fischer 2007, 27.
[30] IFRC 2007, 17.
[31] Fischer 2007, 94.

19.3.3 Availability of Potential Participants

Disaster response missions are often complex operations, with a diverse set of actors displaying little structural interdependence. All the organisations part of the disaster response community on a global scale have legal mandates and/or mission statements that establish the major objectives they are obliged to fulfil. Most of them also apply some kind of standards and/or guidelines to ensure that they act in conformity with and are supportive of humanitarian principles and practices.[32] However, in recent years the proliferation of actors involved in humanitarian assistance has provoked serious problems of overlapping agendas and mandates, with political rivalries and increasing difficulties for coordinating relief efforts. To this end, as noted with regard to the Haiti earthquake, the mission 'evolved on an *ad hoc basis* from mandates or delegated authorities in the panicked aftermath of the quake',[33] resulting in ambiguity of authority that could hamper relief efforts.

19.3.4 'Command-and-Control' Paradigm in Disaster Response Missions

At least where the UN relief mechanism is concerned, it is not always easy to understand who holds general 'command and control' powers over the entire disaster response community. Although the establishment of the OCHA and the ERC/USG has certainly contributed to strengthen of the simplification process within the UN disaster response system, both agencies need to fully respect the mandates of all organisations and entities involved in the emergency mission.[34] Furthermore, they cannot supersede the specific authority of the Receiving State, which retains overall authority and responsibility on the direction, control, co-ordination and supervision of the assistance within its territory.[35] For example, immediately after the tsunami that hit its coastal regions, the Indonesian military

[32] See United Nations 2005, 20. As examples, see the *Emergency Field Handbook, A Guide for UNICEF Staff*, New York, 2005, at: http://www.unicef.org/publications/files/UNICEF_EFH_2005.pdf (accessed 22 February 2012); and International Civil Defence Organization, *Disaster Management Guide*, Geneva, 1998.

[33] Arkedis and Derham 2010, 2.

[34] GA Res. 46/182 above n. 13, para 34. In particular, the ERC has been entrusted with the mandate, *inter alia*, to process requests from affected member States for emergency assistance requiring a coordinated response, as well as to act as the central focal point for governmental, intergovernmental and non-governmental relief activities. It has further to chair the IASC (i.e., the primary mechanism for inter-agency coordination of humanitarian assistance involving key UN and non-UN humanitarian partners) and head the UN Office for the Coordination of Humanitarian Affairs (OCHA).

[35] Nuclear Assistance Convention, above footnote 11, Article 3; 1992 Convention on the Transboundary Effects of Industrial Accidents, Annex X, Article 1.

and government officials announced, on 11 January 2005, restrictions on future foreign relief operations in Aceh, including the establishment of the Indonesian military (the Tentara Nasional Indonesia (TNI)) operational control over all foreign relief operations, a requirement that a TNI officer be on board any foreign aircraft engaged in relief and confinement of foreign aid workers to the towns of the Banda Aceh and Meulaboh unless they receive TNI permission to operate elsewhere.[36]

To minimise existing frictions between local authorities and international assistance, some IDRL instruments including, for example, the Framework Convention on Civil Defence Assistance, specify that the requesting State shall direct and assume responsibility for operations only after prior consultations with the Head of the Civil Defence unit of the supporting State have been made.[37] On the other hand, the assisting party should, where the assistance involves personnel, appoint in consultation with the requesting State the officer in charge who retains immediate operational supervision over the personnel and the equipment provided. The designated officer should exercise such supervision in cooperation with the appropriate authorities of the requesting State.

A 'combined national–international managerial effort'[38] is also required to facilitate field coordination among the national institutions and humanitarian partners involved. In this respect, OCHA On Site Operations Coordination Centre (OSOCC) should act as an interface between the affected country's Local Emergency Management Authority and the international assistance operations.[39] However, different tools could be implemented with the support of domestic authorities. During the response to tropical storm Stan in Guatemala, for example, the CONRED (Coordinadora Nacional para la Reducción de Desastres) was responsible for managing the national emergency as a whole; on the other hand, the General Secretariat of the Executive Branch for Planning and Programming (SEGEPLAN) was established with the mandate, among others, to manage, negotiate and administer the international cooperation. In particular, it liaised directly with the UN system through the pre-existing mechanism of the 'Dialogue Group'.[40]

When disaster response missions are deployed through regional and sub-regional agreements, procedures may vary according to applicable legal framework. For example, Article 26 of the Agreement Establishing the Caribbean Disaster Management Agency (CDEMA) provides that following a request for assistance by any affected participating State, members of the disciplined forces of another

---

[36] See Margesson 2005, 23 and IFRC 2006a, 8.

[37] Framework Convention, above n. 11, Article 4(4).

[38] See UN Guidelines on the Use of Military and Civil Defence Assets in Disaster Relief, Project DPR 213/3 MCDA, May 1994, para 90.

[39] See OSOCC Guidelines, 2nd edition, 2009, section 2.

[40] IFRC 2007, 22. The 'Dialogue Group' has existed since 2004 and includes 13 countries and all the international development agencies, thus representing the international community in Guatemala.

participating State are despatched to any part of the territory of the requesting State.[41] In particular:

> ... the Executive Director shall, subject to the express prior agreement of the competent authorities of the requesting State, designate a Special Coordinator from among the senior officers of such forces, acting after consultation with the Chiefs of Staffs or Commanding Officers of the disciplined forces concerned.

It is further provided that the Special Coordinator shall be charged with responsibility for coordinating the disaster relief efforts of the disciplined forces in the affected State, and that no member of the disciplined forces of a participating State shall be despatched without the express prior consent of the affected State. In the absence of a contrary agreement between the requesting State and the sending State, it is further provided that members of the disciplined forces of the sending State shall be under the control and disciplinary authority of their commanding officer.[42]

With regard to the relationship with the local authorities, it is commonly accepted that the overall direction, control, coordination and supervision of assistance despatched to a requesting State shall fall under the responsibility of the requesting State within its territory. Specifically, CDEMA provides that where the assistance from a sending State involves personnel other than disciplined forces, the sending State shall appoint in consultation with the requesting State the officer in charge who retains immediate operational supervision over personnel, equipment and supplies; with further clarification that the designed officer shall exercise such supervision in cooperation with the competent authorities of the requesting State.[43] Similarly, under the AADMER legal framework it is provided that, upon arrival of the assisting Entity at the disaster site, the Incident Manager of the requesting Party shall conduct an on-site operational briefing for the assisting Entity for the deployment of the assisting Entity's assets. While the responsibility for the overall direction and control of assistance is placed upon the requesting Party; the Assisting Entity shall ensure the compliance with national laws and regulations, as well as conformity with the national incident command system of the affected Party, and designate an officer-in-charge, referred to as the Head of the assistance, to exercise supervision in co-operation with the appropriate domestic authorities. Both the requesting Party and the assisting Entity, through their designated National Focal Points, shall submit to the AHA Centre a report on the status and outcome of the actual provision of assistance within 24–48 h from their arrival at the site of the disaster.[44]

Despite the numerous treaties and agreements concluded at the international, regional and sub-regional levels, bilateral assistance still predominates. There are

---

41 See 2008 Agreement Establishing the Caribbean Disaster Emergency Management Agency, Article 26.

42 Ibid.

43 Ibid., Article 21(2).

44 See *Standard Operating Procedure* (SASOP), above n. 17, section V.

well over 100 bilateral treaties, most of them in Europe, providing procedures for the initiation and termination of assistance and describing modalities for the emergency assistance and emergency team management.[45] While there are, of course, many differences among the various agreements, there is a number of common trends as well.[46]

In all cases, the coordination and management of the rescue and emergency operations is the exclusive responsibility of the authorities of the requesting State. To this end, a few treaties provide that for each operation the requesting State shall inform the assisting State through diplomatic channels about names and functions of the authorities charged with the direction and coordination of the rescue and emergency operations.[47] Any orders addressed to the intervention team shall be directed only to team leaders, who will decide how to implement them and instruct their teams accordingly. Nevertheless, a few treaties specify that the relief team shall work in the territory of the requesting Party under the direction of its leadership,[48] and in some instances it is further provided that the team shall act in accordance with the guidelines that are in effect in its country of origin.[49] Some treaties further provide that the aid units sent to locations of disaster or major emergencies have received special training, in particular in fire fighting, technical assistance, medical and health assistance, rescue and other emergency work.[50]

19.4 Legal Recognition of Disaster Response Missions

If they intend to fully and effectively operate within the affected country, international disaster response missions must obtain recognition of their juridical personality under domestic law. The recognition of legal capacity is often a necessary precondition to many of the activities that are part of a relief effort, including hiring local personnel, opening bank accounts, entering into contracts, acquiring and disposing of property, and being part of legal proceedings.[51] To this end, the IDRL Guidelines call upon affected States to grant eligible assisting

[45] Fischer 2007, 24.

[46] Fischer 2007, 80.

[47] See Convenio entre al Reino de Espana y la Republica Francesa, above n. 19, Article 8(1).

[48] Ibid., Article 8(2); and 1998 Agreement on Cooperation on Disaster Prevention and Management and Civil Protection, France—Malaysia, Article 8(2).

[49] See 1995 Agreement between the Republic of Finland and the Republic of Estonia on cooperation and mutual assistance in cases of accidents, Article 8.

[50] Swiss Federal Council–Philippines Agreement, above n. 19, Article 5(1); 1988 Agreement on cooperation on cooperation between the Kingdom of Spain and the Argentine Republic disaster preparedness and prevention, and mutual assistance in the event of disasters, Article 9.

[51] For more on this see Chap. 23 by Silingardi in this volume.

humanitarian organisations, upon entry or as soon as possible thereafter, 'at least a temporary authorization to legally operate on their territory'.[52]

For UN agencies and other IOs, the achievement of such legal personality is guaranteed by the law of privileges and immunities. However, only the IAEA, UN and its specialised agencies are granted juridical personality according to specific conventions on privileges and immunities.[53] In a 1971 report, the Secretary-General specifically identified the instances in which the provisions of the 1946 Convention on the privileges and immunities of the UN would apply to disaster relief units made available through the UN. Whereas, in particular, the provisions on juridical personality, property, funds, assets and communication facilities would apply automatically only when the disaster relief unit holds UN subsidiary organ status,[54] the provisions related to the immunity of officials from legal process with respect to official acts, and their exemption from taxation and immigration restrictions as well as issuance to UN officials of laissez-passer for speedy travel, would apply automatically regardless of whether the disaster relief unit is a subsidiary organ or not. The same rights would apply to UN officials assigned to work with the unit.[55] Where the provisions of the 1946 Convention do not apply (for instance, where the receiving country is not part of the Convention or where, although the receiving country is part of the Convention, the legal status of the disaster relief unit is separate from that of the United Nations and its members cannot be referred to as experts on missions for the United Nations), it would be up to the receiving country to provide privileges and immunities similar to those accorded under the Convention.[56]

---

[52] See IFRC, *Guidelines for the Domestic Facilitation and Regulation of International Disaster Relief and Initial Recovery Assistance*, Article 20.

[53] 1946 Convention on the Privileges and Immunities of the United Nations; 1947 Convention on the Privileges and Immunities of the Specialised Agencies; 1959 Agreement on the Privileges and Immunities of the International Atomic Energy Agency. For more on privileges and immunities of UN and its specialised agencies, see Zwitter 2011, 61.

[54] Un Doc. E/4994, *Legal Status of Disaster Relief Units Made Available Through the United Nations*, 13 May 1971, reproduced in *United Nations Juridical Yearbook* (1971), 191, para 17 (a). Available at: http://untreaty.un.org/cod/UNJuridicalYearbook/pdfs/english/ByVolume/1971/chpVI.pdf. Accessed 22 February 2012.

[55] Ibid., para 17 (b). The following para 17 (d), states that: 'Similar facilities to those specified in Section 25 shall be accorded to experts and other persons who, though not the holders of United Nations laissez-passer, have a certificate that they are traveling on the business of the United Nations'. Article 6 further provides a number of immunities directly applicable to those persons serving with the unit who could be regarded as experts on missions for the UN.

[56] Ibid., para 19. On this issue, see also Beigbeder 1991, 334 and S/2009/277, above n. 2, 92, citing as example the Swedish Technical Cadre Unit, serving in Peru, which was granted such privileges and immunities by the Government of Peru. See 1970 Agreement between the United Nations, the Government of Peru and the Government of Sweden for the Provision of the Technical Cadre Unit of the Swedish Stand-By-Force for United Nations Service to Assist in Reconstruction of Areas in Peru Devastated as a Result of the Earthquake which Occurred on 31 May 1970, Article 4.

All the other IOs participating in a disaster response mission could generally benefit from this set of rights only to the extent that the contracting parties have so arranged in the constitutive acts, or if such facilities have been agreed upon in specific agreements.[57]

With regard to the assistance provided under specific regional and sub-regional agreements, it is covered by privileges and immunities law only in case of an agreement with the State involved prior to relief operations,[58] or when these rights are set out in a multilateral convention.[59] For example, Article 30 of the CDEMA Agreement provides a wide range of privileges and immunities to CDEMA, as well as to its property and assets (Article 2, Section 3).[60] Article 32 further provides for the inviolability of any CDEMA archives; Article 32 provides that the official correspondence and all other forms of official communications shall be inviolable[61]; and Article 34 finally asserts that CDEMA, its assets, property, income, operations and transactions shall be exempt from all direct taxation, and that goods imported or exported for its official use shall be exempt from all custom duties except for taxes which are no more than charges for services rendered. Other instruments, such as for example the SASOP, only refer to the general provision that the requesting or receiving party shall provide, to the possible extent, local facilities and services for the proper and effective administration of the assistance, and ensure protection of personnel, equipment and materials brought into its territory.[62] Under this perspective, it is also important to note that for many facilities (such as warehouses for relief items) security represents a critical issue. During the response to tropical storm Stan in Guatemala, for example, many relief organisations experienced thefts at the facilities offered by the Guatemalan Government, and one of the affected organisations decided to remove all its goods because security could not be guaranteed.[63]

To reduce the risk for international actors to be withheld of their capability to operate within disaster response missions, the recent Model Act provides that assisting States and relevant regional and international IOs (such as the ONU and

---

[57] See, for example, the 1927 Convention establishing an International Relief Union, Article 10 requiring the contracting parties 'to accord … insofar as possible under the local laws, the most extensive immunities, facilities and exemptions for the purpose of the operation of the IRU'.

[58] 1997 Agreement between the Government of Barbados and the Caribbean Disaster Emergency Response Agency for the Provision of Headquarters for CDERA, Articles 2–8.

[59] This is the case, for example, of the Tampere Convention (Article 5), the AADMER (Article 14), and the Inter-American Convention to Facilitate Disaster Assistance (Article 16).

[60] See CDEMA, above n. 41, Article 30.

[61] In particular, Article 32 further states that 'CDEMA shall have the right to use codes and to despatch and receive correspondence by courier in sealed bags, which shall not be searched or detained unless the competent authorities have reasonable grounds to believe that the sealed bags do not only contain articles, correspondence or documents for the exclusive official use of CDEMA, in which case the bag shall be opened only in the presence of an officer of CDEMA'.

[62] See *Standard Operating Procedure* (*SASOP*), above n. 17, section V(D).

[63] IFRC 2007, 34.

ASEAN) would automatically obtain existing legal personality under the domestic law of the affected country. The same holds true for the components of the International Red Cross and Red Crescent Movement, some having legal personality under international law (the ICRC and IFRC) and others being governed by specific global standards concerning their international operations as agreed by States. It is also assumed that international humanitarian organisations that already operate legally in the affected State and/or have other agreements concerning their legal status in that State would be deemed eligible to receive domestic and international legal facilities and immunities.[64] The remaining international humanitarian organisations and individuals (above all NGOs) would need to be approved as eligible in accordance with the criteria and procedures developed by each State, either in advance of any disaster or after commencement.[65]

More specific rules apply in case the disaster response mission involves the deployment of military and civil defence assets. The Oslo Guidelines provide that the Convention on the Privileges and Immunities of the UN of 1946 shall apply to the MCDA operation,[66] as well as a set of specific rights that the government of the affected State shall grant to the MCDA operation.[67] According to the Oslo Guidelines, the government of the affected State further undertakes to provide without cost to the MCDA operation and in agreement with the Head of the MCDA operation such areas for headquarters, camps or other premises as may be necessary for the conduct of the MCDA operational and administrative activities and for the accommodation of its members, and treat them as being subject to the exclusive control and authority of the Head of the MCDA operation.[68]

19.4.1 NGOs Participation in Disaster Response Missions

Apart from few exceptions,[69] NGOs do not normally work on the basis of a request by the affected State or its consent to an offer. On the contrary, they frequently reach formal agreements with affected States only after the commencement of the disaster operation and they have already arrived in the affected area. As a result,

[64] *Model Act*, above n. 6, Article 23.

[65] Ibid., Article 24.

[66] Oslo Guidelines, above n. 11, sections 3 and 21.

[67] Oslo Guidelines, above n. 11, Annex I, Chapter 4(12).

[68] Ibid., Chapter 4(14)(15). Where such utilities or facilities are not provided free of charge, Section 15 states that 'payment shall be made by the MCDA operation on terms to be agreed upon with the competent authority. The MCDA operation shall be responsible for the maintenance and upkeep of facilities so provided'. Finally, in Section 16 it is provided that 'The MCDA operation shall be given the right, where necessary, to generate electricity for its use and to transmit and distribute such electricity'.

[69] See, the Tampere Convention (Article 21), AADMER (Article 11), and the Inter-American Convention (Articles 2 and 16).

the control by the affected State over the initiation of disaster response by these actors is basically exercised though visa and customs controls and regulations on in-country operations rather than by formal refusals of assistance.[70] The same is true for the International Red Cross and Red Crescent Movement. However, the various components of the Movement may provide support to the National Red Cross or Red Crescent Society in an affected State when that entity requests it (or if it accepts an offer of such support) without a separate approval from the government.[71]

Furthermore, NGOs are not generally granted privileges and immunities under international law, and there is no international regulation for the recognition of their legal personality. The only exception is the Council of Europe's Convention on the Recognition of the Legal Personality of International NGOs of 1986.[72] The process envisaged in its Article 3 could have been a useful model for the recognition of international NGOs registered in another State[73]; however, this convention has only 11 States parties and would be relevant only to disasters occurring within their territory.

In general, foreign NGOs, foreign National Red Cross and Red Crescent Societies (the ICRC and the International Federation are excluded), and foreign private businesses that wish to operate in the affected country as part of a disaster relief mission have three options in gaining domestic legal personality: (1) register with governmental authorities; (2) forge direct relationships with domestic entities, such as preregistered national NGOs or institutions; and, (3) enter a specific headquarters or other status agreement with the government. However, registration procedures are generally complex and time consuming, and at the end of the day they may prove ill-suited to disaster relief activities,[74] whereas the usefulness of an association with a domestic implementing partner has scarcely been explored in

---

[70] For more on this see Chap. 23 by Silingardi in this volume.

[71] See Fischer 2007, 92, citing as the normative basis for providing such direct support to the National Society the 1986 Statutes of the Movement (amended in December 1995); and the 1969 Principles and Rules of Red Cross and Red Crescent Disaster Relief (revised in 1973, 1977, 1981, 1986, and 1995).

[72] 1986 European Convention on the Recognition of the Legal Personality of International Non-Governmental Organisations.

[73] Ibid., Article 3, stating that: 'The proof of acquisition of legal personality and capacity shall be furnished by presenting the NGO's memorandum and articles of association or other basic constitutional instruments, Such instruments shall be accompanied by documents establishing administrative authorisation, registration or any other form of [...official publication by the registering State...] which granted the legal personality and capacity. In a [State] Party which has no publicity procedure, the instrument establishing the NGO shall be duly certified by a competent authority...'.

[74] IFRC 2006b, 12–14; IFRC 2007a, 26–30; IFRC 2007b, 12; IFRC 2009c, 93; IFRC 2011, 38–39. See also Fischer 2007, 126, arguing that 'given the complexity of procedures, some international NGOs simply go without official registration and "hope for the best"'. One of the few exceptions is that of Nepal, whose established practice under the Social Welfare Act, No. 2049, 1992, has been to allow assisting international actors entry without registration during disaster emergency. See Model Act, above n. 6, 89.

practice.[75] One of the few exceptions is represented by the Indonesian Regulation No. 23 of 2008, which allows international institutions or foreign NGOs to participate in disaster management severally, jointly and/or in conjunction with an Indonesian working partner.[76]

Thus, the best way to replace the need for separate registration of NGOs would seem to be signing separate agreements by which the disaster-affected government recognises the legal personality of such organisations under its domestic law, and therefore granting them a number of facilities, privileges and immunities to carry out their functions. However, obtaining such an agreement, as well as expanding an existing one for NGOs already registered and operating in the affected country to cover new situations related to disaster relief, could be time consuming (in some cases, the process can take 6–18 months).[77]

Having chosen none of these three options NGOs can only refer to the general obligation concerning the facilitation of disaster relief operations incorporated in a number of international instruments, mainly of non-binding nature, in support of their request to governments to minimise the registration requirements and consequent delay.[78]

19.5 The Termination of Assistance

International disaster response is 'widely understood to be a temporary reaction to an extraordinary event'.[79] With this perspective, disaster response operations have been generally classified into the following two phases[80]:

- The 'International Disaster Relief Period', which begins immediately after the disaster occurs and includes activities such as, among others, the delivery of food, water and emergency supplies; the restoration of critical lines of communication; and rescue efforts for people trapped in the disaster; and
- The 'International Initial Recovery Period', which shifts the focus on the restoration or improvement of the pre-disaster living conditions of disaster-affected communities, including initiatives to increase resilience to disasters and reduce disaster risks.

---

75 IFRC 2005, 24; IFRC 2006b, 13.

76 Government Regulation of Republic of Indonesia, Number 23 of 28 February 2008 concerning Participation of International Institutions and Foreign Non-Governmental Institutions in Disaster Management, Article 12.

77 IFRC 2009b, 78.

78 Fischer 2007, 362.

79 Ibid., 89.

80 See *Model Act*, above n. 6, Articles 9 and 10.

The necessity to separate the termination of the Disaster Relief Period (phase 1) from that of the International Initial Recovery Period (phase 2) is clear in the IFRC Pilot Model Act. To this end, it provides for a minimum of period of public notice of termination that is shorter for the disaster relief period (45 days instead of 90) because recovery activities 'are more long term and programmatic in nature, and may, therefore, require longer to phase out or, where possible, to hand over to the affected communities.'[81]

It is also possible to add to the classification a third phase, i.e., the 'Reconstruction Phase', which is aimed at providing extensive infrastructure reconstruction, including schools, medical clinics and bridges, on more enduring and stable terms than those involved in the second phase. However, at least with regard to the legal frameworks and special facilities that are expected to facilitate the assistance of international actors in disasters, it has been proposed that a distinction should be made between disaster response (that includes the first two phases) and general development, which is linked to the third phase, when the focus of international assistance shifts to reconstruction.[82]

The problem gets further complicated due to the conduct of some governments, which, in the face of internal political pressure, not only have imposed premature cut-off dates concerning the access or legal facilities of international disaster responders, but have also reverted quite suddenly from the emergency period to the recovery phase.[83] Likewise, international actors have sometimes undertaken insufficient planning with local authorities to take up responsibility when they decide to terminate their operations after a disaster.

According to the IDRL instruments, modalities of termination depend on the legal framework under which international assistance has been activated. There are some instruments, such as, for example, the Inter-American Convention to Facilitate Disaster Assistance, which are silent on this point, and other that limit themselves to express the clause of termination on general terms. For example, the Framework Convention on Civil Defence Assistance only provides that: 'The mission of the Civil Defence Unit of the Supporting State shall come to an end when the crisis for which it was sent is deemed to have ended, or when the Beneficiary State so requests, or the Supporting State so decides'.[84]

However, the major part of IDRL instruments provides that each operation should be terminated only after consultation among the parties. A few treaties specify that consultation to make arrangements for proper conclusion of assistance should take place only after the requesting State or the assisting State have

81 Ibid., 57.

82 Fischer 2007, 89.

83 Ibid., 96; and Model Act, above n. 6, 57.

84 See Framework Convention on Civil Defence Assistance, above footnote 11, Article 4(6).

provided notification of their intention in writing.[85] Both the Tampere Agreement and the IDRL Guidelines further make direct reference to the potential impact on affected persons, providing in relevant part that the affected State and the assisting actor should consult with each other 'bearing in mind the impact of such termination on disaster-affected communities'.[86]

Finally, specific procedures on termination are provided for assistance rendered under regional and sub-regional agreements. The CDEMA Agreement, for example, provides that the Executive Director shall, after consultation with the requesting State, determine the period of response to a disaster and that the requesting or sending State can, at any time, after appropriate consultation and by notification in writing, terminate the receipt or provision of assistance received or provided under the Agreement.[87] According to the AADMER legal framework, as a general rule, the assisting entity shall begin the withdrawal process from the disaster site when the Incident Manager of the requesting or receiving party has determined and declared that either/or the critical situation arising from the disaster emergency is over, the risks faced by the Party arising from the disaster have been overcome, there is no subsequent immediate hazard foreseeable, and when all or most of the victims of the disaster have been rescued. Nevertheless, the assisting entity shall also liaise with the Incident Manager for the withdrawal of its team(s) from the operations when its resources and assets available for effective disaster relief and emergency response have been depleted due to prolonged use during the relief operations. In that case, the assisting entity shall update the AHA Centre about this development through the National Focal Point. Finally, the assisting entity shall submit an exit plan/strategy and debrief reports to the Incident Manager before its final withdrawal and a final report should be sent to the AHA Centre within 2 weeks from the departure from the affected country.[88]

19.6 Conclusions

Disaster response missions are often complex operations, with a diverse set of actors displaying little structural interdependence. However, international disaster response has never been dominated by a 'command and control' paradigm of a highly centralised response, with a few selected authorities issuing orders down the line to both domestic and international responders. As a consequence, a distinguished scholar has clearly pointed out that 'there is no international relief system

[85] See Nuclear Assistance Convention, above n. 11, Article 11; Tampere Convention, above n. 15, Article 6; Convention on the Transboundary Effects of Industrial Accidents, above n. 41, Annex X, Article 10.

[86] Tampere Convention, above n. 11, Article 6; and IDRL Guidelines, above n. 52, Article 12.

[87] See CDEMA Agreement, above n. 41, Article 26.

[88] See *Standard Operating Procedure* (*SASOP*), above n. 17, Chapter V(G).

per se'.[89] In particular, as the disaster scenarios of the last decades have clearly denounced, most of the relief missions do not have clear institutional features, and it is not always easy to understand, at least where the UN relief mechanism is concerned, who holds general 'command and control' powers over the entire disaster response community. When disaster response activities are part of integrated missions, i.e., in the case of emergencies in which there are major political negotiations and/or when UN peace-keeping forces are deployed, there may be three separate and distinct reporting lines: peace-keeping forces, overseen by a Force Commander, humanitarian affairs by the HC and development activities by the RC. In these cases, such as, for example, MINUSTAH in Haiti, it is not uncommon that OCHA suffers from the highly hierarchical UN system, being a peace-keeping mission led by military command where rank and hierarchy carry all the weight, and it is, therefore, unable to affirm its technical leadership over the entire humanitarian community. It is probably true that the absence of clear and precise rules on how international emergency missions should be set up as well as their institutional features (chain of command, mandate, financing, etc.) could have the 'salutary effect to preserve the independence of actors such as the International Red Cross and Red Crescent Movements and NGOs';[90] on the other hand, the continued lack of clarity and the absence of a unified command could hamper the effectiveness of most relief operations and ultimately cripple reconstruction efforts in the long term.[91]

At least whenever they develop under the provision of bilateral treaties and agreements or through (at least some) regional and sub-regional agreements, such as the AADMER and CDEMA, it seems that relief missions do not encounter most of these 'institutional' problems. In both cases, clear mandates are indeed accompanied by sufficiently precise institutional features and supplied through an effective chain of command. However, both bilateral assistance missions and regional and sub-regional agreements share a common weakness in that they have limited geographical reach.

The situation gets further complicated due to the conduct of some governments, which, in the face of internal political pressure, frequently make use of their overall authority and responsibility on the direction and control of the assistance within their territory in contrast with the specific interests of international responders. To quote what an eminent scholar noted 20 years ago, it seems that the international community has not yet been able to develop tools and mechanism through which, on this specific issue, IOs, NGOs, donor governments and affected countries could 'complement rather than compete with each other'.[92]

---

[89] See Beigbeder 1991, 10.

[90] See Fischer 2007, 151.

[91] Arkedis and Derham 2010, 2.

[92] See Beigbeder 1991, 389.

References

Arkedis J, Derham M (2010) Haiti after the quake: nations-building next door, progressive policy institute policy memo. http://progressivefix.com

Beigbeder Y (1991) The role and status of international humanitarian volunteers and organizations: the right and duty to humanitarian assistance. Martinus Nijhoff Publishers, Dodrecht

Bhattacharjee A, Lossio R (2011) Evaluation of OCHA response to the Haiti earthquake, final report. http://ochanet.unocha.org

Fischer D (2007) Law and legal issues in international disaster response: a desk study. International Federation of Red Cross and Red Crescent Societies, Geneva

IFRC (2003) Report on findings from South Asia, Southern Africa and Central Americas

IFRC (2005) Nepal: laws, policies, planning and practices on international disaster response

IFRC (2006a) Legal issues from the international response to the tsunami in Indonesia

IFRC (2006b) Legal issues from the international response to the tsunami in Sri Lanka

IFRC (2006c) Legal issues from the international response to the tsunami in Thailand

IFRC (2007) Legal issues from the international response to tropical storm Stan in Guatemala

Macalister-Smith P (1986) The International Relief Union: reflections on establishing an International Relief Union of July 12, 1927. Legal History Review 54:363–374

Margesson R (2005) Indian Ocean earthquake and tsunami: humanitarian assistance and relief operations, congressional research service report for congress. http://www.fas.org/sgp/crs/row/RL32715.pdf

United Nations (2005) Humanitarian response review. United Nations, New York

Welikala A (2005) Sri Lanka: the post-tsunami declaration of emergency. Centre for Policy Alternatives (CPA). http://www.reliefweb.int/rw/RWB.NSF/db900SID/VBOL

Zwitter A (2011) United Nations' legal framework of humanitarian assistance. In Heintze H-J, Zwitter A (eds) International law and humanitarian assistance: a crosscut through legal issues pertaining to humanitarianism. Springer, Heidelberg, pp 51–69

Chapter 20
Actors, Activities, and Coordination in Emergencies

Giovanni De Siervo

Abstract The last decades witnessed a proliferation of new players in the international humanitarian arena. The increased number of States and non-governmental actors required an additional effort to establish new coordination settings to avoid gaps, overlaps, and duplications. However, as shown by recent emergencies, the issue still remains critical. Starting from the features of the main different actors and highlighting roles and responsibilities, this paper will present the institutional framework of the most important coordination mechanisms that have been developed in recent years.

Keywords Disasters · Relief · International aid · Coordination · Humanitarian actors · United Nations · NGOs · Military

Contents

G. De Siervo (✉)
Department of Civil Protection, Presidenza del Consiglio dei Ministri, 00193, Rome, Italy
e-mail: giovanni.desiervo@protezionecivile.it

A. de Guttry et al. (eds.), *International Disaster Response Law*,
DOI: 10.1007/978-90-6704-882-8_20,

20.1 Defining the Context

Whenever a major disaster strikes, as well as in the case of a humanitarian emergency, coordination 'is probably the most discussed issue'[1] because of the gaps, overlaps, and duplications that are commonly recorded among international actors, and between them and the local actors. Analysts, scholars, and practitioners have studied the topic in-depth. Starting from defining roles and responsibilities, to the development of Standard Operating Procedures and guidelines, everything has been considered and analyzed. However, reality shows that today we still assist to uncoordinated responses to emergencies causing ineffective action by the international community.[2] As a matter of fact it is generally agreed that coordination is the key factor to any successful relief operation. In reality, nobody likes to be coordinated. Coordination in emergencies is an issue also among national actors, but for the purposes of this paper it will be considered mainly with regard to international actors.

The literature has made several different attempts to define coordination, some are very broad: 'the orchestration of efforts of diverse organizations'[3] or 'the orderly and organized direction of activities'.[4] Others are more specific and define the concept as: 'the general elements of interaction between State Parties or their competent bodies, mutual assistance in the provision of technical facilities and equipment and the planning and carrying out of activities related to emergency response',[5] or 'the systematic use of policy instruments to deliver humanitarian assistance in a cohesive and effective manner. Such instruments include: (1) strategic planning; (2) gathering data and managing information; (3) mobilizing resources and assuring accountability; (4) orchestrating a functional division of labor in the field; (5) negotiating and maintaining a serviceable framework with host political authorities; and (6) providing leadership'.[6] Especially the latter

[1] IFRC 2007a, b, 150.

[2] 'There is agreement among humanitarian actors that it is one of the most significant challenges to effective disaster response. An International Federation of Red Cross and Red Crescent Societies (IFRC) survey found that coordination problems were reported by 40—90 % of international and national organizations', IFRC 2007a, b, 150.

[3] Seybolt 1997, 4.

[4] McEntire 1997, 223.

[5] Fischer 2003, 6.

[6] Minear 2002, 20.

definition appears to be the most complete since it clearly identifies the different activities which are crucial, as well as critical, in coordination. The definition is based indeed on the assumption that different actors share an objective and a common strategy which is not always the case, despite the well established and often reiterated guiding humanitarian principles. According to the UN Office for the Coordination of Humanitarian Affairs (OCHA), 'coordination may be defined as actions to harmonize individual responses to maximize impact and achieve synergies'.[7] There should be a common strategic vision among all actors involved and the delivery of aid should be ensured in a complementary fashion, according to the respective roles and capabilities.

The ways to achieve an effective coordination might be very different and they range from authoritative methodologies to systems based on simple exchange of information.

The authoritative methods foresee a clear chain of command and control with a set of well-defined responsibilities. They usually originate from structured systems with a hierarchical organization.

At the extreme opposite there are methods 'by default' where the coordination would be ensured by the simple exchange of information since each actor—by implementing its own mandate—would contribute to reach the final objective.

In between the two extremes lie the methods based on the continuous search for consensus. In these systems a hierarchy is not usually foreseen and all decisions are based on the mutual consent of the parties involved.[8] Each one of those methodologies has pros and cons: the chain of command by defining clear responsibilities would assign to the person or organization in charge the power to enforce coordination with clear benefits for the timing. However, by imposing decisions it would probably create resentment/attrition on the coordinated actor and it would not give the right incentives for any further cooperation. The coordination 'by default' offers a possible option where no one is really in charge, a self-regulated system where the actors agree among themselves on the types of functions and assistance each will provide without adding another layer of bureaucracy. Though in today's reality, where the actors are exponentially increasing and they are constantly fighting sharing the 'market', it appears to be idealistic. The consensus-based systems would allow smoother relations among organizations of different kinds but, at the same time, the search for consensus is a very complex and time-consuming activity that would rely on the leadership of the person, or organization, in charge. Furthermore, in post disaster situations, the word coordination assumes a very specific meaning because the result of non-effective coordination might bring immediate negative impacts on the affected

---

[7] UNDAC 2006, para B.1.

[8] The reference text on this regard is the first evaluation of coordination efforts for the UN Department of Humanitarian Affairs after the genocide in Rwanda in 1994. The report highlighted three broad categories to describe the forms of coordination: 'coordination by command,' 'coordination by consensus,' 'coordination by default'. Donini and Niland 1994, p 13.

population, for this reason the majority of practitioners seem to prefer systems that ensure the possibility of enforcing coordination.

At the international level a centralized approach to disaster relief coordination does not exist. In the framework of the International Disaster Response Law (IDRL) there are a number of tools that seek to improve coordination; however, the international community preferred to address such issues by less formal and non-legally binding means. The League of the Nations—by adopting the Convention and Statutes Establishing an International Relief Union in 1927[9]—tried to impose a centralized approach to international disaster relief coordination through the creation of the International Relief Union.

The Convention entered into force in December 1932, the Union had funding problems since the very beginning and effectively died with the demise of the League of Nations (formally the Secretariat of the IRU closed in 1982). There was not a single major disaster on which the IRU actually took action. Since then, global coordination policies and structures have been mainly developed through non-binding instruments, such as UN General Assembly Resolutions. However, there are some sectoral treaties,[10] and some regional instruments[11] which provide specific coordination roles for particular intergovernmental entities.

The 'landmark' is the 1991 UN General Assembly Resolution 46/182 that set the main principle valid for coordination: 'Each State has the responsibility first and foremost to take care of the victims of natural disasters and other emergencies occurring on its territory. Hence, the affected State has the primary role in the initiation, organization, coordination, and implementation of humanitarian assistance within its territory'.

In principle there is no doubt that coordination responsibility falls on the governments. The international tools and methodologies would only integrate national efforts. However, very often, States lack sound legal and institutional arrangements for the coordination of international actors and the negative consequences of this preparation gap have been evident in recent operations. Furthermore, the national institutions in charge of coordinating post disaster operations usually have to deal with a very challenging environment: infrastructures are often seriously damaged; coordinators are often personally affected by the event; the high pressure by the public opinion and the media is constant. Moreover,

---

[9] According to some scholars: 'The 1927 Convention is the only important multilateral instrument of public international law to have been concerned exclusively with disaster relief, beyond the context of armed conflicts', Macalister-Smith 1981, 147.

[10] 1986 Convention on Assistance in the Case of a Nuclear Accident or Radiological Emergency; 1993 Convention on the Prohibition of the Development, Production, Stockpiling, and Use of Chemical Weapons and on their Destruction Paris, and 1998 Tampere Convention on the Provision of Telecommunication Resources for Disaster Mitigation and Relief Operations.

[11] For example: 1991 *Agreement Establishing the Caribbean Disaster Emergency Response Agency* (CDERA); 2005 *ASEAN Agreement on Disaster Management and Emergency Response*; 1987 *Arab Cooperation Agreement on Regulating and Facilitating Relief Operations*, and EU Council Decision 2001/792/EC establishing the Community Civil Protection Mechanism. For a more comprehensive survey of legal texts refer to Chap. 1 by de Guttry in this volume.

authorities usually have limited knowledge and understanding of the complexity, culture, policies, procedures, and working mechanisms of international relief organizations, and vice versa. In this complex scenario, the massive influx of international actors and means may pose additional burdens on local capabilities. For these reasons the international community, over the years, has developed a non-binding set of tools, codes, guidelines, standard operating procedures, and rules to facilitate the role of the affected State.

The number of actors present on the post disaster stage does not facilitate the task. Traditionally, the national responders belonged to emergency management authorities, public institutions, and civil society, while at the international level the Red Cross and Red Crescent Movement, some NGOs, the UN System, and a few other organizations were operational. Today, the number and kind of actors have drastically increased, the kind of actors has diversified and different philosophies, methodologies, and agendas have appeared on the stage.

20.1.1 Coordination in Disasters and Complex Emergencies

The issue of coordination in emergency situations widely differs according to the kind of crisis that has to be dealt with. Two kinds of emergencies generally require a large-scale international relief operation: natural or man-made disasters and 'complex emergencies'.

In the first case, the affected government has the primary responsibility to manage the relief activities, it has to 'call' the crisis and to ensure coordination; the international actors are expected to act in accordance with its indications and in respect of its sovereignty.

In case of a 'complex emergency',[12] the humanitarian agencies assume direct protection responsibilities of the affected population, due to the breakdown of national authorities, and the coordination mechanisms are mainly internationally driven.

Coordinating disaster response in the aftermath of a natural or man-made disaster is less problematic that in a complex emergency. General principles, criteria, and tools are the same. However, the dynamics of emergency coordination are intrinsically connected to the kind and origin of the disaster, its location and the political, economic, administrative, and cultural situation of the affected country. Successes and failures of coordination depend essentially from the geo-political environment of each affected country. The presence of a stable national authority, with a proper administrative structure and an organized response system would certainly simplify the provision of international support as well as the

[12] A complex emergency is 'a humanitarian crisis in a country, region or society where there is total or considerable breakdown of authority resulting from internal or external conflict and which requires an international response that goes beyond the mandate or capacity of any single agency and/or the ongoing United Nations country program', IASC 2004, p 5.

coordination. On the other hand, political tensions, social unrests, or conflicts would raise major concerns since international humanitarian response to disasters has to be provided according to the recognized humanitarian principles.

Disasters, either natural or man-made, are, to a large extent, unpredictable 'calamitous events or series of events resulting in widespread loss of life, great human suffering and distress, or large-scale material or environmental damage, thereby seriously disrupting the functioning of society'.[13] Especially in the case of a sudden disaster, such as earthquakes or floods, coordination raises different concerns compared to a slow development crisis (such as droughts), at least in the first days after the event. Complex emergencies or slow development crisis are indeed the result of structural problems that require to be addressed by different management methodologies. Large sudden onset disasters overwhelm the normal situation in seconds or hours. For this reason, the response takes place in a unique, high pressure emergency environment with the aim of saving as many lives as possible. In these instances, relief activities revolve around generally straightforward operations, such as search and rescue, triage, medical treatment, provision of water, food, and shelter. Local authorities have to respond in a very short timeframe and they are often overwhelmed by emerging needs that push them to require international assistance. Clearly, the coordination settings in these situations should be specific. Some authors argue that responding to a natural disaster is very different from operating in complex emergencies and slow development crisis, not only because of the emergency environment but because the logics are different.[14] The first case focuses on the phases of rescue and life sustaining activities, while the latter has to deal with relief and rehabilitation phases addressing structural problems. This would not be the case for discussing the theories related to emergency phases and to Linking Relief, Rehabilitation, and Development (LRRD)[15] but it is doubtless that the phases are overlapping causing problems and misunderstandings among actors that have different mandates, priorities, and missions.

---

[13] United Nations International Law Commission, Sixty-first session, Geneva, 4 May-5 June and 6 July-7 August 2009, Protection of persons in the event of disasters, Draft Articles 1–5, Document A/CN.4/629. As described by de Guttry in Chap. 1 in this volume 'The specific elements of the definition of "disaster" can, therefore, be summed up in the following manner: (a) it is a man-made or a natural event; (b) its consequences produce risks or cause significant injuries or widespread damage; (c) persons, property and/or the environment are affected'.

[14] Katoch 2006, 154–158.

[15] For a general overview of the concept http://www.urd.org/spip.php?page=mot&id_mot=36%26lang=en. Accessed 23 February 2012.

20.1.2 'Traditional' and 'New Actors'

Traditionally, international disaster response has been ensured by agencies depending either on States or international organizations.[16] At the same time, the traditional humanitarian organizations such as the Red Cross and Red Crescent Movement have been providing post disaster assistance as well as some Non-Governmental Organizations. All were operating according to widely recognized principles of humanity, neutrality, and impartiality and the main difference among the actors was linked to the status of being governmental or non-governmental organizations. The relatively limited number of entities and their well-known derivation could have facilitated the efforts to coordinate their action although the results were not often positive.

Besides that, in recent years the number and variety of actors in the humanitarian arena have significantly increased[17] making even more complex the coordination task. Especially, non State actors are more and more present in post disaster situations and the number of NGOs has drastically increased at the global level.

Despite this trend, the last decade has witnessed a return to the centrality of the State in disaster relief.[18] This situation reflects the changing geopolitical context and an emerging perception that international humanitarian assistance is no longer the preferred option. Certainly in complex emergencies, as well as in post disaster situations, the affected States tend to reaffirm their national sovereignty and to play a more direct role over the relief operations. Affected States reduce the humanitarian space by limiting the access of international relief organizations and imposing strict controls over their activities. From the 2004 South East Asia tsunami to the 2005 Pakistan earthquake, from Myanmar 2008 Cyclone Nargis to the China 2008 Sichuan earthquake, the number of examples of this trend is growing.[19]

At the international level, governments have also increased their direct presence by using their emergency services or their military resources. This situation may be explained in different ways and several authors have recognized a growing trend to submit the provision of humanitarian support to political considerations.[20]

---

[16] For a more comprehensive analysis of current challenges of disaster relief refer to Chap. 21 by Donini in this volume.

[17] This was recognized by the ECOSOC in 2004: 'the need to ensure that this multiplication of actors does not detract from the effectiveness of the humanitarian response and the neutrality and independence of humanitarian assistance', ECOSOC Res. 2004/50, U.N. Doc. No. E/2004/INF/2/Add.2 (2004) at 134.

[18] As shown by some recent research (Harvey 2010, p 5) by studying the official data of relief international contributions by the European Commission it appears that during the 1970 and 1980s, when humanitarian action was limited by Cold War tensions, the affected States played a much more central role in disaster response because financial resources were channeled directly to their national governments. In the 1990s, however, this contribution fell to 6 % from over 90 % in 1976 while the contribution to NGOs has significantly risen.

[19] Kent 2011, 1.

[20] Global Humanitarian Partnership 2010, p 2; Kent 2011, 2–3.

OECD DAC[21] member governments continue to contribute to the humanitarian and post disaster response and they still remain the major donors at the international level.[22] However, Non-DAC government contributions have recently considerably increased[23] and the donations of the corporate, philanthropic (i.e., 'billantrophy'), or public donations have increased in recent years. Furthermore, the corporate sector[24] is also more and more present in post disaster situations at global level.[25]

The proliferation of actors, in permanent competition for funding and visibility, has brought several authors to consider the relief sector like an enterprise or a real market.[26] This paper does not explore the background and challenges of this crowded 'arena' however, it is important to mention some of the elements that have a direct implication on coordination.

UN GA Resolution 46/182 aims to improve coherence and coordination of aid encouraging both affected and assisting States to channel offers and assistance requests through the UN Emergency Relief Coordinator but this is, clearly, not always the case.

First of all, the funding arrangements which undergo to the different actors bear important consequences because the stakeholders are not always the same. Generally, there is no doubt that, in the first instance, the stakeholders in any post disaster operation should be the local affected population and institutions; however, the relief organizations have growing concerns regarding being accountable to their donors. At the same time, the presence of new donors which are not part of the traditional discussion or coordination constituencies may create additional problems. Private philanthropy, Non-DAC donors, public fundraising are today more and more actively present on the stage and it is difficult to ensure that they will always coordinate their action.

---

[21] Organization for Economic Cooperation and Development—Development Assistance Committee (DAC): 'For 50 years now, the OECD Development Assistance Committee (DAC) has grouped the world's main donors, defining and monitoring global standards in key areas of development'. http://www.oecd.org/, accessed 11 February 2012.

[22] For a detailed analysis of the changing landscape of donors in humanitarian action see Macrae 2003.

[23] 'Of the 10 largest world donors, Saudi Arabia has shown the largest increase of reported contributions in the past four years (2,465 %)'. Stoddard 2010, 22.

[24] See Kent and Burke 2011.

[25] This trend takes origin from the theory of corporate social responsibility, by offering means and know-how to the community, and exponentially increased after the 2004 South East Asia Tsunami. In this respect were recorded very good examples and less positive experiences, because there are sometimes mixed motivations behind the actions of the business sector. However, the corporate sector has a great potential to bring an incredible added value to emergency response but needs to be placed in an overall framework agreed with the humanitarian community. There should be guidelines and rules that need to be undersigned by the business companies prior to deployment.

[26] See Rieff 2000, Minear 2002, Polman 2010.

Another implication is that the different actors are not at all times adequately prepared and do not understand risks and implications of their actions. If, on the one hand, traditional organizations and donors knew and respected principles, guidelines, and methodologies, on the other hand the newcomers are not always aware of the agreed standards and procedures.

Nowadays there is an almost unanimous acceptance of humanitarian principles but, apparently, there are different methods to implement them. Every organization has its own mandate, philosophy, and operational methodology that deeply affect the way the principles are implemented and the operations are carried out.[27] In this respect, it is interesting to notice the number of different coordination constituencies for NGOs. Furthermore, some NGOs or organizations do not commit themselves to participate in coordination arrangements.

There are no possible legal instruments to block any kind of group of people intending to create an entity and to 'access the market'. The only effective check could be implemented by the affected government by setting up domestic legal barriers for the provision of disaster assistance (i.e., access, customs, and registration).

The use of State entities raises very serious, and long debated, concerns related to the nature of the different actors, especially the military. By their own nature, those instruments depend on a government and they are not independent, also if they do not pursue any specific objective. Furthermore, the military follow their own reporting line and a separated chain of command that might exclude them from coordination. The 'integrated mission'[28] concept of the UN is seriously questioned for the risk of submitting humanitarian action to political action undermining the importance of independence/impartiality to political considerations.[29]

Achieving the proper coordination in a situation when different actors have different donors, mandates, and operational methodologies is a real challenge.

---

[27] The Feinstein International Centre of the Tufts University has recognized the following Typology of Humanitarian Actors: '*"Principled-Dunantist"* based on the basic tenets of humanitarianism developed by Henri Dunant. Proponents of principle-centered action argue for a narrower definition of humanitarianism limited to life-saving assistance and protection of civilians, based on core principles of neutrality, impartiality, and independence. *"Pragmatist-Wilsonian"* recognize the importance of principles but place a higher premium on action, even when this means putting core principles in jeopardy. They identify broadly with foreign policy objectives of their home government, whose funds they often use. *"Solidarist"* beyond the provision of assistance and protection they address the root causes of conflict, which are political at the core. *"Faith-based"* the world's major religious traditions, western and non-western alike, embody humanitarian affirmations and obligations. In addition to international faith-based agencies that do not usually engage in proselytizing, there is a wide variety of religious organizations at the local level. Faith-based entities may themselves embody principled, pragmatist, and/or solidarist features.' See Donini et al. 2008, p 11.

[28] See Eide et al. 2005.

[29] See *infra* Sect. 20.2.2.5.

20.2 The Coordination Mechanisms in Place

The lack of proper coordination leads to gaps, overlaps, duplications, increased expenses, and inefficient use of resources beyond incapacity to respond to the affected population needs.

In case of disaster, the affected country is in charge of the coordination of both national and international actors, a challenging task for which several attempts have been made to try to facilitate the effort. The existing international coordination mechanisms at headquarters and national levels are to a large extent UN driven. The recognized role of UN coordination is ensured and it was repeatedly confirmed, at the same time several other tools were developed at regional level or based on the typology of actors.[30]

There is general agreement that to be effective, coordination cannot be implemented only on the spot when aid occurs, but it should be planned in advance and implemented at different levels: at international/strategic level, at national level, and on the spot.

20.2.1 The Host Nation and the Local Emergency Management Authority

As a general rule, the primary duty-bearer with regard to persons affected by disasters is the government of the affected State. Every country has built its own emergency response service developed according to its political, cultural, and social traditions. Civil protection, civil defense, contingency agency, emergency management authorities each organizational systems has its own features, some are in charge of the whole crisis management, in other cases they are in charge of coordination only.[31] Those organizations also have different institutional positions with respect to their governments; in some cases they depend on the ministries for internal affairs, the ministries of security, the prime minister, or the president. Their main task is to organize and implement relief operations on their national territory; their action is mainly focused on coordinating the action of all the different actors involved: ministries, administrations, and civil society. Each country has chosen its coordination methodology, centralized or decentralized to the local level, hierarchical or consensus-based, organized on the basis of sectors or by competences; however, in general it is possible to identify at least the highest

---

[30] See for example, the tools developed by different NGOs constituencies or coordination 'umbrella'. In the framework of the Red Cross Red Crescent Movement, the Agreement on the organization of the international activities of the components of the International Red Cross and Red Crescent Movement ('Seville Agreement') of 1997.

[31] For a more comprehensive analysis of national legal frameworks governing disaster response refer to Chap. 12 by Mancini in this volume.

coordination authority mandated by the national government to ensure the response operations.

In 1971, the UN General Assembly 'invite[d] potential recipient Governments…[t]o appoint a single national disaster relief coordinator to facilitate the relief of international aid in times of emergency'. When the severity of the disaster overwhelms the national response capacities and there is need for an international response, the States have in principle, the duty of requesting and co-ordinating the assistance in their own country.[32] In this case, it is crucial to identify in a very short time who has the mandate for requesting assistance. Relief organizations, both governmental and NGOs are willing to intervene in a timely manner for a number of reasons. First of all, the time factor is crucial for saving life activities, the public opinion attention is very high in the first post disaster phases, the 'humanitarian arena' is very crowded and also for reasons of effectiveness (resources, especially of technical nature, need time to be immediately operational and in some cases, emergency funds can be released only after the event). For these reasons, the agencies need to receive the request as soon as possible. On the other hand, the affected State would need to make a proper needs assessment—which is the key element for an effective response—that takes time.

In an 'ideal' situation the disaster would strike a country with a stable government that would assess the damages; it would call for specific international assistance defining the framework and rules to follow to provide support. Unfortunately, reality is often different. In recent years, in well-organized countries too, we saw how the pressure of the public opinion can affect strong governments. In the aftermath of the Katrina Hurricane emergency, the US President seemed to reject the very idea of foreign assistance, stating on 1 September 2005, that the US would 'rise up and take care of it'.[33] After pressures from political leaders and the media, the position changed and offers of assistance were welcomed.[34]

National governments are usually reluctant to admit of not being able to cope with the effects of a catastrophe, for this reason open requests for assistance do not happen often.[35] More frequently, the requests are transformed into welcoming assistance, for example India after 2001 Gujarat earthquake or Myanmar after 2008 Nargis cyclone.[36]

---

[32] In some cases it is not easy to identify the institution in charge, for example, when the 2005 earthquake struck Pakistan, there was no provision in the national law designating the institution in charge for co-ordinating relief.

[33] Interview to President George W. Bush to ABC 'Good Morning America', reported in 'Foreign governments line up to help after Katrina' Reuters 1 September 2005, http://reliefweb.int/sites/reliefweb.int/files/reliefweb_pdf/node-183522.pdf. Accessed 15 December 2011.

[34] van der Linde 2008, 1.

[35] ALNAP 2010, 22.

[36] After the Gujarat Earthquake, the Indian government publicly welcomed 'acts of solidarity'; in the aftermath of Nargis Cyclone, 'The Government of the Union of Myanmar welcomes international humanitarian assistance', The Tripartite Core Group, Post-Nargis Joint Assessment, 39.

For a country requesting assistance there are a number of options: it can activate the bilateral channel, a multilateral institution (global or regional), or it can combine the different methods (this is the case especially for major catastrophes). After the 2008 Sichuan earthquake, China for example, accepted bilateral assistance or aid through regional organizations but specifically indicated that UNDAC was not requested.

The request timing has a direct impact on the coordination efforts since countries in sudden onset disasters are not often able to prepare a proper needs assessment but end up compiling a standard 'shopping list' of ordinary emergency items. By consequence, there is a supply-driven response; the international actors do not offer supplies and assets according to assessed needs, but according to their availability causing gaps and overlaps. The affected country usually does not have the capability to refuse offers because it receives pressure to accept both domestically and internationally[37]; second, because in the aftermath of a major disaster, the workload required to scrutinize all possible offers is often well beyond the domestic capacity. International organizations and foreign governments normally deal with affected State governments through official offers and requests prior to providing assistance, but this is not common practice of other international actors such as NGOs.

The ability to co-ordinate a situation like the one above described requires good skills, a sound knowledge of the applicable legal framework, the international relief actors, and their dynamics but these are not often present in the national responding communities. Each State should prepare for the possibility of receiving incoming assistance, and there should be a dedicated legislation, but this is not happening in the majority of cases. Regional organizations such as the European Union have invited their members to implement these kinds of instruments in their legislations. The 'Council Conclusions on Host Nation Support'[38] in order to remove any possible obstacle to international assistance to ensure effective disaster response 'Calls on the Member States and the Commission to step up structured work in the field of Host Nation Support' and 'make the necessary arrangements in the existing organizational structure in order to either receive assistance or facilitate the transit of assistance'. The 'Guidelines for the domestic facilitation and regulation of international disaster relief and initial recovery assistance'[39] (the 'IDRL Guidelines'), adopted by at the State parties to the Geneva Conventions at the 30th International Conference of the Red Cross and Red Crescent Movement on 30 November 2007, are meant to assist governments to be better prepared for

[37] Regardless of the fact that Italy did not request intentional assistance in the aftermath of the 2009 L'Aquila earthquake, there were several pressing offers of international assistance coming from various countries and NGOs. Nonetheless, it was officially reported that international offers would be considered only after a proper needs assessment, some NGOs decided anyway to deploy their teams to Italy.

[38] 3051st JUSTICE and HOME AFFAIRS Council meeting, Brussels, 2 and 3 December 2010.

[39] Endorsed by the UN General Assembly in 2008 Res. 63/139, Res. 63/141, and Res. 63/137, IFRC 2007b, IFRC 2008.

the common legal problems in international response operations. Despite these attempts to set up tools fit to manage international aid, nowadays very few countries have developed their own legal and organizational framework.[40]

Once the offer is accepted, the incoming assistance should then be channeled through the existing coordination authorities. The system set up by national government to manage the relief operations is commonly called Local Emergency Management Authority (LEMA). As per the overall national systems, each country has developed it according to its own national organizational culture and methodologies.[41]

National coordination settings should ensure that national and international responses are complementary. In the US, for example, the National Incident Management System (NIMS) is the emergency management doctrine applicable at all administrative levels and across functional discipline to ensure effective resource coordination. It is based on enhanced cooperation and interoperability among responders through a standardized flexible, all-hazards approach to incident management; it also recognizes a clear chain of responsibilities and command. The NIMS Incident Command System became a referral point at the international level. It consists of a standard management hierarchy and procedures for managing temporary incident of any size with a clear chain of command structure.

LEMA should set up dedicated instances and tools to co-ordinate international actors and to make the best possible use of incoming resources. This would also facilitate the national ownership in terms of a co-ordinated response. International actors would have to refer to the national coordination settings. These are the rules that in principle should apply; the practice of recent operations has, however, shown that some international actors deliberately bypass national coordination structures[42] and fail to inform domestic authorities of their activities. At the same time, it is very still rare to find countries that have set up a dedicated coordination system for international aid. Furthermore, there is often a change of coordination settings in the various phases of the response, from the acute emergency period to recovery/ development; in some cases it is smooth, in other instances more abrupt.[43]

Very often, capacity shortcomings—particularly at the level of local government—are a real constraint to effective coordination. In situations like the 2010 Haiti earthquake, another problem also emerges: not only were the people in charge personally affected by the disaster, and they could not produce a proper needs assessment, but they did not have the capability of maintaining their coordination role.[44] The international community in that case had to support the affected country by lending immediate capacity and technical assistance.

---

[40] GAO 2006

[41] In Italy the Augustus methodology and DiComAC concept were developed. OECD 2010, 18, 44.

[42] ALNAP 2010, 23.

[43] Bennett et al. 2006, 40.

[44] Binder and Grünewald 2010, 42.

20.2.2 The United Nations Global Coordination and the Cluster System

In 1971, General Assembly Resolution 2816 (XXVI) called on the Secretary-General to appoint a Disaster Relief Coordinator with the responsibility to 'mobilize, direct and coordinate' the UN response to disasters. In March 1972, the Office of the United Nations Disaster Relief Organization (UNDRO) was established to co-ordinate international relief activities in countries struck by natural or other disasters. It was headed by a Disaster Relief Coordinator who reported directly to the UN Secretary-General. Its main function was to act as catalyst and coordinator of providers of aid and services by matching donor responses with reported needs. It carried out the functions of information coordination center and facilitated the establishment of stockpiles in areas susceptible to natural disasters. The main problems encountered by the Disaster Relief Coordinator and UNDRO were linked to the financial weakness of the office and the difficulties in meeting the objectives.

In 1991, the General Assembly recognized the need to strengthen coordination for rapid response to humanitarian emergencies by adopting the resolution 46/182, which sought to strengthen the 'central and unique role' of the UN to ensure leadership and 'coordinating the efforts of the international community to support the affected countries'. It replaced the Disaster Relief Coordinator with a higher level status of the Under-Secretary-General for Humanitarian Affairs, the 'Emergency Relief Coordinator' (ERC) with responsibility for improving coordination of international assistance both in disaster and conflict emergencies. To perform its tasks it had been assigned a secretariat, the Department of Humanitarian Affairs (DHA) that was established in April 1992, incorporating UNDRO and other UN units. Resolution 46/182 provided to the DHA three new tools to improve the response and the coordination of the international community to emergencies: the Inter-Agency Standing Committee (IASC),[45] the Central Emergency Revolving Fund (CERF),[46] and the Consolidated Inter-Agency Appeals Process (CAP).[47]

DHA, however, was much criticized[48] and it was soon replaced by the Office for the Coordination of Humanitarian Affairs (OCHA), created within the UN Secretariat as a part of the 1998 reform following the 'Renewing the United

[45] IASC is a policy-making body chaired by the ERC and is composed by the executive heads of the humanitarian and development UN agencies, of the International Federation of Red Cross and Red Crescent, ICRC, IOM, and NGO consortia.

[46] The Central Emergency Revolving Fund (CERF) is a quick available source of emergency funding at disposal of operational organizations especially at the initial phases of the emergency.

[47] The Consolidated Inter-Agency Appeals Process (CAP) assesses the needs of critical situations and prepares a comprehensive interagency response strategy.

[48] The role of DHA was not well-defined and there was confusion between its co-ordinating role and its more operational roles. Furthermore, DHA never received adequate funding and human resources. For a more comprehensive analysis of DHA role see Weiss 1998.

Nations: A program for Reform'.[49] OCHA is not directly operational (so seen as more impartial) with the tasks of: 'Mobilize and coordinate effective and principled humanitarian action in partnership with national and international actors in order to alleviate human suffering in disasters and emergencies; Advocate the rights of people in need; Promote preparedness and prevention; Facilitate sustainable solutions'.[50] The operational responsibilities of DHA, as mine action and logistics, were devolved to other UN entities.

In post disaster assistance, the UN Emergency Relief Coordinator is operating mainly through his/her country level representatives, the 'humanitarian coordinators'.

20.2.2.1 Resident Coordinator and Humanitarian Coordinator

To ensure coherence of action and coordination among the different actors, the Resident Coordinator and the United Nation Country team system has been established. The United Nations Resident Coordinator is the highest United Nations official and the chief of the UN diplomatic mission in a country, except when there is an appointed Special Representative of the Secretary-General (SRSG). He/She has the same rank as an Ambassador of a foreign State, is the designated representative of the UN Secretary-General, and leads the United Nations Country Team.[51] The function is usually performed by the Resident Representative of the United Nations Development Program (UNDP).[52]

In case of an emergency, if international humanitarian assistance is required and a separate Humanitarian Coordinator (HC) position is not established, RCs are often called to assume the UN Humanitarian Coordinator[53] role and co-ordinating country-level response to humanitarian crises.

---

[49] UN GA A/51/1950 Renewing the United Nations: A program for Reform, Report from the Secretary-General.

[50] OCHA Mission Statement available at: http://www.unocha.org, accessed 18 February 2012.

[51] The Resident Coordinator system aims at bringing together the different UN agencies to improve the efficiency and effectiveness of operational activities at the country level. It includes all organizations of the United Nations system dealing with operational activities for development, regardless of their formal presence in the country. At country level, RCs are tasked to ensure leadership within the UN system, facilitating the coordination and coherence of all UN operational activities, advocating and promoting the UN global agenda. The UN General Assembly established the concept of a single official to co-ordinate operational activities within the UN system in 1977 (GA Resolution 32/197). The concept has evolved, and the role of the UN Country Team has been reaffirmed in all GA Resolutions (GA Resolutions 47/199, 50/120, 56/201, 59/201 and 62/208) as well as on the Comprehensive Policy Reviews of 1992, 2004 and 2007.

[52] The fact that the Resident Coordinator is wearing more than one hat at the time is criticized. For this reason, it is often stressed that the Resident Coordinator should be independent from any agency, including his/her mother entity, a neutral position *vis à vis* the government, strong humanitarian experience, and a mix of diplomatic and operational skills.

[53] The designation is decided by the UN ERC in consultation with the Inter-Agency Standing Committee. In this function, the Resident Coordinator/Humanitarian Coordinator (RC/HC) is in

The Humanitarian Coordinator plays a crucial role to ensure an effective co-ordinated humanitarian system at country level, particularly in case of natural disasters. The system has a solid normative framework, developed and implemented at inter-agency level and strengthened by the recent Humanitarian Reform.[54] However, coordination is also connected with personal skills[55]: it has to be ensured that Humanitarian Coordinators own adequate expertise by providing them with learning opportunities before and during their appointment. For this reason, a well-functioning support system needs to be in place, both at the country and at the global level.

20.2.2.2 UN Country Team

The UN Country Team (UNCT) includes all the entities of the UN system that carry out operational activities for development, emergency, recovery, and transition.[56] It is composed of all the UN entities that carry out operational activities in a specific country; it is the forum that ensures inter-agency coordination and decision-making at the national level. The UN Country Team is led by the UN Resident Coordinator; it is participatory, collegial, based on consensus and mutual accountability. Its decisions are non-binding. The main purpose of the Country Team is to facilitate all involved agencies to plan and work together to ensure the delivery of tangible results in support for the development agenda. They share assessments, define a common working program, and jointly mobilize resources to ensure a coherent action of the different UN entities. All UNCT members have direct line accountability to their own organization, as well as collegial accountability to the Resident Coordinator.

20.2.2.3 Humanitarian Reform and Cluster Approach

A system composed of multiple autonomous bodies—each dependent on voluntary contributions—obviously lacks strategic leadership and is liable to create gaps and a lower preparedness level.

(Footnote 53 continued)
charge for supporting national efforts and he/she is accountable to the Emergency Relief Coordinator for the strategic and operational coordination of the response of the United Nations Country Team member agencies and relevant humanitarian actors.

[54] See *infra* Sect. 20.2.2.3.

[55] In Haiti, for example, the weak humanitarian leadership was responsible for many of the shortcomings of the response 'As a result, operational agencies did not have a framework for their activities, the military could not be properly assigned tasks and the government could not be sufficiently engaged with and supported'. Binder and Grünewald 2010, 33.

[56] The United Nations Country Team (UNCT) exists in 136 countries, covering all of the 180 countries where there are United Nations programs.

Considering the initial slow implementation and negative results of the international assistance to the Darfur Crisis (a complex emergency) in 2004, the ERC commissioned an independent review of the humanitarian response capacities of the UN, NGOs, International Red Cross and Red Crescent Movement, and other key actors to identify critical gap areas and to make recommendations to address them. Based on the analysis of the 'Humanitarian Response Review', published in April 2005, the basis was set for the 'Humanitarian reform seeks to improve the effectiveness of humanitarian response by ensuring greater predictability, accountability and partnership'.[57] The review highlighted gaps and inconsistencies of the humanitarian response system, especially related to predictability and coordination, and suggested methods to address them. The three main innovations are linked to the cluster approach, a more predictable financing and the strategic leadership.[58]

While financial innovations may play a central role in coordination because they provide adequate, flexible, and predictable resources,[59] as well as the strengthening of the Humanitarian Coordinator function, the more crucial innovation for coordination is the institution of the cluster approach. Starting from the non predictability of humanitarian responses (this was the case that originated the problem in the Darfur case), the Humanitarian Response Review suggested to address the issue by identifying sectoral coordination at global level with a clearly identified lead organization. Following the recommendations, the IASC has identified, in September 2005, nine global clusters with their respective lead organization for the following areas: nutrition/UNICEF, water and sanitation/ UNICEF, health/WHO, camp coordination and management/UNHCR-IOM, emergency shelter UNHCR-IFRC, protection/UNHCR, logistics/WFP, telecommunications/OCHA-UNICEF-WFP, and early recovery/UNDP.[60]

The aim of the cluster approach is to ensure predictable and timely response in crisis. It seeks to improve the partnerships among the different humanitarian actors

---

[57] http://oneresponse.info/COORDINATION/CLUSTERAPPROACH/Pages/Cluster%20Approach.aspx. Accessed 8 February 2012.

[58] Disagreement remains over whether the conceptualization of clusters was a consultative process or not. IASC is the most representative humanitarian forum established, however it cannot claim to represent the full spectrum of humanitarian actors, and there are concerns about the way in which national authorities were included in the elaboration process (ALNAP 2010, p 23). It has been noted that the process was pushed by OCHA and ERC without adequate time for consultation and that the lead had been assigned in advance. Furthermore, 'donors were outside of the original planning of the clusters, and were gradually brought in then funding requirements became apparent', Stoddard et al. 2007, 7.

[59] The Central Emergency Relief Fund provides a minimum amount of flexible and predictable financing for the most urgent life-saving programs that are critically under-funded. The CERF can also be used immediately to provide quick initial funding for rapid response in sudden onset disasters.

[60] Today the number of clusters has been increased by adding some cross-cutting issues like: environment, age, gender, mental health. For further elements http://oneresponse.info/COORDINATION/CLUSTERAPPROACH, accessed 13 February 2012.

(UN agencies, the International Red Cross and Red Crescent Movement, international organizations, and NGOs[61]) to make sure that sufficient capacity at global level is available in all the main sectors/areas of response.[62]

The principle of designating a lead organization at global level meant to address the long lasting issue of sectoral leadership. If it does not mean the existence of a chain of command, the global cluster lead organization is mandated to ensure that response capacity is ready and that assessment, planning, and response activities are carried out in collaboration with partners in accordance with agreed standards and guidelines. It also makes the international humanitarian community a better partner for host governments by identifying a focal point for the specific sector. Furthermore, the cluster leaders also act as the 'provider of last resort'.

The 'provider of last resort' concept represents a commitment of sector leaders to do their utmost to ensure an adequate and appropriate response where there are critical gaps in humanitarian response. The cluster leader in those cases may need to commit itself to filling the gap. Many cluster leaders have reoriented their strategy to cope with new responsibilities (for example UNICEF for Water and Sanitation) because—according to IASC parameters—global cluster leader organizations have to prepare for three emergencies (involving 500,000 affected people each) per year out of which two are simultaneous. According to some analyses, only WFP and UNHCR are ready to do so.[63] At national level the cluster leader can be a different organization from the global one. This depends on the current situation of the country; a global cluster leader might be not present in the country or a different organization might have a specific experience in a specific sector.

Successful implementation of the cluster approach will depend on the participation of all actors in all phases of the crisis, from the needs assessment, to planning, implementation, and ex-post evaluation. The cluster approach is about making the international humanitarian community more organized, achieving more strategic responses, and better prioritization. The aim behind the cluster system was making the 'humanitarian community to work collectively toward an inclusive coordination mechanism to which all stakeholders can feel a sense of belonging'.[64]

The cluster approach serves also to ensure better accountability in international responses to humanitarian emergencies, by clarifying the division of labor among organizations, and better defining their roles and responsibilities within the different sectors of response. Cluster leaders are accountable, at global level, to the

[61] The International Committee of the Red Cross (ICRC), like some NGOs (following of the Dunantist approach), do not take part in the cluster approach, but they co-ordinate with UN to achieve efficient response for the affected people. However, at the global level they participate as an observer in many of the cluster working group meetings.

[62] See IASC 2007.

[63] Stoddard et al. 2007, 13.

[64] Adinolfi et al. 2005, 47.

Emergency Relief Coordinator and at field level they are accountable to Humanitarian Coordinators.

In principle, in case of major 'new' emergencies that require a multi-sectoral response with participation of a wide range of international humanitarian actors, the cluster approach should be applied from the beginning to plan and organize the international response. The activation has to be requested to the Emergency Relief Coordinator by the Humanitarian Coordinator, or Resident Coordinator, after consultation with relevant partners. The ERC in coordination with Global cluster leader ensures agreement at global level and communicates it to HC/RC and partners within 24 h. The HC/RC will then inform the host government and all partners. The cluster approach should be implemented in close co-operation with the host government, the cluster leaders at country level ensure the development and the maintaining of proper links with all relevant local stakeholders. The Inter-Agency Standing Committee (IASC), in 2006, decided that all countries with Humanitarian Coordinators already appointed will implement the cluster approach.

Since its establishment the cluster approach has been employed in a number of emergencies with mixed results. It has shown good potential to improve international coordination but also between the international community and domestic stakeholders. All evaluations of the cluster approach have shown that it did work in slow development emergencies to fill gaps and to solve duplication, as well as managing the newcomers. In sudden onset disasters, the effectiveness of clusters however appears to be limited. The system indeed needs time to be set up and a complete analysis of local structures and capacities should be realized beforehand.

The fact that the cluster system was 'designed' as a gap-filler and is being used as a system in itself raises problems because clusters are process rather than action oriented. Their effectiveness depends on the motivation and ability of the appointed lead agencies to put the resources and effort into making their cluster work, as well as on the willingness of being co-ordinated by all different agencies.

Furthermore, in their current implementation, clusters largely exclude national and local actors. They are coordination settings established for foreign agencies where the use of the English language does not facilitate the integration with the affected State coordination and response mechanisms.

The leadership aspect most crucially differentiates the cluster approach from earlier models of coordination. Having a designated lead agency with responsibility not only for the performance of its own program but for the entire sectoral response represents the most important benefit of this approach.

The Humanitarian reform has also looked at strengthening the Humanitarian Coordinators System. In countries with a Humanitarian Coordinator in place, the UNCT will establish the Humanitarian Country Team when a crisis erupts or chronic vulnerability deteriorates.[65] It is an essential prerequisite for effective

---

[65] Guidance for Humanitarian Country Teams endorsed by the 75th IASC Working Group 18 November 2009.

application of the cluster approach and it is composed of all the main organizations that undertake humanitarian action in the country and that commit themselves to participate to coordination arrangements, these include: UN agencies, the International Organization for Migrations, NGOs, and the Red Cross and Red Crescent movement. The cluster leaders are also represented in the HCT. The main task of HCT is to co-ordinate the humanitarian action in the country and to make sure that it is provided according to humanitarian principles. It operates in the support and coordination of local authorities. It does not replace the UNCT; the two entities coexist because their focus is different.

20.2.2.4 The United Nations Disaster Assessment and Coordination (UNDAC) and the OSOCC Concept

In sudden onset disasters, at least in the first days, it is complex to apply the cluster approach to co-ordinate relief operations because of the timeframe. Clusters can be very useful if already in place, but they need time to be established and adequately trained personnel with knowledge, capabilities, and leadership.

Life-saving activities, typical of the first phases of sudden onset disasters, have to be implemented in a very short time; the media exposure of today's disasters spreads information and facilitates the massive and quick arrival on-site of a multitude of actors. For this reason, other coordination tools were developed in the framework of DHA/OCHA.

Established in 1993, the United Nations Disaster Assessment and Coordination (UNDAC) is a system created to fill in the possible coordination gaps in the first days after the disaster. It is set up by four different elements: staff, methodology, mobilization procedures, and equipment. UNDAC is a roster of experienced emergency managers available to intervene in real time. The roster is managed by OCHA and is composed of professional staff coming from over 40 countries either from national emergency services or international humanitarian organizations. UNDAC teams are regionally organized to make sure that their deployment takes place in a short period of time and by virtue of their knowledge of the region and related specific risks. They are fully equipped and deployable in 12–24 h in every part of the world. The UNDAC team is provided free of charge to the affected country to support the coordination during the initial phases of the disaster through the provision of technical services under the leadership of the RC/HC. The UNDAC team supports the affected country by providing a coordination platform able to support a multi-sectoral assessment and a proper information management. It is activated on request of the affected government or the UN Country team.

UNDAC teams are often invested with the duty of establishing and managing an On Site Coordination Centre (OSOCC). This concept was developed by the International Search and Rescue Advisory Group (INSARAG)[66] guidelines to

[66] See *infra* Sect. 20.3.1.

facilitate coordination of Search and Rescue teams[67] that need special support because of their specific task. Usually, the SAR teams work side by side with UNDAC teams, since they are deployed in the earliest phases of a disaster. The OSOCC concept was recognized to hold an added value in coordination at the early phases of a sudden onset disaster for the coordination of international resources.

The OSOCC guidelines,[68] though mainly dedicated to UNDAC, provide guidance to the first agency arriving on the site of the disaster and request to set up a coordination structure in coordination with OCHA. It is a rapid response tool that cooperates with LEMA in the immediate aftermath of a sudden onset disaster. It is inspired by the Incident Command Centers[69] commonly established at national level. As a rapid response tool, in order to be effective, OSOCC has to be established in the immediate aftermath of the emergency, to be operational simultaneously to the arrival of the first international responders and it is expected to be active until national authorities or traditional UN structures can take over the coordination activities. OSOCC's objectives are: to act as a link between international responders and government of the affected country; to provide a system for co-ordinating and facilitating the international relief activities; to provide an information management platform.

OSOCC responds to a series of concerns: it is a single point of entry for the LEMA managers; second, it offers a focal point for the international community. It provides the physical space and facilities to ensure the essentials of coordination. It facilitates the exchange of information between LEMA and international rescuers; however, OSOCC is not a command center, but a coordination cell where decisions are taken by consensus. To be more effective, the common services (like UNJLC, HIC, UNDSS), usually provided by UN, should be integrated into the OSOCC.

Another important feature of OSOCC is the information management platform: the information gathering on what is happening, who is doing what and where, that would then be disseminated after validation.

The OSOCC guidelines also describe the functioning of the Reception and Departure Centre that should be located at the entry point of international relief teams in order to facilitate their deployment to the affected site and to improve coordination.

Another very useful tool was developed in the framework of UNDAC: the Virtual OSOCC. This Web-based platform provides real-time information management dedicated to relief workers. It is accessible to all and every user can

[67] UNGA Res 57/150, 16 December 2002 'Strengthening the Effectiveness and Coordination of International Urban Search and Rescue Assistance'.

[68] OSOCC guidelines OCHA, 2nd edition 2009.

[69] 'Incident command system provides a flexible core mechanism for co-ordinated and collaborative incident management, whether for incidents where additional resources are required or are provided from different organizations within a single jurisdiction or outside the jurisdiction, or for complex incidents with national implications', US National Incident Management System, Homeland and Security 2008.

upload information and resources. It allows having an overall picture of the activities of all different actors that decide to make use of it.

20.2.2.5 UN Integrated Missions

Integrated missions have come into existence as a development of the UN involvement in peacekeeping and peace-building,[70] in managing 'complex emergencies' that simultaneously call on the political, military, humanitarian, and developmental sides of the UN system. The concept can be defined as an approach through which the UN seeks to support countries to move from a situation of complex emergency to a lasting peace, by using the system-wide available response, within an overall political-strategic management framework. It applies to missions with a Special Representative of the Secretary-General (SRSG) with the overall responsibility of the whole operation both military and humanitarian/development. In these instances, the Humanitarian Coordinator role is given to the same person or to a Deputy SRSG. Such missions institutionalize a permanent and highly visible link between the political instances (SRSG and RC) and the Humanitarian Coordinator.

The integrated missions raise serious criticism and objections from the humanitarian community because it weakens the perception of the UN as neutral and impartial. In those situations, humanitarian action is characterized as just another tool to reach the long-term political objective.

20.2.3 Regional Mechanisms

In parallel with the global mechanisms, several dedicated coordination tools were developed at regional level, for example, in Europe, Latin America, and among NATO countries.

The European Union over the years has developed several different tools to intervene in emergency situations.[71] Moreover, the European Union member countries are among the more active countries in international post disasters operations. For this reason, the issue of coordination assumes a special meaning especially after the innovations of the Lisbon Treaty that, in order to answer to the increasing demand for the EU to become more coherent especially at international level, established the European High Representative of the Union for Foreign Affairs and Security Policy and the External Action Service (EEAS).

The request for a more coherent approach to disaster management among different instruments brought in 2010 the merger of the European Commission services dealing with 'humanitarian aid' and 'European Community Mechanism for Civil Protection' in the same General Directorate Humanitarian Aid and Civil

---

[70] See Weir 2006.

[71] For a detailed analysis of the different instruments see Chap. 6 by Casolari in this volume.

Protection—ECHO. This merger indeed imposed a reinforced co-operation among different actors and operational cultures, and for this reason the European Commission has developed dedicated procedures. Results are encouraging (joint assessments) and a step forward is expected with the new forthcoming EU civil protection legislation.[72]

The European Union also developed a tool aimed at ensuring more strategic coherence and civil–military coordination within EEAS by setting up a Crisis Platform that brings together all EU stakeholders from the EEAS crisis response/management structures and the relevant European Commission services. The Platform allows the EU to use all instruments at its disposal when responding to multidimensional crises: political, diplomatic, military, economic, development, and humanitarian.

In Latin America, four different sub-regional mechanisms were established: the ComitêAndinopara a Prevenção e AtençãoaosDesastres (CAPRADE), the Centro de Coordinaciónpara la Prevención de los DesastresNaturales en América Central (CEPREDENAC), the AgenciaCaribeñapara el Manejo de los Desastres y la Emergencia (CDEMA), and the ReuniónEspecializada de Reducción de Riesgos de DesastresSocionaturales, la Defensa Civil, la Protección Civil y la AsistenciaHumanitaria del MERCOSUR (REHU). Each of them is provided with specific tools and procedures. To ensure action coherence and to improve the synergetic approach and exchange of information among the various bodies active on these issues in Latin America, a special forum has been created: the Foro de coordinaciòn y cooperacion de los mecanismos Sub-regionales de Gestiòn del Riesgo de Desasters de la Amerìca.[73]

The North Atlantic Treaty Organization (NATO) plays a role both as regional organization as well as—due to the specific nature of the organization—civil military coordination.[74]

NATO established a Civil Defence Committee[75] (renamed Civil Protection Committee in 1995) to oversee efforts to provide for the protection of populations.[76] In 1997, the Ministerial Session endorsed a proposal to create a Euro-Atlantic Disaster Response Capability, which called for the establishment of a Euro-Atlantic Disaster Response Coordination Centre (EADRCC) and Euro-Atlantic Disaster Response Unit (EADRU). The following EAPC Policy on 'Enhanced Practical Cooperation in International Disaster Relief' was agreed in 1998. The EARDCC is located at the NATO Headquarters and is the focal point for information sharing among NATO countries. In close consultation with UN-OCHA, it co-ordinates the

---

72 See Chap. 5 by Gestri in this volume.

73 See Chap. 1 by de Guttry in this volume.

74 See *infra* Sect. 20.2.4.1.

75 For the involvement of NATO in civil defense see Alexander 2006, 13.

76 In 1953, the first procedures for 'NATO Cooperation for Disaster Assistance in Peacetime' were adopted. For a more comprehensive analysis see North Atlantic Treaty Organization, NATO's Role in Disaster Assistance 14 (2001).

responses of member countries and ensures close liaison with the organizations involved in international disaster response. EADRU is a non-standing group of volunteer member States available to provide military and/or civilian assets that can be deployed where appropriate in the event of a major emergency.

NATO's involvement in post disaster assistance follows the basic principles: the stricken country remains the responsible party for disaster management; the United Nations retains the primary role in the coordination of international disaster relief operations, the EADRCC role is coordination rather than direction; EADRU members are committed to co-ordinate with the UN and to observe the Oslo Guidelines; EARDCC does not dispatch coordination team in the affected country. In case of a disaster requiring international assistance, it is up to each nation to decide whether to provide assistance or not and, if so, whether to do it through the EADRU or directly.

20.2.4 Working with the Military

Very often, response operations are handled at national level by the military forces of the affected State, so the need to have a clear framework for coordination is critical.[77] Moreover, international military actors are increasingly involved in humanitarian activities[78] both in complex emergencies and post disaster relief operations.[79] Clearly, the issues raised in the two cases are remarkably different.

In natural disaster contexts, the capacity of the military can be an added value to humanitarian agencies. In complex emergencies, however, the use of military assets raises concerns since their presence is guided by political/strategic reasons and it might negatively affect the perception of the local populations regarding humanitarian activities and actors.

Civil–military coordination is needed for a matter of operational effectiveness: it remains difficult due to the very different philosophies, working methods, and organizational cultures.[80]

---

[77] For a comprehensive analysis of civil military relations refer to Chap. 24 by Calvi-Parisetti in this volume.

[78] 'Member States, even those who do not give a primary role to their military forces in domestic response, are now using their military capacity for relief operations on a global basis.' United Nations Press Release, UN Updates Guidelines for International Military Aid in Disaster Relief Operations (Nov. 27, 2006), available at http://www.un.org/apps/news/story.asp?NewsID=20733&Cr=disaster&Cr1=relief. Accessed 9 February 2012.

[79] There are examples of domestic laws facilitating their participation in international disaster relief for example, in 1992, Japan amended its law on international disaster relief to provide a specific role for its military forces. IFRC 2007a, b, 154.

[80] In Pakistan in the aftermath of 2005 earthquake was used a model of 'non-interfering coordination' in which the military shared an open and honest assessment of needs with the humanitarian community and allowed NGOs to choose what operations they would undertake and where. In this model, gaps in humanitarian delivery are 'back-filled' by the army and government agencies.

The first challenge is related to civilian and military actors' lack of knowledge about respective organizational identities. The hierarchical military structure has problems to interact with co-ordinating structures that apply consensus methodologies or 'by default', and the operational language is different too. The high number of civilian organizations with different mandates and methodologies sets an additional problem to military forces that are used to work with a structured set of responsibilities defined in advance such as the rules of engagement.

While many attempts have been made to improve civil–military coordination in international operations over the past decade (at least to improve information sharing) field studies show that *de facto* co-operation remains inadequate, ad hoc, and fragmented.[81] In the 2010 Haiti earthquake emergency, for example, in the early weeks of the response the humanitarian community missed an opportunity to properly give instructions and allocate tasks to the military and set up a common decision-making and coordination forum.[82]

Relatively few existing international legal instruments make specific reference to military assets in relief operations.[83] The primary instrument in this area are the Oslo Guidelines,[84] which call for the use of military assets in disaster relief as exceptional and only as a last resort when the civilian alternative is not adequate or cannot be obtained in a timely manner to meet urgent humanitarian needs.[85]

---

[81] Haugevik and de Carvalho 2007, 7.

[82] Binder and Grünewald 2010, 39.

[83] The ASEAN, CDERA, and BSEC Agreements (1998 *Agreement among the Governments of the Participating States of the Black Sea Economic Co-operation on Collaboration in Emergency Assistance and Emergency Response to Natural and Man-Made Disasters*), the 1995 *Agreement between the Government of the Republic of Finland and the Government of the Republic of Estonia on Co-operation and Mutual Assistance in Cases of Accidents*, and the 1974 *Agreement between Sweden and Norway concerning the Improvement of Rescue Services in Frontier Areas* make specific reference to the use of military.

[84] 'Guidelines on the Use of Military and Civil Defense Assets in Disaster Relief,' known as the 'Oslo Guidelines', first prepared in 1994 by a number of donor States and humanitarian agencies and revised in 2006, available at http://reliefweb.int/node/22924, accessed 14 February 2012. A similar, more restrictive document is dedicated to the complex emergencies 'Guidelines on the Use Of Military and Civil Defense Assets to Support United Nations Humanitarian Activities in Complex Emergencies' ('MCDA Guidelines') of March 2003.

[85] The concept of last resort raises many concerns from several donor countries because they usually apply military resources under civil responsibility and direction in the framework of their civil protection. This situation was recognized by the 2006 revision of the Oslo Guidelines when it was acknowledged in the 'Last resort' paragraph the concept of civil protection by contrast to civil defense. 'However, foreign civil protection assets, when civilian in nature and respecting humanitarian principles, can provide an important direct and indirect contribution to humanitarian actions based on humanitarian needs assessments and their possible advantages in terms of speed, specialization, efficiency and effectiveness, especially in the early phases of relief response the use of civil protection assets should be needs driven, complementary to and coherent whit humanitarian aid operations, respecting the overall coordinating role of the UN', Oslo Guidelines, para 7.

Several analyses show that the Oslo Guidelines are limitedly known and followed, for this reason some work still remains to be done to ensure their wide dissemination.[86]

20.3 Coordination and Relief Standardization

Coordination depends substantially on sharing a common language and following the same standards. In this respect a major issue raised in recent emergencies is the lack of coherence between assets coming from different countries, since different assets might have the same name. For this reason, there are several attempts to set up common standard definitions and rules.

There is the need to tend toward a standardization of the capacities and means offered. On one hand, the language and the operational terminology has to be the same, on the other hand the standards applied need to be the same to ensure coherence and interoperability.

There have been several attempts to do that and it is quite peculiar that there are many different constituencies discussing standards for similar activities.

20.3.1 INSARAG

The International Search and rescue Advisory Group (INSARAG) is an international network of Search and Rescue professionals that provide guidelines and technical standards for Search and Rescue Activities.

INSARAG was created in 1991 in the aftermath of the response to the 1988 Armenian earthquake when the difference of standards and procedures among different SAR teams clearly appeared. Based on their Guidelines, it also foresees an internationally recognized classification for Urban Search and Rescue Team.[87] The OSOCC concept was developed in the INSARAG guidelines as a tool for the coordination on SAR.

20.3.2 EU Civil Protection Modules

In the framework of the European Civil Protection Mechanism,[88] the concept of civil protection modules was developed in the aftermath of the response to the 2004 South East Asia Tsunami. The European Commission and member States

---

86 SIPRI 2008, 14.

87 The Guidelines are available at http://ochanet.unocha.org/p/Documents/INSARAG%20Guidelines%202011-Latest.pdf. Accessed 9 February 2012.

88 For more details see Chap. 5 by Gestri in this volume.

have developed the standards and rules of engagement.[89] The modules are national assets provided on a voluntary basis. Seventeen different typologies of civil protection have been identified: pumping and purification of water, aerial fire fighting (planes and helicopters), urban search and rescue (heavy and medium), medical assistance including medical evacuation (advanced medical posts, field hospital, and aerial evacuation), emergency shelter, CBRN detection and sampling, and search and rescue in CBRN conditions. Tasks, capacities, main components, and deployment times are defined and standardized.

20.3.3 The Sphere Project and other Standardization Initiatives

The increasing number of actors on the field had the positive impact of focussing the attention on quality control and on improving the coordination.

Following the example of IASC, a number of inter-agency initiatives to improve accountability, quality, and performance of humanitarian action were developed. Hundreds of agencies, bilateral and multilateral donors, the UN system, the Red Cross and Red Crescent Movement, NGOs and inter-agency umbrella organizations have participated in, or are members of, one or more of those initiatives.

The Sphere Project[90] is probably the most known and implemented. Launched in 1997 by a group of humanitarian NGOs and the Red Cross and Red Crescent Movement, Sphere has developed a handbook of standards for four sectors (Water/Sanitation and Hygiene Promotion; Food Security; Nutrition and Food Aid; Settlement and non-Food Items and Health Services). Each standard has key indicators and guidance notes.

Among the various initiatives that were developed it is interesting to mention: the Active Learning Network for Accountability and Performance in Humanitarian Action ALNAP, Humanitarian Accountability Partnership—International—HAP, People in Aid, Coordination SUD—Synergie Qualité, Quality COMPAS/Groupe URD, The Emergency Capacity Building Project's Accountability and Impact Measurement Initiative.

All these initiatives aim at improving accountability, quality, and performance in humanitarian action. However, they try to achieve this goal in different ways causing considerable overlaps. If there is no doubt that to improve the relief assistance performances, there is the need to define common standards and codes of best practice; it appears that the number of these initiatives and the effectiveness of their actions still need to be explored.

[89] 2008/73/EC, Euratom and 2010/481/EU, Euratom.

[90] Sphere 2011

The International Organization for Standards (ISO) is also developing standards in response to risks of natural and man-made origin. These standards would include guidelines on 'command, control, coordination and cooperation' in disaster response, in areas such as 'information gathering; information sharing/ information processing; information flows/knowledge flow; interoperability; structures and procedures; decision support; warning [.]'.[91]

20.4 Conclusions

Coordination is probably the key issue in disaster management. The increasing number of actors and their different typologies impose to find tools to avoid gaps, overlaps, and duplications.

To find global binding tools to ensure coordination appears unrealistic. The 'perfect' coordination system does not exist because of conflicting agendas, mandates, or operational methodologies. However, finding a suitable solution aiming at ensuring effective provision of relief support to the affected population and safeguarding at the same time the features of donors and different actors is needed.

Coherence should be ensured between the strategic and the operational level, and among international, national, and local levels. To do that it appears important to invest in preparedness at all different levels.

At country level, a dedicated clear legal and operational framework needs to be defined on the basis of internationally recognized standards.

At all levels, different entities (national and international, governmental and non-governmental) should have available dedicated personnel trained and aware of international principles and dynamics.

At international level, an additional effort should be made to rationalize the existing coordination tools as well as to standardize means and procedures. The number of initiatives and constituencies addressing similar concerns (not always consistent among themselves) raises an additional coordination problem. There is an emerging need for having verifiable and known standards with a clear set of evaluation indicators.

Requests and offers need to be rationalized too. Nowadays States and organizations can receive, at the same time, requests for assistance from different sources without any coordination: affected State, OCHA, regional organizations (EU, ASEAN, NATO). This situation raises an issue of coordination *ab origine*. Moreover, these requests are often addressed to different stakeholders (ministry of external affairs, ministry of interior, ministry of defense) that might decide to intervene autonomously.

[91] International Organization for Standardization, Business Plan—ISO/TC 223: Societal Security (ver. 1, Nov. 24, 2006), at 1.43.

Rescuers should be accountable first of all to their stakeholders, especially the affected population and institutions; the international community has to make an additional effort in identifying the organizations and entities that have the best capacities to cope with the different post disaster phases. This has to be done at all different levels: donors, UN, and NGOs.

Regarding the funding arrangements, efforts should be made to facilitate an inclusion of new donors into international coordination settings.

Both at national and international levels more emphasis should be given to the needs assessment to avoid gaps and overlaps in the response. The urgency of providing humanitarian relief has to be balanced with the need for providing needs-based resources.

Regarding the coordination methodologies, the task to create consensus is a very difficult one to implement. The organization in charge has to devote a lot of resources and to look for coordinators with adequate leadership capabilities. Furthermore, leadership is also connected to the power to enforce other agencies to co-ordinate. Today, no international organization seems to have this power. Sovereignty may play a very important role in this respect; the humanitarian agencies will increasingly need to work alongside the expanding national capabilities of many governments.

The best way to avoid conflicting interests between humanitarian and political/strategic concerns is to reiterate and to reinforce the value of humanitarian principles.

The issue of civil–military coordination raises specific concerns. In complex emergencies, the clear difference of roles and mandates should to be maintained. In case of natural and man-made disasters, the 2006 Oslo Guidelines update—by recognizing the concept of 'civil protection'—seems to offer the right framework to improve the coordination and a more effective use of the military resources.

The role of new technologies may bring a great added value to simplify the work of coordinators, real-time data transfer, Web-based communication, maps. The word coordination assumes a different connotation in a world where it is possible to have information in real time.

The cluster approach has shown good potential to improve international coordination between the international community and domestic stakeholders. Recent evaluations have identified possible gaps and opportunities for improvement, the international community will need to implement them. For the time being it does not appear to be effective in the first days of sudden onset disasters. Furthermore, the number of actors involved in the clusters, especially in major disasters, appears to be a burden to effective coordination. In this regard the tools developed at regional level might play a crucial role. Organizations unable or unwilling to respect the standards should be excluded, even if it is difficult to imagine which institution could enforce that.

References

Adinolfi C et al (2005) Humanitarian response review. An independent report commissioned by the United Nations Emergency Relief Coordinator & Under-Secretary-General for Humanitarian Affairs. Office for the Coordination of Humanitarian Affairs

Alexander D (2006) Globalization of disaster: trends, problems and dilemmas. J Int Aff Spring/Summer 59:1–22

ALNAP (2010) Meeting paper 26th annual meeting. The role of national governments in international humanitarian response to disasters.16–17 Nov 2010, Kuala Lumpur, Malaysia

Bennett J et al (2006) Coordination of international humanitarian assistance in tsunami-affected countries. Tsunami Evaluation Coalition

Binder A, Grünewald F (2010) IASC cluster approach evaluation. 2 phase: Haiti country study. Groupe URD and the Global Public Policy Institute

Donini A et al (2008) Humanitarian agenda 2015: final report. The State of the humanitarian enterprise. Feinstein International Center, Tufts University, Medford, MA

Donini A, Niland N (1994) Rwanda: lessons learned. A report on the coordination of humanitarian activities. United Nations Department of Humanitarian Affairs, New York

Eide E et al (2005) Report on integrated missions: practical perspectives and recommendations. Independent Study for the Expanded UN ECHA

Fischer H (2003) International disaster response law: a preliminary overview and analysis of Existing Treaty Law. IFRC

GAO—United States Government Accountability Office (2006). Hurricane Katrina. Comprehensive policies and procedures are needed to ensure appropriate use of and accountability for international assistance. Washington, D.C. USA

Global Humanitarian Platform (2010) Strengthening partnership for effective humanitarian action. 2–3 Feb 2010. Summary note http://www.globalhumanitarianplatform.org/doc00004251.doc

Grünewald F, Binder A (2010) Inter-agency real-time evaluation in Haiti: 3 months after the earthquake. Groupe URD and the Global Public Policy Institute

Harvey P (2010) The affected state: accepting responsibility. The role of national governments in international humanitarian response to disasters. Meeting report, 26th ALNAP Meeting, pp 4–5

Haugevik K, de Carvalho B (2007) Civil-military Cooperation in multinational and interagency operations discussion paper on operational terminologies and assessment for security in practice no. 2 Norwegian Institute of International Affairs

IASC (2004) Civil military relationship in complex emergencies. An IASC reference paper, Inter-Agency Standing Committee

IASC (2007) Guidance note on using the cluster approach to strengthen humanitarian response, Inter-Agency Standing Committee

IFRC (2007a) Law and legal issues in international disaster response: a desk study. International Federation of the Red Cross and Red Crescent Societies

IFRC (2007b) Annotations to the draft guidelines for the domestic facilitation and regulation of international disaster relief and initial recovery assistance. International Federation of the Red Cross and Red Crescent Societies

IFRC (2008) Introduction to the guidelines for the domestic facilitation and regulation of international disaster relief and initial recovery assistance. International Federation of the Red Cross and Red Crescent Societies

Katoch A (2006) The responders' cauldron: the uniqueness of international disaster response. J Int Aff Spring/Summer 59(2):153–172

Kent R (2011) Narrowing the corridors of humanitarian action, Humanitarian Futures Programme. King's College London, UK

Kent R, Burke J (2011) Commercial and humanitarian engagement in crisis contexts: current trends and future drivers. Humanitarian Futures Programme, King's College London, UK

Macalister-Smith P (1981) The international relief union of 1932. Disasters 5:147–154

Macrae J (ed) (2003) Uncertain power: the changing role of official donors in humanitarian action. Overseas Development Group. http://www.odi.org.uk/work/projects/details.asp?id=1205&title=changing-role-official-donors-humanitarian-assistance#resources
McEntire D (1997) Reflecting on the weaknesses of the international community during the IDNDR: some implications for research and its application'. Disaster Prevent Manage 6(4):221–233
Minear L (2002) The humanitarian enterprise: dilemmas and discoveries. Kumarian Press, Bloomfield
OECD (2010) Review of the Italian National Civil Protection System. OECD International Futures Programme
Polman L (2010) The crisis caravan: what's wrong with humanitarian aid? Metropolitan Books, Henry Holt, New York
Rieff D (2000) Kosovo's humanitarian circus. World Policy J 17(3):25–32
Seybolt T (1997) Coordination in Rwanda: the humanitarian response to genocide and civil war. Working paper series, Cambridge
SIPRI (2008) The effectiveness of foreign military assets in natural disaster response. A report by SIPRI, SIPRI, Stockholm SE
Sphere (2011) Humanitarian charter and minimum standards in disaster response. The Sphere Project
Stoddard A et al (2007) Cluster approach evaluation. Final report, OCHA evaluation and studies section
Stoddard A (2010) The state of the humanitarian system, assessing performance and progress. ALNAP The Tripartite Core Group, Post-Nargis Joint Assessment, pp 37–52. http://www.aseansec.org/21765.pdf
Steets J et al (2010) Cluster approach evaluation 2: synthesis report, IASC cluster approach evaluation 2nd phase. Groupe URD and the Global Public Policy Institute
United Nations (1991) General assembly resolution 46/182. Strengthening of the coordination of humanitarian emergency assistance of the United Nations
United Nations (2003) Guidelines on the use of military and civil defence assets to support United Nations humanitarian activities in complex Emergencies
United Nations (2006) Guidelines on the use of foreign military and civil defence assets in disaster relief—'Oslo guidelines'
United Nations Disaster Assessment and Coordination (UNDAC) (2006) Office for the coordination of humanitarian affairs. UNDAC field hand book
van der Linde D (2008) The politics of disasters: a study in post Katrina international aid. http://www.disasterdiplomacy.org/pb/vanderlinde2008.pdf
Weir E (2006) Conflict and compromise: UN integrated missions and the humanitarian imperative. Kofi Annan Peacekeeping Training Centre Monograph n. 4
Weiss TG (1998) Civilian-military interactions and ongoing UN reforms: DHA's past and OCHA's remaining challenges. Int Peacekeeping 5(4):49–70

Chapter 21
Disasters and the Future of Humanitarian Action: Issues, Trends, and Challenges

Antonio Donini

Abstract Since the end of the Cold War, there has been an unprecedented growth and institutionalization of the international humanitarian enterprise. This growth was to a large extent due to the end of bipolarism and the consequent lifting of inhibitions around military and humanitarian interventions. Accordingly, humanitarian agencies have adapted to a new context that allowed presence 'in' conflict areas, rather than just 'around' conflict. The model was predicated on two assumptions that have now become increasingly questionable: the first was that conflict would continue to be the main driver of disasters and vulnerability; the second was that western-driven approaches to the provision of assistance and protection would continue to be welcome in disaster affected States. After discussing major trends in disasters and disaster response, this chapter questions both these assumptions and provides pointers on the humanitarian challenges of the future.

Keywords Humanitarianism · Humanitarian action · Disasters · Conflict · Sovereignty

Contents

A. Donini (✉)
Feinstein International Center, Tufts University, Boston, MA, USA
e-mail: antonio.donini@tufts.edu

A. de Guttry et al. (eds.), *International Disaster Response Law*, 517
DOI: 10.1007/978-90-6704-882-8_21,

21.1 Introduction

According to the most reliable available data,[1] natural and man-made disasters have been increasing in terms of frequency, size, and number of people affected. Between 1980 and 2011, 15,604 disasters have occurred killing more than 2 million people across the world. While most of these disasters were relatively small scale and only a relatively small number of large disasters catch the attention of the media and public opinion, there is growing awareness of the potentially devastating consequences of the increase in frequency and scope of disasters especially for those areas most vulnerable to climate change and environmental stress. As a consequence, in recent years national budgets for emergency response, disaster preparedness, and mitigation have experienced rapid growth as have the activities of international agencies and NGOs directly involved in policy development related to disasters and in operational disaster response.

In the two decades and a half since the end of the Cold War, there has been an unprecedented growth and institutionalization of the international humanitarian enterprise dealing with crisis and conflict. This growth was to a large extent due to the end of bipolarism and the consequent lifting of inhibitions around military and humanitarian interventions. Accordingly, humanitarian agencies have adapted to a new context that allowed presence 'in' conflict areas, rather than just 'around' conflict. This 'interventionist' model was more or less successfully applied to humanitarian action from Afghanistan to Somalia and from Kosovo to Darfur. The model was predicated on two assumptions that have now become increasingly questionable: the first was that conflict was and would continue to be the main driver of disasters and vulnerability; the second was that western-driven approaches to the provision of assistance and protection would, by and large, continue to be welcome in disaster affected States. Both these assumptions, as we shall see, are increasingly questionable. Both the nature and scale of disasters, and the vulnerability of individuals and communities to sudden and/or prolonged hazard events

[1] The data on the occurrence and effects of natural and technological disasters is from the Centre for Research on the Epidemiology of Disasters (CRED). CRED's Emergency Events Database contains information on over 18,000 disasters in the world from 1900 to present. The database is compiled from various sources, including UN agencies, non-governmental organizations, insurance companies, research institutes and press agencies. An event is classified as a disaster when at least one of the following criteria is fulfilled: ten or more people killed; 100 or more people affected; a declaration of a state of emergency or a call for international assistance was made (http://www.emdat.be/criteria-and-definition: accessed February 25, 2012). EM-DAT data do not include civil war or conflict related man-made disasters.

are rapidly changing. These changes are bound to have a significant impact both on the institutions that provide assistance and protection in disasters as well as on the national and local regimes that will facilitate or constrain the work of humanitarian agencies.

The humanitarian system is geared to, and perhaps getting better at, addressing crises that fit with the post-Cold War model of conflict-intervention-displacement and, sometimes, peace-building. But the external environment is rapidly changing and it is far from clear that the mental and institutional models that are being applied today will be equally applicable in the future. Current trends seem to indicate that there are major systemic changes at play that challenge the existing status quo in the humanitarian enterprise. Two trends in particular need to be highlighted.

The first is that conflict as a variable affecting the need for humanitarian action is on the decline. Recent studies have shown that the end of the Cold War, marked by the collapse of the Soviet Union in 1991, had a dramatic effect on the general level of armed conflict in the global system. The levels of both interstate and societal warfare declined through the 1990s and this trend continues in the early 2000s, falling over 60 % from their peak levels.[2] The decline in the numbers of refugees and IDPs displaced by conflict—a rough proxy indicator of humanitarian vulnerability and need—is less pronounced, but equally significant.[3] The number of displaced peaked at around 45 million in 1991 and has been on a downward trend since.

The second trend is that so-called "natural" disasters—i.e., disasters arising from natural hazard events but often made worse by the way human settlements are organized—are on the increase both in terms of frequency and impact.[4] While the number of earthquakes is relatively stable, there has been an exponential increase in floods and cyclones, most likely linked to an acceleration of the incidence of climate change. Some of the increase may be attributed to improved reporting. However, with growing population and massive urbanization the world's exposure to natural hazards is inevitably increasing. This is particularly true as the strongest population growth is located in coastal areas (with greater exposure to floods, cyclones, tidal waves, and climate change-induced increase in sea level). To make matters worse any land remaining available for urban growth

---

[2] See http://www.systemicpeace.org/conflict.htm (accessed February 25, 2012), particularly Fig. 3, Global Trends in Armed Conflict, 1946–2011. Although the methodologies are different (the definition of 'conflict' being a case in point), the University of British Columbia's 'The Causes of Peace and the Shrinking Costs of War Human Security Report Project 2009/2010' reaches similar conclusions..

[3] http://www.systemicpeace.org/conflict.htm, Fig. 7 (accessed February 25, 2012).

[4] See for example the data series published by the Center for Research on the Epidemiology of Disasters (CRED): http://www.cred.be/publications (accessed February 22, 2012). UN Environment Programme (UNEP) data show an exponential increase in hazardous events since the 1960 s and especially of floods: http://www.grida.no/graphicslib/detail/trends-in-natural-disasters_a899# (accessed February 25, 2012).

is generally risk-prone, for instance flood plains or steep slopes subject to landslides. The economic cost of disasters is also rapidly increasing. One estimate puts the cost in 2011 at US $380 billion, nearly two-thirds higher than in 2005, the previous record year which had recorded losses of US $220 billion.[5]

21.2 The Humanitarian Enterprise in the Early Twenty-First Century

Since the end of the Cold War, there have been major quantitative and qualitative changes in the role and functions of the humanitarian enterprise. From a relatively marginal activity which took place mainly outside theaters of war, it is now center stage. Boosted by the wave of military and so-called humanitarian interventions of the 1990s, humanitarian actors have been bringing assistance (often), protection (with more difficulty) to the farthest borderlands of crisis and conflict. Humanitarian agencies have also become peaceful but powerful vectors of western ideas, culture, and behavior. The growth of the humanitarian system has occurred in parallel to the penetration of the capitalist system to areas that hitherto had not been fully incorporated into the flows of globalization. In many ways, western NGOs have become the capillary vessels of globalization, if not the 'mendicant orders of empire.'[6]

The changes have been both quantitative and qualitative.

21.2.1 Quantitative Changes in Humanitarian Action

Humanitarian action has seen unprecedented growth in the past 20 years. Never has so much money, so many aid workers, so much media attention been devoted to humanitarian issues. The humanitarian enterprise—UN agencies and NGOs combined—now disburses upwards of US $16.7 billion/year. More than $90 billion have been spent in the past 10 years, much of it in the same countries affected by chronic and acute crises.[7] The overall expenditure of OECD/DAC countries—the major contributors to ongoing crises—is also estimated to have increased in 2010 (from US $11.2 billion in 2009 to US $11.8 billion). But the substantial

[5] Munich RE press release 4 January 2012, http://www.munichre.com/en/media_relations/press_releases/2012/2012_01_04_press_release.aspx (accessed February 25, 2012).

[6] Hardt and Negri 2001, 36. On the links between globalization and humanitarian assistance see also Donini 2010.

[7] Unless otherwise indicated, data in this and the following paragraphs are from Development Initiatives 2011.

increases made by just three donors (the United States, Japan and Canada) mask reductions by some of their peers. For example Italy has dropped from $423 to $362 million from 2008 to 2010 or less than $7 per citizen.[8] Thus while the overall international response to humanitarian crises shows an upward trend, many governments are coming under pressure to justify existing levels of aid spending. On the other hand, non-OECD donors—Saudi Arabia, Turkey, United Arab Emirates, and Russia—are playing an increasing role; they were marginal at the turn of the century and account for over $500 million/year in 2010.

The US $16.7 billion is only the visible part of the humanitarian funding iceberg. Not captured are the efforts of individuals, organizations, and governments within crisis-affected countries themselves, which are difficult to estimate but save a substantial number of lives. Also not captured is the response of the military and non-State actors in delivering "humanitarian" assistance.

Governments contributed an estimated US $12.4 billion in response to international humanitarian crises in 2010—the highest volume on record. In 2009, the three largest government/institutional donors of humanitarian aid were the United States (US $4.4 billion), the European Union (US $1.6 billion), and the United Kingdom (US $1 billion). In terms of generosity, however, Luxembourg, Sweden, and Norway contributed the highest shares of gross national income and Luxembourg, Norway, and the United Arab Emirates contributed the most per person.

Private voluntary contributions are estimated to have been in the region of US $4 billion in each of the past 3 years. In 2010, Médecins sans Frontières (MSF) received US $1.1 billion for humanitarian activities from private contributions; this more or less equates to the humanitarian expenditure of the third largest donor, the United Kingdom. World Vision International, the world's largest NGO, raised even more funds but with a higher proportion coming from government sources.

In 2009, Sudan remained the largest single recipient of the international humanitarian response for the fifth consecutive year, with US $1.4 billion. There is a remarkable consistency in the top 'receivers' of humanitarian aid which also include Palestine, Iraq, Afghanistan and the DRC in the pole positions.

In 2009 about two-thirds of all humanitarian assistance went to conflict-affected and post-conflict States. Globally, crises in conflict-affected States are lasting longer. This is blurring the traditional distinction between chronic and acute situations. Some of the top-ranking crises—Somalia, Afghanistan, DRC, Darfur—continue to be both chronic and acute. Humanitarian aid is thus largely long term in nature. Most of the long-term affected countries are in sub-Saharan Africa and are also vulnerable to drought—two sorts of insecurity, two factors that put development gains at risk. To date, few countries show any clear transition from a post-conflict and peacekeeping context to actual peace and reconstruction; only two of the top 20 recipients of international humanitarian aid have clearly moved out of the emergency phase in the past 5 years. ODA expenditure on governance and security is increasing, reaching US $16.6 billion in 2009. Peacekeeping

[8] Development Initiatives 2011, Figs. 6 and 10.

expenditure reached more than US $9 billion in the same year. The data shows how the bulk of peacekeeping funds are spent in the same countries receiving long-term humanitarian assistance.

At the same time, humanitarian assistance is becoming more expensive. The costs of key components of humanitarian food aid are rising as well as those of delivering it. The cost of food increased by more than 40 % between 2007 and 2011. During the same period, oil prices increased by 36 % in real terms. The humanitarian enterprise is still very much focused on response. Data on disaster risk reduction (DRR) shows slowly increasing expenditure, but still to only extremely low levels. Total expenditure on DRR reached just US $835 million in 2009, a mere 0.5 % of total ODA.

The spectacular growth in budgets and funding has resulted in an explosion of the institutionalization of the humanitarian enterprise. Long gone are the days where humanitarian aid workers and their agencies were essentially 'voluntary', nimble and diverse. Now the introduction of standards, norms, guidelines, and mechanisms of accountability has made the system more uniform and predictable. Reforms of the United Nations machinery—the introduction of 'clusters', for example—have increased the predictability of the response, clarified sectoral responsibilities and, at least in theory, fostered more accountability. The industry has also become much more professionalized; for many humanitarian aid workers—and there are an estimated 300,000[9]—working in emergencies has become a career rather than a voluntary mission.

At the same time, the oligopolization of the enterprise has continued apace; northern federations of major NGOs and UN humanitarian agencies define how the enterprise works, what constitutes a crisis and how it should be addressed. The combination of institutionalization, professionalization and the 'network power' resulting from the dominance of standards, technologies and processes developed in the global North shapes the order in which aid agencies and civil society organizations function according to established hierarchical divisions.[10] This results in higher barriers to entry for groups from the South. The humanitarian enterprise remains essentially 'of the North' and the isomorphism—the pressure to conform—has increased: "you" can join "us" but only on "our" terms.

The figures above give an idea of the increase in the size of the global humanitarian effort but they say little about the changing nature of crises and disasters.

---

9 Stoddard et al. 2009

10 On the concept of network power, see Grewal 2008.

21.2.2 Qualitative Changes in Humanitarian Action

While the growth of the humanitarian enterprise is relatively easy to measure, the qualitative changes in the external environment and within the enterprise itself are more open to interpretation. Nevertheless, a number of general points can be highlighted.

The pressures of politics on humanitarian action continue to be an area of concern. Afghanistan, Iraq, Darfur, Somalia, Sri Lanka, and Haiti have been set-backs for principled humanitarianism. The instrumentalization of humanitarian action in support of political and military agendas has resulted in unprecedented levels of cooptation, blurring of lines, and subordination of humanitarianism to politics. While in itself this phenomenon is not new, instrumentalization seems to have become systemic in the sense that UN and donor government policies increasingly see the incorporation of assistance into partisan agendas as the model for crisis response. This takes the shape of integrated missions in the UN and of the 'joined-up' or integrated approaches favored by governments.

The global war on terror (GWOT) has accelerated this process of incorporation of assistance into world ordering processes. If agencies have to choose between being 'for' or 'against', the space for neutral, impartial and independent humanitarian action rapidly shrinks. In extreme cases, the polarization introduced by GWOT results in the criminalization of humanitarian action as in Somalia or Palestine where aid agencies need to certify that none of their assistance is benefiting proscribed groups and thus risk violating anti-terrorist legislation in their home countries. Consequently, aid agencies are becoming more risk averse.

Humanitarianism is also affected by the current wave of interventionism, which is fuelled in part by the International Criminal Court (ICC) and Responsibility to Protect (R2P) agendas. Increasingly, the North's human rights agenda makes the work of humanitarian agencies, which need to negotiate access including with abusive warlords, more difficult and more precarious. Experience in Darfur has shown the perils of mixing the two (13 NGOs were expelled in 2009 because they were perceived as aiding the ICC). The human rights agenda, focused as it is on 'naming and shaming' is resulting in reduced access and space for humanitarian actors in many contexts (Sri Lanka, DRC, Somalia, Afghanistan). The humanitarian enterprise has itself become much more interventionist. Even those humanitarians, who do not see themselves as "force multipliers"[11] of northern world ordering agendas or of stabilization operations,[12] are affected by association. In

[11] Secretary of State Colin Powell famously stated that "NGOs are such a force multiplier for us, such an important part of our combat team"; Remarks to the National Foreign Policy Conference for leaders of US NGOs, US Department of State, Washington DC, 26 October 2001.

[12] "Stability operations are humanitarian relief missions that the military conducts outside the U.S. in pre-conflict, conflict and post-conflict countries, disaster areas or underdeveloped nations, and in coordination with other federal agencies, allied governments and international organizations. The new policy elevates the importance of such military health support in stability operations, called Medical Stability Operations (MSOs), to a DoD priority that is comparable with combat operations," "New DoD Policy Outlines Military Health Support in Global Stability Missions", Press Release, 24 May 2010.

Afghanistan, Iraq, Darfur, Somalia, and elsewhere, aid workers have paid a high price for being seen as taking sides.

The collapse of the asylum and protection regime is an additional area of concern. From refugees to IDPs, the obstacles for those fleeing conflict or persecution are greater. At the same time, access to 'internally stuck persons' (ISPs) who are unable to move, and more generally, dealing with protection issues has become more difficult. On the plus side, deliberate harm to civilians is increasingly questioned by public opinion and civil society in the North, but also in the South as the Arab spring shows.

The humanitarian field is more crowded than ever with the emergence of new traditions (Islamic NGOs and donors), a diversification of donors (Gulf States, Brazil, Cuba/Venezuela, private donors/foundations) and new types of 'humanitarian' action (for profits, Private Security Companies) including military-aid hybrids. The growth of State-centric forms of humanitarian assistance in the South is increasingly challenging the traditional State-avoiding ethos of northern NGOs.

In sum, while expenditure, institutionalization, and professionalization have increased, the humanitarian system is still affected by recurring internal and external pathologies. Internally, the system is beset by the tension between the needs and perspectives of the vulnerable groups it purports to assist and protect and the top-down nature of an enterprise whose rewards systems and network power feed the machine and create more distance between 'outsiders' and 'insiders'.[13] Externally, the tension between principles, pragmatism, and politics, that is, the deliberate politicization and manipulation of humanitarian action has reached new heights: the instrumental use of humanitarian assistance, especially in high profile crises, is now inseparable from western foreign policy objectives.[14]

Moreover, because it is now center stage rather than at the margins and because of the resources and influence that it mobilizes and moves, humanitarian action has crossed the threshold of power. It has transitioned through growth and institutionalization from a powerful discourse of compassion to a discourse of power, from mobilizing myth to overpowering enterprise. At its most extreme, the biopolitical power of giving (or not) is about "bare life": it implies choosing between those "lives that are exposed and lives that are saved,"[15] between who receive little or no assistance and remain in a transient, or more often than not, permanent state of purgatory, and those who for reasons of political or economic expediency are allowed to break out of conflict or crisis. What we have here is a kind of primordial form of instrumentalization that is inherent in the humanitarian relationship.

Moving from the nature of the relationship to its projection on a global plane, we face more questions and challenges. Because it is dominantly an exchange without reciprocity, there is a disconnect (and a growing one in the context of

---

[13] See Donini et al. 2008.

[14] Actually, this is not so new. Henry Kissinger in 1976 stated that: "Disaster relief is becoming increasingly a major instrument of our foreign policy".

[15] Giorgio Agamben, quoted in Fassin, 507.

globalization) between the lofty universalist and principled goals of humanitarianism and the messy reality on the ground. 'There is nothing so ethnocentric, so particularistic, as the claim of universalism'.[16] The cold metal of the water pump provided by the well-meaning principled humanitarian can feel quite different to the 'hapless victim' or to the militant insurgent. Rather than as an expression of compassion or solidarity, it could be seen as redolent of arrogance, alien values or of a history of colonialism and domination.

The issue of better insulation of humanitarian action, if not, ideally at least, a complete separation from partisan politics and stabilization agendas, is likely to remain an unresolved one for some time. The ICRC and other 'Dunantist' humanitarian agencies remain wary of, if not hostile to, the politicization and militarization of aid inherent in stabilization agendas. The majority of the humanitarian enterprise, however,—the UN system and the large federations of NGOs (with the exception of MSF and a few small NGOs that focus only on humanitarian issues)—remain engaged to a larger or smaller degree with 'Wilsonian' agendas, i.e., agendas that link humanitarian action directly or indirectly to the foreign policy objectives of their home countries or their main funding sources.

21.3 Humanitarian Action 2020

If it is true that conflict as a vector of humanitarian need is down, and that vulnerability linked to climate change, natural hazard events, technological and possibly civilization-changing or "black swan" events, is up, this is likely to have major implications for the future of humanitarian action. Current data shows a general increase in climate change-related hazard events, particularly floods and cyclones.[17] If this trend is confirmed in the longer term, non-conflict related disasters are likely to be the future focus of humanitarian agencies.

Climate change is likely to negatively impact food security in both Africa and Asia. In Africa, a shortening of growing seasons and a reduction of land suitable for farming will drive net food production down. If there is no adoption of more advanced agricultural technologies, yields are estimated to fall up to 50 % during the period 2000–2020. South African smallholders are forecast to suffer up to a 90 % decline of income by 2100 as a result of climate change.[18] In Asia, climate change is forecast to cause yield declines of up to 30 % by 2050 mostly through increases in average temperature; a 1 °C increase in average temperature is estimated to cause a 10 % decline in rice yield.[19] Climate change will also reduce land

---

16 Wallerstein 2006, 40.

17 http://www.grida.no/graphicslib/detail/trends-in-natural-disasters_a899# (accessed February 25, 2012). I am indebted to Peter Walker for pointing me to the data in the following paragraphs.

18 Cruz et al. 2007.

19 Cruz et al. 2007.

available for agriculture. According to the International Panel on Climate Change, climate change will trigger a threefold increase in food prices by 2080.[20]

Recent new projections of climate change-associated sea level rise suggest up to a 1.4 m rise by 2100. On present population projections this would displace some 100 million people in Asia, 14 million in Europe, and 8 million each in South America and Africa from coastal settlements. Take a look at a world map and the correlation between costal locations and mega cities becomes all too clear.[21]

Some trends such as increases in sea levels or extreme weather events are more or less predictable, but as important is the lack of predictability associated with climate change. "Climate change does not just cause changes in known hazard risks, but also raises the level of uncertainty, and will generate surprises. Disaster risk reduction and more robust development planning are crucial in adapting to the increasing risks associated with climate change."[22] The humanitarian enterprise will also have to deal with "compound catastrophic events" where disasters, poor or dysfunctional governance, criminality, service breakdown compound the complexity of the crisis in ways we cannot imagine today.

What we really do not know is how society and our systems of governance will react to these increasing levels of stress and uncertainty. In these disaster settings, northern humanitarian agencies will inevitably come to clash with the logic of the State. The comfortable interventionist spirit of northern humanitarians will be increasingly challenged by States and civil society organizations in the south that will have the primary responsibility for responding. It is debatable if our traditional humanitarian approaches are adequate to address such rapidly changing forms of vulnerability and the rising risks they entail in contexts where the State will increasingly provide a framework, benevolent or not, for the work of external agencies.

This has implications for the scope and shape of a humanitarian enterprise that is still based on Cold War and post-Cold War assumptions of what constitutes a "crisis". The enterprise is essentially backward-looking. We are getting better at addressing last year's crisis and perhaps today's. But is the enterprise adapted to the challenges that are likely to come our way in the coming decades? How are we faring in places like Yemen and Syria? Not very well, it seems. How will we fare when a mega multi country disaster such as the 2004 tsunami hits again?

We are already seeing strong affirmations of State sovereignty in countries affected by conflict (Sudan, Sri Lanka) In non-conflict environments the pressure of the State is likely to become even stronger. Because the nature of the crisis will implicate the State directly in the response, we can foresee that there will be more regulation and more pressure to conform to national State-driven agendas. This is not necessarily bad. Gone are the days of free and easy humanitarian

[20] Cruz et al. 2007, 469–506.

[21] Webster et al. 2009, 149.

[22] Van Aalst 2006, 5.

interventionism of NGOs and UN agencies. Having clear normative and legal frameworks for the work of outside agencies is obviously a good thing. Problems will arise when the State is fragile, abusive or hostile to humanitarian principles. Humanitarian actors will also engage inevitably with national militaries (and the international contingents coming to help them). When the State is legitimate, and the external intervention is agreed by all players, there is no reason why civilian and military agencies should not work together with a division of labor that respects their respective ethos and competence.

We can expect new players to become much more active in the relief arena. China and India, Brazil, and Indonesia are likely to bring different perspectives and operational approaches that will challenge the current northern/western functioning of the humanitarian enterprise. It is likely that their assistance will compete with that provided by the established agencies and that it will be much more State-centric than what we are accustomed to. What this means in terms of the protection of at-risk communities and their rights in crisis contexts is as yet unclear. On the positive side, we can expect local groups to be much better informed through the internet and social media and in much better position to demand accountability and transparency in assistance provision both to the State and to outside players.

Southern donors and State actors will also want to be much more directly involved in the governance and standard setting of a humanitarian enterprise that is still very much northern in ethos and funding. We do not know if they will want to change the rules of the existing club or set up one, or several, new ones. We cannot assume that 'our' universal principles will fit 'their' perception of the south's more robust position in the world.

Moreover, even if conflict is on the decline, the settling of tectonic plates leading to a more complex multipolar world is likely to lead to localized and in some cases extremely violent conflicts. Some will no doubt argue that in such asymmetrical conflicts, there is no space for neutrality. Recent crises such as Afghanistan, Pakistan, Iraq, Somalia, still demonstrate the opposite: the shrinking of humanitarian space and the instrumentalization of humanitarian action have had deleterious effects for communities needing assistance, for the security of humanitarian aid workers and for the credibility of their organizations. However, we cannot assume that neutrality as an operational concept will be as welcome in the future. Many States are already saying clearly that they will gladly accept outside humanitarian assistance, but on their own terms. As for protection, the acceptance of the role of outsiders is likely to be even more tenuous.

At the same time, the need for a protected niche for principled humanitarian agencies—such as the ICRC or MSF—will remain. The acceptance of these agencies will be a function of their ability to stay as far as possible out of politics and to focus strictly on life-saving issues. Agencies mixing humanitarian assistance with rights or development or justice agendas will become easy targets for vilification or worse. This may result in a bifurcation between a more modest international humanitarian enterprise, closer in ambition and intent to classical time-tested humanitarian principles and a variety of other approaches to addressing needs in conflict and non-conflict disasters. These other approaches—more politicized or focusing on development, solidarity, and justice agendas, among others—can of course provide a number of useful and necessary services, but strictly speaking they are not humanitarian. In complex, extremely polarized or fraught situations, the traditional principle-based approach would stand a better, or sometime the only, chance of saving and protecting lives than today's increasingly politically driven and militarized forms of relief, on the one hand, and emerging non-western "sovereignty-based" discourses on the other.

21.4 The End of Humanitarianism as a Mobilizing Myth?[23]

The challenges of the future will require change and adaptation in the humanitarian enterprise. Institutions tend to lag behind change in the real world and humanitarian agencies are no exception. Since the end of the Cold War humanitarian action and the principles that underpin it have been used and abused. Wars have been called 'humanitarian' (Kosovo, Sri Lanka). New players such as the military and for-profit agencies have trespassed into the humanitarian arena (Afghanistan, Iraq, Somalia). But despite significant growth and institutionalization, the basic parameters of the humanitarian system, which had last been redefined as the cold War ended, have remained unchanged. If there ever was a golden age of humanitarianism, it is now long gone. A verification of the continued pertinence of these parameters is now urgent.

Is humanitarianism losing its identity? Its moral compass? We lament the increasing conflation between humanitarian and development/political/military agendas; as well as the emergence of "other" humanitarianisms and of humanitarian rejectionists. It is far from clear that humanitarianism as we know it today will it be able to save itself or at least insulate itself more effectively from politicization and incorporation into the North's world ordering agendas—especially in the context of a fast-changing global order in which the West is losing its grip. And it is even less clear that old world humanitarianism will be relevant or acceptable to emerging States and civil societies in the global south and to the likely formidable challenges arising from the conflation of climate change, urbanization, migration, increased vulnerability to food and energy shocks, and the like.

Over the past 20 years humanitarianism has functioned for many young and not so young people in the North as a kind of last (western) frontier. In this it has been similar to the human rights movement. It was a mobilizer of energy. It gave purpose and meaning to people. It functioned as a substitute for "revolution" and other "isms" of the past. Humanitarian engagement used to be essentially voluntary and somewhat marginal. Now it has become a career and its protagonists,

---

[23] On the concept of mobilizing myth as applied to development and related international activities, see Murphy and Augelli 1993.

pundits and prima donnas are part of acclaimed international elites. Increasingly, humanitarian leaders pass through the revolving door of politics and business.[24] In order to succeed, humanitarians are pressed to "act as a business, act like a government".[25] Career progression in large NGOs is not dissimilar from government or business. Everything is structured with endless traffic on email and mobile phones replacing initiative and local responsibility. For better or worse, gone are the days of happy go lucky operationalism and flexibility. Funding systems and reward structures promote professionalization, institutionalization and conformity to the detriment of risk taking and innovation.

The idea of humanitarianism, like the idea of rights, has seized hold of the utopian imagination. Human rights and humanitarianism provided a moral alternative to bankrupt political utopians—a replacement for the universal political projects that shaped much of the dark history of the twentieth century. The human rights and humanitarian movements, resurgent after WWII, and energized after the fall of the Berlin wall, shared the vision that fueled utopian politics—not just the anti-capitalist politics of old-fashioned Communist parties, but also internationalist developmentalism, anticolonialist movements, liberation theology and vain attempts to forge "socialism with a human face." We tend to forget that these movements and the myths they vehiculate are recent and contingent and that they are likely to be challenged by emerging hard-nosed politics and by alternative utopias.

Moreover, success for the humanitarian ideology and discourse came at its own peril because like its human rights cousin, humanitarianism emerged largely in confrontation with power. Humanitarian agencies used to be State-avoiding, but now they increasingly depend on the State directly for funding, or indirectly for patronage, visibility and their own security. States advocate for access for 'their' NGOs and often come to the rescue when they get into trouble. The humanitarian oligarchy mobilizes and moves resources, and interacts with politics at the highest level. Indeed, as mentioned above, many famous humanitarians have become full time politicians (the obverse is less frequent). Whether humanitarians like it or not, humanitarian action has become part of governance. Some would even say that it is part of government. However, in a multipolar or increasingly polarized world, humanitarian power will be increasingly challenged by other forms of succor to the vulnerable

Will humanitarianism go the way of other mobilizing myths? This seems to me to be the key question. The more the humanitarian agenda expands into non-humanitarian territory—development, justice, human rights—the more it risks being sucked into power and politics and perceived as taking sides. Humanitarianism has been the victim of its own success, if not its delusions of grandeur. It is

---

[24] As an example, Andrew Natsios, senior Vice-President of World Vision US, was appointed head of USAID by G.W. Bush. Earlier in his career he had worked for various private companies and in academia. The case of Bernard Kouchner, one of the founders of MSF, who became a minister in both a leftist and rightist French government is also emblematic.

[25] Cooley and Ron 2002.

unclear whether even the more modest Dunantist version will be able to survive unscathed in a global confrontation between western and non-western discourses on the best way of addressing vulnerability to disasters.

The aspiration for a more just and secure world in which individuals can lead meaningful lives in freedom from fear and want is one that humanitarians affirm, whatever they see as their role in bringing about such changes. Even if the loftier agenda of changing the world is not within their purview, as citizens humanitarians are deeply concerned by its state. During the past quarter century, humanitarianism, in addition to the assistance and protection that it has provided to the vulnerable, has functioned as an important mobilizing framework that gives direction and meaning to the lives of hundreds of thousands of dedicated aid workers. Will humanitarianism go the way of its earlier counterparts? Will it be saved or resurrected in a different incarnation?

21.5 Conclusions

I offer two, perhaps temporary, conclusions. First, there remains a need and an opportunity *to build better safety nets for the most vulnerable in conflicts and disasters*, nets that cut across cultures, are principle-based and to the extent possible independent from partisan politics. More can and should be done to promote and protect the universality of humanitarian action and enlarge its global reach and character.

Second, political and structural changes in the wider world are proceeding faster and running deeper than most humanitarians realize. The incorporation of aid in securitization and the rapid emergence of climate change as a vector of vulnerability, among other global forces, may trigger events of an unprecedented magnitude. Serious reform is not yet in the air, but it is unavoidable to adapt an enterprise that is fundamentally still stuck in mental models of yesteryear to a fast-changing complex new world. There must be *a more forthright engagement with change*, building on the bedrock of time-tested principles and creating a humanitarian enterprise that is inclusive, participatory, transparent and accountable and, above all, that is “of the world” rather than “of the north”. Reform, inevitably, will take time. More research, analysis and debate will be required to better grasp what lies ahead. Not engaging vigorously with change and adaptation will not only be a lost opportunity in improving the collective ability to save and protect lives in disasters of a potentially global scale, it might also sound the death knell for humanitarianism as we know it.

References

Cooley A, Ron J (2002) The NGO scramble. Organizational insecurity and the political economy of transnational action. Int Secur 27(1):5–39

Cruz RV, Harasawa M, Lal S, Wu Y, Anokhin B, Punsalmaa Y et al (2007) Asia. In: Parry ML, Canziani OF, Palutikof JP, van der Linden PJ, Hanson CE (eds) Climate change 2007: impacts, adaptation and vulnerability. Contribution of Working Group II to the Fourth assessment report of the intergovernmental panel on climate Change. Cambridge University Press, Cambridge

Development Initiatives (2011) Global Humanitarian Assistance Report 2011. www.devint.org

Donini A et al (2008) Humanitarian action 2015: The state of the humanitarian enterprise. Feinstein International Center, Medford

Donini A (2010) The far side: the meta-functions of humanitarianism in a globalized world. Disasters 34:220–237

Fassin D (2007) Humanitarianism as a politics of life. Public Culture 19:3

Grewal D (2008) Network power: the social dynamics of globalization. Yale University Press, New Haven

Hardt M, Negri A (2001) Empire. Harvard University Press, Cambridge

Murphy C, Augelli E (1993) International institutions, decolonization and development. Int Political Sci Rev 14(1):71–85

Stoddard A, Harmer A, Di Domenico V (2009) Providing aid in insecure environments, 2009 update. Trends in the violence against aid workers and the operational response, Humanitarian Policy Group, ODI

Van Aalst MK (2006) The impacts of climate change on the risk of natural disasters. Disasters 30:5–18

Wallerstein I (2006) European universalism. The rhetoric of power. The New Press, New York

Webster M, Ginnetti J, Walker P, Coppard D, Kent R (2009) The humanitarian response costs of climate change. J. Environ Hazards 8:149–163

Chapter 22
Customs Obstacles to Relief Consignments Under International Disaster Response Law

Giovanna Adinolfi

Abstract Humanitarian assistance and relief in the event of disaster may require the affected State to import the goods and equipment indispensable to satisfy the needs of the population. Severe problems may arise in this phase, precluding the chance to provide immediate aid: customs delays, lack of exemptions from custom duties, charges, restrictions, and ordinary customs procedures are all potential obstacles to prompt and effective assistance. A considerable body of law has been developing to address these issues, yet the existing international legal instruments are considerably heterogeneous, varying in scope and content. The purpose of this study is to analyze the trends followed within such a complex legal framework regarding the application of waivers to ordinary customs barriers and practices for relief consignment, at the same time assessing whether international trade law applies in these circumstances. The legal position of intergovernmental organizations will be taken into account in the light of the privileges conferred upon them by their constitutive agreements. The study concludes with some considerations on the feasibility of an international legal text prescribing the obligation for all States to adopt every measure necessary to facilitate access of relief goods and equipment to territories struck by disaster.

Keywords Obstacles to trade · Custom duties · Quantitative restrictions · Food safety · National legislations · UN aid

---

G. Adinolfi (✉)
Università degli Studi di Milano, 20122 Milan, Italy
e-mail: giovanna.adinolfi@unimi.it

A. de Guttry et al. (eds.), *International Disaster Response Law*,
DOI: 10.1007/978-90-6704-882-8_22,

Contents

22.1 Introductory Remarks

The enjoyment of the right to humanitarian assistance, insofar as its existence is recognized under public international law,[1] or in practical terms, the possibility for populations to receive the aid necessary to ease their suffering in the event of disaster, in many cases can be guaranteed only by access to foreign goods and equipment. In the light of this consideration, the United Nations General Assembly has recognized that 'international relief assistance should supplement national efforts to improve the capacities of developing countries to mitigate the effects of natural disasters expeditiously and effectively and to cope efficiently with all emergencies'.[2] This remark should be expanded to take into account some further concerns, e.g., the disruptive effects of technological disasters or their consequences, like those of natural disasters, in industrialized nations, some of which may also be dramatic (as made clear by Hurricane Katrina in the USA in 2005 or the explosion of nuclear energy facilities after the earthquake in Japan in 2011).

However, when it is necessary to import goods and equipment, further constraints on assistance and relief may emerge, as the implementation of national laws and regulations on customs matters could jeopardize the timely start and deployment of humanitarian efforts.[3] Indeed, the burden arising from the application of customs duties, fees or charges may stop or limit relief consignments. The same situation could result from restrictions on the importation of particular goods, or the implementation of regulations concerning the physical characteristics

---

[1] See Chap. 15 by Creta in this volume.

[2] UN General Assembly res. 46/182, 19 December 1991, para 18.

[3] See IFRC 2007a, 98 ff for the narrative of some events where humanitarian assistance was delayed or prevented by the application of customs regulations.

of products allowed to circulate within the boundaries of a State.[4] In addition, imports are usually subject to the presentation of specific documentation, potentially involving delays in customs clearance.

It is undisputed that by regulating access of foreign products to the national market, States may legitimately pursue public ends of an economic and/or social character. However, in the aftermath of a disaster, the effects of implementing these laws and regulations have to be appraised as well, and the introduction of waivers duly considered.[5]

These issues have been addressed since the very earliest days of international disaster response law as can be evinced from some bilateral agreements concluded by the United States following the Second World War.[6] However, a coherent legal framework prescribing upon States clear obligations on customs matters is still lacking. Hard and soft law instruments have been adopted, and in some instances the latter aim to provide a comprehensive regulation, though they are not binding upon States. The main points of reference are the 1970 World Custom Organization (WCO) Recommendation to Expedite the Forwarding of Relief Consignments in the Event of Disasters,[7] the 2002 UN General Assembly resolution on Strengthening the effectiveness and co-ordination of international urban search and rescue assistance,[8] the Model Rules for Disaster Relief Operations, published in 1982 by UNITAR,[9] the International Federation of the Red Cross and Red Crescent Societies 1977 Measures to expedite international relief, adopted jointly with the UN Economic and Social Council,[10] the 1994 Code of Conduct for the International Red Cross and Red Crescent Movement and NGOs in Disaster Relief, and the IFRC 2007a, b Guidelines for the Domestic Facilitation and Regulation of International Disaster Relief and Initial Recovery Assistance.[11]

As for hard law instruments, for the purposes of the present chapter it would be impossible to consider all the huge number of treaties on relief which entered into force on a bilateral, regional, and universal basis,[12] concluded in many cases as a response to previous natural or man-made disasters. Bilateral treaties are quite

---

[4] For example, on occasion of Hurricane Katrina in 2005, the US customs authorities stopped imports of food from the UK containing British beef, banned since 1997 because of spongiform encephalopathy hitting cattle in that country. See IFRC 2007a, 105 ff.

[5] Delays are not to be discounted even when national authorities concur on an easing of custom formalities and procedures: see Bannon and Fisher 2006, on events related to the imports of relief goods in Sri Lanka after the 2004 tsunami.

[6] See the references in Fisher 2003, 24 f.

[7] See WCO doc. T2-423, June 8, 1970.

[8] UN General Assembly res. 57/150, 16 December 2002, in particular para 3.

[9] el Baradei et al. 1982.

[10] The document is annexed to UN doc. A/32/60.

[11] The last two documents were adopted, at the 26th and 30th International Conferences of the Red Cross and Red Crescent, respectively. Available at www.ifrc.org.

[12] A list of these agreements may be found in the UN Secretariat Memorandum in UN doc. A/CN.4/590/Add.2.

common between European States,[13] with all the deficiencies ensuing from their limited subjective scope. Similar considerations also apply to the bilateral treaties concluded by the UN, specifically concerning its action in emergency situations, whose legal setting does favor humanitarian assistance, but over a limited geographic area.

Regional treaties for disaster relief have come into force in all continents except Africa.[14] Among them, mention must be made of the 1991 Inter-American Convention to Facilitate Disaster Assistance,[15] but counting only five contracting parties, despite being open to the 35 members of the Organization of American States and to any other third country. The 2005 ASEAN Agreement on Disaster Management and Emergency Response,[16] concluded in the aftermath of the 2004 tsunami and earthquake in the Indian Ocean and which entered into force in 2009 for the ten ASEAN member States should also be mentioned. As for Europe, no regional agreement specifically concerning assistance in the event of disaster has been concluded, and co-operation is extensively based on bilateral treaties. Regional frameworks were set up under the aegis of the Council of Europe in 1987, when the EUR-OPA Major Hazards Agreement was adopted, lacking, however, a specific focus on customs matters.[17] In addition, co-operation between the 27 members of the EU is promoted by Article 196 of the Treaty on the Functioning of the European Union, whereby the Union is called upon to promote co-operation between national civil protection authorities and to adopt measures to support and complement members' action, *inter alia*, in responding to natural or man-made disasters occurring within their boundaries. A common mechanism for civil protection was thus established in 2001, whose general purpose is to provide support in the event of major emergencies and to facilitate coordinated intervention by EU member States and the Union itself.[18] However, for customs issues the main legal instruments consist of the EU primary and secondary rules concerning the customs union and trade relationships with third States.

Universal agreements have been finalized over the last decades, but either they concern the movement of specifically defined goods (such as the 1998 Tampere

---

[13] A clear indication of this trend can be inferred looking through the list compiled in the UN Secretariat document cited in the previous note. See also Fisher 2007, 354; for an analysis of general trends followed in bilateral treaties, see Fisher 2003, 29 ff.

[14] IFRC 2007b, 9 and Field 2003.

[15] Available at www.oas.org/juridico/english/treaties/a-54.html. Accessed 5 January 2012.

[16] Available at www.aseansec.org/18441.htm. Accessed 5 January 2012.

[17] See resolution 87(2) of the Council's Committee of Ministers, March 20, 1987. Open to the participation of Council of Europe members and to any other third State, EUR-OPA was conceived as a co-operation mechanism where programs for co-ordinated relief assistance may be discussed and developed. However, as a 'partial agreement' under a Committee resolution of August 2, 1951, it is not an international treaty, but was conceived as an activity of the Council which members are not compelled to participate in. See Chap. 1 by de Guttry in this volume.

[18] See para 4 of the preamble to Council decision 2007/779 of November 8 2007, in *OJEU* L 314, 9 ff. More extensively, see Chaps. 5 by Gestri and 6 by Casolari in this volume.

Convention on the Provision of Telecommunication Resources for Disaster Mitigation and Relief Operations, or the 1990 Istanbul Convention on Temporary Admission, for equipment covering only medical, surgical and laboratory devices) or, when regarding consignments of all goods needed for assistance, they have not yet achieved significant State participation (e.g., the Specific Annexes B.3 and J.5 to the revised 1999 International Convention on the Simplification and Harmonization of Customs Procedures, which came into force in 2006 and were applied by 18 and 15 States, respectively). Furthermore, these instruments may refer to humanitarian assistance in general terms, or be restricted to emergencies in the wake of particular events, as in the case of the 1986 Convention on Assistance in the Case of a Nuclear Accident or Radiological Emergency, concluded after the Chernobyl nuclear disaster. Finally, also treaties concerning international organizations have some relevance, to the extent they recognize privileges and immunities for the movement and access of goods and materials used by these institutions when exercising their competences. A clear example is given by the 1946 Convention on Privileges and Immunities of the United Nations or by its 1947 sister convention on UN specialized agencies.

Taken as a whole, this body of law provides evidence for an interest within the international community in the elaboration of legal instruments aiming to ease support in favor of populations struck by natural or technological disasters, developing rules that go beyond a general duty to provide assistance. They all contribute to specifying in more concrete terms how the primary responsibility to provide aid to affected populations has to be carried out by States having to cope with the disruptive consequences of disasters within their territory, and to frame the general recommendation formulated in 1991 by the General Assembly, according to which 'disaster-prone countries should develop special emergency procedures to expedite the rapid procurement and employment of equipment and relief supplies'.[19] However, notwithstanding the general aim to establish close co-operative links between States, the fragmented character of this regulation cannot be underestimated, from both a subjective and a material point of view.

22.2 Exemptions from the Payment of Customs Duties, Charges or Other Fees Having an Equivalent Effect

The issue of payment by relief actors of duties and similar fees when importing the materials necessary for humanitarian assistance is covered by most instruments referred to in the previous section. The rationale behind this regulation is the need to avoid burdening assistance with additional costs, and to shorten administrative

[19] UN doc. A/RES/46/182, cit., para 30.

procedures. However, some important differences can be identified as to the scope and binding force of the relevant legal texts.[20]

Indeed, in very broad terms, the soft law instruments adopted by the International Federation of Red Cross and Red Crescent Societies explicitly recommend that States in whose territory a disaster has occurred should facilitate the rapid access of all goods of prime necessity and equipment by adopting a waiver of customs taxes, restrictions, and procedures.[21] On the contrary, a restricted approach is followed in the relevant United Nations documents concerning relief consignments, as they include no reference to the suspension of import duties or restrictions. Indeed, UN General Assembly resolution 57/150 simply calls States to simplify or reduce customs and administrative procedures (para 3), while the 1977 Measures to Expedite the Forwarding of Relief Consignments refers only to certain administrative practices (import and export licenses).

A waiver of customs regulations may be found in the 1970 World Customs Organization recommendation, whereby members of both the WCO and the UN, as well as customs unions, are exhorted to allow the 'admission free of import duties and taxes' of relief consignments received as gifts for distribution to victims of a disaster (para 5). Concerning equipment, the recommendation sets a temporary admission regime, applicable on the condition that importers undertake to re-export the materials after use (para 6).[22] The recommendation introduces an important limitation on the beneficiaries of this regime, as they are restricted to organizations approved by the government of the stricken State. In any case, this is a common feature of most of the legal texts discussed here, as they introduce more or less detailed regulation recognizing the primary role of States in taking care of victims of disasters occurring within their boundaries, and in co-ordinating all humanitarian efforts by national and non-national entities, be they intergovernmental, governmental or private institutions. As for the latter, it is usually established that they can provide assistance as long as they have been authorized by the competent national authorities of the assisted State.[23]

A universal stipulation for the waiver of customs duties and taxes may be found in para 6 of Annex J.5 to the Kyoto Convention, formulated in terms quite similar to those of the 1970 WCO recommendation, concerning the imports of goods of

---

[20] In this study, particular attention is drawn to the legal regime of imports of relief goods and equipment. Most treaties and other legal instruments referred to also include provisions addressed to States from whose territory consignments are exported and/or States of transit, aiming to facilitate international assistance also through the relaxation of their customs legislations.

[21] See paras 17 and 18 of the 2007 IFRC Guidelines and para 3 of Annex I to the 1994 Code of Conduct.

[22] It is worth noting that the 1970 WCO recommendation stipulates nothing about the customs regime applied to the equipment when re-exported, in particular with regard to the application of possible export duties by the affected State. This is a general feature of all the instruments discussed here, where no clear prohibition of export duties is provided for. There is, rather, a general obligation to facilitate the departure of materials used during relief operations (see the references in IFRC 2007a, 104).

[23] See Chaps. 10 by Costas Trascasas and 23 by Silingardi in this volume.

prime necessity[24] and equipment indispensable for the operations of disaster relief personnel, in both cases received as gifts. However, the Annex has seen scant participation by WCO members. If this was not the case, the advantages of a broader subjective scope would necessarily be limited. Indeed, even within the framework of an international treaty, such as the Kyoto Convention, admission of relief goods, and equipment free of import duties and other charges, is a mere recommendation whose implementation is considered desirable in view of a progressive harmonization and simplification of customs procedures.[25]

An obligation to waive import duties is provided for in the 1990 Istanbul Convention on Temporary Admission, concluded under the auspices of the WCO. Indeed, Article 2, para 2 binds participating States to grant temporary admission 'with total conditional relief from import duties and taxes'. Like the Kyoto Convention, the rule refers to goods of prime necessity loaned free-of-charge and to certain equipment, in particular medical, surgical and laboratory equipment (Annex B.9). Nevertheless, contrary to the already mentioned WCO acts, gifts and donations are not covered, as the special import regime applies on the condition that items will be re-exported within a specified period of time (Article 7 and Annex B.9, Article 5). Hence, by implication, imports of some essential goods, e.g., foodstuffs, do not come under the scope of the binding legal prescriptions of the Convention.

A further characteristic of disaster response treaties to be taken into consideration pertains to the option conferred upon contracting parties to introduce reservations, hence excluding the efficacy of legal obligations otherwise binding upon them. For example, the 1986 Convention on Assistance in the Case of a Nuclear Accident or Radiological Emergency broadly prescribes the exemption from customs duties and taxes on imports of equipment necessary for assistance (Article 8, para 3). It recognizes, however, that State parties have the freedom to declare upon accession that they do not consider themselves bound by this obligation in whole or in part (Article 8, para 9). Indeed, a large number of the 107 parties to the Convention have adopted reservations or interpretative declarations to exclude them from the scope of the said provision, or to claim to be bound by it under a specific interpretation or some specified conditions.[26]

---

[24] Under both the WCO recommendation and the Kyoto Convention, prime necessity goods include foodstuffs, medicines, clothing, blankets, tents, and prefabricated houses. The Kyoto Convention also refers to vehicles and other means of transport, as well as items for the purifying and storage of water.

[25] See Article 1.c of the Kyoto Convention for a definition of 'recommended practice', as para 6 of Annex J.5 is formally defined.

[26] See, for example, the United Kingdom reservation, according to which, if assistance is provided by a State, Article 8, para 3 applies if that State is itself bound by it in its relations with the United Kingdom. Sri Lanka has declared that the granting of the waiver is subject to applicable national laws and regulations. France has excluded the application of Article 8, para 3. The text of the reservations and declaration is published at www.iaea.org/Publications/Documents/Conventions/cacnare_reserv.pdf. Accessed 5 January 2012.

Most of the limitations of universal hard- and soft-law instruments are absent in regional and bilateral agreements. As for the latter, they include varying regimes for imports of relief materials, covering either goods of prime assistance or equipment, or both.[27] Nevertheless, the positive implications due to their wide material scope are offset by the limited number of States to which they are addressed.

Among regional instruments, the 1991 Inter-American Convention is framed in very general terms (Article V). Similarly, the 2005 ASEAN Agreement sets out a duty-free regime for importing equipment (Article 14), while for goods, Article 8, para 2.b refers to the preparation of operational procedures by contracting parties for regional co-operation covering the facilitation of their trans-boundary movement as well.

For Europe, in addition to the bilateral treaties in force between European States, reference must also be made to the EU legal regime. The abolition of customs duties in trade relationships between EU members, applying also to goods and equipment used in disaster conditions, is generally established by Article 28 of the Treaty on the Functioning of the European Union. As for relief materials imported from third countries into the territory of the Union, some Community Customs Code rules apply. In particular, temporary admission with total relief of duties is provided for 'materials to be used in connection with measures taken to counter the effects of disasters' affecting EU territory. For equipment, specific provisions concern medical, surgical, and laboratory equipment, covered by a temporary importation regime provided that they have been requested by medical institutions facing exceptional circumstances and that they are dispatched on an occasional basis as a loan free-of-charge.[28] As for goods meant for the populations (excluding materials for rebuilding the affected areas), relief from duties is allowed

---

[27] By way of example, see Article 5 of the 1977 Convention on Mutual Assistance in the Event of Disasters or Serious Accident between France and Germany, whereby goods to be distributed to the population (means of emergency aid) or necessary to use the equipment (operational goods) may be imported tax free (para 4); the same rule does not apply to 'items of equipment', i.e., the material and vehicles intended for use by emergency teams, which are covered by a general obligation to facilitate frontier-crossing and by a regime of temporary admission (para 2), with the obligation to re-export at the end of the operation (para 4). The 1988 Agreement on Co-operation between the Kingdom of Spain and the Argentine Republic on Disaster Preparedness and Prevention, and Mutual Assistance in the Event of Disasters is limited to equipment, and its Article XIV.3 prescribes exemption from import duties and taxes. The 1964 Agreement between the United Kingdom and India covers a broader category of materials, including both goods of prime necessity and hospital equipment (Articles I and II), even if it specifically sets obligations only upon the United Kingdom for disaster in India. The prescriptions of the 2004 Agreement on Mutual Assistance in the Case of Disaster or Serious Accidents between Austria and the Kingdom of Jordan have been given a more comprehensive and reciprocal character, requiring the two States to exempt from duties the import of relief items and equipment (Article 6, para 6), defined in Article 2 as 'goods intended for delivery free-of-charge to the affected people living in the requesting state' and as 'materials, particularly technical facilities', respectively.

[28] See Articles 677 and 678 of the EU Commission regulation no. 2454/93, July 2, 1993, in *OJEC* L/253, 1 ff. More extensively see IFRC 2010b, 26 ff.

upon authorization of the EU Commission, and only if they are imported by national authorities, or organizations approved by national authorities, and made available or distributed free-of-charge to disaster victims.[29]

22.3 Waivers to Customs Procedures and Restrictions on Importing of an Economic or Social Character in the Event of Disaster

In order to accelerate and favor humanitarian assistance and relief, a legal framework concerning customs issues should also cover non-tariff barriers, through waivers to quantitative restrictions on importing goods and equipment, complementary to the obligation or recommendation not to impose customs taxes. Such provisions may be found in para 5 of the 1970 WCO recommendation, in Article 6 of Annex J.5 to the Kyoto Convention and in the 1990 Temporary Admission Convention; they could be, and are introduced in a number of bilateral treaties of mutual assistance in case of disaster. In addition, also the 1998 Tampere Convention on telecommunication equipment refers to non-tariff barriers, as its Article 9 was drafted in general terms to cover 'regulatory barriers', including regulations restricting the import of telecommunication equipment. However, the reduction of such barriers is prescribed by the Convention 'when possible' and in conformity with national laws, thus leaving a wide margin of autonomy to contracting parties.

When waivers to the implementation of import restrictions are not mentioned in international agreements applicable between the assisted State and the assisting State, it is worth recalling the general stipulation provided for in the 1994 General Agreement on Tariffs and Trade. This Agreement does not concern support in situations of emergency at all, rather it sets the basic principles and prescriptions for the exchange of goods in the bilateral relationships between the 153 members of the World Trade Organization. However, one of its pillars may be found in Article XI, where a general prohibition for import restrictions is imposed upon WTO members. Although this general stipulation may be waived when specific circumstances occur, it may be of particular importance as a free trade obligation facilitating the trans-boundary movement of goods and equipment, when destined for use in the territory of a State also hit by a disaster.

Facilitating humanitarian assistance could also be promoted by the adoption of rules providing for the simplification of import procedures, for example waiving existent regulation concerning import documentation or speeding up customs clearance. Some instruments of international disaster response law make explicit reference only to these issues, in particular the above-mentioned 2002 UN General Assembly resolution 57/150 and the 1977 Measure to Expedite the Forwarding of

---

[29] See Articles 9 ff of EU Council regulation no. 98/183, in *OJEC* L/105, 1 ff.

Relief Consignments adopted by the WCO and UN Economic and Social Council. The approach followed by multilateral, regional, and bilateral treaties may vary, according to the specific subject covered by their texts, in any case aiming to accelerate customs procedures in order to provide affected populations with the means necessary to satisfy their most urgent needs.[30]

Further regulation on customs procedures may also be found in the 1965 Convention on Facilitation of International Maritime Traffic, whose Annex requires State parties to 'facilitate the arrival and departure of vessels engaged in natural disaster relief work' and, to the greatest extent possible, to 'facilitate the entry and clearance of... cargo' arriving on these vessels.[31] Likewise, Annex 9 to the 1944 Convention on International Civil Aviation prescribes a similar obligation, albeit referring exclusively to relief flights performed by, or on behalf of, States or international organizations recognized by the UN.[32]

A common feature of these regulations, undermining the practical effects of their implementation, is the use of rather vague language in their texts. A mere obligation, if not a recommendation, to 'facilitate' customs clearance does not *per se* impose upon States a clear mode of behavior, and continues to leave a broad margin of discretion in deciding the magnitude of the waiver to daily customs practices to be applied for importing relief consignments. This circumstance is all the more relevant for the ICAO and IMO conventions, considering the high number of their contracting parties and their potential contribution to designing national customs legislation able to speed up humanitarian assistance and relief in the event of disaster.

A further element to be considered, since it may somehow impede or complicate relief consignments, is the regulations enacted by States concerning the quality of products that may enter national markets. Usually, the enactment of these rules is determined by a growing concern within national communities for the need to protect consumers and, in broader terms, to safeguard human, animal, and plant health and life. To find a balance between satisfying this need and, on the other hand, protecting the freedom of individual economic activity, national authorities may give prevalence to the former, thus introducing regulations excluding some products from consumption or identifying the physical characteristics they must have to be placed on the market. These stipulations usually

---

[30] See the 1970 WCO recommendation, paras 6 (for equipment under a temporary admission regime) and 7 (for custom clearance), Articles 2 and 3 (customs clearance and simplified documentation) of Annex J.5 of the Kyoto Convention; Article 4 (simplified documentation) of Annex B.9 to the 1990 Convention on Temporary Admission, Article 9 of the 1998 Tampere Convention, Article 14.b of the 1999 ASEAN Agreement (prescribing a general duty to facilitate import of equipment and materials), Article V of the 1991 Inter-American Convention (envisaging a 'best efforts' obligation to expedite or, if appropriate, dispense with customs formalities). Provisions aiming at the facilitation of customs procedures and formalities are included in all bilateral treaties as well.

[31] See Sections 5.11 and 5.12 in the Annex to the 1965 Convention, as amended.

[32] See the reference in IFRC 2007a, 42 ff.

apply to foreign products as well, whose imports are thus prohibited or made conditional upon compliance with technical standards. Among the latter, sanitary and phytosanitary measures may be used to protect human, animal, or plant life or health from the spread of diseases or disease-causing products.

The adoption of these regulations is subject to the constraints posed by a number of international agreements on trade matters, concluded with the specific purpose of preventing States from introducing unjustifiable obstacles to imports, by enacting legislation setting technical standards. In this regard, the WTO agreements on technical obstacles and on sanitary or phytosanitary measures come into play, as well as some stipulations of the already mentioned 1994 General Agreement on Tariffs and Trade. However, they give WTO members great autonomy in framing national legislation, provided they are consistent with international standards, or scientifically based and not applied in a manner likely to constitute an undue barrier to international trade.

If a disaster has occurred, the legitimate social interests justifying these measures may collide with the pursuit of humanitarian aims, as the strict application of qualitative restrictions to imports may deny relief organizations the use of technical equipment, or individuals access to goods of prime necessity (for example foodstuff) for the satisfaction of their urgent needs.

This issue is not neglected in international disaster response law, even if the instruments containing specific provisions on this come to discrete solutions. For example, the 1970 WCO recommendation explicitly stipulates that its application does not preclude the efficacy of 'prohibitions or restrictions imposed under national laws and regulations on grounds of public morality or order, public security, public hygiene or health or based on veterinary or phytopathological consideration'. The 1990 Istanbul Convention includes a similar provision for the temporary admission of goods of prime necessity and equipment.[33] The approach thus largely respects States' normative and regulatory autonomy, with the result that it is entirely left to their discretion whether to revise the national laws and regulations or to introduce waivers to their application because of the exceptional circumstances following a disaster.

A similar orientation in favor of health and safety can also be inferred from those legal instruments whereby a waiver to import regulations is prescribed or recommended only for 'economic import prohibitions or restrictions'.[34] In these cases, by implication it can be assumed that contracting States refer to regulations forbidding or setting quantitative limits to importing some specific goods in the pursuit of economic aims, such as the protection of national production from foreign competition, and not restrictions with a social aim, such as the protection of health and safety. Compliance with technical standards and similar regulations

---

[33] The Convention on Temporary Admission refers also to restrictions or prohibition introduced on the basis of considerations 'relating to the protection of endangered species of wild fauna and flora, or … to the protection of copyright and industrial property' (Article 19).

[34] See Article 6 of Annex J.5 to the Kyoto Convention; Article 19 of the 1990 Istanbul Convention on Temporary Admission.

is also required by agreements whereby assistance in the event of disaster is to be provided in accordance with the national laws of the assisted States (e.g., the 1999 ASEAN Agreement, Article 13, para 1), thus discounting the possibility that relief actors may request customs clearance for products whose importation is forbidden by those laws, unless their application is suspended or derogations are provided for.

Even those instruments focusing more extensively on the interests of the populations affected by disasters do not fail to weigh up safety and public health concerns, even if trying to find a balance with the equally relevant need to provide effective support to individuals. Indeed, the 2007 IFRC Guidelines call upon assisting States and humanitarian organizations not to use disaster relief and initial recovery goods that may pose a threat to human safety or health (or to the environment) (para 17.4); at the same time, all States involved in disaster relief are recommended to consider whether 'normal requirements regarding fumigation and prohibitions on food imports and exports can be modified or reduced' (para 18.4). Also the 1977 UN-WCO Measures to Expedite International Relief invite States receiving assistance to waive regulations concerning fumigation certificates and restrictions on food imports lest they "impede the admission to relief items essential for the protection of disaster victims" (Recommendation D). However, no criteria for interpreting and implementing these provisions are set, and it becomes quite difficult for relief operators to identify the legal framework within which they are allowed to provide assistance.

Some guidelines could be provided by the standards developed by the Codex Alimentarius Commission, an intergovernmental body established in 1963 by the Food and Agricultural Organization and the World Health Organization with the mandate to formulate technical standards concerning foodstuffs. Among the numerous documents so far adopted, the Code of Ethics for International Trade in Food Including Concessional and Food Aid Transactions must be mentioned.[35] Enacted in 1979 and later revised in 1985 and 2010, the Code sets out some basic principles to be followed by States for the trans-boundary movement of food, based on the assumption that individuals 'are entitled to safe, sound and wholesome food and to protection from unfair trade practices' (para 3.1). As a corollary to this general principle, some more specific provisions recommend that food be traded only if it guarantees the safety of its final consumers. As the Code covers also concessional and food aid transactions, it does not exclude the possibility of applying waivers to existing national legislation. In particular, it is left to the legislation of the importing country, or to decisions of its competent authorities, to allow or to prohibit food not in conformity with the technical requirements imposed by the legislation of the exporting country.

This rule is the result of the 2010 amendment to the Code in its previous version providing that in special circumstances, such as famines and other emergency

[35] See the Codex Alimentarius Commission doc. CAC/RCP 20-1979.

situations, food safety concerns should not be underestimated.[36] As revised, the Code follows a different approach. First, its language is very general, with no reference to food emergencies that may follow natural or technological disasters. In addition, the waiver to standards is framed as an exception to the exporting country legislation forbidding exports and sales on the internal market of food not in conformity with technical standards. Furthermore, the exception may be invoked only if the importing State has given its consent to receive the food. Compliance with standards in force within the importing country is not mentioned, implicitly assuming that when receiving food as aid or on a concessional basis, the competent national authorities may apply national legislation. In conclusion, it is always left to the discretion of the assisted State to decide whether to provide humanitarian assistance allowing the distribution of foodstuffs which, in normal circumstances, would not be made available for consumption under national or foreign legislation.[37]

22.4 The Legal Regime for Importing Goods and Equipment by Intergovernmental Organizations: The United Nations Organisation and its Specialized Agencies

Some stipulations facilitating operations by the United Nations and its specialized agencies (hereinafter, the UN system) may be drawn from the constitutive instruments of these organizations, usually setting out the privileges and immunities they enjoy in the exercise of their functions. The interesting feature of this legal regime is that it pre-exists the humanitarian assistance operations, so no agreement with the affected State has to be concluded to facilitate their deployment, and it applies to all member States of the UN and its specialized agencies, thus contributing to legal certainty in the relationship with the assisted and third States. However, conceived as generally covering these relations as a whole, such rules fail to consider fully the difficulties met in the delivery of relief in favor of populations hit by disasters. Therefore, in more recent decades, new instruments have been developed with the specific purpose of further expediting UN activities.

The legal basis of the UN system's operations lies in Article 105 of the Charter of San Francisco, as well as in the similarly formulated provisions included in the treaties establishing the UN specialized agencies. They stipulate that on each member's territory, these organizations enjoy such privileges and immunities as are necessary for the fulfillment of their purposes. The exercise of the functional immunity thus established has required the adoption of more detailed regulations,

---

[36] See IFRC 2007a, 106 ff.

[37] For example, within the EU no derogations are admitted to the extensive Union regulation concerning food safety, not even when constituting assistance in the event of disaster: see IFRC 2010a, 25.

setting out under which circumstances and under which conditions it may be legitimately enjoyed.

The 1946 Convention on the Privileges and Immunities of the United Nations was negotiated to fill this gap. When it came into force, a body of law was introduced to grant the Organization the legal instruments necessary to pursue its aims without external interference. Among the provisions contained in the Convention, Section 7.b provides that the United Nations, its assets, and other property are 'exempted from customs duties and prohibitions and restrictions on import and export' when they are used in the performance of the UN's official duties. An identical provision is included in Section 9.b of the 1947 Convention on the Privileges and Immunities of the Specialized Agencies of the United Nations, applicable to all intergovernmental institutions which establish a relationship with the UN under Articles 57 and 63 of the Charter of San Francisco.

As a consequence, all equipment and relief materials used within the context of the UN system's relief operations and transported within the territory of States affected by a natural or man-made disaster may freely move across frontiers, without being subject to any tariff or quantitative non-tariff barriers. For example,[38] the combined application of the two conventions allows the implementation of a duty-free regime to the food aid carried out by the United Nations under the World Food Programme, jointly established in 1961 by the UN General Assembly[39] and the Food and Agricultural Organization with the mission to deliver food to people in need, also actively intervening in emergency situations caused by natural disasters.

For our purposes, these Conventions are not without limitations, as they do not specifically cover all the difficulties in customs facilitation and clearance that may emerge in disaster assistance. To fill this gap, in 1994 the UN Office for the Coordination of Humanitarian Affairs devised a Model Customs Facilitation Agreement, approved in 1996 by the WCO. The conclusion of bilateral agreements with States on this basis would speed up import, export and transit of relief consignments within UN-led humanitarian assistance and disaster relief operations.

Article 3 is the core provision of the Model Agreement, providing for facilitation measures to be adopted by the assisted States, as well as by States from whose territory relief consignments are exported or across whose territory they transit. The provision resembles those discussed above, and requires waiving customs duties, taxes and restrictions, and the simplification of customs procedures for importing goods of prime necessity and equipment. In one respect, the conclusion of agreements under this Model would represent a considerable step ahead. Indeed, the Model provides that the facilitation regime for consignments would apply to organizations involved in UN relief operations, including the UN itself, its

[38] For an analysis of UN system involvement in disaster relief operations, see Chap. 19 by Silingardi in this volume.

[39] See UN General Assembly res. 1714 (XVI), December 19, 1961.

specialized agencies, and other governmental, intergovernmental and non-governmental organizations certified by the UN as *bona fide* participants in the operations (Article 2). In case no implementing legislation is required, when humanitarian assistance is carried out on this basis, no other international agreement would be necessary with assisting States or UN specialized agencies, nor would private relief organizations be required to follow the national procedures of the assisted State to benefit from customs privileges. In particular, the latter could carry out their activities with UN certification, thus benefiting from the same advantages recognized to the UN system's components, without having to be authorized by national authorities. Unfortunately, the Model has been used to conclude assistance agreements with a very limited number of States (Honduras, Liberia, Mali, Moldova, Nepal, and Uzbekistan).[40]

22.5 Conclusions

As shown over the previous pages, international disaster response law dealing with custom issues does not form a coherent legal framework imposing clear obligations upon States for the adoption of specifically identified measures. Despite the huge number of treaties so far concluded at bilateral, regional and universal level, the resolutions of the UN General Assembly, and the soft-law instruments adopted within the IFRC and other organizations, States still retain a high degree of discretion in introducing national legislation and regulation to favor access to foreign relief consignments within their territory.

In many cases, international legal provisions are formulated in general terms, such as the obligation 'to facilitate' customs clearance, and when they prescribe the adoption of specifically identified practices (such as exemption from customs duties and taxes), new constraints may emerge, e.g., the limited number of States concerned or the faculty to introduce reservations. The instruments developed in an effort to codify a comprehensive set of rules whose application would facilitate humanitarian assistance and relief have the drawback of being soft law, as in the case of the 1994 and 2007 IFRC's instruments; furthermore the regulation they provide underlines the role of national authorities in providing and co-ordinating assistance, and for some issues relating to customs matters, it is left open to them to decide whether or not to adopt measures that could ease the access of foreign goods and equipment (for example, in applying qualitative requirements for imported products). Finally, the high number of bilateral treaties, though witnessing an increasing awareness within the international community, contributes at the same time to the fragmentation of international disaster response law into a network of bilateral relationships. They vary considerably in scope and content,

[40] See http://www.unocha.org/what-we-do/coordination-tools/logistics-support/customs-facilitation . Accessed 5 January 2012.

and it is hard to infer from a comparative analysis of their texts, and considering other regional and universal agreements, the emergence of customary rules of international law. While it is true that they all provide for at least the exemption from customs duties and equivalent taxes, the recurring character of this stipulation, together with the possibility conferred upon States to lay down reservations, lead one to discount the idea that this treaty practice has favored the emergence of a rule of general international law with the same content.

Notwithstanding recognition by the UN General Assembly of the 'great importance' of international co-operation 'to address emergency situations and to strengthen the response capacity of affected countries' and the 'significant contribution in supplementing national efforts' that can be provided by intergovernmental and non-governmental organizations,[41] international disaster response law still lacks universal consensus relating exclusively to humanitarian assistance and relief in the event of disaster, and regulating customs matters with sufficient detail. Indeed, the multilateral treaties in force have a very limited scope, as they may refer to a particular disaster (as in the 1986 Convention on Assistance in the Case of a Nuclear Accident or Radiological Emergency) or the provision of relief circumscribed to a specific sector (in the case of the 1998 Tampere Convention on the Provision of Telecommunication Resources for Disaster Mitigation and Relief Operations), seemingly reflecting a widespread view within the international community that universal instruments should be narrowly focused.

From this perspective, a considerable difference exists compared with international humanitarian law applicable in the event of international conflict. Indeed, Section III of the Fourth 1949 Geneva Convention, concerning occupied territories, obliges the occupying power to exempt relief consignments (including foodstuffs, medical supplies and clothing) 'from all charges, taxes or customs duties unless these are necessary in the interests of the economy of the territory' (Article 61). As a general obligation included in a multilateral treaty, it is surely applicable to the 194 States which have ratified the Convention. It is questionable whether Article 61 falls within those stipulations 'so fundamental to the respect of the human person and "elementary considerations of humanity"' to be considered binding upon all States, irrespective of their adhesion to the Convention itself.[42] A study by the International Committee of the Red Cross has answered in the affirmative, extending the scope of the provision to all types of conflicts, thus including internal conflicts.[43]

In the past, proposals for the conclusion of a comprehensive agreement concerning assistance in the event of disasters had been put forward, also covering technical aspects, including customs matters.[44] Indeed, in 1984 the UN Secretary

[41] Res. 46/182, para 5.

[42] See *Legality of the Threat or Use of Nuclear Weapons*, Advisory Opinion, *I.C.J. Reports* 1996, 226 ff, para 79.

[43] See Henckaerts and Doswald-Beck 2005, 193 ff.

[44] For a thorough analysis, see Macalister-Smith 1985, 33 ff and Fidler 2005, 463. See also Acconci 2011, 333.

General submitted the text of a Draft Convention on Expediting the Delivery of Emergency Assistance to the Economic and Social Council,[45] but without success. It referred to both natural and man-made disasters, when a legal regime would be applied to speed up relief consignments. Exporting States would be under the obligation to authorize rapidly, and to ensure that documentation requirements did not delay the dispatch of equipment and relief consignments. Assisted States would have had to suspend the application of customs duties, taxes and importing prohibitions or restrictions. As for national technical requirements, exemption from hygiene, health and animal protection regulation was implemented as far as possible and it was stated that their application would delay importation; a general obligation was introduced to simplify and accelerate customs procedures.

Even on the basis of this past experience, the UN Secretary General has on various occasions recommended further development of international initiatives to co-ordinate assistance through the conclusion of a convention also providing a framework for customs matters.[46] However, since the adoption of the 2007 IFRC Guidelines, its approach has changed, as it currently recommends States to use the Guidelines to frame their internal legislation,[47] and at the same time to consider recourse to the Model Custom Facilitation Agreement for the conclusion of international agreements. Thus, the focus is on enacting appropriate national legislation and concluding bilateral agreements. In as far as any common view exists within the international community to follow this path, thus relying extensively on national legislations for the introduction of legal instruments that facilitate the entry of goods of prime necessity and equipment, the efforts of the relevant institutions should be addressed to favoring the development of this legislation in the direction of an extension of customs benefits to all relief organizations, irrespective of their legal, intergovernmental, governmental or private status.[48]

---

[45] UN doc. A/39/267/Add.2 E/1984/96/Add.2, of June 18, 1984.

[46] See UN doc. A/55/82-E/2000/61, para 135.

[47] See UN doc. A/63/277, August 13, 2008, para 72.e; UN doc. A/64/331, August 27, 2009, para 78; UN doc. A/65/356, September 8, 2010, para 83.

[48] The adoption of this approach has been recently endorsed by the IFRC, whose 31st International Conference in November 2011 presented a pilot version of a Model Act for the Facilitation and Regulation of International Disaster Relief and Initial Recovery Assistance (available at www.ifrc.org/en/what-we-do/idrl/model-act-on-idrl/, accessed 5 January 2012), with the purpose of promoting the implementation of the 2007 Guidelines at national level. According to the text, the legal facilities provided for by the Model Act (including those relevant to importing relief goods and equipment—see Articles 29–41), are available to so called 'Eligible Actors', which comprise *de jure* third States, intergovernmental institutions, and national components of the Red Cross and Red Crescent Movement (Article 21, para a.(i–iii)); as for private organizations, they may be made eligible by the assisted State either unilaterally (Article 21, para a.(iv)) or upon request, provided they do not pursue profit aims and have legal personality under international law or a third State legal order (Article 22).

References

Acconci P (2011) Tutela della salute e diritto internazionale. CEDAM, Padova

Bannon V, Fisher D (2006) Legal lessons in disaster relief from the tsunami, the Pakistan earthquake and Hurricane Katrina. ASIL Insights. www.ail.org/insights060315.cfm

el Baradei M et al (1982) Model rules for disaster relief operations, policy and efficacy studies no. 8. United Nations Institute for Training and Research, New York

Fidler DP (2005) Disaster relief and governance after the Indian Ocean tsunami: what role for International Law. Melb J Int Law 6:458–483

Field T-L (2003) International disaster response law in a southern African context, in IFRC International disaster response laws, principles and practice: reflections, prospects and challenges. International Federation of Red Cross and Red Crescent Societies, Geneva, pp 81–90

Fisher H (2003) International disaster response law treaties: trends, patterns and lacunae, in IFRC International disaster response law, principles and practices: reflections, prospects and challenges. International Federation of Red Cross and Red Crescent Societies, Geneva, pp 24–44

Fisher D (2007) Domestic regulation of international humanitarian relief in disasters and armed conflict: a comparative analysis. Int Rev Red Cross 866:345–372

Henckaerts J-M, Doswald-Beck L (2005) Customary International Humanitarian Law, volume I: rules. International Committee of the Red Cross, Geneva

IFRC (2007a) Law and legal issues in international disaster response: a desk study. International Federation of Red Cross and Red Crescent Societies, Geneva

IFRC (2007b) Regional (Africa) survey of disaster response laws, policies and principles. International Federation of Red Cross and Red Crescent Societies, Geneva

IFRC (2010a) Analysis of law in the EU and a selection of member states pertaining to cross-border disaster relief, synthesis report and recommendations. International Federation of Red Cross and Red Crescent Societies, Geneva

IFRC (2010b) Analysis of law in the European Union pertaining to cross-border disaster relief. International Federation of Red Cross and Red Crescent Societies, Geneva

Macalister-Smith P (1985) Disaster relief: reflections on the role of International Law. Zeitschrift für ausländisches öffentliches Recht und Völkerrecht 45:25–43

Chapter 23
The Status of Emergency Workers

Stefano Silingardi

Abstract Without safe, timely, and unhindered access to affected territories, humanitarian organizations and relief personnel cannot give prompt and efficient help to affected populations. To this end, a number of States have concluded bilateral or multilateral agreements (which sometimes evolved through a series of regional agreements) providing for specific types of legal and administrative facilitation. Facilitation measures can also be found in various guidelines, models, and codes of conduct developed by experts or by the humanitarian community, including the IDRL Guidelines. However, today's legal framework is far from clear, and there are many gaps and weaknesses that constrain the IDRL in addressing bureaucratic hurdles that hinder the access of emergency workers to the affected territory and their functioning. The purpose of this chapter is to evaluate the effectiveness as well as the gaps and weaknesses of this body of law. After defining the issue at stake (Sect. 23.1) and analyzing what international law generally provides regarding the obligations of domestic authorities in allowing and facilitating humanitarian assistance in times of disaster (Sect. 23.2), the chapter examines the restrictions on entry into the country of operations (Sect. 23.3), and the restrictions on operations (Sect. 23.4) being faced by relief personnel, with special focus on the issuance of work permits and the recognition of professional qualifications; impediments to their movement; engagement, and termination of locally engaged personnel; opening of bank accounts; and issues of double taxation and insurance coverage. While the specifics on military personnel are further analyzed in Sect. 23.5; Sect. 23.6 is devoted to the analysis of the duties and obligations of disaster relief personnel in relation to relevant international and national laws. The concluding part of the chapter suggests, with a

---

S. Silingardi (✉)
Dipartimento di Giurisprudenza, Università di Modena e Reggio Emilia,
via San Geminiano 3, 41121 Modena, Italy
e-mail: stefano.silingardi@unimore.it

A. de Guttry et al. (eds.), *International Disaster Response Law*,
DOI: 10.1007/978-90-6704-882-8_23,

de lege ferenda perspective, how this complex legal framework could be amended to meet existing and future challenges.

Keywords Privileges and Immunities Law · Disaster relief personnel's rights and obligations during disasters · International and National laws · Military personnel · Civil and Criminal Liability

Contents

23.1 Introduction

As a general rule, disaster relief personnel benefit from only those rights that have been created through special agreements in treaties with receiving States. Several types of legal and administrative facilitation can be found in many bilateral treaties, in numerous multilateral treaties, and in several regional mutual assistance treaties. Yet, throughout the world, the major players involved in relief efforts, such as States, International Organizations (IOs), Non-Governmental Organizations (NGOs), and Non-Governmental Humanitarian Agencies (NGHAs)[1] still

[1] The International Federation of the Red Cross and Red Crescent Societies (IFRC) and the International Committee of the Red Cross (ICRC) have coined the term NGHAs to encompass the various components of the International Red Cross and Red Crescent Movement involved in a

have to go through a lengthy and expensive bureaucratic process before entering the affected territory and carrying out their functions. Before turning to the individual regulatory issues, it is helpful to briefly recall the general provisions of international law concerning the obligations of domestic authorities in allowing and facilitating humanitarian assistance in times of disaster.

Although not directly related to disasters and international humanitarian relief,[2] various bodies of human rights law give protection to many rights relevant in the context of a disaster, such as the right to life, food, water, health, and medical services, among others.[3] What human rights law can do, therefore, is to add an obligation on the affected States to allow access to relief organizations and their staff in times of disaster so as to facilitate their operation whenever required because national authorities failed to take all the necessary actions to protect the affected population.[4] However, this human rights-based approach does not provide for specifying the means that should be employed for facilitation of international relief. Insofar as the issues of co-ordination and facilitation are concerned, the task of regulation rests thus upon the domains of the law on privileges and immunities and IDRL.

23.2 Privileges and Immunities Law

In providing the assistance requested, privileges and immunities law may 'address many of the access and operations issues identified as the most problematic.'[5] However, at least with regard to the *ratione personarum* perspective, the application of this set of rights is not consistent, and one may distinguish among those accorded to State officials, IOs and their personnel, and NGOs and their staff.

Only a few of the bilateral treaties providing procedures for the initiation and termination of assistance have made specific reference to privileges and immunities law with regard to State officials. For example, the 1947 Agreement between United States and China equates the privileges and immunities of the personnel

(Footnote 1 continued)
disaster response. See *The Code of Conduct for the International Red Cross and Red Crescent Movement and Non-Governmental Organisations (NGOs) in Disaster Relief*. Available as annex 2 to The Sphere Project, *Humanitarian Charter and Minimum Standards in Humanitarian Response*, 2011, at: http://www.sphereproject.org. Accessed 22 February 2012.

[2] According to Dinstein 2000, 77 'no general right of humanitarian assistance has actually been crystallized in positive international law.' See also Bothe 2000, 170; and Okere and Makawa 2001, 437.

[3] Fischer 2007, 34, citing as examples, the 1990 African Charter on the Rights and Welfare of the Child, and the International Convention on the Rights of Persons with Disabilities, UN General Assembly Resolution 61/106, U.N. Doc. No. A/RES/61/106 (2007).

[4] Fidler 2007, 251; and Valencia-Ospina 2011, paras 31–38. For more on this see also Chap. 15 by Creta in this volume.

[5] See Fischer 2007, 39.

involved in a relief operation to those of the United States diplomatic personnel in China,[6] and the 1996 Agreement between United States and Belarus to those of the administrative and technical staff personnel under the 1961 Vienna Convention on Diplomatic Relations.[7] Apart from these few exceptions, most bilateral treaties and agreements have provided only for rights similar to the privileges and immunities accorded to State officials, such as exemption from standard immigration restriction, and work permit rules, or immunity from administrative, civilian, and criminal jurisdiction of the requesting State.[8]

Provisions on privileges and immunities are also contained in multilateral treaties directly related to disaster relief activities, both of global and regional relevance. In some cases, these instruments set forth detailed provisions, including rules on precise identification of the beneficiaries of such privileges and immunities and their corresponding obligation to respect the laws of the receiving State. The 1986 Nuclear Assistance Convention and 1998 Tampere Convention, for instance, provide a non-exhaustive list of such rights. These include: immunities from arrest, detention, and legal process; exemptions from taxation, duties or other charges; and immunities from seizure, attachment, or requisition of equipment, materials, and property.[9] Other instruments, such as the 2000 Framework Convention on Civil Defence Assistance, or, at the regional level, the 1963 Nordic Mutual Emergency Assistance Agreement and the 2007 CEPREDENAC Agreement, limit the provision of privileges and immunities to just stating the general principle of permitting the assisting entities to carry out their functions.[10] More

---

[6] See 1947 Agreement concerning the United States relief assistance to the Chinese people (with Exchange of Notes), Article 5.

[7] 1996 Agreement between the Government of the United States of America and the Government Republic of Belarus Regarding Co-operation to Facilitate the Provision of Assistance, Article 2.

[8] As examples, see the 1989 Convention between the Kingdom of Denmark and the Federal Republic of Germany on mutual assistance in the event of disasters or serious accident, Articles 4, 5, and 9; and the 1989 Agreement between the Government of the French Republic and the Swiss Federal Council on mutual assistance in the event of disasters or serious accidents, Articles 6, 7, 11, and 12. See also the 2000 Acuerdo entre el Gobierno del Reino de España y el Gobierno de la Federación de Rusia sobre cooperación en el ámbito de la prevención de catástrofes y asistencia mutua en la mitigación de sus consecuencias, Articles 10–12; and the 1992 Agreement on Cooperation between the Kingdom of Spain and the Argentine Republic on disaster preparedness and prevention, and mutual assistance in the event of disasters, Article 19.

[9] 1986 Convention on Assistance in the Case of a Nuclear Accident or Radiological Emergency, Article 8; 1998 Tampere Convention on the Provision of Telecommunication Resources for Disaster Mitigation and Relief Operations, Articles 5 and 9(5). At the regional level, see 1991 Agreement Establishing the Caribbean Disaster Emergency Response Agency (CDERA), Article 21; and 2008 Agreement Establishing the Caribbean Disaster Emergency Management Agency (CDEMA), Article 27.

[10] 2000 Framework Convention on Civil Defence Assistance, Article 4(a)(5); 1963 Nordic Mutual Assistance Agreement in connection with radiation accidents, Article 6; and 2007 Nuevo Convenio Constitutivo del Centro de Coordinación para la Prevención de los Desastres Naturales en América Central (CEPREDENAC), Article 15.

recently, the new 2008 CDEMA Agreement has started allowing member States to grant fiscal and customs benefits, as well as diplomatic privileges and immunities, on a voluntary basis to the organization and its personnel in accordance with international laws and domestic legislation.[11] Finally, there are some conventions at the regional level, such as the 2005 ASEAN Agreement on Disaster Management and Emergency Response (AADMER) and the 1991 Inter-American Convention to Facilitate Disaster Assistance, which only grant exemptions and facilities to State officials of the assisting States in accordance with the national law of the receiving State.[12]

With regard to IOs, apart from the UN, its specialized agencies and the IAEA, whose privileges and immunities are guaranteed by specific conventions,[13] all the other international and regional IOs, and their personnel, may benefit from privileges and immunities rights only to the extent that they fall within the ambit of application of specific disaster-focused legal instruments. This is the case, for example, with some multilateral conventions and agreements, such as the Tampere Convention (Article 5), the AADMER (Article 14), and the Inter-American Convention to Facilitate Disaster Assistance (Article 16). Provisions on privileges and immunities may also be found in the many bilateral agreements concluded between States and IOs (particularly, the UN and its agencies), which are generally based on the 1946 Convention of the UN and the 1947 Convention of the specialized agencies. Examples of this practice are provided by agreements concluded between Suriname, Dominica and the WHO[14]; between the Federal Republic of Yugoslavia and IOM[15]; between Indonesia and the UN, UNICEF and WHO[16]; between Fiji and UN, UNICEF and UNDP[17]; between Cambodia and WHO and

[11] Nuevo Convenio Constitutivo del Centro de Coordinación para la Prevención de los Desastres Naturales en América Central, above footnote 10, Article 15; and Agreement Establishing the Caribbean Disaster Emergency Management Agency, above footnote 9, Articles 30–34.

[12] 2005 ASEAN Agreement on Disaster Management and Emergency Response (AADMER), Articles 1, 14 and 17; 1991 Inter-American Convention to Facilitate Disaster Assistance, Articles 4 and 16.

[13] 1946 Convention on the Privileges and Immunities of the United Nations; 1947 Convention on the Privileges and Immunities of the Specialized Agencies; and 1959 Agreement on the Privileges and Immunities of the International Atomic Energy Agency.

[14] 1983 Emergency Technical Cooperation Agreement between the PAN American Health Organization and the Government of Suriname in Case of a Major Natural Disaster, Article 8; and 1983 Emergency Technical Cooperation Agreement between the PAN American Health Organization and the Government of Dominica in Case of a Major Natural Disaster, Article 8.

[15] See, as an example, the 1994 Agreement between the Federal Republic of Yugoslavia and the International Organization for Migration on the Privileges and Immunities of this Organization.

[16] IFRC 2005c, 8.

[17] IFRC 2005b, 7.

UNDP[18]; between Laos and UNDP and WFP[19]; and, finally, between Uganda and WFP, UNDP, and UNICEF.[20]

Of some relevance under this topic is also the 2005 Optional Protocol to the Convention on the Safety of United Nations and its Associated Personnel. The 1994 Convention is a criminal law instruments based on the well-known principle *aut dedere aut judicare*, which imposes an obligation on a State hosting a UN operation to protect UN personnel and property (Article 7).[21] This Convention applies only to specific operations and certain categories of personnel. In particular, the operation should be for the purpose of maintaining or restoring international peace and security (i.e., peacekeeping operations), or any other operation where the Security Council or the General Assembly has declared that there exists and exception risk to the safety of the personnel participating in the operation (Article 1). However, the requirement of a declaration of risk by the Security Council or the General Assembly to cover a host of other activities of the UN operations whose personnel were target of attacks was impractical. The Optional Protocol, which is not yet in force, and which would affect only those parties to the Convention that choose to also become party to the protocol, expands the scope of 'operations' to the following without the declaration of risk: (i) delivering humanitarian, political, or deployment assistance in peace building; and (ii) delivering emergency humanitarian assistance (Article, para 1).[22] As a consequence, it makes the Convention applicable to a larger number of UN and associated personnel. In particular, legal protections envisaged in the Convention include the provisions that the host State shall: (i) upon conclusion of specific agreement with UN, grant privileges and immunities for military and police components of the operation (Article 5); (ii) facilitate the unimpeded transit of UN and associated personnel and their equipment to and from the host State (Article 6); (iii) ensure the safety and security of UN and associated personnel (Article 7).

Privileges and immunities similar to those enjoyed by IOs, have also been granted to the ICRC and the International Federation, owing to their unique international mandates, composition, and recognition in the Geneva Conventions and their Additional Protocols.[23] Although they are not governmental organizations in the legal sense, they have concluded with the governments of most countries a number of legal status agreements to carry out their humanitarian functions, including those relating to disaster relief response which grant them privileges and immunities modeled on the lines provided for in the 1947

[18] IFRC 2009a, 52.

[19] IFRC 2009b, 75.

[20] IFRC 2011, 38.

[21] 1994 Convention on the Safety of United Nations and Associated Personnel.

[22] 2005 Optional Protocol to the Convention on the Safety of United Nations and Associated Personnel.

[23] Fischer 2007, 40.

Convention on the specialized agencies.[24] The legal status agreement with the Kingdom of Cambodia, for example, states that members of the delegation 'shall be immune, together with their spouses and relatives of less than eighteen dependent on them, from immigration restrictions and alien registration.' It further gives the organization freedom to 'carry out, on the entire territory of Cambodia, such activities as may be necessary for the exercise of its humanitarian mission,' and gives the members of the delegation freedom of movement and travel.[25] Finally, it seeks consent to open subdelegations in other parts of the country outside the capital.[26]

To conclude with NGOs and their personnel, it is well known that they are not generally granted privileges and immunities under international law.[27] With this perspective, some international instruments on disaster response have been interpreted in such a way as to include NGOs and their personnel among the beneficiaries of privileges and immunities rights. The main examples of this practice are represented by Article 5 of the Tampere Convention and Article 14 of the AADMER, the latter defining 'Assisting Entity' as including, in addition to States and IOs, 'any other entity or persons that offer and/or render assistance to a Receiving Party or a Requesting Party in the event of disaster management.' Other conventions, such as the Inter-American Convention to Facilitate Disaster Assistance, provide explicitly that NGOs shall enjoy the protection of the convention. However, both the AADMER and the Inter-American Convention have limited geographical reach, while the Tampere Convention, though multilateral in nature, has a very specific aim the relevance of which should not be overvalued.

In conclusion, owing to their personal and substantive scope of application, the provisions on privileges and immunities are insufficient to fully protect disaster relief personnel, and hence they need to be supplemented with other legal facilities that are better adapted to the needs of international disaster relief actors and their personnel. Most of these facilities are included in many international instruments, usually referred to as IDRL, which constitute the legal basis for the analysis performed in the sections that follow.

---

[24] Among the few countries that has not signed a Legal Status Agreement with the IFRC, we may mention the Laos Government, IFRC 2009b, 76.

[25] Agreement between the Government of the Kingdom of Cambodia and the International Conference of the Red Cross and Red Crescent Societies (1994), Articles 2(1), 9(1)(c), and (h). For other example of this practice, please see IFRC 2005a, 7, and IFRC 2005b, 9.

[26] Ibid., Article 2(4).

[27] A limited range of privileges and immunities to foreign NGOs are occasionally afforded under domestic laws on disaster relief. This is the case, for example of a recent enacted Indonesian law, see S/2009/277, above footnote 2, 98. For more on this, see Chap. 19 by Silingardi in this volume.

23.3 Restrictions on Entry into the Country of Operations

In 2008, the Government of Sri Lanka became aware that some foreign aid workers (mainly of British, Dutch, and Norwegian NGOs) who started operating in its territory after the 2004 tsunami were too sympathetic to the defeated Tamil Tigers. As a consequence, it enacted new visa rules under which aid workers are granted only 1-year visas and no renewal is given to visas of foreign workers operating in Sri Lanka for more than 3 years.[28] Likewise, in March 2009 the Burmese junta declined to renew the Tripartite Core Group's (TCG) mandate[29]; instead, it reverted to the much more complex previous system.[30] Under this set of rules, international aid workers must apply directly to their respective line ministries, who in turn would submit their applications to the Foreign Affairs Policy Committee (FAPC), which handles all visa applications. However, as there is no single ministry overseeing aid work, aid agencies were required to sign cooperation agreements with individual ministries before applying for visas; international personnel in Myanmar reported that it usually takes 4 months to 2 years to obtain a cooperation agreement with a ministry and another 5 months to obtain a visa.[31] A third restrictive action against disaster relief actors came up on 1 February 2011, when the Government of Pakistan decided to end the special procedures put in place after the 2010 flood and to revert to its regular visa regime. As a consequence, prior to departing from their country, foreign emergency workers were forced to obtain visas from the Pakistani embassy in their country of residence. Furthermore, only 'officials visas' for UN staff or 'NGO visas' for NGO staff are extended by the Ministry of Interior after the person concerned arrives in the country.

However, for relief organizations, bureaucratic restrictions are not only time consuming, often leading to delays in the provision of aid, but also onerous, even leading to the diversion of economic resources meant for the benefit of the affected population.[32] A number of international instruments, both of *hard law* and *soft law*, therefore recommend that disaster-affected States should provide entry visas

---

[28] Page, *Aid workers forced to leave Sri Lanka under strict new visa rules*, June 3, 2009, http://www.timesonline.co.uk/tol/news/world/asia/article6418015.ece. Accessed 22 February 2012.

[29] The TCG was composed with ASEAN at the core, and comprising the Myanmar government, and UN. It was created on 2 March 2008, 1 month after Cyclone Nargis struck Myanmar's Irrawady Delta, and was instrumental in facilitating the granting of entry visas for foreign relief personnel. At: http://www.reliefweb.int/node/399732. Accessed 22 February 2012.

[30] See *As Foreign Aid Workers Leave, Food Security Concerns Grow*, July 22, 2009, which reported that, according to sources close to the TCG, the visa restriction was partly due to the Myanmar's junta anger over Thailand's criticism of the trial against opposition leader Aung San Suu Kyi. Available at: http://irrawaddy.org/article.php?art_id=16383. Accessed 22 February 2012.

[31] *Myanmar: Junta's change of tack obstructs aid work in cyclone-hit Myanmar*. Available at: http://www.reliefweb.int/node/364998. Accessed 22 February 2012.

[32] IFRC 2006a, 12.

for disaster relief personnel without cost and that such visas should be renewable for the time required for the response.

23.3.1 Hard Law: Global Treaties, Regional Law, Bilateral Treaties and Agreements

Facilitation measures for entry into the territory of operation are incorporated in various multilateral and/or global agreements pertaining to specific issues, such as responding to nuclear and industrial accidents,[33] pollution incidents caused by hazardous and noxious substances,[34] civil defence,[35] or providing telecommunication resources for relief operations.[36] However, while on the one hand these rights and duties are only applicable to the disaster situation pertaining to the object of the agreements, on the other hand, most of these agreements have not reached a large number of ratifications. The Framework Convention on Civil Defence Assistance, for example, has only 26 contracting parties,[37] the Convention on the Transboundary Effects of Industrial Accidents only 40,[38] and the Tampere Convention only 43.[39]

Other facilitation measures can be found in numerous networks of regional and subregional organizations dedicated to disaster cooperation, such as the CDEM-A,[40] the AADMER,[41] and the 1991 Inter-American Convention. The latter, in particular, not only provides a general obligation to permit personnel of the assisting State to enter, transit and leave the affected country, but also specifies that each State party 'shall provide such personnel with the necessary documents and facilities, in accordance with its law.'[42] Under the AADMER (Articles 12–14) and the related Standard Operating Procedures (SASOP), the disaster-affected Party, in accordance with its national laws and regulations, and in cooperation with the newly established Centre for Humanitarian Assistance (AHA Centre), shall further

---

[33] Nuclear Accident Convention, above footnote 9, Articles 8 and 9; and 1992 Convention on the Transboundary Effects of Industrial Accidents, Annex X 'Mutual assistance pursuant to Article 12,' Article 6.

[34] 1990 International Convention on Oil Pollution Preparedness, Response and Cooperation, Article 7; and 2000 Protocol on Preparedness, Response, and Cooperation to Pollution Incidents by Hazardous and Noxious Substances, Article 5.

[35] Framework Convention on Civil Defence Assistance, above footnote 10, Article 4.

[36] Tampere Convention, above footnote 9, Article 9.

[37] See at: http://www.icdo.org/files/states-party.pdf. Accessed 22 February 2012.

[38] See at: http://live.unece.org/env/teia/parties.html. Accessed 22 February 2012.

[39] See at: http://www.itu.int/ITU-D/emergencytelecoms/tampere.html. Accessed 22 February 2012.

[40] CDEMA, above footnote 9, Articles 27 and 28.

[41] AADMER, above footnote 12, Article 13.

[42] Inter-American Convention, above footnote 12, Article 7.

facilitate the Customs, Immigration, and Quarantine (CIQ) procedures by using predefined arrangements.[43]

Facilitation measures pertaining to access to the affected country have also been included in some instruments not directly related to disasters. The African Union's Convention for the Protection and Assistance of Internally Displaced Persons in Africa of 2009, for example, commits signatories to be prepared to coordinate international relief and to 'allow rapid and unimpeded passage of … personnel to internally displaced persons,' including those displaced by disaster.[44]

To conclude the *hard law* legal framework, numerous bilateral treaties address issues of facilitating entry. The UN Secretariat Memorandum of 2007 has listed, over the period 1947–2002, nearly 103 bilateral treaties between States and 33 between States and IOs, many of which concluded by European Union (EU) member States.[45] In almost all these treaties, the parties are required to take all the necessary measures to facilitate the entry, stay, and movement—individual or collective—of duly notified personnel on the territory of the affected party, provided the leader of the intervention team has an official paper evidencing his position, the type of unit, and the names of his team members.[46] Most of the treaties further reflect a general intent to ensure that frontier-crossing formalities are minimized, including the exemption of emergency personnel from passport and visa formalities.[47] The 2004 Austria-Jordan Agreement, for example, states in Article 5 that the parties shall 'reduce border formalities to an *absolute minimum* [emphasis added]' and that the members of the intervention team are not required to have a visa or residence permit during their assistance in the requesting State.[48]

Besides their limited geographical reach, the deficiency of both the bilateral and multilateral agreements is that they address mainly, if not exclusively, States and IOs, and not the subjects (such as NGOs) that in the last decades have developed into major players in relief operations.

---

[43] See *Standard Operating Procedure for Regional Standby Arrangements and Coordination of Joint Disaster Relief and Emergency Response Operations* (SASOP), and ANNEX K 'Form 5,' ASEAN Secretariat, November 2009.

[44] 2009 African Union Convention for the Protection and Assistance of Internally Displaced Persons in Africa (Kampala Convention), Article 5(7).

[45] IFRC 2010a, Annex 3, which list at least 33 bilateral agreements between EU member States.

[46] See 2004 Agreement between the Republic of Austria and the Hashemite Kingdom of Jordan on Mutual Assistance in the Case of Disasters or Serious Accidents; 1998 Agreement on Cooperation on Disaster Prevention and Management and Civil Protection, France–Malaysia, Article 9(3); 2000 Agreement between the Government of the Hellenic Republic and the Government of the Russian Federation on cooperation in the field of prevention and response to natural and man-made disasters, Article 9.

[47] See 1987 Agreement between France and Switzerland on mutual assistance in the event of disasters or serious accidents, Article 6(1).

[48] Austria–Jordan Agreement, above footnote 46, Article 5(2).

23.3.2 Soft Law: Resolutions or Declarations of International Bodies, Guidelines, Models, Codes of Conduct

By reason of this ineffectiveness, the issue of access has been further addressed in many non-binding resolutions or declarations of international bodies.[49] For example, the General Assembly (GA) Resolution 46/182 of 1991 calls on both affected and transit States to facilitate the access of humanitarian organizations to disaster-affected countries; similarly, the GA Resolution 57/150 of 2002 calls on States to 'simplify or reduce, as appropriate, the customs and administrative procedures related to the entry, transit, stay and exit of international urban search and rescue teams.'[50] Facilitation measures are also enshrined in guidelines, models, and codes of conducts developed by experts or by the humanitarian community since the early 1980s. Among these are the models and guidelines developed by the International Law Association (ILA),[51] the United Nations Institute for Training and Research (UNITAR),[52] and the Max Planck Institute for Comparative Public Law and International Law.[53] More recently, the *Institut de droit international* (IDI) adopted in 2003 a resolution on humanitarian assistance providing, *inter alia*, that 'when visas or other authorizations are required they shall be promptly given free of charge,' and that States 'adopt laws and regulations and conclude bilateral or multilateral treaties providing for the above-mentioned facilities.'[54]

One of the most important services rendered by the humanitarian community to comprehensively regulate the system of legal facilities for disaster relief personnel is currently represented by the IDRL Guidelines, which were adopted by olution 4 of the 30th International Conference of the Red Cross and Red Crescent Societies in November 2007.[55] The purpose of this instrument is to provide guidance to States interested in improving their domestic legal, policy, and institutional frameworks concerning international disaster relief assistance with specific regard to entry into the country of operation, for example, by recommending that affected

[49] See *Measures to expedite international relief*, resolution 6 adopted at the 23rd International Conference of the Red Cross and Red Crescent, in *Handbook of the International Red Cross and Red Crescent Movement*, (3d ed., 1994), 811–815.

[50] See UN General Assembly Res. 46/182 of 1991, paras 6–7; and UN General Assembly Res. 57/150 of 2002, para 3.

[51] Bothe 1980, 520–527.

[52] United Nations Institute for Training and Research, Model Rules for Disaster Relief Operations, New York, UNITAR, 1982.

[53] Macalister-Smith 1991, para 20.

[54] See Institute of International law, *Resolution on 'Humanitarian Assistance*,' Bruges Session, September 2, 2003, para 7.

[55] IFRC, *Guidelines for the Domestic Facilitation and Regulation of International Disaster Relief and Initial Recovery Assistance*, Article 20.

States 'grant visas ... ideally without costs, renewable within their territory [and to] waive or significantly expedite the provision of such visas.'

More recently, at the end of its 31st International Conference, the IFRC decided to supplement its Guidelines with a new Model Act to provide a tool for States wishing to implement them.[56] With regard to entry into the country of operations, the Model Act encourages States to either use a disaster Personnel Visa, unless national security or public health and safety concerns related to the particular individual preclude it (Article 25), or a disaster personnel visa waiver (alternative Article 25), rather than a tourist visa. During the disaster relief period, such entry visas should be issued to the international personnel upon arrival at the port of entry of the affected State, without any fee for an initial period of 3 months and renewable for a period of up to 6 months. After the termination of this period, but during the 'International Initial Recovery Assistance Period' (i.e., the period following a disaster during which relevant legal facilities are made available to eligible actors for the purpose of restoring or improving the pre-disaster living conditions of disaster-affected communities, including initiatives to increase resilience to disasters, and reduce disaster risk), disaster visas shall be issued following application, prior to travel, to the appropriate embassy, which shall issue them within a specified time.

However, what largely hampers the effectiveness of all these instruments developed by experts or by the humanitarian community is that they stand, from the perspective of international law, in the domain of *soft law*. In other words, they cannot be considered as 'full-fledged' rules of international law but instead can be spelled out only as rules of conduct that are not intended to be legally binding and cannot be enforced in courts. To sustain the IDRL Guidelines, the GA has, for example, adopted four resolutions encouraging States to strengthen their legal and institutional frameworks for disaster relief by taking these Guidelines into account.[57]

23.3.3 Development at the National Level

Under the guidance of Part V, Section 16, of the IDRL Guidelines, a number of countries have amended their laws in the last few years to create specific rules for expeditious, and free-of-charge visa procedures for recovery personnel.

In 2008, Indonesia became the first country to make legislative changes based on the IDRL Guidelines. Indonesian Government Regulation No. 21 provides that foreign personnel assisting disaster management shall have easy access on

[56] *Model Act for the Facilitation and Regulation of International Disaster Relief and initial Recovery Assistance (Pilot Version November 2011).*

[57] See Un General Assembly resolutions 63/137, December 11, 2008, para 6; 63/139, December 11, 2008, para 8; 63/141, December 11, 2008, para 5; and 64/251, January 22, 2010, para 7.

immigration matters, such as the processing and servicing of a visa, entry permit, limited stay permit (for a period not exceeding the period of disaster emergency response), and exit permit.[58]

Likewise, in Panama a new executive decree on immigration was promulgated in August 2008, which included a special visa category for international humanitarian relief personnel 'that come in representation of governmental agencies or properly reputable non-governmental agencies.' They will be exempt from all the requirements stipulated for tourist visas in Articles 17 and 28 of Decree Law No. 3 dated 22 February 2008, except for a letter from the Department of Foreign Affairs that certifies the type and duration of the assistance carried out by the International Agency.[59]

Other changes emerged in New Zealand, when, in 2009, the Ministry of Civil Defence and Emergency Management drew on IDRL Guidelines in developing a set of standard operating procedures for an 'International Assistance Cell' tasked with coordinating and facilitating international relief.[60] In Colombia, the law requires that a special temporary visa be given to 'volunteers, aid workers or NGO personnel, or a person who is duly backed by an international agency or a diplomatic mission in order to perform social welfare work, attendance, testing, observation or humanitarian aid.'[61] Finally, both the most recent draft of Afghanistan's National Disaster Preparedness Law of 2011 and draft of the Kazakhstan's Law on Civil Protection provide systems for the quick issuance of visas for humanitarian purposes.[62]

There are other States that provide for visa waiver. According to Section 11 of the new Norwegian Immigration Act that came into force in 2010, when it is necessary for humanitarian reasons, national considerations, or international obligations, a visa may be issued for a period not exceeding 3 months even if the conditions laid down in Section 10 of the Act ('Schengen visa') are not satisfied.[63] In Mexico, pursuant to the general law on Civil Protection, visas are waived for international relief personnel.[64] Pakistan also adopted the practice of temporary visa waiver during recent disasters (Sect. 23.3)

---

[58] Government Regulation of the Republic of Indonesia, Number 21 of 28 February 2008 concerning Disaster Management, Article 33.

[59] Executive Decree No. 320, of August 8, 2008, Articles 56–58.

[60] National Crisis Management Centre, International Assistance Cell, Standard Operating Procedures, September 2009.

[61] Decree 4000 of 2004 enacting provisions on the issuance of visas, control of foreigners, and other provisions relating to migration, 30 November 2004, Article 41(6).

[62] Draft National Disaster Preparedness law, 2011, Article 42.

[63] Act of 15 May 2008 on the Entry of Foreign Nationals into the Kingdom of Norway and their Stay in the Realm (Immigration Act), section 11. See also Regulations of 15 October 2009 on the Entry of Foreign Nationals into the Kingdom of Norway and their Stay in the Realm (Immigration Act), 14.

[64] General Law on Civil Protection, as amended to April 2006, 24 April 2004.

Moreover, there are some countries that do not have specific provisions about disasters but seem to provide more or less adequate procedures to expedite the entry of foreign relief personnel through their general domestic laws. In Uganda, for example, there are no provisions for expeditious visa issuance or waiver under the existing regulations, but according to an immigration officer, this is unnecessary because obtaining a visa at the port of entry ordinarily does not take more than 10 min.[65] In Guatemala, personnel of IOs who are not under the umbrella of either the UN or a foreign State have been able to obtain longer term visas[66]; in other cases, international relief personnel (especially from unregistered NGOs) are allowed to enter without a visa or with a short-term tourist visa. In Laos, for example, NGOs tend to use tourist visas (which can be obtained at any Laos consulate or embassy abroad in less than 1 week after filling out a simple form and submitting two identification pictures) to avoid lengthy procedures and delays: once in the territory, they commence the process of changing the tourist visa into a courtesy visa.[67] However, this technically does not allow them to work in the country.[68] Further, the visa renewal procedure is time-consuming.[69]

A different perspective prevails under the Schengen arrangements, wherein EU citizens are allowed to move freely throughout the EU without the need for a visa or work permit. Additionally, member States are allowed to exempt the relief personnel of non-EU member States from visa requirements, or the Schengen visa procedures in the event of a national emergency.[70]

However, a recent analysis performed by the IFRC demonstrates that several EU countries prefer not to use this discretionary power, but instead to establish arrangements for entry through bilateral agreements, providing for formalities that vary according to the partner country.[71] Where neither the discretionary exemption nor bilateral or multilateral arrangements apply, it appears that special procedures under national law are employed on an *ad hoc* basis. Bulgaria, which is not yet a full-fledged member of the Schengen area, for example, provides a short-track procedure allowing emergency teams to obtain a visa (a one-time transit visa with a validity term of 36 h and a short-stay visa with a maximum term of 15 days) upon arrival at the border without prior application at the consular representations.[72] In contrast, the Netherlands can exempt the relief personnel of a non-EU

---

[65] IFRC 2011, 49.

[66] IFRC 2007, 33.

[67] IFRC 2009b, 100.

[68] IFRC 2005a, 24.

[69] In Myanmar, for example, most visas are single entry, so if an international aid worker has to leave the country for personal reasons, he or she has no choice but to reapply to get back in. See *Fresh visa headaches for aid workers*, at: http://irinnews.org/Report.aspx?ReportID=85049. Accessed 21 February 2012. See also IFRC 2006a, 16; IFRC 2007, 33; IFRC 2006b, 16.

[70] Council Regulation 539/2001/EC, *OJEC 2001* L081.

[71] IFRC 2010a, 23–24; and IFRC 2010b, 19–20.

[72] IFRC 2010e, 33.

country from visa requirements, but only following the decision of the Ministry of Foreign Affairs.[73]

A special situation is that of the United Kingdom, which is not part of the EU Schengen arrangements. Nationals of the European Economic Area (EEA) do not generally require leave to enter or remain in the UK. However, for foreign aid personnel of third countries the UK has not yet considered the issue, but it is likely that it would be dealt with on a case-by-case basis. In particular, it is left to the Secretary of State (or for immigration officials acting on behalf of the Secretary of State) to exercise the general discretionary power to exempt any person or class of persons (for example, international relief workers) from immigration requirements. Exemption must be made by way of a statutory instrument, and the order so made will be by legislation, which must be laid before the Parliament and published.[74]

23.4 Restrictions on Operations

Once on the ground, emergency workers often have to comply with various additional legal constraints in carrying out their functions.

23.4.1 The Issuance of Work Permits and the Recognition of Professional Qualifications

Under the law of privileges and immunities, the staff of diplomatic missions, consulates, and UN agencies may be generally granted an official visa allowing them to work within the affected territory. Non-governmental personnel, as well as State and IOs officials who are not covered by specific agreements, may not be generally afforded this privilege, and therefore they need a formal certification from the Government before they are allowed to practise. Usually, the authorization takes the form of a work permit or visa, which is most of the time conditional upon registration of the assisting actor under national law.[75] For certain professions involved in disaster-response operations, such as physicians, nurses, pharmacists, and architects as well as for certain types of relevant activities, such

[73] IFRC 2010c, 36.

[74] IFRC 2010d, 51–52.

[75] IFRC 2011, 48–49. For a more detailed comment of this practice see Chap. 19 by Silingardi in this volume.

as driving a motor vehicle or piloting a helicopter, States may further decide that the recognition of foreign certificates and diplomas is required.[76]

However, only a few countries have specific provisions on the recognition of professional qualifications for disaster relief. For example, the Emergencies Act of 2004 in the Australian Capital Territory States that 'where foreign assistance is provided in accordance with a co-operative agreement, overseas professional qualifications will be recognized in the Territory without further need for certification or registration.'[77] Indonesia requires that incoming personnel, particularly those in the professions of health, search and rescue, construction, communications and hydrology, meet the required qualifications according to government needs as mentioned in the 'initiation letter' (request) for foreign assistance.[78]

In case non-specific provisions exist, application will be granted to the provisions of general national laws, which most of the time provide lengthy and confusing procedures largely inadequate to the time frame of disaster response. According to the Working of Aliens Act of 1978, for example, Thailand's legislation provides different types of procedures depending on whether and with whom the organization was registered: those registered with the Thai International Cooperation Agency have sometimes been able to obtain a non-immigrant F visa (for persons performing 'official' duties) and not needed to process a work permit, while organizations registered through the Ministry of Labour typically require a visa *and* work permit.[79] Federal States may also face an additional complication if provincial or lower level governments govern the recognition of foreign qualifications.

However, there are other cases in which the existing national laws and procedures seem to be adequate. For example, in Uganda, international relief providers would be granted on arrival 'Special Passes' that give them immediate but temporary permission to carry out their operations while their work permits are being processed (which usually takes 3 weeks to 1 month).[80]

If domestic laws are fragmented, international guidance on this topic is very limited. Specific provisions concerning work permits and the recognition of foreign professional qualifications are incorporated in only a few international instruments, while some other instruments include provisions broad enough to take them into account.[81] In the former category of instruments, mention may be made of two conventions: the Tampere Convention, which provides that 'Reduction of regulatory barriers may take the form of … recognition of … foreign operating

[76] Fischer 2007, 118–120. According to IFRC 2007, 33, most international staff in Guatemala does not apply for these permits because of the long and bureaucratic procedures.

[77] Emergency Act 2004 (ACT).

[78] *Guidelines on the Role of the International Organizations and Foreign Non-Government Organizations During Emergency Response*, 2011, Chapter II, D.2(a).

[79] IFRC 2006b, 15.

[80] IFRC 2011, 49.

[81] See *Protection of persons in the event of disasters*, Memorandum by the Secretariat (A/CN.4/590), 22 December 2007, 64–66.

licenses;'[82] and the 1984 Draft Convention on Expediting the Delivery of Emergency Assistance, which calls upon the receiving State 'to recognize university degrees, professional certificates and other certificates of competency and licenses held by relief personnel and necessary for the performance of their agreed function.'[83]

States may also decide to abandon lengthy procedure in favor of specific provisions included in bilateral agreements. The 2004 Agreement between Austria and Jordan, for example, States that 'no work permit is required for members of the intervention team and individuals sent for rescue tasks for all of these activities carried out within the framework of assistance.'[84] However, these provisions are only enforceable between the contracting parties.

At the regional level, only a few attempts have been made to facilitate the recognition of professional qualifications. The Balkan Red Cross and Red Crescent Societies recommended in 2004 that Governments 'see that the legal recognition of professional expertise ... is accorded.'[85] Similar provisions were included in the 2000 International Emergency Management Assistance Memorandum of Understanding between a number of States of the United States and provinces of Canada.[86] Likewise, in 2009 ASEAN countries signed the 'ASEAN Mutual Recognition Arrangement on Medical Practitioners,' the main objective of which is to facilitate, in accordance with the domestic regulation in the host country and with the condition set forth in Article 3, the mobility of medical practitioners within ASEAN countries.[87]

A more comprehensive approach to this issue has been taken in the EU context. Through Directive No. 2005/36/EC, EU law provides a procedure for the 'automatic' recognition of professional qualifications possessed by EU citizens when their services are provided on a temporary basis, as in the case of disaster relief and response activities. However, while States are still allowed to take up to 1 month to process the requests,[88] the implementation of this EU legislation by member States continues to be inconsistent despite the mandatory nature of this legislation. The recent analysis performed by the IFRC demonstrates that several EU countries have not included in their domestic legislation the procedure for temporary provision of services. In the Austrian legislation, for example, the procedure for

---

82 Tampere Convention, above footnote 9, Article 9.

83 1984 Draft Convention on expediting the delivery of emergency assistance, Article 7(2)(d).

84 Austria–Jordan Agreement, above footnote 46.

85 2004 Recommended Rules and Practices on Implementation of International Disaster Response Laws, Rules and Principles in the Balkans, part III, para 14.

86 2000 International Emergency Management Assistance Memorandum of Understanding, Article 5.

87 2009 ASEAN Mutual Recognition Arrangement on Medical Practitioners.

88 *OJ 2005* L 255.

recognition of paramedics' qualifications normally takes up to 4 months after the applicant submits all the necessary documents and pays the requisite fees.[89]

As for the recognition of qualifications obtained outside the EU, the member States are free to recognize, in accordance with their rules, professional qualifications acquired outside the territory of the European Union by third country nationals. However, all recognitions should respect the minimum training conditions for certain professions; further, there is no maximum time for processing requests.[90] The IFRC reports indicate that in most member States, unless a specific bilateral or multilateral agreement applies, the procedures associated with recognition might significantly impede the ability of a qualified individual to enter a member State and render his or her services during a disaster.[91]

Finally, some member States further provide for recognition through bilateral agreements or through specific national procedures outside the context of EU legislation. The same Austrian legislation requires that there must be specific legal basis for exempting professionals from the normal requirements; in Germany, exemptions are granted as the situation demands.[92]

To cope with this confusing and extremely fragmented legal framework, the most recent international soft law instruments encourage States to grant personnel of eligible assisting international actors 'any necessary work permits ideally without cost, renewable within their territory, for the time necessary to carry out disaster relief or initial recovery activities.'[93] The Model Act further encourages the preparation of a list of countries and institutions (to be reviewed at least once a year) from which 'certifications will be expected to be particularly trustworthy.'[94]

23.4.2 The Impediments to the Movement of Relief Personnel

The questions of access does not end after crossing the receiving State's borders because some countries may decide, mostly for political or security reasons, to place additional restrictions on the movements of relief personnel. For example, in Laos, the granting of a Memorandum of Understanding (MoU) to permit access to certain areas that are less accessible than others for historically sensitive reasons may be delayed by up to 2 years.[95]

The 'Red Cross/Red Crescent NGO Code of Conduct' recognizes that freedom of movement within the affected territory and equal access to all the victims are

[89] IFRC 2010b, 21.

[90] *OJ 2005* L 255.

[91] IFRC 2010b, 21.

[92] Ibid.

[93] *IDRL Guidelines*, above footnote 55, section 16.

[94] *Model Act*, above footnote 56, 77.

[95] IFRC 2009b, 104.

necessary preconditions for the effectiveness of disaster-response operations.[96] To this end, multiple international instruments suggest the existence on part of the receiving States of an obligation not to unduly limit the access of relief personnel to the disaster area, while some instruments require that they undertake positive steps to facilitate such movement.[97] The 2003 Bruges Resolution of the IDI calls upon the affected States to permit humanitarian personnel 'full and free access to all the victims and ensure the freedom of movement and the protection of personnel.'[98] From this perspective, of some note is the recent GA Resolution (65/133 of 3 March 2011), which, although not binding as such in this respect, calls upon all Governments and parties in complex humanitarian emergencies, 'in conformity with the relevant provisions of international law and national law … to ensure the safe and unhindered access of humanitarian personnel … to efficiently perform their task of assisting affected civilian population.'[99]

In the last few years, provisions allowing easy movement within the affected territory have finally been included in some national laws. In Vietnam, for example, the Governmental Decree No. 64 of 14 May 2008 prohibits any acts of impeding the humanitarian aid of organizations or individuals; the Law on Red Cross Activities No. 11 of the National Assembly, dated 3 June 2008, bans acts of impeding Red Cross activities by organizations or individuals.[100] In Indonesia, Regulation No. 21 of 2008 provides that, besides easy access to the country in the form of visa or entry permit, foreign personnel may have easy access to the disaster area to carry out their aid program.[101]

At the regional level, the only completely satisfactory legal framework is that of the EU law. As part of the free movement of persons principle, based on Title IV TFEU (ex Title III TEC), EU citizens (and workers) are entitled to move freely between the member States without being subject to discrimination, while non-EU citizens have to comply with the basic rules regarding entry. In particular, Directive No. 2004/38/EC provides for the free movement not only of EU citizens but also of non-EU citizens who have some connection to an EU citizen, for example, a spouse, partner, or caregiver.

---

[96] *The Code of Conduct*, above footnote 1, para 1.

[97] See A/CN.4/590, above footnote 81, 78–81.

[98] See Bruges Resolution, above footnote 54, para 7(3).

[99] See GA Res 65/133 (2011), 3 March 2011, para 27.

[100] IFRC 2009c, 139, citing Article 3 of Decree 64/2008/ND-CP on Mobilization, Receipt, Distribution and Use of Sources of Voluntary Donations, and Article 6 of Law no. 11/2008/QH12 on Red Cross Activities.

[101] Governmental Regulation No. 21 of 2008, above footnote 58, Article 34.

23.4.3 The Engagement of Local Personnel

Generally speaking, affected States want the relief actor to hire local personnel, both because the latter have a greater understanding of the relevant political and cultural climate in which they operate, and because, once trained, they may actively contribute to the post-emergency reconstruction, thus strengthening the local capabilities of the affected State.[102] The advantages associated with the engagement of local staff are widely recognized even by relief actors. First, the costs for foreign staff are much higher. Second, through engagement of local personnel, they may evade the many legal constraints that they may otherwise face with regard, *inter alia*, to the obtainment of visas and work permits and the recognition of foreign professional qualifications.

In practice, things are quite different, and many relief actors encounter problems in hiring local staff.[103] Particularly for NGOs, this has often been due to their lack of domestic legal personality[104]; however, they have also encountered difficulties in drafting proper employment contracts because they lack information about domestic legal requirements or because they find such requirements too complicated and time-consuming to apply. Finally, in some instances, they felt that the domestic legislation did not offer acceptable terms and conditions for employees; thus, the NGOs preferred to develop contracts that combined both their own national standards and the domestic standards.[105] Even UN organizations and IOs, which, by virtue of their privileges and immunities, should be able to operate largely outside the rules of domestic labor law, have been hampered by some States that have failed to recognize these privileges with regard to hiring local staff.[106]

International instruments do not generally deal with this issue. The only guidance provided is for military personnel in the MCDA Model Agreement and the NATO EADRU Model Agreement. Using the same language, the two instruments call on affected States to accept that the MCDA operation (or National Element of the EADRU) 'may recruit locally such personnel as it requires.' Upon the request of the Head of the MCDA operation (or National Element of the EADRU), the Government of the receiving State (or of the stricken EAPC nation) 'undertakes to facilitate the recruitment of qualified local staff … and to accelerate the process of

---

[102] See IFRC 2006c, 15, reporting that the Government of Sri Lanka, with the aim to ensure that locals were being employed wherever possible, delayed some visa applications for foreign staff where it felt there were sufficient people with the requisite skills and experience available in-country.

[103] See Fischer 2007, 120. Among States really encouraging the engagement of local staff, see IFRC 2010e, 40, reporting that to hire local personnel in Bulgaria, foreign entities are only required a registration, which is done immediately and the expenses are around 30 Euro.

[104] IFRC 2011, 41. For more on the domestic legal personality of NGOs see Chap. 19 by Silingardi in this volume.

[105] IFRC 2006a, 16–17 See Fischer 2007, 120.

[106] See Fischer 2007, 120.

such recruitment.'[107] The Oslo Guidelines further provide that, unless otherwise specified in the Agreement, 'locally recruited members of the MCDA operation shall enjoy the immunities concerning official acts carried out within the MCDA operation.'

Chap. 3 of the OCHA Field Administrative Manual requires that advertisements for the recruitment of national staff be placed in the local media. However, this notice has not been always followed. In Myanmar, for example, on the one hand OCHA announced vacancies for the database associate posts in a popular English newspaper and circulated these posts within the UN country network; on the other, vacancies for all other national posts were announces in the country's UN network only. As a consequence, while the vacancy announcement in the newspaper attracted 77 candidates, the advertisement circulated within the UN network attracted only 34 candidates.[108]

According to GA Resolution 51/243, dated 15 September 1997, UN agencies may also use gratis personnel on an exceptional and temporary basis, for specialized functions only and not to substitute regular staff. A specific use of this facility has been made by OCHA during the Myanmar operations, by entering into a MoU with nine governments for obtaining standby partners. However, due to the non-recruitment of regular staff to replace standby partners, OCHA relied on the services of two staff members provided by standby partners and one Junior Professional Officer to lead three suboffices for a period between 4 and 10 months, in contravention of the intent of GA Resolution 51/243.[109]

23.4.4 The Opening of Bank Accounts

Having no local bank accounts, humanitarian actors have to open private accounts in personal names, which could be problematic for the receipt of donations in general.[110] However, the existing IDRL instruments do not directly address this issue.[111] The most notable exception is represented by the recent Model Act of 2011, which in Articles 54 and 55 provides a number of facilities concerning currency and banking. It specifically States that the relevant ministry of the affected State shall: (1) facilitate the transit, through the territory, of such funds and currencies by eligible assisting international actors as they deem necessary to

---

[107] *Model Agreement Covering the Status of MCDA,* Annex I to the Oslo Guidelines, para 19; and NATO, *Model Agreement Covering the Status of National Elements of the EADRU on Mission on the Territory of a Stricken Nation*, para 5(6).

[108] OIOS, Internal Audit Division, *Audit Report, OCHA Operations in Myanmar,* 22 September 2009, para 37. Available at: http://usun.state.gov/documents/organization/159811.pdf. Accessed 12 February 2012.

[109] Ibid., para 36.

[110] See, as an example, IFRC 2006b, 19.

[111] Fischer 2007, 126.

provide international disaster relief and initial recovery assistance; (2) make available to eligible assisting international actors the most favorable legal exchange rates to the State's currency that is provided to foreign actors with regard to the funds to be used for the purpose of providing international disaster relief or initial recovery assistance; and (3) permit eligible assisting international actors to open accounts in domestic banks or in domestic branches of international banks.[112]

At the national level, the only instrument providing this kind of facilities is the Indonesian Guideline of 2011, which allows that providers of assistance may carry foreign and rupiah currencies to and from Indonesia according to monetary regulations and obtain legal exchange value in accordance with the disaster emergency operations; it also allows foreign personnel to open personal bank accounts for operational needs and their humanitarian activities, subject to checking with their respective embassies in Indonesia.[113]

23.4.5 Issues of Double Taxation and Insurance Coverage

The risk of being subjected to income tax in the country of operation is actually relevant to only a small section of actors involved in disaster-response activities. On the one hand, under the law on privileges and immunities, UN agencies and other IOs, along with their staff and diplomatic foreign State personnel, are generally exempted from income tax; on the other hand, many States, the IFRC, and some NGOs have entered into bilateral agreements to guard their nationals and staff against double taxation.[114] Other example of this practise can be found in the constitutive acts of some regional and subregional organizations. The CDEMA Agreement, for example, in Article 27 states that requesting States shall grant to the personnel of the sending State or personnel acting on its behalf 'exemption from taxes, duties or other charges, in respect of the performance of their functions in rendering assistance, as is accorded to diplomatic personnel in accordance with international law.'[115] Article 34 further provides that 'no tax shall be levied by Participating States in respect of salaries, other types of emoluments or any other form of payment made by CDEMA to the Executive Director and staff of CDEMA as well as experts performing missions for CDEMA.'

For disaster relief personnel not covered by such guarantees, income tax still remains an area of major concern. Under the tax law of the affected country, donations to foreign NGOs could be, for example, considered as taxable organizational income, and NGOs may be also be asked to deduct and withhold tax from their staff salaries.

---

112 *Model Act*, above footnote 56, Articles 54 and 55.

113 Indonesian Guidelines, above footnote 78, Ch. II, D.1(e)(f).

114 See Fischer 2007, 127.

115 See CDEMA Agreement, above footnote 9, Article 27(2)(c).

The issue of double taxation on disaster relief personnel has never been the object of specific regulation in IDRL instruments probably because it concerns, for the most part, NGOs, which have never sought proper consideration of their domestic legal capacity under international law. However, the recent Model Act presented under the auspices of the IFRC provides income tax exemptions to both international disaster relief actors and their personnel. In particular, it calls upon affected countries to neither treat such personnel as residents (or as having any connection with them) for tax purposes nor subject or require them to pay any taxes, duties, levies, social security contributions and governmental fees, or employment levies having similar effect.[116]

The issue of insurance coverage is much more complex. According to the IFRC desk study, the lack of insurance and medical coverage for the many risks that disaster relief personnel undertake is considered one of the most sensible issues in the discharge of their functions.[117]

Despite its importance, international guidance on this topic is of little use. Among the few exceptions, BSEC Agreement places upon the assisting States the duty to provide insurance to the members of the assistance team. However, it also provides that 'these expenses shall be included into the total bill for the assistance' that will normally be reimbursed by affected States.[118] The issue under discussion has been further handled in some bilateral treaties, such as the Agreement between Spain and Argentina: it provides that members of the emergency teams shall retain the social welfare and social security coverage provided for in the laws of the assisting State throughout their stay in the requesting State and that such personnel shall be entitled, in the requesting State, to all the appropriate emergency benefits, with the expenses being borne by the requested State as if the insured event had occurred in the territory of that State.[119] Other treaties focus on the coverage of free-of-charge medical expenses to disaster relief personnel.[120] The Finland-Estonia Agreement further provides that the assisting party shall insure the relief team in accordance with its regulations, while the requesting party shall reimburse such expenses.[121]

However, the scarce international regulation does not actually ensure that sufficient measures are in place to adequately cover health, disability, and death claims of the personnel of international assisting actors. Especially for NGOs,

---

116 See *Model Act*, above footnote 56, Article 52.

117 See Fischer 2007, 130.

118 1999 Agreement among the Governments of the Participating States of the Black Sea Economic Cooperation (BSEC) on collaboration in Emergency Assistance and Emergency Response to natural and man-made Disasters, Article 13.

119 See Spain–Argentina Agreement, above footnote 8, Article 19.

120 See Acuerdo entre el Gobierno del Reino de España y el Gobierno de la Federación de Rusia, above footnote 8, Article 9.

121 See 1996 Agreement between the Government of the Republic of Finland and the Government of the Republic of Estonia on Cooperation and Mutual Assistance in Cases of Accidents, Article 10.

many problems still remain unsolved, including wide variations in the level of coverage of medical expenses, disability and loss of life, as well as increasing difficulty in obtaining insurance coverage, often with vague and not fully understandable exclusion clauses.

23.5 Special Provisions Concerning the Legal Status of Military Personnel

In the last few decades, foreign military assets (i.e., personnel, equipment, and services of military nature provided by governments with the consent of the affected State) have played a major role in supporting disaster-response operations.[122] During the international response to the Haiti Earthquake, for example, 26 countries provided significant military assets, including field hospitals, troops, military aircraft, hospital ships, cargo ships, port handling equipment, and helicopters.[123] With this perspective, not only civil military co-ordination has been a vital part of disaster relief operations, but also specific provisions concerning the legal status of military personnel became of great relevance.

As a general rule, military assets should be employed by UN humanitarian agencies only as a last resort, i.e., only in the absence of any other civilian alternative to support urgent humanitarian needs within the time required. Although their comparative advantage over civil response in terms of timeliness and effectiveness has been proved beyond doubt,[124] from an international legal standpoint there is currently no clear and satisfactory set of rules concerning the legal status of military assets within the affected country. In particular, many in the humanitarian community harshly criticize the decision to deploy military assets because it concerns the essential attributes of State power and thus may present a challenge to the fundamental principles of impartiality and neutrality that represent the unanimous basis for disaster relief operations.[125]

Given the national security implications, there are some countries, such as China and North Korea, that do not as a rule accept foreign military actors as part of disaster-response operations; instead, they prohibit the signing of Status of Forces Agreements (SOFAs) or other treaties inviting foreign military forces, unless with the legislature's approval. On the other hand, there are some countries that have provided special procedures for facilitating the receipt of (at least some)

---

122 General Assembly GA/111, *Adopting text on bolstering effectiveness of military, civil assets in disaster response*, Sixty-fifth General Assembly Plenary, 107th Meeting (AM), July 1, 2011. On this topic, see also Chap. 24 by Calvi Parisetti in this volume.

123 Bhattacharjee and Lossio 2011, 29.

124 See *The Effectiveness of Foreign Military Assets in Natural Disaster Response, a Report by the Stockholm International Peace Research Institute*, 2008, at 9.

125 Ibid., 32. See also A/CN.4/590, above footnote 81, 114.

military forces. In Australia, for example, members (including civilian members) of the armed forces of countries with whom Australia has a Status of Forces Agreement, members of the armed forces of the Asia–Pacific region and of the Commonwealth, and members of foreign navies have, as a class, been granted special purpose visas. As a consequence, they may enter Australia without an individually issued visa provided they carry their identity papers and movement orders, and in the case of navy crews, provided the ship on which they travel has appropriate authority to enter Australia.[126]

At the global level, the primary resource for States on this question are the Oslo Guidelines on the Use of Foreign Military and Civil Defence Assets in Disaster Relief, which, as a general rule, call upon affected States to facilitate the deployment of Military and Civil Defence Assets (MCDA), ensuring them the waiver of visa requirements, free access to disaster zones and recognition of certificates.[127]

In particular, the Oslo Guidelines make a distinction between individual UN MCDA personnel and foreign MCDA personnel. On the basis of Article 105 of the UN Charter, UN MCDA personnel may be granted, when they are deployed at the request of the UN Office for the Coordination of Humanitarian Affairs (OCHA), the status of experts on mission for the UN according to Article 6 of the UN Convention on the Privileges and Immunities of 1946 and thus may benefit from all the rights concerned.[128] As regards foreign MCDA, the Oslo Guidelines perceive that most of them are mobilized and deployed in a natural disaster bilaterally or under regional or alliance agreements. The main tasks of these agreements are to grant more specific facilitation measures to military assets in each other's territory and to determine both the role that international forces may play in domestic disaster relief and their cooperation with State agencies. If such agreements have not been concluded, it is recommended that States, wishing to act bilaterally, should make use of the 'Model Agreement covering the Status of MCDA' set out in Annex I of the Guidelines.

The Model Agreement is greatly shaped upon the NATO SOFA.[129] In both instruments, members shall be exempt from passport and visa regulations, and from immigration inspection on entering or leaving the territory of a receiving State. They shall also be exempt from any regulations of the receiving State governing the registration and control of aliens; however, they shall not acquire any right to permanent residence or domicile in the affected State. For the purpose of entry and departure, members of the MCDA, as well as members of a force under the NATO SOFA, shall present on demand a personal identity card issued by

---

[126] IFRC 2009a, 82; and IFRC 2010f, 33.

[127] 2006 *Guidelines on The Use of Foreign Military and Civil Defence Assets in Disaster Relief*, (Revision 1.1 November 2007), Article 60.

[128] Ibid., para 30.

[129] 1951 Agreement between the Parties to the North Atlantic Treaty Regarding the Status of Their Forces, Article 3(1).

the sending State, as well as an individual or collective movement order issued by or under the authority of the Head of the operation.[130] The same language appears in the 'NATO EADRU Model Agreement.'[131]

Concerning the operational rights of military personnel, the MCDA Model Agreement and the NATO EADRU Model Agreement state that the government of the affected territory shall accept as valid, without tax or fee, a certificate provided on request by the Head of the MCDA operation (or National Element of the EADRU) in respect of the technical and professional qualifications of any of its members practicing a profession or similar occupation in connection with the operation.[132] From this perspective, the NATO SOFA is narrower as it limits the obligation of the receiving State to accept as valid, without a driving test or fee, the driving permits or licenses issued by the sending States.[133]

A more comprehensive approach for the facilitation and utilization of military and civil assets and capacities has been provided for in certain regional and subregional agreements, such as the ASEAN. Based on the AADMER, the ASEAN developed a number of procedures for deployment of military assets; identification of military personnel, related officials, and vehicle markings; coordination with the Requesting/Receiving Party, and the general obligation of military personnel to respect national laws and regulations, as well as of the Requesting/Receiving Party to provide, to the extent possible, local facilities and services for the proper and effective administration of assistance.[134]

23.6 The Duty to Respect International and National Laws

As a general rule, all international disaster relief actors and their staff shall work in accordance with the principles of humanity, neutrality, and impartiality, which are already included in major international instruments, such as GA Resolution 46/182 and the IDRL Guidelines, as well as in a number of existing domestic disaster management laws and policies,[135] and in specific international standards.[136] Relief entities and their personnel also have to respect the local culture and customs; their activities shall not be used to achieve political or ideological goals, or to interfere in the domestic affairs of the receiving State.

---

[130] Ibid., Article 3(2); and *MCDA Model Agreement*, above footnote 107, para 30.

[131] *NATO EADRU Model Agreement*, above footnote 107, Article 6(8).

[132] *MCDA Model Agreement*, above footnote 107, para 35; and *NATO EADRU Model Agreement*, above footnote 107, Article 6(14).

[133] NATO SOFA, above footnote 129, Article 4.

[134] See *SASOP procedures*, above footnote 43, section 6, 26.

[135] See *Model Act*, above footnote 56, 66, citing as examples the Philippines Disaster Risk Management Act 2010, Article 2; and the Panama's Manual on Procedures for the Foreign Ministry in the Case of Disasters 2009, section 4.

[136] See generally *The Code of Conduct*, above footnote 1, paras 2–5.

From a legal standpoint, disaster relief personnel further have to respect and observe all the laws and regulations of the receiving State as well as the applicable international law,[137] including the human rights of persons affected by disasters and obligations in relation to the protection of refugees and internally displaced persons, and with international humanitarian law where applicable.[138] However, at least when human rights guarantees and protection are concerned, the roles and responsibilities of relief actors in this particular context are generally secondary as they must be seen in relation to the primary duty of the State (or other relevant authorities) to protect the population under their jurisdiction (Sect. 23.2).

The need for compliance with national laws and standards is commonly referred to as 'a key requirement' underlying the provisions of most of the law on disaster relief assistance.[139] In particular, it is included in many international instruments, of both declaratory and regulatory nature,[140] and in almost all the bilateral treaties in force. Some instruments further provide specific recommendations to ensure such compliance. The AAMDER, in particular, places an obligation on the head of the relief-providing organization to ensure observance of national laws and regulations, and on the receiving State to co-operate in ensuring observance.[141]

To fully ensure that the obligations of the international assisting actors and their staff under the IDRL are not in contrast with national laws, several treaties incorporate clauses requiring that certain provisions are applied and interpreted in accordance with national law.[142] For example, the Tampere Convention provides that 'the requesting State Party shall retain the authority to reject all or part of any telecommunication assistance offered pursuant to this Convention in accordance with the requesting State Party's existing national law and policy.'[143] Similarly, the Convention on Assistance in the Case of a Nuclear Accident contains a saving clause in order not to 'prevent compensation or indemnity available under any applicable international agreement or national law of any State.'[144]

---

[137] See, for example, Macalister-Smith 1991, 11; Inter-American Convention, above footnote 12, Article 9(d); Nuclear Accident Convention, above footnote 9, Article 8(7); Tampere Convention, above footnote 9, Article 5(7); IDRL Guidelines, above footnote 55, para 4(1); and, to the extent that military assets are involved, MCDA Model Agreement, above footnote 107, para 5. See also Elucidation of Government Regulation No. 23 of 2008 Concerning Participation of International Institutions and Foreign Non-Governmental Institution in Disaster Management, *Supplement to State Gazette of Republic of Indonesia No. 4830, section 1.*

[138] For a more detailed comment on of the IDRL in relation with other branches of International Law see the Chap. 2 by Venturini in this volume.

[139] A/CN.4/590, above footnote 81, 53.

[140] Among the declaratory text, see GA Res. 46/182, above footnote 47, annex, para 5; Macalister-Smith 1991, paras 9 (b), and 22 (a); *IDRL Guidelines*, above footnote 55, para 4.

[141] AADMER, above footnote 12, Article 13(2).

[142] See A/CN.4/590, above footnote 81, 54–55.

[143] See Tampere Convention, above footnote 9, Article 4(5).

[144] See Nuclear Accident Convention, above footnote 9, Article 10(3).

Other instruments, such as the 2003 Bruges Declaration of the IDI, adopt the opposite view, calling upon States to alter their national law so as to take into account certain provisions of IDRL, for example, concerning facilities relative to humanitarian assistance.[145] A few instruments of national law, including the 2000 Belize Disaster Preparedness and Response Act and the 2006 Saint Lucia Disaster Management Act, share the same view. According to such instruments, the executive authorities of both States may proclaim that a treaty or other international agreement, where relevant to the response to disaster, should be part of the respective domestic law for the duration of any disaster emergency, and that the provisions of that treaty shall for the duration of any disaster emergency, as if enacted in the respective Act.[146]

When assistance is performed outside the above-mentioned legal frameworks, contrasts between international obligations and national laws should be tackled under the rules of general international law on *ad hoc* basis. That means that, at least when *hard law* instruments are concerned, an affected State cannot rely on its own legislation to limit the scope of its international obligations. On the other hand, where *soft law* instruments are concerned the situation is more complex. However, the present author is of the opinion that to minimize the bureaucratic and legal obstacles that affected States can oppose, the disaster-response community (i.e., all the disaster relief actors whose assistance has been activated through a specific legal framework of either multilateral or bilateral nature) should have the legitimate expectation that activities performed in conformity with these obligations shall not be biased under domestic law, even if they are in contrast with specific internal laws or regulations. However, that approach does not cover civil and criminal liability issues for personal injuries and property damages resulting from actions undertaken during the course of responding to a disaster, which are subjected to specific rules.

23.6.1 Civil and Criminal Liability

Issues concerning the civil and criminal liability of disaster relief personnel are not managed in a comprehensive manner through an overarching agreement or a

---

145 A/CN.4/590, above footnote 81, 56, citing the *Resolution on'Humanitarian Assistance,'* above footnote 54, section 7, para 2, which provides that 'States should adopt laws and regulations and conclude bilateral or multilateral treaties providing for facilities relative to humanitarian assistance.'

146 See Belize Disaster Preparedness and Response Act, Chapter 145 (revised edition 2000), Article 29; and Saint Lucia Disaster Management Act, No. 30 of 2006, Article 22. Accessed 22 February 2012.

model in place but are rather regulated through 'a variety of domestic provisions and international arrangements.'[147] Under this perspective, while international instruments focus on inter-State allocation of liability and compensation, issues of individual liability are addressed in numerous domestic laws.[148]

The general trend in all the international instruments in force is to adopt a liability paradigm based on prior allocation. Although the choices may vary across different agreements, that does not lead to a confused fragmentation of liability rules. With this perspective, IOs and their personnel, the IFRC, as recognized by its status agreement, and State officials enjoy immunity from administrative, civilian, and criminal jurisdiction of the host State, at least for acts performed in their official capacity (Sect. 23.2). For other actors, almost all treaties, of both multilateral and bilateral nature, contain provisions calling for a waiver of liability for the assisting States, for their protection against third-party claims, and also for immunity of their personnel. However, these provisions shall not apply in cases of wilful misconduct by the individuals who caused death, injury, loss, or damage.

Only very few instruments break this paradigm, considering the assisting party fully responsible for any illegal act of its personnel, such as, for example, the 1997 Chile-Argentina Agreement.[149] Other instruments apply variations to this paradigm, exclusively with respect to the compensation issue. Decision No. 2004/277/EC envisages that compensation shall be provided by the State of origin of the personnel causing damage,[150] and another instrument places upon both the requested and the requesting States the duty to co-operate in facilitating compensation in case of damage suffered by third parties.[151] Further provisions provide that the requesting State agrees to compensate the assisting State or organization for the death or injury of their personnel.[152]

As for bilateral treaties, at least on the topic of compensation they generally adopt a different approach. Almost all of them indeed provide that the Contracting Parties waive any right that they may have to claim compensation from each other in case of damage to property caused by a member of the relief team in the line of their duty, and any in case of damage to the health or death of a member of the relief team when such an event takes place in relation to the performance of tasks

[147] See United States Defense Threats Reduction Agency, *Foreign Consequence Management Legal Deskbook* (January 2007), at section 4(4), para 1. Available at: http://www.dtra.mil/documents/business/current/FCMLegalDeskbook.pdf. Accessed 22 February 2012.

[148] For more on individual liability and compensation, please see A/CN.4/590, above footnote 81, 137.

[149] 1997 Agreement between the Argentina Republic and the Republic of Chile regarding Cooperation in Case of Catastrophes, Article 9.

[150] 1986 Agreement on Cooperation concerning Rescue Services in the Frontier Areas between Finland and Norway, Article 9.

[151] *OJ 2004* L 87.

[152] Nuclear Accident Convention, above footnote 9, Article 10. See also Fischer 2007, 146.

related to assistance mission.[153] However, some of them allow the receiving State to claim compensation in case the assisting personnel caused such damages knowingly or through gross negligence[154]; and most of them return to the receiving State liability model with regard to the compensation for third-party damage or loss. The Finland–Estonia Agreement further completes this liability paradigm providing that the Party requesting assistance shall provide reimbursement for injuries caused to other persons in its territory by relief personnel of the assisting State, according to the same law that would apply had its employees caused the injury.[155]

For military personnel, issues of liability may be addressed in SOFAs or Visiting Forces Agreements (VFAs). For example, Article 8 of the NATO SOFA completely waives any liability for damage to any property of the Contracting Party caused by a member or an employee of the armed services of the other Contracting Party in the execution of his duties concerning the operation.[156] Under both the NATO EADRU Agreement and the Oslo Guidelines, all members of the emergency teams, including locally recruited personnel, enjoy immunity from legal process in respect of all acts performed in their official capacity, even after they cease to be members of the team. The sending State may exercise its domestic jurisdiction only with respect to crimes or offenses committed by members of the team; for civilian proceedings, one may establish, according to circumstances, whether the proceeding is related to official duties or not. In the former case, the proceeding shall be discontinued and the general immunity shall apply; in the latter, the proceeding may continue. However, both agreements provide that, in case the member of the team is unable because of his official duties or authorized absence to protect his interests, the court of the affected State shall suspend the proceeding but not for more than 90 days.[157] Under this perspective, one can also note that Article 8 of the 1994 Convention on the Safety of the UN and Associated Personnel, which is applicable to emergency relief operations under the provision of the 2005 Optional Protocol, requires that except as otherwise provided in an applicable SOFA, if any UN or associated personnel has been captured or detained

---

[153] See 2004 Agreement between the Government of the Republic of Latvia and the Government of the Republic of Hungary on co-operation and mutual assistance in the event of disasters and other large scale accidents, Article 11. See also 1988 Agreement between the Federal Republic of Germany and the Kingdom of the Netherlands on mutual assistance in the event of disasters, including serious accidents, Article 10; and Spain-Argentina Agreement, above footnote 10, Article 17.

[154] See Spain–Russia Agreement, above footnote 8, Article 13.

[155] See Finland–Estonia Agreement, above footnote 121, Article 11; and Austria-Jordan Agreement, above footnote 47, Article 10.

[156] *NATO SOFA*, above footnote 127, Article 8. Paras 5 and 6 of the same article further provide procedures in dealing with claims by third parties for damages caused by employees of the armed forces in the performance of their official duties and with claims arising from inactions in the performance of official duties.

[157] See *MCDA Model Agreement*, above footnote 107, para 7; *NATO EADRU Model Agreement*, above footnote 107, Article 7(6).

in the course of the performance of their duties and their identity has been established, they shall not be subject to interrogation and they shall be promptly released and returned to the UN or other appropriated authority.[158]

As noted, further rules are found in VFAs. For example, according to Article 6 of the 1998 VFA between United States and Philippines, both Governments waive all claims for damage to property or people arising from military activities covered by the VFA, including disaster relief operations. As regards jurisdiction, Philippine authorities are granted jurisdiction over the US personnel who commit criminal offenses on Philippine territory. However, the United States continues to maintain jurisdictional authority over its personnel with respect to violations of the US law, and it may request personnel accused under Philippine law to be held in custody by the US authorities rather than by Philippine authorities.[159]

23.7 Conclusions

The IDRL has been described as a 'rather scattered and heterogeneous collection of instruments.'[160] In particular, as we have seen, it has a number of gaps and weaknesses that affect its capability to effectively address the many bureaucratic constraints that come up with regard to emergency workers' gaining access to the affected territory and carrying out their functions.

What mainly prevents international law from drawing up a comprehensive legal framework on the rights and duties of disaster relief personnel is that receiving States retain, as a natural appendix to their sovereign authority, the exclusive power to regulate the access of foreign persons and entities into their territory. From this perspective, the preservation of national pride, a perceived ability to be able to deal with disaster internally, mistrust of the motivations behind the provision of international assistance and concerns that international actors would usurp the primary role of the government in responding to disasters are only a few of the reasons that could stand behind the decision of a disaster-affected government to restrict the operation of relief actors.[161]

Once accepted as valid contributors by the affected State, the special rights of aid workers are mainly based, as already seen, on special agreements in treaties; outside the treaties, the assisting States, IOs, and NGOs have to respect the rights of the receiving State.[162] However, besides one sector (i.e., the entry visa

[158] See 1994 Convention on the Safety of UN and Associated Personnel, above footnote 21, Article 8.

[159] 1998 Agreement between the Government of the Republic of the Philippines and the Government of the United States of America Regarding the Treatment of United States Armed Forces Visiting the Philippines, Article 6.

[160] See Fischer 2007, 354.

[161] IFRC 2003, 10.

[162] Jakovljević 2004, 263.

requirements) that tends to be regulated by treaties, there are other clearly identifiable areas that are inadequately regulated or are omitted almost entirely from these agreements. Among others, these areas include: work permits; legal recognition of foreign professional qualifications; recognition of the domestic legal personality of NGOs; rules on the engagement of local staff; the opening of bank accounts and the insurance coverage of disaster relief personnel; double taxation issues and freedom of movement of relief personnel. In all of these areas, the rules vary depending on the laws of the particular State involved, the nationality of the particular aid workers, the international status of their employer, and/or the country from which they begin their travel.[163]

The experience of the last few decades has clearly demonstrated that the most significant results with regard to legal and administrative facilitation for humanitarian organizations and their personnel have been achieved through multilateral efforts at the regional and/or subregional level where the parties are most accustomed to dealing with one another. The EU and ASEAN involvement in disaster relief operations certainly represent the most notable examples of this practice. An alternative solution could be reached by the strengthening of rules in national laws under the guidance of the IDRL Guidelines or through the recent Model Act, which further provides useful tools. However, only a limited number of countries in the last few years have changed their laws in accordance with the IDRL Guidelines, most of them only with regard to the creation of specific rules for expedited or free-of-charge visa procedures for relief personnel. From this perspective, it thus seems essential that the SC and the GA, from a top-down perspective, put constant pressure on States not only to ratify the relevant global conventions but also to effectively ensure the rights of humanitarian organizations and their staff in domestic laws and regulations.

References

Bhattacharjee A, Lossio R (2011) Evaluation of OCHA response to the Haiti earthquake. Final report. http://ochanet.unocha.org

Bothe M (1980) Rapport spécial sur un projet d'accord-type relative aux actions de secours humanitaires. Committee on International Medical and Humanitarian Law, International Law Association, Report on the 59th conference, Belgrade, 1978, pp 520–527

Bothe M (2000) Relief actions. In: Bernhardt R (ed) Encyclopedia of Public International Law, vol 4. Elsevier Science Publishers, Amsterdam, pp 168–174

Dinstein Y (2000) The right to humanitarian assistance in peacetime. Naval War Coll Rev 53:77–92

Fidler DP (2007) Governing catastrophes: security, health and humanitarian assistance. Int Rev Red Cross 89:247–270

[163] In Cambodia, some well-known NGOs tend to receive visas more readily than those that are smaller and relatively unknown. See IFRC 2009a, 70.

Fischer D (2007) Law and legal issues in international disaster response: a desk study. International Federation of Red Cross and Red Crescent Societies, Geneva
IFRC (2003) Report on findings from South Asia, Southern Africa and Central Americas
IFRC (2005a) Nepal: laws, policies, planning and practices on international disaster response
IFRC (2005b) Fiji: laws, policies, planning and practices on international disaster response
IFRC (2005c) Indonesia: laws, policies, planning and practices on international disaster response
IFRC (2006a) Legal issues from the international response to the Tsunami in Indonesia
IFRC (2006b) Legal issues from the international response to the Tsunami in Thailand
IFRC (2006c) Legal issues from the international response to the Tsunami in Sri Lanka
IFRC (2007) Legal issues from the international response to tropical storm Stan in Guatemala
IFRC (2009a) Legal preparedness for responding to disasters and communicable disease emergencies: study report—Cambodia
IFRC (2009b) Legal preparedness for responding to disasters and communicable disease emergencies: study report—Lao PDR
IFRC (2009c) Legal preparedness for responding to disasters and communicable disease emergencies: study report—Vietnam
IFRC (2010a) Analysis of law in the European Union pertaining to cross-border disaster relief
IFRC (2010b) Analysis of law in the EU and a selection of member states pertaining to Cross-Border Disaster relief
IFRC (2010c) Legal aspects of international disaster response in Dutch emergencies and crisis situations, country report by the Netherlands Red Cross
IFRC (2010d) Analysis of law in the United Kingdom pertaining to Cross-Border Disaster Relief, prepared for the British Red Cross by the British Institute of International and Comparative Law
IFRC (2010e) Normative requirements for receipt, originations and transit of disaster relief through the territory of the republic of Bulgaria, prepared for the Bulgarian Red Cross by Interlex, Ltd
IFRC (2010f) Legal preparedness for international disaster response in Australia—laws, policies, planning and practices
IFRC (2011) International Disaster Response Law (IDRL) in Uganda
Jakovljević B (2004) International Disaster Relief Law. Israel Yearb Human Rights 34:251–286
Macalister-Smith P (1991) International guidelines on humanitarian assistance. Max Planck Institute for Comparative Public Law and International Law, Heidelberg
Okere B, Makawa EM (2001) Global solidarity and the international response to disasters. In: Caron Leben (ed) The international aspects of natural and industrial catastrophes. Martinus Nijhoff Publishers, The Hague, pp 429–456
Valencia-Ospina E (2011) Fourth report on the protection of persons in the event of disasters, ILC 63rd session, A/CN.4/643

Chapter 24
The Use of Civil and Military Defense Assets in Emergency Situations

Piero Calvi Parisetti

Abstract The humanitarian landscape has changed considerably during the last two decades. On the one hand, large population displacements as a result of protracted conflict seem to be on a downward trend. On the other, the number of people affected by natural disasters—particularly sudden onset ones related to meteorological hazards—has grown exponentially. With this backdrop, the use of international military and civil defense assets in humanitarian operations has grown significantly. In large-scale sudden onset natural disasters, responding to the needs of affected populations often requires logistical capacity that only military actors, often international military actors, possess. In conflict-related crises, the drive toward deeper integration among the political, security, and humanitarian agendas had a significant impact on the role of the military, expanding they remit more broadly into the delivery of development and humanitarian assistance. This has generated impassioned debate within the humanitarian community, whose principal positions have been that the military are a poor fit for such work, and that co-opting assistance as a tool to achieve local, national, and even international security is not effective. Humanitarians have also argued that blurring the distinction between humanitarian and military, and consequently, other political objectives, not only puts humanitarian staff at risk but, by undermining the key principles of impartiality and neutrality, also endangers the humanitarian enterprise as a whole. The use of military and civil defense assets in emergency situations does not benefit from an internationally recognized binding legal framework. All that is available are two sets of non-binding guidelines developed with the participation of a large number of stakeholders, crucially involving member States, and another two reference documents developed by the Inter-

P. Calvi Parisetti (✉)
Istituto per gli Studi di Politica Internazionale, Via Clerici 5,
20121 Milano, Italy
e-mail: pcalvip@gmail.com

A. de Guttry et al. (eds.), *International Disaster Response Law*,
DOI: 10.1007/978-90-6704-882-8_24,

Agency Standing Committee (IASC) and therefore relevant primarily for the humanitarian community.

Keywords Military and civil defense assets · Humanitarian assistance · Disaster response · Disaster preparedness · Civilian-military coordination · Integrated mission · Humanitarian principles

Contents

24.1 Introduction

The humanitarian need created by large-scale sudden onset disasters can overwhelm the capacity of civilian authorities and traditional humanitarian actors; responding to the needs of affected populations often requires logistical capacity that only military actors, often international military actors, possess. This trend largely began in earnest with the deployment of significant international military assets in support to the humanitarian response to Hurricane Mitch in Central America in 1999 and has continued subsequently with the deployment of air assets for transport, search, and rescue capacities and field hospitals in a range of crises from the Bam earthquake in 2003, the Kashmir earthquake in 2005, and the Indian Ocean tsunami the same year, to the use of UN peacekeeping assets in the humanitarian response to the Haiti earthquake in 2010, and the use of US naval assets in the aftermath of the earthquake and tsunami in Japan in 2011. The role of the military is not limited to the post-disaster response; international military actors also play an important role in supporting disaster preparedness, including building the capacity of national militaries in this area, as demonstrated by Australian military support to Asia Pacific nations.

Increasingly, disaster management is seen as a core task of many national, as well as multilateral, militaries. However, in practice, despite existing guidance on the use of military assets in humanitarian response, their use continues to be a source of tension between international humanitarian and military actors in some contexts. This is particularly the case in contexts such as Cyclone Nargis in 2008, the Haitian earthquake in 2010, the Pakistan floods the same year, where disaster preparedness and response are complicated by pre-existing armed conflict or chronic political violence or instability or ongoing integrated international intervention strategy. The principle of last resort is key to ensuring principled approaches to the use of military assets that are necessary to effectively support, rather than undermine, the humanitarian response. However, there remain real differences between the principles and the practice. Despite much operational level debate, key questions remain regarding international military engagement in such complex situations; how does the role of international military in disaster management change with respect to complex emergencies? How does this impact upon civil–military coordination? Are existing frameworks adequate for governing interaction in such environments?

24.2 An Evolving Operational Landscape

The first decade of this century has seen the emergence of what many now call a "new humanitarian paradigm". This term is used to describe the prevailing trend of dramatic growth in the number of people affected worldwide by sudden onset natural disasters, particularly of hydrometeorological origin. Such growth is supported on the one hand by global trends such as overall population growth, environmental degradation, and urbanization, increasing the vulnerability of larger and larger sectors of the world's population to a range of disasters, and, on the other, by the spectacular growth in the frequency and intensity of meteorological events, fuelled by global warming. Furthermore, population growth and urbanization are also responsible for the sub-trend that sees a significant growth in what we have today known as "urban disasters". In terms of figures, the EM-DAT database,[1] maintained by the University of Louvain in Belgium, has recorded a rise in the number of natural disasters since 1987. In 1988, the year EM-DAT was created, around 240 natural disasters where reported—the record at that time. Since 2000, the annual number has fluctuated between around 380 and around 520, peaking at 550 in 2002 and then leveling off somewhat. Even more significantly, during the same period the number of people yearly affected by natural disasters has grown from around 50 million to over 300 million. In

[1] http://www.emdat.be/natural-disasters-trends, accessed 14 February 2012.

2007, the UN Under-Secretary-General for Humanitarian Affairs, John Holmes, characterized the high incidence of hydrometeorological disasters as a "mega-disaster" linked to climate change.[2] Based on the trends presented by EM-DAT and according to the data provided by the Intergovernmental Panel on Climate Change, the incidence and intensity of climate-related hazards is likely to grow even further in the future.[3] The incidence of geological hazards is harder to predict. However, the global trends outlined above are likely to make such hazards have an even greater human cost.

Critical to the definition of "new humanitarian paradigm" are also the consequences on the population and the nature of the humanitarian response to the growing number of climate-related disasters. It is important to understand how the growth in the number of people affected derives largely from the growth in the *number* of extreme meteorological events. Although some events are indeed huge and affect millions of people at a time, the vast majority of the "new disasters" are of small or medium scale—they have a devastating impact on the local populations but rarely trigger the need for international humanitarian assistance. Furthermore, hydrometeorological hazards result in disasters affecting large numbers of people, but causing relatively few deaths.[4] Lastly, the humanitarian consequences of floods and windstorms are of relatively short duration, especially if compared with chronic, conflict-related crises lasting 20 or 30 years. It is also critical to understand that such disasters are responded to almost exclusively at the local level and many argue that the true role of international assistance vis-à-vis such emerging trends is not in response, but rather in preparedness, developing the capacity of the very local responders who are most likely to be on the forefront when disaster strikes. This is well reflected in a growing number of military-run assistance programs that support local first responders and develop their capacities rather than directly provide assistance once a disaster has happened. Such engagement of international military actors may be in part determined by, or at least is perceived as being part of, a strategy to support domestic political or security objectives. This may include demonstrating the added moral and economic value of national militaries at the time when defense budgets are coming under pressure, or the explicit use of aid to support national security objectives.

The concept of a "new humanitarian paradigm" is introduced in contrast to an "old paradigm" which appears to reflect more the recent history of humanitarian assistance than today's reality. The "old paradigm" refers to wide-ranging international humanitarian assistance rendered in situations of conflict, often protracted, resulting primarily in large-scale population displacements. In such situations, technically defined as Complex Emergencies, the national government is

---

[2] Sir John Holmes in an interview to AFP. See http://www.earthlab.com/articles/climatechange warnsun.aspx

[3] Pachauri and Reisinger 2007.

[4] Inter-Agency Standing Committee (IASC); World Health Organization (WHO). Protecting the health of vulnerable people from the humanitarian consequences of climate change and climate-related disasters 2009.

either altogether absent or has a very limited capacity (and, in some cases, willingness) to provide for the affected population. Virtually, anything the beneficiaries receive in terms of goods and services comes from international assistance through humanitarian organizations, and humanitarian assistance is often critical to the very survival of huge numbers of people. This has been the prevailing face of the humanitarian world for more than 20 years, with chronic crises such as Liberia, Sierra Leone, Cote d'Ivoire, the Great Lakes of central Africa, Angola, Uganda, Sri Lanka, and many others posing basically the same challenges year after year to the humanitarian community. Then, practically at the same time when the new paradigm was becoming increasingly apparent, many of these crises found a positive solution, and the number of Complex Emergencies around the world is today at its lowest since the definition was introduced in the early 1990 s. The nature of the engagement of the international community in these fragile and conflict-affected States also changed significantly, and this also has a major bearing on the nature of the militaries' involvement. Today, for many governments and multilateral organizations, integration, in its various models, is the principal framework for engagement. Whether bilateral or multilateral, integrated interventions commonly seek to combine aid, the promotion of political reform, governance, and rule of law, and military or security engagement in pursuit of one overarching political goal. This has had a significant impact on the role of the military, traditionally very little involved in the "old humanitarian paradigm" crises, expanding their remit more broadly into the delivery of development and humanitarian assistance. This has generated impassioned debate within the humanitarian community, whose principal positions have been that the military are a poor fit for such work, and that co-opting assistance as a tool to achieve local, national, and even international security is not effective. Humanitarians have also argued that blurring the distinction between humanitarian and military, and consequently, other political objectives, not only puts humanitarian staff at risk (since they may be considered as part of a military/political strategy by other belligerents) but, by undermining the key principles of impartiality and neutrality, also endangers the humanitarian enterprise as a whole.

24.3 The Regulatory Framework

Under the 1949 Geneva Convention Relative to the Protection of Civilian Persons in Time of War (GC IV), in cases of occupation, the Occupying Power (OP), to the fullest extent of the means available to it, is legally obliged to provide for and ensure provision of adequate food and medical supplies and health services. When supply is inadequate, the OP shall agree to relief schemes on behalf of the population of the occupied territory. GC IV also clearly recognizes the role of States and impartial humanitarian organizations in undertaking such relief schemes and obliges the OP to facilitate them.[5] In conjunction with these provisions and bearing

[5] Articles 55, 56, 59 and 60 of GC IV.

in mind that the OP is not only composed of military forces, humanitarian organizations have argued that even in cases of occupation, relief schemes should be under civilian control and direction, and to the extent possible in the given circumstances, be carried out by the civilian components of the OP, impartial humanitarian organizations and/or other civilian actors. Hence, the military's primary role in relief, if any, should be one of facilitation, even though it might have a role in directly providing relief and a duty to do so, especially when requested, authorized, and undertaken as an essential last resort in meeting critical needs when civilian means are unavailable.[6]

Apart from these rather unspecific and somewhat controversial prescriptions from the Geneva Convention, the use of civil and military defense assets in humanitarian operations does not benefit from an internationally recognized binding legal framework. All that is available are two sets of non-binding guidelines developed with the participation of a large number of stakeholders, crucially involving States, and another two reference documents developed by the Inter-Agency Standing Committee (IASC)[7] and therefore relevant primarily for the humanitarian community. These are only consensus document and their prescriptions do not constitute an obligation for the IASC members. The rationale for their inclusion in a review of our regulatory framework is therefore relatively thin. They are included in this review as they represent the internal policy reaction of the humanitarian community to changes in the operational landscape and a link with the two sets of guidelines developed by much larger groups of stakeholders.

24.3.1 The Oslo Guidelines

The "Oslo Guidelines" were originally prepared over a period of 2-years beginning in 1992. They were the result of a collaborative effort that culminated in an international conference in Oslo, Norway, in January 1994 and were released in May 1994.[8] They were intended to address the need for principles and standards and to provide improved coordination in the use of military and civil defense assets in response to natural, technological, and environmental emergencies in peacetime.

---

[6] Bessler and Seki 2006, 4–10.

[7] The Inter-Agency Standing Committee (IASC) is the top policy-making body of the humanitarian community, involving the key UN and non-UN humanitarian partners. The IASC was established in June 1992 following United Nations General Assembly Resolution 46/182 on the strengthening of humanitarian assistance. General Assembly Resolution 48/57 affirmed its role as the primary mechanism for inter-agency coordination of humanitarian assistance.

[8] The following States and Organizations were involved in this effort: Argentina, Austria, Belgium, Germany, Indonesia, Italy, Japan, Kenya, the Netherlands, Norway, Russian Federation, Switzerland, United Kingdom of Great Britain and Northern Ireland, United States of America, AFDRU, Brown University's Watson Institute, DHA, European Union/ECHO, ICDO, ICRC, IFRC, INSARAG, NATO, Steering Committee for Humanitarian Response, UNHCR, UN Legal Liaison Office, University of Naples, University of Ruhr, WHO, and Western European Union. Over 180 delegates from 45 States and 25 organizations attended the conference.

A decade later, the unprecedented deployment in 2005 of military forces and assets in support of humanitarian response to natural disasters, following an increasing trend over the past years, confirmed the need to update the 1994 Guidelines. In particular, it was recognized that new impetus was needed to create awareness of the Guidelines, particularly among countries that contribute military and civil defense asset. The Consultative Group on the Use of Military and Civil Defense Assets (MCDA), at its annual meeting in December 2005, tasked UN OCHA's Civil–Military Coordination Section with this revision, to reflect current terminology and organizational changes, following a layout similar to the 2003 "Guidelines on the Use of Military and Civil Defense Assets to Support United Nations Humanitarian Activities in Complex Emergencies" ("MCDA Guidelines"). Norway, Switzerland, and Sweden took the lead in the update, facilitated by OCHA's Civil–Military Coordination Section. The revised Oslo Guidelines were re-launched in November 2006.

The Oslo Guidelines address for the first time a number of fundamental issues which have been revisited, and basically reiterated, by the subsequent documents.

The relationship with the core humanitarian principles of Humanity, Neutrality, and Impartiality is spelt out in para 20. The humanitarian imperative is widely recognized by all humanitarian actors as the basic principle and condition for the delivery of humanitarian assistance. Ensuring that assistance is based on actual needs and delivered by actors that have no political interest or stake in the situation on the ground not only helps to ensure access to people in need of assistance, but also contributes to the safety and long-term perception of humanitarian workers as neutral agents in the field. In addition to this, and following the trend of umpteenth UN General Assembly resolutions, respect for the sovereignty of States is explicitly referred to in para 21.

The principle that MCDA should be used in humanitarian operations only as a measure of last resort is stated quite early in the document, already in Para 5:

> Military and civil defense assets should be seen as a tool complementing existing relief mechanisms in order to provide specific support to specific requirements, in response to the acknowledged "humanitarian gap" between the disaster needs that the relief community is being asked to satisfy and the resources available to meet them. Therefore, foreign military and civil defense assets should be requested only where there is no comparable civilian alternative and only the use of military or civil defense assets can meet a critical humanitarian need. The military or civil defense asset must therefore be unique in capability and availability. However, foreign civil protection assets, when civilian in nature and respecting humanitarian principles, can provide an important direct and indirect contribution to humanitarian actions based on humanitarian needs assessments and their possible advantages in terms of speed, specialization, efficiency and effectiveness, especially in the early phase of relief response.[9] The use of civil protection assets should be needs driven,

[9] This paragraph also draws an important distinction between military and civil defense assents, on the one hand, and foreign civil protection assets on the other. It is interesting to note that several European countries (notably including Italy) insisted on this distinction and strongly advocated for the use of civil protection mechanisms rather than military assets in disaster response. Nonetheless, among these countries France has deployed military assets in response to major natural disasters, including the 2003 earthquake in Bam, Iran; the 2004 Indian Ocean tsunami; and the 2005 earthquake in Pakistan. Belgium and Germany also reported sending military assets in response to only a few, large-scale natural disasters.

> complementary to and coherent with humanitarian aid operations, respecting the overall coordinating role of the UN.

Furthermore, complementarity of MCDA to properly humanitarian assets is detailed in para 24:

> Military and civil defense assets should be seen as a tool complementing existing relief mechanisms in order to provide specific support to specific requirements, in response to the acknowledged "humanitarian gap" between the disaster needs that the relief community is being asked to satisfy and the resources available to meet them.

Paragraph 32 sets out a number of key operational concepts which are basically retained by all other related documents:

i. Requests for MCDA to support UN agencies must be made by the Humanitarian Coordinator/Resident Coordinator, with the consent of the Affected State, and based solely on humanitarian criteria.
ii. MCDA should be employed by UN humanitarian agencies as a last resort, i.e., only in the absence of any other available civilian alternative to support urgent humanitarian needs in the time required.
iii. A UN humanitarian operation using military assets must retain its civilian nature and character. While MCDA may remain under military control, the operation as a whole must remain under the overall authority and control of the responsible humanitarian organization. This does not infer any civilian command and control status over military assets.
iv. Humanitarian work should be performed by humanitarian organizations. Insofar as military organizations have a role to play in supporting humanitarian work, it should, to the extent possible, not encompass direct assistance, in order to retain a clear distinction between the normal functions and roles of humanitarian and military stakeholders.
v. Any use of MCDA should be, at its onset, clearly limited in time and scale and present an exit strategy element that defines clearly how the function it undertakes could, in the future, be undertaken by civilian personnel.
vi. Countries providing MCDA to support UN humanitarian operations should ensure that they respect the UN Codes of Conduct and the humanitarian principles.

The need for the humanitarian effort to remain under civilian control is restated in para 37:

> To be effective, the direction and coordination of the overall humanitarian effort requires the leadership of professional humanitarian staff. As such, UN MCDA should always remain under civilian control.

The key issue of the profile of military personnel and assets involved in humanitarian operations is addressed at several points, and most explicitly in paras 38 and 39:

> In principle, unarmed UN MCDA, accepted as neutral and impartial, and clearly distinguished from other military units, can be used to support the full range of humanitarian

> activities. However, their involvement in direct assistance should be weighed on a case-by-case basis and only if it satisfies the criteria of last resort. Their activities should focus on indirect assistance and infrastructure support missions.
>
> Military and civil defense personnel employed exclusively in the support of UN humanitarian activities should be clearly distinguished from those forces engaged in other military missions, including the military component of peacekeeping missions, peace operations and peace support, and accorded the appropriate protection by the Affected State and any combatants.

The avoidance of excessive reliance on military resources is addressed in para 34:

> ... as a general principle, UN humanitarian agencies must avoid becoming dependent on military resources and member States are encouraged to invest in increased civilian capacity instead of the ad hoc use of military forces to support humanitarian actors.

Nearly half of the Oslo Guidelines are devoted to a rather detailed description of the tasks and reciprocal responsibilities of the stakeholders in the use of MCDA in humanitarian operations. These include the affected State and transit States, the UN Resident Coordinator and/or Humanitarian Coordinator, the UN humanitarian agencies, the UN Office for the Coordination of Humanitarian Affairs and, crucially, the assisting State, and foreign military or civil defense commanders.

24.3.2 *MCDA Guidelines (Guidelines on the Use of Military and Civil Defense Assets to Support United Nations Humanitarian Activities in Complex Emergencies)*

First developed in 2003[10] and revised in January 2006, the MCDA Guidelines are complementary to the Oslo Guidelines, which focus on the use of military and civil defense assets in natural, environmental, and technological disasters. This initiative represents the response from the humanitarian community on the one hand to the increase in the use of militaries not only in supporting humanitarian operations but also in directly providing aid in certain contexts, and on the other to the prevailing drive toward integration between humanitarian, political, and security objectives. The MCDA Guidelines therefore provide indications for the use of international military and civil defense personnel, equipment, supplies and services in support of the United Nations (UN) in pursuit of humanitarian

[10] The MCDA Guidelines were developed with the collaboration of a broad representation of the international humanitarian community, through a Drafting Committee consisting of representatives of Austria, Czech Republic, France, Germany, Italy, Sudan, Switzerland, UK, USA, DPKO, SCHR, UNHCR, UNICEF and WFP, as well as a Review Committee consisting of representatives of Australia, Canada, China, Costa Rica, Denmark, Ecuador, Egypt, Estonia, Finland, Ghana, Greece, India, Japan, Libyan Arab Jamahiriya, Madagascar, Mauritius, Mexico, Netherlands, Norway, Poland, Russian Federation, Sweden, Turkey, Yugoslavia, COE, ECHO, EC, EUMS, ICDO, ICRC, ICVA, INTERACTION, IOM, NATO, OCHA, THW and WHO.

objectives in complex emergencies. It provides guidance on when these resources can be used, how they should be employed, and how UN agencies should interface, organize, and coordinate with international military forces with regard to the use of military and civil defense assets.

The MCDA Guidelines reiterate that humanitarian assistance must be provided in accordance with the basic humanitarian principles of humanity, impartiality, and neutrality (para 22) and stress—particularly relevant in situations of complex emergency[11]—that "The UN seeks to provide humanitarian assistance with full respect for the sovereignty of States" (para 23). Introducing a useful element of analysis, based on the degree of contact with the affected population, international military resources are divided into direct assistance, indirect assistance, and infrastructure support.

Paragraph 23 addresses the key preoccupations of the humanitarian community, by insisting that humanitarian operation using military assets must retain its civilian nature and character and must remain under civilian control and authority. It sets out a number of important standards:

> Requests for military assets must be made by the Humanitarian/Resident Coordinator on the ground, not political authorities, and based solely on humanitarian criteria.

MCDA should be employed by humanitarian agencies as a last resort, i.e. only in the absence of any other available civilian alternative to support urgent humanitarian needs in the time required.

A humanitarian operation using military assets must retain its civilian nature and character. While military assets will remain under military control, the operation as a whole must remain under the overall authority and control of the responsible humanitarian organization. This does not infer any civilian command and control status over military assets.

Humanitarian work should be performed by humanitarian organizations. Insofar as military organizations have a role to play in supporting humanitarian work, it should, to the extent possible, not encompass direct assistance, in order to retain a clear distinction between the normal functions and roles of humanitarian and military stakeholders.

Any use of MCDA should be, at its onset, clearly limited in time and scale and present an exit strategy element that defines clearly how the function it undertakes could, in the future, be undertaken by civilian personnel.

Countries providing military personnel to support humanitarian operations should ensure that they respect the Un Codes of Conduct and the humanitarian principles.

Interestingly, exactly the same concepts are reiterated with only minor differences in language in later sections of the Guidelines, under Operational Standards

---

[11] A complex emergency is defined by the IASC as: "a humanitarian crisis in a country, region, or society where there is total or considerable breakdown of authority resulting from internal or external conflict and which requires an international response that goes beyond the mandate or capacity of any single agency and/or the ongoing United Nations country program.".

for the Use of MCDA (paras 32–49). Precise indications are also given to stress the distinction between military and civilian personnel, specifying, among other things, that "Military personnel providing direct assistance should not be armed and should rely on the security measures of the supported humanitarian agency" (para 40) and that "Under no circumstance will UN MCDA be used to provide security for UN humanitarian activities." (para 43).

UN Humanitarian Civil–Military Coordination (CMCoord) is presented as the essential dialog and interaction between civilian and military actors necessary to protect and promote humanitarian principles, avoid competition, minimize inconsistency, and when appropriate, pursue common goals. This is done through sharing of information and exchange of liaison personnel (paras 50–55).

The final sections of the MCDA Guidelines spell out the operational procedures and the responsibilities of various stakeholders. The UN Emergency Relief Coordinator, in consultation with the Inter-Agency Standing Committee, provides the overall guidance for a particular complex emergency. The UN Resident Coordinator or Humanitarian Coordinator or the Special Representative of the Secretary-General will initiate the request for the use of military and civil defense resources in the field. UN humanitarian agencies will request the use of these assets through the Humanitarian Coordinator or Resident Coordinator who has coordination responsibilities for the complex emergency. OCHA's Military and Civil Defense Unit (MCDU) will process the request, make the necessary arrangements with the Member States, and track the use of these resources. It will maintain a UN Civil–Military Coordination (CMCoord) training program and a roster of UN CMCoord trained liaison personnel for mobilization. The affected State has primary responsibility for providing humanitarian assistance to persons within its borders. UN MCDA shall have at least the same freedom of movement, immunities, privileges, and exemptions afforded to UN humanitarian agencies. Transit States will facilitate the movement of requested UN MCDA in the same manner as they facilitate the movement of UN relief goods and personnel.

24.3.3 Civil–Military Relationship in Complex Emergencies, an IASC Reference Paper, 2004

This paper was endorsed by the IASC Working Group as an IASC Reference Paper in 2004. It complements the MCDA Guidelines of March 2003. The paper is conceived as a non-binding reference for humanitarian practitioners, assisting them in formulating country-specific operational guidelines on civil–military relations for particular complex emergencies. It was also intended to be updated as the environment changes and as new guidance on related issues becomes available.

Part 1 of the paper reviews, in a generic manner, the nature and character of civil–military relations in complex emergencies. Part 2 lists the fundamental humanitarian principles and concepts that must be upheld when coordinating with the military. Part 3, the most substantive one, proposes practical considerations for humanitarian workers engaged in civil–military coordination. Amongst the issues addressed are the establishment of liaison arrangements (paras 32–34); information sharing (paras 35 and 36); use of military assets for humanitarian operations (paras 37–39), basically summarizing the content of the Oslo and MCDA Guidelines; use of military escorts for humanitarian convoys (para 40); joint civil–military relief operations (paras 41 and 42); separate military operations for relief purposes (paras 43–45), and general conduct of humanitarian staff (para 46).

24.3.4 IASC, Guidelines on the Use of Military or Armed Escorts for Humanitarian Convoys, 2001

The text was approved for implementation by the IASC Working Group in May 2001. Part I reviews the broader policy context. It concludes that, due to changes in the nature of conflict and in the nature of humanitarian assistance, military or armed escorts are, in a limited number of cases, necessary. In these cases, they should be used sparingly, and only in accordance with clear guidelines. The substantive Part II consists of two sets of non-binding guidelines determining when and how escorts might be used. The general rule, according to the document, is that humanitarian convoys will not use armed or military escorts. Exceptions to the general rule are considered for a number of circumstances as a last resort, provided that criteria of sovereignty, need, safety, and sustainability are met.

24.4 Unresolved Issues

Although the reference documents reviewed in the previous section strive to make conceptual clarity in a number of critical areas, when looking at the reality of today's humanitarian operations several critical issues remain largely unresolved. To a large extent, this state of affairs does not depend on the non-binding nature or the regulatory framework. At the core, problems arise since humanitarian and military actors have fundamentally different institutional thinking and cultures, characterized by the distinct chain-of-command and clear organizational structures of the military vis-à-vis the diversity of the humanitarian community. Even more importantly, the two groups have different mandates, objectives, working methods, and even vocabularies. These structural differences are particularly evident in the distinct approaches of the military and civilian organizations to direct civilian assistance. The military's approach is informed by security rather than long-term development considerations.[12]

[12] Gourlay 2000.

Humanitarian action in complex emergencies is largely dependent on acceptance by the parties to the conflict. In the real world, despite the clarity of what set forth in guidelines, any operations undertaken jointly by humanitarian agencies and military forces may—and in fact often does—have a negative impact on the perception of the humanitarian agencies' impartiality and neutrality and hence affect their ability to operate effectively throughout a complex emergency. Furthermore, any perception that humanitarian actors may have become affiliated with the military forces within a specific situation could impact negatively on the security of humanitarian staff and their ability to access vulnerable populations. In this respect, for instance, IASC documents make every effort to ensure that every task associated with military provision of assistance is termed "*relief*" instead of "*humanitarian*".

Blurring the lines between humanitarian, political, and military actors has become particularly evident with the adoption of the UN Integrated Missions model, which invests the Special Representative of the Secretary-General with the combined responsibilities of UN peacekeeping Force Commander, UN Resident Coordinator (eminently political), and UN Humanitarian Coordinator (supposedly neutral and impartial). Integration was conceived in order to streamline UN efforts and ensure that the objectives of all UN forces and agencies are directed toward a common overarching goal. If this approach makes good organizational sense, it has drawn fierce criticism on the part of the humanitarian community (particularly the Red Cross and NGOs, but also from sectors of UNHCR and UNICEF).[13] One experience in particular, the use of Provincial Reconstruction Teams (PRTs) under the United Nations Assistance Mission to Afghanistan (UNAMA) is commonly referred to in practitioners' parlance as "the death of humanitarianism". These join civil–military units (50–150 members, of which only 5–10 percent civilians) were tasked to provide both improved security and to facilitate reconstruction and economic development throughout the country. Anecdotal evidence[14] points to extremes of blurring, including severe breaches of the various guidelines such as the deployment of military personnel, armed and in civilian clothes. The practical merger of the military and the "humanitarian" as represented by the PRTs resulted in serious negative consequences for the humanitarian working environment, compensated for by few "hearts and minds" victories. In particular, many (although not all) humanitarian agencies point to a strong relationship between the use of PRTs and the dramatic increase of targeting of NGO staff in security incidents since 2003.[15]

In situations of natural disasters, most of the local actors engaged in humanitarian work are present on the ground long before the arrival of international personnel and will continue their functions after their departure. Whilst this is

[13] For an in-depth analysis of Integrated Missions from a humanitarian perspective see: Weir 2006.

[14] Jakobsen 2005, 37.

[15] Jakobsen footnote 14 above.

largely taken into account by the culture and working methods of the humanitarian community, which engages with local actors by developing their response capacity before the event and then supports them during actual operations, militaries usually intervene in complete autonomy, as if nothing existed before their arrival, thereby creating the potential for tension and distortions.

Questions also remain concerning the overall effectiveness of the use of foreign military assets. In the only comprehensive piece of research available on the subject,[16] the Stockholm International Peace Research Centre (SIPRI) reviews a number of international response operations occurred between 1997 and 2006. Whilst timeliness is seen as the main factor affecting effectiveness, promised military assets slow to arrive and to start operating may actually impede the response by preventing the deployment of civilian alternatives. The appropriateness of military assets is often hampered by the lack of thorough, multi-stakeholder needs and capacity assessments. Some countries that contribute military assets insist on force-protection measures, which both reduce the efficiency of the operation and may intimidate or be resented by local populations. The effectiveness of foreign military assets in disaster relief is also affected by the capacity of local emergency management agencies to coordinate and effectively use the assets during the relief operation.

Furthermore, whilst the Oslo and MCDA Guidelines are quite clear about coordination between civilian humanitarian actors and militaries, this has been one of the greatest challenges created by the increasing deployment of foreign military assets. The differences in cultures, priorities, and operating modes between military personnel and civilian actors have an impact not least on information sharing between the civilian and military spheres.

Lastly, and quite importantly, the costs of deploying military assets are generally higher than for civilian assets. This has been interpreted by some as a breach of the humanitarian principle of impartiality, which prescribes that assistance should be rendered solely according to needs (and therefore not according to political or strategic considerations, as it is often the case in the deployment of military assets for humanitarian purposes). This has also caused concerns that foreign military assets are placing a disproportionate burden on humanitarian funds. This concern is not entirely justified, as several countries have introduced measures whereby their defense ministry covers some or all of the costs of deploying military assets for overseas disaster relief, thereby reducing the impact on humanitarian aid budgets.

[16] SIPRI 2008.

References

Bessler M, Seki K (2006) Civil-Military relations in armed conflict, in liaison. J Civil-Military humanitarian Relief Collab 3(3):4–10

Gourlay C (2000) Partners apart: managing military-civil co-operation in humanitarian interventions, in disarmament forum, peacekeeping: Evolution or extinction? 3

Inter-Agency Standing Committee and World Health Organization (2009) Protecting the health of vulnerable people from the humanitarian consequences of climate change and climate related disasters

Jakobsen PW (2005) PRT IN Afghanistan: successful but not sufficient, danish institute for International studies. 6:37

Pachauri RK, Reisinger A (eds) (2007) Contribution of Working Groups I II and III to The fourth assessment report of the intergovernmental panel on climate change core writing team. IPCC, Geneva

Weir EA (2006) Conflict and compromise: UN Integrated Missions and the UN Imperative Kofi Annan International Training Center Monograph. Accra, Ghana

SIPRI (2008) The effectiveness of foreign military assets in natural disaster response, stockholm

Chapter 25
The Role of International Financial Institutions

Giovanna Adinolfi

Abstract Multilateral and regional financial institutions have adopted numerous instruments designed to provide financial assistance to countries hit by disaster. Their aim is to support immediate relief to populations, as well as recovery and reconstruction. Over the last decades, development banks have extended the scope of their assistance, on the assumption that to overcome emergencies and difficulties due to disaster, the adoption of preventive measures can be as important as post-disaster operations. Consequently, new financial instruments have been introduced, focusing on prevention and disaster risk reduction actions by beneficiaries. All these initiatives may include a component in favor of the least developed countries, to make financial resources available to them on concessional terms. In more recent practice, debt relief programs have also been introduced to reduce the debt of beneficiary countries toward international financial institutions, so that more resources can be allocated to humanitarian assistance, recovery, and reconstruction programs.This chapter will analyze the practice of the International Monetary Fund and the World Bank Group. The analysis will be carried out in the light of the general instruments of financial assistance adopted by these institutions, to explore to what extent positive discrimination is applied in favor of countries affected by disaster. Special emphasis will be placed on whether coordination mechanisms are implemented between these institutions and between them and other actors, both States and other intergovernmental (regional or universal) organizations providing financial assistance. The purpose is to explore whether mechanisms of international governance have emerged in the practice.

Keywords Financial assistance · Loans and grants · Debt relief · Coordination among international financial institutions

G. Adinolfi (✉)
Università degli Studi di Milano, 20122, Milan, Italy
e-mail: giovanna.adinolfi@unimi.it

A. de Guttry et al. (eds.), *International Disaster Response Law*,
DOI: 10.1007/978-90-6704-882-8_25,

Contents

25.1 Introductory Remarks

The role of international financing in the aftermath of disasters is unanimously recognized. Indeed, in most cases, affected States are characterized by a low level of development, and structurally lack the resources necessary to cope with the challenges of economic growth. To subsidize short- and long-term social and economic investments, access to foreign funds is of the uppermost importance. When natural or man-made disasters occur, the scarcity of resources even becomes a major concern, as funds previously meant to finance the development process are likely to be diverted to immediate relief and recovery, with the risk of undermining the results already achieved. At the same time, it could be unfeasible to bear the huge costs of assistance independently, and to provide individuals immediate aid to alleviate their material losses and plan and implement recovery programs, as well as restore infrastructures and productive activities.

For these reasons, international legal texts concerning disaster response extensively recognize the importance of providing financing to affected States,[1] emphasizing the need for cooperation by third States and international

[1] See UNGA doc. A/RES/46/182, December 19, 1991 (establishing a central emergency funding mechanism for humanitarian assistance by the UN system: see Chap. 26 by Palandri in this volume), whose para 21 states that "[o]rganizations and entities of the United Nations system should continue to respond to requests for emergency assistance within their respective mandates". See also the ECOSOC resolution 1993/205, where the Council stressed the importance of adequate financial resources both for relief and for the continuum of development processes in the affected States (para 21).

organizations, with reference to both disaster risk reduction[2] and post-disaster assistance.[3] In this context, international financial institutions (IFIs) may have a role to play for a variety of reasons. First of all, they already have large resources. Gathered through the subscription of quotas or shares by members or raised from the financial markets, these assets could be channeled in favor of States facing the disruptive consequences of disasters. In addition, the practice of these institutions could facilitate the process of disbursing resources, following already existing policies and procedures, with no need to elaborate, adopt, and implement new financial facilities, which could not but be the cause of delays in the delivery of assistance. Finally, most of their practice is informed by a principle of positive discrimination, whereby most vulnerable countries may have access to financing on more favorable terms than those applied to other members. This last consideration is particularly pertinent to our research, considering that for the reasons mentioned above, developing countries are more exposed than others to difficulties due to disaster, and the least developed face even more complex financial constraints.

However, IFIs have been set up in order to meet particular purposes, as set out in their respective establishing treaties. Usually, no reference is made to disasters, but in more general terms they are called upon to provide financial (and technical) support to favor and promote the development and economic growth of their members. Their competences may also be limited to assistance in particular circumstances, which do not nevertheless include emergency situations in the wake of a disaster. Although not precluding the adoption of financial instruments specific to the latter, these normative elements have to be taken into consideration, as they could limit the scope of action of the organization, as discussed in the sections to follow.

A further element constraining the involvement of international financial institutions pertains to the modalities envisaged in their constitutive instruments, whereby assets to be used in financial assistance may be raised. Since in many cases these instruments explicitly or implicitly forbid fund raising from the

---

[2] A comprehensive approach to disaster risk reduction has gained new momentum after the 2005 World Conference on Disaster Reduction, convened in Japan in the aftermath of the earthquake and tsunami in the Indian Ocean of December 2004 (see Chaps. 8 and 9 by Nicoletti and La Vaccara in this volume). In para 13a of the Framework for Action 2005–2015, issued at the end of the conference, States have recognized their primary responsibility for taking measures to reduce disaster risk, but specific mention is also made of 'concerted international cooperation … to stimulate and contribute to developing the … capacities … needed for disaster risk reduction at all levels'. See paras 31–32 on the desirable role to be played by international organizations, including financial institutions.

[3] In addition to the documents mentioned in note 1, see also the UN General Assembly resolution concerning natural disasters, where the organ 'stresses … the importance of strengthening international cooperation, particularly through the effective use of multilateral mechanisms, in the timely provision of humanitarian assistance through all phases of a disaster, from relief and recovery to development, including the provisions of adequate resources' (UN General Assembly doc. A/RES/65/264, January 28, 2011, para 13).

international capital markets, or at any rate limit external funding to official lending by States, the main source of financing lies in the subscription of capital quotas or shares by members when they join. The need to preserve this capital, so that assistance can be provided on a permanent basis, can have a strong effect on the terms of lending or the possibility of making members eligible to grants, and not only loans.

A third aspect to be considered relates to the necessity of the strong coordination of these institutions among themselves, with other donors and financing institutions, and with the affected States as well. For such States, international disaster response law instruments assert that they have the primary *responsibility* for taking care of the victims of disasters occurring within their frontiers, so that it is their role to initiate, organize, coordinate, and implement humanitarian assistance on their territory. The UN General Assembly so stated in 1991, in its resolution 46/182 where the basic principles on humanitarian emergency were formulated.[4] Along the same lines, draft Article 9 approved by the UN International Law Commission's Drafting committee on the protection of persons in the event of disasters inferred the primary role of the affected State in the direction, control, coordination, and supervision of relief from its *duty* 'to ensure the protection of persons and provision of disaster relief and assistance on its territory'.[5] In both UN documents, the reference is to the 'role' of the State in the direction and coordination of assistance. It may not be interpreted as a strict obligation to undertake those activities autonomously, as the State could well lack the capacity to act, because, for example, of the weakening of its institutional ability to respond after a disaster has occurred. The language could be better understood to mean that external actors may not bypass the affected States, and have to seek to coordinate with them. In the case of international financial institutions, this is reflected in all their disaster assistance policies, whose implementation is conditional upon the affected State's national authorities' consent and involvement. However, those authorities may lack response and programing capacity, thus jeopardizing the IFIs' ability to intervene.

At the same time, aid from multiple external sources of financing can lead to uncoordinated support, and thus to gaps and deficiencies in the assistance they provide. Mechanisms for coordination and cooperation among the institutions involved (be they international, national or local, intergovernmental, governmental or private) are thus indispensable, in order to ensure that all the needs of the affected State, from immediate humanitarian assistance to reconstruction, are appropriately satisfied, and this through the action of the most competent institution. However, the creation and implementation of such mechanisms may be quite difficult when the number of actors involved is high, if their competences

---

[4] See para 4 of the annex to the UNGA doc. 46/182, cit. See also the report of the ILC Special Rapporteur on the protection of persons in the event of disasters, in UNGA doc. A/CN.4/629, 31 March 2010, 34 ff.

[5] See UNGA doc. A/CN.4/L.76, 14 July 2010, 9 ff.

overlap, and the constitutive instruments legally circumscribe the scope of cooperation.

In the light of these preliminary considerations, the present contribution aims to put forward a legal analysis of the mechanisms adopted by international financial institutions for assistance in the event of disasters. First, the instruments established by the International Monetary Fund (IMF) will be discussed, underscoring how the scope of action of the Fund, limited to balance of payments assistance, constitutes a legal obstacle to wide-ranging support. The second part looks at the more comprehensive aid from the International Bank for Reconstruction and Development (IBRD) and the International Development Association (IDA), part of the World Bank Group. Particular emphasis is placed on the broader mandate of its institutions. Limitations will be inferred from their respective constitutive treaties, however, as they do not cover involvement in all the phases of pre- and post-disaster assistance, mainly excluding immediate relief. Some final considerations will be developed to discuss the major deficiencies of this practice.

25.2 International Monetary Fund Practice

25.2.1 IMF Financial Support in the Event of Disaster: Main Characteristics and Limitations

According to Article I (v) of the Articles of Agreement of the IMF (hereinafter the Articles), one of the main purposes of the Fund is to make its resources temporarily available to members, to provide them 'with the opportunity to correct maladjustments in their balance of payments'. Introduced in the text of the Articles in 1969, the expression 'temporarily' suggests that IMF members are under an obligation to return the resources obtained from the Fund. Consistently with this assumption, Article V, Section 2.a provides that the IMF's financial assistance takes the form of members purchasing from the Fund foreign currency in exchange for their national currencies, with an obligation to carry out an opposite operation within a specified period of time.

Within this general background, the IMF has been developing practices and policies in favor of members struck by disaster since the 1960s. It has first sought to arrange support in the context of ordinary financial instruments concerning the use of general resources[6] (the so-called credit tranche policy), whose assumption is

[6] The IMF's general resources mainly consist of quotas paid by members at the time of accession (Article II, section 2 and Article III, section 1), together with the assets borrowed by the Fund itself (Article VII, section 1(i)). Even if not forbidden by Article VII, the conclusion of debit contracts with private parties is made impossible by the immunity from civil jurisdiction and execution enjoyed by the IMF under Article IX, sections 3 and 4. As a consequence, the Fund's resources are much more limited than those of multilateral development banks, which do not

that balance of payments difficulties arise because of members' wrong or inopportune macroeconomic measures. Only lately has it been considered appropriate to introduce policies which could be used for events beyond members' control, such as when a disaster has occurred, and to establish facilities to the exclusive benefit of the most economically vulnerable members, i.e., low-income countries, in view of their more pressing needs when hit by a disaster.

The starting point of a legal analysis of this evolution is that the Fund's assistance may not *per se* pursue humanitarian aims, as they are not mentioned in, nor can they be implicitly presumed from, Article I of the Articles. The IMF cannot exercise its competences unless in conformity with its establishing instrument. In particular, Article V, section 3, concerning financial assistance through the general resources, states that a member requesting the Fund's support has to 'represent' that it needs to purchase foreign currency because of its balance of payments or reserve position, or because of a development in its reserves (para b (ii)). Even if external deficit is not a precondition for access to IMF funding, this provision clearly refers to an unfavorable balance of payments and to an increased need for foreign currencies. Similarly, a balance of payments need is provided for in all instruments in favor of low-income members, even if they are not funded through the IMF's general resources, but through assets conferred by contributors and administered by the IMF as a trustee.

Accordingly, the Fund's financial support can only be available where disasters have had a detrimental impact on the balance of payments, either because of the reduced ability of the affected member to export (for example because the disaster has destroyed or highly jeopardized its capital stock and means of production), or an increase in import expenses (as the country may need foreign supplies to provide relief and/or to run recovery and reconstruction programs). It may not be granted to sustain increasing public spending which would not affect the external equilibrium, despite it being necessary to carry out post-disaster and prevention and risk reduction activities.

A further limitation to the Fund's approach regards its exclusive application in cases of natural disaster: never has the IMF Secretariat or the Executive Board favored extending its scope to man-made disasters, and no practice has been moving in this direction. As will be shown later on, the Fund has not adopted a legal definition of 'disaster', thus preserving a wide margin of maneuver to decide whether or not to support members. Only recently a definition has been framed within debt forgiveness initiatives, even if only to limit the Fund's involvement to extremely rare circumstances.

(Footnote 6 continued)
enjoy immunity before national courts under their respective establishing treaties, and obtain most of their financial assets through the emission of bonds into international credit markets.

25.2.2 The Initial IMF Assistance Practice in the Event of Balance of Payment Difficulties Due to Factors Beyond the Control of Members

The very earliest practice of assistance in the wake of natural disasters was conceived in the 1960s within the IMF's credit tranches policy.[7] However, at its inception, it was qualified by some peculiarities, as interested members were exempted from one of the basic assumptions of the policy of conditionality, i.e., the presentation of an economic program determining measures to be implemented to correct the balance of payments need and on whose basis the Fund would then define conditions to be satisfied in order to have access to its financial assistance. By way of illustration, after being simultaneously affected by a reduction of the cultivation of rice due to a Nile flooding, and a decrease in cotton crops because of a plague of cotton leaf worm, in 1962 Egypt presented no economic reform program and, to guarantee the reintegration of resources obtained from the Fund, simply offered gold as a collateral security, in accordance with the then in force Article V, section 4 of the Articles.[8] To avoid the development of a generalized practice that would free members from submitting a stabilization program, and to warrant the revolving character of IMF resources, in 1963 the Executive Board decided that only in exceptional circumstances might it accept gold as a collateral security to purchases of foreign currency, and that a strict time limit of six months would apply to the repurchase of national currencies, thus derogating from the general policy on repurchases and the 3–5 years period at that time prevailing.[9]

The idea that access to the IMF's resources could be granted when balance of payments needs sprang from events beyond members' control (and thus not the outcome of inappropriate economic policies) was formally recognized with the approval of the decision concerning 'compensatory financing'.[10] It provided for the right of members to request assistance within specified amounts to address external disequilibria due to a downturn in export earnings, implicitly even as a consequence of a natural disaster. Members could have recourse to assistance under the general policy on the use of the Fund's resources as well, within wider margins of financing but subject to more stringent conditions[11]; rather, this remained the sole option if the disaster's detrimental effect on the balance of payments was due to an increase in import expenses resulting from the need to

[7] For a synthesis of IMF assistance under the emergency instrument for natural disasters from 1962 to 2011, see IMF 2005, 3 and IMF Factsheet 2011.

[8] See Horsefield 1969a 524 ff.

[9] See decision no. 1543-(63/39) adopted in on July 1, 1963, in Horsefield 1969b, 240 ff.

[10] See decision no. 1477-(63/8) of February 27, 1963 (Horsefield 1969b, 238 ff) as modified in 1966 with a new decision (*ibidem*, 492 ff).

[11] For an analysis of this practice see Gold 1990, 633 ff.

sustain relief and recovery activities, as compensatory financing was limited to a reduction in the value of exports.[12]

25.2.3 IMF Facilities for Assistance in the Event of Natural Disasters

At present, emergency assistance by the IMF is governed by the 2011 Executive Board decision to establish the Rapid Financing Instrument (RFI)[13] under the credit tranche policy, open to all members, and also by the Rapid Credit Facility (RCF) instituted in 2009 under the Poverty Reduction and Growth Trust (PRGT), for the exclusive benefit of low-income members[14] Both represent the finale steps in two parallel processes, whereby the IMF has been framing its support, introducing within its policies also concessional instruments to which particularly fragile and vulnerable countries may be eligible.[15]

As for the support to which all members may accede, after the adoption of compensatory financing, a policy specifically designed to address external imbalances following natural disasters was introduced in 1982, with the endorsement by the Executive Board of the Guidelines on Emergency Natural Disaster Assistance (ENDA).[16] The legal framework underwent a further change in 2009–2011, first with the abolition of compensatory financing,[17] then with the decision to establish the RFI, replacing the ENDA. As for the low-income members, while it is not appropriate here to analyze the path along which the Fund has developed its approach in favor of economic growth and poverty reduction, suffice it to say that the RCF has been introduced with the purpose of facilitating eligible members in gaining access to external financial resources to cope with urgent and short-term balance of payments needs.

Both RFI and RCF assistance may be activated in the event of an urgent balance of payments need that could result in immediate and severe economic disruption.

[12] In order to help members satisfy the food demand of their populations, in 1981 an 'import element' was added to the compensatory financing facility, but limited to balance of payments needs due to an increase in the cost for the imports of cereals: see decision no. 6860-(81/81), in Boughton 2001, 749 ff.

[13] IMF 2011b.

[14] Decision no. 14385-(09/79), adopted July 23, 2009. The text of the Instrument is in IMF 2010b, 183 ff. The list of IMF members eligible for assistance under the Trust is annexed to decision no. 8240-(86/56) SAF, as amended, in IMF 2010b, 495 ff; criteria for eligibility under the Trust are set forth by para 1(A) of decision no. 14521-(10/3), January 11, 2010, ibidem, 498 ff.

[15] A recent analysis of the IMF's role in fragile States may be found in IMF 2011c.

[16] See IMF 2010b, 402 ff.

[17] See decision no. 14282-(09/29), March 24, 2009, in IMF 2010b, 326.

The relevant IMF documents[18] make reference, *inter alia*, to exogenous shocks, i.e., events beyond the control of the authorities of a member, with a significant impact on the economy, comprising, as an illustrative list, natural disasters, terms-of-trade shocks, shocks to demand for exports, or conflict/crisis in neighboring countries. However, the definition given in the RCF decision also qualifies such events as 'sudden', thus, in principle, excluding natural disasters caused by a constant course of less visible events, even if their whole effect would have the same disruptive consequences as a sudden episode.

Quantitative limits have been established for the support members may receive, up to 50 % of a member's quota per year, and to 100 % on a cumulative basis for the RFI, and for an amount equal to 25 % and 75 % of quotas respectively per annum and cumulatively under the RCF. The value of the assistance could be higher for low-income members only insofar as their 'existing and prospective policies are sufficiently strong to address the shock'[19]; a similar condition is provided for repeated access to the RFI, even if with no further criteria if the urgent balance of payments need is primarily due to an exogenous shock.

The increased limit to RFI assistance compared with the ENDA (with a lower annual cap of 25 % of quota) explains a slight strengthening of the conditions attached to it, which was framed to mirror the provisions governing RCF support. Indeed, under both facilities, the requesting member has to represent that it has an urgent need because of its balance of payments or reserve position, or developments in its reserves that if not addressed, would result in severe economic disruption. Only for the RCF is it established that the Fund may not challenge the member's representation prior to the approval of the disbursement (as for all PRGT components) and the member has also to demonstrate that its balance of payments need has not been caused by a withdrawal of credit by other sources of financing.

In both cases, a request for assistance is approved to the extent the Fund is satisfied that the member will cooperate with it to find appropriate solutions to its external imbalance, and, second, that it presents a plan of the policies it intends to pursue in this regard and commits itself not to introduce any measure that could jeopardize its efforts, such as exchange and trade restrictions. A complete macroeconomic and structural program is not required, either because the shock is considered to be of only a limited nature and presumably can be resolved within 1 year, or because the member is unable to present it, as it lacks the institutional capacity necessary for its implementation, or has to tackle the external need with particular urgency. These circumstances justify the IMF decision to confer RFI and RCF support only thorough an outright purchase or loan of foreign currency,[20]

---

[18] See IMF 2011b, para 2.a and decision no. 14385-(09/79), op. cit. n. 14 above, para I.a (iii). See also IMF 2011a, 7, note 8 and IMF 2009, 23, note 47.

[19] See decision no. 14385-(09/79), op. cit. n. 14 above, section II.2.b.

[20] A further differentiation between recourse to RFI and to the RCF component of the PRGT, to be added to those analyzed in the text, pertains to the formal qualification of the transaction between the Fund and the assisted member. In the former it is named 'purchase' of foreign

and to exclude the possibility of adopting an 'arrangement', i.e., an Executive Board's decision whereby the assisted State is assured that it will have access to IMF resources within a specified period of time. However, concerning the conditions attached to the purchases or loans, it is not to be excluded that the approval of the support be made conditional upon the implementation by the member of so-called 'prior action', even if it could be presumed that this would not be the case if emergency assistance is delivered when a natural disaster has occurred, because of the prevailing need to provide immediate relief to the population. Similarly, in order to facilitate decisions for repeated use of the RFI, members could be invited to introduce in their program quantitative or structural targets to be pursued during the period of assistance.

The main differences between RFI and RCF support pertain to the origin of the resources transferred to the assisted members and to the terms of financing.

Regarding the resources used by the IMF, it has to be underlined that the legal basis of the RCF is to be found in Article V, section 2.b of the Articles, and not in Article V, section 3, concerning the use of general resources and on whose basis the RFI has been adopted. Article V, section 2.b states that '[i]f requested, the Fund may decide to perform financial… services, including the administration of resources contributed by members, that are consistent with the purposes of the Fund. Operations involved in the performance of such financial services shall not be on the account of the Fund'. It follows that support for low-income countries in the framework of the PRGT is funded using resources transferred to the Fund by members and other contributors rather than quotas and loans respectively under Articles III and VII. This circumstance implies that balance of payments assistance for eligible members is highly conditioned by the amount of resources the IMF has gathered, through grants or loans in favor of, and notes issued by, the Trust. This amount cannot be unilaterally changed by resorting to an increase in the general resources—in IMF practice employed as a means to strengthen its capacity to help members cope with external imbalance.[21] The same applies to any other trust the Fund decides to establish, which could be, and actually is, of particular relevance for our purposes, as will be made clear in the following pages.

Nevertheless, the exclusion of trusts' activities by Article V, section 3 has another, positive, implication: IMF support may be given through loans, but grants are not excluded, to the possible benefit of low-income members, as they would not be burdened by any obligation to return the foreign currency received by the Fund.

(Footnote 20 continued)
currency (with the obligation for the member to transfer an equivalent amount of national currency to the Fund, to be 'repurchased' afterwards). In the latter, the transaction is qualified as a 'loan' under which the member does not provide the IMF with any national currency.

[21] The only path the IMF might follow to decide to increase the resources under the Trust by itself is the adoption of a decision to sell its gold holdings on the market, acting under Article V, section 12.c and f (ii). However, in recent times it has been followed only once, in 2009, with the purpose to transfer the earnings to the PGRT only in part.

As for the terms of financing, the 2011 decision establishing the RFI does not qualify this facility as a 'special policy' under Article V, section 3.a, as previously provided for the ENDA.[22] This article has been interpreted in the Fund's practice as legitimizing the differentiation of the terms of financing when an IMF policy is designed to overcome specifically identified external payment difficulties. In case of the ENDA, its establishment as a special policy meant that no surcharge was applied to outstanding purchases by the assisted State. The reversal of the decision for the RFI bears with it the consequence that for emergency assistance under the IMF general resources, the same terms of financing concerning charges, surcharges, and repayment periods provided for the credit tranche policy are applied.

Differently, the aid to low-income countries under the Poverty Reduction and Growth Trust is qualified as 'concessional', as more favorable conditions are applied, in consideration of the particular structural weaknesses of these members. Thus, a charge of zero percent per annum is applied, and a longer time period for the repayment of the loan is established, from 5.5 to 10 years after the date of the disbursement.

25.2.4 Debt Relief Initiatives

After the 2010 earthquake in Haiti, the Fund has decided to introduce new financial instruments to provide assistance in the event of natural disasters to meet the particular financial constraints low-income members have to cope with. Indeed, the RCF is well suited to immediate relief, while the post-emergency phase could be supported through access to the Extended Credit Facility, the component of the PRGT designed to help members face balance of payments needs associated with structural macroeconomic imbalances. However, both imply an obligation to repay the loan. For low-income members, more favorable assistance could be advisable, considering their structural lack of financial resources. Accordingly, acting under Article V, section 2.b of the Articles, in order to contribute to the efforts of the international community in favor of Haiti and, more generally, to adopt a general instrument to rely on in any future similar case, the Executive Board has established the Post-Catastrophe Debt Relief Trust Fund (hereinafter the Debt Trust).[23]

---

[22] See decision 12341-(00/117) adopted on November 28, 2000, in IMF 2010b, 401 ff.

[23] See decision no. 14649-(10/64), adopted on June 25, 2010, in IMF 2010b, 302 ff. For some considerations, see IMF 2010a. The Debt Trust complements the already existing trusts established by the Fund for debt relief purposes, i.e., the Heavily Indebted Poor Countries Initiative (adopted in 1996 jointly with the World Bank, to reduce the debt burden upon poor members within the framework of general policies for growth and poverty reduction) and the Multilateral Debt Relief Initiative (established in 2005 together with the World Bank and the African Development Fund, governing the cancellation of all debts due to the Fund at the end of 2004, as a contribution to accelerate the pursuit of the Millennium Development Goals).

States allowed assistance under this trust fund would receive grants for a reduction of the debt due to the IMF so as to free up resources to meet balance of payments needs that could arise for the reconstruction of the national economy and productive capacity. Two different modalities of debt relief have been set up: flow relief, whereby grants would be used for the relief of payments due within 2 years after the disaster, and stock relief, to eliminate all debts to the Fund. It is worth underlining that, from the IMF's perspective, decisions to provide debt relief do not bring about a reduction of the Fund assets, as the payments due from beneficiary members are funded through resources transferred to the Debt Trust both by contributors in the form of grants, loans, deposits, or other types of investments, and by other IMF accounts, at least in the initial phase. Each time a decision for debt relief is approved, an equivalent amount of resources is transferred from the Debt Trust account to other IMF general or administered accounts, to cover the loss due to the missing repurchase or repayment by the beneficiary low-income member.

Because of the extensive nature of the assistance and, at the same time, the exceptional needs to be addressed, specific eligibility criteria have been introduced. The first regards the countries admitted to debt relief, as not all low-income members may be qualified: the Debt Trust's scope is limited to members eligible to the PGRT support and whose annual per capita gross national income is, at the time of the request for debt relief, below the International Development Association operational cutoff (that is the threshold annually established by IDA to determine the countries admitted to its financial assistance) or, for members whose population is below one million, is less than twice the IDA cutoff. Not only has a country to be in the list of members eligible to concessional lending for poverty reduction and growth, but, as that list is revised every 2 years,[24] when requesting debt relief it has still to satisfy the per capita income criterion to be included. In any case, debt relief will be provided irrespective of the ability of the member to have access to the international financial markets on a durable and sustainable basis, the second eligibility criterion established for the PRGT.[25]

Members must also have experienced an event that is covered by the definition of disasters set forth in the Debt Trust decision. This is the first time the IMF has adopted a legal definition of disaster not based on the nature of the event, but on its effects. Indeed, eligible members may take advantage of debt relief if hit by a 'qualifying catastrophic disaster', i.e., an exceptional natural disaster that has affected at least one-third of the population and a large portion of the economy by the destruction of more than a quarter of its productive capacity or because of damages to an amount exceeding 100 % of the gross national product. The

[24] Decision no. 14521-(10/3), op.cit. n. 14 above, para 5.

[25] See n. 14 above.

introduction of this further element of qualification is due to the will of the IMF to limit debt relief to extremely exceptional circumstances, not only in favor of the poorest and most vulnerable members, but exclusively when highly affected by material losses.

Further substantive criteria are established for the two tracks along which members can obtain debt relief. For the flow relief, a balance of payments need must have arisen from the disaster. As long as the Executive Board agrees that a member falls within the subjective scope of application of the debt instrument as well, a grant for temporary debt relief will be provided automatically. A more in-depth evaluation is carried out for the Fund to decide to make the member's existing debt eligible for stock relief. Indeed, the decision may be adopted only 6 months after the disaster has occurred and on the basis of an evaluation of the magnitude and the causes of the external need (which must be substantial and created or exacerbated by the disaster itself). Another criterion is the presumed length of economic recovery efforts (expected still to persist at the end of the 2 years flow relief period), and the level of indebtedness of the affected member, high enough compared to its exports or its gross national product for the freed resources to be critical in coping with the balance of payment need. The criticality requirement is measured also taking into consideration the availability of alternative sources of financing.

This last point leads to a specific element of Debt Trust assistance, which cannot be found in any other IMF financial instrument concerning support in the event of natural disasters. The delivery of stock debt relief is conditional upon the existence of a concerted effort by the international community to provide debt relief, as shown by the participation of other official creditors (States and other international organizations) accounting for at least eighty percent of the outstanding sovereign external debt due at the time of the catastrophe. The IMF does not claim to act in isolation, but is legitimated in approving permanent debt relief if the affected member would benefit by a broad support by creditors. This approach is very similar to the path followed at the time of the establishment of the other two IMF debt relief instruments,[26] where the Fund acted in strict collaboration with a number of multilateral development banks and the main official creditors, providing coordinated aid to support the financial efforts of the poorest countries for their growth and poverty reduction by cancelling debt.

Other strict conditions apply for a stock debt relief decision. Indeed, the Fund must be satisfied not only that the member will cooperate with it in order to find appropriate solutions to its balance of payments need (the standard clause included in all IMF financial instruments for assistance in case of natural disasters), but it has also to determine that it has adopted adequate macroeconomic policies in the

---

[26] See n. 23 above.

six months preceding the decision to disburse stock relief. So, also in this case the obligation to cooperate is complemented by some conditions, even if not pertaining to measures the member has to adopt after the IMF's decision to assist, but to be qualified as *ex ante* conditionality, as it regards the overall national macroeconomic situation prevailing in the period immediately preceding the IMF's decision.

25.3 Multilateral Development Banks: The World Bank Group

Some of the limitations to IMF support for States affected by disaster are unknown in the practice of multilateral development banks. Indeed, their respective constitutive instruments legitimize *de jure* the exercise of broader action and have allowed a profound change in the practice of these institutions in more recent decades, as they evolved from project lender organizations, designed to finance specific investment projects, to full-fledged development institutions. Consistently with this all-encompassing mandate, their activities are carried out within the framework of more comprehensive national strategies for economic and social development and are not forced to give support to ride out a particular difficulty, such as balance of payments needs in the case of the IMF. As a consequence, they are granted a wider margin of maneuver and can assist countries stricken by disasters more comprehensively.

The second element to be taken into consideration in order to appreciate the broader scope of development banks action pertains to the sources of their financial assets. Indeed, they only comprise payments made by members at the time of accession to a limited extent, since these institutions mainly gather funds through the emission of bonds into the international financial markets. Benefiting from a widely recognized creditworthiness, this base of financing permits them to widen their available resources for the profit of members, eligible not only for loans, but also grants, even when donors transfer no or insufficient funds to the multilateral banks for assistance in case of disaster. Trust funds are also used in the practice of development banks, and in more recent times their establishment has warranted the delivery of assistance for large amounts, in most cases to face most serious emergencies.

This section will focus on the financial instruments introduced by the World Bank in support of the members having to cope with the disruptive consequence of natural or man-made disasters. However, the role of regional development banks should not be underestimated, since in the wake of the 2005 Hyogo Declaration and its Framework for Action they all have adopted instruments facilitating their members in acceding to additional financial resources to meet the most urgent short-term needs of populations hit by catastrophic events and to plan and implement recovery and reconstruction initiatives. In recent years, the Inter-

American,[27] Asian,[28] African,[29] and European[30] development banks have introduced and strengthened facilities specifically designed for these purposes, proposing a systematic approach favoring the development of a dialog agenda with members, in a cooperative effort to identify vulnerabilities to man-made and/or natural risks, and to complement their respective development strategies with measures for prevention, disaster risk reduction and mitigation. Simultaneously, financial instruments have been adopted for immediate humanitarian assistance (mainly to sustain the efforts of more specialized national or international organizations, both private and governmental or intergovernmental) and recovery (with the aim of helping restore basic services and infrastructures, thus initiating activities essential for a more comprehensive reconstruction of social and economic life within the affected area).

---

[27] For the Inter-American Development Bank, reference must be made to the Disaster Risk Management Policy (doc. GN-2354-5 of February 23, 2007). On this basis, the Bank manages the Disaster Prevention Sector Facility (doc.GN-2085-3 of March 9, 2001) and the trust Disaster Prevention Fund (doc. GN-2405-3 of March 16, 2006) to support risk reduction and mitigation activities. Post-disaster instruments have been introduced with the twofold purpose of supporting immediate humanitarian assistance and the subsequent recovery in case of natural hazard events, and of helping members to cope with the physical damage due to technological accidents. In this case, the Bank's operations are financed through the Emergency Technical Cooperation (to deliver grants supporting humanitarian assistance by international or local aid organizations) and the Immediate Response Facility for Emergencies Caused by Natural and Unexpected Disasters, introduced in 2003 (see IDB 2007, 15).

[28] Within the Asian Development Bank, the approach to disaster support was comprehensively formulated with the adoption in May 2004 of the Disaster and Emergency Assistance Policy (ADB 2004). With this as its basis, emergency assistance loans are approved for members to smooth short-term assistance in order to help restore basic infrastructures and economic, social and governance activities. These loans have been supplemented by the establishment of the Asia Pacific Disaster Response Fund (ADB 2009), for the provision of grants in the immediate aftermath of natural disasters to face very urgent needs of the affected population. The Bank's ordinary development loans are considered appropriate for the reconstruction phase, incorporating preventive, mitigation, and preparedness activities. However, for specific events, the Bank has decided to create special funds, such as the 2005 Asian Tsunami Fund (ADB 2005), a regional instrument aiming to provide support to governments and aid actors in the countries hit by the December 2004 tsunami in the Indian Ocean through grants to finance investment projects for reconstruction and associated development activities.

[29] In 1974, the African Development Bank established the Special Relief Fund, on whose basis it may approve grants for members in order to help them meet short-term needs when a disaster has occurred within their territories (AfDB 2008). Initially devised for the benefit of States having to face droughts, nowadays the Fund may be used in a variety of situations, including not only natural disasters, but also conflicts and accidents.

[30] As for the European Bank for Reconstruction and Development, established in 1991 to facilitate transition to a market economy for Central and Eastern Europe and Central Asian countries, its financial assistance is provided through loans funded by a group of donor States and the European Union. In disaster situations, its involvement is limited to nuclear safety, so as to address all potential risks arising from the existence of obsolete nuclear sites in the territory of its members. See www.ebrd.com/pages/sector/nuclearsafety.shtml. Accessed 9 January 2012.

25.3.1 *Introduction: The Scope of the 2007 Rapid Responses to Crisis and Emergencies Policy in the Light of the World Bank's Articles of Agreement*

The IBRD's and IDA's (hereinafter, the World Bank, or the Bank)[31] policy regarding disaster assistance was renewed in 2007 with the establishment of a new operational policy, named 'Rapid Response to Crises and Emergencies'.[32] Its adoption was mainly justified by the need to rectify some of the deficiencies of the operational policy previously in force (such as delays in the approval of financing or in the disbursement of loans or grants, and the limited emphasis paid to prevention and mitigation issues). At the same time, the Bank considered it appropriate to adapt the rules to its practice, taking into consideration that it had made its financial assistance available in a variety of situations not covered by the regulation existing at that time.[33]

The purpose of the new policy is 'to address major adverse economic and/or social impacts resulting from an actual or imminent natural or man-made disaster'.[34] No definition is given for the notion of disasters, but it is clear that the scope of the Bank's policy is wider than that of the IMF, limited to natural events. Second, the policy also comprises activities furthering the prevention of disasters and the mitigation of their disruptive effects, in their imminence and, according to a broader perspective, for a systemic reduction of State vulnerability to risk.

Crisis assistance must be consistent with the purposes set out in the agreements establishing the IBRD and IDA. Constituted in 1944 with the main aim of helping countries to overcome the destruction due to the Second World War, the former has progressively shifted its attention to the issue of development.[35] In a similar vein, IDA was established in 1960 specifically 'to promote economic development, increase productivity and thus raise standards of living in the less-developed' members,[36] hence supplementing IBRD activities by focusing its efforts on the most vulnerable countries.[37] The policies adopted by the Bank for the fulfillment of

---

[31] The text of the treaties establishing the IBRD and IDA may be found on the web site www.worldbank.org. Accessed 9 January 2012.

[32] See Operational policy 8.00, *Rapid Response to Crises and Emergencies*, March 2007 (hereinafter OP 8.00), superseding the Operational policy 8.50 *Emergency Recovery Assistance*, August 1995 (hereinafter OP 8.50).

[33] For broader considerations, see World Bank 2007, 2 ff and 5 ff. For example, notwithstanding the 1995 operational policy did not refer to man-made disasters, the Bank provided its financial support in these circumstances as well. See also IEG/World Bank 2006, 55 ff.

[34] See OP 8.00, para 1.a.

[35] See Article I (i) of the IBRD Articles of Agreement.

[36] See Article I of the IDA Articles of Agreement.

[37] As already mentioned, access to IBRD and IDA's resources conforms to a graduation process, based on per capita gross national income. See Operational policy 3.10, Annex D, *IBRD/IDA and Blend Countries: Per Capita Incomes, Lending Eligibility and Repayment Terms*, July 2010. Another criteria followed by the two institutions in defining their credit-eligible members refers

its purposes are informed by the mandate stated in the agreements establishing the two institutions, whereby the encouragement of investments is considered the main channel for promoting economic development,[38] and is pursued through investment operations (to cover the costs of specific economic and social projects)[39] and development policy operations (designed to support structural reforms to a member's economy as a whole, or in a specific sector).[40]

However, the rationale underlying these operations has undergone a steady evolution, and since the 1990s fighting poverty has been the main focus of the development agenda of both institutions.[41] Direct evidence for this progression is provided by Operational policy 1.00, where it is explicitly stated that '[t]he Bank's mission is sustainable poverty reduction'.[42] For our purposes, it must be underlined that the notion of poverty given by the document encompasses 'vulnerability to shocks', together with the lack of opportunities, voice, and representation.

Within this framework, it is unexpected that the World Bank would employ its usual means (financial and technical assistance) to support efforts for relief, recovery and reconstruction in cases of disasters striking its members. The basic assumption is that disasters can, and do, slow down the process of economic development, and their occurrence may justify special financial assistance, to address specific and urgent needs.

(Footnote 37 continued)
to the lack of access to international capital markets (IBRD Articles of Agreement, Article III.4 (ii) and IDA Articles of Agreement, Article V.1.c).

38 See reference n. 35 above and the introductory article of the IDA Articles of Agreement.

39 See Operational policy 10.00, *Investment Lending: Identification to Board Presentation*, June 2004 (hereinafter OP 10.00). See n. 40 below.

40 See Operational policy 8.60, *Development Policy Lending*, August 2004 (hereinafter OP 8.60), para 2. Investment and development policy operations are carried out on the basis of an agreement concluded by the Bank with the borrower, be it a State or a private legal person within one of its members (see IBRD's Articles of Agreement, Article III.4 and IDA's establishing instrument, Article V.2.c; see also Operational policy 7.00, *Lending Operations: Choice of Borrowers and Contractual Agreements*, February 2001). They are named loan or credit agreements in the case of the IBRD and IDA respectively, to which the financial terms and conditions provided by the Operational policy no. 3.10, approved in June 2003, are applied. The main difference between IBRD loans and IDA credits pertains to the rate of interest (next to value markets in the case of the IBRD, and at zero per cent for IDA) and the repayment terms (respectively an average 18 years and up to a maximum 40 years). In the eventuality of a Bank's loan to a private person, a guarantee agreement is concluded with the member in whose territory the funded project is located (IBRD Articles of Agreement, Article III.4 (i) and IDA Articles of Agreement, Article V.2.d), whereby the member State guarantees as primary obligor the payment of the principal of, and of the interests on, the loan. The two institutions may also conclude 'grants agreements', with no obligation for the beneficiary to reimburse the resources it has received. For an extensive legal analysis of the content of these agreements and their legal nature, see Vezzani 2011, 53 ff and 112 ff.

41 See Sihihata 1995, 33 ff.

42 See Operational policy 1.00, *Poverty Reduction*, August 2004, para 1.

25.3.2 Planning and Financing Preventive Measures and Humanitarian Assistance Under the 2007 Bank Policy

First and foremost, the prevention issue has become an integral part of the Bank's approach. Indeed, the text of the 2007 operational policy affirms that programs and procedures intended to reduce the impact of disasters should be an integral part of the documents defining the poverty reduction strategy for each member.[43] The matter is all the more relevant for countries highly exposed to natural or man-made disasters. Hence, in the Poverty Reduction and Strategy Paper (PRSP) (to be compulsorily prepared by States eligible to receive IDA's concessional lending) or in other documents stating the government plans for poverty reduction and economic growth, appropriate consideration should be given to the effects of possible future disasters over both the macroeconomic, structural, and national social policy goals and their consequent external financing needs. At the same time, the Bank is called upon not to ignore those same issues when adopting the 'Country Assistance Strategy' (CAS), where the key areas of its actions are defined in order to effectively support each member's efforts for poverty reduction.[44] In this preliminary phase, where the programmatic basis for future assistance is laid down, a cooperative dialog is triggered between the Bank and its members,[45] so that the implication of vulnerability to disasters can simultaneously form an integral part of the strategy for fighting poverty devised by the members and in the program for financial and technical assistance of the Bank. Consistently, in its investment operations, the Bank is expressly legitimized to direct its loans and grants to support members' initiatives aiming to build and strengthen the capacity of their preparedness for and management of emergencies.[46]

In the process leading to the adoption of a new policy for emergency assistance, one of the main issues to be settled was whether the Bank could have a role in providing humanitarian assistance. Indeed, it was not deemed to be covered by its mandate, which focused on the promotion of investments for production, and not on the financing of expenses for the delivery of immediate relief to the populations affected by disasters. In line with this approach, the operational policy in force up to 2007 ruled that the Bank's objective for emergency assistance was 'to restore assets and production levels in the disrupted economy' and that, focusing on areas

[43] See OP 8.00, para 12.

[44] See Bank procedure 2.11, *Country Assistance Strategy*, November 2010. Assistance strategies are implemented through the Bank's lending operations: for both investment operations and policy-based loans, it is expressly established that they are to be coherent with the strategy adopted for each member (see OP 8.60, para 3 and OP 10.00, para 3.a).

[45] See Bank procedure 2.11, para 1 ('[the Country Strategy Paper] is prepared in consultation with country authorities') and 6 ('[t]he CAS … are developed in close consultation with the government, usually through several ministries and agencies and at various level'). As for PRSP, usually the Bank provides technical and financial assistance to support their design.

[46] See OP 8.00, para 12.

of comparative advantage, it would go to finance investment and productive activities, rather than relief or consumption. Relief operations were thus considered to be outside the Bank's scope of action. They included search and rescue, evacuation, food and water distribution, temporary sanitation and health care, temporary shelter, and restoration of access to transport. It was recognized that they could be better carried out by local groups, the government concerned, bilateral relief programs, nongovernmental organizations (NGOs), and specialized international relief organizations.[47]

However, in the course of the years, the World Bank has become aware that it could not ignore the fact that the assistance provided by each actor operating in a particular emergency is a single part of a more complex process, where the coordination of all organizations involved (local, national or international, public or private) is a necessary precondition for an effective support.[48] As a consequence, the 2007 operational policy, while recognizing that its focus is still on the Bank's core development and economic competences,[49] is open to the provision of relief, even if under strict circumstances. Indeed, it is included in the Bank's action in a specific emergency insofar as the institution participates in partnership with other donors in an integrated program covering activities extending outside its mandate, contributing to their preparation, appraisal, and supervision, and clearly not to their implementation.[50] However, it is not to be excluded that financial support may be made available to other international organizations for the supply of goods, in view of their great expertise in humanitarian aid, and to sustain their interventions in specific instances.[51]

25.3.3 Emergency Recovery Loans and Coordination with Other Institutions

Having defined the modalities of the Bank's involvement in the phase immediately following a disaster, the 2007 operational policy sets the specific activities which could come under its scope.[52] They are carried out via investment operations mainly pertaining to the restoration of physical assets, essential services, means of production, and economic activities, excluding from their aim tackling long-term economic issues, requiring a policy response by the government that could be

[47] OP 8.50, para 2 and footnote 4.

[48] See World Bank 2007, 11 ff.

[49] See OP 8.00, para 1.b.

[50] See OP 8.00, para 5.

[51] See n. 59 below and the accompanying text.

[52] See OP 8.00, para 4.

more appropriately addressed under policy-based lending.[53] Notwithstanding the Bank pursues the aim to support members in the reinstatement of infrastructures and productive assets, through the 2007 policy it may also finance the purchase of goods insofar as they are necessary to implement the economic recovery program adopted by national authorities; the only condition to be satisfied is that it be carried out through procurement procedures satisfying requirements of economy and efficiency.[54]

The main financial instrument for assistance in the event of disaster is the emergency recovery loan[55] to be implemented within 2 or 3 years. Subsidizing investment operations, it can be used to restore productive activities immediately after a disaster, but also in order to strengthen the management and implementation of reconstruction efforts, and to favor the adoption of preventive measures reducing vulnerability to risk. In many respects, the decision for the provision of these loans is adopted in line with the usual terms and procedures followed in ordinary investment lending operations. Indeed, taking into account the Bank's assistance strategy in force at the time of the disaster for the beneficiary member, a loan agreement has to be drafted and negotiated by the Secretariat, and then approved by the Executive Board, coming into force after being signed by both the Bank's representative and the borrower. However, the procedure actually followed is accelerated, to reduce delays, and provide financial assistance within a short time.[56] In addition, the amount to be transferred may cover all expenditure necessary to implement the whole operation,[57] derogating from the ordinary clause whereby Bank financing is limited to a part of the whole spending to be sustained by the borrower.[58]

Some exceptions have also been introduced regarding the beneficiaries of emergency assistance. Indeed, the Bank's support is usually extended to State authorities and private legal persons, in accordance with Article III of IBRD's Articles of Agreement and Article V of IDA's constitutive instrument. However, upon request by a member, alternative agreements for the implementation of emergency response activities may be concluded by the Bank, also providing for the allocation of grants to public or private entities operating within the affected area, or to UN agencies and programs or other international or national agencies, including NGOs.[59] But, the adoption of such alternative instruments is limited to

---

[53] See OP 8.00, para 6. For the distinction between investment operations and development policy operations, see n. 40 above and the accompanying text.

[54] See OP 8.00, para 7.e.

[55] For our purposes, the expression 'loan' also includes IDA's emergency assistance credits.

[56] For more details, see the Bank's Secretariat document in World Bank 2010, complementing the Bank procedure no. 8.00 of March 2007.

[57] See OP 8.00, para 7.c. It is not to be excluded that Bank financing can be used to cover the expenses made by the borrower before the loan/credit or grant arrangements are signed (para 7.d).

[58] See Vezzani 2011, 56.

[59] For example, a grant agreement was made in September 2011 between the World Bank and the United Nations High Commissioner for Refugees (UNHCR). Its adoption has been promoted

cases where exceptional circumstances occur and to the extent that the State has insufficient capacity to implement an emergency response. In line with the principle that the State has a primary role in providing assistance to its population, the projects funded may be limited to early recovery and have to include capacity-building operations to enable a speedy transfer of responsibilities to the interested country.[60]

The same exceptions to ordinary investment operations apply if the Bank decides to make recourse to the other instruments provided for in the 2007 operational policy, i.e., the restructuring of assistance already in place, or similarly the redesigning of investment projects not yet approved, to include recovery and reconstruction activities within their scope. A final component of the World Bank's assistance consists of contingent financing that may be provided for the benefit of high-risk countries considered to have the appropriate institutional and implementation capacity to respond to emergencies. In general terms, reserved to members eligible to receive IBRD's assistance, this 'insurance' instrument may be integrated within a development policy operation to allow the borrower to postpone drawing part of the loan.[61] Within the operational policy for disasters, its use is restricted to finance the purchase of goods included in the emergency recovery program and necessary for assistance, and thus to meet the members' foreign reserves needs.[62]

Investment operations are funded through ordinary capital, including shares as subscribed and paid by member States on the occasion of their accession to the IBRD and IDA, regular replenishments of IDA funds, and the funds borrowed from international capital markets by the issuing of bonds. However, the World Bank also acts through the administration and disbursement of resources allocated to the so-called 'trust funds', with a country-specific, regional or global territorial scope. Indeed, the Bank may accept contributions from sovereign and non-sovereign donors in order to finance activities consistent with the IBRD's and IDA's Articles of Agreement and with the country's strategies. These resources are deposited in trust funds and then bypassed to a recipient to carry out activities over which the Bank preserves an appraisal and supervisory role (recipient-executed trust funds) or used to directly finance the Bank's program (Bank-executed trust funds).[63] Trust funds have been frequently used for natural disasters, also with the

(Footnote 59 continued)
by Ethiopia and Kenya, requesting an alternative agreement whereby the UNHCR would be the recipient of an IDA grant necessary for health and nutrition interventions in the camps situated in the two countries, receiving Somali refugees leaving their territories because of heavy and extensive famine. See the emergency project paper in the World Bank document Report No: 63642-AFR, August 31, 2011 and the Agreement for Grant H735 Conformed, September 19, 2011.

[60] See OP 8.00, para 9.

[61] See OP 8.60, para 21 ff.

[62] See OP 8.00, para 13.

[63] See Operational policy 14.00, *Trust Funds* and the related Bank procedure 14.00 of July 2008.

aim of merging all donors' efforts into a single financial instrument administered by the Bank, and in order to concertedly support national governments in their efforts to tackle the material consequences of a natural or man-made disaster. Recently, initiatives have been established under trust funds for the benefit of Haiti after the earthquake of 2010, and Indonesia in 2006 and 2010.[64]

The need for strong coordination among donors has persuaded the Bank to adopt legal instruments designed to ensure that resources channeled into its trust funds are used for an effective implementation of relief and reconstruction activities in the aftermath of disaster. The Fiduciary Principles Accord concluded in 2008 represents an important step ahead in this direction. As an agreement between the World Bank and some UN programs and agencies involved by their mandate in post-crisis recovery and reconstruction, the Accord was designed to facilitate the transfer of funds from a World Bank trust to the UN system, and vice versa.[65]

25.4 Major Findings: IFIs as Actors of Governance Mechanisms for Relief, Recovery, and Reconstruction in the Event of Disasters?

Over the last years, legal instruments and the practice of international financial institutions have undergone a significant evolution in order to introduce new policies to meet more effectively the needs of countries and populations struck or likely to be struck by natural or man-made disasters. As a consequence, additional resources have been made available to finance a wide range of activities, from disaster prevention and risk reduction to post-catastrophe reconstruction.

As a whole, this complex set of rules and procedures can hardly be considered as shaping a homogeneous and coherent system. The policies of international financial institutions vary considerably in material scope, due to the lack of a common definition of disasters. Some of them intervene only in the case of natural events, others are legitimized to provide financial assistance also when man-made disasters occur, while a third category is involved exclusively in coping with the consequences of technological catastrophe. In addition, there is no previously agreed and deliberate division of competences based on geographic or economic considerations, or on the activities each organization is best suited to finance. Rather, each institution mostly acts autonomously, within its mandate as set out in its constitutive instrument, and more frequently to respond to requests for assistance by its members only after a disaster has occurred.

---

[64] See World Bank 2011, 46 ff and 94.

[65] The text of the Fiduciary Principles Accord may be found on the website www.undg.org. Accessed 9 January 2012.

One of the main deficiencies in the overall legal framework is the lack of an international body with comprehensive competence to coordinate the delivery of financial assistance. Indeed, as underlined by the World Bank, '[t]he primary challenge when responding to emergencies is to identify correctly the priority activities and sequence them in such a way as to address the urgent needs of the most affected without undermining the success of the overall recovery and reconstruction program'[66]; a concerted effort by the international community is thus desirable, in order 'to support a single comprehensive program that provides the appropriate framework for each donor... to focus on the areas in which it is best placed to provide the most effective assistance, taking into account the needs and circumstances of each situation'.[67]

Coherently with this purpose, some initiatives have been adopted within the policies of each institution and more broadly within the United Nations system. Concerning the former, the World Bank has been one of the busier actors, as the 2007 policy on rapid response to crisis and emergency has been integrated by some rules concerning cooperation and coordination with all entities involved in the delivery of assistance, including the Bank's participation (in cooperation with other institutions) in the preparation, appraisal and supervision of integrated support programs also covering activities outside its mandate. Similarly, some instruments have been introduced for more effective coordination with other UN agencies and programs (i.e., the 2008 Fiduciary Principles Accord), in the light of the primary requirement that support operations be carried out by the organization with specific expertise in the field. However, this coordination is limited to cases where assistance is financed through trust funds, and not by the ordinary resources of the institutions. The use of the latter is left to the individual judgment of the pertinent organization, without any interference from other actors in the administration.[68]

Some practice by regional development banks[69] and the IMF may also be considered. In any case, similar 'coordination provisions' are limited in number and scope, and their adoption is *de facto* left to the discretion of the institutions themselves, not being promoted or supervised by any supervisory body.

---

[66] World Bank 2007, para 20.

[67] Ibidem, para 23.

[68] However, through a derogation adopted by the Executive Board, the limits of the 2008 Accord have been overcome in the IDA decision to finance the UNHCR through grants in the delivery of assistance in the refugees' camps in Ethiopia and Kenya (n. 59 above).

[69] See ADB 2004, para 70 (for support by the Asian Development Bank of relief actions by the WFP, UNICEF, the IFRC and UNHCR); ADB 2009, para 12 (whereby assistance through the ADB Disaster Response Fund is granted in strict coordination with the UN humanitarian/resident coordinator); IDB doc. 2354-3, cit., directive B-3 and IDB 2007, 26 (for the coordination of the Inter-American Development Bank with aid organizations to finance their immediate humanitarian assistance); AfDB 2008, para 3.1 (whereby support under the African Development Bank Special Relief Fund may be approved after having received an appeal from the United Nations).

Within the UN system, the coordination of financial assistance for humanitarian aid is promoted by the Central Emergency Response Fund, the Consolidated Appeal Process, and the Flash Appeal, whose scope is however restricted to humanitarian relief in the immediate aftermath of a disaster.[70] Concerted action was favored with the establishment in 1999 of the International Strategy for Disaster Reduction,[71] within whose framework a Global Facility for Disaster Reduction and Recovery was established in 2006, managed by the World Bank. However, it does not operate as a coordinating mechanism among international institutions involved in the implementation of recovery programs, but, thanks to grants by States and other international organizations, it favors the disbursement of additional resources to States stricken by natural disasters. Actually, it is a further mechanism for additional financing.

Within the UN system, a more comprehensive financial assistance approach could be promoted applying the UN Charter provisions regarding specialized agencies. Indeed, both the IMF and the World Bank institutions have concluded an agreement with the United Nations according to Article 63 of the Charter, and are subject to the coordination function of the Social and Economic Council. However, over the last decades, the UN system has been subject to much criticism and many proposals for its amendment have been put forward in order to avoid overlaps and guarantee better coordination among all UN agencies and programs. Insufficient coordination in disaster prevention and response reflects the limits of this system within a given sector.

In addition, participation in the UN system is precluded to all multilateral development banks except the World Bank institutions, due to legal considerations and the will of these institutions to preserve their autonomy. However, it should also be remembered that for some organizations (in particular, the World Trade Organization and the International Atomic Energy Agency) their formal autonomy from the UN system did not prevent their participation in the Chief Executive Board on Coordination, the coordinating mechanism for specialized agencies set up in 1946. The involvement of regional development banks to this forum could hence be pursued granting them observer status, in any case with a view to their participation in the strategic programing and planning of financial assistance to States hit by disasters.

As underlined by the International Court of Justice on occasion of the request by the World Health Organization (WHO) for an advisory opinion on the legitimacy under international law of the use by States of nuclear weapons, the powers of the UN specialized agencies have to be inferred from their constitutive instruments, but they also need to be conceptualized in a broader framework, where consideration of their respective scope of action is of particular

[70] See Chap. 26 by Palandri in this volume.

[71] UN General Assembly doc. A/RES/54/291, December 22, 1999.

significance.[72] This assumption has led the Court to deny its jurisdiction in the particular case, since the conditions set out in Article 96 of the UN Charter for the exercise of advisory functions were not satisfied: the request did not pertain to the WHO functions, whose legitimacy when acting for the promotion of health, according to the Court, is in no way determined by the legality or illegality under international law of the behavior causing the threat to health. Applying the Court's reasoning to the broader context of global governance, where all relevant actors can contribute to overcome emergencies due to disasters, and for an effective delimitation of the competencies of UN agencies and programs, a suitable comprehensive mechanism of coordination is desirable. To effectively tackle emergencies, an appropriate mechanism ought to be established, where financial institutions can intervene in a coordinated way to support the affected State, complementing and supplementing their actions in view of the common purpose of satisfying every need to the benefit of populations.

References

ADB (2004) Disaster Emergency Assistance Policy www.adb.org/documents/policies/disaster_emergency/default.asp

ADB (2005) Asian Tsunami Fund www.adb.org/Documents/Papers/Tsunami/Asian-Tsunami-Fund.pdf

ADB (2009) Establishment of the Asia Pacific disaster response fund www.adb.org/Documents/Others/Asia-Pacific-Disaster-Response.pdf

AfDB (2008) Revised policy guidelines and procedures for emergency relief assistance www.afdb.org/fileadmin/uploads/afdb/Documents/Policy-Documents/REVISED%20POLICY%20GUIDELINES%20AND%20PROCEDURES%20FOR%20EMERGENCY%20RELIEF%20ASSISTANCE%20AND%20GENERAL%20REGULATIONS%20OF%20THE%20SPECIAL%20RELIEF%20FUND.pdf

Boughton JM (2001) Silent revolution. The International Monetary Fund 1979–1989. International Monetary Fund, Washington, DC

Gold J (1990) Natural disasters and other emergencies beyond control: assistance by the IMF. Int Lawyer 24:621–641

Horsefield JK (ed) (1969a) The International Monetary Fund 1945–1965. Twenty years of International Monetary Cooperation, volume I: Chronicle. International Monetary Fund, Washington, DC

Horsefield JK (ed) (1969b) The International Monetary Fund 1945–1965. Twenty Years of International Monetary Cooperation, volume III: Documents, International Monetary Fund, Washington, DC

IDB (2007) From disaster response to prevention. Companion paper to the disaster risk management policy www.iris.edu/hq/files/about_iris/governance/ds/docs/IADB_From_Response_To_Prevention.pdf

IDB (2008) Disaster risk management policy guidelines, idbdocs.iadb.org/wsdocs/getdocument.aspx?docnum = 360026

IEG/World Bank (2006) Hazards of nature, risks to development. An IEG evaluation of World Bank assistance for natural disasters. World Bank, Washington, DC

[72] See *Legality of the Use by a State of Nuclear Weapons in Armed Conflict, Advisory Opinion,* ICJ Rep1996, 66 f. para 26. For a comment, see Klabbers 2009.

IMF (2005) Subsidization of the Fund's emergency assistance for natural disasters to PRGF-eligible members
IMF (2009) A new architecture of facilities for low-income countries www.imf.org/external/np/pp/eng/2009/062609.pdf
IMF (2010a) Proposal for a Post-Catastrophe Debt Relief Trust Fund www.imf.org/external/np/pp/eng/2010/042210.pdf
IMF (2010b) Selected decisions and selected documents of the International Monetary Fund, 35th edn. International Monetary Fund, Washington, DC
IMF (2011a) The Fund's Financing Role—Reform Proposals on Liquidity and Emergency Assistance www.imf.org/external/np/pp/eng/2011/102811.pdf
IMF (2011b) The Fund's Financing Role—Reform Proposals on Liquidity and Emergency Assistance—Decisions www.imf.org/external/np/pp/eng/2011/112111.pdf
IMF (2011c) Macroeconomic and operational challenges in countries in Fragile Situations, www.imf.org/external/np/pp/eng/2011/061511a.pdf
IMF Factsheet (2011) IMF emergency assistance: supporting recovery from natural disasters and armed conflicts www.imf.org/external/np/exr/facts/conflict.htm
Klabbers J (2009) Global governance before the ICJ: Re-reading the WHA opinion. Max Planck Yearb UN Law 13:1–28
Sihihata I F I (1995) The World Bank in a changing World. Selected essays and lectures, vol II. Martinus Nijhoff Publichers, The Hague
Vezzani S (2011) Gli accordi delle Organizzazioni del Gruppo della Banca mondiale. Giappichellli, Torino
World Bank (2007) Toward a new framework for Rapid Bank response to crises and emergencies www.worldbank.org/PROJECTS/Resources/40940-1205169918173/Rapidresponseboardpaper.pdf
World Bank (2010) Rapid response to crises and emergencies: procedural guidelines, www.worldbank.org/OPSMANUAL/Resources/RR_to_Crises_&_Emergencies_Procedural_Guidelines_06_28_2010ReadOnly.docx
World Bank (2011) Directory of programs supported by Trust Funds as of March 31, 2011. The World Bank, Washington, DC

Chapter 26
Funding Arrangements for Disaster Response

Ivana Palandri

Abstract Complex emergencies have changed dramatically. This requires the deployment of new resources so as to ensure a more predictable and timely response. A better prevention capability and timely responses should be supported by sufficient and flexible funding. The humanitarian system has established several mechanisms to improve financing in terms of prevention, equity, and readiness for action. The author focuses attention on current funding instruments adopted at universal, regional, and bilateral levels and on the role played by private parties.

Keywords Funding instruments · Natural disasters · Emergency situations · United Nations · Regional organizations · Bilateral agreements · Private parties

Contents

I. Palandri (✉)
Dipartimento di Giurisprudenza, Università di Modena e Reggio
Emilia via San Geminiano 3, 41121, Modena, Italy
e-mail: ivana.palandri@unimore.it

A. de Guttry et al. (eds.), *International Disaster Response Law*,
DOI: 10.1007/978-90-6704-882-8_26,

26.1 Introduction

Adequate economic resources are an essential requirement for humanitarian aid to be quick and effective, both in the case of natural disasters and in other emergency situations.

To this end, at the global, regional, and local levels a series of mechanisms have been created to finance humanitarian aid. In this context, we will therefore consider instruments put in place by the United Nations system,[1] by some regional organizations (the European Union, the Central American Integration System, CARICOM, ASEAN) and bilaterally between States. Finally, attention will be dedicated to the role played or which could be played by private parties (individuals and organizations) in the financing of humanitarian aid.

26.2 The United Nations System

The need to provide a central funding mechanism for emergencies, complementary to that of organizations and entities of the United Nations, was recognized in 1991 by the UN General Assembly by Resolution 46/182,[2] which requested the Secretary-General to establish, under its authority, "a central emerging revolving fund as a cash-flow mechanism to ensure the rapid and co-ordinated response of the organizations of the system" (para 23). The Fund so established was initially allocated a budget of USD 50 million, to be then fed by voluntary contributions, with an initial consolidated appeal launched by the Secretary-General,[3] known as the Consolidated Appeal Process (CAP).

The Fund's resources are available for UN institutions, its funds and programs, such as UNICEF, UNHCR, UNDP, WFP, as well as specialized agencies

---

[1] This paper does not include the UN financial institutions. On International Monetary Fund see Chap. 25, section 25.2, by Adinolfi in this volume.

[2] A/RES/46/182, 15 December 1991.

[3] "For emergencies requiring a coordinate response, the Secretary-General should ensure that an initial consolidated appeal covering all concerned organizations of the system, prepared in consultation with the affected State, is issued within the shortest possible time and in any event not longer than 1 week". A/RES/46/182, para 31.

(FAO, WHO, etc.). A later GA Resolution,[4] extended the possibility also to the International Organization for Migration (IOM).

Resolution 46/182 establishes the status of Emergency Relief Coordinator (ERC), appointed by the Secretary-General. This status has co-ordinating functions for all the activities carried out by the United Nations in the context of both natural disasters and other emergencies. For our purposes, in particular, the Emergency Relief Coordinator must process urgent requests for assistance, submitted by the Member States concerned, and prepare, in consultation with the government of the affected country, a consolidated appeal to be issued by the Secretary-General. This entails managing, in consultation with the operational organizations concerned, the Central Emerging Revolving Fund and assisting the mobilization of resources; as well as preparing an annual report for the Secretary-General on the co-ordination of humanitarian emergency assistance, to include information on the Central Emerging Revolving Fund and to be submitted to the General Assembly, through the ECOSOC.

A dedicated office—the United Nations Office for the Coordination of Humanitarian Affairs (OCHA)—has absorbed part of already existing services and carries out the tasks of the Emergency Relief Coordinator.

The system established by Resolution 46/182, namely the Fund and the CAP, were the main instruments of the United Nations[5] ensuring an effective and co-ordinated response in the event of humanitarian crises and the main instruments for funding and planning at the disposal of United Nations humanitarian organizations until 2005.

However, the strict provisions regulating the Fund were an obstacle to its use. As a matter of fact, it was expected that the Fund was to be refunded within 6 months of the loans received, which meant that the humanitarian organizations of the United Nations hesitated to resort to this financial instrument, except in cases where they were certain they would receive contributions from donors.

In most cases, in fact, the Fund had only been used in the context of crises that had received extensive media attention (Iraq, Kosovo, Afghanistan), since in such cases the refund was secured through voluntary contributions.

It was therefore necessary to modernize existing instruments[6] to help strengthen the intervention capability of the humanitarian system and to make the financing of these measures more predictable. This reform, introduced in 2005, came into full effect in 2006.

---

[4] A/RES/48/57, 14 December 1993.

[5] In the period between its establishment and 2005 the Fund was allocated about USD 337 million in loans. See Report of the Secretary-General, Improvement of the Central Emerging Revolving Fund, doc. A/60/432, 20 October 2005, para 5.

[6] See Report of the Secretary-General, In Larger Freedom: Towards Development, Security, and Human Rights for All, doc. A/59/2005, 21 March 2005. The proposals advanced by the Secretary-General were accepted by the General Assembly. See A/RES/60/1, 15 September 2005.

26.2.1 *The 2006 Reform: The Central Emergency Response Fund*

With the 2006 reform the Central Emerging Revolving Fund was renamed the Central Emergency Response Fund (CERF).[7] Its work is expected to be evaluated in relation to the realization of three objectives: (1) to promote early action and response and reduce the loss of lives; (2) to enhance response to time-critical requirements based on demonstrable needs; (3) to strengthen core elements of humanitarian response in underfunded crises on the basis of performance indicators proposed by the Emergency Relief Coordinator and evaluated each year by the Advisory Group, an independent body created *ad hoc*.[8]

The system of CERF funding has been strengthened, with the overall goal of reaching the sum of USD 500 million, divided between loans (USD 50 million) and grants, which should reach the amount of USD 450 million.

Member States of the UN, private businesses, foundations, and individuals are strongly encouraged to contribute to the Fund. CERF has also been successful in attracting new and returning donors and an increased number of private and public donations. From an initial number of 52 Member States contributing to the Fund in 2006, the figure reached 122 in 2010.[9]

However, the sum of USD 500 million, despite the increasing number of donors, has never been reached. Even during 2011 effective donations appeared to fall.[10]

UN funds, programs and specialized agencies, and the IOM[11] are eligible grant recipients. NGOs may receive funding indirectly as cooperating partners of UN agencies and, along with humanitarian partners, benefit from CERF funding for common services. OCHA, as a manager of the Fund, may apply for a CERF loan,[12] but it cannot benefit from a CERF grant.

Priority funding is taken from loan component of the Fund. Only if loans are not sufficient, grants will be used.[13]

The grant element is split into two components: rapid response window and underfunded emergencies window.

---

7 A/RES/60/124, 15 December 2005.

8 The Advisory Group has also the task of providing advice to the CERF on rapidity with which the funds should be allocated, the basis of appropriations, to and also on examining the operation of the CERF to in carrying out financial checks and to contributing to the visibility and transparency.

9 OCHA 2010a, 25.

10 See CERF Pledges and contributions 2006–2011, http://ochaonline.un.org/cerfhtml/PC_2006-11_220811.pdf. Accessed 15 February 2012.

11 WFP is the UN agency with the largest share of CERF funding (33 %). See Report of the Secretary-General, Central Emergency Response Fund, doc. A/66/357, 13 September 2011, para 7.

12 In December 2010 a single loan of USD 9,9 million was disbursed to the OCHA and was repaid at the end of June 2011. See doc. A/66/357, para 10.

13 Secretary-General's Bulletin, Establishment and Operation of the Central Emergency Response Fund, ST/SGB/2010/5, 23 April 2010, Sect. 3.

Only a part (2/3) of the total amount of grants is earmarked for early, vital interventions and for up to USD 30 million for every crisis.[14]

The CERF, in fact, mostly provides only for the initial financial aid, since its resources constitute a small proportion of the total funds available for humanitarian purposes in the United Nations system. Most of the interventions, moreover, are funded within the framework of existing procedures (CAP and Flash Appeal).

As regards underfunded emergency interventions, only ½ of the grant component of the Fund is intended for their financing[15] and must be utilized to provide grants to address core emergency humanitarian needs in chronically underfunded emergencies.[16] In principle, the minimum recommended amount allocated to each country is USD 1 million.[17] Grants for underfunded emergencies must be provided in order to promote an equitable response to humanitarian crises across the world and must be based on demonstrable core emergency humanitarian needs. From July 2010 to June 2011, for example, the Fund provided USD 6 million for underfunded emergencies in response to severe drought in Djibouti.[18]

To determine how to best allocate donations intended for this category of interventions, the Emergency Relief Coordinator, on the basis of consultations with interested parties (the Agency Standing Committee,[19] Eligible Organizations, the Resident/Humanitarian Coordinator, humanitarian country teams and the affected State), defines the priority areas of actions to be financed.

Where appropriate, an Eligible Organization could apply for a grant as well as a loan in combination, in order to address such humanitarian needs for a specific program or projects.

In the period July 2010–June 2011 the Emergency Relief Coordinator approved grants for a total of USD 342 million, of which USD 215,6 million was for early interventions and USD 126,5 million for underfunded emergencies. About USD 120 million (35 % of total funding) was used to respond to emergencies caused by natural disasters, particularly in Asia and the Caucasus area.[20]

Also the mechanism of reimbursement of the Fund has been enhanced to facilitate its use by humanitarian organizations. In fact, the reimbursement of loans by the beneficiary is done primarily through a levy on contributions received for the program or project in question; if the operating body does not have sufficient

---

[14] ST/SGB/2010/5, para 4.2.

[15] CERF underfunded grants should mitigate the unevenness and slowness of the voluntary humanitarian contributions system by targeting emergencies that have not attracted or are unlikely to attract sufficient and timely funding for life-saving activities.

[16] ST/SGB/2010/5, para 4.3.

[17] Cf. OCHA, 2010b, 4.

[18] See doc. A/66/357, para 18.

[19] A/RES/46/182, para 38.

[20] See doc. A/66/357 para 4.

contributions to cover the loan,[21] the repayment of the balance is delayed until it has sufficient amounts.[22]

Despite continuous improvements to the operations of CERF, there are a number of outstanding issues, well highlighted in the 5-year evaluation report:[23] a lack of effective co-ordination with other existing funding mechanisms; under-utilization by the operational bodies of the Fund's loans component,[24] which shows what the needs of humanitarian agencies are; the impossibility for NGOs of having direct access to Fund resources, complained of repeatedly by such organizations; the extreme complexity of the procedure for accessing resources of the Fund; the limited rapidity in the allocation of funds; the lack of attractiveness of the Fund which affects its ability to increase voluntary contributions from donors.[25]

26.2.2 The Other Funding Instruments

The Central Emergency Response Fund is definitely the main instrument at the disposal of the UN to finance humanitarian actions, but it is not the only tool. Other forms of financing have been created, in particular the Emergency Response Funds (ERFs) and the Common Humanitarian Funds (CHFs). Both instruments were established *ad hoc* in a given country to respond to humanitarian crises.

The first Emergency Response Fund was established in Angola in 1997 to respond to increasing humanitarian needs caused by years of conflict. When the humanitarian reform process began in 2005 it banked on existing practices on the use of these pooled funding mechanisms for channeling humanitarian assistance.

---

[21] At the beginning of July 2010 there were three existing loans. Of a total of USD 1,4 million loaned to the WHO in Sudan in 2004, USD 1,1 million has now been repaid and of a total of USD 2,660,510 million loaned to the UNPD in Sudan in 2007 only USD 1,644,474 million has been repaid. See doc. A/66/357, para 10.

[22] The ERC "shall make every effort to obtain full reimbursement to the loan element of the Fund in respect of any outstanding advance within 2 years of the date of the advance". ST/SGB/2010/5, para 3.8.

[23] Channel Resources 2011.

[24] The report about the 5-year evaluation recommends that "the CERF loan funds should be reduced to U.S. $ 30 million and the balance transferred to the grant window". Channel Resource 2011, 37.

[25] The key donors appear to be only seven in total. With their donations they account for 80 % of the Fund resources, whereas other donors only contribute in to a limited way extent. Channel Resources 2011, 92 ff. The United Nations General Assembly recently "called upon all member States and invited the private sector and all concerned individuals and institutions to consider increasing their voluntary contributions to the Central Emergency Response Fund [...]". A/RES/65/133, 15 December 2010.

As a result several new Emergency Response Funds were initiated in countries that were subject to complex humanitarian emergencies.[26]

The aim of Emergency Response Funds is to provide rapid and flexible funding to in-country actors to be addressed to unforeseen humanitarian needs. The Funds also provide governments and the private sector with an opportunity to pool their contributions to a specific country to enable timely and reliable humanitarian assistance in response to emergencies.[27]

ERF funding is available to NGOs (which cannot access the CERF) and UN agencies for emergency response (however the majority of funding goes to NGOs).[28]

ERFs are relatively small compared to the Central Emergency Response Fund and the Common Humanitarian Funds.[29] Therefore, funding allocations for projects tend to be small—ranging from UDS 100,000 to USD 500,000—and the mechanism is run in parallel with other humanitarian financing mechanisms, including the CERF and CHFs.

The Emergency Response Funds are usually not included in the Consolidated Appeal Process or similar co-ordination mechanisms, but are in line with the Common Humanitarian Action Plan[30] objectives and identified priorities.

The OCHA manages the Emergency Response Fund in each country and all project applications have to be approved by the Humanitarian Coordinator before they can receive a grant from the fund. The financial administration is in most cases managed by the UNDP.

The Common Humanitarian Funds are a multi-donor, strategic, and predictable funding mechanism.

Their main objective is to enable the Humanitarian Coordinator and the humanitarian community to ensure early and predictable funding to the most critical humanitarian needs, as identified and formulated in a Common Humanitarian Action Plan and for projects included in the CAP. The objective of a CHF is to raise funds through the Consolidated Appeal Process. Nevertheless, for example, only 45 % of the CAP for the Central African Republic for 2010 was funded, against assessed needs of USD 129 million. For this reason in April 2011 the

---

[26] There are currently 16 ERFs in operation. http://ochanet.unocha.org/p/Documents/CHFs%20and%20ERFs%20FundingStatusGraphics%2020Jun2011.pdf Accessed 14 February 2012.

[27] Between 2006 and 2010 the number of donors using the ERFs increased from 6 to 56. In 2010, of the 15 funds that were in operation 13 attracted funding totaling USD 154,3 million, the highest amount to date. Source Global Humanitarian Assistance (GHA) 2011a, 3.

[28] Global Humanitarian Assistance (GHA) 2011a, 10.

[29] In 2010 the fund of Haiti received the largest amount ever received by an ERF, USD 82 million in response to the earthquake.

[30] The Common Humanitarian Action Plan is a strategic plan for humanitarian response in a given country or region. It provides a common analysis of the context in which humanitarian action takes place; an assessment of needs; best, worst, and most likely scenarios; identification of roles and responsibilities; a clear statement of longer term objectives and goals; a framework for monitoring the strategy and revising it if necessary. The Common Humanitarian Action Plan is the foundation for developing a Consolidated Appeal and as such it is part of the CAP.

Emergency Relief Coordinator granted the country USD 5 million from the Central Emergency Response Fund's allocation for underfunded emergencies.[31]

The Common Humanitarian Funds also maintain an Emergency Reserve (a maximum of 10 % of total funding) for responding to unplanned emergency needs outside the CAP.

All humanitarian partners (UN agencies, NGOs, local authorities, etc.) participating in the CAP are eligible to receive CHFs funding.

Allocations from a Common Humanitarian Fund are based on an advisory allocation process that engages sector/cluster groups and other relevant stakeholders at country level in a comprehensive prior exercise.

A Common Humanitarian Fund has two allocation mechanisms: (1) a standard allocation of funding against priority activities within the CAP. It consists of two rounds, one at the beginning of the year[32] and the other mid-year. The allocation process takes 2–6 weeks; (2) an Emergency Reserve for providing rapid response of unforeseen and/or rapid-outset circumstances not addressed through the standard allocation.

CHFs are managed by a Humanitarian Coordinator with support from the OCHA Country Office and a dedicated advisory group. Based on an allocation proposal developed and submitted by sector/cluster groups, the Humanitarian Coordinator, supported by a technical Review Board, takes a final decision on granting Funds.

The UNDP is the financial fund manager of all existing Funds.[33]

In addition to these general tools set up at the central and local levels, in the UN system there are two additional financing channels to initially deal with an emergency: the OCHA Emergency Cash Grant and Pre-positioned Funds and the UNDP Response to Sudden Crisis.

The OCHA Emergency Cash Grant,[34] originates from the UN regular budget, and can be disbursed for relief activities in the immediate aftermath of a disaster in the country requesting or welcoming international assistance.[35] The size of the allocation does not exceed USD 100,000 in the case of a catastrophic event. If the country is included in the OECD/DAC list of aid recipients, the grant can be

---

[31] See Security Council, Report of the Secretary-General on the Situation in the Central African Republic and on the Activities of the United Nations Integrated Peacebuilding Office in that Country, doc. S/2011/311, 16 May 2011, para 44.

[32] The majority of CHFs funds are allocated at the beginning of the year.

[33] Common Humanitarian Funds exists in the Central African Republic (total donation USD 41 million from 2006 to June 2011); the Democratic Republic of Congo (total donation USD 616 million from 2006 to June 2011); Somalia (total donation USD 81 million from 2006 to June 2011); Sudan (total donation USD 869 million from 2006 to June 2011). http://ochanet.unocha.org/p/Documents/CHFs%20and%20ERFs%20FundingStatusGraphics%2020Jun2011.pdf Accessed 14 February 2012.

[34] A/RES/59/141, 17 December 2004.

[35] The OCHA Emergency Cash Grant covers the most pressing needs of the affected populations resulting from natural, environmental, and technological disasters. It cannot be used for rehabilitation or reconstruction activities, establishing co-ordination mechanism or/and recruiting personnel. http://ocha.unog.ch/drptoolkit/FEmergencyCashGrant.html. Accessed 14 February 2012.

supplemented by Pre-positioned Funds[36] (Emergency Grant Reserve) at the OCHA's discretion.[37]

The Resident Coordinator, the Humanitarian Coordinator[38] and the OCHA Field or Regional Office are eligible to request grants. The Government of the affected State can also request them through its Permanent Mission to the UN in Geneva or New York.

If approved, the grant is disbursed within 10 days and should be spent within 2 months.

In response to a sudden crisis the UNDP can make its funds available from its core resources for rapid disbursement on a case-by-case basis. Normally the size of the allocation does not exceed USD 100,000. Their aim is to enable the Resident Coordinator to co-ordinate an effective response to a sudden crisis (disaster or conflict), conduct a needs assessment, initiate an early recovery framework, and establish solid foundations for sustainable recovery.[39]

Only the Relief Coordinator can request the funds.[40]

Finally, we should not forget that all of the various organizations and entities of the United Nations (WFP, WHO, FAO, UNHCR, UNICEF, OCHA, etc.) have funds for emergency interventions,[41] which are used to finance initial needs in accordance with their mission.

26.2.3 Appeal Mechanisms

Basically, the appeal mechanisms to the donor community are twofold: the Consolidated Appeal Process (CAP) and the Flash Appeal. The CAP is a strategic planning and fundraising tool, consisting of a Common Humanitarian Action Plan and a list of project proposals.[42] It is a tool used by aid organizations to plan, implement, and monitor their activities together.

---

[36] Pre-positioned Funds are currently provided by Denmark, Italy, Ireland, the Netherlands, Norway, and the United Kingdom.

[37] Grants from Pre-positioned Funds should not exceed the amount of regular OCHA grants, except in the case of Italy, where the amount can be higher and can be released not only in case the of natural disasters but also for an acute crisis within a complex emergency situation. However, in this particular case, prior to the release of funds, a written request must be sent to the Italian Permanent Mission for approval.

[38] See Chap. 23, section 23.2.3, by Silingardi in this volume.

[39] This includes the recruitment of emergency management personnel to support immediate needs.

[40] IASC 2010, 68.

[41] In 2010 the final global budget of OCHA was USD 263,3 million. Of this total, OCHA sought USD 219 million in voluntary contributions. OCHA 2010a, 33.

[42] See CAP 2011 http://ochanet.unocha.org/p/Documents/CAP_2011_Humanitarian_Appeal_SCREEN.pdf. Accessed 14 February 2012. On the Consolidate Appeals for 2012 see http://www.unocha.org/cap/appeals/by-year/results/taxonomy%3A66. Accessed 14 February 2012.

Humanitarian organizations, working together in the world's crisis regions, have to produce appeals to be presented to the international community and donors.

The CAP is typically launched in November and covers the upcoming calendar year.

All humanitarian partners, including national authorities, can participate in developing the humanitarian response plan. Government consent to issue the appeal is not required, but consultation is essential.

The UN agencies, international organizations, and international and national NGOs and components of the International Red Cross and Red Crescent Movement may include projects in the appeal as long as their projects are in line with the priorities identified in the Common Humanitarian Action Plan.[43] Government bodies of the affected country can be included as partners in a UN or NGO project, but cannot appeal directly for funds.

The Flash Appeals have been set up to respond quickly to a natural disaster or sudden deterioration of a complex emergency situation by raising finance. Their purpose is to provide a co-ordinated humanitarian response for the first 3 (or maximum 6) months of such emergencies.

The Flash Appeal is prepared in consultation with all humanitarian actors (government officials, donors, UN agencies, the International Committee of the Red Cross, members of the International Federation of the Red Cross and Red Crescent Societies, NGOs, etc.).

The Resident Coordinator or the Humanitarian Coordinator, with support from the OCHA, is responsible for the content and quality of the document, which must include an analysis of the context and humanitarian needs[44] and response plans (including specific proposed projects). The Flash Appeal may include projects from UN agencies, international organizations, and NGOs. It may include project partnerships with the Red Cross or Red Crescent National Society of the country of operation. Government bodies cannot appeal for funds directly in a flash appeal, but can be partners in UN or NGO projects.

It usually takes 5 days to prepare and refine the document and only on the sixth day is the appeal officially launched.[45]

In order to make funds available for operational agencies it is necessary to speed up the process of launching the appeal, which means that the document will be based on the needs deemed most urgent in the first phase of the crisis.

Therefore, the document, as well as the projects contained within it, have to be reviewed after the launch of the appeal, on the basis of new information available. Generally, the contents of a Flash Appeal are revised the month after its launch,

---

[43] See footnote 30.

[44] In the case of Tsunami "the original UN Appeal amount of US $ 1.28 billion was a largely arbitrary calculation about the consolidated amount of funds different agencies felt they needed". Flint and Goyder 2006, 30.

[45] IASC 2006, 3–4.

in order to incorporate more information and projects. The Flash Appeal may be developed into or succeeded by a Consolidated Appeal if an inter-agency response is needed beyond 6 months.

26.3 The Regional Instruments

As mentioned in the Introduction some funding mechanisms have also been adopted at regional level to cope with emergencies. In this context, it may be interesting to discuss Europe, Asia, and Central America, as they are the regions where such organizations and mechanisms have grown most. Which means that the analysis is not exhaustive of all of the instruments adopted in the various regional areas.

26.3.1 The European Union

The European Union (EU) at the global level is the second "government contributor" to international humanitarian response.[46]

The financing of humanitarian actions, intended as responses to both natural disasters and complex emergencies, is carried out through the general budget of the EU, with the exception of the European Development Fund (EDF),[47] which is funded by member states. However, instruments have been set up specifically to finance the various emergencies, including the Civil Protection Financial Instrument (CPFI) and the European Union Solidarity Fund (EUSF) and, more generally, a regulation has been adopted for the financing of humanitarian aid.

The Civil Protection Financial Instrument[48] is an instrument to finance rapid response and timely measures for major emergencies, whether these result from natural, industrial, or technological disasters or terrorist acts,[49] inside or outside the EU, where a request is made for assistance in accordance with the EU Civil Protection Mechanism (CPM).[50]

Financial assistance covers actions in the field of the Civil Protection Mechanism to facilitate reinforced co-operation in civil protection assistance interventions; the measures prevent or reduce the effects of an emergency and the actions

---

[46] See Global Humanitarian Assistance (GHA) 2011b, 11.

[47] The European Development Fund is the main instrument for providing EU aid for development co-operation in the ACP countries and OCT. The tenth EDF covers the period from 2008 to 2013 and provides an overall budget of EUR 22.682 million. See Chap. 6, section 6.2.1, by Casolari in this volume.

[48] Council Decision No 2007/162 of 5 March 2007, *OJ L* 71, 10 March 2007.

[49] Article 1 (1).

[50] See Chap. 5, section 5.3, by Gestri in this volume.

to enhance the EU's state of readiness for response to emergencies.[51] Eligible actions are specified in the Decision and include demonstration projects, awareness and dissemination measures, sending and deploying experts, or releasing at short notice adequate means and equipment.[52] In the field of the CPM eligible actions for financial assistance are: dispatching assessment and co-ordination experts along with their supporting equipment, supporting member states in obtaining access to equipment[53] and transport resources, completing the transport provided by member states by financing additional transport resources necessary for ensuring a rapid response to major emergencies.[54] "The total of CPFI co-financing used at the start of the transport provisions up to the end of 2010 amounts to around € 7.5 million, with 2010 and 2011 showing a marked increase in the number of requests for pooling and financial assistance".[55]

Beneficiaries may be natural or legal persons, whether governed by private or public law.[56]

To avoid duplication of efforts and funding, certain areas are not eligible for funding by the CPFI, including the actions and measures included in the Action program in the field of health 2008–2013[57] or the Action program in the field of consumer policy 2007–2013,[58] those implemented outside the EU through the Stability Instrument,[59] those provided for by specific programs on

---

[51] Artiche 1 (2).

[52] Article 4 (1).

[53] For example, a pilot project on stepped-up co-operation between member states to fight forest-fire (EU Forest Fire Tactical Reserve—EUFFTR) was initiated in 2008. The EUFFTR project consisted of two fire-fighting planes (Canadianair). The planes were a supplementary European resource designed to reinforce the overall EU fire-fighting resources and they were available to assist the member states requesting aerial fire-fighting assistance through the Civil Protection Mechanism. The French Ministry of the Interior (the project beneficiary) ensured the deployment of the planes, stationed in Bastia (Corsica). The EUFFTR intervened in six of nine forest-fire emergencies for which the Mechanism is activated in 2009: twice in France and Portugal, once in Italy and Greece. See European Commission, Report on the evaluation of the application of the Civil Protection Mechanism and the Civil Protection Financial Instrument for the years 2007–2009, COM (2011) 696, 10 November 2011, 11–12.

[54] The member states requesting financial support for the assistance with transportation of their assistance shall must reimburse at least 50 % of the EU funds received, not later than 6 months after the intervention (Article 4 (3) lett. a).

[55] COM (2011) 696, 13, para 55. In 2007, there was one request for transport financing of a total value of around EUR 0.03 million; the total value of transport co-financing during 2008 and 2009 stayed at around EUR 0.4 million yearly; in 2010 it reached around EUR 6.6 million, for 55 request, and in 2011 it increased to EUR 10.8 million, for 35 requests.

[56] Article 5.

[57] Decision No 1350/2007 of the European Parliament and of the Council of 23 October 2007, *OJ L* 301, 20 November 2007.

[58] Decision No 1926/2006 of the European Parliament and of the Council of 18 December 2006, *OJ L* 404, 30 December 2006.

[59] Regulation No 1717/2006 of the European Parliament and of the Council of 15 November 2006, *OJ L* 327, 24 November 2006.

terrorism[60] or relating to the maintenance of order and internal security and those covered by humanitarian aid.[61]

Financial assistance under this Instrument may take the form of grants or public procurement contracts.

The total amount for the actions and measures financed by the Financial Instrument for the period 1 January 2007—31 December 2013 is set at EUR 189.8 million.[62]

Actions and measures financed by the Civil Protection Financial Instrument are ancillary in particular to the European Union Solidarity Fund (EUSF).

The EU has established a Solidarity Fund[63] in order to respond in a rapid, efficient, and flexible manner to urgent situations. The Fund will intervene mainly in cases of major natural disasters with serious repercussions on living conditions, the natural environment or the economy, in one or more regions of a member state or a country applying for accession.

A natural disaster is considered as "major" if, in the case of a State, it results in damage estimated either at or over EUR 3 billion (at 2002 prices), or more than 0.6 % of its gross national income. By way of exception, the Solidarity Fund may be mobilized for extraordinary regional disasters resulting in damage inferior to this threshold, which affect the major part of its population, with serious and lasting repercussions on living conditions and the economic stability of the region.[64]

---

[60] Council Decision No 2007/124 of 12 February 2007, *OJ L* 58, 24 February 2007.

[61] Council Regulation No 1257/96 of 20 June 1996, *OJ L* 163, 2/07/1996. Regulation as last amended by Regulation No 219/2009 of the European Parliament and of the Council of 11 March 2009, *OJ L* 87, 31 March 2009.

[62] Within the framework of the reform of the existing financial instrument, in the context of the Multiannual Financial Framework 2014–2020 (see European Commission, EU Budget Proposal—Multiannual Financial Framework 2014–2020, available at http://ec.europa.eu/budget/reform/ Accessed 15 February 2012.), the European Commission presented the proposal to reform the financial instrument for civil protection: Proposal for a Decision of the European Parliament and the Council on a Union Civil Protection Mechanism, COM (2011) 943, 20 December 2011. The proposal merges into a single text which includes both the provisions relating to the functioning of the Civil Protection Mechanism and those relating to the financing its activities. The financial provisions are incorporated in Chapter V (Articles 19–27) of the proposal. The eligible actions are grouped in general actions (Article 20), prevention and preparedness actions (Article 21), response actions (Article 22) and actions linked to equipment, transport resources, and related logistics (Article 23). The provisions relating to the financial assistance for transport under current CPFI are amended and simplified and the proposal introduces revised conditions for financing increasing the co-financing rates up to 85 % of the total eligible cost and up to 100 % in limited cases when certain criteria are met. Actions receiving financial assistance under the proposal not receive assistance from other EU financial instruments.

[63] Council Regulation No 2012/2002 of 11 November 2002, *OJ L* 311, 14 November 2002.

[64] The definition of "extraordinary regional disaster" in the Regulation is rather vague and conditions for activating the Fund under this category are difficult to meet. For this reason the Commission in the course of 2010 accepted nine of the applications and decided that the conditions for mobilizing the Fund were not met in the case of five other applications. See European Commission, European Union Solidarity Fund—Annual Report 2010, COM (2011) 694, 31 October 2011, 6–11.

In these specific cases, the annual amount available is limited to no more than 7.5 % of the annual amount allocated to the Solidarity Fund (i.e., EUR 1 billion[65]).[66]

Assistance from the Fund takes the form of a single and global grant, with no necessary co-financing, complementing the public efforts of the beneficiary State.

No later than 10 weeks after the first damage caused by the disaster, the affected State should submit an application to the Commission for assistance from the Fund. It should provide all possible information on the damage caused by the disaster and its impact on the population and the economy. On the basis of this information, the Commission decides whether the EUSF may be mobilized and, if that is the case, agrees to a grant.[67]

The beneficiary State is responsible for the implementation of the grant.[68]

Overall, between the creation of the Solidarity Fund in 2002 and the end of 2010, 42 applications were approved with financial aid totaling more than EUR 2.4 billion.[69] The requests concerned a variety of different types of natural disasters including storms, flood, mudslides, earthquakes, and forest fires.[70] The most serious case was the 2009 earthquake at L'Aquila in Italy with over EUR 10 billion of damage: the Fund intervened with over EUR 493 million,[71] the highest grant paid out so far.

The EU's humanitarian aid provides emergency assistance to victims of natural disasters, man-made crises (e.g., wars and outbreaks of fighting), or other comparable exceptional circumstances.[72] The aid shall also include actions to prepare for risks or prevent disasters or comparable exceptional circumstances.[73]

---

[65] See Inter-institutional Agreement of 17 May 2006 between the European Parliament, the Council and the Commission on budgetary discipline and sound financial management, *OJ C* 139, 14 June 2006.

[66] Article 2. Intended to finance measures alleviating non-insurable damage in principle, the urgent actions eligible for the Fund are the following: immediate restoration to working order of infrastructure and plant in the fields of energy, drinking water, waste water, telecommunications, transport, health and education; providing temporary accommodation and funding rescue services to meet the immediate needs of the population concerned; immediate securing of preventive infrastructures and measures of immediate protection of the cultural heritage; immediate cleaning up of disaster-stricken areas, including natural zones (Article 3).

[67] See, for example, Decision of the European Parliament and the Council of 15 December 2010, *OJ L* 342, 28 December 2010, 16; Decision of the European Parliament and the Council of 13 December 2011, *OJ L* 4, 7 January 2012, 14.

[68] Correct implementation of EU-funded operations is ensured by several layers of checks and monitoring, at internal level and by external actors.

[69] See European Commission, The future of European Solidarity Fund, COM (2011) 613, 6 October 2011, 16–18.

[70] See COM (2011) 694, 3 ff.

[71] See European Commission, European Solidarity Fund—Annual Report 2009, COM (2011) 136, 23 March 2011, 5-6.

[72] Article 1, Regulation No. 1257/96.

[73] See Chap. 6, section 6.2.1.1, by Casolari in this volume.

The Regulation governs the implementation of all Union operations providing humanitarian assistance to victims whose own authorities are unable to provide effective relief. This is an important aspect of external relations and, by focusing on supplies and services, the policy aims to prevent and alleviate suffering. In order to ensure that policy is both effective and comprehensive, co-ordination between the member states and the Commission is reinforced by co-operation with NGOs and international organizations.

As a short-term measure (lasting a maximum of 6 months), humanitarian aid is primarily intended to save lives during emergencies and their immediate aftermath; to provide the necessary assistance and relief to people affected by the arising occurrence of long-lasting crises, in particular those caused by the outbreaks of fighting or wars; to carry out short-term rehabilitation and reconstruction work, especially on infrastructures and equipments, in the post-emergency phase; to cope with the consequences of population movements (refugees, displaced people and returnees) by means of schemes to assist repatriation and resettlement where appropriate; to ensure preparedness for the risks concerned and use a suitable rapid early-warning and intervention system.[74]

The aid can also be used to finance improvements in its implementation, e.g., preparatory feasibility studies, project evaluation, technical assistance, humanitarian mine-clearance operations, campaigns to increase the understanding of humanitarian issues, and better co-ordination between the EU and member states.[75]

An EU humanitarian aid operation can be initiated at the request of the Commission, NGOs,[76] international organizations, member states or beneficiary countries.[77]

The financial support of the EU in coping with emergencies, managed by DG Humanitarian Aid and Civil Protection (ECHO) of the Commission, is responsible for the actions of civil protection and for humanitarian operations. In 2010, DG ECHO[78] has provided funding amounting overall to EUR 1.114.860 million.[79]

---

[74] Article 2. See, for example, European Commission, Humanitarian Aid Strategy for 2012, SEC (2011) 1426, 21 November 2011.

[75] Article 4.

[76] Eligible NGOs must meet the following criteria: (a) be non-profit making autonomous organizations in a member state of the EU under the law in force in that member state; (b) have their main headquarters in a member state of the EU or in a third country that receives of EU aid.

[77] Article 6.

[78] http://ec.europa.eu/echo/index_en.htm. Accessed 8 February 2012.

[79] See European Commission, Annual Report on the European Union's Humanitarian Aid and Civil Protection Policies and their Implementation in 2010, COM (2011) 343, 10 June 2011, 6.

26.3.2 Central America and the Caribbean Area

In the Central American region, one of the regions most affected by natural disasters, is interesting, for our purposes, to take into account the Coordination Centre for Natural Disaster Prevention in Central America (CEPREDENAC),[80] an institution that belongs to the Central American Integration System (SICA),[81] but with independent legal status,[82] which aims to promote activities, projects, and programs to reduce risks caused by natural and social disasters. To fulfill its objectives, the Centre promotes and co-ordinates international co-operation and exchange of information, practices and technical and scientific assistance in the prevention, and reduction of disasters and disaster response.[83]

Sources of financing of the Centre are the voluntary contributions of member states, which may take the form of financial, human, material, and logistical[84] contributions of any kind, national and international, public or private donations, grants, etc. Amongst these voluntary contributions it is worth mentioning the SICA-Spain Fund, sponsored by the Spanish Agency for International Development Cooperation (AECID), which is the main instrument of co-operation between Spain and the SICA.[85] A line of the Fund is allocated to disaster prevention and risk management and the implementing body of this line is the CEPREDENAC.[86]

The member states may require technical and financial assistance from the Centre. In general the benefits of such assistance are distributed on an equitable basis, but taking into account the real needs of each member state. In June 2010 the Heads of State and Government of SICA member states have approved the new risk management policy[87] and, in order to finance this policy, it was decided to set

[80] In Spanish Centro de Coordinación para la Prevención de los Desastres Naturales en América Central.

[81] In Spanish Sistema de la Integración Centroamericana. Member states of SICA are Belize, Costa Rica, El Salvador, Guatemala, Honduras, Nicaragua and Panama; Associated Member Dominican Republic.

[82] See Article 1, Treaty establishing the CEPREDENAC available at www.sica.int/cepredenac. Accessed 15 February 2012.

[83] Article 4, Treaty establishing the CEPREDENAC.

[84] Article 10 of the General Rules of operation of CEPREDENAC (available at www.sica.int/CEPREDENAC) states, however, that a minimum annual voluntary contribution by member states is determined by the Council of Representatives, the highest decision-making body composed of representatives of member states.

[85] Spain in the period 2005–2009 was the second largest donor after the European Commission, in Central America.

[86] CEPREDENAC in the period 2006–2009 has received a contribution of USD 2,637 million. See AECID, Fondo España-SICA. Memoria de Labores 2006–2009, 12, available at www.sica.int/fes/cepredenac.aspx. Accessed 15 February 2012.

[87] SICA, Política Centroamericana de Gestión Integral de Riesgo de Desastres, available at www.sica.int/cepredenac. Accessed 15 February 2012.

up a "Fondo Centroamericano de Fomento de la Gestión Integral de Riesgos de Desastres". To date, however, the Fund has not yet been established.

In the Caribbean region the Caribbean Community (CARICOM)[88] has in 2009 established the Caribbean Disaster Emergency Management Agency (CDEMA).[89] The Agency focuses its attention on Comprehensive Disaster Management (CDM),[90] a strategy endorsed by all Participating States[91] of the Agency and accepted by the CARICOM.

The Agency has at its disposal the Emergency Assistance Fund, which shall be used to defray expenses incurred in connection with the rendering of assistance in the event of a disaster occurring in a Participating State. Moreover, the Participating States may request contributions to the budget of the Fund,[92] but not the expenses incurred by a sending State in providing assistance to a requesting State.[93]

Participating States shall contribute to the Fund in accordance with a scale of assessment recommended by the Management Committee and approved by the Council. CDEMA may accept contributions to the Fund from external sources.

Even within the CARICOM, as in SICA, there is a bilateral instrument of financial assistance: the Canadian Caribbean Disaster Risk Management Fund, an important component of the Canadian International Development Agency's regional Caribbean Disaster Risk Management Program. The Fund is administered by the Canadian High Commission in Barbados.

The Fund provides assistance to NGOs, voluntary agencies, community groups, and governmental agencies in CARICOM member states, such as CDEMA.

26.3.3 The Association of South-East Asian Nations

Natural disasters are a frequent occurrence in South-East Asia, killing an estimated 350,000 people in the last decade and causing tens of billions of dollars' worth of damage. For this reason, the increase in the resilience of its ten member states is a

---

[88] The member states of CARICOM are Antigua and Barbuda, the Bahamas, Barbados, Belize, Dominica, Grenada, Guyana, Haiti, Jamaica, Montserrat, Saint Lucia, St. Kitt and Nevis, St. Vincent and Grenadine, Suriname, Trinidad and Tobago.

[89] This is the new name of the regional disaster management body formerly known as CDERA, Caribbean Disaster Emergency Response Agency. CDERA was established in 1991.

[90] See http://www.cdema.org/CDMStrategyandProgrammeFramework2007-2012.pdf. Accessed 15 February 2012.

[91] Participating States of CDEMA are all CARICOM member states and Anguilla, British Virgin Islands, Turks, and Caicos Islands.

[92] Article XVIII (3), 2008 Agreement establishing the CDEMA.

[93] Article XXV of the Agreement states that "Except as may otherwise be agreed between them, the expenses incurred by a sending State in providing assistance a requesting State shall be defrayed by the sending State". On the functions of CDEMA see Chap. 23, section 23.3 (b), by Silingardi in this volume.

key priority for the Association of South-East Asian Nations (ASEAN).[94] In July 2005, ASEAN member states signed the ASEAN Agreement on Management and Emergency Response (AADMER), which entered into force on 24 December 2009.

The AADMER is a legally binding agreement. As a regional framework that has been ratified by all member states, it provides mechanisms to reduce loss of life and assets resulting from disasters in South-East Asia.[95] It also aims to facilitate joint responses to disasters through concerted national efforts and intensified regional and international co-operation. The Ministers or Secretaries of the government bodies in charge of disaster management and risk reduction constitute the Conference of Parties (COP),[96] which is responsible for reviewing and evaluating the overall implementation of the Agreement. The ASEAN Committee on Disaster Management (ACDM), made up of the respective national disaster management offices of each ASEAN member states,[97] executes the Agreement.

The Agreement provides a framework for the development of operational procedures[98] to respond collectively and expeditiously to disasters and includes provisions for the movement of relief assistance, utilization of military and civilian personnel in disaster relief[99] and the establishment of a centre to co-ordinate regional disaster response, the ASEAN Co-ordinating Centre for Humanitarian Assistance (AHA Centre).[100]

If a member state needs assistance in the event of a disaster emergency within its territory, it may request assistance from any other member, directly or through the AHA Centre.

For implementation of the Agreement a fund has been established: the ASEAN Disaster Management and Emergency Relief Fund,[101] administered by the ASEAN Secretariat.

---

[94] Member states of ASEAN are Brunei, Cambodia, Indonesia, Lao, Malaysia, Myanmar, Philippines, Singapore, Thailand, and Viet Nam.

[95] "The objective of this Agreement is to provide effective mechanisms to achieve substantial reduction of disaster losses in lives and in the social, economic, and environmental assets of the Parties, and to jointly respond to disaster emergencies through concerted national efforts and intensified regional and international co-operation. This should be pursued in the overall context of sustainable development and in accordance with the provisions of this Agreement" (Article 2 AADMER). The text of the Agreement is available at http://www.asean.org/18441. Accessed 15 February 2012.

[96] Article 21 AADMER.

[97] Article 22 AADMER.

[98] See Standard Operating Procedure for Regional Standby Arrangements and Coordination of Joint Disaster Relief and Emergency Response Operations (SASOP), available at http://www.aseandrr.net/Portals/0/Asean-SASOP.pdf. Accessed 2 February 2012.

[99] See Chap. 23, section 23.3 (a), by Silingardi in this volume.

[100] See Article 20 and Annex AADMER. Web site http://ahacentre.org Accessed 15 February 2012.

[101] Article 24 AADMER.

Member states shall contribute to the Fund, in accordance with the decisions of the COP. The Fund is open to contributions from other sources, such as international organizations, regional financial institutions, and international donor community.

The Fund will be used to provide necessary resources to support the operational budget of the AHA Centre (by regular annual contributions from member States), to provide emergency funds to support urgent needs as well as other emergency activities and to support the implementation of activities under the AADMER Work Programme[102] (voluntary contributions).

26.4 Bilateral Agreements

At a bilateral level, apart from the specific agreements on co-operation in case of disasters, which determine in large part only the allocation of costs to deploy and associated functioning of an emergency mission,[103] most funding for prevention, mitigation and response to emergencies arises under the more general co-operation agreements. These agreements provide, in fact, the different forms of co-operation (technical co-operation, financial co-operation, humanitarian assistance, and emergency assistance). For examples include the 2007 Agreement for Economic and Technical Cooperation between United States of America and Burundi coverings economic, technical, humanitarian, and related assistance that may be provided by the USA in Burundi[104]; and the 2008 Agreement on Development Co-operation between Italy and Albania coverings technical and financial co-operation, humanitarian, and emergency assistance.[105] The cooperation agreements also set out financial instruments that can be used to fund cooperation activities (grants, aid loans, provisions of equipment, materials,[106] etc.). Moreover, cooperation agreements establish whether the humanitarian and emergency assistance can be financed outside the cooperation agreement[107] and who the beneficiaries beyond the State can be.

---

[102] See AADMER Work Programme for 2010–2015 available at http://www.aseandrr.net/Portals/0/AADMER-work-programme-final.pdf. Accessed 15 February 2012.

[103] See Chap. 1, section 1.3, by de Guttry in this volume.

[104] Article 1. The text of the Agreement is available at http://www.state.gov/documents/organization/108889.pdf Accessed 14 February 2012.

[105] Article 6 (1). The text of the Agreement is available at http://itra.esteri.it/itrapgm/Visualizza.asp?ID=49233) Accessed 15 February 2012.

[106] See, for example, Article 2 (3) letters d) and e) of the 1991 Agreement between Australia and Pakistan on Development Cooperation, available at http://www.austlii.edu.au/au/other/dfat/treaties/1991/35.html Accessed 14 February 2012; Article II of the 1974 Agreement on Economic and Technical Cooperation between France and Congo, available at http://basedoc.diplomatie.gouv.fr/exl-php/util/documents/accede_document.php. Accessed 14 February 2012.

[107] See, for example, Article 6 (3) Italy-Albania Agreement.

Under the new trend to conclude bilateral agreements between States and international organizations,[108] within the framework of cooperation agreements we can find, for instance, the 2006 Scientific Cooperation Agreement between Italy and the Caribbean Community (CARICOM) on Cooperation in Hydro-Meteorological Monitoring, Natural Disaster Prevention and Early Warning.[109] It stipulates that all costs for the implementation of activities envisaged in the Agreement are to be borne by the Italian State (Article 5). A further example is the 2000 Cooperation Agreement between European Community and the People's Republic of Bangladesh on Partnership and Development',[110] in accordance to with the EU has contributed more than EUR 100 million in disaster-related actions.[111] Amongst the bilateral agreements between States and international organizations which are specific to the prevention of and response to disasters and the provision of financial support, we find the 1998 Agreement between Italy and UN/Economic Commission for Latin America and the Caribbean (ECLAC) on Disaster Prevention in Latin America and in the Caribbean,[112] whereby the Italian government puts at the disposal of the ECLAC financial resources for a range of activities (laid down in Annex A) in the field of disaster prevention and mitigation; and the 2004 Joint Declaration of Cooperation between Italy and UNESCO on Emergency Actions in Countries affected by Conflicts or Natural Disaster for the Safeguarding, Rehabilitation, and Protection of Cultural and Natural Heritage[113] which establishes a financial assistance by the Italian Government to UNESCO to respond to specific emergency situations, as a result of damage and/or destruction of cultural and natural heritage.

26.5 Private Parties

In addition to humanitarian assistance from governments and international organizations, funding from private sources contributes to emergency responses.[114] The main private donors are individuals, private foundations, private companies, trusts, and corporations.[115]

---

[108] See Chap. 1, section 1.3, by de Guttry in this volume.

[109] The Agreement is not in force. The text is available at http://itra.esteri.it/itrapgm/Visualizza.asp?ID=48895. Accessed 14 February 2012.

[110] *OJ L* 118, 27 April 2001, 48 ff.

[111] See European Commission, Country Strategy Paper for Bangladesh 2007–2013, 33, available at http://eeas.europa.eu/bangladesh/csp/csp_07_13_en.pdf. Accessed 14 February 2012.

[112] *GURI* 16 January 1995, No. 12.

[113] *GURI* 14 March 2005, No. 60.

[114] See, for example, World Economic Forum 2010.

[115] In certain contexts the support from private donors can be particularly significant where it can equal or even exceed the support given by government donors, for example in Haiti in 2010.

Foundations can play a significant role, as they often succeed in attracting large sums due to their visibility (use of social networks), or the fame of the person they are named after (for example, the William J. Clinton Foundation or the Bill and Melinda Gates Foundation) or the people who created them (actors/actresses, the world of culture, etc.). Some of these foundations have, amongst their objectives, the prevention of and response to disasters,[116] while others have even been especially set up for a specific purpose.[117]

The funds raised from foundations come largely from donations made by private citizens[118] and are generally allocated to humanitarian organizations, UN agencies, NGOs, the International Red Cross, and Red Crescent Movements.[119]

The funds can also be used directly in the field by the foundations themselves. The fact that the foundations and private companies operate directly in the field is criticized by traditional humanitarian actors, as they do not always guarantee the fundamental humanitarian principles of neutrality and impartiality.[120]

The contributions to individuals, as well as in addition to cash, can also be of a material nature, especially in the first emergency phase following a disaster which may involve a number of problems associated with the transport of such goods in the country concerned if the foundation does not have an organization able to undertake the transport and distribution on site, meaning that most of the goods collected would be lost.[121]

---

[116] See, for example, The Patterson Foundation Disaster Relief Initiative, http://disaster.thepattersonfoundation.org/?p=287; Shafqat Human Development Foundation's mission is to provide help to people who became victims of natural disasters http://www.shafqatfoundation.org/. Accessed 15 February 2012.

[117] See J/P HRO (Haitian Relief Organization) founded after the January 2010 earthquake in Haiti by Sean Penn, http://www.jphro.org/. Accessed 14 February 2012.

[118] The source of funding affects the type, duration, and scope of assistance delivered, as well as the potential outcomes.

[119] In the case of Tsunami 2004 the majority of private donations have gone to NGOs and Red Cross Movement. See Flint and Goyder 2006, 17.

[120] "In addition to the traditional humanitarian NGOs and international humanitarian organizations, private foundations and companies are playing an increasing role [...]. This larger number of actors brings a variety of motivation, interest and practices. Reaffirming the humanitarian principles of neutrality and non-discrimination becomes all the more important". European Commission, Annual Report on the European Union's Humanitarian Aid and Civil Protection Policies and their Implementation in 2010, COM (2011) 343, 10 June 2011, 2. See moreover Good Humanitarian Donorship, Principles & Good Practices of GHD, available at http://www.goodhumanitariandonorship.org/gns/principles-good-practice-ghd/overview.aspx. Accessed 15 February 2012; OCHA-World Economic Forum, Guiding Principles for Public–Private Collaboration for Humanitarian Action, available at http://www.agire.it/filemanager/cms_agire/image/Come_agire/Principles_for_Public-Private_Collaboration_for_Humanitarian_Action.pdf. Accessed 15 February 2012.

[121] See United States-Centre for International Disaster Information, Guidelines for appropriate international disaster donations, available at http://www.cidi.org/guidelines. Accessed 14 February 2012.

Therefore, one can conclude that if the private parties can play an important role in fundraising, it is equally important for donors to make sure that they comply with the fundamental humanitarian principles enshrined in the General Assembly Resolution 46/182 and that they are capable of fulfilling the objectives pursued.

In the absence of an ability to meet such requirements, I believe that donation to traditional humanitarian actors remains the only viable alternative for donors.

Furthermore, it should be noted that the increasing privatization might progressively weaken the possibilities of using existing multilateral institutions and their funding mechanism and, consequently, their chances of opportunities for intervention.

26.6 Concluding Remarks

The analysis has revealed that much of the system for financing emergency response is based on voluntary contributions, more or less structured, whether they are from States, private entities, or individuals. The only exception is the European Union, which devotes a portion of its annual budget to such activities without the need for donors.

The current financial crisis is affecting the level of voluntary contributions, and consequently the resources available to respond to emergencies. This is due to the fact that even many of the traditional donor States are now experiencing economic difficulties, as proved by the available data.[122]

Financing emergencies requires vast new resources of capital, both private and public. In particular, it requires mobilizing more public funds. Governments and international organizations should increase the resources allocated to disaster risk reduction and integrate resilience planning into their development budgets and strategies.

What would be appropriate is greater co-ordination between the various financing mechanism, so as not to waste resources.

The available resources are, in the opinion of the present author, also affected by the long-standing practice in some countries of NGOs and also UN local agencies relying on donations by SMS. While this may increase the number of donors, unfortunately it will not increase the amount of the total donations, which are relatively low.[123]

---

[122] See Global Humanitarian Assistance (GHA) 2011b, 16; Namibia Flash Appeal http://fts.unocha.org/reports/daily/ocha_R1_A931___1109240209.pdf. Accessed 12 February 2012.

[123] For example, private donations to the OCHA have decreased over the period 2007–2010. See OCHA Donor Ranking, available at http://ochanet.unocha.org/p/Documents/Donor%20Ranking%204%20years%20as%20at%2015%20Feb%202011.pdf Accessed 15 February 2012.

References

Channel Resources (2011) 5-Year evaluation of the central emergency response fund. Synthesis report: final draft http://ochanet.unocha.org/p/Documents/110726%20CERF%20Evaluation%20Report%20Final.pdf

Flint M, Goyder H (2006) Funding the tsunami response http://www.sida.se/Document/Import/pdf/Funding-the-Tsunami-Response1.pdf

OCHA (2010a) Annual report http://ochanet.unocha.org/p/Documents/OCHA_2010AR.pdf

OCHA (2010b) Guidelines. CERF underfunded emergencies window: procedures and criteria http://ochanet.unocha.org/p/Documents/CERF%20UFE%20Procedures%20and%20Criteria%2018%20March%202010.pdf

Global Humanitarian Assistance (GHA) (2011a) Emergency response funds (ERFs). Profile http://www.globalhumanitarianassistance.org/wp-content/uploads/2011/08/ERF-profile-final.pdf

Global Humanitarian Assistance (GHA) (2011b) Report 2011 http://www.globalhumanitarianassistance.org/reports

Inter-Agency Standing Committee (IASC) (2006) Guidelines for flash appeals http://www.humanitarianappeal.net

Inter-Agency Standing Committee (IASC) (2010) Handbook for RCs and HCs on emergency preparedness and response http://www.humanitarianinfo.org/iasc

World Economic Forum (2010) Engineering & construction disaster resource partnership. A new private-public partnership model for disaster response http://www3.weforum.org/docs/WEF_EN_DisasterResourcePartnership_Report_2010.pdf

Chapter 27
Disasters and Corruption, Corruption as Disaster

Enrico Calossi, Salvatore Sberna and Alberto Vannucci

Abstract This chapter analyzes the role played by corruption in post-disaster contexts. Data show growth in both natural and man-made disasters and in humanitarian response provided by bilateral and multilateral donors. These events have become more frequent and also cause more deaths. Moreover, the data demonstrate a strong relation between the impact of these disasters on the standards of living and the prior level of corruption of the country. The severity of disasters is a consequence of corruption, but the opportunities for corruption are also increased in post-disaster situations. Several factors contribute to frustrating the transparency and accountability of decision-making processes during humanitarian crises. We include all these factors in a "formula of corruption". Despite the growing importance of this issue, the international community has responded to these crucial problems only tentatively. We review those international treaties that have addressed the issue of corruption at the international level. These treaties are preliminary instruments to fight corruption, even if they are not specifically designed to fight this plague in post-disaster contexts. This lack of institutional response has caused civil society and NGOs to take independent measures. For this reason, several NGOs have recommended the implementation of further action in order to map and prevent corruption.

Keywords Disaster · International aid · Corruption · Moral costs · Civil society · Mortality · Democracy

---

E. Calossi · S. Sberna · A. Vannucci (✉)
University of Pisa, 56126, Pisa, Italy
e-mail: vannucci@sp.unipi.it

E. Calossi
e-mail: enrico.calossi@sp.unipi.it

S. Sberna
e-mail: salvatore.sberna@sp.unipi.it

A. de Guttry et al. (eds.), *International Disaster Response Law*,
DOI: 10.1007/978-90-6704-882-8_27,

Contents

27.1 Introduction

Natural and man-made disasters generate a complex chain of actions involving a plurality of institutional and societal actors.[1] Emergency situations after disasters typically demand a prompt humanitarian response, giving relief to the more urgent needs of the affected people. Following immediate aid, other vital measures aimed at reconstructing the basic urban and infrastructure assets, as well as at promoting a restoration of acceptable levels of civil and economic activities, are similarly undertaken. In this process, a large amount of resources—money, food, shelter, water, sanitation, drugs, etc.—are collected, transferred, allocated, and distributed, following extraordinary decision-making processes and involving the participation of many foreign as well as national and local organizations and institutions.

In this contribution, we analyze the opportunities for corruption and the effects that this phenomenon tends to produce within the policy-making process which shapes the context for humanitarian responses to natural and man-made disasters. In the first section, we analyze trends in natural/man-made disasters and in international aid provided by bilateral and multilateral donors. The emerging importance of such events, and their dramatic impact on the standards of living for countries worldwide, are demonstrated by the data. The effects of these events are not explained only by the frequency and magnitude of their occurrence. On the contrary, economic (income) and institutional (corruption) variables are crucial in explaining differences in the death

[1] This chapter is the product of the joint effort of the authors. For the records, Enrico Calossi wrote the final version of Sect. 27.4, Salvatore Sberna Sect. 27.2, Alberto Vannucci Sect. 27.3. Introduction and conclusions have been written jointly.

rates and destructiveness of disasters across countries, as shown by recent empirical research. The assessment of this link is a necessary step before analyzing the relation between corruption and international aid. The prior level of corruption needs to be taken into account to predict the impact of relief aid. In the second section, we address this problem theoretically and provide a general scheme for the analysis of the relationship between international aid and corruption in emergency situations. Do relief interventions encourage good governance or are there some variables that influence opportunities and incentive to bribery in these exceptional circumstances? In the third part, we provide a review of those treaties which deal with corruption at international level. These treaties are considered important as preliminary instruments by civil society and NGOs in order to fight corruption, but are still not sufficient. Some NGOs, like Transparency International, emphasize the necessity to implement a more precise mapping of the phenomenon in order to prevent corruption in humanitarian aid more effectively. Finally, some conclusive remarks will be presented.

27.2 Disasters and International Aid: Trends and Empirical Evidence

27.2.1 Disasters and International Aid: Patterns and Trends

According to EM-DAT data,[2] disasters have been increasing in recent years, affecting a larger number of people. Between 1980 and 2011, 15,604 disasters have occurred, killing more than 2 million people in different countries.[3] Almost all disasters throughout the world have caught the attention of media, world public opinion, national governments, and international organizations. As a consequence, in recent years budgets for emergency, humanitarian reconstruction, and relief aid have increased impressively as has the number of international agencies and NGOs directly involved in humanitarian and relief field operations. Before addressing theoretically the question of some patterns in emergency situations becoming

[2] The data on the occurrence and effects of natural and technological disasters come from the Centre for Research on the Epidemiology of Disasters (CRED). CRED has maintained the Emergency Events Database EM-DAT which contains information of over 18,000 mass disasters in the world from 1900 to present. The database is compiled from various sources, including UN agencies, non-governmental organizations, insurance companies, research institutes and press agencies. An event is classified as a disaster when at least one of the following criteria is fulfilled: 10 or more people were killed; 100 or more people were affected; a declaration of a state of emergency or a call for international assistance was made (http://www.emdat.be/criteria-and-definition, accessed 13 February 2012). EM-DAT data do not include other made-man disasters as those caused by civil wars or conflicts.

[3] According to EM-DATA, between 1980 and 2011, 9,006 natural disasters and 6,598 technological disasters occurred. Total casualties have been estimated at more than 2 millions from natural disasters, and at 250,000 people from technological disasters.

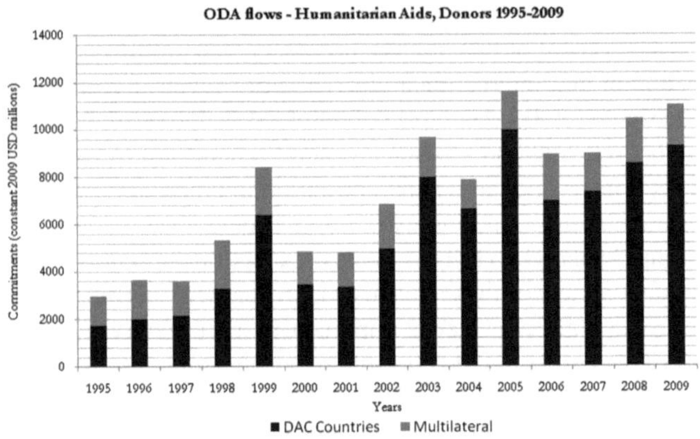

Fig. 27.1 Humanitarian aid (ODA flows) by donors for the period 1995–2010 (OECD Statistics)

incentives to corruption, we present some data about the amount of international aid provided by bilateral and multilateral donors for relief interventions. Then we give some empirical evidence about the relevance of corruption in predicting the effects of disasters, since some recent findings show that corruption affects both disaster prevention and international response.

If the level of corruption raises the likelihood of damage and casualties resulting from disasters, the magnitude of the disaster can already predict the amount of international aid provided by foreign donors. This is a crucial point, because in a globalized world, the bigger the disaster the greater the international aid that will be provided for relief and reconstruction. Therefore, it is not by coincidence that we see impressive growth as we look at the trends in humanitarian aid in the last 30 years. The response of countries and international organizations to these kinds of events has changed in recent years. International aid provided to help emergency relief and reconstruction has rapidly grown (see Fig. 27.1).

According to OECD data on Official Development Assistance,[4] from 1995 to 2009 commitments for emergency response have increased by 400 %; there are similar trends in reconstruction relief (+150 %) and disaster prevention (645.9 USD million in 2009) (Fig. 27.2). Table 27.1 reports aggregate data on ODA by donors for the years 1995–2009. However, no complete data exist about the amount of resources provided for emergency purposes by bilateral, multilateral and private donors. This is only a portion of the total amount of resources provided to countries

[4] According to OECD, the sector "Humanitarian Aid" consists of emergency and distress relief in cash or in kind, including emergency response, relief food aid, short-term reconstruction relief and rehabilitation, disaster prevention and preparedness. It excludes aid to refugees in donor countries. The data cover flows from all bilateral and multilateral donors (DAC countries and EU institutions) and refer to developing countries or territories eligible to receive official development assistance (ODA).

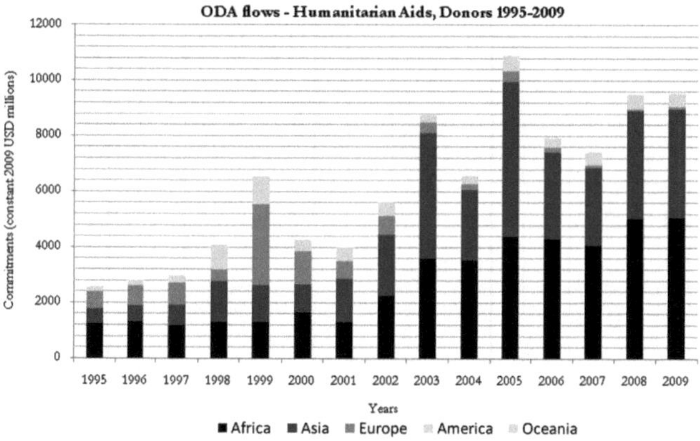

Fig. 27.2 Recipients of humanitarian aid (ODA flows) sorted by regions for the period 1995–2010 (OECD Statistics)

that have called on the international community for assistance. If we consider other bilateral and multilateral donors (UN, IMF, WB), and especially private and NGO donations, this amount would rise to an extraordinary level. Looking at ODA flows, Africa and Asia are the regions that received the largest amount of relief aid. In relation to casualties from disasters Fig. 27.3 clearly shows that more humanitarian aid was provided to those countries which experienced higher level of deaths from disasters. They are also the regions with higher levels of corruption, and in many cases this is associated with the lowest standards in democratic accountability. Figure 27.3 clearly illustrates that countries with higher levels of corruption (left side of the graph) are more likely to receive international aid.[5] These findings need more accurate analysis, as several factors affect this correlation. It is important to take into account that ODA flows are directed to developing countries that are normally also highly corrupt. In any case, the figure confirms that international aid targets primarily countries which were already highly corrupt before disasters occurred, therefore their impact will be affected by such conditions.

By their very nature, some types of disasters, such as earthquake, are associated with the highest number of victims, even though storms and floods are the most frequent natural disasters accounting, respectively for 26 and 34 % of natural hazards. However, Table 27.2 provides a list of the six disasters which caused most deaths in the period 1980–2012. Haiti, Indonesia, Myanmar, Pakistan are displayed in the upper rows of the table with the highest mortality from disasters. Therefore, looking at the list of countries we can intuitively say that a certain relationship exists at country level between casualties from disasters and socioeconomic

[5] We measure corruption using the Transparency International Corruption Perceptions Index (CPI). The CPI measures the degree to which public sector corruption is perceived to exist in 178 countries around the world. It scores countries on a scale from 10 (very clean) to 0 (highly corrupt).

Table 27.1 ODA flows in humanitarian aid disaggregated by sector for the period 1995–2010. Commitments (constant 2009 USD millions)* (OECD Statistics)

(A) *Reconstruction relief and rehabilitation*

Donors	1995	1996	1997	1998	1999	2000	2001	2002	2003	2004	2005	2006	2007	2008	2009
DAC countries	93.8	81.0	135.8	99.3	219.1	221.0	160.6	308.4	1459.3	455.5	1573.7	879.7	828.1	593.9	671.6
Non-DAC countries															13.3
Multilateral, total	229.6	75.4	69.3	178.1	132.7	131.3	180.9	164.3	501.4	289.2	379.2	576.6	268.6	178.1	147.0
Total, all	323.4	156.3	205.1	277.5	351.7	352.3	341.5	472.6	1960.7	744.7	1952.9	1456.4	1096.7	772.0	832.0

(B) *Disaster prevention and preparedness*

Donors	2004	2005	2006	2007	2008	2009
DAC countries		8.4	40.1	137.2	261.1	513.8
Multilateral, total	5.6	13.5	14.0	129.1	105.7	132.1
Total, all	5.6	21.9	54.1	266.3	366.9	645.9

(C) *Emergency response*

Donors	1995	1996	1997	1998	1999	2000	2001	2002	2003	2004	2005	2006	2007	2008	2009
DAC countries	1624.3	1895.4	1930.3	3147.9	6052.8	3087.5	3081.8	4520.1	6230.8	6111.1	8205.7	6027.0	6368.0	7709.5	8120.3
Non-DAC countries															121.5
Multilateral, total	916.4	1540.6	1340.1	1784.3	1776.0	1163.9	1174.6	1595.9	1016.2	883.7	1171.6	1282.6	1217.8	1629.7	1468.4
Total, all	2540.7	3435.9	3270.4	4932.2	7828.8	4251.4	4256.4	6116.1	7246.9	6994.9	9377.3	7309.6	7585.9	9339.2	9710.2

Humanitarian aid (A + B + C)

Donors	1995	1996	1997	1998	1999	2000	2001	2002	2003	2004	2005	2006	2007	2008	2009
DAC countries	1753.4	2009.6	2135.9	3298.0	6409.7	3457.3	3357.0	4979.1	7989.7	6636.5	9962.9	6994.6	7356.2	8554.7	9305.7
Non-DAC countries															134.8
Multilateral, total	1231.9	1644.3	1444.1	2042.6	1983.2	1398.6	1480.2	1872.8	1690.0	1239.7	1636.0	1969.1	1627.8	1908.8	1747.6
Total, all	2985.3	3653.8	3580.0	5340.6	8392.9	4855.8	4837.2	6851.9	9679.7	7876.2	11598.9	8963.7	8984.0	10463.5	11188.0

* DAC members are Australia, Austria, Belgium, Canada, Denmark, Finland, France, Germany, Greece, Ireland, Italy, Japan, Korea, Luxembourg, New Zealand, Norway, Portugal, Spain, Sweden, Switzerland, United Kingdom, United States, European Union Institutions.

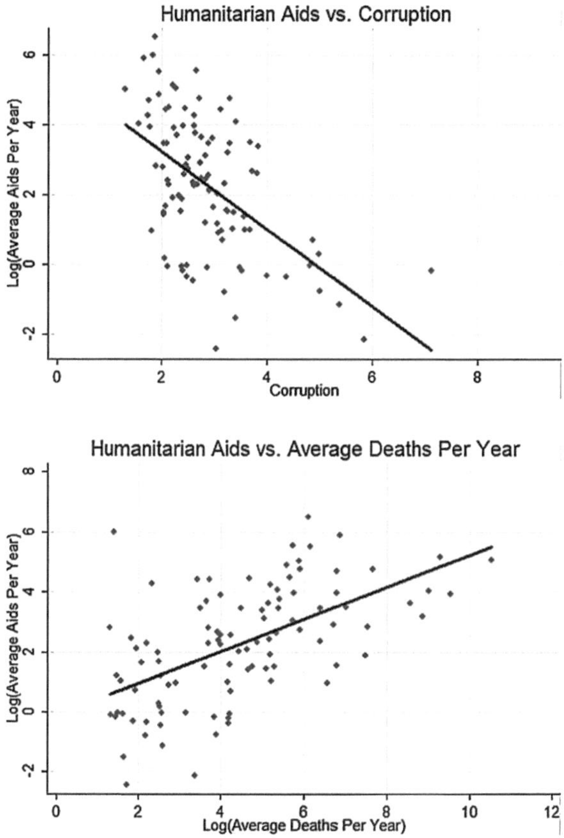

Fig. 27.3 Humanitarian aid, deaths from disasters and corruption for the period 1995–2010 ["EM-DAT: The OFDA/CRED International Disaster Database www.em-dat.net—Université Catholique de Louvain—Brussels—Belgium"; Transparency International Corruption Perceptions Index (CPI)]

variables such as GDP or institutional ones such as corruption. This evidence is also supported by the fact that disasters occur equally both in clean and corrupt countries. The flat regression line presented in Fig. 27.4 indicates that cleaner nations do not experience fewer of these shocks. Other studies have found that no significant correlation exists between the occurrence of natural disaster and per capita income of a country.[6] What really changes is the impact of such events, and destructiveness of disasters can be also explained by certain economic and institutional variables at country level. In the next paragraph, we will attempt to evaluate the relationship between disasters and corruption, and then between corruption and international aid reviewing the results of some recent empirical studies.

[6] Kahn 2005, 275.

Table 27.2 Top 10 most important disasters for the period 1980–2012 sorted by numbers of killed at the country level ("EM-DAT: The OFDA/CRED International Disaster Database www.em-dat.net—Université Catholique de Louvain—Brussels—Belgium")

Disaster	Date	No killed
1. Haiti, earthquake	12/01/2010	222,570
2. Indonesia, earthquake	26/12/2004	165,708
3. Myanmar, storm	02/05/2008	138,366
4. China P Rep, earthquake	12/05/2008	87,476
5. Pakistan, earthquake	08/10/2005	73,338
6. Venezuela, flood	15/12/1999	30,000

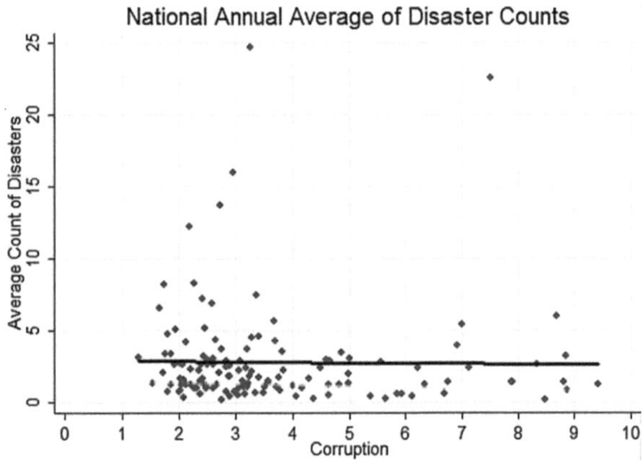

Fig. 27.4 National annual average of disaster counts and corruption in public sector ["EM-DAT: The OFDA/CRED International Disaster Database www.em-dat.net—Université Catholique de Louvain—Brussels—Belgium"; Transparency International Corruption Perceptions Index (CPI)]

27.2.2 Corruption, Disaster, International Aid: Some Empirical Evidences

While natural disasters may not be preventable, it is possible to prevent the suffering they cause. It is commonly said, in fact, that earthquakes do not kill people; collapsing buildings do.[7] Some recent studies have identified various negative effects of corruption on disaster prevention and reconstruction.[8] These studies have empirically evaluated the importance of income, geography and institutional capacity when countries experience natural disasters, and whether such variables explain differences in casualties and damages from natural shocks across countries. On the other hand, no cross-country analyses exist about the impact of international aid on endogenous corruption in post-natural disaster contexts. Relying on international data, some studies found that corruption lowers investment.[9] In a

[7] Anbarci et al. (2005, 2007).

[8] Ambraseys and Bilham 2011.

[9] Mauro 1995; Pellegrini and Gerlagh 2004. For a cross-national study on the causes of corruption, see Treisman (2000)

Table 27.3 Natural disasters sorted by type (1980–2012) ("EM-DAT: The OFDA/CRED International Disaster Database www.em-dat.net—Université Catholique de Louvain—Brussels—Belgium")

Disaster type	Number	Sample %
Drought	467	4.7
Earthquake (seismic activity)	799	8.1
Epidemic	1,166	11.8
Extreme temperature	388	3.9
Flood	3,382	34.1
Insect infestation	77	0.8
Mass movement wet	520	5.2
Storm	2,651	26.7
Volcano	152	1.5
Wildfire	313	3.2
Total	9,915	100

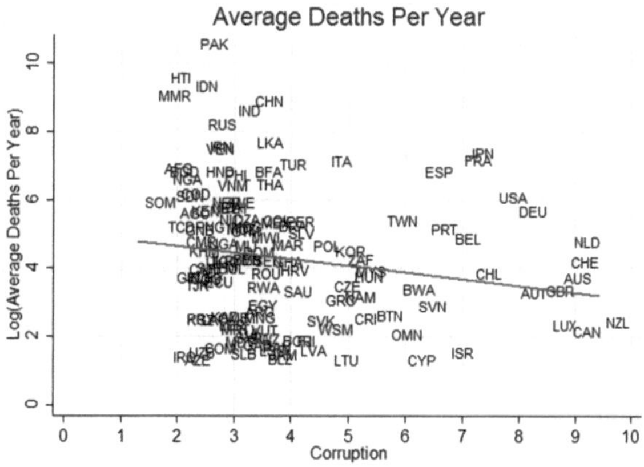

Fig. 27.5 Average deaths per year ["EM-DAT: The OFDA/CRED International Disaster Database www.em-dat.net—Université Catholique de Louvain—Brussels—Belgium"; Transparency International Corruption Perceptions Index (CPI)]

seminal study on foreign aid and corruption, Alesina and Weder[10] found that there is no evidence that foreign aid goes disproportionally to less corrupt governments. According to some measures of aid, more corrupt governments receive more foreign aid than less corrupt ones, after controlling for several other determinants of aid. The line in Fig. 27.3 depicts this relationship. It would seem that bilateral and multilateral donors are not sensitive to the level of corruption of the receiving countries, thus corruption does not influence aid flows.[11] No further analyses have yet tested the same relationship in the case of relief aid and natural disasters. It remains to be investigated whether corrupt countries receive less relief aid than less corrupt counterparts. Furthermore, no answers have been provided about the impact of foreign aid on corruption. Existing data on corruption do not permit us to

[10] Alesina and Weder 2002.

[11] Alesina and Weder 2002.

gage accurately changes in corruption levels over time against changes in received aid. However, Alesina and Weder[12] did not find any evidence that foreign aid reduces corruption, even though they correctly say that "it is not quite clear what the determinants of corruption are, thus it is unclear what one should control for in evaluating the effect of aid on corruption" (Table 27.3).

For this reason, in the attempt to propose a tentative evaluation of the post-shock aid impact that takes into account the endogeneity of corruption and other socioeconomic variables, it is crucial to understand the importance of income, institutional capacity, and corruption when countries experience natural disasters.

In particular, some studies have found that richer nations suffer fewer deaths from natural disaster.[13] The explanation for this is based on the perception that richer nations are able to reduce their natural-disaster risk exposure through effective regulation, planning, and by providing quality infrastructure and quality emergency management Kahn[14] found a very strong effect of income distribution on disaster mortality. A richer nation had the same death count from natural disasters if its income Gini coefficient was 1 standard deviation higher or its GDP per capita was $6,500 lower. In a post-disaster context, the income distribution might also have a negative impact. Foreign aid, instead of reaching the poor might be appropriated by the rich, since the latter are more likely to be educated and involved in aid management.

The quality of institutions is strongly correlated with development. This is why institutions play a relevant role in reducing natural-disaster deaths. Kahn[15] shows that less democratic nations suffer higher national death counts from disasters. This mechanism has been studied by Anbarci et al.,[16] who found that public sector corruption is positively related to earthquake deaths, controlling for factors such as earthquake frequency and magnitude, distance from population centers, and a country's level of development. Government corruption could cause higher mortality through the lack of enforcement of building codes, infrastructure quality, and zoning. Therefore, these studies provide evidence for the idea that "when a major quake strikes these substandard structures, the conspiracy extends from builder and public official to an often lethal one between people and nature".[17] The relationship between corruption and deaths from disaster is shown in Fig. 27.5, where we present a cross-national graph. The figure graphs a negative trend between deaths and quality of government. However, what is still missing in this literature is the analysis of the post-disaster relationship between corruption and international aid. On the other hand, abundant evidence exists about corruption cases in emergency situations involving both national and foreign actors.

---

12 Alesina and Weder 2002.

13 Kahn 2005.

14 Kahn 2005.

15 Kahn 2005.

16 Anbarci et al. 2007.

17 Anbarci et al. 2007, 226.

According to NGOs, the distribution of materials (especially food) is considered one of the key stages where corruption risks are more frequent. For example, in a survey conducted in Bangladesh by Transparency International in 2008 respondents made the following observations:

> "a) Selection of agencies in a non-transparent way through individual and personal relationship; b) Local government structures involved in corrupt practices when they select beneficiaries and distribute relief goods; c) Supporters of the ruling political party being given priority in roadside shelters following flooding d) NGOs having to bribe government officials to receive funds from government programs, and government officials taking bribes from NGOs to select them as partner NGOs; e) Creation of fake names and addresses of recipients of relief by government officials f) Politicians pressing on government officials to distribute relief goods to party members. When this was refused the member of parliament ordered the distribution to be stopped".[18]

Low accountability of local partners is often the main cause of corruption in foreign aid management. This is a crucial point because co-operation with these actors cannot be avoided. In 2000, a study on the unintended consequences of humanitarian assistance in Sudan noted:

> "In Government of Sudan areas, there is a complex system of relief committees and structures which present lists of needs to agencies in the areas of health, education, water and training. The pressure on local resources from influxes of displaced southerners creates opportunities for government officials, who determine needs and access in Government of Sudan areas of Operation Lifeline Sudan operation to control and profit from relief inputs. Thus the Wau relief committee, for example, received two tons of sorghum, half a ton of pulses and 16 gallons of oil for every distribution they facilitated. Relief inputs are negotiated more through compromises struck between agencies and the organs of government than in accordance with the actual needs of displaced people".[19]

In many cases, not all eligible groups receive foreign aid. Most of the time ethnic or political minorities are intentionally excluded and not targeted by relief operation. Clientelism also affects distribution policies implemented by local authorities. For example, the first schools to receive assistance from feeding programs in Sierra Leone allegedly had some family/special ties with members of assessment teams.[20] A recent study of needs assessment process in Ethiopia states that aid was more negotiated than assessed. The study found that Emergency Food Security Assessment practice was not correct because it did not follow a consistent frame, but it gave increased discretionary power to lower level government officials.[21]

Local actors could also make strategic complaints that they were excluded from aid disbursements, in order to damage aid agencies' reputations and to extort more resources. In Sierra Leone, there is evidence that local chiefs use accusations of corruption as part of a strategy to gain power against NGOs retaining access to foreign aid management. False accusations were moved from local authorities to

[18] Ewins et al. 2006, 7.

[19] Duffield et al. 2000, 33

[20] Fanthorpe 2003.

[21] Ewins et al. 2006, 30.

an NGO which was working in partnership with a food pipeline agency. They accused NGO field staff of forcing beneficiaries to pay in order to receive food, but the accusations were proved to be false.[22]

Evidence shows that corruption survives emergency events, unintentionally fueled by foreign interventions, and potentially flourishes in the absence of effective State controls. In the next section, we focus on this relationship, by singling out the main variables influencing corruption in those countries that experience natural or man-made disasters.

27.3 Disasters and Opportunities for Corruption

27.3.1 Factors Favoring Corruption During Humanitarian Crisis

There is a clear tradeoff between the rapidity of the response offered by international agencies and local actors, which is essential in emergency situations arising from natural or man-made disasters, and the possibility of an accountable and transparent decision-making process in the allocation of the resources essential to satisfy the basic needs and the re-establishment of an acceptable degree of well being of the population. For instance: the participation of actors in the rescue and distributional choiccs; thc sctup and implementation of competitive procedures in the allocation of the collected resources; the definition of priorities and standards of delivery; the societal; and institutional control over the allocation and the financial records of relief resources; all such processes—which favor a clear attribution of responsibilities and the sanctioning of improper behavior—require an amount of time which decreases as the number of decision makers involved falls, the discretionary power given to them increases, and the procedural constraints and ex-ante controls are weakened.

Several factors contribute to obstructing transparency and accountability of decision-making processes during humanitarian crisis. Among them are:

(a) the time pressure in emergency operations, requiring quick decisions based on inadequate information and a limited procedural base;
(b) the exceptional, or even unique, nature of the situation under which humanitarian interventions are promoted and managed also hinders ex-post audits, owing to the lack of terms of reference to evaluate their results and effectiveness;

---

[22] Fanthorpe 2003.

(c) the considerable quantity of financial and in-kind resources at stake, which—especially in low-income countries—may encourage misappropriation[23];
(d) the emergency recruitment of the local staff and management, which can reduce their loyalty and ability to fulfill their duties[24];
(e) the high media and public opinion pressure for quick aid action;
(f) the fragility of State institutions and weakness of the public service, sometimes beset by the same factors which caused the humanitarian crisis, and the difficulty of exercising effective control or to enforcing respect for the law;
(g) the large number of public and private actors—intergovernmental agencies, donor and recipient governments at local and national level, NGOs, etc.—converging at the same time in the same context to deal with the emergency, each following its own rules and procedures, increasing the complexity of any co-ordination or audit activity[25];
(h) the asymmetrical power relationship between the beneficiaries, the agents and the donors, resulting in low levels of transparency to disaster-affected populations.[26]

Such conditions, which are common to virtually all humanitarian interventions, tend to increase the probability of poor outcomes in aid interventions and favor corruption. Actors which exercise some kind of power in similar decision-making processes, experience a lower risk of being caught and sanctioned for their misbehavior and corrupt practices. Moreover, public reporting is discouraged by the very nature of intervention, since "the potential for proven corruption to alienate donors or the taxpaying public also militates against corruption—and therefore effective controls".[27] The scale, cost, and quality of the relief operations can therefore be undermined by the primary concern of providing quick aid and support to suffering people, causing inefficient as well as ineffective procurement and distribution of resources.

Corruption is one of the factors which can induce actors involved in decision making, allocation and control to put personal gain before the duties of their official role. As a consequence, a set of negative effects can be observed.[28] A factor

---

[23] As Hees et al. 2007, 4 observe: "Emergency aid amounts to around US $6–7 billion annually, just from Official Development Assistance, not including private donations. In exceptional circumstances such as the recent Asian tsunami, it is estimated that close to US $14 billion was pledged for emergency aid for tsunami victims alone. Such large sums of money make humanitarian aid vulnerable to corruption".

[24] Ewins et al. 2006.

[25] Hees et al. 2007.

[26] Ewins et al. 2006, 13.

[27] Schultz and Søreide 2006, 4.

[28] We do not consider here the possibility of "beneficial" bribery, sometimes defined as such due the necessity to balance corruption and humanitarian imperative: "The process of delivering relief is characterized by a tension between addressing humanitarian imperatives and accessing to vulnerable populations, particularly in conflicts. At its simplest, the dilemma is expressed in whether to pay or not a bribe at a checkpoint in order to allow relief to reach needy populations"

to be considered alongside generalized waste of resources and poor-quality implementation of aid policies is the misallocation of funds. In decision making, corrupt agents, will tend to pay inflated prices for goods and services of lower quality, and to define priorities in the allocation of resources according to the bribes they can expect. Projects will be funded simply when the agents expect to collect higher bribes at a lower risk, not according to the expected social benefit of the projects. Moreover, especially when bribes are calculated as a fixed percentage of the value of the resources supplied or contracted, investments in useless assets will be made by corrupt agents merely to maximize the rent of corruption.[29] Such assets are partly converted into bribes offered to decision makers and brokers, and partly distributed in accordance with "willingness to pay", kinship, clientelistic or other arbitrary criteria, not meeting the real priority of needs of the population. Victims of natural disasters or conflict may then be deprived of crucial life-saving assets. Substandard—in the worst case, useless—commodities may be supplied at higher prices. An inequitable distribution of assistance, diverted away from the affected communities, may also contribute to an increase in the disproportion of income.[30] Moreover, an increase in power asymmetries may also result from the massive misappropriation of funds channeled into the country diverted from political gate-keepers and reinvested in their political own careers; similarly, the undue advantage for corrupting firms in accumulating capital hinders the market process. Finally, the adverse reputational effect of corruption scandals on the activity of institutional donors is another long-lasting, negative effect of such practices, which tends to reduce the trust of the public in humanitarian efforts.[31]

27.3.2 Toward a Definition of Corruption

In order to single out those conditions and mechanisms which may foster corruption in humanitarian response to disasters we have to circumscribe the phenomenon. Surprisingly enough, there is no unequivocal and commonly accepted definition of what corruption is. While corruption is commonly defined as "abuse

(Footnote 28 continued)
(Ewins et al. 2006, 5). If corruption can serve—especially in LDCs—as a market substitute to circumvent burdensome regulation and officials' arbitrariness, its benefits are a "second-best" solution only from a very limited point of view, socially outweighed by its harmful effects: Klitgaard 1988; Cremer 1998.

[29] della Porta and Vannucci 2012.

[30] For a survey of the literature on the effects of corruption see Lambsdorf 2007.

[31] Willitts-King and Harvey 2005, 2. The fear for a negative reputational effect may explain why "corruption remains a taboo topic among humanitarian agency staff, which inhibits the effectiveness of measures ad whistle-blowing mechanisms and analysis of current control system" (Transparency International 2010, xi).

of entrusted power for private gain",[32] the problem of singling out the standards against which such "abuse" or violation can be assessed remains open to discussion: formal norms, public interests, public opinion standards are among them. Legal systems in donor and recipient countries typically provide different regulation of similar conducts, while *misuse of power for private benefit* can in itself assume different forms and content. Beside corruption in a stricter sense, embezzlement, favoritism, nepotism, clientelism, cronyism, vote buying, fraud, extortion, or inefficiency and waste of resources are often used synonymously describing improper relationships involving public administrators.[33] Different phenomena indeed, which require different explanations and policies to prevent or combat them.

From our point of view there is a risk of *conceptual stretching* in the adoption of a similar "almost-all encompassing" definition of corruption. Moreover, the conception of abuse or corruption diverges within and among cultures, often with substantial differences from the donor to recipient country and law.[34] For example, sexual favors or other non-monetary, informal benefits offered to the agents managing aid resources may not be perceived and sanctioned as illegal and corrupt acts. In this murky environment, several practices may in fact have an ambiguous legal status, and interested actors can take advantage of the existence of such "grey areas", cultivating hidden relations and contacts with agents participating in the humanitarian decision-making process.

In order to avoid (or at least reduce) similar ambiguities, we may differentiate the basic constitutive components of corruption by adopting a principal-agent scheme.[35] There are different kinds of illicit, dysfunctional, or malfunctioning humanitarian operations, and corruption is but one of them. The principal-agent approach offers a clear way to conceptualize the logic of corruption. In formal terms, corruption can be defined as: the *illegal* and therefore *hidden violation* of an explicit or implicit contract that states a delegation of responsibility from a *principal* to an *agent* who has the legal authority, as well as the official and informal obligation to use his discretionary power, capacity and information to pursue the principal's interests. The violation occurs when the agent exchanges these resources in a *(corrupt) transaction* with a *client*, the *briber* (a contractor, a final beneficiary, another employee, an agent belonging to another agency, etc.),

[32] This is the operational definition provided by Transparency International, leading NGO in anticorruption. Cf. http://www.transparency.org/news_room/faq/corruption_faq, accessed 21 February 2012.

[33] See for instance Kreidler 2006, 1, who encompasses nepotism, bribery, kick-backs or cuts, theft and diversion as alternative forms of corruption.

[34] Transparency International 2010, xi. Ewin et al. 2006, 22 notice that "respondents to the survey in Uganda and Pakistan frequently mentioned local authorities using bribes to complement their salaries, but did not see this as corrupt. Respondents also had different perceptions of the meaning of corruption, influenced by issues of gender, ethics and religion".

[35] Cf. among others Banfield (1975), della Porta and Vannucci (1999, 2012), Lambsdorff (2007).

for which the agent receives as a reward an amount of money—the bribe—or other items of value.

Any agent entrusted by public organizations (governments, public companies or agencies, etc.) or private ones (companies, NGOs, etc.) with the power to manage resources in the process of humanitarian action after natural or man-made disasters also has private interests that may not coincide with those of his “principal”. Moreover, he can usually hide information on the characteristics and content of his tasks and activities, which have to respond to local, contingent, idiosyncratic emergency conditions. This is the reason why, in delegating power and responsibilities to the agent, the principal lays down rules and procedures that limit his range of discretion, and develops various mechanisms of legal, administrative, social, political, or contractual control and enforcement of any abuse. For instance, most agencies operating in humanitarian aid after disaster, including NGOs, donors, and government offices, “have written procurement procedures. Typically, these procedures reflect best practices in international competitive bidding (…). Corruption represents a violation of these procedures and the principles behind them”.[36] Among the rules posed by the principal, there is the prohibition of accepting payments or other rewards from actors for the accomplishment of delegated tasks, as this would increase the risk of the agent disregarding the interests of the principal. We consider corruption, the distortion of relations between agent and principal induced by a third actor: the exchange relationship with the briber causes/prompts the agent to avoid the constraints imposed by norms and procedures. By offering money or other rewards, the briber succeeds in obtaining from the agent favorable decisions, reserved information, and protection.[37]

In the transaction between the agent and the briber *property rights* to *rents* created through the humanitarian relief operations are shared between the two: the agent modifies to the advantage of the briber the foreseen allotment of funds, water, medicine, shelter, services, etc., obtaining as a reward a portion of the value. In general terms, a rent may be created and allocated by the agent through the following actions: acquisition of commodities paid for at more than their market price; the selling or the licensing of use of assets for at a lower price than their market price; the use of control or enforcement activities that attribute power to selectively impose costs or reduce the value of private goods.[38] By means of a hidden transaction, the briber and the corrupt agent share between them the rent thus created.

---

[36] Schultz and Søreide 2006, 9.

[37] della Porta and Vannucci 2012, 6.

[38] Rose-Ackerman 1978, 61–3.

27.3.3 Approaches to Corruption: A Synthetic Formula

Several factors should be taken into consideration to explain and qualify the risks of corruption in humanitarian operations after disasters. To put it simply, there are three main theoretical approaches in the literature on corruption, focusing on different though not irreconcilable variables. The *cultural* perspective looks at the differences in cultural traditions, social norms and interiorized values which shape individuals' moral preferences and consideration of his social role. Individuals belonging to different societies and organizations are *pushed* toward corruption by the nature of their internalized values and by social pressures. They tend to make less use of opportunities for illegal enrichment the higher their (and their peer group's) moral standards—and vice versa.[39]

The *economic* approach emphasizes the crucial role of economic incentives and opportunities to engage in corrupt activities. Corruption is considered the outcome of rational individual choices, and its spread is influenced by the structure of expected costs and rewards. As with other behaviors involving deviation from laws and/or informal norms, the individual decision to participate in corrupt exchanges depends on the expected risk of being reported and punished, the severity of the potential penal and administrative penalties, and the expected rewards as compared with available alternatives.

A third *neo-institutional* approach considers not only *external* variables—moral values or economic incentives—but also the *endogenous* dynamics of corrupt networks.[40] Once a certain organizational texture and 'cultural adaptation' to corruption has developed, informal codes and governance structures provide internal stability and enforcement mechanisms to illegal dealings in specific areas of public activity, reducing uncertainty among partners in relationships which thus appear more lucrative and less morally censurable. The coevolution of economic incentives and cultural values, in other words, is path dependent: the heritage of corruption in the past produces increasing returns in subsequent periods by neutralizing moral barriers; by creating more profitable opportunities rooted in formal procedures and decision-making processes; by providing informal norms, organizational shields and mechanisms of protection against external intrusion by the authorities and internal friction among corrupt actors.[41]

A synthetic expression of the main variables can be expressed with the following formula[42]:

[39] Pizzorno 1992, 46.

[40] A neo-institutional approach to the analysis of corruption has been adopted, among others, by Husted (1994), della Porta and Vannucci (1999, 2012), Lambsdorff (2007).

[41] della Porta and Vannucci 2012, 219–22.

[42] This formula restates Klitgaard's one (1988, 75), which summed up the basic assumption of the rational choice theory, to include also the cultural and institutional dimension. The list of potential corruption generators (or constraints) here also includes *H*, standing for hidden (that is,

$$C_t = f(R;\ D;\ H;\ -A;\ -\mathrm{Mc};\ C_{t-1,t-2,\ldots})$$

The diffusion of Corruption at a certain time t (C_t) is a function of:

i. *Rents*, i.e., State assets, spending budget, foreign aid, natural resources, regulation creating monopolistic positions, and any other resource which can generate rents. The probability of corruption is proportional to the amount of such rents, which makes their hidden appropriation more attractive for those offering and accepting bribes.

ii. *Discretion* in the exercise of the power attributed to agents to decide how to collect, create or allocate rents and resources. Probability of corruption will increase when individual agents have wider discretion in deciding who will benefit from their decisions, since in this case the corrupt exchange can be affected with reduced risk.

iii. *Hidden information*, i.e., the capacity to use as a resource in the corrupt exchange confidential information which can influence the allocation of rents. The less transparent the decision-making process, the stronger the incentives to corruption, which becomes more difficult to detect. Bribes can be paid by the briber to the corrupt agent to gain access to confidential, privileged information, which has a value since it increases the probability of gaining access to an economic rent.

iv. *Accountability*, i.e., the efficacy of State and social control over agents' conduct. The more effective the mechanisms and institutional arrangements to hold agents responsible for their actions and to sanction them in case of violation, the less probable will be their involvement in corrupt exchanges.

v. *Moral costs*, i.e., the individual's moral aversion to corruption, reflecting customs, attitudes, cultural norms, and informal constraints shaping values and preferences. Moral costs structure the preferences which affect corruption choices: they represent the loss of utility that results from "engaging in an illegal action".[43] The higher the moral cost for a given agent, the stronger will be his "preference for law-fulfillment" (that is, the kind of *psychological suffering* associated with the violation of legal norms), influenced by his personal preferences as well as by the values and informal codes prevailing in the organization where he has been socialized, will be; and the lower the expected benefit from bribery. Considered as *given* in economic models, moral costs of corruption may vary significantly both among countries and—taking a long view—with time.

(Footnote 42 continued)
not publicly available) information; Mc, standing for Moral costs; $C_{t-1,\ t-2,\ldots}$, standing for the "heritage" of corruption in previous periods.

[43] Rose-Ackerman 1978, 113; della Porta and Vannucci 2005.

vi. *Corruption in prior periods*, reflecting the existence of structures of "internal governance" of corruption networks which developed in the past. The influence of the legacy of pre-existing bribery operates through several mechanisms, which makes involvement in corrupt exchanges less risky and more profitable. Widespread corruption generates 'skills of illegality', governance structures and informal norms whose strength is based on adaptive expectations and co-ordination effects. Moreover, the shadow of past corruption may also influence its spread in the present through the intentional activities of actors implicated in corruption networks, who can obstruct judges' inquiries and strengthen expectations of impunity through reforms favouring corruption.

27.3.4 Corruption and Anticorruption in Humanitarian Relief Actions

Without going into details, the *corruption formula* presented above may provide a framework for both the research agenda on mechanisms of corruption in the humanitarian relief after disasters and a general guide for anticorruption measures. A crucial aspect of disaster response is in fact the primary concern for urgent delivery, allocation and distribution to the affected population of considerable amounts of resources within a loose institutional, law and procedural context. All these elements have an impact on opportunities, incentives and constraints of corrupt exchanges.

As a consequence of natural and man-made disasters, networks are created among different actors. The decision-making process through which assistance relief is contracted between these actors and finally delivered affects the nature and chances of corruption risk. Humanitarian action is undertaken by a variety of donor organizations, NGOs, bilateral and multilateral agencies, Red Cross agencies, private contractors, and military forces. All these actors operate according to different norms and guidelines, and rely on different sources of funding (donor governments, appeals made by aid agencies to the general public, private corporations, or foundations). Even the power and accountability of these actors can vary significantly. The contact between actors coming from richer countries (usually providing relief) and those from poorer countries is in itself a source of possible corruption. It is a fact that the largest number of disasters (with the greatest need for relief) is located in countries with high levels of corruption.[44] The simple fact that the staff of foreign NGOs or humanitarian agencies is paid much more than local personnel arouses suspicion of waste and misconduct in public

[44] Ewins et al. 2006.

opinion.[45] This profligacy may be easily perceived as a form of corruption, particularly by local actors, and may create an environment where the moral costs are lowered and corruption in itself is more likely to take place. Usually, if not always, emergency management absorbs vast sums of money (see also Sect. 3), at least according to the recipient's standards.[46] The mobilization of large amount of resources and funds in humanitarian operations multiplies the rents allocated by public and private agencies, generating an exceptional, sometimes once-in-a-lifetime opportunity for potential givers and accepters of bribes to take profit from this abnormal, often unique situation.

Wide discretion give to a small set of agents is the rule in emergency decision making, since the *proceduralization* of the process and the participation of a plurality of actors would increase time needed and transaction costs, slowing down the distribution of aid. As a rule, "in emergencies, procurement officials normally exercise high levels of discretion in terms of identifying beneficiary needs".[47] The *need for speed* "can mean agencies do not comply with procedures designed to minimize the risks of corruption, for example a tendering process" (Ewins et al. 2006, 13).

The legal and normative constraints shaping the framework for emergency operations—as already observed—are usually quite loose, since State institutions and public bureaucracy are often weak or weakened by the disaster itself. The extraordinariness of the situation does not permit ordinary procedures to be followed; "fast-track" measures enabling agents to respond quickly and flexibly to contingent demands are activated, therefore hampering both ex-ante and ex-post monitoring and evaluation processes. Incentives to corruption are then stronger, owing to the weakness of auditing and diminished accountability of agents for decisions and management of financial and material resources in emergency conditions.

Moreover, as a by-product, privileged information on specific aspects of allocation mechanisms and decision making will be more valuable. Knowing beforehand what the donor agencies and governments will require in procurement procedures, or the criteria and mechanisms under which resources will be allocated, guarantee bribers a competitive advantage. Opaqueness in decision making will therefore encourage directing information toward willing bribers.

Moral cost is another crucial element to be considered, reflecting the basic elements of the cultural environment of both donor and recipient countries, whose agents respond to social norms, internalized beliefs, such as *esprit de corps* and the

---

[45] For example, in Pakistan, the Transparency International survey identified 'foreign donor officials staying in 5 star hotels and charging it to disaster relief accounts' as a form of corruption. (Ewins et al. 2006).

[46] As Ewins et al. 2006 notice, there is "a tendency for disaster response either high-profile, with a proliferation of organizations, large amounts of funding and huge co-ordination challenge, or 'forgotten', with extremely limited resources and capabilities". Needless to say, the first environment is considerably more corruption-prone.

[47] Schultz and Søreide 2006, 13.

"public spiritedness" of officials, political culture, and public attitudes toward illegality. Agents operating on behalf of governments, NGOs, companies or other organizations involved in the humanitarian efforts may therefore make their choices according to very different ethical standards. Their average professional integrity—"that is, the degree to which a staff member's attitude and behavior aligns with the goals and achievements of the institution that they represent"[48]—has a crucial importance in determining the risks of corruption in the relief operations after disasters. We may expect, for instance, that higher moral costs will deter corruption in NGOs, Red Cross, and other bilateral and multilateral agencies when agents have been recruited on the basis of integrity and truthfulness and have been socialized to these values. Moreover, in this case peer control and stigma are added to the threat of incurring legal sanctions. On the other hand, urgency, the necessity quickly to find local personnel, usually hired on short-term contracts, to manage large-scale operations may induce a selection of agents poorly motivated and qualified agents who have lower moral standards.

Finally, the perceived pre-crisis level of corruption influences the risk of corruption in subsequent emergency management. High levels of past corruption may facilitate the development of new hidden exchanges.[49] Several mechanisms come into play: pre-existing corruption networks and trust relationships, established practices and informal rules stating the level of bribes to be paid to agents and brokers, the "know-how" acquired by skilled corruption practitioners, robust expectation that corruption cannot be avoided. All these converge to increase the expected benefit of new corrupt transactions.[50] Most countries affected by disasters, as we have shown in Sect. 3, are actually characterized by high levels of perceived corruption.[51] A bidirectional causal nexus may exist between the two phenomena: poor governance in the political sphere—also expressed by high levels of perceived corruption—may degenerate into internal conflicts or civil war. In war and post-war contexts, moreover, corrupting contractors benefiting from international emergency aid may have a hidden interest in sustaining the conflict economy.[52]

In the following section, a survey of measures proposed by international organizations and NGOs to reduce the risk of corruption in critical emergency situations will be presented and briefly discussed. Such mechanisms operate through variables included in the corruption formula illustrated above: implementing participation by local communities and feedback mechanisms, improving the transparency and traceability of aid flows, introducing independent monitoring

---

48 Schultz and Søreide 2006, 10.

49 Ewins et al. 2006, 17.

50 In Indonesia, for example, "following the 2004 tsunami, assessment teams were informed that 'incentive payments' of 10 % add-on to the bid, were a normal and accepted practice" (Schultz and Søreide 2006, 13–4).

51 Cremer 1998, Willitts-King and Harvey 2005, Savage et al. 2007.

52 Schultz and Søreide 2006, 8.

mechanisms,[53] promoting consistent standard and "best practice" procedures for procurement, supporting the professionalization of procurement officers, supporting specialized courses on humanitarian aid.[54] Such measures—among others—tend to reduce discretion and hidden information and to increase accountability and moral costs of agents in emergency decision making. The target of dismantling internal "governance structures" of deep-rooted, long-lasting corruption may instead be fostered through strategies aimed at breaking down trust links between those giving and accepting bribes, guaranteeing certainty of rights to beneficiaries of aid policies, etc.[55]

27.4 International Organizations' and NGOs' Reactions to Corruption in Humanitarian Actions

In general terms, the increasing concern of various actors—governments, NGOs, international organizations—at the negative effects of corruption in relief operations after disasters has not yet been translated into any relevant reform of the norms and procedures regulating them. As we illustrate in the following section, the alarm at the perverse effects of corruption and the difficulties in eradicating it still lacks any coherent and wide-ranging institutional response. For this reason, corruption in a post-disaster context is not dealt with by specific juridical instruments but through more general treaties. In this chapter we provide an overview of these treaties.

27.4.1 International Anticorruption Treaties Pre-2000

In the last 15 years, the issue of corruption has been taken up by several international organizations, following the 1997 OECD Convention on Combating bribery of foreign public officials in international business transactions.[56] The OECD Convention, which at the present has been ratified by the 34 OECD member countries, as well as Argentina, Brazil, Bulgaria, and South Africa, focuses on the "supply-side" of international corrupt exchange and may provide a

53 Transparency International 2005.

54 Schultz and Søreide 2006.

55 della Porta and Vannucci 2012, 264.

56 Firms and agents from non-OECD countries, however, enjoy a competitive advantage in illegal activities not being exposed to the risk of prosecution and sanctioning for corruption crimes according to their national law.

general legal framework also covering some specific phases within humanitarian responses.[57] As stated in its Article 1(1):

> "Each Party shall take such measures as may be necessary to establish that a criminal offence under its law for any person intentionally to offer, promise or give any undue pecuniary or other advantage, whether directly or through intermediaries, to a foreign public official, for that official or for a third party, in order that the official act or refrain from acting in relation to the performance of official duties, in order to obtain or retain business or other improper advantage in the conduct of international business".

Misconduct in humanitarian activities can therefore be prosecuted by the donor countries which have adopted the OECD anti-bribery Convention only when *national* agents and companies have illegal dealings with officials of the recipient country.

This convention can be considered as the paramount international treaty dedicated to fighting corruption. In particular, its most innovative aspect is that it criminalizes bribery of foreign civil servant of third countries. In addition, the convention aims its attempt to fight corruption at other four separate areas.

(a) It categorizes the earnings from international corruption as a *money laundering offence* (Article 7).
(b) All the countries were obliged to enforce the accountability of companies and to forbid accounting practices used in order to bribe foreign public officials or to hide such bribery. Thus, the establishment of *off-the-books accounts* and similar practices used to conceal bribery was to be forbidden by signatory countries (Article 8).
(c) Since foreign bribery engages actors in different jurisdictions and international financial channels are often used to perform or hide international bribery, the Convention prescribes *international co-operation* and mutual legal support between countries and the exchange of information. Even extradition is to be made easier in relation to offences governed by the Convention and practices of seizure and confiscation of the proceeds of corruption are to be adopted (Articles 9–10).
(d) Signatory countries are required to co-operate in a review process to monitor and promote the full implementation of the Convention (Article 12).

The OECD Convention was preceded by the treaty under the aegis of the Organization of American States. The impact of the "Inter-American Convention Against Corruption" (IACAC), which was approved in 1996 and came into force in 1997, was only regional, and some of its commitments were less precise than those of the OECD Convention. However, the IACAC prohibits the corruption of government official of another State, but for "any State Party that has not established transnational bribery as an offense shall, insofar as its laws permit, provide

---

[57] For a survey of conventions and other instruments developed at the global, international, regional, and subregional level to fight corruption see http://www.transparency.org/global_priorities/international_conventions/conventions_instruments, accessed 22 February 2012.

assistance and co-operation with respect to this offense as provided in this Convention" (Article 7). Moreover, the IACAC introduces (Article 3), among many other obligations, commitments which are relevant to the present contribution, i.e.: (a) the establishment of systems for registering the income, assets, and liabilities of public officials; (b) the institution of open, equal, efficient systems of procurement of goods and services; (c) the abolition of tax facilities for any individual or corporation for expenditures made in violation of the anti-corruption laws.

As already stated in the previous section, the 1997 Convention gave to firms and agents from non-OECD countries a competitive advantage in illegal activities. This situation led the OECD members to seek a broader agreement to fill the gap between OECD and non-OECD companies.

At the European level, the first step was the "Convention on the Fight against Corruption involving Officials of the European Communities or Officials of member States of the European Union" adopted by Council of the European Union in 1997, but it was limited to the civil servants of the EU.

27.4.2 International Anti-Corruption Treaties Post-2000

Other important acts adopted by the Council of Europe are the "Criminal Law Convention" (which came into force in 2002), the "Civil Law Convention on Corruption" (which came into force in 2003) and the "Protocol on Corruption" (which came into force in 2005). The process of ratification is still far from being concluded as to date 41 countries have ratified the first document, 33 the second, and 19 the third one, eligible parties being all 46 members of the Council of Europe and six non-member States invited to join (Belarus, Canada, Holy See, Japan, Mexico, USA).

The obligations of the parties to the Council of Europe Convention directly reflect the duties of the OECD convention. Corruption is criminalized not only if it involves foreign officials but also members of assemblies and officials of international organizations: proceeds of corruption are considered money laundering, off-the-books accounts are prohibited, and international co-operation among the States is prescribed. The monitoring of the convention is directly assigned to the GRECO.[58]

Other regional organizations also adopted their own international treaties against corruption. In 2001, "Anti-Corruption Action Plan" was developed as part of the anti-corruption initiative for Asia and the Pacific adopted by the Asian

---

[58] The Group of States against Corruption (GRECO) was established in 1999 by the Council of Europe to monitor States' compliance with the organization's anti-corruption standards. By 2012 GRECO comprises 49 member States (48 European States and the United States of America). GRECO holds observer status to the Organization for Economic Cooperation and Development (OECD) and the United Nations—represented by the United Nations Office on Drugs and Crime (UNODC).

Development Bank (ADB) and the Organization for Economic Co-operation and Development (OECD). It establishes a non-binding structure of action for Asia–Pacific countries in relation to the public sector, the private sector, and civil society. Twenty-eight countries had endorsed the plan as of November 2007. Recognizing that corruption is a dangerous problem with deleterious effects on social welfare, political stability, and economic growth, the action plan indicates the participating countries' objectives and describes how reform will be implemented.

In 2001, thirteen countries of the Southern African Development Community (SADC) adopted the "Protocol against Corruption". It became operational in July 2005, after its ratification by two-thirds of the SADC membership, providing both preventive and enforcement mechanisms. The purpose of the Protocol is to promote the development of anti-corruption mechanisms at the national level; to promote co-operation in the fight against corruption by State parties; to harmonize anti-corruption national legislation in the region. The Protocol provides, as other treaties do, *preventive measures and mechanisms* (Article 4); the *criminalization* of the bribery of foreign officials (Article 6); the confiscation of the proceeds of corruption as measures against *money laundering* (Article 8). The Protocol also intended to make it more difficult for corrupt agents to export bribe money to one of the SADC countries. Moreover, the Protocol can be a legal basis for *extradition* in the absence of a bilateral extradition treaty (Article 9). The Protocol also provides for legal co-operation and assistance among State parties (Article 10).

At the end of 2001 another African regional organization, the Economic Community of West African States (ECOWAS) adopted a "Protocol on the fight against corruption". The Protocol obliges States Parties to adopt the necessary legislative measures to criminalize illicit gains, false accounting, and the laundering of the gains of corruption; to ensure the protection of victims; and to provide legal co-operation to one another. The Protocol further calls upon signatory countries to harmonize their national anti-corruption laws, to adopt effective preventive measures against corruption, and to introduce proportionate and dissuasive sanctions. The protocol criminalizes the active and passive bribery in the public and private sectors but does not refer directly to the corruption of foreign officials.

In 2003, the AU "Convention on Preventing and Combating Corruption" was adopted by the heads of State at the African Union Summit held in Maputo (Mozambique) on 11 July and came into force on 5 August 2006. Some NGOs, such as Transparency International, were given observer status and participated actively in the experts' meetings and made written and oral submissions. The AU Convention provides a complete framework and covers a range of criminal offenses including bribery (domestic or foreign), appropriation of property by civil servants, trading in influence, illicit enrichment, money laundering, and concealment of property. It makes provisions on prevention, regional co-operation, criminalization, mutual legal support, and recovery of assets. It covers both public sector and private sector corruption, both supply and demand side. It was the first treaty to contain compulsory provisions about corruption between private parties and transparency in political party funding. Other notable elements of the Convention are the obligatory requirements of public declaration of assets by designated civil servants and the restrictions on their immunity. The treaty also gives particular consideration to the need for the media to have free access to information. The Follow-Up Mechanism involves an Advisory Board on Corruption within the African Union (Article 22). This is assigned a range of functions, including research and storage of information, advice to governments, and regular reporting to the Executive Council on the progress of signatory States in implementing the Convention, drawing on annual reports to the Board by the various countries.

Apart from the provisions already mentioned, the AU Convention contains a number of provisions specifically linked to the African context, making it unique among regional anti-corruption conventions—most of them cannot be found even in the later UN convention. In particular, it encourages signatory countries to create mechanisms to promote *participation by the private sector* (Article 11) in the fight against unfair competition, respect for tender procedures and property rights; it provides minimum guarantees of a fair trial. Moreover, the AU Convention calls on signatory States to collaborate with the countries of origin of multinational companies to criminalize and punish the practice of clandestine commissions and other forms of corrupt dealings in international trade, encouraging countries to take legislative measures to combat corruption of public officials by *freezing their foreign accounts,* and the facilitation of the repatriation of stolen or illegally acquired monies to the countries of origin (Articles 16 and 17).

In 2005, the United Nations Convention against Corruption (UNCAC) came into force, after being adopted in 2003. It is a unique instrument among other conventions, not only in its geographic reach but also in the range and depth of its obligations. The treaty was discussed over a 2-year period at the United Nations office in Vienna by representatives of more than 100 countries.

The secretariat for the negotiations was the United Nations Office on Drugs and Crime (UNODC). Delegates of civil society organizations, including Transparency International, also participated in this development. The text of the Convention was presented for approval by the General Assembly on 31 October 2003. States were then invited to sign it, starting with a signing conference in Merida, Mexico on 9–10 December 2003.[59] The UNCAC was initially signed by 111 States. The thirtieth ratification, required to make the treaty binding, was made on 15 September 2005, making the actual date of coming into force 14 December 2005.

The UNCAC dedicates its first section to (a) *preventive measures* (Article 5) stating extensive provisions on the ways, means and standards for preventive measures in the public and private sectors. In the second section, the UNCAC calls for (b) *criminalization* of a broad variety of offenses, and a definition of the public official. Furthermore, it includes offenses relating both to the public sector, even for foreign officials (Article 16), and the private sector (Article 21). The UNCAC

[59] Since then the ninth of December has represented the International Anti-Corruption Day.

also requires an (c) *international co-operation* (chapter IV) framework which has the potential to improve common law enforcement support. The provisions on (d) *technical co-operation and information exchange* (Article 50) are crucial to the overall composition and balance of the UNCAC. These take account of the need for "enhanced financial and technical assistance" to developing countries and countries in transition to help them implement the Convention. Without such assistance, some countries will not be in a position to implement UNCAC requirements. UNCAC provides for an (e) *implementation mechanism* under the auspices of the Conference of States Parties (Article 62). The first Conference is to be convened within a year after entry into force of the treaty and regularly thereafter. The duties of the Conference comprise: reviewing periodically the realization of the treaty; making recommendations to improve the Convention and its implementation; using relevant information generated by other international; and regional instruments; putting into effect supplementary review mechanisms and establishing any review body deemed necessary to assess the measures taken by States Parties (and difficulties encountered) to implement the Convention.

Since the second half of the first decade of the twenty-first century every country on the globe can apply at least one, and in many cases two legal instruments to fight corruption in humanitarian relief operations. Table 27.4 summarizes the current existing international treaties, which can be useful to address corruption in post-disaster contexts.

27.4.3 NGOs' Response to Corruption in Humanitarian Aid

The collaboration between States has been a crucial first step in fighting corruption in relief operations; but there are other efforts that could be made to combat this plague. Besides States, NGOs have also played an important role in humanitarian actions after disasters. For this reason, during the drafting stage of some international treaties (for example: the AU Convention and the UNCAC) NGOs have been involved in the preliminary work and consulted as experts. But these are not the only actions by NGOs to fight corruption.

In 2005, Transparency International (TI), which is an NGO primarily devoted to support anti-corruption policies, led joint research with other NGOs to lay the foundation for two publications. The aim was to map the risks of relief operations and to propose solutions to prevent corruption in their execution. There were examples of substantial diversion of aid resources recently reported in Afghanistan, Iraq, Liberia, and Somalia; but the idea for these publications came from the huge relief operation following the Asian tsunami, when the amount of resources collected produced apprehension about opportunities for corruption.

In response to this concern, in 2005 TI launched the first phase of the research to diagnose corruption risks specific to humanitarian actions, and to develop a set

Table 27.4 Treaties addressing corruption at the international level

Year of signature	Entry into force	Name	Organization	Geographic extension	Criminalization of corruption of foreign officials	Other innovative commitments
1996	1997	Inter-American Convention Against Corruption (IACAC)	Organisation of American States	Americas	No	Yes
1997	1997	Convention on the Fight against Corruption involving Officials of the European Communities or Officials of Member States of the European Union	European Union	Europe	No	Yes
1997	1999	Convention on the Bribery of Foreign Public Officials in International Business Transactions	Organisation for Economic Co-operation and Development	Developed	countries	Yes
Yes						
1998	2002	Criminal Law Convention	Council of Europe	Europe	Yes	No
1999	2003	Civil Law Convention	Council of Europe	Europe	Yes	No
2001	2001	Anti-Corruption Action Plan for Asia–Pacific	Asian Development Bank (ADB) and Organisation for Economic Co-operation and Development (OECD)	Asia - Pacific	No	No
2001	2005	Protocol against Corruption	Southern African Development Community	Southern Africa	Yes	Yes
2001	2001	Protocol on the Fight against Corruption	ECOWAS	Western Africa	No	No
2003	2005	Protocol on Corruption	Council of Europe	Europe	Yes	No
2003	2006	Convention on Preventing and Combating Corruption	African Union	Africa	No	Yes
2003	2005	Convention against Corruption	United Nations	World	Yes	Yes

Assistance Process	Corruption Risk Example
1. Initial assessment, decision to respond and program design	1.a Elites bribe/influence those conducting the assessment to inflate needs and/or to favour specific groups 1.b Response selected to enhance personal or organizational reputation rather than based on needs
2. Fundraising and allocation of funding	2.a Double funding: allocating the same overhead expenditure to two or more projects
3. Establishment of offices and operations / Agreements to work with local organizations	3.a Agency staff invent partners or demand kickbacks
4. Procurement and logistics	4.a Goods which are sub-standard or do not meet the original specification are accepted and ultimately paid for through kickbacks, bribes, collusion
5. Targeting and registration of specific beneficiaries	5.a Powerful individuals within the community manipulate the beneficiary lists 5.b Beneficiaries have to bribe agency staff, local elites or authorities to maintain their place in a distribution line or receive goods 5.c Manipulation of monitoring reports/information to attract further resources
6. Implementation / distribution	6.a Reports falsified to hide corruption 6.b Disposal of assets to favored people
7. Project monitoring, reporting, evaluation and program closure	7.a Monitoring, reporting or evaluations falsified to hide evidence of corruption that was found

Fig. 27.6 Map of corruption risks in humanitarian assistance (Ewins et al. 2006, p. 26)

of good practices. The first, diagnostic phase culminated in 2006 with the publication of the report "Mapping the Risks of Corruption in Humanitarian Action".[60] The second phase was carried out during 2007–2008 by a joint team from the Feinstein International Center (FIC) of Tufts University, the Humanitarian Policy Group (HPG) of the Overseas Development Institute, and TI, in co-operation with some leading international non-governmental humanitarian organizations (Action Aid, Catholic Relief Services, CARE International, Islamic Relief Worldwide,

60 Ewins et al. 2006.

Lutheran World Federation, Save the Children USA, World Vision International), through interviews with agency managers and staff. The report "Preventing Corruption in Humanitarian Assistance: Final Research Report"[61] is a handbook, offering a menu of good practices and tools for preventing and detecting corruption in humanitarian operations.

No phase of the humanitarian intervention is immune to corruption, but any phase faces different kinds of risk, related to the complex structure of resources allocated through procedures and contracts that represents the basis of humanitarian assistance.[62] Presenting the various aspects of the process in tabular form, it tries to map the areas where different kinds of corruption may exist, pointing to the various instruments and techniques that need to be developed in order to minimize corruption. In particular, corruption risks have to be mapped according to the different stages of a relief response, from assessment and fundraising to procurement, targeting, distribution, and evaluation.

An example of this mapping exercise is given by Fig. 27.6. This illustrates the typical process of humanitarian assistance that is used as a framework to develop a set of tables which map overall corruption risks.

Heel[63] describes policies and processes that could create *an organizational environment* supporting transparency, integrity and accountability. Specific corruption risks are faced by public servants during the various support *functions* that constitute the core of every humanitarian program, such as supply chain management and finance. Moreover, at different *stages* of the program cycle, from the needs assessment to the post-distribution phase, three key elements have to be considered: (a) the "*corruption risks*" (b) the situations to be *"watched out"*, and (c) *"prevention measures"*. Looking at some of these stages, operational conditions to be watched out can be analyzed through the lens of the variables expressed in the "corruption formula", as presented in the previous section.

For example, looking at the stage entitled "manipulated selection of local partners agencies",[64] the presence of "*potential partners who don't have physical offices or clear governance structures*" is considered a "red-flag" situation to "be watched out". Local partners are not effectively held accountable. Moreover, the recruitment of *"partners with staff who appear to come from the same family"* could reduce the *"moral costs"* of corruption, since the sense of duty toward relatives can be stronger than formal obligations toward the humanitarian organization: corrupting or stealing for the benefit of one's family can be subjectively considered as morally justifiable, though illicit, behavior. "Partners unable to give references for previous work" are to be considered a risky case, since this element could be an indication of "*corruption in prior periods*".

---

[61] Hees et al. 2007.

[62] Ewins et al. 2006.

[63] Hees et al. 2007.

[64] Hees et al. 2007, 123.

On the other hand, several preventive measures proposed in the handbook may positively influence the "corruption formula". For instance, "*setting firm criteria, in accordance with our organizational culture*" is intended to reduce discretion in decision making; "*remember that your partners can affect your own image and reputation*" aims at increasing –accountability in the management of aid, thus strengthening reciprocal control.

At the present time, a considerable number of juridical instruments allows for more effective prosecution of corruption in post-disaster relief operations. These international treaties, if effectively implemented at national level, may be useful in the effort to fight corruption. The importance of prevention strategy has on the other hand been stressed by operating agencies, especially NGOs. Analysis of corruption risks, sharing of information, open discussion, and co-ordinated action are the best strategies for implementing agencies' zero-tolerance policies on corruption in humanitarian action, improving accountability, quality performance, and good management.

Even if some humanitarian agencies feel that focusing on possible corruption risks may distract already overstretched management capacity from more important issues:

> "mitigating many of these corruption risks is essentially about good management. At a more fundamental level, it is also about greater levels of accountability and transparency to disaster affected populations. This is where the real challenges lie: in having committed staff at all levels who believe in the humanitarian objectives of the organization, and disaster-affected populations who understand what they are meant to be receiving, can participate in its planning and implementation and can complain if relief is corruptly abused. Investing in this would result not only in greater potential to minimize corruption, but also in more substantive accountability and consequently more effective humanitarian action."[65]

27.5 Conclusions

According to statistics, disasters have been increasing in recent years, affecting a larger number of people. Budgets for emergency humanitarian reconstruction and relief have been impressively increased, as has the number of international agencies and NGOs directly involved in humanitarian field operations. The evidence reported in the first section of this chapter justifies the growing awareness of institutions and civil society of the growing relevance of these events. The international community has become more effective in its interventions, and there is usually little delay in relief and reconstruction efforts, which channel large amounts of resources into damaged zones. However, the press and NGOs have questioned the sincere intentions of these interventions, and have asked whether

---

[65] Ewins et al. 2006, 71.

aid policies really result in both good governance and development, or, instead, whether they are wasted in inefficient public consumption and other opaque practices, worsening endogenous corruption. The concentration of foreign resources in emergency situations is an important determinant of rampant corruption. This element has an adverse effect on the quality of relief assistance. The effect of corruption can be disastrous in itself, increasing mortality and hampering relief in such exceptional situations.

In recent years, the international community and civil society have shown a growing awareness of the pernicious influence of corruption in post-disaster situations. A legal framework was set up through several international treaties which have, among other things, criminalized corruption of third State officials. From a juridical point of view, however, there has been no attempt to address expressly the issue of corruption in humanitarian actions, specifically considering the risks of abuses in intervention after disasters. The contribution of several NGOs—with a leading role played by Transparency International—in the assessment of corruption risks and in the formulation of voluntary tools to improve societal monitoring and participation can be seen as the first step toward a "bottom-up" approach toward anti-corruption in after-disaster management, leading to permanent inclusion of such issues on the agenda of donor and recipient States as well as of international organizations.

References

Alesina A, Weder B (2002) Do corrupt governments receive less foreign aid? Am Econ Rev 92:1126–1137

Ambraseys N, Bilham R (2011) Corruption kills. Science 469:153–155

Anbarci N, Escaleras M, Register C (2005) Earthquake fatalities: the interaction of nature and political economy. J Public Econ 89:1907–1933

Anbarci N, Escaleras M, Register C (2007) Public sector corruption and major earthquakes: a potentially deadly interaction. Public Choice 132:209–230

Banfield EC (1975) Corruption as a feature of governmental organisation. J Law Econ 18(3):587–605

Cremer G (1998) On the problem of misuse in emergency aid. J Human Assist. http://sites.tufts.edu/jha/archives/131. Accessed 23 Feb 2012

della Porta D, Vannucci A (1999) Corrupt exchanges. Aldine De Gruyter, New York

della Porta D, Vannucci A (2005) The moral (and immoral) costs of corruption. In: von Alemann U (ed) Dimensionen politischer Korruption. Wiesbaden, Vs Verlag, pp 109–134

della Porta D, Vannucci A (2012) The hidden order of corruption: an institutional approach. Farnham, Ashgate

Duffield M et al (2000) Sudan: the unintended consequences of humanitarian assistance, field evaluation study, report to the European community humanitarian office. Trinity College, Dublin

Ewins P, Harvey P, Savage K, Jacobs A (2006) Mapping the risks of corruption in humanitarian action, Overseas Development Institute and Management Accounting for NGOs, Report for Transparency international and the U4 Anti-corruption Resource Centre, July. http://www.odi.org.uk/resources/details.asp?id=607&title=mapping-risks-corruption-humanitarian-action

Fanthorpe R (2003) Humanitarian aid in post-war Sierra Leone: the politics of moral economy. In Collinson P (ed) Power, livelihoods and conflict: case studies in political economy analysis for humanitarian action, HPG Report 13, Overseas Development Institute
Hees RG, Ahlendorf M, Rozo M (2007) Prevention of corruption in emergency procurement: an imperative for the humanitarian community. Aid Trade Rev, IAT03-18/2
Husted B (1994) Honor among thieves: a transaction-cost interpretation of corruption in the third world. Bus Ethics Quart 4(1):17–27
Kahn M (2005) The death toll from natural disasters: the role of income, geography, and institutions. Rev Econ Stat 87:271–284
Klitgaard R (1988) Controlling corruption. University of California Press, Berkeley
Kreidler C (2006) Corruption as an internal problem for emergency operations. J Human Assist. http://sites.tufts.edu/jha/archives/30
Lambsdorff J (2007) Institutional economics of corruption and reform. Cambridge University Press, Cambridge
Mauro P (1995) Corruption and growth. Quart J Econom 110(3):681–712. (MIT Press)
Pellegrini L, Gerlagh R (2004) Corruption's effect on growth and its transmission channels. Kyklos 57(3):429–456
Pizzorno A (1992) La corruzione nel sistema politico. In: dela Porta D (ed) Lo scambio occulto. Bologna, Il Mulino, pp 13–74
Rose-Ackerman S (1978) Corruption: a study in political economy. Academic Press, New York
Savage K, Delesgues L, Martin E (2007) Corruption perceptions and risks in humanitarian assistance: an Afghanistan case study. HPG Working Paper, July. http://www.odi.org.uk/resources/docs/4162.pdf
Schultz J, Søreide T (2006) Corruption in emergency procurement, CMI Institute, U4 Issue, n. 7
Transparency International (2005) Curbing corruption in tsunami relief operations. Asia Development Bank, Manila
Transparency International (2010) Preventing corruption in humanitarian operations. http://www.transparency.org/news_room/in_focus/2010/hum_handbook
Treisman D (2000) The causes of corruption: a cross-national study. J Public Econ 76:399–457
Willitts-King B, Harvey P (2005) Managing the risks of corruption in humanitarian relief operations, Humanitarian Policy Group, Overseas Development Institute, March. http://www.odi.org.uk/resources/docs/1977.pdf

Chapter 28
Natural and Man-Made Disasters: Challenges and International Perspectives for Insurance

Giuseppe Turchetti, Sara Cannizzo and Leopoldo Trieste

Abstract Catastrophic risks are not statistical independent. Natural and man-made events have a low frequency, making very difficult to estimate the probability of occurrence. A single catastrophic event involves a very large number of people and properties simultaneously, making insufficient the traditional techniques of risk diversification usually adopted by insurers when they underwrite risks. Both the Hurricane Katrina in 2005—the most costly natural catastrophic event—and the World Trade Center terroristic attack in September 11, 2001—the most costly man-made catastrophic event—are examples of mega disasters violating the rules of insurability of risks and require a global answer from the insurance sector. To be efficient, a catastrophic risk financing system should involve a co-presence of private and public actors: insurers, reinsurers, and governments. Governments should border their actions on promoting competitive developed insurance markets, and on incentivizing a higher penetration of catastrophic insurance.

Keywords Natural Catastrophes · Man-made Disasters · Frequency · Pure risks · Catastrophic Insurance · Catastrophic Insurance Penetration · Catastrophic risks financing system

---

G. Turchetti (✉) · S. Cannizzo · L. Trieste
Scuola Superiore Sant'Anna, Piazza Martiri della Libertà, 33, I-56127, Pisa, Italy
e-mail: g.turchetti@sssup.it

S. Cannizzo
e-mail: s.cannizzo@sssup.it

L. Trieste
e-mail: l.trieste@sssup.it

A. de Guttry et al. (eds.), *International Disaster Response Law*,
DOI: 10.1007/978-90-6704-882-8_28,

Contents

28.1 Introduction

Natural catastrophes—like severe storms, tornadoes, earthquakes—mega events having a human component in diffusion—as floods caused by an excessive urbanization along rivers, famines, epidemics, human errors in nuclear power plants, and disasters with a complete human cause—such as terroristic attacks—are characterized by an expected and sometimes inestimable impact on lives, environment, and wealth.

These events dramatically show what *uncertainty* means: we have no consistent tools to estimate the probability of their occurrence. Tornadoes, earthquakes, nuclear disasters show that we live in a both uncertain and risky world.

The problem of high uncertain events with high severity is not just theoretical. How can society bear the weight of damages generated by these events? Is there a way to insure people, companies, and States? Is there a premium that an insurer considers fair to ask for covering losses generated by catastrophic events? May moral hazard still play a role in case of catastrophic events? How can insurance companies underwrite risks worldwide for future disasters?

These themes are becoming increasingly important as current and future trends show how catastrophic events are growing both in frequency and intensity.

Many factors may increase the frequency of disasters with no reduction in the uncertainty of prediction.[1] These factors could even raise the complexity of the phenomenon changing the actors involved in finding the solutions.

---

[1] The European Environment Agency (EEA) reported that the number and impact of disasters increased due to: increase of human activities and economic assets placed in risky areas, better reporting, and possibly climate changes (EEA 2010).

Globalization is the first element: the list of dramatic events gets longer. Moreover, systems are more interconnected and more influenced by behaviors, variables and conditions coming from different, and far regions. This means that we have more information on the elements that influence catastrophic events, but we have also more complex system of old and new variables to manage. This complexity cannot be completely dominated.

A second but thorny element is *climate change*. Weather and climate directly and indirectly cause natural disasters all over the world, dealing with geophysical events, hydrological events, and meteorological events.

In this complex and rapidly evolving scenario, the insurance industry has to manage really difficult responsibilities, issues, and challenges.

This chapter is organized as follows: the two pivotal dimensions in the insurance mechanism—frequency of the events and severity of losses—are analyzed in Sects. 28.2 and 28.3, respectively. In Sect. 28.4 we debate, through some examples, about who pays for the huge difference between total and insured losses provoked by natural catastrophes and man-made disasters highlighted in Sect. 28.3. The issues presented in the first four sections constitute the necessary framework for analyzing, in Sect. 28.5, catastrophe insurance in more detail and for describing possible technical solutions useful to face the problems emerged. A final section presents some concluding remarks.

28.2 Frequency of Catastrophic Events

28.2.1 Frequency of Natural and Man-Made Disasters

The first relevant problem in insuring natural catastrophes and man-made disasters is that the frequency of these events is relatively low if compared with other risks (e.g., car accidents). Our knowledge of temporal distribution of disasters is insufficient to find some regularity, at least robust enough to predict future events.

However, the regional distribution of natural catastrophes is less complicated. For example, the map of seismic areas is fairly reliable in indicating risk of earthquakes. We do not know *when* and exactly *where* an earthquake may occur, but we can say if earthquake is more likely to happen in a particular region rather than in another.

Natural catastrophes (i.e., loss events triggered by natural forces) and man-made disasters or *technical* disasters (i.e., loss events associated with human activities) seem to follow different trends.

In the period 1970–2010 were registered 3,842 natural catastrophes with 2,382,087 victims and 5,267 man-made disasters with 256,041victims, respectively.[2] Table 28.1 presents the description statistics of catastrophic events

[2] Events occurred all over the world.

Table 28.1 Summary statistics for 1970–2010 natural and man-made disasters all over the world (original data Swiss Re, *sigma* No 1/2011)

	Min (year)	1st quartile	Median	Mean (standard deviation)	3rd quartile	Max (year)
Natural cats	29 (1973)	46.00	106.00	93.71 (44.40)	135.00	167 (2010)
Man-made cats	61 (1984)	81.00	130.00	128.50 (51.78)	163.00	258 (2005)

discriminating between natural catastrophes and man-made disasters. The series of natural catastrophes in the last 40 years shows a mean value of 93.71 cases a year, a median value of 106 case, a first quartile[3] of 46 and third quartile of 135; the distribution of man-made disasters shows a mean value of 128.5 cases a year, a median value of 130 cases, with a first quartile of 61 and third quartile of 163. Figure 28.1a shows the frequency distribution of the number of man-made disasters, and Fig. 28.1b shows the frequency distribution of the number of natural catastrophes. The two series are far from normal and symmetric distributions, when mean and median coincide. For this reason, we suggest to discuss in terms of median and quartile values. This means that the measure of central value for natural catastrophic events is 106[4] instead of 93.71, and first quartile and third quartile better measure the dispersion of values as for median[5] value than standard deviation as for mean value (Table 28.1).

28.2.2 *Victims of Natural and Man-Made Disasters*

Analyzing the impact of catastrophic disasters in terms of victims, also the two series of the number of victims from natural and man-made catastrophes in the last 40 years are far from normal and symmetric distribution, as Fig. 28.2a and b show.

In the last 40 years, mean value of natural catastrophes is 58,100 victims a year and median value is 15,390 victims a year, a first quartile of 10,560, and third quartile of 46,730; as regards man-made disasters, mean value is 6,245 victims a year and median value is 6,082, a first quartile of 4,325, and third quartile of 7,340 (Table 28.2).

Both data of natural and man-made catastrophes suggest that there are no significant relationships between victims and the number of cases; i.e., often some sporadic events may provoke a large number of victims. A very low and positive correlation (0.38, p value = 0.02) between the number of events and victims is

[3] The quartile values cut in four equal parties the distribution of events: over the first quartile there are the 75 % of events, and over the third quartile there are the 25 % of events.

[4] The middle value cutting in two equal parties the distribution of natural catastrophes is 106 events a year, and for man-made catastrophes the middle value is 130 events a year.

[5] Measured by the interquartile range: about 89 for natural events, and 82 for man-made disasters.

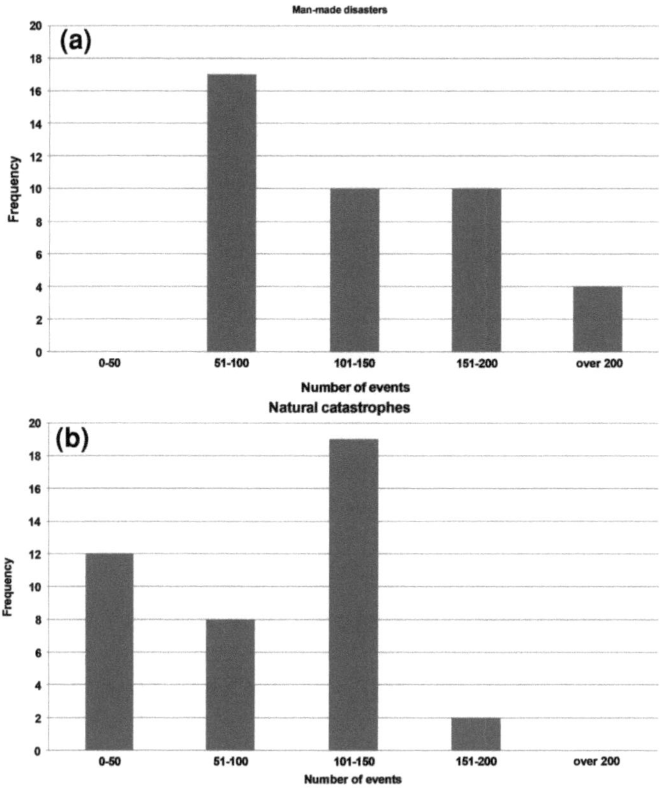

Fig. 28.1 **a** Distribution of number of events in man-made disasters, over 1970–2010 (original data from Swiss Re, *sigma* No 1/2011) **b** Distribution of number of events in natural catastrophes, over 1970–2010 (original data from Swiss Re, *sigma* No 1/2011)

shown considering man-made disasters. However, these correlations seems just indicate a "direction" rather than having a specific sense since the distribution of the series is not normal.

Catastrophes are "unique" events by definition, i.e., different natural or man-made disasters cannot be sufficiently comparable. Evidence for this last finding is the number of victims and the economic losses involved in catastrophic events. It is interesting to note that there is not a correlation between victims and losses; there is not a significant and unbiased correlation between the number of disasters and human and economic losses.

28.2.3 Nuclear Accidents

The relative low frequency of catastrophic events is mostly observed for civil nuclear accidents.

Table 28.2 Summary statistics for 1970–2010 victims in natural and man-made disasters (original data Swiss Re, *sigma* No 1/2011)

Victims	Min (year)	1st quartile	Median	Mean (standard deviation)	3rd quartile	Max (year)
Natural cats	3,858 (1975)	10,560	15,390	58,100 (93,381.26)	46,730	371,063 (1970)
Man-made cats	2,493 (1984)	4,325	6,082	6,245 (2,726.06)	7,340	17,881 (1979)

Considering accidents with an assigned INES[6] level equal or bigger than four (disaster with local, wider, serious effects), this list enumerates few cases. In the period 1952–2011, the only INES 6 nuclear accident is the case of 1957 Kyshtym (Russia). The INES 5 rank accounts four episodes: Fukushima (2011), Three Mile Island (1979), U.S. Windscale Pile (UK), and the Canadian Chalk River (1952). Nuclear accidents with INES 4 were been five: Fleurus (2006), Tokaimura (1999), Tomsk (1993), Saint Laurent des Eaux (1980), and Jaslovské Bohunice (1977).

28.3 Economic Impact of Catastrophic Events

28.3.1 Insured Losses for Natural and Man-Made Disasters

A second essential variable in insuring catastrophic events is the severity of losses. Losses cannot be completely supported by insurance sector or governments alone as they may concur to cause risk of insolvency or GDP reduction, and a strong rise in deficit levels.

As shown in Table 28.3 over 1970–2010, the problem of the increasing in costs is generated by natural catastrophes rather than man-made disasters.

The variability of the total insured losses for catastrophes is well explained by the series of insured losses caused by weather-related natural catastrophes and man-made disasters. On the contrary, earthquakes and tsunami insured losses register a relatively low change in the years. A feasible explanation is that weather-related natural catastrophes may have a higher probability to obtain an insurance coverage. In period 2006–2010 the major insured losses regard floods, earthquakes, droughts, bush fires, colds, and frosts, as shown in Table 28.4.

Losses for cold and frost catastrophes registered the lowest annual percentage variations. In contrast, the most variable expenditures for insured damages are referred to floods and earthquakes.

Figure 28.3 shows the composition of insured losses and its recent trend over 2006–2010. In 2006, natural disasters insured losses were about 74.5 % of total

[6] International Nuclear Events Scale (INES) ranks nuclear accidents by severity (from 1 to 7). Level seven has been assigned to the Chernobyl disaster (IEA 2008).

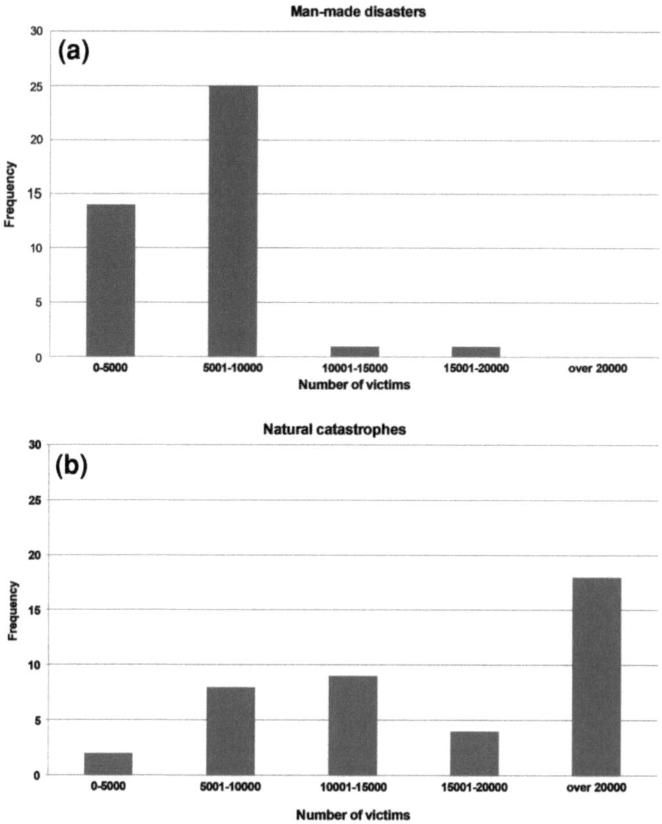

Fig. 28.2 **a** Distribution of number of victims 1970–2010 in man-made disasters (original data from Swiss Re, *sigma* No 1/2011) **b** Distribution of number of victims 1970–2010 natural catastrophes (original data from Swiss Re, *sigma* No 1/2011)

insured losses. This percentage increased during all 2006–2010 period. Consequently, man-made disasters registered a different trend. Their weight on the total insured losses decreased from 25.6 % in 2006 to 8.3 % in 2010.

A further remark on earthquake events: this kind of catastrophes has a very low frequency facing the idea that the risk is very low too. The latest events during the last 2 years showed that the major part of the world is subject to this kind of disasters, and the insurance penetration rate is very low. Earthquake in Japan in 2011 had economic losses of 5.4 % of GDP with an insurance contribution for reconstruction of about 17 %; earthquake in Chile in 2010 caused economic losses as 18.6 % of GDP with a 27 % ratio of insurance industry contribution; finally, Haiti earthquake registered economic losses for 121 % of GDP and only a 1 % of insurance contribution.[7]

[7] Swiss Re, *sigma*, January 2012.

Table 28.3 Summary statistics for 1970–2010 insured losses for some catastrophes (original data source: Swiss Re, *sigma* No 1/2011) (USD million at 2010 prices)

Insured Losses	Min (year)	1st quartile	Median	Mean (standard deviation)	3rd quartile	Max (year)
Weather-related nat. cats	470 (1971)	3,960	9,740	15,590 (19,520)	20,020	112,800 (2005)
Earthquakes	0.00	0.00	150	1,350 (3,760)	620	20,640
Man-made disasters	1,670 (1971)	3,220	4,190	5,340 (4,550)	6,110	31,280 (2001)

As regards losses resulting by terroristic attacks,[8] the last 20 years list of the most costly attacks in terms of insured losses presents: September 11, 2001 bringing about 2,982 victims, and accounting about USD 23 billion[9] at 2010 prices; IRA attacks bomb in 1992, 1993, 1996[10] caused over USD 3.29 billion; Oklahoma City bomb attack in 1996[11] caused USD 117 million; USD 104 million due to the 2008 attack in Mumbai.[12]

28.3.2 Is There a Relationship Between Human and Economic Losses?

The analyzed data also suggest that there is not a direct and immediate relationship between victims and economic implications of catastrophic events. Insured losses seem to be more positively related to the number of events rather than to the number of human losses.

28.3.3 Nuclear Disasters, Safety, and Economic Losses

One of the cases in which economic, human, and health-environmental losses are difficult to assess is nuclear accident. Elements that should be considered in these

[8] The examples consider a broad list of terroristic attacks. Indeed, a more accurate definition of *terrorism* should exclude cases of serial killers or attacks that cannot share the definition of terrorism as "the unlawful use of force and violence against persons or property to intimidate or coerce a government, the civilian population, or any segment thereof, in furtherance of political or social objectives" (U.S. 28 Code of Federal Regulation, Sect. 0.85).

[9] Losses in 2010 dollars.

[10] In a total of 6 fatalities.

[11] Causing 166 victims.

[12] Guy Carpenter 2011, 6.

Table 28.4 Major insured losses according to natural catastrophe category—Years 2006–2010 [*original data source* Swiss Re, *sigma* No 1/2011, *sigma* No 1/2010, *sigma* No 2/2009, *sigma* No 1/2008, *sigma* No 7/2007 (USD million at 2010 prices: losses were transformed to 2010 values with the Consumer Price Index, available from http://stats.oecd.org, accessed January 17, 2012)]

Natural catastrophes	n.	Victims	Insured loss(USD m)	Natural catastrophes	n.	Victims	Insured loss (USD m)
Floods				Droughts, bush fires, heat waves			
2006	58	7,217	1,063	2006	5	2,259	130
2007	53	5,798	6,324	2007	7	745	1,376
2008	44	3,184	2,084	2008	2	32	506
2009	46	2,696	1,694	2009	8	603	1,776
2010	69	11,027	6,393	2010	9	56,276	10
Storms				Cold, Frost			
2006	47	4,600	8,933	2006	12	1,617	1,470
2007	57	6,729	15,039	2007	10	487	987
2008	62	141,91	39,757	2008	7	1,750	1,594
2009	51	3,188	13,765	2009	6	538	595
2010	63	1,702	20,126	2010	10	1,024	397
Earthquakes				Hail			
2006	8	5,880	86	2006	1	28	1,111
2007	9	636	459	2007	8	20	254
2008	12	87,829	427	2008	7	10	772
2009	12	1,699	619	2009	3	7	4,264
2010	13	227,05	12,943	2010	5	19	0

estimates are direct damages, expenditures realized for actions to mitigate the consequences of radiation diffusion, for social, animal, food protection, and health care provision, for radio-ecological activities, for researching, and monitoring the level of radiation. Then there are also opportunity costs due to the abandon of contaminated fields, by the closure of agriculture and industrial activities. Moreover, we should also consider the long run costs of energy by the loss of power if reactors are shut down. For instance, we have not a precise estimate of damages provoked by the Chernobyl accident. Just Belarus has estimated a loss of USD 235 billion over 30 years.[13]

28.3.4 *Insured Losses and Insurance Coverage in Different Regions*

According to preliminary estimates from Swiss Re,[14] 2011 will be recognized as the year with the highest catastrophe-related economic losses in history with about

[13] Report of Belarus Foreign Ministry 2009, 2.

[14] Swiss Re, *sigma,* December 2011.

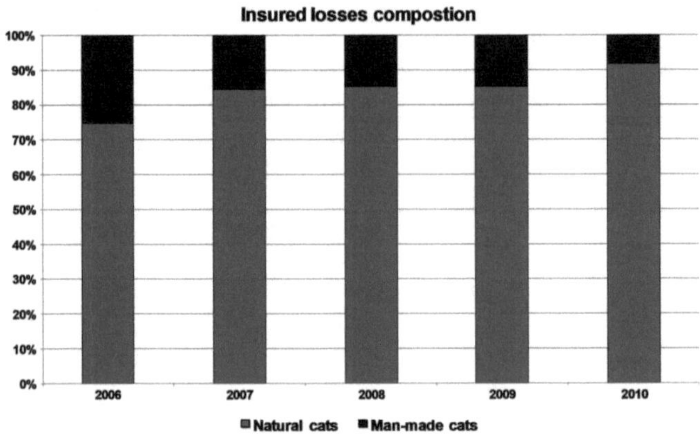

Fig. 28.3 Insured losses composition and its trend over 2006-2010 (original data from Swiss Re, *sigma*)

USD 350 billion. Losses for insurance companies related to insured catastrophes (property and business interruption, excluding life insurance losses, and liability) are about USD 108 billion (30.86 % of the total economic losses). The major losses for these events are been the earthquake and tsunami in Japan (USD 35 billion), the tsunami in New Zealand (from 12 billion USD), the floods in Thailand (from 8 to 11 USD billion of economic losses), and severe storms and tornadoes in Alabama and Missouri (USD 14 billion).

In 2010, natural and man-made catastrophes cost the society about over than USD 218 billion (0.31 % of GDP) all over the world: the percentage of 34 % has been determined in Asia (0.28 % of GDP), 24.5 % in Latin America and Caribbean (1.10 % of GDP), 16.5 % in Europe (0.19 % of GDP), 9.3 % North America(0.13 % of GDP), 6 % Oceania/Australia (0.95 % of GDP), 0.2 % Africa (0.02 % of GDP), and 9.5 % for catastrophes happened over Seas/Space. As regards insured losses, the North America region has the 74,6 % ratio of insured losses to economic losses, Oceania/Australia has the 67,5 % of insured losses, Africa rate is 36,8 %, Europe region has a 17,9 % of insured losses ratio, Latin America, and Caribbean have the 16,8 % insured losses, Asia 3 % ratio, and Seas/Space a 7,9 %.[15]

28.4 Who Pays the Difference Between Total Losses and Insured Losses?

A gap is observed between the total economic losses involved in natural and man-made catastrophes and the amount of insured losses. Who does actually pay the difference between total losses and insured losses? Governments, International and

[15] Swiss Re, *sigma* No 1/2011.

Financial Organizations, International Funds through humanitarian programs, and individuals pay the difference.

A study focused on the impact of natural catastrophes on fiscal sustainability of governments distinguishing between middle/high-income countries and low-income countries over 1975–2008.[16] As regards middle/high-income countries, the results seem to say that *climatic events* have a clear negative impact on government budgets as deficit increase (25 % in real terms), but *geological disasters* have a insignificant influence in change of the level of the deficit. For high-income countries, natural disasters have not significant impact on GDP, both expenditures and revenues increase but have an insignificant impact on deficit, meaning that these countries can moderate the shocks without deficit spending. While in middle-income countries only geological disasters have an impact on GDP causing a decline, and on the fiscal side, expenditures increase, and have a significant negative impact on deficit after climatic disasters. In lower-middle-income countries, deficit increase after climatic disasters further reduces their ability to repay as these countries have a lower capacity to manage governments expenditures in an efficient and effective way.

The study also compares countries according to the insurance penetration degree,[17] about the real consequences of shocks over 1975–2008, reported in Fig. 28.4. As shown, panel A refers to countries with low insurance penetration and panel B refers to high insurance penetration countries. After climatic and geological disasters, countries in panel A have a larger reduction of GDP (first column) than countries with high insurance penetration (panel B) and suffer a consistent deficit increase (second column of panel A); while in countries with high insurance penetration government expenditures and revenues increase together (third and fourth column of panel B) but resulting in a small change in deficit level (second column panel B). Interpreting these data, in high insurance penetration countries, insurers can recover productivity capacity with little efforts by governments budgets, and the increasing expenditures and revenues suggest redistributive fiscal efforts.

After disasters, financial, and insurance developed markets may offer a solid support in financing damages and reconstruction, as a small impact on GDP without an important deficit expansion may demonstrate.

28.5 The Role and Challenges of Insurers in Catastrophic Risks

Insurance provides protection against risks. Companies and individuals buy insurance in order to satisfy their need of safety. Under risk conditions, they decide to transfer the losses linked to an event to the insurer.

[16] Meleckly and Raddatz 2011.

[17] The degree of insurance penetration is measured by the total value of premiums to GDP.

Panel A. Countries with Low Insurance Penetration

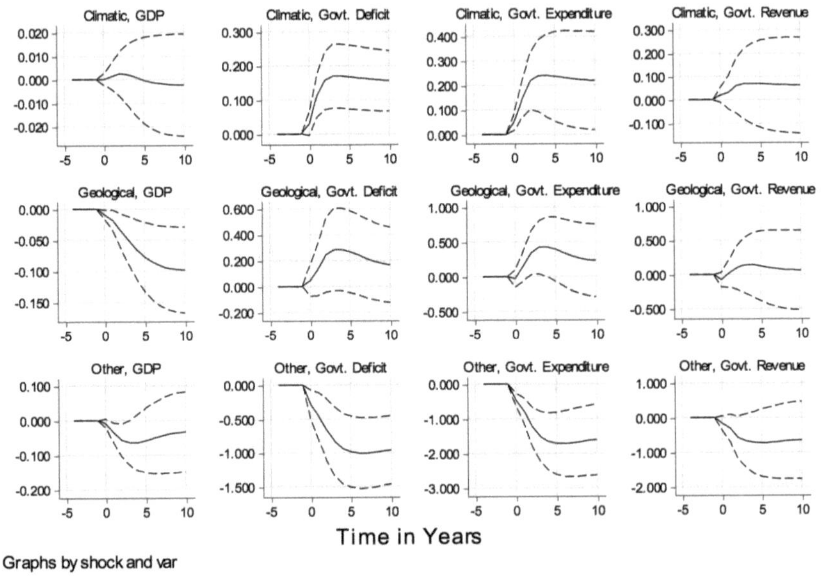

Panel B. Countries with High Insurance Penetration

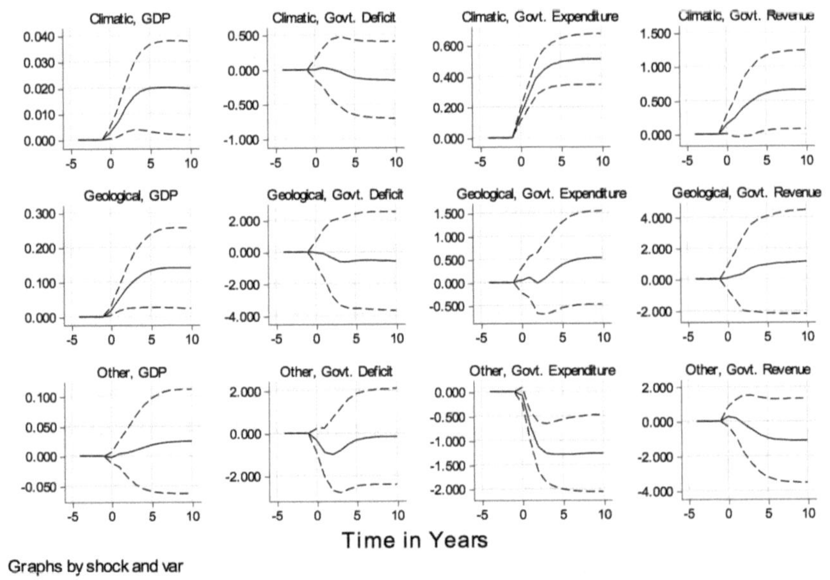

Fig. 28.4 Cumulative impulse response functions (IRFs) for countries with low insurance penetration (*panel* A) and countries with high insurance penetration (*panel* B) (Melecky and Raddatz 2011, public disclosure authorized)

Classifying risks in categories, we may find *pure risk* and *speculative risk*. A pure risk refers to situations in which there are only two probabilities, a loss or a neutral condition. For example, the fire of a building or being victim of theft. Speculative risk, on the contrary, refers to situations in which either losses or profits are verifiable. Buying shares on the Stock Exchange or betting on horses races are typical speculative risks. Insurance companies insure pure risks.

An additional and equally important classification is between *fundamental risks* and *particular risks*.[18] Fundamental risks refer to events affecting the whole economy, or a relevant part of it, or to events affecting a large number of individuals, such as wars, floods, earthquakes, nuclear, and environmental disasters. On the contrary, particular risks refer to individuals not to a community. Therefore, catastrophic risks are fundamental risks.

Pure risks are insurable by an insurer under some important conditions. Assuming risks from individuals and companies, the insurer makes the pooling of risks sharing the losses happening to the few to the entire number of policyholders. First, it needs a very large number of exposure units that are subject to the same risk, in order to benefit from the law of large numbers properties and to make an accurate prediction of the probability of future losses, and of the expected loss. Probability of loss and the severity of expected loss are the most important elements allowing the insurer to price a risk and to provide coverage against it. Second, risks must be statistical independent—that means losses not occur simultaneously and from the same source, and losses should be accidental and non-intentional, determinable, and measurable.

Catastrophic risks are not statistically independent. A single catastrophic event involves a very large number of people and properties simultaneously, making insufficient the traditional techniques of risk diversification usually adopted by insurers when they underwrite risks: this kind of events is *locally dependent*.[19]

A locally dependent event with low frequency and very high severity could become *globally independent* and *globally insurable* through the reinsurance market, which allows pooling these risks with other independent risks in other regions of the world. The risk of flood in a US State and the risk of flood in France are independent risks, which reinsurance companies could manage. Both the Hurricane Katrina in 2005, the most costly natural catastrophic event, and the World Trade Center terroristic attack in September 11 2001, the most costly man-made catastrophic event, are examples of mega disasters violating the rules of insurability of risks and require a global answer from the insurance sector. Traditional insurers ask for *reinsurance solutions* as the main tool for managing catastrophic risks. In several cases, reinsurance solutions alone are not sufficient to sustain mega catastrophic events and to cover their losses. Introducing risk-adjusted securities, mega catastrophic events become diversifiable across financial

[18] Rejda 1995, 4–19.

[19] Cummins 2006, 342–345 and Cummins 2007, 182–184.

markets and having a low correlation with security revenues are attractive for investors.

Catastrophic risks:

- Have a low frequency;
- Have a very high severity of loss: large-scale earthquakes strike a big area and large number of properties;
- May have a very large deviation of the actual insurance loss from the expected insurance loss;
- Usually involve a localized geographic region;
- Have a restricted and insufficient historical data collection making to insurers very difficult to estimate the probability of a catastrophic event.

In catastrophic insurance: some specialist consulting companies develop probabilistic simulating models assessing the risk of loss from each event like hurricane, cyclones, floods, and earthquakes.

Premium. Two are the principal hypotheses to determine the price, the premium, for a natural catastrophic insurance coverage. The first one may be a free mechanism based on the property value insured and directly proportional to the risk insured. The second one, a semi-free premium system operating a price differentiation based on the type of building, on the measures of prevention, and on the adopted building technologies instead of the country severity of risk. Not to distinguish according to the country severity of risk may have a positive influence in increasing the individual responsibilities of insured, and may help the diffusion of insurance. The semi-free premium needs support to be efficient. For example, a system transferring to a public entity/public fund/public reinsurer the catastrophic risk or making a consortium for the pooling of risks. In addition, a consortium may have more influence on reinsurance markets. The *annual expected loss*, the *administrative and distribution expenses*, and the *cost of capita*l compose the price—the premium.[20] The expected loss frequency and the expected loss severity make up the annual expected loss; it represents the pure risk, the minimum amount of premium the insurer needs to cover the future loss. The probability distribution of losses is approximately estimated by the "exceedance probability curve," an expression of the likelihood that the losses exceed a specific amount. Usually, the cost of capital is the opportunity cost of investing capital into the insurance business instead of into an alternative investment and represents a compensation for the insurer for bearing the risk.

Loss estimation. The lack of data collection referring to losses caused by catastrophic events does not allow a reliable assessment of future expected losses with traditional techniques, in particular for very rare events. In order to compensate for information shortage insurers make appraisals for reconstruction costs based on provisional models and simulation models.

[20] Cummins and Mahul 2009, 27–74.

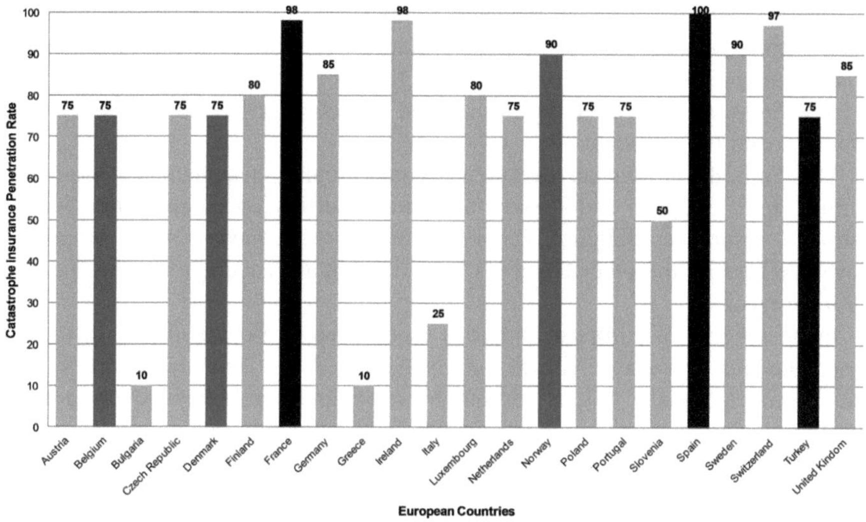

Fig. 28.5 An overview of catastrophe insurance penetration rates in Europe (*original data source* CEA, Position paper 2011)

Intermediation, underwriting, policy management. Intermediation, underwriting, and policy management are functions that should be carried out by insurance companies in order to get scale economies and efficiency, as catastrophic insurance is usually included into property insurance covering fire or theft for residential, commercial, industrial properties, and homes.

To be efficient, a catastrophic risk financing system should involve a co-presence of private and public actors: insurers, private reinsurers, governments. Governments in addition to give loans to the poor and disadvantaged victims of catastrophic disaster, should also border their actions on promoting competitive insurance markets and on incentivizing a higher penetration of catastrophic insurance.[21]

A large competitive catastrophic insurance market may provide better covering solutions for these kinds of events within a private–public partnership. Various covering solutions have been adopted all over the world to protect against losses from natural catastrophic risks.

Compulsory cover. A compulsory property insurance system covering all the houses and private buildings against fire and natural catastrophic losses could be introduced by enlarging fire insurance already existing. In this scenario, each private building should have protection with a small premium paid by the property owner; franchises and hypothesis of self coverage exclusions for small losses are useful for reducing the costs of claims and promoting the adoption of risk prevention behaviors by insured.

[21] Cummins and Mahul 2009, 75–80.

Semi-compulsory cover. In the semi-compulsory insurance proposal, a natural catastrophic coverage may be added to voluntary fire insurance policy for houses and private buildings including business activities.

A Voluntary Cover. Leaving insurer and householder free to haggle over the premium and the coverage.

The Fig. 28.5 shows an overview of catastrophic insurance penetration in Europe. France, Spain, and Turkey, have a compulsory coverage system for catastrophic insurance; Belgium, Denmark, and Norway, have a semi-compulsory coverage system; the other countries have a voluntary coverage system for catastrophic risks.

In the majority of European countries major insured risks are: flood, storm, hail, landslide, fire; in some countries earthquake risk is not included. Turkey is an exception: earthquake risk is insured by a compulsory policy covering every dwelling inside the boundaries of municipalities, although a voluntary system for the other catastrophic risks. Also in other European countries it is observable a double coverage purchase system: compulsory for a specific risk and voluntary or semi-compulsory for the remaining catastrophic risks. United Kingdom adopted a voluntary system but most mortgages require home owners to have flood insurance. Switzerland has a compulsory coverage for fire insurance with natural catastrophic cover included and an optional purchase for business interruption. Norway has a compulsory system for catastrophic risks attached to fire policies and optional via separate insurance cover for hail, frost, and forest fire risks.

Fifteen countries do not have a public institution with reinsurance functions. Austria has a public fund reimbursing for a percentage of several flood, avalanche, earthquake, landslide, and hurricane or hail disasters. In France, the public reinsurer Caisse Centrale de Réassurance works as reinsurer for the insurance market in catastrophic events.

New financing techniques of risk-linked securities like catastrophic risk bond (*CAT bonds*) are important instruments for assessing and transferring risks. CAT bonds have been successfully introduced in 1994 by Hannover Re into financial markets. These devices are a kind of asset called *event-linked bonds*. A CAT bond emission covers events having a probability of occurrence of 0.01 % or less, meaning that having a return period of 100 years this kind of catastrophic events are not reinsurable. In the CAT bond structure, there is an embedded call option linked to the occurrence of the event. The cash flow raised by the issue of the bonds is invested in low risk profile securities, such as treasury bonds. If the event happens, the investors do not receive the principal, and proceeds of the financial operation are reversed to insurers for covering the claims. If catastrophic event does not happen, the principal returns to investors when bond expires. Generally, CAT bonds have a maturity of 1–5 years. The functioning of this kind of bonds allows investing the fixed returns on swaps, immunizing the investors from interest

[22] Cummins and Weiss 2009, 522-527 and Cummins 2008, 25–28.

rate risk, and credit risk. For this reason, CAT bonds have very low correlation with returns of security markets and are very attractive for investors.[22]

28.6 Concluding Remarks

Uncertainty is the condition of lack of knowledge about a system, a process, or an event. Uncertainty about a catastrophic risk refers to: the event generation, the local intensity, the exposure, historical data, claims data, frequency, severity of losses, and so on.

Insuring natural and man-made catastrophe risks raises some important problems. Puzzles originate by the fact that natural and man-made disasters have a low frequency, making very difficult to estimate the probability of occurrence. Unfortunately, in catastrophic events deviations among actual losses, that could be very high, and expected losses, are very large. For this reasons, insurers share risks with international reinsurance companies.

A catastrophic risk financing system to be efficient should involve different actors: insurers, reinsurers, and governments. Usually, the role of governments is to work for the creation of funds, the concession of loans with low interest rate, and the implementation of measures for loss prevention. In recent years, alternative risk transfer solutions using the diversification capability of international financial markets have been adopted. The intrinsic characteristics of natural and man-made catastrophic risks require specific insurance answers; compulsory insurance, semi-compulsory insurance, and voluntary system are examples of covering solutions.

The issues that the insurance industry, the governments, the society, and the whole international community are facing in preventing, managing, and financing catastrophic risks are really challenging and should be addressed with a more structured, coordinated, and long lasting strategy.

References

Belarus Foreign Ministry (2009) Chernobyl disaster. http://chernobyl.undp.org/english/docs/belarus_23_anniversary.pdf. Accessed 17 Jan 2012

CEA (2011) Insurance of natural catastrophes in Europe, Position paper. http://www.cea.eu/uploads/Modules/Publications/climate-change-2011-web.pdf. Accessed 17 Jan 2012

Cummins JD (2006) Should the government provide insurance for catastrophes? Fed Reserv Bank St. Louis Rev 88(4):337–379

Cummins JD (2007) Reinsurance for natural and man-made catastrophes in United States: current state of the market and regulatory reforms. Risk Manag Insur Rev 10(2):179–220

Cummins JD (2008) CAT bonds and others risk-linked securities: state of the market and recent developments. Risk Manag Insur Rev 11(1):23–47

Cummins JD, Mahul O (2009) Catastrophe risk financing in developing countries. Principles of public intervention, The World Bank. http://siteresources.worldbank.org/FINANCIALSECTOR/Resources/CATRISKbook.pdf. Accessed 17 Jan 2012

Cummins JD, Weiss MA (2009) Convergence of insurance and financial markets: hybrid and securitized risk-transfer solutions. J Risk Insur 76(3):493–545

EEA (2010) Mapping the impacts of natural hazards and technological accidents in Europe, technical report. http://www.eea.europa.eu/publications/mapping-the-impacts-of-natural Accessed 17 Jan 2012

Guy Carpenter (2011) Terrorism. Terror market continues to provide abundant cover, Marsh&McLennan report

IEA (2008) INE The nuclear and radiological event scale, http://www.iaea.org/Publications/Factsheets/English/ines.pdf. Accessed 17 Jan 2012

Meleckly M, Raddatz C (2011) How do governments respond after catastrophes? Natural-disaster shocks and the fiscal stance. Policy research working paper series 5564, The World Bank. Public disclosure authorized. Accessed 17 Jan 2012

Rejda GE (1995) Principles of risk management and insurance. Harper Collins College Publishers, New York

Swiss Re (2012) Lessons from recent major earthquakes, January 2012

Swiss Re (2011) Sigma preliminary estimates, news release December 2011. http://media.swissre.com/documents/news_release_sigma_preliminary_estimates_Dec_2011.pdf. Accessed 17 Jan 2012

Swiss Re (2011) *Sigma* No 1

Swiss Re (2010) *Sigma* No 1

Swiss Re (2009) *Sigma* No 2

Swiss Re (2008) *Sigma* No 1

Swiss Re (2007) *Sigma* No 2

Chapter 29
Conclusions

Natalino Ronzitti

As has been pointed out in the Resolution of the *Institut de droit international* adopted at the 2003 Bruges session, for the purpose of humanitarian assistance disasters may be divided into three categories: (a) disasters of natural origin, (b) man-made disasters of technological origin, (c) disasters caused by armed conflicts or violence. The Bruges resolution encompasses all the three categories of disasters, while the ILC which codifies the law of humanitarian assistance has concentrated its work on the first two, i.e., natural and man-made disasters, pointing out that disasters caused by armed conflicts are of a special nature. One may add the concept of humanitarian assistance has developed in connection with war, with the adoption of conventions on humanitarian law which have achieved universal standing. In part, but only in part, this is true also for man-made disasters and, in the absence of conventional regulation, the applicable rules may be found in the law governing international responsibility. However, the regulation of humanitarian assistance in case of natural disaster has not yet been universally codified. Even domestic law does not offer enough guidance to construe general principles of law to be applied.

Individuals and entire populations should be the beneficiaries of humanitarian assistance, but it is difficult to construe the right to humanitarian assistance as a human right and to determine the subject against whom such right should be claimed.

As the chapters of this book demonstrate, IDRL is more an issue pertaining to soft law or conventional law than to customary international law, and the question is whether there is a duty to provide humanitarian assistance based on well-established provisions of customary international law. Neither State practice nor *opinio iuris* support the existence of such a custom. On the other hand, one may

N. Ronzitti (✉)
Istituto Affari Internazionali, Via Angelo Brunetti, 9, 00186, Rome, Italy
e-mail: n.ronzitti@iai.it

A. de Guttry et al. (eds.), *International Disaster Response Law*,
DOI: 10.1007/978-90-6704-882-8_29,

specify a number of principles, some of them lying at the very foundation of international law, which may be applied in the event of a disaster, bearing in mind that the same principles do not apply in the case of natural disasters, man-made disasters of technological origin, or those caused by an armed conflict.

One may refer to the following set of principles.

a. Non-intervention: the question is often asked whether the mere offer of assistance constitutes intervention. This is not a real issue. International law prohibits dictatorial or coercive intervention, and the mere offer of assistance does not constitute intervention prohibited by international law. On the contrary, it is to be valued and cannot be considered an unfriendly act.
b. Territorial sovereignty: aid may be delivered, provided that the territorial State gives its consent to the delivery of humanitarian assistance on its territory, in particular when the humanitarian aid is provided by peacekeeping forces or by humanitarian organizations protected by foreign armed forces. The law of armed conflict, including Articles 69–71 of the Protocol I additional to the 1949 Geneva Conventions, make relief action in occupied territory or in the territory under the control of a party to the conflict, conditional upon the consent of the occupying power or the party controlling the territory where humanitarian aid is to be delivered.
c. Is the territorial State free to withhold its consent? In principle, yes. An example would be military security in an occupied territory. This is paramount. However, security reasons cannot constitute an excuse for negating consent, if they are not supported by real exigencies. Accordingly, consent might be refused only in case of imperative military necessity, and the territorial sovereign should state the reasons why it is refused. The doctrine of responsibility to protect (R2P) might be used in construing an obligation to give consent, as explained below.
d. There is no obligation under international law to give aid, unless States are duty bound by a treaty provision. A prime example is the solidarity clause enshrined in Article 222 of the TFEU. The Union and its member States have the duty to co-operate and render assistance at the request of political authorities of the State in which the calamitous event occurred. It may consist not only in a terrorist attack, but also in a natural or man-made disaster.
e. Can the doctrine of the R2P be of any help? According to the present author the doctrine of R2P cannot be construed as a right to enter foreign territory without the consent of the territorial State or without UNSC authorization. This doctrine mainly means that the State has the obligation to protect its own population. The R2P is not without effect for our issue, even though it is understood within this narrow meaning. One may figure out a duty of the territorial State to ask assistance and a duty of the same State not to refuse external aid and/or raise arbitrary conditions for allowing the relief personnel to enter its territory. The same is true, mutatis mutandis, for consent termination. It cannot arbitrarily be withheld. The duty to seek assistance may also come out from the obligations enshrined in the International Covenant on Economic, Social and Cultural

Rights such as the right to food, clothing and housing (Article 11). Since the territorial State is coping with severe difficulties it has the duty to call for external aid in order to implement its obligations. Unlike the duty to call for assistance, the right to seek assistance falls within the liberty of the concerned sovereign. It goes without saying that the UNSC may authorize an action in the territory of the State where the disaster occurred, provided that the situation constitutes a threat to peace and international security. The SC enjoys considerable latitude in qualifying a situation as a threat to peace under Article 39 of the UN Charter. There is little precedent on the issue of disasters which are man-made and do not have an effect across boundaries. A UN Force was dispatched to Haiti in 2004 in the context of the overthrow of the head of State then in the exercise and the establishment of a dictatorial regime, and it was also maintained after the earthquake in 2010: the UN helped in the country's reconstruction. The trigger point was not the humanitarian emergency, but the domestic political situation, a classic case of UN intervention.

f. Is there any right of the endangered State to claim assistance? And if yes, from whom? The right to assistance may derive from a treaty provision such as Article 222 of the TFEU mentioned above. It may also be derived from the law of State responsibility if the disaster has been caused by a neighboring State, for instance a nuclear explosion.
g. The law of international responsibility provides further guidance. A state of necessity, for instance, may be claimed to intervene in foreign territory if the calamitous event produces very dangerous consequences for a neighboring State. Take, for example, the destruction of a dam and a resulting flood across the frontier. If the territorial State is unable or unwilling to take the necessary steps to deal with the danger, the neighboring State may intervene in foreign territory. The law of the sea offers the example of severe pollution coming from the high seas and threatening the coastal State, which is entitled to take the necessary measures against a polluting foreign flag.
h. Does a human rights perspective offer a better solution? Article 6 of the International Covenant on Civil and Political Rights sets out the right to life, as does its companion Article of the European Convention on Human Rights (Article 2). Both provisions cannot be derogated or suspended according to the clause on public emergency threatening the life of the nation, which permits taking derogatory measures. Article 6 of the International Covenant on Civil and Political Rights has been interpreted by General Comment No. 6 as encompassing the obligation to take the necessary measures to protect such a right. The problem is to establish how a State ravaged by a natural disaster of a great magnitude may fulfill that duty. Right to life is an individual right which can be enforced vis-à-vis the State having jurisdiction over the territory where the disaster occurred Often the State in question is a poor country which does not have the necessary means for giving assistance and relief. Claiming a right to be guaranteed by the international community is nonsense according to present-day international law. Individuals may have a right vis-à-vis their own State, but they are merely beneficiaries of external aid. At present, the

international community does not guarantee any right which the individual may claim from a foreign State, unless a specific set of rules has been established. Since human rights also apply in wartime, the occupying power is obliged to guarantee right to life. As to man-made disasters, the relevant conventions often provide a right for individuals under the rules they set out, and the ILC draft Articles on International liability in case of loss from cross-boundary harm arising out of hazardous activities establishes a right to prompt and adequate compensation for those who have suffered harm (Article 6).

Man-made disasters are often the cause for persons living in poor countries to flee from their territory. The 1951 Refugee Convention is not applicable, and the principle of non-refoulement, which has acquired the status of customary law, is also not relevant, unless the disaster is accompanied by hazster a political situation and the refugees are obliged to flee territory owing to a threat to their life because of their race, religion, political opinion or membership of a particular social group. New conventional law is required based on the principle of humanity that applies in peace as well as in war, as stated by the ICJ in the Corfu Channel case. For instance, the practice of giving temporary protection should become a common standard.

In conclusion, a norm of customary international law covering all disasters situations, independently of their origin and nature, does not yet exist, nor it is possible to predict future developments in this regard. Assistance and relief should be regulated by conventional law, and the solidarity clause enshrined in Article 222 of the TFEU is a good example, taking into account that economic considerations and funding are paramount. As far as customary international law is concerned, the evolution of IDRL should develop from the principle of humanity. At present, the interpreter has to rely on a set of principles which have been developed in connection with several sectors of international law and which might also be applied to IDRL.

Appendices

International Treaties

Universal

1856 Paris Declaration Respecting Maritime Law, 16 April 1865
1912 International Sanitary Convention, 17 January 1912
1926 Slavery Convention, 25 September 1926
1927 Convention Establishing an International Relief Union, 12 July 1927
1930 Convention Concerning Forced or Compulsory Labour, 30 June 1930
1944 Articles of Agreement of the International Monetary Fund, 22 July 1944
1944 Convention on International Civil Aviation, 7 December 1944
1945 Charter of the United Nations, 26 June 1945
1946 Convention on Privileges and Immunities of the United Nations, 13 February 1946
1946 WHO Constitution, 22 July 1946
1947 General Agreement on Tariffs and Trade, 30 October 1947
1947 Convention on the Privileges and Immunities of the Specialized Agencies, 21 November 1947
1948 Convention on the Prevention and Punishment of the Crime of Genocide, 9 December 1948
1949 Convention (I) for the Amelioration of the Condition of the Wounded and Sick in Armed Forces in the Field, 12 August 1949
1949 Convention (II) for the Amelioration of the Condition of Wounded, Sick and Shipwrecked Members of Armed Forces at Sea, 12 August 1949
1949 Convention (III) relative to the Treatment of Prisoners of War, 12 August 1949
1949 Convention (IV) relative to the Protection of Civilian Persons in Time of War, 12 August 1949
1949 Convention for the Suppression of the Traffic in Persons and of the Exploitation of the Prostitution of Others, 2 December 1949
1951 Convention Relating to the Status of Refugees, 28 July 1951
1956 Supplementary Convention on the Abolition of Slavery, the Slave Trade, and Institutions and Practices Similar to Slavery, 30 April 1956
1959 Agreement on the Privileges and Immunities of the International Atomic Energy Agency, of 1 July 1959

A. de Guttry et al. (eds.), *International Disaster Response Law*,

DOI: 10.1007/978-90-6704-882-8,

1960 Convention on Third Party Liability in the Field of Nuclear Energy, 29 July 1960

1961 Customs Convention on the Temporary Importation of Professional Equipment, 8 June 1961

1962 Convention on Consent to Marriage, Minimum Age for Marriage and Registration of Marriages, 10 December 1962

1963 Vienna Convention on Consular Relation, 24 April 1963

1963 Vienna Convention on civil liability for nuclear damage, 21 May 1963

1964 Additional Protocol amending the Convention on Third Party Liability in the Field of Nuclear Energy of 29 July 1960, 28 January 1964

1965 Convention on Facilitation of International Maritime Traffic, 9 April 1965

1965 International Convention on the Elimination of All Forms of Racial Discrimination, 21 December 1965

1966 International Covenant on Civil and Political Rights, 16 December 1966

1966 International Covenant on Economic, Social and Cultural Rights, 16 December 1966

1967 Protocol relating to the Status of Refugees, 31 January 1967

1969 WHO International Health Regulations, 25 July 1969

1969 Vienna Convention on the Law of Treaties, 23 May 1969

1969 International Convention Relating to Intervention on the High Seas in Cases of Oil Pollution Casualties, 29 November 1969

1970 Agreement between the United Nations, the Government of Peru and the Government of Sweden for the Provision of the Technical Cadre United of the Swedish Stand-By Force for United Nations Service to Assist in Reconstruction of areas in Peru Devastated as a Result of the Earthquake which Occurred on 31 May 1970, 29 July 1970

1972 Convention on the Prevention of Marine Pollution by Dumping of Wastes and Other Matter, 13 November 1972

1973 International Convention on the Simplification and Harmonization of Customs Procedures (Kyoto Convention), 18 May 1973

1977 Convention on Civil Liability for Oil Pollution Damage resulting from Exploration for and Exploitation of Seabed Mineral Resources, 1 May 1977

1977 Protocol Additional to the Geneva Conventions of 12 August 1949, and relating to the Protection of Victims of International Armed Conflicts (Protocol I), 8 June 1977

1977 Protocol Additional to the Geneva Conventions of 12 August 1949, and relating to the Protection of Victims of Non-International Armed Conflicts (Protocol II), 8 June 1977

1979 Convention on the Physical Protection of Nuclear Material, 26 October 1979

1979 Convention on Long-range Transboundary Air Pollution, 13 November 1979

1979 Convention on the Elimination of All Forms of Discrimination against Women, 18 December 1979

1980 Convention on the Civil Aspects of International Child Abductions, 25 October 1980

1982 Protocol amending the Convention on Third Party Liability in the Field of Nuclear Energy of 29 July 1960, 16 November 1982

1982 United Nations Convention on the Law of the Sea, 10 December 1982

1984 Convention Against Torture and Other Cruel, Inhuman or Degrading Treatment or Punishment, 10 December 1984

1985 Vienna Convention for the Protection of the Ozone Layer, 22 March 1985

1985 Agreement on the Conservation of Nature and Natural Resources, 9 July 1985

1986 Convention on Assistance in the Case of a Nuclear Accident or Radiological Emergency, 26 September 1986

1986 Convention on the Early Notification of a Nuclear Accident, 26 September 1986

1987 EUR-OPA Major Hazards Agreement, 20 March 1987

1987 Montreal Protocol on Substances that Deplete the Ozone Layer, 16 September 1987

1988 Convention on the Suppression of Unlawful Acts against the Safety of Maritime Navigation, 10 March 1988

1988 Protocol for the Suppression of Unlawful Acts against the Safety of Fixed Platforms Located on the Continental Shelf, 10 March 1988

1988 Joint Protocol Relating to the Application of the Vienna Convention and the Paris Convention, 21 September 1988

1989 Agreement on Cooperation Across State Frontiers to Prevent or Limit Damage to Persons or Property or to the Environment in the case of Accidents, 20 January 1989

1989 Basel Convention on the Control of Transboundary Movement of Hazardous Wastes and their disposal, 22 March 1989

1989 Indigenous and Tribal Peoples Convention, 27 June 1989

1989 Convention on the Rights of the Child, 20 November 1989

1990 Convention on Temporary Admission (Istanbul Convention), 26 June 1990

1990 International Convention on Oil Pollution Preparedness, Response and Cooperation, 30 November 1990

1990 International Convention on the Protection of the Rights of All Migrant Workers and Members of their Families, 18 December 1990

1991 Convention on Environmental Impact Assessment in a Transboundary Context (Espoo Convention), 25 February 1991

1992 Convention on the Protection and Use of Transboundary Watercourses and International Lakes, 17 March 1992

1992 Convention on the Transboundary Effects of Industrial Accidents, 17 March 1992

1992 United Nations Framework Convention on Climate Change, 9 May 1992

1992 Co-operation Agreement on the Forecast, Prevention and Mitigation of Natural and Technological Disasters, 18 July 1992

1992 International Convention on Civil Liability for Oil Pollution Damage, 27 November 1992

1993 Convention on the Prohibition of the Development, Production, Stockpiling and Use of Chemical Weapons and on their Destruction, 13 January 1993

1993 Convention on the Protection of Children and Co-operation in Respect of Inter-Country Adoptions, 29 May 1993

1993 Prevention of Major Industrial Accidents Convention, 22 June 1993

1994 Convention on Nuclear Safety, 17 June 1994

1994 United Nations Convention to Combat Desertification in those Countries Experiencing Serious Drought and/or Desertification, Particularly in Africa, 14 October 1994

1994 Convention on the Safety of United Nations and Associated Personnel, 9 December 1994

1996 International Convention on Liability and Compensation for Damage in Connection with the Carriage of Hazardous and Noxious Substances by Sea, 3 May 1996

1997 Convention on the Law of the Non-Navigational Uses of International Watercourses, 21 May 1997

1997 International Civil Aviation Organization (ICAO), Annex 9 to the Convention on International Civil Aviation: International Standards and Recommended Practices—Facilitation (10th edition), 31 August 1997

1997 Convention on Supplementary Compensation for Nuclear Damage, 12 September 1997

1997 Protocol to Amend the Vienna Convention on Civil Liability for Nuclear Damage, 12 September 1997

1997 Joint Convention on the Safety of Spent Fuel Management and on the Safety of Radioactive Waste Management, 29 September 1997

1997 OECD Convention on Combating bribery of foreign public officials in international business transactions, 21 November 1997

1997 Kyoto Protocol to the United Nations Framework Convention on Climate Change, 11 December 1997

1997 International Convention for the Suppression of Terrorist Bombing, 15 December 1997

1998 Framework Agreement on Cooperation between the European Economic Community and the Cartagena Agreement and its member countries, 1 May 1998

1998 Tampere Convention on the Provision of Telecommunication Resources for Disaster Mitigation and Relief Operations, 18 June 1998

1998 Rome Statute of the International Criminal Court, 17 July 1998

1998 Convention on the Protection of Environment through Criminal Law, 4 November 1998

1999 Food Aid Convention, 13 April 1999

1999 Worst Forms of Child Labour Convention, 17 June 1999

1999 Protocol of Amendment to the International Convention on the Simplification and Harmonization of Customs Procedures of 18 May 1973, 26 June 1999

1999 Optional Protocol to the Convention on the Elimination of All Forms of Discrimination against Women, 6 October 1999

1999 Protocol on Liability and Compensation for Damage Resulting from Transboundary Movements of Hazardous Wastes and their Disposal, 10 December 1999

2000 Protocol on Preparedness, Response and Co-operation to pollution Incidents by Hazardous and Noxious Substances, 15 March 2000

2000 Charter on Cooperation to Achieve the Coordinated Use of Space Facilities in the Event of Natural or Technological Disasters, 25 April 2000

2000 Framework Convention in Civil Defence Assistance, 22 May 2000

2000 Optional Protocol to the Convention on the Rights of the Child on the sale of children, child prostitution and child pornography, 25 May 2000

2000 Optional Protocol to the Convention on the Rights of the Child on the involvement of children in armed conflict, 25 May 2000

2000 Protocol to Prevent, Suppress and Punish Trafficking in Persons, Especially Women and Children, Supplementing the United Nations Convention against Transnational Organized Crime, 15 November 2000

2001 International Convention on Civil Liability for Bunker Oil Pollution Damage, 23 March 2001

2001 Stockholm Convention on Persistent Organic Pollutants, 22 May 2001

2001 International Treaty on Plant Genetic Resources for Food and Agriculture, 3 November 2001

2003 Protocol on Strategic Environmental Assessment, 21 May 2003

2003 United Nations Convention Against Corruption, 31 October 2003

2005 WHO International Health Regulations, 23 May 2005

2005 International Convention for the Suppression of Acts of Nuclear Terrorism, 13 April 2005

2005 Amendment to the Convention on the Physical Protection of Nuclear Material, 8 July 2005

2005 Optional Protocol to the Convention on the Safety of United Nations and Associated Personnel, 8 December 2005

2006 Convention on the Rights of Persons with Disabilities, 13 December 2006

2011 Agreement on Co-operation on Aeronautical and Maritime Search and Rescue in the Arctic, 12 May 2011

Regional

1950 European Convention for the Protection of Human Rights and Fundamental Freedoms, 4 November 1950

1951 Agreement between the Parties to the North Atlantic Treaty regarding the Status of their Forces, 19 June 1951

1952 Protocol No. 1 to the European Convention on Human Rights, 20 March 1952

1963 Nordic Mutual Assistance Agreement in connection with radiation accidents, 17 October 1963

1969 American Convention on Human Rights, 22 November 1969

1975 International aid and trade agreement between the ACP (African Caribean and Pacific Countries) group and the European Union aimed at supporting the "ACP states' efforts to achieve comprehensive, self reliant and self-sustained development" (Lomé Convention), 28 February 1975

1976 Convention for the Protection of the Marine Environment and the Coastal Region of the Mediterranean, 16 February 1976

1976 Protocol concerning cooperation in combating pollution of the Mediterranean Sea by oil and other harmful substances in cases of emergency, 16 February 1976

1980 European Outline Convention on transfrontier co-operation between territorial communities or authorities, 21 May 1980

1981 Convention for Co-operation in the Protection and Development of the Marine and Coastal Environment of the West and Central African Region, 23 March 1981

1981 African Charter of Human and People's Rights, 27 June 1981

1983 Convention for the Protection and Development of the Marine Environment of the Wider Caribbean Region, 24 March 1983

1983 Protocol No. 6 to the Convention for the Protection of Human Rights and Fundamental Freedoms concerning the Abolition of the Death Penalty, 28 April 1983

1983 Agreement for Cooperation in Dealing with Pollution of the North Sea by Oil and other Harmful Substances, 13 September 1983

1985 Convention for the Protection, Management and Development of the Marine and Coastal Environment of the Eastern African Region, 21 June 1985

1986 European Convention on the Recognition of the Legal Personality of International Non-Governmental Organisations, 24 April 1986

1987 Arab Cooperation Agreement on Regulating and Facilitating Relief Operations, 3 September 1987

1990 African Charter on the Rights and Welfare of the Child, 11 July 1990

1990 Cooperation Agreement for the Protection of the Coasts and Waters of the North-East Atlantic Against Pollution, Spain–France–Morocco–Portugal–European Economic Community, 17 October 1990

1991 Inter-American Convention to Facilitate Disaster Assistance, 7 June 1991

1991 Agreement establishing the Caribbean Disaster Emergency Response Agency CDERA, 22 September 1991

1991 Protocol on Environmental Protection to the Antarctic Treaty, 4 October 1991

1992 Treaty on European Union (Maastricht Treaty), 7 February 1992

1992 Convention on the protection of the marine environment of the Baltic Sea, 9 April 1992

1992 Convention on the Protection of the Black Sea Against Pollution, 21 April 1992

1992 Convention for the Protection of the marine Environment of the North-East Atlantic (OSPAR Convention), 22 September 1992

1993 Agreement on co-operation and interaction in the field of study of earthquakes and forecasting of seismic danger of the countries of the CIS, 1993

1993 Intergovernmental agreement on interaction in the field of the prevention and reduction of consequences of natural and technological disasters—participants of CIS countries, 1993

1994 Inter-American Convention on International Traffic in Minors, 18 March 1994

1994 Inter-American Convention on the Prevention, Punishment and Eradication of Violence against Women, 9 June 1994

1994 Convention on cooperation for the protection and sustainable use of the river Danube, 29 June 1994

1994 Protocol for the Protection of the Mediterranean Sea against Pollution Resulting from Exploration and Exploitation of the Continental Shelf and the Seabed and its Subsoil (Offshore Protocol), 14 October 1994

1995 Agreement between the Governments of the Republic of Kazakhstan, the Kyrgyz Republic and the Republic of Uzbekistan on co-operation and interaction in the field of research on earthquakes and forecasting of seismic danger, 1995

1996 Agreement on interaction of the States—participants of the Commonwealth of the Independent States in case of evacuation of their citizens from third countries in the event of the occurrence of natural disasters, 1996

1996 Inter-American Convention Against Corruption, 29 March 1996

1997 Convention on the Fight against Corruption involving Officials of the European Communities or Officials of Member States of the European Union, 26 May 1997

1998 Agreement between the Republic of Kazakhstan, Kyrgyz Republic, Republic of Tajikistan and Republic of Uzbekistan about co-operation in the field of prevention and liquidation of emergencies, 1998

1998 Agreement among the Governments of the Participating States of the Black Sea Economic Cooperation (BSEC) on collaboration in Emergency Assistance and Emergency Response to natural and man-made Disasters, 15 April 1998

1999 Council of Europe Criminal Law Convention on Corruption, 27 January 1999

1999 Agreement Between Member States and Associate Members of the Association of Caribbean States for Regional Cooperation on Natural Disasters, 17 April 1999

1999 Council of Europe Civil Law Convention on Corruption, 4 November 1999

2000 Partnership Agreement Between the Members of the African, Caribbean and Pacific Group of States of the One Part, and the European Community and its Member States, of the Other Part (Cotonou Agreement), 23 June 2000

2000 Charter of Fundamental Rights of the European Union, 2 October 2000

2001 Southern African Development Community (SADC) Protocol against Corruption, 14 August 2001

2001 ECOWAS Protocol on the Fight Against Corruption, 21 December 2001

2002 SAARC Convention on Preventing and Combating Trafficking in Women and Children for Prostitution, 5 January 2002

2002 Protocol to the Barcelona Convention for the Protection of the Mediterranean Sea against Pollution, concerning cooperation in preventing pollution from ships and, in cases of emergency, combating pollution of the Mediterranean Sea, 25 January 2002

2002 Protocol No. 13 to the Convention for the Protection of Human Rights and Fundamental Freedoms, concerning the abolition of the death penalty in all circumstances, 3 May 2002

2002 Nordic public health preparedness agreement, 14 June 2002

2003 Agreement between the European Atomic Energy Community (Euratom) and non-member States of the European Union on the participation of the latter in the Community arrangements for the early exchange of information in the event of radiological emergency (Ecurie), 29 January 2003

2003 Protocol to the African Charter on Human and People's Rights on the Rights of Women in Africa, 11 July 2003

2003 African Union Convention on Preventing and Combating Corruption, 11 July 2003

2003 Framework Convention for the Protection of the Marine Environment of the Caspian Sea, 4 November 2003

2004 Arab Charter on Human Rights, 22 May 2004

2004 Protocolo Adicional al Acuerdo Marco sobre Medio Ambiente del MERCOSUR en Materia de Cooperación y Asistencia ante Emergencias Ambientales, 7 July 2004

2004 Treaty establishing a Constitution for Europe, 29 October 2004

2005 Council of Europe Convention on Action against Trafficking in Human Beings, 15 May 2005

2005 ASEAN Agreement on Disaster Management and Emergency Response, 26 July 2005

2005 Additional Protocol to the Agreement among the Governments of the Participating States of the Black Sea Economic Cooperation (BSEC) on Collaboration in Emergency Assistance and Emergency Response to Natural and Man-Made Disasters of 1998, 20 October 2005

2006 Inter-institutional Agreement between the European Parliament, the Council and the Commission on budgetary discipline and sound financial management, 17 May 2006

2006 Protocol on the Protection and Assistance to Internally Displaced Persons to the Pact on Security, Stability and Development in the Great Lakes region, 30 November 2006

2007 Nuevo Convenio Constitutivo del Centro de Coordinación para la Prevención de los Desastres Naturales en América Central (CEPREDENAC), 12 July 2007

2007 Council of Europe Convention on the Protection of Children against Sexual Exploitation and Sexual Abuse, 25 October 2007

2007 Treaty on the Functioning of the European Union, 13 December 2007

2008 Protocol on Integrated Coastal Zone Management in the Mediterranean to the Convention for the Protection of the Marine Environment and the Coastal Region of the Mediterranean, 21 January 2008

2008 Agreement establishing the CDEMA, 2 July 2008

2009 ASEAN Mutual Recognition Arrangement on Medical Practitioners, 26 February 2009

2009 Convention for the Protection and Assistance of Internally Displaced Persons (IDPs) in Africa (Kampala Convention), 22 October 2009

Bilateral

1947 Agreement concerning the United States relief assistance to the Chinese people (with Exchange of Notes), 27 October 1947

1955 Exchange of Notes Constituting an Agreement between the United States of America and the Republic of Korea relating to Duty-free Entry and Exemption from Internal Taxation of Relief and Equipment, 22 April and 2 May 1955

1959 Convention on Mutual Assistance between French and Spanish Fire and Emergency Services, 14 July 1959

1962 Agreement between Luxembourg and France on the mutual assistance of rescue services, 10 December 1962

1970 Agreement on Mutual Assistance between the French and Monegasque Relief and Civil Defence Services, 16 April 1970

1974 Agreement on Economic and Technical Cooperation between France and Congo, 1 January 1974

1977 Convention on Mutual Assistance in the Event of Disasters or Serious Accidents, France–Germany, 3 February 1977

1981 Convention on Mutual Assistance in Case of Catastrophes or Serious Accidents, Belgium–France, 21 April 1981

1983 Emergency Technical Cooperation Agreement between the PAN American Health Organization and the Government of Suriname in Case of a Major Natural Disaster, 3 January 1983

1985 Agreement between the Kingdom of Denmark and the Federal Republic of Germany on mutual assistance in the event of disasters or serious accident, 16 May 1985

1986 Agreement between Argentina and Brasil on the Early Notification and Mutual Assistance in the Case of a Nuclear Accident or Radiological Emergency, 10 December 1986

1987 Agreement between France and Switzerland on reciprocal assistance in case of disasters or major accidents, 14 January 1987

1987 Agreement on technical cooperation and mutual assistance in the field of civil defence, Spain–Morocco, 21 January 1987

1988 Agreement on Cooperation on Disaster Preparedness and Prevention, and Mutual Assistance in the Event of Disasters, Argentina–Spain, 3 June 1988

1988 Agreement between the Federal Republic of Germany and the Kingdom of the Netherlands on mutual assistance in the event of disasters, including serious accidents, 7 June 1988

1989 Agreement between the Government of the French Republic and the Swiss Federal Council on mutual assistance in the event of disasters or serious accidents, 27 July 1989

1991 Agreement between Australia and Pakistan on Development Cooperation, 13 July 1991

1992 Protocol between the Kingdom of Spain and the Portuguese Republic on Technical Cooperation and Mutual Assistance in the Field of Civil Defence, 9 March 1992

1992 Convention in the Area of the Prediction and Prevention of Major Risks and on Mutual Assistance in the Event of Natural or Man-Made Disasters, France–Italy, 16 September 1992

1994 Agreement between the Federal Republic of Yugoslavia and the International Organization for Migration on the Privileges and Immunities of this Organization, 1994

1994 Agreement between the Government of the Kingdom of Cambodia and the International Federation of the Red Cross and Red Crescent Societies, 1994

1994 Agreement between the Government of the Republic of Kazakhstan and the Government of the Russian Federation on co-operation in the field of prevention of industrial failures, accidents, acts of nature and the reduction of their consequences, 1994

1994 Agreement by and between the Government of the Finnish Republic and the Government of the Russian Federation about Cooperation to avert disasters and to prevent their consequences, 9 August 1994

1995 Agreement of Joint Control on Forest Fire between the Government of the People's Republic of China and the Government of the Russian Federation, 26 June 1995

1995 Agreement between the Government of the Republic of Finland and the Government of the Republic of Estonia on Cooperation and Mutual Assistance in Cases of Accidents, 26 June 1995

1996 Agreement between the Government of the United States of America and the Government Republic of Belarus Regarding Cooperation to Facilitate the Provision of Assistance, 18 July 1996

1997 Agreement between the Government of Barbados and the Caribbean Disaster Emergency Response Agency for the Provision of Headquarters for CDERA, 1997

1997 Agreement between the Republic of Argentina and the Republic of Chile on co-operation in case of catastrophes, 8 August 1997

1998 Agreement between Italy and UN/Economic Commission for Latin America and the Caribbean (ECLAC) on Disaster Prevention in Latin America and in the Caribbean, 5 February 1988

1998 Agreement Between the Government of the Republic of the Philippines and the Government of the United States of America Regarding the Treatment of United States Armed Forces Visiting the Philippines, 10 February 1998

1998 Agreement on Cooperation on Disaster Prevention and Management and Public Safety, France–Malaysia, 25 May 1998

1999 Wildfire protection Agreement between the Department of the Interior and the Department of Agriculture of the United States of America and the Secretariat of Environment, Natural Resources and Fisheries of the United Mexican States for the Common Border, 4 June 1999

1999 Agreement between the European Community and the Swiss Confederation on the Carriage of Goods and Passengers by Rail and Road, 21 June 1999

2000 Agreement between the Government of the Hellenic Republic and the Government of the Russian Federation on Co-operation in the Field of Prevention and Response to Natural and Man-Made Disasters, 21 February 2000

2000 Cooperation Agreement between European Community and the People's Republic of Bangladesh on Partnership and Development, 22 May 2000

2000 Acuerdo entre el Gobierno del Reino de España y el Gobierno de la Federación de Rusia sobre cooperación en el ámbito de la prevención de catástrofes y asistencia mutua en la mitigación de sus consecuencias, 14 June 2000

2000 International Emergency Management Assistance Memorandum of Understanding between United States and Canada, 18 July 2000

2000 Agreement between the Government of the Federal Democratic Republic of Ethiopia and the Government of the State of Eritrea, 12 December 2000

2001 Wildfire Arrangement between the Department of the Interior and the Department of Agriculture of the United States of America and the National Rural Fire Authority of New Zealand, 2001

2001 Convenio entre el Reino de España y la República Francesa en materia de protección y de seguridad civil, 11 October 2001

2001 Protocol of Intentions between the Government of the United States of America and the Republic of the Philippines Concerning Cooperation and Disaster Prevention and Management, 20 November 2001

2004 Agreement between the Republic of Austria and the Hashemite Kingdom of Jordan on Mutual Assistance in the Case of Disasters or Serious Accidents, 13 March 2004

2004 Agreement between the Government of the Republic of Latvia and the Government of the Republic of Hungary on co-operation and mutual assistance in the event of disasters and other large-scale accidents, 21 August 2004

2006 Scientific Co-operation Agreement on Co-operation in Hydro-Meteorological Monitoring, Natural Disaster Prevention and Early Warning between Italy and the Caribbean Community CARICOM, 6 April 2006

2006 Memorandum of Understanding between the China Earthquake Administration and the Italian Civil Protection Department on Cooperation in the field of Seismic Risk Mitigation and Emergency Management, 21 April 2006

2007 Administrative agreement between Italy and France on Transboundary cooperation in mountainous areas in situations of emergency, 19 March 2007

2007 Memorandum of Understanding between Italy and Venezuela on bilateral cooperation in civil protection issues, 21 March 2007

2007 Agreement for Economic and Technical Cooperation between United States of America and Burundi coverings economic, technical, humanitarian and related assistance that may be provided by the USA in Burundi, 12 December 2007

2008 Memorandum of Understanding between the General Secretariat of the League of Arab States and the United Nations International Strategy for Disaster Reduction, 26 August 2008

2008 Agreement on Development Cooperation between Italy and Albania covering technical and financial cooperation, humanitarian and emergency assistance, 2 December 2008

2010 Agreement between the European Union and the Republic of Serbia establishing a framework for the participation of the Republic of Serbia in European Union crisis management operations, 20 December 2010

2011 Framework Agreement between the United States of America and the European Union on the participation of the United States of America in European Union crisis management operations, 17 May 2011

Other International Instruments

United Nations

UNGA

1948 UNGA Resolution 217 (III), 10 December 1948
1961 UNGA Resolution 1714 (XVI), 19 December 1961
1963 UNGA Resolution 1904 (XVIII), 20 November 1963
1965 UNGA Resolution 2131(XX), 21 December 1965
1967 UNGA Resolution 2263 (XXII), 7 November 1967
1970 UNGA Resolution 2625(XXV), 24 October 1970
1971 UNGA Resolution 2816 (XXVI), 14 December 1971
1971 UNGA Resolution 2856 (XXVI), 20 December 1971
1977 UNGA Resolution 32/197, 20 December 1977
1981 UNGA Resolution 36/103, 9 December 1981
1983 UNGA Resolution 38/202, 20 December 1983
1988 UNGA Resolution 43/131, 8 December 1988
1989 UNGA Resolution 44/236, 22 December 1989
1990 UNGA Resolution 45/100, 14 December 1990
1991 UNGA Resolution 46/91, 16 December 1991
1991 UNGA Resolution 46/119, 17 December 1991
1991 UNGA Resolution 46/182, 19 December 1991
1992 UNGA Resolution 47/133, 18 December 1992
1992 UNGA Resolution 47/135, 18 December 1992
1992 UNGA Resolution 47/199, 22 December 1992
1993 UNGA A/CONF.157/23 Vienna Declaration and Programme of Action, 12 July 1993
1993 UNGA Resolution 48/57, 14 December 1993
1995 UNGA Resolution 50/120, 20 December 1995
1999 UNGA Resolution 54/219, 22 December 1999
2000 UNGA Resolution 55/2, 8 September 2000
2001 UNGA Resolution 56/151, 19 December 2001

A. de Guttry et al. (eds.), *International Disaster Response Law*,
DOI: 10.1007/978-90-6704-882-8,

2001 UNGA Resolution 56/201, 21 December 2001
2002 UNGA Resolution 57/150, 16 December 2002
2004 UNGA Resolution 59/141, 2 December 2004
2004 UNGA Resolution 59/201, 20 December 2004
2005 UNGA Resolution 60/1, 16 September 2005
2005 UNGA Resolution 60/124, 15 December 2005
2005 UNGA Resolution 60/147, 16 December 2005
2005 UNGA Resolution 60/195, 22 December 2005
2007 UNGA Resolution 61/295, 2 October 2007
2007 UNGA Resolution 62/67, 6 December 2007
2007 UNGA Resolution 62/208, 19 December 2007
2008 UNGA Resolution 63/117, 10 December 2008
2008 UNGA Resolution 63/137, 11 December 2008
2008 UNGA Resolution 63/139, 11 December 2008
2008 UNGA Resolution 63/141, 11 December 2008
2008 UNGA Resolution 63/245, 24 December 2008
2010 UNGA Resolution 64/250, 22 January 2010
2010 UNGA Resolution 64/251, 22 January 2010
2010 UNGA Resolution 65/133, 15 December 2010
2010 UNGA Resolution 65/157, 20 December 2010
2011 UNGA Resolution 65/264, 28 January 2011
2011 UNGA, Adopting text on bolstering effectiveness of military, civil assets in disaster response, reaffirms principles of neutrality, independence, 1 July 2011

UNSC

UNSC Resolution 687, 3 April 1991
1991 UNSC Resolution 688, 5 April 1991
1992 UNSC Resolution 770, 13 August 1992
1992 UNSC Resolution 794, 3 December 1992
1994 UNSC Resolution 925, 8 June 1994
1994 UNSC Resolution 929, 22 June 1994
1996 UNSC Resolution 1080, 15 November 1996
1997 UNSC Resolution 1101, 28 March 1997
1997 UNSC Resolution 1114, 19 June 1997
2001 UNSC Resolution 1373, 28 September 2001
2002 UNSC Resolution 1315, 16 January 2002
2004 UNSC Resolution 1540, 28 April 2004
2006 UNSC Resolution 1706, 31 August 2006
2007 UNSC Resolution 1769, 31 July 2007
2010 UNSC Resolution 1966, 22 December 2010
2011 UNSC Resolution 1970, 26 February 2011
2011 UNSC Resolution 1973, 17 March 2011

ECOSOC

1985 ESCOSOC Resolution 1985/17, 28 May 1985

1993 ECOSOC Resolution 1993/205, 12 February 1993

1994 ECOSOC Resolution 1994/31, 27 July 1994

2004 ECOSOC Resolution 2004/50, 8 April 2004

2008 ECOSOC Resolution 2008/36, 25 July 2008

2009 ECOSOC Resolution 2009/3, 22 July 2009

ICCPR/Human Rights Committee

1982 UN Human Rights Committee, CCPR General Comment 6, The right to life (Article 6), 30 April 1982

1989 UN Human Rights Committee, CCPR General Comment 17, Rights of the child (Article 24), 7 April 1989

1994 UN Human Rights Committee, CCPR General Comment 24, Issues relating to reservations made upon ratification or accession to the Covenant or the Optional Protocols thereto, or in relation to declarations under Article 41 of the Covenant, 4 November 1994

2001 UN Human Rights Committee, CCPR General Comment 29: Article 4: Derogations during a State of Emergency, 31 August 2001

2004 UN Human Rights Committee, CCPR General Comment 31: Nature of the General Legal Obligation Imposed on States Parties to the Covenant, 26 May 2004

2007 UN Human Rights Committee, CCPR General comment 32, Article 14, Right to equality before courts and tribunals and to fair trial, 23 August 2007

ICESCR/Committee on Economic, Social and Cultural Rights

1990 CESCR General Comment 3, The nature of States parties obligations (Article 2, para 1), 14 December 1990

1998 CESCR, General Comment 9, The domestic application of the Covenant, 3 December 1998

1999 CESCR, General Comment 12, The right to adequate food, 12 May 1999

2000 CESCR, General Comment 14, the rights to the highest attainable standard of health, 11 August 2000

2001 CESCR, Statement E/C.12/2001/10, 4 May 2001

2003 CESCR, General Comment No. 15 (2002), The right to water (Articles 11 and 12 of the International Covenant on Economic, Social and Cultural Rights), 20 January 2003

UN Commission on Human Rights

1984 UN Commission on Human Rights, The Siracusa Principles on the Limitation and Derogation Provisions in the International Covenant on Civil and Political Rights, 28 September 1984

2005 UN Commission on Human Rights, Principles on housing and property restitution for refugees and displaced persons, E/CN.4/Sub.2/2005/17, 28 June 2005

Committee on the Rights of the Child

2011 Committee on the Rights of the Child, General Comment N. 13, The right of the child to freedom from all forms of violence, 18 April 2011

Committee on the Rights of Persons with Disabilities

2009 UN Committee on the Rights of Persons with Disabilities, Guidelines on treaty-specific document to be submitted by states parties under Article 35, para 1, of the Convention on the Rights of Persons with Disabilities, CRPD/C/2/3, 18 November 2009

ILC

2001 International Law Commission, Draft Articles on Responsibility of States for Internationally Wrongful Acts, November 2001

2008 International Law Commission, Memorandum of the Secretariat, Protection of Persons in the Event of Disasters, 31 March 2008

2008 International Law Commission, Preliminary report of the Special Rapporteur on the protection of persons in the event of disasters, 5 May 2008

2009, International Law Commission, Second report of the Special Rapporteur on the protection of persons in the event of disasters, 7 May 2009

2010 International Law Commission, Third report of the Special Rapporteur on the protection of persons in the event of disasters, 31 March 2010

2011 International Law Commission Draft Articles on the Responsibility of International Organizations, 26 April 2011

2011, International Law Commission, Fourth report of the Special Rapporteur on the protection of persons in the event of disasters, 11 May 2011

Other UN Documents

1972 Declaration of the United Nations Conference on the Human Environment, 16 June 1972

1978 UNESCO Declaration on Race and Racial Prejudice, 27 November 1978

2000 UN Global Compact Principles, 26 July 2000

2005 United Nations World Conference on Disaster Reduction, Hyogo Declaration, 22 January 2005

2005 United Nations World Conference on Disaster Reduction, Hyogo Framework for Action 2005–2015: Building the Resilience of Nations and Communities to Disasters, 22 January 2005

2005 UN Sub-Commission on the Promotion and Protection of Human Rights, Principles on Housing and Property Restitution for Refugees and Displaced Persons, 28 June 2005

2011 Sixty-fourth World Health Assembly, Strengthening national health emergency and disaster management capacities and resilience of health systems, 24 May 2011

2011 Report of the Special Rapporteur on Trafficking in Persons, Especially Women and Children, A/HRC/17/35, 13 April 2011

Regional

European Union

Council of the European Union

1987 Resolution 87/C 176/01 of the Council and the representatives of the Governments of the Member States, meeting within the Council of 25 June 1987 on the introduction of Community cooperation on civil protection, 25 June 1987

1989 Resolution 89/C 44/03 of the Council and the representatives of the Governments of the Member States, meeting within the Council of 13 February 1989 on the new developments in Community cooperation on civil protection, 13 February 1989

1990 Resolution 90/C 315/01 of the Council and the representatives of the Governments of the Member States, meeting within the Council of 23 November 1990 on Community cooperation on civil protection, 23 November 1990

1991 Resolution 91/C 198/01 of the Council and the representatives of the Governments of the Member States, meeting within the Council of 8 July 1991 on improving mutual aid between Member States in the event of natural or technological disasters 8 July 1991

1994 Resolution 94/C 313/01 of the Council and the representatives of the Governments of the Member States, meeting within the Council of 31 October 1994 on strengthening Community cooperation on civil protection, 31 October 1994

1995 Decision 95/553/EC of the Representatives of the Governments of the Member States meeting within the Council of 19 December 1995 regarding protection for citizens of the European Union by diplomatic and consular representations, 19 December 1995

1996 Council Regulation (EC) No 1257/96 concerning humanitarian aid, 20 June 1996

1996 Decision 96/409/CFSP of the Representatives of the Governments of the Member States, meeting within the Council of 25 June 1996 on the establishment of an emergency travel document, 25 June 1996

1997 Council Decision 98/22/EC establishing a Community Action Programme in the field of Civil Protection, 19 December 1997

1999 Council Decision 1999/847/EC establishing a Community action programme in the field of civil protection, 9 December 1999

2001 Council Regulation (EC) 539/2001 listing the third countries whose nationals must be in possession of visas when crossing the external borders and those whose nationals are exempt from that requirement, 15 March 2001

2001 Euratom, Council Decision 2001/792/EC establishing a Community mechanism to facilitate reinforced cooperation in civil protection assistance interventions, 23 October 2001

2001 Resolution 2001/C 82/01 of the Council and of the Governments of the Member States, meeting within the Council of 26 February 2001 on strengthening the capabilities of the European Union in the field of civil protection, 26 February 2001

2002 Council Regulation (EC) 2012/2002 establishing the European Union Solidarity Fund, 11 November 2002

2005 Council Joint Action 2005/643/CFSP on the European Union Monitoring Mission in Aceh (Indonesia), 9 September 2005

2007 Council Regulation (Euratom) 300/2007 establishing an Instrument for Nuclear Safety Cooperation, 19 February 2007

2007 Council Decision 2007/124 establishing for the period 2007 to 2013, as part of General Programme on Security and Safeguarding Liberties, the Specific Programme 'Prevention,

Preparedness and Consequence Management of Terrorism and other Security related risks', 12 February 2007

2007 Council Decision 2007/162/EC establishing a Civil Protection Financial Instrument, 5 March 2007

2007 Council Decision 2007/779/EC establishing a Community Civil Protection Mechanism, 8 November 2007

2008 Council of the European Union, Council Conclusions 16474/08 calling for civil protection capabilities to be enhanced by a European mutual assistance system building on the civil protection civil approach, 28 November 2008

2008 Council of the European Union, European Union guidelines 2008/C 317/06 on the implementation of the consular Lead State concept, 12 December 2008

2008 Joint Statement 2008/C 25/01 by the Council and the Representatives of the Governments of the Member States meeting within the Council, the European Parliament and the European Commission, European Consensus on Humanitarian Aid, 30 January 2008

2010 Council Decision 2010/131/EU on setting up the Standing Committee on operational cooperation on internal security, 25 February 2010

2010 Council of the European Union, Guidelines 15613/10 on consular protection of EU citizens in third countries, 5 November 2010

2010 Council of the European Union, Conclusions on the Communication from the Commission to the European Parliament and the Council—Towards a stronger European disaster response: the role of civil protection and humanitarian assistance, 14 December 2010

2010 Council of the European Union, Decision 2010/427/EU establishing the organisation and functioning of the European External Action Service, 26 July 2010

2011 Council of the European Union, Decision 2011/210/CFSP on a European Union military operation in support of humanitarian assistance operation in response to the crisis situation in Libya (EUFOR Libya), 1 April 2011

European Council

2010 European Council, The Stockholm Programme—An open and secure Europe serving and protecting citizens, 2010/C 115/01, 4 May 2010

European Parliament

1997 European Parliament Resolution B4-0504 and 0536/97 on the situation in Congo-Brazzaville, 12 June 1997

1999 European Parliament Resolution A4-0242/1999 on the role of the Union in the world: Implementation of the common foreign and security policy for 1998, 5 May 1999

2011 European Parliament resolution 2011/2072 on facing the challenges of the safety of offshore oil and gas activities, 13 September 2011

2011 European Parliament, Resolution 2011/2023 on 'Towards a stronger European disaster response: the role of civil protection and humanitarian assistance', 27 September 2011

European Commission

2003 Commission Decision 2004/277/EC, Euratom laying down rules for the implementation of Council Decision 2001/792/EC, Euratom establishing a Community mechanism to facilitate reinforced cooperation in civil protection assistance interventions, 29 December 2003

2007 Commission Decision 2008/73/EC, Euratom amending Decision 2004/277/EC, Euratom as regards rules for the implementation of Council Decision 2007/779/EC, Euratom establishing a Community civil protection mechanism, 20 December 2007

2007 European Commission Recommendation of 5 December 2007 on reproducing the text of Article 20 TEC in passports, 5 December 2007

2010 Commission Decision 2010/481/EU, Euratom amending Decision 2004/277/EC, Euratom as regards rules for the implementation of Council Decision 2007/779/EC, Euratom establishing a Community civil protection mechanism, 29 July 2010

2011 European Commission Proposal for a Regulation of the European Parliament and of the Council on Safety of Offshore Oil and Gas Prospection, Exploration and Production Activities, 27 October 2011

2011 Commission Proposal for a Decision of the European Parliament and of the Council on a Union Civil Protection Mechanism, 20 December 2011

Other EU Documents

2004 Directive 2004/35/EC of the European Parliament and the Council on environmental liability with regard to the prevention and remedying of environmental damage, 21 April 2004

2006 Joint framework for EU cooperation and coordination in relation to emergencies in Japan, 2006

2006 Decision 1926/2006 of the European Parliament and of the Council establishing a programme of Community action in the field of consumer policy (2007–2013), 18 December 2006

2006 Regulation (EC) 1717/2006 of the European Parliament and of the Council establishing an Instrument for Stability, 15 November 2006

2007 Opinion 2007/C 161/21 of the European Economic and Social Committee on the Green Paper on diplomatic and consular protection of Union citizens in third countries, 14 March 2007

2007 Decision 1350/2007/EC of the European Parliament and of the Council establishing a second programme of Community action in the field of health, 23 October 2007

2011 European Union, Committee of the Regions, Opinion on 'Towards a stronger European disaster response', 11 May 2011

African Union

1999 African Commission on Human and Peoples' Rights, Res. 41 (XXVI) 99: Resolution on the Rights to a fair Trial and Legal Assistance in Africa, 15 November 1999

2010 African Union Executive Council Decision EX.CL/589(XVII) on the Report of the second Ministerial Conference on Disaster Risk Reduction, 16 April 2010

ICRC/IFRC

1969 XXI International Conference of the Red Cross, Declaration of principles for international humanitarian relief to the civilian population in disaster situations, resolution 26, September 1969

1969 XXI International Conference of the Red Cross, Principles and Rules for Red Cross and Red Crescent Disaster Relief, September 1969

1977 XXIII International Conference of the Red Cross and Red Crescent, Measures to expedite international relief, resolution 6, 1977

1986 XXV International Conference of the Red Cross, Statutes of the International Red Cross and Red Crescent Movement, October 1986, as amended by the XXVI International Conference of the Red Cross and Red Crescent in December 1995 and by the XXIX International Conference of the Red Cross and Red Crescent in June 2006

1997 Agreement on the organization of the international activities of the components of the International Red Cross and Red Crescent Movement, 27 November 1997

Other Documents

1970 World Custom Organization, Recommendation of the Customs co-operation Council to Expedite the Forwarding of Relief Consignments in the Event of Disasters, 8 June 1970

1981 Universal Islamic Declaration of Human Rights, 19 September 1981

1982 Pan Caribbean Disaster Preparedness and Prevention Project, 17 February 1982

1984 International Law Association, Paris Minimum Standards of Human Rights Norms In a State of Emergency, 1 September 1984

1990 Institute for Human Rights at Åbo Akademi University, Turku/Åbo Finland, Declaration of minimum humanitarian standards, 2 December 1990

1994 Qatar International Law Conference, Doha Declaration on Priorities for progressive Development of International Law in the United Nations Decade of International Law to meet the Challenges of the 21st century, 25 March 1994

1994 World Conference on Natural Disaster Reduction, Yokohama Strategy and Plan of Action for a Safer World. Guidelines for Natural Disaster Prevention, Preparedness and Mitigation, 27 May 1994

1999 Guatemala Declaration, 20th Ordinary Meeting of the Presidents of Central America, the Dominican Republic and Belize, 18 and 19 October 1999

2001 ADB/OECD, Anti-Corruption Action Plan for Asia and the Pacific, November 2001

2002 Andean Council of Foreign Ministers, decision No. 529, Creating the Andean Committee for Disaster Prevention and Response (CAPRADE), 7 June 2002

2002 Second World Assembly on Ageing, Madrid Plan of Action on Ageing, April 2002

2003 Institute of International Law, Resolution of the Sixteenth Commission on Humanitarian Assistance, 2 September 2003

2004 Inter-Agency Standing Committee, Civil-Military Relationship in Complex Emergencies—An IASC Reference Paper, 28 June 2004

2005 13th Asia–Pacific Economic Cooperation Leaders' Meeting, Busan Declaration, 18–19 November 2005

2005 13th SAARC Summit, Dhaka Declaration, 13 November 2005

2005 Association of Caribbean States, Summit of Heads of State and/or Government, Declaration of Panama, 29 July 2005

2007 OAS General Assembly Resolution 2314 On Natural Disaster Reduction, Risk Management and Assistance in Natural and Other Disaster Situations, 5 June 2007

2009 AADMER Standard Operating Procedure for Regional Standby Arrangements and Coordination of Joint Disaster Relief and Emergency Response Operations (SASOP), 2009

2010 OSPAR Recommendation 2010/18 on the prevention of significant acute oil pollution from offshore drilling activities, 24 September 2010

2010 EUR-OPA Resolution 2010–1 of the Committee of Permanent Correspondents 'Working together in Europe and the Mediterranean for the Prevention of Disasters, Preparedness and Response: Priorities for Action', 28 September 2010

2011 Declaration by the IAEA Ministerial Conference on Nuclear Safety, 20 June 2011

Guidelines and Codes of Conduct

1978 UNEP Environmental Law Guidelines and Principles on Shared Natural Resources, May 1978

1979 Codex Alimentarius Commission, Code of Ethics for International Trade in Food Including Concessional and Food Aid Transactions, December 1979 (revised in 1985 and 2010)

1982 UNITAR, Model Rules for Disaster Relief Operations, 1982

1985 Codex Alimentarius Commission, Amendment to the Code of Ethics for International Trade in Food Including Concessional and Food Aid Transactions, July 1985

1993 International Institute of Humanitarian Law, Guiding Principles on the Right to Humanitarian Assistance, April 1993

1994 OCHA Guidelines on the Use of Foreign Military and Civil Defence Assets In Disaster Relief (Oslo Guidelines), May 1994

1994 Code of Conduct for the International Red Cross and Red Crescent Movement and Non-Governmental Organizations (NGOs) in Disaster Relief, 31 December 1994

1996 OCHA Model Customs Facilitation Agreement, April 1996

1996 CRC, General Guidelines for Periodic Reports, CRC/C/58, 20 November 1996

1997 Sphere Project, 1997

2003 OCHA Guidelines On The Use of Military and Civil Defence Assets To Support United Nations Humanitarian Activities in Complex Emergencies, March 2003

2003 International Meeting on Good Humanitarian Donorship, Principles and good practice of humanitarian Donorship, 17 June 2003

2004 OCHA Guiding Principles on Internal Displacement, September 2004

2004 Balkan National Societies meeting on IDRL, Implementation of International Disaster Response Laws, Rules and Principles in the Balkans, Recommended Rules and Practices, 26 September 2004

2004 IAEA Code of Conduct on the Safety of Research Reactors, 24 September 2004

2005 United Nations Principles on Housing and Property Restitution for Refugees and Displaced Persons (*Pinheiro Principles*), 28 June 2005

2006 OCHA Guidelines on The Use of Military and Civil Defence Assets In Disaster Relief—“Oslo Guidelines”, 27 November 2006

2007 IFRC Guidelines for the Domestic Facilitation and Regulation of International Disaster Relief and Initial Recovery Assistance, 30 November 2007

2008 UNEP Guidelines for the Determination of Liability and Compensation for Damage Resulting from Pollution of the Marine Environment in the Mediterranean Sea Area, 18 January 2008

A. de Guttry et al. (eds.), *International Disaster Response Law*,
DOI: 10.1007/978-90-6704-882-8,

2008 Brookings-Bern Project on Internal Displacement, Human Rights and Natural Disasters. Operational Guidelines and Field Manual on Human Rights Protection in Situations of Natural Disaster, March 2008

2009 UNEP Draft Guidelines for the Development of Domestic Legislation on Liability, Response Action and Compensation for Damage Caused by Activities Dangerous to the Environment, 11 November 2009

2011 ISAC Operational Guidelines on the Protection of Persons in Situations of Natural Disasters, 10 January 2011

2011 Sphere Handbook, Humanitarian Charter and Minimum Standards in Humanitarian Response, 2011

2011 IFRC Model Act for the Facilitation and Regulation of International Disaster Assistance, Pilot Version, November 2011

Table of Cases

Universal

Permanent Court of International Justice

1927 Judgment, The Lotus Case (France v. Turkey), 7 September 1927

International Court of Justice

1969 Judgment, North Sea Continental Shelf Cases (Federal Republic of Germany v. Denmark; Federal Republic of Germany v. Netherlands), 20 February 1969

1970 Judgment, Barcelona Traction, Light and Power Company, Limited (Belgium v. Spain), 5 February 1970

1986 Judgment, Military and Paramilitary Activities in and against Nicaragua (Nicaragua v. United States of America), 27 June 1986

1996 Advisory Opinion, Legality of the Threat or Use of Nuclear Weapons, 8 July 1996

1997 Judgment, Gabčíkovo-Nagymaros Project (Hungary v. Slovakia), 25 September 1997

2004 Advisory Opinion, Legal Consequences of the Construction of a Wall in the Occupied Palestinian Territory, 9 July 2004

International Criminal Court

Prosecutor v. Katanga and Ngudjolo Chui, Pre-Trial Chamber I, Decision on the confirmation of charges, 30 September 2008

ICTR

Prosecutor v. Akayesu, Judgment, 2 September 1998

Prosecutor v. Kambanda, Judgment and Sentence, 4 September 1998

Prosecutor v. Kayishema, Judgment, Trial Chamber, 1 June 2001

Prosecutor v. Rutaganira, Judgment, Trial Chamber, 14 March 2005

A. de Guttry et al. (eds.), *International Disaster Response Law*,

DOI: 10.1007/978-90-6704-882-8,

ICTY

Prosecutor v. Tadić, Decision on the Defence Motion for Interlocutory Appeal on Jurisdiction, 2 October 1995

Prosecutor v. Karadžić and Mladić, Review of Indictment pursuant to Rule 61, 11 July 1996

Prosecutor v. Delalić (Celebici case), Judgment, Trial Chamber, 16 November 1996

Prosecutor v. Kunarac et al., Judgment, Appeals Chamber, 12 June 2002

Prosecutor v. Milošević, Decision on Motion for Judgment of Acquittal, Trial Chamber, 16 June 2004

UN Human Rights Committee

Lansman et al. v. Finlad, Communication No. 511/1992, 8 November 1994

Regional

African Commission on Human and People's Rights

Commission Nationale des Droits de l'Homme et des Libertés v. Chad, Communication No. 74/92, decision adopted during the 18th Ordinary session, 2–11 October 1995

Jawara v. the Gambia, 11 May 2000

The Social and Economic Rights Action Center and the Center for Economic and Social Rights v. Nigeria, 13–27 October 2001

European Commission of Human Rights

De Becker v. Belgium, Report of 8 January 1960

Denmark, Norway, Sweden and the Netherlands v. Greece (Greek Case), Report of 5 November 1969

Cyprus v. Turkey, Report of 10 July 1976

European Court of Human Rights

Lawless v. Ireland (Lawless case), Judgment of 1 July 1961

Golder v. The United Kingdom, Judgment of 21 February 1975

Ireland v. The United Kingdom, Judgment of 18 January 1978

Silver and Others v. The United Kingdom, Judgment of 24 September 1982

Soering v. The United Kingdom, Judgment of 7 July 1989

Brannigan and Mc Bride v. The United Kingdom, Judgment of 25 May 1993

Aksoy v. Turkey, Judgment of 18 December 1996

Findlay v. The United Kingdom, Judgment of 25 February 1997

Sakik and Others v. Turkey, Judgment of 27 November 1997

Cirklar v. Turkey, Judgment of 28 October 1998

Brogan v. The United Kingdom, Judgment of 29 November 1998

Z and Others v. The United Kingdom, Judgment of 10 May 2001

Marshall v. The United Kingdom, Decision on admissibility of 10 July 2001
Öneryıldız v. Turkey [GC], Judgment of 30 November 2004
Isayeva v. Russia, Judgment of 15 November 2007
Budayeva and Others v. Russia, Judgment of 20 March 2008

Court of Justice of the European Union

Portuguese Republic v. Council of the European Union, Judgment of 3 December 1996
Grzelczyk v. Centre public d'aide sociale d'Ottignies-Louvain-la-Neuve, Judgment of 20 September 2001
Commission of the European Communities v. Ireland, Judgment of 30 May 2006
Commission of the European Communities v. Council of the European Union, Judgment of 20 May 2008
European Parliament v. Council of the European Union, Judgment of 6 November 2008

Inter-American Commission on Human Rights

Advisory Opinion on Habeas Corpus in Emergency Situations, 30 January 1987
Advisory Opinion on Judicial Guarantees in States of Emergency, 6 October 1987
Sanchez et al. ("Operation Gatekeeper") v. United States, 27 October 2005

National Courts

United States District Court, Eastern District of Louisiana, Claire Brou, et al., v. Federal Emergency Management Agency, et al., 15 August 2006
United States District Court, Eastern District of Louisiana, Robinson et al., v. United States, 18 November 2009
Colombia, Judgment T-830/09 of the Constitutional Court of Colombia, 19 November 2009

Index

A. de Guttry et al. (eds.), *International Disaster Response Law*,
DOI: 10.1007/978-90-6704-882-8,